TUFF STUFF'S
Baseball Memorabilia
Price Guide

TUFF STUFF'S
Baseball Memorabilia Price Guide

Jim Warren II
Dennis Madigan
Melanie Haynie
Jerry Shaver

Editorial Director: Larry Canale
Managing Editor: John Harrington
Copy Editor/Proofreader: Sean Ryan
Contributing Writers/Research: Matt Smith, Jeremy Zucker
Designers: Abe Longmire, Michael Pederson
Data Entry: Emilie Ferrell, Suzy Partch

Tuff Stuff Books
Richmond, Va.
A division of Landmark Specialty Publications Inc.

The authors assume full responsibility for the facts and information contained in this book.

ISBN: 0-930625-24-2
Library of Congress Catalog Number: 98-60763

Manufactured in the United States of America

Published by
Tuff Stuff Books
Richmond, Va.
A division of Landmark Specialty Publications Inc.

Cover Design: Tim Roberts, Rick Kidd
Cover Photograph: Imgaes Unlimited, Herbert Cosby
Front cover photo: Reggie Jackson Signed Baseball, Hank Aaron store model bat, 1944 Bob Prichard model glove, 1968 Topps Roberto Clemente, 1964 Topps Mickey Mantle, 1980s Boston Red Sox pennant

ACKNOWLEDGMENTS

It seemed like a good idea at the time.

When *Tuff Stuff* magazine's senior price guide editor, Jim Warren, called the staff together last summer and proposed that we compile a complete and comprehensive guide to baseball memorabilia, we jumped at the chance. He had barely finished outlining the idea when we started fighting over who got to write which sections. We hammered out a formal proposal for the powers that be, and headed off to the Cleveland National Sports Collectors Convention to begin our research.

As time passed, and the information began to pile up, and the deadline loomed ever closer, one thing quickly became clear: There's no way four people can write a book like this. Cramming 130–plus years of baseball memorabilia information between two covers is an impossible task.

Of course, eventually we did write it—you're holding the proof. But it never could have been completed without countless hours of hard work from many knowledgeable and talented people. The four of us might be listed as the authors, but don't let that fool you. Without the people listed below, we never would have gotten beyond p. 3.

First of all, we'd like to thank Phil Wood for writing the foreword as well as providing the information used in compiling our Baseball Jerseys chapter. Phil is one of the most knowledgeable people in the hobby, and he's a great guy to work with. Thanks, Phil, for all of your time and expertise.

This project would never have gotten off the ground without a tremendous amount of support from folks at both Tuff Stuff Publications and its parent company, Landmark Communications. Our thanks especially go to Rick Spears, president of Landmark Specialty Publications, and Frank Finn, president of Tuff Stuff Publications, for all of their guidance, leadership, and patience throughout the long process of bringing this book to press.

We'd also like to thank Allan Miller, Ted Jones, Elizabeth Smith, and Tracy Anderson of Antique Trader Books for their constant support. There's a world of difference between producing a comprehensive book and a monthly magazine, and without the expertise of these people we never could have made the transition.

And, of course, we couldn't have done it without *Tuff Stuff* editor-in-chief Larry Canale. Larry was with us through every step of the process, and without his constant nagging—er, *encouragement*—we never could have seen the project through to completion. Thanks, L.C.

In any book, the writers are simply the first step in a long, involved process, and the following folks lent considerable time, talent, and energy to the final product. Special thanks to John Harrington, managing editor of *Tuff Stuff's* fantasy sports magazines, *Tuff Stuff's Sports Figures,* and Classic Collectibles Online, for coordinating this project and keeping things running smoothly. Thanks also to Sean Ryan for making sure everything was readable; Jeremy Zucker for all of his assistance in researching and compiling information; Matt Smith for his work on the pennants and posters sections; and Emilie Ferrell and Suzy Partch for the hours they spent typing in checklist after checklist after checklist. Also, many thanks to designer Abe Longmire for his tremendous patience in both scanning the hundreds of images in this book and bearing with us as we re-wrote seemingly dozens of pages once they were already designed. Thanks also to Abe's design partner, Mike Pederson, for plowing through many of these pages during the proofing stage.

And finally, we'd especially like to thank all of the people involved in the hobby who gave us advice, information, artwork, and everything else we asked for. Without the contributions of these folks, there would be an awful lot of white space between the covers of this book. Thanks to Ron Oser, Bill Mastro, and the folks at Auction Universe for providing a wealth of recent auction data used to compile prices.

Thanks to memorabilia experts Joe Phillips, for all of his expertise in the area of gloves, and Joy Schreiber, for her invaluable assistance in the areas of tickets and programs. And, thanks to Ralph and Terry Kovell for lending their considerable expertise to this project. Thanks also to Kevin Keating and Mille Koleth, authors of the soon-to-be-published *Negro Leagues Autograph Guide,* for their assistance in compiling vintage autograph prices. And to Roger Radford, who not only drops by the office to give us a hand, but who always brings plenty of candy with him when he does.

Special thanks to Brian Cahill and the folks at Score Board, and Don Garrett Jr., and Jackie Davis for providing us with numerous items from their collections to use for artwork. We'd also like to thank all of the baseball card manufacturers—Upper Deck, Topps, Fleer, Pacific, and Pinnacle—for their information and assistance.

Thanks also to the folks at the following auction houses for use of their fine photography:
- Scott M. Goodman Sports World
- Leland's
- Leslie Hindman Auctioneers
- Mastro Fine Sports Auctions and Mastro & Steinbach
- North Shore Sports
- Oregon Trails
- Robert Edward Auctions
- Ron Oser Auctions
- Sotheby's
- Superior Galleries.

We'd also like to thank our stable of baseball price guide contributors—the folks in the trenches with us every month—for providing their invaluable expertise in helping compile prices: Julie Alexander, Matt Wozniak, Steve Marlowe, Tim and Mary Page, Cal Stottlar, Ray Guidry, Steve Mencik, Bill Edwards, Steve Ungrey, Joe Sperling, William Bryda, Bob Barca, Earle Parish, Tom Webb, Brad Boe, Brad Loper, and Stanley Lyon.

And last but not least, we'd like to thank everyone else at Tuff Stuff Publications for putting up with us while we worked on this book. Without everyone pitching in and taking up our slack, we never could have given this project the time and attention it deserved. Thanks, guys.

—Jim Warren II, Dennis Madigan, Melanie Haynie, Jerry Shaver
April 20, 1998

TABLE OF CONTENTS

Foreword 8
By Phil Wood

Introduction 10

Chapter 1 12
  Autographs
                              Hall of Fame Players 15
                              Active Players 43
                              Retired Players 56
                              Managers and Announcers 68

Chapter 2 70
  Multi-Signed Items
                              Milestone Autographs 70
                              All-Star Team-Signed Balls 74
                              World Series Team-Signed Balls 76
                              Team-Signed Balls 80

Chapter 3 100
  Jerseys

Chapter 4 104
  Publications
                              Baseball Digest 104
                              Baseball Magazine 110
                              Sport 114
                              Sports Illustrated 118
                              Street & Smith 126
                              Life, Newsweek, Time....................................128
                              Media Guides 130
                              Yearbooks..146
                              Books 158

Chapter 5 176
  Programs, Press Pins, Tickets
                              All-Star Programs..177
                              World Series Programs 178
                              LCS/Division Series Programs......................180
                              Special Programs and Tickets.......................182
                              All-Star Press Pins 185
                              World Series Press Pins 186
                              Phantom Press Pins.......................................188
                              Hall of Fame Press Pins 189
                              All-Star Tickets 190
                              World Series Tickets 192
                              LCS/Division Series Tickets..........................194

Chapter 6 196
  Figures
                         Bobbin' Heads 197
                         Corinthians 199
                         Hartland 200
                         Gartlan 201
                         Starting Lineup 202
                         SAM 221
                         Sports Impressions 222
                         Salvino 224
                         Miscellaneous Figures 225

Chapter 7 227
  Plates

Chapter 8 232
  Limited Edition Cards
                         Limited Edition Cards 232
                         Baseball Medallions 236

Chapter 9 248
  Pennants & Posters
                         Pennants 248
                         Posters 251

Chapter 10 252
  Stadium Memorabilia

Chapter 11 257
  Cereal Boxes

Chapter 12 260
  Cans & Bottles

Chapter 13 264
  Baseball Games

Chapter 14 276
  Baseball Movies

Chapter 15 283
  Auction Results

Chapter 16 294
  Cards
                         Vintage/Tobacco Cards 295
                         Modern Era Trading Cards 302

About the Authors 384

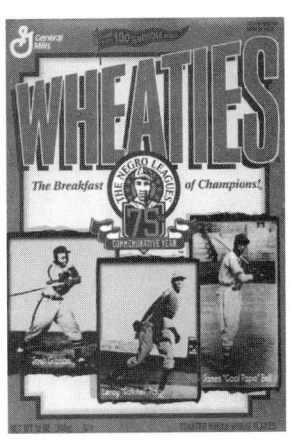

FOREWORD

By Phil Wood

Time travel. Theorized by Albert Einstein, hypothesized by H.G. Wells, a motion picture phenomenon featuring Michael J. Fox and Doc Brown's DeLorean. Who hasn't dreamt of going back in time to right a wrong, witness history, or see for themselves if they really don't make 'em like they used to?

Quantum physics holds that real time travel is possible, if only in theory—something to do with being able to travel faster than the speed of light, or something equally fantastic. Baseball collectors, however, will tell you that going back in time can be a daily occurrence, if your passion for the sport is in line with a similar passion for the hobby.

Wrap your fingers around a vintage team-signed ball from the 1950s. Let the accumulated DNA of the 25 or so men who originally handled the sphere soak through your fingertips and into your consciousness. BOOM! You're back in the days of 16 teams in the majors and "16 Tons" on the radio. "I Like Ike." The Edsel. Drive-Ins. Warren Giles runs the National League, and foreign styles rule the runways. Coke was still nothing more than "the pause that refreshes."

Slip into a 1940s vintage flannel uniform. Close your eyes. POOF! You're watching Ward Bond on the silver screen and buying war bonds in the lobby. Those old pots and pans may be headed for the scrap metal drive, but you've managed to save your Play Balls and scorecards from the paper drive. Your actual drive is now shift-free thanks to something called an "automatic" transmission.

Collecting baseball memorabilia is as old as the sport itself. We've always been a nation of collectors, even though we didn't know it until the 1970s when the so-called "organized" hobby came of age. Apparently, it's the reason God made attics and basements, shoeboxes and steamer trunks. Thousands of hard-core baseball fans discovered they were also hard-core collectors, needing only to move what was stashed away in the attic into a more prominent spot in the living room.

Unlike baseball cards, which our moms frequently dispensed with while we were either away at college or just not paying attention, the game's ephemera—i.e., stuff that didn't come wrapped with gum—made its way into desk drawers and cubbyholes. It's a peculiar irony that so much vintage material survives today, since so much of it was originally intended to be used and discarded. I'm convinced that our moms figured out if something couldn't be stuck through the spokes of our bikes with a clothes pin, it must be worth keeping.

Beginning a collection of baseball memorabilia is easy. The hard part is stopping. Once you get started, you discover potential new collectibles every day of your life. To wit:

Walk down any city street during the summer time, and you'll likely see a newspaper vending box. There's a good chance that box will have a cardboard sign stuck in the front of it, advertising the paper's coverage of the local nine. It might even picture a specific player. Already you're thinking, "Wouldn't that look great autographed and in a frame...." And while I'm not advocating thievery, suffice it to say that the newspaper people fully expect those signs to disappear. They're thrilled that you'd want to hang an ad for their product in your house. And don't forget the newspaper itself. Historic newsprint can punch up any collection of baseball memorabilia.

Go into any grocery store in North America. Walk down the aisles with your eyes open and you'll see product after product featuring baseball players or scenes on the packaging. Most are cereal boxes, but whatever the product, they're all highly collectible.

Open your mailbox. If you're a sports fan of any serious nature, you subscribe to *Sports Illustrated*, *Sport*, *Baseball Digest*, or any one of a number of time-honored national sports publications. They may seem like simple periodicals with limited shelf lives now, but hang onto them for a few years and you've suddenly got a decent collection.

Are there pitfalls to collecting baseball memorabilia? Absolutely. But the book you're holding in your hands right now will go a long way toward helping you avoid those occasional bumps in the road. Think of it as an itinerary for a journey through time, space, and the odd wad of cash.

Speaking of economics, I'd also like to suggest that if you really want to stretch those dollars, you make sure your knowledge of the game itself consists of more than knowing the basics. It's not like remembering the math tables in elementary school. Know who's in the Hall of Fame and who's not (Dizzy and Dazzy are, Daffy isn't). Know who's deceased and who's not (Jackie and Uncle Robby are, B. Robby and F. Robby aren't).

Know that the Washington Nationals were in the American League, and the Chicago American Giants were in the Negro National League. Get the picture? You'll find that your overall enjoyment of baseball is enhanced by the hobby, and vice versa.

Finally, a word about the best aspect of collecting: friendship. The relationships struck through years of collecting will last a lifetime. Literally overnight, you'll discover you've got friends all over the country. You'll realize there's a reason to shop around for the best deal on long distance calling. Before you know it, you'll have a genuine need for an address book beyond those random slips of paper in your wallet.

I'll leave you with the words a sportswriter penned long ago: "Baseball is the greatest game God ever gave man the opportunity to invent." The hobby it spawned parallels that praise.

—May 1998

INTRODUCTION

The *American Heritage Dictionary* defines memorabilia as "1. Objects valued for their historical significance. 2. Events or experiences worthy of remembrance." Of course, it's up to the individual to determine which objects are significant or which events deserve remembering. For baseball collectors, it pretty much comes down to anything and everything having to do with playing, watching, or experiencing baseball.

And we do mean anything. From vintage, store-model little league gloves to *Peanuts* comic strips featuring Charlie Brown pitching; from miniature stadium replicas to the pill bottles from Mickey Mantle's medicine cabinet; any object even remotely connected to baseball is fair game for collectors.

That makes compiling a complete guide to baseball memorabilia a tough assignment. Obviously, we couldn't include everything. The corresponding tome would require about 100 volumes and have a cover price close to the average annual income of a family of four. What we have included are some of the most interesting and popular collectibles from baseball's long and storied history. And while some readers may be disappointed by what's not here, we trust that most of you will be thrilled with the wealth of information contained in these pages.

We begin with the most comprehensive guide to baseball autographs that *Tuff Stuff* has ever produced. Autographs may be the fastest growing form of baseball collecting, and it seems that young and old alike enjoy the experience of getting a player's, manager's, or even an announcer's signature.

Our expanded autograph list includes current stars, retired players, and the best of the best, Hall of Famers. For readers who are used to *Tuff Stuff's* monthly autograph coverage, have no fear. We've added many players to the lineup, as well as listing prices for the latest autograph phenomenon, mini-helmets. Plus we've included a section on collecting signatures of some of the game's best managers, announcers, commissioners, and owners.

And just when you thought the autograph section was complete, we include listings for multi-signed items, including memorabilia autographed by members of the 500 Home Run Club, the 3,000 Hit Club, and the 300 Win Club. We give you the rundown on who belongs to each group, including newer members like Eddie Murray and Paul Molitor, as well as up-to-date pricing for balls, bats, and other items signed by all the members of several of baseball's elite milestone clubs.

Plus, we provide a comprehensive listing of team-signed baseballs from every ballclub for every year from 1920-1997. The list includes the most prominent players from each squad—the names to look for when purchasing a team-signed ball—as well as pricing information. We've also provided similar lists for All-Star game and World Series team-signed balls—from 1920 to last year's Fall Classic.

Game-worn uniforms have become a big part of baseball collecting and we have an expert to help. We called on Phil Wood, a leading authority on jersey collecting, to guide you on what to look for when purchasing authentic player uniforms.

Then we turn our attention to baseball publications. Ever wonder what all those magazines stacked in your closet might be worth? We have the answer. *Baseball Digest, Baseball Magazine, Sport, Sports Illustrated, The Sporting News, Street & Smith,* and other titles such as *Life, Time,* and *Newsweek* have followed the game of baseball from its earliest days. Look for updated and accurate prices for each baseball issue of each magazine.

Along the same line, team-issued media guides are not only a great source of information, they have also become a collectible mainstay. We include year-by-year listings for each team, for every year it has issued a media guide. The same is true for team yearbooks, another popular collectible. Again, look for complete year-by-year listings for each team.

And what collector's library would be complete without books? We dug deep to uncover a wealth of baseball literature, from relatively common favorites like Hank Aaron's *I Had A Hammer* to obscure first editions like W. P. Kinsella's *Shoeless Joe Jackson Comes to Iowa.*

The next chapter goes into detail about one of the most accessible baseball artifacts: game programs. Almost every fan buys one at the ballpark, and programs have become popular collectibles. We've included listings for regular-season programs, as well as those from every All-Star and World Series game. Of course, you can't even get into the park without a ticket, and we provide pricing for ticket stubs as well. Also, check out our additional listings for programs and tickets from some of baseball's most memorable moments, from Don Larsen's perfect World Series game to Cal Ripken Jr.'s 2,131st consecutive game.

Press Pins also have their place in the hobby. Want to know what's out there, and what they're worth on the open market? Know what a phantom press pin is? How about Hall of Fame pins? This chapter gives you the scoop.

Then we move into the world of figures, plates, and limited-edition cards and coins. Sports figures have long been a mainstay in the hobby. From the earliest Bobbin' Heads and Hartland statues; to low-end plastic favorites like Kenner Starting Lineups and Corinthian Headliners; to expensive, limited-edition, autographed pieces from Gartlan or Sports Impressions, we've got the lowdown on baseball's most collectible figurines. We've also provided information on the best limited-edition collectible baseball plates from the Bradford Exchange, Gartlan, Hackett, and Sports Impressions.

Highland Mint cards rushed into the market in the early 1990s and haven't looked back. These replicas of actual cards from manufacturers like Topps and Pinnacle are produced in bronze, silver, and gold editions. As soon as the cards took off in the hobby, Highland Mint started to produce similar coins. Like the cards, these are limited editions cast in bronze, silver, or gold. Chapter eight goes to great lengths to provide a complete checklist, production numbers, and of course, accurate pricing for items from Highland Mint, Enviromint, Upper Deck, Premier Instant Replay, and others.

The next few chapters delve into highly specialized collectibles. Pennants and posters are often found on a child's wall, but are they valuable? Some are. We'll give you all the information you need to know about collecting pennants and posters, including pricing of the best examples from major manufacturers.

One of the strangest avenues for baseball collectors is stadium memorabilia—not souvenirs you buy at the ballpark, but actual seats, signs, or even bricks from the game's most cherished arenas. Check out our list of dozens of items from different stadiums—from infield dirt to the outfield wall, we've got it all.

Chapter 11 looks at cereal box collecting. Sure, these boxes are great to chase, but can you eat the stuff? And how many are out there? Which brands have featured which players? We've got the answers.

Cans and bottles are another popular form of food-related baseball collectibles. From RC Cola to Ted Williams Root Beer, we've got listings for all of the most popular commemorative cans and bottles, as well as tips on preserving and storing your collection.

And what better way to enjoy the game of baseball than with a baseball game? This chapter provides tons of information about baseball-related board, card, and pinball games from the turn of the century to the present. And if that's not enough, check out our listing of baseball video games, from Atari's archaic 2600 Baseball to EA Sports' Triple Play '98.

Then we head to Hollywood for a comprehensive look at baseball-related movie memorabilia. As long as there have been movies, there have been baseball movies, and we provide an in-depth look at memorabilia from the earliest silent films to the latest million-dollar blockbusters. From posters to costumes to props, there's a little something for every fan of baseball films.

Our final chapter is devoted to baseball cards. Each set that we list in *Tuff Stuff* will also be listed here, along with quality ratings, descriptions, current prices, and artwork. Plus we've added prices, checklists, and artwork for dozens of pre-war card sets, including the most popular tobacco issues.

So there you have it. A complete look at baseball memorabilia from past to present. It's a lot of information to absorb, but baseball's been around a long time. So check it out and let us know what you think. We hope you enjoy this book as much as we've enjoyed bringing it to you—and as much as we all enjoy the hobby that inspired it.

Jerry Shaver
Melanie Haynie
Dennis Madigan
Jim Warren II

Chapter 1

AUTOGRAPHS

As long as there have been professional baseball players, there have been baseball fans collecting their autographs. There's something uniquely personal about an autograph—it adds an "I was there" element to the item it adorns, and often represents a collector's rare brush with a hero of the game.

Since the early days, the signatures of ballplayers have been coveted. From Babe Ruth and Walter Johnson in the first part of the century, through Mickey Mantle and Ted Williams in baseball's Golden Age, to Cal Ripken Jr. and Mark McGwire today, autographs have been a mainstay in the hobby.

However, the hobby itself has changed greatly.

Early autograph "cuts" and shouts of "Hey mister, will you sign my ball?" have been replaced by superstars sitting at tables in front of lines a mile long, signing anything and everything for fans asking "How much?"

Nevertheless, securing a superstar's "John Hancock" is often just as thrilling today as it was in the past.

THROUGH THE YEARS

Before the days of mail-order autographs and supershows, fans had to be creative in getting the sigs of their favorite players. The standard medium for this effort from the 1800s through the mid-1900s resulted in signatures called "cuts."

A "cut" is the most primitive form of autograph and is generally the easiest to find, thus the least expensive. Signatures were called cuts because they were cut from a letter, check, program, autograph book, or scrap of paper. The signature was then matted and framed with a photo of the player. Autographs of legendary players from the early part of the century like Babe Ruth and Lou Gehrig are most often found on cuts.

Beyond cuts, there are numerous other items that have become particular favorites of autograph collectors:

• Before the autograph explosion of the 1980s, 3x5 index cards were popular items. An easy alternative to bulky baseballs and bats, index cards have remained prominent in the hobby. Similar to cuts, signed index cards are great for framing with photos or preserving in an album. Look for older players to be more prominent on index cards and the values to be modestly higher than cut signatures.

• 8x10 photos are among the autograph standards for today's athletes. The clarity of the photo is important for older players, and larger photos (16x20 and up) may command a premium. Photos can be action shots or portraits—both are collectible. Signed photos are easy to preserve in albums or frame and display.

• If there's been one staple in the autograph market throughout the century, an official league baseball is it. Whether it's signed by only one player or by an entire team, an autographed baseball makes for a terrific collectible. Of all the balls used in America's favorite sports, baseballs are the best for autographs—they're small enough to display but large enough to write on, have a smooth writing surface, and work well with a ballpoint pen.

• With the onslaught of autograph shows in the late 1980s, bats became popular high-end items among autograph collectors. Bats can be attractively displayed, but should be kept in clear plastic tubes to protect both the wood and the sig. Most athletes on the show circuit charge more to sign a bat than they do for other items, so the values for signed bats tend to rise as well.

• From 1946–64, the Hall of Fame issued commemorative black-and-white postcards of each of its members. Each postcard pictures a player's plaque that hangs on the wall in Cooperstown. Because these cards were issued for such a limited time, they're tough to find autographed and command a steep price.

After 1964, the Hall of Fame replaced the black-and-white plaque cards with gold editions. These postcards are much more plentiful and are easily preserved in plastic sleeves.

• Signed Perez-Steele Postcards are hot items with limited edition collectors. Only 10,000 postcards are produced of each player. The first set was issued in 1980, and new cards are released every two years for the Hall of Fame's newest inductees. The number of autographed postcards will vary depending on the player.

• Signed Perez-Steele Great Moments were first introduced in 1985 with production runs of 5,000 sets, which are periodically updated. These cards are larger than regular Perez-Steele Postcards and feature action photography. Eight series of cards are in circulation, with the last being produced in 1992.

• Signed Perez-Steele Celebration Cards were produced to commemorate the 50th anniversary of the Hall of Fame in 1989. A total of 10,000 44-card sets were produced. Players in the set include Hank Aaron, Mickey Mantle, and Ted Williams.

BUILDING A COLLECTION

The best way to get autographs is still to catch players at the ballpark. Players often sign before and after games. Your best bet is to have your items ready, hang around close to the dugout or bullpen, and most of all, be polite.

If you can't regularly get to the ballpark, you'll find many retired and current players signing autographs at card shows. Yes, you'll usually have to pay a fee for the autograph, but this is still a great way to build your collection. You get a chance to spend a few moments with the player, and by getting the autograph in person, you have no doubts about its authenticity.

A third way to get signatures is through the mail. Many players still sign via the mail, provided you include a self-addressed, stamped envelope (SASE) with your (polite) request. Some players charge a fee or ask for a donation to a charity or cause they're involved with in exchange for the autograph. Be patient, be prepared for some setbacks, and don't blindly send off your most treasured collectibles—many players take a while (several months) to answer their mail, and sometimes your requests will be returned unsigned or not returned at all.

As with baseball cards, networking and trading are also great ways to enhance your autograph collection. Swap signatures with friends or become part of a group that seeks out hard-to-find autographs. Use the Internet to your advantage—it's a great way to connect with autograph collectors around the world.

If you really want to get serious about autographs, head to Florida or Arizona in February and March. Spring training is a great place to interact with players and grab multiple signatures. Players are usually more relaxed and are more willing to take the time to sign for fans. This is also a great opportunity to put together team-signed baseballs and secure autographs from former players that may be instructors or coaches during the spring.

CERTIFICATES OF AUTHENTICITY

If you go to a show signing, more often than not the promoter will supply a Certificate of Authenticity with the item, verifying that the autograph is real.

Many items that are bought from outside sources like catalogs or mail-order dealers also come with certificates of authenticity. It's best to remember, though, that a certificate is only as legitimate as the person providing

it. Certificates can be forged just as easily as the autographs themselves.

This doesn't mean you should ignore the certificates when they're offered, but the best advice is to do business with someone you know and trust. If this isn't possible, do some research. Learn what a certain player's autograph looks like, and compare it to the one you're considering. Forgeries are the most serious problem in the autograph hobby, and collectors must proceed with caution.

The bigger the star, the greater the temptation for an unscrupulous dealer to sell fakes. Big-name players like Mickey Mantle and Ted Williams have their names forged so often and with such accuracy that it's virtually impossible to tell the difference between a fake and the real deal.

Forgeries are nothing new to the hobby. It's a poorly-kept secret that bat boys and clubhouse attendants forged autographs for the stars as long as 50 years ago. Since then, autopens, rubber stamps, and other instruments have contributed to the problem. If you're not getting your autographs in person, be selective and make sure you trust the person with whom you are dealing. If the dealer can't remember where the gem came from, or has a story that sounds too good to be true, hold on to your cash.

STORAGE

Now that you've amassed an autograph collection, you need to protect and display the items you've had signed.

Signed baseballs are best kept and displayed in cubes or some type of holder designed for multiple baseballs. Cubes are ideal for team-signed balls, allowing you to view all sides of the ball.

Photos, cards, magazines, and other flat items are best kept in binders with clear plastic sleeves, which protect your collection while allowing you to show it off at the same time.

Bats are a little tougher to display because of their size. You should put autographed bats in clear plastic tubes. Racks have been designed to display large items like bats, but they can still be difficult to show.

Autographed hats, jerseys, and other types of equipment need to be kept in cases, though their size hinders their attractiveness for display purposes. No matter what you want to display, keep the autographs out of direct sunlight and extreme heat, which can cause that signatures to fade over time.

One last note. Autographs are valuable and need to be treated that way. Insure your collection just as you would other valuable keepsakes in your home. If the unthinkable ever happens, you'll be glad you did.

OFFICIAL BASEBALLS

All official American League and National League baseballs include a signature stamp of the league president. This is especially important for authenticating older autographs. For example, it would be impossible for Babe Ruth to have signed an American League baseball with Joseph E. Cronin's signature stamped on it, because Cronin didn't become league president until 1959, 23 years after Ruth died. Below is a complete list of league presidents and the time they served. Any baseballs not including these names are considered unofficial balls.

American League

(1901-1927) Byron B. Johnson
(1927-1931) Ernest S. Barnard
(1931-1959) William Harridge
(1959-1973) Joseph E. Cronin
(1974-1983) Leland S. McPhail Jr.
(1984-1993) Robert W. Brown
(1994-present) Gene Budig

National League

(1918-1934) John A. Heydler
(1934-1951) Ford C. Frick
(1951-1969) Warren C. Giles
(1970-1986) Charles S. Feeney
(1986-1989) A. Bartlett Giamatti
(1989-1993) William D. White
(1994-present) Leonard Coleman

AUTOGRAPH LEGEND

1. Signature—Signatures have value even if they aren't on items considered collectible or suitable for display. They are often referred to as "cuts" because collectors cut them from original sources (documents, autograph books, etc.) and matte/frame them along with a photo or other attractive item. Values are for clear, uninscribed signatures in ink.

2. Signed 3x5 cards—Before the explosive '80s, collecting signatures on 3x5 cards was extremely popular. Index cards have been used for autographs since the early 1900s. Values decrease 15-25 percent for signatures on the lined side of the card.

3. Signed Photo—8x10 color photos are the standard for modern players. For older players, the clarity and quality of the photograph and signature are more important than the size. Values are for uninscribed photos with clear signatures in ink.

4. Signed Baseball—Prices for modern players are based on single-signed official balls in Near Mint condition with the signatures in ballpoint pen on the sweet spot. Pre-1940s prices are based on single-signed (in ink) balls, Excellent or better. Most single-signed balls from the past, except Ruth, are signed on a side panel. Clarity and boldness of the signature and condition of the ball are factors for grading.

5. Signed Bats—This medium was not widely available to autograph collectors until players began signing at card shows. Values are for signed game-model bats; deduct 15-20 percent for a generic, no-name bat.

6. Signed Black and White Plaques—Postcards issued by the Hall of Fame picturing the member's Cooperstown plaque. The B&Ws were issued during the years 1946-1964. Values are for front-signed plaques.

7. Signed Gold Plaques—Modern gold or yellow postcards issued by the Hall. Similar to the B&W postcards, these replaced the B&Ws in 1964 and the HOF has continued to print them to date. Most collectors prefer the signature across the top of the front of the card, and values are for cards signed in this manner.

8. Signed Perez-Steele Postcards—Only 10,000 of these attractive postcards were printed of each Hall of Famer. Of course, the number that have been autographed will vary from player to player. Perez-Steele Galleries issues updates as new members are inducted into the Hall.

9. Signed Perez-Steele Great Moments—First offered in 1985 with 5,000 numbered sets, these cards are periodically updated. The cards are oversized and typically show the player in action.

10. Signed Perez-Steele Celebration Cards—These were offered in 1989 to celebrate the 50th anniversary of the Hall of Fame. There were 10,000 sets produced, with 44 boxed cards completing the set. An attractive book was included as part of the set.

11. Store model glove—Player model gloves that were sold at retail outlets and made in the USA, based on excellent condition. A slight percentage decrease for child sizes and a slight increase for models matching the hand of the player (left-handed glove for left-handed player).

12. Mini-helmets—In 1997, Riddell released replica mini-helmets for all 30 Major League teams. These helmets have quickly become a mainstay in the autograph hobby. Prices are for helmets signed in either Sharpie or paint pen.

HALL OF FAME AUTOGRAPHS

Any baseball autograph collection worth its salt includes players who have reached the Hall of Fame. Why? Because those players represent the best of the best, the most successful (and usually the most popular) players to ever play the game.

When it comes to the sigs of Hall of Famers, some are naturally harder to find than others. The toughest ones are the players who passed away many years ago, including Cap Anson, Jake Beckley, Dan Brouthers, and Alexander Cartwright. It's virtually impossible to find these players' autographs on anything but a cut or a 3x5 card. Collectors pay a steep premium for these players, but their addition will enhance any collection.

At the other end of the spectrum are the handful of living Hall of Famers who appear frequently on the autograph show circuit. In fact, many of these players will go on to earn far more for signing at shows than they ever did as players. Regulars on the show loop include Bob Feller, Hank Aaron, Ernie Banks, and Brooks Robinson. These numerous appearances keep the autograph values somewhat moderate for players with the impeccable credentials of an Aaron or a Banks.

Many collectors also write to players via the Hall of Fame or a foundation address. The success rate for certain players is good, especially if you donate money to their charities. Other players, like Joe DiMaggio and Ted Williams, don't sign through the mail, period. If you do choose to send something through the mail, be patient. Some players can take a while to respond.

N/A indicates that the item for a player isn't known to exist.
* indicates that an item is known or suspected to exist but no pricing information is available.

Aaron, Hank (1934-)

Year inducted:	1982
Cut:	$15.00
3x5 card:	20.00
Photo:	30.00
Ball:	45.00
Bat:	175.00
B&W Plaque:	N/A
Gold Plaque:	20.00
Signed Perez-Steele:	30.00
Unsigned Perez-Steele:	15.00
Great Moments:	30.00
Celebration Card:	25.00
Store model glove:	65.00
Mini-helmet:	45.00

Alexander, Grover Cleveland (1887-1950)

Year Inducted:	1938
Cut:	$300.00
3x5 card:	450.00
Photo:	900.00
Ball:	5,000.00
Bat:	N/A
B&W Plaque:	1,000.00
Gold Plaque:	N/A
Signed Perez-Steele:	N/A
Unsigned Perez-Steele:	10.00
Great Moments:	N/A
Celebration Card:	N/A
Store model glove:	400.00
Mini-helmet:	N/A

Alston, Walter (1911-1984)

Year Inducted:	1983
Cut:	$15.00
3x5 card:	40.00
Photo:	150.00
Ball:	700.00
Bat:	N/A
B&W Plaque:	N/A
Gold Plaque:	85.00
Signed Perez-Steele:	750.00
Unsigned Perez-Steele:	20.00
Great Moments:	N/A
Celebration Card:	N/A
Store model glove:	N/A
Mini-helmet:	N/A

Anson, Adrian "Cap" (1852-1922)

Year Inducted:	1939
Cut:	$1,000.00
3x5 card:	1,500.00
Photo:	3,500.00
Ball:	17,000.00
Bat:	N/A
B&W Plaque:	N/A
Gold Plaque:	N/A
Signed Perez-Steele:	N/A
Unsigned Perez-Steele:	5.00
Great Moments:	N/A
Celebration Card:	N/A
Store model glove:	N/A
Mini-helmet:	N/A

Aparicio, Luis (1934-)

Year Inducted:	1984
Cut:	$5.00
3x5 card:	8.00
Photo:	15.00
Ball:	25.00
Bat:	100.00
B&W Plaque:	N/A
Gold Plaque:	12.00
Signed Perez-Steele:	20.00
Unsigned Perez-Steele:	15.00
Great Moments:	20.00
Celebration Card:	20.00
Store model glove:	50.00
Mini-helmet:	25.00

Appling, Luke (1909-1991)

Year Inducted:	1964
Cut:	$5.00
3x5 card:	10.00
Photo:	30.00
Ball:	75.00
Bat:	200.00
B&W Plaque:	N/A
Gold Plaque:	15.00
Signed Perez-Steele:	40.00
Unsigned Perez-Steele:	20.00
Great Moments:	N/A
Celebration Card:	N/A
Store model glove:	100.00
Mini-helmet:	N/A

Ashburn, Richie (1927-1997)

Year Inducted:	1995
Cut:	$5.00
3x5 card:	10.00
Photo:	15.00
Ball:	25.00
Bat:	85.00
B&W Plaque:	N/A
Gold Plaque:	12.00
Signed Perez-Steele:	30.00
Unsigned Perez-Steele:	10.00
Great Moments:	N/A
Celebration Card:	N/A
Store model glove:	50.00
Mini-helmet:	25.00

Averill, Earl (1902-1983)

Year Inducted:	1975
Cut:	$5.00
3x5 card:	15.00
Photo:	85.00
Ball:	450.00
Bat:	N/A
B&W Plaque:	N/A
Gold Plaque:	25.00
Signed Perez-Steele:	450.00
Unsigned Perez-Steele:	8.00
Great Moments:	N/A
Celebration Card:	N/A
Store model glove:	100.00
Mini-helmet:	N/A

Baker, Frank "Home Run" (1886-1963)

Year Inducted:	1955
Cut:	$100.00
3x5 card:	250.00
Photo:	800.00
Ball:	3,600.00
Bat:	N/A
B&W Plaque:	700.00
Gold Plaque:	N/A
Signed Perez-Steele:	N/A
Unsigned Perez-Steele:	5.00
Great Moments:	N/A
Celebration Card:	N/A
Store model glove:	1,200.00
Mini-helmet:	N/A

Bancroft, Dave (1891-1972)

Year Inducted:	1971
Cut:	$50.00
3x5 card:	100.00
Photo:	250.00
Ball:	2,800.00
Bat:	N/A
B&W Plaque:	N/A
Gold Plaque:	600.00
Signed Perez-Steele:	N/A
Unsigned Perez-Steele:	5.00
Great Moments:	N/A
Celebration Card:	N/A
Store model glove:	650.00
Mini-helmet:	N/A

Banks, Ernie (1931-)

Year Inducted:	1977
Cut:	$10.00
3x5 card:	15.00
Photo:	25.00
Ball:	35.00
Bat:	135.00
B&W Plaque:	N/A
Gold Plaque:	15.00
Signed Perez-Steele:	30.00
Unsigned Perez-Steele:	15.00
Great Moments:	25.00
Celebration Card:	20.00
Store model glove:	85.00
Mini-helmet:	50.00

Barlick, Al (1915-1995)

Year Inducted:	1989
Cut:	$8.00
3x5 card:	10.00
Photo:	15.00
Ball:	30.00
Bat:	100.00
B&W Plaque:	N/A
Gold Plaque:	12.00
Signed Perez-Steele:	20.00
Unsigned Perez-Steele:	5.00
Great Moments:	20.00
Celebration Card:	N/A
Store model glove:	N/A
Mini-helmet:	N/A

Barrow, Ed (1868-1953)

Year Inducted:	1953
Cut:	$60.00
3x5 card:	160.00
Photo:	400.00
Ball:	3,300.00
Bat:	N/A
B&W Plaque:	1,700.00
Gold Plaque:	N/A
Signed Perez-Steele:	N/A
Unsigned Perez-Steele:	5.00
Great Moments:	N/A
Celebration Card:	N/A
Store model glove:	N/A
Mini-helmet:	N/A

Beckley, Jake (1867-1918)

Year Inducted:	1971
Cut:	$1,200.00
3x5 card:	1,700.00
Photo:	3,500.00
Ball:	N/A
Bat:	N/A
B&W Plaque:	N/A
Gold Plaque:	N/A
Signed Perez-Steele:	N/A
Unsigned Perez-Steele:	5.00
Great Moments:	N/A
Celebration Card:	N/A
Store model glove:	N/A
Mini-helmet:	N/A

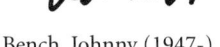

Bell, James "Cool Papa" (1903-1991)

Year Inducted:	1974
Cut:	$10.00
3x5 card:	15.00
Photo:	60.00
Ball:	175.00
Bat:	400.00
B&W Plaque:	N/A
Gold Plaque:	30.00
Signed Perez-Steele:	80.00
Unsigned Perez-Steele:	25.00
Great Moments:	80.00
Celebration Card:	50.00
Store model glove:	600.00
Mini-helmet:	N/A

Bench, Johnny (1947-)

Year Inducted:	1989
Cut:	$10.00
3x5 card:	15.00
Photo:	28.00
Ball:	35.00
Bat:	130.00
B&W Plaque:	N/A
Gold Plaque:	22.00
Signed Perez-Steele:	30.00
Unsigned Perez-Steele:	5.00
Great Moments:	30.00
Celebration Card:	30.00
Store model glove:	50.00
Mini-helmet:	45.00

Bender, Charles "Chief" (1884-1954)

Year Inducted:	1953
Cut:	$100.00
3x5 card:	250.00
Photo:	450.00
Ball:	3,500.00
Bat:	N/A
B&W Plaque:	1,200.00
Gold Plaque:	N/A
Signed Perez-Steele:	N/A
Unsigned Perez-Steele:	5.00
Great Moments:	N/A
Celebration Card:	N/A
Store model glove:	800.00
Mini-helmet:	N/A

Berra, Yogi (1925-)

Year Inducted:	1972
Cut:	$8.00
3x5 card:	10.00
Photo:	25.00
Ball:	35.00
Bat:	175.00
B&W Plaque:	N/A
Gold Plaque:	18.00
Signed Perez-Steele:	30.00
Unsigned Perez-Steele:	15.00
Great Moments:	25.00
Celebration Card:	20.00
Store model glove:	85.00
Mini-helmet:	40.00

Bottomley, Jim (1900-1959)

Year Inducted:	1974
Cut:	$150.00
3x5 card:	300.00
Photo:	400.00
Ball:	2,700.00
Bat:	N/A
B&W Plaque:	N/A
Gold Plaque:	N/A
Signed Perez-Steele:	N/A
Unsigned Perez-Steele:	5.00
Great Moments:	N/A
Celebration Card:	N/A
Store model glove:	400.00
Mini-helmet:	N/A

Boudreau, Lou (1917-)

Year Inducted:	1970
Cut:	$8.00
3x5 card:	10.00
Photo:	15.00
Ball:	25.00
Bat:	100.00
B&W Plaque:	N/A
Gold Plaque:	6.00
Signed Perez-Steele:	25.00
Unsigned Perez-Steele:	15.00
Great Moments:	20.00
Celebration Card:	15.00
Store model glove:	50.00
Mini-helmet:	35.00

Bresnahan, Roger (1879-1944)

Year Inducted:	1945
Cut:	$500.00
3x5 card:	650.00
Photo:	1,200.00
Ball:	6,000.00
Bat:	N/A
B&W Plaque:	N/A
Gold Plaque:	N/A
Signed Perez-Steele:	N/A
Unsigned Perez-Steele:	5.00
Great Moments:	N/A
Celebration Card:	N/A
Store model glove:	1,200.00
Mini-helmet:	N/A

Brock, Lou (1939-)

Year Inducted:	1985
Cut:	$8.00
3x5 card:	10.00
Photo:	20.00
Ball:	25.00
Bat:	125.00
B&W Plaque:	N/A
Gold Plaque:	10.00
Signed Perez-Steele:	20.00
Unsigned Perez-Steele:	15.00
Great Moments:	20.00
Celebration Card:	N/A
Store model glove:	150.00
Mini-helmet:	40.00

Brouthers, Dan (1858-1932)

Year Inducted:	1945
Cut:	$1,200.00
3x5 card:	1,700.00
Photo:	5,000.00
Ball:	8,000.00
Bat:	N/A
B&W Plaque:	N/A
Gold Plaque:	N/A
Signed Perez-Steele:	N/A
Unsigned Perez-Steele:	5.00
Great Moments:	N/A
Celebration Card:	N/A
Store model glove:	N/A
Mini-helmet:	N/A

Brown, Mordecai "Three Finger" (1876-1948)

Year Inducted:	1949
Cut:	$300.00
3x5 card:	500.00
Photo:	900.00
Ball:	5,500.00
Bat:	N/A
B&W Plaque:	N/A
Gold Plaque:	N/A
Signed Perez-Steele:	N/A
Unsigned Perez-Steele:	5.00
Great Moments:	N/A
Celebration Card:	N/A
Store model glove:	1,200.00
Mini-helmet:	N/A

Bulkeley, Morgan (1837-1922)

Year Inducted:	1937
Cut:	$800.00
3x5 card:	1,200.00
Photo:	4,000.00
Ball:	N/A
Bat:	N/A
B&W Plaque:	N/A
Gold Palque:	N/A
Signed Perez-Steele:	N/A
Unsigned Perez-Steele:	5.00
Great Moments:	N/A
Celebration Card:	N/A
Store model glove:	N/A
Mini-helmet:	N/A

Bunning, Jim (1931-)

Year Inducted:	1996
Cut:	$5.00
3x5 card:	7.00
Photo:	20.00
Ball:	35.00
Bat:	75.00
B&W Plaque:	N/A
Gold Plaque:	15.00
Signed Perez-Steele:	30.00
Unsigned Perez-Steele:	10.00
Great Moments:	*
Celebration Card:	*
Store model glove:	40.00
Mini-helmet:	40.00

Burkett, Jesse (1868-1953)

Year Inducted:	1946
Cut:	$450.00
3x5 card:	700.00
Photo:	1,000.00
Ball:	5,500.00
Bat:	N/A
B&W Plaque:	1,500.00
Gold Plaque:	N/A
Signed Perez-Steele:	N/A
Unsigned Perez-Steele:	5.00
Great Moments:	N/A
Celebration Card:	N/A
Store model glove:	*
Mini-helmet:	N/A

Campanella, Roy (1921-1993)

Year Inducted:	1969
Cut:	$300.00
3x5 card:	400.00
Photo:	700.00
Ball:	3,500.00
Bat:	N/A
B&W Plaque:	N/A
Gold Plaque:	N/A
Signed Perez-Steele:	N/A
Unsigned Peerz Steele:	N/A
Great Moments:	N/A
Celebration Card:	N/A
Store model glove:	85.00
Mini-helmet:	N/A

Campanella, Roy (Post-accident)

Year Inducted:	1969
Cut:	$100.00
3x5 card:	150.00
Photo:	250.00
Ball:	400.00
Bat:	600.00
B&W Plaque:	N/A
Gold Plaque:	250.00
Signed Perez-Steele:	175.00
Unsigned Perez-Steele:	30.00
Great Moments:	200.00
Celebration Card:	200.00
Store model glove:	N/A
Mini-helmet:	N/A

Carew, Rod (1945-)

Year Inducted:	1991
Cut:	$7.00
3x5 card:	10.00
Photo:	20.00
Ball:	28.00
Bat:	125.00
B&W Plaque:	N/A
Gold Plaque:	20.00
Signed Perez-Steele:	25.00
Unsigned Perez-Steele:	5.00
Great Moments:	25.00
Celebration Card:	N/A
Store model glove:	85.00
Mini-helmet:	40.00

Carey, Max (1890-1976)

Year Inducted:	1961
Cut:	$7.00
3x5 card:	15.00
Photo:	125.00
Ball:	750.00
Bat:	N/A
B&W Plaque:	75.00
Gold Plaque:	60.00
Signed Perez-Steele:	N/A
Unsigned Perez-Steele:	5.00
Great Moments:	N/A
Celebration Card:	N/A
Store model glove:	350.00
Mini-helmet:	N/A

Carlton, Steve (1944-)

Year Inducted:	1994
Cut:	$7.00
3x5 card:	10.00
Photo:	20.00
Ball:	25.00
Bat:	90.00
B&W Plaque:	N/A
Gold Plaque:	25.00
Signed Perez-Steele:	30.00
Unsigned Perez-Steele:	8.00
Great Moments:	N/A
Celebration Card:	N/A
Store model glove:	85.00
Mini-helmet:	40.00

Cartwright, Alexander (1820-1892)

Year Inducted:	1938
Cut:	$600.00
3x5 card:	750.00
Photo:	3,000.00
Ball:	N/A
Bat:	N/A
B&W Plaque:	N/A
Gold Plaque:	N/A
Signed Perez-Steele:	N/A
Unsigned Perez-Steele:	5.00
Great Moments:	N/A
Celebration Card:	N/A
Store model glove:	N/A
Mini-helmet:	N/A

Chadwick, Henry (1824-1908)

Year Inducted:	1938
Cut:	$1,000.00
3x5 card:	1,200.00
Photo:	3,200.00
Ball:	N/A
Bat:	N/A
B&W Plaque:	N/A
Gold Plaque:	N/A
Signed Perez-Steele:	N/A
Unsigned Perez-Steele:	5.00
Great Moments:	N/A
Celebration Card:	N/A
Store model glove:	N/A
Mini-helmet:	N/A

Chance, Frank (1877-1924)

Year Inducted:	1946
Cut:	$600.00
3x5 card:	750.00
Photo:	2,000.00
Ball:	7,000.00
Bat:	N/A
B&W Plaque:	N/A
Gold Plaque:	N/A
Signed Perez-Steele:	N/A
Unsigned Perez-Steele:	5.00
Great Moments:	N/A
Celebration Card:	N/A
Store model glove:	1,200.00
Mini-helmet:	N/A

Chandler, A.B. "Happy" (1898-1991)

Year Inducted:	1982
Cut:	$8.00
3x5 card:	12.00
Photo:	35.00
Ball:	100.00
Bat:	300.00
B&W Plaque:	N/A
Gold Plaque:	18.00
Signed Perez-Steele:	20.00
Unsigned Perez-Steele:	20.00
Great Moments:	N/A
Celebration Card:	20.00
Store model glove:	N/A
Mini-helmet:	N/A

Oscar Charleston (signature)

Charleston, Oscar (1896-1954)

Year Inducted:	1976
Cut:	$600.00
3x5 card:	1,000.00
Photo:	3,000.00
Ball:	7,000.00
Bat:	N/A
B&W Plaque:	N/A
Gold Plaque:	N/A
Signed Perez-Steele:	N/A
Unsigned Perez-Steele:	5.00
Great Moments:	N/A
Celebration Card:	N/A
Store model glove:	800.00
Mini-helmet:	N/A

Chesbro, Jack (1874-1931)

Year Inducted:	1946
Cut:	$600.00
3x5 card:	750.00
Photo:	2,000.00
Ball:	10,000.00
Bat:	N/A
B&W Plaque:	N/A
Gold Plaque:	N/A
Signed Perez-Steele:	N/A
Unsigned Perez-Steele:	5.00
Great Moments:	N/A
Celebration Card:	N/A
Store model glove:	1,200.00
Mini-helmet:	N/A

Clarke, Fred (1872-1960)

Year Inducted:	1945
Cut:	$100.00
3x5 card:	200.00
Photo:	400.00
Ball:	3,000.00
Bat:	N/A
B&W Plaque:	350.00
Gold Plaque:	N/A
Signed Perez-Steele:	N/A
Unsigned Perez-Steele:	5.00
Great Moments:	N/A
Celebration Card:	N/A
Store model glove:	*
Mini-helmet:	N/A

Clarkson, John (1861-1909)

Year Inducted:	1963
Cut:	$1,200.00
3x5 card:	2,000.00
Photo:	2,500.00
Ball:	N/A
Bat:	N/A
B&W Plaque:	N/A
Gold Plaque:	N/A
Signed Perez-Steele:	N/A
Unsigned Perez-Steele:	5.00
Great Moments:	N/A
Celebration Card:	N/A
Store model glove:	*
Mini-helmet:	N/A

Roberto Clemente (signature)

Clemente, Roberto (1934-1972)

Year Inducted:	1973
Cut:	$150.00
3x5 card:	200.00
Photo:	350.00
Ball:	2,200.00
Bat:	N/A
B&W Plaque:	N/A
Gold Plaque:	N/A
Signed Perez-Steele:	N/A
Unsigned Perez-Steele:	45.00
Great Moments:	N/A
Celebration Card:	N/A
Store model glove:	60.00
Mini-helmet:	N/A

Cobb, Ty (1886-1961)

Year Inducted:	1936
Cut:	$300.00
3x5 card:	400.00
Photo:	1,200.00
Ball:	2,600.00
Bat:	N/A
B&W Plaque:	1,000.00
Gold Plaque:	N/A
Signed Perez-Steele:	N/A
Unsigned Perez-Steele:	60.00
Great Moments:	N/A
Celebration Card:	N/A
Store model glove:	1,500.00
Mini-helmet:	N/A

Cochrane, Mickey (1903-1962)

Year Inducted:	1947
Cut:	$75.00
3x5 card:	150.00
Photo:	350.00
Ball:	2,000.00
Bat:	N/A
B&W Plaque:	500.00
Gold Plaque:	N/A
Signed Perez-Steele:	N/A
Unsigned Perez-Steele:	10.00
Great Moments:	N/A
Celebration Card:	N/A
Store model glove:	350.00
Mini-helmet:	N/A

Collins, Eddie (1887-1951)

Year Inducted:	1939
Cut:	$100.00
3x5 card:	175.00
Photo:	400.00
Ball:	5,000.00
Bat:	N/A
B&W Plaque:	550.00
Gold Plaque:	N/A
Signed Perez-Steele:	N/A
Unsigned Perez-Steele:	5.00
Great Moments:	N/A
Celebration Card:	N/A
Store model glove:	550.00
Mini-helmet:	N/A

Collins, Jimmy (1870-1943)

Year Inducted:	1945
Cut:	$500.00
3x5 card:	950.00
Photo:	1,500.00
Ball:	6,000.00
Bat:	N/A
B&W Plaque:	N/A
Gold Plaque:	N/A
Signed Perez-Steele:	N/A
Unsigned Perez-Steele:	5.00
Great Moments:	N/A
Celebration Card:	N/A
Store model glove:	800.00
Mini-helmet:	N/A

Combs, Earle (1899-1976)

Year Inducted:	1970
Cut:	$15.00
3x5 card	40.00
Photo:	350.00
Ball:	2,000.00
Bat:	N/A
B&W Plaque:	N/A
Gold Plaque:	100.00
Signed Perez-Steele:	N/A
Unsigned Perez-Steele:	10.00
Great Moments:	N/A
Celebration Card:	N/A
Store model glove:	400.00
Mini-helmet:	N/A

Comiskey, Charles (1859-1931)

Year Inducted:	1939
Cut:	$375.00
3x5 card:	450.00
Photo:	1,200.00
Ball:	8,000.00
Bat:	N/A
B&W Plaque:	N/A
Gold Plaque:	N/A
Signed Perez-Steele:	N/A
Unsigned Perez-Steele:	5.00
Great Moments:	N/A
Celebration Card:	N/A
Store model glove:	N/A
Mini-helmet:	N/A

Conlan, Jocko (1899-1989)

Year Inducted:	1974
Cut:	$5.00
3x5 card:	10.00
Photo:	35.00
Ball:	90.00
Bat:	250.00
B&W Plaque:	N/A
Gold Plaque:	15.00
Signed Perez-Steele:	60.00
Unsigned Perez-Steele:	10.00
Great Moments:	N/A
Celebration Card:	150.00
Store model glove:	N/A
Mini-helmet:	N/A

Connolly, Tom (1870-1961)

Year Inducted:	1953
Cut:	$275.00
3x5 card:	350.00
Photo:	900.00
Ball:	7,000.00
Bat:	N/A
B&W Plaque:	1,200.00
Gold Plaque:	N/A
Signed Perez-Steele:	N/A
Unsigned Perez-Steele:	5.00
Great Moments:	N/A
Celebration Card:	N/A
Store model glove:	N/A
Mini-helmet:	N/A

Connor, Roger (1857-1931)

Year Inducted:	1976
Cut:	$1,000.00
3x5 card:	1,700.00
Photo:	2,500.00
Ball:	8,000.00
Bat:	N/A
B&W Plaque:	N/A
Gold Plaque:	N/A
Signed Perez-Steele:	N/A
Unsigned Perez-Steele:	5.00
Great Moments:	N/A
Celebration Card:	N/A
Store model glove:	N/A
Mini-helmet:	N/A

Coveleski, Stan (1889-1984)

Year Inducted:	1969
Cut:	$5.00
3x5 card:	10.00
Photo:	80.00
Ball:	450.00
Bat:	*
B&W Plaque:	N/A
Gold Plaque:	20.00
Signed Perez-Steele:	300.00
Unsigned Perez-Steele:	10.00
Great Moments:	N/A
Celebration Card:	N/A
Store model glove:	800.00
Mini-helmet:	N/A

Crawford, Sam (1880-1968)

Year Inducted:	1957
Cut:	$65.00
3x5 card	90.00
Photo:	250.00
Ball:	2,500.00
Bat:	N/A
B&W Plaque:	250.00
Gold Plaque:	200.00
Signed Perez-Steele:	N/A
Unsigned Perez-Steele:	5.00
Great Moments:	N/A
Celebration Card:	N/A
Store model glove:	600.00
Mini-helmet:	N/A

Cronin, Joe (1906-1984)

Year Inducted:	1956
Cut:	$10.00
3x5 card:	25.00
Photo:	100.00
Ball:	550.00
Bat:	*
B&W Plaque:	60.00
Gold Plaque:	35.00
Signed Perez-Steele:	700.00
Unsigned Perez-Steele:	20.00
Great Moments:	N/A
Celebration Card:	N/A
Store model glove:	100.00
Mini-helmet:	N/A

Cummings, Candy (1848-1924)

Year Inducted:	1939
Cut:	$1,500.00
3x5 card:	1,700.00
Photo:	4,500.00
Ball:	N/A
Bat:	N/A
B&W Plaque:	N/A
Gold Plaque:	N/A
Signed Perez-Steele:	N/A
Unsigned Perez-Steele:	5.00
Great Moments:	N/A
Celebration Card:	N/A
Store model glove:	N/A
Mini-helmet:	N/A

Cuyler, Kiki (1899-1950)

Year Inducted:	1968
Cut:	$150.00
3x5 card:	175.00
Photo:	400.00
Ball:	3,500.00
Bat:	N/A
B&W Plaque:	N/A
Gold Plaque:	N/A
Signed Perez-Steele:	N/A
Unsigned Perez-Steele:	5.00
Great Moments:	N/A
Celebration Card:	N/A
Store model glove:	150.00
Mini-helmet:	N/A

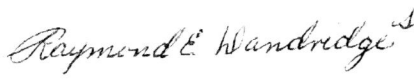

Dandridge, Ray (1913-1994)

Year Inducted:	1987
Cut:	$5.00
3x5 card:	10.00
Photo:	20.00
Ball:	60.00
Bat:	175.00
B&W Plaque:	N/A
Gold Plaque:	12.00
Signed Perez-Steele:	20.00
Unsigned Perez-Steele:	5.00
Great Moments:	20.00
Celebration Card:	20.00
Store model glove:	650.00
Mini-helmet:	N/A

Day, Leon (1916-1995)

Year Inducted:	1995
Cut:	$10.00
3x5 card:	20.00
Photo:	50.00
Ball:	100.00
Bat:	125.00
B&W Plaque:	N/A
Gold Plaque:	N/A
Signed Perez-Steele:	N/A
Unsigned Perez-Steele:	10.00
Great Moments:	N/A
Celebration Card:	N/A
Store model glove	*
Mini-helmet:	N/A

Dean, Jay "Dizzy" (1911-1974)

Year Inducted:	1953
Cut:	$75.00
3x5 card:	100.00
Photo:	275.00
Ball:	800.00
Bat:	N/A
B&W Plaque:	150.00
Gold Plaque:	135.00
Signed Perez-Steele:	N/A
Unsigned Perez-Steele:	40.00
Great Moments:	N/A
Celebration Card:	N/A
Store model glove:	600.00
Mini-helmet:	N/A

Delahanty, Ed (1867-1903)

Year Inducted:	1945
Cut:	$1,500.00
3x5 card:	2,000.00
Photo:	4,000.00
Ball:	N/A
Bat:	N/A
B&W Plaque:	N/A
Gold Plaque:	N/A
Signed Perez-Steele:	N/A
Unsigned Perez-Steele:	5.00
Great Moments:	N/A
Celebration Card:	N/A
Store model glove:	800.00
Mini-helmet:	N/A

Dickey, Bill (1907-1993)

Year Inducted:	1954
Cut:	$8.00
3x5 card:	15.00
Photo:	50.00
Ball:	150.00
Bat:	500.00
B&W Plaque:	45.00
Gold Plaque:	35.00
Signed Perez-Steele:	80.00
Unsigned Perez-Steele:	20.00
Great Moments:	60.00
Celebration Card:	50.00
Store model glove:	85.00
Mini-helmet:	N/A

Dihigo, Martin (1905-1971)

Year Inducted:	1977
Cut:	$650.00
3x5 card:	800.00
Photo:	1,500.00
Ball:	4,000.00
Bat:	N/A
B&W Plaque:	N/A
Gold Plaque:	N/A
Signed Perez-Steele:	N/A
Unsigned Perez-Steele:	5.00
Great Moments:	N/A
Celebration Card:	N/A
Store model glove:	800.00
Mini-helmet:	N/A

DiMaggio, Joe (1914-)

Year Inducted:	1955
Cut:	$25.00
3x5 card:	60.00
Photo:	100.00
Ball:	200.00
Bat:	1,200.00
B&W Plaque:	135.00
Gold Plaque:	90.00
Signed Perez-Steele:	350.00
Unsigned Perez-Steele:	75.00
Great Moments:	N/A
Celebration Card:	N/A
Store model glove:	350.00
Mini-helmet:	225.00

Doby, Larry (1924-)

Year Inducted:	1998
Cut:	$5.00
3x5 Card:	8.00
Photo:	12.00
Ball:	25.00
Bat:	75.00
B&W Plaque:	N/A
Gold Plaque:	N/A
Signed Perez-Steele:	N/A
Unsigned Perez-Steele:	N/A
Great Moments:	N/A
Celebration Card:	N/A
Store model glove:	N/A
Mini-helmet:	N/A

Doerr, Bobby (1918-)

Year Inducted:	1986
Cut:	$5.00
3x5 card:	7.00
Photo:	10.00
Ball:	20.00
Bat:	85.00
B&W Plaque:	N/A
Gold Plaque:	6.00
Signed Perez-Steele:	15.00
Unsigned Perez-Steele:	10.00
Great Moments:	15.00
Celebration Card:	15.00
Store model glove:	75.00
Mini-helmet:	30.00

Drysdale, Don (1936-1993)

Year Inducted:	1984
Cut:	$7.00
3x5 card:	10.00
Photo:	30.00
Ball:	75.00
Bat:	200.00
B&W Plaque:	N/A
Gold Plaque:	25.00
Signed Perez-Steele:	35.00
Unsigned Perez-Steele:	15.00
Great Moments:	N/A
Celebration Card:	N/A
Store model glove:	50.00
Mini-helmet:	N/A

Duffy, Hugh (1866-1954)

Year Inducted:	1945
Cut:	$300.00
3x5 card:	400.00
Photo:	750.00
Ball:	3,500.00
Bat:	N/A
B&W Plaque:	900.00
Gold Plaque:	N/A
Signed Perez-Steele:	N/A
Unsigned Perez-Steele:	5.00
Great Moments:	N/A
Celebration Card:	N/A
Store model glove:	800.00
Mini-helmet:	N/A

Durocher, Leo (1905-1992)

Year Inducted:	1994
Cut:	$15.00
3x5 card:	25.00
Photo:	50.00
Ball:	125.00
Bat:	400.00
B&W Plaque:	N/A
Gold Plaque:	N/A
Signed Perez-Steele:	N/A
Unsigned Perez-Steele:	5.00
Great Moments:	N/A
Celebration Card:	N/A
Store model glove:	85.00
Mini-helmet:	N/A

Evans, Billy (1864-1956)

Year Inducted:	1973
Cut:	$225.00
3x5 card:	350.00
Photo:	500.00
Ball:	4,000.00
Bat:	N/A
B&W Plaque:	N/A
Gold Plaque:	N/A
Signed Perez-Steele:	N/A
Unsigned Perez-Steele:	5.00
Great Moments:	N/A
Celebration Card:	N/A
Store model glove:	N/A
Mini-helmet:	N/A

Evers, Johnny (1883-1947)

Year Inducted:	1946
Cut:	$300.00
3x5 card:	400.00
Photo:	1,200.00
Ball:	6,000.00
Bat:	N/A
B&W Plaque:	1,100.00
Gold Plaque:	N/A
Signed Perez-Steele:	N/A
Unsigned Perez-Steele:	5.00
Great Moments:	N/A
Celebration Card:	N/A
Store model glove:	700.00
Mini-helmet:	N/A

Ewing, William "Buck" (1859-1906)

Year Inducted:	1939
Cut:	$1,000.00
3x5 card:	2,400.00
Photo:	4,000.00
Ball:	N/A
Bat:	N/A
B&W Plaque:	N/A
Gold Plaque:	N/A
Signed Perez-Steele:	N/A
Unsigned Perez-Steele:	5.00
Great Moments:	N/A
Celebration Card:	N/A
Store model glove:	1,200.00
Mini-helmet:	N/A

Faber, Urban "Red" (1888-1976)

Year Inducted:	1964
Cut:	$15.00
3x5 card:	35.00
Photo:	100.00
Ball:	1,800.00
Bat:	N/A
B&W Plaque:	N/A
Gold Plaque:	85.00
Signed Perez-Steele:	N/A
Unsigned Perez-Steele:	5.00
Great Moments:	N/A
Celebration Card:	N/A
Store model glove:	650.00
Mini-helmet:	N/A

Feller, Bob (1918-)

Year Inducted:	1962
Cut:	$5.00
3x5 card:	10.00
Photo:	12.00
Ball:	20.00
Bat:	75.00
B&W Plaque:	20.00
Gold Plaque:	7.00
Signed Perez-Steele:	20.00
Unsigned Perez-Steele:	15.00
Great Moments:	20.00
Celebration Card:	N/A
Store model glove:	50.00
Mini-helmet:	30.00

Ferrell, Rick (1905-1995)

Year Inducted:	1984
Cut:	$5.00
3x5 card:	7.00
Photo:	20.00
Ball:	40.00
Bat:	125.00
B&W Plaque:	N/A
Gold Plaque:	8.00
Signed Perez-Steele:	30.00
Unsigned Perez-Steele:	15.00
Great Moments:	20.00
Celebration Card:	20.00
Store model glove:	350.00
Mini-helmet:	N/A

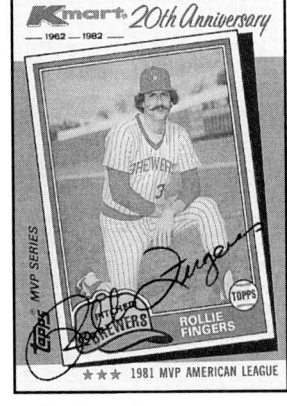

Fingers, Rollie (1946-)

Year Inducted:	1992
Cut:	$5.00
3x5 card:	7.00
Photo:	12.00
Ball:	20.00
Bat:	75.00
B&W Plaque:	N/A
Gold Plaque:	8.00
Signed Perez-Steele:	20.00
Unsigned Perez-Steele:	5.00
Great Moments:	20.00
Celebration Card:	N/A
Store model glove:	85.00
Mini-helmet:	30.00

Flick, Elmer (1876-1971)

Year Inducted:	1963
Cut:	$20.00
3x5 card:	50.00
Photo:	250.00
Ball:	2,500.00
Bat:	N/A
B&W Plaque:	300.00
Gold Plaque:	450.00
Signed Perez-Steele:	N/A
Unsigned Perez-Steele:	5.00
Great Moments:	N/A
Celebration Card:	N/A
Store model glove:	1,200.00
Mini-helmet:	N/A

Ford, Edward "Whitey" (1926-)

Year Inducted:	1974
Cut:	$10.00
3x5 card:	15.00
Photo:	20.00
Ball:	30.00
Bat:	100.00
B&W Plaque:	N/A
Gold Plaque:	12.00
Signed Perez-Steele:	35.00
Unsigned Perez-Steele:	15.00
Great Moments:	30.00
Celebration Card:	N/A
Store model glove:	75.00
Mini-helmet:	40.00

Foster, Bill (1904-1978)

Year Inducted:	1996
Cut:	$25.00
3x5 card:	*
Photo:	*
Ball:	*
Bat:	*
B&W Plaque:	N/A
Gold Plaque:	N/A
Signed Perez-Steele:	N/A
Unsigned Perez-Steele:	5.00
Great Moments:	N/A
Celebration Card:	N/A
Store model glove:	*
Mini-helmet:	N/A

Foster, Andrew "Rube" (1888-1976)

Year Inducted:	1981
Cut:	$2,000.00
3x5 card:	3,800.00
Photo:	5,500.00
Ball:	13,000.00
Bat:	N/A
B&W Plaque:	N/A
Gold Plaque:	N/A
Signed Perez-Steele:	N/A
Unsigned Perez-Steele:	5.00
Great Moments:	N/A
Celebration Card:	N/A
Store model glove:	N/A
Mini-helmet:	N/A

Fox, Nelson "Nellie" (1927-1975)

Year Inducted:	1997
Cut:	$100.00
3x5 card:	150.00
Photo:	250.00
Ball:	2,000.00
Bat:	*
B&W Plaque:	*
Gold Plaque:	*
Signed Perez-Steele:	*
Unsigned Perez-Steele:	5.00
Great Moments:	*
Ceebration Cards:	*
Store model glove:	*
Mini-helmet:	N/A

Foxx, Jimmie (1907-1967)

Year Inducted:	1951
Cut:	$200.00
3x5 card:	275.00
Photo:	500.00
Ball:	3,000.00
Bat:	N/A
B&W Plaque:	525.00
Gold Plaque:	2,500.00
Signed Perez-Steele:	N/A
Unsigned Perez-Steele:	15.00
Great Moments:	N/A
Celebration Card:	N/A
Store model glove:	400.00
Mini-helmet:	N/A

Frick, Ford (1894-1978)

Year Inducted:	1970
Cut:	$15.00
3x5 card:	40.00
Photo:	100.00
Ball:	800.00
Bat:	N/A
B&W Plaque:	N/A
Gold Plaque:	135.00
Signed Perez-Steele:	N/A
Unsigned Perez-Steele:	5.00
Great Moments:	N/A
Celebration Card:	N/A
Store model glove:	N/A
Mini-helmet:	N/A

Frisch, Frank (1898-1973)

Year Inducted:	1947
Cut:	$15.00
3x5 card:	40.00
Photo:	175.00
Ball:	1,700.00
Bat:	N/A
B&W Plaque:	100.00
Gold Plaque:	150.00
Signed Perez-Steele:	N/A
Unsigned Perez-Steele:	20.00
Great Moments:	N/A
Celebration Card:	N/A
Store model glove:	150.00
Mini-helmet:	N/A

Galvin, James "Pud" (1856-1902)

Year Inducted:	1965
Cut:	$1,300.00
3x5 card:	2,500.00
Photo:	3,000.00
Ball:	12,000.00
Bat:	N/A
B&W Plaque:	N/A
Gold Plaque:	N/A
Signed Perez-Steele:	N/A
Unsigned Perez-Steele:	5.00
Great Moments:	N/A
Celebration Card:	N/A
Store model glove:	800.00
Mini-helmet:	N/A

Gehrig, Lou (1903-1941)

Year Inducted:	1939
Cut:	$650.00
3x5 card:	800.00
Photo:	2,000.00
Ball:	5,000.00
Bat:	N/A
B&W Plaque:	N/A
Gold Plaque:	N/A
Signed Perez-Steele:	N/A
Unsigned Perez-Steele:	50.00
Great Moments:	N/A
Celebration Card:	N/A
Store model glove:	1,500.00
Mini-helmet:	N/A

Chas. Gehringer

Gehringer, Charlie (1903-1993)

Year Inducted:	1949
Cut:	$5.00
3x5 card:	10.00
Photo:	40.00
Ball:	100.00
Bat:	250.00
B&W Plaque:	40.00
Gold Plaque:	25.00
Signed Perez-Steele:	70.00
Unsigned Perez-Steele:	20.00
Great Moments:	40.00
Celebration Card:	40.00
Store model glove:	150.00
Mini-helmet:	N/A

Gibson, Bob (1935-)

Year Inducted:	1981
Cut:	$7.00
3x5 card:	12.00
Photo:	18.00
Ball:	25.00
Bat:	100.00
B&W Plaque:	N/A
Gold Plaque:	12.00
Signed Perez-Steele:	20.00
Unsigned Perez-Steele:	10.00
Great Moments:	N/A
Celebration Card:	N/A
Store model glove:	85.00
Mini-helmet:	35.00

Josh Gibson

Gibson, Josh (1911-1947)

Year Inducted:	1972
Cut:	$700.00
3x5 card:	800.00
Photo:	1,200.00
Ball:	6,500.00
Bat:	N/A
B&W Plaque:	N/A
Gold Plaque:	N/A
Signed Perez-Steele:	N/A
Unsigned Perez-Steele:	5.00
Great Moments:	N/A
Celebration Card:	N/A
Store model glove:	1,500.00
Mini-helmet:	N/A

Giles, Warren (1896-1979)

Year Inducted:	1979
Cut:	$20.00
3x5 card:	40.00
Photo:	125.00
Ball:	1,000.00
Bat:	*
B&W Plaque	N/A
Gold Plaque:	N/A
Signed Perez-Steele:	N/A
Unsigned Perez-Steele:	5.00
Great Moments:	N/A
Celebration Card:	N/A
Store model glove:	N/A
Mini-helmet:	N/A

Gomez, Vernon "Lefty" (1908-1989)

Year Inducted:	1972
Cut:	$8.00
3x5 card:	15.00
Photo:	40.00
Ball:	150.00
Bat:	400.00
B&W Plaque:	N/A
Gold Plaque:	20.00
Signed Perez-Steele:	80.00
Unsigned Perez-Steele:	20.00
Great Moments:	50.00
Celebration Card:	N/A
Store model glove:	85.00
Mini-helmet:	N/A

Goslin, Leon "Goose" (1900-1971)

Year Inducted:	1968
Cut:	$50.00
3x5 card:	70.00
Photo:	300.00
Ball:	2,700.00
Bat:	N/A
B&W Plaque:	N/A
Gold Plaque:	3,000.00
Signed Perez-Steele:	N/A
Unsigned Perez-Steele:	10.00
Great Moments:	N/A
Celebration Card:	N/A
Store model glove:	150.00
Mini-helmet:	N/A

Greenberg, Hank (1911-1986)

Year Inducted:	1956
Cut:	$20.00
3x5 card:	35.00
Photo:	125.00
Ball:	600.00
Bat:	*
B&W Plaque:	75.00
Gold Plaque:	70.00
Signed Perez-Steele:	325.00
Unsigned Perez-Steele:	20.00
Great Moments:	N/A
Celebration Card:	N/A
Store model glove:	300.00
Mini-helmet:	N/A

Griffith, Clark (1869-1955)

Year Inducted:	1946
Cut:	$135.00
3x5 card:	150.00
Photo:	350.00
Ball:	2,200.00
Bat:	N/A
B&W Plaque:	600.00
Gold Plaque:	N/A
Signed Perez-Steele:	N/A
Unsigned Perez-Steele:	10.00
Great Moments:	N/A
Celebration Card:	N/A
Store model glove:	N/A
Mini-helmet:	N/A

Grimes, Burleigh (1893-1985)

Year Inducted:	1964
Cut:	$8.00
3x5 card:	12.00
Photo:	60.00
Ball:	225.00
Bat:	*
B&W Plaque:	N/A
Gold Plaque:	20.00
Signed Perez-Steele:	160.00
Unsigned Perez-Steele:	10.00
Great Moments:	N/A
Celebration Card:	N/A
Store model glove:	650.00
Mini-helmet:	N/A

Grove, Robert "Lefty" (1900-1975)

Year Inducted:	1947
Cut:	$25.00
3x5 card:	40.00
Photo:	200.00
Ball:	1,300.00
Bat:	N/A
B&W Plaque:	125.00
Gold Plaque:	100.00
Signed Perez-Steele:	N/A
Unsigned Perez-Steele:	25.00
Great Moments:	N/A
Celebration Card:	N/A
Store model glove:	250.00
Mini-helmet:	N/A

Hafey, Charles "Chick" (1903-1973)

Year Inducted:	1971
Cut:	$35.00
3x5 card:	50.00
Photo:	175.00
Ball:	1,500.00
Bat:	N/A
B&W Plaque:	N/A
Gold Plaque:	600.00
Signed Perez-Steele:	N/A
Unsigned Perez-Steele:	10.00
Great Moments:	N/A
Celebration Card:	N/A
Store model glove:	400.00
Mini-helmet:	N/A

Haines, Jesse (1893-1978)

Year Inducted:	1970
Cut:	$35.00
3x5 card:	40.00
Photo:	125.00
Ball:	950.00
Bat:	N/A
B&W Plaque:	N/A
Gold Plaque:	75.00
Signed Perez-Steele:	N/A
Unsigned Perez-Steele:	10.00
Great Moments:	N/A
Celebration Card:	N/A
Store model glove:	350.00
Mini-helmet:	N/A

Hamilton, Billy (1866-1940)

Year Inducted:	1961
Cut:	$500.00
3x5 card:	750.00
Photo:	2,500.00
Ball:	5,500.00
Bat:	N/A
B&W Plaque:	N/A
Gold Plaque:	N/A
Signed Perez-Steele:	N/A
Unsigned Perez-Steele:	5.00
Great Moments:	N/A
Celebration Card:	N/A
Store model glove:	800.00
Mini-helmet:	N/A

Hanlon, Ned (1857-1937)

Year Inducted:	1996
Cut:	*
3x5 card:	*
Photo:	*
Ball:	*
Bat:	*
B&W Plaque:	N/A
Gold Plaque:	N/A
Signed Perez-Steele:	N/A
Unsigned Perez-Steele:	N/A
Great Moments:	5.00
Celebration Card:	N/A
Store model glove:	N/A
Mini-helmet:	N/A

Harridge, Will (1883-1971)

Year Inducted:	1972
Cut:	$85.00
3x5 card:	125.00
Photo:	300.00
Ball:	2,500.00
Bat:	N/A
B&W Plaque:	N/A
Gold Plaque:	N/A
Signed Perez-Steele:	N/A
Unsigned Perez-Steele:	5.00
Great Moments:	N/A
Celebration Card:	N/A
Store model glove:	N/A
Mini-helmet:	N/A

Harris, Stanley "Bucky" (1896-1977)

Year Inducted:	1975
Cut:	$25.00
3x5 card:	40.00
Photo:	200.00
Ball:	1,200.00
Bat:	N/A
B&W Plaque:	N/A
Gold Plaque:	150.00
Signed Perez-Steele:	N/A
Unsigned Perez-Steele:	10.00
Great Moments:	N/A
Celebration Card:	N/A
Store model glove:	150.00
Mini-helmet:	N/A

Hartnett, Charles "Gabby" (1900-1972)

Year Inducted:	1955
Cut:	$30.00
3x5 card:	60.00
Photo:	250.00
Ball:	2,000.00
Bat:	N/A
B&W Plaque:	200.00
Gold Plaque:	325.00
Signed Perez-Steele:	N/A
Unsigned Perez-Steele:	5.00
Great Moments:	N/A
Celebration Card:	N/A
Store model glove:	200.00
Mini-helmet:	N/A

Heilmann, Harry (1894-1951)

Year Inducted:	1952
Cut:	$250.00
3x5 card:	350.00
Photo:	500.00
Ball:	2,500.00
Bat:	N/A
B&W Plaque:	N/A
Gold Plaque:	N/A
Signed Perez-Steele:	N/A
Unsigned Perez-Steele:	5.00
Great Moments:	N/A
Celebration Card:	N/A
Store model glove:	250.00
Mini-helmet:	N/A

Herman, Billy (1909-1992)

Year Inducted:	1975
Cut:	$5.00
3x5 card:	7.00
Photo:	25.00
Ball:	50.00
Bat:	175.00
B&W Plaque:	N/A
Gold Plaque:	12.00
Signed Perez-Steele:	20.00
Unsigned Perez-Steele:	20.00
Great Moments:	20.00
Celebration Card:	20.00
Store model glove:	100.00
Mini-helmet:	N/A

Hooper, Harry (1887-1974)

Year Inducted:	1971
Cut:	$15.00
3x5 card:	20.00
Photo:	150.00
Ball:	1,200.00
Bat:	N/A
B&W Plaque:	N/A
Gold Plaque:	115.00
Signed Perez-Steele:	N/A
Unsigned Perez-Steele:	5.00
Great Moments:	N/A
Celebration Card:	N/A
Store model glove:	800.00
Mini-helmet:	N/A

Hornsby, Rogers (1896-1963)

Year Inducted:	1942
Cut:	$150.00
3x5 card:	200.00
Photo:	500.00
Ball:	2,500.00
Bat:	N/A
B&W Plaque:	650.00
Gold Plaque:	N/A
Signed Perez-Steele:	N/A
Unsigned Perez-Steele:	15.00
Great Moments:	N/A
Celebration Card:	N/A
Store model glove:	250.00
Mini-helmet:	N/A

Hoyt, Waite (1899-1984)

Year Inducted:	1969
Cut:	$10.00
3x5 card:	15.00
Photo:	80.00
Ball:	450.00
Bat:	*
B&W Plaque:	N/A
Gold Plaque:	30.00
Signed Perez-Steele:	450.00
Unsigned Perez-Steele:	10.00
Great Moments:	N/A
Celebration Card:	N/A
Store model glove:	550.00
Mini-helmet:	N/A

Hubbard, Cal (1900-1977)

Year Inducted:	1976
Cut:	$30.00
3x5 card:	60.00
Photo:	250.00
Ball:	1,000.00
Bat:	N/A
B&W Plaque:	N/A
Gold Plaque:	500.00
Signed Perez-Steele:	N/A
Unsigned Perez-Steele:	5.00
Great Moments:	N/A
Celebration Card:	N/A
Store model glove:	N/A
Mini-helmet:	N/A

Hubbell, Carl (1903-1988)

Year Inducted:	1947
Cut:	$10.00
3x5 card:	12.00
Photo:	40.00
Ball:	175.00
Bat:	*
B&W Plaque:	35.00
Gold Plaque:	20.00
Signed Perez-Steele:	80.00
Unsigned Perez-Steele:	25.00
Great Moments:	40.00
Celebration Card:	N/A
Store model glove:	350.00
Mini-helmet:	N/A

Huggins, Miller (1879-1929)

Year Inducted:	1964
Cut:	$700.00
3x5 card:	1,000.00
Photo:	1,500.00
Ball:	6,000.00
Bat:	N/A
B&W Plaque:	N/A
Gold Plaque:	N/A
Signed Perez-Steele:	N/A
Unsigned Perez-Steele:	10.00
Great Moments:	N/A
Celebration Card:	N/A
Store model glove:	N/A
Mini-helmet:	N/A

Hulbert, William (1832-1882)

Year Inducted:	1995
Cut:	*
3x5 card:	*
Photo:	N/A
Ball:	N/A
Bat:	N/A
B&W Plaque:	N/A
Gold Plaque:	N/A
Signed Perez-Steele:	N/A
Unsigned Perez-Steele:	5.00
Great Moments:	N/A
Celebration Card:	N/A
Store model glove:	N/A
Mini-helmet:	N/A

Hunter, Jim "Catfish" (1946-)

Year Inducted:	1987
Cut:	$5.00
3x5 card:	7.00
Photo:	12.00
Ball:	20.00
Bat:	75.00
B&W Plaque:	N/A
Gold Plaque:	8.00
Signed Perez-Steele:	20.00
Unsigned Perez-Steele:	10.00
Great Moments:	15.00
Celebration Card:	15.00
Store model glove:	50.00
Mini-helmet:	30.00

Irvin, Monte (1919-)

Year Inducted:	1973
Cut:	$5.00
3x5 card:	7.00
Photo:	10.00
Ball:	20.00
Bat:	85.00
B&W Plaque:	N/A
Gold Plaque:	7.00
Signed Perez-Steele:	20.00
Unsigned Perez-Steele:	15.00
Great Moments:	20.00
Celebration Card:	15.00
Store model glove:	250.00
Mini-helmet:	30.00

Jackson, Reggie (1946-)

Year Inducted:	1993
Cut:	$10.00
3x5 card:	20.00
Photo:	35.00
Ball:	55.00
Bat:	175.00
B&W Plaque:	N/A
Gold Plaque:	25.00
Signed Perez-Steele:	60.00
Unsigned Perez-Steele:	15.00
Great Moments:	N/A
Celebration Card:	N/A
Store model glove:	100.00
Mini-helmet:	65.00

Jackson, Travis (1903-1987)

Year Inducted:	1982
Cut:	$7.00
3x5 card:	15.00
Photo:	80.00
Ball:	350.00
Bat:	*
B&W Plaque:	N/A
Gold Plaque:	35.00
Signed Perez-Steele:	80.00
Unsigned Perez-Steele:	20.00
Great Moments:	N/A
Celebration Card:	N/A
Store model glove:	125.00
Mini-helmet:	N/A

Jenkins, Ferguson (1943-)

Year Inducted:	1991
Cut:	$5.00
3x5 card:	7.00
Photo:	12.00
Ball:	20.00
Bat:	75.00
B&W Plaque:	N/A
Gold Plaque:	10.00
Signed Perez-Steele:	15.00
Unsigned Perez-Steele:	5.00
Great Moments:	15.00
Celebration Card:	N/A
Store model glove:	75.00
Mini-helmet:	30.00

Jennings, Hugh (1869-1928)

Year Inducted:	1945
Cut:	$500.00
3x5 card:	900.00
Photo:	1,000.00
Ball:	6,000.00
Bat:	N/A
B&W Plaque:	N/A
Gold Plaque:	N/A
Signed Perez-Steele:	N/A
Unsigned Perez-Steele:	5.00
Great Moments:	N/A
Celebration Card:	N/A
Store model glove:	800.00
Mini-helmet:	N/A

Johnson, Ban (1864-1931)

Year Inducted:	1937
Cut:	$200.00
3x5 card:	250.00
Photo:	500.00
Ball:	3,500.00
Bat:	N/A
B&W Plaque:	N/A
Gold Plaque:	N/A
Signed Perez-Steele:	N/A
Unsigned Perez-Steele:	5.00
Great Moments:	N/A
Celebration Card:	N/A
Store model glove:	N/A
Mini-helmet:	N/A

Johnson, Judy (1900-1989)

Year Inducted:	1975
Cut:	$5.00
3x5 card:	10.00
Photo:	60.00
Ball:	200.00
Bat:	*
B&W Plaque:	N/A
Gold Plaque:	25.00
Signed Perez-Steele:	90.00
Unsigned Perez-Steele:	20.00
Great Moments:	*
Celebration Card:	N/A
Store model glove:	*
Mini-helmet:	N/A

Johnson, Walter (1887-1946)

Year Inducted:	1936
Cut:	$425.00
3x5 card:	500.00
Photo:	1,000.00
Ball:	3,500.00
Bat:	N/A
B&W Plaque:	*
Gold Plaque:	N/A
Signed Perez-Steele:	N/A
Unsigned Perez-Steele:	25.00
Great Moments:	N/A
Celebration Card:	N/A
Store model glove:	400.00
Mini-helmet:	N/A

Joss, Addie (1880-1911)

Year Inducted:	1978
Cut:	$1,500.00
3x5 card:	2,500.00
Photo:	3,900.00
Ball:	10,000.00
Bat:	N/A
B&W Plaque:	N/A
Gold Plaque:	N/A
Signed Perez-Steele:	N/A
Unsigned Perez-Steele:	5.00
Great Moments:	N/A
Celebration Card:	N/A
Store model glove:	*
Mini-helmet:	N/A

Kaline, Al (1934-)

Year Inducted:	1980
Cut:	$5.00
3x5 card:	7.00
Photo:	15.00
Ball:	25.00
Bat:	100.00
B&W Plaque:	N/A
Gold Plaque:	12.00
Signed Perez-Steele:	25.00
Unsigned Perez-Steele:	15.00
Great Moments:	25.00
Celebration Card:	20.00
Store model glove:	50.00
Mini-helmet:	35.00

Keefe, Tim (1857-1933)

Year Inducted:	1964
Cut:	$600.00
3x5 card:	800.00
Photo:	2,000.00
Ball:	7,000.00
Bat:	N/A
B&W Plaque:	N/A
Gold Plaque:	N/A
Signed Perez-Steele:	N/A
Unsigned Perez-Steele:	5.00
Great Moments:	N/A
Celebration Card:	N/A
Store model glove:	750.00
Mini-helmet:	N/A

Keeler, Willie (1872-1923)

Year Inducted:	1939
Cut:	$1,000.00
3x5 card:	2,000.00
Photo:	3,000.00
Ball:	8,000.00
Bat:	N/A
B&W Plaque:	N/A
Gold Plaque:	N/A
Signed Perez-Steele:	N/A
Unsigned Perez-Steele:	5.00
Great Moments:	N/A
Celebration Card:	N/A
Store model glove:	*
Mini-helmet:	N/A

Kell, George (1922-)

Year Inducted:	1983
Cut:	$5.00
3x5 card:	7.00
Photo:	10.00
Ball:	25.00
Bat:	75.00
B&W Plaque:	N/A
Gold Plaque:	6.00
Signed Perez-Steele:	15.00
Unsigned Perez-Steele:	15.00
Great Moments:	20.00
Celebration Card:	15.00
Store model glove:	50.00
Mini-helmet:	35.00

Kelley, Joe (1871-1943)

Year Inducted:	1971
Cut:	$800.00
3x5 card:	1,000.00
Photo:	1,500.00
Ball:	8,000.00
Bat:	N/A
B&W Plaque:	N/A
Gold Plaque:	N/A
Signed Perez-Steele:	N/A
Unsigned Perez-Steele:	5.00
Great Moments:	N/A
Celebration Card:	N/A
Store model glove:	*
Mini-helmet:	N/A

Kelly, George (1895-1984)

Year Inducted:	1973
Cut:	$8.00
3x5 card:	15.00
Photo:	75.00
Ball:	350.00
Bat:	*
B&W Plaque:	N/A
Gold Plaque:	30.00
Signed Perez-Steele:	325.00
Unsigned Perez-Steele:	15.00
Great Moments:	N/A
Celebration Card:	N/A
Store model glove:	400.00
Mini-helmet:	N/A

Kelly, Michael "King" (1857-1894)

Year Inducted:	1945
Cut:	$2,000.00
3x5 card:	3,500.00
Photo:	5,000.00
Ball:	N/A
Bat:	N/A
B&W Plaque:	N/A
Gold Plaque:	N/A
Signed Perez-Steele:	N/A
Unsigned Perez-Steele:	5.00
Great Moments:	N/A
Celebration Card:	N/A
Store model glove:	1,200.00
Mini-helmet:	N/A

Killebrew, Harmon (1936-)

Year Inducted:	1984
Cut:	$5.00
3x5 card:	10.00
Photo:	20.00
Ball:	25.00
Bat:	125.00
B&W Plaque:	N/A
Gold Plaque:	12.00
Signed Perez-Steele:	25.00
Unsigned Perez-Steele:	20.00
Great Moments:	25.00
Celebration Card:	20.00
Store model glove:	65.00
Mini-helmet:	35.00

Kiner, Ralph (1922-)

Year Inducted:	1975
Cut:	$5.00
3x5 card:	7.00
Photo:	15.00
Ball:	20.00
Bat:	85.00
B&W Plaque:	N/A
Gold Plaque:	10.00
Signed Perez-Steele:	25.00
Unsigned Perez-Steele:	15.00
Great Moments:	20.00
Celebration Card:	20.00
Store model glove:	50.00
Mini-helmet:	30.00

Klein, Chuck (1904-1958)

Year Inducted:	1980
Cut:	$200.00
3x5 card:	300.00
Photo:	500.00
Ball:	3,000.00
Bat:	N/A
B&W Plaque:	N/A
Gold Plaque:	N/A
Signed Perez-Steele:	N/A
Unsigned Perez-Steele:	10.00
Great Moments:	N/A
Celebration Card:	N/A
Store model glove:	250.00
Mini-helmet:	N/A

Klem, Bill (1874-1951)

Year Inducted:	1953
Cut:	$400.00
3x5 card:	600.00
Photo:	1,200.00
Ball:	3,500.00
Bat:	N/A
B&W Plaque:	N/A
Gold Plaque:	N/A
Signed Perez-Steele:	N/A
Unsigned Perez-Steele:	5.00
Great Moments:	N/A
Celebration Card:	N/A
Store model glove:	N/A
Mini-helmet:	N/A

Koufax, Sandy (1935-)

Year Inducted:	1972
Cut:	$10.00
3x5 card:	15.00
Photo:	50.00
Ball:	65.00
Bat:	175.00
B&W Plaque:	N/A
Gold Plaque:	30.00
Signed Perez-Steele:	75.00
Unsigned Perez-Steele:	40.00
Great Moments:	60.00
Celebration Card:	N/A
Store model glove:	250.00
Mini-helmet:	75.00

Lajoie, Napoleon (1874-1959)

Year Inducted:	1937
Cut:	$250.00
3x5 card:	350.00
Photo:	900.00
Ball:	4,500.00
Bat:	N/A
B&W Plaque:	750.00
Gold Plaque:	N/A
Signed Perez-Steele:	N/A
Unsigned Perez-Steele:	5.00
Great Moments:	N/A
Celebration Card:	N/A
Store model glove:	1,500.00
Mini-helmet:	N/A

Landis, Kenesaw Mountain (1866-1944)

Year Inducted:	1944
Cut:	$225.00
3x5 card:	300.00
Photo:	650.00
Ball:	3,500.00
Bat:	N/A
B&W Plaque:	N/A
Gold Plaque:	N/A
Signed Perez-Steele:	N/A
Unsigned Perez-Steele:	5.00
Great Moments:	N/A
Celebration Card:	N/A
Store model glove:	N/A
Mini-helmet:	N/A

Lasorda, Tom (1927-)

Year Inducted:	1997
Cut:	$8.00
3x5 card:	10.00
Photo:	20.00
Ball:	35.00
Bat:	100.00
B&W Plaque:	N/A
Gold Plaque:	20.00
Signed Perez-Steele:	*
Unsigned Perez-Steele:	5.00
Great Moments:	*
Celebration Card:	*
Store model glove:	*
Mini-helmet:	45.00

Lazzeri, Tony (1903-1946)

Year Inducted:	1991
Cut:	$275.00
3x5 card:	450.00
Photo:	700.00
Ball:	4,000.00
Bat:	N/A
B&W Plaque:	N/A
Gold Plaque:	N/A
Signed Perez-Steele:	N/A
Unsigned Perez-Steele:	5.00
Great Moments:	N/A
Celebration Card:	N/A
Store model glove:	400.00
Mini-helmet:	N/A

Lemon, Bob (1920-)

Year Inducted:	1976
Cut:	$5.00
3x5 card:	7.00
Photo:	12.00
Ball:	20.00
Bat:	75.00
B&W Plaque:	N/A
Gold Plaque:	6.00
Signed Perez-Steele:	20.00
Unsigned Perez-Steele:	15.00
Great Moments:	20.00
Celebration Card:	20.00
Store model glove:	50.00
Mini-helmet:	30.00

Leonard, Walter "Buck" (1907-)

Year Inducted:	1972
Cut:	$5.00
3x5 card:	7.00
Photo:	25.00
Ball:	40.00
Bat:	125.00
B&W Plaque:	N/A
Gold Plaque:	10.00
Signed Perez-Steele:	40.00
Unsigned Perez-Steele:	15.00
Great Moments:	25.00
Celebration Card:	25.00
Store model glove:	*
Mini-helmet:	50.00

Lindstrom, Fred (1905-1981)

Year Inducted:	1976
Cut:	$12.00
3x5 card:	20.00
Photo:	150.00
Ball:	700.00
Bat:	N/A
B&W Plaque:	N/A
Gold Plaque:	40.00
Signed Perez-Steele:	*
Unsigned Perez-Steele:	5.00
Great Moments:	N/A
Celebration Card:	N/A
Store model glove:	400.00
Mini-helmet:	N/A

Lloyd, John (1884-1964)

Year Inducted:	1977
Cut:	$700.00
3x5 card:	750.00
Photo:	1,200.00
Ball:	7,000.00
Bat:	N/A
B&W Plaque:	N/A
Gold Plaque:	N/A
Signed Perez-Steele:	N/A
Unsigned Perez-Steele:	5.00
Great Moments:	N/A
Celebration Card:	N/A
Store model glove:	500.00
Mini-helmet:	N/A

Lombardi, Ernie (1908-1977)

Year Inducted:	1986
Cut:	$30.00
3x5 card:	50.00
Photo:	300.00
Ball:	1,400.00
Bat:	N/A
B&W Plaque:	N/A
Gold Plaque:	N/A
Signed Perez-Steele:	N/A
Unsigned Perez-Steele:	5.00
Great Moments:	N/A
Celebration Card:	N/A
Store model glove:	150.00
Mini-helmet:	N/A

Lopez, Al (1908-)

Year Inducted:	1977
Cut:	$5.00
3x5 card:	10.00
Photo:	35.00
Ball:	80.00
Bat:	225.00
B&W Plaque:	N/A
Gold Plaque:	30.00
Signed Perez-Steele:	75.00
Unsigned Perez-Steele:	20.00
Great Moments:	60.00
Celebration Card:	45.00
Store model glove:	100.00
Mini-helmet:	100.00

Lyons, Ted (1900-1986)

Year Inducted:	1955
Cut:	$8.00
3x5 card:	10.00
Photo:	75.00
Ball:	225.00
Bat:	*
B&W Plaque:	35.00
Gold Plaque:	30.00
Signed Perez-Steele:	225.00
Unsigned Perez-Steele:	10.00
Great Moments:	N/A
Celebration Card:	N/A
Store model glove:	150.00
Mini-helmet:	N/A

Mack, Connie (1862-1956)

Year Inducted:	1937
Cut:	$100.00
3x5 card:	150.00
Photo:	350.00
Ball:	1,000.00
Bat:	N/A
B&W Plaque:	600.00
Gold Plaque:	N/A
Signed Perez-Steele:	N/A
Unsigned Perez-Steele:	5.00
Great Moments:	N/A
Celebration Card:	N/A
Store model glove:	800.00
Mini-helmet:	N/A

MacPhail, Larry (1890-1975)

Year Inducted:	1978
Cut:	$60.00
3x5 card:	175.00
Photo:	400.00
Ball:	1,700.00
Bat:	N/A
B&W Plaque:	N/A
Gold Plaque:	N/A
Signed Perez-Steele:	N/A
Unsigned Perez-Steele:	5.00
Great Moments:	N/A
Celebration Card:	N/A
Store model glove:	N/A
Mini-helmet:	N/A

Mantle, Mickey (1931-1995)

Year Inducted:	1974
Cut:	$60.00
3x5 card:	90.00
Photo:	150.00
Ball:	200.00
Bat:	1,500.00
B&W Plaque:	N/A
Gold Plaque:	75.00
Signed Perez-Steele:	350.00
Unsigned Perez-Steele:	75.00
Great Moments:	200.00
Celebration Card:	175.00
Store model glove:	150.00
Mini-helmet:	N/A

Manush, Heinie (1901-1971)

Year Inducted:	1964
Cut:	$30.00
3x5 card:	60.00
Photo:	300.00
Ball:	2,200.00
Bat:	N/A
B&W Plaque:	N/A
Gold Plaque:	275.00
Signed Perez-Steele:	N/A
Unsigned Perez-Steele:	5.00
Great Moments:	N/A
Celebration Card:	N/A
Store model glove:	100.00
Mini-helmet:	N/A

Maranville, Walter "Rabbit" (1891-1954)

Year Inducted:	1954
Cut:	$150.00
3x5 card:	250.00
Photo:	350.00
Ball:	2,000.00
Bat:	N/A
B&W Plaque:	*
Gold Plaque:	N/A
Signed Perez-Steele:	N/A
Unsigned Perez-Steele:	5.00
Great Moments:	N/A
Celebration Card:	N/A
Store model glove:	350.00
Mini-helmet:	N/A

Marichal, Juan (1937-)

Year Inducted:	1983
Cut:	$8.00
3x5 card:	10.00
Photo:	18.00
Ball:	28.00
Bat:	85.00
B&W Plaque:	N/A
Gold Plaque:	12.00
Signed Perez-Steele:	20.00
Unsigned Perez-Steele:	15.00
Great Moments:	20.00
Celebration Card:	15.00
Store model glove:	75.00
Mini-helmet:	35.00

Marquard, Richard "Rube" (1889-1980)

Year Inducted:	1971
Cut:	$10.00
3x5 card:	15.00
Photo:	150.00
Ball:	700.00
Bat:	N/A
B&W Plaque:	N/A
Gold Plaque:	45.00
Signed Perez-Steele:	*
Unsigned Perez-Steele:	5.00
Great Moments:	N/A
Celebration Card:	N/A
Store model glove:	1,200.00
Mini-helmet:	N/A

Mathews, Eddie (1931-)

Year Inducted:	1978
Cut:	$8.00
3x5 card:	12.00
Photo:	20.00
Ball:	30.00
Bat:	100.00
B&W Plaque:	N/A
Gold Plaque:	10.00
Signed Perez-Steele:	20.00
Unsigned Perez-Steele:	15.00
Great Moments:	20.00
Celebration Card:	15.00
Store model glove:	85.00
Mini-helmet:	40.00

Mathewson, Christy (1880-1925)

Year Inducted:	1936
Cut:	$1,000.00
3x5 card:	1,400.00
Photo:	3,000.00
Ball:	13,000.00
Bat:	N/A
B&W Plaque:	N/A
Gold Plaque:	N/A
Signed Perez-Steele:	N/A
Unsigned Perez-Steele:	15.00
Great Moments:	N/A
Celebration Card:	N/A
Store model glove:	1,500.00
Mini-helmet:	N/A

Mays, Willie (1931-)

Year Inducted:	1979
Cut:	$15.00
3x5 card:	20.00
Photo:	30.00
Ball:	50.00
Bat:	200.00
B&W Plaque:	N/A
Gold Plaque:	25.00
Signed Perez-Steele:	60.00
Unsigned Perez-Steele:	40.00
Great Moments:	30.00
Celebration Card:	N/A
Store model glove:	125.00
Mini-helmet:	60.00

McCarthy, Joe (1887-1978)

Year Inducted:	1957
Cut:	$15.00
3x5 card:	25.00
Photo:	150.00
Ball:	1,000.00
Bat:	N/A
B&W Plaque:	80.00
Gold Plaque:	50.00
Signed Perez-Steele:	N/A
Unsigned Perez-Steele:	10.00
Great Moments:	N/A
Celebration Card:	N/A
Store model glove:	*
Mini-helmet:	N/A

McCarthy, Tom (1863-1922)

Year Inducted:	1946
Cut:	$1,500.00
3x5 card:	2,000.00
Photo:	4,000.00
Ball:	N/A
Bat:	N/A
B&W Plaque:	N/A
Gold Plaque:	N/A
Signed Perez-Steele:	N/A
Unsigned Perez-Steele:	5.00
Great Moments:	N/A
Celebration Card:	N/A
Store model glove:	750.00
Mini-helmet:	N/A

McCovey, Willie (1938-)

Year Inducted:	1986
Cut:	$8.00
3x5 card:	12.00
Photo:	25.00
Ball:	30.00
Bat:	150.00
B&W Plaque:	N/A
Gold Plaque:	12.00
Signed Perez-Steele:	20.00
Unsigned Perez-Steele:	8.00
Great Moments:	25.00
Celebration Card:	20.00
Store model glove:	100.00
Mini-helmet:	40.00

McGinnity, Joe (1871-1929)

Year Inducted:	1946
Cut:	$800.00
3x5 card:	1,500.00
Photo:	5,000.00
Ball:	9,000.00
Bat:	N/A
B&W Plaque:	N/A
Gold Plaque:	N/A
Signed Perez-Steele:	N/A
Unsigned Perez-Steele:	5.00
Great Moments:	N/A
Celebration Card:	N/A
Store model glove:	1,200.00
Mini-helmet:	N/A

McGowan, Bill (1896-1954)

Year Inducted:	1992
Cut:	$300.00
3x5 card:	400.00
Photo:	2,000.00
Ball:	5,000.00
Bat:	N/A
B&W Plaque:	N/A
Gold Plaque:	N/A
Signed Perez-Steele:	N/A
Unsigned Perez-Steele:	5.00
Great Moments:	N/A
Celebration Card:	N/A
Store model glove:	*
Mini-helmet:	N/A

McGraw, John (1873-1934)

Year Inducted:	1937
Cut:	$500.00
3x5 card:	750.00
Photo:	1,500.00
Ball:	6,000.00
Bat:	N/A
B&W Plaque:	N/A
Gold Plaque:	N/A
Signed Perez-Steele:	N/A
Unsigned Perez-Steele:	5.00
Great Moments:	N/A
Celebration Card:	N/A
Store model glove:	*
Mini-helmet:	N/A

McKechnie, Bill (1886-1965)

Year Inducted:	1962
Cut:	$75.00
3x5 card:	150.00
Photo:	350.00
Ball:	2,000.00
Bat:	N/A
B&W Plaque:	300.00
Gold Plaque:	*
Signed Perez-Steele:	N/A
Unsigned Perez-Steele:	5.00
Great Moments:	N/A
Celebration Card:	N/A
Store model glove:	250.00
Mini-helmet:	N/A

Medwick, Joe (1911-1975)

Year Inducted:	1968
Cut:	$25.00
3x5 card:	45.00
Photo:	200.00
Ball:	1,700.00
Bat:	N/A
B&W Plaque:	N/A
Gold Plaque:	125.00
Signed Perez-Steele:	N/A
Unsigned Perez-Steele:	10.00
Great Moments:	N/A
Celebration Card:	N/A
Store model glove:	100.00
Mini-helmet:	N/A

Mize, Johnny (1913-1993)

Year Inducted:	1981
Cut:	$7.00
3x5 card:	12.00
Photo:	35.00
Ball:	60.00
Bat:	175.00
B&W Plaque:	N/A
Gold Plaque:	12.00
Signed Perez-Steele:	20.00
Unsigned Perez-Steele:	20.00
Great Moments:	30.00
Celebration Card:	20.00
Store model glove:	100.00
Mini-helmet:	N/A

Morgan, Joe (1943-)

Year Inducted:	1990
Cut:	$5.00
3x5 card:	7.00
Photo:	15.00
Ball:	25.00
Bat:	100.00
B&W Plaque:	N/A
Gold Plaque:	12.00
Signed Perez-Steele:	20.00
Unsigned Perez-Steele:	5.00
Great Moments:	20.00
Celebration Card:	N/A
Store model glove:	75.00
Mini-helmet:	35.00

Musial, Stan (1920-)

Year Inducted:	1969
Cut:	$12.00
3x5 card:	20.00
Photo:	35.00
Ball:	50.00
Bat:	150.00
B&W Plaque:	N/A
Gold Plaque:	25.00
Signed Perez-Steele:	80.00
Unsigned Perez-Steele:	60.00
Great Moments:	80.00
Celebration Card:	50.00
Store model glove:	100.00
Mini-helmet:	60.00

Newhouser, Hal (1921-)

Year Inducted:	1992
Cut:	$5.00
3x5 card:	7.00
Photo:	12.00
Ball:	20.00
Bat:	75.00
B&W Plaque:	N/A
Gold Plaque:	8.00
Signed Perez-Steele:	20.00
Unsigned Perez-Steele:	5.00
Great Moments:	15.00
Celebration Card:	N/A
Store model glove:	85.00
Mini-helmet:	30.00

Nichols, Charles "Kid" (1869-1953)

Year Inducted:	1949
Cut:	$200.00
3x5 card:	300.00
Photo:	500.00
Ball:	3,200.00
Bat:	N/A
B&W Plaque:	1,000.00
Gold Plaque:	N/A
Signed Perez-Steele:	N/A
Unsigned Perez-Steele:	5.00
Great Moments:	N/A
Celebration Card:	N/A
Store model glove:	*
Mini-helmet:	N/A

Niekro, Phil (1939-)

Year Inducted:	1997
Cut:	$5.00
3x5 card:	10.00
Photo:	15.00
Ball:	22.00
Bat:	75.00
B&W Plaque:	N/A
Gold Plaque:	20.00
Signed Perez-Steele:	N/A
Unsigned Perez-Steele:	5.00
Great Moments:	N/A
Celebration Card:	N/A
Store model glove:	75.00
Mini-helmet:	30.00

O'Rourke, Jim (1850-1919)

Year Inducted:	1945
Cut:	$1,500.00
3x5 card:	2,500.00
Photo:	3,500.00
Ball:	10,000.00
Bat:	N/A
B&W Plaque:	N/A
Gold Plaque:	N/A
Signed Perez-Steele:	N/A
Unsigned Perez-Steele:	5.00
Great Moments:	N/A
Celebration Card:	N/A
Store model glove:	N/A
Mini-helmet:	N/A

Ott, Mel (1909-1958)

Year Inducted:	1951
Cut:	$200.00
3x5 card:	275.00
Photo:	500.00
Ball:	3,500.00
Bat:	N/A
B&W Plaque:	650.00
Gold Plaque:	N/A
Signed Perez-Steele:	N/A
Unsigned Perez-Steele:	15.00
Great Moments:	N/A
Celebration Card:	N/A
Store model glove:	75.00
Mini-helmet:	N/A

Paige, Leroy "Satchel" (1906-1982)

Year Inducted:	1971
Cut:	$40.00
3x5 card:	80.00
Photo:	200.00
Ball:	900.00
Bat:	N/A
B&W Plaque:	N/A
Gold Plaque:	140.00
Signed Perez-Steele:	3,500.00
Unsigned Perez-Steele:	45.00
Great Moments:	N/A
Celebration Card:	N/A
Store model glove:	1,200.00
Mini-helmet:	N/A

Palmer, Jim (1945-)

Year Inducted:	1990
Cut:	$5.00
3x5 card:	10.00
Photo:	18.00
Ball:	25.00
Bat:	100.00
B&W Plaque:	N/A
Gold Plaque:	10.00
Signed Perez-Steele:	20.00
Unsigned Perez-Steele:	5.00
Great Moments:	25.00
Celebration Card:	N/A
Store model glove:	75.00
Mini-helmet:	30.00

Pennock, Herb (1894-1948)

Year Inducted:	1948
Cut:	$175.00
3x5 card:	200.00
Photo:	350.00
Ball:	2,500.00
Bat:	N/A
B&W Plaque:	N/A
Gold Plaque:	N/A
Signed Perez-Steele:	N/A
Unsigned Perez-Steele:	10.00
Great Moments:	N/A
Celebration Card:	N/A
Store model glove:	400.00
Mini-helmet:	N/A

Perry, Gaylord (1938-)

Year Inducted:	1991
Cut:	$5.00
3x5 card:	7.00
Photo:	12.00
Ball:	20.00
Bat:	75.00
B&W Plaque:	N/A
Gold Plaque:	10.00
Signed Perez-Steele:	15.00
Unsigned Perez-Steele:	5.00
Great Moments:	15.00
Celebration Card:	N/A
Store model glove:	75.00
Mini-helmet:	30.00

Plank, Edward (1875-1926)

Year Inducted:	1946
Cut:	$1,500.00
3x5 card:	2,200.00
Photo:	3,200.00
Ball:	8,000.00
Bat:	N/A
B&W Plaque:	N/A
Gold Plaque:	N/A
Signed Perez-Steele:	N/A
Unsigned Perez-Steele:	5.00
Great Moments:	N/A
Celebration Card:	N/A
Store model glove:	1,200.00
Mini-helmet:	N/A

Radbourne, Charles "Hoss" (1854-1897)

Year Inducted:	1939
Cut:	$2,000.00
3x5 card:	2,500.00
Photo:	3,200.00
Ball:	N/A
Bat:	N/A
B&W Plaque:	N/A
Gold Plaque:	N/A
Signed Perez-Steele:	N/A
Unsigned Perez-Steele:	5.00
Great Moments:	N/A
Celebration Card:	N/A
Store model glove:	N/A
Mini-helmet:	N/A

Reese, Harold "Pee Wee" (1918-)

Year Inducted:	1984
Cut:	$10.00
3x5 card:	15.00
Photo:	30.00
Ball:	50.00
Bat:	175.00
B&W Plaque:	N/A
Gold Plaque:	22.00
Signed Perez-Steele:	40.00
Unsigned Perez-Steele:	15.00
Great Moments:	35.00
Celebration Card:	35.00
Store model glove:	100.00
Mini-helmet:	35.00

Rice, Sam (1890-1974)

Year Inducted:	1963
Cut:	$20.00
3x5 card:	40.00
Photo:	150.00
Ball:	1,500.00
Bat:	N/A
B&W Plaque:	150.00
Gold Plaque:	140.00
Signed Perez-Steele:	N/A
Unsigned Perez-Steele:	5.00
Great Moments:	N/A
Celebration Card:	N/A
Store model glove:	400.00
Mini-helmet:	N/A

Rickey, Branch (1881-1965)

Year Inducted:	1967
Cut:	$175.00
3x5 card:	200.00
Photo:	750.00
Ball:	2,500.00
Bat:	N/A
B&W Plaque:	N/A
Gold Plaque:	N/A
Signed Perez-Steele:	N/A
Unsigned Perez-Steele:	5.00
Great Moments:	N/A
Celebration Card:	N/A
Store model glove:	N/A
Mini-helmet:	N/A

Rixey, Eppa (1891-1963)

Year Inducted:	1963
Cut:	$60.00
3x5 card:	100.00
Photo:	350.00
Ball:	3,500.00
Bat:	N/A
B&W Plaque:	N/A
Gold Plaque:	N/A
Signed Perez-Steele:	N/A
Unsigned Perez-Steele:	5.00
Great Moments:	N/A
Celebration Card:	N/A
Store model glove:	300.00
Mini-helmet:	N/A

Rizzuto, Phil (1917-)

Year Inducted:	1994
Cut:	$7.00
3x5 card:	10.00
Photo:	18.00
Ball:	25.00
Bat:	100.00
B&W Plaque:	N/A
Gold Plaque:	12.00
Signed Perez-Steele:	30.00
Unsigned Perez-Steele:	15.00
Great Moments:	N/A
Celebration Card:	N/A
Store model glove:	50.00
Mini-helmet:	35.00

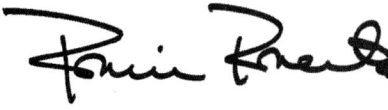

Roberts, Robin (1926-)

Year Inducted:	1976
Cut:	$5.00
3x5 card:	7.00
Photo:	12.00
Ball:	20.00
Bat:	75.00
B&W Plaque:	N/A
Gold Plaque:	8.00
Signed Perez-Steele:	20.00
Unsigned Perez-Steele:	15.00
Great Moments:	15.00
Celebration Card:	N/A
Store model glove:	50.00
Mini-helmet:	30.00

Robinson, Brooks (1937-)

Year Inducted:	1983
Cut:	$7.00
3x5 card:	10.00
Photo:	15.00
Ball:	25.00
Bat:	100.00
B&W Plaque:	N/A
Gold Plaque:	8.00
Signed Perez-Steele:	20.00
Unsigned Perez-Steele:	15.00
Great Moments:	15.00
Celebration Card:	15.00
Store model glove:	60.00
Mini-helmet:	30.00

Robinson, Frank (1935-)

Year Inducted:	1982
Cut:	$7.00
3x5 card:	12.00
Photo:	22.00
Ball:	30.00
Bat:	125.00
B&W Plaque:	N/A
Gold Plaque:	12.00
Signed Perez-Steele:	25.00
Unsigned Perez-Steele:	15.00
Great Moments:	25.00
Celebration Card:	N/A
Store model glove:	75.00
Mini-helmet:	40.00

Robinson, Jackie (1919-1972)

Year Inducted:	1962
Cut:	$175.00
3x5 card:	300.00
Photo:	700.00
Ball:	2,500.00
Bat:	N/A
B&W Plaque:	600.00
Gold Plaque:	700.00
Signed Perez-Steele:	N/A
Unsigned Perez-Steele:	30.00
Great Moments:	N/A
Celebration Card:	N/A
Store model glove:	350.00
Mini-helmet:	N/A

Robinson, Wilbert (1863-1934)

Year Inducted:	1945
Cut:	$700.00
3x5 card:	750.00
Photo:	2,000.00
Ball:	6,000.00
Bat:	N/A
B&W Plaque:	N/A
Gold Plaque:	N/A
Signed Perez-Steele:	N/A
Unsigned Perez-Steele:	5.00
Great Moments:	N/A
Celebration Card:	N/A
Store model glove:	800.00
Mini-helmet:	N/A

Roush, Edd (1893-1988)

Year Inducted:	1962
Cut:	$8.00
3x5 card:	10.00
Photo:	75.00
Ball:	160.00
Bat:	*
B&W Plaque:	80.00
Gold Plaque:	30.00
Signed Perez-Steele:	80.00
Unsigned Perez-Steele:	15.00
Great Moments:	N/A
Celebration Card:	N/A
Store model glove:	300.00
Mini-helmet:	N/A

Ruffing, Charles "Red" (1904-1986)

Year Inducted:	1967
Cut:	$20.00
3x5 card:	35.00
Photo:	125.00
Ball:	500.00
Bat:	*
B&W Plaque:	N/A
Gold Plaque:	100.00
Signed Perez-Steele:	350.00
Unsigned Perez-Steele:	10.00
Great Moments:	N/A
Celebration Card:	N/A
Store model glove:	150.00
Mini-helmet:	N/A

Rusie, Amos (1871-1942)

Year Inducted:	1977
Cut:	$700.00
3x5 card:	750.00
Photo:	2,000.00
Ball:	5,000.00
Bat:	N/A
B&W Plaque:	N/A
Gold Plaque:	N/A
Signed Perez-Steele:	N/A
Unsigned Perez-Steele:	5.00
Great Moments:	N/A
Celebration Card:	N/A
Store model glove:	650.00
Mini-helmet:	N/A

Ruth, George Herman "Babe" (1895-1948)

Year Inducted:	1936
Cut:	$700.00
3x5 card:	1,000.00
Photo:	2,500.00
Ball:	4,200.00
Bat:	N/A
B&W Plaque:	4,500.00
Gold Plaque:	N/A
Signed Perez-Steele:	N/A
Unsigned Perez-Steele:	80.00
Great Moments:	N/A
Celebration Card:	N/A
Store model glove:	900.00
Mini-helmet:	N/A

Schalk, Ray (1892-1970)

Year Inducted:	1955
Cut:	$45.00
3x5 card:	75.00
Photo:	350.00
Ball:	1,700.00
Bat:	N/A
B&W Plaque:	450.00
Gold Plaque:	300.00
Signed Perez-Steele:	N/A
Unsigned Perez-Steele:	5.00
Great Moments:	N/A
Celebration Card:	N/A
Store model glove:	200.00
Mini-helmet:	N/A

Schmidt, Mike (1949-)

Year Inducted:	1995
Cut:	$10.00
3x5 card:	15.00
Photo:	40.00
Ball:	55.00
Bat:	160.00
B&W Plaque:	N/A
Gold Plaque:	40.00
Signed Perez-Steele:	75.00
Unsigned Perez-Steele:	15.00
Great Moments:	N/A
Celebration Card:	N/A
Store model glove:	75.00
Mini-helmet:	65.00

Schoendienst, Red (1923-)

Year Inducted:	1989
Cut:	$5.00
3x5 card:	7.00
Photo:	12.00
Ball:	25.00
Bat:	85.00
B&W Plaque:	N/A
Gold Plaque:	10.00
Signed Perez-Steele:	20.00
Unsigned Perez-Steele:	5.00
Great Moments:	20.00
Celebration Card:	N/A
Store model glove:	40.00
Mini-helmet:	30.00

Seaver, Tom (1944-)

Year Inducted:	1992
Cut:	$10.00
3x5 card:	15.00
Photo:	30.00
Ball:	40.00
Bat:	125.00
B&W Plaque:	N/A
Gold Plaque:	25.00
Signed Perez-Steele:	40.00
Unsigned Perez-Steele:	8.00
Great Moments:	35.00
Celebration Card:	N/A
Store model glove:	75.00
Mini-helmet:	50.00

Sewell, Joe (1898-1990)

Year Inducted:	1977
Cut:	$5.00
3x5 card:	8.00
Photo:	30.00
Ball:	80.00
Bat:	200.00
B&W Plaque:	N/A
Gold Plaque:	15.00
Signed Perez-Steele:	60.00
Unsigned Perez-Steele:	15.00
Great Moments:	N/A
Celebration Card:	40.00
Store model glove:	400.00
Mini-helmet:	N/A

Simmons, Al (1902-1956)

Year Inducted:	1953
Cut:	$175.00
3x5 card:	325.00
Photo:	500.00
Ball:	2,800.00
Bat:	N/A
B&W Plaque:	800.00
Gold Plaque:	N/A
Signed Perez-Steele:	N/A
Unsigned Perez-Steele:	10.00
Great Moments:	N/A
Celebration Card:	N/A
Store model glove:	200.00
Mini-helmet:	N/A

Sisler, George (1893-1973)

Year Inducted:	1939
Cut:	$25.00
3x5 card:	50.00
Photo:	175.00
Ball:	1,200.00
Bat:	N/A
B&W Plaque:	135.00
Gold Plaque:	125.00
Signed Perez-Steele:	N/A
Unsigned Perez-Steele:	10.00
Great Moments:	N/A
Celebration Card:	N/A
Store model glove:	250.00
Mini-helmet:	N/A

Slaughter, Enos (1916-)

Year Inducted:	1985
Cut:	$5.00
3x5 card:	7.00
Photo:	10.00
Ball:	20.00
Bat:	85.00
B&W Plaque:	N/A
Gold Plaque:	6.00
Signed Perez-Steele:	20.00
Unsigned Perez-Steele:	15.00
Great Moments:	20.00
Celebration Card:	20.00
Store model glove:	50.00
Mini-helmet:	30.00

DUKE SNIDER
1980 – HALL OF FAME

Snider, Edwin "Duke" (1926-)

Year Inducted:	1980
Cut:	$8.00
3x5 card:	12.00
Photo:	20.00
Ball:	30.00
Bat:	125.00
B&W Plaque:	N/A
Gold Plaque:	10.00
Signed Perez-Steele:	25.00
Unsigned Perez-Steele:	15.00
Great Moments:	25.00
Celebration Card:	25.00
Store model glove:	60.00
Mini-helmet:	40.00

Spahn, Warren (1921-)

Year Inducted:	1973
Cut:	$5.00
3x5 card:	7.00
Photo:	15.00
Ball:	20.00
Bat:	85.00
B&W Plaque:	N/A
Gold Plaque:	8.00
Signed Perez-Steele:	20.00
Unsigned Perez-Steele:	15.00
Great Moments:	20.00
Celebration Card:	20.00
Store model glove:	85.00
Mini-helmet:	30.00

Spalding, Albert (1850-1915)

Year Inducted:	1939
Cut:	$750.00
3x5 card:	1,750.00
Photo:	1,800.00
Ball:	12,000.00
Bat:	N/A
B&W Plaque:	N/A
Gold Plaque:	N/A
Signed Perez-Steele:	N/A
Unsigned Perez-Steele:	5.00
Great Moments:	N/A
Celebration Card:	N/A
Store model glove:	750.00
Mini-helmet:	N/A

Speaker, Tris (1888-1958)

Year Inducted:	1937
Cut:	$200.00
3x5 card:	275.00
Photo:	500.00
Ball:	3,000.00
Bat:	N/A
B&W Plaque:	600.00
Gold Plaque:	N/A
Signed Perez-Steele:	N/A
Unsigned Perez-Steele:	10.00
Great Moments:	N/A
Celebration Card:	N/A
Store model glove:	1,500.00
Mini-helmet:	N/A

Stargell, Willie (1940-)

Year Inducted:	1988
Cut:	$5.00
3x5 card:	7.00
Photo:	10.00
Ball:	20.00
Bat:	85.00
B&W Plaque:	N/A
Gold Plaque:	8.00
Signed Perez-Steele:	15.00
Unsigned Perez-Steele:	5.00
Great Moments:	15.00
Celebration Card:	15.00
Store model glove:	65.00
Mini-helmet:	30.00

Stengel, Casey (1890-1975)

Year Inducted:	1966
Cut:	$40.00
3x5 card:	80.00
Photo:	150.00
Ball:	1,000.00
Bat:	N/A
B&W Plaque:	N/A
Gold Plaque:	100.00
Signed Perez-Steele:	N/A
Unsigned Perez-Steele:	15.00
Great Moments:	N/A
Celebration Card:	N/A
Store model glove:	800.00
Mini-helmet:	N/A

Sutton, Don (1945-)

Year Inducted:	1998
Cut:	$5.00
3x5 card:	7.00
Photo:	12.00
Ball:	25.00
Bat:	75.00
B&W Plaque:	N/A
Gold Plaque:	N/A
Signed Perez-Steele:	N/A
Unsigned Perez-Steele:	N/A
Great Moments:	N/A
Celebration Card:	N/A
Store model glove:	65.00
Mini-helmet:	35.00

Terry, Bill (1896-1989)

Year Inducted:	1954
Cut:	$7.00
3x5 card:	10.00
Photo:	50.00
Ball:	160.00
Bat:	*
B&W Plaque:	30.00
Gold Plaque:	25.00
Signed Perez-Steele:	80.00
Unsigned Perez-Steele:	25.00
Great Moments:	N/A
Celebration Card:	N/A
Store model glove:	300.00
Mini-helmet:	N/A

Thompson, Sam (1860-1922)

Year Inducted:	1974
Cut:	$1,200.00
3x5 card:	3,250.00
Photo:	6,000.00
Ball:	10,000.00
Bat:	N/A
B&W Plaque:	N/A
Gold Plaque:	N/A
Signed Perez-Steele:	N/A
Unsigned Perez-Steele:	5.00
Great Moments:	N/A
Celebration Card:	N/A
Store model glove:	800.00
Mini-helmet:	N/A

Tinker, Joe (1880-1948)

Year Inducted:	1946
Cut:	$300.00
3x5 card:	400.00
Photo:	1,200.00
Ball:	6,000.00
Bat:	N/A
B&W Plaque:	1,000.00
Gold Plaque:	N/A
Signed Perez-Steele:	N/A
Unsigned Perez-Steele:	5.00
Great Moments:	N/A
Celebration Card:	N/A
Store model glove:	1,200.00
Mini-helmet:	N/A

Traynor, Harold "Pie" (1899-1972)

Year Inducted:	1948
Cut:	$100.00
3x5 card:	130.00
Photo:	300.00
Ball:	1,200.00
Bat:	N/A
B&W Plaque:	450.00
Gold Plaque:	450.00
Signed Perez-Steele:	N/A
Unsigned Perez-Steele:	5.00
Great Moments:	N/A
Celebration Card:	N/A
Store model glove:	150.00
Mini-helmet:	N/A

Vance, Clarence "Dazzy" (1891-1961)

Year Inducted:	1955
Cut:	$200.00
3x5 card:	300.00
Photo:	750.00
Ball:	3,200.00
Bat:	N/A
B&W Plaque:	600.00
Gold Plaque:	N/A
Signed Perez-Steele:	N/A
Unsigned Perez-Steele:	5.00
Great Moments:	N/A
Celebration Card:	N/A
Store model glove:	200.00
Mini-helmet:	N/A

Vaughn, Joseph "Arky" (1912-1952)

Year Inducted:	1985
Cut:	$150.00
3x5 card:	250.00
Photo:	650.00
Ball:	3,500.00
Bat:	N/A
B&W Plaque:	N/A
Gold Plaque:	N/A
Signed Perez-Steele:	N/A
Unsigned Perez-Steele:	5.00
Great Moments:	N/A
Celebration Card:	N/A
Store model glove:	400.00
Mini-helmet:	N/A

Veeck, Bill (1914-1986)

Year Inducted:	1991
Cut:	$40.00
3x5 card:	75.00
Photo:	250.00
Ball:	2,000.00
Bat:	N/A
B&W Plaque:	N/A
Gold Plaque:	N/A
Signed Perez-Steele:	N/A
Unsigned Perez-Steele:	5.00
Great Moments:	N/A
Celebration Card:	N/A
Store model glove:	N/A
Mini-helmet:	N/A

Waddell, George "Rube" (1876-1914)

Year Inducted:	1946
Cut:	$1,000.00
3x5 card:	1,500.00
Photo:	4,500.00
Ball:	12,500.00
Bat:	N/A
B&W Plaque:	N/A
Gold Plaque:	N/A
Signed Perez-Steele:	N/A
Unsigned Perez-Steele:	5.00
Great Moments:	N/A
Celebration Card:	N/A
Store model glove:	1,200.00
Mini-helmet:	N/A

Wagner, John Peter "Honus" (1874-1955)

Year Inducted:	1936
Cut:	$300.00
3x5 card:	400.00
Photo:	800.00
Ball:	4,000.00
Bat:	N/A
B&W Plaque:	1,200.00
Gold Plaque:	N/A
Signed Perez-Steele:	N/A
Unsigned Perez-Steele:	15.00
Great Moments:	N/A
Celebration Card:	N/A
Store model glove:	1,500.00
Mini-helmet:	N/A

Wallace, Bobby (1873-1960)

Year Inducted:	1953
Cut:	$225.00
3x5 card:	300.00
Photo:	700.00
Ball:	4,500.00
Bat:	N/A
B&W Plaque:	800.00
Gold Plaque:	N/A
Signed Perez-Steele:	N/A
Unsigned Perez-Steele:	5.00
Great Moments:	N/A
Celebration Card:	N/A
Store model glove:	1,200.00
Mini-helmet:	N/A

Walsh, Ed (1881-1959)

Year Inducted:	1946
Cut:	$150.00
3x5 card:	200.00
Photo:	400.00
Ball:	3,600.00
Bat:	N/A
B&W Plaque:	350.00
Gold Plaque:	N/A
Signed Perez-Steele:	N/A
Unsigned Perez-Steele:	5.00
Great Moments:	N/A
Celebration Card:	N/A
Store model glove:	1,200.00
Mini-helmet:	N/A

Waner, Lloyd (1906-1982)

Year Inducted:	1967
Cut:	$15.00
3x5 card:	20.00
Photo:	125.00
Ball:	500.00
Bat:	N/A
B&W Plaque:	N/A
Gold Plaque:	30.00
Signed Perez-Steele:	3,500.00
Unsigned Perez-Steele:	15.00
Great Moments:	N/A
Celebration Card:	N/A
Store model glove:	150.00
Mini-helmet:	N/A

Waner, Paul (1903-1965)

Year Inducted:	1952
Cut:	$100.00
3x5 card:	125.00
Photo:	300.00
Ball:	2,500.00
Bat:	N/A
B&W Plaque:	350.00
Gold Plaque:	N/A
Signed Perez-Steele:	N/A
Unsigned Perez-Steele:	5.00
Great Moments:	N/A
Celebration Card:	N/A
Store model glove:	300.00
Mini-helmet:	N/A

Ward, Monte (1860-1925)

Year Inducted:	1964
Cut:	$1,000.00
3x5 card:	1,500.00
Photo:	3,000.00
Ball:	12,000.00
Bat:	N/A
B&W Plaque:	N/A
Gold Plaque:	N/A
Signed Perez-Steele:	N/A
Unsigned Perez-Steele:	5.00
Great Moments:	N/A
Celebration Card:	N/A
Store model glove:	1,500.00
Mini-helmet:	N/A

Weaver, Earl (1930-)

Year Inducted:	1996
Cut:	$5.00
3x5 card:	7.00
Photo:	15.00
Ball:	25.00
Bat:	75.00
B&W Plaque:	N/A
Gold Plaque:	30.00
Signed Perez-Steele:	30.00
Unsigned Perez-Steele:	10.00
Great Moments:	*
Celebration Card:	*
Store model glove:	*
Mini-helmet:	35.00

Weiss, George (1895-1972)

Year Inducted:	1971
Cut:	$40.00
3x5 card:	85.00
Photo:	300.00
Ball:	3,500.00
Bat:	N/A
B&W Plaque:	N/A
Gold Plaque:	N/A
Signed Perez-Steele:	N/A
Unsigned Perez-Steele:	5.00
Great Moments:	N/A
Celebration Card:	N/A
Store model glove:	N/A
Mini-helmet:	N/A

Welch, Mickey (1859-1941)

Year Inducted:	1973
Cut:	$1,700.00
3x5 card:	2,750.00
Photo:	4,000.00
Ball:	8,500.00
Bat:	N/A
B&W Plaque:	N/A
Gold Plaque:	N/A
Signed Perez-Steele:	N/A
Unsigned Perez-Steele:	5.00
Great Moments:	N/A
Celebration Card:	N/A
Store model glove:	N/A
Mini-helmet:	N/A

William Wells

Wells, Willie (1905-1989)

Year Inducted:	1997
Cut:	$750.00
3x5 card:	*
Photo:	*
Ball:	*
Bat:	*
B&W Plaque:	N/A
Gold Plaque:	N/A
Signed Perez-Steele:	N/A
Unsigned Perez-Steele:	5.00
Great Moments:	N/A
Celebration Card:	N/A
Store model glove:	*
Mini-helmet:	N/A

Wheat, Zack (1888-1972)

Year Inducted:	1959
Cut:	$50.00
3x5 card:	80.00
Photo:	200.00
Ball:	1,600.00
Bat:	N/A
B&W Plaque:	200.00
Gold Plaque:	350.00
Signed Perez-Steele:	N/A
Unsigned Perez-Steele:	10.00
Great Moments:	N/A
Celebration Card:	N/A
Store model glove:	1,200.00
Mini-helmet:	N/A

Wilhelm, Hoyt (1923-)

Year Inducted:	1985
Cut:	$5.00
3x5 card:	7.00
Photo:	10.00
Ball:	20.00
Bat:	75.00
B&W Plaque:	N/A
Gold Plaque:	8.00
Signed Perez-Steele:	20.00
Unsigned Perez-Steele:	15.00
Great Moments:	15.00
Celebration Card:	N/A
Store model glove:	250.00
Mini-helmet:	30.00

Williams, Billy (1938-)

Year Inducted:	1987
Cut:	$5.00
3x5 card:	7.00
Photo:	10.00
Ball:	20.00
Bat:	85.00
B&W Plaque:	N/A
Gold Plaque:	8.00
Signed Perez-Steele:	15.00
Unsigned Perez-Steele:	5.00
Great Moments:	15.00
Celebration Card:	15.00
Store model glove:	75.00
Mini-helmet:	30.00

Williams, Ted (1918-)

Year Inducted:	1966
Cut:	$40.00
3x5 card:	60.00
Photo:	100.00
Ball:	200.00
Bat:	750.00
B&W Plaque:	N/A
Gold Plaque:	60.00
Signed Perez-Steele:	300.00
Unsigned Perez-Steele:	75.00
Great Moments:	250.00
Celebration Card:	175.00
Store model glove:	125.00
Mini-helmet:	225.00

Willis, Vic (1876-1947)

Year Inducted:	1995
Cut:	$300.00
3x5 card:	450.00
Photo:	800.00
Ball:	N/A
Bat:	N/A
B&W Plaque:	N/A
Gold Plaque:	N/A
Signed Perez-Steele:	N/A
Unsigned Perez-Steele:	5.00
Great Moments:	N/A
Celebration Card:	N/A
Store model glove:	N/A
Mini-helmet:	N/A

Wilson, Lewis "Hack" (1900-1948)

Year Inducted:	1979
Cut:	$300.00
3x5 card:	400.00
Photo:	800.00
Ball:	4,500.00
Bat:	N/A
B&W Plaque:	N/A
Gold Plaque:	N/A
Signed Perez-Steele:	N/A
Unsigned Perez-Steele:	15.00
Great Moments:	N/A
Celebration Card:	N/A
Store model glove:	400.00
Mini-helmet:	N/A

Wright, George (1847-1937)

Year Inducted:	1937
Cut:	$800.00
3x5 card:	1,200.00
Photo:	2,800.00
Ball:	8,500.00
Bat:	N/A
B&W Plaque:	N/A
Gold Plaque:	N/A
Signed Perez-Steele:	N/A
Unsigned Perez-Steele:	5.00
Great Moments:	N/A
Celebration Card:	N/A
Store model glove:	N/A
Mini-helmet:	N/A

Wright, Harry (1835-1895)

Year Inducted:	1953
Cut:	$1,200.00
3x5 card:	2,000.00
Photo:	3,600.00
Ball:	N/A
Bat:	N/A
B&W Plaque:	N/A
Gold Plaque:	N/A
Signed Perez-Steele:	N/A
Unsigned Perez-Steele:	5.00
Great Moments:	N/A
Celebration Card:	N/A
Store model glove:	N/A
Mini-helmet:	N/A

Wynn, Early (1920-)

Year Inducted:	1972
Cut:	$5.00
3x5 card:	7.00
Photo:	15.00
Ball:	25.00
Bat:	75.00
B&W Plaque:	N/A
Gold Plaque:	10.00
Signed Perez-Steele:	25.00
Unsigned Perez-Steele:	15.00
Great Moments:	20.00
Celebration Card:	N/A
Store model glove:	50.00
Mini-helmet:	40.00

Yastrzemski, Carl (1939-)

Year Inducted:	1989
Cut:	$8.00
3x5 card:	12.00
Photo:	25.00
Ball:	35.00
Bat:	125.00
B&W Plaque:	N/A
Gold Plaque:	20.00
Signed Perez-Steele:	35.00
Unsigned Perez-Steele:	5.00
Great Moments:	30.00
Celebration Card:	25.00
Store model glove:	50.00
Mini-helmet:	45.00

Yawkey, Tom (1903-1976)

Year Inducted:	1980
Cut:	$100.00
3x5 card:	150.00
Photo:	400.00
Ball:	2,200.00
Bat:	N/A
B&W Plaque:	N/A
Gold Plaque:	N/A
Signed Perez-Steele:	N/A
Unsigned Perez-Steele:	5.00
Great Moments:	N/A
Celebration Card:	N/A
Store model glove:	N/A
Mini-helmet:	N/A

Young, Cy (1867-1955)

Year Inducted:	1937
Cut:	$300.00
3x5 card:	350.00
Photo:	700.00
Ball:	3,500.00
Bat:	N/A
B&W Plaque:	1,000.00
Gold Plaque:	N/A
Signed Perez-Steele:	N/A
Unsigned Perez-Steele:	10.00
Great Moments:	N/A
Celebration Card:	N/A
Store model glove:	350.00
Mini-helmet:	N/A

Youngs, Ross (1897-1927)

Year Inducted:	1972
Cut:	$1,000.00
3x5 card:	1,500.00
Photo:	2,500.00
Ball:	7,000.00
Bat:	N/A
B&W Plaque:	N/A
Gold Plaque:	N/A
Signed Perez-Steele:	N/A
Unsigned Perez-Steele:	5.00
Great Moments:	N/A
Celebration Card:	N/A
Store model glove:	800.00
Mini-helmet:	N/A

ACTIVE PLAYERS

Active players are charged with carrying the torch for the National Pastime, and every collector wants signatures from today's biggest stars. Unlike Hall of Famers who go months at a time without mention in the media, today's stars like Ken Griffey Jr. and Cal Ripken are in the paper and on television every day.

Unfortunately for collectors, it's these same everyday demands on today's players that make their autographs so tough to get. Even in the off-season, many players want nothing more than to get away from the game for a few months.

Also, many of today's stars don't make the rounds on the show circuit, making their sigs that much harder to acquire. Unlike retired players who have the time and use the shows to supplement their income, today's stars

don't need the money and value their time too much to spend an afternoon signing autographs at a show for a few thousand dollars.

The best time to get the autographs of current players is during spring training. The teams are all together, and the atmosphere is more relaxed than during the season so players are generally more willing to sign. If you can't make it to Florida or Arizona in person, the end of the winter is a good time to start mailing requests to players in care of their respective teams' spring training headquarters. You'll find the response rate is better in spring training than it is during the season.

The following list includes autograph prices on several items for an extensive selection of popular active players. For definitions of the items see p. 14.

Alomar, Roberto
Card:	8.00
Photo:	18.00
Ball:	25.00
Mini-helmet:	45.00
Model bat:	80.00
Jersey:	200.00

Alomar, Sandy
Card:	7.00
Photo:	15.00
Ball:	22.00
Mini-helmet:	40.00
Model bat:	75.00
Jersey:	180.00

Alou, Moises
Card:	5.00
Photo:	15.00
Ball:	22.00
Mini-helmet:	45.00
Model bat:	75.00
Jersey:	150.00

Alvarez, Wilson
Card:	4.00
Photo:	12.00
Ball:	18.00
Mini-helmet:	40.00
Model bat:	65.00
Jersey:	125.00

Anderson, Brady
Card:	8.00
Photo:	18.00
Ball:	25.00
Mini-helmet:	45.00
Model bat:	80.00
Jersey:	190.00

Anderson, Garrett
Card:	5.00
Photo:	12.00
Ball:	20.00
Mini-helmet:	40.00
Model bat:	65.00
Jersey:	150.00

Appier, Kevin
Card:	5.00
Photo:	15.00
Ball:	22.00
Mini-helmet:	40.00
Model bat:	70.00
Jersey:	125.00

Baerga, Carlos
Card:	5.00
Photo:	12.00
Ball:	20.00
Mini-helmet:	40.00
Model bat:	65.00
Jersey:	150.00

Bagwell, Jeff
Card:	12.00
Photo:	22.00
Ball:	30.00
Mini-helmet:	60.00
Model bat:	100.00
Jersey:	225.00

Baines, Harold
Card:	5.00
Photo:	10.00
Ball:	22.00
Mini-helmet:	40.00
Model bat:	80.00
Jersey:	175.00

Beck, Rod
Card:	5.00
Photo:	12.00
Ball:	18.00
Mini-helmet:	40.00
Model bat:	65.00
Jersey:	125.00

Bell, Derek
Card:	5.00
Photo:	12.00
Ball:	20.00
Mini-helmet:	40.00
Model bat:	70.00
Jersey:	125.00

Bell, Jay
Card:	5.00
Photo:	15.00
Ball:	25.00
Mini-helmet:	45.00
Model bat:	75.00
Jersey:	125.00

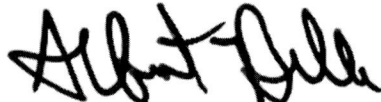

Belle, Albert
Card:	15.00
Photo:	25.00
Ball:	40.00
Mini-helmet:	75.00
Model bat:	150.00
Jersey:	300.00

Benes, Alan
Card:	5.00
Photo:	12.00
Ball:	20.00
Mini-helmet:	40.00
Model bat:	65.00
Jersey:	125.00

Benes, Andy
Card:	6.00
Photo:	12.00
Ball:	22.00
Mini-helmet:	40.00
Model bat:	65.00
Jersey:	150.00

Berroa, Geronimo
Card:	5.00
Photo:	12.00
Ball:	18.00
Mini-helmet:	40.00
Model bat:	70.00
Jersey:	125.00

DANTE BICHETTE
1995 N.L. HOME RUN CHAMP

Bichette, Dante
Card:	8.00
Photo:	15.00
Ball:	25.00
Mini-helmet:	45.00
Model bat:	80.00
Jersey:	200.00

Biggio, Craig
Card:	8.00
Photo:	18.00
Ball:	25.00
Mini-helmet:	45.00
Model bat:	80.00
Jersey:	200.00

Blauser, Jeff
Card:	5.00
Photo:	12.00
Ball:	20.00
Mini-helmet:	40.00
Model bat:	70.00
Jersey:	125.00

Boggs, Wade
Card:	10.00
Photo:	20.00
Ball:	35.00
Mini-helmet:	55.00
Model bat:	90.00
Jersey:	220.00

Bonds, Barry
Card:	12.00
Photo:	25.00
Ball:	35.00
Mini-helmet:	55.00
Model bat:	100.00
Jersey:	250.00

Bonilla, Bobby
Card:	7.00
Photo:	15.00
Ball:	25.00
Mini-helmet:	45.00
Model bat:	70.00
Jersey:	180.00

Bottalico, Rickey
Card:	4.00
Photo:	12.00
Ball:	18.00
Mini-helmet:	40.00
Model bat:	65.00
Jersey:	125.00

Brown, Kevin
Card:	7.00
Photo:	15.00
Ball:	22.00
Mini-helmet:	40.00
Model bat:	65.00
Jersey:	175.00

Buhner, Jay
Card:	7.00
Photo:	15.00
Ball:	25.00
Mini-helmet:	45.00
Model bat:	80.00
Jersey:	200.00

Burks, Ellis
Card:	5.00
Photo:	15.00
Ball:	25.00
Mini-helmet:	45.00
Model bat:	80.00
Jersey:	125.00

Burnitz, Jeromy
Card:	5.00
Photo:	15.00
Ball:	22.00
Mini-helmet:	40.00
Model bat:	70.00
Jersey:	125.00

Cameron, Mike
Card: 5.00
Photo: 15.00
Ball: 25.00
Mini-helmet: 40.00
Model bat: 70.00
Jersey: 125.00

Caminiti, Ken
Card: 7.00
Photo: 15.00
Ball: 25.00
Mini-helmet: 45.00
Model bat: 75.00
Jersey: 180.00

Canseco, Jose
Card: 8.00
Photo: 15.00
Ball: 25.00
Mini-helmet: 45.00
Model bat: 80.00
Jersey: 200.00

Carter, Joe
Card: 8.00
Photo: 15.00
Ball: 25.00
Mini-helmet: 45.00
Model bat: 80.00
Jersey: 200.00

Castilla, Vinny
Card: 7.00
Photo: 15.00
Ball: 22.00
Mini-helmet: 40.00
Model bat: 70.00
Jersey: 175.00

Cirillo, Jeff
Card: 4.00
Photo: 15.00
Ball: 20.00
Mini-helmet: 40.00
Model bat: 70.00
Jersey: 125.00

Clark, Tony
Card: 7.00
Photo: 15.00
Ball: 22.00
Mini-helmet: 45.00
Model bat: 75.00
Jersey: 180.00

Clark, Will
Card: 8.00
Photo: 20.00
Ball: 30.00
Mini-helmet: 45.00
Model bat: 75.00
Jersey: 200.00

Clemens, Roger
Card: 20.00
Photo: 30.00
Ball: 50.00
Mini-helmet: 75.00
Model bat: 125.00
Jersey: 300.00

Cone, David
Card: 8.00
Photo: 15.00
Ball: 25.00
Mini-helmet: 50.00
Model bat: 75.00
Jersey: 200.00

Cordova, Marty
Card: 5.00
Photo: 15.00
Ball: 22.00
Mini-helmet: 40.00
Model bat: 70.00
Jersey: 125.00

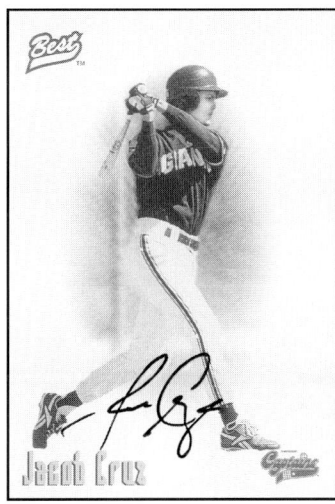

Cruz, Jacob
Card: 4.00
Photo: 10.00
Ball: 15.00
Mini-helmet: 35.00
Model bat: 60.00
Jersey: 125.00

Cruz, Jose Jr.
Card: 10.00
Photo: 20.00
Ball: 35.00
Mini-helmet: 50.00
Model bat: 80.00
Jersey: 200.00

Damon, Johnny
Card: 5.00
Photo: 15.00
Ball: 22.00
Mini-helmet: 40.00
Model bat: 70.00
Jersey: 125.00

Davis, Chili
Card: 6.00
Photo: 15.00
Ball: 22.00
Mini-helmet: 40.00
Model bat: 75.00
Jersey: 125.00

Delgado, Carlos
Card:	6.00
Photo:	15.00
Ball:	22.00
Mini-helmet:	40.00
Model bat:	70.00
Jersey:	125.00

DeShields, Delino
Card:	5.00
Photo:	15.00
Ball:	22.00
Mini-helmet:	40.00
Model bat:	70.00
Jersey:	125.00

Dunwoody, Todd
Card:	5.00
Photo:	12.00
Ball:	20.00
Mini-helmet:	35.00
Model bat:	65.00
Jersey:	125.00

Durham, Ray
Card:	5.00
Photo:	15.00
Ball:	22.00
Mini-helmet:	40.00
Model bat:	70.00
Jersey:	125.00

Drabek, Doug
Card:	5.00
Photo:	15.00
Ball:	22.00
Mini-helmet:	40.00
Model bat:	65.00
Jersey:	125.00

Dykstra, Len
Card:	5.00
Photo:	10.00
Ball:	20.00
Mini-helmet:	40.00
Model bat:	70.00
Jersey:	150.00

Eckersley, Dennis
Card:	10.00
Photo:	20.00
Ball:	30.00
Mini-helmet:	55.00
Model bat:	90.00
Jersey:	225.00

Edmonds, Jim
Card:	6.00
Photo:	12.00
Ball:	20.00
Mini-helmet:	40.00
Model bat:	75.00
Jersey:	175.00

Erstad, Darin
Card:	8.00
Photo:	18.00
Ball:	25.00
Mini-helmet:	45.00
Model bat:	75.00
Jersey:	180.00

Estes, Shawn
Card:	5.00
Photo:	15.00
Ball:	22.00
Mini-helmet:	40.00
Model bat:	65.00
Jersey:	125.00

Fassero, Jeff
Card:	4.00
Photo:	12.00
Ball:	18.00
Mini-helmet:	40.00
Model bat:	65.00
Jersey:	125.00

Fielder, Cecil
Card:	8.00
Photo:	20.00
Ball:	30.00
Mini-helmet:	50.00
Model bat:	80.00
Jersey:	180.00

Finley, Chuck
Card:	5.00
Photo:	15.00
Ball:	22.00
Mini-helmet:	40.00
Model bat:	65.00
Jersey:	125.00

Finley, Steve
Card:	5.00
Photo:	15.00
Ball:	22.00
Mini-helmet:	40.00
Model bat:	70.00
Jersey:	125.00

Fryman, Travis
Card:	7.00
Photo:	15.00
Ball:	25.00
Mini-helmet:	45.00
Model bat:	70.00
Jersey:	175.00

Galarraga, Andres
Card:	10.00
Photo:	20.00
Ball:	30.00
Mini-helmet:	55.00
Model bat:	90.00
Jersey:	225.00

Gant, Ron
Card:	5.00
Photo:	15.00
Ball:	22.00
Mini-helmet:	40.00
Model bat:	75.00
Jersey:	125.00

Garciaparra, Nomar
Card:	15.00
Photo:	25.00
Ball:	35.00
Mini-helmet:	60.00
Model bat:	100.00
Jersey:	250.00

Gilkey, Bernard
Card:	4.00
Photo:	12.00
Ball:	20.00
Mini-helmet:	40.00
Model bat:	70.00
Jersey:	125.00

Glavine, Tom
Card: 8.00
Photo: 18.00
Ball: 28.00
Mini-helmet: 50.00
Model bat: 80.00
Jersey: 200.00

Gonzalez, Alex
Card: 5.00
Photo: 15.00
Ball: 20.00
Mini-helmet: 40.00
Model bat: 65.00
Jersey: 125.00

Gonzalez, Juan
Card: 10.00
Photo: 20.00
Ball: 30.00
Mini-helmet: 60.00
Model bat: 100.00
Jersey: 225.00

Gooden, Dwight
Card: 7.00
Photo: 15.00
Ball: 25.00
Mini-helmet: 45.00
Model bat: 70.00
Jersey: 150.00

Goodwin, Tom
Card: 4.00
Photo: 12.00
Ball: 18.00
Mini-helmet: 40.00
Model bat: 65.00
Jersey: 125.00

Grace, Mark
Card: 8.00
Photo: 15.00
Ball: 28.00
Mini-helmet: 45.00
Model bat: 80.00
Jersey: 200.00

Green, Shawn
Card: 5.00
Photo: 15.00
Ball: 22.00
Mini-helmet: 40.00
Model bat: 75.00
Jersey: 125.00

Greene, Todd
Card: 5.00
Photo: 12.00
Ball: 18.00
Mini-helmet: 30.00
Model bat: 60.00
Jersey: 125.00

Greer, Rusty
Card: 7.00
Photo: 15.00
Ball: 22.00
Mini-helmet: 45.00
Model bat: 75.00
Jersey: 175.00

Grieve, Ben
Card: 10.00
Photo: 20.00
Ball: 30.00
Mini-helmet: 50.00
Model bat: 100.00
Jersey: 185.00

Griffey, Ken Jr.
Card: 25.00
Photo: 35.00
Ball: 50.00
Mini-helmet: 90.00
Model bat: 175.00
Jersey: 350.00

Grissom, Marquis
Card: 5.00
Photo: 15.00
Ball: 22.00
Mini-helmet: 40.00
Model bat: 70.00
Jersey: 125.00

Grudzielanek, Mark
Card: 4.00
Photo: 12.00
Ball: 20.00
Mini-helmet: 40.00
Model bat: 65.00
Jersey: 125.00

Guerrero, Vladimir
Card: 7.00
Photo: 15.00
Ball: 25.00
Mini-helmet: 45.00
Model bat: 85.00
Jersey: 175.00

Guillen, Jose
Card: 7.00
Photo: 15.00
Ball: 22.00
Mini-helmet: 45.00
Model bat: 70.00
Jersey: 175.00

Gwynn, Tony
Card: 15.00
Photo: 25.00
Ball: 40.00
Mini-helmet: 65.00
Model bat: 125.00
Jersey: 250.00

Hamilton, Joey
Card: 4.00
Photo: 12.00
Ball: 18.00
Mini-helmet: 40.00
Model bat: 65.00
Jersey: 125.00

Hammonds, Jeffrey
Card: 6.00
Photo: 15.00
Ball: 25.00
Mini-helmet: 45.00
Model bat: 70.00
Jersey: 150.00

Helton, Todd
Card: 5.00
Photo: 12.00
Ball: 20.00
Mini-helmet: 45.00
Model bat: 75.00
Jersey: 125.00

Henderson, Rickey
Card: 15.00
Photo: 22.00
Ball: 35.00
Mini-helmet: 60.00
Model bat: 100.00
Jersey: 225.00

Hentgen, Pat
Card: 5.00
Photo: 15.00
Ball: 22.00
Mini-helmet: 40.00
Model bat: 65.00
Jersey: 125.00

Hermansen, Chad
Card: 5.00
Photo: 12.00
Ball: 18.00
Mini-helmet: 35.00
Model bat: 60.00
Jersey: 125.00

Hernandez, Livan
Card: 7.00
Photo: 15.00
Ball: 25.00
Mini-helmet: 45.00
Model bat: 75.00
Jersey: 175.00

Hernandez, Roberto
Card: 5.00
Photo: 15.00
Ball: 22.00
Mini-helmet: 40.00
Model bat: 65.00
Jersey: 125.00

Hershiser, Orel
Card: 8.00
Photo: 15.00
Ball: 25.00
Mini-helmet: 45.00
Model bat: 80.00
Jersey: 180.00

Higginson, Bobby
Card: 4.00
Photo: 12.00
Ball: 20.00
Mini-helmet: 40.00
Model bat: 70.00
Jersey: 125.00

Hoiles, Chris
Card: 5.00
Photo: 12.00
Ball: 20.00
Mini-helmet: 40.00
Model bat: 70.00
Jersey: 125.00

Hoffman, Trevor
Card: 4.00
Photo: 15.00
Ball: 22.00
Mini-helmet: 40.00
Model bat: 65.00
Jersey: 125.00

Hollandsworth, Todd
Card: 5.00
Photo: 15.00
Ball: 25.00
Mini-helmet: 40.00
Model bat: 65.00
Jersey: 125.00

Hundley, Todd
Card: 7.00
Photo: 15.00
Ball: 22.00
Mini-helmet: 40.00
Model bat: 75.00
Jersey: 175.00

Hunter, Brian
Card: 7.00
Photo: 15.00
Ball: 22.00
Mini-helmet: 40.00
Model bat: 70.00
Jersey: 175.00

Irabu, Hideki
Card: 7.00
Photo: 20.00
Ball: 30.00
Mini-helmet: 50.00
Model bat: 80.00
Jersey: 150.00

Isringhausen, Jason
Card: 5.00
Photo: 12.00
Ball: 22.00
Mini-helmet: 40.00
Model bat: 65.00
Jersey: 150.00

Jaha, John
Card: 4.00
Photo: 12.00
Ball: 18.00
Mini-helmet: 40.00
Model bat: 70.00
Jersey: 125.00

Jefferies, Gregg
Card:	5.00
Photo:	12.00
Ball:	22.00
Mini-helmet:	40.00
Model bat:	70.00
Jersey:	150.00

Jeter, Derek
Card:	18.00
Photo:	30.00
Ball:	45.00
Mini-helmet:	75.00
Model bat:	140.00
Jersey:	300.00

Johnson, Charles
Card:	7.00
Photo:	15.00
Ball:	22.00
Mini-helmet:	45.00
Model bat:	75.00
Jersey:	175.00

Johnson, Lance
Card:	4.00
Photo:	12.00
Ball:	20.00
Mini-helmet:	40.00
Model bat:	65.00
Jersey:	125.00

Johnson, Randy
Card:	18.00
Photo:	30.00
Ball:	45.00
Mini-helmet:	75.00
Model bat:	125.00
Jersey:	275.00

Jones, Andruw
Card:	12.00
Photo:	20.00
Ball:	30.00
Mini-helmet:	50.00
Model bat:	85.00
Jersey:	200.00

Jones, Bobby
Card:	4.00
Photo:	12.00
Ball:	18.00
Mini-helmet:	40.00
Model bat:	65.00
Jersey:	125.00

Jones, Chipper
Card:	15.00
Photo:	25.00
Ball:	40.00
Mini-helmet:	65.00
Model bat:	125.00
Jersey:	250.00

Jones, Doug
Card:	4.00
Photo:	12.00
Ball:	18.00
Mini-helmet:	40.00
Model bat:	65.00
Jersey:	125.00

Jordan, Brian
Card:	5.00
Photo:	15.00
Ball:	22.00
Mini-helmet:	40.00
Model bat:	75.00
Jersey:	125.00

Joyner, Wally
Card:	5.00
Photo:	15.00
Ball:	25.00
Mini-helmet:	45.00
Model bat:	70.00
Jersey:	125.00

Justice, David
Card:	12.00
Photo:	20.00
Ball:	30.00
Mini-helmet:	55.00
Model bat:	90.00
Jersey:	200.00

Karros, Eric
Card:	7.00
Photo:	15.00
Ball:	22.00
Mini-helmet:	45.00
Model bat:	70.00
Jersey:	175.00

Kendall, Jason
Card:	5.00
Photo:	15.00
Ball:	22.00
Mini-helmet:	40.00
Model bat:	70.00
Jersey:	125.00

Kent, Jeff
Card:	5.00
Photo:	15.00
Ball:	22.00
Mini-helmet:	40.00
Model bat:	70.00
Jersey:	125.00

Key, Jimmy
Card:	6.00
Photo:	15.00
Ball:	25.00
Mini-helmet:	45.00
Model bat:	70.00
Jersey:	150.00

Kile, Darryl
Card:	5.00
Photo:	15.00
Ball:	22.00
Mini-helmet:	40.00
Model bat:	65.00
Jersey:	125.00

King, Jeff
Card:	5.00
Photo:	15.00
Ball:	25.00
Mini-helmet:	40.00
Model bat:	75.00
Jersey:	125.00

Klesko, Ryan
Card:	7.00
Photo:	15.00
Ball:	25.00
Mini-helmet:	45.00
Model bat:	80.00
Jersey:	180.00

Knoblauch, Chuck
Card:	10.00
Photo:	20.00
Ball:	28.00
Mini-helmet:	50.00
Model bat:	85.00
Jersey:	200.00

Konerko, Paul
Card:	5.00
Photo:	12.00
Ball:	20.00
Mini-helmet:	45.00
Model bat:	70.00
Jersey:	125.00

Kotsay, Mark
Card:	5.00
Photo:	12.00
Ball:	20.00
Mini-helmet:	40.00
Model bat:	65.00
Jersey:	125.00

Lankford, Ray
Card:	7.00
Photo:	15.00
Ball:	22.00
Mini-helmet:	45.00
Model bat:	75.00
Jersey:	180.00

Lansing, Mike
Card:	4.00
Photo:	12.00
Ball:	18.00
Mini-helmet:	40.00
Model bat:	70.00
Jersey:	125.00

Larkin, Barry
Card:	8.00
Photo:	15.00
Ball:	25.00
Mini-helmet:	45.00
Model bat:	80.00
Jersey:	200.00

Lee, Travis
Card:	8.00
Photo:	20.00
Ball:	30.00
Mini-helmet:	50.00
Model bat:	85.00
Jersey:	150.00

Leiter, Al
Card:	5.00
Photo:	15.00
Ball:	25.00
Mini-helmet:	40.00
Model bat:	65.00
Jersey:	125.00

Lofton, Kenny
Card:	10.00
Photo:	18.00
Ball:	28.00
Mini-helmet:	50.00
Model bat:	85.00
Jersey:	200.00

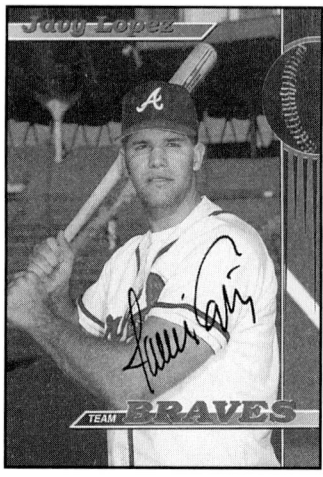

Lopez, Javy
Card:	8.00
Photo:	15.00
Ball:	25.00
Mini-helmet:	45.00
Model bat:	75.00
Jersey:	180.00

Maddux, Greg
Card:	22.00
Photo:	35.00
Ball:	55.00
Mini-helmet:	90.00
Model bat:	150.00
Jersey:	325.00

Martin, Al
Card:	4.00
Photo:	12.00
Ball:	20.00
Mini-helmet:	40.00
Model bat:	70.00
Jersey:	125.00

Martinez, Edgar
Card:	8.00
Photo:	15.00
Ball:	25.00
Mini-helmet:	45.00
Model bat:	80.00
Jersey:	200.00

Martinez, Pedro
Card:	8.00
Photo:	15.00
Ball:	25.00
Mini-helmet:	45.00
Model bat:	80.00
Jersey:	200.00

Martinez, Ramon
Card:	5.00
Photo:	15.00
Ball:	22.00
Mini-helmet:	40.00
Model bat:	70.00
Jersey:	150.00

Martinez, Tino
Card:	10.00
Photo:	20.00
Ball:	30.00
Mini-helmet:	55.00
Model bat:	90.00
Jersey:	200.00

McDonald, Ben
Card:	7.00
Photo:	15.00
Ball:	25.00
Mini-helmet:	45.00
Model bat:	65.00
Jersey:	150.00

McDowell, Jack
Card:	7.00
Photo:	15.00
Ball:	25.00
Mini-helmet:	45.00
Model bat:	65.00
Jersey:	150.00

McGriff, Fred
Card:	12.00
Photo:	22.00
Ball:	35.00
Mini-helmet:	60.00
Model bat:	100.00
Jersey:	225.00

McGwire, Mark
Card:	15.00
Photo:	28.00
Ball:	40.00
Mini-helmet:	75.00
Model bat:	125.00
Jersey:	275.00

McRae, Brian
Card:	5.00
Photo:	15.00
Ball:	22.00
Mini-helmet:	40.00
Model bat:	70.00
Jersey:	125.00

Mesa, Jose
Card:	5.00
Photo:	12.00
Ball:	20.00
Mini-helmet:	40.00
Model bat:	65.00
Jersey:	125.00

Molitor, Paul
Card:	15.00
Photo:	25.00
Ball:	40.00
Mini-helmet:	65.00
Model bat:	125.00
Jersey:	225.00

Mondesi, Raul
Card:	10.00
Photo:	20.00
Ball:	30.00
Mini-helmet:	50.00
Model bat:	85.00
Jersey:	200.00

Morandini, Mickey
Card:	4.00
Photo:	12.00
Ball:	18.00
Mini-helmet:	40.00
Model bat:	70.00
Jersey:	125.00

Mussina, Mike
Card:	12.00
Photo:	20.00
Ball:	35.00
Mini-helmet:	55.00
Model bat:	90.00
Jersey:	225.00

Myers, Randy
Card:	5.00
Photo:	12.00
Ball:	20.00
Mini-helmet:	40.00
Model bat:	65.00
Jersey:	125.00

Nagy, Charles
Card:	5.00
Photo:	12.00
Ball:	20.00
Mini-helmet:	40.00
Model bat:	65.00
Jersey:	125.00

Neagle, Denny
Card:	7.00
Photo:	15.00
Ball:	22.00
Mini-helmet:	45.00
Model bat:	75.00
Jersey:	180.00

Nen, Robb
Card:	5.00
Photo:	15.00
Ball:	25.00
Mini-helmet:	40.00
Model bat:	70.00
Jersey:	125.00

Nilsson, Dave
Card:	4.00
Photo:	15.00
Ball:	20.00
Mini-helmet:	40.00
Model bat:	70.00
Jersey:	125.00

Nixon, Otis
Card:	5.00
Photo:	12.00
Ball:	20.00
Mini-helmet:	40.00
Model bat:	65.00
Jersey:	125.00

Nomo, Hideo
Card: 15.00
Photo: 25.00
Ball: 45.00
Mini-helmet: 70.00
Model bat: 125.00
Jersey: 275.00

Olerud, John
Card: 7.00
Photo: 15.00
Ball: 25.00
Mini-helmet: 45.00
Model bat: 70.00
Jersey: 150.00

O'Neill, Paul
Card: 12.00
Photo: 18.00
Ball: 25.00
Mini-helmet: 50.00
Model bat: 85.00
Jersey: 200.00

Ordoñez, Rey
Card: 5.00
Photo: 15.00
Ball: 22.00
Mini-helmet: 40.00
Model bat: 65.00
Jersey: 125.00

Orie, Kevin
Card: 4.00
Photo: 12.00
Ball: 18.00
Mini-helmet: 40.00
Model bat: 70.00
Jersey: 125.00

Palmeiro, Rafael
Card: 7.00
Photo: 15.00
Ball: 25.00
Mini-helmet: 45.00
Model bat: 75.00
Jersey: 180.00

Palmer, Dean
Card: 5.00
Photo: 15.00
Ball: 25.00
Mini-helmet: 40.00
Model bat: 75.00
Jersey: 125.00

Park, Chan Ho
Card: 5.00
Photo: 15.00
Ball: 25.00
Mini-helmet: 45.00
Model bat: 70.00
Jersey: 150.00

Pettitte, Andy
Card: 12.00
Photo: 20.00
Ball: 35.00
Mini-helmet: 55.00
Model bat: 90.00
Jersey: 200.00

Percival, Troy
Card: 4.00
Photo: 12.00
Ball: 18.00
Mini-helmet: 40.00
Model bat: 65.00
Jersey: 125.00

Piazza, Mike
Card: 20.00
Photo: 30.00
Ball: 50.00
Mini-helmet: 80.00
Model bat: 150.00
Jersey: 300.00

Radke, Brad
Card: 5.00
Photo: 15.00
Ball: 25.00
Mini-helmet: 40.00
Model bat: 70.00
Jersey: 125.00

Raines, Tim
Card: 7.00
Photo: 15.00
Ball: 25.00
Mini-helmet: 45.00
Model bat: 75.00
Jersey: 150.00

Ramirez, Manny
Card: 8.00
Photo: 15.00
Ball: 25.00
Mini-helmet: 45.00
Model bat: 80.00
Jersey: 200.00

Renteria, Edgar
Card: 5.00
Photo: 12.00
Ball: 20.00
Mini-helmet: 40.00
Model bat: 70.00
Jersey: 125.00

Reynolds, Shane
Card: 5.00
Photo: 15.00
Ball: 22.00
Mini-helmet: 40.00
Model bat: 65.00
Jersey: 125.00

Ripken, Cal
Card: 25.00
Photo: 40.00
Ball: 65.00
Mini-helmet: 100.00
Model bat: 200.00
Jersey: 375.00

Rivera, Mariano
Card:	5.00
Photo:	15.00
Ball:	22.00
Mini-helmet:	40.00
Model bat:	70.00
Jersey:	125.00

Rodriguez, Alex
Card:	15.00
Photo:	30.00
Ball:	45.00
Mini-helmet:	70.00
Model bat:	140.00
Jersey:	275.00

Rodriguez, Ivan
Card:	10.00
Photo:	18.00
Ball:	30.00
Mini-helmet:	55.00
Model bat:	90.00
Jersey:	200.00

Rolen, Scott
Card:	7.00
Photo:	18.00
Ball:	25.00
Mini-helmet:	45.00
Model bat:	75.00
Jersey:	200.00

Saberhagen, Bret
Card:	6.00
Photo:	12.00
Ball:	25.00
Mini-helmet:	45.00
Model bat:	65.00
Jersey:	150.00

Salmon, Tim
Card:	7.00
Photo:	15.00
Ball:	25.00
Mini-helmet:	45.00
Model bat:	75.00
Jersey:	200.00

Sanders, Reggie
Card:	5.00
Photo:	15.00
Ball:	22.00
Mini-helmet:	40.00
Model bat:	75.00
Jersey:	125.00

Saunders, Tony
Card:	4.00
Photo:	12.00
Ball:	18.00
Mini-helmet:	35.00
Model bat:	65.00
Jersey:	125.00

Schilling, Curt
Card:	7.00
Photo:	15.00
Ball:	22.00
Mini-helmet:	40.00
Model bat:	70.00
Jersey:	175.00

Segui, David
Card:	4.00
Photo:	12.00
Ball:	20.00
Mini-helmet:	40.00
Model bat:	70.00
Jersey:	125.00

Shaw, Jeff
Card:	4.00
Photo:	12.00
Ball:	18.00
Mini-helmet:	40.00
Model bat:	65.00
Jersey:	125.00

Sheffield, Gary
Card:	10.00
Photo:	20.00
Ball:	30.00
Mini-helmet:	50.00
Model bat:	90.00
Jersey:	200.00

Simon, Randall
Card:	4.00
Photo:	10.00
Ball:	15.00
Mini-helmet:	30.00
Model bat:	60.00
Jersey:	125.00

Smoltz, John
Card:	7.00
Photo:	15.00
Ball:	25.00
Mini-helmet:	50.00
Model bat:	75.00
Jersey:	200.00

Snow, J.T.
Card:	5.00
Photo:	15.00
Ball:	22.00
Mini-helmet:	40.00
Model bat:	75.00
Jersey:	125.00

Sorrento, Paul
Card:	4.00
Photo:	12.00
Ball:	18.00
Mini-helmet:	35.00
Model bat:	65.00
Jersey:	125.00

Sosa, Sammy
Card:	12.00
Photo:	20.00
Ball:	30.00
Mini-helmet:	50.00
Model bat:	100.00
Jersey:	225.00

Sprague, Ed
Card:	4.00
Photo:	12.00
Ball:	18.00
Mini-helmet:	35.00
Model bat:	65.00
Jersey:	125.00

Strawberry, Darryl
Card:	8.00
Photo:	15.00
Ball:	28.00
Mini-helmet:	50.00
Model bat:	90.00
Jersey:	150.00

Steinbach, Terry
Card:	5.00
Photo:	15.00
Ball:	22.00
Mini-helmet:	40.00
Model bat:	65.00
Jersey:	125.00

Surhoff, B.J.
Card:	5.00
Photo:	15.00
Ball:	20.00
Mini-helmet:	40.00
Model bat:	75.00
Jersey:	125.00

FRANK THOMAS
2-TIME A.L. MVP

Thomas, Frank
Card:	22.00
Photo:	35.00
Ball:	50.00
Mini-helmet:	90.00
Model bat:	160.00
Jersey:	325.00

Thome, Jim
Card:	10.00
Photo:	20.00
Ball:	30.00
Mini-helmet:	50.00
Model bat:	80.00
Jersey:	200.00

Thompson, Justin
Card:	4.00
Photo:	12.00
Ball:	20.00
Mini-helmet:	40.00
Model bat:	65.00
Jersey:	125.00

Tomko, Brett
Card:	5.00
Photo:	12.00
Ball:	20.00
Mini-helmet:	40.00
Model bat:	65.00
Jersey:	125.00

Tucker, Michael
Card:	5.00
Photo:	15.00
Ball:	22.00
Mini-helmet:	40.00
Model bat:	70.00
Jersey:	125.00

Vaughn, Mo
Card:	10.00
Photo:	20.00
Ball:	30.00
Mini-helmet:	55.00
Model bat:	100.00
Jersey:	200.00

Valentin, John
Card:	5.00
Photo:	12.00
Ball:	18.00
Mini-helmet:	40.00
Model bat:	70.00
Jersey:	125.00

Ventura, Robin
Card:	6.00
Photo:	15.00
Ball:	25.00
Mini-helmet:	40.00
Model bat:	75.00
Jersey:	125.00

Vizquel, Omar
Card:	5.00
Photo:	15.00
Ball:	22.00
Mini-helmet:	40.00
Model bat:	70.00
Jersey:	125.00

Wagner, Billy
  Card: 5.00
  Photo: 12.00
  Ball: 20.00
  Mini-helmet: 40.00
  Model bat: 65.00
  Jersey: 125.00

Walker, Larry
  Card: 10.00
  Photo: 20.00
  Ball: 30.00
  Mini-helmet: 55.00
  Model bat: 100.00
  Jersey: 220.00

Wetteland, John
  Card: 5.00
  Photo: 15.00
  Ball: 22.00
  Mini-helmet: 45.00
  Model bat: 65.00
  Jersey: 125.00

White, Devon
  Card: 5.00
  Photo: 15.00
  Ball: 22.00
  Mini-helmet: 40.00
  Model bat: 70.00
  Jersey: 125.00

White, Rondell
  Card: 5.00
  Photo: 15.00
  Ball: 25.00
  Mini-helmet: 40.00
  Model bat: 75.00
  Jersey: 125.00

Wohlers, Mark
  Card: 5.00
  Photo: 12.00
  Ball: 20.00
  Mini-helmet: 40.00
  Model bat: 65.00
  Jersey: 125.00

Williams, Bernie
  Card: 10.00
  Photo: 20.00
  Ball: 30.00
  Mini-helmet: 55.00
  Model bat: 90.00
  Jersey: 200.00

MATT WILLIAMS

Williams, Matt
  Card: 8.00
  Photo: 15.00
  Ball: 25.00
  Mini-helmet: 45.00
  Model bat: 80.00
  Jersey: 200.00

Wilson, Paul
  Card: 6.00
  Photo: 15.00
  Ball: 22.00
  Mini-helmet: 40.00
  Model bat: 65.00
  Jersey: 125.00

Womack, Tony
  Card: 5.00
  Photo: 15.00
  Ball: 22.00
  Mini-helmet: 40.00
  Model bat: 70.00
  Jersey: 125.00

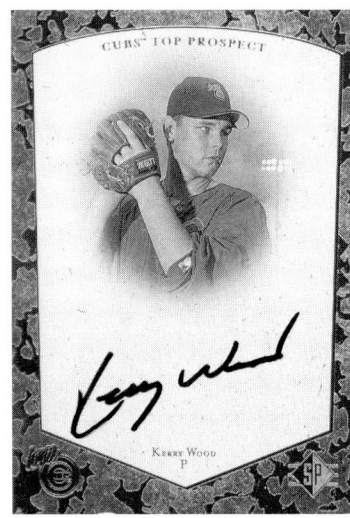

Wood, Kerry
  Card: 8.00
  Photo: 15.00
  Ball: 25.00
  Mini-helmet: 40.00
  Model bat: 75.00
  Jersey: 150.00

Wright, Jaret
  Card: 6.00
  Photo: 15.00
  Ball: 25.00
  Mini-helmet: 40.00
  Model bat: 70.00
  Jersey: 125.00

Young, Eric
  Card: 5.00
  Photo: 15.00
  Ball: 22.00
  Mini-helmet: 40.00
  Model bat: 70.00
  Jersey: 125.00

RETIRED PLAYERS

This list includes many retired players whose contributions to the game make them of significant interest to collectors. A "†" indicates the player is deceased. A "*" indicates that an autographed item isn't known to exist, or is so rare that it's difficult to price. For example: Sandy Amoros died in 1992, and the first baseball mini-helmets weren't released until 1997, making it impossible for him to have signed one.

Abrams, Cal†
Card:	$6.00
Photo:	12.00
Ball:	22.00
Mini-helmet:	*
Model bat:	75.00
Jersey:	125.00

Adcock, Joe
Card:	$8.00
Photo:	15.00
Ball:	25.00
Mini-helmet:	45.00
Model bat:	75.00
Jersey:	125.00

Agee, Tommie
Card:	$5.00
Photo:	10.00
Ball:	20.00
Mini-helmet:	40.00
Model bat:	75.00
Jersey:	125.00

Allen, Dick
Card:	$8.00
Photo:	15.00
Ball:	25.00
Mini-helmet:	45.00
Model bat:	100.00
Jersey:	150.00

Amoros, Sandy†
Card:	$15.00
Photo:	35.00
Ball:	85.00
Mini-helmet:	*
Model bat:	75.00
Jersey:	125.00

Bando, Sal
Card:	$5.00
Photo:	10.00
Ball:	20.00
Mini-helmet:	40.00
Model bat:	75.00
Jersey:	125.00

Bauer, Hank
Card:	$6.00
Photo:	12.00
Ball:	25.00
Mini-helmet:	45.00
Model bat:	75.00
Jersey:	125.00

Belanger, Mark
Card:	$5.00
Photo:	10.00
Ball:	20.00
Mini-helmet:	40.00
Model bat:	75.00
Jersey:	125.00

Bell, Buddy
Card:	$5.00
Photo:	10.00
Ball:	20.00
Mini-helmet:	40.00
Model bat:	75.00
Jersey:	125.00

Bell, George
Card:	$5.00
Photo:	10.00
Ball:	25.00
Mini-helmet:	45.00
Model bat:	75.00
Jersey:	125.00

Bell, Gus†
Card:	$10.00
Photo:	25.00
Ball:	50.00
Mini-helmet:	*
Model bat:	75.00
Jersey:	125.00

Berg, Moe†
Card:	*
Photo:	$400.00
Ball:	1,200.00
Mini-helmet:	*
Model bat:	*
Jersey:	*

Blair, Paul
Card:	$6.00
Photo:	12.00
Ball:	22.00
Mini-helmet:	45.00
Model bat:	75.00
Jersey:	125.00

Blue, Vida
Card:	$8.00
Photo:	15.00
Ball:	25.00
Mini-helmet:	45.00
Model bat:	75.00
Jersey:	150.00

Blyleven, Bert
Card:	$8.00
Photo:	12.00
Ball:	25.00
Mini-helmet:	45.00
Model bat:	75.00
Jersey:	150.00

Bonds, Bobby
Card:	$8.00
Photo:	15.00
Ball:	25.00
Mini-helmet:	45.00
Model bat:	85.00
Jersey:	150.00

Bouton, Jim

Card:	$5.00
Photo:	10.00
Ball:	22.00
Mini-helmet:	45.00
Model bat:	75.00
Jersey:	125.00

Bowa, Larry

Card:	$5.00
Photo:	10.00
Ball:	22.00
Mini-helmet:	45.00
Model bat:	75.00
Jersey:	125.00

Boyer, Clete

Card:	$5.00
Photo:	10.00
Ball:	20.00
Mini-helmet:	40.00
Model bat:	75.00
Jersey:	125.00

Boyer, Ken†

Card:	35.00
Photo:	80.00
Ball:	325.00
Mini-helmet:	*
Model bat:	*
Jersey:	*

Branca, Ralph

Card:	$6.00
Photo:	12.00
Ball:	22.00
Mini-helmet:	45.00
Model bat:	75.00
Jersey:	125.00

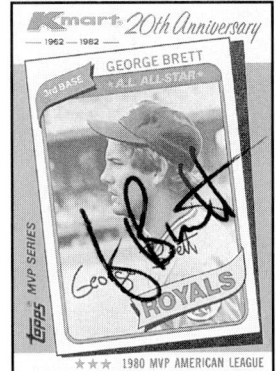

Brett, George

Card:	$15.00
Photo:	35.00
Ball:	50.00
Mini-helmet:	75.00
Model bat:	150.00
Jersey:	250.00

Brown, Bobby

Card:	$8.00
Photo:	15.00
Ball:	30.00
Mini-helmet:	50.00
Model bat:	75.00
Jersey:	125.00

Buckner, Bill

Card:	$8.00
Photo:	12.00
Ball:	25.00
Mini-helmet:	45.00
Model bat:	100.00
Jersey:	175.00

Burdette, Lew

Card:	$5.00
Photo:	10.00
Ball:	20.00
Mini-helmet:	40.00
Model bat:	75.00
Jersey:	125.00

Burgess, Smoky†

Card:	$15.00
Photo:	30.00
Ball:	150.00
Mini-helmet:	*
Model bat:	*
Jersey:	*

Burroughs, Jeff

Card:	$5.00
Photo:	10.00
Ball:	20.00
Mini-helmet:	40.00
Model bat:	75.00
Jersey:	125.00

Cabell, Enos

Card:	$5.00
Photo:	10.00
Ball:	20.00
Mini-helmet:	40.00
Model bat:	75.00
Jersey:	125.00

Callison, Johnny

Card:	$5.00
Photo:	10.00
Ball:	20.00
Mini-helmet:	40.00
Model bat:	75.00
Jersey:	125.00

Campaneris, Bert

Card:	$5.00
Photo:	10.00
Ball:	20.00
Mini-helmet:	40.00
Model bat:	75.00
Jersey:	125.00

Carey, Andy

Card:	$5.00
Photo:	10.00
Ball:	22.00
Mini-helmet:	45.00
Model bat:	75.00
Jersey:	125.00

Carrasquel, Chico

Card:	$6.00
Photo:	12.00
Ball:	25.00
Mini-helmet:	45.00
Model bat:	75.00
Jersey:	125.00

Carter, Gary

Card:	$10.00
Photo:	15.00
Ball:	25.00
Mini-helmet:	45.00
Model bat:	100.00
Jersey:	175.00

Carty, Rico
Card:	$8.00
Photo:	15.00
Ball:	25.00
Mini-helmet:	50.00
Model bat:	75.00
Jersey:	125.00

Cash, Norm†
Card:	$25.00
Photo:	45.00
Ball:	275.00
Mini-helmet:	*
Model bat:	*
Jersey:	*

Cavarretta, Phil
Card:	$8.00
Photo:	18.00
Ball:	40.00
Mini-helmet:	60.00
Model bat:	75.00
Jersey:	125.00

Cedeño, Cesar
Card:	$7.00
Photo:	12.00
Ball:	25.00
Mini-helmet:	45.00
Model bat:	75.00
Jersey:	125.00

Cepeda, Orlando
Card:	$8.00
Photo:	12.00
Ball:	25.00
Mini-helmet:	45.00
Model bat:	85.00
Jersey:	125.00

Cey, Ron
Card:	$5.00
Photo:	10.00
Ball:	25.00
Mini-helmet:	45.00
Model bat:	75.00
Jersey:	125.00

Chambliss, Chris
Card:	$5.00
Photo:	10.00
Ball:	20.00
Mini-helmet:	40.00
Model bat:	75.00
Jersey:	125.00

Chance, Dean
Card:	$5.00
Photo:	10.00
Ball:	20.00
Mini-helmet:	40.00
Model bat:	75.00
Jersey:	125.00

Clark, Jack
Card:	$6.00
Photo:	12.00
Ball:	22.00
Mini-helmet:	45.00
Model bat:	75.00
Jersey:	125.00

Colavito, Rocky
Card:	$10.00
Photo:	18.00
Ball:	40.00
Mini-helmet:	60.00
Model bat:	100.00
Jersey:	150.00

Coleman, Jerry
Card:	$5.00
Photo:	10.00
Ball:	22.00
Mini-helmet:	45.00
Model bat:	75.00
Jersey:	125.00

Concepcion, Dave
Card:	$7.00
Photo:	15.00
Ball:	25.00
Mini-helmet:	45.00
Model bat:	75.00
Jersey:	150.00

Conigliaro, Tony†
Card:	$75.00
Photo:	150.00
Ball:	550.00
Mini-helmet:	*
Model bat:	*
Jersey:	*

Connors, Chuck†
Card:	$20.00
Photo:	50.00
Ball:	100.00
Mini-helmet:	*
Model bat:	*
Jersey:	*

Cooper, Cecil
Card:	$7.00
Photo:	10.00
Ball:	22.00
Mini-helmet:	45.00
Model bat:	75.00
Jersey:	150.00

Crandall, Del
Card:	$5.00
Photo:	10.00
Ball:	25.00
Mini-helmet:	45.00
Model bat:	75.00
Jersey:	125.00

Crosetti, Frank
Card:	$8.00
Photo:	15.00
Ball:	30.00
Mini-helmet:	50.00
Model bat:	75.00
Jersey:	125.00

Cruz, Jose
Card:	$7.00
Photo:	15.00
Ball:	25.00
Mini-helmet:	45.00
Model bat:	75.00
Jersey:	150.00

Cuellar, Mike
Card:	$7.00
Photo:	15.00
Ball:	25.00
Mini-helmet:	45.00
Model bat:	75.00
Jersey:	125.00

Dark, Alvin
Card:	$5.00
Photo:	10.00
Ball:	20.00
Mini-helmet:	40.00
Model bat:	75.00
Jersey:	125.00

Davis, Tommy

Card:	$5.00
Photo:	10.00
Ball:	20.00
Mini-helmet:	40.00
Model bat:	75.00
Jersey:	125.00

Davis, Willie

Card:	$5.00
Photo:	10.00
Ball:	20.00
Mini-helmet:	40.00
Model bat:	75.00
Jersey:	125.00

Dawson, Andre

Card:	$10.00
Photo:	20.00
Ball:	35.00
Mini-helmet:	60.00
Model bat:	100.00
Jersey:	200.00

Dempsey, Rick

Card:	$6.00
Photo:	10.00
Ball:	20.00
Mini-helmet:	40.00
Model bat:	75.00
Jersey:	125.00

Dent, Bucky

Card:	$7.00
Photo:	10.00
Ball:	20.00
Mini-helmet:	40.00
Model bat:	75.00
Jersey:	150.00

DiMaggio, Dom

Card:	$10.00
Photo:	20.00
Ball:	75.00
Mini-helmet:	100.00
Model bat:	100.00
Jersey:	150.00

Downing, Brian

Card:	$6.00
Photo:	10.00
Ball:	20.00
Mini-helmet:	40.00
Model bat:	75.00
Jersey:	125.00

Dropo, Walt

Card:	$5.00
Photo:	10.00
Ball:	22.00
Mini-helmet:	45.00
Model bat:	75.00
Jersey:	125.00

Ennis, Del†

Card:	$5.00
Photo:	10.00
Ball:	22.00
Mini-helmet:	*
Model bat:	75.00
Jersey:	125.00

Erskine, Carl

Card:	$6.00
Photo:	12.00
Ball:	25.00
Mini-helmet:	45.00
Model bat:	75.00
Jersey:	125.00

Evans, Darrell

Card:	$7.00
Photo:	10.00
Ball:	22.00
Mini-helmet:	45.00
Model bat:	75.00
Jersey:	125.00

Evans, Dwight

Card:	$8.00
Photo:	15.00
Ball:	25.00
Mini-helmet:	50.00
Model bat:	100.00
Jersey:	150.00

Face, Elroy

Card:	$5.00
Photo:	10.00
Ball:	25.00
Mini-helmet:	45.00
Model bat:	75.00
Jersey:	125.00

Fidrych, Mark

Card:	$6.00
Photo:	10.00
Ball:	20.00
Mini-helmet:	40.00
Model bat:	75.00
Jersey:	125.00

Fisk, Carlton

Card:	$15.00
Photo:	25.00
Ball:	40.00
Mini-helmet:	65.00
Model bat:	125.00
Jersey:	200.00

Flanagan, Mike

Card:	$7.00
Photo:	10.00
Ball:	20.00
Mini-helmet:	40.00
Model bat:	75.00
Jersey:	125.00

Flood, Curt†

Card:	$10.00
Photo:	25.00
Ball:	45.00
Mini-helmet:	60.00
Model bat:	85.00
Jersey:	150.00

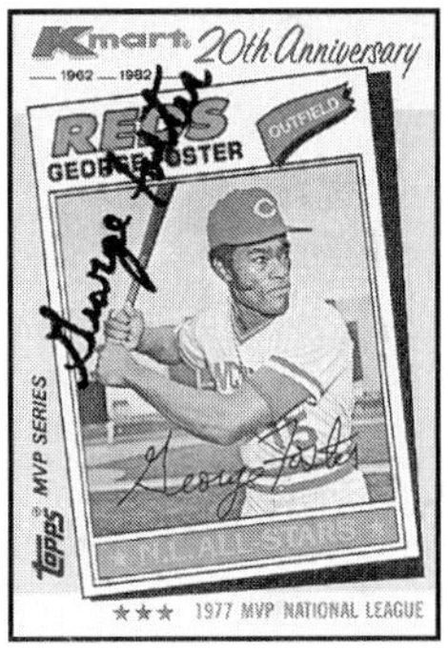

Foster, George

Card:	$7.00
Photo:	10.00
Ball:	25.00
Mini-helmet:	45.00
Model bat:	100.00
Jersey:	150.00

Furillo, Carl†

Card:	$20.00
Photo:	70.00
Ball:	325.00
Mini-helmet:	*
Model bat:	*
Jersey:	*

Garagiola, Joe

Card:	$6.00
Photo:	12.00
Ball:	25.00
Mini-helmet:	45.00
Model bat:	75.00
Jersey:	125.00

Garcia, Mike†
Card: $20.00
Photo: 60.00
Ball: 600.00
Mini-helmet: *
Model bat: *
Jersey: *

Garvey, Steve
Card: $8.00
Photo: 12.00
Ball: 25.00
Mini-helmet: 50.00
Model bat: 100.00
Jersey: 150.00

Gibson, Kirk
Card: $8.00
Photo: 12.00
Ball: 25.00
Mini-helmet: 50.00
Model bat: 100.00
Jersey: 150.00

Gilliam, Jim†
Card: $20.00
Photo: 70.00
Ball: 700.00
Mini-helmet: *
Model bat: *
Jersey: *

Gordon, Joe†
Card: $25.00
Photo: 100.00
Ball: 1300.00
Mini-helmet: *
Model bat: *
Jersey: *

Gossage, Rich
Card: $8.00
Photo: 15.00
Ball: 25.00
Mini-helmet: 45.00
Model bat: 75.00
Jersey: 125.00

Gray, Pete
Card: $10.00
Photo: 20.00
Ball: 35.00
Mini-helmet: 55.00
Model bat: 75.00
Jersey: 125.00

Griffey, Ken Sr.
Card: $8.00
Photo: 12.00
Ball: 25.00
Mini-helmet: 45.00
Model bat: 100.00
Jersey: 150.00

Groat, Dick
Card: $5.00
Photo: 10.00
Ball: 20.00
Mini-helmet: 40.00
Model bat: 75.00
Jersey: 125.00

Guidry, Ron
Card: $8.00
Photo: 15.00
Ball: 25.00
Mini-helmet: 45.00
Model bat: 75.00
Jersey: 150.00

Haddix, Harvey†
Card: $10.00
Photo: 25.00
Ball: 60.00
Mini-helmet: *
Model bat: 75.00
Jersey: 125.00

Harrelson, Bud
Card: $5.00
Photo: 10.00
Ball: 22.00
Mini-helmet: 45.00
Model bat: 75.00
Jersey: 125.00

Harrelson, Ken
Card: $6.00
Photo: 12.00
Ball: 25.00
Mini-helmet: 45.00
Model bat: 75.00
Jersey: 125.00

Henrich, Tommy
Card: $6.00
Photo: 12.00
Ball: 25.00
Mini-helmet: 45.00
Model bat: 75.00
Jersey: 125.00

Herman, Babe†
Card: $20.00
Photo: 50.00
Ball: 300.00
Mini-helmet: *
Model bat: *
Jersey: *

Hernandez, Keith
Card: $8.00
Photo: 15.00
Ball: 25.00
Mini-helmet: 50.00
Model bat: 100.00
Jersey: 150.00

Herzog, Whitey
Card: $8.00
Photo: 15.00
Ball: 30.00
Mini-helmet: 50.00
Model bat: 75.00
Jersey: 125.00

Hodges, Gil†
Card:	$70.00
Photo:	300.00
Ball:	1,200.00
Mini-helmet:	*
Model bat:	*
Jersey:	*

Horton, Willie
Card:	$5.00
Photo:	10.00
Ball:	22.00
Mini-helmet:	45.00
Model bat:	75.00
Jersey:	125.00

Hough, Charlie
Card:	$7.00
Photo:	12.00
Ball:	22.00
Mini-helmet:	40.00
Model bat:	75.00
Jersey:	125.00

Houk, Ralph
Card:	$5.00
Photo:	12.00
Ball:	22.00
Mini-helmet:	40.00
Model bat:	75.00
Jersey:	125.00

Howard, Elston†
Card:	$100.00
Photo:	300.00
Ball:	1,200.00
Mini-helmet:	*
Model bat:	*
Jersey:	*

Howard, Frank
Card:	$7.00
Photo:	12.00
Ball:	22.00
Mini-helmet:	40.00
Model bat:	100.00
Jersey:	150.00

Hrbek, Kent
Card:	$8.00
Photo:	12.00
Ball:	28.00
Mini-helmet:	50.00
Model bat:	100.00
Jersey:	150.00

Hubbs, Ken†
Card:	$20.00
Photo:	200.00
Ball:	650.00
Mini-helmet:	*
Model bat:	*
Jersey:	*

Jackson, Bo
Card:	$10.00
Photo:	20.00
Ball:	30.00
Mini-helmet:	50.00
Model bat:	125.00
Jersey:	175.00

Jackson, Joe†
Card:	*
Photo:	$10,000.00
Ball:	30,000.00
Mini-helmet:	*
Model bat:	*
Jersey:	*

Jensen, Jackie†
Card:	$20.00
Photo:	75.00
Ball:	300.00
Mini-helmet:	*
Model bat:	*
Jersey:	*

John, Tommy
Card:	$8.00
Photo:	15.00
Ball:	20.00
Mini-helmet:	45.00
Model bat:	75.00
Jersey:	150.00

Jones, Cleon
Card:	$5.00
Photo:	10.00
Ball:	20.00
Mini-helmet:	40.00
Model bat:	75.00
Jersey:	125.00

Kaat, Jim
Card:	$8.00
Photo:	12.00
Ball:	25.00
Mini-helmet:	45.00
Model bat:	75.00
Jersey:	175.00

Kingman, Dave
Card:	$6.00
Photo:	12.00
Ball:	25.00
Mini-helmet:	45.00
Model bat:	100.00
Jersey:	150.00

Kluszewski, Ted†
Card:	$20.00
Photo:	60.00
Ball:	200.00
Mini-helmet:	*
Model bat:	*
Jersey:	*

Koosman, Jerry
Card:	$8.00
Photo:	12.00
Ball:	25.00
Mini-helmet:	45.00
Model bat:	75.00
Jersey:	150.00

Kubek, Tony
Card:	$10.00
Photo:	20.00
Ball:	40.00
Mini-helmet:	60.00
Model bat:	100.00
Jersey:	175.00

Kuenn, Harvey†
Card:	$15.00
Photo:	40.00
Ball:	275.00
Mini-helmet:	*
Model bat:	*
Jersey:	*

Larsen, Don

Card:	$6.00
Photo:	12.00
Ball:	20.00
Mini-helmet:	40.00
Model bat:	75.00
Jersey:	150.00

LeFlore, Ron

Card:	$5.00
Photo:	10.00
Ball:	20.00
Mini-helmet:	40.00
Model bat:	75.00
Jersey:	125.00

Lolich, Mickey

Card:	$5.00
Photo:	10.00
Ball:	20.00
Mini-helmet:	40.00
Model bat:	75.00
Jersey:	125.00

Lonborg, Jim

Card:	$6.00
Photo:	12.00
Ball:	25.00
Mini-helmet:	45.00
Model bat:	75.00
Jersey:	125.00

Lopat, Ed†

Card:	$15.00
Photo:	50.00
Ball:	175.00
Mini-helmet:	*
Model bat:	*
Jersey:	*

Lopes, Davey

Card:	$6.00
Photo:	10.00
Ball:	20.00
Mini-helmet:	40.00
Model bat:	75.00
Jersey:	125.00

Lowenstein, John

Card:	$5.00
Photo:	10.00
Ball:	20.00
Mini-helmet:	40.00
Model bat:	75.00
Jersey:	125.00

Luzinski, Greg

Card:	$5.00
Photo:	10.00
Ball:	20.00
Mini-helmet:	40.00
Model bat:	75.00
Jersey:	125.00

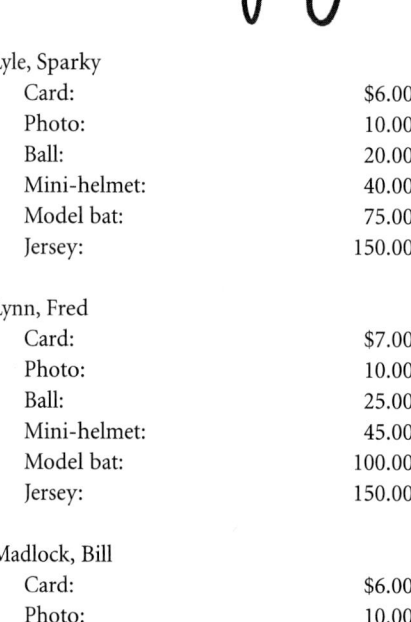

Lyle, Sparky

Card:	$6.00
Photo:	10.00
Ball:	20.00
Mini-helmet:	40.00
Model bat:	75.00
Jersey:	150.00

Lynn, Fred

Card:	$7.00
Photo:	10.00
Ball:	25.00
Mini-helmet:	45.00
Model bat:	100.00
Jersey:	150.00

Madlock, Bill

Card:	$6.00
Photo:	10.00
Ball:	20.00
Mini-helmet:	40.00
Model bat:	100.00
Jersey:	150.00

Maglie, Sal†

Card:	$20.00
Photo:	50.00
Ball:	250.00
Mini-helmet:	*
Model bat:	*
Jersey:	*

Malzone, Frank

Card:	$5.00
Photo:	10.00
Ball:	22.00
Mini-helmet:	45.00
Model bat:	75.00
Jersey:	125.00

Marion, Marty

Card:	$7.00
Photo:	12.00
Ball:	25.00
Mini-helmet:	45.00
Model bat:	75.00
Jersey:	125.00

Maris, Roger†

Card:	$150.00
Photo:	350.00
Ball:	1,000.00
Mini-helmet:	*
Model bat:	*
Jersey:	*

Marshall, Mike

Card:	$25.00
Photo:	100.00
Ball:	250.00
Mini-helmet:	*
Model bat:	*
Jersey:	*

Martin, Billy†
Card:	$15.00
Photo:	65.00
Ball:	200.00
Mini-helmet:	*
Model bat:	*
Jersey:	*

Matthews, Gary
Card:	$5.00
Photo:	10.00
Ball:	20.00
Mini-helmet:	40.00
Model bat:	75.00
Jersey:	125.00

Mattingly, Don
Card:	$10.00
Photo:	25.00
Ball:	50.00
Mini-helmet:	75.00
Model bat:	125.00
Jersey:	250.00

Mazeroski, Bill
Card:	$8.00
Photo:	12.00
Ball:	20.00
Mini-helmet:	45.00
Model bat:	100.00
Jersey:	150.00

McCarver, Tim
Card:	$7.00
Photo:	15.00
Ball:	25.00
Mini-helmet:	50.00
Model bat:	100.00
Jersey:	150.00

McDougald, Gil
Card:	$8.00
Photo:	15.00
Ball:	25.00
Mini-helmet:	45.00
Model bat:	75.00
Jersey:	125.00

McDowell, Sam
Card:	$5.00
Photo:	10.00
Ball:	20.00
Mini-helmet:	40.00
Model bat:	75.00
Jersey:	125.00

McGraw, Tug
Card:	$8.00
Photo:	15.00
Ball:	22.00
Mini-helmet:	45.00
Model bat:	75.00
Jersey:	150.00

McLain, Denny
Card:	$5.00
Photo:	10.00
Ball:	20.00
Mini-helmet:	40.00
Model bat:	75.00
Jersey:	150.00

McNally, Dave
Card:	$8.00
Photo:	15.00
Ball:	25.00
Mini-helmet:	45.00
Model bat:	75.00
Jersey:	125.00

McRae, Hal
Card:	$8.00
Photo:	15.00
Ball:	25.00
Mini-helmet:	45.00
Model bat:	85.00
Jersey:	125.00

Minoso, Minnie
Card:	$6.00
Photo:	12.00
Ball:	28.00
Mini-helmet:	45.00
Model bat:	75.00
Jersey:	125.00

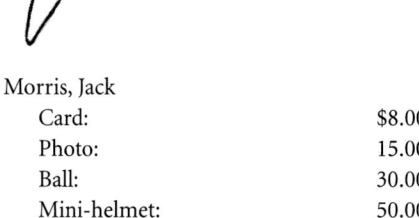

Morris, Jack
Card:	$8.00
Photo:	15.00
Ball:	30.00
Mini-helmet:	50.00
Model bat:	75.00

Munson, Thurman†
Card:	$200.00
Photo:	350.00
Ball:	1,200.00
Mini-helmet:	*
Model bat:	*
Jersey:	*

Murcer, Bobby
Card:	$6.00
Photo:	12.00
Ball:	25.00
Mini-helmet:	45.00
Model bat:	75.00
Jersey:	125.00

Murphy, Dale
Card:	$8.00
Photo:	15.00
Ball:	28.00
Mini-helmet:	50.00
Model bat:	100.00
Jersey:	150.00

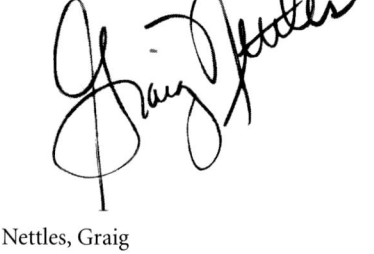

Murray, Eddie
Card:	$25.00
Photo:	50.00
Ball:	75.00
Mini-helmet:	100.00
Model bat:	200.00
Jersey:	250.00

Nettles, Graig
Card:	$5.00
Photo:	10.00
Ball:	22.00
Mini-helmet:	45.00
Model bat:	100.00
Jersey:	150.00

Newcombe, Don
Card:	$5.00
Photo:	10.00
Ball:	22.00
Mini-helmet:	45.00
Model bat:	75.00
Jersey:	125.00

Niekro, Joe
Card:	$5.00
Photo:	10.00
Ball:	20.00
Mini-helmet:	40.00
Model bat:	75.00
Jersey:	125.00

O'Doul, Lefty†
Card:	$70.00
Photo:	150.00
Ball:	1,500.00
Mini-helmet:	*
Model bat:	*
Jersey:	*

Oh, Sadaharu
Card:	$20.00
Photo:	35.00
Ball:	125.00
Mini-helmet:	*
Model bat:	*
Jersey:	*

Oliva, Tony
Card:	$8.00
Photo:	12.00
Ball:	25.00
Mini-helmet:	45.00
Model bat:	100.00
Jersey:	150.00

Parker, Dave
Card:	$5.00
Photo:	12.00
Ball:	28.00
Mini-helmet:	50.00
Model bat:	100.00
Jersey:	150.00

Pepitone, Joe
Card:	$5.00
Photo:	10.00
Ball:	20.00
Mini-helmet:	40.00
Model bat:	75.00
Jersey:	125.00

Perez, Tony
Card:	$7.00
Photo:	12.00
Ball:	28.00
Mini-helmet:	50.00
Model bat:	100.00
Jersey:	150.00

Perry, Jim
Card:	$6.00
Photo:	12.00
Ball:	22.00
Mini-helmet:	45.00
Model bat:	75.00
Jersey:	125.00

Pesky, Johnny
Card:	$6.00
Photo:	12.00
Ball:	22.00
Mini-helmet:	45.00
Model bat:	75.00
Jersey:	125.00

Pierce, Billy
Card:	$5.00
Photo:	10.00
Ball:	22.00
Mini-helmet:	45.00
Model bat:	75.00
Jersey:	125.00

Piersall, Jimmy
Card:	$8.00
Photo:	15.00
Ball:	30.00
Mini-helmet:	55.00
Model bat:	75.00
Jersey:	125.00

Pinson, Vada†
Card:	$15.00
Photo:	35.00
Ball:	50.00
Mini-helmet:	*
Model bat:	100.00
Jersey:	150.00

Powell, Boog
Card:	$5.00
Photo:	10.00
Ball:	25.00
Mini-helmet:	45.00
Model bat:	85.00
Jersey:	125.00

Puckett, Kirby
Card:	$12.00
Photo:	25.00
Ball:	50.00
Mini-helmet:	75.00
Model bat:	125.00
Jersey:	200.00

Randolph, Willie
Card:	$6.00
Photo:	12.00
Ball:	25.00
Mini-helmet:	45.00
Model bat:	75.00
Jersey:	125.00

Raschi, Vic†
Card:	$20.00
Photo:	50.00
Ball:	275.00
Mini-helmet:	*
Model bat:	*
Jersey:	*

Reynolds, Allie†
Card:	$10.00
Photo:	25.00
Ball:	70.00
Mini-helmet:	*
Model bat:	75.00
Jersey:	125.00

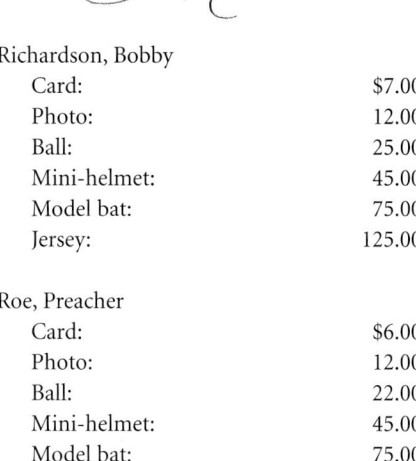

Rice, Jim
Card:	$8.00
Photo:	15.00
Ball:	25.00
Mini-helmet:	45.00
Model bat:	100.00
Jersey:	150.00

Richard, J.R.
Card:	$8.00
Photo:	15.00
Ball:	28.00
Mini-helmet:	45.00
Model bat:	75.00
Jersey:	125.00

Richardson, Bobby
Card:	$7.00
Photo:	12.00
Ball:	25.00
Mini-helmet:	45.00
Model bat:	75.00
Jersey:	125.00

Roe, Preacher
Card:	$6.00
Photo:	12.00
Ball:	22.00
Mini-helmet:	45.00
Model bat:	75.00
Jersey:	125.00

Rose, Pete
Card:	$10.00
Photo:	20.00
Ball:	35.00
Mini-helmet:	65.00
Model bat:	100.00
Jersey:	200.00

Rosen, Al
Card:	$6.00
Photo:	12.00
Ball:	25.00
Mini-helmet:	45.00
Model bat:	75.00
Jersey:	125.00

Ryan, Nolan
Card:	$15.00
Photo:	30.00
Ball:	50.00
Mini-helmet:	80.00
Model bat:	125.00
Jersey:	200.00

Sandberg, Ryne
Card:	$10.00
Photo:	30.00
Ball:	45.00
Mini-helmet:	65.00
Model bat:	125.00
Jersey:	200.00

Sain, Johnny

Card:	$6.00
Photo:	12.00
Ball:	20.00
Mini-helmet:	40.00
Model bat:	75.00
Jersey:	125.00

Santo, Ron

Card:	$8.00
Photo:	15.00
Ball:	25.00
Mini-helmet:	45.00
Model bat:	100.00
Jersey:	150.00

Score, Herb

Card:	$7.00
Photo:	15.00
Ball:	25.00
Mini-helmet:	45.00
Model bat:	75.00
Jersey:	125.00

Shantz, Bobby

Card:	$5.00
Photo:	10.00
Ball:	25.00
Mini-helmet:	45.00
Model bat:	75.00
Jersey:	125.00

Simmons, Ted

Card:	$5.00
Photo:	12.00
Ball:	25.00
Mini-helmet:	45.00
Model bat:	85.00
Jersey:	125.00

Skowron, Bill "Moose"

Card:	$5.00
Photo:	10.00
Ball:	20.00
Mini-helmet:	40.00
Model bat:	75.00
Jersey:	125.00

Smith, Lee

Card:	$6.00
Photo:	15.00
Ball:	28.00
Mini-helmet:	45.00
Model bat:	75.00
Jersey:	150.00

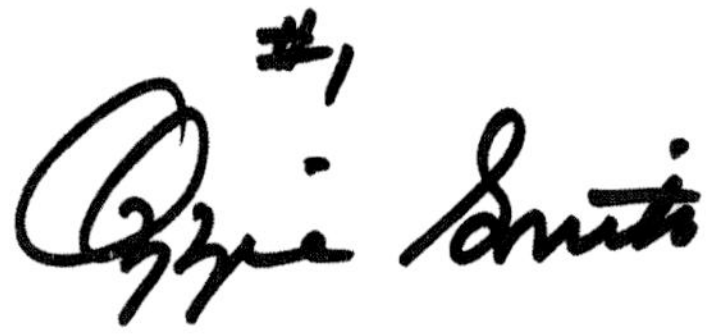

Smith, Ozzie

Card:	$10.00
Photo:	20.00
Ball:	30.00
Mini-helmet:	50.00
Model bat:	100.00
Jersey:	175.00

Smith, Reggie

Card:	$6.00
Photo:	12.00
Ball:	25.00
Mini-helmet:	45.00
Model bat:	85.00
Jersey:	125.00

Stanky, Eddie

Card:	$6.00
Photo:	12.00
Ball:	25.00
Mini-helmet:	45.00
Model bat:	75.00
Jersey:	125.00

Staub, Rusty

Card:	$6.00
Photo:	12.00
Ball:	25.00
Mini-helmet:	45.00
Model bat:	85.00
Jersey:	125.00

Stewart, Dave

Card:	$5.00
Photo:	12.00
Ball:	25.00
Mini-helmet:	45.00
Model bat:	75.00
Jersey:	125.00

Stottlemyre, Mel

Card:	$5.00
Photo:	10.00
Ball:	20.00
Mini-helmet:	40.00
Model bat:	75.00
Jersey:	125.00

Sutter, Bruce

Card:	$6.00
Photo:	12.00
Ball:	22.00
Mini-helmet:	45.00
Model bat:	75.00
Jersey:	125.00

Thomson, Bobby

Card:	$5.00
Photo:	12.00
Ball:	30.00
Mini-helmet:	50.00
Model bat:	70.00
Jersey:	125.00

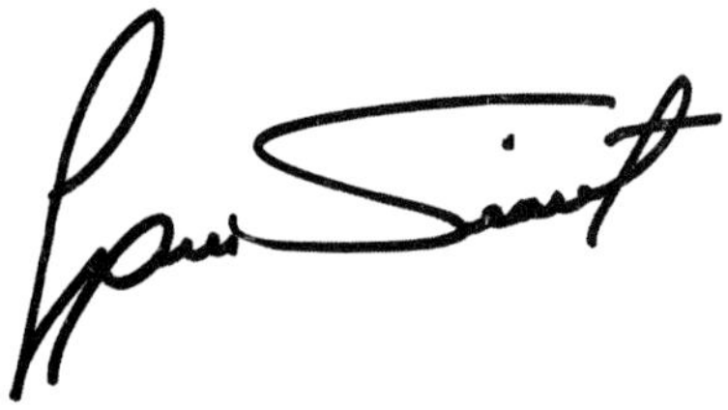

Tiant, Luis

Card:	$8.00
Photo:	15.00
Ball:	25.00
Mini-helmet:	45.00
Model bat:	75.00
Jersey:	125.00

Trammell, Alan

Card:	$10.00
Photo:	20.00
Ball:	35.00
Mini-helmet:	55.00
Model bat:	125.00
Jersey:	175.00

Uecker, Bob
  Card: $10.00
  Photo: 20.00
  Ball: 35.00
  Mini-helmet: 55.00
  Model bat: 75.00
  Jersey: 125.00

Vander Meer, Johnny†
  Card: $10.00
  Photo: 18.00
  Ball: 35.00
  Mini-helmet: 60.00
  Model bat: *
  Jersey: *

Vernon, Mickey
  Card: $5.00
  Photo: 10.00
  Ball: 25.00
  Mini-helmet: 45.00
  Model bat: 75.00
  Jersey: 125.00

Whitaker, Lou
  Card: $8.00
  Photo: 15.00
  Ball: 28.00
  Mini-helmet: 50.00
  Model bat: 100.00
  Jersey: 175.00

Wills, Maury
  Card: $8.00
  Photo: 15.00
  Ball: 28.00
  Mini-helmet: 45.00
  Model bat: 75.00
  Jersey: 125.00

Winfield, Dave
  Card: $15.00
  Photo: 35.00
  Ball: 45.00
  Mini-helmet: 75.00
  Model bat: 150.00
  Jersey: 200.00

Wood, Joe†
  Card: $20.00
  Photo: 120.00
  Ball: 600.00
  Mini-helmet: *
  Model bat: *
  Jersey: *

Woodling, Gene
  Card: $6.00
  Photo: 12.00
  Ball: 25.00
  Mini-helmet: 45.00
  Model bat: 75.00
  Jersey: 125.00

Wynn, Jimmy
  Card: $5.00
  Photo: 10.00
  Ball: 22.00
  Mini-helmet: 40.00
  Model bat: 75.00
  Jersey: 125.00

Yost, Eddie
  Card: $5.00
  Photo: 10.00
  Ball: 20.00
  Mini-helmet: 40.00
  Model bat: 75.00
  Jersey: 125.00

Yount, Robin
  Card: $15.00
  Photo: 30.00
  Ball: 45.00
  Mini-helmet: 65.00
  Model bat: 150.00
  Jersey: 200.00

MANAGERS AND ANNOUNCERS

While the men who call the shots—managers, announcers, commisioners, and owners—aren't as popular in the hobby as superstar players like Mickey Mantle and Joe DiMaggio, they are still an important part of baseball history. The following list includes current and former managers, as well as other men who helped shape the game from out-side the white lines. We've also included several of the biggest names in baseball announcing, men whose gift of gab has enlivened many a ballgame. Prices are for 8x10 photos and official league baseballs. A "†" denotes the personality is deceased. A "*" indicates that an autogrpahed item isn't known to exist, or is so rare that it's difficult to price.

Don Baylor

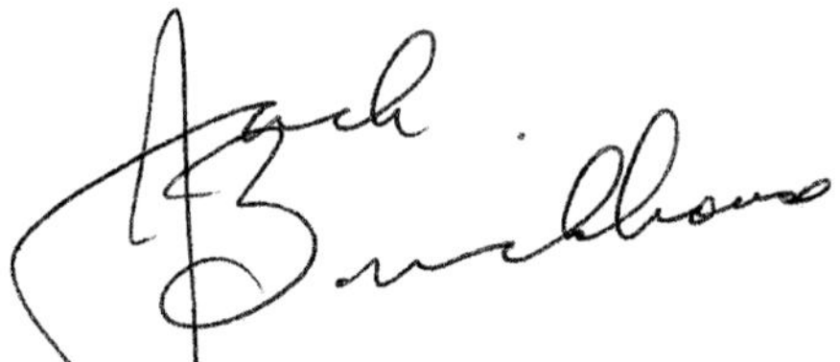

Jack Brickhouse

Bowie Kuhn

Name		Price	Name		Price
Anderson, Sparky	Photo:	$15.00	Eckert, William†	Photo:	*
	Ball:	25.00		Ball:	*
Allen, Mel†	Photo:	25.00	Finley, Charles O.†	Photo:	20.00
	Ball:	40.00		Ball:	30.00
Alou, Felipe	Photo:	12.00	Francona, Terry	Photo:	10.00
	Ball:	22.00		Ball:	20.00
Autry, Gene	Photo:	75.00	Fregosi, Jim	Photo:	12.00
	Ball:	100.00		Ball:	20.00
Baker, Dusty	Photo:	15.00	Garner, Phil	Photo:	12.00
	Ball:	22.00		Ball:	22.00
Barber, Red†	Photo:	25.00	Gaston, Cito	Photo:	12.00
	Ball:	40.00		Ball:	20.00
Barney, Rex†	Photo:	25.00	Giamatti, Bartlett A.†	Photo:	40.00
	Ball:	40.00		Ball:	100.00
Baylor, Don	Photo:	15.00	Hargrove, Mike	Photo:	15.00
	Ball:	25.00		Ball:	25.00
Bell, Buddy	Photo:	10.00	Harwell, Ernie	Photo:	25.00
	Ball:	20.00		Ball:	35.00
Bochy, Bruce	Photo:	10.00	Herzog, Whitey	Photo:	15.00
	Ball:	20.00		Ball:	25.00
Boone, Bob	Photo:	12.00	Howe, Art	Photo:	12.00
	Ball:	22.00		Ball:	22.00
Brickhouse, Jack	Photo:	15.00	Johnson, Davey	Photo:	15.00
	Ball:	25.00		Ball:	25.00
Buck, Jack	Photo:	15.00	Johnson, Ted	Photo:	10.00
	Ball:	22.00		Ball:	20.00
Caray, Harry†	Photo:	25.00	Kelly, Tom	Photo:	15.00
	Ball:	40.00		Ball:	25.00
Collins, Terry	Photo:	10.00	Kuhn, Bowie	Photo:	20.00
	Ball:	20.00		Ball:	40.00
Cox, Bobby	Photo:	15.00	La Russa, Tony	Photo:	22.00
	Ball:	25.00		Ball:	30.00
Dierker, Larry	Photo:	10.00	Lamont, Gene	Photo:	15.00
	Ball:	15.00		Ball:	22.00

Leyland, Jim	Photo: Ball:	15.00 25.00	Showalter, Buck	Photo: Ball:	15.00 25.00	
Manuel, Jerry	Photo: Ball:	10.00 20.00	Steinbrenner, George	Photo: Ball:	15.00 25.00	
Martin, Billy†	Photo: Ball:	75.00 200.00	Tanner, Chuck	Photo: Ball:	10.00 18.00	
Mauch, Gene	Photo: Ball:	15.00 25.00	Thompson, Chuck	Photo: Ball:	12.00 20.00	
McKeon, Jack	Photo: Ball:	10.00 20.00	Torre, Joe	Photo: Ball:	15.00 25.00	
McNamara, John	Photo: Ball:	10.00 18.00	Turner, Ted	Photo: Ball:	10.00 20.00	
Miller, Ray	Photo: Ball:	10.00 20.00	Ueberroth, Peter	Photo: Ball:	25.00 35.00	
Muser, Tony	Photo: Ball:	10.00 20.00	Valentine, Bobby	Photo: Ball:	12.00 22.00	
Oates, Johnny	Photo: Ball:	12.00 20.00	Veeck, Bill†	Photo: Ball:	40.00 100.00	
O'Malley, Walter†	Photo: Ball:	* 100.00	Vincent, Fay	Photo: Ball:	25.00 35.00	
Piniella, Lou	Photo: Ball:	15.00 28.00	Virdon, Bill	Photo: Ball:	10.00 18.00	
Riggleman, Jim	Photo: Ball:	10.00 20.00	Williams, Dick	Photo: Ball:	12.00 22.00	
Russell, Bill	Photo: Ball:	12.00 22.00	Williams, Jimy	Photo: Ball:	10.00 15.00	
Scully, Vin	Photo: Ball:	15.00 25.00	Zimmer, Don	Photo: Ball:	15.00 22.00	
Selig, Bud	Photo: Ball:	20.00 30.00				

Walter O'Malley

Joe Torre

Bill Veeck

MULTI-SIGNED ITEMS

MILESTONE AUTOGRAPHS

There are certain revered performance milestones in every sport, and baseball is no exception. Great players become defined by their accomplishments, like ripping 3,000 hits, blasting 500 home runs, or winning 300 games. These benchmarks traditionally ensure a player's place in the Hall of Fame.

Naturally, players reaching these milestones are among the sport's most collectible. Here's a rundown of the members of some of baseball's most renowned milestone clubs, and what to look for when obtaining collectibles autographed by everyone in each group.

"500 Home Run Club Poster"
(Signed by 11)
$600-$700

500 HOME RUNS

Only 15 players in major league history have reached this remarkable plateau. Babe Ruth, Jimmie Foxx, and Mel Ott were the first to eclipse the mark. Acquiring items signed by any of these three players is extremely difficult because they all died long before collecting autographs became popular.

There is no known item bearing the signatures of all 15 members. Most collectors today consider a 500 home run item complete if it includes everyone except the original three—Ruth, Foxx, and Ott. Of the remaining 12, Mickey Mantle and Ted Williams are the next two hardest autographs to obtain. Mantle passed away in 1995, and Williams limits himself to just one or two appearances a year. While both of these players were readily accessible in the 1980s, they have become two of the most highly sought-after autographs in the hobby.

The remaining members of the 500 HR club appear regularly on the autograph circuit.

The most common items to be signed by club members are baseballs. Most players will readily sign a ball at a very reasonable price. Bats have become an increasingly difficult item to acquire. Williams stopped signing bats a long time ago, and most of the other players charge a large premium for signing them.

In recent years, several popular special edition prints and posters have been issued. In 1989, Ron Lewis created a lithograph of the 11 living 500 home run hitters (Eddie Murray didn't join the club until 1996). This is an attractive poster that is readily available. In '96, Doo S. Oh created a new poster that included Murray and removed Mantle. Both posters had limited print runs, and are popular unsigned as well.

The items listed below are priced without Babe Ruth, Jimmie Foxx, or Mel Ott autographs. For single-signed items please refer to the Hall of Fame Autograph section.

500 HR Club Ball
(Signed by 11 members)

500 HR Club Photo
(Signed by 11 members)
$500-$600

500 HR Club Bat
(Signed by 11 members)

Official American or National League Baseball

Signed	$750.00
Signed (w/o Mickey Mantle)	500.00
Signed (w/o Eddie Murray)	700.00

Baseball Bat

Signed	$3,500.00
Signed (w/o Mickey Mantle)	1,500.00
Signed (w/o Ted Williams)	1,800.00
Signed (w/o Eddie Murray)	3,300.00

1989 Lewis Lithograph Limited Edition of 100

Signed	$3,200.00

Murray not featured on lithograph

1989 Lewis Poster Limited Edition of 5,000

Signed	$2,000.00
Unsigned	75.00

Murray not featured on poster

1996 Oh Poster Limited Edition of 5,000

Signed	$1,500.00
Unsigned	50.00

Craig Pursley Painting 40x28

Signed	$3,000.00

500 HOME RUN CLUB

Hank Aaron (755)	Jimmie Foxx (534)
Babe Ruth (714)	Willie McCovey (521)
Willie Mays (660)	Ted Williams (521)
Frank Robinson (586)	Ernie Banks (512)
Harmon Killebrew (573)	Eddie Mathews (512)
Reggie Jackson (563)	Mel Ott (511)
Mike Schmidt (548)	Eddie Murray (504)
Mickey Mantle (536)	

3,000 HITS

The 3,000-Hit Club is another exclusive group, with only 20 players checking in. While many members of the club are alive and signing regularly, a number have long since passed away. Collectors consider 3,000 hit items complete without the signatures of Ty Cobb, Tris Speaker, Honus Wagner, Eddie Collins, Nap Lajoie, Paul Waner, and Roberto Clemente.

Clemente autographs are unique because he was killed in a plane crash after collecting his 3,000th hit in the final game of 1972. Expect to pay top dollar for items autographed by any of these deceased players.

Pete Rose, Hank Aaron, and others are regulars on the show scene. Below are prices for items signed by the 13 living members.

All items listed below do not include autographs of Ty Cobb, Tris Speaker, Honus Wagner, Eddie Collins, Nap Lajoie, Paul Waner, or Roberto Clemente. For single-signed items please refer to the Hall of Fame Autograph section.

3,000 Hit Club Bat
(Signed by 8 members)

Official American or National League Baseball

Signed	$550.00

Baseball Bat

Signed	1,200.00

1995 Lewis Poster Limited Edition

Signed	800.00
Unsigned	25.00

Murray and Molitor not featured on poster

1997 Oh Poster Limited Edition of 4,000

Signed	900.00
Unsigned	25.00

3,000 HIT CLUB	
Pete Rose (4,256)	Nap Lajoie (3,242)
Ty Cobb (4,189)	Paul Molitor (3,178)*
Hank Aaron (3,771)	George Brett (3,154)
Stan Musial (3,630)	Paul Waner (3,152)
Tris Speaker (3,514)	Robin Yount (3,142)
Carl Yastrzemski (3,419)	Dave Winfield (3,110)
Honus Wagner (3,415)	Rod Carew (3,053)
Eddie Collins (3,312)	Lou Brock (3,023)
Willie Mays (3,283)	Al Kaline (3,007)
Eddie Murray (3,255)	Roberto Clemente (3,000)
* Still active; total through 1997.	

500 HOME RUNS & 3,000 HITS

Perhaps the most exclusive multi-signed item bears only three signatures. Hank Aaron, Willie Mays, and Eddie Murray are the only players in baseball history to amass both 3,000 hits and 500 home runs.

Both Aaron and Mays have been active on the autograph circuit for years, and Murray has joined them since his retirement.

Hank Aaron

Willie Mays

Eddie Murray

Official American or National League Baseball

Signed	$150.00

Baseball Bat

Signed	400.00

300 WINS

Only 20 players in baseball history have achieved this milestone. Many of baseball's all-time pitching records are held by men who pitched in the early days of baseball. Only eight of the 20 players in the 300 win club are living today, making it the hardest milestone to complete. For those collectors trying to attain signatures of the living legends, a pitching rubber is a popular item to have signed.

All items listed below are considered complete with just the eight living players—Warren Spahn, Steve Carlton, Nolan Ryan, Don Sutton, Phil Niekro, Gaylord Perry, Tom Seaver, and Early Wynn. For single-signed items on the deceased players, refer to the Hall of Fame Autograph section.

300 Game Winners Ball
(Signed by all 8 living)

300 Game Winners Litho
(Anthony Brunelli 1994)

Official American or National League Baseball

Signed	$500.00

Baseball Bat

Signed	750.00

Pitching Rubber

Signed	500.00

1994 Brunelli Lithograph

Signed	1,000.00
Unsigned	50.00

300 GAME WINNERS

Cy Young (511)	Eddie Plank (326)
Walter Johnson (417)	Nolan Ryan (324)
Pete Alexander (373)	Don Sutton (324)
Christy Mathewson (373)	Phil Niekro (318)
Warren Spahn (363)	Gaylord Perry (314)
Kid Nichols (361)	Tom Seaver (311)
Jim Galvin (360)	Charley Radbourn (309)
Tim Keefe (342)	Mickey Welch (307)
Steve Carlton (329)	Lefty Grove (300)
John Clarkson (328)	Early Wynn (300)

OTHER POPULAR ITEMS

This 1998 Baseball Kings poster by Ron Lewis, limited to 5,000 prints, pictures the career leaders in four major statistical categories: Pete Rose (hits), Nolan Ryan (strikeouts), Hank Aaron (home runs), and Rickey Henderson (stolen bases).

Official American or National League Baseball

Signed	$200.00

Baseball Bat

Signed	325.00

1998 Baseball Kings Poster Limited Edition of 150

Signed	575.00
Unsigned	25.00

ALL-STAR TEAM SIGNED BASEBALLS

Collectors looking for one single item that includes the signatures of many of baseball's biggest stars from any given era should look no further than an All-Star team-signed ball.

The first All-Star Game, held in Chicago in 1933, showcased stars like Babe Ruth and Lou Gehrig. Since then, the Midsummer Classic has become an annual gathering of the game's greatest and most popular players. An All-Star team-signed ball is a great way to get the autographs of several stars on one piece. Below is a list of values for AL and NL team-signed balls by year, including several key names to look for on the ball. The price assumes the ball has all the key signatures.

AUTOGRAPHED ALL-STAR TEAM BASEBALLS

1933 American League All-Star Team

1936 American League All-Star Team

1940 American League All-Star Team

1985 National League All-Star Team

Year	League	Key Signatures	Price
1933	American	Cronin, Foxx, Gehrig, Grove, Mack, Ruth	$7,500.00
1933	National	Frisch, Hubbell, McGraw, Traynor, Waner	3,000.00
1934	American	Cronin, Foxx, Gehrig, Ruth, Simmons	7,500.00
1934	National	Hubbell, Ott, Traynor, Vaughan, Waner	2,500.00
1935	American	Cronin, Foxx, Gehrig, Gomez, Hornsby	5,000.00
1935	National	Frisch, Ott, Terry, Vaughan	1,800.00
1936	American	Cronin, DiMaggio, Foxx, Gehrig, McCarthy	6,000.00
1936	National	Dean, Hubbell, Medwick, Ott, Traynor, Vaughan	1,500.00
1937	American	Averill, Foxx, DiMaggio, Gehrig, Gomez	5,500.00
1937	National	Dean, Frisch, Harder, Ott, Vaughan	2,000.00
1938	American	Cronin, Foxx, DiMaggio, Gehrig	5,500.00
1938	National	Durocher, Frisch, Lombardi, Ott, Vaughan	1,500.00
1939	American	DiMaggio, Feller, Foxx, Gehrig, Ruffing	5,000.00
1939	National	Derringer, Mize, Ott, Vaughan	1,700.00
1940	American	Cronin, DiMaggio, Feller, Foxx, Ruffing, Williams	700.00
1940	National	Derringer, Herman, Ott, Vaughan	2,000.00
1941	American	DiMaggio, Feller, Foxx, Keltner, Williams	750.00
1941	National	Derringer, Hubbell, Mize, Ott, Vaughan	800.00
1942	American	Boudreau, Chandler, DiMaggio, Rizzuto, Williams	600.00
1942	National	Frisch, McKechnie, Medwick, Ott, Reese, Vaughan	900.00
1943	American	Appling, Doerr, McCarthy, Newhouser, Stephens	500.00
1943	National	Frisch, Musial, Marion, Ott, Sewell, Vander Meer	600.00
1944	American	Boudreau, Cronin, Doerr, McCarthy, Newhouser	500.00
1944	National	Cavarretta, Musial, Ott, Wagner	600.00
1945	No game played	—	—
1946	American	DiMaggio, Doerr, Feller, Keller, Williams	550.00
1946	National	Mize, Musial, Reese, Sewell, Slaughter	650.00
1947	American	Boudreau, DiMaggio, Doerr, Williams	650.00
1947	National	Mize, Musial, Ott, Slaughter, Spahn	650.00
1948	American	Berra, DiMaggio, Doerr, Evers, Raschi, Williams	600.00
1948	National	Branca, Kiner, Mize, Musial, Ott, Sain, Slaughter	650.00
1949	American	Berra, DiMaggio, Doby, Lemon, Williams	600.00
1949	National	Campanella, Kiner, Musial, Newcombe, Robinson	700.00
1950	American	Berra, DiMaggio, Rizzuto, Williams	750.00
1950	National	Campanella, Kiner, Musial, Robinson, Snider	700.00
1951	American	Berra, DiMaggio, Rizzuto, Williams	650.00
1951	National	Campanella, Kiner, Musial, Robinson, Slaughter	750.00
1952	American	Bauer, Berra, Kell, Mantle, Paige	1,000.00
1952	National	Campanella, Kiner, Musial, Robinson, Snider	700.00
1953	American	Berra, Mantle, Mize, Paige, Rizzuto, Williams	800.00
1953	National	Campanella, Mathews, Musial, Robinson, Snider	650.00
1954	American	Doby, Fox, Ford, Lemon, Mantle, Williams	700.00
1954	National	Campanella, Hodges, Musial, Robinson, Spahn	700.00
1955	American	Berra, Doby, Ford, Mantle, Williams	700.00
1955	National	Aaron, Banks, Campanella, Mathews, Musial	800.00
1956	American	Berra, Ford, Martin, Mantle, Williams	550.00
1956	National	Aaron, Banks, Campanella, Musial	600.00

Year	League	Key Signatures	Price
1957	American	Fox, Killebrew, Mantle, Williams, Wynn	700.00
1957	National	Aaron, Banks, Mathews, Mays, Musial	500.00
1958	American	Berra, Ford, Mantle, Martin, Williams	600.00
1958	National	Aaron, Banks, Mays, Musial, Spahn	600.00
1959	American	Berra, Ford, Killebrew, Mantle, Williams	500.00
1959*	American	Berra, Kaline, Mantle, Maris, Williams	550.00
1959	National	Aaron, Banks, Drysdale, Musial	450.00
1959*	National	Aaron, Banks, Musial, Spahn	450.00
1960†	American	Berra, Fox, Mantle, Maris, Williams	700.00
1960†	National	Banks, Clemente, Mays, Musial	700.00
1961	American	Berra, Killebrew, Mantle, Maris	600.00
1961*	American	Berra, Cash, Colavito, Mantle, Maris	600.00
1961	National	Aaron, Clemente, Mathews, Musial	500.00
1961*	National	Aaron, Clemente, Mathews, Musial	500.00
1962	American	Berra, Mantle, Maris, Wilhelm	500.00
1962*	American	Kaline, Mantle, Maris, B. Robinson	500.00
1962	National	Aaron, Banks, Clemente, Drysdale	500.00
1962*	National	Aaron, Banks, Clemente, Mays, Musial	500.00
1963	American	Kaline, Killebrew, Yastrzemski	400.00
1963	National	Aaron, Clemente, Mays, Musial	450.00
1964	American	Ford, Howard, Mantle, B. Robinson	400.00
1964	National	Aaron, Clemente, Koufax, Mays, Torre	800.00
1965	American	Kaline, Killebrew, Oliva, B. Robinson	400.00
1965	National	Aaron, Banks, Clemente, Koufax, Rose	550.00
1966	American	Hunter, B. Robinson, F. Robinson	450.00
1966	National	Aaron, Clemente, Morgan, Stargell	500.00
1967	American	Carew, Hunter, Mantle, Yastrzemski	450.00
1967	National	Aaron, Banks, Clemente, Rose, Seaver	500.00
1968	American	Carew, Killebrew, Mantle, Oliva, Tiant	500.00
1968	National	Aaron, Carlton, Mays, Seaver	400.00
1969	American	Carew, Howard, Jackson, Williams	400.00
1969	National	Aaron, Banks, Carlton, Clemente, Mays	500.00
1970	American	Carew, Hunter, Palmer, Yastrzemski	400.00
1970	National	Aaron, Clemente, Gibson, Perry, Rose	500.00
1971	American	Carew, Jackson, Munson, F. Robinson	500.00
1971	National	Aaron, Bench, Clemente, Jenkins, Mays	500.00
1972	American	Carew, Fisk, Palmer, Perry, Ryan	350.00
1972	National	Aaron, Clemente, Gibson, Mays, Seaver	500.00
1973	American	Fingers, Fisk, Hunter, Munson, Ryan	400.00
1973	National	Aaron, Bench, Morgan, Rose, Seaver	375.00
1974	American	Allen, Fingers, Munson, Murcer, Perry	400.00
1974	National	Aaron, Brock, Morgan, Rose, Schmidt	400.00
1975	American	Aaron, Jackson, Munson, Yastrzemski	400.00
1975	National	Brock, Garvey, Rose, Seaver, Sutton	350.00
1976	American	Brett, Fisk, Jackson, Lynn, Munson	425.00
1976	National	Foster, Garvey, Rose, Schmidt, Seaver	350.00
1977	American	Brett, Jackson, Munson, Palmer	450.00
1977	National	Garvey, Morgan, Rose, Seaver, Sutton	350.00
1978	American	Carew, Guidry, Jackson, Martin, Palmer	350.00
1978	National	Bench, Fingers, Niekro, Rose, Sutter	350.00
1979	American	Brett, Carew, Jackson, Lynn, Ryan	350.00
1979	National	Bench, Carlton, Parker, Rose, Schmidt	350.00
1980	American	Brett, Carew, John, Lynn, Molitor	300.00
1980	National	Carlton, Carter, Richard, Rose, Schmidt	300.00
1981	American	Brett, Carew, Jackson, Morris, Winfield	350.00
1981	National	Carter, Parker, Rose, Ryan, Schmidt	350.00
1982	American	Brett, Carew, Jackson, Murray, Yount	350.00
1982	National	Carlton, Carter, Rose, Schmidt, Smith	325.00
1983	American	Brett, Lynn, Rice, Ripken, Winfield	325.00

Year	League	Key Signatures	Price
1983	National	Bench, Carter, Murphy, Schmidt, Smith	350.00
1984	American	Brett, Carew, Jackson, Murray, Ripken	325.00
1984	National	Gooden, Gwynn, Murphy, Schmidt	325.00
1985	American	Brett, Fisk, Henderson, Morris, Ripken	325.00
1985	National	Murphy, Rose, Ryan, Sandberg, Smith	300.00
1986	American	Brett, Clemens, Ripken, Winfield	350.00
1986	National	Gwynn, Murphy, Sandberg, Schmidt	300.00
1987	American	McGwire, Puckett, Ripken, Saberhagen	300.00
1987	National	Gwynn, Hershiser, Schmidt, Smith	300.00
1988	American	Brett, Clemens, Ripken, Winfield	250.00
1988	National	Cone, Gooden, Maddux, Smith	250.00
1989	American	B. Jackson, Puckett, Ripken, Ryan	250.00
1989	National	Clark, Gwynn, Schmidt, Smoltz	250.00
1990	American	Canseco, Eckersley, Griffey Jr., Ripken	250.00
1990	National	Bonds, Dawson, Gwynn, O. Smith	250.00
1991	American	Boggs, Clemens, Griffey Jr., Ripken	200.00
1991	National	Glavine, Gwynn, Murray, O. Smith	200.00
1992	American	Clemens, Griffey, Ripken, Ventura	200.00
1992	National	Glavine, Gwynn, Maddux, Walker	225.00
1993	American	Belle, Boggs, Griffey, Puckett, Ripken	200.00
1993	National	Bonds, Glavine, Piazza, Sandberg	225.00
1994	American	Griffey, Johnson, Mussina, Ripken	250.00
1994	National	Bagwell, Gwynn, Maddux, Piazza	250.00
1995	American	Griffey, Ripken, Rodriguez, Thomas	250.00
1995	National	Biggio, Maddux, Nomo, Piazza	250.00
1996	American	Griffey, McGwire, Ripken, Vaughn	250.00
1996	National	Bonds, Jones, Maddux, Piazza, Smith	250.00
1997	American	Clemens, Griffey, McGwire, Ripken	250.00
1997	National	Bagwell, Gwynn, Maddux, Walker	250.00

* Indicates 2nd game, † Indicates both games

WORLD SERIES TEAM-SIGNED BASEBALLS

Unlike All-Star team-signed balls, balls signed by every member of a World Series team aren't necessarily loaded with superstars. Nonetheless, the fact that these squads made it to baseball's biggest stage makes their team-signed balls among the most sought-after in the hobby.

Again, these baseballs should be official American or National League balls signed in blue or black ballpoint pen. Every member of the team—including the manager and coaching staff—should be represented, preferably with the manager and/or the best player signing on the sweet spot. The values below assume that all the big-name players are present. We begin our list with the 1920 World Series because so few team-signed balls are known to exist from prior seasons.

1949 World Series Yankees

1951 World Series Yankees

1953 World Series Yankees

1954 World Series Giants

Year	W/L	Team	Key Signatures	NM Price
1920	Winner	Cleveland Indians	Bagby, Caldwell, Chapman, Coveleski, Gardner, Jamieson, O'Neill, J. Sewell, Smith, Speaker, Wambsganss	$2,000.00
	Loser	Brooklyn Dodgers	Grimes, Konetchy, Marquard, Myers, Pfeffer, W. Robinson, Wheat	1,500.00
1921	Winner	New York Giants	Bancroft, Barnes, Burns, Frisch, Kelly, McGraw, Meusel, Nehf, Smith, Snyder, Toney, Youngs	2,500.00
	Loser	New York Yankees	Baker, Hoyt, Huggins, Mays, Meusel, Pipp, Ruth, Shawkey, Ward	3,500.00
1922	Winner	New York Giants	Bancroft, Barnes, Frisch, Kelly, McGraw, Meusel, Nehf, Stengel, Snyder, Youngs	2,500.00
	Loser	New York Yankees	Baker, Bush, Hoyt, Huggins, Meusel, Pipp, Ruth, Schang, Shawkey	2,800.00
1923	Winner	New York Yankees	Bush, Gehrig, Hoyt, Huggins, Jones, Meusel, Pennock, Pipp, Ruth, Ward, Witt	3,000.00
	Loser	New York Giants	Bancroft, Frisch, Jackson, Kelly, McGraw, Meusel, Ryan, Stengel, Youngs	2,500.00
1924	Winner	Washington Senators	Goslin, Harris, Johnson, Judge, Rice, Zachery	1,800.00
	Loser	New York Giants	Barnes, Frisch, Gowdy, Jackson, Kelly, McGraw, Meusel, Snyder, Terry Wilson, Youngs	2,200.00
1925	Winner	Pittsburgh Pirates	Barnhart, Carey, Cuyler, Grantham, McKechnie, Meadows, Smith, Traynor, Wright	1,000.00
	Loser	Washington Senators	Coveleski, Goslin, Harris, Johnson, Judge, Rice	1,500.00
1926	Winner	St. Louis Cardinals	Alexander, Bell, Blades, Bottomley, Douthit, Hafey, Haines, Hornsby, Rhem, Southworth	1,800.00
	Loser	New York Yankees	Combs, Hoyt, Huggins, Gehrig, Lazzeri, Meusel, Pennock, Ruth	4,000.00
1927	Winner	New York Yankees	Combs, Hoyt, Huggins, Gehrig, Lazzeri, Meusel, Moore, Pennock, Ruth	18,000.00
	Loser	Pittsburgh Pirates	Barnhart, Cronin, Cuyler, Grantham, Groh, Harris, Hill, Kremer, Traynor, L. Waner, P. Waner	900.00
1928	Winner	New York Yankees	Combs, Durocher, Gehrig, Hoyt, Huggins, Lazzeri, Meusel, Pipgras, Pennock, Ruth	10,000.00
	Loser	St. Louis Cardinals	Alexander, Bottomley, Frisch, Hafey, Haines, Maranville, McKechnie	2,000.00
1929	Winner	Philadelphia Athletics	Cochrane, Collins, Cronin, Earnshaw, Foxx, Grove, Haas, Mack, Miller, Simmons	1,000.00
	Loser	Chicago Cubs	Cuyler, Hartnett, Hornsby, Malone, McCarthy, Root, Wilson	1,000.00
1930	Winner	Philadelphia Athletics	Cochrane, Collins, Dykes, Foxx, Grove, Mack, Miller, Simmons	1,000.00
	Loser	St. Louis Cardinals	Adams, Bottomley, Douthit, Frisch, Gelbert, Grimes, Hafey, Haines, Street, Watkins, Wilson	1,000.00
1931	Winner	St. Louis Cardinals	Cochrane, Earnshaw, Foxx, Grove, Hoyt, Mack, Simmons	1,000.00
	Loser	Philadelphia Athletics	Mack, Foxx, Simmons, Cochrane, Grove, Earnshaw, Hoyt	1,500.00
1932	Winner	New York Yankees	Allen, Combs, Dickey, Gehrig, Gomez, Lazzeri, McCarthy, Ruffing, Ruth, Sewell	4,000.00
	Loser	Chicago Cubs	Bush, Cuyler, Grimes, Grimm, Hartnett, Herman, Hornsby, Moore, Stephenson, Warneke	900.00
1933	Winner	New York Giants	Hubbell, Jackson, Ott, Schumacher, Terry, Vergez	1,000.00
	Loser	Washington Senators	Cronin, Crowder, Goslin, Kuhel, Manush, Myer, Whitehill	800.00
1934	Winner	St. Louis Cardinals	Collins, D. Dean, P. Dean, Durocher, Frisch, Haines, Martin, Medwick	1,000.00
	Loser	Detroit Tigers	Bridges, Cochrane, Gehringer, Goslin, Greenberg, Rowe	850.00
1935	Winner	Detroit Tigers	Bridges, Cochrane, Gehringer, Goslin, Greenberg, Rowe	700.00
	Loser	Chicago Cubs	Cuyler, Demaree, Galan, Grimm, Hack, Hartnett, Herman, Klein, Lee, Lindstrom, Warneke	700.00

Year	W/L	Team	Key Signatures	NM Value
1936	Winner	New York Yankees	Dickey, DiMaggio, Gehrig, Gomez, Lazzeri, McCarthy, Pearson, Ruffing	2,000.00
	Loser	New York Giants	Hubbell, Jackson, Leiber, Mancuso, Moore, Ott, Terry	700.00
1937	Winner	New York Yankees	Dickey, DiMaggio, Gehrig, Gomez, Lazzeri, McCarthy, Ruffing	2,000.00
	Loser	New York Giants	Bartell, Hubbell, Leiber, Melton, Moore, Ott, Ripple, Terry	700.00
1938	Winner	New York Yankees	Dickey, DiMaggio, Gehrig, Gomez, McCarthy, Ruffing	1,500.00
	Loser	Chicago Cubs	Bryant, Dean, Garbark, Grimm, Hack, Hartnett, Herman, Lazzeri, Lee, Reynolds	750.00
1939	Winner	New York Yankees	Dickey, DiMaggio, Gomez, Keller, McCarthy, Rolfe, Ruffing, Selkirk	1,500.00
	Loser	Cincinnati Reds	Derringer, Goodman, Lombardi, McCormick,Walters	400.00
1940	Winner	Cincinnati Reds	Derringer, Lombardi, McCormick, Ripple, Walters, Werber	450.00
	Loser	Detroit Tigers	Averill, Gehringer, Greenberg, McCosky, Newsom, Rowe, York	500.00
1941	Winner	New York Yankees	Dickey, DiMaggio, Gomez, McCarthy, Rizzuto, Ruffing	1,000.00
	Loser	Brooklyn Dodgers	Camilli, Durocher, Herman, Higbe, Medwick, Reese, Reiser, Wyatt	600.00
1942	Winner	St. Louis Cardinals	Slaughter, Musial, W. Cooper, M. Cooper, Beazley	750.00
	Loser	New York Yankees	Dickey, DiMaggio, Gomez, Gordon, McCarthy, Rizzuto, Ruffing	1,000.00
1943	Winner	New York Yankees	Chandler, Dickey, Johnson, Keller, McCarthy, Russo	750.00
	Loser	St. Louis Cardinals	M.Cooper, W. Cooper, Lanier, Musial	450.00
1944	Winner	St. Louis Cardinals	M.Cooper, W. Cooper, Hopp, Marion, Musial	450.00
	Loser	St. Louis Browns	Kreevich, Kramer, McQuinn, Potter, Stephens	350.00
1945	Winner	Detroit Tigers	Cramer, Greenberg, Newhouser, Trout, York	350.00
	Loser	Chicago Cubs	Cavarretta, Grimm, Hack, Johnson, Nicholson, Pafko, Wyse	350.00
1946	Winner	St. Louis Cardinals	Garagiola, Kurowski, Musial, Pollet, Schoendienst, Slaughter, Walker	700.00
	Loser	Boston Red Sox	Cronin, DiMaggio, Doerr, Ferriss, Hughson, Pesky, Williams	700.00
1947	Winner	New York Yankees	Berra, DiMaggio, Henrich, McQuinn, Reynolds, Rizzuto, Shea	1,000.00
	Loser	Brooklyn Dodgers	Branca, Furillo, Hatten, Hodges, Reese, Robinson, Snider, Stankey, Vaughan	1,000.00
1948	Winner	Cleveland Indians	Bearden, Boudreau, Feller, Gordon, Keltner, Lemon, Mitchell, Paige	500.00
	Loser	Boston Braves	Dark, B. Elliott, Heath, Holmes, Sain, Spahn, Stankey	500.00
1949	Winner	New York Yankees	Bauer, Berra, DiMaggio, Henrich, Raschi, Rizzuto, Reynolds, Stengel	1,200.00
	Loser	Brooklyn Dodgers	Branca, Campanella, Connors, Furillo, Hodges, Newcombe, Reese, Robinson, Snider	1,000.00
1950	Winner	New York Yankees	Bauer, Berra, DiMaggio, Ford, Henrich, Mize, Raschi, Rizzuto, Stengel	1,000.00
	Loser	Philadelphia Phillies	Ashburn, Ennis, Hammer, Konstanty, Roberts, Simmons	400.00
1951	Winner	New York Yankees	Bauer, Berra, DiMaggio, Jensen, Mantle, McDougald, Mize, Raschi, Rizzuto, Stengel	4,000.00
	Loser	New York Giants	Dark, Durocher, Irvin, Jansen, Maglie, Mays, Thomson	750.00
1952	Winner	New York Yankees	Bauer, Berra, Mantle, Martin, Mize, Raschi, Reynolds, Rizzuto, Stengel	1,000.00
	Loser	Brooklyn Dodgers	Avila, Easter, Doby, Feller, Garcia, Lemon, Mitchell, Rosen, Wynn	900.00
1953	Winner	New York Yankees	Bauer, Berra, Ford, Mantle, Martin, Mize, Raschi, Rizzuto, Stengel	1,000.00
	Loser	Brooklyn Dodgers	Doby, Feller, Garcia, Lopez, Lemon, Mitchell, Rosen, Westlake, Wynn	900.00
1954	Winner	New York Giants	Antonelli, Dark, Durocher, Irvin, Mueller, Mays, Wilhelm	1,000.00
	Loser	Cleveland Indians	Avila, Doby, Feller, Garcia, Lemon, Lopez, Rosen, Wynn	450.00
1955	Winner	Brooklyn Dodgers	Alston, Campanella, Erskine, Furillo, Gilliam, Hodges, Koufax, Newcombe, Podres, Reese, Snider, Robinson, Zimmer	3,000.00
	Loser	New York Yankees	Bauer, Berra, Ford, Howard, Larsen, Mantle, Stengel	1,200.00
1956	Winner	New York Yankees	Bauer, Berra, Ford, Howard, Larsen, Mantle, Martin, Skowron, Stengel	1,200.00
	Loser	Brooklyn Dodgers	Alston, Campanella, Drysdale, Erskine, Furillo, Gilliam, Hodges, Koufax, Newcombe, Reese, Robinson, Snider	900.00
1957	Winner	Milwaukee Braves	Aaron, Adcock, Burdette, Mathews, Schoendienst, Spahn	1,200.00
	Loser	New York Yankees	Bauer, Berra, Ford, Howard, Larsen, Kubek, Mantle, Skowron, Stengel, Sturdivant	1,000.00
1958	Winner	New York Yankees	Berra, Ford, Howard, Kubek, Larsen, Mantle, Stengel, Turley	1,000.00
	Loser	Milwaukee Braves	Aaron, Adcock, Burdette, Mathews, Schoendienst, Spahn	700.00
1959	Winner	Los Angeles Dodgers	Alston, Drysdale, Gilliam, Hodges, Howard, Koufax, Snider, Wills, Zimmer	700.00
	Loser	Chicago White Sox	Aparicio, Cash, Fox, Kluszewski, Lopez, Shaw, Wynn	750.00
1960	Winner	Pittsburgh Pirates	Clemente, Friend, Groat, Law, Mazeroski, Stuart, Vernon	1,500.00
	Loser	New York Yankees	Berra, Ford, Howard, Kubek, Mantle, Maris, Skowron, Stengel	700.00
1961	Winner	New York Yankees	Berra, Ford, Howard, Kubek, Mantle, Maris	2,000.00
	Loser	Cincinnati Reds	Coleman, Freese, Jay, O'Toole, Pinson, Robinson	1,200.00
1962	Winner	New York Yankees	Berra, Ford, Howard, Kubek, Mantle, Maris, Terry, Tresh	750.00
	Loser	San Francisco Giants	Cepeda, Marichal, Mays, McCormick, McCovey	500.00
1963	Winner	Los Angeles Dodgers	Alston, T. Davis, W. Davis, Drysdale, Gilliam, Koufax, Wills	550.00
	Loser	New York Yankees	Berra, Ford, Howard, Kubek, Mantle, Maris, Terry, Tresh	700.00

Year	W/L	Team	Key Signatures	NM Value
1964	Winner	St. Louis Cardinals	Boyer, Brock, Flood, Gibson, Groat, McCarver, White	500.00
	Loser	New York Yankees	Berra, Ford, Howard, Kubek, Mantle, Maris, Stottlemyre, Tresh	500.00
1965	Winner	Los Angeles Dodgers	Alston, W. Davis, Drysdale, Gilliam, Lefebvre, Koufax, Wills	500.00
	Loser	Minnesota Twins	Grant, Kaat, Killebrew, Oliva, Versalles	350.00
1966	Winner	Baltimore Orioles	Aparicio, Blair, Blefary, Johnson, McNally, Palmer, Powell, B. Robinson, F. Robinson	350.00
	Loser	Los Angeles Dodgers	Alston, T. Davis, W. Davis, Drysdale, Koufax, Sutton, Wills	350.00
1967	Winner	St. Louis Cardinals	Brock, Carlton, Cepeda, Flood, Gibson, Maris, McCarver, Schoendienst	400.00
	Loser	Boston Red Sox	Conigliaro, Lonborg, Lyle, Petrocelli, Scott, Williams, Yastrzemski	800.00
1968	Winner	Detroit Tigers	Cash, Freehan, Kaline, Lolich, McLain	500.00
	Loser	St. Louis Cardinals	Brock, Carlton, Cepeda, Flood, Gibson, Maris, McCarver, Schoendienst	350.00
1969	Winner	New York Mets	Agee, Hodges, Koosman, Kranepool, Ryan, Seaver, Swoboda	2,500.00
	Loser	Baltimore Orioles	Blair, Cuellar, McNally, B. Robinson, F. Robinson, Cueller, Palmer, Powell, Weaver	300.00
1970	Winner	Baltimore Orioles	Blair, Cueller, McNally, B. Robinson, F. Robinson, Palmer, Powell, Weaver	325.00
	Loser	Cincinnati Reds	Anderson, Bench, Carbo, Concepcion, May, McRae, Perez, Rose	600.00
1971	Winner	Pittsburgh Pirates	Blass, Clemente, Mazeroski, Oliver, Sanguillen, Stargell	550.00
	Loser	Baltimore Orioles	Cueller, Dobson, McNally, B. Robinson, F. Robinson, Palmer, Powell, Weaver	300.00
1972	Winner	Oakland Athletics	Bando, Blue, Campaneris, Fingers, Hunter, Jackson, Williams	400.00
	Loser	Cincinnati Reds	Anderson, Bench, Concepcion, Foster, McRae, Morgan, Perez, Rose	300.00
1973	Winner	Oakland Athletics	Bando, Blue, Campaneris, Fingers, Hunter, Jackson, Williams	450.00
	Loser	New York Mets	Berra, Koosman, Kranepool, Mays, Milner, Seaver, Staub	400.00
1974	Winner	Oakland Athletics	Bando, Blue, Campaneris, Fingers, Hunter, Jackson, Williams	450.00
	Loser	Los Angeles Dodgers	Alston, Buckner, Cey, Garvey, John, Lopes, Russell, Sutton, Wynn	300.00
1975	Winner	Cincinnati Reds	Anderson, Bench, Concepcion, Foster, Griffey, Morgan, Perez, Rose	500.00
	Loser	Boston Red Sox	Carbo, Cooper, Evans, Fisk, Lee, Lynn, Petrocelli, Rice, Tiant, Wise, Yastrzemski	350.00
1976	Winner	Cincinnati Reds	Anderson, Bench, Concepcion, Foster, Griffey, Morgan, Perez, Rose, Zachary	500.00
	Loser	New York Yankees	Chambliss, Hunter, Lyle, Martin, Munson, Nettles, Randolph	800.00
1977	Winner	New York Yankees	Guidry, Hunter, Jackson, Lyle, Martin, Munson, Nettles, Piniella	750.00
	Loser	Los Angeles Dodgers	Baker, Cey, Garvey, John, Lasorda, Lopes, Russell, Smith, Sutton	300.00
1978	Winner	New York Yankees	Gossage, Guidry, Hunter, Jackson, Lyle, Martin, Munson, Piniella	700.00
	Loser	Los Angeles Dodgers	Baker, Cey, Garvey, John, Lasorda, Lopes, Russell, Smith, Sutton	250.00
1979	Winner	Pittsburgh Pirates	Blyleven, Candelaria, Madlock, Parker, Stargell, Tekulve	300.00
	Loser	Baltimore Orioles	Flanagan, D. Martinez, Murray, Palmer, Singleton, Weaver	200.00
1980	Winner	Philadelphia Phillies	Boone, Bowa, Carlton, Luzinski, Rose, Schmidt, Trillo	300.00
	Loser	Kansas City Royals	Brett, Leonard, McRae, Otis, Porter, Quisenberry, White, Wilson	250.00
1981	Winner	Los Angeles Dodgers	Baker, Cey, Garvey, Guerrero, Lasorda, Lopes, Russell, Sax, Valenzuela	325.00
	Loser	New York Yankees	Gossage, Guidry, Jackson, John, Murcer, Nettles, Piniella, Winfield	400.00
1982	Winner	St. Louis Cardinals	Andujar, Hernandez, Kaat, McGee, O. Smith, Sutter	350.00
	Loser	Milwaukee Brewers	Caldwell, Cooper, Fingers, Molitor, Oglivie, Thomas, Vuckovich, Yount	350.00
1983	Winner	Baltimore Orioles	Altobelli, Boddicker, D. Martinez, Murray, Palmer, C. Ripken Jr.	450.00
	Loser	Philadelphia Phillies	Carlton, Denny, Morgan, Perez, Rose, Schmidt	250.00
1984	Winner	Detroit Tigers	Anderson, Gibson, Evans, Hernandez, Johnson, Morris, Parrish, Trammell, Whitaker	500.00
	Loser	San Diego Padres	Garvey, Gossage, Gwynn, Nettles	250.00
1985	Winner	Kansas City Royals	Brett, Howser, McRae, Saberhagen, Quisenberry, White, Wilson	400.00
	Loser	St. Louis Cardinals	Clark, Coleman, McGee, O. Smith, Tudor	250.00
1986	Winner	New York Mets	Carter, Dykstra, Gooden, Hernandez, D. Johnson, Mitchell, Strawberry, Wilson	400.00
	Loser	Boston Red Sox	Baylor, Boggs, Boyd, Buckner, Clemens, Evans, D. Henderson, Hurst, Rice, Seaver	300.00
1987	Winner	Minnesota Twins	Blyleven, Brunansky, Gaetti, Hrbek, Kelly, J. Niekro, Puckett, Reardon, Viola	400.00
	Loser	St. Louis Cardinals	Clark, Coleman, McGee, O. Smith, Tudor	200.00
1988	Winner	Los Angeles Dodgers	Gibson, Guerrero, Hershiser, Lasorda, Sax, Valenzuela	250.00
	Loser	Oakland Athletics	Canseco, Eckersley, La Russa, McGwire, Steinbach, Stewart, Weiss	225.00
1989	Winner	Oakland Athletics	Canseco, Eckersley, R. Henderson, La Russa, McGwire, Steinbach, Stewart, Weiss	300.00
	Loser	San Francisco Giants	Butler, Clark, Mitchell, Williams	225.00
1990	Winner	Cincinnati Reds	Davis, Dibble, Larkin, Morris, Myers, O'Neill, Piniella, Rijo, Sabo	300.00
	Loser	Oakland Athletics	Canseco, Eckersley, R. Henderson, La Russa, McGwire, Stewart, Welch	225.00
1991	Winner	Minnesota Twins	Aguilera, Davis, Erickson, Hrbek, Kelly, Knoblauch, Morris, Puckett, Tapani	400.00
	Loser	Atlanta Braves	Avery, Blauser, Cox, Gant, Glavine, Justice, Pendleton, Smoltz, Wholers	250.00
1992	Winner	Toronto Blue Jays	Alomar, Borders Carter, Cone, Gaston, Key, Morris, Olerud, Stieb, Stottlemyre, Winfield, White	400.00
	Loser	Atlanta Braves	Avery, Cox, Gant, Glavine, Justice, Pendleton, Reardon, Sanders, Smoltz	300.00

**1955 World Series
Dodgers**

**1960 World Series
Pirates**

**1961 World Series
Yankees**

**1977 World Series
Yankees**

Year	W/L	Team	Key Signatures	NM Value
1993	Winner	Toronto Blue Jays	Alomar, Carter, Gaston, Henderson, Hentgen, Key, Molitor, Morris, Olerud, Stottlemyre, Stewart, White	400.00
	Loser	Philadelphia Phillies	Daulton, Dykstra, Green, Hollins, Kruk, Schilling, Williams	250.00
1994			No World Series	
1995	Winner	Atlanta Braves	Avery, Cox, Glavine, Grissom, C. Jones, Justice, Klesko, Lopez, Maddux, McGriff, Smoltz, Wohlers	400.00
	Loser	Cleveland Indians	Alomar, Baerga, Belle, Hershiser, Lofton, D. Martinez, Mesa, Murray, Nagy, Ramirez, Thome	350.00
1996	Winner	New York Yankees	Boggs, Cone, Jeter, Martinez, Pettitte, Rivera, Torre, Wetteland, Williams	600.00
	Loser	Atlanta Braves	Cox, Glavine, C. Jones, Justice, Klesko, Lopez, Maddux, McGriff, Smoltz, Wohlers	300.00
1997	Winner	Florida Marlins	Bonilla, Brown, Fernandez, Hernandez, Johnson, Leyland, Nen, Renteria, Sheffield	500.00
	Loser	Cleveland Indians	Alomar, Grissom, Hershiser, Ramirez, Thome, Vizquel, Williams	300.00

TEAM SIGNED BASEBALLS

1931 New York Yankees

1932 St. Louis Cardinals

1939 New York Giants

1954 New York Giants

Atlanta Braves

Year	Key Signatures	Price
1966	Aaron, F. Alou, Mathews, P. Niekro, Torre	$350.00
1967	Aaron, F. Alou, Boyer, Carty, P. Niekro, Torre	200.00
1968	Aaron, F. Alou, Boyer, P. Niekro, Torre	250.00
1969	Aaron, F. Alou, Boyer, Carty, Cepeda, Evans, P. Niekro, Wilhelm	250.00
1970	Aaron, Boyer, Cepeda, Evans, P. Niekro, Wilhelm	150.00
1971	Aaron, Boyer, Cepeda, Evans, P. Niekro, Versalles, Williams	150.00
1972	Aaron, Baker, Cepeda, Evans, Mathews, P. Niekro, Williams	150.00
1973	Aaron, Baker, Evans, Johnson, Mathews, P. Niekro	150.00
1974	Aaron, Baker, Evans, Johnson, Mathews, P. Niekro	175.00
1975	Baker, Evans, Johnson, P. Niekro	100.00
1976	Bristol, Gaston, P. Niekro	85.00
1977	Burroughs, Matthews, P. Niekro	75.00
1978	Burroughs, Cox, Horner, Murphy, P. Neikro	85.00
1979	Burroughs, Cox, Horner, Murphy, P. Neikro	100.00
1980	Burroughs, Chambliss, Cox, Horner, Murphy, P. Niekro	100.00
1981	Butler, Chambliss, Cox, Horner, Murphy, P. Niekro, Perry	125.00
1982	Butler, Chambliss, Horner, Murphy, P. Niekro, Torre	125.00
1983	Butler, Chambliss, Horner, Murphy, P. Niekro, Torre	80.00
1984	Chambliss, Horner, Murphy, Torre	75.00
1985	Chambliss, Horner, Murphy, Sutter	75.00
1986	Griffey, Horner, Murphy	75.00
1987	Griffey, Murphy, Z. Smith	75.00
1988	Gant, Glavine, Murphy, Sutter	75.00
1989	Blauser, Gant, Glavine, Murphy, Smoltz	125.00
1990	Avery, Blauser, Cox, Gant, Glavine, Justice, Murphy, Smoltz	150.00
1991	Avery, Blauser, Cox, Gant, Glavine, Justice, Pendleton, Smoltz	250.00
1992	Avery, Cox, Gant, Glavine, Justice, Pendleton, Sanders, Smoltz	300.00
1993	Avery, Cox, Gant, Glavine, Justice, Maddux, McGriff, Pendleton, Sanders, Smoltz	250.00
1994	Avery, Cox, Glavine, Jones, Justice, Klesko, Lopez, Maddux, McGriff, Sanders, Smoltz	275.00
1995	Avery, Cox, Glavine, C. Jones, Justice, Klesko, Lopez, Maddux, McGriff, Smoltz, Wohlers	400.00
1996	Cox, Glavine, C. Jones, Justice, Klesko, Lopez, Maddux, McGriff, Smoltz, Wohlers	300.00
1997	Cox, Glavine, C. Jones, Klesko, Lopez, Maddux, McGriff, Smoltz, Wohlers	250.00

Baltimore Orioles

Year	Key Signatures	Price
1954	Larsen, Stephens, Turley	$200.00
1955	Abrams, Miranda, Richards, Triandos	200.00
1956	Kell, Richards, Triandos	225.00
1957	Kell, Richards, Triandos	250.00
1958	Pappas, Richards, B. Robinson, Triandos, Wilhelm	200.00
1959	Pappas, Richards, B. Robinson, Triandos, Wilhelm	200.00
1960	Estrada, Gentile, Pappas, Richards, B. Robinson, Triandos, Wilhelm	200.00
1961	Barber, Gentile, Powell, Richards, B. Robinson, Triandos, Wilhelm	200.00
1962	Gentile, Pappas, Powell, Roberts, B. Robinson, Wilhelm	200.00
1963	Aparicio, Barber, Gentile, Pappas, Powell, Roberts, B. Robinson	225.00
1964	Aparicio, Bunker, Piniella, Pappas, Powell, Roberts, B. Robinson	250.00
1965	Aparicio, Barber, Blair, Blefary, Palmer, Powell, Roberts, B. Robinson	225.00
1966	Aparicio, Blair, Blefary, Johnson, McNally, Palmer, Powell, B. Robinson, F. Robinson	350.00
1967	Aparicio, Blair, Blefary, Johnson, Powell, B. Robinson, F. Robinson	250.00
1968	Blair, Blefary, Johnson, McNally, Powell, B. Robinson, F. Robinson, Weaver	200.00
1969	Blair, Cuellar, McNally, Palmer, Powell, B. Robinson, F. Robinson, Weaver	300.00
1970	Blair, Cueller, McNally, Palmer, Powell, B. Robinson, F. Robinson, Weaver	325.00
1971	Cueller, Dobson, McNally, Palmer, Powell, B. Robinson, F. Robinson, Weaver	300.00

1972	Baylor, Cueller, McNally, Palmer, Powell, Robinson, Weaver	150.00
1973	Bumbry, Cueller, McNally, Palmer, Powell, Robinson, Weaver	200.00
1974	Baylor, Blair, Cueller, McNally, Palmer, Powell, Robinson, Weaver	250.00
1975	Baylor, Cueller, May, Palmer, B. Robinson, Singleton, Weaver	200.00
1976	Cueller, Jackson, May, Palmer, Robinson, Singleton, Weaver	200.00
1977	D. Martinez, Murray, Palmer, Robinson, Singleton, Weaver	125.00
1978	Flanagan, D. Martinez, Murray, Palmer, Singleton, Weaver	150.00
1979	Flanagan, D. Martinez, Murray, Palmer, Singleton, Weaver	200.00
1980	Flanagan, D. Martinez, Murray, Palmer, Singleton, Stone, Weaver	200.00
1981	Flanagan, D. Martinez, Murray, Palmer, Singleton, Weaver	125.00
1982	Flanagan, D. Martinez, Murray, Palmer, C. Ripken Jr., Weaver	125.00
1983	Altobelli, Boddicker, D. Martinez, Murray, Palmer, C. Ripken Jr.	450.00
1984	Boddicker, Flanagan, D. Martinez, Murray, Palmer, C. Ripken Jr.	200.00
1985	Lynn, D. Martinez, Murray, C. Ripken Jr., Weaver	85.00
1986	Boddicker, Lynn, D. Martinez, Murray, C. Ripken Jr., Weaver	100.00
1987	Knight, Lynn, Murray, C. Ripken Jr., C. Ripken Sr., Sheets	85.00
1988	Lynn, Murray, C. Ripken Jr., C. Ripken Sr., F. Robinson	100.00
1989	Anderson, C. Ripken Jr., F. Robinson, Tettleton	100.00
1990	Anderson, Finley, McDonald, C. Ripken Jr., F. Robinson	100.00
1991	Anderson, Evans, Oates, C. Ripken Jr., F. Robinson	85.00
1992	Anderson, Mussina, Oates, C. Ripken Jr., Sutcliffe	115.00
1993	Anderson, Baines, Mussina, C. Ripken Jr., Sutcliffe, Valenzuela	115.00
1994	Anderson, Baines, McDonald, Mussina, Palmeiro, C. Ripken Jr.	125.00
1995	Anderson, Baines, Brown, Mussina, Palmeiro, C. Ripken Jr.	150.00
1996	Alomar, Anderson, Mussina, Palmeiro, C. Ripken Jr.	150.00
1997	Alomar, Anderson, Mussina, Myers, Palmeiro, C. Ripken Jr.	150.00

Boston Braves

Year	Key Signatures	Price
1920	Boeckel, Mann, Maranville, Oeschger, Powell	$900.00
1921	Barbare, Boeckel, Cruise, Oeschger, Powell, Southworth	500.00
1922	Barbare, Boeckel, Marquard, Powell, Southworth	500.00
1923	Boeckel, Marquard, McInnis, Powell, Southworth	500.00
1924	Bancroft, Barnes, Mann, Marquard, Powell, Tierney	800.00
1925	Bancroft, Barnes, Burrus, Mann, Marquard	800.00
1926	Bancroft, Benton, Brown, Burrus, Mann	400.00
1927	Bancroft, Brown, Burrus, Fournier, Richbourg	400.00
1928	Burrus, Clark, Hornsby, Richbourg, Sisler, Smith	400.00
1929	Clark, Evers, Harper, Maranville, Richbourg, Sisler	300.00
1930	Berger, Clark, Maranville, McKechnie, Richbourg, Sisler	600.00
1931	Berger, Brandt, Maranville, McKechnie, Schulmerich	400.00
1932	Berger, Brandt, Maranville, McKechnie, Schulmerich	400.00
1933	Berger, Cantwell, Maranville, McKechnie, Moore, Schulmerich	400.00
1934	Berger, Brandt, Frankhouse, McKechnie, Whitney	350.00
1935	Berger, Frankhouse, McKechnie, Ruth	1,200.00
1936	Berger, Cuccinello, Jordan, MacFayden, McKechnie, Moore	300.00
1937	Berger, V. DiMaggio, Fette, McKechnie, Moore, Turner	300.00
1938	Cooney, Cuccinello, V. DiMaggio, Lopez, Stengel	450.00
1939	Cooney, Cuccinello, Hassett, Lopez, Simmons, Stengel, West	350.00
1940	Cooney, Cuccinello, Hassett, Lopez, Miller, Stengel	600.00
1941	Cooney, Hassett, Stengel, P. Waner, West	350.00
1942	Cooney, Lombardi, Sain, Spahn, Stengel, P. Waner, West	900.00
1943	Holmes, McCarthy, Stengel	300.00
1944	Holmes, Nieman, Tobin	250.00
1945	Holmes, Nieman, Workman	225.00
1946	Herman, Holmes, Sain, Spahn	300.00
1947	B. Elliot, Holmes, Sain, Spahn	300.00
1948	Dark, B. Elliot, Heath, Holmes, Sain, Spahn, Stankey	500.00
1949	Dark, B. Elliot, Holmes, Sain, Spahn, Stankey	300.00

1950	B. Elliot, Gordon, Holmes, Jethro, Sain, Spahn	250.00
1951	B. Elliot, Gordon, Jethro, Sain, Spahn	225.00
1952	Gordon, Jethro, Mathews, Spahn	300.00

Boston Red Sox

Year	Key Signatures	Price
1920	Barrow, Hendryx, Hooper, Hoyt, Jones, McInnis, Pennock	$1,000.00
1921	Duffy, Hendryx, Jones, Pennock, Pratt	750.00
1922	Burns, Duffy, Harris, Pennock, Pratt	650.00
1923	Boone, Burns, Chance, Ehmke, Harris	1,200.00
1924	Boone, Ehmke, Harris, Ruffing, Veach	450.00
1925	Boone, Carlyle, Ehmke, Prothro, Ruffing	400.00
1926	Carlyle, Ehmke, Jacobson, Ruffing, Tobin	400.00
1927	Jacobson, Myer, Rothrock, Ruffing, Tobin	400.00
1928	Morris, Myer, Rothrock, Ruffing, K. Williams	1,500.00
1929	Morris, Rothrock, Ruffing, K. Williams	600.00
1930	Morris, Rothrock, Ruffing, Webb	300.00
1931	Berry, MacFayden, Morris, Rothrock, Webb	250.00
1932	Alexander, R.Johnson, Jolley, Webb	300.00
1933	Alexander, R. Ferrell, Hodapp, R. Johnson, Jolley	300.00
1934	R. Ferrell, W. Ferrell, Grove, Harris, R. Johnson, Pennock	450.00
1935	Cronin, R. Ferrell, W. Ferrell, Grove, R. Johnson	400.00
1936	Cramer, Cronin, R. Ferrell, W. Ferrell, Foxx, Grove, Manush	500.00
1937	Chapman, Cramer, Cronin, Doerr, Foxx, Grove, Higgins, Wilson	450.00
1938	Chapman, Cramer, Cronin, Doerr, Foxx, Grove, Higgins	750.00
1939	Cramer, Cronin, Doerr, Foxx, Grove, Williams	500.00
1940	Cramer, Cronin, DiMaggio, Doerr, Foxx, Grove, Williams	800.00
1941	Cronin, DiMaggio, Doerr, Foxx, Grove, Newsome, Williams	600.00
1942	Cronin, DiMaggio, Doerr, Hughson, Pesky, Williams	450.00
1943	Cronin, Doerr, Hughson	400.00
1944	Cronin, Doerr, Hughson, Johnson	300.00
1945	Camilli, Cronin, Ferriss, Johnson	250.00
1946	Cronin, DiMaggio, Doerr, Ferriss, Hughson, Pesky, Williams	700.00
1947	Cronin, DiMaggio, Dobson, Doerr, Ferriss, Pesky, Williams	300.00
1948	DiMaggio, Doerr, McCarthy, Pesky, Stephens, Williams	300.00
1949	DiMaggio, Doerr, McCarthy, Parnell, Pesky, Stephens, Williams	300.00
1950	DiMaggio, Doerr, McCarthy, Parnell, Pesky, Stephens, Williams	300.00
1951	Boudreau, DiMaggio, Doerr, Evers, Kell, Parnell, Pesky, Williams	250.00
1952	Boudreau, D. DiMaggio, Evers, Goodman, Kell, Parnell, Stephens	250.00
1953	Boudreau, Goodman, Kell, Parnell, Piersall, Williams	450.00
1954	Boudreau, Goodman, Jensen, Kell, Piersall, Williams	450.00
1955	Goodman, Jensen, Sullivan, Williams, Zauchin	250.00
1956	Brewer, Jensen, Piersall, Vernon, Williams	350.00
1957	Jensen, Piersall, Vernon, Williams	225.00
1958	Jensen, Runnels, Williams	400.00
1959	Jensen, Runnels, Williams	200.00
1960	Runnels, Wertz, Williams	400.00
1961	Jensen, Malzone, Runnels, Schwall, Yastrzemski	200.00
1962	Malzone, Raditz, Runnels, Yastrzemski	200.00
1963	Monbouquette, Pesky, Radatz, Stuart, Yastrzemski	200.00
1964	Conigliaro, Herman, Pesky, Radatz, Stuart, Yastrzemski	250.00
1965	Conigliaro, Herman, Lonborg, Petrocelli, Yastrzemski	250.00
1966	Conigliaro, Herman, Lonborg, Petrocelli, Scott, Yastrzemski	250.00
1967	Conigliaro, Lonborg, Lyle, Petrocelli, Scott, Williams, Yastrzemski	800.00
1968	Lonborg, Lyle, Petrocelli, Scott, D. Williams, Yastrzemski	175.00
1969	Conigliaro, Lonborg, Lyle, Petrocelli, D. Williams, Yastrzemski	300.00
1970	Conigliaro, Lyle, Petrocelli, Yastrzemski	150.00
1971	Aparicio, Conigliaro, Fisk, Lyle, Petrocelli, Tiant, Yastrzemski	150.00
1972	Aparicio, Fisk, Petrocelli, Tiant, Yastrzemski	200.00

1943 St. Louis Browns

1948 Brooklyn Dodgers

1949 Brooklyn Dodgers

1950 Brooklyn Dodgers

Year	Key Signatures	Price
1973	Aparicio, Cepeda, Evans, Fisk, Lee, Petrocelli, Tiant, Yastrzemski	150.00
1974	Carbo, Cooper, Evans, Fisk, Lee, Marichal, Petrocelli, Tiant, Yastrzemski	200.00
1975	Carbo, Cooper, Evans, Fisk, Lee, Lynn, Petrocelli, Rice, Tiant, Wise, Yastrzemski	350.00
1976	Cooper, Evans, Fisk, Jenkins, Lynn, Petrocelli, Rice, Tiant, Yastrzemski, Zimmer	250.00
1977	Carbo, Evans, Fisk, Hobson, Jenkins, Lynn, Rice, Scott, Tiant, Yastrzemski, Zimmer	150.00
1978	Eckersley, Evans, Fisk, Hobson, Lynn, Rice, Tiant, Torrez, Yastrzemski, Zimmer	125.00
1979	Eckersley, Evans, Fisk, Hobson, Lynn, Rice, Torrez, Yastrzemski, Zimmer	150.00
1980	Eckersley, Evans, Fisk, Lynn, Perez, Rice, Yastrzemski, Zimmer	150.00
1981	Eckersley, Evans, Lansford, Perez, Rice, Yastrzemski	125.00
1982	Boggs, Eckersley, Evans, Lansford, Perez, Rice, Yastrzemski	200.00
1983	Armas, Boggs, Eckersley, Evans, Rice, Yastrzemski	175.00
1984	Armas, Boggs, Buckner, Clemens, Eckersley, Evans, Rice	100.00
1985	Armas, Boggs, Boyd, Buckner, Clemens, Evans, Rice	75.00
1986	Baylor, Boggs, Boyd, Buckner, Clemens, Evans, Rice, Seaver	300.00
1987	Baylor, Boggs, Buckner, Burks, Clemens, Evans, Greenwell, Rice	100.00
1988	Boggs, Burks, Clemens, Evans, Greenwell, Hurst, Rice	100.00
1989	Boggs, Burks, Clemens, Esasky, Evans, Greenwell, Rice, L. Smith	100.00
1990	Boddicker, Boggs, Burks, Clemens, Greenwell, Evans	125.00
1991	Boggs, Burks, Clark, Clemens, Greenwell, Reardon, Vaughn	100.00
1992	Boggs, Clemens, Greenwell, Hobson, Vaughn	100.00
1993	Clemens, Dawson, Greenwell, Hobson, Valentin, Vaughn	80.00
1994	Clemens, Dawson, Greenwell, Hobson, Valentin, Vaughn	125.00
1995	Canseco, Clemens, Greenwell, Valentin, Vaughn	120.00
1996	Clemens, Valentin, Vaughn	125.00
1997	Garciaparra, Valentin, Vaughn	120.00

Brooklyn Dodgers

Year	Key Signatures	Price
1920	Grimes, Konetchy, Marquard, Myers, Pfeffer, W. Robinson, Wheat	$1,500.00
1921	Griffith, Grimes, Johnston, Robinson, Schmandt, Wheat	1,000.00
1922	DeBerry, T. Griffith, Grimes, Johnston, Myers, Robinson, Ruether, Vance, Wheat	1,200.00
1923	Fournier, Grimes, Johnston, Robinson, Vance, Wheat	1,300.00
1924	Brown, Fournier, Grimes, High, Robinson, Vance, Wheat	1,200.00
1925	Brown, Cox, Fournier, Grimes, Robinson, Stock, Taylor, Vance, Wheat	1,200.00
1926	Carey, Fournier, Grimes, Herman, Maranville, Petty, Robinson, Vance, Wheat	1,500.00
1927	Carey, Herman, Robinson, Vance	1,000.00
1928	Bancroft, Bissonette, Carey, Hendrick, Herman, Lopez, Robinson, Vance	1,000.00
1929	Bancroft, Bressler, Carey, Clark, Frederick, Gilbert, Herman, Robinson, Vance	1,000.00
1930	Bissonette, Frederick, Herman, Lopez, Robinson, Vance, Wright	900.00
1931	Bissonette, Clark, Lombardi, Lopez, O'Doul, Robinson, Vance	1,000.00
1932	Carey, Clark, Kelly, Lopez, O'Doul, Stripp, Taylor, Vance, Wilson, Wright	750.00
1933	Carey, Frederick, Lopez, Mungo, O'Doul, Wilson, Wright	800.00
1934	Boyle, Cuccinello, Koenecke, Leslie, Lopez, Mungo, Stengel, Stripp, Wilson,	450.00
1935	Leslie, Lopez, Mungo, Stengel, Stripp	400.00
1936	Bordagaray, Hassett, Lindstrom, Mungo, Stengel, Stripp	400.00
1937	Grimes, Hassett, Hoyt, Manush, Phelps	400.00
1938	Camilli, Cuyler, Durocher, Grimes, Hoyt, Manush, Phelps	2,500.00
1939	Camilli, Durocher, Hamlin	350.00
1940	Camilli, Durocher, Fitzsimmons, Medwick, Reese	700.00
1941	Camilli, Durocher, Herman, Higbe, Medwick, Reese, Reiser, Wyatt	600.00
1942	Camilli, Durocher, French, Herman, Medwick, Reese, Reiser, Vaughan, Wyatt	500.00
1943	Durocher, Herman, Hodges, Medwick, Vaughan, Walker, L. Waner, P. Waner, Wyatt	500.00
1944	Durocher, Galan, Stankey, Walker	400.00
1945	Branca, Durocher, Galan, Olmo, Rosen, Stankey, Walker	300.00
1946	Durocher, Furillo, Higbe, Medwick, Reese, Stankey,	450.00
1947	Branca, Furillo, Hatten, Hodges, Reese, Robinson, Snider, Stankey, Vaughan	1,000.00
1948	Branca, Campanella, Durocher, Furillo, Hodges, Reese, Robinson, Roe, Snider	800.00
1949	Branca, Campanella, Connors, Furillo, Hodges, Newcombe, Reese, Robinson, Snider	1,000.00
1950	Campanella, Erskine, Furillo, Hodges, Newcombe, Reese, Robinson, Roe, Snider	750.00

1951	Branca, Campanella, Erskine, Hodges, Newcombe, Reese, Robinson, Snider	600.00
1952	Campanella, Erskine, Furillo, Hodges, Podres, Reese, Robinson, Snider	900.00
1953	Campanella, Erskine, Furillo, Gilliam, Hodges, Reese, Robinson, Snider	900.00
1954	Alston, Campanella, Erskine, Furillo, Gilliam, Hodges, Lasorda, Newcombe, Podres, Reese, Robinson, Snider	1,400.00
1955	Alston, Campanella, Erskine, Furillo, Gilliam, Hodges, Koufax, Newcombe, Podres, Reese, Snider, Robinson, Zimmer	3,000.00
1956	Alston, Campanella, Drysdale, Erskine, Furillo, Gilliam, Hodges, Koufax, Newcombe, Reese, Robinson, Snider	900.00
1957	Alston, Campanella, Drysdale, Furillo, Gilliam, Hodges, Koufax, Newcombe, Podres, Reese, Snider, Zimmer	1,000.00

California Angels

Year	Key Signatures	Price
1965	Adcock, Chance, Fregosi	$150.00
1966	Adcock, Chance, Fregosi	100.00
1967	Fregosi, Johnstone, Mincher	100.00
1968	Davalillo, Fregosi, Reichardt	125.00
1969	Fregosi, Johnstone, Wilhelm	100.00
1970	Fregosi, Johnstone, Wright	100.00
1971	Conigliaro, Fregosi, Messersmith	125.00
1972	Pinson, Rivers, Ryan, Wright	125.00
1973	Pinson, F. Robinson, Ryan, Singer	125.00
1974	Rivers, F. Robinson, Ryan, Tannana, Williams	125.00
1975	Rivers, Ryan, Tannana, Williams	250.00
1976	B. Bonds, Ryan, Tannana, Williams	150.00
1977	Baylor, B. Bonds, Grich, Ryan, Tannana	150.00
1978	Baylor, Bostock, Fregosi, Lansford, Rudi, Ryan, Tannana	100.00
1979	Baylor, Carew, Fregosi, Lansford, Ryan, Tannana	150.00
1980	Baylor, Carew, Fregosi, Lansford, Tannana	100.00
1981	Baylor, Carew, Fregosi, Grich, Lynn	75.00
1982	Baylor, Boone, Carew, Grich, Jackson, Lynn, Mauch	150.00
1983	Boone, Carew, Grich, Jackson, John, Lynn	100.00
1984	Boone, Carew, Downing, Grich, Jackson, John, Lynn	100.00
1985	Boone, Carew, Downing, Grich, Jackson, John, Sutton	100.00
1986	Boone, DeCinces, Downing, Grich, Jackson, Joyner, Sutton	75.00
1987	Boone, Buckner, DeCinces, Downing, Joyner, Sutton, White	75.00
1988	Armas, Boone, Buckner, Davis, Downing, Finley, Joyner, White	75.00
1989	Abbott, Blyleven, Davis, Finley, Joyner, White	70.00
1990	Abbott, Bichette, Blyleven, Davis, Finley, Joyner, Langston, White, Winfield	100.00
1991	Abbott, Finley, Joyner, Langston, Winfield	60.00
1992	Abbott, Blyleven, Finley, Langston	75.00
1993	Davis, Finley, Langston, Salmon, Snow	75.00
1994	Davis, Edmonds, Finley, Langston, Salmon, Snow	95.00
1995	Anderson, Davis, Edmonds, Finley, Langston, Phillips, Salmon, L. Smith, Snow	125.00
1996	Anderson, Edmonds, Erstad, Finley, Salmon	120.00
1997	Anderson, Edmonds, Erstad, Finley, Salmon	120.00

Chicago Cubs

Year	Key Signatures	Price
1920	Alexander, Flack, Hollocher, Robertson	$1,200.00
1921	Alexander, Barber, Evers, Flack, Grimes, Maisel	1,500.00
1922	Aldridge, Alexander, Grimes, Hartnett, Miller, O'Farrell	1,000.00
1923	Aldridge, Alexander, Grimes, Hartnett, Miller, O'Farrell, Statz	900.00

1924	Alexander, Grantham, Hartnett, Heathcote, Kaufman	900.00
1925	Alexander, Freigau, Grimm, Hartnett, Jahn, Maranville	1,000.00
1926	Adams, Hartnett, McCarthy, Root, Stephenson, Wilson	1,100.00
1927	Grimm, Hartnett, McCarthy, Root, Stephenson, Webb, Wilson	600.00
1928	Cuyler, Hartnett, Malone, McCarthy, Stephenson, Wilson	600.00
1929	Cuyler, Hartnett, Hornsby, Malone, McCarthy, Root, Wilson	1,000.00
1930	Cuyler, Grimm, Hartnett, Hornsby, Malone, McCarthy, Wilson	1,200.00
1931	Cuyler, English, Grimm, Hartnett, Herman, Hornsby, Taylor, Wilson	1,000.00
1932	Bush, Cuyler, Grimes, Grimm, Hartnett, Herman, Hornsby, Moore, Stephenson, Warneke	900.00
1933	Bush, Cuyler, Grimes, Grimm, Hartnett, Herman, Stephenson	500.00
1934	Cuyler, Grimm, Hack, Hartnett, Herman, Klein, Warneke	500.00
1935	Cuyler, Demaree, Galan, Grimm, Hack, Hartnett, Herman, Klein, Lee, Lindstrom, Warneke	700.00
1936	Demaree, Grimm, Hartnett, Herman, Klein, Lindstrom, Warneke	400.00
1937	Carleton, Demaree, French, Hartnett, Herman, Galan, Grimm	500.00
1938	Bryant, Dean, Garbark, Grimm, Hack, Hartnett, Herman, Lazzeri, Lee, Reynolds	750.00
1939	Dean, Galan, Hartnett, Herman, Lee, Leiber	350.00
1940	Dean, Hartnett, Herman, Leiber, Nicholson, Passeau	250.00
1941	Dean, Hack, Nicholson	250.00
1942	Cavarretta, Foxx, Hack, Nicholson, Novikoff, Passeau	300.00
1943	Cavarretta, Goodman, Nicholson, Stanky	300.00
1944	Cavarretta, Dallessandro, Foxx, Grimm, Nicholson, Pafko	250.00
1945	Cavarretta, Grimm, Hack, Johnson, Nicholson, Pafko, Wyse	350.00
1946	Grimm, Hack, Waitkus	250.00
1947	Cavarretta, Grimm, Nicholson, Pafko	250.00
1948	Grimm, Nicholson, Pafko, Schmitz	250.00
1949	Burgess, Frisch, Grimm, Pafko, Sauer	300.00
1950	Frisch, Pafko, Sauer	250.00
1951	Burgess, Connors, Frisch, Pafko, Sauer	250.00
1952	Baumholtz, Fondy, Hacker, Sauer	250.00
1953	Banks, Baumholtz, Fondy, Garagiola, Kiner, Sauer	250.00
1954	Banks, Garagiola, Kiner, Sauer	400.00
1955	Banks, Hack, Sauer	200.00
1956	Banks, Hack, Irvin	225.00
1957	Banks, Drabowsky, Long	200.00
1958	Banks, Long, Thomson	225.00
1959	Averill, Banks, Dark, Long, Thomson, Williams	200.00
1960	Ashburn, Banks, Boudreau, Grimm, Santo, Williams, Zimmer	200.00
1961	Ashburn, Banks, Brock, Santo, Williams, Zimmer	225.00
1962	Banks, Brock, Hubbs, Santo, Williams	225.00
1963	Banks, Brock, Ellsworth, Hubbs, Santo, Williams	200.00
1964	Banks, Brock, Jackson, Kessinger, Santo, Williams	200.00
1965	Banks, Kessinger, Santo, Williams	125.00
1966	Banks, Durocher, Jenkins, Kessinger, Santo	150.00
1967	Banks, Durocher, Jenkins, Kessinger, J. Niekro, Santo, Williams	150.00
1968	Banks, Durocher, Jenkins, Kessinger, J. Niekro, Santo, Williams	150.00
1969	Banks, Durocher, Hands, Jenkins, Kessinger, Santo, Williams	200.00
1970	Banks, Durocher, Hickman, Jenkins, Santo, Wilhelm, Williams	200.00
1971	Banks, Durocher, Jenkins, Santo, Williams	125.00
1972	Durocher, Jenkins, Santo, Williams	125.00
1973	Jenkins, Monday, Williams	100.00
1974	Kessinger, Madlock, Monday, Williams	100.00
1975	Cardenal, Kessinger, Madlock, Monday	100.00
1976	Madlock, Monday, Sutter	75.00
1977	Buckner, Murcer, Reuschel, Sutter, Trillo	75.00
1978	Buckner, Kingman, Murcer, Sutter	75.00

1950 New York Yankees

1951 New York Yankees

1952 Brooklyn Dodgers

1953 Brooklyn Dodgers

Year	Key Signatures	Price
1979	Buckner, Kingman, Murcer, Sutter	75.00
1980	Buckner, Kingman, Sutter	75.00
1981	Bonds, Buckner, Durham, L. Smith	75.00
1982	Buckner, Durham, Hernandez, Jenkins, Sandberg, L. Smith	100.00
1983	Bowa, Buckner, Cey, Durham, Jenkins, Sandberg, L. Smith	125.00
1984	Bowa, Cey, Durham, Eckersley, Sandberg, L. Smith, Sutcliffe	225.00
1985	Bowa, Cey, Dunston, Durham, Eckersley, Sandberg, L. Smith, Sutcliffe	75.00
1986	Cey, Dunston, Durham, Eckersley, Palmeiro, Sandberg, Sutcliffe	85.00
1987	Dawson, Dunston, Durham, Maddux, Palmeiro, Sandberg, Sutcliffe	75.00
1988	Dawson, Dunston, Gossage, Grace, Maddux, Palmeiro, Sandberg, Sutcliffe, Zimmer	75.00
1989	Dawson, Dunston, Grace, Maddux, Sandberg, Sutcliffe, Zimmer	200.00
1990	Dawson, Dunston, Grace, Maddux, Sandberg, Zimmer	125.00
1991	Bell, Dawson, Dunston, Grace, Maddux, Sandberg, Sutcliffe, Zimmer	100.00
1992	Dawson, Grace, Maddux, Sandberg, Sosa	125.00
1993	Grace, Myers, Sandberg, Sosa	85.00
1994	Dunston, Grace, Myers, Sandberg Sosa	95.00
1995	Dunston, Grace, McRae, Myers, Sosa	125.00
1996	Grace, Sandberg, Sosa	120.00
1997	Grace, Johnson, Orie, Sandberg, Sosa	125.00

Chicago White Sox

Year	Key Signatures	Price
1920	Cicotte, E. Collins, Faber, Felsch, Jackson, Kerr, Leibold, Risberg, Weaver, Williams	$1,500.00
1921	E. Collins, Faber, Hooper, Kerr, Schalk, Sheely, Strunk	900.00
1922	E. Collins, Evers, Faber, Falk, Hooper, Mostil, Schalk, Sheely	1,500.00
1923	E. Collins, Faber, Falk, Hooper, Lyons, Schalk, Sheely	1,000.00
1924	E. Collins, Evers, Faber, Falk, Hooper, Lyons, Mostil, Schalk, Sheely, Thurston	1,500.00
1925	E. Collins, Faber, Falk, Hooper, Lyons, Schalk, Sheely	1,200.00
1926	Barrett, E. Collins, Faber, Falk, Lyons, Mostil, Schalk, Sheely	800.00
1927	Clancy, Faber, Falk, Lyons, Metzler, Schalk	450.00
1928	Faber, Kamm, Lyons, Metzler, Schalk, Walsh	1,200.00
1929	Faber, Lyons, Reynolds, Shires, Walsh	1,000.00
1930	Appling, Faber, Jolley, Lyons, Reynolds, Walsh, Watwood	350.00
1931	Appling, Blue, Faber, Lyons	300.00
1932	Appling, Faber, Lyons	400.00
1933	Appling, Faber, Lyons, Simmons, Swanson	450.00
1934	Appling, Bonura, Conlan, Lyons, Simmons	450.00
1935	Appling, Bonura, Conlan, Lyons, Simmons, Stratton	400.00
1936	Appling, Bonura, Kennedy, Lyons, Stratton	350.00
1937	Appling, Bonura, Lyons, Stratton	350.00
1938	Appling, Hayes, Lyons, Steinbacher, Stratton, Walker	350.00
1939	Appling, Kuhel, Lyons, McNair, Walker	300.00
1940	Appling, Kuhel, Lyons, Solters, Wright	250.00
1941	Appling, Lee, Lyons, Wright	300.00
1942	Appling, Lyons, Wright	300.00
1943	Appling, Grove, Hodgin	300.00
1944	Hodgin, Schalk, Trosky	250.00
1945	Appling, Lee, Lopat	250.00
1946	Appling, Caldwell, Lopat, Lyons	300.00
1947	Appling, Lopat, Lyons, Wright, York	250.00
1948	Appling, Lyons, Michaels, Wight	250.00
1949	Appling, Michaels, Wight	250.00
1950	Appling, Fox, Zernial	250.00
1951	Fox, Minoso, Robinson	250.00
1952	Fox, Minoso, Robinson	250.00
1953	Fox, Minoso, Trucks	300.00
1954	Fox, Kell, Minoso, Trucks	250.00
1955	Donovan, Dropo, Fox, Kell, Minoso, Trucks	225.00
1956	Aparicio, Fox, Kell, Minoso, Pierce	250.00

Year	Key Signatures	Price
1957	Aparicio, Fox, Lopez, Minoso, Pierce	225.00
1958	Aparicio, Cash, Fox, Lopez, Pierce, Wynn	200.00
1959	Aparicio, Cash, Fox, Kluszewski, Lopez, Shaw, Wynn	750.00
1960	Aparicio, Fox, Kluszewski, Lopez, Minoso, Score, Sievers, Wynn	350.00
1961	Aparicio, Fox, Larsen, Lopez, Minoso, Pierce, Sievers, Smith, Wynn	200.00
1962	Aparicio, DeBusschere, Fox, Herbert, Lopez, Peters, Wynn	250.00
1963	DeBusschere, Fox, Lopez, Peters, Wilhelm	175.00
1964	Lopez, Peters, Wilhelm	125.00
1965	John, Lopez, Wilhelm	150.00
1966	Agee, John, Stanky, Wilhelm	200.00
1967	Agee, Boyer, Colavito, John, Stanky, Wilhelm	125.00
1968	Aparicio, John, Lopez	125.00
1969	Aparicio, John, Lopez, Melton	150.00
1970	Aparicio, John, Melton	150.00
1971	John, Melton, Wood	125.00
1972	Allen, Gossage, Wood	100.00
1973	Melton, Tanner, Wood	100.00
1974	Allen, Gossage, Kaat, Santo, Wood	100.00
1975	Gossage, Kaat, Wood	100.00
1976	Dent, Garr, Gossage, Lemon	75.00
1977	Gamble, Lemon, Stone, Zisk	75.00
1978	Doby, Lemon, Stone	75.00
1979	Bannister, La Russa, Lemon, Trout, Washington	100.00
1980	Baines, La Russa, Lemon	75.00
1981	Baines, Fisk, Hoyt, La Russa, Lemon, Luzinski	100.00
1982	Baines, Fisk, Hoyt, La Russa, Luzinski, Lyle	100.00
1983	Baines, Fisk, Hoyt, Kittle, Koosman, La Russa, Luzinski	175.00
1984	Baines, Fisk, Kittle, La Russa, Luzinski, Seaver	75.00
1985	Baines, Fisk, Guillen, Kittle, La Russa, Seaver	100.00
1986	Baines, Bonilla, Fisk, Guillen, Kittle, La Russa,	100.00
1987	Baines, Calderon, Fisk	100.00
1988	Baines, Fisk, McDowell, Thigpen	75.00
1989	Baines, Fisk, McDowell, Thigpen	75.00
1990	Baines, Fernandez, Fisk, McDowell, Sosa, Thigpen, Thomas, Ventura	75.00
1991	Fernandez, Fisk, McDowell, Sosa, Thigpen, Thomas, Ventura	125.00
1992	Fernandez, Fisk, McDowell, Thigpen, Thomas, Ventura	85.00
1993	Fernandez, Jackson, McDowell, Thomas, Ventura	175.00
1994	Fernandez, Hernandez, McDowell, Thomas, Ventura	125.00
1995	Durham, Fernandez, Hernandez, Thomas, Ventura	125.00
1996	Alvarez, Durham, Fernandez, Hernandez, Thomas, Ventura	125.00
1997	Alvarez, Belle, Durham, Hernandez, Thomas, Ventura	150.00

Cincinnati Reds

Year	Key Signatures	Price
1920	Daubert, Ring, Roush	$700.00
1921	Bressler, Daubert, Duncan, Groh, Marquard, Rixey, Roush	750.00
1922	Daubert, Duncan, Hargrave, Harper, Pinelli, Rixey, Roush	600.00
1923	Donohue, Duncan, Hargrave, Luque, Rixey, Roush	500.00
1924	Critz, Mays, Pinelli, Rixey, Roush, Walker	500.00
1925	Donohue, Hargrave, Rixey, Roush, Walker	450.00
1926	Donahue, Mays, Pipp, Rixey, Roush, Walker	450.00
1927	Hargrave, Kelly, Lucas, Rixey	400.00
1928	Allen, Kelly, Rixey	600.00
1929	Dressen, Gooch, Kelly, Lucas, Rixey, Swanson	1,000.00
1930	Cuccinello, Durocher, Heilmann, Kelly, Rixey, Walker	1,200.00
1931	Cuccinello, Durocher, Heilman, Hendrick, Rixey, Roush, Stripp	400.00
1932	Durocher, Hafey, Heilman, Hendrick, Herman, Lombardi, Rixey	600.00

Year	Key Signatures	Price
1933	Bottomley, Hafey, Lombardi	500.00
1934	Bottomley, Hafey, Lombardi	450.00
1935	Bottomley, Cuyler, Derringer, Hafey, Herman, Lombardi	500.00
1936	Cuyler, Hafey, Herman, Lombardi, Scarsella	400.00
1937	Cuyler, Hafey, Lombardi	400.00
1938	Berger, Derringer, Lombardi, McCormick, Vander Meer	350.00
1939	Derringer, Goodman, Lombardi, McCormick, Walters	400.00
1940	Derringer, Lombardi, McCormick, Walters	450.00
1941	Lombardi, McCormick, Vander Meer, Walters, L. Waner	500.00
1942	McCormick, Vander Meer, Walters	300.00
1943	McCormick, Riddle, Vander Meer	250.00
1944	McCormick, Tipton, Walters	300.00
1945	McKechnie, Miller, Walters	300.00
1946	McKechnie, Vander Meer, Walters	250.00
1947	Blackwell, Galan, Young	250.00
1948	Kluszewski, Sauer, Vander Meer	250.00
1949	Cooper, Kluszewski, Vander Meer	250.00
1950	Adcock, Blackwell, Kluszewski	250.00
1951	Adcock, Blackwell, Kluszewski	225.00
1952	Adcock, Hornsby, Kluszewski	300.00
1953	Bell, Hornsby, Kluszewski	350.00
1954	Kluszewski, Post, Temple	250.00
1955	Bell, Burgess, Kluszewski, Post	250.00
1956	Bell, Kluszewski, Post, Robinson	300.00
1957	Bell, Kluszewski, Post, Robinson	300.00
1958	Newcombe, Pinson, Robinson	250.00
1959	Bell, Newcombe, Pinson, Robinson	400.00
1960	Bell, Martin, Newcombe, Pinson, Post, Robinson	300.00
1961	Coleman, Freese, Jay, O'Toole, Pinson, Robinson	1,200.00
1962	Coleman, Jay, Pinson, Purkey, Robinson	350.00
1963	Harper, Maloney, Pinson, Robinson, Rose	225.00
1964	Perez, Pinson, Robinson, Rose	225.00
1965	Ellis, Johnson, Maloney, Perez, Pinson, Robinson, Rose	300.00
1966	Harper, Helms, Johnson, Perez, Pinson, Rose	150.00
1967	Bench, May, Pinson, Rose	200.00
1968	Bench, May, Pinson, Rose, Perez	200.00
1969	Bench, May, Perez, Rose	225.00
1970	Anderson, Bench, Carbo, Concepcion, May, McRae, Perez, Rose	600.00
1971	Anderson, Bench, Concepcion, Foster, May, McRae, Perez, Rose	225.00
1972	Anderson, Bench, Concepcion, Foster, McRae, Morgan, Perez, Rose	300.00
1973	Anderson, Bench, Concepcion, Foster, Griffey, Morgan, Perez, Rose	300.00
1974	Anderson, Bench, Concepcion, Foster, Morgan, Perez, Rose	300.00
1975	Anderson, Bench, Concepcion, Foster, Griffey, Morgan, Perez, Rose	500.00
1976	Anderson, Bench, Concepcion, Foster, Griffey, Morgan, Perez, Rose, Zachary	500.00
1977	Anderson, Bench, Concepcion, Foster, Griffey, Morgan, Rose, Seaver	150.00
1978	Anderson, Bench, Concepcion, Foster, Griffey, Morgan, Rose, Seaver	175.00
1979	Bench, Concepcion, Foster, Griffey, Knight, Morgan, Seaver	150.00
1980	Bench, Concepcion, Foster, Griffey, Knight, Seaver	100.00
1981	Bench, Concepcion, Foster, Griffey, Knight, Seaver	100.00
1982	Bench, Concepcion, Seaver	100.00
1983	Bench, Concepcion, Soto	100.00
1984	Concepcion, Davis, Parker, Perez, Rose, Soto	100.00
1985	Browning, Concepcion, Davis, Franco, Parker, Perez, Rose	100.00

1953 New York Giants

**1955 Detroit Tigers
(w/ Ted Williams)**

1955 Brooklyn Dodgers

1955 New York Yankees

Year	Key Signatures	Price
1986	Concepcion, Davis, Franco, Parker, Perez, Rose	75.00
1987	Concepcion, Davis, Franco, Larkin, O'Neill, Parker, Rose	85.00
1988	Concepcion, Davis, Franco, Jackson, Larkin, O'Neill, Rose, Sabo	100.00
1989	Davis, Franco, Griffey, Larkin, O'Neill, Rose, Sabo	75.00
1990	Davis, Dibble, Larkin, Morris, Myers, O'Neill, Piniella, Sabo	300.00
1991	Davis, Dibble, Larkin, Morris, O'Neill, Piniella, Sabo	75.00
1992	Charlton, Dibble, Larkin, Morris, O'Neill, Piniella, Rijo, Sabo, Sanders, Morris,	85.00
1993	Dibble, Johnson, Larkin, Morris, Perez, Rijo, Sabo, Sanders,	45.00
1994	Brantley, Johnson, Larkin, Morris, D. Sanders, R. Sanders	65.00
1995	Brantley, Gant, Johnson, Larkin, Morris, R. Sanders	125.00
1996	Brantley, Larkin, R. Sanders	100.00
1997	Green, Larkin, R. Sanders, Shaw	100.00

Cleveland Indians

Year	Key Signatures	Price
1920	Bagby, Caldwell, Chapman, Coveleski, Gardner, Jamieson, O'Neill, J. Sewell, Smith, Speaker, Wambsganss	$2,000.00
1921	Coveleski, Gardner, Jamieson, O'Neill, J. Sewell, Speaker	1,000.00
1922	Coveleski, Jamieson, McGinnis, O'Neill, J. Sewell, Speaker, Uhle	800.00
1923	Coveleski, Jamieson, J. Sewell, Speaker, Summa, Uhle	1,000.00
1924	Burns, Coveleski, Jamieson, Myatt, J. Sewell, Shaute, Speaker	900.00
1925	Buckeye, Burns, McNulty, J. Sewell, Speaker, Uhle	750.00
1926	Burns, J. Sewell, Speaker, Summa, Uhle	700.00
1927	Burns, Fonseca, Jamieson, Miller, J. Sewell	400.00
1928	Fonseca, Hodapp, Jamieson, J. Sewell	400.00
1929	Averill, Falk, Ferrell, Fonseca, Hodapp, J.Sewell, L. Sewell	400.00
1930	Averill, Ferrell, Hodapp, Jamieson, Morgan, Porter, J. Sewell, L. Sewell	400.00
1931	Averill, Ferrell, Morgan, Porter	300.00
1932	Averill, Cissell, Ferrell, Porter, Vosmik	300.00
1933	Averill, Johnson, Porter, Vosmik	1,000.00
1934	Averill, Hale, Harder, Johnson, Knickerbocker, Trosky, Vosmik	1,000.00
1935	Averill, Hale, Harder, Johnson, Trosky, Vosmik	1,000.00
1936	Allen, Averill, Hale, Sullivan, Trosky, Weatherly	300.00
1937	Averill, Campbell, Feller, Pytlak, Solters, Trosky	325.00
1938	Averill, Boudreau, Feller, Heath, Keltner, Pytlak, Trosky	350.00
1939	Boudreau, Feller, Hale, Keltner, Trosky	300.00
1940	Boudreau, Feller, Smith, Trosky, Weatherly	300.00
1941	Boudreau, Feller, Heath	300.00
1942	Bagby, Boudreau, Fleming	250.00
1943	Bagby, Boudreau, Heath, Smith	250.00
1944	Boudreau, Gromek, Reynolds	350.00
1945	Boudreau, Gromek, Reynolds	300.00
1946	Boudreau, Edwards, Feller, Lemon, Reynolds	300.00
1947	Boudreau, Feller, Lemon, Mitchell	300.00
1948	Bearden, Boudreau, Feller, Gordon, Keltner, Lemon, Mitchell, Paige	500.00
1949	Boudreau, Doby, Feller, Gordon, Lemon, Mitchell, Vernon, Wynn	250.00
1950	Boudreau, Easter, Doby, Feller, Lemon, Mitchell, Rosen, Wynn	300.00
1951	Avila, Easter, Doby, Feller, Lemon, Lopez, Rosen, Wynn	300.00
1952	Avila, Easter, Doby, Feller, Garcia, Lemon, Mitchell, Rosen, Wynn	400.00
1953	Doby, Feller, Garcia, Lemon, Lopez, Mitchell, Rosen, Westlake, Wynn	250.00
1954	Avila, Doby, Feller, Garcia, Lemon, Lopez, Rosen, Wynn	450.00
1955	Colavito, Doby, Feller, Kiner, Lemon, Lopez, Rosen, Score, Smith, Wertz, Wynn	400.00
1956	Colavito, Feller, Lemon, Lopez, Rosen, Score, Wertz, Wynn	350.00
1957	Colavito, Lemon, Maris, Wertz, Wilhelm, Wynn	500.00
1958	Colavito, Doby, Gordon, Lemon, Maris, Minoso, Vernon, Wilhelm	250.00
1959	Colavito, Gordon, Martin, Minoso, Perry, Score	200.00
1960	Asporomonte, Kuenn, Perry, Piersall	200.00
1961	Kirkland, McDowell, Perry, Piersall	150.00
1962	Donavan, McDowell, Romano	150.00

Year	Key Signatures	Price
1963	Adcock, Alvis, Francona	125.00
1964	John, McDowell, Tiant	125.00
1965	Colavito, McDowell, Tiant, Wagner	250.00
1966	Colavito, McDowell, Tiant	150.00
1967	Adcock, McDowell, Tiant	125.00
1968	Dark, McDowell, Tiant	125.00
1969	Dark, Harrelson, McDowell, Tiant	100.00
1970	Dark, McDowell, Nettles, Pinson	100.00
1971	Chambliss, Dark, McDowell, Nettles, Pinson	125.00
1972	Bell, Chambliss, Nettles, Perry	125.00
1973	Chambliss, Gamble, Perry	100.00
1974	Gamble, G. Perry, J. Perry	125.00
1975	Eckersley, G. Perry, Powell, F. Robinson	200.00
1976	Bell, Eckersley, Powell, F. Robinson	100.00
1977	Bell, Eckersley, F. Robinson, Thornton	150.00
1978	Bell, Thornton, Torborg	85.00
1979	Bonds, Hargrove, Harrah, Thornton	75.00
1980	Barker, Charboneau, Hargrove, Harrah	75.00
1981	Blyleven, Hargrove, Harrah	75.00
1982	Blyleven, Hargrove, Harrah, Sutcliffe, Thornton	75.00
1983	Blyleven, Franco, Harrah, Sutcliffe,	75.00
1984	Blyleven, Butler, Carter, Franco, Thornton	75.00
1985	Blyleven, Butler, Carter, Franco, Nixon	70.00
1986	Carter, Franco, P. Niekro	75.00
1987	Carlton, Carter, Franco, P. Niekro, Snyder	100.00
1988	Carter, Franco, Snyder	75.00
1989	Belle, Carter, D. Jones, Orosco	75.00
1990	Alomar, Baerga, Belle, Hernandez	50.00
1991	Alomar, Baerga, Belle, Nagy	65.00
1992	Alomar, Baerga, Belle, Lofton, Nagy	100.00
1993	Alomar, Baerga, Belle, Lofton, Nagy, Thome	125.00
1994	Alomar, Baerga, Belle, Lofton, D. Martinez, Morris, Murray, Nagy, Ramirez, Thome	175.00
1995	Alomar, Baerga, Belle, Hershiser, Lofton, D. Martinez, Mesa, Murray, Nagy, Ramirez, Thome	350.00
1996	Alomar, Belle, Lofton, Hershiser, Mesa, Nagy, Ramirez, Thome	200.00
1997	Alomar, Grissom, Hershiser, Ramirez, Thome, Vizquel, Williams	300.00

Colorado Rockies

Year	Key Signatures	Price
1993	Baylor, Bichette, Castilla, Galarraga, Hayes	$150.00
1994	Baylor, Bichette, Burks, Castilla, Galarraga, Hayes, Weiss	150.00
1995	Baylor, Bichette, Burks, Castilla, Galarraga, Walker, Weiss	125.00
1996	Baylor, Bichette, Burks, Castilla, Galarraga, Walker, Weiss	125.00
1997	Baylor, Bichette, Burks, Castilla, Galarraga, Walker, Weiss	125.00

Detroit Tigers

Year	Key Signatures	Price
1920	Cobb, Heilmann, Jennings, Veach	$2,000.00
1921	Bassler, Blue, Cobb, Heilmann, Jones, Veach	1,000.00
1922	Bassler, Blue, Cobb, Heilmann, Rigney, Veach	1,000.00
1923	Blue, Cobb, Daus, Heilmann, Manush, Rigney	1,200.00
1924	Bassler, Blue, Cobb, Gehringer, Heilmann, Manush, Pratt	1,200.00
1925	Blue, Cobb, Gehringer, Heilmann, Manush, Wingo	1,100.00
1926	Cobb, Fothergill, Gehringer, Heilmann, Manush	1,000.00
1927	Collins, Fothergill, Gehringer, Heilmann, Manush	500.00
1928	Gehringer, Heilmann, Rice	400.00
1929	Alexander, Gehringer, Harris, Heilmann, Johnson, Rice	400.00
1930	Alexander, Gehringer, Harris, Hoyt, McManus, Stone	400.00
1931	Alexander, Gehringer, Harris, Hoyt, Rogell, Stone	400.00
1932	Gehringer, Harris, Walker	400.00
1933	Gehringer, Greenberg, Harris	500.00
1934	Bridges, Cochrane, Gehringer, Goslin, Greenberg, Rowe	850.00
1935	Cochrane, Gehringer, Goslin, Greenberg	700.00
1936	Bridges, Cochrane, Gehringer, Goslin, Greenberg, Simmons	450.00
1937	Cochrane, Gehringer, Goslin, Greenberg, York	550.00
1938	Cochrane, Gehringer, Greenberg, Walker	600.00
1939	Averill, Bridges, Gehringer, Greenberg	500.00
1940	Averill, Gehringer, Greenberg, McCosky, Newsom, Rowe, York	500.00
1941	Benton, Gehringer, McCosky, Radcliff, York	500.00
1942	Newhouser, Trucks, York	350.00
1943	Cramer, Newhouser, Trout, Trucks, York	250.00
1944	Newhouser, Trout, Wakefield, York	300.00
1945	Greenberg, Newhouser, York	350.00
1946	Greenberg, Kell, Newhouser, Trucks,	300.00
1947	Kell, Newhouser, Trucks,	300.00
1948	Cramer, Kell, Newhouser, Trucks	300.00
1949	Evers, Kell, Newhouser, Trucks, Wertz	250.00
1950	Evers, Groth, Kell, Newhouser, Wertz	350.00
1951	Kell, Trucks, Wertz	300.00
1952	Dropo, Gray, Wertz	250.00
1953	Boone, Dropo, Kuenn	250.00
1954	Boone, Dropo, Kaline, Kuenn	400.00
1955	Boone, Kaline, Kuenn	225.00
1956	Boone, Kaline, Kuenn, Lary	250.00
1957	Boone, Bunning, Kaline, Kuenn	225.00
1958	Bunning, Kaline, Kuenn, Martin	200.00
1959	Bunning, Kaline, Kuenn	200.00
1960	Bunning, Cash, Colavito, Kaline	300.00
1961	Bunning, Cash, Colavito, Kaline	300.00
1962	Bunning, Cash, Colavito, Kaline	150.00
1963	Cash, Colavito, Kaline, Lolich	150.00
1964	Cash, Kaline, Lolich, McLain	175.00
1965	Cash, Kaline, Lolich, McLain	150.00
1966	Cash, Kaline, Lolich, McLain	150.00
1967	Cash, Freehan, Kaline, Lolich, McLain	200.00
1968	Cash, Freehan, Kaline, Lolich, McLain	500.00
1969	Cash, Freehan, Kaline, Lolich, McLain	150.00
1970	Cash, Freehan, Kaline, Lolich, J. Niekro	125.00
1971	Cash, Freehan, Kaline, Lolich, Martin, J. Niekro	200.00
1972	Cash, Freehan, Kaline, Lolich, Martin	200.00
1973	Cash, Freehan, Kaline, Lolich, Martin, Northrup	175.00
1974	Freehan, Horton, Kaline, Lefore, Lolich	150.00
1975	Freehan, Horton, Lefore, Lolich	100.00
1976	Fidrych, Freehan, Horton, Lefore, Staub	125.00
1977	Fidrych, Lefore, Staub	125.00
1978	Lefore, Morris, Parrish, Staub, Trammell, Whitaker	125.00
1979	Anderson, Morris, Parrish, Staub, Trammell, Whitaker	120.00
1980	Anderson, Gibson, Morris, Parrish, Trammell, Whitaker	125.00
1981	Anderson, Gibson, Morris, Parrish, Trammell, Whitaker	125.00
1982	Anderson, Gibson, Morris, Parrish, Trammell, Whitaker	125.00
1983	Anderson, Gibson, Morris, Parrish, Trammell, Whitaker	150.00
1984	Anderson, Evans, Gibson, Hernandez, Johnson, Morris, Parrish, Trammell, Whitaker	500.00
1985	Anderson, Gibson, Morris, Parrish, Trammell, Whitaker	100.00
1986	Anderson, Gibson, Morris, Parrish, Trammell, Whitaker	125.00
1987	Anderson, Gibson, Morris, Trammell, Whitaker	200.00
1988	Anderson, Morris, Trammell, Whitaker	100.00

1956 New York Yankees

1958 Cleveland Indians

1958 New York Yankees

1958 Washington

1989	Anderson, Lynn, Morris, Trammell, Whitaker	75.00
1990	Anderson, Fielder, Fryman, Morris, Trammell, Whitaker	100.00
1991	Anderson, Fielder, Fryman, Gullickson, Tettleton, Trammell, Whitaker	100.00
1992	Anderson, Fielder, Fryman, Tettleton, Whitaker	85.00
1993	Anderson, Fielder, Fryman, Gibson, Trammell, Whitaker	90.00
1994	Anderson, Davis, Fielder, Fryman, Gibson, Trammell, Whitaker	95.00
1995	Anderson, Fielder, Fryman, Gibson, Higginson, Trammell, Whitaker	100.00
1996	Clark, Fryman, Higginson	100.00
1997	Clark, Fryman, Higginson, Hunter, Jones, Thompson	100.00

Florida Marlins

Year	Key Signatures	Price
1993	Conine, Destrade, Harvey, Hough, Santiago, Sheffield, Weiss	$150.00
1994	Conine, NenSantiago, Sheffield	75.00
1995	Conine, Dawson, Johnson, Nen, Sheffield	150.00
1996	Brown, Conine, Johnson, Nen, Sheffield	125.00
1997	Bonilla, Brown, Fernandez, Hernandez, Johnson, Leyland, Nen, Renteria, Sheffield	500.00

Houston Astros

Year	Key Signatures	Price
1965	Morgan, Staub, Wynn	$200.00
1966	Morgan, Staub, Wynn	125.00
1967	Mathews, Morgan, Staub, Wynn	125.00
1968	Dierker, Staub, Wynn	125.00
1969	Dierker, Morgan, Wynn	100.00
1970	Cedeno, Dierker, Morgan, Wynn	100.00
1971	Cedeno, Dierker, Morgan	100.00
1972	Cedeno, Dierker, Durocher, May, Wynn	75.00
1973	Cedeno, Durocher, Wynn	100.00
1974	Cedeno, Dierker, Wilson	100.00
1975	Cedeno, Cruz, J. Niekro, Richard	75.00
1976	Cedeno, J. Niekro, Richard	75.00
1977	Cedeno, Cruz, J. Niekro, Richard	75.00
1978	Cedeno, Cruz, J. Niekro, Richard	75.00
1979	Cedeno, Cruz, J. Niekro, Richard	85.00
1980	Cedeno, Cruz, Morgan, J. Niekro, Richard, Ryan	150.00
1981	Cedeno, Cruz, J. Niekro, Ryan, Sutton	125.00
1982	Cruz, J. Niekro, Ryan, Sutton	100.00
1983	Cruz, J. Niekro, Ryan, Scott	125.00
1984	Cruz, J. Niekro, Ryan, Scott	75.00
1985	Cruz, Davis, J. Niekro, Ryan, Scott	100.00
1986	Cruz, Davis, Ryan, Scott	100.00
1987	Caminiti, Cruz, Davis, Ryan, Scott	125.00
1988	Davis, Ryan, Scott	100.00
1989	Biggio, Caminiti, Davis, Scott	50.00
1990	Biggio, Caminiti, Davis, Scott	50.00
1991	Bagwell, Biggio, Caminiti, Finley, Harnisch, Kile, Schilling	65.00
1992	Bagwell, Biggio, Caminiti, Finley, Jones, Kile,	40.00
1993	Bagwell, Biggio, Caminiti, Drabek, Finley, Kile, Swindell	40.00
1994	Bagwell, Biggio, Caminiti, Drabek, Finley, Kile, Reynolds	50.00
1995	Bagwell, Bell, Biggio, Hampton, Hunter, Kile, Reynolds	125.00
1996	Bagwell, Bell, Biggio, Hampton, Hunter, Kile, Reynolds	125.00
1997	Bagwell, Bell, Biggio, Hampton, Kile, Reynolds, Wagner	125.00

Houston Colt .45s

Year	Key Signatures	Price
1962	Aspromonte, Mejias	400.00
1963	Aspromonte, Staub	225.00
1964	Aspromonte, Fox, Staub	250.00

1963	Adcock, Alvis, Francona	125.00
1964	John, McDowell, Tiant	125.00
1965	Colavito, McDowell, Tiant, Wagner	250.00
1966	Colavito, McDowell, Tiant	150.00
1967	Adcock, McDowell, Tiant	125.00
1968	Dark, McDowell, Tiant	125.00
1969	Dark, Harrelson, McDowell, Tiant	100.00
1970	Dark, McDowell, Nettles, Pinson	100.00
1971	Chambliss, Dark, McDowell, Nettles, Pinson	125.00
1972	Bell, Chambliss, Nettles, Perry	125.00
1973	Chambliss, Gamble, Perry	100.00
1974	Gamble, G. Perry, J. Perry	125.00
1975	Eckersley, G. Perry, Powell, F. Robinson	200.00
1976	Bell, Eckersley, Powell, F. Robinson	100.00
1977	Bell, Eckersley, F. Robinson, Thornton	150.00
1978	Bell, Thornton, Torborg	85.00
1979	Bonds, Hargrove, Harrah, Thornton	75.00
1980	Barker, Charboneau, Hargrove, Harrah	75.00
1981	Blyleven, Hargrove, Harrah	75.00
1982	Blyleven, Hargrove, Harrah, Sutcliffe, Thornton	75.00
1983	Blyleven, Franco, Harrah, Sutcliffe,	75.00
1984	Blyleven, Butler, Carter, Franco, Thornton	75.00
1985	Blyleven, Butler, Carter, Franco, Nixon	70.00
1986	Carter, Franco, P. Niekro	75.00
1987	Carlton, Carter, Franco, P. Niekro, Snyder	100.00
1988	Carter, Franco, Snyder	75.00
1989	Belle, Carter, D. Jones, Orosco	75.00
1990	Alomar, Baerga, Belle, Hernandez	50.00
1991	Alomar, Baerga, Belle, Nagy	65.00
1992	Alomar, Baerga, Belle, Lofton, Nagy	100.00
1993	Alomar, Baerga, Belle, Lofton, Nagy, Thome	125.00
1994	Alomar, Baerga, Belle, Lofton, D. Martinez, Morris, Murray, Nagy, Ramirez, Thome	175.00
1995	Alomar, Baerga, Belle, Hershiser, Lofton, D. Martinez, Mesa, Murray, Nagy, Ramirez, Thome	350.00
1996	Alomar, Belle, Lofton, Hershiser, Mesa, Nagy, Ramirez, Thome	200.00
1997	Alomar, Grissom, Hershiser, Ramirez, Thome, Vizquel, Williams	300.00

Colorado Rockies

Year	Key Signatures	Price
1993	Baylor, Bichette, Castilla, Galarraga, Hayes	$150.00
1994	Baylor, Bichette, Burks, Castilla, Galarraga, Hayes, Weiss	150.00
1995	Baylor, Bichette, Burks, Castilla, Galarraga, Walker, Weiss	125.00
1996	Baylor, Bichette, Burks, Castilla, Galarraga, Walker, Weiss	125.00
1997	Baylor, Bichette, Burks, Castilla, Galarraga, Walker, Weiss	125.00

Detroit Tigers

Year	Key Signatures	Price
1920	Cobb, Heilmann, Jennings, Veach	$2,000.00
1921	Bassler, Blue, Cobb, Heilmann, Jones, Veach	1,000.00
1922	Bassler, Blue, Cobb, Heilmann, Rigney, Veach	1,000.00
1923	Blue, Cobb, Daus, Heilmann, Manush, Rigney	1,200.00
1924	Bassler, Blue, Cobb, Gehringer, Heilmann, Manush, Pratt	1,200.00
1925	Blue, Cobb, Gehringer, Heilmann, Manush, Wingo	1,100.00
1926	Cobb, Fothergill, Gehringer, Heilmann, Manush	1,000.00
1927	Collins, Fothergill, Gehringer, Heilmann, Manush	500.00
1928	Gehringer, Heilmann, Rice	400.00
1929	Alexander, Gehringer, Harris, Heilmann, Johnson, Rice	400.00
1930	Alexander, Gehringer, Harris, Hoyt, McManus, Stone	400.00

1931	Alexander, Gehringer, Harris, Hoyt, Rogell, Stone	400.00
1932	Gehringer, Harris, Walker	400.00
1933	Gehringer, Greenberg, Harris	500.00
1934	Bridges, Cochrane, Gehringer, Goslin, Greenberg, Rowe	850.00
1935	Cochrane, Gehringer, Goslin, Greenberg	700.00
1936	Bridges, Cochrane, Gehringer, Goslin, Greenberg, Simmons	450.00
1937	Cochrane, Gehringer, Goslin, Greenberg, York	550.00
1938	Cochrane, Gehringer, Greenberg, Walker	600.00
1939	Averill, Bridges, Gehringer, Greenberg	500.00
1940	Averill, Gehringer, Greenberg, McCosky, Newsom, Rowe, York	500.00
1941	Benton, Gehringer, McCosky, Radcliff, York	500.00
1942	Newhouser, Trucks, York	350.00
1943	Cramer, Newhouser, Trout, Trucks, York	250.00
1944	Newhouser, Trout, Wakefield, York	300.00
1945	Greenberg, Newhouser, York	350.00
1946	Greenberg, Kell, Newhouser, Trucks,	300.00
1947	Kell, Newhouser, Trucks,	300.00
1948	Cramer, Kell, Newhouser, Trucks	300.00
1949	Evers, Kell, Newhouser, Trucks, Wertz	250.00
1950	Evers, Groth, Kell, Newhouser, Wertz	350.00
1951	Kell, Trucks, Wertz	300.00
1952	Dropo, Gray, Wertz	250.00
1953	Boone, Dropo, Kuenn	250.00
1954	Boone, Dropo, Kaline, Kuenn	400.00
1955	Boone, Kaline, Kuenn	225.00
1956	Boone, Kaline, Kuenn, Lary	250.00
1957	Boone, Bunning, Kaline, Kuenn	225.00
1958	Bunning, Kaline, Kuenn, Martin	200.00
1959	Bunning, Kaline, Kuenn	200.00
1960	Bunning, Cash, Colavito, Kaline	300.00
1961	Bunning, Cash, Colavito, Kaline	300.00
1962	Bunning, Cash, Colavito, Kaline	150.00
1963	Cash, Colavito, Kaline, Lolich	150.00
1964	Cash, Kaline, Lolich, McLain	175.00
1965	Cash, Kaline, Lolich, McLain	150.00
1966	Cash, Kaline, Lolich, McLain	150.00
1967	Cash, Freehan, Kaline, Lolich, McLain	200.00
1968	Cash, Freehan, Kaline, Lolich, McLain	500.00
1969	Cash, Freehan, Kaline, Lolich, McLain	150.00
1970	Cash, Freehan, Kaline, Lolich, J. Niekro	125.00
1971	Cash, Freehan, Kaline, Lolich, Martin, J. Niekro	200.00
1972	Cash, Freehan, Kaline, Lolich, Martin	200.00
1973	Cash, Freehan, Kaline, Lolich, Martin, Northrup	175.00
1974	Freehan, Horton, Kaline, Lefore, Lolich	150.00
1975	Freehan, Horton, Lefore, Lolich	100.00
1976	Fidrych, Freehan, Horton, Lefore, Staub	125.00
1977	Fidrych, Lefore, Staub	125.00
1978	Lefore, Morris, Parrish, Staub, Trammell, Whitaker	125.00
1979	Anderson, Morris, Parrish, Staub, Trammell, Whitaker	120.00
1980	Anderson, Gibson, Morris, Parrish, Trammell, Whitaker	125.00
1981	Anderson, Gibson, Morris, Parrish, Trammell, Whitaker	125.00
1982	Anderson, Gibson, Morris, Parrish, Trammell, Whitaker	125.00
1983	Anderson, Gibson, Morris, Parrish, Trammell, Whitaker	150.00
1984	Anderson, Evans, Gibson, Hernandez, Johnson, Morris, Parrish, Trammell, Whitaker	500.00
1985	Anderson, Gibson, Morris, Parrish, Trammell, Whitaker	100.00
1986	Anderson, Gibson, Morris, Parrish, Trammell, Whitaker	125.00
1987	Anderson, Gibson, Morris, Trammell, Whitaker	200.00
1988	Anderson, Morris, Trammell, Whitaker	100.00

1989	Anderson, Lynn, Morris, Trammell, Whitaker	75.00
1990	Anderson, Fielder, Fryman, Morris, Trammell, Whitaker	100.00
1991	Anderson, Fielder, Fryman, Gullickson, Tettleton, Trammell, Whitaker	100.00
1992	Anderson, Fielder, Fryman, Tettleton, Whitaker	85.00
1993	Anderson, Fielder, Fryman, Gibson, Trammell, Whitaker	90.00
1994	Anderson, Davis, Fielder, Fryman, Gibson, Trammell, Whitaker	95.00
1995	Anderson, Fielder, Fryman, Gibson, Higginson, Trammell, Whitaker	100.00
1996	Clark, Fryman, Higginson	100.00
1997	Clark, Fryman, Higginson, Hunter, Jones, Thompson	100.00

1956 New York Yankees

Florida Marlins

Year	Key Signatures	Price
1993	Conine, Destrade, Harvey, Hough, Santiago, Sheffield, Weiss	$150.00
1994	Conine, NenSantiago, Sheffield	75.00
1995	Conine, Dawson, Johnson, Nen, Sheffield	150.00
1996	Brown, Conine, Johnson, Nen, Sheffield	125.00
1997	Bonilla, Brown, Fernandez, Hernandez, Johnson, Leyland, Nen, Renteria, Sheffield	500.00

Houston Astros

Year	Key Signatures	Price
1965	Morgan, Staub, Wynn	$200.00
1966	Morgan, Staub, Wynn	125.00
1967	Mathews, Morgan, Staub, Wynn	125.00
1968	Dierker, Staub, Wynn	125.00
1969	Dierker, Morgan, Wynn	100.00
1970	Cedeno, Dierker, Morgan, Wynn	100.00
1971	Cedeno, Dierker, Morgan	100.00
1972	Cedeno, Dierker, Durocher, May, Wynn	75.00
1973	Cedeno, Durocher, Wynn	100.00
1974	Cedeno, Dierker, Wilson	100.00
1975	Cedeno, Cruz, J. Niekro, Richard	75.00
1976	Cedeno, J. Niekro, Richard	75.00
1977	Cedeno, Cruz, J. Niekro, Richard	75.00
1978	Cedeno, Cruz, J. Niekro, Richard	75.00
1979	Cedeno, Cruz, J. Niekro, Richard	85.00
1980	Cedeno, Cruz, Morgan, J. Niekro, Richard, Ryan	150.00
1981	Cedeno, Cruz, J. Niekro, Ryan, Sutton	125.00
1982	Cruz, J. Niekro, Ryan, Sutton	100.00
1983	Cruz, J. Niekro, Ryan, Scott	125.00
1984	Cruz, J. Niekro, Ryan, Scott	75.00
1985	Cruz, Davis, J. Niekro, Ryan, Scott	100.00
1986	Cruz, Davis, Ryan, Scott	100.00
1987	Caminiti, Cruz, Davis, Ryan, Scott	125.00
1988	Davis, Ryan, Scott	100.00
1989	Biggio, Caminiti, Davis, Scott	50.00
1990	Biggio, Caminiti, Davis, Scott	50.00
1991	Bagwell, Biggio, Caminiti, Finley, Harnisch, Kile, Schilling	65.00
1992	Bagwell, Biggio, Caminiti, Finley, Jones, Kile,	40.00
1993	Bagwell, Biggio, Caminiti, Drabek, Finley, Kile, Swindell	40.00
1994	Bagwell, Biggio, Caminiti, Drabek, Finley, Kile, Reynolds	50.00
1995	Bagwell, Bell, Biggio, Hampton, Hunter, Kile, Reynolds	125.00
1996	Bagwell, Bell, Biggio, Hampton, Hunter, Kile, Reynolds	125.00
1997	Bagwell, Bell, Biggio, Hampton, Kile, Reynolds, Wagner	125.00

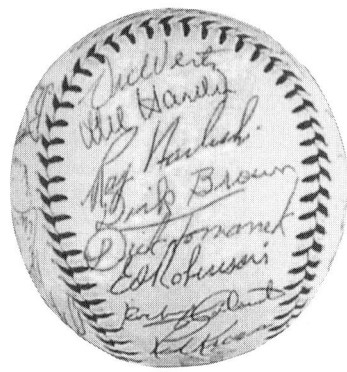

1958 Cleveland Indians

1958 New York Yankees

1958 Washington

Houston Colt .45s

Year	Key Signatures	Price
1962	Aspromonte, Mejias	400.00
1963	Aspromonte, Staub	225.00
1964	Aspromonte, Fox, Staub	250.00

Kansas City Athletics

Year	Key Signatures	Price
1956	Boudreau, Simpson, Slaughter	$250.00
1957	Boudreau, Martin, Trucks	225.00
1958	Cerv, Maris	500.00
1959	Cerv, Maris, Tuttle	300.00
1960	Bauer, Herzog, Throneberry	200.00
1961	Bauer, Howser, Nuxhall, Throneberry	150.00
1962	Bauer, Howser, Tartabull	150.00
1963	Drabowsky, Harrelson, Tartabull	200.00
1964	Campaneris, Colavito, Gentile	200.00
1965	Campaneris, Harrelson, Hunter	300.00
1966	Campaneris, Hunter, Odom	125.00
1967	Appling, Hunter, Odom	200.00

Kansas City Royals

Year	Key Signatures	Price
1969	Drabowsky, Fiore, Piniella	$325.00
1970	Lemon, Otis, Piniella	150.00
1971	Drago, Lemon, Otis, Piniella	100.00
1972	Lemon, Mayberry, Otis, Piniella	100.00
1973	Mayberry, McRae, Otis, Piniella	250.00
1974	Brett, Busby, Mayberry, McRae, Otis, Pinson	125.00
1975	Brett, Herzog, Killebrew, Mayberry, McRae, Pinson	150.00
1976	Brett, Herzog, Leonard, Mayberry, Otis, White	150.00
1977	Brett, Cowens, Herzog, Leonard, Mayberry, McRae, Otis, White	200.00
1978	Brett, Herzog, Leonard, McRae, Otis, Porter, White, Wilson	150.00
1979	Brett, Herzog, McRae, Otis, Porter, Quisenberry, White, Wilson	125.00
1980	Brett, Leonard, McRae, Otis, Porter, Quisenberry, White, Wilson	250.00
1981	Aikens, Brett, Howser, McRae, Otis, Quisenberry, White, Wilson	100.00
1982	Aikens, Brett, Howser, McRae, Otis, Quisenberry, White, Wilson	100.00
1983	Aikens, Brett, Howser, McRae, Otis, Quisenberry, White, Wilson	100.00
1984	Brett, Howser, McRae, Saberhagen, Quisenberry, White, Wilson	125.00
1985	Brett, Howser, McRae, Saberhagen, Quisenberry, White, Wilson	400.00
1986	Brett, Howser, Jackson, McRae, Saberhagen, Quisenberry, White	75.00
1987	Brett, Jackson, Saberhagen, Seitzer, Tartabull, Quisenberry, White	100.00
1988	Brett, Buckner, Jackson, Montgomery, Saberhagen, White, Wilson	125.00
1989	Brett, Buckner, Gordon, Jackson, Montgomery, Saberhagen	125.00
1990	Appier, Brett, Jackson, McRae, Montgomery, Saberhagen, White	100.00
1991	Appier, Brett, Gibson, McRae, Montgomery, Saberhagen	100.00
1992	Appier, Brett, Jefferies, Joyner, B. McRae, H. McRae, Montgomery	85.00
1993	Appier, Brett, Cone, Joyner, B. McRae, H. McRae, Montgomery	125.00
1994	Appier, Cone, Hamelin, Joyner, B. McRae, Montgomery	95.00
1995	Appier, Boone, Damon, Gaetti, Goodwin, Joyner, Montgomery	90.00
1996	Appier, Damon, Montgomery	90.00
1997	Appier, Bell, Damon, King, Montgomery	90.00

Los Angeles Angels

Year	Key Signatures	Price
1961	Averill, L. Thomas, Yost	$250.00
1962	Chance, Fregosi, L. Thomas	200.00
1963	Chance, Fregosi, L. Thomas	125.00
1964	Adcock, Chance, Fregosi	100.00

Los Angeles Dodgers

Year	Key Signatures	Price
1958	Alston, Drysdale, Furillo, Gilliam, Hodges, Koufax, Reese, Snider	500.00
1959	Alston, Drysdale, Gilliam, Hodges, Howard, Koufax, Snider, Wills, Zimmer	700.00
1960	Alston, T. Davis, Drysdale, Gilliam, Hodges, Koufax, Snider, Wills	450.00
1961	Alston, T. Davis, W. Davis, Drysdale, Hodges, Koufax, Snider, Wills	300.00
1962	Alston, T. Davis, W. Davis, Drysdale, Gilliam, Koufax, Snider, Wills	300.00
1963	Alston, T. Davis, W. Davis, Drysdale, Gilliam, Koufax, Wills	550.00
1964	Alston, T. Davis, W. Davis, Drysdale, Gilliam, Koufax, Wills	300.00
1965	Alston, W. Davis, Drysdale, Gilliam, Koufax, Lefebvre, Wills	500.00
1966	Alston, T. Davis, W. Davis, Drysdale, Koufax, Sutton, Wills	350.00
1967	Alston, Davis, Drysdale, Sutton	250.00
1968	Alston, K. Boyer, Davis, Drysdale, Sutton, Versalles	150.00
1969	Alston, Davis, Parker, Russell, Sizemore, Sutton, Wills	225.00
1970	Alston, Davis, Mota, Russell, Sutton, Wills	200.00
1971	Alston, Buckner, Davis, Downing, Garvey, Russell, Sutton, Wills	225.00
1972	Alston, Buckner, Davis, Garvey, John, Robinson, Russell, Sutton	225.00
1973	Alston, Buckner, Cey, Davis, Garvey, John, Lopes, Russell, Sutton	150.00
1974	Alston, Buckner, Cey, Garvey, John, Lopes, Russell, Sutton, Wynn	300.00
1975	Alston, Buckner, Cey, Garvey, John, Lopes, Russell, Sutton	150.00
1976	Alston, Baker, Buckner, Cey, Garvey, John, Lasorda, Lopes, Russell, Sutton	125.00
1977	Baker, Cey, Garvey, John, Lasorda, Lopes, Russell, Smith, Sutton	300.00
1978	Baker, Cey, Garvey, John, Lasorda, Lopes, Russell, Smith, Sutton	250.00
1979	Baker, Cey, Garvey, Lasorda, Lopes, Russell, Sutcliffe, Sutton	125.00
1980	Baker, Cey, Garvey, Lasorda, Lopes, Russell, Sutcliffe, Sutton	125.00
1981	Baker, Cey, Garvey, Lasorda, Lopes, Russell, Sax, Valenzuela	325.00
1982	Baker, Cey, Garvey, Lasorda, Lopes, Russell, Sax, Valenzuela	125.00
1983	Baker, Lasorda, Russell, Sax, Stewart, Valenzuela, Welch	160.00
1984	Guerrero, Hershiser, Lasorda, Sax, Valenzuela	150.00
1985	Hershiser, Lasorda, Russell, Sax, Valenzuela	100.00
1986	Hershiser, Lasorda, Madlock, Russell, Sax, Valenzuela	100.00
1987	Guerrero, Hershiser, Lasorda, Sax, Valenzuela	100.00
1988	Gibson, Guerrero, Hershiser, Lasorda, Sax, Valenzuela	250.00
1989	Gibson, Hershiser, Lasorda, R. Martinez, Murray, Valenzuela	150.00
1990	Gibson, Lasorda, R. Martinez, Murray, Valenzuela	100.00
1991	Butler, Carter, Hershiser, Lasorda, R. Martinez, Murray, Strawberry	75.00
1992	Butler, Hershiser, Karros, Lasorda, R. Martinez, Strawberry	80.00
1993	Hershiser, Karros, Lasorda, P. Martinez, R. Martinez, Piazza, H. Rodriguez	150.00
1994	Butler, Hershiser, Karros, Lasorda, Martinez, Mondesi, Piazza, H. Rodriguez	150.00
1995	Butler, Karros, Lasorda, Martinez, Mondesi, Nomo, Piazza, Valdes	150.00
1996	Hollandsworth, Karros, Martinez , Mondesi, Nomo, Piazza	175.00
1997	Hollandsworth, Karros, Martinez, Mondesi, Nomo, Park, Piazza	175.00

Milwaukee Braves

Year	Key Signatures	Price
1953	Adcock, Burdette, Grimm, Mathews, Spahn	$350.00
1954	Aaron, Adcock, Burdette, Grimm, Mathews, Spahn	300.00
1955	Aaron, Adcock, Burdette, Grimm, Mathews, Spahn	350.00
1956	Aaron, Adcock, Burdette, Grimm, Mathews, Spahn	350.00
1957	Aaron, Adcock, Burdette, Mathews, Schoendienst, Spahn	1,200.00
1958	Aaron, Adcock, Burdette, Mathews, Schoendienst, Spahn	700.00
1959	Aaron, Adcock, Burdette, Mathews, Schoendienst, Spahn	400.00
1960	Aaron, Adcock, Burdette, Mathews, Schoendienst, Spahn	350.00
1961	Aaron, Adcock, Burdette, Mathews, Spahn, Torre	225.00
1962	Aaron, Adcock, Burdette, Mathews, Spahn, Torre	350.00
1963	Aaron, Burdette, Mathews, Spahn, Torre	200.00
1964	Aaron, Carty, Mathews, Spahn, Torre	200.00
1965	Aaron, Mathews, P. Niekro, Torre	300.00

1959 Chicago White Sox

1961 New York Yankees

1962 New York Mets

1962 New York Yankees

Milwaukee Brewers

Year	Key Signatures	Price
1970	Downing, Harper, Pattin	$150.00
1971	Briggs, Harper, May	100.00
1972	Briggs, Lonborg, Scott	100.00
1973	Colborn, Porter, Scott, Thomas	100.00
1974	Porter, Scott, Yount	175.00
1975	Aaron, Porter, Scott, Thomas, Yount	250.00
1976	Aaron, Scott, Thomas, Yount	125.00
1977	Bando, Cooper, Yount	100.00
1978	Caldwell, Cooper, Molitor, Oglivie, Thomas, Yount	100.00
1979	Caldwell, Cooper, Molitor, Oglivie, Thomas, Yount	200.00
1980	Cooper, Molitor, Oglivie, Thomas, Yount	100.00
1981	Cooper, Fingers, Molitor, Oglivie, Thomas, Vuckovich, Yount	125.00
1982	Cooper, Fingers, Molitor, Oglivie, Thomas, Vuckovich, Yount	350.00
1983	Cooper, Molitor, Oglivie, Sutton, Thomas, Yount	150.00
1984	Cooper, Fingers, Oglivie, Sutton, Yount	125.00
1985	Cooper, Fingers, Molitor, Oglivie, Vuckovich, Yount	75.00
1986	Cooper, Higuera, Molitor, Oglivie, Yount	75.00
1987	Cooper, Higuera, Molitor, Surhoff, Yount	75.00
1988	Higuera, Molitor, Surhoff, Yount	75.00
1989	Bosio, Molitor, Sheffield, Surhoff, Vaughn, Yount	100.00
1990	Molitor, Parker, Sheffield, Surhoff, Vaughn, Yount	75.00
1991	Bichette, Molitor, Sheffield, Surhoff, Vaughn, Yount	100.00
1992	Bichette, Eldred, Garner, Listach, Molitor, Nilsson, Surhoff, Vaughn, Yount	60.00
1993	Garner, Hamilton, Jaha, Listach, Nilsson, Surhoff, Vaughn, Yount	50.00
1994	Eldred, Garner, Jaha, Nilsson, Surhoff, Valentin, Vaughn	85.00
1995	Garner, Jaha, Nilsson, Surhoff, Valentin, Vaughn	75.00
1996	Cirillo, Garner, Jaha, Nilsson, Valentin, Vaughn	75.00
1997	Cirillo, Garner, Jaha, Nilsson, Valentin, Vaughn	75.00

Minnesota Twins

Year	Key Signatures	Price
1961	Kaat, Killebrew, Martin, Versalles	$250.00
1962	Kaat, Killebrew, Versalles	225.00
1963	Kaat, Killebrew, Versalles	225.00
1964	Kaat, Killebrew, Oliva, Versalles	225.00
1965	Kaat, Killebrew, Oliva, Versalles	350.00
1966	Kaat, Killebrew, Oliva, Versalles	200.00
1967	Carew, Kaat, Killebrew, Oliva, Versalles	325.00
1968	Carew, Kaat, Killebrew, Oliva	225.00
1969	Carew, Kaat, Killebrew, Nettles, Oliva	325.00
1970	Blyleven, Carew, Kaat, Killebrew, Oliva, Perry, Tiant	300.00
1971	Blyleven, Carew, Kaat, Killebrew, Oliva, Perry	125.00
1972	Blyleven, Carew, Kaat, Killebrew	150.00
1973	Blyleven, Carew, Kaat, Killebrew, Oliva	125.00
1974	Blyleven, Carew, Killebrew, Oliva	150.00
1975	Blyleven, Carew, Oliva	250.00
1976	Blyleven, Bostock, Campbell, Carew	100.00
1977	Bostock, Carew, Hisle	100.00
1978	Carew, Marshall, Smalley	100.00
1979	Koosman, Marshall, Smalley	75.00
1980	Koosman, Landreaux, Smalley	75.00
1981	Castino, Koosman, Smalley	75.00
1982	Brunansky, Gaetti, Hrbek, Viola	75.00
1983	Brunansky, Gaetti, Hrbek, Viola	75.00
1984	Brunansky, Gaetti, Hrbek, Puckett, Viola	125.00
1985	Blyleven, Brunansky, Gaetti, Hrbek, Puckett, Viola	100.00
1986	Blyleven, Brunansky, Gaetti, Hrbek, Puckett, Viola	100.00

1987	Brunansky, Gaetti, Hrbek, J. Niekro, Puckett, Reardon, Viola	400.00
1988	Blyleven, Carlton, Gaetti, Hrbek, Puckett, Reardon, Viola	75.00
1989	Gaetti, Hrbek, Puckett, Reardon, Viola	75.00
1990	Aguilera, Erickson, Gaetti, Hrbek, Puckett, Tapani	75.00
1991	Aguilera, Davis, Erickson, Hrbek, Knoblauch, Morris, Puckett	400.00
1992	Aguilera, Erickson, Hrbek, Knoblauch, Puckett, Tapani	85.00
1993	Aguilera, Erickson, Hrbek, Knoblauch, Puckett, Tapani, Winfield	100.00
1994	Aguilera, Erickson, Hrbek, Knoblauch, Puckett, Tapani, Winfield	110.00
1995	Aguilera, Cordova, Erickson, Knoblauch, Puckett, Radke	90.00
1996	Cordova, Erickson, Knoblauch, Puckett, Radke	100.00
1997	Aguilera, Cordova, Knoblauch, Radke	90.00

Montreal Expos

Year	Key Signatures	Price
1969	Bailey, Jones, Staub	$350.00
1970	Bailey, Morton, Staub	125.00
1971	Bailey, Marshall, Staub	100.00
1972	Bailey, Marshall, McCarver, Singleton, Torrez	125.00
1973	Bailey, Marshall, McCarver, Singleton	80.00
1974	Bailey, W. Davis, Singleton, Torrez	100.00
1975	Carter, Murray, Parrish	100.00
1976	Carter, Parrish, Thornton	100.00
1977	Carter, Dawson, Perez	100.00
1978	Carter, Dawson, Grimsley, Perez, Valentin	100.00
1979	Carter, Dawson, Parrish, Perez	125.00
1980	Carter, Dawson, Parrish	125.00
1981	Carter, Dawson, Raines, Reardon, Wallach,	150.00
1982	Carter, Dawson, Oliver, Raines, Reardon, Rogers, Wallach	100.00
1983	Carter, Dawson, Oliver, Raines, Reardon	100.00
1984	Carter, Dawson, Raines, Reardon, Rose	125.00
1985	Dawson, Raines, Reardon, Smith, Wallach	65.00
1986	Galarraga, Dawson, Raines, Reardon, Wallach	75.00
1987	Galarraga, D. Martinez, Raines, Wallach	100.00
1988	Galarraga, D. Martinez, Raines, Wallach	75.00
1989	Galarraga, Langston, D. Martinez, Raines, Wallach	100.00
1990	Galarraga, Grissom, D. Martinez, Raines, Walker, Wallach	75.00
1991	Fassero, Galarraga, Grissom, D. Martinez, Walker, Wallach	60.00
1992	F. Alou, M. Alou, Carter, Galarraga, Grissom, Walker, Wetteland	50.00
1993	F. Alou, M. Alou, Grissom, Hill, Lansing, Walker, Wetteland	50.00
1994	F. Alou, M. Alou, Grissom, Lansing, Martinez, Walker, Wetteland	60.00
1995	F. Alou, M. Alou, Grudzielanek, Lansing, Martinez, Segui, White	90.00
1996	F. Alou, M. Alou, Grudzielanek, Lansing, Martinez, Segui, White	90.00
1997	F. Alou, Grudzielanek, Guerrero, Lansing, Martinez, Segui, White	80.00

New York Giants

Year	Key Signatures	Price
1920	Bancroft, Barnes, Frisch, Kelly, McGraw, Nehf, Toney, Youngs	$2,200.00
1921	Bancroft, Barnes, Burns, Frisch, Kelly, McGraw, Meusel, Nehf, Smith, Snyder, Toney, Youngs	2,500.00
1922	Bancroft, Barnes, Frisch, Kelly, McGraw, Meusel, Nehf, Snyder, Stengel, Youngs	2,500.00
1923	Bancroft, Frisch, Jackson, Kelly, McGraw, Meusel, Ryan, Stengel, Youngs	2,500.00
1924	Barnes, Frisch, Gowdy, Jackson, Kelly, McGraw, Meusel, Snyder, Terry, Wilson, Youngs	2,200.00
1925	Frisch, Jackson, Kelly, Lindstrom, McGraw, Meusel, Terry, Wilson, Youngs	2,200.00
1926	Frisch, Jackson, Kelly, Lindstrom, McGraw, Meusel, Ott, Terry, Tyson, Youngs	2,200.00

1927	Grimes, Harper, Hornsby, Jackson, Lindstrom, McGraw, Roush, Terry	2,200.00
1928	Benton, Fitzsimmons, Hogan, Hubbell, Jackson, Lindstrom, McGraw, O'Doul, Ott, Reese, Roush, Terry, Welsh	4,500.00
1929	Hubbell, Jackson, Lindstrom, McGraw, Ott, Roush, Terry	1,200.00
1930	Fitzsimmons, Hogan, Hubbell, Jackson, Leach, Lindstrom, McGraw, Ott, Roush, Terry	1,500.00
1931	Fitzsimmons, Hogan, Hubbell, Jackson, Leach, Lindstrom, McGraw, Ott, Terry, Walker	1,200.00
1932	Hogan, Hoyt, Hubbell, Jackson, Leach, Lindstrom, McGraw, Ott, Terry, Walker	1,200.00
1933	Hubbell, Jackson, Ott, Schumacher, Terry, Vergez	1,000.00
1934	Hubbell, Jackson, Moore, Ott, Schumacher, Terry	450.00
1935	Hubbell, Jackson, Leiber, Moore, Ott, Schumacher, Terry	750.00
1936	Hubbell, Jackson, Leiber, Mancuso, Moore, Ott, Terry	700.00
1937	Bartell, Hubbell, Leiber, Melton, Moore, Ott, Ripple, Terry	700.00
1938	Danning, Hubbell, Leiber, Melton, Moore, Ott, Ripple, Terry	500.00
1939	Bonura, Danning, Demaree, Hubbell, Moore, Ott, Terry	500.00
1940	Danning, Demaree, Hubbell, Moore, Ott, Terry, Young	500.00
1941	Bartell, Danning, Hartnett, Hubbell, Moore, Ott, Terry, Young	500.00
1942	Adams, Bartell, Danning, Hubbell, Mize, Ott	700.00
1943	Adams, Lombardi, Mancuso, Medwick, Ott, Witek	400.00
1944	Adams, Lombardi, Mancuso, Medwick, Ott, Voiselle, Weintraub	500.00
1945	Adams, Lombardi, Mungo, Ott, Voiselle, Weintraub	450.00
1946	Cooper, Lombardi, Marshall, Mize, Ott, Voiselle	600.00
1947	Cooper, Lombardi, Jansen, Marshall, Mize, Ott, Thomsom	450.00
1948	Durocher, Gordon, Jansen, Marshall, Mize, Ott, Thomsom	500.00
1949	Durocher, Gordon, Jansen, Marshall, Mize, Thomson	400.00
1950	Dark, Durocher, Irvin, Jansen, Maglie, Thompson, Thomson	400.00
1951	Dark, Durocher, Irvin, Jansen, Maglie, Mays, Thomson	750.00
1952	Dark, Durocher, Irvin, Maglie, Mays, Thomson, Wilhelm	400.00
1953	Dark, Durocher, Irvin, Mueller, Thompson, Thomson, Wilhelm	350.00
1954	Antonelli, Dark, Durocher, Irvin, Mueller, Mays, Wilhelm	1,000.00
1955	Antonelli, Durocher, Irvin, Mays, Thompson, Wilhelm	500.00
1956	Antonelli, Dark, Mays, Schoendienst, Thompson, White	450.00
1957	Antonelli, Gomez, Grissom, Mays, Saur, Schoendienst	300.00

New York Mets

Year	Key Signatures	Price
1962	Ashburn, Stengel, Thomas, Throneberry, Woodling	$400.00
1963	Hickman, Hodges, Jackson, Kranepool, Snider, Stengel, Thomas	350.00
1964	Hickman, Jackson, Kranepool, Smith, Stengel, Thomas	400.00
1965	Hickman, Kranepool, McGraw, Spahn, Stengel, Swoboda	325.00
1966	Boyer, Kranepool, McGraw, Swoboda	225.00
1967	Boyer, Davis, Harrelson, Kranepool, Seaver, Swoboda	400.00
1968	Hodges, Koosman, Kranepool, Ryan, Seaver, Swoboda	650.00
1969	Agee, Hodges, Koosman, Kranepool, Ryan, Seaver, Swoboda	2,500.00
1970	Agee, Clendenon, Hodges, Koosman, Kranepool, Ryan, Seaver, Swoboda	325.00
1971	Agee, Hodges, Koosman, Kranepool, McGraw, Ryan, Seaver	275.00
1972	Agee, Berra, Hodges, Koosman, Kranepool, Matlack, Mays, Seaver, Staub	250.00
1973	Berra, Koosman, Kranepool, Mays, Milner, Seaver, Staub	400.00
1974	Berra, Koosman, Kranepool, Matlack, Milner, Seaver, Staub	150.00
1975	Berra, Grote, Kingman, Koosman, Kranepool, Seaver, Staub	125.00
1976	Grote, Kingman, Koosman, Kranepool, Matlack, Seaver, Torre	150.00
1977	Kingman, Koosman, Kranepool, Matlack, Seaver, Torre	125.00
1978	Koosman, Mazzilli, Montanez, Torre	100.00
1979	Mazzilli, Swan, Torre, Youngblood	100.00

1963 Kansas City Royals

1963 New York Yakees

1964 Cincinnati Reds

1969 Montreal Expos

1980	Mazzilli, Reardon, Swan, Torre, Wilson, Youngblood	100.00
1981	Kingman, Mazzilli, Staub, Torre, Youngblood	125.00
1982	Brooks, Foster, Kingman, Staub, Swan, Wilson, Youngblood	100.00
1983	Foster, Hernandez, Kingman, Staub, Strawberry, Seaver, Wilson	125.00
1984	Foster, Gooden, Hernandez, D. Johnson, Strawberry, Wilson	150.00
1985	Carter, Foster, Gooden, Hernandez, D. Johnson, Strawberry, Wilson	200.00
1986	Carter, Foster, Gooden, Hernandez, D. Johnson, Mitchell, Strawberry, Wilson	400.00
1987	Carter, Gooden, Hernandez, D. Johnson, H. Johnson, Strawberry, Wilson	150.00
1988	Carter, Cone, Gooden, Hernandez, D. Johnson, H. Johnson, Strawberry, Wilson	125.00
1989	Carter, Cone, Gooden, Hernandez, Jefferies, D. Johnson, H. Johnson, Strawberry	125.00
1990	Cone, Franco, Gooden, Jefferies, D. Johnson, H. Johnson, Strawberry, Viola	125.00
1991	Cone, Franco, Gooden, Jefferies, Johnson, McReynolds, Viola	75.00
1992	Bonilla, Cone, Franco, Gooden, Johnson, Murray	85.00
1993	Bonilla, Franco, Gooden, Johnson, Kent, Murray	75.00
1994	Bonilla, Burnitz, Franco, Gooden, Jones, Kent, Saberhagen, Segui	75.00
1995	Bonilla, Brogna, Franco, Hundley, Isringhausen, Jones, Kent, Pulsipher, Saberhagen	100.00
1996	Franco, Hundley, Isringhausen, Jones, Pulsipher	100.00
1997	Franco, Gilkey, Husky, Jones, Olerud, Ordonez, Reed	100.00

New York Yankees

Year	Key Signatures	Price
1920	Huggins, Mays, Meusel, Pratt, Ruth, Shawkey, Quinn	$3,000.00
1921	Baker, Hoyt, Huggins, Mays, Meusel, Pipp, Ruth, Shawkey, Ward	3,500.00
1922	Baker, Bush, Hoyt, Huggins, Meusel, Pipp, Ruth, Schang, Shawkey	2,800.00
1923	Bush, Gehrig, Hoyt, Huggins, Jones, Meusel, Pennock, Pipp, Ruth, Ward, Witt	3,000.00
1924	Combs, Dugan, Gehrig, Hoyt, Huggins, Meusel, Pennock, Pipp, Ruth	3,500.00
1925	Combs, Hoyt, Huggins, Gehrig, Meusel, Pennock, Pipp, Ruth	3,500.00
1926	Combs, Hoyt, Huggins, Gehrig, Lazzeri, Meusel, Pennock, Ruth	4,000.00
1927	Combs, Hoyt, Huggins, Gehrig, Lazzeri, Meusel, Moore, Pennock, Ruth	18,000.00
1928	Combs, Durocher, Gehrig, Hoyt, Huggins, Lazzeri, Meusel, Pipgras, Pennock, Ruth	10,000.00
1929	Combs, Dickey, Durocher, Gehrig, Hoyt, Huggins, Lazzeri, Pennock, Ruth, Wells	3,500.00
1930	Chapman, Combs, Dickey, Gehrig, Gomez, Hoyt, Lazzeri, Pennock, Ruffing, Ruth	3,000.00
1931	Chapman, Combs, Dickey, Gehrig, Gomez, Lazzeri, McCarthy, Ruffing, Ruth, Sewell	4,000.00
1932	Allen, Combs, Dickey, Gehrig, Gomez, Lazzeri, McCarthy, Ruffing, Ruth, Sewell	4,000.00
1933	Allen, Combs, Dickey, Gehrig, Gomez, Lazzeri, McCarthy, Ruffing, Ruth, Sewell	3,500.00
1934	Combs, Dickey, Gehrig, Gomez, Lazzeri, McCarthy, Ruffing, Ruth	3,000.00
1935	Combs, Dickey, Gehrig, Gomez, Lazzeri, McCarthy, Ruffing	1,500.00
1936	Dickey, DiMaggio, Gehrig, Gomez, Lazzeri, McCarthy, Pearson, Ruffing	2,000.00
1937	Dickey, DiMaggio, Gehrig, Gomez, Lazzeri, McCarthy, Ruffing	2,000.00
1938	Dickey, DiMaggio, Gehrig, Gomez, McCarthy, Ruffing	1,500.00
1939	Dickey, DiMaggio, Gomez, Keller, McCarthy, Rolfe, Ruffing, Selkirk	1,500.00
1940	Dickey, DiMaggio, McCarthy, Ruffing	550.00
1941	Dickey, DiMaggio, Gomez, McCarthy, Rizzuto, Ruffing	1,000.00
1942	Dickey, DiMaggio, Gomez, Gordon, McCarthy, Rizzuto, Ruffing	1,000.00
1943	Chandler, Dickey, Keller, McCarthy	750.00
1944	Etten, Lindell, Martin, McCarthy	350.00
1945	Etten, McCarthy, Ruffing	250.00
1946	Chandler, Dickey, DiMaggio, Henrich, Keller, McCarthy, Rizzuto	800.00
1947	Berra, DiMaggio, Henrich, McQuinn, Reynolds, Rizzuto, Shea	1,000.00
1948	Berra, DiMaggio, Henrich, Raschi, Rizzuto	650.00
1949	Bauer, Berra, DiMaggio, Henrich, Raschi, Rizzuto, Reynolds, Stengel	1,200.00
1950	Bauer, Berra, DiMaggio, Ford, Henrich, Mize, Raschi, Rizzuto, Stengel	1,000.00
1951	Bauer, Berra, DiMaggio, Jensen, Mantle, McDougald, Mize, Raschi, Rizzuto, Stengel	4,000.00
1952	Bauer, Berra, Mantle, Martin, Mize, Raschi, Reynolds, Rizzuto, Stengel	1,000.00
1953	Bauer, Berra, Ford, Mantle, Martin, Mize, Raschi, Rizzuto, Stengel	1,000.00
1954	Bauer, Berra, Ford, Grim, Mantle, Rizzuto, Stengel	1,000.00
1955	Bauer, Berra, Ford, Howard, Larsen, Mantle, Stengel	1,000.00
1956	Bauer, Berra, Ford, Howard, Larsen, Mantle, Martin, Skowron, Stengel	1,200.00
1957	Bauer, Berra, Ford, Howard, Larsen, Kubek, Mantle, Skowron, Stengel, Sturdivant	1,000.00

1958	Berra, Ford, Howard, Kubek, Larsen, Mantle, Stengel, Turley	1,000.00
1959	Berra, Ford, Howard, Kubek, Larsen, Mantle, Slaughter, Stengel	500.00
1960	Berra, Ford, Howard, Kubek, Mantle, Maris, Skowron, Stengel	700.00
1961	Berra, Ford, Howard, Kubek, Mantle, Maris	2,000.00
1962	Berra, Ford, Howard, Kubek, Mantle, Maris, Terry, Tresh	750.00
1963	Berra, Ford, Howard, Kubek, Mantle, Maris, Terry, Tresh	700.00
1964	Berra, Ford, Howard, Kubek, Mantle, Maris, Stottlemyre, Tresh	500.00
1965	Ford, Howard, Mantle, Maris, Stottlemyre, Tresh	450.00
1966	Howard, Mantle, Maris, Stottlemyre, Tresh	500.00
1967	Howard, Mantle, Stottlemyre, Tresh	375.00
1968	Bahnsen, Mantle, Stottlemyre, Tresh	250.00
1969	Murcer, Pepitone, Stottlemyre	250.00
1970	Munson, Murcer, Stottlemyre, White	325.00
1971	Munson, Murcer, Stottlemyre	350.00
1972	Lyle, Munson, Murcer, Stottlemyre	225.00
1973	Lyle, McDowell, Munson, Murcer, Nettles, Stottlemyre	225.00
1974	Chambliss, Lyle, Munson, Murcer, Nettles, Piniella, Stottlemyre	225.00
1975	Bonds, Chambliss, Hunter, Lyle, Martin, Munson, Nettles, Piniella	350.00
1976	Chambliss, Hunter, Lyle, Martin, Munson, Nettles, Randolph	800.00
1977	Guidry, Hunter, Jackson, Lyle, Martin, Munson, Nettles, Piniella	750.00
1978	Gossage, Guidry, Hunter, Jackson, Lyle, Martin, Munson, Piniella	700.00
1979	Gossage, Guidry, Hunter, Jackson, John, Martin, Munson, Nettles	200.00
1980	Gossage, Guidry, Jackson, John, Murcer, Nettles, Piniella, Tiant	225.00
1981	Gossage, Guidry, Jackson, John, Murcer, Nettles, Piniella, Winfield	400.00
1982	Gossage, Griffey, Guidry, John, Murcer, Nettles, Piniella, Winfield	125.00
1983	Baylor, Gossage, Guidry, Martin, Mattingly, Nettles, Winfield	225.00
1984	Baylor, Berra, Guidry, Mattingly, Niekro, Winfield	150.00
1985	Baylor, Guidry, Henderson, Martin, Mattingly, Niekro, Winfield	150.00
1986	Guidry, Henderson, Mattingly, Niekro, Righetti, Winfield	150.00
1987	Guidry, Henderson, John, Mattingly, Piniella, Winfield	150.00
1988	Henderson, John, Martin, Mattingly, Piniella, Winfield	200.00
1989	Henderson, Mattingly, Sax, Winfield	150.00
1990	Dent, Mattingly, Righetti, Sax	150.00
1991	Mattingly, Sax, Williams	100.00
1992	Mattingly, Showalter, Tartabull, Williams	90.00
1993	Boggs, Key, Mattingly, O'Neill, Showalter, Tartabull, Williams	115.00
1994	Abbott, Boggs, Key, Mattingly, O'Neill, Showalter, Williams	125.00
1995	Boggs, Cone, Mattingly, O'Neill, Showalter, Williams, Wetteland	95.00
1996	Boggs, Cone, Jeter, Martinez, Pettitte, Torre, Williams, Wetteland	600.00
1997	Boggs, Cone, Martinez, Pettitte, Torre, Williams	250.00

Oakland Athletics

Year	Key Signatures	Price
1968	Bando, Campaneris, Hunter, Jackson, Odom	$250.00
1969	Bando, Campaneris, Fingers, Hunter, Jackson, Odom	300.00
1970	Bando, Campaneris, Fingers, Hunter, Jackson, Odom	200.00
1971	Bando, Blue, Campaneris, Fingers, Hunter, Jackson, Odom	225.00
1972	Bando, Blue, Campaneris, Fingers, Hunter, Jackson, Williams	400.00
1973	Bando, Blue, Campaneris, Fingers, Hunter, Jackson, Williams	450.00
1974	Bando, Blue, Campaneris, Fingers, Hunter, Jackson, Williams	450.00
1975	Bando, Blue, Campaneris, Fingers, Jackson, Rudi	300.00
1976	Bando, Baylor, Blue, Campaneris, Fingers	125.00
1977	Allen, Armas, Blue	75.00
1978	Armas, Page, Revering	75.00
1979	Armas, Henderson, Revering	100.00
1980	Armas, Henderson, Martin, Norris	175.00
1981	Armas, Henderson, Martin	150.00
1982	Armas, Henderson, Lopes, Martin	175.00
1983	Henderson, Lansford, Lopes	75.00

1984	Henderson, Kingman, Lansford, Lopes, Morgan	100.00
1985	Baker, Lansford, Kingman, Sutton, Tettleton	75.00
1986	Baker, Canseco, Kingman, Lansford, La Russa, Stewart, Tettleton	125.00
1987	Canseco, Eckersley, La Russa, McGwire, Steinbach, Stewart	125.00
1988	Canseco, Eckersley, La Russa, McGwire, Steinbach, Stewart, Weiss	225.00
1989	Canseco, Eckersley, R. Henderson, La Russa, McGwire, Steinbach	300.00
1990	Canseco, Eckersley, R. Henderson, La Russa, McGwire, Welch	225.00
1991	Canseco, Eckersley, R. Henderson, La Russa, Steinbach, Stewart	100.00
1992	Canseco, Eckersley, R. Henderson, La Russa, McGwire, Steinbach	150.00
1993	Eckersley, R. Henderson, La Russa, McGwire, Sierra, Steinbach	75.00
1994	Eckersley, R. Henderson, La Russa, McGwire, Sierra, Steinbach	110.00
1995	Eckersley, Giambi, R. Henderson, La Russa, McGwire, Stottlemyre	75.00
1996	Giambi, McGwire, Steinbach	75.00
1997	Giambi, McGwire, Stairs, Taylor	75.00

Philadelphia Athletics

Year	Key Signatures	Price
1920	Mack, T. Walker, Witt	$850.00
1921	Mack, T. Walker, Witt	700.00
1922	Galloway, Hauser, Mack, Miller, Rommel	600.00
1923	Hauser, Mack, Miller	600.00
1924	Hauser, Lamar, Mack, Miller, Simmons	800.00
1925	Cochrane, Grove, Lamar, Mack, Miller, Rommel, Simmons	1,700.00
1926	Cochrane, French, Mack, Simmons	1,500.00
1927	Cobb, Cochrane, Collins, Foxx, French, Grove, Mack, Simmons, Wheat	2,800.00
1928	Bishop, Cobb, Cochrane, Collins, Foxx, Grove, Hale, Mack, Miller, Simmons, Speaker, Quinn	1,500.00
1929	Cochrane, Collins, Cronin, Earnshaw, Foxx, Grove, Haas, Mack, Miller, Simmons	1,000.00
1930	Cochrane, Collins, Dykes, Foxx, Grove, Mack, Miller, Simmons	1,000.00
1931	Cochrane, Earnshaw, Foxx, Grove, Hoyt, Mack, Simmons	1,500.00
1932	Cochrane, Foxx, Grove, Haas, Mack, Simmons	600.00
1933	Cochrane, Foxx, Grove, Johnson, Higgins, Mack	500.00
1934	Cramer, Foxx, Higgins, Johnson, Mack	400.00
1935	Cramer, Foxx, Johnson, Mack, Moses	400.00
1936	Finney, Johnson, Mack, Moses	300.00
1937	Johnson, Mack, Moses	300.00
1938	Johnson, Mack, Moses	500.00
1939	Hayes, Johnson, Mack, Moses	350.00
1940	Hayes, Johnson, Mack, Moses	400.00
1941	Chapman, Collins, Mack, Moses, Siebert	450.00
1942	Johnson, Knickerbocker, Mack	400.00
1943	Estalella, Flores, Mack	300.00
1944	Hayes, Kell, Mack	350.00
1945	Estalella, Kell, Mack	300.00
1946	Mack, McCosky, Valo	350.00
1947	Mack, Marchildon, Valo	300.00
1948	Mack, Majeski, Valo	300.00
1949	Chapman, Fox, Kellner, Mack, Valo	300.00
1950	Dillinger, Lehner, Mack, Valo	350.00
1951	Fain, Shantz, Zernial	300.00
1952	Fain, Shantz, Zernial	250.00
1953	Philley, Robinson, Zernial	250.00
1954	Finigan, Renna, Zernial	300.00

1969 New York Mets

1959 San Francisco Giants

1970 New York Mets

1972 Atlanta Braves

Philadelphia Phillies

Year	Key Signatures	Price
1920	Meusel, Rixey, Stengel, Wheat, Williams	$1,000.00
1921	Bruggy, Konetchy, Meusel, Williams	500.00
1922	Henline, Lee, Walker, Williams	400.00
1923	Henline, Holke, Mokan, Tierney, Williams	400.00
1924	Harper, Holke, Williams, Wrightstone	400.00
1925	Harper, Hawks, Williams, Wrightstone	400.00
1926	Carlson, Leach, Mokan, Williams, Wilson	350.00
1927	Leach, Thompson, Williams, Wrightstone	350.00
1928	Klein, Leach, Whitney	2,500.00
1929	Hurst, Klein, O'Doul, Sothern, Thevenow, Thompson, Whitney	400.00
1930	Davis, Hurst, Klein, O'Doul, Whitney	600.00
1931	Arlet, Davis, Hurst, Klein, Mallon	400.00
1932	Bartell, Davis, Hurst, Klein, Lee	350.00
1933	Davis, Fullis, Klein, Schulmerich	350.00
1934	Allen, Bartell, Chiozza, Moore, Todd	250.00
1935	Allen, Camilli, Moore	750.00
1936	Camilli, Klein, Moore	250.00
1937	Camilli, Klein, Whitney	250.00
1938	Arnovich, Klein, Weintraub	300.00
1939	Arnovich, Davis, Suhr	250.00
1940	Higbe, May, Rizzo	250.00
1941	Bragan, Etten, Litwhiler	500.00
1942	Etten, Litwhiler, Waner	650.00
1943	Barrett, Northey, Rowe	500.00
1944	Adams, Northey, Schanz	400.00
1945	V. DiMaggio, Foxx, Wasdell	800.00
1946	Ennis, Northey, Rowe	250.00
1947	Leonard, Rowe, Walker	300.00
1948	Ashburn, Leonard, Roberts, Rowe, Sisler	400.00
1949	Ashburn, Meyer, Roberts, Sisler,	400.00
1950	Ashburn, Ennis, Konstanty, Roberts, Simmons	400.00
1951	Ashburn, Jones, Roberts	250.00
1952	Ashburn, Ennis, Roberts	250.00
1953	Ashburn, Ennis, Roberts	250.00
1954	Ashburn, Ennis, Roberts	225.00
1955	Antonelli, Ashburn, Ennis, Roberts	350.00
1956	Ashburn, Haddix, Lopata, Roberts	200.00
1957	Ashburn, Roberts, Sanford	300.00
1958	H. Anderson, Ashburn, Roberts	300.00
1959	H. Anderson, Ashburn, Freese, Roberts	350.00
1960	Callison, Herrera, Roberts	125.00
1961	Demeter, Gonzalez, Mauch	125.00
1962	Callison, Demeter, Mahaffey, Mauch, Sievers	125.00
1963	Callison, Culp, Demeter, Sievers	125.00
1964	Allen, Bunning, Callison	125.00
1965	Allen, Bunning, Callison	200.00
1966	Allen, Bunning, Uecker, White	125.00
1967	Allen, Bunning, White	125.00
1968	Allen, Short, White	100.00
1969	Allen, Hisle, Wise	125.00
1970	Bowa, Bunning, Johnson, McCarver	125.00
1971	Bowa, Bunning, Johnson, McCarver, Montanez	125.00
1972	Bowa, Carlton, Luzinski	150.00
1973	Boone, Bowa, Carlton, Luzinski, Schmidt	150.00
1974	Boone, Bowa, Carlton, Luzinski, Schmidt	125.00
1975	Allen, Boone, Carlton, Luzinski, Schmidt	125.00
1976	Allen, Boone, Bowa, Carlton, Kaat, Luzinski, McCarver, Schmidt	150.00

1977	Boone, Bowa, Carlton, Kaat, Luzinski, McCarver, Schmidt	150.00
1978	Boone, Bowa, Carlton, Kaat, Luzinski, Schmidt	125.00
1979	Boone, Bowa, Carlton, Luzinski, Rose, Schmidt, Trillo	150.00
1980	Boone, Bowa, Carlton, Luzinski, Rose, Schmidt, Trillo	300.00
1981	Boone, Bowa, Carlton, Lyle, Rose, Schmidt, Trillo	125.00
1982	Carlton, Rose, Schmidt, Trillo	150.00
1983	Carlton, Denny, Morgan, Perez, Rose, Schmidt	250.00
1984	Carlton, Hayes, Schmidt, Virgil	125.00
1985	Denny, Hayes, Schmidt, Virgil	75.00
1986	Carlton, Daulton, Schmidt	85.00
1987	Bedrosian, Hayes, Parrish, Samuel, Schmidt	75.00
1988	Parrish, Samuel, Schmidt	100.00
1989	Daulton, Dykstra, Hayes, Schmidt	75.00
1990	Daulton, Dykstra, Kruk, Murphy	50.00
1991	Daulton, Dykstra, Kruk, Murphy	60.00
1992	Daulton, Dykstra, Hollins, Kruk, Schilling	100.00
1993	Daulton, Dykstra, Green, Hollins, Kruk, Schilling, Williams	250.00
1994	Daulton, Dykstra, Hollins, Kruk, Schilling	250.00
1995	Daulton, Dykstra, Hollins, Schilling	75.00
1996	Daulton, Dykstra, Schilling, Stocker	75.00
1997	Bottalico, Brogna, Daulton, Rolen, Schilling, Stocker	75.00

Pittsburgh Pirates

Year	Key Signatures	Price
1920	Carey, Cooper, McKechnie	$800.00
1921	Bigbee, Carey, Cooper, Cuthsaw, Maranville	1,000.00
1922	Bigbee, Carey, Cooper, Gooch, Maranville, McKechnie, Russell, Tierney, Traynor	1,300.00
1923	Barnhart, Carey, Grimm, Maranville, McKechnie, Morrison, Traynor	1,200.00
1924	Carey, Cooper, Cuyler, Maranville, McKechnie, Traynor	1,000.00
1925	Barnhart, Carey, Cuyler, Grantham, McKechnie, Meadows, Smith, Traynor, Wright	1,000.00
1926	Carey, Cuyler, Grantham, Kremer, McKechnie, Meadows, Smith, Traynor, Waner, Wright	1,000.00
1927	Barnhart, Cronin, Cuyler, Grantham, Groh, Harris, Hill, Kremer, Traynor, L. Waner, P. Waner	900.00
1928	Brickel, Grantham, Grimes, Traynor, L. Waner, P. Waner, Wright	400.00
1929	Bartell, Comorosky, Grantham, Grimes, Traynor, L. Waner, P. Waner	700.00
1930	Bartell, Comorosky, Grantham, Kremer, Suhr, Traynor, L. Waner, P. Waner	600.00
1931	Grantham, Meine, Traynor, L.Waner, P. Waner	500.00
1932	Traynor, Vaughn, L.Waner, P. Waner	600.00
1933	Hoyt, Lindstrom, Piet, Traynor, Vaughan, L.Waner, P. Waner	700.00
1934	Grimes, Hoyt, Lindstrom, Suhr, Traynor, Vaughan, L. Waner, P. Waner	750.00
1935	Hoyt, Suhr, Traynor, Vaughan, L. Waner, P. Waner	600.00
1936	Brubaker, Hoyt, Suhr, Traynor, Vaughan, L.Waner, P. Waner	550.00
1937	Suhr, Todd, Traynor, Vaughan, L. Waner, P. Waner	500.00
1938	Brown, Rizzo, Traynor, Vaughan, L. Waner, P. Waner	800.00
1939	Fletcher, Traynor, Vaughan, L. Waner, P. Waner	700.00
1940	DiMaggio, Fletcher, Frisch, Lopez, Sewell, Vaughan, L. Waner, P. Waner	750.00
1941	DiMaggio, Frisch, Lopez, Sewell, Vaughan	750.00
1942	DiMaggio, Frisch, Lopez, Sewell	800.00
1943	DiMaggio, Elliott, Frisch, Lopez, Sewell	300.00
1944	Dahlgren, DiMaggio, Elliott, Frisch, Lopez, Russell, Sewell	350.00
1945	Elliott, Frisch, Lopez, Sewell	700.00

1946	Frisch, Kiner, Lopez, Sewell	850.00
1947	Greenberg, Herman, Kiner, Sewell	250.00
1948	Kiner, Murtaugh, Sewell	325.00
1949	Hopp, Kiner, Westlake	400.00
1950	Hopp, Kiner, Westlake	250.00
1951	Dickson, Garagiola, Kiner	300.00
1952	Garagiola, Groat, Kiner	250.00
1953	Abrams, Kiner, Thomas	250.00
1954	Gordon, Littlefield, Thomas	150.00
1955	Clemente, Groat, Thomas	225.00
1956	Clemente, Mazeroski, Thomas, Virdon	750.00
1957	Clemente, Friend, Groat, Mazeroski, Thomas	900.00
1958	Clemente, Friend, Groat, Kluszewski, Mazeroski, Thomas	700.00
1959	Clemente, Friend, Groat, Kluszewski, Mazeroski, Stuart	700.00
1960	Clemente, Friend, Groat, Law, Mazeroski, Stuart, Vernon	1,500.00
1961	Clemente, Friend, Groat, Mazeroski, Stuart	750.00
1962	Clemente, Clendenon, Friend, Groat, Mazeroski, Stargell	650.00
1963	Clemente, Clendenon, Friend, Mazeroski, Stargell	600.00
1964	Clemente, Clendenon, Friend, Mazeroski, Mota, Stargell	600.00
1965	Clemente, Mazeroski, Mota, Stargell	1,300.00
1966	Clemente, Clendenon, Mazeroski, Stargell	1,000.00
1967	Clemente, Mazeroski, Stargell, Wills	500.00
1968	Bunning, Clemente, Mazeroski, Stargell, Wills	550.00
1969	Bunning, Clemente, Mazeroski, Oliver, Stargell	450.00
1970	Clemente, Mazeroski, Oliver, Stargell	700.00
1971	Clemente, Mazeroski, Oliver, Stargell	550.00
1972	Clemente, Oliver, Stargell	600.00
1973	Briles, Oliver, Stargell	125.00
1974	Oliver, Parker, Stargell	150.00
1975	Candelaria, Oliver, Parker, Stargell	150.00
1976	Candelaria, Oliver, Parker, Stargell, Tekulve	150.00
1977	Gossage, Oliver, Parker, Stargell, Tekulve	150.00
1978	Blyleven, Candelaria, Parker, Stargell, Tekulve	150.00
1979	Blyleven, Candelaria, Madlock, Parker, Stargell, Tekulve	300.00
1980	Blyleven, Candelaria, Madlock, Parker, Stargell, Tekulve	175.00
1981	Madlock, Parker, Tekulve, Tiant	100.00
1982	Candelaria, Madlock, Parker, Tekulve	125.00
1983	Candelaria, Madlock, Parker, Tekulve	75.00
1984	Candelaria, Madlock, Tekulve	75.00
1985	Candelaria, Madlock, Pena	75.00
1986	Bonds, Bonilla, Leyland	75.00
1987	Bonds, Bonilla, Drabek, Leyland, Van Slyke	100.00
1988	Bonds, Bonilla, Drabek, Leyland, Van Slyke	75.00
1989	Bonds, Bonilla, Drabek, Leyland, Van Slyke	100.00
1990	Bonds, Bonilla, Drabek, King, Leyland, Van Slyke	125.00
1991	Bonds, Bonilla, Drabek, King, Leyland, Smiley	125.00
1992	Bonds, Drabek, King, Leyland, Neagle, Van Slyke	125.00
1993	Bell, King, Leyland, Van Slyke	95.00
1994	Bell, King, Leyland, Martin, Neagle, Van Slyke	85.00
1995	Bell, King, Leyland, Martin, Neagle	80.00
1996	Bell, Kendall, King, Leyland, Martin	75.00
1997	Guillen, Kendall, Martin, Womack	75.00

San Diego Padres

Year	Key Signatures	Price
1969	Gaston, J. Niekro, Podres	$225.00
1970	Colbert, Dobson, Gaston	125.00
1971	Colbert, Gaston, Kirby	125.00
1972	Colbert, Gaston, Kirby, Zimmer	100.00

1972 Texas Rangers

1973 New York Mets

1975 New York Mets

1976 Los Angeles

1973	Colbert, Gaston, Grubb, Zimmer	125.00
1974	Gaston, Grubb, McCovey, Winfield	100.00
1975	Grubb, Jones, McCovey, Winfield	100.00
1976	Jones, McCovey, Metzger, Winfield	100.00
1977	Fingers, Hendrick, Kingman, Winfield	125.00
1978	Fingers, G. Perry, O. Smith, Winfield	150.00
1979	Fingers, G. Perry, O. Smith, Winfield	150.00
1980	Fingers, O. Smith, Winfield	100.00
1981	Howard, Kennedy, Salazar, O. Smith	75.00
1982	Gwynn, Kennedy, Lollar	100.00
1983	Garvey, Gwynn, Kennedy	125.00
1984	Garvey, Gossage, Gwynn, Nettles	250.00
1985	Garvey, Gossage, Gwynn, Nettles	85.00
1986	Garvey, Gossage, Gwynn, Kruk, Nettles, Roberts	75.00
1987	Gossage, Gwynn, Kruk, Santiago	60.00
1988	Alomar, Gwynn, Kruk, Santiago	75.00
1989	Alomar, Clark, Gwynn, Santiago	75.00
1990	Alomar, Carter, Clark, Gwynn, Lynn, Santiago	75.00
1991	Fernandez, Gwynn, McGriff	75.00
1992	Gwynn, McGriff, Sheffield	100.00
1993	Ashby, An. Benes, Gwynn, McGriff, Sheffield	80.00
1994	Ashby, An. Benes, Gwynn	80.00
1995	Ashby, An. Benes, Caminiti, Gwynn, Hamilton	100.00
1996	Ashby, Caminiti, Gwynn, Joyner, Valenzuela	125.00
1997	Ashby, Caminiti, Finley, Gwynn	125.00

San Francisco Giants

Year	Key Signatures	Price
1958	Cepeda, Mays, McCormick	$500.00
1959	Cepeda, Jones, Mays, McCormick, McCovey	300.00
1960	Cepeda, Mays, McCormick, McCovey	300.00
1961	Cepeda, Marichal, Mays, McCormick, McCovey	300.00
1962	Cepeda, Marichal, Mays, McCormick, McCovey	500.00
1963	Cepeda, Larsen, Marichal, Mays, McCovey	300.00
1964	Cepeda, Marichal, Mays, McCovey, Perry, Snider	250.00
1965	Marichal, Mays, McCovey, Perry	300.00
1966	Marichal, Mays, McCovey, Perry	225.00
1967	Marichal, Mays, McCormick, McCovey, Perry	225.00
1968	Bonds, Marichal, Mays, McCormick, McCovey, Perry	225.00
1969	Bonds, Marichal, Mays, McCormick, McCovey, Perry	200.00
1970	Bonds, Marichal, Mays, McCovey, Perry	200.00
1971	Bonds, Kingman, Marichal, Mays, McCovey, Perry	250.00
1972	Bonds, Kingman, Marichal, McCovey	250.00
1973	Bonds, Bryant, Kingman, Marichal, Mathews, McCovey	125.00
1974	Bonds, Kingman, Mathews	75.00
1975	Joshua, Mathews, Murcer	75.00
1976	Evans, Mathews, Murcer	75.00
1977	Clark, Evans, Madlock, McCovey	100.00
1978	Blue, Clark, Evans, Madlock, McCovey	100.00
1979	Blue, Clark, Madlock, McCovey	150.00
1980	Blue, Clark, Evans	100.00
1981	Blue, Clark, Evans, Morgan	75.00
1982	Clark, Davis, Evans, Leonard, Morgan, Robinson	75.00
1983	Clark, Davis, Evans, Leonard, Robinson	75.00
1984	Baker, Clark, Davis, Leonard, Oliver, Robinson	75.00
1985	Blue, Davis, Leonard	75.00
1986	Blue, Clark, Davis, Krukow, Thompson	75.00
1987	Clark, Davis, Mitchell, Williams	125.00
1988	Butler, Clark, Mitchell	75.00

1989	Butler, Clark, Mitchell, Williams	225.00
1990	Butler, Clark, Mitchell, Williams	100.00
1991	Clark, McGee, Mitchell, Williams	50.00
1992	Clark, Clayton, McGee, Williams	110.00
1993	Baker, Bonds, Burkett, Clark, Clayton, McGee, Swift, Williams	150.00
1994	Baker, Beck, Bonds, Clayton, McGee, Williams	150.00
1995	Baker, Beck, Bonds, Williams	125.00
1996	Baker, Beck, Bonds, Williams	125.00
1997	Baker, Beck, Bonds, Estes, Kent, Snow	125.00

Seattle Mariners

Year	Key Signatures	Price
1978	Cruz, Reynolds, Roberts	$75.00
1979	Cruz, Horton, Jones	75.00
1980	Bochte, Cruz, Wills	75.00
1981	Cruz, Henderson, Zisk	75.00
1982	Cruz, Henderson, Perry, Zisk	75.00
1983	Cruz, Henderson, Perry, Zisk	75.00
1984	Davis, Henderson, Langston	75.00
1985	Langston, Presley, Thomas	75.00
1986	Langston, Reynolds, Tartabull	75.00
1987	Davis, Langston, Reynolds,	75.00
1988	Buhner, Davis, Langston, Reynolds,	75.00
1989	Buhner, Griffey Jr. Johnson, Martinez, Vizquel	200.00
1990	Buhner, Griffey Jr., Johnson, Martinez, Vizquel	100.00
1991	Buhner, Griffey Jr., Johnson, Martinez, Vizquel	100.00
1992	Buhner, Griffey Jr., Johnson, E. Martinez, T. Martinez, Vizquel	115.00
1993	Buhner, Griffey Jr., Johnson, E. Martinez, T. Martinez, Piniella, Vizquel	100.00
1994	Buhner, Griffey Jr., Johnson, E. Martinez, T. Martinez, Piniella	100.00
1995	Buhner, Griffey Jr., Johnson, E. Martinez, T. Martinez, Piniella	150.00
1996	Buhner, Griffey Jr., Johnson, E. Martinez, Rodriguez, Piniella	175.00
1997	Buhner, Griffey Jr., Johnson, E. Martinez, Rodriguez, Piniella	175.00

Seattle Pilots

Year	Key Signatures	Price
1969	Harper, Hovley, Mincher	500.00

St. Louis Browns

Year	Key Signatures	Price
1920	Jacobson, Shocker, Sisler, Tobin, Williams	$650.00
1921	Jacobson, Shocker, Sisler, Tobin, Williams	500.00
1922	Jacobson, McManus, Severeid, Shocker, Sisler, Tobin, Williams	600.00
1923	Jacobson, McManus, Severeid, Shocker, Tobin, Williams	450.00
1924	Jacobson, McManus, Robertson, Severeid, Shocker, Sisler, Williams	500.00
1925	Jacobson, Rice, Sisler, Williams	550.00
1926	Miller, Rice, Schang, Sisler, Williams	450.00
1927	Miller, Schang, Sisler, Williams	550.00
1928	Blue, Crowder, Manush	600.00
1929	Ferrell, Kress, Manush, Schulte	400.00
1930	Ferrell, Goslin, Kress, Manush	450.00
1931	Ferrell, Goslin, Kress, Melillo, Schulte	400.00
1932	Burns, Ferrell, Goslin, Scharien	400.00
1933	Campbell, Hornsby, West	500.00
1934	Hemsley, Hornsby, West	500.00
1935	Andrews, Hornsby, Solters, West	600.00
1936	Bell, Bottomley, Clift, Hornsby	600.00
1937	Bell, Clift, Hornsby, Vosmik, West	550.00

1938	Almada, Clift, Kress, McQuinn	250.00
1939	Clift, Laabs, McQuinn	250.00
1940	Clift, Judnich, Radcliff	225.00
1941	Clift, Cullenbine, Ferrell, Judnich	300.00
1942	Ferrell, Judnich, Laabs	300.00
1943	Ferrell, Stephens, Sundra	300.00
1944	Kreevich, Potter, Stephens	350.00
1945	Muncrief, Potter, Stephens	700.00
1946	Kramer, Laabs, Stephens	250.00
1947	Heath, Judnich, Stephens	300.00
1948	Moss, Priddy, Zarilla	300.00
1949	Dillinger, Graham, Sievers	250.00
1950	Garver, Linhardt, Sievers	225.00
1951	Coleman, Garver, Wood	500.00
1952	Hornsby, Nieman, Paige	400.00
1953	Larsen, Marion, Paige, Trucks, Wertz	400.00

St. Louis Cardinals

Year	Key Signatures	Price
1920	Doak, Fournier, Haines, Hornsby, Rickey, Stock	$1,500.00
1921	Clemons, Dillhoefer, Doak, Fournier, Haines, Hornsby, Mann, McHenry, Rickey, Smith, Stock	1,200.00
1922	Bottomley, Haines, Hornsby, Rickey, Schultz, Smith, Stock, Toporcer	1,500.00
1923	Bottomley, Haines, Hornsby, Myers, Rickey, Smith	1,500.00
1924	Blades, Bottomley, Hafey, Haines, Hornsby, Rickey	1,500.00
1925	Blades, Bottomley, Hafey, Haines, Hornsby, Mueller, Rickey	1,500.00
1926	Alexander, Bell, Blades, Bottomley, Douthit, Hafey, Haines, Hornsby, Rhem, Southworth	1,800.00
1927	Alexander, Bottomley, Frisch, Hafey, Haines	1,500.00
1928	Alexander, Bottomley, Frisch, Hafey, Haines, Maranville, McKechnie	2,000.00
1929	Alexander, Bottomley, Douthit, Frisch, Hafey, Haines, High, Johnson, McKechnie, Orsatti, Wilson	1,200.00
1930	Adams, Bottomley, Douthit, Frisch, Gelbert, Grimes, Hafey, Haines, Street, Watkins, Wilson	1,000.00
1931	Bottomley, Frisch, Grimes, Hafey, Haines, Hallahan	1,000.00
1932	Bottomley, Collins, Dean, Frisch, Martin, Orsatti, Watkins	600.00
1933	Collins, Dean, Durocher, Frisch, Haines, Hornsby, Martin, Medwick, Vance	1,200.00
1934	Collins, Davis, D. Dean, P. Dean, Durocher, Frisch, Martin, Medwick, Orsatti	1,000.00
1935	Collins, D. Dean, P. Dean, Durocher, Frisch, Haines, Martin, Medwick	500.00
1936	D. Dean, P. Dean, Durocher, Frisch, Haines, Martin, Medwick, Mize	550.00
1937	Dean, Durocher, Frisch, Martin, Medwick, Mize, Padgett	500.00
1938	Frisch, Martin, Medwick, Mize, Slaughter	500.00
1939	Martin, Medwick, Mize, Slaughter	450.00
1940	Martin, Medwick, Mize, Slaughter	400.00
1941	Brown, Hopp, Mize, Slaughter	400.00
1942	Beazley, Cooper, Musial, Slaughter	750.00
1943	M.Cooper, W. Cooper, Musial	450.00
1944	M.Cooper, W. Cooper, Hopp, Marion, Musial	450.00
1945	Adams, Barrett, Brecheen, Buckhart, Kurowski, Schoendienst	300.00
1946	Garagiola, Kurowski, Musial, Pollet, Schoendienst, Slaughter, Walker	700.00
1947	Garagiola, Medwick, Munger, Musial, Schoedienst, Slaughter	350.00

1986 New York Mets

1990 San Fransico Giants

1990 Cincinnati Reds

1996 New York Yankees

1948	Musial, Schoendienst, Slaughter	350.00
1949	Garagiola, Musial, Pollet, Schoendienst, Slaughter	300.00
1950	Garagiola, Musial, Schoendienst, Slaughter	300.00
1951	Musial, Schoendienst, Slaughter	300.00
1952	Musial, Schoendienst, Slaughter	300.00
1953	Haddix, Musial, Schoendienst, Slaughter, Staley	250.00
1954	Haddix, Musial, Schoendienst	200.00
1955	Boyer, Haddix, Musial, Schoendienst, Virdon	250.00
1956	Boyer, Dixon, Moon, Musial	250.00
1957	Boyer, Musial, Wilhelm	250.00
1958	Boyer, Flood, Musial	200.00
1959	Boyer, Flood, McDaniel, Musial, White	200.00
1960	Boyer, Flood, Musial, White	300.00
1961	Boyer, Flood, Gibson, Musial, White	300.00
1962	Boyer, Flood, Gibson, Musial, White	300.00
1963	Boyer, Flood, Gibson, Groat, McCarver, Musial, White	400.00
1964	Boyer, Brock, Flood, Gibson, Groat, McCarver, White	500.00
1965	Boyer, Brock, Flood, Gibson, McCarver, Schoendienst, White	325.00
1966	Brock, Cepeda, Flood, Gibson, McCarver, Schoendienst	300.00
1967	Brock, Carlton, Cepeda, Flood, Gibson, Maris, McCarver, Schoendienst	400.00
1968	Brock, Carlton, Cepeda, Flood, Gibson, Maris, McCarver, Schoendienst	350.00
1969	Brock, Carlton, Flood, Gibson, McCarver, Pinson, Schoendienst, Simmons, Torre	150.00
1970	Allen, Brock, Carlton, Gibson, Schoendienst, Simmons, Torre	175.00
1971	Brock, Carlton, Gibson, Schoendienst, Simmons, Torre	200.00
1972	Brock, Gibson, Schoendienst, Simmons, Torre	150.00
1973	Brock, Gibson, McCarver, Schoendienst, Simmons, Torre	125.00
1974	Brock, Gibson, McBride, Schoendienst, Simmons, Torre	150.00
1975	Brock, Gibson, Hernandez, Schoendienst, Simons	125.00
1976	Brock, Hernandez, Schoendienst, Simmons	150.00
1977	Brock, Hernandez, Simmons	100.00
1978	Boyer, Brock, Hernandez, Simmons	150.00
1979	Boyer, Brock, Hernandez, Simmons	150.00
1980	Bonds, Hendrick, Hernandez, Kaat, Schoendienst, Simmons	100.00
1981	Hernandez, Kaat, Sutter	125.00
1982	Hernandez, Kaat, McGee, O. Smith, Sutter	350.00
1983	Hernandez, McGee, O. Smith, Sutter	125.00
1984	McGee, O. Smith, Sutter	125.00
1985	Clark, Coleman, McGee, O. Smith	250.00
1986	Clark, Coleman, McGee, O. Smith	100.00
1987	Clark, Coleman, McGee, O. Smith	200.00
1988	Coleman, Guerrero, McGee, O. Smith	65.00
1989	Coleman, Guerrero, McGee, O. Smith	100.00
1990	Coleman, Guerrero, McGee, O. Smith, Torre, Zeile	65.00
1991	Gilkey, Guerrero, Lankford, L. Smith, O. Smith, Torre, Zeile	55.00
1992	Galarraga, Gilkey, Jordan, Lankford, L. Smith, O. Smith, Torre, Zeile	75.00
1993	Gilkey, Jefferies, Jordan, Lankford, O. Smith, Torre, Zeile	50.00
1994	Gilkey, Jefferies, Jordan, Lankford, O. Smith, Torre, Zeile	65.00
1995	Gilkey, Jordan, Lankford, O. Smith, Torre, Zeile	125.00
1996	Jordan, Lankford, O. Smith, Stottlemyre	125.00
1997	Eckersley, DeShields, Jordan, Lankford, La Russa, McGwire, Stottlemyre	125.00

Texas Rangers

Year	Key Signatures	Price
1972	Harrah, Howard, Williams	$200.00
1973	Burroughs, Harrah, Martin	100.00
1974	Burroughs, Hargrove, Harrah, Jenkins, Martin	125.00
1975	Burroughs, Hargrove, Harrah, Jenkins, Martin, Perry	150.00
1976	Burroughs, Blyleven, Hargrove, Harrah, Perry	100.00

1977	Blyleven, Harrah, Perry	75.00
1978	Bonds, Harrah, Jenkins, Oliver	100.00
1979	Bell, Jenkins, Lyle, Oliver	75.00
1980	Bell, Jenkins, Lyle, Oliver, Perry, Staub	100.00
1981	Bell, Jenkins, Oliver	75.00
1982	Bell, Hough, Parrish	75.00
1983	Bell, Hough, Parrish	75.00
1984	Bell, Hough, Parrish	75.00
1985	Harrah, Hough, Parrish	75.00
1986	Hough, Incavigila, Parrish, Sierra	75.00
1987	Hough, Incavigila, Parrish, Sierra	75.00
1988	Hough, Incavigila, Sierra	65.00
1989	Baines, Brown, Franco, Palmeiro, Russell, Ryan, Sierra, Witt	100.00
1990	Baines, Brown, Franco, Palmeiro, Ryan, Sierra, Witt	100.00
1991	Franco, Gonzalez, Palmeiro, Palmer, Rodriguez, Ryan, Sierra	75.00
1992	Brown, Gonzalez, Palmeiro, Palmer, Rodriguez, Ryan, Sierra	125.00
1993	Brown, Gonzalez, Palmeiro, Palmer, Rodriguez, Ryan	125.00
1994	Brown, Canseco, Clark, Gonzalez, Greer, Palmer, Rodriguez	125.00
1995	Clark, Gonzalez, Greer, Palmer, Rodriguez	125.00
1996	Clark, Gonzalez, Greer, Palmer, Rodriguez, Wetteland	125.00
1997	Clark, Gonzalez, Greer, Palmer, Rodriguez, Wetteland	125.00

Toronto Blue Jays

Year	Key Signatures	Price
1977	Bailor, Fairly, Howell	$150.00
1978	Cerone, Maybery, Upshaw	100.00
1979	Ainge, Griffin, Maybery, Stieb	75.00
1980	Maybery, Moseby, Stieb, Whitt	75.00
1981	Bell, Garcia, Stieb	75.00
1982	Barfield, Cox, Stieb	75.00
1983	Barfield, Cox, Stieb	75.00
1984	Barfield, Bell, Cox, Fernandez, Key, Stieb	125.00
1985	Barfield, Bell, Cox, Fernandez, Key, Stieb	125.00
1986	Barfield, Bell, Fernandez, Key, Stieb	75.00
1987	Barfield, Bell, Fernandez, Fielder, Henke, Key, McGriff, Stieb	100.00
1988	Barfield, Bell, Fernandez, Fielder, Key, McGriff, Stieb, Stottlemyre	75.00
1989	Bell, Fernandez, Gaston, Key, McGriff, Stieb, Stottlemyre	100.00
1990	Bell, Fernandez, Gaston, Gruber, Key, Olerud, McGriff, Stieb, Stottlemyre	75.00
1991	Alomar, Carter, Gaston, Key, Olerud, Stieb, Stottlemyre, White	100.00
1992	Alomar, Carter, Gaston, Key, Morris, Olerud, Stieb, Stottlemyre, Winfield, White	400.00
1993	Alomar, Carter, Gaston, Henderson, Hentgen, Key, Molitor, Morris, Olerud, Stottlemyre, Stewart, White	400.00
1994	Alomar, Carter, Delgado, Gaston, Hentgen, Molitor, Olerud, Stewart, Stottlemyre, White	125.00
1995	Alomar, Carter, Cone, Gaston, Hentgen, Molitor, Sprague, White	100.00
1996	Carter, Gaston, Gonzalez, Hentgen, Sprague	100.00
1997	Carter, Clemens, Delgado, Gaston, Gonzalez, Green, Hentgen	120.00

Washington Senators

Year	Key Signatures	Price
1920	Griffith, Harris, Johnson, Judge, Milan, Rice	$1,600.00
1921	Gharrity, Harris, Johnson, Judge, Rice, Shanks	1,200.00
1922	Goslin, Harris, Johnson, Judge, Rice	1,200.00
1923	Goslin, Harris, Johnson, Judge, Leibold, Rice, Ruel	1,200.00
1924	Goslin, Harris, Johnson, Judge, Rice	1,800.00
1925	Coveleski, Goslin, Harris, Johnson, Judge, Rice	1,500.00
1926	Coveleski, Goslin, Harris, Johnson, Judge, McNeely, Myer, Rice	1,000.00

1927	Coveleski, Goslin, Hadley, Harris, Johnson, Judge, Lisenbee, Rice, Ruel, Speaker	1,500.00
1928	Barnes, Cronin, Goslin, Harris, Jones, Judge, Reeves, Rice	1,500.00
1929	Cronin, Goslin, Johnson, Judge, Myer, Rice	1,500.00
1930	Cronin, Goslin, Johnson, Judge, Manush, Marberry, Myer, Rice	1,800.00
1931	Cronin, Crowder, Johnson, Manush, Marberry, Rice, West	1,500.00
1932	Cronin, Crowder, Johnson, Manush, Marberry, Reynolds, Rice	1,500.00
1933	Cronin, Crowder, Goslin, Kuhel, Manush, Myer, Whitehill	800.00
1934	Cronin, Kuhel, Manush, Whitehill	350.00
1935	Bolton, Harris, Manush, Myer, Powell, Travis	350.00
1936	Chapman, Harris, Stone, Travis	300.00
1937	Almada, Ferrell, Harris, Lewis, Simmons, Stone, Travis	400.00
1938	Case, Ferrell, Harris, Myer, Simmons, Travis	400.00
1939	Case, Ferrell, Harris, Leonard, Lewis, Vernon, Wright	300.00
1940	Ferrell, Harris, Lewis	300.00
1941	Harris, Travis, Vernon	300.00
1942	Harris, Vernon, Wynn	250.00
1943	Candini, Spence, Vernon, Wynn	250.00
1944	Ferrell, Spence, Wynn	250.00
1945	Ferrell, Lewis, Wolff	250.00
1946	Grace, Leonard, Vernon, Wynn	250.00
1947	Spence, Vernon, Wynn	250.00
1948	Scarborough, Vernon, Wynn	300.00
1949	Robinson, Scarborough, Yost	250.00
1950	Noren, Vernon, Yost	250.00
1951	Coan, Noren, Vernon, Yost	175.00
1952	Jensen, Vernon, Yost	250.00
1953	Busby, Jensen, Porterfield, Vernon	200.00
1954	Morrero, Sievers, Vernon, Yost	200.00
1955	Sievers, Vernon, Yost	300.00
1956	Lemon, Runnels, Sievers, Yost	200.00
1957	Lemon, Sievers, Yost	200.00
1958	Lemon, Pearson, Sievers	200.00
1959	Allison, Killebrew, Lemon, Pascual	200.00
1960	Killebrew, Lemon, Pascual	225.00
1961	Green, Vernon, Woodling	150.00
1962	Hinton, Piersall, Vernon	175.00
1963	Hodges, King, Lock, Minoso	125.00
1964	Hodges, Lock, Osteen	300.00
1965	Hodges, Howard, McCormick	150.00
1966	Hodges, Howard, Valentine	150.00
1967	Hodges, Howard, McMullen	225.00
1968	Howard, McMullen, Pascual	125.00
1969	Bosman, Epstein, Howard, Williams	200.00
1970	Bosman, Epstein, Howard, Williams	175.00
1971	Harrah, Howard, McLain, Williams	225.00

Chapter 3

JERSEYS

**Sandy Koufax
1964**

**Ken Griffey Jr.
1993**

**Ernie Banks
1971**

BASEBALL JERSEYS

Collecting baseball cards is a lot of fun—no doubt about it. But in more than a century of professional baseball, you've never seen one of those little 2½ by 3½-inch pieces of cardboard take the field. Game-used uniforms, on the other hand, literally give collectors a piece of the action.

There's no more personal slice of our national pastime than the very shirts off the players' backs. Uniforms display better than cards, don't require a rigid plastic holder or a number "grade," and can turn a rather bland collection of cardboard into something that can give a charge to even a non-collector. The Baseball Hall of Fame in Cooperstown has a great collection of cards, but the fans who make the journey tend to linger longer at the uniform displays. Also, the brisk sale of replica jerseys confirms that baseball shirts are where it's at.

Collecting game-worn baseball uniforms can be a frustrating, and rather rewarding and educational experience. Expensive? Yes. Risky? Absolutely. Exciting? You better believe it. But before you get started, there are a few things you need to know.

YOU WEAR IT WELL

Shortly after bat first met ball came the concept of teams, and shortly thereafter, leagues. In time, the game's pioneers recognized the need to outfit players in suitable athletic apparel. There were no synthetics, so the choices were between available natural fibers. Cotton was plentiful, but wouldn't stand up to rough play. Silk was too pricey and also lacked durability. Wool, on the other hand, was plentiful, cheap, and sturdy. So wool, or more specifically wool flannel, became the fabric of choice for baseball uniforms.

As the game evolved, so did the equipment, including uniforms. In time, the 100 percent wool flannel was replaced by a blend of wool and cotton. Later, with the advent of synthetics, nylon and rayon were added to the blend. The result was a fabric that was breathable, fairly lightweight, and extremely durable. Flannel would rule the roost until July 16, 1970, when the Pittsburgh Pirates opened Three Rivers Stadium, taking the field in the first 100 percent polyester double-knit uniforms ever worn in the major leagues. There were a handful of experiments with alternate fabrics in the decades leading up to that event (the 1940 Chicago Cubs, 1956

**Lou Boudreau
1960**

**Hugh Casey
1946**

Cincinnati Reds, and 1963 Kansas City A's all tried vests that were predominantly nylon), but none caught on like polyester.

By 1973, every major league team was wearing double-knit uniforms. Since then, we've seen the return of nylon by some teams, either in a mesh (used for batting practice/ warm-up shirts) or in a Russell Athletic–manufactured knit fabric called "Intera" which breathes— something 100 percent polyester cannot do.

REAL RARITIES

When the sports collecting hobby experienced its first major surge in the mid-1970s, you could count the number of serious uniform collectors in this country on your fingers and toes. More than 20 years ago, cards were plentiful and relatively inexpensive, so the idea of spending $25 or more on a game-used jersey was still somewhat foreign to the average hobbyist. At the original Philadelphia show at Spring Garden College, Iowa dealer John Douglas set up with a sizable number of 1960s vintage Philadelphia Phillies' flannels, with prices starting at $25. He didn't sell out that weekend—even in the Phils' home city. Why should he? At the same show, complete card sets of certain years could be had for that much or a little more, and the appellations "superstar" and "rookie card" were yet to come.

In the early days of shirt collecting, the emphasis was on double-knits. They had been around for only a couple of years, and dealers were charging a premium for the newer material. Flannels often went ignored, or ended up as throw-ins to complete trades. The only real

**Hank Aaron
1963**

exceptions were shirts of defunct teams. Obviously, there wouldn't be any genuine double-knit Washington Senators, Houston Colt .45s, etc., uniforms, although the dollar difference was minimal 20 years ago—outside of Brooklyn Dodgers material. It took a while, but in the middle 1980s an idea swept through the hobby. If double-knit jerseys are here to stay, then logically there is a limited universe of flannel uniforms.

Literally overnight, the price structure shifted. Knits were suddenly far more affordable, and flannels, even those shirts of fairly common players, were commanding much higher prices. Demand was, and continues to be, much higher for "all-original" major league flannels than knits.

Today, there are several hundred serious shirt collectors out there, though the number still pales in comparison to the number of card collectors. The total would increase by leaps and bounds if more hobbyists would think about it. Take, for example, the 1993 Topps Finest Refractor of Cal Ripken Jr. There are 240 of them in existence, and each booked for more than $2,000 this past spring. Yet, with that same $2,000, you can start a uniform collection that will impress your friends far more than any little piece of cardboard ever will.

Check out newer card issues that already book for three figures in recent price guides. Then look at how many different cards a player might appear on these days—some players who debuted in this decade already have as many as 1,000 cards. In contrast, a 20-year player averages only around 100 uniforms during his career, so it's quite apparent which item is rarer.

So why, given their rarity and affordability, aren't there many more

**Lou Gehrig
1938**

**Harmon Killebrew
1967**

uniform collectors? The answer is simple: fear.

Buying baseball cards, even vintage cards, is a fairly straightforward proposition. You pay your money, you get your card(s), and authenticity is rarely an issue. Sure, you hear about dealers selling counterfeits, trimmed cards, or restored cards, but it's more of a minor annoyance than a huge hobbywide problem. Uniforms, on the other hand, like autographs, have a major image problem based on ironclad authenticity. To be blunt, there are a lot of bogus uniforms on the market, although if you use your head instead of your heart, you can avoid a lot of misery.

REQUIRED READING

Starting a uniform collection is easy; stopping is the difficult part. Once you've acquired a few, you want more and more. Here's a rundown of a few reference materials that might be helpful if you decide to take up uniform collecting:

• *Baseball Uniforms of the 20th Century*, by Marc Okkonen, published by Sterling. The original hardback from 1991 can still be found in some bookstores, both new and used. The softcover update that came out in 1993 is a little tougher to find. Either one should set you back around $20.

• *Baseball by the Numbers*, by Mark Stang and Linda Harkness, published in 1996 by Scarecrow Press ([800] 462-6420). This book gives the uniform numbers of every team of this century through the 1992 season. It's a big book, since each team is listed by year, and each player is indexed both alphabetically and numerically. It seems pricey at

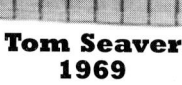

**Tom Seaver
1969**

$85, but it can save you far more time and money spent researching a particular player or number.

• *Diamond Duds*, a bimonthly newsletter for collectors of Major League Baseball uniforms, published by Pearl Publications Group, P.O. Box 10153, Silver Spring, Md. 20904-0153; subscriptions are $20 a year. The only publication of its kind, it also sponsors an annual show that predominantly features equipment.

Your next step is to try to network with some veteran uniform collectors. This may be a little more difficult, depending on where you live, but knowing someone who has been down this road of the hobby can make a big difference. Being able to examine someone's collection before taking the plunge yourself can be a real primer for the novice. Also, a serious collector should be able to make specific dealer recommendations. Several dealers offer free or inexpensive illustrated catalogs, so try to get on as many mailing lists as you can since there's nothing wrong with comparison shopping.

In addition, there are several terms in the uniform-collecting hobby, so be sure you familiarize yourself with all of them.

INSIDE TIPS

Before you start writing checks and running up your phone bill, here are a few words of wisdom you should heed:

• Pick a theme for your collection. That is, go after a shirt from every team, or various style shirts from your favorite team, or uniforms from specific players you find appealing. You get the picture. It's easy to put together an attractive collection of shirts—even

**Fergie Jenkins
1983**

**Ted Williams
1957**

**Pete Rose
1964**

all-original flannels—on a budget.

• Always remember that there are far more superstar knits on the market than could possibly have been worn by the respective player. This is the easiest place to get burned, since it's easy to fake so-called "good game use" on any uniform. If you're going after stars, deal with individuals who have made bulk purchases from the teams, who've got the utility infielders' shirts along with the MVPs. There are "stories" with many shirts offered for sale that are frequently just that: stories. If it's too good to be true, it probably isn't.

A word to the wise regarding letters of authenticity (LOAs): No authentication service can give you a 100 percent ironclad guarantee. (We're referring specifically to third party authenticators, as opposed to a company like MeiGray that's more of a registry, based purely on its obtaining the uniforms directly from the teams from resale.) The letters of some authenticators are void once you sell the item. Some authenticators are hung up on the phrase "shows good game use," when in fact they've never played the game themselves or had postgame lockerroom access.

Too many authenticators will write letters for whatever is submitted to them, whether their own expertise extends to that particular genre of uniform. You'll also find authenticators who will charge a fee based upon what they think a shirt is worth, a clear conflict of interest.

If you purchase a uniform from a dealer offering an LOA, make sure you reserve the right to get a second opinion, and to get your money back if you're not satisfied, within a reasonable amount of time. It's frequently not the dealer's fault if something turns out to be inauthentic, so don't jump down someone's throat if there's no clear intent to defraud. Just don't be afraid to ask tough questions, and remember that skepticism is a very healthy thing. If the answer starts to sound like fiction, it just may be.

One last thing: Be prepared for your non-collecting friends who are baseball fans to be absolutely blown away by your collection. No doubt about it: Every baseball fan at some point pictures himself in a big-league uniform. They'll want to try 'em on and get their picture taken. Can't do that with a card.

UNIFORM-SPEAK

If you're thinking of collecting uniforms, try to become familiar with some of the common shirt collector lingo. Here's a brief list of terms used by uniform collectors and dealers:

All original: This refers to a uniform that has undergone no changes since it was originally issued to the player.

Restored: This indicates that something, like a name on the back or a patch, was removed at some point, but has been restored to look original.

NOB: Player's name is on the back.

NIC: Player's name is stitched in the shirt's collar, either directly on the fabric or on a separate strip of fabric.

NIT: Player's name is stitched into the tail of the shirt—again, either directly or on a separate strip of fabric.

NYT: Indicates lack of year tag, either through wear or because it never had one to start with.

Flagtag: A type of year/set tag that's sewn onto the shirt by one edge, leaving the other edge to flap like a flag.

Salesman's sample: Most manufacturers make up shirts of star players who wear their merchandise, complete with tags, correct size, etc. They are nothing more than replicas, but frequently end up being sold as the real deal.

You'll also hear occasional references to things like "tails cut," which indicates that the player at some point shortened the shirttail for personal comfort, or "extra length," which means the player ordered the shirt with longer-than-normal shirttails.

Chapter 4

PUBLICATIONS

BASEBALL DIGEST

Baseball Digest is the oldest active and continuously published magazine devoted to baseball. The magazine was founded in 1942 by Herbert F. Simmons, a member of the Baseball Writers Association of America, as a collection of baseball articles from around the country. The original cover price was just 15 cents. Today, the magazine carries a $2.99 cover price and measures 7½ by 5¼ inches. It's published by Century Sports Network. In the early years, Baseball Digest printed only ten issues a year—typically not issuing a November or December issue. Starting in 1969, Baseball Digest released 12 issues annually.

Baseball Digest has a comparatively small following among publications collectors, and the secondary values of most issues are lower than those for other baseball pubs. As magazines gain popularity, the values of Baseball Digest back issues should grow as well.

The following prices are for magazines in Excellent/Near-Mint condition.

**Hit & Run
August 1942**

**Hank Aaron
April 1974**

**Jim Hunter
April 1975**

**Thurman Munson
February 1977**

Year	Month	Cover	Price
1942	August	Hit and run	$250.00
1942	October	Pete Reiser	100.00
1942	November	Double play	75.00
1942	December	Joe DiMaggio/Billy Southworth	125.00
1943	February	At bat in Iceland	25.00
1943	March	Back to school	10.00
1943	April	Get two	10.00
1943	May	Catching a popup	20.00
1943	July	Play at second base	10.00
1943	August	Safe at the plate	10.00
1943	September	Stan Musial	40.00
1943	October	Spud Chandler	10.00
1943	November	Johnny Lindell	10.00
1944	February	Bill Johnson	15.00
1944	March	Bill Nicholson/Rip Sewell	15.00
1944	April	Dixie Ward	15.00
1944	May	Lou Boudreau	20.00
1944	July	Vern Stephens	10.00
1944	August	Bucky Walters	15.00
1944	September	Charlie Grimm	10.00
1944	October	Walker Cooper	10.00
1944	November	Marty Marion	10.00
1945	February	Hal Newhouser	15.00

Year	Month	Cover	Price	Year	Month	Cover	Price
1945	March	George McQuinn	15.00	1951	January	Yogi Berra/Whitey Ford	15.00
1945	April	Dixie Walker	15.00	1951	February	Gil Hodges	10.00
1945	May	Bill Voiselle	15.00	1951	March	Eddie Yost	10.00
1945	July	Hank Borowy	15.00	1951	April	Joe DiMaggio	25.00
1945	August	Tommy Holmes	15.00	1951	May	George Earnshaw	10.00
1945	September	Stan Hack	15.00	1951	June	Ted Williams	25.00
1945	October	Hank Greenberg	15.00	1951	July	Irv Noren	10.00
1945	November	Al Lopez	15.00	1951	August	Nellie Fox/Paul Richards	15.00
1946	February	Charlie Keller	15.00	1951	September	Stan Musial	15.00
1946	March	Play at the Plate	10.00	1951	October	Gil McDougald	10.00
1946	April	Bobby Doerr	15.00	1951	November	Charlie Dressen	10.00
1946	May	Bob Feller	15.00	1952	January	Eddie Lopat/Phil Rizzuto	10.00
1946	July	Joe DiMaggio/Ted Williams	50.00	1952	February	Eddie Stanky	10.00
1946	August	Joe Cronin	15.00	1952	March	Sid Gordon	10.00
1946	September	Hank Wyse	15.00	1952	April	Mike Garcia	10.00
1946	October	Dave Ferriss	15.00	1952	May	George Staley	10.00
1946	November	Johnny Pesky/Red Schoendienst	15.00	1952	June	Pee Wee Reese	10.00
1947	February	Bucky Harris	10.00	1952	July	Ted Kluszewski	10.00
1947	March	Johnny Rigney	10.00	1952	August	Bobby Shantz	10.00
1947	April	Johnny Van Cuyk	10.00	1952	September	Sal Maglie	10.00
1947	May	Hank Greenberg/Billy Herman	10.00	1952	October	Carl Erskine	10.00
1947	July	Lou Boudreau/Joe Gordon	15.00	1952	November	Duke Snider	10.00
1947	August	Buddy Kerr	10.00	1953	January	Robin Roberts	10.00
1947	September	Ewell Blackwell	10.00	1953	February	Eddie Mathews	15.00
1947	October	Joe DiMaggio	50.00	1953	March	Billy Martin	15.00
1947	November	Ralph Lapointe	10.00	1953	April	Hornsby/Mantle/Musial	25.00
1948	January	Joe Page	10.00	1953	May	Carl Furillo	10.00
1948	February	Leo Durocher/Branch Rickey	10.00	1953	June	Bob Lemon	10.00
1948	March	Ennis/Hubbard/Meyer	10.00	1953	July	Dorish/Kellner/Logan	10.00
1948	April	Joe McCarthy	10.00	1953	August	Robin Roberts	10.00
1948	May	Art Houtteman	10.00	1953	September	O'Connell/Strickland/Trucks	10.00
1948	June	Willard Marshall	10.00	1953	October	Casey Stengel	10.00
1948	July	Ralph Kiner	10.00	1954	January	Billy Martin	10.00
1948	August	Lou Boudreau	10.00	1954	March	Jimmy Piersall	10.00
1948	September	Stan Musial	25.00	1954	April	Whitey Ford	10.00
1948	October	Hank Sauer	10.00	1954	May	Harvey Kuenn	10.00
1948	November	Paul Fagen	10.00	1954	June	Eddie Mathews/Bobbie Morgan	10.00
1949	January	Jim Hegan	10.00	1954	July	Bob Turley	10.00
1949	February	Red Rolfe	10.00	1954	August	Bob Keegan	10.00
1949	March	Ted Williams	25.00	1954	September	Willie Mays	10.00
1949	April	Joe DiMaggio	25.00	1954	October	World Series	10.00
1949	May	Play at the plate	10.00	1954	November	Dusty Rhodes	10.00
1949	June	Robin Roberts	15.00	1955	January	Ralph Kiner	10.00
1949	July	Johnny Groth	10.00	1955	March	Rookies of '55	10.00
1949	August	Frankie Frisch	10.00	1955	April	Alvin Dark	10.00
1949	September	Vic Raschi	10.00	1955	May	Bob Lemon/Don Mueller	10.00
1949	October	Mel Parnell/Birdie Tebbets	10.00	1955	June	Bobby Avila	10.00
1949	November	Tommy Henrich/Allie Reynolds	10.00	1955	July	Bill Skowron	10.00
1950	January	Richie Ashburn/Roy Smalley	15.00	1955	August	Roy McMillian/Al Smith	10.00
1950	February	Dave Koslo	10.00	1955	September	Don Newcombe	10.00
1950	March	50 Baseball Rules	10.00	1955	October	Walt Alston/Tommy Byrne	10.00
1950	April	Bob Feller	15.00	1955	November	Johnny Podres	10.00
1950	May	Dark/Kramer/Stankey	10.00	1956	February	Al Kaline	10.00
1950	June	Joe DiMaggio	25.00	1956	March	Rookie report	15.00
1950	July	Phil Rizzuto	10.00	1956	April	Luis Aparicio	10.00
1950	August	Dick Sisler	10.00	1956	May	Mike Higgins	10.00
1950	September	Art Houtteman/Larry Jansen	10.00	1956	June	Clem Labine	10.00
1950	October	Hoot Evans	10.00	1956	July	Mickey Mantle	25.00
1950	November	Jim Konstanty	10.00	1956	August	Dale Long	10.00

Year	Month	Cover	Price	Year	Month	Cover	Price
1956	September	Yogi Berra	15.00	1962	August	20 home runs	8.00
1956	October	World Series	10.00	1962	September	Rich Rollins	8.00
1956	November	Don Larson	15.00	1962	October	Tom Tresh/Frank Howard	8.00
1957	January	Robin Roberts	10.00	1963	January	Ralph Terry	8.00
1957	March	Scouting Reports	10.00	1963	February	Ty Cobb/Maury Wills	8.00
1957	April	Farrell/Scheffing/Tighe	10.00	1963	March	Scouting reports	10.00
1957	May	Don Blasingame	10.00	1963	April	Rosters	8.00
1957	June	Breaking up double play	10.00	1963	May	Drysdale/Dean/Grove	8.00
1957	July	Don Hosak	10.00	1963	June	Al Kaline	8.00
1957	August	Stan Musial	15.00	1963	July	Jim O'Toole	8.00
1957	September	Bobby Shantz	10.00	1963	August	Jim Bouton	8.00
1957	October	Babe Ruth	10.00	1963	September	Denny LeMaster	8.00
1958	January	Lew Burdette	10.00	1963	October	Al Downing	8.00
1958	February	Lindy McDaniel	10.00	1964	January	Dodgers' aces	8.00
1958	March	Scouting reports	10.00	1964	February	Roger Maris	10.00
1958	April	Willie Mays/Duke Snider	10.00	1964	March	Scouting reports	8.00
1958	May	Ted Williams	20.00	1964	April	Sandy Koufax	10.00
1958	June	Stan Musial	25.00	1964	May	Harmon Killebrew	8.00
1958	July	Warren Spahn	10.00	1964	June	Tommy Davis/Carl Yastrzemski	8.00
1958	August	Bob Turley	10.00	1964	July	Jim Maloney	8.00
1958	September	Pete Runnels	10.00	1964	August	Dave Nicholson	8.00
1958	October	World Series	10.00	1964	September	Dennis Bennett/Willie Smith	8.00
1959	January	Jensen/Roberts/Truly	10.00	1964	October	Miracle Braves	8.00
1959	February	Baseball's Darling Daughters	10.00	1965	January	Dick Groat	8.00
1959	March	Scouting reports	10.00	1965	February	Winter trades	8.00
1959	April	Ernie Banks	10.00	1965	March	Scouting reports	8.00
1959	May	Juan Pizarro	10.00	1965	April	Which tag is phoney?	8.00
1959	June	Antonelli/Landis/Pascual	10.00	1965	May	Bill Freehan	8.00
1959	July	Vada Pinson	10.00	1965	June	Tony Conigliaro	8.00
1959	August	Hoyt Wilhem	10.00	1965	July	Yankees Six Mistakes	10.00
1959	September	Rocky Colavito/Roy Face	10.00	1965	August	Don Drysdale	8.00
1959	October	World Series	10.00	1965	September	Pete Ward/Joe Morgan	8.00
1960	January	John Roseboro/Larry Sherry	8.00	1965	October	Biggest World Series mysteries	8.00
1960	February	Harvey Kuenn	8.00	1966	January	Sandy Koufax	10.00
1960	March	Scouting reports	8.00	1966	February	Willie Mays	8.00
1960	April	Jim Landis/Charlie Neal	8.00	1966	March	Scouting reports	8.00
1960	May	Early Wynn	8.00	1966	April	Rosters	8.00
1960	June	Bunning/Francona/McDaniel	8.00	1966	May	Sam McDowell	8.00
1960	July	Vern Law	8.00	1966	June	Should the rules be changed?	8.00
1960	August	Dick Gary/Dick Stuart	8.00	1966	July	Juan Marichal	8.00
1960	September	Ron Hansen	8.00	1966	August	Gene Alley/Bill Mazeroski	8.00
1960	October	Dick Groat	8.00	1966	September	George Scott	8.00
1961	January	Bill Virdon	8.00	1966	October	World Series	8.00
1961	February	Ralph Houk	8.00	1967	January	Bunker/Drabowsky/Palmer	8.00
1961	March	Scouting reports	8.00	1967	February	Allison/Drysdale/Mathews	10.00
1961	April	Tony Kubek/Al Sprangler	8.00	1967	March	Scouting reports	8.00
1961	May	Glenn Hobbie	8.00	1967	April	Rosters	8.00
1961	June	Earl Battey	8.00	1967	May	Roger Maris	10.00
1961	July	Wally Moon	8.00	1967	June	Gaylord Perry/Juan Marichal	8.00
1961	August	Norm Cash	8.00	1967	July	Denny McLain	8.00
1961	September	Whitey Ford	8.00	1967	August	Joe Horlen	8.00
1961	October	Koufax/Mantle/Maris/Robinson	25.00	1967	September	Tim McCarver	8.00
1962	January	Elston Howard/Ralph Terry	8.00	1967	October	World Series	8.00
1962	February	Joey Jay	8.00	1968	January	Bob Gibson	8.00
1962	March	Scouting reports	8.00	1968	February	Billy Williams	8.00
1962	April	Orlando Cepeda	8.00	1968	March	Scouting reports	8.00
1962	May	Jim Landis	8.00	1968	April	Rosters	8.00
1962	June	Mickey Mantle	25.00	1968	May	Rod Carew/Jay Johnstone	8.00
1962	July	Dick Donavan	8.00	1968	June	Cookie Rojas/Nellie Briles	8.00

Year	Month	Cover	Price	Year	Month	Cover	Price
1968	July	Jerry Koosman	8.00	1973	August	Allen/May/Melton	5.00
1968	August	Andy Kosco	8.00	1973	September	Ken Holtzman	5.00
1968	September	Matty Alou/Ken Harrelson	8.00	1973	October	Bill Russell	5.00
1968	October	World Series	8.00	1973	November	Jose Cardenal	5.00
1969	January	Lou Brock/Bill Freehan	8.00	1973	December	Willie Stargell	5.00
1969	February	Mickey Mantle	25.00	1974	January	World Series	5.00
1969	March	Scouting reports	8.00	1974	February	Bobby Bonds	5.00
1969	April	Rosters	8.00	1974	March	Bobby Grich	5.00
1969	May	Al Lopez	8.00	1974	April	Hank Aaron	5.00
1969	June	Ernie Banks	8.00	1974	May	Ted Sizemore	5.00
1969	July	Tony Conigiliaro	8.00	1974	June	Felix Millan	5.00
1969	August	Frank Robinson	8.00	1974	July	Brooks Robinson	5.00
1969	September	Brushback Tragedy	8.00	1974	August	Gaylord Perry	5.00
1969	October	World Series	8.00	1974	September	Tommy John	5.00
1969	November	Future superstars	8.00	1974	October	Richie Allen	5.00
1969	December	Tom Seaver	10.00	1974	November	Bando/Campaneris/Jackson	8.00
1970	January	Harmon Killebrew	5.00	1974	December	Lou Brock	5.00
1970	February	Joe Pepitone	5.00	1975	January	Rollie Fingers	5.00
1970	March	Gene Alley	5.00	1975	February	Steve Garvey	5.00
1970	April	Tony Perez	5.00	1975	March	Jeff Burroughs	5.00
1970	May	Roberto Clemente	10.00	1975	April	Jim "Catfish" Hunter	5.00
1970	June	Mel Stottlemyre	5.00	1975	May	Mike Schmidt	8.00
1970	July	Ken Holtzman	5.00	1975	June	Rod Carew	5.00
1970	August	Sal Bando	5.00	1975	July	Nolan Ryan	15.00
1970	September	Tony Perez	5.00	1975	August	Rick Monday	5.00
1970	October	Jim Palmer	5.00	1975	September	Johnny Bench	5.00
1970	November	Johnny Bench	5.00	1975	October	Vida Blue	5.00
1970	December	Billy Williams	5.00	1975	November	Fred Lynn	5.00
1971	January	Brooks Robinson	5.00	1975	December	Joe Morgan	5.00
1971	February	Sal Bando/Juan Marichal	5.00	1976	January	Pete Rose	5.00
1971	March	Carl Yastrzemski	5.00	1976	February	Jim Palmer	5.00
1971	April	Bob Gibson	5.00	1976	March	George Brett	5.00
1971	May	Willie Mays	5.00	1976	April	Carlton Fisk	5.00
1971	June	Tony Oliva	5.00	1976	May	Frank Tanana	5.00
1971	July	Hank Aaron	5.00	1976	June	Rick Manning	5.00
1971	August	Vida Blue	5.00	1976	July	Bill Madlock	5.00
1971	September	Joe Pepitone	5.00	1976	August	Randy Jones	5.00
1971	October	World Series	5.00	1976	September	Larry Bowa	5.00
1971	November	Bobby Murcer	5.00	1976	October	Mickey Rivers	5.00
1971	December	Joe Torre	5.00	1976	November	Mark Fidrych	5.00
1972	January	Steve Blass	5.00	1976	December	Joe Morgan	5.00
1972	February	Earl Williams	5.00	1977	January	World Series	5.00
1972	March	Frank Robinson	5.00	1977	February	Thurman Munson	5.00
1972	April	Bill Melton	5.00	1977	March	Amos Otis	5.00
1972	May	Rosters	5.00	1977	April	Mark Fidrych	5.00
1972	June	Reggie Jackson	8.00	1977	May	John Montefusco	5.00
1972	July	Richie Allen	5.00	1977	June	Steve Carlton	5.00
1972	August	Bud Harrelson	5.00	1977	July	Dave Parker	5.00
1972	September	Roberto Clemente	10.00	1977	August	Ivan DeJesus/Manny Trillo	5.00
1972	October	World Series	5.00	1977	September	Carl Yastrzemski	5.00
1972	November	Carlton Fisk	5.00	1977	October	Steve Garvey	5.00
1972	December	Richie Allen	5.00	1977	November	Bump Wills	5.00
1973	January	Pete Rose	5.00	1977	December	George Foster	5.00
1973	February	Cesar Cedeño	5.00	1978	January	Reggie Jackson	5.00
1973	March	Harmon Killebrew	5.00	1978	February	Willie McCovey	5.00
1973	April	Don Kessinger	5.00	1978	March	Rod Carew	5.00
1973	May	Nolan Ryan	15.00	1978	April	Tom Seaver	10.00
1973	June	Tom Seaver	10.00	1978	May	Cesar Cedeño	5.00
1973	July	Pete Rose	5.00	1978	June	Garry Templeton	5.00

Year	Month	Cover	Price	Year	Month	Cover	Price
1978	July	Dave Kingman	5.00	1983	June	Cal Ripken Jr.	5.00
1978	August	Jim Rice	5.00	1983	July	Tony Peña	5.00
1978	September	Ron Guidry	5.00	1983	August	Dave Stieb	5.00
1978	October	Rich Gale/Clint Hurdle	5.00	1983	September	Chris Chambliss	5.00
1978	November	Reggie Smith	5.00	1983	October	Ron Kittle	5.00
1978	December	Dave Parker	5.00	1983	November	Steve Carlton	5.00
1979	January	World Series	5.00	1983	December	Carlton Fisk	5.00
1979	February	Dave Winfield	5.00	1984	January	Rick Dempsey	5.00
1979	March	Greg Luzinski	5.00	1984	February	Wade Boggs	5.00
1979	April	Rich Gossage	5.00	1984	March	Dale Murphy	5.00
1979	May	Jack Clark	5.00	1984	April	Mike Boddicker	5.00
1979	June	Steve Garvey	5.00	1984	May	Andre Dawson	5.00
1979	July	Al Oliver	5.00	1984	June	Lance Parrish	5.00
1979	August	Bill Buckner	5.00	1984	July	Bill Madlock	5.00
1979	September	Tommy John	5.00	1984	August	Leon Durham	5.00
1979	October	Mike Schmidt	5.00	1984	September	Gwynn/Martinez/McReynolds	5.00
1979	November	Omar Moreno	5.00	1984	October	Ryne Sandberg	5.00
1979	December	George Brett	5.00	1984	November	Keith Hernandez	5.00
1980	January	World Series	5.00	1984	December	Mark Langston	5.00
1980	February	Paul Molitor	5.00	1985	January	Alan Trammell	5.00
1980	March	Gary Carter	5.00	1985	February	Don Mattingly	5.00
1980	April	Willie Stargell	5.00	1985	March	Frank Viola	5.00
1980	May	Don Baylor	5.00	1985	April	Jack Morris	5.00
1980	June	J.R. Richard/Nolan Ryan	5.00	1985	May	Tony Gwynn	5.00
1980	July	Baumgarten/Burns/Trout	5.00	1985	June	Dwight Gooden	5.00
1980	August	Ken Landreaux	5.00	1985	July	Bruce Sutter	5.00
1980	September	Steve Carlton	5.00	1985	August	Pete Rose	5.00
1980	October	Reggie Jackson	5.00	1985	September	Lee Smith	5.00
1980	November	Joe Charboneau	5.00	1985	October	Ron Guidry	5.00
1980	December	George Brett	5.00	1985	November	Pedro Guerrero	5.00
1981	January	Tug McGraw	5.00	1985	December	Dwight Gooden	5.00
1981	February	Eddie Murray	5.00	1986	January	Willie McGee	5.00
1981	March	Rickey Henderson	5.00	1986	February	Bret Saberhagen	5.00
1981	April	Mike Schmidt	5.00	1986	March	Tom Browning	5.00
1981	May	Gary Carter	5.00	1986	April	Harold Baines	5.00
1981	June	Cecil Cooper	5.00	1986	May	Darryl Strawberry	5.00
1981	July	Carlton Fisk	5.00	1986	June	Eddie Murray	5.00
1981	August	Fernando Valenzuela	5.00	1986	July	Bert Blyleven	5.00
1981	September	Danny Darwin	5.00	1986	August	Roger Clemens	10.00
1981	October	Ron Davis	5.00	1986	September	Gary Carter	5.00
1981	November	Pete Rose	5.00	1986	October	Jose Canseco/Wally Joyner	5.00
1981	December	Tim Raines	5.00	1986	November	Bill Doran	5.00
1982	January	Steve Garvey	5.00	1986	December	Roger Clemens/Teddy Higuera	5.00
1982	February	Carney Lansford	5.00	1987	January	Wade Boggs/Don Mattingly	5.00
1982	March	Rollie Fingers	5.00	1987	February	Sid Fernandez	5.00
1982	April	Dave Winfield	5.00	1987	March	Mike Scott	5.00
1982	May	Nolan Ryan	15.00	1987	April	Chris Brown	5.00
1982	June	Jerry Reuss	5.00	1987	May	Pete O'Brien	5.00
1982	July	Salome Barojas	5.00	1987	June	Eric Davis/Jody Davis	5.00
1982	August	Dale Murphy	5.00	1987	July	Mike Witt	5.00
1982	September	Rickey Henderson	5.00	1987	August	Rickey Henderson	5.00
1982	October	Robin Yount	5.00	1987	September	Jack Clark/Ozzie Smith	5.00
1982	November	Kent Krbek	5.00	1987	October	Mark McGwire	5.00
1982	December	Lonnie Smith/Ozzie Smith	5.00	1987	November	George Bell	5.00
1983	January	Darrell Porter	5.00	1987	December	Kevin Seitzer	5.00
1983	February	Mario Soto	5.00	1988	January	Andre Dawson	5.00
1983	March	Doug DeCinces	5.00	1988	February	Frank Viola	5.00
1983	April	Willie McGee	5.00	1988	March	Jimmy Key	5.00
1983	May	Pete Vuckovich	5.00	1988	April	Kevin McReynolds/Mike Pagliarulo	5.00

Year	Month	Cover	Price	Year	Month	Cover	Price
1988	May	Eric Davis	5.00	1993	April	Jose Canseco	3.00
1988	June	Royals Pitchers	5.00	1993	May	Curt Schilling	3.00
1988	July	Andy Van Slyke	5.00	1993	June	Robin Ventura	3.00
1988	August	Dave Winfield	5.00	1993	July	Juan Gonzalez	3.00
1988	September	Greg Maddux	5.00	1993	August	Barry Bonds	3.00
1988	October	Kirby Puckett	5.00	1993	September	Joe Carter	3.00
1988	November	Jose Canseco	5.00	1993	October	John Kruk	3.00
1988	December	Tony Gwynn	5.00	1993	November	Frank Thomas	6.00
1989	January	Jose Canseco	5.00	1993	December	Mike Piazza	6.00
1989	February	Orel Hershiser	5.00	1994	January	Paul Molitor	3.00
1989	March	Greg Jefferies	5.00	1994	February	Randy Johnson	3.00
1989	April	Kirk Gibson	5.00	1994	March	Greg Maddux	3.00
1989	May	Cory Snider	5.00	1994	April	Carlos Baerga	3.00
1989	June	Fred McGriff	5.00	1994	May	Lenny Dykstra	3.00
1989	July	Will Clark	5.00	1994	June	Rafael Palmeiro	3.00
1989	August	Nolan Ryan	12.00	1994	July	Lance Johnson	3.00
1989	September	Bo Jackson	5.00	1994	August	Matt Williams	3.00
1989	October	Dave Stewart	5.00	1994	September	Kirby Puckett	3.00
1989	November	Howard Johnson	5.00	1994	October	Ozzie Smith	3.00
1989	December	Jerome Walton/Dwight Smith	5.00	1994	November	Jimmy Key	3.00
1990	January	Abbott/Clark/Ryan	8.00	1994	December	Bob Hamelin	3.00
1990	February	Ruben Sierra	5.00	1995	January	Jeff Bagwell	3.00
1990	March	Ken Griffey Jr.	12.00	1995	February	Tony Gwynn	3.00
1990	April	Canseco/McGwire/Steinbach	5.00	1995	March	Raul Mondesi	3.00
1990	May	Gibson/Strawberry/Winfield	5.00	1995	April	Kenny Lofton	3.00
1990	June	Mark Grace	5.00	1995	May	Don Mattingly	3.00
1990	July	Bill Geren/Lou Whitaker	5.00	1995	June	Fred McGriff	3.00
1990	August	Bobby Bonilla/Frank Viola	5.00	1995	July	Cal Ripken Jr.	8.00
1990	September	Rickey Henderson	5.00	1995	August	Eddie Mathews	3.00
1990	October	Ozzie Guillen	5.00	1995	September	John Valentin	3.00
1990	November	Cecil Fielder	5.00	1995	October	Barry Larkin	3.00
1990	December	Sandy Alomar/Dave Justice	5.00	1995	November	Mickey Mantle	15.00
1991	January	Bob Welch	3.00	1995	December	Hideo Nomo	3.00
1991	February	Chris Sabo	3.00	1996	January	Albert Belle	3.00
1991	March	Ray Lankford	3.00	1996	February	Tom Glavine	3.00
1991	April	Charlton/Dibble/Myers	3.00	1996	March	Tim Salmon	3.00
1991	May	Darryl Strawberry	3.00	1996	April	Dante Bichette	3.00
1991	June	Tim Raines	3.00	1996	May	Edgar Martinez	3.00
1991	July	Kevin Mitchell	3.00	1996	June	Roberto Alomar	3.00
1991	August	Roger Clemens	3.00	1996	July	Mike Piazza	3.00
1991	September	Robin Yount	3.00	1996	August	Jason Giambi	3.00
1991	October	Cal Ripken Jr.	8.00	1996	September	Harold Baines	3.00
1991	November	Rafael Palmeiro	3.00	1996	October	John Smoltz	3.00
1991	December	Chuck Knoblauch	3.00	1996	November	Mark McGwire	3.00
1992	January	Steve Avery	3.00	1996	December	Derek Jeter	3.00
1992	February	Kirby Puckett	3.00	1997	January	Alex Rodriguez	3.00
1992	March	'92 rookies	3.00	1997	February	Ken Caminiti	3.00
1992	April	Frank Thomas	3.00	1997	March	Andruw Jones	3.00
1992	May	Wade Boggs	3.00	1997	April	Ken Griffey Jr.	3.00
1992	June	Dan Gladden/Greg Olson	3.00	1997	May	Albert Belle/Frank Thomas	3.00
1992	July	Howard Johnson	3.00	1997	June	Brown/Fernandez/A. Leiter	3.00
1992	August	Mark McGwire	3.00	1997	July	Ivan Rodriguez	3.00
1992	September	Juan Guzman	3.00	1997	August	Larry Walker	3.00
1992	October	Kirby Puckett	3.00	1997	September	Roger Clemens	3.00
1992	November	Dennis Eckersley/Tom Glavine	3.00	1997	October	Tino Martinez	3.00
1992	December	Pat Listach	3.00	1997	November	Chipper Jones	3.00
1993	January	Roberto Alomar	3.00	1997	December	Nomar Garciaparra	3.00
1993	February	Gary Sheffield	3.00	1998	January	Tony Gwynn	3.00
1993	March	Tim Wakefield	3.00				

BASEBALL MAGAZINE

Baseball Magazine started publication in 1908 and was considered the country's premier publication on the sport for most of the first half of the century. The magazine began to lose its appeal as competitors like *The Sporting News, Sport,* and *Sports Illustrated* grabbed market share. Ultimately, 1953 was the beginning of the end for *Baseball Magazine.* Only eight issues were published that year, followed by four each in '54 and '55, five in '56, and two final issues in 1957. An attempt was made to revive the magazine in 1964 and '65. But a lack of interest forced *Baseball Magazine*

to vanish for good after its April 1965 issue.

Baseball Magazine is the most expensive of all baseball publications in the hobby. Finding a Near-Mint issue is almost impossible because the magazine was produced so long ago and because very few fans saved their issues. We don't list cover subjects because most of the covers are drawings of the game, teams, or the fans. Very few actual players are depicted on the cover. The prices below reflect magazines in Excellent condition.

Baseball Magazine May 1908

Baseball Magazine September 1910

Baseball Magazine March 1912

Year	Month	Price	Year	Month	Price
1908	May	$2,500.00	1912	April	200.00
1908	June	1,000.00	1912	May	200.00
1908	July	800.00	1912	June	250.00
1908	August	600.00	1912	July	250.00
1908	September	800.00	1912	August	350.00
1908	October	500.00	1912	September	250.00
1908	November	600.00	1912	October	250.00
1908	December	400.00	1912	November	300.00
1909	January	300.00	1912	December	300.00
1909	February	300.00	1913	January	150.00
1909	March	300.00	1913	February	150.00
1909	April	300.00	1913	March	175.00
1909	May	300.00	1913	April	150.00
1909	June	300.00	1913	May	175.00
1909	July	300.00	1913	June	150.00
1909	August	300.00	1913	July	150.00
1909	September	300.00	1913	August	150.00
1909	October	300.00	1913	September	150.00
1909	November	450.00	1913	October	150.00
1909	December	450.00	1913	November	250.00
1910	January	300.00	1913	December	250.00
1910	February	250.00	1914	January	150.00
1910	March	250.00	1914	February	150.00
1910	April	250.00	1914	March	150.00
1910	May	250.00	1914	April	150.00
1910	June	250.00	1914	May	150.00
1910	July	250.00	1914	June	150.00
1910	August	250.00	1914	July	150.00
1910	September	300.00	1914	August	150.00
1910	October	300.00	1914	September	150.00
1910	November	350.00	1914	October	150.00
1910	December	350.00	1914	November	200.00
1911	January	200.00	1914	December	300.00
1911	February	250.00	1915	January	250.00
1911	March	200.00	1915	February	150.00
1911	April	250.00	1915	March	200.00
1911	May	200.00	1915	April	275.00
1911	June	200.00	1915	May	125.00
1911	July	200.00	1915	June	150.00
1911	August	200.00	1915	July	100.00
1911	September	200.00	1915	August	100.00
1911	October	200.00	1915	September	100.00
1911	November	300.00	1915	October	100.00
1911	December	300.00	1915	November	175.00
1912	January	200.00	1915	December	175.00
1912	February	200.00	1916	January	200.00
1912	March	400.00	1916	February	150.00

Year	Month	Price	Year	Month	Price	Year	Month	Price	Year	Month	Price
1916	March	800.00	1921	February	100.00	1926	February	50.00	1931	January	50.00
1916	April	125.00	1921	March	90.00	1926	March	50.00	1931	February	50.00
1916	May	100.00	1921	April	100.00	1926	April	50.00	1931	March	50.00
1916	June	100.00	1921	May	75.00	1926	May	50.00	1931	April	50.00
1916	July	150.00	1921	June	75.00	1926	June	50.00	1931	May	50.00
1916	August	300.00	1921	August	90.00	1926	July	50.00	1931	June	50.00
1916	September	125.00	1921	September	90.00	1926	August	70.00	1931	July	50.00
1916	October	125.00	1921	October	250.00	1926	September	50.00	1931	August	50.00
1916	November	150.00	1921	November	100.00	1926	October	120.00	1931	September	50.00
1916	December	300.00	1921	December	100.00	1926	November	90.00	1931	October	50.00
1917	January	125.00	1922	January	60.00	1926	December	250.00	1931	November	60.00
1917	February	125.00	1922	February	60.00	1927	January	250.00	1931	December	60.00
1917	March	150.00	1922	March	60.00	1927	February	50.00	1932	January	50.00
1917	April	75.00	1922	April	100.00	1927	March	50.00	1932	February	50.00
1917	May	75.00	1922	May	60.00	1927	April	50.00	1932	March	60.00
1917	June	125.00	1922	June	60.00	1927	May	50.00	1932	April	50.00
1917	July	75.00	1922	July	60.00	1927	June	50.00	1932	May	50.00
1917	August	75.00	1922	August	60.00	1927	July	50.00	1932	June	50.00
1917	September	125.00	1922	September	60.00	1927	August	75.00	1932	July	50.00
1917	October	75.00	1922	October	60.00	1927	September	300.00	1932	August	50.00
1917	November	150.00	1922	November	100.00	1927	October	50.00	1932	September	50.00
1917	December	150.00	1922	December	100.00	1927	November	90.00	1932	October	50.00
1918	January	75.00	1923	January	60.00	1927	December	100.00	1932	November	60.00
1918	February	100.00	1923	February	60.00	1928	January	80.00	1932	December	65.00
1918	March	75.00	1923	March	60.00	1928	February	50.00	1933	January	45.00
1918	April	100.00	1923	April	60.00	1928	March	50.00	1933	February	60.00
1918	May	75.00	1923	May	60.00	1928	April	50.00	1933	March	45.00
1918	June	75.00	1923	June	90.00	1928	May	50.00	1933	April	45.00
1918	July	75.00	1923	July	120.00	1928	June	50.00	1933	May	45.00
1918	August	75.00	1923	August	60.00	1928	July	50.00	1933	June	45.00
1918	September	75.00	1923	September	60.00	1928	August	75.00	1933	July	45.00
1918	October	125.00	1923	October	60.00	1928	September	50.00	1933	August	60.00
1918	November	100.00	1923	November	90.00	1928	October	50.00	1933	September	80.00
1918	December	75.00	1923	December	250.00	1928	November	60.00	1933	October	60.00
1919	January	200.00	1924	January	70.00	1928	December	75.00	1933	November	70.00
1919	February	75.00	1924	February	60.00	1929	January	50.00	1933	December	50.00
1919	March	75.00	1924	March	75.00	1929	February	50.00	1934	January	200.00
1919	April	75.00	1924	April	60.00	1929	March	50.00	1934	February	45.00
1919	May	100.00	1924	May	60.00	1929	April	50.00	1934	March	40.00
1919	June	75.00	1924	June	60.00	1929	May	50.00	1934	April	50.00
1919	July	75.00	1924	July	60.00	1929	June	50.00	1934	May	40.00
1919	August	75.00	1924	August	90.00	1929	July	50.00	1934	June	40.00
1919	September	75.00	1924	September	60.00	1929	August	50.00	1934	July	40.00
1919	October	75.00	1924	October	60.00	1929	September	50.00	1934	August	50.00
1919	November	100.00	1924	November	75.00	1929	October	50.00	1934	September	40.00
1919	December	200.00	1924	December	75.00	1929	November	60.00	1934	October	80.00
1920	January (No Issue)	—	1925	January	60.00	1929	December	75.00	1934	November	60.00
1920	February	60.00	1925	February	60.00	1930	January	50.00	1934	December	60.00
1920	March	60.00	1925	March	90.00	1930	February	50.00	1935	January	40.00
1920	April	400.00	1925	April	90.00	1930	March	50.00	1935	February	40.00
1920	May	60.00	1925	May	60.00	1930	April	50.00	1935	March	40.00
1920	June	250.00	1925	June	60.00	1930	May	50.00	1935	April	150.00
1920	July	75.00	1925	July	60.00	1930	June	50.00	1935	May	150.00
1920	August	75.00	1925	August	60.00	1930	July	60.00	1935	June	40.00
1920	September	75.00	1925	September	60.00	1930	August	50.00	1935	July	40.00
1920	October	250.00	1925	October	60.00	1930	September	50.00	1935	August	40.00
1920	November	150.00	1925	November	100.00	1930	October	50.00	1935	September	60.00
1920	December	150.00	1925	December	100.00	1930	November	60.00	1935	October	40.00
1921	January	200.00	1926	January	100.00	1930	December	60.00	1935	November	150.00

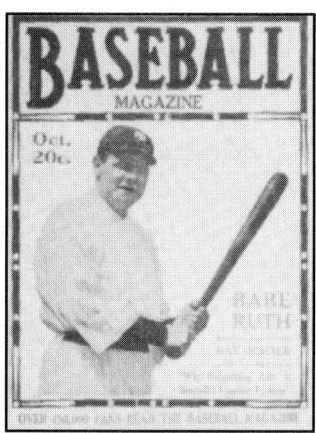

Baseball Magazine October 1920

Baseball Magazine October 1921

Baseball Magazine August 1951

Year	Month	Price	Year	Month	Price
1935	December	40.00	1940	November	50.00
1936	January	40.00	1940	December	25.00
1936	February	40.00	1941	January	25.00
1936	March	40.00	1941	February	25.00
1936	April	40.00	1941	March	25.00
1936	May	40.00	1941	April	25.00
1936	June	40.00	1941	May	25.00
1936	July	50.00	1941	June	25.00
1936	August	60.00	1941	July	25.00
1936	September	40.00	1941	August	50.00
1936	October	40.00	1941	September	25.00
1936	November	60.00	1941	October	25.00
1936	December	40.00	1941	November	50.00
1937	January	35.00	1941	December	30.00
1937	February	35.00	1942	January	35.00
1937	March	35.00	1942	February	35.00
1937	April	35.00	1942	March	20.00
1937	May	35.00	1942	April	20.00
1937	June	35.00	1942	May	30.00
1937	July	35.00	1942	June	20.00
1937	August	35.00	1942	July	20.00
1937	September	100.00	1942	August	20.00
1937	October	35.00	1942	September	20.00
1937	November	50.00	1942	October	20.00
1937	December	35.00	1942	November	40.00
1938	January	35.00	1942	December	20.00
1938	February	35.00	1943	January	20.00
1938	March	35.00	1943	February	20.00
1938	April	35.00	1943	March	20.00
1938	May	75.00	1943	April	20.00
1938	June	30.00	1943	May	20.00
1938	July	30.00	1943	June	20.00
1938	August	40.00	1943	July	20.00
1938	September	30.00	1943	August	20.00
1938	October	30.00	1943	September	20.00
1938	November	60.00	1943	October	20.00
1938	December	30.00	1943	November	20.00
1939	January	30.00	1943	December	35.00
1939	February	30.00	1944	January	20.00
1939	March	30.00	1944	February	20.00
1939	April	30.00	1944	March	20.00
1939	May	30.00	1944	April	20.00
1939	June	75.00	1944	May	20.00
1939	July	75.00	1944	June	20.00
1939	August	150.00	1944	July	20.00
1939	September	30.00	1944	August	20.00
1939	October	40.00	1944	September	20.00
1939	November	100.00	1944	October	20.00
1939	December	100.00	1944	November	20.00
1940	January	25.00	1944	December	35.00
1940	February	25.00	1945	January	16.00
1940	March	25.00	1945	February	16.00
1940	April	25.00	1945	March	16.00
1940	May	25.00	1945	April	16.00
1940	June	25.00	1945	May	16.00
1940	July	25.00	1945	June	16.00
1940	August	25.00	1945	July	16.00
1940	September	25.00	1945	August	16.00
1940	October	75.00	1945	September	16.00

Year	Month	Price	Year	Month	Price
1945	October	16.00	1950	September	12.00
1945	November	16.00	1950	October	12.00
1945	December	20.00	1950	November	12.00
1946	January	30.00	1950	December	20.00
1946	February	20.00	1951	January	12.00
1946	March	16.00	1951	February	12.00
1946	April	16.00	1951	March	12.00
1946	May	16.00	1951	April	12.00
1946	June	16.00	1951	May	20.00
1946	July	25.00	1951	June	15.00
1946	August	16.00	1951	July	12.00
1946	September	16.00	1951	August	200.00
1946	October	40.00	1951	September	12.00
1946	November	20.00	1951	October	12.00
1946	December	30.00	1951	November	18.00
1947	January	16.00	1951	December	25.00
1947	February	16.00	1952	January	15.00
1947	March	16.00	1952	February	50.00
1947	April	16.00	1952	March	12.00
1947	May	16.00	1952	April	12.00
1947	June	30.00	1952	May	12.00
1947	July	16.00	1952	June	12.00
1947	August	16.00	1952	July	25.00
1947	September	16.00	1952	September	12.00
1947	October	16.00	1952	October	12.00
1947	November	25.00	1952	November	15.00
1947	December	30.00	1953	April	12.00
1948	January	16.00	1953	May	12.00
1948	February	16.00	1953	June	12.00
1948	March	16.00	1953	July	25.00
1948	April	16.00	1953	August	12.00
1948	May	16.00	1953	September	12.00
1948	June	16.00	1953	October	25.00
1948	July	16.00	1953	November	20.00
1948	August	40.00	1954	August	12.00
1948	September	16.00	1954	September	12.00
1948	October	25.00	1954	October	15.00
1948	November	16.00	1954	November	12.00
1948	December	20.00	1955	March	20.00
1949	January	25.00	1955	May	12.00
1949	February	16.00	1955	June	12.00
1949	March	16.00	1955	July	12.00
1949	April	16.00	1956	May	15.00
1949	May	50.00	1956	June	20.00
1949	June	16.00	1956	July	25.00
1949	July	16.00	1956	August	12.00
1949	August	16.00	1956	October	15.00
1949	September	16.00	1957	May	18.00
1949	October	16.00	1957	September	12.00
1949	November	16.00	1964	November	10.00
1949	December	25.00	1964	December	12.00
1950	January	12.00	1965	January	10.00
1950	February	12.00	1965	February	10.00
1950	March	12.00	1965	March	10.00
1950	April	12.00	1965	April	10.00
1950	May	25.00			
1950	June	12.00			
1950	July	12.00			
1950	August	12.00			

Baseball Magazine September 1954

Baseball Magazine December 1964

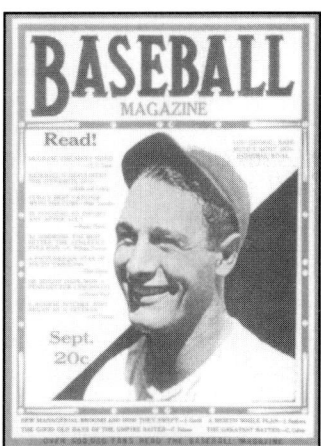

Baseball Magazine September 1927

SPORT MAGAZINE

Among memorabilia collectors, *Sport* magazine is second only to *Sports Illustrated* in popularity. The oldest continuously published magazine devoted to sports, the monthly publication was considered the best sports magazine on the market until the early '70s, when the quality of the editorial content began to lag.

One of the big reasons for the early popularity of *Sport* was the spectacular photography of Ozzie Sweet, whose images brought the covers and pages of the magazine to life. Many fans cut up their *Sport* magazines to display Sweet's work.

The prices below are for baseball-related *Sport* magazines in Excellent condition up to 1980 and in Near-Mint from 1980 to the present. The autograph price represents a magazine signed by the athlete on the cover. For covers featuring multiple personalities, the autographed price is for an issue signed by all pictured players. Keep in mind that some issues don't show an autographed price—either the player pictured had already passed away, making it impossible for him to have signed, or the cover featured an artist's rendition of the game, but no particular player.

**Jackie Robinson
August 1949**

**Mickey Mantle
April 1953**

**Lew Burdette
March 1958**

Year	Month	Cover	Price	Signed
1946	September	Joe DiMaggio	$400.00	$600.00
1947	April	Leo Durocher	35.00	60.00
1947	June	Bob Feller	40.00	60.00
1947	July	Joe Cronin/Ed Dyer	40.00	200.00
1947	August	Ted Williams	60.00	250.00
1947	September	Joe & Dom DiMaggio	80.00	350.00
1948	April	Ted Williams	50.00	250.00
1948	May	Babe Ruth	65.00	—
1948	August	Stan Musial	50.00	75.00
1948	September	Joe DiMaggio/Ted Williams	100.00	500.00
1948	October	Lou Gehrig	65.00	—
1949	February	Lou Boudreau	25.00	50.00
1949	April	Bob Feller	40.00	50.00
1949	May	Enos Slaughter	30.00	50.00
1949	June	Hal Newhouser	25.00	40.00
1949	July	Lou Bourdreau/Joe Gordon	25.00	75.00
1949	August	Jackie Robinson	50.00	750.00
1949	September	Joe DiMaggio	80.00	300.00
1949	October	Christy Mathewson	35.00	—
1950	April	Casey Stengel	24.00	275.00
1950	May	Ralph Kiner	25.00	50.00
1950	June	Bob Lemon	25.00	50.00
1950	July	Stan Musial	45.00	60.00
1950	September	Don Newcombe	20.00	40.00
1950	October	World Series	20.00	—
1951	April	Baseball painting	20.00	—
1951	May	Baseball Jubilee	30.00	—
1951	August	Yogi Berra	30.00	50.00
1951	September	Ted Williams	45.00	250.00
1951	October	Jackie Robinson	45.00	750.00
1952	March	Gil McDougald	18.00	40.00
1952	April	Chico Carrasquel	15.00	25.00
1952	May	Alvin Dark	15.00	25.00
1952	June	Ralph Kiner	20.00	35.00
1952	July	Stan Musial	40.00	60.00
1952	August	Allie Reynolds	18.00	40.00
1952	October	Pee Wee Reese/Jackie Robinson	60.00	800.00
1952	November	Agganis/Reynolds/Robinson/Walker	20.00	700.00
1953	February	Bobby Shantz	18.00	30.00
1953	April	Mickey Mantle	90.00	300.00
1953	May	Bob Lemon	15.00	30.00
1953	June	Hank Bauer	15.00	25.00
1953	August	Warren Spahn	20.00	40.00
1953	September	Robin Roberts	20.00	35.00
1953	October	Roy Campanella	30.00	325.00

Year	Month	Cover	Price	Signed
1953	November	Johnny Lattner/Phil Rizzuto	30.00	60.00
1954	February	Ed Mathews	25.00	45.00
1954	March	Casey Stengel	20.00	250.00
1954	April	Don Newcombe	18.00	30.00
1954	May	Ted Kluszewski	18.00	90.00
1954	July	Stan Musial	35.00	60.00
1954	August	Minnie Minoso	18.00	35.00
1954	September	Duke Snider	30.00	50.00
1954	October	Al Rosen	18.00	30.00
1955	February	Alvin Dark	12.00	25.00
1955	April	Bob Turley	12.00	25.00
1955	May	Bobby Thomson	12.00	25.00
1955	August	Paul Richards	12.00	25.00
1955	September	Duke Snider	35.00	50.00
1955	October	Yogi Berra	25.00	50.00
1956	March	Walter Alston	12.00	175.00
1956	April	Larry Doby	12.00	30.00
1956	May	Bob Lemon	12.00	25.00
1956	June	Willie Mays	30.00	75.00
1956	July	Ted Williams	36.00	250.00
1956	October	Mickey Mantle	60.00	250.00
1957	March	Mickey Mantle	50.00	250.00
1957	April	Ed Mathews	15.00	35.00
1957	May	Campy/Kluszewski/Roberts/Spahn	15.00	450.00
1957	June	Early Wynn	15.00	30.00
1957	July	Al Kaline	24.00	45.00
1957	August	Joe Adcock	20.00	35.00
1957	September	Duke Snider	30.00	50.00
1958	January	Antonelli/Durocher/Mays/Reese/ Robinson/Snider	15.00	700.00
1958	March	Lou Burdette	12.00	25.00
1958	April	Nellie Fox	25.00	250.00
1958	May	Yogi Berra	18.00	40.00
1958	June	Willie Mays	20.00	60.00
1958	July	Herb Score	12.00	25.00
1958	August	Billy Martin	12.00	90.00
1958	September	Eddie Mathews	15.00	30.00
1958	October	Bob Turley	10.00	20.00
1959	March	Al Kaline	20.00	45.00
1959	May	Hank Bauer/Gil Hodges	12.00	325.00
1959	June	Mickey Mantle/Ted Williams	40.00	500.00
1959	July	Don Newcombe/Jimmy Piersall	10.00	35.00
1959	August	Colavito/Mantle/Mathews/Mays	25.00	325.00
1959	September	Stan Musial/Ted Williams	35.00	275.00
1959	October	Warren Spahn	20.00	40.00
1960	March	Chamberlain/Mays/Robinson	15.00	425.00
1960	April	Duke Snider	15.00	35.00
1960	May	Harmon Killebrew/Willie McCovey	15.00	65.00
1960	June	Don Drysdale	12.00	75.00
1960	July	Luis Aparicio/Frank Howard	10.00	40.00
1960	August	Mickey Mantle	30.00	240.00
1960	September	Colavito/Foxx/Mays	20.00	600.00
1960	October	Babe Ruth/Larry Sherry	16.00	25.00
1960	November	Roger Maris	30.00	500.00
1961	April	Frank Howard	8.00	20.00
1961	May	Dick Groat/Mickey Mantle	12.00	240.00
1961	June	Willie Mays	16.00	60.00
1961	August	Warren Spahn	12.00	30.00
1961	September	Joe DiMaggio/Mickey Mantle	40.00	450.00
1961	October	Wally Moon	8.00	20.00
1962	February	Roger Maris	30.00	500.00
1962	April	Norm Cash/Vada Pinson	8.00	30.00
1962	May	Baseball Sluggers	12.00	—
1962	June	Hank Aaron	14.00	50.00
1962	July	Mickey Mantle	30.00	225.00
1962	September	Ken Boyer/Stan Musial	16.00	140.00
1962	October	Willie Mays	12.00	50.00
1962	November	Tommy Davis/Jim Taylor	8.00	40.00
1963	February	Maury Wills	10.00	25.00
1963	April	Wilt Chamberlain/Stan Musial	10.00	140.00
1963	May	Yogi Berra/Mickey Mantle	30.00	250.00
1963	June	Maury Wills	10.00	25.00
1963	July	Rocky Colavito/Al Kaline	20.00	60.00
1963	August	Willie Mays	12.00	50.00
1963	September	Sandy Koufax	20.00	70.00
1963	October	Mickey Mantle	25.00	225.00
1963	November	Whitey Ford	10.00	30.00
1964	February	Sandy Koufax	10.00	60.00
1964	May	Warren Spahn	10.00	30.00
1964	July	Davis/Tresh/Yastrzemski	8.00	60.00
1964	August	Joe DiMaggio/Willie Mays	30.00	275.00
1964	September	Mickey Mantle	30.00	225.00
1964	October	Willie Mays	20.00	60.00
1964	November	Harmon Killebrew	12.00	30.00
1965	April	Dean Chance	6.00	30.00
1965	May	Sandy Koufax	12.00	60.00
1965	June	Willie Mays	10.00	50.00
1965	August	Mickey Mantle	20.00	225.00
1965	September	DiMaggio/Gehrig/F. Robinson	16.00	240.00
1965	October	Sandy Koufax/Maury Wills	10.00	75.00
1966	April	Paul Hornung/Willie Mays	10.00	75.00
1966	May	Maury Wills	8.00	25.00
1966	July	Mickey Mantle	20.00	225.00
1966	August	Frank Robinson	8.00	30.00
1966	September	Willie Mays	16.00	50.00
1966	October	Sandy Koufax	12.00	60.00
1967	February	Frank Robinson	8.00	30.00
1967	May	Mickey Mantle	20.00	225.00
1967	June	Willie Mays	10.00	50.00
1967	July	Richie Allen/Jim Ryun	8.00	30.00
1967	August	Roberto Clemente	25.00	325.00
1967	September	Pete Rose	20.00	40.00
1967	October	Orlando Cepeda/Johnny Unitas	20.00	65.00
1968	February	Carl Yastrzemski	12.00	30.00
1968	May	Willie Mays	10.00	50.00
1968	June	Carl Yastrzemski	10.00	30.00
1968	July	Hank Aaron	10.00	35.00
1968	August	Pete Rose	10.00	30.00
1968	September	Don Drysdale	10.00	60.00
1969	April	Mickey Mantle	40.00	225.00
1969	May	Cobb/DiMaggio/Koufax/Mays/Ruth	15.00	325.00
1969	June	Ted Williams	10.00	225.00
1969	July	Tony Conigliaro	12.00	150.00
1969	December	McLain/Orr/Simpson/Unseld	10.00	140.00
1970	February	Lew Alcindor/Gil Hodges	6.00	400.00
1970	May	Tom Seaver	9.00	35.00
1970	June	Harmon Killebrew	9.00	30.00
1970	August	Hank Aaron	10.00	40.00

**Billy Martin
August 1958**

**Joe DiMaggio/
Mickey Mantle
September 1961**

**Yogi Berra/
Mickey Mantle
May 1963**

**Mickey Mantle
September 1964**

Year	Month	Cover	Price	Signed
1970	September	Johnny Bench	15.00	40.00
1971	May	Flood/McLain/Williams	10.00	250.00
1971	June	Boog Powell	6.00	25.00
1971	July	Carl Yastrzemski	6.00	30.00
1971	September	Willie Mays	15.00	50.00
1971	October	Vida Blue	6.00	25.00
1972	June	Brooks Robinson	6.00	30.00
1972	August	Tom Seaver	9.00	35.00
1972	September	Frank Robinson	6.00	30.00
1972	October	Johnny Bench	18.00	40.00
1973	April	Steve Carlton	12.00	35.00
1973	August	Bobby Murcer	6.00	20.00
1973	September	Gaylord Perry	6.00	20.00
1973	October	Pennant Time	6.00	—
1974	May	Hank Aaron	15.00	40.00
1974	June	Pete Rose	9.00	30.00
1974	October	Reggie Jackson	9.00	50.00
1975	May	Frank Robinson	6.00	30.00
1975	July	Bobby Bonds	9.00	25.00
1975	August	Billy Martin	9.00	90.00
1976	April	Steve Garvey	9.00	25.00
1976	May	Tom Seaver	9.00	35.00
1976	August	Joe Morgan/Pete Rose	9.00	50.00
1977	July	Mark Fidrych	6.00	20.00
1977	October	Rod Carew	6.00	30.00
1978	April	Rich Gossage/Jim Hunter	6.00	30.00
1978	May	Graig Nettles	6.00	20.00
1978	July	Jim Rice	6.00	20.00
1978	August	Tom Seaver	9.00	35.00
1978	October	Carl Yastrzemski	9.00	25.00
1979	April	Pete Rose	9.00	30.00
1979	May	Ron Guidry	6.00	20.00
1979	June	Dave Parker	6.00	20.00
1979	July	Graig Nettles	6.00	20.00
1979	July	J.R. Richard	6.00	20.00
1979	October	Reggie Jackson	9.00	40.00
1980	April	Nolan Ryan	15.00	50.00
1980	May	Lou Piniella	6.00	25.00
1980	May	George Brett	12.00	40.00
1980	July	Gorman Thomas	4.00	15.00
1980	September	Tommy John	4.00	20.00
1981	April	Tug McGraw	6.00	20.00
1981	April	George Brett	8.00	40.00
1981	May	Billy Martin	6.00	80.00
1981	May	Mike Schmidt	4.00	45.00
1981	June	Don Sutton	4.00	25.00
1981	June	Dave Parker	4.00	20.00
1981	July	Goose Gossage	4.00	20.00
1981	July	Bruce Sutter	4.00	20.00
1982	April	Fernando Valenzuela	4.00	20.00
1982	May	Reggie Jackson	6.00	40.00
1982	June	Tom Seaver	6.00	30.00
1982	July	Billy Martin	4.00	80.00
1983	March	Top 100 salaries	4.00	—
1983	April	Steve Garvey	4.00	20.00
1983	May	Steve Carlton	5.00	25.00
1983	June	Gary Carter/Mike Schmidt	6.00	65.00
1983	July	Reggie Jackson	6.00	40.00
1984	March	Salaries	4.00	—

Year	Month	Cover	Price	Signed	Year	Month	Cover	Price	Signed
1984	April	Cal Ripken Jr.	8.00	60.00	1989	July	Jose Canseco	4.00	25.00
1984	June	Dale Murphy	4.00	20.00	1989	October	Doc Gooden/Dan Marino	6.00	115.00
1984	July	Managers	4.00	—	1990	March	Bo Jackson	5.00	25.00
1985	March	Gary Carter	4.00	25.00	1990	April	Canseco/Hershiser/Joyner	3.00	60.00
1985	April	Dwight Gooden	6.00	20.00	1990	May	Baseball preview	3.00	—
1985	May	George Brett	8.00	40.00	1990	June	Top 100 salaries	3.00	—
1985	June	Keith Hernandez/Gary Matthews	4.00	30.00	1990	July	Will Clark	3.00	20.00
1985	July	Kirk Gibson	4.00	20.00	1990	September	Bo Jackson	4.00	25.00
1986	April	Bret Saberhagen	4.00	20.00	1990	October	100 best players in sports	3.00	—
1986	April	Dwight Gooden	4.00	20.00	1991	March	Ken Griffey Jr.	4.00	55.00
1986	May	George Brett	6.00	35.00	1991	April	Baseball preview	3.00	—
1986	June	Top 100 salaries	4.00	—	1991	May	H. Johnson/Kelly/Reardon	3.00	40.00
1987	March	Clemens/Jordan/Schmidt	8.00	300.00	1991	May	Dunston/M. Perez/Saberhagen	3.00	35.00
1987	April	Darryl Strawberry	4.00	20.00	1991	June	Darryl Strawberry	3.00	20.00
1987	June	Top 100 salaries	4.00	—	1992	April	Butler/E. Davis/Strawberry	3.00	40.00
1987	July	Dave Parker/Mike Schmidt	4.00	65.00	1992	May	Cal Ripken Jr.	6.00	50.00
1988	March	Jefferies/Lovell/McDowell	4.00	30.00	1993	March	Dave Winfield	3.00	25.00
1988	April	Don Zimmer	4.00	15.00	1993	April	Barry Bonds	3.00	35.00
1988	April	Will Clark/Keith Hernandez	4.00	40.00	1994	April	Barry Bonds	3.00	35.00
1988	June	Top 100 salaries	4.00	—	1994	May	Mike Piazza	3.00	40.00
1989	March	Orel Hershiser	4.00	20.00	1995	January	Frank Thomas	3.00	40.00
1989	April	Baseball preview	4.00	—	1995	April	Michael Jordan (White Sox)	8.00	200.00
1989	June	Top 100 salaries	4.00	—					

**Mickey Mantle
April 1969**

**Joe Morgan/
Pete Rose
August 1976**

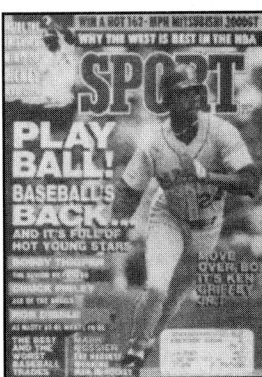

**Ken Griffey Jr.
March 1991**

SPORTS ILLUSTRATED

With more than 3 million weekly readers, *Sports Illustrated* is the godfather of American sports publications. Since the first issue—featuring "Night Baseball in Milwaukee" and the Braves' Eddie Mathews—rolled off the presses on August 16, 1954, *SI* has issued hundreds of baseball covers picturing virtually all of the game's biggest stars from the last 45 years.

Because of its brilliant action cover shots and tendency to feature strong single images, *SI* is especially popular with autograph collectors. The magazines are widespread and fairly inexpensive to collect, and they look terrific when signed with a blue or black Sharpie.

The prices below are for Near-Mint copies of the magazine, which often means that the mailing label is still intact. (Because the vast majority of *Sports Illustrateds* have subscriber mailing labels attached, and because the labels are tough to remove cleanly, the presence of the labels doesn't take much away from the magazines' value.)

On covers with multiple stars, the autograph price is for an issue signed by everyone pictured—adjust the price accordingly if not everyone featured has signed. Issues without autograph prices feature either deceased athletes who could not have signed, or artist's renditions that don't picture a specific or recognizable athlete.

Willie Mays
June 4, 1962

Al Kaline
May 11, 1964

Lou Brock
October 16, 1967

Year	Issue	Cover	Price	Autographed
1954	8/16	Eddie Mathews	$175.00	$225.00
1954	8/23	Masters of Golf (Mantle cards enclosed)	300.00	—
1955	4/11	Day/Durocher/Mays	125.00	300.00
1955	4/18	B. Lopez/Al Rosen	50.00	75.00
1955	5/30	Herb Score	20.00	40.00
1955	6/27	Duke Snider	60.00	90.00
1955	7/11	Yogi Berra	35.00	60.00
1955	8/1	Ted Williams	150.00	350.00
1955	8/15	Ed Mathews	25.00	50.00
1955	8/22	Don Newcombe	15.00	30.00
1955	9/26	Walter Alston	20.00	225.00
1956	1/2	Johnny Podres	40.00	60.00
1956	3/5	Cardinals at spring training (w/Musial)	35.00	75.00
1956	4/9	'56 Baseball Issue	25.00	—
1956	4/23	Billy Martin	20.00	125.00
1956	5/14	Al Kaline/Harvey Kuenn	25.00	150.00
1956	6/18	Mickey Mantle	125.00	350.00
1956	6/25	Warren Spahn	45.00	65.00
1956	7/9	All-Star preview	30.00	—
1956	7/16	Bell/Kluszewski/Post	30.00	130.00
1956	7/30	Joe Adcock	15.00	25.00
1956	8/20	Eddie Mathews	35.00	50.00
1956	9/10	Whitey Ford	45.00	20.00
1956	10/1	Mickey Mantle	50.00	250.00
1957	3/4	Mickey Mantle	65.00	275.00
1957	4/15	1957 Baseball Special	30.00	—
1957	4/22	Wally Moon	15.00	35.00
1957	5/13	Billy Pierce	15.00	20.00
1957	6/3	Clem Labine	15.00	40.00
1957	7/8	Stan Musial/Ted Williams	75.00	300.00
1957	7/22	Hank Bauer	20.00	40.00
1957	9/9	Roy McMillan	12.00	20.00
1957	9/30	World Series scouting report	20.00	—
1958	3/3	Braves at Spring training	15.00	—
1958	3/17	Sal Maglie	20.00	75.00
1958	3/31	Roy Sievers	20.00	40.00
1958	4/14	1958 baseball issue	25.00	—
1958	4/21	Del Crandall	25.00	50.00
1958	5/5	Gil McDougald	20.00	40.00
1958	5/19	Richie Ashburn	25.00	60.00
1958	6/2	Eddie Mathews	30.00	50.00
1958	6/23	Jackie Jensen	15.00	125.00
1958	7/7	All-Star preview	35.00	600.00
1958	7/28	Frank Thomas	15.00	35.00
1959	3/2	Fred Haney/Casey Stengel	17.00	375.00

Year	Issue	Cover	Price	Autographed
1959	4/13	Willie Mays	25.00	75.00
1959	5/4	Bob Turley	12.00	25.00
1959	6/15	Dodger Stadium	10.00	—
1959	8/10	Luis Aparicio/Nellie Fox	35.00	200.00
1959	9/28	Chicago White Sox	30.00	—
1960	3/7	Artist's view of spring training	10.00	—
1960	4/11	1960 baseball issue	20.00	—
1960	6/6	Red Schoendienst	25.00	40.00
1960	7/4	Comiskey Park	15.00	—
1960	7/18	Candlestick Park	20.00	—
1960	8/8	Dick Groat	25.00	35.00
1960	10/10	Vernon Law	20.00	30.00
1961	3/6	Miquel Cueller/Raul Sanchez	6.00	25.00
1961	4/10	1961 baseball issue	20.00	—
1961	.5/15	Cookie Lavagetto	15.00	65.00
1961	6/26	Ernie Broglio/Willie Mays	10.00	75.00
1961	7/31	Umpire	5.00	—
1961	10/2	Roger Maris	40.00	650.00
1961	10/9	Joey Jay	25.00	40.00
1962	3/5	Casey Stengel	15.00	225.00
1962	4/9	Frank Lary	30.00	45.00
1962	4/30	Luis Aparicio	25.00	45.00
1962	6/4	Willie Mays	40.00	80.00
1962	7/2	Mickey Mantle	85.00	300.00
1962	7/30	Ken Boyer	12.00	125.00
1962	8/20	Don Drysdale	25.00	125.00
1962	10/1	1962 World Series	15.00	—
1963	3/4	Sandy Koufax	30.00	80.00
1963	4/8	1963 baseball preview	30.00	—
1963	4/29	Art Mahaffey	20.00	30.00
1963	6/3	Bob Hope	25.00	60.00
1963	6/24	Roy Face	15.00	30.00
1963	7/22	Dick Groat	20.00	35.00
1963	9/2	Ron Fairly	15.00	10.00
1963	9/30	Whitey Ford	25.00	50.00
1964	3/2	Yogi Berra/Casey Stengel	20.00	250.00
1964	4/13	Sandy Koufax	35.00	85.00
1964	5/11	Al Kaline	30.00	50.00
1964	5/25	Frank Howard	15.00	25.00
1964	7/6	Alvin Dark	15.00	25.00
1964	8/10	Johnny Callison	20.00	35.00
1964	8/31	Brooks Robinson	25.00	45.00
1965	3/1	Bo Belinsky/Jim Bunning	20.00	40.00
1965	4/19	Baseball preview	20.00	—
1965	5/17	Bill Veeck	10.00	110.00
1965	6/21	Mickey Mantle	70.00	275.00
1965	7/12	Maury Wills	15.00	30.00
1965	8/9	Juan Marichal	30.00	50.00
1965	8/23	Tony Oliva	15.00	25.00
1965	10/4	World Series: Twins/Dodgers	10.00	—
1965	12/20	Sandy Koufax	35.00	85.00
1966	2/28	Leo Durocher/Eddie Stanky	15.00	140.00
1966	4/18	Dick Groat	20.00	35.00
1966	5/23	Sam McDowell	10.00	20.00
1966	6/6	Sonny Jackson/Joe Morgan	15.00	60.00
1966	7/11	Andy Etchebarren	10.00	20.00
1966	9/5	Harry Walker	10.00	25.00
1966	9/26	Gaylord Perry	25.00	40.00
1966	10/10	Brooks and Frank Robinson	35.00	85.00

**Rookies
March 11, 1968**

**Ted Williams
March 17, 1969**

**Billy Martin
July 21, 1969**

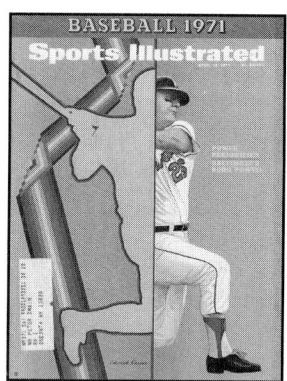

**Boog Powell
April 12, 1971**

**Jerry Grote
June 21, 1971**

**Willie Mays
May 22, 1972**

Year	Issue	Cover	Price	Autographed
1967	3/13	Jim Nash	10.00	20.00
1967	4/17	Maury Wills	12.00	15.00
1967	5/8	Ken Berry/Mickey Mantle	20.00	250.00
1967	5/15	Alston/Drysdale/Koufax/Wills	15.00	275.00
1967	6/5	Al Kaline	20.00	40.00
1967	7/3	Roberto Clemente	35.00	650.00
1967	7/31	The spitball	10.00	—
1967	8/21	Carl Yastrzemski	35.00	65.00
1967	9/4	Tim McCarver	15.00	25.00
1967	10/15	Lou Brock	15.00	35.00
1967	12/25	Carl Yastrzemski	30.00	60.00
1968	3/11	Top rookies (J. Bench)	30.00	90.00
1968	4/15	Baseball preview	10.00	30.00
1968	5/7	Ron Swoboda	9.00	20.00
1968	5/27	Pete Rose	30.00	50.00
1968	6/17	Don Drysdale	20.00	125.00
1968	7/8	Ted Williams	15.00	225.00
1968	7/29	Denny McLain	20.00	10.00
1968	8/19	Curt Flood	10.00	40.00
1968	9/2	Ken Harrelson	12.00	25.00
1968	9/23	Denny McLain	25.00	50.00
1968	10/7	Lou Brock/Bob Gibson	30.00	300.00
1969	3/17	Ted Williams	15.00	225.00
1969	4/14	Bill Freehan	15.00	30.00
1969	5/19	Walt Alston	15.00	250.00
1969	6/30	Ron Santo	15.00	30.00
1969	7/7	Reggie Jackson	30.00	75.00
1969	7/21	Billy Martin	15.00	100.00
1969	8/18	Henry Aaron	30.00	60.00
1969	9/8	Ernie Banks/Pete Rose	25.00	75.00
1969	10/5	Frank Robinson	15.00	35.00
1969	10/20	World Series: Mets/Orioles (B. Robinson)	20.00	40.00
1969	12/22	Tom Seaver	35.00	60.00
1970	2/23	Denny McLain	10.00	20.00
1970	3/23	Dick Allen	15.00	35.00
1970	4/13	Jerry Koosman	8.00	25.00
1970	5/25	Henry Aaron	20.00	50.00
1970	6/20	Tony Coniglaro	15.00	200.00
1970	7/13	Johnny Bench	20.00	45.00
1970	7/27	Willie Mays	20.00	60.00
1970	9/7	Bud Harrelson	10.00	15.00
1970	9/29	Danny Murtaugh	10.00	100.00
1970	10/19	World Series: Reds/Orioles	9.00	75.00
1971	3/22	Wes Parker	10.00	25.00
1971	4/12	Boog Powell	10.00	15.00
1971	5/3	Dave Duncan/Jim Fregosi	7.00	35.00
1971	5/31	Vida Blue	12.00	25.00
1971	6/21	Jerry Grote	7.00	25.00
1971	7/5	Alex Johnson	6.00	20.00
1971	8/2	Willie Stargell	15.00	35.00
1971	8/30	Ferguson Jenkins	15.00	35.00
1971	9/27	Maury Wills	10.00	15.00
1971	10/18	Frank Robinson	15.00	40.00
1972	3/13	Johnny Bench	15.00	40.00
1972	3/27	Vida Blue	10.00	25.00
1972	4/10	Joe Torre	10.00	25.00
1972	5/1	Willie Davis	6.00	20.00
1972	5/22	Willie Mays	15.00	55.00
1972	6/12	Dick Allen	8.00	25.00

Year	Issue	Cover	Price	Autographed
1972	7/3	Steve Blass	6.00	20.00
1972	8/21	Sparky Lyle	6.00	20.00
1972	9/25	Carlton Fisk	15.00	40.00
1972	10/23	Catfish Hunter	10.00	30.00
1973	3/12	Bill Melton	6.00	20.00
1973	4/9	Steve Carlton	10.00	30.00
1973	4/30	Chris Speier	9.00	20.00
1973	6/4	Wilbur Wood	7.00	20.00
1973	7/2	Ron Blomberg/Bobby Murcer	9.00	40.00
1973	7/30	Carlton Fisk	10.00	35.00
1973	8/20	Claude Osteen/Bill Russell	6.00	45.00
1973	9/24	Danny Murtaugh	6.00	100.00
1973	10/22	Bert Campaneris/John Milner	7.00	35.00
1974	3/18	Babe Ruth	7.00	—
1974	4/8	Pete Rose	15.00	40.00
1974	4/15	Henry Aaron	25.00	55.00
1974	5/27	Jim Wynn	6.00	20.00
1974	6/17	Reggie Jackson	9.00	45.00
1974	7/1	Rod Carew	12.00	20.00
1974	7/22	Lou Brock	12.00	30.00
1974	8/12	Mike Marshall	6.00	35.00
1974	10/7	Catfish Hunter	12.00	25.00
1974	10/21	Rollie Fingers	12.00	100.00
1975	3/3	Reds at spring training	10.00	75.00
1975	4/7	Steve Garvey	20.00	35.00
1975	6/2	Billy Martin	7.00	80.00
1975	6/16	Nolan Ryan	30.00	60.00
1975	7/7	Fred Lynn	15.00	30.00
1975	7/21	Jim Palmer/Tom Seaver	10.00	60.00
1975	8/11	The boom in baseball	3.00	—
1975	10/6	Reggie Jackson	9.00	45.00
1975	10/20	Johnny Bench/Luis Tiant	12.00	50.00
1975	11/3	Johnny Bench/Will McEnaney	7.00	40.00
1975	12/22	Pete Rose	25.00	50.00
1976	3/15	Bill Veeck	5.00	100.00
1976	4/12	Joe Morgan	20.00	40.00
1976	5/3	Mike Schmidt	15.00	45.00
1976	5/31	Yankees/Red Sox	12.00	50.00
1976	6/21	George Brett	15.00	45.00
1976	6/28	Bowie Kuhn	4.00	60.00
1976	7/12	Randy Jones	5.00	20.00
1976	8/30	Reggie Jackson	15.00	50.00
1976	10/11	George Foster	12.00	35.00
1976	11/1	Johnny Bench	15.00	40.00
1977	3/14	Tommy Lasorda	5.00	30.00
1977	3/28	Bump Wills	5.00	20.00
1977	4/11	Joe Rudi	5.00	20.00
1977	5/2	Reggie Jackson	8.00	40.00
1977	5/30	Dave Parker	8.00	50.00
1977	6/6	Mark Fidrych	8.00	25.00
1977	6/27	Tom Seaver	10.00	30.00
1977	7/18	Rod Carew/Ted Williams	5.00	225.00
1977	8/15	Sadaharu Oh	15.00	65.00
1977	8/29	Greg Luzinski	5.00	15.00
1977	10/24	Bill Russell/Thrumon Munson	15.00	225.00
1978	3/20	Clint Hurdle	5.00	15.00
1978	4/10	Rod Carew/George Foster	8.00	50.00
1978	4/24	Mark Fidrych	10.00	20.00
1978	7/31	Billy Martin	8.00	80.00

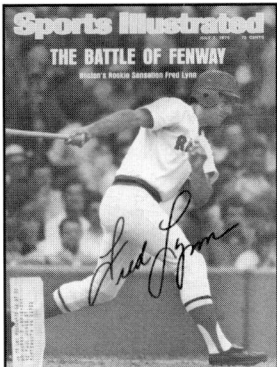

Fred Lynn
July 7, 1975

Bill Russell/
Thurman Munson
October 24, 1977

JimRice/Dave Parker
April 9, 1979

**Doug DeCinces/
Phil Garner
October 22, 1979**

**Steve Carlton
July 21, 1980**

**Kent Hrbek
July 5, 1982**

Year	Issue	Cover	Price	Autographed
1978	8/7	Pete Rose	15.00	40.00
1978	10/23	Lee Lacy	6.00	20.00
1979	3/5	Spring training	10.00	—
1979	3/19	Harry Chappas	5.00	15.00
1979	4/9	Dave Parker/Jim Rice	10.00	40.00
1979	4/30	George Bamberger	5.00	20.00
1979	5/28	Pete Rose	10.00	30.00
1979	6/18	Earl Weaver	5.00	20.00
1979	7/23	Nolan Ryan	20.00	50.00
1979	8/27	Baseball's Golden Oldies	7.00	130.00
1979	10/22	Doug DeCinces/Phil Garner	7.00	40.00
1980	3/24	Kirk Gibson	6.00	25.00
1980	4/7	Keith Hernandez	6.00	20.00
1980	6/9	Darrell Porter	5.00	20.00
1980	7/21	Steve Carlton	15.00	35.00
1980	8/4	Reggie Jackson	10.00	45.00
1980	8/18	J.R. Richard	12.00	35.00
1980	8/25	Orioles/Yankees	10.00	40.00
1980	10/6	Gary Carter	10.00	30.00
1980	10/27	Mike Schmidt	7.00	35.00
1981	1/5	Dave Winfield	10.00	35.00
1981	3/2	J.R. Richard	10.00	25.00
1981	3/16	Rollie Fingers	6.00	25.00
1981	4/13	George Brett/Mike Schmidt	12.00	65.00
1981	4/27	Keough/Kingman/Langford/McCatty/Norris	5.00	60.00
1981	5/18	Fernando Valenzuela	5.00	25.00
1981	6/8	Greg Luzinski	4.00	20.00
1981	6/22	The Strike	3.00	—
1981	7/27	Tom Seaver	10.00	25.00
1981	8/10	George Brett/Mike Schmidt	10.00	60.00
1981	8/17	Gary Carter	7.00	25.00
1981	10/26	Graig Nettles	5.00	20.00
1981	11/2	World Series: Dodgers/Yankees	5.00	25.00
1982	3/15	Reggie Jackson	10.00	45.00
1982	4/12	Steve Garvey	10.00	30.00
1982	5/17	Gaylord Perry	5.00	25.00
1982	7/5	Kent Hrbek	7.00	20.00
1982	7/19	Pete Rose/Carl Yastrzemski	7.00	60.00
1982	8/9	Dale Murphy	6.00	25.00
1982	9/6	Rickey Henderson	10.00	35.00
1982	10/11	Robin Yount	10.00	25.00
1982	10/25	Lee Smith/Robin Yount	10.00	50.00
1983	3/14	Morgan/Perez/Rose	12.00	75.00
1983	4/4	Gary Carter	6.00	25.00
1983	4/18	Tom Seaver	6.00	25.00
1983	4/25	Steve Garvey	6.00	20.00
1983	6/13	Rod Carew	8.00	25.00
1983	7/4	Dale Murphy	8.00	20.00
1983	7/18	Andre Dawson/Dave Stieb	8.00	35.00
1983	10/3	Steve Carlton	10.00	30.00
1983	10/24	Rick Dempsey	3.00	20.00
1984	3/12	George Brett	10.00	40.00
1984	4/2	Yogi Berra	10.00	30.00
1984	4/16	Rich Gossage/Graig Nettles	5.00	35.00
1984	4/23	Darryl Strawberry	6.00	25.00
1984	5/28	Alan Trammell	9.00	30.00
1984	6/11	Leon Durham	3.00	20.00
1984	8/27	Pete Rose	6.00	25.00
1984	9/24	Dwight Gooden/Rick Sutcliffe	3.00	35.00

Year	Issue	Cover	Price	Autographed
1984	10/22	Alan Trammell	9.00	30.00
1985	3/4	Mike Schmidt	10.00	40.00
1985	3/18	Fred Lynn	5.00	20.00
1985	3/25	Mays/Mantle/Ueberroth	5.00	325.00
1985	4/15	Dwight Gooden	5.00	20.00
1985	5/6	Billy Martin	5.00	80.00
1985	7/8	Fernando Valenzuela	5.00	20.00
1985	8/5	Pedro Guerrero	5.00	15.00
1985	8/19	Pete Rose	9.00	30.00
1985	9/2	Dwight Gooden	6.00	20.00
1985	9/23	Ozzie Smith	10.00	30.00
1985	10/28	Ozzie Smith	8.00	40.00
1985	11/4	Kansas City wins the World Series	6.00	—
1985	12/10	Kirk Gibson	6.00	20.00
1986	4/14	Wade Boggs	5.00	25.00
1986	5/12	Roger Clemens	5.00	30.00
1986	7/14	Bo Jackson	10.00	30.00
1986	7/28	Rickey Henderson	5.00	25.00
1986	8/4	Oil Can Boyd	5.00	15.00
1986	8/25	Ron Darling	5.00	15.00
1986	10/6	Darryl Strawberry	5.00	20.00
1986	10/20	Doug Decinces/Bobby Grich	6.00	25.00
1986	10/27	Gary Carter/Jim Rice	6.00	20.00
1986	11/3	Ray Knight	5.00	20.00
1987	3/9	The Ripkens: Billy/Cal Jr./Cal Sr.	15.00	125.00
1987	4/6	Joe Carter/Cory Snyder	4.00	30.00
1987	4/20	Major League Salaries	4.00	—
1987	4/27	Rob Deer	5.00	15.00
1987	5/11	Reggie Jackson	10.00	40.00
1987	5/25	Eric Davis	5.00	20.00
1987	7/6	A Day in the Life of Baseball	5.00	—
1987	7/13	Don Mattingly/Darryl Strawberry	5.00	50.00
1987	7/20	Andre Dawson	5.00	15.00
1987	8/17	Alan Trammell	5.00	20.00
1987	9/27	Ozzie Smith	7.00	25.00
1987	10/5	Lloyd Moseby	5.00	15.00
1987	10/19	Greg Gagne	5.00	15.00
1987	10/26	Dan Gladden	5.00	15.00
1987	11/2	Twins win the World Series	9.00	—
1988	3/7	Kirk Gibson	5.00	15.00
1988	3/14	Pam Postema	3.00	20.00
1988	4/4	Will Clark/Mark McGwire	10.00	60.00
1988	5/2	Billy Ripken	5.00	20.00
1988	5/9	Pete Rose	7.00	25.00
1988	6/6	Coaches who lost their Jobs	4.00	30.00
1988	7/11	Darryl Strawberry	5.00	20.00
1988	7/18	Casey at the Bat	5.00	—
1988	9/26	Dwight Evans	7.00	20.00
1988	10/17	Jose Canseco	6.00	25.00
1988	10/31	Orel Hershiser	6.00	20.00
1988	12/19	Orel Hershiser	10.00	25.00
1989	3/6	Wade Boggs	5.00	25.00
1989	4/1	Pete Rose	5.00	25.00
1989	4/3	Benito Santiago	5.00	20.00
1989	5/1	Nolan Ryan	10.00	40.00
1989	5/8	Jon Peters	4.00	15.00
1989	6/12	Bo Jackson	5.00	20.00
1989	7/3	Pete Rose	5.00	25.00
1989	7/10	Rick Reuschel	5.00	15.00

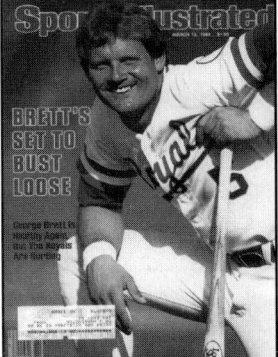

**George Brett
March 12, 1984**

**Darryl Strawberry/
Don Mattingly
July 13, 1987**

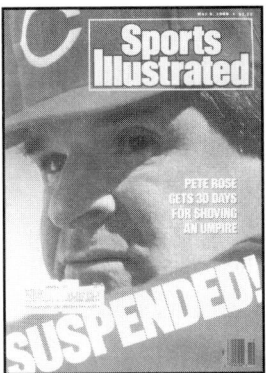

**Pete Rose
May 9, 1988**

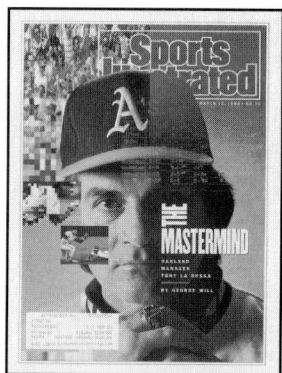

**Tony La Russa
March 12, 1990**

**Mickey Mantle/
Roger Maris
May 27, 1991**

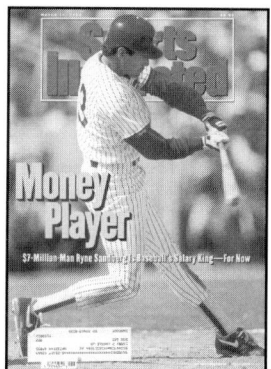

**Ryne Sandberg
March 16, 1992**

Year	Issue	Cover	Price	Autographed
1989	7/24	Greg Jefferies	6.00	20.00
1989	10/16	Rickey Henderson	6.00	30.00
1989	10/30	World Series earthquake	5.00	—
1990	3/12	Tony La Russa	3.00	15.00
1990	4/16	Ted Williams	10.00	225.00
1990	5/7	Ken Griffey Jr.	10.00	50.00
1990	5/28	Will Clark	5.00	25.00
1990	6/4	Lenny Dykstra	5.00	20.00
1990	7/9	Darryl Strawberry	4.00	20.00
1990	7/23	Narciso Elrira	1.00	12.00
1990	8/20	Jose Canseco	5.00	20.00
1990	10/1	Bobby Bonilla	4.00	20.00
1990	10/22	Dennis Eckersley	4.00	20.00
1990	10/29	Chris Sabo	4.00	15.00
1991	3/4	Darryl Strawberry	3.00	20.00
1991	4/15	Nolan Ryan	15.00	45.00
1991	5/13	Roger Clemens	4.00	35.00
1991	5/27	Mickey Mantle/Roger Maris	10.00	200.00
1991	7/1	Orel Hershiser	5.00	20.00
1991	7/29	Cal Ripken Jr.	12.00	50.00
1991	9/30	Ramon Martinez	3.00	20.00
1991	10/21	Kirby Puckett	7.00	25.00
1991	10/28	Dan Gladden/Gregg Olson	5.00	20.00
1991	11/4	World Series	3.00	—
1992	3/16	Ryne Sandberg	5.00	25.00
1992	4/6	Kirby Puckett	5.00	25.00
1992	4/27	Deion Sanders	4.00	25.00
1992	5/4	Barry Bonds	6.00	25.00
1992	5/18	Errors	2.00	—
1992	6/1	Mark McGwire	3.00	25.00
1992	7/6	Steve Palermo	2.00	15.00
1992	8/24	Deion Sanders	4.00	25.00
1992	10/5	George Brett	5.00	30.00
1992	10/19	Dave Winfield	5.00	30.00
1992	10/26	John Smoltz	8.00	20.00
1992	11/2	Blue Jays	4.00	—
1992	12/28	Willie Mays	10.00	50.00
1993	3/1	George Steinbrenner	3.00	25.00
1993	3/22	Dwight Gooden	3.00	20.00
1993	4/5	David Cone	3.00	20.00
1993	5/3	Joe DiMaggio	8.00	225.00
1993	5/24	Barry Bonds	4.00	25.00
1993	7/5	Mike Piazza	4.00	25.00
1993	7/19	Bob Gibson/Denny McLain	5.00	35.00
1993	9/27	Ron Gant	3.00	20.00
1993	11/1	Joe Carter	5.00	20.00
1994	3/14	Michael Jordan (White Sox)	7.00	150.00
1994	4/4	Ken Griffey Jr.	7.00	60.00
1994	4/4	Ken Griffey Jr. (Canadian Issue)	25.00	75.00
1994	4/18	Mickey Mantle	7.00	200.00
1994	5/23	Braves vs Mets	4.00	—
1994	6/6	Ken Griffey Jr.	7.00	60.00
1994	7/18	Mike Mussina	4.00	20.00
1994	8/8	Frank Thomas	6.00	45.00
1994	8/16	Eddie Mathews	6.00	20.00
1995	2/27	Darryl Stawberry	3.00	20.00
1995	5/1	Cal Ripken Jr.	5.00	60.00
1995	6/5	Matt Williams	3.00	20.00
1995	7/10	Hideo Nomo	5.00	30.00

Year	Issue	Cover	Price	Autographed
1995	8/7	Cal Ripken Jr.	8.00	60.00
1995	8/14	Greg Maddux	5.00	45.00
1995	8/21	Mickey Mantle	7.00	—
1995	9/11	Cal Ripken Jr.	5.00	60.00
1995	10/2	Mo Vaughn	4.00	20.00
1995	10/16	Ken Griffey Jr.	5.00	55.00
1995	11/6	Greg Maddux	5.00	45.00
1995	12/19	Cal Ripken Jr.	5.00	60.00
1996	3/18	Jay Buhner and son	2.00	20.00
1996	4/1	Manny Ramirez	3.00	20.00
1996	5/6	Albert Belle	3.00	20.00
1996	5/20	Marge Schott	3.00	15.00
1996	7/8	Alex Rodriguez	3.00	30.00
1996	8/19	Al Simmons	3.00	—
1996	10/14	Roberto Alomar	3.00	25.00
1996	10/21	Derek Jeter	3.00	30.00
1996	11/4	Joe Girardi/John Wetteland	3.00	30.00
1996	11/25	Ted Williams	3.00	200.00
1997	2/24	Derek Jeter/Alex Rodriguez	3.00	50.00
1997	3/31	Randy Johnson	3.00	30.00
1997	5/5	Jackie Robinson	3.00	—
1997	7/28	Tony Gwynn	3.00	40.00
1997	8/11	Ivan Rodriguez	3.00	30.00
1997	11/3	Florida Marlins (Edgar Renteria)	3.00	20.00

**Jay Buhner
March 18, 1998**

**Alex Rodriguez
July 8, 1996**

STREET & SMITH

S treet & Smith's Official Yearbook is considered the most comprehensive baseball annual on the market. The in-depth editorial content is so extensive that it appeals to both casual and hard-core fans. At first, *Street & Smith* was issued once per year, but the frequency increased to thrice yearly in 1963. Today, Street & Smith issues just one magazine per year, with several different regional covers.

Most covers have one single image, which makes the magazine perfect for autograph hounds. Although *Street & Smith* isn't as popular as *Sports Illustrated*, many baseball fans enjoy collecting the magazine. But only the most devoted collector chases all the regional covers issued today.

The prices below are for magazines in Excellent condition through 1980, and in Near-Mint condition from 1980 to the present. The autographed price is for an issue signed by the player pictured on the cover. For issues with multiple players on the cover the autographed price reflects a signature from all players pictured. Adjust the price accordingly if you're missing some sigs. Issues don't have autograph prices if the player pictured has already passed away, making it impossible for him to sign, or if the cover featured an artist's rendition of the game, but no particular player.

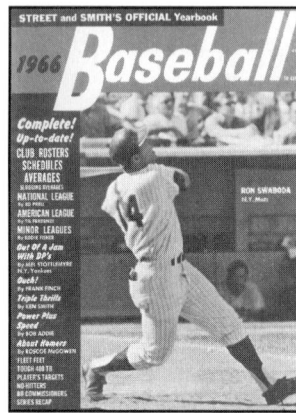

Ron Swoboda 1966

Mike Flanagan 1980

Mike Schmidt 1981

Year	Cover	Price	Signed
1941	Bob Feller	$200.00	$225.00
1942	Howard Pollett	120.00	150.00
1943	Play at the plate	100.00	—
1944	Joe McCarthy	100.00	250.00
1945	N.Y. Giants	100.00	—
1946	Dick Fowler	100.00	125.00
1947	Leo Durocher	75.00	125.00
1948	Joe DiMaggio	125.00	225.00
1949	Lou Boudreau	75.00	100.00
1950	Joe DiMaggio/Ted Williams	125.00	600.00
1951	Joe DiMaggio/Ralph Kiner	125.00	350.00
1952	Stan Musial	100.00	125.00
1953	Mickey Mantle	150.00	350.00
1954	Eddie Mathews	90.00	120.00
1955	Yogi Berra	90.00	120.00
1956	Mickey Mantle/Duke Snider	100.00	325.00
1957	Berra/Larsen/Mantle	100.00	350.00
1958	Bob Buhl/Lew Burdette	75.00	125.00
1959	Burdette/Mantle/Spahn	70.00	325.00
1960	Luis Aparicio/Nellie Fox	60.00	325.00
1961	Dick Groat	50.00	60.00
1962	Roger Maris	60.00	350.00
1963	Don Drysdale	50.00	120.00
1963	Stan Musial	50.00	75.00
1963	Tom Tresh	40.00	60.00
1964	Mickey Mantle	75.00	275.00
1964	Sandy Koufax	50.00	100.00
1964	Warren Spahn	50.00	75.00
1965	Brooks Robinson	50.00	75.00
1965	Ken Boyer	40.00	120.00
1965	Dean Chance	40.00	50.00
1966	Rocky Colavitio	50.00	65.00
1966	Ron Swoboda	30.00	40.00
1966	Sandy Koufax	40.00	90.00
1967	Andy Etchebarren	35.00	50.00
1967	Juan Marichal	35.00	50.00
1967	Harmon Killebrew	35.00	60.00
1968	Orlando Cepeda	35.00	50.00
1968	Jim McGlothin	35.00	45.00
1968	Jim Lonborg	35.00	45.00
1969	Bob Gibson/Denny McLain	35.00	65.00
1970	Tom Seaver	40.00	70.00
1970	Bill Singer	30.00	40.00
1970	Harmon Killebrew	30.00	50.00

Year	Cover	Price	Signed	Year	Cover	Price	Signed
1971	Johnny Bench	30.00	50.00	1988	Mark McGwire/Benito Santiago	10.00	40.00
1971	Gaylord Perry	30.00	45.00	1988	George Bell	10.00	25.00
1971	Boog Powell	25.00	40.00	1989	Jose Canseco	10.00	30.00
1972	Roberto Clemente	40.00	—	1989	Kevin McReynolds	10.00	20.00
1972	Vida Blue	20.00	35.00	1989	Mike Greenwell	10.00	30.00
1972	Joe Torre	20.00	35.00	1989	Orel Hershiser	10.00	25.00
1973	Steve Carlton	20.00	50.00	1990	50th Anniversary	5.00	—
1973	Johnny Bench	20.00	45.00	1991	Lou Piniella	5.00	20.00
1973	Reggie Jackson	25.00	60.00	1991	Ryne Sandberg	5.00	35.00
1974	Hank Aaron	25.00	50.00	1991	Ramon Martinez	5.00	25.00
1974	Pete Rose	20.00	40.00	1991	Dave Justice	5.00	20.00
1974	Nolan Ryan	35.00	75.00	1991	Ken Griffey Jr.	5.00	50.00
1975	Jim "Catfish" Hunter	15.00	30.00	1991	Doug Drabek	5.00	20.00
1975	Mike Marshall	15.00	25.00	1991	Kelly Gruber	5.00	20.00
1975	Lou Brock	15.00	30.00	1991	Nolan Ryan	5.00	50.00
1976	Fred Lynn	15.00	30.00	1992	Roger Clemens	5.00	40.00
1976	Joe Morgan	15.00	30.00	1992	Roberto Alomar	5.00	30.00
1976	Davey Lopez	15.00	30.00	1992	Terry Pendleton	5.00	20.00
1977	Mark Fidrych	15.00	25.00	1992	Bobby Bonilla	5.00	25.00
1977	Randy Jones	15.00	25.00	1992	Fielder/Larkin/Sandberg/Thomas	5.00	100.00
1977	Thurman Munson	25.00	275.00	1992	Bagwell/Sierra/Smith	5.00	60.00
1978	Reggie Jackson	20.00	50.00	1992	Abbott/Butler/Canseco/Clark	5.00	50.00
1978	Steve Garvey	15.00	25.00	1992	Kirby Puckett	5.00	40.00
1978	Rod Carew	15.00	30.00	1993	Roger Clemens	5.00	40.00
1979	J.R. Richard	15.00	30.00	1993	Jim Abbott	5.00	20.00
1979	Burt Hooton	15.00	25.00	1993	Dennis Eckersley	5.00	25.00
1979	Ron Guidry	15.00	25.00	1993	Darryl Strawberry	5.00	20.00
1980	Mike Flanagan	15.00	25.00	1993	Tom Glavine	5.00	30.00
1980	Brian Downing	15.00	25.00	1993	Barry Larkin	5.00	30.00
1980	Joe Niekro	15.00	30.00	1993	Ryne Sandberg	5.00	35.00
1981	Mike Schmidt	15.00	50.00	1993	Roberto Alomar	5.00	25.00
1981	Rickey Henderson	15.00	50.00	1994	Aaron Sele	5.00	20.00
1981	George Brett	15.00	50.00	1994	Lenny Dykstra	5.00	20.00
1982	Rich Gossage/Pete Rose	15.00	50.00	1994	Carlos Baerga	5.00	20.00
1982	Nolan Ryan	25.00	60.00	1994	Frank Thomas	5.00	50.00
1982	Rollie Fingers/Tom Seaver	15.00	55.00	1994	Paul Molitor	5.00	30.00
1983	Robin Yount	15.00	45.00	1994	Dave Justice	5.00	25.00
1983	Steve Carlton	15.00	35.00	1994	Barry Bonds	5.00	40.00
1983	Doug DeCinces	15.00	25.00	1994	Mike Piazza	5.00	50.00
1983	Phil Niekro	15.00	35.00	1995	Roger Clemens	5.00	40.00
1984	Rick Dempsey/Scott McGregor	15.00	45.00	1995	Jimmy Key/Bret Saberhagen	5.00	30.00
1984	Carlton Fisk	15.00	35.00	1995	Barry Larkin/Kenny Lofton	5.00	50.00
1984	Dale Murphy	15.00	30.00	1995	Frank Thomas	5.00	50.00
1984	Pedro Guerrero	15.00	25.00	1995	Moises Alou/Joe Carter	5.00	40.00
1985	Dwight Gooden	10.00	25.00	1995	Greg Maddux	5.00	50.00
1985	Tigers Celebrate	10.00	—	1995	Matt Williams	5.00	25.00
1985	Steve Garvey	10.00	20.00	1995	Tony Gwynn	5.00	35.00
1986	Dwight Gooden/Don Mattingly	10.00	50.00	1995	Gary Sheffield	5.00	25.00
1986	Royals Celebrate	10.00	—	1995	Andres Galarraga	5.00	25.00
1986	Jesse Barfield/Ernie Whitt	10.00	30.00	1995	Jeff Bagwell	5.00	40.00
1987	Gary Carter/Jesse Orosco	10.00	40.00	1995	Cal Ripken Jr.	5.00	50.00
1987	Roger Clemens	10.00	40.00	1995	Lenny Dykstra	5.00	20.00
1987	Mike Scott	10.00	20.00	1995	Mike Piazza	5.00	50.00
1987	Wally Joyner	10.00	20.00	1995	Cecil Fielder	5.00	20.00
1987	Joe Carter	10.00	25.00	1996	Mo Vaughn	5.00	35.00
1988	Jeff Reardon	10.00	20.00	1996	Paul O'Neill	5.00	25.00
1988	Ozzie Smith	10.00	30.00	1996	Cal Ripken Jr.	5.00	50.00
1988	Don Mattingly	10.00	40.00	1996	Sammy Sosa	5.00	30.00
1988	Dale Murphy	10.00	25.00	1996	Kenny Lofton	5.00	30.00

Year	Cover	Price	Signed	Year	Cover	Price	Signed
1996	Greg Maddux	5.00	50.00	1997	Chipper Jones	5.00	40.00
1996	Ken Griffey Jr.	5.00	50.00	1997	Gary Sheffield	5.00	25.00
1996	Dante Bichette	5.00	20.00	1997	Juan Gonzalez/Brian Jordan	5.00	40.00
1996	Hideo Nomo	5.00	30.00	1997	Albert Belle/Sammy Sosa	5.00	50.00
1997	Mo Vaughn	5.00	35.00	1997	Ellis Burks	5.00	20.00
1997	Bernard Gilkey/Derek Jeter	5.00	40.00	1997	Alex Rodriguez	5.00	40.00
1997	Brady Anderson	5.00	20.00	1997	Ken Caminiti/Todd Hollandsworth	5.00	40.00
1997	Barry Larkin/Jim Thome	5.00	50.00	1997	Roger Clemens/Henry Rodriguez	5.00	60.00

LIFE, NEWSWEEK, AND TIME

**Life Magazine
May 1, 1939 & September 1, 1941**

LIFE

Life doesn't have a huge following among sports collectors, but don't blame that on the lack of great cover shots. Some of the best players in baseball have graced the cover of this magazine devoted to vivid pictures. The Joe DiMaggio issue from 1939 and the Mickey Mantle cover from 1956 are tremendously popular among autograph collectors. Ted Williams, Jackie Robinson, Roy Campanella, and Sandy Koufax round out an impressive list of baseball immortals who have appeared on *Life* covers. Issues of *Life* are more common than other magazines, keeping the prices lower for collectors on the secondary market. *Life* is still published monthly and continues to be a benchmark for great photographs.

Year	Month	Cover	Price	Signed
1938	April	John Winsett	$20.00	$60.00
1939	May	Joe DiMaggio	100.00	300.00
1940	April	John Rucker	15.00	50.00
1941	September	Ted Williams	100.00	300.00
1946	April	Charles Barrett	15.00	60.00
1948	April	Dodger rookies	10.00	—
1949	August	Joe DiMaggio	60.00	250.00
1950	May	Jackie Robinson	40.00	350.00
1953	June	Roy Campanella	40.00	350.00
1953	September	Casey Stengel	25.00	350.00
1956	June	Mickey Mantle	60.00	250.00
1957	October	Braves Motorcade	20.00	—
1958	April	Willie Mays	25.00	75.00
1958	July	Roy Campanella	40.00	350.00
1961	August	Mickey Mantle/Roger Maris	50.00	800.00
1962	April	Richard Burton (w/Mantle cards)	125.00	—
1962	September	Don Drysdale	20.00	125.00

Year	Month	Cover	Price	Signed
1963	August	Sandy Koufax	25.00	75.00
1965	July	Mickey Mantle	40.00	240.00
1967	September	Carl Yastrzemski	25.00	50.00
1969	September	Jerry Koosman	15.00	25.00

NEWSWEEK

Newsweek has a rich history of baseball covers. Connie Mack, Babe Ruth, and Ted Williams are among the more popular cover subjects that collectors have chased since the magazine's first baseball cover in 1933. Despite a fairly large circulation, issues of *Newsweek* can be tough to find because so many readers discarded last week's issue when the new one arrived.

Incidentally, the 1934 cover of Babe Ruth could have been signed by "The Bambino" shortly before he died, making for a truly unique collectible.

Year	Month	Cover	Price	Signed
1933	April	Carl Hubbell	$60.00	$100.00
1933	September	Connie Mack	40.00	400.00
1933	September	Clark Griffith	40.00	400.00
1933	December	Judge Kenesaw Landis	40.00	700.00
1934	February	Babe Ruth	75.00	2,500.00
1934	March	Mel Ott	40.00	550.00
1934	October	Mickey Cochrane	60.00	400.00
1935	April	Judge Kenesaw Landis	50.00	700.00
1936	October	Carl Hubbell	50.00	100.00
1937	October	Carl Hubbell	30.00	80.00
1938	April	Rudy York	20.00	—
1938	October	Gabby Hartnett/Joe McCarthy	30.00	450.00
1939	June	Abner Doubleday	50.00	—
1946	September	Ted Willliams	50.00	250.00
1947	June	Bob Feller	40.00	60.00
1947	October	Brooklyn World Series	30.00	—
1948	April	Joe McCarthy/Bill Southworth	30.00	200.00
1949	August	Branch Rickey	25.00	750.00
1950	April	Mel Parnell	15.00	20.00
1952	March	Dodgers Spring Training	12.00	—
1954	October	Bob Feller/Bob Lemon	30.00	70.00
1955	October	World Series	20.00	—
1956	June	Mickey Mantle	60.00	260.00
1957	July	Stan Musial	40.00	70.00
1959	August	Casey Stengel	25.00	225.00
1961	August	Mickey Mantle/Roger Maris	20.00	750.00
1965	April	The Astrodome	10.00	—
1965	October	Sandy Koufax	20.00	60.00
1973	August	Hank Aaron/Babe Ruth	20.00	50.00
1975	June	Nolan Ryan	20.00	50.00

Assortment of Time Magazines

TIME

Perhaps the most sought-after baseball cover of *Time* is the July 1936 issue featuring Joe DiMaggio. Autograph collectors consider this issue a staple of DiMaggio collectibles. As with *Newsweek*, many readers threw out their issues of *Time* when a new issue arrived, resulting in scarcity in the hobby today. Collectors can expect to pay upward of $500 for the 1925 issue with Hall of Famer Goerge Sisler on the cover. But not every baseball-related issue of *Time* will cost you a fortune. In 1995 Time honored Cal Ripken Jr. for breaking Lou Gehrig's consecutive game played record. This issue can usually be found for $5 on the secondary market.

Year	Month	Cover	Price	Signed
1925	March	George Sisler	$500.00	$800.00
1927	March	Connie Mack	250.00	650.00
1928	July	Rogers Hornsby	200.00	600.00
1929	July	Jimmy Foxx	150.00	450.00
1929	October	W. Wrigley Jr.	100.00	400.00
1930	August	W. Robinson	125.00	350.00
1932	March	Gabby Street	100.00	300.00
1932	September	Colonel Jacob Ruppert	75.00	350.00
1934	July	Lefty Gomez	75.00	225.00
1935	April	Dizzy Dean	75.00	300.00
1935	October	Mickey Cochrane	75.00	400.00
1936	July	Joe Dimaggio	450.00	700.00
1936	October	Lou Gehrig/Carl Hubbell	250.00	1,500.00
1937	April	Bob Feller	100.00	125.00
1938	August	Happy Chandler	65.00	200.00
1945	July	Mel Ott	50.00	300.00
1947	April	Leo Durocher	40.00	250.00
1947	September	Jackie Robinson	85.00	400.00
1948	October	Joe Dimaggio	200.00	400.00
1949	September	Stan Musial	150.00	200.00
1950	April	Ted Williams	200.00	400.00
1951	October	Bert Lahr	30.00	75.00
1952	April	Eddie Stanky	35.00	75.00
1953	July	Mickey Mantle	125.00	375.00
1954	July	Willie Mays	200.00	250.00
1955	June	Gwen Verdon	25.00	75.00
1955	July	Augusta Bush	25.00	75.00
1955	August	Roy Campanella	65.00	325.00
1955	October	Casey Stengel	40.00	250.00

Year	Month	Cover	Price	Signed
1956	May	Robin Roberts	40.00	75.00
1957	July	Berdie Tebbetts	25.00	75.00
1958	April	Walter O'Malley	25.00	175.00
1959	August	Rocky Colavito	30.00	75.00
1964	September	Hank Bauer	30.00	50.00
1966	June	Juan Marichal	40.00	60.00
1967	October	Carl Yastrzemski	25.00	50.00
1968	September	Denny McLain	30.00	50.00
1969	September	New York Mets	30.00	—
1971	August	Vida Blue	25.00	40.00
1972	July	Johnny Bench	25.00	50.00
1974	June	Reggie Jackson	30.00	75.00
1975	August	Charles Finley	15.00	125.00
1976	April	Babe Ruth	10.00	—
1977	July	Rod Carew	15.00	40.00
1981	May	Billy Martin	15.00	100.00
1985	August	Pete Rose	15.00	30.00
1986	April	Dwight Gooden	5.00	20.00
1989	July	Pete Rose	5.00	25.00
1992	January	Ted Turner	5.00	25.00
1994	August	Strike	5.00	—
1995	September	Cal Ripken Jr. (corner)	5.00	60.00

**Time Magazine
June 3, 1974**

MEDIA GUIDES

oster sheets and roster booklets were the first "media guides." They were issued to journalists in the 1920s to provide player information to be used in radio broadcasts and newspaper stories. These original guides provided little more than a complete roster and some player biographies and statistics, and were avilable only to ballpark insiders. It wasn't until much later that the guides were sold to the public.

Over the years, the original booklets have evolved into 4x9-inch books with several hundred pages full of stats, including information about team executives, players, minor league affiliates, prospects, team history, and spring training and post-season results. There's so much information—the 1998 Chicago White Sox media guide includes 10 pages on Frank Thomas alone—that the guides are popular with collectors and the general public. In fact, media guides are the most popular team-issued publications among collectors.

Most recent guides are readily available and give fans a chance to get to know their favorite team. Guides from the past 10 years can usually be found for the cover price or slightly more. Guides from the first half of the century, before the advent of mass production and distribution, are of course harder to find and more expensive. Collectors should also look out for media guides from a team's first season, from the first year in a new city or new ballpark, or with star players on the cover.

The list below includes original roster sheets, roster booklets, and media guides in Excellent condition.

Atlanta Braves

Year	Cover	Price
1966	Baseball scene	$40.00
1967	Felipe Alou	35.00
1968	Baseball scene	30.00
1969	Baseball scene	25.00
1970	Hank Aaron	20.00
1971	Baseball scene	20.00
1972	Baseball scene	15.00
1973	Baseball scene	15.00
1974	Baseball scene	10.00
1975	Baseballs	10.00
1976	Dave Bristol	10.00
1977	Cap	10.00
1978	Fulton County Stadium	10.00
1979	Phil Niekro	10.00
1980	Baseball/stadium	8.00
1981	Bob Horner/Dale Murphy	8.00
1982	Joe Torre	6.00
1983	Bedrosian/Murphy/Niekro/Torre	6.00
1984	Teamlogo	6.00
1985	Dale Murphy/Bruce Sutter	6.00
1986	Bobby Cox/Chuck Tanner	6.00
1987	Uniform	6.00
1988	Dale Murphy	8.00
1989	Gant/Glavine/Perry/Smith/Thomas	10.00
1990	25th Anniversary	10.00
1991	Ron Gant/David Justice	10.00
1992	Greg Olson/John Smoltz	10.00
1993	N.L. Champions	10.00
1994	Maddux/McGriff/Justice/Glavine	7.00
1995	30th Season in Atlanta	8.00
1996	World Series trophy	5.00
1997	Maddux/Smoltz/Glavine jerseys	5.00

Baltimore Orioles

Year	Cover	Price
1954	Mascot	$100.00
1955	Mascot	100.00
1956	Mascot	100.00
1957	Mascot	100.00
1958	Mascot	100.00
1959	Mascot	100.00
1960	Mascot	100.00
1961	Mascot	75.00
1962	Mascot	80.00
1963	Mascot	75.00
1964	Mascot	75.00
1965	Hank Bauer	40.00
1966	Mascot	40.00
1967	Dave McNally/Brooks Robinson	40.00
1968	Memorial Stadium	40.00
1969	Baseball scene	25.00
1970	Dugout	25.00
1971	World Series celebration	20.00
1972	Mascot with pennants	15.00
1973	Player	10.00
1974	Players	10.00
1975	Baseball scene	10.00
1976	Team logo	10.00
1977	Palmer/May/Belanger	15.00
1978	Earl Weaver	12.00
1979	25th Anniversary caps	10.00
1980	Baseball scene	6.00

Year	Cover	Price
1981	Locker room	6.00
1982	Team logo/mascot	6.00
1983	Frank and Brooks Robinson	8.00
1984	World Series	6.00
1985	Bumbry/Palmer/Singleton	7.00
1986	Eddie Murray/Cal Ripken Jr.	8.00
1987	Cal Ripken Sr.	6.00
1988	Team logo	10.00
1989	Uniforms	10.00
1990	Baseball scenes	10.00
1991	Stadium	10.00
1992	Camden Yards	10.00
1993	Camden Yards	10.00
1994	150 Years of Baseball in Baltimore	7.00
1995	Cal Ripken Jr.	20.00
1996	Davey Johnson	5.00
1997	Cartoon	5.00

Boston Braves

Year	Cover	Price
1927	Roster sheet	$125.00
1928	Roster sheet	100.00
1929	Roster sheet	100.00
1930	Roster sheet	100.00
1931	Roster booklet—Mascot	100.00
1932	Roster booklet—Mascot	100.00
1933	Roster booklet—Mascot	100.00
1934	Roster booklet—Mascot	100.00
1935	Roster booklet—Mascot	100.00
1936	Roster booklet	75.00
1937	Roster booklet	75.00
1938	Roster booklet—Bees Baseball	75.00
1939	Roster booklet	75.00
1940	Roster booklet—Casey Stengel	75.00
1941	Roster booklet—Casey Stengel	60.00
1942	Roster booklet—Mascot	60.00
1943	Roster booklet—Mascot	60.00
1944	Roster booklet—bat, flag	60.00
1945	Roster booklet—Mascot	60.00
1946	Roster booklet—Billy Southworth	60.00
1947	Roster booklet—Billy Southworth	75.00
1948	Roster booklet—Bob Elliot	75.00
1949	Roster booklet—Billy Southworth	75.00
1950	Roster booklet—Team logo	75.00
1951	Roster booklet	75.00
1952	Roster booklet—baseball, Mascot	75.00

Boston Red Sox

Year	Cover	Price
1927	Roster sheet	$125.00
1928	Roster sheet	100.00
1929	Roster sheet	100.00
1930	Roster sheet	100.00
1931	Roster sheet	100.00
1932	Roster sheet	100.00
1933	Roster sheet	100.00
1934	Roster booklet	150.00
1935	Roster booklet	100.00
1936	Roster booklet	75.00
1937	Roster booklet	75.00
1938	Roster booklet	75.00
1939	Roster booklet—Jimmie Foxx	70.00
1940	Roster booklet—Team logo	70.00
1941	Roster booklet—Fenway Park	60.00
1942	Roster booklet—Bats	60.00
1943	Batting cage	60.00
1944	Roster booklet	60.00
1945	Roster booklet	60.00
1946	Baseball scene	60.00
1947	Roster booklet—World Series pennant	60.00
1948	Roster booklet—Joe McCarthy	60.00
1949	Roster booklet	60.00
1950	Mascot	50.00
1951	Players	125.00
1952	Fenway Park	125.00
1953	Team logo	125.00
1954	Team logo	125.00
1955	Team logo	125.00
1956	Team logo	100.00
1957	Baseball scene	100.00
1958	Reporters	80.00
1959	Player	80.00
1960	Player	80.00
1961	Glove	100.00
1962	Carl Yastrzemski	100.00
1963	Johnny Pesky	60.00
1964	Team logo	60.00
1965	Team logo	75.00
1966	Team logo	40.00
1967	Team logo	40.00
1968	Pennant	40.00
1969	100th Anniversary	40.00
1970	Fenway Park	15.00
1971	Players	15.00
1972	Fans	10.00
1973	Baseball scene	10.00

1974	Darrell Johnson	10.00
1975	Fenway park	10.00
1976	Pennant	10.00
1977	Don Zimmer	10.00
1978	Carl Yastrzemski/Jim Rice	15.00
1979	Jim Rice	12.00
1980	Carl Yastrzemski	12.00
1981	Ralph Houk	6.00
1982	Ralph Houk	6.00
1983	Dwight Evans/Bob Stanley	6.00
1984	Wade Boggs/Jim Rice	8.00
1985	Tony Armas	6.00
1986	Boggs/Boyd/Buckner/Gedman	8.00
1987	Roger Clemens/John McNamara	6.00
1988	Dwight Evans/Roger Clemens	8.00
1989	Joe Morgan	10.00
1990	Fenway Park	10.00
1991	Ellis Burks/Tony Peña	10.00
1992	Roger Clemens/Butch Hobson	10.00
1993	Baseball	10.00
1994	Mo Vaughn	7.00
1995	Team logo	5.00
1996	Mo Vaughn	5.00
1997	Mo Vaughn	5.00

Brooklyn Dodgers

Year	Cover	Price
1927	Roster sheet	$125.00
1928	Roster booklet—Team name	150.00
1929	Roster booklet—Team name	100.00
1930	Roster booklet—Team name	100.00
1931	Roster booklet—Team name	100.00
1932	Roster booklet—Team name	100.00
1933	Roster booklet—Team name	100.00
1934	Roster booklet—Team name	100.00
1935	Roster booklet—Team name	100.00
1936	Roster booklet—Team name	75.00
1937	Roster booklet—Team name	75.00
1938	Roster booklet—Team name	75.00
1939	100th Anniversary	75.00
1940	50th Anniversary in Brooklyn	75.00
1941	Airplane	85.00
1942	"V"	65.00
1943	Roster booklet	65.00
1944	Roster booklet	65.00
1945	Roster booklet	65.00
1946	Roster booklet	65.00
1947	Roster booklet	65.00
1948	Roster booklet	65.00
1949	Roster booklet	150.00
1950	The Bum	125.00
1951	The Bum	125.00
1952	(Unavailable)	125.00
1953	The Bum	125.00
1954	(Unavailable)	125.00
1955	Walter Alston	125.00
1956	Walter Alston	100.00
1957	Walter Alston	100.00

California Angels

Year	Cover	Price
1966	Anaheim Stadium	$60.00
1967	Anaheim	35.00
1968	Anaheim Stadium	25.00
1969	AL West	25.00
1970	Press box	15.00
1971	Four Players	15.00
1972	Del Rice	12.00
1973	Nolan Ryan	20.00
1974	Anaheim Stadium	10.00
1975	Dick Williams	10.00
1976	Angels baseball cards	10.00
1977	Frank Tanana	12.00
1978	Tanana/Ryan/Rudi	15.00
1979	Anaheim Stadium	12.00
1980	Don Baylor	7.00
1981	Equipment	6.00
1982	Team logo	7.00
1983	Reggie Jackson	8.00
1984	Reggie Jackson	7.00
1985	(Unavailable)	6.00
1986	DeCinces/Schofield/Downing	6.00
1987	Donnie Moore	6.00
1988	Wally Joyner/Brian Downing	10.00
1989	All-Star Game	10.00
1990	Wally Joyner/Chuck Finley	10.00
1991	Baseball scene	10.00
1992	Bryan Harvey	10.00
1993	Uniforms	10.00
1994	Tim Salmon	7.00
1995	Anaheim Stadium	5.00
1996	Anderson/Edmonds/Salmon	5.00
1997	Anderson/Edmonds/Salmon	5.00

Chicago Cubs

Year	Cover	Price
1927	Roster booket	$175.00
1928	Roster booket	150.00
1929	Roster booket	150.00
1930	Roster booket	100.00
1931	Roster booket—Rogers Hornsby	100.00
1932	Roster booket—Rogers Hornsby	125.00
1933	Roster booket—mascot	100.00
1934	Roster booket—mascot	100.00
1935	Roster booket—mascot	115.00
1936	Roster booket—mascot	75.00
1937	Roster booket—mascot	75.00
1938	Roster booket—mascot	85.00
1939	Roster booket—mascot	65.00
1940	Roster booklet	65.00
1941	Roster booket—Jimmy Wilson	65.00
1942	Roster booklet	65.00
1943	Roster booklet	65.00
1944	Roster booklet	65.00
1945	Roster booklet	75.00
1946	Roster booket—Charlie Grimm	65.00
1947	Roster booket—mascot	65.00
1948	Roster booklet	100.00
1949	Roster booklet	100.00
1950	Roster booklet	100.00
1951	Roster booklet	100.00
1952	(Unavailable)	100.00
1953	(Unavailable)	100.00
1954	(Unavailable)	75.00
1955	(Unavailable)	75.00
1956	(Unavailable)	75.00
1957	(Unavailable)	75.00
1958	Team logo	75.00
1959	Team logo	60.00
1960	Team logo	40.00
1961	Team logo	40.00
1962	Team logo	40.00
1963	Team logo	40.00
1964	Team logo	40.00
1965	Team logo	40.00
1966	Team logo	25.00
1967	Team logo	25.00
1968	Team logo	25.00
1969	Team logo	25.00
1970	Team logo	20.00
1971	Team logo	20.00
1972	Team logo	15.00
1973	Team logo	15.00
1974	Team logo	10.00
1975	Team logo	10.00
1976	Team logo	10.00
1977	Team logo	8.00
1978	Team logo	8.00
1979	Team logo	8.00
1980	Team logo	7.00
1981	Team logo	7.00
1982	Team logo	7.00
1983	Wrigley Field	7.00
1984	Autographed baseballs	6.00
1985	Frey/Green/Sandberg/Sutcliffe	10.00
1986	Ryne Sandberg	12.00
1987	Billy Williams	10.00
1988	Andre Dawson	10.00
1989	Wrigley Field	10.00
1990	Wrigley Field	10.00
1991	Ryne Sandberg	12.00
1992	Wrigley Field	10.00
1993	Wrigley Field	10.00
1994	Sandberg/Grace/Sosa	7.00
1995	Collage	5.00
1996	Brian McRae	5.00
1997	Sammy Sosa	5.00

Chicago White Sox

Year	Cover	Price
1927	Roster sheet	$125.00
1928	Roster sheet	100.00
1929	Roster sheet	100.00
1930	Roster sheet	100.00
1931	Roster sheet	100.00
1932	Roster sheet	100.00
1933	Roster sheet—Team name	100.00
1934	Roster booklet—Team name	100.00
1935	Roster booklet—Team name	75.00
1936	Roster booklet—Team name	75.00
1937	Roster booklet—Team name	75.00
1938	Roster booklet—Team name	75.00
1939	Roster booklet—Team name	75.00
1940	Roster booklet—Team name	75.00
1941	Roster booklet—Ted Lyons	60.00
1942	Roster booklet—Jimmy Dykes	60.00
1943	Roster booklet—"Buy more war bonds"	60.00
1944	Roster booklet—"Back the attack"	60.00
1945	Roster booklet	60.00
1946	Roster booklet—Team name	50.00
1947	Roster booklet—Ted Lyons	100.00
1948	Roster booklet—mascot	100.00
1949	Roster booklet—Team name	100.00
1950	Luke Appling	100.00
1951	Paul Richards	100.00
1952	Carrasquel/Fox/Minoso/Rogovin	100.00
1953	Baseball scene	100.00
1954	Mascot	100.00
1955	Mascot	100.00

1956	Mascot	100.00
1957	Mascot	80.00
1958	Mascot	80.00
1959	Mascot	80.00
1960	Mascot	75.00
1961	Team name	60.00
1962	Baseball scene	60.00
1963	Baseball scene	60.00
1964	Baseball scene	60.00
1965	Baseball scene	40.00
1966	Baseball scene	30.00
1967	Baseball scene	20.00
1968	Baseball scene	20.00
1969	Baseball scene	15.00
1970	Baseball scene	10.00
1971	Chuck Tanner	10.00
1972	Baseball scene	10.00
1973	Allen/Tanner/Wood	10.00
1974	Team logo	10.00
1975	AL 75th Anniversary	6.00
1976	Team logo	6.00
1977	Team logo	6.00
1978	Team logo	6.00
1979	Don Kessinger	6.00
1980	Crowd	6.00
1981	Baseball scene	6.00
1982	Team logo	6.00
1983	Press Box equipment	6.00
1984	Scoreboard	6.00
1985	Comiskey Park	6.00
1986	Aparicio/Appling/Guillen	7.00
1987	New uniform	6.00
1988	Baseball scene	6.00
1989	Former Players	6.00
1990	Comiskey Park 80 years	10.00
1991	Catcher's mask, bat	10.00
1992	Team logo	10.00
1993	Team logo	10.00
1994	Thomas/McDowell/Lamont	7.00
1995	Comiskey Park	6.00
1996	Thomas/Fernandez/Guillen	5.00
1997	(Unavailable)	5.00

Cincinnati Reds

Year	Cover	Price
1927	Roster sheet	$125.00
1928	Roster sheet	100.00
1929	Roster sheet	100.00
1930	Roster sheet—Team logo	100.00
1931	Roster sheet—Team logo	100.00
1932	Roster booklet—Team logo	100.00
1933	Roster booklet	100.00
1934	Roster booklet—Team name	100.00
1935	Roster booklet—Team logo	100.00
1936	Roster booklet—Team logo	75.00
1937	Roster booklet—Team logo	75.00
1938	Roster booklet—Bill McKechnie	75.00
1939	1869 Team	75.00
1940	Team logo	75.00

1941	Champions pennant	125.00
1942	Team logo	125.00
1943	Team logo	125.00
1944	Team logo	125.00
1945	Baseball	125.00
1946	Baseball scene	125.00
1947	Baseball	125.00
1948	Team logo	125.00
1949	City/team logo	125.00
1950	Reporter	100.00
1951	75th Anniversary	100.00
1952	Team logo	100.00
1953	(Unavailable)	100.00
1954	(Unavailable)	100.00
1955	Mascot	100.00
1956	Birdie Tebbetts	100.00
1957	Schedule	100.00
1958	Mascot	100.00
1959	Mayo Smith	100.00
1960	Fred Hutchinson	75.00
1961	Fred Huthinson/Bill DeWitt	75.00
1962	Mascot	75.00
1963	Mascot	75.00
1964	Mascot	60.00
1965	Mascot	60.00
1966	Mascot	60.00
1967	(Unavailable)	60.00
1968	(Unavailable)	35.00
1969	100th Anniversary	75.00
1970	Caps	30.00
1971	Pete Rose Jr.	30.00
1972	Baseball scene	20.00
1973	Sparky Anderson	20.00
1974	Jack Billingham/Don Gullett	15.00
1975	Johnny Bench	15.00
1976	Joe Morgan	20.00
1977	Johnny Bench	20.00
1978	George Foster	15.00
1979	John McNamara	15.00
1980	Riverfront Stadium	8.00
1981	Baseball scene	8.00
1982	Uniform	8.00
1983	Russ Nixon	8.00
1984	Team logo	8.00
1985	Riverfront Stadium	8.00
1986	Pete Rose	10.00
1987	NL logos	8.00
1988	All-Star Game	8.00
1989	Bats	8.00
1990	Lou Piniella	10.00
1991	World Series trophy	10.00
1992	Equipment	10.00
1993	Locker	10.00
1994	Team logo	7.00
1995	Riverfront Stadium	5.00
1996	Knight/Morris/Boone	5.00
1997	Larkin/Boone/Sanders	5.00

Cleveland Indians

Year	Cover	Price
1927	Roster sheet	$125.00
1928	Roster sheet	100.00
1929	Roster sheet	100.00
1930	Roster sheet	100.00
1931	Roster sheet	100.00
1932	Roster booklet	100.00
1933	Roster booklet	100.00
1934	Roster booklet	100.00
1935	Roster booklet	100.00
1936	Roster booklet—Mascot	75.00
1937	Roster booklet—Mascot	75.00
1938	Roster booklet—Mascot	75.00
1939	Roster booklet—Mascot	75.00
1940	Roster booklet—Mascot	75.00
1941	Roster booklet—Mascot	75.00
1942	Roster booklet—Lou Boudreau	60.00
1943	Roster booklet—Lou Boudreau	60.00
1944	Roster booklet—Mascot	60.00
1945	Roster booklet—Mascot	60.00
1946	Roster booklet—Lou Boudreau	60.00
1947	Roster booklet—Mascot	60.00
1948	Mascot	125.00
1949	Mascot	100.00
1950	Mascot	100.00
1951	Mascot	100.00
1952	Garcia/Wynn/Lemon/Feller	100.00
1953	Reporters	100.00
1954	Al Rosen	100.00
1955	Mascot	100.00
1956	Mascot	100.00
1957	Kirby Farrell	75.00
1958	Bobby Bragan/Frank Lane	75.00
1959	Rocky Colavito	75.00
1960	Tito Francona	75.00
1961	Jim Perry	75.00
1962	Mascot	75.00
1963	Uniform	75.00
1964	Mascot	75.00
1965	Mascot	30.00
1966	Baseball	30.00
1967	Cleveland Stadium	30.00
1968	Baseball	25.00
1969	100th Anniversary	25.00
1970	Mascot	20.00
1971	Cap	20.00
1972	Baseball scene	20.00

1973	Team logo	10.00
1974	Team logo	10.00
1975	Frank Robinson	10.00
1976	Baseball	10.00
1977	Baseball scene	8.00
1978	Baseball and glove	7.00
1979	Team logo	7.00
1980	Fireworks	7.00
1981	Team logo	7.00
1982	Cleveland Stadium	7.00
1983	Team logo	7.00
1984	Memorabilia	7.00
1985	Bert Blyleven/Andre Thornton	7.00
1986	Uniforms	5.00
1987	Joe Carter	7.00
1988	Uniform	6.00
1989	Candiotti/Farrell/Jones/Swindell	10.00
1990	90 Years of Cleveland baseball	10.00
1991	Jacoby/Jones/Alomar	10.00
1992	60 Years at Cleveland Stadium	10.00
1993	Memorabilia	10.00
1994	Belle/Lofton/Baerga	7.00
1995	Jacobs Field	5.00
1996	Players	5.00
1997	All-Star logo/Cleveland skyline	5.00

Colorado Rockies

Year	Cover	Price
1993	(Unavailable)	$20.00
1994	Coors Field	10.00
1995	Coors Field	15.00
1996	Coors Field	5.00
1997	Baseball scenes	5.00

Detroit Tigers

Year	Cover	Price
1927	Roster sheet	$125.00
1928	Roster sheet	100.00
1929	Roster sheet	100.00
1930	Roster sheet	100.00
1931	Roster booklet	100.00
1932	Roster booklet	100.00
1933	Roster booklet—Mascot	100.00
1934	Roster booklet—Mascot	100.00
1935	Roster booklet—Mascot	100.00

1936	Roster booklet—Mascot	75.00
1937	Roster booklet—Mascot	75.00
1938	Mascot	75.00
1939	Mascot	75.00
1940	Mascot	75.00
1941	Briggs stadium	60.00
1942	Briggs Stadium	60.00
1943	Mascot	60.00
1944	Mascot	60.00
1945	Mascot	60.00
1946	Mascot	50.00
1947	Mascot	50.00
1948	Mascot	150.00
1949	Mascot	150.00
1950	Mascot	150.00
1951	Mascot	150.00
1952	Mascot	150.00
1953	Mascot	150.00
1954	Mascot	100.00
1955	Mascot	100.00
1956	Al Kaline	100.00
1957	Frank Lary	100.00
1958	Jim Bunning	100.00
1959	Mascot	100.00
1960	Mascot	75.00
1961	Tiger stadium	75.00
1962	Team logo	60.00
1963	Team logo	60.00
1964	Team logo	40.00
1965	Team logo	30.00
1966	Mascot	30.00
1967	Mascot	30.00
1968	Mascot	30.00
1969	Mascot	25.00
1970	Mascot	20.00
1971	Mascot	15.00
1972	Mascot	10.00
1973	Mascot	10.00
1974	Mascot	10.00
1975	Mascot	10.00
1976	Mascot	10.00
1977	Mascot	10.00
1978	Mascot	10.00
1979	Team logo	10.00
1980	Mascot	5.00
1981	Mascot	5.00
1982	Team logo	5.00
1983	Greenberg and Gehringer uniforms	5.00
1984	Mascot	5.00
1985	World Series trophy	5.00
1986	Mascot	5.00
1987	Mascot	5.00
1988	Alan Trammell	5.00
1989	Team logo	10.00
1990	Uniform	10.00
1991	(Unavailable)	10.00
1992	Alan Trammell/Lou Whitaker	10.00
1993	Players	10.00
1994	Team logo	7.00
1995	Baseballs	5.00

1996	Buddy Bell	5.00
1997	Stripes	5.00

Florida Marlins

Year	Cover	Price
1993	Team logo	$20.00
1994	Mascot	10.00
1995	Team logo	15.00
1996	Mascot	5.00
1997	Team logo	5.00

Houston Astros

Year	Cover	Price
1965	Team logo	$75.00
1966	Catcher's mask	60.00
1967	Astroturf	40.00
1968	Astrodome	40.00
1969	Baseball Anniversary	25.00
1970	Roster	20.00
1971	Locker room	20.00
1972	Ball and bat	15.00
1973	Zodiac signs	12.00
1974	Orange	10.00
1975	Equipment	10.00
1976	Bicentennial logo	10.00
1977	Baseball scene	7.00
1978	(Unavailable)	7.00
1979	(Unavailable)	7.00
1980	Baseball scene	6.00
1981	Team logo	6.00
1982	20th Anniversary in Houston	6.00
1983	Nolan Ryan	6.00
1984	Equipment	6.00
1985	Jersey	6.00
1986	Memorabilia	10.00
1987	Mike Scott/Hal Lanier	10.00
1988	Bill Doran	10.00
1989	Glenn Davis	10.00
1990	Team logo	10.00
1991	Helmet/bat/ball	10.00
1992	Craig Biggio/Pete Harnisch	10.00
1993	Luis Gonzalez/Jeff Bagwell	10.00
1994	Cap	7.00
1995	Jeff Bagwell	5.00
1996	Craig Biggio	5.00
1997	Biggio/Bell/Bagwell	5.00

Houston Colt .45's

Year	Cover	Price
1962	Team logo	$150.00
1963	Team logo	100.00
1964	Baseball scene	100.00

Kansas City Athletics

Year	Cover	Price
1955	K.C. Municipal Stadium	$75.00
1956	Mascot	75.00
1957	Mascot	75.00
1958	Mascot	75.00
1959	Baseball	75.00
1960	Baeball/Cap	75.00
1961	K.C. Municipal Stadium	60.00
1962	(Unavailable)	60.00
1963	Baseball scene	60.00
1964	Team logo	60.00
1965	Team logo	25.00
1966	Team logo	25.00
1967	Team logo	25.00

Kansas City Royals

Year	Cover	Price
1969	Team logo	$60.00
1970	Baseball scene	20.00
1971	Bat rack	20.00
1972	Royals Stadium	20.00
1973	Baseball scene	15.00
1974	Royals Stadium	15.00
1975	Baseball scene	12.00
1976	Whitey Herzog	10.00
1977	Baseball scene	6.00
1978	Baseball scene	6.00
1979	AL West Champions	6.00
1980	Scoreboard	6.00
1981	Baseball scene	6.00
1982	Baseball scene	6.00
1983	Statue	6.00
1984	George Brett	8.00
1985	Scoreboard	6.00
1986	World Series trophy	6.00
1987	Baseball scene	6.00
1988	Fireworks	10.00
1989	Equipment	10.00
1990	Baseball scene	10.00
1991	George Brett	12.00
1992	Equipment	10.00
1993	25th Anniversary	10.00
1994	Kevin Appier/Jeff Montgomery	7.00
1995	Magazine covers	7.00
1996	Players	5.00
1997	25th Anniversary of Kaufman Stadium	5.00

Los Angeles Angels

Year	Cover	Price
1961	Player	$75.00
1962	Baby	75.00
1963	Bill Rigney	60.00
1964	Baseball scene	60.00
1965	Dean Chance	40.00

Los Angeles Dodgers

Year	Cover	Price
1958	Walter Alston	$75.00
1959	L.A. Coliseum	75.00
1960	Dodger Stadium	30.00
1961	Dodger Stadium	30.00
1962	Airplane	50.00
1963	T. Davis/Drysdale/Koufax/Wills	50.00
1964	Baseball scene	40.00
1965	Championship pennants	40.00
1966	Mascot	40.00
1967	Mascot	40.00
1968	Walter Alston	25.00
1969	100th Anniversary	25.00
1970	W. Davis/Osteen/Singer/Sizemore	25.00
1971	Baseball scene	20.00
1972	Baseball scene	20.00
1973	Baseball scene	10.00
1974	Baseball scene	10.00
1975	Steve Garvey	12.00
1976	Buckner/Cey/Garvey/Lopes/Sutton	14.00
1977	Tom Lasorda	12.00
1978	Baker/Cey/Garvey/Smith	14.00
1979	Dodger Stadium	6.00
1980	Team logo	6.00
1981	Baseball scenes	7.00

1982	Steve Howe/Steve Yeager	8.00
1983	Sax/Guerrero/Valenzuela	8.00
1984	Fireworks	6.00
1985	Bill Russell	7.00
1986	Baseball scene	6.00
1987	Dodger Stadium	10.00
1988	Baseballs	10.00
1989	World Series trophy	10.00
1990	100th Anniversary	10.00
1991	Team name	10.00
1992	Dodger Stadium	10.00
1993	Eric Karros	10.00
1994	Mike Piazza/Eric Karros	7.00
1995	Dodger Stadium	5.00
1996	Karros/Piazza/Mondesi/Nomo	5.00
1997	Rookies of the Year	5.00

Milwaukee Braves

Year	Cover	Price
1953	Florida	$125.00
1954	(Unavailable)	125.00
1955	(Unavailable)	125.00
1956	(Unavailable)	125.00
1957	(Unavailable)	100.00
1958	(Unavailable)	100.00
1959	(Unavailable)	100.00
1960	Pennant and Mascot	75.00
1961	Pennant and Mascot	75.00
1962	Pennant and Mascot	75.00
1963	Pennant and Mascot	75.00
1964	Aaron/Alou/Mathews/Spahn	75.00
1965	Felipe Alou/Bobby Bragan	75.00

Milwaukee Brewers

Year	Cover	Price
1971	Newspaper	$40.00
1972	Wisconsin	10.00
1973	Del Crandall/George Scott	12.00
1974	Mascot	10.00
1975	Mascot	10.00
1976	Glove	10.00
1977	Robin Yount	15.00
1978	Larry Hisle	10.00
1979	George Bamberger	10.00
1980	Cooper/Lezcano/Thomas	6.00
1981	Cooper/Oglivie/Yount	8.00
1982	Rollie Fingers	8.00
1983	Kuenn/Vuckovich/Yount	8.00
1984	County Stadium	6.00
1985	Uniform	6.00
1986	Baseball scene	6.00
1987	Ted Higuera	6.00
1988	Baseball scene	6.00
1989	20th Anniversary	10.00
1990	Baseball scene	10.00
1991	Team logo	10.00
1992	Phil Garner	10.00
1993	Pat Listach	10.00

1994	25th Anniversary	7.00
1995	Bob Uecker	8.00
1996	Stadium	5.00
1997	Shovel	5.00

Minnesota Twins

Year	Cover	Price
1961	Metropolitan Stadium	$150.00
1962	Metropolitan Stadium	75.00
1963	Baseball scene	75.00
1964	Baseball	75.00
1965	All-Star Game	40.00
1966	Stadium	25.00
1966	Baseball scene	40.00
1967	Uniform	30.00
1968	Baseball scene	30.00
1969	Metropolitan Stadium	20.00
1970	Rod Carew	20.00
1971	Jim Perry	20.00
1972	Reporters	20.00
1973	Rod Carew	20.00
1974	Baseballs	10.00
1975	Rod Carew/Ty Cobb	15.00
1976	Rod Carew/Harmon Killebrew	15.00
1977	Old media guides	10.00
1978	Rod Carew	10.00
1979	Metropolitan Stadium	6.00
1980	Baseball cards	6.00
1981	Bats/caps/uniforms	6.00
1982	Metrodome	6.00
1983	Kent Hrbek	7.00
1984	Uniforms	6.00
1985	All-Star Game	6.00
1986	25th Anniversary	6.00
1987	Gary Gaetti/Kirby Puckett	8.00
1988	World Series trophy	10.00
1989	Kirby Puckett/Frank Viola	10.00
1990	Carew/Oliva/Puckett	10.00
1991	Rod Carew/Harmon Killebrew	10.00
1992	World Series trophy	10.00
1993	Kirby Puckett	10.00
1994	Autographs	7.00
1995	Uniform/bat/glove	6.00
1996	Rookies of the Year	5.00
1997	Team logo	5.00

 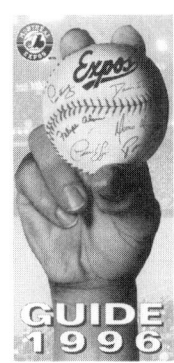

Montreal Expos

Year	Cover	Price
1969	Team logo	$75.00
1970	Jarry Park	40.00
1971	Baseballs	20.00
1972	Jarry Park	20.00
1973	Montreal	10.00
1974	Gene Mauch	10.00
1975	Baseball scene	10.00
1976	Baseball scene	10.00
1977	Cash/McEnaney/Perez/D. Williams	6.00
1978	Gary Carter/Andre Dawson	10.00
1979	Team logo	6.00
1980	Locker	6.00
1981	Pennant	6.00
1982	Baseball scene	6.00
1983	Baseball scene	6.00
1984	Caps	6.00
1985	Olympic Stadium	6.00
1986	Baseball	6.00
1987	Olympic Stadium	10.00
1988	20th Anniversary bat	10.00
1989	High-five	10.00
1990	Team logo	10.00
1991	Team logo	10.00
1992	Dennis Martinez	10.00
1993	25th Anniversary	10.00
1994	New logo	7.00
1995	Felipe Alou	5.00
1996	Autographed baseball	5.00
1997	Baseball scene	5.00

New York Giants

Year	Cover	Price
1927	Roster booklet—Team name	$150.00
1928	Roster booklet—Team name	100.00
1929	Roster booklet—Team name	100.00
1930	Roster booklet—Team name	100.00
1931	Roster booklet—Team name	100.00
1932	Roster booklet—Team name	100.00
1933	Roster booklet—Team name	125.00
1934	Roster booklet—Team name	100.00
1935	Roster booklet—Team name	100.00
1936	Team name	85.00
1937	Team name	85.00
1938	Team name	75.00
1939	New York World's Fair	75.00
1940	Team name	75.00
1941	Team name	60.00
1942	Team name	60.00
1943	Team name	60.00
1944	Team name	60.00
1945	Team name	60.00
1946	Team name	150.00
1947	Baseballs	150.00
1948	Baseballs	150.00
1949	Baseballs	150.00
1950	Polo Grounds	125.00
1951	Team logo	125.00
1952	Leo Durocher	125.00
1953	Polo Grounds	125.00
1954	Team logo	125.00
1955	Team name	125.00
1956	Caps	125.00
1957	Caps	125.00

New York Mets

Year	Cover	Price
1962	First year	$500.00
1963	Mascot	150.00
1964	Shea Stadium	100.00
1965	Mascot	100.00
1966	(Unavailable)	100.00
1967	Donald Grant/George Weiss	100.00
1968	Gil Hodges	100.00
1969	Gil Hodges	100.00
1970	Baseball scene	75.00
1971	Scoreboard	50.00
1972	Tom Seaver	50.00
1973	Yogi Berra	50.00
1974	NL Champs pennant	50.00
1975	Mets management	20.00
1976	Joe Frazier	20.00
1977	Uniform	20.00
1978	Team logo/cap/glove	20.00
1979	Willie Mays	15.00
1980	Team logo	15.00
1981	New York City	15.00
1982	Locker	15.00
1983	Tom Seaver	15.00
1984	Davey Johnson	15.00
1985	Tom Seaver	15.00
1986	Dwight Gooden/Shea Stadium	15.00
1987	World Series ring	15.00
1988	25th Anniversary	15.00
1989	Frank Cashen/Howard Johnson	15.00
1990	Howard Johnson	15.00
1991	Bud Harrelson	15.00
1992	Bonilla/Murray/Saberhagen/Torborg	15.00
1993	Uniform	15.00
1994	Dwight Gooden	7.00
1995	Shea Stadium	7.00
1996	Organization of the Year trophy	5.00
1997	Hundley/Franco/Gilkey	5.00

New York Yankees

Year	Cover	Price
1927	Roster sheet	$175.00
1928	Roster sheet	150.00
1929	Roster sheet	150.00
1930	Roster sheet	150.00
1931	Roster sheet	150.00
1932	Roster booklet	200.00
1933	Roster booklet	100.00
1934	Roster booklet	100.00
1935	Roster booklet	100.00
1936	Roster booklet—Joe McCarthy	100.00
1937	Roster booklet—Joe McCarthy	100.00
1938	Roster booklet—Joe McCarthy	100.00
1939	Roster booklet—Joe McCarthy	100.00
1940	Roster booklet—Joe McCarthy	75.00
1941	Roster booklet—Joe McCarthy	65.00
1942	Joe McCarthy	65.00
1943	(Unavailable)	65.00
1944	(Unavailable)	65.00
1945	"V"	65.00
1946	Team logo	65.00
1947	Team logo	50.00
1948	Team logo	50.00
1949	Team logo	150.00
1950	Team logo	150.00
1951	Team logo	150.00
1952	Team logo	150.00
1953	Team logo	150.00
1954	Team logo	150.00
1955	Team logo	150.00
1956	Team logo	150.00
1957	Team logo	150.00
1958	Team logo	150.00
1959	Team logo	150.00
1960	Yankee Stadium	100.00
1961	Team logo	100.00
1962	Team logo	100.00
1963	Team logo	100.00
1964	Yogi Berra	75.00
1965	Team logo	40.00
1966	Yankee Stadium	40.00
1967	Team logo	40.00
1968	Yankee Stadium	40.00
1969	Glove/cap	40.00
1970	Mel Stottlemyre	25.00
1971	Baseball scene	20.00
1972	Bobby Murcer/Roy White	20.00

Year	Cover	Price
1973	Yankee Stadium	20.00
1974	Whitey Ford/Mickey Mantle	25.00
1975	Bobby Bonds/Catfish Hunter	20.00
1976	Yankee Stadium	20.00
1977	Chris Chambliss/Thurman Munson	25.00
1978	Reggie Jackson/Babe Ruth	25.00
1979	Goose Gossage/Thurman Munson	20.00
1980	Dick Howser/Gene Michael	15.00
1981	Team logo	20.00
1982	Team logo	5.00
1983	Billy Martin	8.00
1984	Dave Righetti	6.00
1985	Don Mattingly	7.00
1986	Guidry/Henderson/Mattingly/Niekro	7.00
1987	Lou Piniella	15.00
1988	Team logo	15.00
1989	Dallas Green	15.00
1990	Bat and ball	15.00
1991	Maas/Mattingly/Meulens/Sax	15.00
1992	Great moments	15.00
1993	(Unavailable)	4.00
1994	Players	7.00
1995	Babe Ruth 100th birthday	5.00
1996	Memorabilia	5.00
1997	Players	5.00

Oakland Athletics

Year	Cover	Price
1968	Oakland Stadium	$25.00
1969	Bando/Campaneris/Hunter	20.00
1970	Baseball scene	20.00
1971	Team logo	15.00
1972	Team logo	15.00
1973	Team logo	15.00
1974	Team logo	15.00
1975	Team logo	15.00
1976	Team logo	10.00
1977	Team logo	10.00
1978	Team logo	10.00
1979	Team logo	10.00
1980	Team logo	6.00
1981	"Billy Ball"	7.00
1982	Spikes	6.00
1983	Jukebox	6.00
1984	Reporters	6.00
1985	Memorabilia	6.00
1986	Baseballs	10.00
1987	All-time team	10.00

1988	Baseball scene	10.00
1989	Canseco/Eckersley/Weiss	10.00
1990	World Series trophy	10.00
1991	Memorabilia	10.00
1992	25th Anniversary	10.00
1993	Dennis Eckersley	10.00
1994	Players	7.00
1995	Team logo	5.00
1996	Baseballs	5.00
1997	Mark McGwire	5.00

Philadelphia Athletics

Year	Cover	Price
1928	Roster sheet	$125.00
1929	Roster sheet	125.00
1930	Roster sheet—mascot	100.00
1931	Roster sheet—mascot	100.00
1932	Roster booklet—mascot	125.00
1933	Roster booklet—mascot	100.00
1934	Roster booklet—mascot	100.00
1935	Roster booklet—mascot	100.00
1936	Mascot	75.00
1937	Mascot	75.00
1938	Mascot	75.00
1939	Mascot	75.00
1940	Mascot	75.00
1941	Baseball	75.00
1942	(Unavailable)	50.00
1943	Mascot	60.00
1944	Mascot	60.00
1945	(Unavailable)	60.00
1946	Connie Mack	60.00
1947	(Unavailable)	60.00
1948	Baseball	60.00
1949	(Unavailable)	100.00
1950	Connie Mack	100.00
1951	(Unavailable)	100.00
1952	Mascot	100.00
1953	(Unavailable)	100.00
1954	Eddie Joost	100.00

1992 MEDIA GUIDE

Philadelphia Phillies

Year	Cover	Price
1927	Roster sheet	$125.00
1928	Roster sheet	100.00
1929	Roster sheet	100.00
1930	Roster sheet—Team logo	100.00
1931	Roster sheet	100.00
1932	Roster booklet—Team logo	100.00
1933	Phillies Golden Anniversary	100.00
1934	Roster booklet—Team logo	100.00
1935	Roster booklet—Team logo	100.00
1936	Roster booklet—Team logo	75.00
1937	Roster booklet—Team logo	75.00
1938	Roster booklet	75.00
1939	Roster booklet	75.00
1940	Roster booklet	75.00
1941	Roster booklet	60.00
1942	Soldier	60.00
1943	Roster booklet	60.00
1944	Roster booklet	60.00
1945	Roster booklet	60.00
1946	Roster booklet—Shibe park	60.00
1947	Roster booklet—Shibe park	60.00
1948	Roster booklet—Shibe park	60.00
1949	Roster booklet	60.00
1950	(Unavailable)	150.00
1951	(Unavailable)	50.00
1952	Shibe Park	50.00
1953	Baseball scene	50.00
1954	Robin Roberts	50.00
1955	"Get Set To Go In '55"	50.00
1956	Crowd	40.00
1957	Crowd	40.00
1958	Crowd	40.00
1959	Team logo	40.00
1960	Team logo	40.00
1961	Team logo	40.00
1962	(Unavailable)	20.00
1963	(Unavailable)	20.00
1964	Cap	150.00
1965	Cap	100.00
1966	Cap	100.00
1967	Cap	75.00
1968	Cap	75.00
1969	Cap	50.00
1970	Team logo	50.00
1971	Frank Luchessi	35.00
1972	Team logo	35.00
1973	Steve Carlton/Cy Young Award	25.00
1974	Baseball scene	20.00
1975	Baseball scene	20.00
1976	Baseball scene	15.00
1977	Division Champs pennant	15.00
1978	Fireworks	15.00
1979	Team logo	15.00
1980	Baseball	10.00
1981	World Series trophy	10.00
1982	Basket of baseballs	10.00
1983	100th Anniversary logo	10.00
1984	NL Champions trophy	10.00
1985	Baseball scene	10.00
1986	Home plate	10.00
1987	Mike Schmidt	15.00
1988	Steve Bedrosian/Mike Schmidt	15.00
1989	Nick Leyva/Lee Thomas	15.00
1990	Ashburn/Carlton/Roberts/Schmidt	15.00

1991	Catcher's mask	15.00
1992	Memorabilia	15.00
1993	League leaders	15.00
1994	Jim Fregosi	7.00
1995	25th Anniversary of Veterans Stadium	5.00
1996	All-Star logo	5.00
1997	Terry Francona	5.00

Pittsburgh Pirates

Year	Cover	Price
1927	Roster sheet	$175.00
1928	Roster sheet	100.00
1929	Roster sheet	125.00
1930	Roster sheet—Mascot	100.00
1931	Roster sheet—Mascot	100.00
1932	Roster booklet—Mascot	125.00
1933	Roster booklet—Mascot	100.00
1934	Roster booklet—Mascot	100.00
1935	Roster booklet—Mascot	80.00
1936	Mascot	75.00
1937	Mascot	75.00
1938	Mascot	75.00
1939	100th Anniversary	75.00
1940	Mascot	75.00
1941	Mascot	60.00
1942	"Remember Pearl Harbor"	60.00
1943	"Buy war bonds, stamps"	60.00
1944	Mascot	60.00
1945	Mascot	60.00
1946	"Buy victory bonds"	60.00
1947	Billy Herman	60.00
1948	William Meyer	60.00
1949	40th Anniversary	60.00
1950	Baseballs	50.00
1951	Team logo	125.00
1952	Baseballs	125.00
1953	Fred Haney	125.00
1954	Honus Wagner statue	125.00
1955	Baseball diamond	125.00
1956	Mascot	125.00
1957	Mascot	100.00
1958	Danny Murtaugh	100.00
1959	Mascot	100.00
1960	Mascot	75.00
1961	Mascot	75.00
1962	Baseball scene	75.00
1963	Baseballs	75.00

1964	Team logo	50.00
1965	Harry Walker	50.00
1966	Mascot	50.00
1967	Mascot	45.00
1968	Larry Sheppard	35.00
1969	Forbes Field	25.00
1970	Three Rivers Stadium	25.00
1971	Danny Murtaugh	25.00
1972	World Series celebration	25.00
1973	Clemente memorial	35.00
1974	Three Rivers Stadium	10.00
1975	Championship star	10.00
1976	Rennie Stennett	10.00
1977	Baseball scene	6.00
1978	(Unavailable)	6.00
1979	Uniforms	10.00
1980	Willie Stargell	9.00
1981	Team logo	6.00
1982	Cap	6.00
1983	Team logo	6.00
1984	Bill Madlock	6.00
1985	Tony Peña	6.00
1986	Three Rivers Stadium	10.00
1987	100th Anniversary logo	10.00
1988	Memorabilia	10.00
1989	Bonilla/LaValliere/Van Slyke	10.00
1990	Bonds/Bonilla/Drabek/Van Slyke	10.00
1991	NL Champions	10.00
1992	Doug Drabek/Don Slaught	10.00
1993	Jim Leyland	10.00
1994	Three Rivers Stadium	7.00
1995	(Unavailable)	5.00
1996	Cap	5.00
1997	Uniforms/caps/ logos	5.00

San Diego Padres

Year	Cover	Price
1969	Preston Gomez	$75.00
1970	Jack Murphy Stadium	15.00
1971	Jack Murphy Stadium	15.00
1972	Padres vs. Dodgers, July 3,1971	15.00
1973	Nate Colbert	12.00
1974	Baseball scene	8.00
1975	Baseball scene	8.00
1976	Randy Jones	8.00
1977	Randy Jones/Butch Metzger	6.00
1978	Baseball scene	6.00
1979	Roger Craig	6.00
1980	Jerry Coleman/Dave Winefield	8.00
1981	Frank Howard	7.00
1982	Dick Williams	6.00
1983	Memorabilia	6.00
1984	Ray Kroc memorabilia	10.00
1985	NL Champions trophy	10.00
1986	Team logo	10.00
1987	Larry Bowa	10.00
1988	Tony Gwynn/Benito Santiago	10.00
1989	Stadium	10.00
1990	Baseball scene	10.00

1991	Uniform/ball/glove	10.00
1992	All-Star Game	10.00
1993	Gary Sheffield/Fred McGriff	10.00
1994	San Diego	7.00
1995	Gwynn/Caminiti/Finley	5.00
1996	Tony Gwynn	5.00
1997	Pitchers	5.00

San Francisco Giants

Year	Cover	Price
1958	Candlestick Park	$150.00
1959	Baseball scene	100.00
1960	Team logo	80.00
1961	Baseball scene	80.00
1962	Baseball scene	60.00
1963	Candlestick Park	60.00
1964	Candlestick Park	60.00
1965	Candlestick Park	60.00
1966	Team logo	50.00
1967	Team logo	40.00
1968	Team logo	35.00
1969	Team logo	35.00
1970	Willie Mays/Willie McCovey	25.00
1971	"Year of the Fox"	20.00
1972	"Best in the West"	20.00
1973	Candlestick Park	15.00
1974	Mathews/Bryant/Bonds	15.00
1975	Team logo	15.00
1976	Team logo	10.00
1977	Joe Altobelli/John Montefusco	10.00
1978	Baseball scene	6.00
1979	Vida Blue/Jack Clark	6.00
1980	On deck circle	6.00
1981	Golden Gate Bridge	6.00
1982	25th Anniversary	6.00
1983	Team logo	6.00
1984	Team logo	6.00
1985	Team logo	6.00
1986	Team logo	6.00
1987	Team logo	6.00
1988	Team logo	10.00
1989	Team logo	10.00
1990	Team logo	10.00
1991	Team logo	10.00
1992	Uniform	10.00
1993	Team logo	10.00

1994	Dusty Baker	7.00
1995	Barry Bonds/Matt Williams	5.00
1996	Barry Bonds/Matt Williams	5.00
1997	40 years in San Francisco	5.00

Seattle Mariners

Year	Cover	Price
1977	Kingdome	$30.00
1978	Baseball	10.00
1979	Kingdome	10.00
1980	Equipment	6.00
1981	Maury Wills	7.00
1982	Team logo	6.00
1983	Gaylord Perry	8.00
1984	Team logo	6.00
1985	Beattie/Davis/Henderson/Langston	7.00
1986	Memorabilia	6.00
1987	Team logo	6.00
1988	Bat	10.00
1989	Kingdome	10.00
1990	AL Baseballs	10.00
1991	Highlights	10.00
1992	Logo	10.00
1993	Kingdome	10.00
1994	Cap	7.00
1995	Team logo	5.00
1996	AL West Championship	5.00
1997	Ken Griffey Jr./Alex Rodriguez	5.00

Seattle Pilots

Year	Cover	Price
1969	Team logo	$125.00
1970	Team logo	100.00

St. Louis Browns

Year	Cover	Price
1927	Roster booklet—Team name	$150.00
1928	Roster booklet—Team name	125.00
1929	Roster booklet	125.00
1930	Roster booklet	125.00
1931	Roster booklet—Sportsman's Park	125.00
1932	Roster booklet—Sportsman's Park	100.00
1933	Roster booklet—Sportsman's Park	100.00
1934	Roster booklet	100.00
1935	Roster booklet	100.00
1936	Roster booklet—Rogers Hornsby	80.00
1937	Roster booklet—Team logo	75.00
1938	Roster booklet	75.00

1939	Roster booklet	75.00
1940	Roster booklet—Fred Haney	75.00
1941	Roster booklet—Statue	60.00
1942	Roster booklet	60.00
1943	Roster booklet—Team logo	60.00
1944	Roster booklet	100.00
1945	(Unavailable)	150.00
1946	Roster booklet—Team logo	150.00
1947	Baseball	150.00
1948	"Meet the Brownies"	150.00
1949	(Unavailable)	150.00
1950	Team logo	150.00
1951	Team logo	150.00
1952	Mascot	150.00
1953	Mascot	150.00

St. Louis Cardinals

Year	Cover	Price
1926	Roster sheet	$200.00
1927	Roster sheet	125.00
1928	Roster sheet	125.00
1929	Roster sheet	100.00
1930	Roster sheet—Team logo	115.00
1931	Roster sheet	115.00
1932	Roster booklet—Team logo	125.00
1933	Roster booklet—Team logo	125.00
1934	Roster booklet—Team logo	115.00
1935	Roster booklet—Team logo	100.00
1936	Roster booklet—Team logo	75.00
1937	Roster booklet—Team logo	75.00
1938	Roster booklet	75.00
1939	Roster booklet—Team logo	75.00
1940	Roster booklet—Team logo	75.00
1941	Roster booklet—Team logo	75.00
1942	Roster booklet—Statue of Liberty	75.00
1943	Roster booklet—flag	75.00
1944	Roster booklet—"V"	75.00
1945	Roster booklet—Team logo	75.00
1946	Roster Booklet	75.00
1947	Roster booklet—Team logo	60.00
1948	Roster booklet—Team logo	60.00
1949	Roster booklet—Team logo	60.00
1950	Players	150.00
1951	26th Anniversary of World Champs	125.00
1952	Team logo	125.00
1953	Mascot	125.00
1954	Team logo	125.00
1955	Team logo	125.00
1956	Team logo	100.00
1957	Team logo	100.00
1958	Mascot	75.00
1959	Stan Musial	100.00
1960	Mascot	75.00
1961	Broglio/McDaniel/Sadecki/Simmons	75.00
1962	Stan Musial	60.00
1963	Baseball scene	60.00
1964	Boyer/Groat/Javier/White	60.00
1965	Team logo	60.00
1966	Busch Stadium	60.00

1967	Busch Stadium	40.00
1968	World Series trophy	55.00
1969	Bob Gibson	45.00
1970	Joe Torre	20.00
1971	Bob Gibson/Joe Torre	25.00
1972	Red Schoendienst/Joe Torre	20.00
1973	Brock/Gibson/Simmons/Torre	20.00
1974	Uniform/cap	15.00
1975	Lou Brock	15.00
1976	Busch Stadium	12.00
1977	Lou Brock/Vern Rapp	7.00
1978	Equipment	7.00
1979	St. Louis Arch	7.00
1980	Keith Hernandez	7.00
1981	Whitey Herzog	7.00
1982	Whitey Herzog	7.00
1983	World Series celebration	7.00
1984	Baseball scene	6.00
1985	Busch Stadium	10.00
1986	Coleman/Herzog/McGee	10.00
1987	Whitey Herzog	10.00
1988	N.L. Champions	10.00
1989	Whitey Herzog	10.00
1990	Team logo	8.00
1991	Joe Torre	10.00
1992	Todd Zeile	10.00
1993	Team logo	10.00
1994	Bats/homeplate	7.00
1995	Mascot	5.00
1996	Tony La Russa	5.00
1997	Busch Stadium	5.00

Texas Rangers

Year	Cover	Price
1972	Team logo	$30.00
1973	Burke/Herzog/Short	20.00
1974	Billy Martin	15.00
1975	Hargrove/Jenkins/Martin	15.00
1976	Toby Harrah	6.00
1977	Equipment	6.00
1978	Billy Hunter	6.00
1979	Baseball	6.00
1980	Catcher	6.00
1981	Fireworks	6.00
1982	Team logo	6.00
1983	Glove	6.00
1984	Buddy Bell	6.00
1985	Cap	6.00

Year	Cover	Price
1986	Arlington Stadium	6.00
1987	Bobby Valentine	10.00
1988	Team logo	10.00
1989	Uniform	10.00
1990	Home plate	10.00
1991	Nolan Ryan	15.00
1992	Julio Franco	10.00
1993	Arlington Stadium	10.00
1994	Jersey	7.00
1995	Ballpark at Arlington	5.00
1996	Ballpark at Arlington	5.00
1997	Juan Gonzalez	5.00

Toronto Blue Jays

Year	Cover	Price
1977	Exhibition Stadium	$45.00
1978	Baseball scene	15.00
1979	Baseball scene	15.00
1980	Alfredo Griffin	10.00
1981	Equipment	10.00
1982	Bobby Cox	10.00
1983	Equipment	10.00
1984	Baseball scene	10.00
1985	Team logo	10.00
1986	10th Anniversary	10.00
1987	Bell/Barfield/Fernandez	10.00
1988	George Bell	10.00
1989	Fred McGriff	12.00
1990	Fred McGriff/Kelly Gruber	12.00
1991	Dave Stieb	10.00
1992	Roberto Alomar	12.00
1993	World Series trophy	10.00
1994	World Championship rings	7.00
1995	Team logo	5.00
1996	Team logo	5.00
1997	(Unavailable)	5.00

Washington Senators

Year	Cover	Price
1928	Roster sheet	$125.00
1929	Roster sheet	100.00
1930	Roster sheet	100.00
1931	Roster sheet	100.00
1932	Roster booklet	100.00
1933	Roster booklet—Capitol Building	100.00
1934	Roster booklet—Capitol Building	100.00
1935	Roster booklet—Capitol Building	100.00
1936	Capitol Building	75.00
1937	Capitol Building	75.00
1938	Capitol Building	75.00
1939	Capitol Building	75.00
1940	Capitol Building	75.00
1941	Capitol Building	75.00
1942	Capitol Building	75.00
1943	Capitol Building	75.00
1944	Capitol Building	60.00
1945	Capitol Building	60.00
1946	Capitol Building	60.00

Year	Cover	Price
1947	Capitol Building	50.00
1948	Capitol Building	50.00
1949	Capitol Building	50.00
1950	Capitol Building	50.00
1951	Capitol Building	50.00
1952	Capitol Building	50.00
1953	Capitol/bat/baseball	50.00
1954	Capitol/bat/baseball	50.00
1955	Capitol/bat/baseball	50.00
1956	Reporter	40.00
1957	Mascot	40.00
1958	Golden anniversary of BBWAA	40.00
1959	Mascot	40.00
1960	Baseball scene	75.00
1961	Doherty/Quesada/Vernon	60.00
1962	Stadium	60.00
1963	Stadium	40.00
1964	Stadium	40.00
1965	Stadium	30.00
1966	Stadium	30.00
1967	Baseball scene	30.00
1968	Baseball scene	30.00
1969	Frank Howard	25.00
1970	Ted Williams	25.00
1971	Stadium	20.00

YEARBOOKS

With more pictures and general content than media guides, yearbooks appeal to the casual baseball fan. In addition to player biographies similar to those found in media guides, yearbooks often include lengthy team histories.

Yearbooks haven't proven as popular as media guides with fans or collectors, which may be why several teams didn't produce them in the 1980s. The prices below are for specimens in excellent condition. Yearbooks from 1994 to the present typically sell for the $5.00 cover price.

Atlanta Braves

Year	Cover	Price
1966	Hank Aaron/Eddie Mathews	$50.00
1967	Baseball scene	30.00
1968	Baseball scene	25.00
1969	Baseball scene	25.00
1970	Baseball scene	20.00
1971	Hank Aaron/Babe Ruth	20.00
1972	Five Players	20.00
1973	Player	20.00
1974	Hank Aaron/Babe Ruth	20.00
1975	Four Players	20.00
1976	Aaron/Cepeda/Niekro	20.00
1977	Hank Aaron	15.00
1978	Burdette/Niekro/Spahn	15.00
1979	Gene Garber	15.00
1980	Bobby Cox/Bob Horner	15.00
1981	Bob Horner/Dale Murphy	15.00
1982	Aaron/Horner/Spahn	15.00
1983	Phil Niekro	12.00
1984	Aaron/Horner/Murphy	12.00
1985	Hank Aaron/Dale Murphy	10.00
1986	Dale Murphy/Chuck Tanner	10.00
1987	Dale Murphy	10.00
1988	Braves Illustrated	10.00
1989	no yearbook issued	—
1990	25 years in Atlanta	10.00
1991	no yearbook issued	—
1992	NL Champions	10.00
1993	no yearbook issued	—
1994	(cover subject unavailable)	5.00
1995	(cover subject unavailable)	5.00
1996	(cover subject unavailable)	5.00
1997	(cover subject unavailable)	5.00

Baltimore Orioles

Year	Cover	Price
1954	Mascot	$350.00
1955	Mascot swinging bat	175.00
1956	Mascot leaning on bat	175.00
1957	Mascot pitching	175.00
1958	Mascot	175.00
1959	Mascot	125.00
1960	Mascot	125.00
1961	Mascot	100.00
1962	Jim Gentile	100.00
1963	Pitcher	100.00
1964	Player	100.00
1965	Bauer/Bunker/B. Robinson	100.00
1966	Blefary/Powell/B. Robinson/F. Robinson	75.00
1967	Frank Robinson	75.00
1968	Brooks and Frank Robinson	40.00
1969	Dave McNally	40.00
1970	Boog Powell	35.00
1971	Brooks Robinson/Jim Palmer	20.00
1972	Palmer/McNally/Cuellar	20.00
1973	Player	20.00
1974	Orioles jukebox	20.00
1975	(cover subject unavailable)	15.00
1976-79	no yearbook issued	—
1980	Mascot	10.00
1981	Players	10.00
1982	Frank Robinson/Earl Weaver	10.00
1983	Brooks Robinson	10.00
1984	30th Anniversary	10.00
1985	no yearbook issued	—
1986	Murray/Ripken/B. Robinson/F. Robinson	10.00
1987-92	no yearbook issued	—
1993	Camden Yards	10.00
1994	(cover subject unavailable)	5.00
1995	(cover subject unavailable)	5.00
1996	(cover subject unavailable)	5.00
1997	(cover subject unavailable)	5.00

Boston Braves

Year	Cover	Price
1946	(cover subject unavailable)	$300.00
1947	Billy Southworth	200.00
1948	no yearbook issued	—
1949	no yearbook issued	—
1950	Braves logo	175.00
1951	Braves Field	150.00
1952	Players	150.00

Boston Red Sox

Year	Cover	Price
1951	Fenway Park	$275.00
1952	Baseball scene	200.00
1953	no yearbook issued	—
1954	no yearbook issued	—
1955	Player	150.00
1956	Team owners	100.00
1957	Fenway Park	125.00
1958	Players and fans	75.00
1959	Player	75.00
1960	Gary Geiger	75.00
1961	Player	75.00
1962	Carl Yastrzemski	75.00
1963	(cover subject unavailable)	50.00
1964	(cover subject unavailable)	50.00
1965	Dick Radatz	50.00
1966	Fenway Park	50.00
1967	Conigliaro/Scott/Yastrzemski	75.00
1968	Lonborg/D. Williams/Yastrzemski	40.00
1969	Fenway Park	40.00
1970	Lyle/Petrocelli/Yastrzemski	40.00
1971	Petrocelli/Scott/Yastrzemski	20.00
1972	Carl Yastrzemski	20.00
1973	Carlton Fisk	25.00
1974	Carlton Fisk/Thurman Munson	15.00
1975	Fisk/Foxx/Williams/Yastremski	15.00
1976	Fred Lynn	15.00
1977	Carl Yastrzemski	15.00
1978	Jim Rice/Carl Yastrzemski	15.00
1979	Jim Rice	15.00
1980	Fred Lynn	10.00
1981	Eckersley/Rice/Yastrzemski	10.00
1982	Evans/Lansford/Rice/Yastrzemski	10.00
1983	Carl Yastrzemski	10.00
1984	Jim Rice	10.00
1985	Tony Armas	10.00
1986	Wade Boggs	10.00
1987	Roger Clemens	10.00
1988	Wade Boggs/Rogers Clemens	10.00
1989	Dwight Evans	10.00
1990	Ellis Burk/Mike Greenwell	10.00
1991	Burks/Clemens/Peña	10.00
1992	Clemens/Reardon/Viola	10.00
1993	Roger Clemens	10.00
1994	(cover subject unavailable)	5.00
1995	(cover subject unavailable)	5.00
1996	(cover subject unavailable)	5.00
1997	(cover subject unavailable)	5.00

Brooklyn Dodgers

Year	Cover	Price
1941	Catcher	$300.00
1947	Player sliding into third	250.00
1948	no yearbook issued	—
1949	NL Champions	350.00
1950	Player drawing	300.00
1951	Bum drawing	250.00
1952	Bum drawing	225.00
1953	Bum drawing	200.00
1954	Bum drawing	250.00
1955	Bum drawing	400.00
1956	Bum drawing	250.00
1957	Bums with pennants drawing	200.00

California Angels

Year	Cover	Price
1966	Anaheim Stadium	$75.00
1967	Team logo	25.00
1968-82	no yearbook issued	—
1983	Carew/Jackson/Lynn	12.00
1984	Anaheim Stadium	12.00
1985	25th Anniversary	12.00
1986-91	no yearbook issued	—
1992	Abbott/Finley/Harvey/Langston	10.00
1993	Nolan Ryan	10.00
1994	(cover subject unavailable)	5.00
1995	(cover subject unavailable)	5.00
1996	(cover subject unavailable)	5.00
1997	(cover subject unavailable)	5.00

Chicago Cubs

Year	Cover	Price
1934	Batter drawing	$800.00
1935-38	no yearbook issued	
1939	(cover subject unavailable)	300.00
1941	(cover subject unavailable)	250.00
1942	(cover subject unavailable)	250.00
1948	Team logo	150.00
1949	Team logo	75.00
1950	Cubs cap	75.00
1951	Red glove	75.00
1952	Team logo	75.00
1953	Team logo	60.00
1954	Team logo	60.00
1955	Team logo	60.00
1956	(cover subject unavailable)	100.00
1957	Player head	125.00
1958-84	no yearbook issued	—
1985	Wrigley Field	10.00
1986	Ryne Sandberg	10.00
1987	Ryne Sandberg/Billy Williams	10.00
1988	Andre Dawson	10.00
1989	(cover subject unavailable)	10.00
1990	Bats	10.00
1991	Ryne Sandberg	10.00
1992	Wrigley Field scoreboard	10.00
1993	Mark Grace	10.00
1994	(cover subject unavailable)	5.00
1995	(cover subject unavailable)	5.00
1996	(cover subject unavailable)	5.00
1997	(cover subject unavailable)	5.00

Chicago White Sox

Year	Cover	Price
1951	(cover subject unavailable)	$350.00
1952	(cover subject unavailable)	250.00
1953	Comisky Park	200.00
1954	Player	150.00
1955	Player	100.00
1956	Baseball scene	100.00
1957	Player	80.00
1958	Player	80.00
1959	Cartoon head	100.00
1960	Player	75.00
1961	Player	50.00
1962	Player	40.00
1963	Player	40.00
1964	Comisky Park	40.00
1965	Uniform	40.00
1966	Baseball scene	40.00
1967	Baseball scene	25.00
1968	Baseball scene	25.00
1969	Tommy John	25.00
1970	Baseball scene	40.00
1971-81	no yearbook issued	—
1982	Fisk/La Russa/Luzinski	10.00
1983	Carlton Fisk	10.00
1984	Hoyt/Kittle/La Russa/Luzinski	10.00
1985-89	no yearbook issued	—
1990	Comisky Park	8.00
1991	Comisky Park	8.00
1992	Team logo	8.00
1993	Cooperstown Collection	8.00
1994	(cover subject unavailable)	5.00
1995	(cover subject unavailable)	5.00
1996	(cover subject unavailable)	5.00
1997	(cover subject unavailable)	5.00

Cincinnati Reds

Year	Cover	Price
1919	Pitcher drawing	$1,500.00
1919	Diamond die-cut with Pat Moran	2,000.00
1947	(cover subject unavailable)	400.00
1948	Ewell Blackwell/Ray Lamanno	250.00
1949	Harry Gumbert/Bucky Walters	250.00
1950	no yearbook issued	—
1951	75th Anniversary of NL	150.00
1952	Crosley Field	150.00
1953	Mascot	100.00
1954	Mascot	100.00
1955	Mascot	100.00
1956	Mascot	100.00
1957	Mascot	100.00
1958	Mascot	50.00
1959	Johnny Vander Meer	50.00
1960	Eppa Rixey	50.00
1961	Mascot	50.00
1962	Mascot	50.00
1963	Mascot	75.00
1964	Mascot	40.00
1965	Mascot	40.00
1966	Mascot	30.00
1967	Mascot	30.00
1968	Team-signed baseball	25.00
1969	Bench/Perez/Rose	25.00
1970	Johnny Bench	25.00
1971	Anderson/Bench/Rose	15.00
1972	Johnny Bench/Tony Perez	15.00
1973	Johnny Bench/Joe Morgan	15.00
1974	Pete Rose	20.00
1975	Joe Morgan	20.00
1976	Morgan/Perez/Rose	12.00
1977	Morgan/Foster/Bench	12.00
1978	Pete Rose	12.00
1979	Bench/Foster/Griffey/Perez	12.00
1980	Equipment	10.00
1981	Riverfront Stadium	10.00
1982	Stadium seat	10.00
1983	Player and fans	10.00
1984	Equipment	10.00
1985	Pete Rose/Ty Cobb	10.00
1986	no yearbook issued	—
1987	E. Davis/Rose/Parker	12.00
1988	All-Star logo	10.00
1989	Team logo	10.00
1990	Player and fans	10.00
1991	World Series trophy	10.00
1992	Equipment	10.00
1993	Barry Larkin's jersey	10.00
1994	(cover subject unavailable)	5.00
1995	(cover subject unavailable)	5.00
1996	(cover subject unavailable)	5.00
1997	(cover subject unavailable)	5.00

Cleveland Indians

Year	Cover	Price
1948	Team logo	$175.00
1949	Team logo	75.00
1950	Cleveland Municipal Stadium	60.00
1951	Team logo	75.00
1952	Team logo	75.00
1953	Umpire	100.00
1954	Doby/Lemon/Rosen/Wynn	100.00
1955	Mascot	100.00
1956	Mascot	100.00
1957	Mascot	125.00
1958	Herb Score	300.00
1959	Team logo	250.00
1960	Jim Perry	100.00
1961	(cover subject unavailable)	100.00
1962	(cover subject unavailable)	100.00
1963	(cover subject unavailable)	100.00
1964	Mascot	75.00
1965	Uniforms	75.00
1966	Sam McDowell	75.00
1967	(cover subject unavailable)	75.00
1968	Baseball	40.00
1969	Baseball scene	40.00
1970	Sam McDowell	30.00
1971	Baseball scene	15.00
1972	Baseball scene	15.00
1973	Jim Perry	15.00
1974-83	no yearbook issued	—
1984	Julio Franco/Rick Sutcliffe	10.00
1985-88	no yearbook issued	—
1989	Team-signed baseball	10.00
1990	90th Anniversary	10.00
1991	Alomar/Chambliss/Score	10.00
1992	Sandy Alomar/Mike Hargrove	10.00
1993	no yearbook issued	—
1994	(cover subject unavailable)	5.00
1995	(cover subject unavailable)	5.00
1996	(cover subject unavailable)	5.00
1997	(cover subject unavailable)	5.00

Detroit Tigers

Year	Cover	Price
1934	Batter and mascot head	$1,000.00
1935-38	no yearbook issued	—
1939	(cover subject unavailable)	750.00
1940-54	no yearbook issued	—
1955	Catcher drawing	300.00
1956	no yearbook issued	—
1957	Baseball scene	200.00
1958	Ty Cobb	200.00
1959	Batter drawing	150.00
1960	Tiger Stadium	125.00
1961	Mascot	125.00
1962	Mascot	125.00
1963	Mascot	125.00
1964	Mascot	100.00
1965	Bill Freehan	100.00
1966	Willie Horton	75.00
1967	Denny McLain	50.00
1968	Al Kaline	50.00
1969	World Series trophy	50.00
1970	Equipment	25.00
1971	Horton/Kaline/Martin	25.00
1972	Mickey Lolich	15.00
1973	Baseball scene	15.00
1974	Baseball scene	15.00
1975	Ron LeFlore	15.00
1976	75th Anniversary	15.00
1977	Fidrych/LeFlore/Staub	15.00
1978	(cover subject unavailable)	15.00
1979	Alan Trammell/Lou Whitaker	15.00
1980	Morris/Trammell/Whitaker	15.00
1981	Morris/Trammell/Whitaker	15.00
1982	Kirk Gibson	12.00
1983	Charlie Gehringer/Hank Greenberg	12.00
1984	Morris/Trammell/Whitaker	12.00
1985	World Championship Trophy	12.00
1986	Sparky Anderson	10.00
1987	Mascot	10.00
1988	Mascot	10.00
1989	(cover subject unavailable)	10.00
1990	Mascot	10.00
1991	Fielder/Whitaker/Trammell	10.00
1992	Sparky Anderson/Casey Stengel	10.00
1993	no yearbook issued	—
1994	(cover subject unavailable)	5.00
1995	(cover subject unavailable)	5.00
1996	(cover subject unavailable)	5.00
1997	(cover subject unavailable)	5.00

Houston Astros

Year	Cover	Price
1965	Astrodome	$100.00
1966	Astrodome	75.00
1967-81	no yearbook issued	—
1982	Nolan Ryan	15.00
1983-91	no yearbook issued	—
1992	Luis Gonzalez	10.00
1993-97	no yearbook issued	

Houston Colt .45s

Year	Cover	Price
1962	Baseball and pistol	$200.00
1963	(cover subject unavailable)	150.00
1964	(cover subject unavailable)	150.00

Kansas City Athletics

Year	Cover	Price
1955	Baseball scene	$175.00
1956	Mascot with birthday cake	150.00
1957	Kansas City Municipal Stadium	150.00
1958	Player diving back to first drawing	150.00
1959	Kansas City Municipal Stadium	150.00
1960	Team logo	125.00
1961	Baseball	125.00
1962	Team logo	125.00
1963	(cover subject unavailable)	75.00
1964	Baseball scene	75.00
1965	Donkey	75.00
1966	(cover subject unavailable)	60.00
1967	Player	60.00

Kansas City Royals

Year	Cover	Price
1969	Pitcher	$50.00
1970	Amos Otis/Lou Piniella	15.00
1971	Amos Otis/Lou Piniella	15.00
1972	Catcher's mitt	15.00
1973	John Mayberry/Paul Splittorf	15.00
1974	Otis/Mayberry/Splittorff	15.00
1975	Killebrew/Mayberry/McRae	15.00
1976-82	no yearbook issued	—
1983	Statue	10.00
1984	Equipment	10.00
1985	Division Championship	10.00

1986	World Series ring	10.00
1987	Royals Championship pennants	10.00
1988	Royals Stadium	10.00
1989	Locker	10.00
1990	Baseball scene	10.00
1991	Kauffman Stadium scoreboard	10.00
1992	(cover subject unavailable)	10.00
1993	Equipment	10.00
1994	(cover subject unavailable)	5.00
1995	(cover subject unavailable)	5.00
1996	(cover subject unavailable)	5.00
1997	(cover subject unavailable)	5.00

Los Angeles Angels

Year	Cover	Price
1961	(cover subject unavailable)	$150.00
1962	Mascot	100.00
1963	(cover subject unavailable)	50.00
1964	Baseball scene	40.00
1965	Baseball scene	40.00

Los Angeles Dodgers

Year	Cover	Price
1958	Team-signed baseball	$300.00
1959	Player sliding into second draawing	200.00
1960	Dodger Stadium	75.00
1961	Dodger Stadium	75.00
1962	Map of Los Angeles	40.00
1963	Maury Wills	50.00
1964	1963 World Champions banner	25.00
1965	Dodger Stadium	35.00
1966	Walter Alston	25.00
1967	Player juggling crowns drawing	20.00
1968	Don Drysdale/Sandy Koufax	20.00
1969	MLB Centennial 1869-1969	20.00
1970	Mascot	20.00
1971	Dodger Stadium	20.00
1972	Dodger Stadium	20.00
1973	Walter Alston/Maury Wills	25.00
1974	Jimmy Wynn	20.00
1975	Steve Garvey	18.00
1976	Davey Lopes	18.00
1977	Players	12.00
1978	Cey/Garvey/Lasorda	15.00
1979	Tom Lasorda	12.00
1980	Baseball cards	12.00
1981	Dusty Baker/Steve Garvey	12.00
1982	World Series Trophy	12.00
1983	25th Anniversary	12.00
1984	Tom Lasorda	10.00
1985	Garvey/Russell/Valenzuela	10.00
1986	Guerrero/Hershiser/Marshall	10.00
1987	Past yearbook covers	10.00
1988	(cover subject unavailable)	10.00
1989	World Series Trophy	10.00
1990	Dodgers greats	10.00
1991	(cover subject unavailable)	8.00
1992	Dodger greats	8.00

1993	Orel Hershiser/Tommy Lasorda	8.00
1994	(cover subject unavailable)	5.00
1995	(cover subject unavailable)	5.00
1996	(cover subject unavailable)	5.00
1997	(cover subject unavailable)	5.00

Milwaukee Braves

Year	Cover	Price
1953	Baseball scene	$225.00
1954	Fans	125.00
1955	Fans and stadium	100.00
1956	Fans	150.00
1957	Team logo	100.00
1958	World Champion banners	100.00
1959	Mascot	100.00
1960	Mascot	60.00
1961	Player	65.00
1962	Team logo	60.00
1963	Player	50.00
1964	Aaron/Mathews/Spahn/Torre	50.00
1965	Felipe Alou/Bobby Bragan	50.00

Milwaukee Brewers

Year	Cover	Price
1970	Player	$75.00
1971-78	no yearbook issued	—
1979	Larry Hisle	10.00
1980	Gorman Thomas	10.00
1981	Fingers/Molitor/Yount	10.00
1982	Fans	10.00
1983	Robin Yount	10.00
1984	County Stadium	10.00
1985	George Bamberger	10.00
1986	Locker room	10.00
1987	Baseball cards	10.00
1988	Paul Molitor	10.00
1989	Hank Aaron	12.00
1990	Team logo	10.00
1991	Paul Molitor	10.00
1992	Molitor/Gantner/Yount	10.00
1993	no yearbook issued	—

1994	(cover subject unavailable)	5.00
1995	(cover subject unavailable)	5.00
1996	(cover subject unavailable)	5.00
1997	(cover subject unavailable)	5.00

Minnesota Twins

Year	Cover	Price
1961	Player and Minnesota drawing	225.00
1962	Metropolitan Stadium	125.00
1963	Harmon Killebrew	125.00
1964	Glove and baseball	100.00
1965	Team-signed baseball	75.00
1966	Tony Oliva	75.00
1967	Kaat/Killebrew/Oliva	50.00
1968	Jim Kaat/Harmon Killebrew	40.00
1969	Carew/Killebrew/Oliva	40.00
1970	Rod Carew	25.00
1971	Carew/Killebrew/Oliva	25.00
1972	Harmon Killebrew/Tony Oliva	15.00
1973	Frank Quilici	15.00
1974	Rod Carew	15.00
1975	Rod Carew	15.00
1976	Rod Carew	15.00
1977	Past yearbook covers	12.00
1978	Rod Carew	12.00
1979	Batting Helmet	12.00
1980	Baseball cards	10.00
1981	Rod Carew	10.00
1982	Metrodome	10.00
1983	no yearbook issued	—
1984	no yearbook issued	—
1985	(cover subject unavailable)	10.00
1986	25th Anniversary	10.00
1987	Uniforms	10.00
1988	World Champions	10.00
1989	Gaetti/Puckett/Reardon/Viola	10.00
1990	Carew/Oliva/Puckett	10.00
1991	Uniforms	10.00
1992	World Series trophy	10.00
1993	no yearbook issued	—
1994	(cover subject unavailable)	5.00
1995	(cover subject unavailable)	5.00
1996	(cover subject unavailable)	5.00
1997	(cover subject unavailable)	5.00

Montreal Expos

Year	Cover	Price
1969	Larry Jaster	$75.00
1970	Nine pictures	50.00
1971	(cover subject unavailable)	50.00
1972	Psychedelic drawing	50.00
1973-81	no yearbook issued	—
1982	All-Star logo	10.00
1983	Carter/Dawson/Oliver	10.00
1984	Dawson/Raines/Rose	10.00
1985	Baseball	10.00
1986	(cover subject unavailable)	10.00
1987-97	no yearbook issued	—

New York Giants

Year	Cover	Price
1887	"Sketches of the NY Baseball Club"	$1,500.00
1947	(cover subject unavailable)	200.00
1948	no yearbook issued	—
1949	no yearbook issued	—
1950	no yearbook issued	—
1951	Fielder and giant baseball	175.00
1952	Leo Durocher drawing	175.00
1953	Polo Grounds	125.00
1954	Player drawing	250.00
1955	Mascot drawing	250.00
1956	Basball cap	125.00
1957	Play at second	125.00

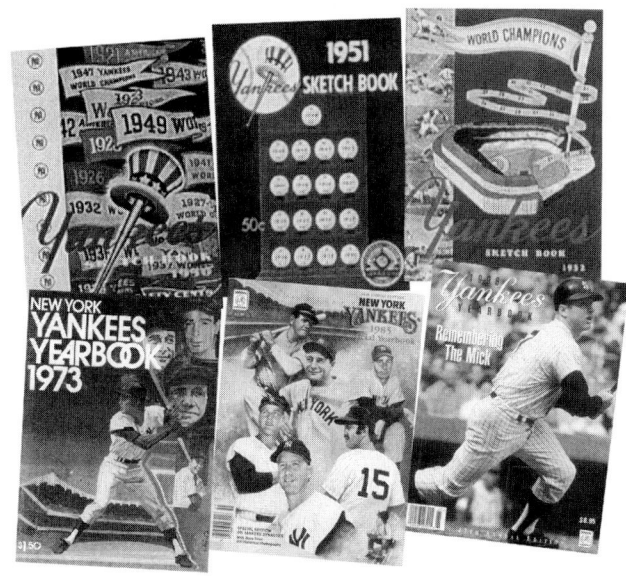

New York Mets

Year	Cover	Price
1962	Baby with team logo	$400.00
1963	(cover subject unavailable)	150.00
1964	Shea Stadium and drawing	100.00
1965	(cover subject unavailable)	75.00
1966	Child with banner drawing	75.00
1967	(cover subject unavailable)	75.00
1968	Gil Hodges drawing	75.00
1969	Shea stadium with floating heads	150.00
1970	World Champions	50.00
1971	Baseball scene	50.00
1972	Harrelson/McGraw/Seaver	15.00
1973	Willie Mays/Tom Seaver	25.00
1974	NL Championhips pennant	25.00
1975	Tom Seaver	25.00
1976	Mascot	20.00
1977	Jerry Koosman	20.00
1978	Baseball scene	20.00
1979	Team logo	15.00
1980	Lee Mazzilli	25.00
1981	Joe Torre	12.00
1982	George Foster/George Bamberger	12.00
1983	Foster/Seaver/Wilson	12.00
1984	Hernandez/Orosco/Strawberry	12.00
1985	Gooden/Hernandez/D. Johnson	25.00
1986	25th Anniversary	10.00
1987	World Champions	10.00
1988	Gooden/D. Johnson/Strawberry	10.00
1989	Carter/Gooden/Strawberry	10.00
1990	Players	10.00
1991	Shea Stadium	10.00
1992	Bonilla/Murray/Saberhagen/Torborg	10.00
1993	Shea Stadium	10.00
1994	(cover subject unavailable)	5.00
1995	(cover subject unavailable)	5.00
1996	(cover subject unavailable)	5.00
1997	(cover subject unavailable)	5.00

New York Yankees

Year	Cover	Price
1950	Past Championship pennants	$400.00
1951	Baseballs on shelves	300.00
1952	Yankee Stadium	275.00
1953	Infielder	200.00
1954	Drawing	175.00
1955	Players	300.00
1956	Mickey Mantle	300.00
1957	Player	300.00
1958	Player	150.00
1959	(cover subject unavailable)	150.00
1960	Drawing	150.00
1961	Yankee Stadium	150.00
1962	Yankee Stadium	150.00
1963	Drawing	100.00
1964	(cover subject unavailable)	100.00
1965	(cover subject unavailable)	75.00
1966	Signed baseballs	75.00
1967	Mickey Mantle	75.00
1968	Mickey Mantle/Mel Stottlemyre	75.00
1969	Mickey Mantle/Mel Stottlemyre	75.00
1970	Mickey Mantle/Mel Stottlemyre	75.00
1971	Bobby Murcer/Roy White	40.00
1972	Murcer/Stottlemyre/White	40.00
1973	DiMaggio/Gehrig/Mantle/Murcer/Ruth	40.00
1974	Bobby Murcer/Thurman Munson	40.00
1975	Past yearbook covers	25.00
1976	Yankee Stadium	25.00
1977	Chris Chambliss	25.00
1978	World Series trophy	25.00
1979	World Series Champions	25.00
1980	Yankee Stadium	15.00
1981	Big Apple	15.00
1982	Winfield/Gossage/Guidry	15.00
1983	Billy Martin	10.00
1984	Yankee greats	10.00
1985	Gehrig/Maris/Mantle/Ruth	10.00
1986	Players	10.00

1987	Gehrig/Mantle/Mattingly	10.00
1988	Clark/Mattingly/Randolph	10.00
1989	Yankee memorabilia	10.00
1990	Don Mattingly	10.00
1991	Players	10.00
1992	Don Mattingly	10.00
1993	Team photo	10.00
1994	(cover subject unavailable)	5.00
1995	(cover subject unavailable)	5.00
1996	(cover subject unavailable)	5.00
1997	(cover subject unavailable)	5.00

Oakland Athletics

Year	Cover	Price
1968	Oakland Coliseum	$75.00
1969	Connie Mack	50.00
1970	Jackson/Monday/Odom	25.00
1971	Sal Bando/Bert Campaneris	25.00
1972	Vida Blue/Dick Williams	25.00
1973	Fingers/Hunter/Rudi/Williams	25.00
1974	World Championship trophies	25.00
1975	"Keep it Alive in '75"	25.00
1976	Bicentennial	20.00
1977	Team logo	20.00
1978	no yearbook issued	—
1979	Team logo	20.00
1980	no yearbook issued	—
1981	no yearbook issued	—
1982	Billy Martin	15.00
1983	Baseball cards	15.00
1984-97	no yearbook issued	—

Philadelphia Athletics

Year	Cover	Price
1949	Connie Mack	$100.00
1950	Connie Mack	100.00
1951	Mascot	100.00
1952	Mascot	100.00
1953	Mascot	125.00
1954	Baseball scene	100.00

Philadelphia Phillies

Year	Cover	Price
1915	Pat Moran	$1,500.00
1949	Batter after swing	350.00
1950	Player drawing	200.00
1951	Player drawing	400.00
1952	Connie Mack Stadium	125.00
1953	Player	125.00
1954	Mascot	125.00
1955	Player	150.00
1956	Richie Ashburn/Robin Roberts	150.00
1957	Basball cap	100.00
1958	Baseball cap	100.00
1959	Team logo	100.00
1960	Players	100.00
1961	(cover subject unavailable)	100.00
1962	Team logo	75.00
1963	Team logo	75.00
1964	Jim Bunning	75.00
1965	Richie Allen/Jim Bunning	50.00
1966	Connie Mack Stadium	50.00
1967	Child eating hot dog	50.00
1968	Phillie ballplayers	50.00
1969	Connie Mack Stadium	50.00
1970	Veterans Stadium	40.00

1971	Veterans Stadium	40.00
1972	Veterans Stadium	40.00
1973	Steve Carlton	40.00
1974	Steve Carlton/Larry Bowa	25.00
1975	Steve Carlton/Mike Schmidt	25.00
1976	Steve Carlton/Mike Schmidt	25.00
1977	Larry Bowa	15.00
1978	Steve Carlton/Mike Schmidt	15.00
1979	Carlton/Rose/Schmidt	15.00
1980	Carlton/Rose/Schmidt	20.00
1981	World Series ring	20.00
1982	Carlton/Rose/Schmidt	12.00
1983	Centennial	12.00
1984	Steve Carlton/Mike Schmidt	12.00
1985	Carlton/Hayes/Samuel/Schmidt	10.00
1986	Mike Schmidt	10.00
1987	Juan Samuel/Mike Schmidt	10.00
1988	Veterans Stadium	10.00
1989	V. Hayes/Jordan/Schmidt	10.00
1990	Equipment	10.00
1991	Veterans Stadium	10.00
1992	Dykstra/Daulton/Kruk	10.00
1993	Dykstra/Daulton/Kruk	10.00
1994	(cover subject unavailable)	5.00
1995	(cover subject unavailable)	5.00
1996	(cover subject unavailable)	5.00
1997	(cover subject unavailable)	5.00

 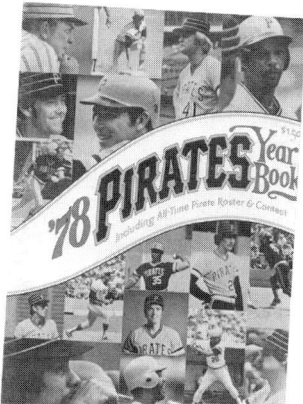

Pittsburgh Pirates

Year	Cover	Price
1910	Pirate with bat, sitting on baseball	$2,500.00
1951	Forbes Field and crossed bats	350.00
1952	Pirate sitting on ball	175.00
1953	(cover subject unavailable)	150.00
1954	Statue	150.00
1955	Mascot	125.00
1956	Mascot	125.00
1957	Mascot	125.00
1958	Mascot	100.00
1959	Mascot	75.00
1960	Pirate in boat	75.00
1961	Mascot	75.00

1962	Team logo	75.00
1963	Mascot	75.00
1964	Baseball scene	75.00
1965	Harry Walker	75.00
1966	Forbes Field	75.00
1967	Roberto Clemente/Bill Mazeroski	75.00
1968	Roberto Clemente/Willie Stargell	50.00
1969	Forbes Field	50.00
1970	Three Rivers Stadium	75.00
1971	Three Rivers Stadium	75.00
1972	Roberto Clemente/Willie Stargell	20.00
1973	Roberto Clemente/Willie Stargell	20.00
1974	Dave Parker/Willie Stargell	15.00
1975	(cover subject unavailable)	10.00
1976	Yosemite Sam	10.00
1977	Baseball cards	10.00
1978	(cover subject unavailable)	10.00
1979	Dave Parker	10.00
1980	(cover subject unavailable)	10.00
1981	Lacy/Madlock/Rhoden	10.00
1982	Willie Stargell/Bill Madlock	10.00
1983	Chuck Tanner	10.00
1984	Brown/Madlock/Peña/Ray	10.00
1985	Bill Mazeroski	10.00
1986	Brown/Leland/Peña/Ray	10.00
1987	Centennial	10.00
1988	Bonds/Bonilla/Van Slyke	10.00
1989	Team logo	10.00
1990	Equipment	10.00
1991	(cover subject unavailable)	10.00
1992	Equipment	10.00
1993	Jay Bell	10.00
1994	(cover subject unavailable)	5.00
1995	(cover subject unavailable)	5.00
1996	(cover subject unavailable)	5.00
1997	(cover subject unavailable)	5.00

San Diego Padres

Year	Cover	Price
1969	Jack Murphy Stadium	$100.00
1970-78	no yearbook issued	—
1979	Dave Winfield	15.00
1980	Dave Winfield	15.00
1981	no yearbook issued	—
1982	(cover subject unavailable)	12.00
1983	Steve Garvey/Dick Williams	12.00
1984	Garvey/Templeton/Williams	12.00
1985	Baseball cap and Championship ring	12.00
1986	Equipment	12.00
1987-91	no yearbook issued	—
1992	Fernandez/Gwynn/Santiago	10.00
1993	25th Anniversary	10.00
1994	(cover subject unavailable)	5.00
1995	(cover subject unavailable)	5.00
1996	(cover subject unavailable)	5.00
1997	(cover subject unavailable)	5.00

San Francisco Giants

Year	Cover	Price
1958	Player with books drawing	$300.00
1959	Baseball scene	100.00
1960	Al Dark	50.00
1961	Basball cap	50.00
1962	NL Champions	50.00
1962	Mid-Season Edition	50.00
1963	Team pennant	40.00
1964	Candlestick Park	40.00
1965	Baseball scene	40.00
1966	Willie Mays	40.00
1967	Juan Marichal/Willie Mays	40.00
1968	Willie Mays	30.00
1969	Bonds/Mays/McCovey	30.00
1970	Willie Mays/Willie McCovey	25.00
1971	Willie McCovey	25.00
1972	Willie Mays	20.00
1973	Bonds/Marichal/Spier	20.00
1974	Rookies	15.00
1975	Mike Caldwell/Gary Matthews	15.00
1976	(cover subject unavailable)	15.00
1977-79	no yearbook issued	—
1980	Mascot	12.00
1981	Frank Robinson	10.00
1982	(cover subject unavailable)	10.00
1983	Frank Robinson	10.00
1984	Equipment	10.00
1985	(cover subject unavailable)	10.00
1986-91	no yearbook issued	—
1992	Will Clark	10.00
1993-97	no yearbook issued	—

Seattle Mariners

Year	Cover	Price
1977	(cover subject unavailable)	$50.00
1978-84	no yearbook issued	—
1985	Beattie/Davis/Langston	10.00
1986-97	no yearbook issued	—

Seattle Pilots

Year	Cover	Price
1969	Team logos	$200.00

St. Louis Browns

Year	Cover	Price
1944	(cover subject unavailable)	$300.00
1945	(cover subject unavailable)	250.00
1946	(cover subject unavailable)	250.00
1947	(cover subject unavailable)	250.00
1948	(cover subject unavailable)	200.00
1949	(cover subject unavailable)	200.00
1950	Team name (wire bound)	200.00
1951	Team logo	200.00
1952	(cover subject unavailable)	300.00
1953	(cover subject unavailable)	200.00

St. Louis Cardinals

Year	Cover	Price
1927	World's Champions	$1,200.00
1951	Mascot	250.00
1952	Player and soldier drawing	175.00
1953	Stan Musial	175.00
1954	Red Schoendienst	100.00
1955	Player	75.00
1956	Player	75.00
1957	Player	75.00
1958	Player	75.00
1959	Stan Musial	75.00
1960	Player	50.00
1961	Ted Simmons/?????? Sadecki	50.00
1962	Stan Musial	50.00
1963	Stan Musial	50.00
1964	Boyer/Groat/Javier/White	50.00
1965	Bob Gibson	50.00
1966	Busch Stadium	75.00
1967	World Champions	75.00
1968	Busch Stadium	50.00
1969	Brock/Flood/Gibson	50.00
1970	Drawings	25.00
1971	Brock/Gibson/Torre	25.00
1972	Player	25.00
1973	Player	25.00
1974	Ted Simmons/Joe Torre	25.00
1975	Lou Brock/Bob Gibson	25.00
1976	Centennial	25.00
1977	Lou Brock/Ty Cobb	15.00
1978	no yearbook issued	—
1979	Mascot	12.00
1980	Keith Hernandez/Ted Simmons	10.00
1981-87	no yearbook issued	—
1988	Team photo	10.00
1989	Vince Coleman/Todd Worrell	10.00
1990	Whitey Herzog	10.00
1991	Lee Smith	12.00
1992	Guerrero/Lankford/Jose/Moore/Musial/Slaughter	10.00
1993	Ozzie Smith	12.00
1994	(cover subject unavailable)	5.00
1995	(cover subject unavailable)	5.00
1996	(cover subject unavailable)	5.00
1997	(cover subject unavailable)	5.00

Texas Rangers

Year	Cover	Price
1976	Cowgirl	$30.00
1977	Team-signed basball	15.00
1978	(cover subject unavailable)	15.00
1979	Ferguson Jenkins/Al Oliver	15.00
1980	Arlington Stadium	15.00
1981	Player	10.00
1982	Team logo	10.00
1983	no yearbook issued	—
1984	George Wright	10.00
1985	Equipment	10.00
1986	no yearbook issued	—
1987	no yearbook issued	—
1988	Ruben Sierra	10.00
1989	no yearbook issued	—
1990	Equipment	10.00
1991	20th Anniversary	10.00
1992	Nolan Ryan	10.00
1993	Arlington Stadium	10.00
1994	(cover subject unavailable)	5.00
1995	(cover subject unavailable)	5.00
1996	(cover subject unavailable)	5.00
1997	(cover subject unavailable)	5.00

Toronto Blue Jays

Year	Cover	Price
1977	(cover subject unavailable)	$50.00
1978	no yearbook issued	—
1979	(cover subject unavailable)	15.00
1980	(cover subject unavailable)	15.00
1981	Jim Clancy/Ernie Whitt	15.00
1982	Martinez/Moseby/Whitt	10.00
1983	Team logo	10.00
1984	Exhibition Stadium	10.00
1985	Team logo	10.00
1986	Baseball and Bat	10.00
1987	Barfield/Clancy/Whitt	10.00
1988	Player	10.00
1989	(cover subject unavailable)	10.00
1990	George Bell	10.00
1991	Drawing	10.00
1992	Roberto Alomar	10.00
1993	World Championship trophy	10.00
1994	(cover subject unavailable)	5.00
1995	(cover subject unavailable)	5.00
1996	(cover subject unavailable)	5.00
1997	(cover subject unavailable)	5.00

Washington Senators

Year	Cover	Price
1947	(cover subject unavailable)	$400.00
1948	no yearbook issued	—
1949	(cover subject unavailable)	350.00
1950	(cover subject unavailable)	300.00
1951	no yearbook issued	—
1952	Player	100.00
1953	The Capitol	100.00
1954	Bob Porterfield/Mickey Vernon	75.00
1955	Mascot	75.00
1956	Clark Griffith drawing	100.00
1957	Players	100.00
1958	Roy Sievers	100.00
1959	(cover subject unavailable)	75.00
1960	Harmon Killebrew drawing	75.00
1961	Team name	150.00
1962	Washington Stadium	75.00
1963	(cover subject unavailable)	75.00
1964	(cover subject unavailable)	50.00
1965	Player	50.00
1966	Baseball scene	25.00
1967	Capitol and Washington Monument	25.00
1968	Player	25.00
1969	Ted Williams	50.00

BASEBALL BOOKS

Once among the least expensive collectibles, baseball books have risen in both popularity and value in recent years. And why not? They make great items for autographing—either by the author or the subject—and they give collectors some insight into many aspects of the game and its best players.

In addition to simple supply and demand, several factors go into determining the value of a book. First editions are far more valuable than subsequent printings. Condition is also important. Consider the condition of both the book and its dust jacket when trying to determine a value.

The following list is by no means comprehensive, but should offer collectors a snapshot of some of the more popular titles among book collectors. The price given is for a first edition printing, with the book and original dust jacket in Excellent condition. Subtract about 50 percent if the book is missing its dust jacket and 25 percent for a second edition. (Note that not every book listed was issued with a dust jacket.)

Title	Author(s)	Publisher	Year	Price
Aaron	Henry Aaron/Furman Bisher	Crowell	1974	$25.00
Aaron R.F.	Henry Aaron/Furman Bisher	World	1968	65.00
A Ball Player's Career	Adrian C. Anson	Era Publishing Co.	1900	500.00
A Baseball Century	Gerald Couzens	Lippincott & Crowell	1980	20.00
A Baseball Century: The First 100 Years of the NL	various	Macmillan	1976	25.00
A Century of Baseball Lore	John Thorn	Galahad	1980	20.00
A Complete History of the Negro Leagues	Mark Ribowsky	Carol Publishing	1997	16.00
A Day in the Bleachers	Arnold Hano	Crowell	1955	72.00
Adios to Ghost	Christy Walsh	self published	1937	100.00
A Dream Season	Gary Carter/John Hough Jr.	Harcourt, Brace, Jovanovich	1986	10.00
A False Spring	Pat Jordan	Dodd & Mead	1975	45.00
After the Miracle	Maury Allen	Watts	1989	20.00
A.G. Spalding and the Rise of Baseball	Peter Levine	Oxford	1985	30.00
A Hand in Sport	Willard Mullin	Barnes	1958	90.00
Al Kaline and the Detroit Tigers	Hal Butler	Regnery	1973	55.00
Al Kaline Story, The	Al Hirshberg	Messner	1964	60.00
All About Baseball	George Sullivan	Putnam	1989	10.00
All the Home Run Kings	A. Daley	Putnam	1972	10.00
All Time All Stars of Black Baseball	James Riley	TK Publishers	1983	120.00
Alston and the Dodgers	Walter Alston	Doubleday	1966	16.00
Always on the Offense	Mike Schmidt	Atheneum	1982	35.00
A Man and His Diamonds	Charles Whitehead	Vantage Press	1980	125.00
Amazing Baseball Teams	Dane Wolf	unknown	1976	10.00
Amazing Mets, The	Jerry Mitchell	Grosset & Dunlap	1970	35.00
Amazing: The Miracle of the Mets	Joseph Durso	Houghton	1970	10.00
American Baseball	David Voight	U. of Oklahoma	1968	20.00
American Boy's Book of Sports and Games, The	unknown	Dick & Fitzgerald	1864	250.00
American Diamond, The	Branch Rickey	Simon & Schuster	1965	150.00
American League Story, The	Lee Allen	Hill & Wang	1962	40.00
American League, The	Donald Honig	Crown	1983	32.00
America's Dizzy Dean	Curtis Smith	Bethany Press	1978	20.00
America's National Game	A. G. Spalding	A. G. Spalding & Bros.	1911	800.00
America Through Baseball	David Voight	Nelson-Hall	1976	30.00
Andy Pafko: The Solid Man	John Hoffman	Barnes	1951	65.00
A Pitcher's Story	Juan Marichal	Doubleday	1967	30.00
A Portrait in Words and Pictures	Dick Johnson	Walker	1991	40.00
Armchair Book of Baseball	John Thorn	Scribner's	1985	15.00
Artful Dodger, The	Tommy Lasorda/David Fisher	Arbour House	1985	20.00
Art of Hitting .300, The	Charlie Lau/Alfred Glossbrenner	Hawthorn	1980	25.00
Art of Pitching, The	Tom Seaver/Lee Lowenfish	Hearst	1984	15.00
A Scrapbook History of Baseball	Jordan Deutsch	Bobbs-Merrill	1975	25.00
A Season in the Sun	Roger Kahn	Harper & Row	1977	50.00
Ask Dale Murphy	Dale Murphy/Curtis Patton	Algoquin	1987	12.50
A Stranger to the Game	Bob Gibson/Lonnie Wheeler	Viking	1994	50.00
At Fenway: Dispatches From Red Sox Nation	Dan Shaughnessy	Crown	1996	14.00
A Thinking Man's Guide to Baseball	Leonard Koppett	Dutton	1967	18.00

Athletic Sports in America	Harry Clay Palmer/Frank Richter	Houghton	1889	300.00
A Tiger in His Time	David Jordan	Diamond	1990	15.00
A Year at a Time	Walter Alston	Word	1976	20.00
Babe: The Legend Comes to Life	Robert Creamer	Simon & Schuster	1974	35.00
Babe and I, The	Claire Ruth	Prentice-Hall	1959	25.00
Babe in Red Stockings, The	Kerry Keene et al	Sagamore	1997	20.00
Babe Ruth	Tom Meany	Barnes	1947	50.00
Babe Ruth	Martin Welden	Crowell	1948	100.00
Babe Ruth and the American Dream	Ken Sobel	Random House	1974	60.00
Babe Ruth As I Knew Him (pb)	Waite Hoyt	Dell	1948	100.00
Babe Ruth Story, The	Babe Ruth/Bob Considine	Dutton	1948	200.00
Babe Ruth, His Story in Baseball	Lee Allen	Putnam	1966	17.50
Babe Ruth: Baseball Boy	Guernsey Van Riper	Bobbs-Merrill	1954	35.00
Babe Ruth: His Life and Legend	Kal Wagenheim	Praeger	1974	45.00
Babe Ruth: Idol of the American Boy	Dan Daniel	Whitman	1930	80.00
Babe Ruth: Sultan of Swat	Lois P. Nicholson	Goodwood	1994	20.00
Babe Ruth-Baseball Boy	Guernsey Van Riper	Bobbs-Merrill	1954	25.00
Babe Ruth's America	Robert Smith	Crowell	1974	40.00
Babe Ruth's Baseball Advice	Babe Ruth	Rand-McNally	1936	200.00
Babe Ruth's Baseball Book for 1932	Babe Ruth	Syndicate	1932	300.00
Babe Ruth's Big Book of Baseball	Babe Ruth	Reilly & Lee	1935	150.00
Babe Ruth's Own Book of Baseball	Babe Ruth	Putnam	1928	75.00
Babe: The Legend Comes To Life	Robert Creamer	Simon & Schuster	1974	60.00
Backstage at the Mets	Lindsey Nelson/Al Hirshberg	Viking	1966	30.00
Ball Four	Jim Bouton	World	1970	40.00
Balldom: The Britannica of Baseball	George Moreland	Balldom	1914	150.00
Ballparks, The	Bill Shannon/George Kalinsky	Hawthorn	1975	75.00
Ballplayers Are Human Too	Ralph Houk	Putnam	1962	25.00
Baltimore Orioles, The	Fred Lieb	Putnam	1955	300.00
Bang the Drum Slowly	Mark Harris	Knopf	1956	150.00
Ban Johnson	Gene Murdock	Greenwood	1982	60.00
Baseball	D. E. Jesse	Ronald	1939	15.00
Baseball America	Donald Honig	Macmillan	1982	20.00
Baseball: America's National Game	A. G. Spalding	American Sports	1911	600.00
Baseball And Mr. Spalding	Arthur Bartlett	Farrar Straus & Young	1951	35.00
Baseball And The Cold War	H. Senzel	Harcourt Brace	1977	25.00
Baseball: An Illustrated History	Ken Burns/Geoffrey Ward	Knopf	1994	60.00
Baseball: An Informal History	Douglas Wallop	Norton	1969	25.00
Baseball As I Have Known It	Fred Lieb	Coward McCann	1977	60.00
Baseball Between the Lines	Donald Honig	Coward McCann	1976	45.00
Baseball Complete	Russ Hodges	Rudolph Field	1952	30.00
Baseball Confidential	Arthur Mann	McKay	1951	48.00
Baseball Days: From the Sandlot to the Show	Bill Littlefield	Bulfinch	1993	10.00
Baseball Diamond in the Rough	Irving Leitner	Criterion	1972	30.00
Base Ball 1845-1871	Seymour Church	unknown	1902	1,200.00
Baseball Encylopedia, The (w/case)	Joe Reichler	Macmillan	1969	60.00
Baseball Extra	Frank Graham	Barnes	1954	35.00
Baseball For Everyone	Joe DiMaggio	Whittlesey House	1948	60.00
Baseball From the Newspaper Accounts	Preston D. Orem	unknown	1961	80.00
Baseball Has Done It	Jackie Robinson	Lippincott	1964	25.00
Baseball—How to Become a Player	John Mongomery Ward	Athletic Publishing Co.	1888	2,000.00
Baseball I Gave You All The Best Years of My Life	Richard Grossinger/Kevin Kerrane	North Atlantic	1977	50.00
Baseball Immortals	Ed Buckholder	Christopher	1955	100.00
Baseball in America	Karen Mullarkey	Collins	1991	40.00
Baseball in Cincinnati	Harry Ellard	Johnson & Hardin	1907	1,500.00
Baseball Is a Funny Game	Joe Garagiola	Lippincott	1960	30.00
Baseball Legends	A. G. Garbec	Gallery Books	1988	20.00
Baseball My Way	Joe Morgan	Atheneum	1976	30.00
Baseball Personalities	Jimmy Powers	Field	1949	25.00
Baseball Players Do Amazing Things	M. Cebuiash	Random House	1973	20.00

A Ball Player's Career

A Stranger to the Game

Baseball Rockies Who Made Good	M. G. Bonner	Knopf	1954	35.00
Baseball Stars of 1962 (pb)	Ray Robinson	Pyramid Books	1962	15.00
Baseball Story, The	Fred Lieb	Putnam	1950	72.00
Baseball Techniques Illustrated	various	Ronald Press	1951	15.00
Baseball: The Fan's Game	Mickey Cochrane	Funk & Wagnall's	1939	150.00
Baseball Through a Knothole	Bill Borst	Krank	1980	15.00
Baseball Treasures	Douglas Congdon-Martin	Schiffer	1992	50.00
Baseball When the Grass was Real	Donald Honig	Coward McCann	1975	35.00
Baseball's Best	Martin Appel	McGraw Hill	1977	30.00
Baseball's Best	Tom Meany	Watts	1964	28.00
Baseball's Famous First Baseman	Ira Smith	Barnes	1956	35.00
Baseball's Famous Outfielders	Ira Smith	Barnes	1954	35.00
Baseball's Famous Pitchers	Ira Smith	Barnes	1954	30.00
Baseball's 50 Greatest Games	Lowell Reidenbaugh	The Sporting News	1986	20.00
Baseball's Golden Age	Charles Conlon/N. & C. McCabe	Harry N. Abrams	1997	25.00
Baseball's Great Experiment	Jules Tygiel	Oxford	1983	32.00
Baseball's Great Tragedy	Bob McGarigle	Expostion	1972	90.00
Baseball's Greatest Catchers	Al Hirshberg	Putnam	1966	30.00
Baseball's Greatest Drama	Joseph Krueger	Classic	1945	40.00
Baseball's Greatest Hitters	Tom Meany	Barnes	1950	60.00
Baseball's Greatest Lineup	Christy Walsh	Barnes	1952	50.00
Baseball's Greatest Managers	Edwin Pope	Doubleday	1960	20.00
Baseball's Greatest Pitchers	Tom Meany	Barnes	1951	60.00
Baseball's Greatest Pitchers	Milton Shapiro	Messner	1969	40.00
Baseball's Greatest Records, Streaks and Feats	Harvey Frommer	Atheneum	1983	15.00
Baseball's Greatest Rivalry	Harvey Frommer	Atheneum	1982	20.00
Baseball's Greatest Sluggers	B. Libby	Random House	1973	15.00
Baseball's Greatest Teams	Tom Meany	Barnes	1949	40.00
Baseball's Hall of Fame Cooperstown	Joe Happel	unknown	1986	10.00
Baseball's Most Valuable Players	G. Vecsey	Random House	1966	30.00
Baseball's 100	Maury Allen	A&W	1981	20.00
Baseball's 10 Greatest Teams	Donald Honig	Macmillan	1982	25.00
Baseball's 25 Greatest Pennant Races	Lowell Reidenbaugh	The Sporting News	1987	32.00
Baseball's Unforgettable Games	Joe Reichler/Ben Olan	Ronald	1960	40.00
Baseball Uniforms of the 20th Century	Marc Okkonen	Sterling	1991	25.00
Baseball: Vol. 1, The Early Years	Harold Seymour	Oxford	1960	100.00
Baseball: Vol. 2, The Golden Age	Harold Seymour	Oxford	1960	75.00
Baseball: Vol. 3, The People's Game	Harold Seymour	Oxford	1960	75.00
Baseball Wit	B. Adler	Crown	1986	15.00
Bats	Davey Johnson/Peter Golenbock	Putnam	1986	45.00
Batting	Carl Yastrzemski/Al Hirshberg	Viking	1972	25.00
Batting Cleanup, Bill Conlin	Kevin Kerrane	Temple UP	1997	25.00
Beating the Bushes	Frank Dolson	Icarus Pr.	1982	25.00
Behind the Mask	Bill Freehan	World	1970	30.00
Behind the Mask	Dave Pallone/Alan Steinberg	Viking	1990	12.50
Best of Baseball, The	Sidney Offit	Putnam	1956	72.00
Best Seats in Baseball, But You have to Stand, The	Lee Gutkind	Dial	1975	35.00
Between The Lines	Steve Howe	Masters	1989	12.50

Beyond the Sixth Game	Peter Gammons	Houghton Mifflin	1985	25.00
Big Red Machine, The	Bob Hertzel	Prentice-Hall	1976	25.00
Bill James Guide to Baseball Managers	Bill James	Scribner	1997	15.00
Bill James Historical Baseball Abstract, The	Bill James	Villard	1986	50.00
Bill Veeck A Baseball Legend	Gerald Eskenazi	McGraw Hill	1988	20.00
Billy	Billy Williams/Irv Haag	Rand McNally	1974	45.00
Billy Ball	Billy Martin/Phil Pepe	Doubleday	1987	25.00
Billy Martin	Gene Schoor	Doubleday	1980	17.50
Billy Sunday: The Man and His Message	William T. Ellis	Winston	1914	160.00
Bingo Long Traveling All Stars and Motor Kings	William Brashler	Harper & Row	1973	100.00
Black Diamonds	John Holway	Meckler	1989	20.00
Blackball Stars	John Holway	Meckler	1988	35.00
Bleachers: A Summer in Wrigley Field	Lonnie Wheeler	Contemporary	1988	30.00
Bleep!	Larry Bowa/Barry Bloom	Bonus	1988	20.00
Bless You Boys	Sparky Anderson/Dan Ewald	Contemporary	1984	15.00
Blooper Man, The	Elson Smith	J. Pohl	1981	25.00
Bo Knows Bo	Bo Jackson/Dick Schaap	Doubleday	1990	15.00
Bo: Pitching & Wooing	Maury Allen	Dial	1973	18.00
Bob Allison Story, The	Hal Butler	Messner	1967	50.00
Bob Feller	Gene Schoor	Doubleday	1962	60.00
Bob Lemon: The Work Horse	Ed McAuley	Barnes	1951	60.00
Bobby Bonds Rising Superstar	G. Sullivan	Putnam	1976	30.00
Bobby Richardson Story, The	Bobby Richardson	Revell	1965	20.00
Bobby Shant	Ed Delaney	Barnes	1953	50.00
Book of American Pastimes, The	Charles Peverelly	self published	1866	2,500.00
Book of Baseball, The	William Patten/Walker McSpadden	Collier	1911	600.00
Book of Major League Baseball Clubs, The	Ed Fitzgerald	Barnes	1952	60.00
Born to Play Ball	Willie Mays/Charles Einstein	Putnam	1955	55.00
Boston Braves	Harold Khese	Putnam	1948	80.00
Boston Red Sox	Tom Meany et al	Barnes	1956	50.00
Boston Red Sox, The	Fred Lieb	Putnam	1947	70.00
Box Socials	W. P. Kinsella	Harper/Collins	1993	20.00
Boys of Fairport, The	Noah Brooks	Scribner's	1898	90.00
Boys of Summer, The	Roger Kahn	H & R	1972	50.00
Boys Who Would Be Cubs, The	Joseph Bosco	Morrow	1990	20.00
Branch Rickey	Murray Polner	Atheneum	1982	45.00
Branch Rickey, American in Action	Arthur Mann	Houghton Mifflin	1957	36.00
Braves, the Pick and the Shovel, The	Al Hirshberg	Waverly House	1948	100.00
Breakout	Ron Leflore/Jim Hawkins	Harper & Row	1978	15.00
Breakthrough to the Big League	Jackie Robinson/Alfred Duckett	Harper & Row	1965	35.00
Broadcasters, The	Red Barber	Dial	1970	30.00
Bronx Zoo, The	Sparky Lyle/Peter Golenbock	Crown	1979	30.00
Brooklyn Dodgers, The	Frank Graham	Putnam	1945	80.00
Brooklyn's Dodgers	Carl E. Prince	Oxford UP	1996	15.00
Brooks Robinson Story, The	Jack Zanger	Messner	1967	15.00
Bums: An Oral History Of The Brooklyn Dodgers	Peter Golenbock	Putnam	1984	25.00
Bums No More!	Stewart Wolpin	St. Martin's	1995	15.00
Bury My Heart at Wrigley Field	Larry Names	Sportsbook	1990	12.00
Bush League	Robert Obojski	Macmillan	1975	48.00
Busting 'Em	Ty Cobb	Clode	1914	1,000.00
Cal Ripken Jr. Count Me In	Cal Ripken Jr./Greg Brown	Taylor	1995	15.00
Calvin: Baseball's Last Dinosaur	Jon Kerr	Brown	1990	40.00
Can't Anybody Here Play This Game?	Jimmy Breslin	Viking	1963	40.00
Carew	Rod Carew/Ira Berkow	Simon & Schuster	1979	25.00
Casey	Joseph Durso	Prentice-Hall	1967	30.00
Casey at the Bat	Casey Stengel/Harry T. Paxton.	Random House	1962	40.00
Casey Stengel	Frank Graham	John Day	1958	20.00
Casey Stengel	Norman MacLean	Drake	1976	30.00
Casey Stengel: Baseball's Greatest Manager	Gene Schoor	Messner	1953	35.00
Casey Stengel's Secrets	Clay Felker	Walker	1961	40.00

America's National Game

The Babe in Red Stockings

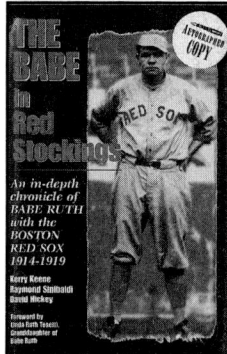

Catch You Later	Johnny Bench/William Brashler	Harper & Row	1979	30.00
Catch: A Major League Life	Ernie Whitt/Greg Cable	McGraw Hill	1988	27.50
Catcher Was a Spy, The	Nicholas Dawidoff	Pantheon	1994	17.00
Catching	Elston Howard	Viking	1966	25.00
Catfish	Jim "Catfish" Hunter/Armen Keteyian	McGraw Hill	1988	10.00
Catfish Hunter	Irwin Stambler	Putnam	1976	20.00
Catfish, Million Dollar Pitcher	Bill Libby	Coward McCann	1976	12.50
Celebrant, The	Eric Rolfe Greenberg	U. of Nebraska	1983	75.00
Chadwick's Baseball Manual	Henry Chadwick	American News Co.	1889	300.00
Champagne and Baloney	Tom Clark	Harper & Row	1976	17.50
Champions of the Bat	Milton Shapiro	Messner	1967	30.00
Charlie Hustle	Pete Rose/Bob Hertzel	Prentice-Hall	1975	35.00
Charlie O and the Angry A's	Bill Libby	Doubleday	1975	20.00
Chicago Cubs	Jim Enright	Macmillan	1975	30.00
Chicago Cubs, The	Warren Brown	Putnam	1946	80.00
Chicago White Sox, The	Warren Brown	Putnam	1952	90.00
Chin Music	James McManus	Crown	1985	25.00
Christy Mathewson	Gene Schoor	Messner	1953	90.00
Chrysanthemum and the Bat, The	Robert Whiting	Dodd & Mead	1977	50.00
Cincinnati Game, The	Lonnie Wheeler/John Baskin	Orange Frazer Press	1988	50.00
Cincinnati Reds, The	Lee Allen	Putnam	1948	100.00
Cincinnati Reds, The	Ritter Collett	Jordan-Powers	1976	125.00
Clemente	Kal Wagenheim	Praeger	1973	48.00
Cleon	Cleon Jones	Coward McCann	1970	25.00
Cleveland Indians, The	Franklin Lewis	Putnam	1949	80.00
Clowning Through Baseball	Al Schacht	Barnes	1941	80.00
Collision At Home Plate	James Reston Jr.	Burlingame	1991	20.00
Colorado Rockies: The Inaugural Season	Clarkson, Rich	Fulcrum	1993	45.00
Comeback, The	Ryne Duren	Lorenz	1978	36.00
Commy	G. W. Axelson	Reilly & Lee	1919	600.00
Confessions from Left Field	Raymond Mungo	Dutton	1983	20.00
Connie Mack	Fred Lieb	Putnam	1945	60.00
Connie Mack's Baseball Book	Connie Mack	Knopf	1950	50.00
Cooperstown: Where Legends Live Forever	Lowell Reidenbaugh	The Sporting News	1983	20.00
Country Hardball	Enos Slaughter/Kevin Reid	Tudor	1981	45.00
Covering All the Bases	Lou Boudreau/Russell Schneider	Sagamore	1993	35.00
Covering the Bases	Benedict Cosgrove	Chronicle	1997	15.00
Covering the Outfield	Terry Moore	Ziff-Davis	1948	40.00
Crash	Dick Allen/Tom Whitaker	Ticknor & Fields	1989	20.00
Crooked Pitch, The	Martin Quigley	Algoquin	1984	35.00
Cubs of 69, The	Rick Tally	Contemporary	1989	20.00
Curious Case of Sidd Finch	George Plimpton	Macmillan	1987	15.00
Curse of Rocky Colavito, The	Terry Pluto	Simon & Schuster	1994	15.00
Curse of the Bambino, The	Dan Shaughnessy	Dutton	1990	25.00
Damn Yankee	Maury Allen	Times	1980	20.00
Darryl	Darryl Strawberry/Art Rust	Bantam	1992	12.50
Dave Winfield: 23 Million Dollar Man	Gene Schoor	Stein & Day	1982	30.00
Day With the Giants	Laraine Day	Doubleday	1952	30.00

Days of Mr. McGraw, The	Joseph Durso	Prentice-Hall	1969	35.00
Decline and Fall of the New York Yankees, The	Jack Mann	unknown	1967	25.00
Detroit Tigers	Joe Falls	Macmillan	1975	40.00
Detroit Tigers, The	Fred Lieb	Putnam	1946	60.00
Diamond Dreams	Walter Iooss/Tom Boswell	Little, Brown & Company	1996	50.00
Diamonds Are Forever	Peter Gordon	Chronicle	1987	40.00
Diamonds in the Rough	David Hanneman	Diamond	1989	12.50
Diamonds in the Rough	Ken Rappoport	Tempo	1979	10.00
Diamonds of the Rough	Joel Zoss/John Bowman	Macmillan	1989	30.00
Diamonds: The Evolution of the Ballpark	Michael Gershman	Houghton Mifflin	1993	40.00
Diary of a Yankee Hater	Bob Marshall	Watts	1981	7.50
DiMaggio Albums, The	Richard Whittingham	Putnam	1982	30.00
Dixie Association	Donald Hays	Simon & Schuster	1984	30.00
Dixon Cornbelt League, The	W. P. Kinsella	Harper/Collins	1993	25.00
Dizziest Season, The	G. H. Fleming	Morrow	1984	40.00
Dizzy Baseball	Dizzy Dean	Greenberg	1952	40.00
Dizzy Dean Story, The	Milton Shapiro	Messner	1963	70.00
Dock Ellis on the Country of Baseball	Donald Hall/Dock Ellis	Coward McCann	1976	20.00
Dodger Daze and Knights	Tommy Holmes	McKay	1953	90.00
Dodgers and Me, The	Leo Durocher	Ziff-Davis	1948	50.00
Dodgers Encyclopedia, The	William F. McNeil	Sports Publications Inc.	1997	40.00
Dodgers Move West, The	Neil Sullivan	Oxford University Press	1987	25.00
Dodgers, The	John Durant	Hastings House	1948	120.00
Dodgers! The First 100 Years	Stanley Cohen	Bird Lane Press	1990	30.00
Dodgers' Way to Play Baseball, The	Al Campanis	Dutton	1954	60.00
Don Baylor	Don Baylor/Claire Smith	St. Martin	1989	20.00
Don Drysdale Story, The	Milton Shapiro	Messner	1964	75.00
Don't Knock the Rock	Gordon Cobbledick	World	1966	60.00
Double X: Jimmie Foxx Baseball's Forgotton Slugger	Bob Gorman	Holy Name Society	1990	15.00
Down to the Wire	Jeff Miller	Taylor	1992	12.50
Duke of Flatbush, The	Duke Snider/Bill Gillbert	Zebra	1988	30.00
Duke Snider Story, The	Irwin Winehouse	Messner	1964	20.00
Dwight Gooden: Strikeout King	Nathan Aaseng	Lerner	1988	10.00
Dynasty	Peter Golenbock	Prentice-Hall	1975	30.00
Earl of Baltimore, The	Terry Pluto	New Century	1982	25.00
Early Innings	Dean Sullivan/Benjamin Rader	U. of Nebraska	1995	25.00
Eddie Mathews and the National Pastime	Eddie Mathews/Bob Buege	Douglas American	1994	45.00
Education of a Baseball Player	Mickey Mantle	Simon & Schuster	1967	40.00
Eight Men Out	Eliot Asinof	Holt, Rinehart, Winston	1963	50.00
El Tiante	Luis Tiant/Joe Fitzgerald	Doubleday	1976	20.00
Endless Summers	Jack Torry	Diamond	1995	15.00
Even the Browns	William Mead	Contemporary	1978	30.00
Every Diamond Doesn't Sparkle	Fresco Thomson	unknown	1964	25.00
Ewell Blackwell	Lou Smith	Barnes	1951	75.00
Explosion	Mark Gallagher	Arbor House	1987	60.00
Expos Inside Out, The	Dan Turner	McClelland & Steward	1983	35.00
Extra Innings	Frank Robinson	McGraw Hill	1988	25.00
Fairport Nine, The	Noah Brooks	Scribner's	1880	600.00
Famous Baseball Stars	Bill Gutman	Dodd & Mead	1973	45.00
Fan, The	Peter Abrahams	Warner	1995	25.00
Fear Strikes Out	Jim Piersall/Al Hirshberg	Atlantic, Little, Brown	1957	30.00
Ferguson Jenkins: The Quiet Winner	Stanley Pashko	Putnam	1975	55.00
Fernando!	Mike Littwin	Bantam	1981	10.00
Fielding	Malcom Child	unknown	1953	25.00
Fireballers, The	J. Newcombe	Putnam	1964	20.00
Fireside Book of Baseball, The	Charles Einstein	Simon & Schuster	1956	75.00
Fireside Book of Baseball, The 2nd	Charles Einstein	Simon & Schuster	1958	90.00
Fireside Book of Baseball, The 3rd	Charles Einstein	Simon & Schuster	1968	150.00
Five O'Clock Comes Early	Bob Welch/George Vescey	Morrow	1982	32.00
Five O'Clock Lightning	Tommy Henrich	Birch Lane	1992	45.00

The Book of Baseball

Chadwick's Baseball Manual

Five Seasons	Roger Angell	Simon & Schuster	1977	18.00
Five Straight Errors on Ladies Day	Walter Nagle	Caxton	1965	70.00
Frank: The First Year	Frank Robinson	Holt, Reinhart, Winston	1976	30.00
Frank Frisch: The Fordham Flash	Frank Frisch/Roy Stockton	Doubleday	1962	50.00
Frank Howard: The Gentle Giant	Al Hirshberg	Putnam	1973	35.00
Frank Robinson: The Making of a Manager	Russell Schneider	Coward, McCann, Geoghegan	1976	25.00
Fred Lynn, The Hero From Boston	Ed Dolan/Richard Lyttle	Icarus Pr.	1982	25.00
Fred Lynn, Young Star	Bill Libby	Putnam	1977	40.00
From Behind the Plate	Johnny Bench	Prentice-Hall	1972	35.00
From Cobb to Catfish	John Kuenster	Rand McNally	1975	25.00
From Ghetto to Glory	Bob Gibson/Phil Pepe	Prentice-Hall	1968	30.00
From Sandlot to Big League	Connie Mack	Knopf	1960	30.00
From Sandlots to League President	Al Hirshberg	Messner	1962	70.00
Fundamentals of Baseball	C. D. Wardlaw	Scribner's	1924	100.00
Further Adventures of Slugger McBatt, The	W. P. Kinsella	Houghton Mifflin	1988	50.00
Gabby Hartnett Story, The	James Murphy	Expostion	1983	40.00
Game of Baseball, The	Gil Hodges/Frank Slocum	Crown	1969	40.00
Gamer, The	Gary Carter	Word	1993	40.00
Games, Asterisks and People	Ford C. Frick	Crown	1973	30.00
Garvey	Steve Garvey/Skip Rozin	Times	1986	20.00
Gary Carter's Iron Mask	Robert Montgomery	Troll	1991	15.00
Gashouse Gang, The	Robert E. Hood	Morrow	1976	18.00
Gashouse Gang, The	J. Roy Stockton	Barnes	1945	60.00
George Brett Story, The	John Garrity	Putnam	1981	65.00
George Foster Story, The	George Foster/Malka Drucker	Holiday House	1979	25.00
Get That Nigger Off The Field	Arthur Rust, Jr.	Delacorte Press	1976	90.00
Giants of San Francisco, The	Art Rosenbaum/Bob Stevens	Coward McCann	1963	40.00
Giants and the Dodgers, The	Lee Allen	Putnam	1964	60.00
Giants, The-Memories and Memorabilia	Bruce Chadwick/David Spindel	Abbeville Press	1993	25.00
Gil Hodges Story, The	Milton Shapiro	Messner	1960	60.00
Gil Hodges: The Quite Man	Marino Amoruso	Erickson	1991	25.00
Ginger Kid, The	Irving Stein	Brown and Benchmark	1992	12.50
Girls of Summer, The	Lois Browne	Harper/Collins	1992	17.50
Glory Days With The Dodgers	John Roseboro	Atheneum	1978	30.00
Glory Fades Away: 19th Century World Series	Jerry Lansche	Taylor Publishing	1991	30.00
Glory of Their Times, The	Lawrence Ritter	Macmillan	1966	35.00
Go-Go White Sox, The	Dave Condon	Coward McCann	1960	60.00
Good Enough to Dream	Roger Kahn	Doubleday	1985	15.00
Good Infield Play	Lou Boudreau	Ziff-Davis	1948	45.00
Good Timing (pb)	Stuart Broomer	ECW	1994	12.00
Great American Novel, The	Phillip Roth	Holt, Rinehart, Winston	1973	15.00
Great Baseball Managers	Charles Cleveland	Crowell	1950	24.00
Great Baseball Mystery, The	Victor Luhrs	Barnes	1966	60.00
Great Encyclopedia of 19th-Century Baseball, The	David Nemec	Donald Fine	1997	50.00
Great Infielders of the Major Leagues	D. Klein	Random House	1972	20.00
Great Moments in Baseball	D. Klein	Cowles	1971	15.00
Great Moments in Baseball	anonymous	Beekman	1990	40.00
Great Moments in Baseball History	Matt Christopher	Little, Brown	1996	10.00

Title	Author	Publisher	Year	Price
Great Negro Baseball Stars	A. S. "Doc" Young	Barnes	1953	120.00
Great No Hit Games of the Major Leagues	F. Graham	Random House	1967	25.00
Great Pennant Races of the Major Leagues	F. Graham	Random House	1967	15.00
Great Rookies of the Major Leagues	J. Brosnan	Random House	1966	20.00
Great Time Coming	David Faulkner	Simon & Schuster	1995	15.00
Greatest American Leaguers	Al Hirshberg	Putnam	1970	30.00
Greatest Cardinals of Them All	John Devaney	Putnam	1968	25.00
Greatest Game Every Played, The	Jerry Izenberg	Holt	1987	25.00
Greatest of All, The	John Mosedale	Dial	1974	75.00
Green Cathedrals	P. Lowry	Addison Wesley	1992	20.00
Green Diamonds	Jay Acton	Zebra	1993	15.00
Guidry	Ron Guidry/Peter Golenbock	Prentice-Hall	1980	15.00
Hack	Robert Boone	Highland Press	1978	60.00
Hank Aaron 715	Pat Reshen	Arco	1974	30.00
Hank Aaron Story, The	Milton Shapiro	Messner	1961	15.00
Hardball	Bob Elliot/George Bell	Key Porter	1990	35.00
Hardball	Bowie Kuhn	Times	1987	50.00
Hardball: A Season in the Projects	Daniel Coyle	Putnam	1993	12.50
Harmon Killebrew Story, The	Hal Butler	Messner	1966	15.00
Harmon Killebrew: Baseball's Superstar	Dr. Wayne Anderson, Jr.	Deseret	1971	48.00
Hawk	Al Hirshberg/Ken Harrelson	Viking	1969	25.00
Heart of the Order	Tony Ardizzone	Holt	1986	20.00
Heart of the Order, The	Tom Boswell	Doubleday	1989	20.00
Henry Aaron: A Quiet Superstar	Al Hirshberg	Putnam	1969	35.00
Heroes Behind the Mask	Milton Shapiro	Messner	1969	30.00
Heroes, Plain Folks, and Skunks	Happy Chandler	Bonus	1989	25.00
Heroes of Baseball	Robert Smith	World	1952	45.00
Heroes of the Bullpen	Milton Shapiro	Messner	1967	30.00
Heroes of the Major Leagues	Alexander Peters	Random House	1967	20.00
Hidden Game of Baseball, The	John Thorn/Pete Palmer	Doubleday	1984	40.00
High Hard One, The	Kirby Higbe	Viking	1967	75.00
Hit and Run	Harold Sherman	Grosset & Dunlap	1929	40.00
Hitting the Aaron Way	Hank Aaron	Prentice-Hall	1974	20.00
Home Game	Paul Quarrington	Doubleday Canada	1983	30.00
Home Games	Bobby Bouton/Nancy Marshall	St. Martin	1983	15.00
Home Run Heard Around the World, The	Ray Robinson	Harper/Collins	1991	15.00
Home Run Story	Zander Hollander	Norton	1966	30.00
Honus: The Life and Times of a Baseball Hero	William Hageman	Sagamore	1996	23.00
Hot Stove League, The	Lee Allen	Barnes	1955	240.00
How I Hit	Mickey Mantle	self published	1956	100.00
How I Hit	Johnny Mize/Murray Kaufman	Holt	1953	40.00
How Life Imitates the World Series	Tom Boswell	Doubleday	1982	25.00
How to Play Baseball	unknown	Thomas Crowell	1913	60.00
How to Play the Outfield	unknown	American Sports Publishing	1917	200.00
How to Play Winning Baseball	Arthur Mann	Grossett & Dunlap	1953	30.00
How to Steal a Pennant	Maury Wills/Don Freeman	Putnam	1976	12.50
How to Watch Baseball Like a Pro	Tim McCarver/Danny Perry	Villard	1998	25.00
Hustle: The Myth, Life and Lies of Pete Rose	Michael Sokoloven	Simon & Shuster	1990	17.50
Hustler's Handbook, The	Bill Veeck/Ed Linn	Putnam	1965	65.00
I Don't Care if I Never Come Back	Art Hill	Simon & Schuster	1980	25.00
I Had a Hammer	Hank Aaron/Lonnie Wheeler	Harper/Collins	1991	20.00
I Love This Game	Kirby Puckett/Mike Bryan	Harper/Collins	1993	12.50
I Managed Good, But Boy Did They Play Bad	Jim Bouton	Playboy	1973	20.00
I Never Had it Made	Jackie Robinson	Putnam	1972	25.00
I'd Rather Be A Yankee	John Tullius	Macmillan	1986	28.00
If At First	Keith Hernandez/Mike Bryan	McGraw Hill	1986	20.00
If I Never Get Back	Darryl Brock	Crown	1990	25.00
If They Don't Win It's a Shame	Dave Rosenbaum	McGregor	1998	25.00
I'm Glad You Didn't Take it Personally	Jim Bouton	Morrow	1971	18.00
Image of Their Greatness, The	Lawrence Ritter/Donald Honig	Crown	1979	35.00

Commy

The Girls of Summer

Imperfect Diamond, The	Lee Lowenfish	Stein & Day	1980	20.00
Impossible Dream, The	Bill McSweeney	Coward McCann	1968	30.00
Incredible Giants, The	Tom Meany et al	Barnes	1955	60.00
Inside Corner-Talks with Tom Seaver	Joel Cohen	Atheneum	1974	30.00
Inside Pitch	Roger Craig/Vern Plagenhoef	Eerdman's	1984	12.50
Inside Pitching	Ferguson Jenkins	Henry Regnery	1972	25.00
Inside the Yankees	Ed Linn	Ballantine	1978	7.50
Invisible Men	Donn Rogosin	Atheneum	1985	60.00
Iowa Baseball Confederacy, The	W. P. Kinsella	Houghton Mifflin	1986	55.00
Iron Horse	Ray Robinson	Norton	1990	17.50
Iron Man: The Cal Ripken Story	Harvey Rosenfeld	St. Martin's	1995	20.00
It Looked Like Forever	Mark Harris	McGraw Hill	1979	25.00
It Pays to Steal	Maury Wills/Steve Gardner	Prentice-Hall	1963	10.00
It's Anybody's Ball Game	Joe Garagiola	Contemporary	1988	10.00
It's Good to Be Alive	Roy Campanella	Little, Brown	1959	35.00
It's What You Learn After You Know It All...	Earl Weaver	Doubleday	1982	45.00
I Was Right on Time	O'Neal/Conrads/Wulf	Simon & Schuster	1996	20.00
Jackie Jensen Story, The	Al Hirshberg	Messner	1960	40.00
Jackie Robinson	Bill Roeder	Barnes	1950	120.00
Jackie Robinson of the Brooklyn Dodgers	Milton Shapiro	Messner	1965	20.00
Jackie Robinson Story, The	Arthur Mann	FJ Low	1950	55.00
Jackie Robinson-A Life Remembered	Maury Allen	Watts	1987	25.00
Jackie Robinson-Baseball Gallant Fighter	Sam & Beryl Epstein	Garrand	1974	45.00
Jersey Game, The	James DiClerico/Barry Pavelec	Rutgers University Press	1991	15.00
Jim Konstanty	Frank Yeutter	Barnes	1951	48.00
Jim Palmer, Great Comeback Competitor	Joel Cohen	Putman	1978	15.00
Jocko	Jocko Conlan/Robert Creamer	Lippincott	1967	30.00
Jock's Itch, The	Tom House	Contemporary	1989	15.00
Joe and Marilyn	Roger Kahn	Morrow	1986	30.00
Joe DiMaggio	George DeGregorio	Scarborough	1983	50.00
Joe DiMaggio	Gene Schoor	Doubleday	1980	32.00
Joe DiMaggio: Baseball's Yankee Clipper	Jack B. Moore	Praeger	1987	55.00
Joe DiMaggio: The Golden Year 1941	Al Silverman	Prentice-Hall	1969	50.00
Joe DiMaggio: Yankee Clipper	Tom Meany	Barnes	1951	100.00
Joe Morgan: A Life in Baseball	Joe Morgan/Joe Falkner	Norton	1993	15.00
Joe, You Coulda Made Us Proud	Joe Pepitone	Playboy	1975	18.00
John McGraw	Charles Alexander	Viking	1988	25.00
Johnny Bench-Catching and Power Hitting	Johnny Bench/John Sammis	Viking	1975	15.00
Johnny Bench-King of the Catchers	Lou Sabin	Putnam	1977	10.00
Jolly Cholly's Story	Charlies Grimm	Regnery	1969	40.00
Josh Gibson	William Brashler	Harper & Row	1978	125.00
Joy in Mudville	George Vecsey	McCall	1970	15.00
Judge Landis and 25 Years of Baseball	J.G. Taylor Spink	Crowell	1947	40.00
July 2, 1903	Mike Sowell	Macmillan	1992	30.00
Kansas City Athletics, The	Ernest Mehl	Holt	1956	60.00
Kid From Cuba, The	James Terzian	Doubleday	1967	30.00
Kiner's Korner	Ralph Kiner	Arbour House	1987	25.00
Kings of the Diamond	Lee Allen/Tom Meany	Putnam	1965	25.00

Kings of the Hill	Nolan Ryan	Harper/Collins	1992	18.00
Kirby Puckett: Fan Favorite	Ann Bauleke	Lerner	1993	15.00
Kiss it Goodby	Shelby Whitefield	Abelard Schuman	1973	30.00
Knuckleballs	Phil Niekro/Tom Bird	Freundlich	1986	20.00
Knuckler: The Phil Niekro Story	Wilfred Binette	Hallux Bros	1970	40.00
Koufax	Sandy Koufax/Ed Linn	Viking	1966	60.00
Lady in the Lockerroom	Susan Fornoff	Sagamore	1993	12.50
Last .400 Hitter, The	John Holway	William C. Brown	1991	20.00
Last to First	Larry Fox	Harper & Row	1970	30.00
Last Yankee, The	David Falkner	Simon & Schuster	1992	15.00
Late Innings	Roger Angell	Simon & Schuster	1982	35.00
Life of Roberto Clemente, The	Paul Robert Walker	Harcourt, Brace, Jovanovich	1988	15.00
Life That Ruth Built, The	Marshall Smelser	Quadrangle	1975	75.00
Lightning in a Bottle	Herbert Crehan	Branden	1992	17.50
Light's On!	David Pietrusza	Scarecrow Press	1997	22.00
Like Nobody Else	Ferguson Jenkins	Regnery	1973	40.00
Long Season, The	Jim Brosnan	Harper & Row	1960	70.00
Lords of Baseball, The	Harold Parrott	Praeger	1976	50.00
Lords of the Realm	John Helyar	Villard	1994	20.00
Los Angeles Dodgers, The	Frank Finch	Jordan	1977	30.00
Los Angeles Dodgers: An Illustrated History, The	Richard Whittingham	Harper	1982	15.00
Los Angeles Dodgers, The	Paul Zimmerman	Coward McCann	1960	30.00
Lose With a Smile	Ring Lardner	Schribner's	1933	175.00
Lou Gehrig: A Quiet Hero	Frank Graham	Putnam	1942	60.00
Lou Gehrig: Courageous Star	Robert Rubin	Putnam	1979	50.00
Lou Gehrig: The Iron Horse of Baseball	Richard Hubler	Houghton Mifflin	1941	80.00
Lou Gehrig: Pride of the Yankees	Paul Gallico	Grosset & Dunlap	1942	75.00
Louisville Slugger	Jan Aarow	Pantheon	1984	30.00
Love Letters to the Mets	Bill Adler	Simon & Schuster	1965	50.00
Low & Outside	Ira Smith/Allen Smith	Doubleday	1949	30.00
Lucky To Be a Yankee	Joe DiMaggio	Rudolph Field	1946	35.00
Mackman, The	Jerome Romanowski	self published	1979	30.00
Magnificent Yankees, The	Tom Meany	Barnes	1952	60.00
Main Spark, The	Sparky Anderson	Doubleday	1978	15.00
Man in the Crowd: Confessions of a Sport Addict	Stanly Cohen	Random House	1981	15.00
Man in the Dugout, The	Donald Honig	Follett	1977	25.00
Man Who Invented Baseball, The	Harold Peterson	Scribners	1973	30.00
Man Who Made Milwaukee Famous, The	Don Money	Apage	1976	30.00
Man Who Stole First Base, The	Eric Nadel	Taylor	1989	12.50
Man, Stan Musial, Then and Now, The	Stan Musial/Bob Broeg	Bethany	1977	50.00
Marge Schott Unleashed	Mike Bass	Sagamore	1993	10.00
Maybe I'll Pitch Forever	Satchel Paige	Doubleday	1962	35.00
Mays, Mantle, Snider	Donald Honig	Macmillan	1987	40.00
McGraw of the Giants	Frank Graham	Putnam	1944	40.00
Me and DiMaggio	C. Lehmann-Haupt	Simon & Schuster	1986	25.00
Me and the Spitter	Gaylord Perry	Saturday Review Press	1974	36.00
Mel Ott Story, The	Milton Shapiro	Messner	1959	45.00
Men At Work	George Will	Macmillan	1990	15.00
Men in Blue, The	Larry Gerlach	Viking	1980	45.00
Men of Autumn, The	Dom Forker	Taylor	1989	20.00
Men of the Reds Machine	Ritter Collett	Landfall	1976	35.00
Mets From Mobile, The	A. S. Young	Harcourt, Brace & World	1970	40.00
Mets Will Win the Pennant, The	William Cox	Putnam	1964	50.00
Mick, The	Mickey Mantle	Doubleday	1985	25.00
Mickey Mantle Album, The	Howard Liss	Hawthorn	1966	100.00
Mickey Mantle of the Yankees	Gene Schoor	Putnam	1958	10.00
Mickey Mantle Story, The	Mickey Mantle	Holt	1953	120.00
Mickey Mantle: Mr. Yankee	Al Silverman	Putnam	1963	50.00
Mickey Mantle-The Indispensable Yankee (pb)	Dick Schapp	Bartholomew	1961	10.00
Mickey Mantle Yankee Slugger	Milton Shapiro	Messner	1962	80.00

Honus: The Life and Times of a Baseball Hero

Marge Schott Unleashed

Title	Author	Publisher	Year	Price
Milwaukee Braves, a Baseball Eulogy, The	Bob Buege	Douglas	1988	25.00
Milwaukee Braves, The	Harold Kaese	Putnam	1954	100.00
Milwaukee's Miracle Braves	Tom Meany et al	Barnes	1954	50.00
Minors, The	Neil Sullivan	St. Martin	1990	17.50
Miracle at Coogan's Bluff	Thomas Kiernan	Crowell	1975	40.00
Miracle in Atlanta	Furman Bisher	World	1966	20.00
Miracle Man: Nolan Ryan	Nolan Ryan	Word	1992	10.00
Miracle New York Yankees, The	Phil Rizzuto/Al Silverman	Coward, McCann	1962	40.00
Misfits!	Thomas Hetrick	McFarland	1991	25.00
Moe Berg: Athlete, Scholar, Spy	Lewis Kaufman	Little, Brown	1974	90.00
More Modern Baseball Stars	Bill Gutman	Dodd, Mead & Co.	1987	25.00
Mostly Baseball	Tom Meany et al	Barnes	1958	40.00
Mr. Baseball	David Lipman	Putnam	1966	50.00
Mr. Cub	Ernie Banks/Jim Ernright	Follet	1971	50.00
Mr. October	Maury Allen	Times	1981	20.00
Mr. Ump	Babe Pinelli/Joe King	Westminister	1953	45.00
Murderers Row	G. H. Fleming	Morrow	1985	80.00
My Baseball Diary	James Farrell	Barnes	1957	60.00
My Baseball Scrapbook	Bob Broeg	River City	1983	45.00
My Favorite Summer	Mickey Mantle	Doubleday	1991	15.00
My Fifty Years in Baseball	Ed Barrow/James Kahn	Coward McCann	1951	75.00
My Giants	Russ Hodges	Doubleday	1963	20.00
My Greatest Baseball Game	Don Schiffer	Barnes	1950	45.00
My Greatest Day in Baseball	John Carmichael	Barnes	1945	35.00
My Kind of Baseball	Rogers Hornsby	McKay	1953	90.00
My Life and Baseball	Felipe Alou	Word	1967	16.00
My Life In and Out of Baseball	Willie Mays/Charles Einstein	Dutton	1966	15.00
My Life in Baseball: The True Record	Ty Cobb/Al Stump	Doubleday	1961	65.00
My Life is Baseball	Frank Robinson/Al Silverman	Doubleday	1968	20.00
My Luke and I	Eleanor Gehrig/Joseph Durso	Crowell	1976	15.00
My Nine Innings	Lee MacPhail	Meckler	1989	25.00
My Own Particular Screwball	Al Schacht	Doubleday	1955	60.00
My 66 Years in the Big Leagues	Connie Mack	Winston	1950	60.00
My Story	Jackie Robinson	Greenberg	1948	120.00
My Thirty Years in Baseball	John McGraw	Boni & Livelight	1923	500.00
My Turn At Bat	Ted Williams	Simon & Shuster	1969	35.00
My Ups and Downs in Baseball	Orlando Cepeda/Charles Einstein	Putnam	1968	30.00
My War with Baseball	Roger Hornsby	Coward McCann	1962	70.00
Nails	Lenny Dykstra/Marty Noble	Doubleday	1987	25.00
National Game, The	Alfred H. Spink	National Game Publishing	1910	800.00
National League Story, The	Lee Allen	Hill & Wang	1961	40.00
National League, The	Donald Honig	Crown	1983	32.00
Natural, The	Bernard Malamud	Harcourt Brace	1952	2,000.00
Negro Baseball Leagues: A Photographic History	Phil Dixon	Amereon	1992	50.00
Neighborhood of Baseball, The	Barry Gifford	Dutton	1981	20.00
New Baseball Reader, The	Charles Einstein	Viking	1991	20.00
New York City Baseball 1947-1957	Harvey Frommer	Macmillan	1980	40.00
New York Giants	Frank Graham	Putnam	1952	150.00

Title	Author	Publisher	Year	Price
New York Mets, The	Donald Honig	Crown	1986	28.00
New York Mets: The Whole Sory	Leonard Koppett	Macmillan	1970	35.00
New York Yankees	Frank Graham	Putnam	1943	100.00
New York Yankees, The	Donald Honig	Crown	1987	28.00
Nice Guys Finish Last	Leo Durocher	Simon & Schuster	1975	35.00
Nine Innings	Dan Okrent	Ticknor & Fields	1985	15.00
1937 Newark Bears	Ronald Mayer	William Wise	1980	48.00
1947: When All Hell Broke Loose In Baseball	Red Barber	Doubleday	1982	40.00
Nineteenth Century Baseball: 1871 Through 1900	Marshall Wright	Jefferson McFarland	1996	38.00
No Big Deal	Mark Fidrych	Lippincott	1977	25.00
No Cheering in the Press Box	Jerome Holtzman	Rinehart & Winston	1974	30.00
No Joy in Mudville	David Andreano	Schenkman	1965	25.00
Nobody's Perfect	Denny McLain/Dave Diles	Dial	1975	20.00
Nolan Ryan: Fireballer	Bill Libby	Putnam	1975	35.00
Nolan Ryan's Pitcher's Bible (pb)	Nolan Ryan/Tom House	Simon & Schuster	1991	15.00
Now Pitching Bob Feller	Bob Feller	Birch Lane	1990	15.00
Now Wait a Minute Casey	Maury Allen	Doubleday	1965	25.00
Number One	Billy Martin/Peter Golenbock	Delacorte	1980	20.00
October 1964	David Halberstam	Villard	1994	15.00
Off Base Confessions of a Thief	Rickey Henderson/John Shea	Harper/Collins	1992	15.00
Official Encyclopedia of Baseball, The	Hy Turkin	Barnes	1951	30.00
Official History of the NL	Chaarles Segar	Jay	1951	72.00
Oh, Baby, I Love It	Tim McCaver/Ray Robinson	Villard	1987	12.50
O Holy Cow! The Selected Verse of Phil Rizzuto	Hart Seely/Tom Peyer	Ecco	1993	10.00
Old Ball Game, The	David Phillips	Regnery	1975	30.00
On the Run	Maury Wills/Mike Celizic	Caroll & Graf	1991	25.00
Once a Bum, Always a Dodger	Don Drysdale	St. Martin's	1990	20.00
Once More Around the Park	Roger Angell	Ballantine	1991	20.00
Once Upon the Polo Grounds	L. Shecter	Dial	1970	10.00
One Armed Wonder	William Kashatus	McFarlnd	1995	15.00
One For The Record	George Plimpton	Harper & Row	1974	20.00
100 Greatest Baseball Players of All Time, The	Lawrence Ritter/Donald Honig	Crown	1981	20.00
100 Years of Baseball	Lee Allen	Bartholomew House	1950	30.00
One Last Round for the Shuffler	Tom Clark	Truck Books	1979	40.00
One Strike Away	Dan Shaughnessy	Beaufort	1987	25.00
Only the Ball Was White	Robert Peterson	Prentice-Hall	1970	180.00
Only Ticket Off the Island, The	Gare Joyce	Lester & Orpen Dennys	1990	40.00
Only Way I Know, The	Cal Ripken Jr/Mike Bryan	Viking	1997	23.00
Orlando Cepeda	Bob Stevens/Richard Keller	Woodford	1987	25.00
Other Game, The	Nolan Ryan	Word	1977	45.00
Our Base Ball Club	Noah Brooks	Dutton	1884	450.00
Our Game	Charles Alexander	Holt	1991	17.50
Out of Left Field	Bob Adelman/Susan Hall	Two Continents	1976	25.00
Out of My League	George Plimpton	Harper & Row	1961	25.00
Out Of the Blue	Orel Hershiser/Jerry Jenkins	Wolgemuth & Hyatt	1989	15.00
Over The Edge	Jay Johnstone	Contemporary	1987	25.00
Pee Wee Reese Story, The	Gene Schoor	Messner	1956	40.00
Pen Men	Bob Cairns	St. Martin	1992	10.00
Pennant Race	Jim Brosnan	Harper	1962	50.00
Perfect Game, The	Tom Seaver	Dutton	1970	12.50
Perfect Yankee, The	Don Larsen/Mark Shaw	Sagamore	1996	20.00
Pete Rose Story, The	Pete Rose	World	1970	24.00
Pete Rose: Mr. .300	Keith Brandt	Putnam	1977	12.50
Pete Rose: My Life in Baseball	Pete Rose	Doubleday	1979	35.00
Pete Rose: My Story	Pete Rose/Roger Kahn	Macmillan	1989	20.00
Pete Rose: They Call Him Charlie Hustle	Bill Libby	Putnam	1972	45.00
Phil Regan	Phil Regan/James Hefley	Zondervan	1968	65.00
Phil Rizzuto	Joe Trimble	Barnes	1951	50.00
Phil Rizzuto: A Yankee Tradition	Dan Hirshberg	Sagamore	1993	60.00
Philadelphia Phillies, The	Allen Lewis	JCP	1981	60.00

The Only Way I Know

The Only Way I Know
CAL RIPKEN, JR.

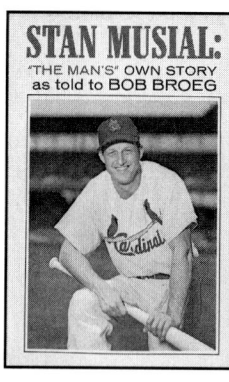

STAN MUSIAL:
"THE MAN'S" OWN STORY
as told to BOB BROEG

Stan Musial:
The Man's Own Story

Philadelphia Phillies, The	Fred Lieb/Stan Baumgartner	Putnam	1953	270.00
Phillip K. Wrigley	Paul Angell	Randy McNally	1975	65.00
Physics of Baseball, The	Robert Kemp Adair	Harper & Row	1990	15.00
Pictorial Base Ball Album	unknown	Mussey & Harper	1888	4,000.00
Pictorial History of the Dodgers	Gene Schoor	Leisure	1984	32.00
Picture History of the Boston Red Sox	George Sullivan	Bobbs-Merrill	1979	35.00
Pine Tarred and Feathered	Jim Kaplan	Algonquin	1985	17.50
Pinstriped Summers	D. Lally	Arbor	1985	10.00
Pinstripe Pandemonium	Geoffrey Stokes	Harper & Row	1984	10.00
Pioneers of Baseball	Robert Smith	Little, Brown	1978	30.00
Pirates, The	Lou Sahadi	Times	1980	25.00
Pitch that Killed, The	Mike Sowell	Macmillan	1989	20.00
Pitcher, The	John Thorn/John Holway	Prentice-Hall	1987	25.00
Pitchers Do Get Lonely	Ira Berkow	Atheneum	1988	15.00
Pitchin' Man	Satchel Paige	Cleveland New	1948	35.00
Pitching in a Pinch	Christy Mathewson	Putnam	1912	600.00
Pitching in a Pinch	Jim Palmer	Atheneum	1975	18.00
Pitching to Win	Bob Feller	Grosett & Dunlap	1952	30.00
Pitching with Tom Seaver	Tom Seaver	Prentice-Hall	1973	40.00
Pittsburgh Pirates, The	Fred Lieb	Putnam	1948	120.00
Play Ball	John Feinstein	Villard	1993	12.50
Play Ball: Stories of the Ball Field	Mike Kelly	Emery & Hughes	1888	4,000.00
Player-Manager	Lou Boudreau/Ed Fitzgerald	Little, Brown	1949	40.00
Playing Around	Donald Hall	Little, Brown	1974	30.00
Playing the Game	Stanley Harris	Stokes	1925	75.00
Politics of Glory, The	Bill James	Macmillan	1994	25.00
Pride Against Prejudice	Joseph Thomas Moore	Praeger	1988	12.50
Primitive Baseball: The First Quarter-Century	Harvey Frommer	Atheneum	1988	10.00
Professional Baseball Franchises	Peter Filichia	Facts on File	1993	16.00
Prophet of the Sandlots	Mark Winegardner	Atlantic Monthly	1990	25.00
Psychologist at Bat, The	David Tracy	Sterling	1951	50.00
Putting It All Together	Brooks Robinson	Hawthorn	1971	45.00
Quality of Courage, The	Mickey Mantle	Doubleday	1964	50.00
Ralph Kiner: The Heir Apparent	Tom Meany	Barnes	1951	40.00
Real Babe Ruth, The	Dan Daniel	Spink	1949	80.00
Real Grass, Real Heroes	Dom DiMaggio/Bill Gilbert	Zebra	1990	15.00
Real McGraw, The	Blanche McGraw	McKay	1953	35.00
Red Sox, the Bean & the Cod, The	Al Hirshberg	Waverly House	1947	120.00
Reggie	Reggie Jackson/Mike Lupica	Villard	1984	16.00
Reggie Jackson Story, The	Bill Libby	Lothrop	1979	20.00
Reggie Jackson, the $3 Million Man	Maury Allen	Harvey	1978	15.00
Reggie: A Season With A Superstar	Reggie Jackson	Playboy	1975	45.00
Relief Pitcher, The	John Thorn	Dutton	1979	25.00
Remeberances of Swings Past	Ron Luciano/Dave Fisher	Bantam	1988	10.00
Return of Billy the Kid, The	Smith/Norman/Lewis	Coward McCann	1977	17.50
Rex Barney's Thank Youuuu for 50 years in Baseball	Rex Barney/Norman Macht	Tidewater	1993	35.00
Richie Ashburn Story, The	Joe Archibald	Messner	1962	60.00
Richter's History and Records of Base Ball	Francis Richter	unknown	1914	1,000.00

Rickey and Robinson	Harvey Frommer	Macmillan	1982	32.00
Roberto Clemente	Roberto Clemente/Ira Miller	Grosset & Dunlap	1973	25.00
Roberto Clemente, Batting King	Arnold Hano	Putnam	1968	20.00
Roberto Clemente Pride of the Pirates	Jerry Brondfield	Garrard	1976	25.00
Rocket Man	Roger Clemens/Peter Gammons	Greene	1987	35.00
Rod Carew's Art & Science of Hitting	Rod Carew	Penguin	1986	25.00
Roger Maris At Bat	Roger Maris/Jim Ogle	Duell, Sloan, Pearce	1962	60.00
Roger Maris: A Man for All Seasons	Maury Allen	Donald Fine	1986	20.00
Roger Maris: A Title to Fame	Harvey Rosenfeld	Praire House	1991	15.00
Ron Santo	Jim Brosnan	Putnam	1974	70.00
Ron Santo: For Love of Ivy	Ron Santo/Randy Minkoff	Bonus	1993	50.00
Rookie	Dwight Gooden	Doubleday	1985	25.00
Rookie	Richard Woodley	Doubleday	1985	27.50
Rookies, The	Ed Walton	Stein & Day	1982	12.50
Roy Campanella	Dick Young	Barnes	1952	60.00
Roy Campanella: Man of Courage	Gene Schoor	Putnam	1959	45.00
Rusty Staub of the Expos	John Robertson	Prentice-Hall	1971	45.00
Ruth Marini of the Dodgers	Mel Cebulash	Lerner	1983	15.00
Ryno!	Ryne Sandberg/Fred Mitchell	Contemporary	1985	25.00
Sadaharu Oh	Sadaharu Oh/David Falkner	Times	1984	28.00
Safe at Home	Sharon Hargrove	Texas A & M	1989	17.50
Sal Maglie Story, The	Milton Shapiro	Messner	1957	40.00
San Francisco Giants, The	Joe King	Prentice-Hall	1958	30.00
Sandlot Seasons	Rob Ruck	U. of Illinios	1987	48.00
Sandy Koufax	Jerry Mitchell	Grosett	1966	35.00
Sandy Koufax, Strikeout King	Arnold Hano	Putnam	1964	30.00
Sandy Koufax Album, The	Howard Liss	Hawthorn	1966	36.00
Sax!	Steve Sax/Steve Delsohn	Contemporary	1986	20.00
Say Hey	Willie Mays/Lou Sahadi	Simon & Schuster	1988	25.00
Say It Ain't So Joe!	Donald Gropman	Little, Brown	1979	60.00
Science of Hitting, The	Ted Williams	Simon & Schuster	1986	12.00
Scooter, The	Gene Schoor	Scribner's	1982	20.00
Screwball	Tug McGraw/Joe Durso	Houghton Mifflin	1974	25.00
Season of Dreams	Tom Kelly	Voyager Press	1992	17.50
Season Ticket	Roger Angell	Houghton Mifflin	1988	15.00
Seatle Pilots Story, The	Carson Van Lindt	Marabou	1993	10.00
Seaver	Gene Schoor	Contemporary	1986	15.00
Second to None	Ryne Sandberg	Bonus	1995	50.00
Secrets of Big League Play	R. Smith	Random House	1965	10.00
Seeing it Through	Tony Conigliaro	Macmillan	1970	35.00
Seventh Babe	Jerome Charyn	Arbor House	1979	35.00
Seventh Game	Roger Kahn	NAL	1982	15.00
Shoeless Joe	W. P. Kinsella	Houghton Mifflin	1982	300.00
Shoeless Joe and Ragtime Baseball	Harvey Frommer	Taylor	1992	15.00
Shoeless Joe Jackson Comes to Iowa	W. P. Kinsella	Oberon Press	1980	750.00
Short Season, The	David Falkner	Times	1986	45.00
Sixty-One	Tony Kubek/Terry Pluto	Macmillan	1987	16.00
Slick	Whitey Ford/Phil Pepe	Morrow	1987	45.00
Slugging It Out in Japan	Warren Cromartie/Robert Whiting	Kodansha International	1991	20.00
Snap Me Perfect	Darrell Porter/Williams Deerfield	Nelson	1984	10.00
Some Are Called Clowns	Bill Heward	Crowell	1974	60.00
Sometimes You See It Coming	Kevin Baker	Crown	1993	15.00
Sparky!	Sparky Anderson/Dan Ewald	Prentice-Hall	1990	40.00
Spartan Seasons	Richard Goldstein	Macmillan	1980	20.00
St. Louis Cardinals, The	Fred Lieb	Putnam	1944	100.00
Stan Musial-Baseball's Durable Man	Ray Robinson	Putnam	1963	40.00
Stan Musial Story, The	Gene Schoor	Messner	1955	60.00
Stan Musial: The Man	Tom Meany	Barnes	1951	100.00
Stan Musial: The Man's Own Story	Stan Musial/Bob Broeg	Doubleday	1964	70.00
Stan Musial-The Man	Irv Goodman	Nelson	1961	30.00

Thurman Munson

Touching Second

Star Pitchers of the Major Leagues	Bill Libby	Random House	1977	10.00
Stars of the Series	Joseph Gies/John Shoemaker	Crowell	1964	30.00
Stealing Home	Phillip O'Connor	Knopf	1979	35.00
Stealing is My Game	Lou Brock/Franz Schulze	Prentice-Hall	1976	50.00
Stengel: His Life and Times	Robert Creamer	Simon & Schuster	1984	32.00
Story of Baseball, The	John Rosenburg	Random House	1964	25.00
Story of Bobby Shantz, The	Bobby Shantz	Lippincott	1953	50.00
Story of Jim Bunning	Jim Bunning	Lippincott	1965	40.00
Story of My Life, The	Hank Greenberg/Ira Berkow	Times Books	1989	30.00
Stroy of Roberto Clemente, All-Star Hero, The (pb)	Jim O'Connor	Dell	1991	8.00
Story of the World Series, The	Fred Lieb	Putnam	1949	60.00
Story Of Ty Cobb, The	Gene Schoor	Messner	1952	75.00
Story of Yogi Berra, The	Gene Schoor	Doubleday	1976	45.00
Strange But True Baseball Stories	Bill Libby	Random House	1971	20.00
Stranger to the Game	Bob Gibson/Lonnie Wheeler	Viking	1994	10.00
Streak: Joe DiMaggio and the Summer of 1941	Michael Seidel	McGraw Hill	1988	20.00
Strike Him Out	H. Sherman	Goldsmith	1931	40.00
Strikeout	Denny McLain/Mike Nahrstedt	The Sporting News	1988	30.00
Strikeout Story	Bob Feller	Grosset & Dunlap	1947	40.00
Strike Two	Ron Luciano/David Fisher	Bantam	1984	10.00
Strike Zone	Jim Bouton	Viking	1994	15.00
Suitors of Spring, The	Pat Jordan	Dodd & Mead	1973	10.00
Summer Game, The	Roger Angell	Viking	1972	40.00
Summer of '49	David Halberstam	Morrow	1989	10.00
Super Scout	Jim Russo/Bob Hammel	Bonus	1992	15.00
Superstars and Screwballs	Richard Goldstein	Dutton	1991	15.00
Superstars of Baseball	Bob Broeg	The Sporting News	1971	30.00
Sweat Seasons	Dom Forker	Taylor	1990	20.00
Sweet Lou	Lou Piniella/Allen Maury	Putnam	1986	20.00
Take Time for Paradise	A. Bartlett Giamatti	Summit	1989	15.00
Tales From the Dugout	Mike Shannon	Contempory	1997	20.00
Talkin' Baseball	Phil Pepe	Ballentine	1998	20.00
Taylor Spink: The Legend and the Man	C. C. Johnson Spink	The Sporting News	1973	100.00
Team that Wouldn't Die, The	Hal Bodley	Serendipity	1981	45.00
Ted Double Duty Radcliff	Kyle McNary	McNary	1994	30.00
Ted Simmons Story, The	Jim Brosnan	Putnam	1977	30.00
Ted Williams	Arthur Sampson	Barnes	1950	45.00
Ted Williams Story, The	Gene Schoor	Messner	1954	60.00
Ted Williams: A Baseball Life	Michael Seidel	Contemporary	1991	25.00
Ted Williams' Hit List, The	Ted Williams/Jim Prime	Masters Press	1996	18.00
Ted Williams: Hitting Unlimited	Tom Meany	Barnes	1951	100.00
Ted Williams: Seasons of the Kid	Richard Cramer	Prentice-Hall	1991	45.00
Ted Williams: The Golden Years 1957	Edwin Pope	Prentice-Hall	1970	50.00
Temporary Insanity	Jay Johnstone	Contemporary	1985	20.00
Ten Best Years of Baseball, The	Harold Rosenthal	Contemporary	1979	20.00
Texas Rangers: The Authorized History	Eric Nadel	Taylor	1997	30.00
That Old Ball Game	David Phillips	Regnery	1975	60.00
They Call Me Sarge	Fred Mitchell/Gary Mathewson	Bonus	1985	15.00

They Kept Me Loyal to the Yankees	Victor Debs	Rutledge	1993	25.00
They Played the Game	Harry Grayson	Barnes	1944	40.00
Third Base Is My Home	Brooks Robinson	Word	1974	30.00
Three Men on Third	Ira Smith/Allen Smith	Doubleday	1951	25.00
Thrill of the Grass, The (pb)	W. P. Kinsella	Peguin Canada	1984	50.00
Thrilling Story of Joe DiMaggio, The	Gene Schoor	Fell	1951	120.00
Throwing Heat	Nolan Ryan	Doubleday	1988	15.00
Thurman Munson	Thurman Munson/Martin Appel	Coward McCann	1978	40.00
Thurman Munson, Pressure Player	Bill Libby	Putnam	1978	25.00
Times At Bat	Arthur Daley	Random	1950	20.00
Tigers of '68: Baseball's Last Real Champions	George Cantor	Taylor	1997	15.00
Tiger Wore Spikes, The	John McCallum	Barnes	1956	60.00
To Everything a Season	Bruce Kuklick	Princeton Up	1991	20.00
Together We Were Eleven Foot Nine	Jim Palmer/Jim Dale	Andrews & McMeel	1996	15.00
Tom Seaver of the Mets	George Sullivan	Putnam	1971	20.00
Tom Seaver: Portrait of a Pitcher	Tom Seaver/Malka Drucker	Holiday House	1978	20.00
Tomahawked	Bill Zack	Simon & Shuster	1993	15.00
Tommorow I'll Be Perfect	Dave Stieb/Kevin Boland	Doubleday	1986	45.00
Tommy Davis Story, The	Patrick Russell	Doubleday	1969	75.00
Tommy John Story, The	Tommy & Sally John/Joe Muser	Revell	1978	30.00
Tony Conigliaro	Robert Rubin	Putnam	1971	15.00
Tony!	Tony Gwynn/Jim Geschke	Contemporary	1986	25.00
Tony O!	Tony Oliva/Bob Fowler	Hawthorn	1973	60.00
Total Baseball	John Thorn	Warner	1989	25.00
Touching Second	Johnny Evers	Reilly & Britton	1910	300.00
Treat 'Em Rough	Ring Lardner	Bobbs-Merrill	1918	150.00
Triumph Born of Tragedy	Andre Thornton/Al Janssen	Harvest House	1983	25.00
Truth Hurts, The	Jimmy Piersall	Contemporary	1984	12.50
Tuned to Baseball	Ernie Harwell	Diamond	1985	20.00
Twelve More Sport Immortals	Ernest Heyn	Bartholomew House	1951	30.00
Twelve Sport Immortals	Ernest Heyn	Bartholomew House	1949	30.00
20th Century Baseball Chronicle	David Nemec/Stephen Hanks	Tormont	1992	40.00
Twenty-Four Inch Home Run, The	Michael Bryson	Contemporary	1990	15.00
Twenty Years Too Soon	Quincy Trouppe	Simon & Schuster	1977	20.00
26th Man, The	Steve Fireovid	Macmillan	1991	20.00
Two Spectacular Seasons	William Mead	Macmillan	1990	12.50
Ty Cobb	Charles Alexander	Oxford	1984	50.00
Ty Cobb	John McCallum	Praeger	1975	50.00
Ty Cobb: The Idol of Baseball Fandom	Sverre Braathen	Avondale	1928	900.00
Ty Cobb: The Greatest	Robert Rubin	Putnam	1978	75.00
Ultimate Baseball Book, The	Daniel Okrent/Harris Lewine	Houghton Mifflin	1979	50.00
Umpire Story, The	James Kahn	Putnam	1953	85.00
Unforgettable Season, The	G. H. Fleming	HR & W	1981	40.00
Universal Baseball Association, Inc., The	Robert Coover	Random House	1968	10.00
Up From the Minor Leagues	Donald Honig	Cowles	1970	40.00
Veeck as in Wreck	Bill Veeck/Ed Linn	Putnam	1962	50.00
Vida Blue: Coming Up Again	Don Kowet	Putnam	1974	15.00
Vida, His Own Story	Vida Blue/Bill Libby	Prentice-Hall	1972	15.00
View from the Dugout	Ed Richter	Chilton	1964	27.50
Views of Sport	Red Smith	Knopf	1954	36.00
Voices from the Great Black BaseballLeagues	John Holway	Dodd Mead	1975	125.00
Voices of the Game	Curtis Smith	Diamond	1987	30.00
Wait 'Til Next Year	Christopher Jennison	Norton	1974	40.00
Wait Till I Make the Show	Bob Ryan	Little, Brown	1974	25.00
Wait Till Next Year	Jackie Robinson	Random House	1960	40.00
Walter Johnson	Roger Treat	Messner	1948	200.00
Walter Johnson, Baseball's Big Train	Henry Thomas	Phenom	1995	25.00
Want to be a Baseball Champion	Ethan Allen	General Mills	1946	45.00
Warren Spahn, Immortal Southpaw (pb)	Al Silverman	Bartholomew	1961	15.00
Warren Spahn Story, The	Milton Shapiro	Messner	1962	18.00

Ty Cobb: The Idol of Baseball Fandom

Willie's Time

Washington Senators	Morris Bealle	Columbia Pubs.	1947	200.00
Washington Senators, The	Shirley Povich	Putnam	1954	240.00
Washingotn's Expansion Senators	James Hartley	Corduroy Press	1998	25.00
Way It Is, The	Curt Flood	Trident	1971	30.00
Weaver On Strategy	Earl Weaver/Terry Pluto	Collier	1984	25.00
We Won Today	Kathleen Parker	Doubleday	1977	36.00
What's the Matter With the Red Sox?	Al Hirshberg	Dodd Mead	1973	40.00
When in Doubt, Fire the Manager	John Underwood/Alvin Dark	Dutton	1980	30.00
When the Cheering Stops	Lee Heiman	Macmillan	1990	15.00
When the Yankees, Giants and Dodgers Ruled...	Roger Kahn	Ticknor & Fields	1993	15.00
Where Have You Gone Joe Dimaggio?	Maury Allen	Dutton	1975	15.00
White Rat	Whitey Herzog/Kevin Horrigan	Harper & Row	1987	10.00
White Sox: A Pictorial History, The	Richard Whittingham	Contemporary	1982	40.00
White Sox Encyclopedia, The	Richard Lindberg/Mark Fletcher	Temple Up	1997	60.00
Whitey and Mickey	W. Ford/Mantle/Durso	Viking	1977	15.00
Whitey Ford Story, The	Milton Shapiro	Messner	1962	40.00
Whiz Kids, The	Harry Paxton	McKay	1950	180.00
Who Was Roberto?	Phil Musick	Doubleday	1974	60.00
Who's on Third	Richard Lindberg	Icarus	1983	40.00
Who's Who in Professional Baseball	Gene Karst/Martin Jones	Arlington House	1973	40.00
Why Time Begins on Opening Day	Thomas Boswell	Doubleday	1984	30.00
Wild and Outside	Stefan Farsis	Walker	1995	25.00
Wild, High and Tight	Peter Golenbock	St. Martin	1994	15.00
Willie Horton Story, The	Hal Butler	Messner	1970	25.00
Willie Mays	Arnold Hano	Grosset & Dunlap	1970	10.00
Willie Mays	Sullivan	Putnam	1973	25.00
Willie Mays Album, The	Howard Liss	Hawthorn	1966	100.00
Willie Mays: Coast to Coast Giant	Charles Einstein	Putnam	1963	60.00
Willie Mays: My Life In and Out of Baseball	Willie Mays/Charles Einstein	Dutton	1966	30.00
Willie Mays Story, The	Milton Shapiro	Messner	1960	60.00
Willie Mays Story, The	Ken Smith	Greenberg	1954	180.00
Willie Mays: Baseball Superstar	Sam & Beryl Epstein	Garrand	1975	12.50
Willie Mays: Coast to Coast Giant	Charles Einstein	Putnam	1963	50.00
Willie Stargell	Bill Libby	Putnam	1973	10.00
Willie Stargell: An Autobiography	Willie Stargell	Harper & Rowe	1984	25.00
Willie's Time	Charles Einstein	Lippincott	1979	30.00
Winfield-A Player's Life	Dave Winfield/Tom Parker	Norton	1988	30.00
Winning	Earl Weaver	Morrow	1972	20.00
Wit and Wisdom of Yogi Berra, The	Phil Pepe	Hawthorn	1974	25.00
Wizard	Ozzie Smith	Contemporary	1982	25.00
World Champion Pittsburgh Pirates, The	Dick Groat/Bill Surface	Coward McCann	1961	50.00
World Series, The	Lee Allen	Dutton	1969	30.00
World Series Classics	Bill Gutman	Random House	1973	20.00
Wrigleyville	Peter Golenbock	St. Martin's	1996	15.00
Wrong Stuff, The	Billy Lee/Dick Lally	Viking	1984	12.50
Yankee Batboy	Joe Carrieri/Zander Hollander	Prentice-Hall	1955	32.00
Yankee Doodles	Milton Gross	House of Kent	1948	60.00
Yankee Stadium: 50 Years of Drama	Joseph Durso	Houghton Mifflin	1972	45.00

Yankee Story, The	Tom Meany	Dutton	1960	60.00
Yankee Stranger	Dorothy Harshman/Ed Figueroa	Exposition Press	1982	20.00
Yankees: An Illustrated History	George Sullivan/John Powers	Prentice-Hall	1982	35.00
Yankees, The	John Durant	Hastings House	1949	120.00
Yaz	Carl Yastrzemski/Al Hirshberg	Viking	1968	40.00
Yaz: Baseball, the Wall and Me	Carl Yastrzemski/Gerald Eskenazi	Doubleday	1990	15.00
Year of the Tiger	Jerry Green	Coward, McCann, Geoghegan	1969	40.00
Year They Called Off the World Series, The	Benton Stark	Avery	1991	15.00
Year the Mets Lost Last Place, The	Paul Zimmerman	World	1969	30.00
Yogi	Yogi Berra/Ed Fitzgerald	Doubleday	1961	40.00
Yogi Berra	Joe Trimble	Barnes	1952	50.00
Yogi Berra Story, The	Gene Roswell	Messner	1958	35.00
Yogi Berra: The Muscle Man	Ben Epstein	Barnes	1951	200.00
Yogi Book, The	Yogi Berra	Workman	1998	25.00
Yogi, It Ain't Over	Yogi Berra/Tom Horton	McGraw Hill	1989	12.50
You Can't Beat the Hours	Mel Allen/Ed Fitzgerald	Harper & Row	1964	40.00
You Can't Hit the Ball with the Bat on Your Shoulder	Bobby Bragan/Jeff Guinn	Summit	1992	25.00
You Could Look It Up	Maury Allen	Times	1979	18.00
You Gotta Have Wa	Robert Whiting	Macmillan	1989	20.00
You Know Me Al	Ring Lardner	Doran	1916	800.00
Young Pitcher, The	Zane Grey	Grosset & Dunlap	1911	60.00

Chapter 5

PROGRAMS, PRESS PINS, & TICKETS

PROGRAMS

Collectors are always looking for remembrances of games they attended. Some of the least expensive and storage-friendly event-related collectibles are game programs. With rosters, feature stories, and other information, programs are terrific for recalling the specifics of a special day at the ballpark.

Available from games as far back as the 1850s, programs have varied in size and cover subject but have remained one of the fixtures in the collections of baseball fans. Today's programs feature more historical information, including team statistics, along with the current player bios, and of course, tons of advertising. In general, unscored programs carry a higher premium than editions in which the game has been scored.

Below is a list of prices for Excellent to Near Mint programs from regular season games in each decade. Programs found in Near-Mint condition from the early 1900s command a premium due to their scarcity.

Between 1876 and 1900 there was only one professional baseball league, and the number of teams ranged from eight to 12 in any given year. During this time most teams underwent several city and nickname changes.

Exceptions to the price ranges below include teams that made the playoffs or teams that included a number of future Hall of Famers. For example, teams like the 1960s Baltimore Orioles, the 1920s New York Yankees, and the 1970s Cincinnati Reds and Oakland A's carry a higher premium for regular season programs. Programs from regular season Yankee games in the 1920s have sold for as much as $125.

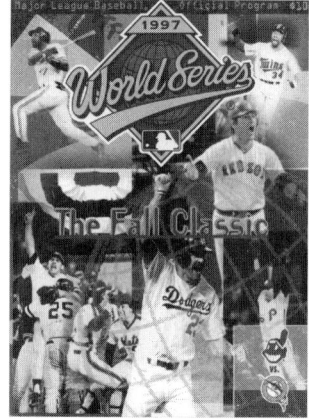

Year	Price Range
pre–1900s*	$250.00-750.00
1900–1910	150.00-400.00
1911–1920	50.00-200.00
1921–1930	25.00-75.00
1931–1940	18.00-40.00
1941–1950	15.00-35.00
1951–1960	10.00-20.00
1961–1970	8.00-18.00
1971–1980	6.00-10.00
1981–1990	4.00-8.00
1991–present	3.00-6.00

ALL-STAR PROGRAMS

All-Star programs were first issued for the inaugural 1933 game, and have been produced every year since, except for 1945 when the All-Star Game was not played. Two different programs were issued from 1959–62, to correspond with each of the two All-Star Games that were played during these seasons. Although World Series programs are the most popular among collectors, a 1944 Pittsburgh All-Star Game program in Near Mint condition attracted a winning bid of $1,358 in a 1998 auction. In the same auction, a collector purchased a Near Mint 1961 San Francisco All-Star program, one of the rarest from that decade, for a bargain $348.

Year	Stadium	Price
1933	Chicago White Sox	$2,500.00
1934	New York Giants	3,000.00
1935	Cleveland	550.00
1936	Boston Braves	3,000.00
1937	Washington	850.00
1938	Cincinnati	1,000.00
1939	New York Yankees	900.00
1940	St. Louis Cardinals	900.00
1941	Detroit	750.00
1942	New York Giants	4,000.00
1943	Philadelphia Athletics	650.00
1944	Pittsburgh	1,000.00
1945	No Game Played	—
1946	Boston Red Sox	1,000.00
1947	Chicago Cubs	500.00
1948	St. Louis Browns	500.00
1949	Brooklyn	900.00
1950	Chicago White Sox	500.00
1951	Detroit	200.00
1952	Philadelphia Phillies	200.00
1953	Cincinnati	250.00
1954	Cleveland	250.00
1955	Milwaukee	175.00
1956	Washington	175.00
1957	St. Louis	225.00
1958	Baltimore	200.00
1959	Pittsburgh	225.00
1959	Los Angeles	100.00
1960	Kansas City	175.00
1960	New York Yankees	100.00
1961	San Francisco	450.00
1961	Boston	300.00
1962	Washington	200.00
1962	Chicago Cubs	175.00
1963	Cleveland	125.00
1964	New York Mets	200.00
1965	Minnesota	125.00
1966	St. Louis	200.00
1967	California	175.00
1968	Houston	125.00
1969	Washington	80.00
1970	Cincinnati	150.00
1971	Detroit	200.00
1972	Atlanta	45.00
1973	Kansas City	175.00
1974	Pittsburgh	45.00
1975	Milwaukee	65.00
1976	Philadelphia	30.00
1977	New York Yankees	25.00

Year	Stadium	Price
1978	San Diego	50.00
1979	Seattle	25.00
1980	Los Angeles	40.00
1981	Cleveland	20.00
1982	Montreal	40.00
1983	Chicago White Sox	25.00
1984	San Francisco	15.00
1985	Minnesota	15.00
1986	Houston	15.00
1987	Oakland	15.00
1988	Cincinnati	20.00
1989	California	12.00
1990	Chicago Cubs	15.00
1991	Toronto	20.00
1992	San Diego	15.00
1993	Baltimore	15.00
1994	Pittsburgh	10.00
1995	Texas	10.00
1996	Philadelphia	10.00
1997	Cleveland	10.00

**1942 All-Star Game
New York**

**1955 All-Star Game
Milwaukee**

**1940 All-Star Game
St. Louis**

**1959 All-Star Game
Pittsburgh**

WORLD SERIES PROGRAMS

World Series programs have been issued every year since 1903, except for 1904 and 1994 when there was no World Series. Prior to 1974, each team printed its own program for the Fall Classic. Since then, the programs have been collaborative efforts between the two teams, albeit with different covers.

Generally, the program from the team that wins the series is slightly more valuable than the runner-up's issue. An exception to that rule is 1948, when Series champ Cleveland experienced a boom at the box office and let the presses run on programs. Meanwhile, the Boston Braves were scarcely noticed in Beantown, and printed comparatively few programs. Consequently, the Braves' edition of the '48 Series program is worth about $50 more than Cleveland's.

Telephone and online auctions are terrific sources for both new and vintage programs. In a 1998 auction, a lot of 10 World Series programs dating from 1936-1949, all in excellent condition, sold for a mere $978. In the same auction, a lot of 15 World Series programs from the 1950s brought $1,149. In late 1997, a collection of 104 World Series programs brought just under $14,000 at auction.

**1912
Red Sox vs. Giants**

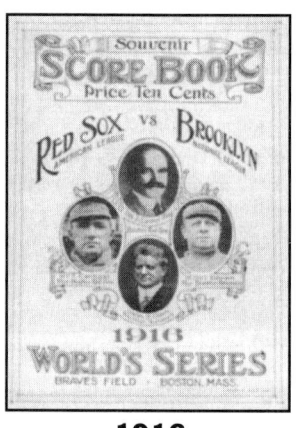

**1916
Red Sox vs. Dodgers**

**1921
Giants vs. Yankees**

Year		Team	Price	Year		Team	Price
1903	Winner	Boston Red Sox	$25,000.00	1926	Winner	St. Louis Cardinals	1,500.00
1903	Loser	Pittsburgh Pirates	20,000.00	1926	Loser	New York Yankees	1,200.00
1904	—	Series Not Played	—	1927	Winner	New York Yankees	2,500.00
1905	Winner	New York Giants	12,000.00	1927	Loser	Pittsburgh Pirates	4,500.00
1905	Loser	Philadelphia Athletics	1,000.00	1928	Winner	New York Yankees	2,000.00
1906	Winner	Chicago White Sox	10,000.00	1928	Loser	St. Louis Cardinals	1,000.00
1906	Loser	Chicago Cubs	9,000.00	1929	Winner	Philadelphia Athletics	1,200.00
1907	Winner	Chicago Cubs	9,000.00	1929	Loser	Chicago Cubs	1,000.00
1907	Loser	Detroit Tigers	8,000.00	1930	Winner	Philadelphia Athletics	1,000.00
1908	Winner	Chicago Cubs	9,000.00	1930	Loser	St. Louis Cardinals	750.00
1908	Loser	Detroit Tigers	8,000.00	1931	Winner	St. Louis Cardinals	650.00
1909	Winner	Pittsburgh Pirates	10,000.00	1931	Loser	Philadelphia Athletics	650.00
1909	Loser	Detroit Tigers	8,000.00	1932	Winner	New York Yankees	1,200.00
1910	Winner	Philadelphia Athletics	10,000.00	1932	Loser	Chicago Cubs	900.00
1910	Loser	Chicago Cubs	8,000.00	1933	Winner	New York Giants	800.00
1911	Winner	Philadelphia Athletics	4,000.00	1933	Loser	Washington Senators	700.00
1911	Loser	New York Giants	4,000.00	1934	Winner	St. Louis Cardinals	600.00
1912	Winner	Boston Red Sox	2,500.00	1934	Loser	Detroit Tigers	500.00
1912	Loser	New York Giants	4,000.00	1935	Winner	Detroit Tigers	700.00
1913	Winner	Philadelphia Athletics	4,000.00	1935	Loser	Chicago Cubs	500.00
1913	Loser	New York Giants	2,500.00	1936	Winner	New York Yankees	400.00
1914	Winner	Boston Braves	3,000.00	1936	Loser	New York Giants	350.00
1914	Loser	Philadelphia Athletics	2,500.00	1937	Winner	New York Yankees	400.00
1915	Winner	Boston Red Sox	3,000.00	1937	Loser	New York Giants	350.00
1915	Loser	Philadelphia Phillies	7,000.00	1938	Winner	New York Yankees	400.00
1916	Winner	Boston Red Sox	3,500.00	1938	Loser	Chicago Cubs	350.00
1916	Loser	Brooklyn Dodgers	3,000.00	1939	Winner	New York Yankees	350.00
1917	Winner	Chicago White Sox	5,000.00	1939	Loser	Cincinnati Reds	300.00
1917	Loser	New York Giants	2,500.00	1940	Winner	Cincinnati Reds	350.00
1918	Winner	Boston Red Sox	10,000.00	1940	Loser	Detroit Tigers	325.00
1918	Loser	Chicago Cubs	8,000.00	1941	Winner	New York Yankees	300.00
1919	Winner	Cincinnati Reds	3,000.00	1941	Loser	Brooklyn Dodgers	400.00
1919	Loser	Chicago White Sox	10,000.00	1942	Winner	St. Louis Cardinals	250.00
1920	Winner	Cleveland Indians	4,000.00	1942	Loser	New York Yankees	225.00
1920	Loser	Brooklyn Dodgers	5,000.00	1943	Winner	New York Yankees	200.00
1921	Winner	New York Giants	1,600.00	1943	Loser	St. Louis Cardinals	225.00
1921	Loser	New York Yankees	1,200.00	1944	Winner	St. Louis Cardinals	200.00
1922	Winner	New York Giants	1,600.00	1944	Loser	St. Louis Browns	350.00
1922	Loser	New York Yankees	1,200.00	1945	Winner	Detroit Tigers	350.00
1923	Winner	New York Yankees	1,600.00	1945	Loser	Chicago Cubs	200.00
1923	Loser	New York Giants	1,200.00	1946	Winner	St. Louis Cardinals	175.00
1924	Winner	Washington Senators	1,200.00	1946	Loser	Boston Red Sox	150.00
1924	Loser	New York Giants	1,500.00	1947	Winner	New York Yankees	250.00
1925	Winner	Pittsburgh Pirates	4,500.00	1947	Loser	Brooklyn Dodgers	250.00
1925	Loser	Washington Senators	1,000.00	1948	Winner	Cleveland Indians	125.00

Year		Team	Price	Year		Team	Price
1948	Loser	Boston Braves	175.00	1978	Winner	New York Yankees	18.00
1949	Winner	New York Yankees	200.00	1978	Loser	Los Angeles Dodgers	15.00
1949	Loser	Brooklyn Dodgers	250.00	1979	Winner	Pittsburgh Pirates	15.00
1950	Winner	New York Yankees	175.00	1979	Loser	Baltimore Orioles	15.00
1950	Loser	Philadelphia Phillies	150.00	1980	Winner	Philadelphia Phillies	15.00
1951	Winner	New York Yankees	175.00	1980	Loser	Kansas City Royals	20.00
1951	Loser	New York Giants	150.00	1981	Winner	Los Angeles Dodgers	18.00
1952	Winner	New York Yankees	175.00	1981	Loser	New York Yankees	15.00
1952	Loser	Brooklyn Dodgers	250.00	1982	Winner	St. Louis Cardinals	25.00
1953	Winner	New York Yankees	175.00	1982	Loser	Milwaukee Brewers	15.00
1953	Loser	Brooklyn Dodgers	250.00	1983	Winner	Baltimore Orioles	25.00
1954	Winner	New York Giants	250.00	1983	Loser	Philadelphia Phillies	20.00
1954	Loser	Cleveland Indians	200.00	1984	Winner	Detroit Tigers	15.00
1955	Winner	Brooklyn Dodgers	250.00	1984	Loser	San Diego Padres	12.00
1955	Loser	New York Yankees	150.00	1985	Winner	Kansas City Royals	20.00
1956	Winner	New York Yankees	150.00	1985	Loser	St. Louis Cardinals	12.00
1956	Loser	Brooklyn Dodgers	275.00	1986	Winner	New York Mets	15.00
1957	Winner	Milwaukee Braves	150.00	1986	Loser	Boston Red Sox	12.00
1957	Loser	New York Yankees	100.00	1987	Winner	Minnesota Twins	15.00
1958	Winner	New York Yankees	125.00	1987	Loser	St. Louis Cardinals	12.00
1958	Loser	Milwaukee Braves	175.00	1988	Winner	Los Angeles Dodgers	15.00
1959	Winner	Los Angeles Dodgers	125.00	1988	Loser	Oakland A's	12.00
1959	Loser	Chicago White Sox	200.00	1989	Winner	Oakland A's	12.00
1960	Winner	Pittsburgh Pirates	150.00	1989	Loser	San Francisco Giants	12.00
1960	Loser	New York Yankees	100.00	1990	Winner	Cincinnati Reds	15.00
1961	Winner	New York Yankees	150.00	1990	Loser	Oakland A's	12.00
1961	Loser	Cincinnati Reds	125.00	1991	Winner	Minnesota Twins	12.00
1962	Winner	New York Yankees	100.00	1991	Loser	Atlanta Braves	10.00
1962	Loser	San Francisco Giants	175.00	1992	Winner	Toronto Blue Jays	15.00
1963	Winner	Los Angeles Dodgers	75.00	1992	Loser	Atlanta Braves	10.00
1963	Loser	New York Yankees	60.00	1993	Winner	Toronto Blue Jays	15.00
1964	Winner	St. Louis Cardinals	125.00	1993	Loser	Philadelphia Phillies	10.00
1964	Loser	New York Yankees	75.00	1994	—	Series Not Played	—
1965	Winner	Los Angeles Dodgers	50.00	1995	Winner	Atlanta Braves	10.00
1965	Loser	Minnesota Twins	100.00	1995	Loser	Cleveland Indians	12.00
1966	Winner	Baltimore Orioles	125.00	1996	Winner	New York Yankees	20.00
1966	Loser	Los Angeles Dodgers	50.00	1996	Loser	Atlanta Braves	12.00
1967	Winner	St. Louis Cardinals	100.00	1997	Winner	Florida Marlins	15.00
1967	Loser	Boston Red Sox	100.00	1997	Loser	Cleveland Indians	8.00
1968	Winner	Detroit Tigers	200.00				
1968	Loser	St. Louis Cardinals	125.00				
1969	Winner	New York Mets	100.00				
1969	Loser	Baltimore Orioles	75.00				
1970	Winner	Baltimore Orioles	60.00				
1970	Loser	Cincinnati Reds	60.00				
1971	Winner	Pittsburgh Pirates	100.00				
1971	Loser	Baltimore Orioles	55.00				
1972	Winner	Oakland A's	75.00				
1972	Loser	Cincinnati Reds	65.00				
1973	Winner	Oakland A's	75.00				
1973	Loser	New York Mets	30.00				
1974	Winner	Oakland A's	25.00				
1974	Loser	Los Angeles Dodgers	30.00				
1975	Winner	Cincinnati Reds	25.00				
1975	Loser	Boston Red Sox	25.00				
1976	Winner	Cincinnati Reds	20.00				
1976	Loser	New York Yankees	20.00				
1977	Winner	New York Yankees	18.00				
1977	Loser	Los Angeles Dodgers	18.00				

**1942
Yankees vs.
Cardinals**

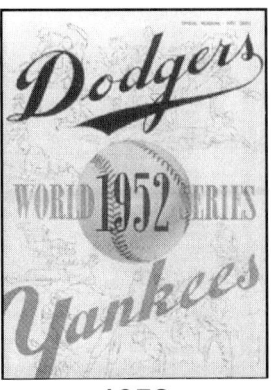

**1952
Dodgers vs.
Yankees**

**1961
Yankees vs. Reds**

**1933
Giants vs. Senators**

**1984
Tigers vs. Padres**

LEAGUE CHAMPIONSHIP SERIES PROGRAMS

The best-of-five League Championship series was initiated in 1969 and expanded to best-of-seven in 1985. With these additional playoff games came the usual parade of collectibles, including programs.

These items, and their Division serires counterparts, are the least popular of the post-season game programs. As with World Series programs, the programs from the winning team are generally more valuable.

AMERICAN LEAGUE

Year		Team	Price
1969	Winner	Baltimore Orioles	$65.00
1969	Loser	Minnesota Twins	125.00
1970	Winner	Baltimore Orioles	25.00
1970	Loser	Minnesota Twins	100.00
1971	Winner	Baltimore Orioles	25.00
1971	Loser	Oakland A's	10.00
1972	Winner	Oakland A's	20.00
1972	Loser	Detroit Tigers	75.00
1973	Winner	Oakland A's	10.00
1973	Loser	Baltimore Orioles	35.00
1974	Winner	Oakland A's	250.00
1974	Loser	Baltimore Orioles	20.00
1975	Winner	Boston Red Sox	50.00
1975	Loser	Oakland A's	40.00
1976	Winner	New York Yankees	15.00
1976	Loser	Kansas City Royals	12.00
1977	Winner	New York Yankees	15.00
1977	Loser	Kansas City Royals	10.00
1978	Winner	New York Yankees	15.00
1978	Loser	Kansas City Royals	10.00
1979	Winner	Baltimore Orioles	75.00
1979	Loser	California Angels	8.00
1980	Winner	Kansas City Royals	10.00
1980	Loser	New York Yankees	8.00
1981	Winner	1st Half East Winner-New York	10.00
1981	Loser	2nd Half East Winner-Milwaukee	40.00
1981	Winner	1st Half West Winner-Oakland	10.00
1981	Loser	2nd Half West Winner-Kansas	30.00
1981	Winner	New York Yankees	10.00
1981	Loser	Oakland A's	10.00
1982	Winner	Milwaukee Brewers	75.00
1982	Loser	California Angels	8.00
1983	Winner	Baltimore Orioles	20.00
1983	Loser	Chicago White Sox	15.00
1984	Winner	Detroit Tigers	8.00
1984	Loser	Kansas City Royals	20.00
1985	Winner	Kansas City Royals	30.00
1985	Loser	Toronto Blue Jays	25.00
1986	Winner	Boston Red Sox	10.00
1986	Loser	California Angels	25.00
1987	Winner	Minnesota Twins	15.00
1987	Loser	Detroit Tigers	12.00
1988	Winner	Oakland A's	100.00
1988	Loser	Boston Red Sox	10.00
1989	Winner	Oakland A's	25.00
1989	Loser	Toronto Blue Jays	20.00
1990	Winner	Oakland A's	25.00
1990	Loser	Boston Red Sox	20.00
1991	Winner	Minnesota Twins	25.00
1991	Loser	Toronto Blue Jays	20.00

Year		Team	Price
1992	Winner	Toronto Blue Jay	25.00
1992	Loser	Oakland A's	20.00
1993	Winner	Toronto Blue Jays	25.00
1993	Loser	Chicago White Sox	20.00
1994	—	Series Not Held	—
1995	Winner	Cleveland Indians	20.00
1995	Loser	Seattle Mariners	15.00
1996	Winner	New York Yankees	20.00
1996	Loser	Baltimore Orioles	10.00
1997	Winner	Cleveland Indians	15.00
1997	Loser	Baltimore Orioles	10.00

NATIONAL LEAGUE

Year		Team	Price
1969	Winner	New York Mets	$200.00
1969	Loser	Atlanta Braves	20.00
1970	Winner	Cincinnati Reds	75.00
1970	Loser	Pittsburgh Pirates	200.00
1971	Winner	Pittsburgh Pirates	200.00
1971	Loser	San Francisco Giants	1,000.00
1972	Winner	Cincinnati Reds	20.00
1972	Loser	Pittsburgh Pirates	40.00
1973	Winner	New York Mets	75.00
1973	Loser	Cincinatti Reds	100.00
1974	Winner	Los Angeles Dodgers	200.00
1974	Loser	Pittsburgh Pirates	150.00
1975	Winner	Cincinnati Reds	15.00
1975	Loser	Pittsburgh Pirates	15.00
1976	Winner	Cincinnati Reds	75.00
1976	Loser	Philadelphia Phillies	12.00
1977	Winner	Los Angeles Dodgers	50.00
1977	Loser	Philadelphia Phillies	10.00
1978	Winner	Los Angeles Dodgers	15.00
1978	Loser	Philadelphia Phillies	12.00
1979	Winner	Pittsburgh Pirates	15.00
1979	Loser	Cincinnati Reds	12.00
1980	Winner	Philadelphia Phillies	15.00
1980	Loser	Houston Astros	35.00
1981	Winner	2nd Half East Winner-Montreal	20.00
1981	Loser	1st Half East Winner-Philadelphia	15.00
1981	Winner	1st Half West Winner-Los Angeles	10.00
1981	Loser	2nd Half West Winner-Houston	15.00
1981	Winner	Los Angeles Dodgers	15.00
1981	Loser	Montreal Expos	30.00
1982	Winner	St. Louis Cardinals	25.00
1982	Loser	Atlanta Braves	12.00
1983	Winner	Philadelphia Phillies	15.00
1983	Loser	Los Angeles Dodgers	75.00
1984	Winner	San Diego Padres	25.00
1984	Loser	Chicago Cubs	15.00
1985	Winner	St. Louis Cardinals	25.00

1985	Loser	Los Angeles Dodgers	50.00
1986	Winner	New York Mets	25.00
1986	Loser	Houston Astros	10.00
1987	Winner	St. Louis Cardinals	10.00
1987	Loser	San Francisco Giants	30.00
1988	Winner	Los Angeles Dodgers	10.00
1988	Loser	New York Mets	8.00
1989	Winner	San Francisco Giants	15.00
1989	Loser	Chicago Cubs	12.00
1990	Winner	Cincinnati Reds	20.00
1990	Loser	Pittsburgh Pirates	12.00
1991	Winner	Atlanta Braves	25.00

1991	Loser	Pittsburgh Pirates	20.00
1992	Winner	Atlanta Braves	25.00
1992	Loser	Pittsburgh Pirates	20.00
1993	Winner	Philadelphia Phillies	20.00
1993	Loser	Atlanta Braves	15.00
1994	—	Series Not Held	—
1995	Winner	Atlanta Braves	20.00
1995	Loser	Cincinnati Reds	15.00
1996	Winner	Atlanta Braves	15.00
1996	Loser	St. Louis Cardinals	10.00
1997	Winner	Florida Marlins	25.00
1997	Loser	Atlanta Braves	10.00

DIVISION SERIES PROGRAMS

In 1994, each league expanded, and the system of determining the League Championship series teams was no longer cut and dry. With three division champions in each league, a fourth party—in the form of a wild card team—gained the chance to upset the top dog and head to the World Series. Unfortunately, in 1994 the owners were forced to cancel the remainder of the season, and the post season, including the World Series, for only the second time in baseball history. Thus, the Division Series debuted in the 1995 season.

AMERICAN LEAGUE

Year		Team	Price
1995	Winner	Cleveland Indians	25.00
1995	Loser	Boston Red Sox	15.00
1995	Winner	Seattle Mariners	25.00
1995	Loser	New York Yankees	15.00
1996	Winner	Baltimore Orioles	20.00
1996	Loser	Cleveland Indians	12.00
1996	Winner	New York Yankees	20.00
1996	Loser	Texas Rangers	12.00
1997	Winner	Cleveland Indians	15.00
1997	Loser	New York Yankees	10.00
1997	Winner	Baltimore Orioles	15.00
1997	Loser	Seattle Mariners	10.00

NATIONAL LEAGUE

Year		Team	Price
1995	Winner	Atlanta Braves	25.00
1995	Loser	Colorado Rockies	25.00
1995	Winner	Cincinnati Reds	25.00
1995	Loser	Los Angeles Dodgers	15.00
1996	Winner	Atlanta Braves	20.00
1996	Loser	Los Angeles Dodgers	12.00
1996	Winner	St. Louis Cardinals	20.00
1996	Loser	San Diego Padres	12.00
1997	Winner	Atlanta Braves	15.00
1997	Loser	Houston Astros	10.00
1997	Winner	Florida Marlins	20.00
1997	Loser	San Francisco Giants	10.00

AUTOGRAPHED PROGRAMS

With the popularity of autographs reaching an all-time high, obtaining the signature of a player pictured on a program can greatly enhance the program's value. For display purposes, it's best that the player sign on the cover, but don't rule out the possibility of having the player sign inside the program, around his biographical information. Since the mid-'70s, the instrument of choice has generally been a blue or black Sharpie; prior to that, ball point pens were the most popular. The ultimate challenge for collectors is to get a regular season, All-Star, World Series, or League Championship series program signed by an entire team.

1946
All-Star Program
(signed by Enos Slaughter)

1982
Oneonta Yankees
(signed by John Elway)

1986
All-Star Program
(signed by 15 HOF'ers)

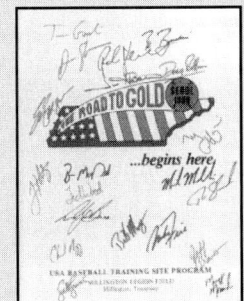

1988
U.S. Olympic Team
(signed by Team Members)

SPECIAL PROGRAMS AND TICKETS

Programs and tickets from landmark games warrant a premium above the values of other regular-season programs and tickets from the same year. These include games in which a record was broken, a no-hitter was thrown, or a milestone was reached.

The tickets from the games in which Cal Ripken Jr. tied and broke the consecutive games record weren't torn at the gate, so only full tickets are available. The same is true of Eddie Murray's 500th home run game. For other games, particularly those that took place decades ago, full tickets are scarce, so a value for the stubs is given. These tickets are denoted with an (S) after the value.

The following price list includes programs and tickets from some monumental games in baseball history.

**Pete Rose's
4,192nd Hit Game**

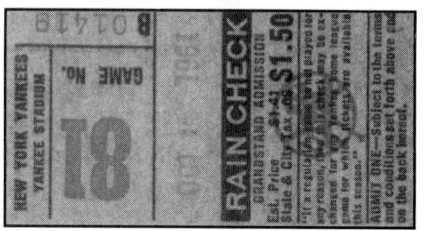

**Roger Maris's
61st Home Run Game**

**Carl Yastrzemski
3,000th Hit Game**

ALL-TIME LEADERS

Date	Game/Player	Ticket	Program
7/1/41	Joe Dimaggio ties consecutive games w/hit record	$650.00 (S)	$400.00
7/2/41	Joe Dimaggio breaks consecutive games w/hit record	1,000.00 (S)	800.00
7/17/41	Joe Dimaggio's hitting streak ends	2,500.00	700.00
9/26/61	Roger Maris hits record tying 61st home run	600.00 (S)	250.00
10/1/61	Roger Maris hits record 61st home run	1,000.00 (S)	1000.00
4/1/74	Hank Aaron ties all-time home run record	600.00	100.00
4/8/74	Hank Aaron breaks all-time home run record	1,500.00	100.00
4/27/83	Nolan Ryan breaks all-time strikeout record	200.00	20.00
9/11/85	Pete Rose breaks all-time hit record	250.00	30.00
5/1/91	Rickey Henderson break all-time stolen base record	150.00	20.00
9/5/95	Cal Ripken Jr. ties all-time consecutive games played record	100.00	15.00
9/6/95	Cal Ripken Jr. breaks all-time consecutive games played record	200.00	20.00
9/6/95	Cal Ripken Jr. 2,131 consecutive games (commemorative)	100.00	30.00
6/14/96	Cal Ripken Jr. breaks world consecutive games played record	35.00	20.00

3,000th HIT GAMES

Date	Game/Player	Ticket	Program
9/30/72	Roberto Clemente	$1000.00	$75.00
5/5/78	Pete Rose	200.00	20.00
9/12/79	Carl Yastrzemski	100.00	20.00
8/4/85	Rod Carew	100.00	15.00
9/9/92	Robin Yount	150.00	22.00
9/30/92	George Brett	200.00	22.00
9/16/93	Dave Winfield	55.00	20.00
6/30/95	Eddie Murray	50.00	15.00
9/16/96	Paul Molitor	30.00	12.00

**Mike Schmidt's
500th Home Run Game**

500th HOME RUN GAMES

Date	Game/Player	Ticket	Program
5/12/70	Ernie Banks	$200.00	$25.00
6/30/78	Willie McCovey	150.00	12.00
9/17/84	Reggie Jackson	175.00	25.00
4/18/87	Mike Schmidt	150.00	15.00
9/6/96	Eddie Murray	100.00	12.00

**Nolan Ryan's
300th Win Game
Commemorative Program**

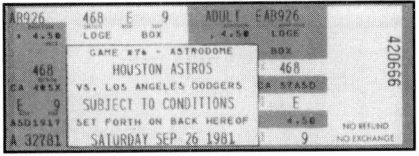

**Nolan Ryan's
5th No-Hit Game**

**Don Larsen's
World Series
Perfect Game**

**Willie Mays'
Famous Catch**

300th WIN GAMES

Date	Game/Player	Ticket	Program
5/6/82	Gaylord Perry	$100.00	$12.00
9/23/83	Steve Carlton	80.00	12.00
8/4/85	Tom Seaver	150.00	18.00
10/6/85	Phil Niekro	100.00	12.00
6/18/86	Don Sutton	100.00	12.00
7/30/90	Nolan Ryan	125.00	15.00
7/30/90	Nolan Ryan (commemorative)	n/a	20.00

NO-HIT GAMES

Date	Game/Player	Ticket	Program
5/15/73	Nolan Ryan-California	$800.00	$100.00
7/15/73	Nolan Ryan-California	700.00	75.00
9/28/74	Nolan Ryan-California	400.00	75.00
6/1/75	Nolan Ryan-California	400.00	75.00
5/30/77	Dennis Eckersley-Cleveland	125.00	30.00
6/16/78	Tom Seaver-Cincinnati	125.00	30.00
9/26/81	Nolan Ryan-Houston	800.00	100.00
6/2/90	Randy Johnson-Seattle	150.00	30.00
6/11/90	Nolan Ryan-Texas	125.00	40.00
5/1/91	Nolan Ryan-Texas	225.00	75.00
7/28/91	Dennis Martinez-Montreal	25.00	8.00
9/8/93	Darryl Kile-Houston	25.00	8.00
9/17/96	Hideo Nomo-Los Angeles	35.00	8.00
5/14/96	Dwight Gooden-New York Yankees	25.00	8.00
5/11/96	Al Leiter-Florida	25.00	8.00

PERFECT GAMES

Date	Game/Player	Ticket	Program
10/8/56	Don Larson-Yankees (World Series)	$500.00 (S)	$400.00
9/9/65	Sandy Koufax-Dodgers	400.00 (S)	100.00
5/8/68	Jim "Catfish" Hunter-Oakland	250.00	50.00
5/15/81	Len Barker-Cleveland	25.00	10.00
9/30/84	Mike Witt-California	25.00	10.00
9/16/88	Tom Browning-Cincinnati	25.00	10.00
7/28/91	Dennis Martinez-Montreal	25.00	8.00
7/28/94	Kenny Rogers-Texas	25.00	8.00

WORLD SERIES SPECIALS

Date	Game/Player	Ticket	Program
9/29/54	Willie Mays catch	$1,000.00	$350.00
10/21/75	Carlton Fisk's HR in 12th inning of Game 6	100.00	55.00
10/18/77	Reggie Jackson hits 3 consecutive HRs in Game 6	125.00	55.00
10/25/86	Buckner boots grounder in Game 6	75.00	20.00
10/15/88	Kirk Gibson's pinch-hit home run Game 1	50.00	20.00

Lou Gehrig Memorial Day

Babe Ruth Day

Roger Maris' First Game

**Last Game
at Ebbetts Field**

**Roy Campanella
Exhibition Game**

Stan Musial's Last Game

**Roger Clemens
20 Strikeouts**

SPECIAL REGULAR SEASON GAMES

Date	Game	Ticket	Program
4/18/23	First game at Yankee Staium	$800.00 (S)	$800.00
7/4/41	Lou Gehrig Memorial Day	1,500.00	100.00
4/15/47	Jackie Robinson's first Dodgers games	1,000.00	500.00
4/27/47	Babe Ruth Day	1,000.00	200.00
10/1/51	Bobby Thomson's "Shot Heard Around the World"	800.00 (S)	750.00
4/30/52	Ted Williams Day	800.00	400.00
4/16/57	Roger Maris' first game	700.00	100.00
9/24/57	Last game at Ebbets Field	2,000.00	1,500.00
5/7/59	Exhibition game honoring Roy Campanella	450.00	100.00
9/29/59	Playoff between Los Angeles and Milwaukee Game 2	250.00	50.00
4/10/62	First game at Dodger Stadium	900.00	150.00
4/13/62	New York Mets first home game (Polo Grounds)	900.00	200.00
10/3/62	Playoff between Los Angeles and San Francisco Game 3	200.00	40.00
4/8/63	Pete Rose's first major league game	500.00	200.00
9/29/63	Stan Musial's last game	450.00	400.00
4/8/69	San Diego Padres' first game (San Diego Stadium)	700.00	150.00
4/14/69	Montreal Expos' first home game	250.00	60.00
6/8/69	Mickey Mantle Day	1,000.00	100.00
6/30/70	First game at Riverfront Stadium	150.00	35.00
10/1/70	Last game at Shibe Park	300.00 (S)	80.00
4/6/77	Seattle Mariners' first game	75.00	20.00
4/7/77	Toronto Blue Jays' first game	100.00	50.00
10/2/78	Bucky Dent's three-run homer in playoff vs. Red Sox	200.00	50.00
8/1/79	Thurman Munson's last game	400.00 (S)	25.00
4/18/81	Tom Seaver's 3,000th strikeout	125.00	25.00
7/24/83	George Brett pine tar incident	250.00	20.00
4/29/86	Roger Clemens strikes out 20 batters	125.00	25.00
9/22/89	Nolan Ryan's 5,000th strikeout	100.00	18.00
9/14/90	Ken Griffey Sr. and Jr. hit back-to-back home runs	50.00	15.00
4/6/92	First game at Camden Yards	40.00	20.00
4/5/93	Colorado Rockies' first game	100.00	20.00
4/5/93	Florida Marlins' first game	85.00	30.00
4/5/93	Florida Marlins' first game commemorative ticket (2,500 made)	150.00	n/a
4/9/93	Colorado Rockies' first home game	85.00	25.00
9/22/93	Nolan Ryan's last game pitched	35.00	10.00
4/4/94	First game at Jacobs Field	75.00	20.00
9/18/96	Roger Clemens strikes out 20 batters	45.00	15.00
4/15/97	Jackie Robinson Day (Shea Stadium)	25.00	10.00

Beginning in 1911, press pins were given to the members of the media as passes into the press boxes during All-Star and World Series games. Pins distributed prior to World War II are scarce and thus have the most value today. Along with limited production runs and elegant designs, the fact that the pins were never sold to the general public helps augment the value of these "gifts."

Interest in these collectibles is generally lower than that of tickets and programs from the same monumental events, though there may be a rebirth of hobby interest in this area. Recently, a lot of seven World Series pins, including the 1922 Giants and 1944 Cardinals, was sold at auction for $4,025, while an assortment of 75 World Series and All-Star pins from the mid-'30s to the mid-'40s went for $8,625.

ALL-STAR PRESS PINS

The first All-Star Game was played at Comiskey Park in Chicago on July 6, 1933, but the first All-Star press pin wasn't issued until 1938. There were no pins issued in 1939, '40, '42, or '44, and there was no All-Star Game in 1945. Pins have been issued every year since 1946. Production numbers are believed to be lower than those for World Series pins, due to the fact that more media coverage is given to the crowning event at the end of the season.

While there was no standard edition All-Star pin issued in 1939 a special press pin was pressed to commemorate Lou Gehrig and his incredible "iron man" streak of consecutive games played, which came to a halt on May 22 of that year at 2,130 games. The pin, which was presented to Gehrig, was entered into auction in 1990 by the family that provided care for Gehrig before his death.

Year	Site	Value	Year	Site	Value
1938	Cincinnati	$7,500.00	1975	Milwaukee	75.00
1941	Detroit	1,000.00	1976	Philadelphia	100.00
1943	Philadelphia	1,300.00	1977	New York (Yankees)	75.00
1946	Boston	800.00	1978	San Diego	75.00
1947	Chicago (Cubs)	1,000.00	1979	Seattle	100.00
1948	St. Louis	1,500.00	1980	Los Angeles	50.00
1949	Brooklyn	525.00	1981	Cleveland	65.00
1950	Chicago (White Sox)	275.00	1982	Montreal	60.00
1951	Detroit	300.00	1983	Chicago (White Sox)	35.00
1952	Philadelphia	300.00	1984	San Francisco	50.00
1953	Cincinnati	425.00	1985	Minnesota	40.00
1954	Cleveland	250.00	1986	Houston	100.00
1955	Milwaukee	175.00	1987	Oakland	80.00
1956	Washington	325.00	1988	Cincinnati	100.00
1957	St. Louis	300.00	1989	California	50.00
1958	Baltimore	450.00	1990	Chicago	110.00
1959	Los Angeles	125.00	1991	Toronto	100.00
1959	Pittsburgh	250.00	1992	San Diego	95.00
1960	Kansas City	250.00	1993	Baltimore	95.00
1960	New York (Yankees)	350.00	1994	Pittsburgh	115.00
1961	Boston	350.00	1995	Texas	115.00
1961	San Francisco	450.00	1996	Philadelphia	115.00
1962	Chicago (Cubs)	325.00	1997	Cleveland	125.00
1962	Washington	300.00			
1963	Cleveland	150.00			
1964	New York (Mets)	175.00			
1965	Minnesota	100.00			
1966	St. Louis	80.00			
1967	California	75.00			
1968	Houston	110.00			
1969	Washington	100.00			
1970	Cincinnati	75.00			
1971	Detroit	125.00			
1972	Atlanta	100.00			
1973	Kansas City	80.00			
1974	Pittsburgh	125.00			

1963 Cleveland Indians

1971 Detroit Tigers

1958 Baltimore Orioles

1960 New York Yankees

WORLD SERIES PRESS PINS

In 1911, both teams participating in the World Series issued press pins to the media. That trend has continued each year, except in 1918 when the Chicago Cubs failed to issue a pin, and in 1921-23, when one pin represented both New York clubs. Generally, the pin of the winning team commands a higher price than that from the Series runner-up. Other factors elevating the demand for particular pins include limited production runs and elaborate designs. In 1997, the Florida Marlins stepped up to the plate and delivered a classy gold pin resembling their logo with "First World Series" inscribed at the bottom, while the Cleveland Indians' '97 pin was similar to the pin the Tribe issued in '95.

1913
New York Giants

1923
New York Yankees/Giants

1924
New York Giants

1927
Pittsburgh Pirates

1927
New York Yankees

1931
Philadelphia Athletics

1939
Cincinnati Reds

1945
Chicago Cubs

Year	Team	Value
1911	Philadelphia Athletics	$14,000.00
1911	New York Giants	8,500.00
1912	Boston Red Sox	3,000.00
1912	New York Giants	9,500.00
1913	Philadelphia Athletics	6,000.00
1913	New York Giants	4,500.00
1914	Philadelphia Athletics	5,000.00
1914	Boston Braves	4,000.00
1915	Boston Red Sox	3,500.00
1915	Philadelphia Phillies	7,500.00
1916	Boston Red Sox	4,500.00
1916	Brooklyn Dodgers	4,000.00
1917	Chicago White Sox	6,000.00
1917	New York Giants (ribbon)	6,000.00
1917	New York Giants (metal)	1,500.00
1918	Boston Red Sox	5,500.00
1919	Chicago White Sox	10,000.00
1919	Cincinnati Reds	2,200.00
1920	Cleveland Indians (enamel)	1,200.00
1920	Cleveland Indians (celluloid)	1,500.00
1920	Brooklyn Dodgers	3,000.00
1921	New York Yankees/Giants	3,000.00
1922	New York Yankees/Giants	3,000.00
1923	New York Yankees/Giants	2,000.00
1924	Washington Senators	1,250.00
1924	New York Giants	1,300.00
1925	Washington Senators	1,000.00
1925	Pittsburgh Pirates	1,300.00
1926	New York Yankees	1,800.00
1926	St. Louis Cardinals	1,400.00
1927	New York Yankees	4,000.00
1927	Pittsburgh Pirates	1,500.00
1928	New York Yankees	2,000.00
1928	St. Louis Cardinals	1,000.00
1929	Philadelphia Athletics	1,250.00
1929	Chicago Cubs	2,000.00
1930	Philadelphia Athletics	3,500.00
1930	St. Louis Cardinals	450.00
1931	Philadelphia Athletics	450.00
1931	St. Louis Cardinals	400.00
1932	New York Yankees	750.00
1932	Chicago Cubs	1,250.00
1933	Washington Senators	500.00
1933	New York Giants	500.00
1934	Detroit Tigers	425.00
1934	St. Louis Cardinals	450.00
1935	Detroit Tigers	600.00
1935	Chicago Cubs	2,000.00
1936	New York Yankees	800.00
1936	New York Giants	375.00
1937	New York Yankees	700.00

Year	Team	Value
1937	New York Giants	400.00
1938	New York Yankees	525.00
1938	Chicago Cubs	1,400.00
1939	New York Yankees	450.00
1939	Cincinnati Reds	300.00
1940	Detroit Tigers	500.00
1940	Cincinnati Reds	350.00
1941	New York Yankees	450.00
1941	Brooklyn Dodgers	350.00
1942	New York Yankees	350.00
1942	St. Louis Cardinals	2,000.00
1943	New York Yankees	400.00
1943	St. Louis Cardinals	2,000.00
1944	St. Louis Browns	500.00
1944	St. Louis Cardinals	525.00
1945	Detroit Tigers	400.00
1945	Chicago Cubs	475.00
1946	Boston Red Sox	350.00
1946	St. Louis Cardinals	425.00
1947	New York Yankees	500.00
1947	Brooklyn Dodgers	400.00
1948	Cleveland Indians	500.00
1948	Boston Braves	500.00
1949	New York Yankees	350.00
1949	Brooklyn Dodgers	350.00
1950	New York Yankees	250.00
1950	Philadelphia Phillies	225.00
1951	New York Yankees	200.00
1951	New York Giants	175.00
1952	New York Yankees	300.00
1952	Brooklyn Dodgers	400.00
1953	New York Yankees	300.00
1953	Brooklyn Dodgers	300.00
1954	Cleveland Indians	300.00
1954	New York Giants	200.00
1955	New York Yankees	250.00
1955	Brooklyn Dodgers	325.00
1956	New York Yankees	175.00
1956	Brooklyn Dodgers	1,500.00
1957	New York Yankees	200.00
1957	Milwaukee Braves	200.00
1958	New York Yankees	180.00
1958	Milwaukee Braves	250.00
1959	Chicago White Sox	200.00
1959	Los Angeles Dodgers	250.00
1960	New York Yankees	200.00
1960	Pittsburgh Pirates	250.00
1961	New York Yankees	300.00
1961	Cincinnati Reds	150.00
1962	New York Yankees	175.00
1962	San Francisco Giants	300.00
1963	New York Yankees	200.00
1963	Los Angeles Dodgers	175.00
1964	New York Yankees	175.00
1964	St. Louis Cardinals	175.00
1965	Minnesota Twins	100.00
1965	Los Angeles Dodgers	125.00
1966	Baltimore Orioles	175.00
1966	Los Angeles Dodgers	100.00

Year	Team	Value
1967	Boston Red Sox	170.00
1967	St. Louis Cardinals	110.00
1968	Detroit Tigers	125.00
1968	St. Louis Cardinals	90.00
1969	Baltimore Orioles	125.00
1969	New York Mets	300.00
1970	Baltimore Orioles	115.00
1970	Cincinnati Reds	100.00
1971	Baltimore Orioles	125.00
1971	Pittsburgh Pirates	150.00
1972	Oakland A's	200.00
1972	Cincinnati Reds	150.00
1973	Oakland A's	300.00
1973	New York Mets	200.00
1974	Oakland A's	300.00
1974	Los Angeles Dodgers	95.00
1975	Boston Red Sox	175.00
1975	Cincinnati Reds	180.00
1976	New York Yankees	150.00
1976	Cincinnati Reds	175.00
1977	New York Yankees	200.00
1977	Los Angeles Dodgers	125.00
1978	New York Yankees	150.00
1978	Los Angeles Dodgers	100.00
1979	Baltimore Orioles	125.00
1979	Pittsburgh Pirates	75.00
1980	Kansas City Royals	140.00
1980	Philadelphia Phillies	100.00
1981	New York Yankees	125.00
1981	Los Angeles Dodgers	100.00
1982	Milwaukee Brewers	100.00
1982	St. Louis Cardinals	50.00
1983	Baltimore Orioles	115.00
1983	Philadelphia Phillies	100.00
1984	Detroit Tigers	50.00
1984	San Diego Padres	50.00
1985	Kansas City Royals	125.00
1985	St. Louis Cardinals	110.00
1986	Boston Red Sox	110.00
1986	New York Mets	125.00
1987	Minnesota Twins	110.00
1987	St. Louis Cardinals	100.00
1988	Oakland A's	50.00
1988	Los Angeles Dodgers	75.00
1989	Oakland A's	90.00
1989	San Francisco Giants	100.00
1990	Oakland A's	95.00
1990	Cincinnati Reds	125.00
1991	Minnesota Twins	100.00
1991	Atlanta Braves	115.00
1992	Toronto Blue Jays	125.00
1992	Atlanta Braves	100.00
1993	Toronto Blue Jays	125.00
1993	Philadelphia Phillies	100.00
1995	Atlanta Braves	150.00
1995	Cleveland Indians	125.00
1996	New York Yankees	175.00
1996	Atlanta Braves	125.00
1997	Florida Marlins	175.00
1997	Cleveland Indians	150.00

**1947
New York Yankees**

**1948
Cleveland Indians**

**1958
Milwaukee Braves**

**1966
Baltimore Orioles**

PHANTOM PRESS PINS

In order to have press pins ready for distribution by the start of the World Series, teams in contention must make the decision to produce them during the regular season. Organizations have pins designed and produced in hopes that the team will make it to the Fall Classic. Phantom pins are pins that are made for teams that fall short of the World Series.

**1938
Pittsburgh Pirates**

Year	Team	Value	Year	Team	Value
1935	St. Louis Cardinals	$550.00	1979	Montreal Expos	75.00
1938	Pittsburgh Pirates	900.00	1979	Houston Astros	2,250.00
1944	Detroit Tigers	600.00	1980	Houston Astros	200.00
1945	St. Louis Cardinals	550.00	1981	Chicago Cubs	200.00
1946	Brooklyn Dodgers	275.00	1981	Oakland A's	85.00
1948	Boston Red Sox	1,500.00	1981	Philadelphia Phillies	75.00
1948	New York Yankees	1,500.00	1982	Los Angeles Dodgers	150.00
1949	Boston Red Sox	1,400.00	1983	Chicago White Sox	50.00
1949	St. Louis Cardinals	700.00	1983	Milwaukee Brewers	250.00
1950	Brooklyn Dodgers	2,000.00	1983	Pittsburgh Pirates	275.00
1951	Brooklyn Dodgers	350.00	1984	Chicago Cubs	165.00
1951	Cleveland Indians	1,500.00	1985	Toronto Blue Jays	200.00
1952	New York Giants	435.00	1986	California Angels	200.00
1955	Chicago White Sox	1,500.00	1986	Houston Astros	150.00
1955	Cleveland Indians	750.00	1987	Boston Red Sox	250.00
1956	Milwaukee Braves	150.00	1987	Detroit Tigers	130.00
1959	Milwaukee Braves	500.00	1987	New York Mets	225.00
1959	San Francisco Giants	500.00	1987	New York Yankees	200.00
1960	Baltimore Orioles	1,500.00	1987	San Francisco Giants	100.00
1960	Chicago White Sox	750.00	1988	Boston Red Sox	100.00
1963	St. Louis Cardinals	150.00	1990	Boston Red Sox	75.00
1964	Baltimore Orioles	900.00	1990	Pittsburgh Pirates	350.00
1964	Chicago White Sox	1,000.00	1994	San Francisco Giants	125.00
1964	Cincinnati Reds	100.00			
1964	Cincinnati Reds (brooch)	150.00			
1964	Philadelphia Phillies	40.00			
1965	San Francisco Giants	175.00			
1966	Pittsburgh Pirates	500.00			
1966	San Francisco Giants	800.00			
1967	Chicago White Sox	85.00			
1967	Minnesota Twins	50.00			
1967	San Francisco Giants	1,200.00			
1969	Atlanta Braves	75.00			
1969	Minnesota Twins	100.00			
1969	San Francisco Giants	250.00			
1970	California Angels	500.00			
1970	Chicago Cubs	450.00			
1971	Oakland A's (large)	750.00			
1971	Oakland A's (small)	150.00			
1971	San Francisco Giants	175.00			
1972	Chicago White Sox	1,000.00			
1972	Pittsburgh Pirates	750.00			
1974	Texas Rangers	500.00			
1975	Oakland A's	450.00			
1976	Philadelphia Phillies	75.00			
1977	Boston Red Sox	95.00			
1978	Cincinnati Reds	100.00			
1978	Milwaukee Brewers	75.00			
1978	Pittsburgh Pirates	100.00			
1978	San Francisco Giants	40.00			
1979	California Angels	250.00			

HALL OF FAME PRESS PINS

Hall of Fame press pins, first introduced in 1982, pay homage to the players inducted into the Hall. Each pin bears the year and the names of the players who were inducted. Also, in 1962, there was a luncheon held for Jackie Robinson, in honor of his induction to the Hall. Reportedly, less than 500 pewter pins were handed out to the attendees of the party. This pin is valued somewhere in the neighborhood of $2,000.

In, 1990, two major companies, IBM and Manufacturer's Hanover, came up with the idea of issuing Retroactive Hall of Fame press pins to commemorate players inducted before 1982. The first edition recognized the first five players inducted into the Hall of Fame in 1936. These two companies continued releasing retroactive pins in 1991, commemorating the 1937 inductees. In 1992, IBM connected with Chemical Bank and began issuing two pins a year in order to cover every year up to the current pins. Chase Bank became the sole sponsor in 1996 and began issuing three pins annually in 1997. The pins are limited to a production run of 500, 350 of which go to the players and their families, with the remaining 150 making it into the hands of the sponsoring companies' top executives.

Hall of Fame Press Pins

Year Released	Year Inducted	Players	NM Price
1982	1982	Aaron, Chandler, T. Jackson, F. Robinson	$450.00
1983	1983	Alston, Kell, Marichal, B. Robinson	350.00
1984	1984	Aparicio, Drysdale, Ferrell, Killebrew, Reese	175.00
1985	1985	Brock, Slaughter, Vaughan, Wilhelm	175.00
1986	1986	Doerr, Lombardi, McCovey	160.00
1987	1987	Dandridge, Hunter, B. Williams	350.00
1988	1988	Stargell	350.00
1989	1989	Barlick, Bench, Schoendienst, Yastrzemski	400.00
1989	1989	50th Anniversary Medallion	775.00
1990	1990	Palmer, Morgan	275.00
1991	1991	Carew, Jenkins, Perry, Lazeri	200.00
1992	1992	Seaver, Newhouser, Fingers, McGowan	325.00
1993	1993	R. Jackson	325.00
1994	1994	Durocher, Rizzuto, Carlton	300.00
1995	1995	Schmidt, Ashburn, Day, Hulbert, Willis	400.00
1996	1996	Bunning, Weaver, Hanlon, B. Foster	300.00
1997	1997	Lasorda, Niekro, Fox, Wells	300.00

Retroactive Hall of Fame Press Pins

Year Released	Year Inducted	Players	NM Price
1990	1936	Cobb, Mathewson, W. Johnson, Ruth, Wagner	$650.00
1991	1937	LaJoie, Speaker, Young, Buckley, B. Johnson, McGraw, Mack, G. Wright	550.00
1992	1938	Alexander, Cartwright, Chadwick	375.00
1992	1955	DiMaggio, Hartnett, Lyons, Vance, Baker, Schalk	375.00
1993	1939	Collins, Gehrig, Keeler, Sisler	350.00
1993	1939	Anson, Comiskey, Cummings, Ewing, Radbourn	350.00
1994	1942	Hornsby	375.00
1994	1966	Stengel, T. Williams	375.00
1995	1944	Landis	375.00
1995	1969	Campanella, Coveleski, Hoyt, Musial	375.00
1996	1945	Bresnahan, Brouthers, Clarke, Collins, Duffy, Jennings, K. Kelly, O'Rourke, W. Robinson	350.00
1996	1974	Bell, Bottomly, Conlan, Ford, Mantle, Thompson	350.00
1997	1946	Burkett, Chance, Chesbro, Evers, Griffith, T. McCarthy, McGinnity, Plank, Tinker, Waddell, Walsh	325.00
1997	1962	Feller, McKechnnie, J. Robinson, Roush	325.00
1997	1972	Berra, J. Gibson, Gomel, Harridge, Koufax, Leonard, Wynn, Youngs	325.00

REGULAR SEASON TICKETS

Tickets are among the most common mementos from a day at the ballpark. Many collectors stuff the stubs into a wallet or purse to keep as a souvenir, so most are in Fair condition at best. Full or unused tickets are considered to be in Excellent condition, since they have seen little wear or tear, and these tickets carry a higher premium—about two to three times the value of stubs.

In recent years, some ballparks, like Cleveland's Jacobs Field, have entered the electronic age. Fans attending "The Jake" leave with full tickets, because attendants use electronic devices, much like the scanners found in supermarkets—to scan the tickets—rather than tearing them. Obviously, this has created a surplus of present-day tickets that aren't torn.

Like souvenir programs, pre-1900 tickets found in Excellent condition command a premium, and the tickets and stubs that generate the most collector interest are those from World Series, All-Star, League Championship, and Division Series games. Ticket values for each of these events are included in their own special sections. Values of tickets from some of baseball's more memorable games—one-game playoffs, player milestones, and the like—are listed under the Specialty Programs and Tickets section.

Below is a list of prices for ticket stubs from regular season games, listed by decade. Remember that unless otherwise noted, all stubs are assumed to be in Excellent condition.

1932
Regular Season
Chicago

1941
Regular Season
Cleveland

1969
Regular Season
Montreal

1974
Regular Season
Atlanta

Year	Price
pre-1900s*	$40.00-60.00
1900-1910	30.00-40.00
1911-1920	25.00-30.00
1921-1930	18.00-25.00
1931-1940	18.00-20.00
1941-1950	15.00-18.00
1951-1960	10.00-15.00
1961-1970	8.00-10.00
1971-1980	5.00-8.00
1981-1990	4.00-6.00
1991-present	3.00-5.00

Pre-1900 tickets and stubs are available from only a very limited number of teams.

There can be a wide range in values even among tickets from the same team in the same era. For instance, tickets from the 1960-64 Chicago White Sox feature player photographs, and range in value from $5 for common players to $20 for Luis Aparicio.

ALL-STAR TICKETS

In 1933, a crowd of over 47,000 fans packed Chicago's Comisky Park to watch the best players from the American League take on the best from the National League. Since then, the All-Star game has become an annual event, canceled only once—in 1945, due to wartime restrictions. From 1959-62, baseball experimented with two All-Star games—one held in an American League park and one in a National League park—but the idea was scrapped after just four years.

Tickets to the Midsummer Classic usually have a different look than those for regular-season games. A 1936 ticket from Braves Field in Boston, for example, features a picture of each member of the Advisory Council, while 1948 tickets take on the color of the host team, the St. Louis Browns.

Full tickets from both the '39 and '48 All-Star games grabbed a winning bid of $463 in a 1997 auction, but such specimens are rare, and collectors generally have to be content with stubs.

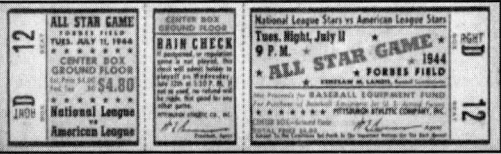

1944 All-Star Game

1940 All-Star Game

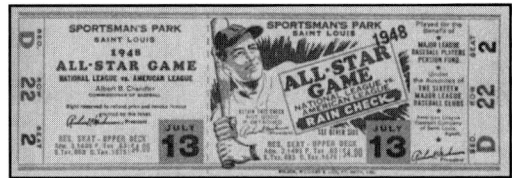

1948 All-Star Game

Year	Host City	Price	Year	Host City	Price	Year	Host City	Price
1933	Chicago (White Sox)	800.00	1957	St. Louis	45.00	1977	New York (Yankees)	25.00
1934	New York (Giants)	225.00	1958	Baltimore	105.00	1978	San Diego	20.00
1935	Cleveland	185.00	1959	Pittsburgh	70.00	1979	Seattle	25.00
1936	Boston (Braves)	300.00	1959	Los Angeles	150.00	1980	Los Angeles	25.00
1937	Washington	215.00	1960	Kansas City	30.00	1981	Cleveland	20.00
1938	Cincinnati	160.00	1960	New York (Yankees)	25.00	1982	Montreal	85.00
1939	New York (Yankees)	225.00	1961	San Francisco	25.00	1983	Chicago (White Sox)	45.00
1940	St. Louis (Cardinals)	90.00	1961	Boston	50.00	1984	San Francisco	18.00
1941	Detroit	90.00	1962	Washington	55.00	1985	Minnesota	20.00
1942	New York (Giants)	110.00	1962	Chicago (Cubs)	40.00	1986	Houston	18.00
1943	Philadelphia (Athletics)	115.00	1963	Cleveland	30.00	1987	Oakland	20.00
1944	Pittsburgh	160.00	1964	New York (Mets)	40.00	1988	Cincinnati	25.00
1945	No Game Played	—	1965	Minnesota	25.00	1989	California	25.00
1946	Boston (Red Sox)	90.00	1966	St. Louis	70.00	1990	Chicago (Cubs)	50.00
1947	Chicago (Cubs)	120.00	1967	California	75.00	1991	Toronto	50.00
1948	St. Louis (Browns)	110.00	1968	Houston	60.00	1992	San Diego	20.00
1949	Brooklyn	90.00	1969	Washington	50.00	1993	Baltimore	45.00
1950	Chicago (White Sox)	75.00	1970	Cincinnati	45.00	1994	Pittsburgh	50.00
1951	Detroit	65.00	1971	Detroit	18.00	1995	Texas	60.00
1952	Philadelphia (Phillies)	70.00	1972	Atlanta	18.00	1996	Philadelphia	40.00
1953	Cincinnati	110.00	1973	Kansas City	22.00	1997	Cleveland*	40.00
1954	Cleveland	135.00	1974	Pittsburgh	45.00			
1955	Milwaukee	120.00	1975	Milwaukee	18.00		*Tickets from this All-Star game were not torn.*	
1956	Washington	80.00	1976	Philadelphia	18.00			

WORLD SERIES TICKETS

In 1903, the Pittsburgh Pirates of the National League played the American League's Boston Red Sox in a best-of-nine series to determine an overall champion of baseball. The next year, the New York Giants refused to play Boston, so no series was held. The World Series returned the following year as a best-of-seven contest, and has remained so to this day, except in the years of 1919-1921, when it reverted to the best-of-nine format.

Since its inception, the World Series has been cancelled only one other time. After overcoming the absence of its biggest stars during the war years, and even the San Francisco earthquake of 1989, the Fall Classic couldn't survive the labor dispute of 1994. Realizing on September 14 that there was no hope of salvaging the season, baseball's owners decided to call off the 1994 World Series, one of the darkest chapters in the history of the game.

As with programs, tickets to games held in the Series winner's home park generally carry a higher premium than those from the loser's home field.

1917 World Series

1935 World Series

1958 World Series

Year		Team	Price	Year		Team	Price
1903	Winner	Boston Red Sox	3,500.00	1921	Loser	New York Yankees	400.00
1903	Loser	Pittsburgh Pirates	3,000.00	1922	Winner	New York Giants	425.00
1904		Series Not Played	—	1922	Loser	New York Yankees	400.00
1905	Winner	New York Giants	1,500.00	1923	Winner	New York Yankees	425.00
1905	Loser	Philadelphia A's	1,200.00	1923	Loser	New York Giants	400.00
1906	Winner	Chicago White Sox	1,200.00	1924	Winner	Washington Senators	400.00
1906	Loser	Chicago Cubs	1,100.00	1924	Loser	New York Giants	375.00
1907	Winner	Chicago Cubs	1,200.00	1925	Winner	Pittsburgh Pirates	450.00
1907	Loser	Detroit Tigers	1,000.00	1925	Loser	Washington Senators	375.00
1908	Winner	Chicago Cubs	1,200.00	1926	Winner	St. Louis Cardinals	350.00
1908	Loser	Detroit Tigers	1,000.00	1926	Loser	New York Yankees	275.00
1909	Winner	Pittsburgh Pirates	1,200.00	1927	Winner	New York Yankees	450.00
1909	Loser	Detroit Tigers	1,000.00	1927	Loser	Pittsburgh Pirates	300.00
1910	Winner	Philadelphia A's	825.00	1928	Winner	New York Yankees	350.00
1910	Loser	Chicago Cubs	800.00	1928	Loser	St. Louis Cardinals	275.00
1911	Winner	Philadelphia A's	825.00	1929	Winner	Philadelphia A's	275.00
1911	Loser	New York Giants	750.00	1929	Loser	Chicago Cubs	250.00
1912	Winner	Boston Red Sox	1,000.00	1930	Winner	Philadelphia A's	275.00
1912	Loser	New York Giants	900.00	1930	Loser	St. Louis Cardinals	225.00
1913	Winner	Philadelphia A's	800.00	1931	Winner	St. Louis Cardinals	250.00
1913	Loser	New York Giants	700.00	1931	Loser	Philadelphia A's	250.00
1914	Winner	Philadelphia A's	800.00	1932	Winner	New York Yankees	350.00
1914	Loser	Boston Braves	800.00	1932	Loser	Chicago Cubs	275.00
1915	Winner	Boston Red Sox	700.00	1933	Winner	New York Giants	275.00
1915	Loser	Philadelphia Phillies	600.00	1933	Loser	Washington Senators	150.00
1916	Winner	Boston Red Sox	725.00	1934	Winner	St. Louis Cardinals	200.00
1916	Loser	Brooklyn Dodgers	1,000.00	1934	Loser	Detroit Tigers	175.00
1917	Winner	Chicago White Sox	700.00	1935	Winner	Detroit Tigers	225.00
1917	Loser	New York Giants	550.00	1935	Loser	Chicago Cubs	200.00
1918	Winner	Boston Red Sox	600.00	1936	Winner	New York Yankees	250.00
1918	Loser	Chicago Cubs	550.00	1936	Loser	New York Giants	200.00
1919	Winner	Cincinnati Reds	1,000.00	1937	Winner	New York Yankees	225.00
1919	Loser	Chicago White Sox	2,500.00	1937	Loser	New York Giants	175.00
1920	Winner	Cleveland Indians	550.00	1938	Winner	New York Yankees	200.00
1920	Loser	Brooklyn Dodgers	500.00	1938	Loser	Chicago Cubs	175.00
1921	Winner	New York Giants	425.00	1939	Winner	New York Yankees	200.00

Year		Team	Price	Year		Team	Price
1939	Loser	Cincinnati Reds	180.00	1969	Winner	New York Mets	100.00
1940	Winner	Cincinnati Reds	100.00	1969	Loser	Baltimore Orioles	50.00
1940	Loser	Detroit Tigers	90.00	1970	Winner	Baltimore Orioles	60.00
1941	Winner	New York Yankees	150.00	1970	Loser	Cincinnati Reds	40.00
1941	Loser	Brooklyn Dodgers	125.00	1971	Winner	Pittsburgh Pirates	40.00
1942	Winner	St. Louis Cardinals	150.00	1971	Loser	Baltimore Orioles	35.00
1942	Loser	New York Yankees	125.00	1972	Winner	Oakland A's	50.00
1943	Winner	New York Yankees	140.00	1972	Loser	Cincinnati Reds	35.00
1943	Loser	St. Louis Cardinals	100.00	1973	Winner	Oakland A's	50.00
1944	Winner	St. Louis Cardinals	100.00	1973	Loser	New York Mets	40.00
1944	Loser	St. Louis Browns	125.00	1974	Winner	Oakland A's	50.00
1945	Winner	Detroit Tigers	100.00	1974	Loser	Los Angeles Dodgers	40.00
1945	Loser	Chicago Cubs	85.00	1975	Winner	Cincinnati Reds	50.00
1946	Winner	St. Louis Cardinals	100.00	1975	Loser	Boston Red Sox	20.00
1946	Loser	Boston Red Sox	70.00	1976	Winner	Cincinnati Reds	40.00
1947	Winner	New York Yankees	140.00	1976	Loser	New York Yankees	25.00
1947	Loser	Brooklyn Dodgers	125.00	1977	Winner	New York Yankees	35.00
1948	Winner	Cleveland Indians	125.00	1977	Loser	Los Angeles Dodgers	30.00
1948	Loser	Boston Braves	100.00	1978	Winner	New York Yankees	35.00
1949	Winner	New York Yankees	125.00	1978	Loser	Los Angeles Dodgers	30.00
1949	Loser	Brooklyn Dodgers	100.00	1979	Winner	Pittsburgh Pirates	45.00
1950	Winner	New York Yankees	125.00	1979	Loser	Baltimore Orioles	20.00
1950	Loser	Philadelphia Phillies	115.00	1980	Winner	Philadelphia Phillies	35.00
1951	Winner	New York Yankees	125.00	1980	Loser	Kansas City Royals	30.00
1951	Loser	New York Giants	100.00	1981	Winner	Los Angeles Dodgers	30.00
1952	Winner	New York Yankees	125.00	1981	Loser	New York Yankees	20.00
1952	Loser	Brooklyn Dodgers	115.00	1982	Winner	St. Louis Cardinals	40.00
1953	Winner	New York Yankees	125.00	1982	Loser	Milwaukee Brewers	35.00
1953	Loser	Brooklyn Dodgers	115.00	1983	Winner	Baltimore Orioles	30.00
1954	Winner	New York Giants	100.00	1983	Loser	Philadelphia Phillies	15.00
1954	Loser	Cleveland Indians	75.00	1984	Winner	Detroit Tigers	40.00
1955	Winner	Brooklyn Dodgers	125.00	1984	Loser	San Diego Padres	35.00
1955	Loser	New York Yankees	115.00	1985	Winner	Kansas City Royals	40.00
1956	Winner	New York Yankees†	125.00	1985	Loser	St. Louis Cardinals	35.00
1956	Loser	Brooklyn Dodgers	115.00	1986	Winner	New York Mets	50.00
1957	Winner	Milwaukee Braves	100.00	1986	Loser	Boston Red Sox	35.00
1957	Loser	New York Yankees	85.00	1987	Winner	Minnesota Twins	50.00
1958	Winner	New York Yankees	100.00	1987	Loser	St. Louis Cardinals	40.00
1958	Loser	Milwaukee Braves	75.00	1988	Winner	Los Angeles Dodgers	35.00
1959	Winner	Los Angeles Dodgers	90.00	1988	Loser	Oakland A's	30.00
1959	Loser	Chicago White Sox	85.00	1989	Winner	Oakland A's	35.00
1960	Winner	Pittsburgh Pirates	100.00	1989	Loser	San Francisco Giants	15.00
1960	Loser	New York Yankees	50.00	1990	Winner	Cincinnati Reds	50.00
1961	Winner	New York Yankees	75.00	1990	Loser	Oakland A's	15.00
1961	Loser	Cincinnati Reds	60.00	1991	Winner	Minnesota Twins	40.00
1962	Winner	New York Yankees	75.00	1991	Loser	Atlanta Braves	20.00
1962	Loser	San Francisco Giants	70.00	1992	Winner	Toronto Blue Jays	35.00
1963	Winner	Los Angeles Dodgers	60.00	1992	Loser	Atlanta Braves	20.00
1963	Loser	New York Yankees	50.00	1993	Winner	Toronto Blue Jays	30.00
1964	Winner	St. Louis Cardinals	90.00	1993	Loser	Philadelphia Phillies	18.00
1964	Loser	New York Yankees	50.00	1994		Series Not Played	—
1965	Winner	Los Angeles Dodgers	50.00	1995	Winner	Atlanta Braves	12.00
1965	Loser	Minnesota Twins	40.00	1995	Loser	Cleveland Indians	10.00
1966	Winner	Baltimore Orioles	50.00	1996	Winner	New York Yankees	15.00
1966	Loser	Los Angeles Dodgers	40.00	1996	Loser	Atlanta Braves	12.00
1967	Winner	St. Louis Cardinals	90.00	1997	Winner	Florida Marlins	12.00
1967	Loser	Boston Red Sox	60.00	1997	Loser	Cleveland Indians*	10.00
1968	Winner	Detroit Tigers	110.00				
1968	Loser	St. Louis Cardinals	100.00				

† *Tickets from Game 5 priced in the Specialty Tickets and Programs section.*

* *Tickets from these World Series games were not torn.*

LEAGUE CHAMPIONSHIP TICKETS

In 1969, the American and National Leagues expanded to 12 teams apiece. With the expansion came the creation of two divisions in each league and the need for a round of playoffs leading up to the World Series. The League Championship Series were originally best-of-five, but the format switched to best-of-seven in 1985.

The formula was altered slightly in 1981, due to a mid-season players' strike. At the end of the regular season, each division's first-half and second-half champions held a best-of-three playoff to advance to the League Championship Series. In 1994, another strike caused the cancellation of the both the LCS and World Series.

Like World Series tickets, LCS tickets from the winning team's park tend to be worth more than those from the opposing team's.

AMERICAN LEAGUE

Year		Team	Price
1969	Winner	Baltimore Orioles	40.00
1969	Loser	Minnesota Twins	30.00
1970	Winner	Baltimore Orioles	30.00
1970	Loser	Minnesota Twins	25.00
1971	Winner	Baltimore Orioles	30.00
1971	Loser	Oakland A's	25.00
1972	Winner	Oakland A's	28.00
1972	Loser	Detroit Tigers	20.00
1973	Winner	Oakland A's	28.00
1973	Loser	Baltimore Orioles	25.00
1974	Winner	Oakland A's	28.00
1974	Loser	Baltimore Orioles	25.00
1975	Winner	Boston Red Sox	22.00
1975	Loser	Oakland A's	18.00
1976	Winner	New York Yankees	20.00
1976	Loser	Kansas City Royals	18.00
1977	Winner	New York Yankees	20.00
1977	Loser	Kansas City Royals	18.00
1978	Winner	New York Yankees	20.00
1978	Loser	Kansas City Royals	18.00
1979	Winner	Baltimore Orioles	15.00
1979	Loser	California Angels	10.00
1980	Winner	Kansas City Royals	12.00
1980	Loser	New York Yankees	10.00
1981	Winner	New York Yankees	15.00
1981	Loser	Oakland A's	12.00
1982	Winner	Milwaukee Brewers	12.00
1982	Loser	California Angels	10.00
1983	Winner	Baltimore Orioles	10.00
1983	Loser	Chicago White Sox	8.00
1984	Winner	Detroit Tigers	20.00
1984	Loser	Kansas City Royals	10.00
1985	Winner	Kansas City Royals	12.00
1985	Loser	Toronto Blue Jays	10.00
1986	Winner	Boston Red Sox	18.00
1986	Loser	California Angels	10.00
1987	Winner	Minnesota Twins	18.00
1987	Loser	Detroit Tigers	15.00
1988	Winner	Oakland A's	18.00
1988	Loser	Boston Red Sox	10.00
1989	Winner	Oakland A's	18.00
1989	Loser	Toronto Blue Jays	8.00
1990	Winner	Oakland A's	12.00
1990	Loser	Boston Red Sox	8.00
1991	Winner	Minnesota Twins	12.00
1991	Loser	Toronto Blue Jays	8.00
1992	Winner	Toronto Blue Jays	10.00

Year		Team	Price
1992	Loser	Oakland A's	8.00
1993	Winner	Toronto Blue Jays	15.00
1993	Loser	Chicago White Sox	10.00
1994		Series Not Held	—
1995	Winner	Cleveland Indians	15.00
1995	Loser	Seattle Mariners	12.00
1996	Winner	New York Yankees	15.00
1996	Loser	Baltimore Orioles	10.00
1997	Winner	Cleveland Indians*	15.00
1997	Loser	Baltimore Orioles	10.00

Tickets from these ALCS games were not torn.

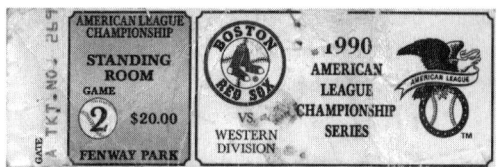

1990 AL Playoff

NATIONAL LEAGUE

Year		Team	Price
1969	Winner	New York Mets	40.00
1969	Loser	Atlanta Braves	20.00
1970	Winner	Cincinnati Reds	40.00
1970	Loser	Pittsburgh Pirates	30.00
1971	Winner	Pittsburgh Pirates	30.00
1971	Loser	San Francisco Giants	20.00
1972	Winner	Cincinnati Reds	40.00
1972	Loser	Pittsburgh Pirates	30.00
1973	Winner	New York Mets	30.00
1973	Loser	Cincinnati Reds	30.00
1974	Winner	Los Angeles Dodgers	25.00
1974	Loser	Pittsburgh Pirates	22.00
1975	Winner	Cincinnati Reds	35.00
1975	Loser	Pittsburgh Pirates	22.00
1976	Winner	Cincinnati Reds	35.00
1976	Loser	Philadelphia Phillies	28.00
1977	Winner	Los Angeles Dodgers	25.00
1977	Loser	Philadelphia Phillies	22.00
1978	Winner	Los Angeles Dodgers	25.00
1978	Loser	Philadelphia Phillies	22.00
1979	Winner	Pittsburgh Pirates	35.00
1979	Loser	Cincinnati Reds	30.00
1980	Winner	Philadelphia Phillies	22.00
1980	Loser	Houston Astros	18.00
1981	Winner	Los Angeles Dodgers	20.00
1981	Loser	Montreal Expos	12.00

Year		Team	Price	Year		Team	Price
1982	Winner	St. Louis Cardinals	18.00	1990	Winner	Cincinnati Reds	12.00
1982	Loser	Atlanta Braves	8.00	1990	Loser	Pittsburgh Pirates	8.00
1983	Winner	Philadelphia Phillies	22.00	1991	Winner	Atlanta Braves	15.00
1983	Loser	Los Angeles Dodgers	18.00	1991	Loser	Pittsburgh Pirates	8.00
1984	Winner	San Diego Padres	18.00	1992	Winner	Atlanta Braves	15.00
1984	Loser	Chicago Cubs	12.00	1992	Loser	Pittsburgh Pirates	10.00
1985	Winner	St. Louis Cardinals	18.00	1993	Winner	Philadelphia Phillies	18.00
1985	Loser	Los Angeles Dodgers	15.00	1993	Loser	Atlanta Braves	6.00
1986	Winner	New York Mets	12.00	1994		Series Not Held	—
1986	Loser	Houston Astros	10.00	1995	Winner	Atlanta Braves	15.00
1987	Winner	St. Louis Cardinals	16.00	1995	Loser	Cincinnati Reds	12.00
1987	Loser	San Francisco Giants	12.00	1996	Winner	Atlanta Braves	15.00
1988	Winner	Los Angeles Dodgers	25.00	1996	Loser	St. Louis Cardinals	10.00
1988	Loser	New York Mets	12.00	1997	Winner	Florida Marlins	18.00
1989	Winner	San Francisco Giants	18.00	1997	Loser	Atlanta Braves	8.00
1989	Loser	Chicago Cubs	12.00				

DIVISION SERIES TICKETS

As baseball continued to grow in the 1990s, each league expanded to three divisions, creating the need for another round of playoffs to determine who would appear in the LCS. The Division Series was scheduled to begin in 1994, but the eighth work stoppage in baseball history, which lasted from August 12, 1994 to March 31, 1995, changed those plans. Instead, all post-season games were cancelled, and the inaugural best-of-five Division Series were postponed until 1995.

AMERICAN LEAGUE

Year		Team	Price
1995	Winner	Cleveland Indians	15.00
1995	Loser	Boston Red Sox	10.00
1995	Winner	Seattle Mariners	18.00
1995	Loser	New York Yankees	10.00
1996	Winner	Baltimore Orioles	15.00
1996	Loser	Cleveland Indians	12.00
1996	Winner	New York Yankees	15.00
1996	Loser	Texas Rangers	10.00
1997	Winner	Cleveland Indians*	15.00
1997	Loser	New York Yankees	8.00
1997	Winner	Baltimore Orioles	15.00
1997	Loser	Seattle Mariners	10.00

* Tickets from these Division Series games were not torn.

NATIONAL LEAGUE

Year		Team	Price
1995	Winner	Atlanta Braves	15.00
1995	Loser	Colorado Rockies	15.00
1995	Winner	Cincinnati Reds	15.00
1995	Loser	Los Angeles Dodgers	10.00
1996	Winner	Atlanta Braves	15.00
1996	Loser	Los Angeles Dodgers	10.00
1996	Winner	St. Louis Cardinals	15.00
1996	Loser	San Diego Padres	8.00
1997	Winner	Atlanta Braves	10.00
1997	Loser	Houston Astros	8.00
1997	Winner	Florida Marlins	15.00
1997	Loser	San Francisco Giants	8.00

AUTOGRAPHED TICKETS

While tickets aren't generally considered a premium item to have autographed—especially since their size usually allows for only one signature—they are often the only option for collectors who happen to run into a player before, during, or after a ballgame. If you don't happen to have a ball or an 8x10 handy, a ticket stub will do the trick. And since they're small, tickets are relatively easy to store or display.

Ideally, a player from the home team who had a great game is the perfect choice to autograph a ticket, but this isn't always the case. If Ken Griffey Jr. goes 0-for-4 while Dan Wilson slugs a grand slam, Griffey's is still the autograph to get.

Chapter 6

FIGURES

BOBBIN' HEADS

The original Bobbin' Heads were made in Japan in the 1960s and '70s. The papier-maché figures, with spring-loaded, bobbing heads originally retailed for $1–$3, and were marketed at stadiums and other outlets across the country. These figures weren't especially popular when they were first released, and thus didn't sell too well.

But over the past decade, Bobbin' Heads have been redis-covered by collectors. The fragile material is easily damaged and many figures today are found with cracks and chipped paint. The lack

1961-62 Roger Maris

of figures in mint condition has caused prices to skyrocket over the past couple of years.

Most pieces are generic team figures with a either a boy head or the head of the team mascot. Many team Bobbin' Heads can be found with variations in labels, logos, base shape, and color.

The figures listed below are combined in "sets" determined by base color and release date. For each set we list the team, the type of head, the relative scarcity of the piece (see sidebar), and the current secondary market price for pieces in mint condition.

SCARCITY

Every Bobbin' Head is rated on its scarcity relative to other Bobbin' Head figures. Common figures are the easiest to find and are ideal for collectors entering the hobby. Difficult and scarce figures are harder to find and command a premium. The rare and very rare figures are almost impossible to find. Only the most dedicated Bobbin' Head collectors attempt to add these to their collections.

C	Common
D	Difficult
S	Scarce
R	Rare
VR	Very Rare

1960-61 New York Yankees

1960-61 Baseball

	NM Price
Complete Set (18)	$2,400.00

Quality Rating ★★★

This is the first run of Bobbin' Heads released. All 14 major league teams are represented, plus four minor league teams. All of the bases are square, though the colors vary from team to team.

Team	Head	Scarcity	Mint
Baltimore Orioles	Mascot	R	$250.00
Boston Red Sox	Boy	S	250.00
Chicago Cubs	Boy	R	200.00
Cincinnati Reds	Mascot	S	225.00

Team	Head	Scarcity	Mint
Detroit Tigers	Boy	S	200.00
Houston Colt .45s	Boy	S	175.00
Los Angeles Angels	Boy	C	100.00
Minnesota Twins	Boy	C	50.00
New York Mets	Boy	S	150.00
New York Yankees	Boy	D	125.00
Pittsburgh Pirates	Boy	S	150.00
San Francisco Giants	Boy	S	100.00
Washington Senators	Boy	VR	500.00
Minor League			
Hawaii Islanders	Boy	VR	300.00
Portland Beavers	Boy	R	150.00
Seattle Raniers	Boy	VR	250.00
Tacoma Giants	Boy	R	200.00

Team	Head	Scarcity	Mint
Anaheim Angels	Boy	D	$200.00
Baltimore Orioles	Mascot	R	325.00
Boston Red Sox	Boy	D	200.00
Chicago Cubs	Mascot	S	300.00
Chicago White Sox	Boy	S	200.00
Cincinnati Reds	Mascot	VR	750.00
Cleveland Indians	Mascot	R	350.00
Detroit Tigers	Mascot	S	200.00
Houston Colts			
(white uniform)	Boy	D	200.00
(blue uniform)	Boy	VR	1,000.00
Kansas City A's	Boy	S	300.00
Los Angeles Angels	Boy	D	150.00
Los Angeles Dodgers	Boy	D	150.00
Milwaukee Braves	Mascot	S	250.00
Minnesota Twins	Boy	R	400.00
New York Mets	Boy	R	300.00
New York Yankees	Boy	S	200.00
Philadelphia Phillies	Boy	D	150.00
Pittsburgh Pirates	Mascot	VR	750.00
St. Louis Cardinals	Mascot	R	300.00
San Francisco Giants	Boy	R	300.00
Washington Senators	Boy	S	250.00
Minor League			
Spokane Indians	Mascot	VR	300.00

**1961-62
Mickey Mantle**

1961-62 Baseball Caricatures

	NM Price
Complete Set (7)	$4,000.00

Quality Rating ★★★

These figures appear on either round or square white bases. Although most stand about seven inches tall, 4½-inch versions of Mickey Mantle and Roger Maris were produced. The Willie Mays figure can be found with both light and dark skin tone. The light colored Mays is the easiest of the caricatures to find, while Roberto Clemente is the hardest.

Player	Team	Scarcity	Mint
Clemente, Roberto	Pirates	VR	$1,500.00
Mantle, Mickey			
(large)	Yankees	VR	600.00
(small)	Yankees	VR	1,200.00
Maris, Roger			
(large)	Yankees	VR	500.00
(small)	Yankees	VR	800.00
Mays, Willie			
(dark skin)	Giants	VR	600.00
(light skin)	Giants	R	350.00

1961-62 Baseball

	NM Price
Complete Set (22)	$6,500.00

Quality Rating ★★★

Each Bobber in the series came with a round white base. The hardest figures to find are the Cincinnati Reds, Pittsburgh Pirates, and the blue variation of the Houston Colts.

1961-62 Baseball Miniatures

	NM Price
Complete Set (20)	$5,000.00

Quality Rating ★★★

These Bobbers are similar to the regular issue except they measure only four inches in height. All figures stand on a round white base, and most contain a magnet in the base.

Team	Head	Scarcity	Mint
Baltimore Orioles	Mascot	R	$300.00
Boston Red Sox	Boy	R	350.00
Chicago Cubs	Mascot	R	400.00
Chicago White Sox	Boy	S	250.00
Cincinnati Reds	Mascot	R	350.00
Cleveland Indians	Mascot	R	300.00
Detroit Tigers	Mascot	S	250.00
Houston Colts	Boy	S	200.00
Kansas City A's	Boy	S	200.00
Los Angeles Angels	Boy	D	175.00
Los Angeles Dodgers	Boy	D	150.00
Milwaukee Braves	Mascot	R	400.00
Minnesota Twins	Boy	S	200.00
New York Mets	Boy	R	300.00
New York Yankees	Boy	R	300.00
Philadelphia Phillies	Boy	R	225.00
Pittsburgh Pirates	Mascot	R	350.00
St. Louis Cardinals	Mascot	R	350.00
San Francisco Giants	Boy	R	325.00
Washington Senators	Boy	R	275.00

1962-64 "Green" Baseball

			NM Price
Complete Set (20)			$2,000.00

Quality Rating ★★★

All of these Bobbers feature round green bases. The Houston Colts doll has a gun in his hand instead of a bat. The Boston Red Sox figure can be found with both red and white hats.

Team	Head	Scarcity	Mint
Baltimore Orioles	Mascot	S	150.00
Boston Red Sox			
(red hat)	Boy	S	150.00
(white hat)	Boy	D	100.00
Chicago Cubs	Mascot	R	300.00
Chicago White Sox	Boy	C	75.00
Cincinnati Reds	Mascot	S	125.00
Cleveland Indians	Mascot	D	125.00
Detroit Tigers	Mascot	D	125.00
Houston Colts	Boy	R	300.00
Kansas City A's	Boy	S	200.00
Los Angeles Angels	Boy	D	125.00
Los Angeles Dodgers	Boy	C	100.00
Milwaukee Braves	Mascot	S	200.00
Minnesota Twins	Boy	C	100.00
New York Mets	Boy	D	120.00
New York Yankees	Boy	D	150.00
Philadelphia Phillies	Boy	D	100.00
Pittsburgh Pirates	Mascot	S	150.00
St. Louis Cardinals	Mascot	S	150.00
San Francisco Giants	Boy	D	100.00
Washington Senators	Boy	S	250.00

1962-64 Baseball

			NM Price
Complete Set (19)			$10,000.00

Quality Rating ★★★

This is similar to the green series except that each Bobber is black. Again these figures stand on round green bases. All of these figures are very rare and extremely difficult to find.

Team	Head	Scarcity	Mint
Baltimore Orioles	Boy	VR	$700.00
Boston Red Sox	Boy	VR	1,500.00
Chicago Cubs	Boy	VR	600.00
Chicago White Sox	Boy	VR	650.00
Cincinnati Reds	Boy	VR	1,000.00
Cleveland Indians	Boy	VR	1,000.00
Detroit Tigers	Boy	VR	700.00
Houston Colts	Boy	VR	2,000.00
Kansas City A's	Boy	VR	1,000.00
Los Angeles Angels	Boy	VR	1,000.00

Team	Head	Scarcity	Mint
Los Angeles Dodgers	Boy	VR	600.00
Milwaukee Braves	Boy	VR	1,000.00
Minnesota Twins	Boy	VR	400.00
New York Mets	Boy	VR	800.00
New York Yankees	Boy	VR	1,200.00
Philadelphia Phillies	Boy	VR	600.00
Pittsburgh Pirates	Boy	VR	500.00
St. Louis Cardinals	Boy	VR	500.00
San Francisco Giants	Boy	VR	500.00

1965-72 Baseball

			NM Price
Complete Set (28)			$3,000.00

Quality Rating ★★★

This is the easiest series to complete of all of the Bobbin' Heads. Each figure stands on a round gold base.

Team	Head	Scarcity	Mint
Atlanta Braves	Mascot	C	$75.00
Baltimore Orioles	Mascot	D	125.00
Boston Red Sox	Boy	D	125.00
California Angels	Boy	D	100.00
Chicago Cubs	Mascot	D	125.00
Chicago White Sox	Boy	C	75.00
Cincinnati Reds	Mascot	D	125.00
Cleveland Indians	Mascot	S	150.00
Detroit Tigers	Mascot	D	125.00
Houston Astros	Boy	C	75.00
Kansas City Royals	Boy	C	75.00
Los Angeles Angels	Boy	C	75.00
Los Angeles Dodgers	Boy	C	75.00
Milwaukee Brewers	Boy	C	75.00
Minnesota Twins	Boy	D	100.00
Montreal Expos	Boy	C	75.00
New York Mets	Boy	C	75.00
New York Yankees	Boy	D	125.00
Oakland A's			
(yellow)	Boy	C	50.00
(white)	Boy	S	150.00
Philadelphia Phillies	Boy	C	75.00
Pittsburgh Pirates	Mascot	D	100.00
St. Louis Cardinals	Mascot	D	125.00
San Diego Padres	Boy	VR	700.00
San Francisco Giants	Boy	C	75.00
Seattle Pilots	Boy	R	300.00
Texas Rangers	Boy	S	125.00
Washington Senators	Boy	R	250.00
Minor League			
Hawaii Islanders	Boy	VR	300.00
Denver Bears	Mascot	VR	400.00

CORINTHIAN HEADLINERS

orinthian Marketing first entered the sports figure market in 1996 with its Headliners brand of three-inch figurines with oversized heads. Corinthian debuted a football set in '96, then issued sets for all four major sports leagues—including baseball—in 1997.

The first baseball cases shipped in early spring, and over the course of the '97 season Corinthian added several players to the set. The additions included uniform variations for Jose Canseco, who appeared in the uniforms of both the Oakland A's and Boston Red Sox, and Kenny Lofton, in the uniforms of both the Cleveland Indians and Atlanta Braves.

Corinthian's plan was to issue a line of low-end sports figures to compete with the popular Kenner Starting Lineups. Headliners were distributed at most of the major retail outlets across the country, including Kmart, Wal-Mart, Toys "R" Us, Target, and KayBee toy stores. Unfortunately, most of the figures sat on shelves, and the heavy supply prevented a strong secondary market from developing. Most collectors show little interest in these figures, and most Headliners currently sell for little more than the original $3.99 retail price. The prices listed below are for pieces in their original package and in mint condition.

1997 BASEBALL

Player	Team	Mint Price
Complete Set (33)		$175.00
Alomar, Roberto	Orioles	5.00
Belle, Albert	Indians	5.00
Bonds, Barry	Giants	4.00
Boggs, Wade	Yankees	5.00
Caminiti, Ken	Padres	5.00
Canseco, Jose	Athletics	5.00
Canseco, Jose	Red Sox	8.00
Dykstra, Lenny	Phillies	5.00
Galarraga, Andres	Rockies	4.00
Griffey Jr., Ken	Mariners	15.00
Gwynn, Tony	Padres	5.00
Hershiser, Orel	Indians	4.00
Johnson, Randy	Mariners	5.00
Jones, Chipper	Braves	10.00
Justice, Dave	Indians	8.00

Player	Team	Mint Price
Karros, Eric	Dodgers	5.00
Larkin, Barry	Reds	5.00
Lofton, Kenny	Braves	5.00
Lofton, Kenny	Indians	8.00
McGriff, Fred	Braves	5.00
McGwire, Mark	Athletics	8.00
Molitor, Paul	Twins	4.00
Mondesi, Raul	Dodgers	4.00
Nomo, Hideo	Dodgers	7.00
O'Neill, Paul	Yankees	5.00
Piazza, Mike	Dodgers	6.00
Ripken Jr., Cal	Orioles	10.00
Rodriguez, Ivan	Rangers	4.00
Sandberg, Ryne	Cubs	5.00
Sheffield, Gary	Marlins	5.00
Thomas, Frank	White Sox	75.00
Vaughn, Mo	Red Sox	5.00
Williams, Matt	Indians	4.00

HARTLAND FIGURES

Hartland Plastics, of Hartland, Wis., produced collectible figurines for more than 40 years. Through a variety of ownership changes, factory moves, bizarre disappearances, and natural disasters, the Hartland name has survived. And although the possibility of future Hartland production looks grim at the moment, the brand's legendary resiliency has been its trademark throughout a long and storied history.

In 1958, Hartland released its first baseball series. The eight-inch figures were distributed at ballpark concession stands, where they sold for $2 each. The company continued its baseball production through the early '60s.

Figures were packaged in two different types of boxes—one solid and one with a cellophane window on the front. The pieces came with a variety of accessories, including bats, catcher's gear, and tags featuring the player's nickname and facsimile autograph.

During this time, Hartland produced many variations of its pieces. At least 11 players were produced with magnets attached to their feet or bases, intended to make the figures stick to car dashboards. Whether or not other figures produced at the same time, like Duke Snider or Dick Groat, came in magnet versions, is unknown. Other well-known variations include Eddie Mathews with or without red trim around his Braves logo, the Hank Aaron high-step and flat-footed versions, and a gold Mickey Mantle used to make a lamp.

In 1987, Dallas attorney William Alley bought the rights to Hartland's baseball properties and reprinted many of the baseball figures from the 1950s. Alley expanded the line in 1990, creating new pieces of Roberto Clemente, Lou Gehrig, Dizzy Dean, Whitey Ford, Bob Feller, and Ty Cobb. The production run for the figures was announced at 10,000 each, but it's estimated that the actual numbers were far lower.

Alley's company also created a tableau entitled "The Confrontation," which depicted manager Sparky Anderson arguing with an umpire. Only 20 "Confrontation" pieces are known to exist, 10 of which remain in their original packaging because of a dispute with the company that produced the boxes. "The Confrontation" is one of the rarest and most valuable Hartland figures ever produced, priced at upwards of $2,500.

After several ownership changes, Steven Manufacturing began production under the USA Hartland name and issued what came to be known as the "Missouri Hartlands." Steven developed several new figurines, including Nolan Ryan (in both home and away Rangers jerseys), Cy Young, Honus Wagner, and another tableau entitled "Safe at Second."

In July of 1993, USA Hartland was in the midst of producing a new Carl Yastrzemski figure when the Great Missouri Flood completely destroyed the factory. All of the molds were lost in the disaster, and the company folded later that year.

Of the original Hartland baseball figures, Groat was the shortest-printed and is the most difficult to find. Other scarce pieces include Rocky Colavito, Harmon Killebrew, Roger Maris, Don Drysdale, and Snider. Aside from "The Confrontation," the most difficult recent piece to obtain is Yastrzemski, because most of his figures were destroyed in the flood.

Roberto Clemente

1960

Player	Team	Mint
Aaron, Hank	Braves	$350.00
Aparicio, Luis	White Sox	350.00
Banks, Ernie	Cubs	350.00
Berra, Yogi	Yankees	250.00
Colavito, Rocky	Tigers	1,250.00
Drysdale, Don	Dodgers	500.00
Fox, Nellie	White Sox	250.00
Groat, Dick	Pirates	1,750.00
Killebrew, Harmon	Twins	750.00
Mantle, Mickey	Yankees	400.00
Maris, Roger	Yankees	500.00
Mathews, Eddie	Braves	250.00
Mays, Willie	Giants	300.00
Musial, Stan	Cardinals	300.00
Ruth, Babe	Yankees	300.00
Snider, Duke	Dodgers	600.00
Spahn, Warren	Braves	250.00
Williams, Ted	Red Sox	350.00
Batboy		250.00
Minor Leaguer		200.00

1990

Player	Team	Size	Mint
Aaron, Hank	Braves	10,000	$100.00
Aparicio, Luis	White Sox	10,000	75.00
Banks, Ernie	Cubs	10,000	75.00
Berra, Yogi	Yankees	10,000	100.00
Colavito, Rocky	Tigers	10,000	50.00
Drysdale, Don	Dodgers	10,000	75.00
Fox, Nellie	White Sox	10,000	60.00
Groat, Dick	Pirates	10,000	60.00
Killebrew, Harmon	Twins	10,000	75.00
Mantle, Mickey	Yankees	10,000	125.00
Maris, Roger	Yankees	10,000	125.00
Mathews, Eddie	Braves	10,000	100.00
Mays, Willie	Giants	10,000	100.00
Musial, Stan	Cardinals	10,000	60.00
Ruth, Babe	Yankees	10,000	60.00
Snider, Duke	Dodgers	10,000	60.00
Spahn, Warren	Braves	10,000	50.00
Williams, Ted	Red Sox	10,000	100.00
Batboy		2,500	200.00
Minor Leaguer		2,000	200.00

1993

Player	Team	Mint
Clemente, Roberto	Pirates	$100.00
Ford, Whitey	Yankees	100.00
Ryan, Nolan (home)	Rangers	75.00
Ryan, Nolan (away)	Rangers	75.00
Wagner, Honus	Pirates	150.00
Yastrzemski, Carl	Red Sox	400.00
Young, Cy	Indians	150.00
"Safe at Second"		150.00

Hartland "Dallas"

Player	Team	Mint
Clemente, Roberto	Pirates	$125.00
Cobb, Ty	Tigers	1,000.00
Dean, Dizzy	Cardinals	250.00
Feller, Bob	Indians	2,000.00
Ford, Whitey	Yankees	100.00
Gehrig, Lou	Yankees	400.00
Umpire		100.00
"The Confrontation"		2,500.00

GARTLAN

Gartlan U.S.A. was founded by Bob Gartlan in 1985. Most of the players in this line of fine porcelain figures were produced in both eight- and five-inch (mini) versions. The large figures feature authentic autographs on the nameplate, while the smaller figures include facsimile signatures. Production runs vary from piece to piece. Most of the mini figures had production runs of 10,000, while the larger figures were more limited.

Pete Rose led off the Gartlan line in 1985 with an eight-inch signed pewter figure limited to 4,192 pieces—the number of hits that broke Ty Cobb's all-time record. Today, Gartlan figures are some of the most popular in the hobby, with the eight-inch signed pieces attracting the most attention from collectors.

For a handful of players, Gartlan issued artist's proof figures that are more limited than either of the other series. The artist's proofs include the artist's signature along with that of the athlete.

Like other figure manufacturers, Gartlan started a collector's club for its loyal customers. A number of pieces were made available only to club members; these pieces are especially hard to find today.

Player	Team	Edition Size	Mint Price
Aaron, Hank			
(signed)	Braves	1,982	$150.00
(mini)	Braves	10,000	40.00
(commemorative)	Braves	755	280.00
(club)	Braves	N/A	100.00
Aparicio, Luis			
(signed)	White Sox	1,984	100.00
(mini)	White Sox	10,000	40.00
Barlick, Al			
(signed)	(umpire)	1,989	125.00
Bell, "Cool Papa"			
(signed)	Grays	1,499	125.00
Bench, Johnny			
(signed)	Reds	1,989	250.00
(mini)	Reds	10,000	50.00
(artist's proof)	Reds	250	450.00
Berra, Yogi			
(signed)	Yankees	2,150	225.00
(mini)	Yankees	10,000	50.00
(artist's proof)	Yankees	250	350.00
Brett, George			
(signed)	Royals	2,250	200.00
(mini)	Royals	10,000	40.00
(club)	Royals	N/A	100.00
Carew, Rod			
(signed)	Twins	1,991	125.00
(mini)	Twins	10,000	40.00
Carlton, Steve			
(signed)	Phillies	3,290	175.00
(mini)	Phillies	10,000	40.00
(artist's proof)	Phillies	500	400.00
Dandridge, Ray			
(signed)	Eagles	1,987	125.00
DiMaggio, Joe			
(signed)	Yankees	2,214	800.00
(signed)	Yankees	325	1,750.00
(artist's proof)	Yankees	12	6,000.00
Fisk, Carlton			
(signed)	White Sox	1,972	150.00
(mini)	White Sox	10,000	40.00
(artist's proof)	White Sox	300	350.00
Ford, Edward "Whitey"			
(signed)	Yankees	2,360	125.00
(mini)	Yankees	10,000	40.00
(artist's proof)	Yankees	250	350.00
Griffey Jr., Ken			
(signed)	Mariners	2,360	200.00
(mini)	Mariners	10,000	40.00
Irvin, Monte			
(signed)	Giants	1,973	100.00
(mini)	Giants	10,000	40.00
Kiner, Ralph			
(signed)	Pirates	1,975	100.00
(mini)	Pirates	10,000	40.00
Leonard, Walter "Buck"			
(signed)	Grays	1,972	125.00
Mathews, Eddie			
(signed)	Braves	1,978	150.00
(mini)	Braves	10,000	40.00
Musial, Stan			
(signed)	Cardinals	1,969	225.00
(mini)	Cardinals	10,000	40.00
(artist's proof)	Cardinals	300	300.00
(pewter)	Cardinals	500	850.00
Rose, Pete			
(platinum)	Reds	4,192	700.00
(mini)	Reds	10,000	75.00
Schmidt, Mike			
(signed)	Phillies	1,987	750.00
(mini)	Phillies	10,000	40.00
(artist's proof)	Phillies	20	1,500.00
(club)	Phillies	N/A	125.00
Seaver, Tom			
(signed)	Mets	1,992	125.00
(mini)	Mets	10,000	40.00
Spahn, Warren			
(signed)	Braves	1,973	125.00
(mini)	Braves	10,000	40.00
Strawberry, Darryl			
(signed)	Mets	2,500	100.00
(mini)	Mets	10,000	40.00
Thomas, Frank			
(signed)	White Sox	1,994	200.00
(mini)	White Sox	10,000	40.00
Williams, Ted			
(signed)	Red Sox	2,654	350.00
(mini)	Red Sox	10,000	50.00
(artist's proof)	Red Sox	250	800.00
Yastrzemski, Carl			
(signed)	Red Sox	1,989	250.00
(mini)	Red Sox	10,000	80.00
(artist's proof)	Red Sox	250	400.00

KENNER STARTING LINEUP

Kenner is the acknowledged leader in the low-end sports figure market. Since 1988, the Starting Lineup brand has grown from a simple line of athlete action figures into one of the most popular sports collectibles.

It all started when Pat McInally—then a punter and wide receiver for the Cincinnati Bengals—was selling a condominium to Kenner marketing director Bruce Stein. McInally was known for his tireless work with children's charities, and Stein asked for ideas for a new toy line. McInally, who noticed that most action figures on the market depicted fictional characters like G.I. Joe, thought a line of action figures of sports stars would be successful.

Thus, Kenner Starting Lineup figures were born—plastic models of stars in all major sports, attractively packaged with a collector card. After securing all the necessary licenses, Kenner offered its first set: 1988 Baseball.

The initial distribution plan was to release all-star cases, including the game's biggest stars, nationwide, with regional cases, packed with lesser-known players, distributed locally.

Kenner used this distribution plan until 1990 before switching to a more conventional national release schedule. Today, Kenner issues three or four different case assortments per set through all of the major national retail toy and department stores.

The company's first few releases included large checklists of pieces, and collectors had a tough time completing their sets. Unlike trading cards, which are released in similar numbers across a set, Kenner issued its figures based on popularity. The biggest stars were produced in larger quantities than the lesser-known players.

The size of the regional market also dictated the number of cases produced for each team. This distribution made it tough for collectors to find some of their favorite players. Those who didn't complete their sets usually needed a minor star or a "common" player not issued in their area.

Kenner's initial regional distribution helped lay the foundation for the hobby as it is known today. Collectors who wanted complete sets, or who wanted players not available in their area, were forced to trade with other collectors to get the pieces they needed. This led to the rapid development of the secondary market.

Some of today's most popular players weren't considered major stars in 1988, and finding their early pieces may be difficult. For example, even though Tony Gwynn is now considered one of the top stars in the game, his pieces from '88 and '89 are extremely hard to find in any condition—let alone Mint.

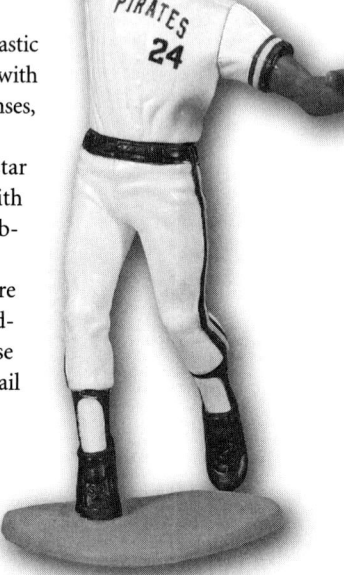

**1990
Barry Bonds**

GRADING

Kenner figures are graded in four categories—Mint, Near-Mint, Lesser, and Distressed.

Mint—A piece with no signs of any flaws—a perfect piece in perfect packaging. All figures are priced in Mint condition.

Near-Mint—A piece with only a minor flaw, such as a slight curl in the cardboard, a frayed edge, or sightly faded color. A Near-Mint figure can't have

a crease in the cardboard or a dent in the protective plastic bubble.

Lesser—A piece that has a small crease, a dent in the bubble, or a broken hang tab.

Distressed—A piece showing extreme wear, but with no damage to the card or the figure. Most Distressed pieces are removed from the packaging and sold as open figures.

KENNER STARTING LINEUP

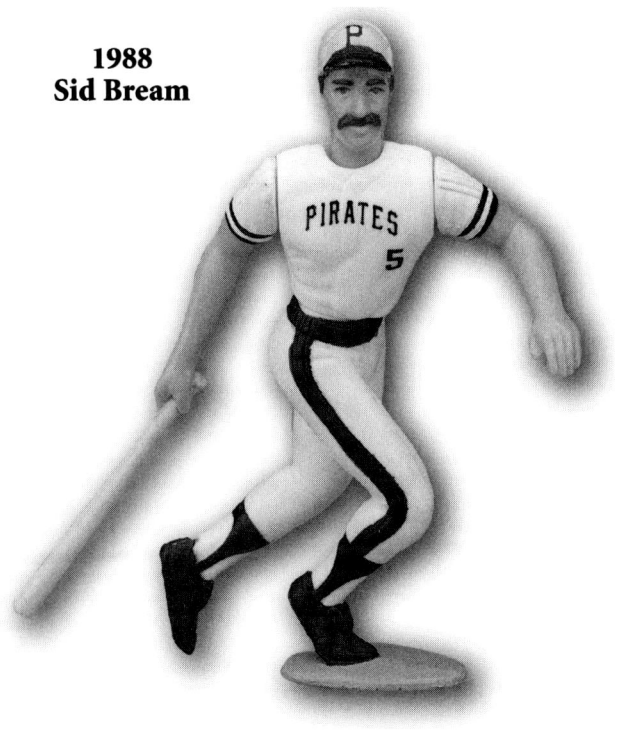

1988
Sid Bream

1988 BASEBALL

	NM Price
Complete Set (124)	$3,100.00
5-Player Stand w/box	60.00
5-Player Stand w/o box	40.00
Blue Collector's Showcase	50.00
All-Star Autographed Baseball	40.00

Quality Rating ★★★

The premier set, identified by the red-bordered card, is difficult to complete because many of the regional players are hard to find. The top pieces include Ripken, Ryan, and Bonds. Most figures can be found with and without a mail-in offer for a facsimile autographed baseball.

Player	Team	Mint Price	Card Price	Figure Price
Ashby, Alan	Astros	$18.00	$4.00	$6.00
Baines, Harold	White Sox	15.00	4.00	5.00
Bass, Kevin	Astros	12.00	3.00	4.00
Bedrosian, Steve	Phillies	15.00	4.00	5.00
Bell, Buddy	Reds	18.00	4.00	6.00
Bell, George	Blue Jays	20.00	5.00	7.00
Boddicker, Mike	Orioles	18.00	4.00	6.00
Boggs, Wade	Red Sox	35.00	8.00	12.00
Bonds, Barry	Pirates	75.00	20.00	25.00
Bonilla, Bobby	Pirates	20.00	5.00	7.00
Bream, Sid	Pirates	12.00	3.00	4.00
Brett, George	Royals	75.00	18.00	25.00
Brown, Chris	Padres	10.00	2.50	3.50
Brunansky, Tom	Twins	22.00	5.00	7.00
Burks, Ellis	Red Sox	40.00	8.00	12.00

Player	Team	Mint Price	Card Price	Figure Price
Canseco, Jose	Athletics	32.00	7.00	10.00
Carter, Gary	Mets	20.00	5.00	7.00
Carter, Joe	Indians	35.00	8.00	12.00
Clark, Jack	Yankees	17.00	4.00	5.00
Clark, Will	Giants	27.00	6.00	8.00
Clemens, Roger	Red Sox	50.00	12.00	16.00
Coleman, Vince	Cardinals	10.00	2.50	3.50
Daniels, Kal	Reds	15.00	4.00	5.00
Davis, Alvin	Mariners	12.00	3.00	4.00
Davis, Eric	Reds	10.00	2.50	3.50
Davis, Glenn	Astros	12.00	3.00	4.00
Davis, Jody	Cubs	14.00	3.00	4.00
Dawson, Andre	Cubs	20.00	6.00	8.00
Deer, Rob	Brewers	16.00	4.00	5.00
Downing, Brian	Angels	12.00	3.00	4.00
Dunne, Mike	Pirates	10.00	2.50	3.50
Dunston, Shawon	Cubs	15.00	4.00	5.00
Durham, Leon	Cubs	14.00	3.00	4.00
Dykstra, Lenny	Mets	20.00	4.00	6.00
Evans, Dwight	Red Sox	20.00	5.00	7.00
Fisk, Carlton	White Sox	65.00	12.00	20.00
Franco, John	Reds	16.00	4.00	5.00
Franco, Julio	Indians	18.00	4.00	6.00
Gaetti, Gary	Twins	15.00	4.00	5.00
Gooden, Dwight	Mets	10.00	2.50	3.50
Griffey Sr., Ken	Braves	25.00	5.00	8.00
Guerrero, Pedro	Dodgers	10.00	2.50	3.50
Guillen, Ozzie	White Sox	17.00	4.00	5.00
Gwynn, Tony	Padres	175.00	40.00	75.00
Hall, Mel	Indians	12.00	3.00	4.00
Hatcher, Billy	Astros	14.00	3.00	4.00
Hayes, Von	Phillies	15.00	4.00	5.00
Henderson, Rickey	Yankees	20.00	3.00	5.00
Hernandez, Keith	Mets	15.00	4.00	5.00
Hernandez, Willie	Tigers	14.00	3.00	4.00
Herr, Tom	Cardinals	10.00	2.50	3.50
Higuera, Ted	Brewers	15.00	4.00	5.00
Hough, Charlie	Rangers	18.00	4.00	6.00
Hrbek, Kent	Twins	15.00	4.00	5.00
Incaviglia, Pete	Rangers	18.00	4.00	6.00
Johnson, Howard	Mets	14.00	3.00	4.00
Joyner, Wally	Angels	12.00	3.00	4.00
Kennedy, Terry	Orioles	15.00	4.00	5.00
Kruk, John	Padres	25.00	5.00	7.00
Langston, Mark	Mariners	30.00	7.50	10.00
Lansford, Carney	Athletics	20.00	5.00	7.00
Leonard, Jeffrey	Giants	15.00	4.00	5.00
Lynn, Fred	Orioles	20.00	5.00	7.00
Maldonado, Candy	Giants	12.00	3.00	4.00
Marshall, Mike	Dodgers	14.00	3.00	4.00
Mattingly, Don	Yankees	35.00	8.00	10.00
McGee, Willie	Cardinals	16.00	4.00	5.00
McGwire, Mark	Athletics	90.00	15.00	35.00
McReynolds, Kevin	Mets	15.00	4.00	5.00

Player	Team	Mint Price	Card Price	Figure Price
Molitor, Paul	Brewers	60.00	12.00	20.00
Moore, Donnie	Angels	20.00	5.00	7.00
Morris, Jack	Tigers	24.00	5.00	7.00
Murphy, Dale	Braves	14.00	3.00	4.00
Murray, Eddie	Orioles	95.00	12.00	25.00
Nokes, Matt	Tigers	12.00	3.00	4.00
O'Brien, Pete	Rangers	12.00	3.00	4.00
Oberkfell, Ken	Braves	12.00	3.00	4.00
Parker, Dave	Athletics	25.00	7.50	10.00
Parrish, Larry	Rangers	12.00	3.00	4.00
Phelps, Ken	Mariners	12.00	3.00	4.00
Presley, Jim	Mariners	12.00	3.00	4.00
Puckett, Kirby	Twins	70.00	18.00	25.00
Quisenberry, Dan	Royals	16.00	4.00	5.00
Raines, Tim	Expos	14.00	3.00	4.00
Randolph, Willie	Yankees	14.00	3.00	4.00
Rawley, Shane	Phillies	12.00	3.00	4.00
Reardon, Jeff	Twins	25.00	6.00	8.00
Redus, Gary	White Sox	12.00	3.00	4.00
Reuschel, Rick	Giants	12.00	3.00	4.00
Rice, Jim	Red Sox	24.00	5.00	7.00
Righetti, Dave	Yankees	15.00	4.00	5.00
Ripken Jr., Cal	Orioles	375.00	50.00	75.00
Rose, Pete	Reds	70.00	16.00	20.00
Ryan, Nolan	Astros	325.00	80.00	100.00
Saberhagen, Bret	Royals	20.00	5.00	7.00
Samuel, Juan	Phillies	12.00	3.00	4.00
Sandberg, Ryne	Cubs	80.00	17.50	24.00
Santiago, Benito	Padres	20.00	5.00	7.00
Sax, Steve	Dodgers	13.00	3.00	4.00
Schmidt, Mike	Phillies	70.00	17.50	24.00
Scott, Mike	Astros	10.00	2.50	3.50
Seitzer, Kevin	Royals	14.00	3.00	4.00
Sierra, Ruben	Rangers	30.00	8.00	12.00
Smith, Ozzie	Cardinals	80.00	18.00	25.00
Smith, Zane	Braves	12.00	3.00	4.00
Snyder, Cory	Indians	12.00	3.00	4.00
Strawberry, Darryl	Mets	10.00	2.50	3.50
Stubbs, Franklin	Dodgers	12.00	3.00	4.00
Surhoff, B.J.	Brewers	20.00	4.00	5.00
Sutcliffe, Rick	Cubs	17.00	4.00	5.00
Tabler, Pat	Indians	12.00	3.00	4.00
Tartabull, Danny	Royals	17.00	4.00	5.00
Trammell, Alan	Tigers	20.00	5.00	7.00
Valenzuela, Fernando	Dodgers	10.00	2.50	3.50
Van Slyke, Andy	Pirates	28.00	6.00	8.00
Viola, Frank	Twins	18.00	4.00	6.00
Virgil, Ozzie	Braves	12.00	3.00	4.00
Walker, Greg	White Sox	12.00	3.00	4.00
Whitaker, Lou	Tigers	24.00	5.00	7.00
White, Devon	Angels	30.00	7.50	10.00
Winfield, Dave	Yankees	50.00	10.00	15.00
Witt, Mike	Angels	12.00	3.00	4.00
Worrell, Todd	Cardinals	18.00	4.00	6.00
Yount, Robin	Brewers	75.00	18.00	24.00

1988 Canadian figures

	NM Price
Complete Set (11)	$500.00

Quality Rating ★★

Hasbro of Canada issued an 11-player set. The packaging is similar to the American version, except for the bilingual text. Very few figures made it into the U.S., making this set almost impossible to find.

Player	Team	Mint Price	Card Price	Figure Price
Bell, George	Blue Jays	$35.00	$5.00	$7.00
Brett, George	Royals	75.00	18.00	25.00
Boggs, Wade	Red Sox	50.00	8.00	12.00
Carter, Gary	Mets	35.00	5.00	7.00
Clemens, Roger	Red Sox	100.00	10.00	15.00
Dawson, Andre	Cubs	35.00	6.00	8.00
Henderson, Rickey	Yankees	35.00	3.00	5.00
Mattingly, Don	Yankees	50.00	8.00	10.00
Raines, Tim	Expos	35.00	3.00	4.00
Strawberry, Darryl	Mets	35.00	2.50	3.50
Winfield, Dave	Yankees	75.00	10.00	15.00

1989 Bobby Bonilla

1989 BASEBALL

	NM Price
Complete Set (168)	$4,000.00

Quality Rating ★★★★

This issue can be identified by its green-bordered cards, and like the '88 set, it's very difficult to complete. The Angels' team is one of baseball's hardest team sets to find. The '89 Ripken is harder to find than the '88 piece, and the Maddux is one of baseball's hottest figures.

Player	Team	Mint Price	Card Price	Figure Price
Alomar, Roberto (R)	Padres	$475.00	$100.00	$150.00

Player	Team	Mint Price	Card Price	Figure Price	Player	Team	Mint Price	Card Price	Figure Price
Anderson, Brady (R)	Orioles	200.00	40.00	70.00	Hayes, Von	Phillies	12.00	3.00	4.00
Baines, Harold	White Sox	15.00	4.00	5.00	Henderson, Rickey	Yankees	15.00	4.00	5.00
Barrett, Marty (R)	Red Sox	14.00	3.00	4.00	Henneman, Mike (R)	Tigers	10.00	2.50	3.50
Bass, Kevin	Astros	10.00	2.50	3.50	Hernandez, Keith	Mets	12.00	3.00	4.00
Bedrosian, Steve	Phillies	12.00	3.00	4.00	Hershiser, Orel (R)	Dodgers	20.00	5.00	7.00
Bell, George	Blue Jays	12.00	3.00	4.00	Higuera, Ted	Brewers	20.00	5.00	7.00
Berryhill, Damon (R)	Cubs	12.00	3.00	4.00	Howell, Jack (R)	Angels	100.00	25.00	35.00
Boggs, Wade	Red Sox	30.00	6.00	8.00	Hrbek, Kent	Twins	14.00	3.00	4.00
Bonds, Barry	Pirates	70.00	12.00	20.00	Incaviglia, Pete	Rangers	12.00	3.00	4.00
Bonilla, Bobby	Pirates	16.00	4.00	5.00	Jackson, Bo (R)	Royals	25.00	6.00	8.00
Bradley, Phil (R)	Phillies	22.00	5.00	7.00	Jackson, Danny (R)	Reds	14.00	3.00	4.00
Braggs, Glen (R)	Brewers	12.00	3.00	4.00	Jacoby, Brook (R)	Indians	10.00	2.50	3.50
Brantley, Mickey (R)	Mariners	12.00	3.00	4.00	James, Chris (R)	Phillies	12.00	3.00	4.00
Brett, George	Royals	70.00	17.50	24.00	James, Dion (R)	Braves	15.00	4.00	5.00
Brookens, Tom (R)	Tigers	12.00	3.00	4.00	Jefferies, Greg (R)	Mets	32.00	8.00	10.00
Brunansky, Tom	Cardinals	12.00	3.00	4.00	Jones, Doug (R)	Indians	18.00	4.00	6.00
Buechele, Steve (R)	Rangers	18.00	4.00	6.00	Joyner, Wally	Angels	14.00	3.00	4.00
Burks, Ellis	Red Sox	25.00	4.00	8.00	Kruk, John	Padres	30.00	6.00	10.00
Butler, Brett (R)	Giants	20.00	5.00	7.00	Langston, Mark	Mariners	26.00	6.00	8.00
Calderon, Ivan (R)	White Sox	18.00	4.00	6.00	Lansford, Carney	Athletics	20.00	5.00	7.00
Canseco, Jose	Athletics	24.00	4.00	7.00	Larkin, Barry (R)	Reds	75.00	10.00	15.00
Carter, Gary	Mets	18.00	4.00	6.00	Laudner, Tim (R)	Twins	15.00	4.00	5.00
Carter, Joe	Indians	20.00	5.00	7.00	LaValliere, Mike (R)	Pirates	10.00	2.50	3.50
Clark, Will	Giants	22.00	5.00	7.00	Leiter, Al (R)	Yankees	15.00	3.00	4.00
Clemens, Roger	Red Sox	35.00	7.50	10.00	Lemon, Chet (R)	Tigers	14.00	3.00	4.00
Coleman, Vince	Cardinals	10.00	2.50	3.50	Lind, Jose (R)	Pirates	20.00	5.00	7.00
Cone, David (R)	Mets	50.00	10.00	15.00	Maddux, Greg (R)	Cubs	375.00	100.00	200.00
Daniels, Kal	Reds	12.00	3.00	4.00	Maldonado, Candy	Giants	12.00	3.00	4.00
Davis, Alvin	Mariners	15.00	4.00	5.00	Marshall, Mike	Dodgers	10.00	2.50	3.50
Davis, Chili (R)	Angels	140.00	35.00	45.00	Mattingly, Don	Yankees	27.00	6.00	8.00
Davis, Eric	Reds	10.00	2.50	3.50	McGee, Willie	Cardinals	15.00	4.00	5.00
Davis, Glenn	Astros	10.00	2.50	3.50	McGwire, Mark	Athletics	50.00	8.00	12.00
Davis, Mark (R)	Padres	30.00	7.50	10.00	McReynolds, Kevin	Mets	18.00	4.00	6.00
Dawson, Andre	Cubs	20.00	5.00	7.00	Mitchell, Kevin (R)	Giants	20.00	5.00	7.00
Deer, Rob	Brewers	10.00	2.50	3.50	Molitor, Paul	Brewers	35.00	8.00	12.00
Diaz, Bo (R)	Reds	14.00	3.00	4.00	Morris, Jack	Tigers	20.00	5.00	7.00
Doran, Billy (R)	Astros	20.00	5.00	7.00	Murphy, Dale	Braves	15.00	4.00	5.00
Drabek, Doug (R)	Pirates	30.00	7.50	10.00	Myers, Randy (R)	Mets	18.00	4.00	6.00
Dunston, Shawon	Cubs	15.00	4.00	5.00	Nokes, Matt (R)	Tigers	10.00	2.50	3.50
Dykstra, Lenny	Mets	30.00	7.50	10.00	Pagliarulo, Mike (R)	Yankees	10.00	2.50	3.50
Eckersley, Dennis (R)	Athletics	90.00	20.00	30.00	Parker, Dave	Athletics	25.00	6.00	8.00
Elster, Kevin (R)	Mets	12.00	3.00	4.00	Pasqua, Dan (R)	White Sox	15.00	4.00	5.00
Fletcher, Scott (R)	Rangers	12.00	3.00	4.00	Pena, Tony (R)	Cardinals	18.00	4.00	6.00
Franco, John	Reds	12.00	3.00	4.00	Pendleton, Terry (R)	Cardinals	25.00	6.00	8.00
Gaetti, Gary	Twins	12.00	3.00	4.00	Perez, Melido (R)	White Sox	30.00	6.00	8.00
Gant, Ron (R)	Braves	175.00	30.00	40.00	Perry, Gerald (R)	Braves	16.00	4.00	5.00
Gibson, Kirk (R)	Dodgers	12.00	3.00	4.00	Plesac, Dan (R)	Brewers	10.00	2.50	3.50
Gladden, Dan (R)	Twins	14.00	3.00	4.00	Puckett, Kirby	Twins	60.00	12.00	16.00
Gooden, Dwight	Mets	10.00	2.50	3.50	Quinones, Rey (R)	Mariners	18.00	4.00	6.00
Grace, Mark (R)	Cubs	40.00	8.00	12.00	Raines, Tim	Expos	11.00	3.00	4.00
Greenwell, Mike (R)	Red Sox	10.00	2.50	3.50	Ray, Johnny (R)	Angels	120.00	30.00	40.00
Gubicza, Mark (R)	Royals	10.00	2.50	3.50	Reardon, Jeff	Twins	30.00	7.50	10.00
Guerrero, Pedro	Cardinals	10.00	2.50	3.50	Reynolds, Harold (R)	Mariners	20.00	5.00	7.00
Guillen, Ozzie	White Sox	24.00	5.00	7.00	Rice, Jim	Red Sox	16.00	4.00	5.00
Gwynn, Tony	Padres	400.00	100.00	175.00	Righetti, Dave	Yankees	16.00	4.00	5.00
Hall, Albert (R)	Braves	14.00	3.00	4.00	Ripken Jr., Cal	Orioles	400.00	100.00	150.00
Hall, Mel	Indians	12.00	3.00	4.00	Russell, Jeff (R)	Rangers	18.00	4.00	6.00
Hatcher, Billy	Astros	10.00	2.50	3.50	Saberhagen, Bret	Royals	16.00	4.00	5.00

Player	Team	Mint Price	Card Price	Figure Price
Sabo, Chris (R)	Reds	20.00	5.00	7.00
Salazar, Luis (R)	Tigers	15.00	4.00	5.00
Samuel, Juan	Phillies	10.00	2.50	3.50
Sandberg, Ryne	Cubs	50.00	12.00	16.00
Santiago, Benito	Padres	25.00	6.00	8.00
Schmidt, Mike	Phillies	60.00	15.00	20.00
Schofield, Dick (R)	Angels	120.00	30.00	40.00
Scioscia, Mike (R)	Dodgers	20.00	5.00	7.00
Scott, Mike	Astros	10.00	2.50	3.50
Seitzer, Kevin	Royals	12.00	3.00	4.00
Sheets, Larry (R)	Orioles	12.00	3.00	4.00
Shelby, John (R)	Dodgers	10.00	2.50	3.50
Sierra, Ruben	Rangers	30.00	7.50	10.00
Slaught, Don (R)	Yankees	12.00	3.00	4.00
Smith, Dave (R)	Astros	10.00	2.50	3.50
Smith, Lee (R)	Red Sox	70.00	15.00	20.00
Smith, Ozzie	Cardinals	50.00	10.00	15.00
Smith, Zane	Braves	12.00	3.00	4.00
Snyder, Cory	Indians	12.00	3.00	4.00
Stanicek, Pete (R)	Orioles	10.00	2.50	3.50
Steinbach, Terry (R)	Athletics	20.00	5.00	7.00
Stewart, Dave (R)	Athletics	25.00	6.00	8.00
Stillwell, Kurt (R)	Royals	12.00	3.00	4.00
Strawberry, Darryl	Mets	10.00	2.50	3.50
Surhoff, B.J.	Brewers	18.00	4.00	6.00
Sutcliffe, Rick	Cubs	16.00	4.00	5.00
Sutter, Bruce (R)	Braves	30.00	7.50	10.00
Swindell, Greg (R)	Indians	20.00	4.00	6.00
Tabler, Pat	Royals	13.00	3.00	4.00
Tartabull, Danny	Royals	12.00	3.00	4.00
Thigpen, Bobby (R)	White Sox	30.00	7.50	10.00
Thompson, Milt (R)	Phillies	15.00	4.00	5.00
Thompson, Robby (R)	Giants	15.00	4.00	5.00
Trammell, Alan	Tigers	15.00	4.00	5.00
Treadway, Jeff (R)	Reds	40.00	8.00	12.00
Uribe, Jose (R)	Giants	12.00	3.00	4.00
Valenzuela, Fernando	Dodgers	14.00	3.00	4.00
Van Slyke, Andy	Pirates	16.00	4.00	5.00
Viola, Frank	Twins	10.00	2.50	3.50
Walk, Bob (R)	Pirates	12.00	3.00	4.00
Walker, Greg	White Sox	18.00	4.00	6.00
Weiss, Walt (R)	Athletics	32.00	8.00	10.00
Welch, Bob (R)	Athletics	20.00	5.00	7.00
Whitaker, Lou	Tigers	20.00	5.00	7.00
White, Devon	Angels	140.00	40.00	60.00
Winfield, Dave	Yankees	30.00	7.50	10.00
Witt, Mike	Angels	120.00	40.00	50.00
Worrell, Todd	Cardinals	14.00	3.00	4.00
Wynne, Marvell (R)	Padres	32.00	8.00	10.00
Young, Gerald (R)	Astros	12.00	3.00	4.00
Yount, Robin	Brewers	75.00	18.00	24.00

1989 Canadian figures

	NM Price
Complete Set (20)	$1,500.00

Quality Rating ★★

George Bell and Tim Raines are the most plentiful pieces because they were the only two players from Canadian teams. Again, only a handful of figures ever reached the U.S. The Ripken piece is extremely difficult to find.

Player	Team	Mint Price	Card Price	Figure Price
Bell, George	Blue Jays	$35.00	$3.00	$4.00
Boggs, Wade	Red Sox	50.00	6.00	8.00
Canseco, Jose	Athletics	50.00	4.00	7.00
Carter, Gary	Mets	35.00	4.00	6.00
Clemens, Roger	Red Sox	100.00	7.50	10.00
Davis, Eric	Reds	35.00	2.50	3.50
Dawson, Andre	Cubs	35.00	5.00	7.00
Gaetti, Gary	Twins	35.00	3.00	4.00
Gibson, Kirk	Dodgers	35.00	3.00	4.00
Gooden, Dwight	Mets	35.00	2.50	3.50
Greenwell, Mike	Red Sox	35.00	2.50	3.50
Henderson, Rickey	Yankees	35.00	4.00	5.00
Joyner, Wally	Angels	35.00	3.00	4.00
Mattingly, Don	Yankees	50.00	6.00	8.00
McGwire, Mark	Athletics	50.00	4.00	6.00
Raines, Tim	Expos	35.00	3.00	4.00
Ripken Jr., Cal	Orioles	1,000.00	100.00	150.00
Sabo, Chris	Reds	35.00	5.00	7.00
Schmidt, Mike	Phillies	100.00	18.00	24.00
Scott, Mike	Astros	35.00	2.50	3.50
Smith, Ozzie	Cardinals	100.00	10.00	15.00
Strawberry, Darryl	Mets	35.00	2.50	3.50
Trammell, Alan	Tigers	35.00	4.00	5.00
Valenzuela, Fernando	Dodgers	35.00	3.00	4.00

1989 Baseball Greats

	NM Price
Complete Set (10)	$450.00

Quality Rating ★★★

This legends set continues to be popular with collectors. The Ruth and Gehrig figures can be found in three different versions. We list prices for each individual player and card, as well as the "mint in box" price for the pair.

Player	Team	Mint Price	Card Price	Figure Price
Banks/Williams		$40.00	—	—
Banks, Ernie	Cubs	—	$7.00	$12.00
Williams, Billy	Cubs	—	3.00	4.00
Bench/Rose		60.00	—	—
Bench, Johnny	Reds	—	5.00	10.00
Rose, Pete	Reds	—	7.00	12.00
Drysdale/Jackson		60.00	—	—
Drsydale, Don	Dodgers	—	4.00	10.00
Jackson, Reggie	Athletics	—	8.00	14.00
Mantle/DiMaggio		90.00	—	—
Mantle, Mickey	Yankees	—	12.00	20.00
DiMaggio, Joe	Yankees	—	8.00	15.00
Matthews/Aaron		50.00	—	—
Mathews, Eddie	Braves	—	3.00	6.00
Aaron, Hank	Braves	—	7.00	12.00

Player	Team	Mint Price	Card Price	Figure Price
Mays/McCovey		45.00	—	—
Mays, Willie	Giants	—	7.00	12.00
McCovey, Willie	Giants	—	2.00	5.00
Musial/Gibson		40.00	—	—
Musial, Stan	Cardinals	—	6.00	10.00
Gibson, Bob	Cardinals	—	4.00	8.00
Ruth/Gehrig (white/gray)		55.00	—	—
Ruth, Babe	Yankees	—	6.00	12.00
Gehrig, Lou	Yankees	—	6.00	12.00
Ruth/Gehrig (white/white)		70.00	—	—
Ruth, Babe	Yankees	—	6.00	12.00
Gehrig, Lou	Yankees	—	6.00	12.00
Ruth/Gehrig (gray/white)		45.00	—	—
Ruth, Babe	Yankees	—	6.00	12.00
Gehrig, Lou	Yankees	—	6.00	12.00
Stargell/Clemente		55.00	—	—
Stargell, Willie	Pirates	—	2.00	4.00
Clemente, Roberto	Pirates	—	10.00	15.00
Yastremzki/Aaron		90.00	—	—
Yastrzemski, Carl	Red Sox	—	12.00	20.00
Aaron, Hank	Braves	—	7.00	12.00

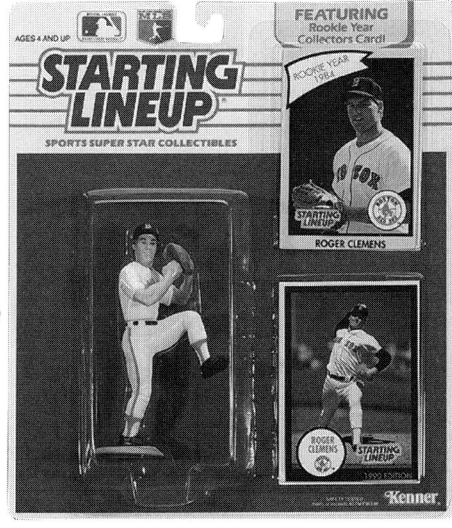

1990 Roger Clemens

1990 BASEBALL

	NM Price
Complete Set (87)	$1,600.00

Quality Rating ★★★

The figures of Jose Canseco, Bo Jackson, Nolan Ryan, and Jerome Walton were issued in the regular and extended cases. Each figure can be found with or without an extended sticker. We list all four players in both sections. The Maddux piece is still one of the hottest in the hobby. Each piece comes with two cards; the listed price is for each individual card.

Player	Team	Mint Price	Card Price	Figure Price
Anderson, Allan (R)	Twins	$12.00	$3.00	$4.00
Backman, Wally (R)	Twins	15.00	4.00	5.00
Ballard, Jeff (R)	Orioles	12.00	3.00	4.00

Player	Team	Mint Price	Card Price	Figure Price
Barfield, Jesse (R)	Yankees	10.00	2.50	3.50
Bedrosian, Steve	Giants	10.00	2.50	3.50
Benzinger, Todd (R)	Reds	14.00	3.00	4.00
Berryhill, Damon	Cubs	12.00	3.00	4.00
Boggs, Wade	Red Sox	20.00	3.00	5.00
Bonds, Barry	Pirates	60.00	16.00	20.00
Bonilla, Bobby	Pirates	15.00	4.00	5.00
Bosio, Chris (R)	Brewers	15.00	4.00	5.00
Burks, Ellis	Red Sox	15.00	4.00	5.00
Canseco, Jose	Athletics	16.00	4.00	5.00
Clark, Will				
(batting)	Giants	20.00	5.00	7.00
(power)	Giants	22.00	5.00	7.00
Clemens, Roger	Red Sox	28.00	6.00	8.00
Coleman, Vince	Cardinals	10.00	2.50	3.50
Darling, Ron (R)	Mets	10.00	2.50	3.50
Davis, Eric	Reds	12.00	3.00	4.00
Dawson, Andre	Cubs	18.00	4.00	6.00
Dibble, Rob (R)	Reds	16.00	4.00	5.00
Dykstra, Lenny	Phillies	25.00	6.00	8.00
Eckersley, Dennis	Athletics	60.00	12.00	20.00
Esasky, Nick (R)	Red Sox	24.00	5.00	7.00
Gaetti, Gary	Twins	12.00	3.00	4.00
Galarraga, Andres (R)	Expos	30.00	7.50	10.00
Gibson, Kirk	Dodgers	10.00	2.50	3.50
Gooden, Dwight	Mets	12.00	3.00	4.00
Grace, Mark				
(batting)	Cubs	18.00	4.00	5.00
(power)	Cubs	22.00	5.00	7.00
Greenwell, Mike	Red Sox	10.00	2.50	3.50
Griffey Jr., Ken				
(R, sliding)	Mariners	110.00	25.00	40.00
Guerrero, Pedro	Cardinals	10.00	2.50	3.50
Hayes, Von	Phillies	10.00	2.50	3.50
Henderson, Dave (R)	Athletics	13.00	3.00	4.00
Henderson, Rickey	Athletics	15.00	4.00	5.00
Herr, Tom	Phillies	10.00	2.50	3.50
Hershiser, Orel	Dodgers	15.00	4.00	5.00
Hrbek, Kent	Twins	12.00	3.00	4.00
Jackson, Bo	Royals	12.00	3.00	4.00
Jefferies, Greg	Mets	15.00	4.00	5.00
Johnson, Howard	Mets	12.00	3.00	4.00
Jordan, Rickey (R)	Phillies	12.00	3.00	4.00
Kelly, Roberto (R)	Yankees	15.00	4.00	5.00
Larkin, Barry	Reds	60.00	6.00	14.00
Maddux, Greg	Cubs	450.00	150.00	200.00
Magrane, Joe (R)	Cardinals	10.00	2.50	3.50
Mattingly, Don				
(bat in hand)	Yankees	20.00	5.00	7.00
(power)	Yankees	24.00	5.00	7.00
McGriff, Fred (R)	Blue Jays	50.00	10.00	16.00
McGwire, Mark	Athletics	40.00	8.00	12.00
McReynolds, Kevin	Mets	10.00	2.50	3.50
Mitchell, Kevin	Giants	12.00	3.00	4.00
Molitor, Paul	Brewers	28.00	6.00	8.00
Murray, Eddie	Dodgers	200.00	50.00	75.00
Nokes, Matt	Tigers	15.00	4.00	5.00
O'Neill, Paul (R)	Reds	30.00	7.50	10.00

Player	Team	Mint Price	Card Price	Figure Price
Oquendo, Jose (R)	Cardinals	10.00	2.50	3.50
Pettis, Gary	Tigers	20.00	5.00	7.00
Puckett, Kirby	Twins	40.00	8.00	12.00
Randolph, Willie	Dodgers	14.00	3.00	4.00
Reed, Jody (R)	Red Sox	15.00	4.00	5.00
Reuschel, Rick	Giants	12.00	3.00	4.00
Righetti, Dave	Yankees	10.00	2.50	3.50
Ripken Jr., Cal	Orioles	180.00	45.00	60.00
Ryan, Nolan	Rangers	54.00	12.00	18.00
Sabo, Chris	Reds	12.00	3.00	4.00
Samuel, Juan	Mets	12.00	3.00	4.00
Sandberg, Ryne	Cubs	35.00	8.00	12.00
Sax, Steve	Yankees	10.00	2.50	3.50
Scott, Mike	Astros	10.00	2.50	3.50
Sheffield, Gary (R)	Brewers	35.00	8.00	10.00
Smiley, John (R)	Pirates	13.00	3.00	4.00
Smith, Ozzie	Cardinals	40.00	7.50	10.00
Stewart, Dave	Athletics	15.00	4.00	5.00
Strawberry, Darryl				
(batting)	Mets	10.00	2.50	3.50
(fielding)	Mets	10.00	2.50	3.50
Sutcliffe, Rick	Cubs	14.00	3.00	4.00
Tettleton, Mickey (R)	Orioles	20.00	5.00	7.00
Trammell, Alan	Tigers	14.00	3.00	4.00
Van Slyke, Andy	Pirates	20.00	5.00	7.00
Viola, Frank	Mets	12.00	3.00	4.00
Whitaker, Lou	Tigers	15.00	4.00	5.00
Williams, Mitch	Cubs	15.00	4.00	5.00
Winfield, Dave	Yankees	45.00	10.00	15.00
Yount, Robin	Brewers	70.00	17.50	24.00
Walton, Jerome (R)	Cubs	10.00	2.50	3.50

Extended Set

	NM Price
Complete Set (9)	$250.00

Quality Rating ★★

Kenner's increase in popularity led to issuing the first extended set. It's obviously led by Griffey, but the Carter piece is a sleeper with just one per case. Figures can be found with or without an extended sticker. The jumping Griffey is harder to find than the sliding, because it was released in the Extended series.

Player	Team	Mint Price	Card Price	Figure Price
Abbott, Jim (R)	Angels	$15.00	$3.00	$5.00
Alomar Jr., Sandy (R)	Indians	24.00	4.00	6.00
Canseco, Jose	Athletics	16.00	4.00	5.00
Carter, Joe	Padres	35.00	8.00	12.00
Griffey Jr., Ken				
(jumping)	Mariners	125.00	30.00	40.00
Jackson, Bo	Royals	12.00	3.00	4.00
McDonald, Ben (R)	Orioles	20.00	3.00	5.00
Ryan, Nolan	Rangers	54.00	12.00	18.00
Walton, Jerome (R)	Cubs	10.00	2.50	3.50

1991 Doug Drabek

1991 BASEBALL

	NM Price
Complete Set (46)	$450.00
Mail-in Poster	10.00

Quality Rating ★★

This set is easily identified by the coin that accompanies each figure. The coin sells for about 25% of the listed card price. The extended figures can be found with either a steel or an aluminum coin. All of the regular figures have a steel coin. The Ryan piece was released in both the regular and the Extended cases, but the back of his card was updated for the Extended piece.

Player	Team	Mint Price	Card Price	Figure Price
Abbott, Jim	Angels	$15.00	$4.00	$5.00
Alomar Jr., Sandy	Indians	16.00	4.00	5.00
Armstrong, Jack (R)	Reds	14.00	3.00	4.00
Bonds, Barry	Pirates	30.00	7.50	10.00
Bonilla, Bobby	Pirates	14.00	3.00	4.00
Browning, Tom	Reds	10.00	2.50	3.50
Canseco, Jose	Athletics	14.00	3.00	4.00
Clark, Will	Giants	16.00	4.00	5.00
Davis, Eric	Reds	8.00	1.50	2.50
Dawson, Andre	Cubs	10.00	2.00	3.00
DeShields, Delino (R)	Expos	10.00	2.00	3.00
Drabek, Doug	Pirates	16.00	4.00	5.00
Dunston, Shawon	Cubs	12.00	3.00	4.00
Dykstra, Lenny	Phillies	15.00	4.00	5.00
Fielder, Cecil (R)	Tigers	15.00	3.00	4.00
Franco, John	Mets	10.00	2.50	3.50
Gooden, Dwight	Mets	9.00	1.50	2.50
Grace, Mark	Cubs	12.00	3.00	4.00
Griffey Jr., Ken				
(batting)	Mariners	35.00	6.00	10.00
Gruber, Kelly (R)	Blue Jays	10.00	2.50	3.50
Guillen, Ozzie	White Sox	15.00	4.00	5.00
Henderson, Rickey	Athletics	10.00	2.50	3.50

Player	Team	Mint Price	Card Price	Figure Price
Jackson, Bo	Royals	10.00	2.50	3.50
Jefferies, Greg	Mets	13.00	3.00	4.00
Johnson, Howard	Mets	10.00	2.50	3.50
Kelly, Roberto	Yankees	10.00	2.50	3.50
Larkin, Barry	Reds	24.00	4.00	6.00
Maas, Kevin (R)	Yankees	9.00	1.50	2.50
Magadan, Dave (R)	Mets	9.00	1.50	2.50
Martinez, Ramon (R)	Dodgers	15.00	3.00	4.00
Mattingly, Don	Yankees	18.00	4.00	6.00
McDonald, Ben	Orioles	12.00	3.00	4.00
McGwire, Mark	Athletics	24.00	4.00	6.00
Mitchell, Kevin	Giants	10.00	2.50	3.50
Puckett, Kirby	Twins	25.00	5.00	7.00
Ryan, Nolan	Rangers	45.00	10.00	15.00
Sabo, Chris	Reds	8.00	1.50	2.50
Sandberg, Ryne	Cubs	30.00	7.50	10.00
Santiago, Benito	Padres	12.00	3.00	4.00
Sax, Steve	Yankees	12.00	3.00	4.00
Stewart, Dave	Athletics	13.00	3.00	4.00
Strawberry, Darryl	Mets	10.00	2.50	3.50
Trammell, Alan	Tigers	16.00	4.00	5.00
Viola, Frank	Mets	11.00	3.00	4.00
Williams, Matt (R)	Giants	35.00	8.00	12.00
Zeile, Todd (R)	Cardinals	15.00	4.00	6.00

Extended Set

	NM Price
Complete Set (10)	$150.00

Quality Rating ★★
The popularity of Griffey and Ryan is the only thing that keeps this set afloat. The back of the Ryan card is different than the regular issue.

Player	Team	Mint Price	Card Price	Figure Price
Bell, George	Cubs	$10.00	$1.50	$2.50
Coleman, Vince	Mets	10.00	1.50	2.50
Davis, Glenn	Orioles	10.00	2.50	3.50
Griffey Jr., Ken (running.)	Mariners	40.00	10.00	15.00
Griffey Sr., Ken	Mariners	22.00	5.00	7.00
Jackson, Bo	White Sox	18.00	4.00	6.00
Justice, Dave	Braves	28.00	7.50	10.00
Raines, Tim	White Sox	13.00	3.00	4.00
Ryan, Nolan	Rangers	45.00	10.00	15.00
Strawberry, Darryl	Dodgers	10.00	2.50	3.50

1991 Baseball Headline

	NM Price
Complete Set (7)	$180.00

Quality Rating ★★★
Kenner's first Headline series is led by Griffey and Ryan. Despite the limited production run, these figures remain unpopular with collectors.

Player	Team	Mint Price	Card Price	Figure Price
Canseco, Jose	Athletics	$18.00	n/a	$6.00
Clark, Will	Giants	20.00	n/a	8.00
Griffey Jr., Ken	Mariners	60.00	n/a	16.00
Henderson, Rickey	Athletics	18.00	n/a	6.00
Jackson, Bo	Royals	15.00	n/a	5.00
Mattingly, Don	Yankees	40.00	n/a	14.00
Ryan, Nolan	Rangers	60.00	n/a	20.00

1992 BASEBALL

	NM Price
Complete Set (37)	$500.00
Give-away Poster	10.00

Quality Rating ★★★
This issue includes a poster and a card with each figure. The poster sells for 25% of the listed card price. The rookie selection includes Thomas, Gonzalez, and Belle. Like the Griffey rookie, the Extended Thomas is harder to find than the regular one.

Player	Team	Mint Price	Card Price	Figure Price
Alomar, Roberto	Blue Jays	$25.00	$4.00	$6.00
Bell, George	Cubs	8.00	1.50	2.50
Belle, Albert (R)	Indians	50.00	8.00	12.00
Biggio, Craig (R)	Astros	12.00	2.50	3.50
Bonds, Barry	Pirates	24.00	6.00	5.00
Calderon, Ivan	Expos	8.00	1.50	2.50
Canseco, Jose	Athletics	12.00	3.00	4.00
Clark, Will	Giants	15.00	4.00	5.00

Player	Team	Mint Price	Card Price	Figure Price
Clemens, Roger	Red Sox	20.00	4.00	5.00
Dibble, Rob (R)	Reds	8.00	1.50	2.50
Erickson, Scott (R)	Twins	10.00	2.00	3.00
Fielder, Cecil	Tigers	10.00	2.50	3.50
Finley, Chuck (R)	Angels	8.00	1.50	2.50
Glavine, Tom (R)	Braves	32.00	6.00	8.00
Gonzalez, Juan (R)	Rangers	40.00	7.50	10.00
Griffey Jr., Ken				
(bat in hand)	Mariners	35.00	6.00	10.00
(swinging)	Mariners	35.00	6.00	10.00
Gwynn, Tony	Padres	28.00	5.00	7.00
Henderson, Dave	Athletics	7.00	1.00	2.00
Henderson, Rickey	Athletics	10.00	2.50	3.50
Jackson, Bo				
(running)	White Sox	9.00	1.50	2.50
(bat in hand)	White Sox	10.00	2.50	3.50
Johnson, Howard	Mets	10.00	2.50	3.50
Jose, Felix (R)	Cardinals	13.00	3.00	4.00
Justice, Dave	Braves	15.00	4.00	5.00
Maas, Kevin	Yankees	8.00	1.50	2.50
Martinez, Ramon	Dodgers	8.00	1.50	2.50
McGriff, Fred	Padres	20.00	5.00	7.00
McRae, Brian (R)	Royals	9.00	1.50	2.50
Ripken Jr., Cal	Orioles	75.00	18.00	24.00
Ryan, Nolan	Rangers	30.00	7.50	10.00
Sabo, Chris	Reds	8.00	1.50	2.50
Sandberg, Ryne	Cubs	18.00	4.00	6.00
Sierra, Ruben	Rangers	14.00	3.00	4.00
Strawberry, Darryl	Dodgers	10.00	2.50	3.50
Thomas, Frank				
(fielding)	White Sox	45.00	10.00	15.00
Williams, Matt (R)	Giants	15.00	5.00	7.00

Extended Set

	NM Price
Complete Set (9)	$150.00

Quality Rating ★★

The popularity of the Seaver piece may have led to the release of the Cooperstown Collection. Another Thomas rookie leads this issue.

Player	Team	Mint Price	Card Price	Figure Price
Avery, Steve (R)	Braves	$10.00	$2.00	$3.00
Bonilla, Bobby	Mets	10.00	2.50	3.50
Davis, Eric	Dodgers	8.00	1.50	2.50
Puckett, Kirby	Twins	20.00	4.00	7.00
Saberhagen, Bret	Mets	8.00	1.50	2.50
Seaver, Tom	Mets	20.00	4.00	7.00
Tartabull, Danny	Yankees	10.00	1.00	2.00
Thomas, Frank				
(batting)	White Sox	70.00	16.00	20.00
Van Poppel, Todd	Athletics	10.00	4.00	4.00

1992 Baseball Headline

	NM Price
Complete Set (7)	$140.00

Quality Rating ★★★

As with the '91 series, these Headliners don't generate much collector attention. Only the biggest names like Griffey and Ryan seem to sell.

Player	Team	Mint Price	Card Price	Figure Price
Brett, George	Royals	$36.00	n/a	$15.00
Fielder, Cecil	Tigers	15.00	n/a	5.00
Griffey Jr., Ken	Mariners	40.00	n/a	20.00
Henderson, Rickey	Athletics	15.00	n/a	5.00
Jackson, Bo	White Sox	12.00	n/a	5.00
Ryan, Nolan	Rangers	40.00	n/a	20.00
Sandberg, Ryne	Cubs	32.00	n/a	15.00

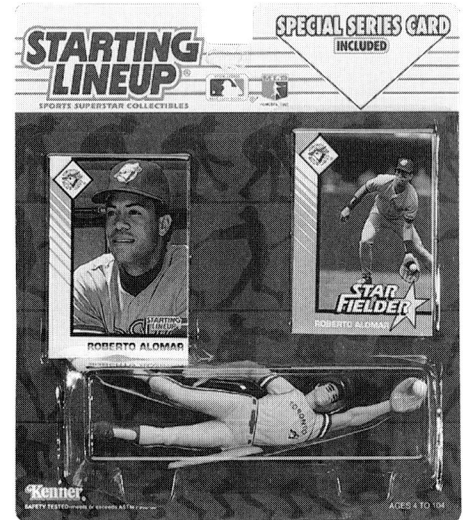

1993 Robereto Alomar

1993 BASEBALL

	NM Price
Complete Set (38)	$400.00

Quality Rating ★★★

This is a nice set that includes the rookies of Jeff Bagwell, Kevin Brown, and Larry Walker. Most collectors seem to overlook the regular set and go for the extended pieces. Each piece comes with two cards; the listed price is for each individual card.

Player	Team	Mint Price	Card Price	Figure Price
Alomar, Roberto	Blue Jays	$10.00	$2.00	$3.00
Baerga, Carlos (R)	Indians	10.00	2.00	3.00
Bagwell, Jeff (R)	Astros	40.00	12.00	16.00
Bonds, Barry	Pirates	15.00	3.00	4.00
Brown, Kevin (R)	Rangers	15.00	2.00	5.00
Canseco, Jose	Rangers	15.00	3.00	4.00
Clark, Will	Giants	8.00	1.50	2.50
Clemens, Roger	Red Sox	16.00	3.00	4.00
Cone, David	Blue Jays	10.00	1.50	2.50
Fryman, Travis (R)	Tigers	8.00	1.50	2.50
Glavine, Tom	Braves	32.00	6.00	8.00
Gonzalez, Juan	Rangers	20.00	4.00	5.00

Player	Team	Mint Price	Card Price	Figure Price
Griffey Jr., Ken	Mariners	30.00	7.00	10.00
Grissom, Marquis (R)	Expos	12.00	2.00	3.00
Guzman, Juan	Blue Jays	8.00	1.50	2.50
Karros, Eric (R)	Dodgers	16.00	4.00	5.00
Kelly, Roberto	Yankees	6.00	1.00	2.00
Kruk, John	Phillies	12.00	3.00	4.00
Lankford, Ray (R)	Cardinals	10.00	1.00	2.00
Larkin, Barry	Reds	15.00	1.50	2.50
Mack, Shane (R)	Twins	6.00	1.00	2.00
McDowell, Jack (R)	White Sox	9.00	1.50	2.50
McGriff, Fred	Padres	15.00	4.00	5.00
McGwire, Mark	Athletics	20.00	3.00	5.00
Mussina, Mike (R)	Orioles	25.00	5.00	7.00
Palmer, Dean (R)	Rangers	9.00	1.50	2.50
Pendleton, Terry	Braves	6.00	1.00	2.00
Puckett, Kirby	Twins	15.00	4.00	5.00
Ripken Jr., Cal	Orioles	35.00	8.00	12.00
Roberts, Bip (R)	Reds	9.00	1.50	2.50
Ryan, Nolan	Rangers	36.00	8.00	12.00
Sandberg, Ryne	Cubs	15.00	4.00	5.00
Sheffield, Gary	Padres	9.00	1.50	2.50
Smoltz, John (R)	Braves	50.00	6.00	8.00
Thomas, Frank	White Sox	20.00	5.00	7.00
Van Slyke, Andy	Pirates	6.00	1.00	2.00
Ventura, Robin (R)	White Sox	15.00	2.50	3.50
Walker, Larry (R)	Expos	35.00	7.00	9.00

Extended Set

		NM Price
Complete Set (7)		$350.00

Quality Rating ★★★★

This is arguably the best extended set Kenner has issued. The Ryan retirement and the Maddux piece are two of the more popular baseball figures of all time.

Player	Team	Mint Price	Card Price	Figure Price
Bonds, Barry	Giants	$15.00	$3.00	$5.00
Fisk, Carlton	White Sox	20.00	4.00	7.00
Jackson, Bo	White Sox	10.00	2.50	3.50
Maddux, Greg	Braves	160.00	40.00	75.00
Neid, David (R)	Rockies	12.00	3.00	4.00
Ryan, Nolan (retire)	Rangers	160.00	40.00	75.00
Santiago, Benito	Marlins	10.00	2.50	3.50

1993 Baseball Headline

		NM Price
Complete Set (8)		$175.00

Quality Rating ★★★

In the beginning, collectors only had a mild interest in the Headline series, which may be why this was Kenner's last Headline set. The Ripken could be a sleeper because the headline touts his approach of Lou Gehrig's record, which has now been broken.

Player	Team	Mint Price	Card Price	Figure Price
Abbott, Jim	Angels	$14.00	n/a	$5.00
Alomar, Roberto	Blue Jays	15.00	n/a	5.00
Glavine, Tom	Braves	20.00	n/a	10.00
McGwire, Mark	Athletics	30.00	n/a	15.00
Ripken Jr., Cal	Orioles	50.00	n/a	20.00
Ryan, Nolan	Angels	45.00	n/a	20.00
Sanders, Deion	Braves	20.00	n/a	8.00
Thomas, Frank	White Sox	30.00	n/a	15.00

1993 BASEBALL STADIUM STARS

	NM Price
Complete Set (6)	$175.00

Quality Rating ★★★

This is Kenner's first Stadium Stars issue and, like the Headline series, does not attract much collector attention.

Player	Team	Mint Price	Card Price	Figure Price
Clemens, Roger	Red Sox	$25.00	n/a	$10.00
Fielder, Cecil	Tigers	20.00	n/a	10.00
Griffey Jr., Ken	Mariners	35.00	n/a	15.00
Ryan, Nolan	Rangers	50.00	n/a	25.00
Sandberg, Ryne	Cubs	30.00	n/a	15.00
Thomas, Frank	White Sox	50.00	n/a	25.00

1994
Jay Bell

1994 BASEBALL

				NM Price
Complete Set (57)				$450.00

Quality Rating ★★★
Piazza leads the rookie crop, but don't overlook Johnson, Rodriguez, and M. Vaughn. The Extended series, like previous issues, is produced in smaller quantities than the regular issue.

Player	Team	Mint Price	Card Price	Figure Price
Appier, Kevin (R)	Royals	$8.00	$1.00	$2.00
Avery, Steve	Braves	8.00	1.50	2.50
Baerga, Carlos	Indians	8.00	1.50	2.50
Bagwell, Jeff	Astros	20.00	4.00	6.00
Bell, Derek (R)	Padres	8.00	1.50	2.50
Bell, Jay (R)	Pirates	8.00	1.50	2.50
Belle, Albert	Indians	12.00	3.00	4.00
Boggs, Wade	Yankees	8.00	1.50	2.50
Bonds, Barry	Giants	8.00	1.50	2.50
Burkett, John (R)	Giants	7.00	1.00	2.00
Carter, Joe	Blue Jays	7.00	1.00	2.00
Clemens, Roger	Red Sox	12.00	2.50	3.50
Cone, David	Royals	10.00	2.50	3.50
Curtis, Chad (R)	Angels	8.00	1.50	2.50
Daulton, Darren (R)	Phillies	8.00	1.50	2.50
Deshields, Delino	Dodgers	8.00	2.00	3.00
Fernandez, Alex (R)	White Sox	14.00	2.50	4.00
Fielder, Cecil	Tigers	7.00	1.00	2.00
Galarraga, Andres	Rockies	10.00	2.50	3.50
Grace, Mark	Cubs	8.00	1.00	2.00
Greene, Tommy (R)	Phillies	8.00	1.50	2.50
Griffey Jr., Ken	Mariners	28.00	5.00	7.00
Harper, Brian (R)	Brewers	8.00	1.50	2.50
Harvey, Brian (R)	Marlins	8.00	3.00	4.00
Hayes, Charlie (R)	Angels	8.00	1.50	2.50
Hoiles, Chris (R)	Orioles	8.00	1.50	2.50
Hollins, Dave (R)	Phillies	8.00	1.50	2.50
Jefferies, Greg	Cardinals	7.00	1.00	2.00
Johnson, Randy (R)	Mariners	35.00	5.00	10.00
Justice, Dave	Braves	10.00	2.50	3.50
Karros, Eric	Dodgers	8.00	2.50	3.50
Key, Jimmy (R)	Yankees	10.00	3.00	4.00
Kile, Darryl (R)	Astros	10.00	1.50	2.50
Knoblauch, Chuck (R)	Twins	14.00	1.50	2.50
Langston, Mark	Angels	8.00	1.50	2.50
Mattingly, Don	Yankees	10.00	2.00	3.00
Merced, Orlando (R)	Pirates	8.00	1.50	2.50
Molitor, Paul	Blue Jays	10.00	3.00	4.00
Mussina, Mike	Orioles	10.00	3.00	4.00
Olerud, John (R)	Blue Jays	10.00	2.00	3.00
Phillips, Tony (R)	Tigers	7.00	1.00	2.00
Piazza, Mike (R)	Dodgers	55.00	10.00	15.00
Rijo, Jose (R)	Reds	8.00	1.50	2.50
Ripken Jr., Cal	Orioles	50.00	8.00	12.00
Rodriguez, Ivan (R)	Rangers	15.00	4.00	5.00
Salmon, Tim (R)	Angels	12.00	2.00	3.00
Sandberg, Ryne	Cubs	20.00	4.00	5.00
Schilling, Curt (R)	Phillies	10.00	1.50	2.50
Sheffield, Gary	Marlins	7.00	1.00	2.00

Player	Team	Mint Price	Card Price	Figure Price
Snow, J.T. (R)	Angels	16.00	3.00	4.00
Thomas, Frank	White Sox	18.00	4.00	5.00
Thompson, Robby	Giants	7.00	1.00	2.00
Vaughn, Greg (R)	Brewers	10.00	1.00	2.00
Vaughn, Mo (R)	Red Sox	16.00	3.00	4.00
Ventura, Robin	White Sox	7.00	1.00	2.00
Williams, Matt	Giants	10.00	2.50	3.50
Winfield, Dave	Twins	10.00	3.00	4.00

Extended Set

	NM Price
Complete Set (8)	$140.00

Quality Rating ★★
The extended series offers power hitters Palmiero and Gonzalez. Like the other extended sets, this is produced in smaller quantities than the regular issues. The key figure is the Lofton rookie.

Player	Team	Mint Price	Card Price	Figure Price
Carlton, Steve	Phillies	$20.00	$3.00	$4.00
Clark, Will	Rangers	12.00	4.00	5.00
Dykstra, Lenny	Phillies	12.00	3.00	4.00
Gonzalez, Juan	Rangers	25.00	4.00	5.00
Lofton, Kenny (R)	Indians	65.00	12.00	20.00
McGriff, Fred	Braves	15.00	3.00	4.00
Palmerio, Rafael	Orioles	25.00	4.00	5.00
Sheffield, Gary (power.)	Marlins	12.00	3.00	4.00

1994 Baseball Stadium Stars

	NM Price
Complete Set (8)	$180.00

Quality Rating ★★★★
Only the Jackson and Sanders figures seem to generate any collector interest. Most figures can still be purchased at retail prices.

Player	Team	Mint Price	Card Price	Figure Price
Bonds, Barry	Giants	$20.00	n/a	$10.00
Clark, Will	Giants	18.00	n/a	8.00
Eckersley, Dennis	Athletics	18.00	n/a	8.00
Glavine, Tom	Braves	25.00	n/a	10.00
Gonzalez, Juan	Rangers	25.00	n/a	10.00
Jackson, Bo	White Sox	50.00	n/a	20.00
Puckett, Kirby	Twins	20.00	n/a	10.00
Sanders, Deion	Braves	40.00	n/a	20.00

1994 Cooperstown

	NM Price
Complete Set (8)	$100.00

Quality Rating ★★★★
The Cooperstown Collection was extremely popular when it was

released. Although it has now lost some of its popularity, it's still a great set. The Jackson and Wagner figures are short printed. A variation on the Robinson—wearing #44 instead of #42—is known to exist, but it's unknown how many were made.

Player	Team	Mint Price	Card Price	Figure Price
Cobb, Ty	Tigers	$14.00	$2.00	$2.00
Gehrig, Lou	Yankees	14.00	2.00	2.00
Jackson, Reggie	Yankees	30.00	5.00	9.00
Mays, Willie	Giants	14.00	2.00	2.00
Robinson, Jackie				
(#42)	Dodgers	14.00	2.00	2.00
(#44)	Dodgers	400.00	4.00	175.00
Ruth, Babe	Red Sox	14.00	2.00	2.00
Wagner, Honus	Pirates	30.00	5.00	9.00
Young, Cy	Red Sox	14.00	2.00	2.00

1995 BASEBALL

	NM Price
Complete Set (58)	$400.00

Quality Rating ★★★
This set receives only mild interest from collectors despite several good rookies, including Bichette, Lopez, Mondesi, and Klesko.

Player	Team	Mint Price	Card Price	Figure Price
Abbott, Jim	Angels	$10.00	$3.00	$4.00
Alou, Moises (R)	Expos	12.00	3.00	4.00
Baerga, Carlos	Indians	8.00	2.50	3.50
Bagwell, Jeff	Astros	12.00	2.50	3.50
Belle, Albert	Indians	10.00	2.50	3.50
Berroa, Geranimo (R)	A's	10.00	3.00	4.00
Bichette, Dante (R)	Rockies	16.00	4.00	5.00
Bonds, Barry	Giants	10.00	2.50	3.50
Buhner, Jay (R)	Mariners	16.00	4.00	5.00
Canseco, Jose	Athletics	10.00	2.50	3.50
Carr, Chuck (R)	Marlins	10.00	3.00	4.00
Carter, Joe	Blue Jays	8.00	1.50	2.50
Cedeno, Andujar (R)	Astors	10.00	4.00	5.00
Clark, Will	Giants	8.00	1.50	2.50
Clemens, Roger	Red Sox	14.00	3.00	4.00
Conine, Jeff (R)	Marlins	10.00	2.50	3.50
Cooper, Scott (R)	Cardinals	10.00	4.00	5.00
Daulton, Darren	Phillies	10.00	2.50	3.50
Delgado, Carlos (R)	Blue Jays	15.00	4.00	5.00
Fielder, Cecil	Tigers	8.00	1.50	2.50
Floyd, Cliff (R)	Expos	8.00	4.00	5.00
Franco, Julio	Indians	8.00	1.50	2.50
Griffey Jr., Ken	Mariners	28.00	4.00	8.00
Gonzalez, Juan	Rangers	10.00	3.00	4.00
Gwynn, Tony	Padres	15.00	1.50	2.50
Hamelin, Bob (R)	Royals	10.00	3.00	4.00
Hammonds, Jeffrey	Orioles	15.00	4.00	5.00
Johnson, Randy	Mariners	15.00	4.00	5.00
Kent, Jeff (R)	Mets	12.00	4.00	5.00
King, Jeff (R)	Pirates	13.00	3.00	4.00
Klesko, Ryan (R)	Braves	35.00	5.00	7.00

Player	Team	Mint Price	Card Price	Figure Price
Knoblauch, Chuck	Twins	10.00	1.50	2.50
Kruk, John	Phillies	10.00	2.50	3.50
Lankford, Ray	Cardinals	8.00	1.50	2.50
Larkin, Barry	Reds	12.00	3.00	5.00
Lopez, Javier (R)	Braves	30.00	5.00	7.00
Martin, Al (R)	Pirates	10.00	2.50	3.50
McRae, Brian	Royals	8.00	1.50	2.50
Molitor, Paul	Blue Jays	8.00	1.50	2.50
Mondesi, Raul (R)	Dodgers	32.00	8.00	12.00
Mussina, Mike	Orioles	8.00	1.50	2.50
Neel, Troy (R)	A's	10.00	2.50	3.50
Nilsson, Dave (R)	Brewers	10.00	2.50	3.50
Olerud, John	Blue Jays	8.00	1.50	2.50
O'Neill, Paul	Reds	10.00	2.50	3.50
Piazza, Mike	Dodgers	25.00	4.00	8.00
Puckett, Kirby	Twins	10.00	2.50	3.50
Ripken Jr., Cal	Orioles	35.00	8.00	12.00
Salmon, Tim	Angels	10.00	2.50	3.50
Sanders, Deion	Braves	8.00	1.50	2.50
Sanders, Reggie (R)	Reds	10.00	2.50	3.50
Sosa, Sammy (R)	Cubs	15.00	3.00	4.00
Tettleton, Mickey	Orioles	8.00	1.50	2.50
Thomas, Frank	White Sox	12.00	2.50	3.50
Van Slyke, Andy	Pirates	10.00	2.50	3.50
Vaughn, Mo	Red Sox	10.00	1.50	2.50
Wilkins, Rick (R)	Cubs	10.00	2.50	3.50
Williams, Matt	Giants	10.00	1.50	2.50

Extended Set

	NM Price
Complete Set (9)	$300.00

Quality Rating ★★
This extended set is more popular than the regular set. The Alex Rodriguez rookie is still hot, plus you get the Ripken streak piece, Lofton, Ramirez, and Piazza. The Schmidt figure was also found in Clover stores without the extended sticker.

Player	Team	Mint Price	Card Price	Figure Price
Canseco, Jose	Red Sox	$10.00	$4.00	$5.00
Greer, Rusty	Rangers	15.00	4.00	5.00
Lofton, Kenny	Indians	55.00	10.00	25.00
Pagnozzi, Tom	Cardinals	10.00	4.00	5.00
Piazza, Mike	Dodgers	25.00	6.00	8.00
Ramirez, Manny	Indians	70.00	10.00	20.00
Ripken Jr., Cal	Orioles	100.00	20.00	40.00
Rodriguez, Alex	Mariners	110.00	25.00	40.00
Schmidt, Mike	Phillies	16.00	4.00	5.00

1995 Ken Griffey Jr.

1995 Baseball Stadium Stars

	NM Price
Complete Set (10)	$250.00

Quality Rating ★★★★

The Maddux and Johnson figures are popular among collectors. There is very little interest in the others, including the Daulton short-printed piece.

Player	Team	Mint Price	Card Price	Figure Price
Daulton, Darren	Phillies	$30.00	n/a	$15.00
Dykstra, Lenny	Phillies	25.00	n/a	10.00
Griffey, Jr., Ken	Mariners	35.00	n/a	15.00
Johnson, Randy	Mariners	65.00	n/a	30.00
Justice, Dave	Braves	24.00	n/a	10.00
Maddux, Greg	Braves	60.00	n/a	25.00
McGwire, Mark	Athletics	40.00	n/a	20.00
Thomas, Frank	White Sox	30.00	n/a	15.00
Vaughn, Mo	Red Sox	30.00	n/a	15.00

1995 Baseball Cooperstown

	NM Price
Complete Set (10)	$100.00

Quality Rating ★★★★

After a quick start the Cooperstown Collection has slowed down in the hobby. The Killebrew and Mathews are short-printed pieces. The Ruth figure is his alleged "called shot."

Player	Team	Mint Price	Card Price	Figure Price
Carew, Rod	Twins	$10.00	$2.00	$3.00
Dean, Dizzy	Cardinals	10.00	2.00	3.00
Drysdale, Don	Dodgers	10.00	2.00	3.00
Feller, Bob	Indians	10.00	2.00	3.00
Ford, Whitey	Yankees	10.00	2.00	3.00
Gibson, Bob	Cardinals	10.00	2.00	3.00
Killebrew, Harmon	Twins	15.00	3.00	4.00

Player	Team	Mint Price	Card Price	Figure Price
Mathews, Eddie	Braves	15.00	3.00	4.00
Paige, Satchel	Indians	10.00	2.00	3.00
Ruth, Babe	Yankees	12.00	2.00	3.00

1996
Chipper Jones

1996 BASEBALL

	NM Price
Complete Set (69)	$750.00

Quality Rating ★★★★

This set contains another good crop of rookies including Jones, Nomo, and Jeter, as well as veteran players Caminiti and Martinez. The Jones rookie has become the hottest piece of any of the '96 issues.

Player	Team	Mint Price	Card Price	Figure Price
Alomar, Roberto	Orioles	$10.00	$1.50	$2.50
Bagwell, Jeff				
(white bat)	Astros	15.00	2.50	5.00
(black bat)	Astros	10.00	2.50	3.00
Belle, Albert	Indians	10.00	2.50	3.00
Biggio, Craig	Astros	8.00	1.50	2.50
Bonds, Barry	Giants	8.00	1.50	2.50

Player	Team	Mint Price	Card Price	Figure Price
Bones, Ricky (R)	Brewers	10.00	2.50	3.50
Brogna, Rico (R)	Mets	10.00	2.50	3.50
Caminiti, Ken (R)	Padres	20.00	1.50	2.50
Castilla, Vinny (R)	Rockies	12.00	1.50	2.50
Clark, Will	Rangers	8.00	1.50	2.50
Cone, David	Yankees	10.00	1.50	2.50
Cordero, Wil (R)	Red Sox	10.00	2.50	3.00
Cordova, Marty (R)	Twins	12.00	2.50	3.00
Dunston, Shawon	Cubs	8.00	1.50	2.50
Dysktra, Lenny	Phillies	8.00	1.50	2.50
Edmonds, Jim (R)	Angels	10.00	2.50	3.00
Eisenreich, Jim (R)	Phillies	8.00	1.50	2.50
Gaetti, Gary	Royals	8.00	1.50	2.50
Gant, Ron	Reds	8.00	1.50	2.50
Griffey Jr., Ken	Mariners	20.00	4.00	5.00
Grisson, Marquis	Braves	12.00	2.50	3.00
Guillen, Ozzie	White Sox	8.00	1.50	2.50
Hunter, Brian (R)	Astros	10.00	2.50	3.00
Jeter, Derek (R)	Yankees	80.00	15.00	25.00
Johnson, Charles (R)	Marlins	10.00	2.50	3.00
Jones, Chipper (R)	Braves	175.00	30.00	75.00
Maddux, Greg	Braves	40.00	7.00	10.00
Manto, Jeff (R)	Orioles	10.00	2.50	3.00
Martinez, Edgar (R)	Mariners	15.00	3.00	4.00
McGriff, Fred	Braves	8.00	1.50	2.50
McGwire, Mark	Athletics	12.00	1.50	3.00
Mondesi, Raul	Dodgers	10.00	2.50	3.00
Murray, Eddie	Indians	12.00	2.50	3.00
Nomo, Hideo				
(R, gray)	Dodgers	50.00	10.00	25.00
(R, white)	Dodgers	50.00	10.00	25.00
O'Neill, Paul	Yankees	8.00	1.50	2.50
Piazza, Mike	Dodgers	18.00	3.00	4.00
Puckett, Kirby	Twins	10.00	1.50	2.50
Ripken Jr., Cal				
(diving)	Orioles	30.00	7.50	12.00
(diving w/sliding card)	Orioles	30.00	7.50	12.00
(sliding)	Orioles	30.00	7.50	12.00
(sliding w/diving card)	Orioles	30.00	7.50	12.00
Rodriguez, Ivan	Rangers	10.00	1.50	2.50
Sanders, Deion	Reds	8.00	1.50	2.50
Smith, Ozzie	Cardinals	12.00	2.50	3.00
Sosa, Sammy	Cubs	8.00	1.50	2.50
Steinbach, Terry	Athletics	8.00	1.50	2.50
Thomas, Frank	White Sox	15.00	3.00	4.00
Thome, Jim (R)	Indians	25.00	6.00	10.00
Thompson, Ryan (R)	Mets	8.00	1.50	2.50
Valentin, John (R)	Red Sox	8.00	1.50	2.50
Vaughn, Mo	Red Sox	8.00	1.50	2.50
Walker, Larry	Rockies	15.00	3.00	5.00
White, Rondell (R)	Expos	12.00	3.00	4.00
Williams, Matt	Giants	10.00	1.50	2.50

Extended Set

	NM Price
Complete Set (16)	$180.00

Quality Rating ★★
This is Kenner's largest extended set. The Griffey and Mattingly figures are in the new standing pose.

Player	Team	Mint Price	Card Price	Figure Price
Alou, Moises	Expos	$10.00	$2.50	$3.00
Anderson, Garrett (R)	Angeles	12.00	3.50	4.00
Baerga, Carlos	Indians	10.00	2.50	3.00
Bichette, Dante	Rockies	12.00	3.00	4.00
Carter, Joe	Blue Jays	10.00	2.50	3.00
Conine, Jeff	Marlins	10.00	2.50	3.00
Curtis, Chad	Tigers	10.00	2.00	3.00
Gonzalez, Juan	Rangers	20.00	3.00	4.00
Griffey Jr., Ken (standing)	Mariners	40.00	7.50	10.00
Justice, Dave	Braves	15.00	2.50	3.00
Karros, Eric	Dodgers	10.00	2.50	3.00
Larkin, Barry	Reds	15.00	2.50	3.00
Mattingly, Don (standing)	Yankees	16.00	5.00	6.00
Morris, Hal (R)	Reds	8.00	1.50	2.50
Neagle, Denny (R)	Pirates	20.00	3.00	5.00
Palmeiro, Rafael	Orioles	12.00	1.50	3.00

1996 Baseball Stadium Stars

	NM Price
Complete Set (11)	$225.00

Quality Rating ★★★
Kenner increased the size of its Stadium Stars set to 11 players, including the first Ripken piece. Unfortunately, they could not get the rights to depict Camden Yards, Jacobs Field, or Dodger Stadium. Thus the figures of Ripken, Belle, and Piazza appear on Veterans Stadium, site of the '96 All-Star game.

Player	Team	Mint Price	Card Price	Figure Price
Belle, Albert	Indians	$20.00	n/a	$10.00
Buhner, Jay	Mariners	25.00	n/a	10.00
Canseco, Jose	Red Sox	20.00	n/a	10.00
Daulton, Darren	Phillies	20.00	n/a	10.00
Grace, Mark	Cubs	20.00	n/a	10.00
Knoblauch, Chuck	Twins	20.00	n/a	10.00
Lopez, Javey	Braves	35.00	n/a	15.00
Piazza, Mike	Dodgers	35.00	n/a	15.00
Ripken, Cal	Orioles	55.00	n/a	25.00
Ventura, Robin	White Sox	20.00	n/a	10.00
Williams, Matt	Giants	20.00	n/a	10.00

1996 Cooperstown

		NM Price
Complete Set (14)		$175.00

Quality Rating ★★★★

Ten of the figures were available nationwide. The Ashburn piece was only available at Clover stores. The Carew, Carlton and Killebrew were only available at regional shows across the country. The Carew was from the National in Anahiem, Carlton at Fanfest in Philadelphia, and Killebrew at the Tuff Stuff show in Richmond. It is estimated that Kenner released approximately 10,000 Carew, 7,500 Carlton, and 3,500 Killebrew figures.

Player	Team	Mint Price	Card Price	Figure Price
Aaron, Hank	Braves	$20.00	$3.00	$3.50
Alexander, Grover	Phillies	10.00	3.00	3.50
Ashburn, Richie (Clover)	Phillies	20.00	5.00	7.00
Carew, Rod (National)	Angels	30.00	10.00	14.00
Carlton, Steve (Fanfest)	Phillies	30.00	6.00	10.00
Clemente, Roberto	Pirates	16.00	3.00	3.50
Foxx, Jimmy	Yankees	15.00	3.00	3.50
Greenberg, Hank	Tigers	10.00	3.00	3.50
Hornsby, Rogers	Cardinals	15.00	3.00	3.50
Killebrew, Harmon (Tuff Stuff)	Senators	25.00	6.00	8.00
Morgan, Joe	Reds	10.00	3.00	3.50
Ott, Mel	Tigers	10.00	3.00	3.50
Roberts, Robin	Phillies	15.00	3.00	5.00
Robinson, Jackie	Dodgers	16.00	3.00	5.00

1996 Cooperstown 12" Figures

		NM Price
Complete Set (6)		$125.00

Quality Rating ★★★

These 12-inch figures have not been as popular as Kenner expected. All of these pieces can be found for less than the $20 issue price.

Player	Team	Mint Price	Card Price	Figure Price
Cobb, Ty	Tigers	$15.00	n/a	$7.00
Gehrig, Lou	Yankees	15.00	n/a	7.00
Ruth, Babe (KayBee)	Red Sox	15.00	n/a	7.00
(regular)	Yankees	15.00	n/a	7.00
Wagner, H. (Toys R Us)	Pirates	15.00	n/a	7.00
Young, Cy		15.00	n/a	7.00

1997 Frank Thomas

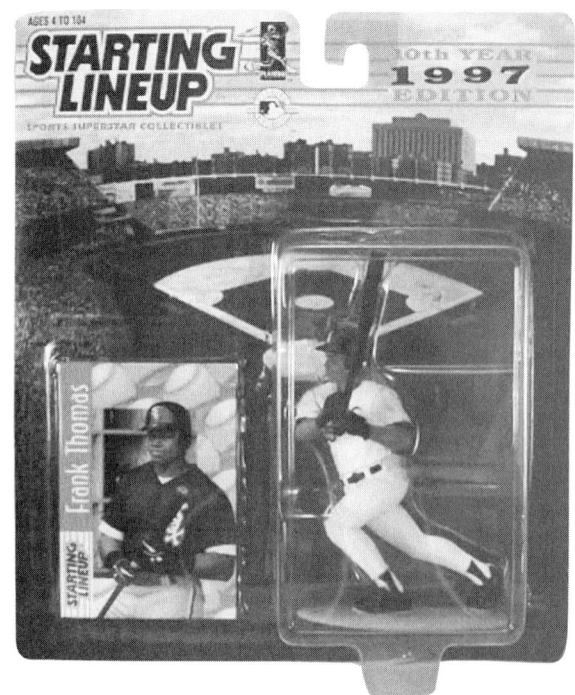

1997 BASEBALL

		NM Price
Complete Set (54)		$500.00

Quality Rating ★★★

This series' packaging is the best Kenner has ever used. Again player selection is good. There are several short print players from both the American and National Leagues.

Player	Team	Mint Price	Card Price	Figure Price
Alomar, Roberto	Orioles	$10.00	$2.00	$3.00
Anderson, Brady	Orioles	16.00	3.00	5.00
Bagwell, Jeff	Astros	10.00	2.00	3.00
Bell, Derek	Astros	8.00	2.00	3.00
Belle, Albert	Indians	12.00	3.00	4.00
Bichette, Dante	Rockies	10.00	2.00	3.00
Burks, Ellis	Rockies	12.00	2.00	3.00
Bonds, Barry	Giants	12.00	3.00	4.00
Brosius, Scott (R)	Athletics	8.00	2.00	3.00
Clemens, Roger	Red Sox	15.00	3.00	4.00
Damon, Johnny (R)	Royals	10.00	2.00	3.00
Finley, Steve (R)	Padres	10.00	2.00	3.00
Glavine, Tom	Braves	15.00	3.00	4.00
Greer, Rusty	Rangers	8.00	2.00	3.00
Griffey Jr., Ken	Mariners	20.00	5.00	7.00
Hundley, Todd (R)	Mets	16.00	4.00	5.00
Isringhausen, Jason (R)	Mets	10.00	3.00	4.00
Jaha, John (R)	Brewers	12.00	2.00	3.00
Johnson, Randy	Mariners	15.00	3.00	4.00
Jones, Chipper	Braves	30.00	5.00	6.00
Jordan, Brian (R)	Cardinals	10.00	2.00	3.00
Joyner, Wally	Royals	8.00	2.00	3.00
Kendall, Jason (R)	Pirates	12.00	3.00	4.00
Klesko, Ryan	Braves	15.00	3.00	5.00
Lopez, Javier	Braves	14.00	2.00	3.00

Player	Team	Mint Price	Card Price	Figure Price
Martinez, Tino (R)	Mariners	30.00	6.00	10.00
McRae, Brian	Cubs	8.00	2.00	3.00
Mesa, Jose (R)	Indians	10.00	2.00	3.00
Molitor, Paul	Twins	10.00	2.00	3.00
Mondesi, Raul	Dodgers	10.00	2.00	3.00
Nomo, Hideo	Dodgers	16.00	3.00	4.00
Ordonez, Ray (R)	Mets	20.00	3.00	4.00
Park, Chan Ho (R)	Dodgers	15.00	3.00	4.00
Piazza, Mike	Dodgers	12.00	3.00	4.00
Ramirez, Manny	Indians	15.00	3.00	5.00
Ripken Jr., Cal	Orioles	16.00	4.00	6.00
Rodriguez, Alex	Mariners	20.00	5.00	7.00
Rodriguez, Henry (R)	Expos	14.00	2.00	3.00
Rodriguez, Ivan	Rangers	12.00	3.00	4.00
Sandberg, Ryne	Cubs	10.00	2.00	3.00
Sanders, Reggie	Reds	10.00	2.00	3.00
Smoltz, John	Braves	18.00	2.00	5.00
Snow, J.T.	Angles	12.00	3.00	4.00
Thomas, Frank	White Sox	12.00	3.00	4.00
Valdes, Ismael (R)	Dodgers	15.00	2.00	3.00
White, Devon	Marlins	10.00	2.00	3.00
Williams, Bernie (R)	Yankees	18.00	2.00	3.00
Williams, Matt	Padres	10.00	2.00	3.00

Extended Figures

	NM Price
Complete Set (14)	$160.00

Quality Rating ★★★

Kenner has a strong lineup. The Jones, Clark, and Pettite rookies are popular pieces, but don't overlook Jeter and Rodriguez.

Player	Team	Mint Price	Card Price	Figure Price
Belle, Albert	White Sox	$10.00	$2.00	$3.00
Bottalico, Rickey (R)	Phillies	10.00	2.00	3.00
Caminiti, Ken	Padres	10.00	2.00	3.00
Clark, Tony (R)	Tigers	20.00	5.00	7.00
Clemens, Roger	Blue Jays	12.00	3.00	4.00
Eckersley, Dennis	Cardinals	10.00	2.00	3.00
Jeter, Derek	Yankess	18.00	4.00	6.00
Jones, Andrew (R)	Braves	35.00	5.00	10.00
McGwire, Mark	Athletics	12.00	3.00	4.00
Mussina, Mike	Orioles	10.00	2.00	3.00
Pettite, Andy (R)	Yankees	20.00	4.00	5.00
Rodriguez, Alex	Mariners	18.00	4.00	6.00
Sanders, Deion	Reds	10.00	2.00	3.00
Williams, Matt	Indians	10.00	2.00	3.00

1997 Baseball Stadium Stars

	NM Price
Complete Set (7)	$140.00

Quality Rating ★★★

Kenner decided to change this set by only using HOFers. The Jenkins figure is the short-print.

Player	Team	Mint Price	Card Price	Figure Price
Aaron, Hank	Braves	$20.00	n/a	$10.00
Jenkins, Ferguson	Cubs	25.00	n/a	10.00
Kaline, Al	Tigers	20.00	n/a	10.00
Mantle, Mickey	Yankees	30.00	n/a	15.00
Ruth, Babe	Yankees	25.00	n/a	12.00
Schmidt, Mike	Philies	20.00	n/a	10.00
Yastrzemski, Carl	Red Sox	20.00	n/a	10.00

1997 Baseball Classic Doubles

	NM Price
Complete Set (10)	$250.00

Quality Rating ★★★

Classic Doubles is a takeoff on the old Baseball Greats series. An active player is pitted against a baseball legend. The Maddux/Young piece is the short-print.

Player	Team	Mint Price	Card Price	Figure Price
Aaron/Robinson		$20.00	—	—
Aaron, Hank	Braves	—	$3.00	$5.00
Robinson, Jackie	Dodgers	—	3.00	5.00
Bonds/Bonds		20.00	—	—
Bonds, Barry	Giants	—	3.00	5.00
Bonds, Bobby		—	2.00	4.00
Griffey Jr./Griffey Sr.		25.00	—	—
Griffey Sr., Ken	Reds	—	2.00	4.00
Griffey Jr., Ken	Mariners	—	4.00	6.00
Johnson/Ryan		30.00	—	—
Johnson, Randy	Mariners	—	3.00	5.00
Ryan, Nolan	Rangers	—	5.00	7.00
Maddux/Young		50.00	—	—
Maddux, Greg	Braves	—	5.00	8.00
Young, Cy		—	4.00	6.00
Mantle/Maris		45.00	—	—
Mantle, Mickey	Yankees	—	7.00	10.00
Maris, Roger	Yankees	—	4.00	5.00
McGwire/Maris		25.00	—	—
Maris, Roger	Yankees	—	4.00	5.00
McGwire, Mark	Athletics	—	4.00	5.00
Nomo/Drysdale		25.00	—	—
Drysdale, Don	Dodgers	—	3.00	5.00
Nomo, Hideo	Dodgers	—	3.00	5.00
Ripken/Robinson		25.00	—	—
Ripken Jr., Cal	Orioles	—	4.00	6.00
Robinson, Brooks	Orioles	—	3.00	5.00
Thomas/Ruth		25.00	—	—
Ruth, Babe	Yankees	—	4.00	6.00
Thomas, Frank	White Sox	—	4.00	6.00
Doby/Robinson		25.00	—	—
Doby, Larry	Indians	—	2.00	3.00
Robinson, Jackie	Dodgers	—	3.00	5.00

1997 Baseball 12"

			NM Price
Complete Set (4)			$80.00

Quality Rating ★★★

These figures are similar to '96's 12" Cooperstown figures. The Cooperstown set wasn't that popular with collectors becuase of the retired player selection, but the Griffey piece from this set has done well.

Player	Team	Mint Price	Card Price	Figure Price
Griffey Jr., Ken	Mariners	$45.00	n/a	$20.00
Maddux, Greg	Braves	35.00	n/a	15.00
Piazza, Mike	Dodgers	35.00	n/a	15.00
Ripken Jr., Cal	Orioles	35.00	n/a	15.00

1997 Baseball Freeze Frame

			NM Price
Complete Set (6)			$125.00

Quality Rating ★★★

This set was designed after the Nolan Ryan Club piece, with each player depicted in three different poses. These pieces were available only at Toys 'R' Us. The figure price is for each individual piece.

Player	Team	Mint Price	Card Price	Figure Price
Bichette, Dante	Rockies	$25.00	n/a	$5.00
Gonzalez, Juan	Rangers	25.00	n/a	5.00
Griffey Jr., Ken	Mariners	45.00	n/a	7.00
Jones, Chipper	Braves	45.00	n/a	7.00
Piazza, Mike	Dodgers	25.00	n/a	5.00
Thomas, Frank	White Sox	25.00	n/a	5.00

1997 Cooperstown

			NM Price
Complete Set (10)			$175.00

Quality Rating ★★★

This has an all new cast including the first woman baseball player—Dottie Kamenshek. The Jackie Robinson figure was available only at Los Angeles Dodger home games.

Player	Team	Mint Price	Card Price	Figure Price
Bench, Johnny	Reds	$10.00	$2.00	$3.00
Fingers, Rollie	Athletics	10.00	2.00	3.00
Gibson, Josh	Grays	10.00	2.00	3.00
Johnson, Walter	Senators	12.00	3.00	4.00
Kamenshek, Dottie	Peaches	10.00	2.00	3.00
Mantle, Mickey	Yankees	20.00	4.00	6.00
Robinson, Brooks	Orioles	15.00	3.00	4.00
Robinson, Jackie	Dodgers	75.00	10.00	5.00
Snider, Duke	Dodgers	10.00	2.00	3.00
Wilhelm, Hoyt	White Sox	10.00	2.00	3.00
Yastzremski, Carl	Red Sox	10.00	2.00	3.00

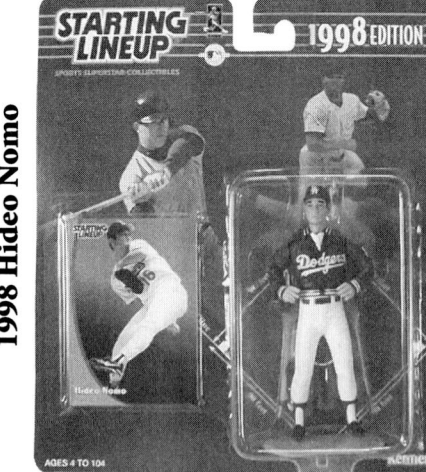

1998 Hideo Nomo

1998 BASEBALL

			NM Price
Complete Set (39)			$350.00

Quality Rating ★★★

Garciaparra and Rivera lead a weak group of rookies. Baseball is a slow mover compared to the other sports. The Chicago Cubs gave away a Mark Grace figure on April 19, 1998, and a Sammy Sosa figure on July 23rd at Wrigley field.

Player	Team	Mint Price	Card Price	Figure Price
Belle, Albert	White Sox	$8.00	$2.00	$3.00
Biggio, Craig	Astros	10.00	2.00	3.00
Bonds, Barry	Giants	10.00	2.00	3.00
Brown, Kevin	Marlins	8.00	2.00	3.00
Canseco, Jose	Athletics	10.00	2.00	3.00
Clark, Will	Rangers	8.00	2.00	3.00
Erstad, Darin (R)	Angels	10.00	2.00	3.00
Galarraga, Andres	Rockies	8.00	2.00	3.00
Garciaparra, Nomar (R)	Red Sox	50.00	10.00	15.00
Glavine, Tom	Braves	15.00	3.00	4.00
Gonzalez, Juan	Rangers	10.00	2.00	3.00
Grace, Mark	Cubs	10.00	2.00	3.00
Grace, Mark (Cubs)	Cubs	—	—	—
Griffey Jr., Ken	Mariners	20.00	4.00	6.00
Grudzielanek, Mark (R)	Expos	10.00	2.00	3.00
Gwynn, Tony	Padres	12.00	2.00	3.00
Higginson, Bob (R)	Tigers	12.00	2.00	3.00
Hill, Glenallen (R)	Giants	10.00	2.00	3.00
Jeter, Derek	Yankees	15.00	3.00	5.00
Jones, Chipper	Braves	25.00	4.00	6.00
Justice, Dave	Indians	10.00	2.00	3.00
Knoblauch, Chuck	Twins	12.00	3.00	4.00
Lankford, Ray	Cardinals	8.00	2.00	3.00
Larkin, Barry	Reds	10.00	2.00	3.00
Morandini, Mickey (R)	Phillies	10.00	2.00	3.00
Newfield, Marc (R)	Brewers	10.00	2.00	3.00
Nomo, Hideo	Dodgers	10.00	2.00	3.00
Palmeiro, Rafael	Orioles	10.00	2.00	3.00
Piazza, Mike	Dodgers	15.00	3.00	4.00
Ripken Jr., Cal	Orioles	15.00	3.00	4.00
Rivera, Mariano (R)	Yankees	24.00	4.00	6.00

Player	Team	Mint Price	Card Price	Figure Price
Rodriguez, Alex	Mariners	15.00	3.00	4.00
Sanders, Deion	Reds	12.00	2.00	3.00
Sheffield, Gary	Marlins	10.00	2.00	3.00
Sosa, Sammy (Cubs)	Cubs	—	—	—
Sprague, Ed (R)	Toronto	10.00	2.00	3.00
Thomas, Frank	White Sox	15.00	3.00	4.00
Thome, Jim	Indians	10.00	2.00	3.00
Vaughn, Mo	Red Sox	10.00	2.00	3.00
Walker, Larry	Rockies	12.00	2.00	3.00
Williams, Bernie	Yankees	10.00	2.00	3.00

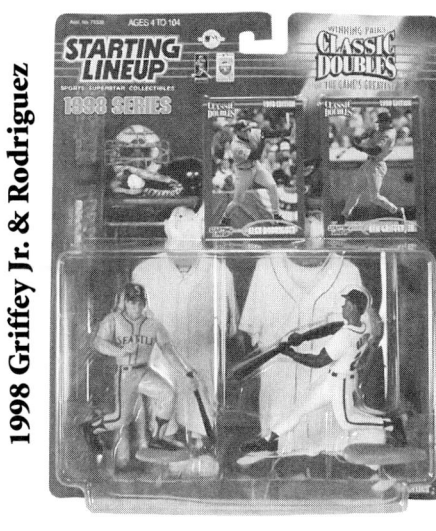

1998 Griffey Jr. & Rodriguez

Kenner Classic Doubles

NM Price

Complete Set (10) $200.00

Quality Rating ★★★★
This set is only mildly popular with collectors The Ruth/Maris and Griffey/A-Rod pieces lead the pack.

Player	Team	Mint Price	Card Price	Figure Price
Griffey Jr./Rodriguez		$25.00	—	—
Griffey Jr., Ken	Mariners	—	$3.00	$5.00
Rodriguez, Alex	Mariners	—	3.00	5.00
Ordonez/Jeter		24.00	—	—
Ordonez, Rey	Mets	—	2.00	4.00
Jeter, Derek	Yankees	—	3.00	5.00
Belle/Thomas		20.00	—	—
Belle, Albert	White Sox	—	2.00	4.00
Thomas, Frank	White Sox	—	3.00	5.00
Rodriguez/Piazza		24.00	—	—
Rodriguez, Ivan	Rangers	—	2.00	4.00
Piazza, Mike	Dodgers	—	3.00	5.00
Canseco/McGwire		20.00	—	—
Canseco, Jose	Athletics	—	2.00	4.00
McGwire, Mark	Athletics	—	2.00	4.00
Ruth/Maris		25.00	—	—
Ruth, Babe	Yankees	—	3.00	5.00
Maris, Roger	Yankees	—	3.00	5.00

Player	Team	Mint Price	Card Price	Figure Price
Ryan/Johnson		24.00	—	—
Ryan, Nolan		—	3.00	5.00
Johnson, Walter		—	3.00	5.00
Hunter/Jackson		20.00	—	—
Hunter, "Catfish"	Athletics	—	2.00	4.00
Jackson, Reggie	Athletics	—	3.00	5.00
Berra/Munson		20.00	—	—
Berra, Yogi	Yankees	—	2.00	4.00
Munson, Thurman	Yankees	—	3.00	5.00
Bench/Morgan		20.00	—	—
Bench, Johnny	Reds	—	2.00	4.00
Morgan, Joe	Reds	—	—	—

1998 Kenner Freeze Frame

NM Price

Complete Set (6) $120.00

Quality Rating ★★★★
This set offers six new players. Jeter, Ripken, and A-Rod lead the way.

Player	Team	Mint Price	Card Price	Figure Price
Bagwell, Jeff	Astros	$20.00	N/A	$10.00
Bonds, Barry	Giants	20.00	N/A	10.00
Jeter, Derek	Yankees	24.00	N/A	12.00
Maddux, Greg	Braves	20.00	N/A	10.00
Ripken Jr., Cal	Orioles	24.00	N/A	12.00
Rodriguez, Alex	Mariners	24.00	N/A	12.00

1998 Cooperstown

NM Price

Complete Set (11) $90.00

Quality Rating ★★★★
Kenner has a fresh lineup of faces. The Clemente piece is popular and Speaker is the short-print.

Player	Team	Mint Price	Card Price	Figure Price
Berra, Yogi	Yankees	$8.00	$2.00	$3.00
Brock, Lou	Cardinals	8.00	2.00	3.00
Campanella, Roy	Yankees	8.00	2.00	3.00
Clemente, Roberto	Pirates	12.00	3.00	4.00
Leonard, Buck		8.00	2.00	3.00
Niekro, Phil		8.00	2.00	3.00

Player	Team	Mint Price	Card Price	Figure Price
Palmer, Jim	Orioles	10.00	2.00	3.00
Robinson, Frank	Orioles	8.00	2.00	3.00
Seaver, Tom	Mets	8.00	2.00	3.00
Spahn, Warren	Braves	8.00	2.00	3.00
Speaker, Tris		15.00	4.00	5.00

1998 John Smoltz

1998 Baseball Stadium Stars

	NM Price
Complete Set (7)	$140.00

Quality Rating ★★★
Kenner changed this issue from actual stadiums to a generic baseball diamond. This allows Kenner to choose any player without worrying about stadium licensing.

Player	Team	Mint Price	Card Price	Figure Price
Belle, Albert	White Sox	$20.00	n/a	$10.00
Griffey Jr., Ken	Mariners	24.00	n/a	12.00
Piazza, Mike	Dodgers	24.00	n/a	12.00
Ripken Jr., Cal	Orioles	24.00	n/a	12.00
Rodriguez, Alex	Mariners	25.00	n/a	12.00
Smoltz, John	Braves	20.00	n/a	10.00
Williams, Bernie	Yankees	20.00	n/a	10.00

1989 One-on-One

	NM Price
Complete Set (4)	$175.00

Quality Rating ★★★
This is one of Kenner's more popular non-regular issues. We list the prices for the mint in box and an opened figure, as well as the price for each individual card.

Player	Team	Mint Price	Card Price	Figure Price
Canseco/Trammell		$40.00	—	$20.00
Canseco, Jose	Athletics	—	5.00	—
Trammell, Alan	Tigers	—	2.50	—
Carter/Davis		40.00	—	20.00
Carter, Gary	Mets	—	4.00	—
Davis, Eric	Reds	—	4.00	—

Player	Team	Mint Price	Card Price	Figure Price
Mattingly/Boggs		72.00	—	35.00
Mattingly, Don	Yankees	—	6.00	—
Boggs, Wade	Red Sox	—	6.00	—
Sandberg/Coleman		50.00	—	25.00
Sandberg, Ryne	Cubs	—	7.00	—
Coleman, Vince	Cardinals	—	2.00	—

OAKLAND ATHLETICS

Team Lineups

Player	Team	Mint Price	Card Price	Figure Price
1990 Award Winners		$40.00	n/a	$20.00
1991 Award Winners		65.00	n/a	30.00
Boston Red Sox	Red Sox	65.00	n/a	30.00
Chicago Cubs	Cubs	65.00	n/a	30.00
Detroit Tigers	Tigers	65.00	n/a	30.00
N.Y. Mets	Mets	65.00	n/a	30.00
N.Y. Yankees	Yankees	125.00	n/a	60.00
Oakland A's	A's	130.00	n/a	60.00
St. Louis Cardinals	Cardinals	75.00	n/a	35.00

Cal Ripken Convention Piece

Kenner Convention

Player	Team	Mint Price	Card Price	Figure Price
Ripken Jr., Cal (1996)				
(Cincinnati)	Orioles	$40.00	$7.50	$15.00
(Dallas)	Orioles	40.00	7.50	15.00
(Santa Clara)	Orioles	40.00	7.50	15.00
(New Jersey)	Orioles	40.00	7.50	15.00
Bench, Johnny (1997)				
(Cincinnati)	Reds	10.00	2.00	3.00

Sports Accessories, Memorabilia (SAM)

Mark Parrish and Mark Skigen founded Sports Accessories, Memorabilia (SAM) in 1992. Unlike the original papier-mâché bobbin' heads, these figures are made of porcelain. SAM issued caricatures of players with oversized heads, with just a couple of generic bobbers.

Most of these figures had production runs between 3,000 and 5,000. SAM continues to issue a few players every couple of months. Currently there are 60 bobbers, and most of them sell for less than $100, except for the few figures that include autographs.

Player	Team	Mint Price	Player	Team	Mint Price
A.L. All-Star	—	$40.00	Musial, Stan	Cardinals	50.00
N.L. All-star	—	40.00	Nomo, Hideo	Dodgers	50.00
Alomar, Roberto	Orioles	50.00	Nomo, Hideo (signed)	Dodgers	100.00
Banks, Ernie	Cubs	50.00	Palmer, Jim	Orioles	55.00
Bench, Johnny	Reds	45.00	Palmer, Jim (signed)	Orioles	100.00
Berra, Yogi	Yankees	45.00	Paige, Satchel	Monarchs	50.00
Brett, George	Royals	50.00	Perez, Tony	Reds	50.00
Carew, Rod	Twins	45.00	Perry, Gaylord	—	50.00
Carlton, Steve	Philies	50.00	Puckett, Kirby	Twins	55.00
Carter, Gary	Expos	45.00	Puckett, Kirby (signed)	Twins	200.00
Clemens, Roger	Red Sox	50.00	Ripken, Cal (home)	Orioles	75.00
Clemente, Roberto	Pirates	75.00	Ripken, Cal (away)	Orioles	50.00
Cobb, Ty	Tigers	50.00	Ripken, Cal (home-signed)	Orioles	250.00
Drysdale, Don	Dodgers	50.00	Ripken, Cal (away-signed)	Orioles	250.00
Fingers, Rollie	Athletics	55.00	Robinson, Brooks	Orioles	50.00
Ford, Whitey	Yankees	50.00	Rose, Pete	Reds	50.00
Gehrig, Lou	Yankees	50.00	Ruth, Babe	Yankees	80.00
Gibson, Bob	Cardinals	55.00	Ryan, Nolan	Angels	60.00
Griffey Jr., Ken	Mariners	50.00	Ryan, Nolan	Astros	60.00
Gwynn, Tony	Padres	50.00	Ryan, Nolan	Mets	60.00
Jackson, Martinez	Negro League	50.00	Ryan, Nolan	Rangers	60.00
Jackson, Reggie	Yankees	65.00	Seaver, Tom	Mets	40.00
Jeter, Derek	Yankees	50.00	Schmidt, Mike	Phillies	55.00
Jordan, Michael	Birm. Barons	110.00	Snider, Duke	Dodgers	50.00
Mantle, Mickey	Yankees	110.00	Stargell, Willie	Pirates	50.00
Maris, Roger	Yankees	60.00	Williams, Ted	Red Sox	70.00
Mays, Willie	Giants	65.00	Yastrzemski, Carl	Red Sox	60.00
Morgan, Joe	Reds	50.00			

SPORTS IMPRESSIONS

Sports Impressions was founded in 1987 by Joe Timmerman. Most of the early figures were produced in large quantities and without autographs. In 1991, Enesco, manufacturer of the popular Precious Moments figures and other porcelain collectibles, bought Sports Impressions and changed the company's philosophy. They began producing more limited runs that included the autographs of the featured players.

Enesco's Sports Impressions line falls in the middle of the sports figures market. They're nicer than most of the low-end sports figures, but when Salvino entered the market with a higher priced product that more accurately depicted the players, Sports Impressions began losing its appeal. In 1996 Enesco issued its last sports figures, and today there's little demand for Sports Impressions. Collectors tend to opt for the more popular Starting Lineup brand, or the high-end Salvino figures.

**7" Duke Snider
Sports Impressions**

Player		Team	Ht.	Mint
Aaron, Hank	(regular)	Braves	5"	$40.00
	(500 HR)	Braves	7"	75.00
	(signed)	Braves	7"	195.00
Alomar, Roberto	(signed)	Blue Jays	7"	125.00
Banks, Ernie	(regular)	Cubs	5"	40.00
	(500 HR)	Cubs	7"	75.00
Bench, Johnny	(regular)	Reds	6"	70.00
	(signed)	Reds	7"	125.00
Boggs, Wade	(regular)	Red Sox	7"	60.00
Bonds, Barry	(regular)	Pirates	8"	120.00
Branca, Ralph	(signed)	Dodgers	7"	100.00
Canseco, Jose	(regular)	Athletics	10"	125.00
	(regular)	Athletics	7"	100.00
	(swinging)	Athletics	5"	50.00
	(batting)	Athletics	5"	40.00
Carew, Rod	(regular)	Twins	9"	75.00
Carlton, Steve	(regular)	Phillies	9"	100.00
Carter, Gary	(regular)	Mets	7"	50.00
Clark, Will	(regular)	Giants	10"	125.00
	(regular)	Giants	7"	70.00
	(regular)	Giants	5"	30.00

Player		Team	Ht.	Mint
Clemens, Roger	(regular)	Red Sox	5½"	60.00
	(signed)	Red Sox	7"	125.00
	(regular)	Red Sox	7"	75.00
Cobb, Ty	(regular)	Tigers	7"	80.00
Davis, Eric	(regular)	Reds	7"	40.00
	(regular)	Reds	5"	20.00
Dawson, Andre	(regular)	Cubs	7"	50.00
Dykstra, Lenny	(regular)	Phillies	7"	75.00
	(regular)	Phillies	5"	35.00
Feller, Bob	(regular)	Indians	7"	60.00
Foxx, Jimmie	(500 HR)	Athletics	7"	100.00
Garvey, Steve	(regular)	Dodgers	7"	40.00
	(regular)	Dodgers	5"	30.00
Gehrig, Lou	(regular)	Yankees	7"	125.00
Gibson, Kirk	(regular)	Dodgers	7"	40.00
Glavine, Tom	(signed)	Braves	8"	125.00
Gooden, Dwight	(regular)	Mets	10"	75.00
	(regular)	Mets	7"	60.00
	(regular)	Mets	5"	35.00
Greenwell, Mike	(regular)	Red Sox	7"	40.00
	(regular)	Red Sox	5"	30.00

Player		Team	Ht.	Mint	Player		Team	Ht.	Mint
Griffey Jr., Ken	(regular)	Mariners	7"	120.00	Morgan, Joe	(regular)	Reds	7"	120.00
	(regular)	Mariners	5"	60.00		(regular)	Reds	5"	30.00
Gwynn, Tony	(regular)	Padres	7"	60.00	Munson, Thurman	(regular)	Yankees	10"	125.00
	(regular)	Padres	5"	35.00		(regular)	Yankees	7"	70.00
Henderson, Rickey	(regular)	Athletics	8"	100.00		(regular)	Yankees	5"	35.00
	(AP)	Athletics	8"	200.00	Ott, Mel	(500 HR)	Giants	7"	80.00
Hernandez, Keith	(regular)	Mets	7"	40.00	Piazza, Mike	(signed)	Dodgers	7"	125.00
Hershiser, Orel	(regular)	Dodgers	7"	40.00	Puckett, Kirby	(regular)	Twins	7"	70.00
	(regular)	Dodgers	5"	30.00		(regular)	Twins	5"	35.00
Jackson, Bo	(regular)	Royals	10"	80.00	Ripken Jr., Cal	(regular)	Orioles	7"	125.00
	(regular)	Royals	7"	75.00		(regular)	Orioles	5"	40.00
	(regular)	Royals	5"	25.00	Robinson, Brooks	(regular)	Orioles	7"	70.00
Jackson, Reggie	(500 HR)	Athletics	7"	100.00		(regular)	Orioles	5"	35.00
	(regular)	Angels	7"	80.00	Robinson, Frank	(500 HR)	Orioles	7"	75.00
	(regular)	Yankees	7"	120.00	Robinson, Jackie	(regular)	Dodgers	7"	75.00
	(regular)	Yankees	9"	125.00		(regular)	Dodgers	5"	30.00
	(signed)	Athletics	8"	150.00	Ruth, Babe	(500 HR)	Yankees	7"	100.00
	(regular)	Yankees	5"	40.00		(Club)	Yankees	4"	45.00
Jefferies, Gregg	(regular)	Mets	7"	40.00	Ryan, Nolan	(regular)	Rangers	10"	125.00
Johnson, Howard	(regular)	Mets	7"	50.00		(signed '93)	Rangers	8"	300.00
	(regular)	Mets	5"	30.00		(no auto. '93)	Rangers	8"	125.00
Justice, Dave	(signed)	Braves	8"	150.00		(farewell, signed)	Rangers	8"	250.00
Kaline, Al	(regular)	Tigers	7"	60.00		(farewell)	Rangers	8"	125.00
Killebrew, Harmon	(500 HR)	Twins	7"	80.00		(AP)	Rangers	7"	200.00
Langston, Mark	(regular)	Angels	7"	50.00		(regular)	Mets	5"	100.00
Mantle, Mickey	(regular)	Yankees	6"	250.00		(regular)	Astros	5"	75.00
	(signed)	Yankees	8"	500.00		(regular)	Angels	5"	75.00
	(regular)	Yankees	8"	200.00		(regular)	Rangers	5"	75.00
	(500 HR)	Yankees	7"	125.00		(mini)	Rangers	5"	40.00
	(regular)	Yankees	5"	50.00		(regular)	Rangers	15"	125.00
	(club)	Yankees	5"	75.00		(AP)	Rangers	15"	350.00
	(regular)	Yankees	7"	200.00		(signed)	Rangers	7"	195.00
	(regular)	Yankees	10"	225.00	Sandberg, Ryne	(regular)	Cubs	6"	50.00
	(regular)	Yankees	15"	200.00		(signed)	Cubs	7"	150.00
	(AP)	Yankees	15"	300.00	Schmidt, Mike	(signed)	Phillies	8"	200.00
Mathews, Eddie	(500 HR)	Braves	7"	100.00		(regular)	Phillies	8"	100.00
Mattingly, Don	(regular)	Yankees	10"	120.00		(500 HR)	Phillies	7"	100.00
	(var.)	Yankees	7"	300.00	Seaver, Tom	(regular)	Mets	9"	75.00
	(regular)	Yankees	7"	100.00		(regular)	Mets	7"	70.00
	(signed)	Yankees	8"	150.00		(regular)	Mets	5"	35.00
	(regular)	Yankees	6"	75.00	Snider, Duke	(regular)	Dodgers	7"	70.00
	(fielding)	Yankees	5"	50.00		(regular)	Dodgers	5"	35.00
	(batting)	Yankees	5"	40.00	Strawberry, Darryl	(regular)	Dodgers	7"	60.00
	(regular)	Yankees	15"	100.00		(regular)	Dodgers	5"	30.00
	(AP)	Yankees	15"	300.00	Thomson, Bobby	(signed)	Giants	7"	100.00
Mays, Willie	(500 HR)	Giants	7"	70.00	Trammell, Alan	(regular)	Tigers	7"	60.00
	(catch)	Giants	7"	70.00		(swing)	Tigers	5"	30.00
	(regular)	Giants	5"	40.00	Van Slyke, Andy	(regular)	Pirates	7"	50.00
McCovey, Willie	(regular)	Giants	7"	100.00	Ventura, Robin	(signed)	White Sox	8"	100.00
McGwire, Mark	(regular)	Athletics	9½"	125.00	Viola, Frank	(regular)	Twins	7"	50.00
	(regular)	Athletics	7"	75.00	Wagner, Honus		Tigers	7"	70.00
	(regular)	Athletics	5"	35.00	Williams, Ted	(500 HR)	Red Sox	7"	100.00
McReynolds, Kevin	(regular)	Mets	7"	40.00		(regular)	Red Sox	10"	125.00
Mitchell, Kevin	(regular)	Giants	7"	70.00		(regular)	Red Sox	5"	50.00
	(regular)	Giants	5"	30.00	Winfield, Dave		Blue Jays	7"	60.00
Molitor, Paul	(regular)	Brewers	7"	70.00	Young, Cy	(regular)	Indians	7"	70.00

SALVINO

Salvino Inc. was founded by brothers Rick and Wayne Salvino in 1988, with the goal of offering the most realistic-looking sports figures in the hobby. Since then, Salvino has become the leader in high-end porcelain sports figures and statues. Sandy Koufax and Don Drysdale were the first two figures released, and the success of these pieces allowed Salvino to expand its player selection into other sports.

Most Salvino figures come with the featured player's autograph on the base, an enhancement that helped the company rapidly gain a foothold in the market. Of all of the Salvino figures, the Mickey Mantle pieces are the most popular with collectors.

Player		Team	Size	Mint
Campanella, Roy		Dodgers	2,000	$395.00
	(SE)	Dodgers	200	575.00
Clemente, Roberto		Pirates	1,750	125.00
Drysdale, Don		Dodgers	2,500	185.00
	(AP)	Dodgers	300	400.00
Griffey Jr., Ken		Mariners	2,500	185.00
Henderson, Rickey	(HU)	Athletics	600	275.00
	(AU)	Athletics	600	275.00
	(SE)	Athletics	550	375.00
Jackson, Reggie		Yankees	1,500	275.00
Koufax, Sandy		Dodgers	2,500	195.00
	(AP)	Dodgers	500	250.00
		Dodgers	368	750.00
Mantle, Mickey	(field)	Yankees	682	1,000.00
	(bat)	Yankees	682	1,000.00
	(HU)	Yankees	950	750.00
	(AU)	Yankees	950	600.00
	(HU, #6)	Yankees	368	1,600.00
	(HU, #7)	Yankees	368	1,600.00
		Yankees	2,000	125.00
Maris, Roger		Yankees	2,000	125.00
Martin, Billy		Yankees	2,000	125.00
Mays, Willie	(NY)	Giants	750	395.00
	(SF)	Giants	750	395.00
	(HU)	Giants	368	600.00
Robinson, Brooks		Orioles	1,000	275.00
Snider, Duke	(HU)	Dodgers	1,000	275.00
	(AU)	Dodgers	1,000	275.00

Salvino Price Guide Key	
AU	Away Uniform
AP	Artist Proof
HU	Home Uniform
SE	Special Edition

Ken Griffey Jr.

MISCELLANEOUS SPORTS FIGURES

In addition to the major manufacturers, several other companies have issued a limited number of baseball figures over the years. These figures range from high-end statues—like the Art of Sport—to Hallmark ornaments, to low-end figures like Microstars. Some are still involved in the figure market, while others have come and gone. Here's the skinny on the remaining available baseball figures.

ART OF SPORT

British manufacturer Endurance Ltd. entered the figure market with its Art of Sport line of golf, cricket, and boxing figures issued in England. Their line of figures recently became available in the U.S., when the company issued its first baseball figure—Baltimore star Cal Ripken Jr. The Ripken piece, along with the follow-up Ken Griffey Jr. release, was well received in the hobby.

Cal Ripken Jr.

Player	Team	Edition	Mint Price
Ripken Jr., Cal			
(unsigned)	Orioles	4,515	$200.00
(signed)	Orioles	500	425.00
Griffey Jr., Ken			
(unsigned)	Mariners	1,500	225.00
(signed)	Mariners	500	450.00

HALLMARK ORNAMENTS

Greeting card giant Hallmark recently expanded its popular line of collectible ornaments with the addition of sports personalities. The "Baseball Heroes" series made its debut in 1994, with a Babe Ruth piece. Hallmark released three more ornaments in the series, with Jackie Robinson being the last before the line was retired.

A second baseball series, entitled "At the Ballpark," debuted in 1996 with Nolan Ryan, and continued last year with Hank Aaron.

"At the Ballpark"

Player	Team	Mint Price
Ryan, Nolan ('96 w/MLB logo)	Rangers	$30.00
Ryan, Nolan ('96 w/o MLB logo)	Rangers	30.00
Aaron, Hank ('97)	Braves	15.00

Baseball Heroes

Player	Team	Mint Price
Ruth, Babe ('94)	Yankees	$45.00
Gehrig, Lou ('95)	Yankees	25.00
Paige, Satchel ('96)	Kansas City	16.00
Robinson, Jackie ('97)	Dodgers	13.00

MICROSTARS

MicroStars was a short-lived venture, lasting little more than two years before going out of business. The company hit the market with a 14-figure baseball set in 1995. The set of two-inch figures included some of the biggest stars in the game, and the unique packaging allowed collectors to remove and later replace the figures without damaging the box. The baseball set was MicroStars' last, and today it draws little interest from collectors.

	Mint Price
Complete Set (14)	**$40.00**

Player	Team	Price
Bagwell, Jeff	Astros	$3.00
Belle, Albert	Indians	3.00
Bonds, Barry	Giants	3.00
Clark, Will	Rangers	3.00
Clemens, Roger	Red Sox	3.00
Dykstra, Lenny	Phillies	3.00
Griffey Jr., Ken	Mariners	4.00
Key, Jimmy	Yankees	3.00
Molitor, Paul	Blue Jays	3.00
Piazza, Mike	Dodgers	4.00
Puckett, Kirby	Twins	3.00
Ripken Jr., Cal	Orioles	5.00
Sanders, Deion	Reds	3.00
Thomas, Frank	White Sox	4.00

PROSPORT CREATIONS

Figures from Prosport Creations look similar to figures from Sports Impressions. Unfortunately, most of the pieces don't look like the players they represent. Consequently, the line never caught on with collectors, and the company disappeared from the hobby in the early '90s.

Baseball
(AP—Artist's Proof)

Player		Team	Ht.	Mint Price
Ashburn, Richie				
	(signed)	Phillies	9"	$50.00
	(AP)	Phillies	9"	100.00
	(mini)	Phillies	5"	35.00
Carew, Rod				
	(signed)	Twins	9"	75.00
	(AP)	Twins	9"	100.00
Dickey, Bill				
	(facsimile sig.)	Yankees	9"	50.00
	(AP)	Yankees	9"	100.00
	(mini)	Yankees	5"	35.00
Ford, Whitey				
	(signed)	Yankees	9"	75.00
	(AP)	Yankees	9"	100.00
	(mini)	Yankees	5"	35.00
Garvey, Steve				
	(signed)	Dodgers	9"	100.00
	(AP)	Dodgers	9"	150.00
Gibson, Bob				
	(signed)	Cardinals	9"	60.00
	(AP)	Cardinals	9"	100.00
	(mini)	Cardinals	5"	35.00
Gwynn, Tony				
	(signed)	Padres	9"	100.00
	(AP)	Padres	9"	150.00
Jenkins, Ferguson				
	(signed)	Cubs	9"	75.00
	(signed AP)	Cubs	9"	100.00
Killebrew, Harmon				
	(signed)	Twins	9"	150.00
	(signed AP)	Twins	9"	200.00
Mathews, Eddie				
	(signed)	Braves	9"	100.00
	(signed AP)	Braves	9"	150.00
Palmer, Jim				
	(signed)	Orioles	9"	75.00
	(signed AP)	Orioles	9"	150.00
	(mini)	Orioles	5"	35.00
Robinson, Brooks				
	(signed)	Orioles	9"	100.00
	(signed AP)	Orioles	9"	150.00
Smith, Ozzie				
	(signed)	Cardinals	9"	125.00
	(signed AP)	Cardinals	9"	175.00
Stargell, Willie				
	(signed)	Pirates	9"	100.00
	(signed AP)	Pirates	9"	125.00

RACING CHAMPIONS

Racing Champions recently teamed with *Sports Illustrated* to issue a series of eight-inch pewter figures. Each figure comes with a replica *Sports Illustrated* cover. The first figure debuted in 1997, and the second reached the market six months later. Mickey Mantle is the latest baseball player in the series.

Player	Team	Mint Price
Thomas, Frank	White Sox	$25.00
Griffey Jr., Ken	Mariners	25.00
Mantle, Mickey	Yankees	25.00

ROMITO ENTERPRISES

Long-time sports figure dealer Rick Romito started his own line of prestige pieces in 1996. The first player, Roberto Clemente, was issued in two different poses. The second series included Walter Johnson and Jackie Robinson. Despite high-quality production, initial sales were slow, but the figures seem to be catching on in the hobby.

Player	Team	Edition	Mint Price
Clemente, Roberto			
Roberto at 3,000	Pirates	1,000	$90.00
Roberto at Forbes	Pirates	1,000	170.00
Johnson, Walter	Senators	500	150.00
Robinson, Jackie	Dodgers	1,000	150.00

Walter Johnson

Jackie Robinson

Chapter 7

PLATES

BRADFORD EXCHANGE

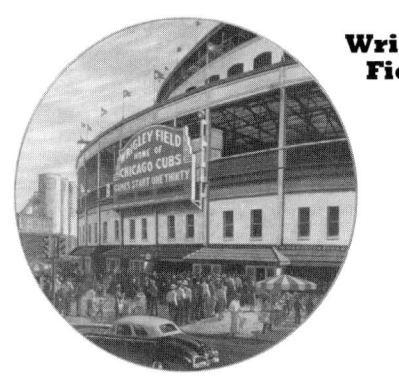

Wrigley Field

J. Roderick MacArthur introduced collectible plates to the United States, when he formed the Bradford Exchange to help collectors all over the world buy and trade collectible plates. Today, the Bradford Exchange manufactures and distributes a wide variety of plates. Although most of their releases feature stars from the entertainment field, they have issued several sports plates with a number of themes.

500 Home Run Club

Plate	Price
Mickey Mantle	$40.00
Ted Williams	40.00

Baseball Record Breakers

Plate	Price
Yogi Berra	$40.00
Lou Gehrig	40.00
Cal Ripken Jr.	40.00
Mike Schmidt	40.00

Classic Ballparks

Plate	Price
Fenway Park	$50.00
Wrigley Field	50.00
Yankee Stadium	50.00

Great Moments in Baseball

Plate	Price
Dizzy Dean: World Series Shutout	$40.00
Joe DiMaggio: The Steak	50.00
Carl Hubbell: The 1934 All-Star	40.00
Ralph Kiner: The Home Run	50.00
Don Larsen: Perfect World Series Game	40.00
Billy Martin: The Rescue Catch	40.00
Bill Mazeroski: Winning Home Run	40.00
Stan Musial: 5-Homer Double-Header	50.00
Satchel Paige: Greatest Games	40.00
Jackie Robinson: Saved Pennant	50.00
Enos Slaughter: The Mad Dash	50.00
Bobby Thomson: The Shot Heard 'Round the World	40.00

Immortals of the Diamonds

Plate	Price
The Georgia Peach, Ty Cobb	$50.00
The Pride of the Yankees, Lou Gehrig	50.00
The Sultan of Swat, Babe Ruth	60.00
The Winningest Pitcher, Cy Young	60.00

Legends of Baseball

Plate	Price
Grover Alexander	$50.00
Ty Cobb: The Georgia Peach	60.00
Mickey Cochrane: Black Mike	50.00
Jimmie Foxx: The Beast	40.00
Lou Gehrig: The Luckiest Man	60.00
Lefty Grove: His Greatest Season	50.00
Rogers Hornsby: The .424 Season	50.00
Shoeless Joe Jackson: Where Triples Die	60.00
Walter Johnson: The Shutout	40.00
Christy Mathewson: 1905 World Series	40.00
Mel Ott: Master Melvin	50.00
Babe Ruth: The Called Shot	75.00
Tris Speaker: The Gray Eagle	40.00
Pie Traynor: Pittsburgh Champ	50.00
Honus Wagner: The Flying Dutchman	50.00
Cy Young: The Perfect Game	60.00

Lost Ballparks

Plate	Price
Ebbetts Field	$100.00
Forbes Field	75.00
Polo Grounds	75.00
Shibe Park	75.00

Mickey Mantle Collection

Plate	Price
500th Home Run	$50.00
1956 World Series	60.00
1961 Home Run Chase	60.00
Bronx Bomber	50.00
The Oklahoma Kid	60.00
Triple Crown Season	50.00

Superstars of Baseball

Plate	Price
Don Drysdale	$35.00
Bob Gibson	35.00
Al Kaline	35.00
Harmon Killebrew	35.00
Willie Mays	35.00
Frank Robinson	35.00
Maury Wills	35.00
Carl Yastrzemski	35.00

Take Me Out to the Ball Game

Plate	Price
Briggs Stadium	$50.00
Cleveland Stadium	60.00
Comiskey Park	60.00
County Stadium	75.00
Ebbetts Field	60.00
Fenway Park	75.00
Forbes Field	60.00
Memorial Stadium	75.00
Polo Grounds	60.00
Shibe Park	60.00
Wrigley Field	60.00
Yankee Stadium	75.00

GARTLAN U.S.A.

Gartlan U.S.A.'s first memorabilia effort was a line of porcelain sports figures. The success of the figurines led Gartlan to create a line of commemorative sports plates. Gartlan has produced plates in three sizes—a small 3¼-inch plate, an 8½-inch plate, and a large 10¼-inch plate. Along with the different sizes, most plates have an Artist's Proof version. These are usually 10¼-inches and are signed by both the player and the artist. Production runs on the AP plates usually number less than 100.

Gartlan has also offered a few plates directly through its club. Only collectors enrolled in the club received offers for the special plates, and Gartlan produced only enough to cover the orders it received. These club-only plates can be very difficult to find on the secondary market.

The edition size refers to the number of plates produced. A "—" indicates that Gartlan has not released a final production run.

Player	Size	Edition	Issue Price	Current Price
Luis Aparicio	Signed 10¼"	1,984	$69.95	$75.00
	8½"	10,000	29.95	30.00
	3¼"	—	14.95	20.00
Al Barlick	3¼"	—	14.95	20.00
	Club Plate 1990	Club only	34.00	110.00
Johnny Bench	Signed 10¼"	1,989	100.00	300.00
	3¼"	—	14.95	35.00
	Artist's Proof plate	100	100.00	395.00
Yogi Berra	Signed 10¼"	2,150	99.95	175.00
	8½"	10,000	29.95	35.00
	3¼"	—	14.95	20.00
	Artist's Proof plate	250	175.00	175.00
George Brett	Signed 10¼"	2,000	100.00	450.00
	3¼"	—	14.95	20.00
	Artist's Proof plate	24	225.00	750.00
Rod Carew	Signed 10¼"	950	69.95	175.00
	8½"	10,000	29.95	30.00
	3¼"	—	14.95	20.00

Player	Size	Edition	Issue Price	Current Price
Carlton Fisk	Signed 10¼"	950	89.95	175.00
	8½"	10,000	29.95	35.00
	3¼"	—	14.95	20.00
	Artist's Proof plate	300	175.00	175.00
Whitey Ford	Signed 10¼"	2,360	69.95	75.00
	8½"	10,000	29.95	35.00
	3¼"	—	14.95	20.00
	Artist's Proof plate	250	175.00	175.00
Ken Griffey Jr.	Signed 10¼"	1,989	99.95	175.00
	8½"	10,000	29.95	40.00
	3¼"	—	14.95	25.00
	Club Plate 1992	Club only	30.00	75.00
Reggie Jackson	3¼"	—	14.95	25.00
	Artist's Proof plate	44	175.00	450.00
Pete Rose (Diamond)	Signed 10¼"	950	195.00	400.00
	3¼"	—	19.00	25.00
	Club Plate 1989	Club only	34.00	150.00
	A.P. Farewell Plate	50	300.00	500.00
Pete Rose (Platinum)	Signed 10¼"	4,192	100.00	625.00
	3¼"	—	19.00	25.00
Mike Schmidt	Signed 10¼"	1,987	100.00	750.00
	3¼"	—	14.95	25.00
	A.P. Plate	56	150.00	600.00
Tom Seaver	Signed 10¼"	1,992	89.95	150.00
	8½"	10,000	29.95	35.00
	3¼"	—	14.95	20.00
Darryl Strawberry	Signed 10¼"	2,500	69.95	125.00
	8½"	10,000	39.95	40.00
	3¼"	—	14.95	20.00
Frank Thomas	Signed 10¼"	1,994	124.95	150.00
	8½"	10,000	29.95	35.00
	3¼"	—	14.95	25.00
Carl Yastrzemski	Signed 10¼"	950	99.95	225.00
	8½"	10,000	29.95	35.00
	3¼"	—	14.95	20.00

HACKETT

Hackett American issued a handful of 8½-inch full-color baseball plates during the mid-1980s. The plates—other than the Babe Ruth, Ty Cobb, and Dwight Gooden issues—were all hand-signed by the player depicted. Hackett issued two different Reggie Jackson plates. The scarcity of these plates has made them some of the more desired and valuable sports plates in the hobby.

Plate	Price
Hank Aaron signed	$350.00
Steve Carlton signed	350.00
Gary Carter signed	175.00
Roger Clemens signed	600.00
Ty Cobb unsigned	100.00
Whitey Ford signed	300.00
Steve Garvey signed	225.00
Dwight Gooden unsigned	100.00
Reggie Jackson, Paluso	900.00
Reggie Jackson, Alexander	700.00
Wally Joyner signed	295.00
Harmon Killebrew signed	325.00
Sandy Koufax signed	400.00
Eddie Mathews signed	300.00
Willie Mays signed	300.00
Pete Rose	45.00
Babe Ruth unsigned	100.00
Nolan Ryan signed	800.00
Tom Seaver signed	325.00
Tom Seaver 300	250.00
Don Sutton signed	325.00

SPORTS IMPRESSIONS

Nolan Ryan

Sports Impressions has issued a wide variety of plates in addition to its line of figures. Most players have plates in three variations. The most common version is the mini-plate, with no released production run. The more popular plates with collectors are the 10¼-inch plates, which had production runs ranging from 2,000–10,000, depending on the player. The Gold Edition is the most limited of all of the plates, with production runs of no more than 2,500. Sports Impressions also released a series of theme plates. A "—" indicates that Sports Impressions didn't release production numbers.

Mike Schmidt

Mark McGwire

Ted Williams

Player	Size	Edition	Price
Wade Boggs	Mini Plate	—	$20.00
	Gold Edition	1,000	125.00
	10¼"	2,000	20.00
Jose Canseco	10¼"	10,000	50.00
	Gold Edition	2,500	125.00
	Mini Plate	—	20.00
Gary Carter	Mini Plate	—	20.00
	Gold Edition	1,000	125.00
	10¼"	2,000	50.00
Will Clark	10¼"	10,000	65.00
	Gold Edition	2,500	125.00
	Mini Plate	—	20.00
Roberto Clemente	10¼"	10,000	75.00
	Mini Plate	—	20.00
Andre Dawson	10¼"	10,000	50.00
	Gold Edition	1,000	125.00
	Mini Plate	—	20.00
Lenny Dykstra	10¼"	10,000	50.00
	Gold Edition	1,000	125.00
	Mini Plate	—	20.00
Bob Feller	10¼"	10,000	50.00
	Gold Edition	2,500	125.00
	Mini Plate	—	20.00
Lou Gehrig	10¼"	10,000	125.00
	Mini Plate	—	20.00
Kirk Gibson	Mini Plate	—	20.00
	Gold Edition	2,500	125.00
	10¼"	10,000	75.00
Dwight Gooden	Gold Edition	3,500	125.00
	Mini Plate	—	125.00
K. Griffey Sr. & K. Griffey Jr.	Gold Edition	1,991	125.00
	Mini Plate	—	25.00
Rickey Henderson	Gold Edition	1,990	125.00
	Mini Plate	—	20.00
Keith Hernandez	10¼"	2,000	50.00
	Gold Edition	1,000	175.00
	Mini Plate	—	20.00
Orel Hershiser	10¼"	10,000	65.00
	Gold Edition	2,500	125.00
	Mini Plate	—	20.00
Greg Jefferies	Mini Plate	—	20.00
	Gold Edition	3,500	125.00

Player	Size	Edition	Price
Al Kaline	10¼"	10,000	50.00
	Gold Edition	1,000	125.00
	Mini Plate	—	20.00
Mickey Mantle "Life of a Legend"	12"	1,968	195.00
Mickey Mantle "Switch Hitter"	Mini Plate	—	20.00
Mickey Mantle "Mickey 7"	Gold Edition	1,500	200.00
Don Mattingly (Player of the Year)	Mini Plate	—	20.00
	10¼"	5,000	60.00
	Gold Edition	2,500	125.00
Don Mattingly (23)	Mini Plate	—	20.00
	10¼"	—	50.00
	Gold Edition	1,991	125.00
Don Mattingly "Yankees Pride"	Mini Plate	—	20.00
	Gold Edition	—	150.00
Willie Mays "The Golden Years"	8½"	5,000	125.00
	Mini Plate	—	20.00
Willie Mays "Famous Catch"	Gold Edition	2,500	150.00
	Mini Plate	—	20.00
Mark McGwire	Gold Edition	2,500	125.00
	Mini Plate	—	20.00
Paul Molitor	Gold Edition	1,000	125.00
	Mini Plate	—	20.00
Joe Morgan	Gold Edition	1,990	150.00
	Mini Plate	—	20.00
Thurman Munson	10¼"	10,000	50.00
	Mini Plate	—	20.00
Stan Musial	Gold Edition	1,963	150.00
	Mini Plate	—	20.00
Brooks Robinson	Gold Edition	1,000	50.00
	Mini Plate	—	20.00
Jackie Robinson	Gold Edition	1,965	150.00
	Mini Plate	—	20.00
Babe Ruth	10¼"	10,000	200.00
	Mini Plate	—	20.00
Nolan Ryan "5,000 Ks"	Gold Edition	5,000	150.00
	Mini Plate	—	20.00
Nolan Ryan "300 Wins"	Gold Edition	1,990	150.00
	Mini Plate	—	20.00
Tom Seaver	Gold Edition	3,311	150.00
	Mini Plate	—	20.00
Duke Snider "Boys of Summer"	Gold Edition	1,500	125.00
	10¼"	5,000	50.00

	Mini Plate	—	20.00
Darryl Strawberry	Gold Edition	3,500	125.00
Alan Trammell	Gold Edition	1,000	125.00
	10¼"	10,000	50.00
	Mini Plate	—	50.00
Honus Wagner	10¼"	10,000	75.00
	Mini Plate	—	20.00
Ted Williams	Gold Edition	1,960	150.00
	Mini Plate	—	20.00
Frank Viola	Mini Plate	—	20.00
	Gold Edition	2,500	125.00
Cy Young	10¼"	10,000	75.00
	Mini Plate	—	20.00

Darryl Strawberry

Dwight Gooden

Theme Plates

Theme	Size	Edition	Price
Boggs/Williams/Yastrzemski "Fenway Tradition"			
	12"	1,000	$200.00
Mantle/Mays/Snider "The Golden Years"			
	12"	1,000	200.00
Mantle/Mays/Snider "Greatest Centerfielders"			
	Gold Edition	3,500	150.00
	Mini Plate	—	20.00
Mantle/Mays/Snider	10¼"	3,500	75.00
	Gold Edition	1,500	150.00
	Mini Plate	—	20.00
Robinson/Williams/Mantle/Yastrzemski "Living Triple Crown"			
	Gold Edition	1,000	150.00
	10¼"	10,000	65.00
	Mini Plate	—	20.00
Ryan/Carlton/Seaver "Kings of Ks"	12"	1,990	195.00
Brooklyn Dodgers "Dem Bums"	10¼"	1,000	50.00
	Mini Plate	—	20.00
Yankees "Living Triple Crown"	Mini Plate	—	—
	10¼"	—	—
	Gold Edition	—	—
"Yankees Tradition"	Mini Plate	—	20.00
	10¼"	10,000	65.00
Brooklyn Dodgers "Wait till next Year"	10¼"	5,000	75.00
	Mini Plate	—	20.00
Yankee Stadium	10½"	5,000	75.00
	Mini Plate	—	20.00

LIMITED EDITION BASEBALL CARDS

HIGHLAND MINT

In 1992, Highland Mint issued reproductions of popular trading cards in bronze and silver. The cards are etched in remarkable detail to look exactly like the player's rookie card and recent-year issues. The cards retailed for $50 (bronze) and $235 (silver), but the prices didn't stay that low for long. Cards that sold out of the bronze and silver editions were reproduced in an extremely limited gold edition that retailed for $500 and also quickly grew in value.

The original license allowed for the reproduction only of Topps cards. In 1994, Pinnacle got into the mix, and in 1995, Highland Mint replicat-ed an Upper Deck card of Michael Jordan playing baseball. This Jordan card was Highland Mint's last card release, as collector demand shifted to the company's less expensive line of coins.

In 1995, Highland Mint experimented with mini-cards, releasing a Cal Ripken Jr. and Lou Gehrig double mini-set to coincide with the con-secutive game record held by Gehrig and about to be broken by Ripken. The set went over so well that four other pairings were introduced, includ-ing Greg Maddux and Cy Young, commemorating Maddux's fourth straight Cy Young Award.

Roger Clemens

Ken Griffey Jr.

Kirby Puckett

Lou Gehrig/Cal Ripken Jr. Mini-Set

Year	Player	Card	Gold Mintage	Gold Price	Silver Mintage	Silver Price	Bronze Mintage	Bronze Price
1992	Alomar, Roberto	'88 Topps	—	—	214	$325.00	928	$80.00
1994	Bagwell, Jeff	'92 Pinnacle	—	—	750	250.00	2,500	75.00
1994	Banks, Ernie	'54 Topps	—	—	437	350.00	920	75.00
1994	Bench, Johnny	'69 Topps	—	—	500	400.00	1,384	80.00
1992	Bonds, Barry	'86 Topps	—	—	596	400.00	2,677	100.00
1992	Brett, George	'75 Topps	—	—	999	325.00	3,560	80.00
1992	Clark, Will	'86 Topps	—	—	150	450.00	1,044	90.00
1992	Clemens, Roger	'85 Topps	—	—	432	350.00	1,789	90.00

Year	Player	Card	Gold Mintage	Gold Price	Silver Mintage	Silver Price	Bronze Mintage	Bronze Price
1992	Gonzalez, Juan	'90 Topps	—	—	365	300.00	1,899	80.00
1992	Griffey Jr., Ken	'92 Topps	500	1,300.00	1,000	600.00	5,000	150.00
1995	Jordan, Michael	'94 Upper Deck	500	1,200.00	1,000	800.00	5,000	160.00
1994	Justice, Dave	'90 Topps	—	—	265	300.00	1,396	75.00
1994	Maddux, Greg	'92 Pinnacle	—	—	750	300.00	2,500	80.00
1994	Mantle, Mickey	'92 Pinnacle	500	1,300.00	1,000	800.00	5,000	180.00
1992	Mattingly, Don	'84 Topps	—	—	414	350.00	1,550	75.00
1994	Molitor, Paul	'79 Topps	—	—	260	350.00	639	125.00
1993	Piazza, Mike	'93 Topps	374	1,000.00	750	500.00	2,500	100.00
1992	Puckett, Kirby	'85 Topps	—	—	359	500.00	1,723	125.00
1992	Ripken Jr., Cal	'92 Topps	—	—	1,000	800.00	4,065	225.00
1992	Robinson, Brooks	'57 Topps	—	—	796	350.00	2,043	75.00
1992	Robinson, Brooks (Signed)		—	—	150	400.00	350	150.00
1992	Ryan, Nolan	'92 Topps	—	—	999	1,200.00	5,000	250.00
1994	Ryan, Nolan	'92 Pinnacle	500	1,200.00	1,000	600.00	5,000	175.00
1994	Salmon, Tim	'93 Topps	—	—	264	300.00	768	100.00
1992	Sandberg, Ryne	'92 Topps	—	—	430	325.00	1,932	80.00
1994	Sanders, Deion	'89 Topps	—	—	187	250.00	668	60.00
1994	Schmidt, Mike	'74 Topps	—	—	500	350.00	1,641	75.00
1992	Smith, Ozzie	'79 Topps	—	—	211	400.00	1,088	100.00
1992	Thomas, Frank	'92 Topps	500	1,500.00	1,000	600.00	5,000	150.00
1992	Winfield, Dave	'74 Topps	—	—	266	325.00	1,216	75.00
1994	Yastrzemski, Carl	'60 Topps	—	—	500	300.00	1,072	75.00
1992	Yount, Robin	'75 Topps	—	—	349	300.00	1.564	75.00
1996	Griffey/Thomas (mini-set)		500	350.00	1,000	250.00	5,000	110.00
1996	Johnson/Ryan (mini-set)		—	—	500	175.00	2,500	85.00
1996	Maddux/Young (mini-set)		—	—	500	175.00	2,500	85.00
1996	Piazza/Campanella (mini-set)		—	—	500	150.00	2,500	75.00
1995	Ripken Jr./Gehrig (mini-set)		375	700.00	500	400.00	2,500	180.00

BLEACHERS

Bleachers began releasing 23 Karat Gold Cards in 1993. The first cards were a tribute to a legend, Nolan Ryan, and the recognition of a future star, Ken Griffey Jr. In 1995, Bleachers joined dozens of other manufacturers in celebrating the record-breaking streak of Cal Ripken Jr. by issuing two cards. Other milestones honored by Bleachers include Eddie Murray's 500 home run and 3,000 hit plateau, and Griffey's chase of Roger Maris' record 61 home runs in a season. Most of these cards carry a sugested retail price of $30.

Year	Player	Mintage	Price
1993	Griffey Jr., Ken #1 (Mega Star)	10,000	$30.00
1993	Ryan, Nolan #1 (27 Seasons)	10,000	30.00
1993	Ryan, Nolan #2 (Strikeout King)	5,714	90.00
1995	Griffey Jr., Ken #2 (silver/gold)	10,000	30.00
1995	Ripken Jr., Cal #1 (Iron Man)	75,000	30.00
1995	Ripken Jr., Cal/Gehrig, Lou (Iron Men)	20,000	30.00
1995	Thomas, Frank	10,000	30.00
1996	Ford, Whitey	25,000	30.00
1996	Mantle, Mickey #1 (Baseball's All-Time Great)	25,000	30.00
1996	Mantle, Mickey #2 (MVP)	10,000	30.00
1996	Mantle, Mickey #3 (Triple Crown)	10,000	30.00
1996	Mantle, Mickey #4 (#7)	10,000	30.00
1996	Mantle, Mickey #5 (Commerce Comet)	10,000	30.00
1996	Mantle, Mickey (Diamond Star)	10,000	30.00
1996	Murray, Eddie #1 (500 HRs)	10,000	30.00
1996	Murray, Eddie #2 (3,000 Hits & 500 HRs)	5,000	30.00
1996	Ripken Jr., Cal #2 (World Record)	10,000	30.00
1996	Ripken Jr., Cal (Diamond Star)	21,310	30.00

Year	Player	Mintage	Price
1996	Ripken Jr., Cal (Japanese)	10,000	30.00
1996	Rodriguez, Alex (black facsimile autograph)	5,000	30.00
1996	Rodriguez, Alex (pearl facsimile autograph)	5,000	30.00
1996	Ryan, Nolan (Diamond Star)	10,000	30.00
1996	Ryan, Nolan (laser cut Diamond Star)	10,000	30.00
1996	Thomas, Frank (Diamond Star)	10,000	30.00
1996	Williams, Ted	25,000	30.00
1996	Williams, Ted (Diamond Star)	10,000	30.00
1997	Clemente, Roberto (Diamond Star)	10,000	30.00
1997	Gehrig, Lou/Ruth, Babe (Avon)	50,000	30.00
1997	Griffey Jr., Ken #3 (triple image)	10,000	30.00
1997	Griffey Jr., Ken #4 (name in teal)	10,000	30.00
1997	Griffey Jr., Ken w/Chasing 62 HRs logo #1	4,997	40.00
1997	Griffey Jr., Ken w/Chasing 62 HRs logo #2	4,997	40.00
1997	Griffey Jr., Ken w/Chasing 62 HRs logo #3	4,997	40.00
1997	Jeter, Derek	10,000	30.00
1997	Ruth, Babe (Diamond Star)	10,000	30.00

GULFSTREAM MINT: SPORTSTRIKES

Gulfstream Mint issued metal baseball cards, called ingots, for two players, Mickey Mantle and Frank Thomas. Both players came in two editions—gold and silver—with mintages of 150 and 750, respectively. The cards are etched in great detail by Susan Wagner, sculptor of Hall of Fame plaques since 1984, and feature a facsimile autograph on both the card and the front of the display box. Each card is encased in a four-screw screw-down holder, which rests in a velvet-lined box. Cards are individually numbered, and registration was available through the company until Gulfstream ceased operation in 1997.

Year	Player	Gold Mintage	Gold Price	Silver Mintage	Silver Price	Set Price
1996	Mantle, Mickey	150	$725.00	750	$400.00	$1,125.00
1996	Thomas, Frank	150	700.00	750	375.00	1,000.00

HOBBY EDITIONS

Hobby Editions was formed by a former employee of Gulfstream Mint who retained the rights to distribute the Keeper Series porcelain replica cards. Each card in the 10-card set is a replica of the player's Topps rookie card, with production limited to 500 sets. Each card is protected in a screw-down holder and display box, and carries a retail price of $70. Mickey Mantle is included in this set, and a bonus card redeemable for one of 50 "Finders" series Mantle cards is inserted at a rate of one in 10 Keeper series cards.

**Joe Jackson
Vintage Keeper**

In 1997, Hobby Editions released a new line called the Vintage Keeper Series consisting of porcelain cards replicating the 1914 Cracker Jack set, with a production run of 150 each. The first card issued was Shoeless Joe Jackson, with Tris Speaker, Honus Wagner, and Ty Cobb following. In addition, there is a "Finders" series Honus Wagner T206 replica limited to 120 cards.

Keeper Series

Year	Player	Mintage	Price
1997	Griffey Jr., Ken ('89 Topps Traded)	500	$100.00
1997	Jeter, Derek ('93 Topps)	500	85.00
1997	Jones, Andruw ('97 Topps)	500	70.00
1997	Jones, Chipper ('91 Topps)	500	90.00
1997	Mantle, Mickey ('52 Topps)	500	125.00
1997	Puckett, Kirby ('85 Topps)	500	75.00
1997	Ripken Jr., Cal ('82 Topps Traded)	500	90.00
1997	Robinson, Jackie ('52 Topps)	500	75.00
1997	Thomas, Frank ('90 Topps)	500	90.00
1997	Williams, Ted ('54 Topps)	500	75.00

Vintage Keeper Series

Year	Player	Mintage	Price
1997	Alexander, Grover Cleveland	150	$75.00
1997	Cobb, Ty	150	90.00
1997	Jackson, Joe	150	75.00
1997	Johnson, Walter	150	75.00
1997	Lajoie, Napoleon	150	75.00
1997	Mathewson, Christy	150	75.00
1997	Speaker, Tris	150	75.00
1997	Wagner, Honus	150	125.00

PREMIER INSTANT REPLAY

Premier Instant Replay cards feature motion prints in a 6¼- by 7¼-inch frame. Each print in the 30-card set showcases a career highlight from players like Ken Griffey Jr., Cal Ripken Jr., and Nomar Garciaparra, and they retail for $7 a piece.

Year	Player	Mintage	Price	Year	Player	Mintage	Price
1997	Alomar, Roberto	5,000	$10.00	1997	Gwynn, Tony	5,000	12.00
1997	Bagwell, Jeff	5,000	12.00	1997	Hollandsworth, Todd	5,000	8.00
1997	Belle, Albert	5,000	12.00	1997	Jeter, Derek	5,000	20.00
1997	Bonds, Barry	5,000	12.00	1997	Jones, Andruw	5,000	15.00
1997	Clark, Tony	5,000	12.00	1997	Jones, Andruw (WS home run)	5,000	15.00
1997	Erstad, Darin	5,000	10.00	1997	Jones, Chipper	5,000	20.00
1997	Garciaparra, Nomar	5,000	15.00	1997	Jordan, Brian	5,000	8.00
1997	Gonzalez, Juan	5,000	12.00	1997	Maddux, Greg	5,000	15.00
1997	Griffey Jr., Ken	5,000	22.00	1997	McGwire, Mark	5,000	15.00
1997	Guerrero, Vladimir	5,000	12.00	1997	Piazza, Mike	5,000	15.00

Year	Player	Mintage	Price	Year	Player	Mintage	Price
1997	Ramirez, Manny	5,000	11.00	1997	Sheffield, Gary	5,000	12.00
1997	Ripken Jr., Cal	5,000	20.00	1997	Sosa, Sammy	5,000	10.00
1997	Rodriguez, Alex	5,000	20.00	1997	Thomas, Frank	5,000	22.00
1997	Rolen, Scott	5,000	12.00	1997	Vaughn, Mo	5,000	12.00
1997	Sandberg, Ryne	5,000	10.00	1997	Young, Dimitri	5,000	8.00

PROMINT

Promint tried to repeat the success of Highland Mint with its own line of gold-etched cards, featuring a lower price point and larger print run. The cards weren't as thick as Highland Mint's, and Promint used its own card design instead of forming a relationship with an existing manufacturer. Unfortunately these cards never caught on with collectors. Today most cards can be found for around the original issue price of $29.95.

**1994
Ken Griffey Jr.**

Year	Player	Promo Mintage	Promo Price	Card Mintage	Card Price
1993	Ryan, Nolan (Gold Sig.)	1,000	$150.00	50,000	$50.00
1993	#1 Ryan, Nolan	250	200.00	50,000	40.00
1993	#2 Bonds, Bobby	1,000	100.00	50,000	30.00
1993	#3 Ryan, Nolan (Anniversary)	1,000	100.00	50,000	30.00
1993	#4 Puckett, Kirby	1,000	100.00	50,000	30.00
1993	#5 Brett, George	1,000	110.00	50,000	40.00
1994	#6 Thomas, Frank	1,000	110.00	50,000	40.00
1994	#7 Griffey Jr., Ken	1,000	125.00	50,000	50.00
1994	#8 Piazza, Mike	1,000	100.00	50,000	30.00
1994	#9 Clemens, Roger	1,000	100.00	50,000	35.00
1994	#10 Bagwell, Jeff	1,000	100.00	50,000	30.00
1994	Ruth, Babe (Diamond)	100	500.00	25,000	150.00
1995	#11 Mattingly, Don	1,000	100.00	50,000	30.00
1995	#12 Smith, Ozzie	1,000	100.00	50,000	30.00
1995	#13 Gwynn, Tony	1,000	110.00	50,000	35.00
1995	#14 Belle, Albert	1,000	100.00	50,000	30.00
1995	#15 Maddux, Greg	1,000	115.00	50,000	40.00
1995	#16 Ripken Jr., Cal	1,000	115.00	50,000	45.00
1995	#17 Sanders, Deion	1,000	100.00	50,000	30.00
1995	#18 Fielder, Cecil	1,000	100.00	50,000	30.00
1995	#19 Nomo, Hideo	1,000	110.00	50,000	40.00
1995	#20 Bichette, Dante	1,000	100.00	50,000	30.00
1995	#21 Vaughn, Mo	1,000	100.00	50,000	30.00
1995	#22 Canseco, Jose	1,000	100.00	50,000	30.00
1996	#23 Sandberg, Ryne	1,000	100.00	50,000	30.00
1996	#24 McGwire, Mark	1,000	125.00	50,000	50.00
1996	#25 Griffey Jr., Ken	1,000	125.00	50,000	50.00
1996	#26 Murray, Eddie	1,000	100.00	50,000	30.00

UPPER DECK

Upper Deck issued two single gold baseball cards through its Upper Deck Authenticated division. These cards were produced by Authentic Images for Upper Deck, and the design was unlike Upper Deck's regular card releases. A poor marketing effort prevented these cards from becoming popular in the hobby. Currently Upper Deck has no plans for additional cards.

Year	Player	Mintage	Price
1996	Griffey Jr., Ken "The Natural"	1,996	$150.00
1996	Nomo, Hideo "Rookie of the Year"	1,996	150.00

BASEBALL MEDALLIONS

Ken Griffey Jr. Enviromint

Ken Griffey Jr. Highland Mint Magnum Series

Barry Bonds Highland Mint

Ken Griffey Jr. Highland Mint

Cal Ripken Jr. Highland Mint

HIGHLAND MINT

In 1994, Highland Mint built on the success of its limited edition cards with a line of sports medallions. The scheme was the same, in that the company started with bronze and silver editions and didn't offer gold until later. The bronze mintage was 25,000 with a retail price of $9.99, while silver's numbers were 5,000 and $19.95. The gold line—the Gold Signature Series—featured silver coins with gold overlays of the featured players. Mintage was 1,500 of each, retailing for $49.95. All three of these products came encased in hard plastic capsules in velvet-lined jewelery boxes.

At the outset, the coins were red hot—medallion prices were rising within weeks of release. To further capitalize on the popularity, Highland Mint started offering collectors something different: jumbo medallions. The Magnum Series kicked off with Cal Ripken Jr. and Ken Griffey Jr., each depicted on bronze and silver medallions 2.5 inches in diameter—more than twice the size of the regular medallions. Each coin was packaged in a velvet box that opened like a book. Mintage was 3,500 bronze ($35 retail) and 750 silver ($150 retail). Like the cards, when bronze and

silver sold out, gold versions were introduced (375 mintage, $250 apiece).

In 1997, Highland Mint pounded the market with several new series, most in response to the success of these in other sports. Sets of two and three medallions encased in one box were issued. Bronze medallions with matching phone cards were introduced late in '97. The most popular of the new issues was the Elite Series. Griffey led the charge for these 44-millimeter medallions, issued in bronze (5,000 mintage), silver (2,500), and gold signature versions (1,000). Retail prices were $20, $40, and $80 respectively. As a bonus, 500 of the bronze medallions were replaced with gold-plated coins. Secondary market values have risen to the same level as the gold signature versions.

The player selection for all the series is stocked with baseball's big boys, the hottest rookies, and some of the biggest names from the past. The coins are individually numbered and are licensed by Major League Baseball. Each of the medallions and sets comes with a numbered certificate of authenticity, matching the number on the coin(s).

Year	Player	Gold Mintage	Gold Price	Silver Mintage	Silver Price	Bronze Mintage	Bronze Price
1996	Alomar, Roberts	—	—	5,000	$30.00	—	—
1994	Bagwell, Jeff	—	—	5,000	30.00	25,000	$12.00
1995	Belle, Albert	—	—	5,000	25.00	—	—
1994	Boggs, Wade	—	—	5,000	25.00	—	—
1994	Bonds, Barry	—	—	5,000	30.00	—	—
1995	Bonds, Barry (Gold Signature)	1,500	$85.00	—	—	—	—
1995	Canseco, Jose	—	—	5,000	20.00	—	—
1995	Clark, Will	—	—	5,000	20.00	—	—
1994	Clemens, Roger	—	—	5,000	40.00	—	—
1996	Fielder, Cecil	—	—	5.000	20.00	—	—
1994	Griffey Jr., Ken	—	—	5,000	50.00	25,000	30.00
1995	Griffey Jr., Ken (Gold Signature)	1,500	125.00	—	—	—	—
1996	Griffey Jr., Ken (Magnum)	375	300.00	750	200.00	5,000	90.00

Year	Player	Gold Mintage	Gold Price	Silver Mintage	Silver Price	Bronze Mintage	Bronze Price
1997	Griffey Jr., Ken (Elite Ser.)	1,000	100.00	2,500	55.00	4,500	30.00
1997	Griffey Jr., Ken (Elite Series, Gold Plated)	500	100.00	—	—	—	—
1997	Griffey Jr., Ken (Medallion/Phone card)	—	—	—	—	2,500	45.00
1995	Gwynn, Tony	—	—	5,000	30.00	—	—
1997	Irabu, Hideki	—	—	5,000	20.00	—	—
1996	Jeter, Derek	—	—	5,000	30.00	25,000	15.00
1996	Jeter, Derek (Gold Signatuere)	1,500	85.00	—	—	—	—
1997	Jeter, Derek (Medallion/Phone card)	—	—	—	—	2,500	40.00
1997	Jones, Andruw	—	—	5,000	30.00	—	—
1995	Jones, Chipper	—	—	5,000	40.00	25,000	20.00
1996	Jones, Chipper (Gold Signatuere)	1,500	85.00	—	—	—	—
1997	Jones, Chipper (Medallion/Phone card)	—	—	—	—	2,500	40.00
1997	Jones, Chipper (Elite Series)	1,000	80.00	2,500	40.00	4,500	25.00
1997	Jones, Chipper (Elite Series, Gold Plated)	500	80.00	—	—	—	—
1994	Maddux, Greg	—	—	5,000	35.00	25,000	18.00
1995	Maddux, Greg (Gold Signatuere)	1,500	90.00	—	—	—	—
1997	Maddux, Greg (Medallion/Phone card)	—	—	—	—	2,500	40.00
1994	Mattingly, Don	—	—	5,000	30.00	25,000	15.00
1997	Mantle, Mickey	—	—	—	—	25,000	20.00
1997	Mantle, Mickey (Medallion/Phone card)	—	—	—	—	2,500	60.00
1998	Mantle, Mickey (Medallion/Motion card)	—	—	—	—	2,500	80.00
1998	Mantle, Mickey (Elite Series)	1,000	80.00	2,500	40.00	4,500	25.00
1997	McGwire, Mark	—	—	5,000	30.00	—	—
1997	Mondesi, Raul	—	—	5,000	20.00	—	—
1996	Murray, Eddie	—	—	5,000	25.00	—	—
1995	Nomo, Hideo	1,500	60.00	5,000	30.00	—	—
1994	Piazza, Mike	—	—	5,000	30.00	25,000	15.00
1994	Piazza, Mike (Gold Signatuere)	1,500	125.00	—	—	—	—
1997	Piazza, Mike (Medallion/Phone card)	—	—	—	—	2,500	35.00
1995	Puckett, Kirby	—	—	5,000	30.00	—	—
1996	Puckett, Kirby (Gold Signatuere)	1,500	70.00	—	—	—	—
1994	Ripken Jr., Cal	—	—	5,000	70.00	25,000	20.00
1995	Ripken Jr., Cal (Gold Signatuere)	1,500	125.00	—	—	—	—
1996	Ripken Jr., Cal (RB)	—	—	—	—	15,000	20.00
1996	Ripken Jr., Cal (Magnum)	375	350.00	750	200.00	3,000	100.00
1997	Ripken Jr., Cal (Elite Series)	1,000	90.00	2,500	50.00	4,500	35.00
1997	Ripken Jr., Cal (Elite Series, Gold Plated)	500	85.00	—	—	—	—
1997	Ripken Jr., Cal (Medallion/Phone card)	—	—	—	—	2,500	45.00
1995	Rodriguez, Alex	—	—	5,000	35.00	25,000	20.00
1996	Rodriguez, Alex (Gold Signatuere)	1,500	80.00	—	—	—	—
1997	Rodriguez, Alex (Magnum)	—	—	750	150.00	3,000	65.00
1997	Rodriguez, Alex (Elite Series)	1,000	80.00	2,500	40.00	4,500	30.00
1997	Rodriguez, Alex (Elite Series, Gold Plate)	500	80.00	—	—	—	—
1997	Rodriguez, Alex (Medallion/Phone card)	—	—	—	—	2,500	40.00
1996	Ruth, Babe (Magnum)	375	250.00	750	150.00	3,500	60.00
1997	Ruth, Babe (Magnum/Motion Card)	—	—	1,000	60.00	—	—
1996	Ryan, Nolan (Magnum)	—	—	750	175.00	3,500	70.00
1996	Sandberg, Ryne	—	—	5,000	25.00	—	—
1995	Smith, Ozzie	—	—	5,000	30.00	—	—
1994	Thomas, Frank	—	—	5,000	50.00	25,000	20.00
1995	Thomas, Frank (Gold Signatuere)	1,500	125.00	—	—	—	—
1997	Thomas, Frank (Magnum)	—	—	750	150.00	3,000	60.00
1997	Thomas, Frank (Medallion/Phone card)	—	—	—	—	2,500	40.00
1997	Thomas, Frank (Elite Series)	1,000	80.00	2,500	40.00	4,500	30.00
1997	Thomas, Frank (Elite Series, Gold Plated)	500	80.00	—	—	—	—
1996	Vaughn, Mo	—	—	5,000	20.00	—	—
1994	Matching Pairs Set (9)	—	—	500	500.00	—	—
1995	Matching Pairs Set (9)	—	—	500	325.00	—	—

Year	Player	Gold Mintage	Gold Price	Silver Mintage	Silver Price	Bronze Mintage	Bronze Price
1995	Matching Pairs Set (9)	—	—	100	300.00	—	—
1997	Albert Belle/Frank Thomas Set (2)	—	—	—	—	2,500	30.00
1997	Ken Griffey Jr./Alex Rodriguez (2)	—	—	—	—	2,500	30.00
1997	Young Guns (Jeter, Jones, Rodriguez)	—	—	—	—	2,500	40.00
1997	Pinstripe Heroes (Mantle, Mattingly, Jeter)	—	—	2,500	40.00	—	—
1997	Home Run Heroes (McGwire, Griffey, Jr.)	1,500	50.00	—	—	—	—
1997	Southern Pride (C. Jones, Maddux, A. Jones)	—	—	2,500	35.00	—	—
1997	Pacific Power (Rodriguez, Johnson, Griffey, Jr.)	—	—	2,500	35.00	—	—

Elite Series Proof Set

In addition to the three medallions issued for each player in the Elite Series, Highland Mint offered proof sets containing each of the three medallions, with matching numbers. Retail price for each of the 350 sets was $150.

Year	Player	Mintage	Price
1997	Griffey Jr., K.	350	$185.00
1997	Jones, C.	350	160.00
1998	Mantle, M.	350	175.00
1997	Ripken Jr., C.	350	185.00
1997	Rodriguez, A.	350	175.00
1997	Thomas, F.	350	175.00

HOBBY EDITIONS

Like Highland Mint, Hobby Editions also expanded from cards to medallions. The Chosen Few player medallions are also the work of Baseball Hall of Fame sculptor Susan Wagner. In addition to her work with the Hall, Wagner also sculpted the bronze statue of Roberto Clemente that was unveiled at the 1994 All-Star Game in Pittsburgh.

The player selection in the Chosen Few series includes sluggers Ken Griffey Jr. and Frank Thomas and newcomers Alex Rodriguez and Derek Jeter. Each release entailed 1,000 bronze, 500 silver, and 250 gold, with 50 proof sets including one of each medallion. Issue prices were $19, $35, $55, and $130, respectively.

Year	Player	Gold Mintage	Gold Price	Silver Mintage	Silver Price	Bronze Mintage	Bronze Price
1997	Griffey Jr., Ken	250	$90.00	500	$50.00	1,000	$30.00
1997	Jeter, Derek	250	65.00	500	40.00	1,000	20.00
1997	Jones, Chipper	250	80.00	500	45.00	1,000	25.00
1997	Maddux, Greg	250	55.00	500	40.00	1,000	20.00
1997	Piazza, Mike	250	65.00	500	40.00	1,000	20.00
1997	Ripken Jr., Cal	250	80.00	500	45.00	1,000	25.00
1997	Rodriguez, Alex	250	55.00	500	40.00	1,000	20.00
1997	Thomas, Frank	250	65.00	500	40.00	1,000	20.00

Chosen Few Medallion Proof Sets

Year	Player	Mintage	Price
1997	Griffey Jr., Ken	50	$140.00
1997	Jeter, Derek	50	130.00
1997	Jones, Chipper	50	135.00
1997	Maddux, Greg	50	130.00
1997	Piazza, Mike	50	130.00
1997	Ripken Jr., Cal	50	135.00
1997	Rodriguez, Alex	50	130.00
1997	Thomas, Frank	50	130.00

CHICAGOLAND PROCESSING ENVIROMINT

Chicagoland first produced medallions in 1985. The company named its product Enviromint because the silver medallions are made from recycled silver taken from film scraps. Each coin issued commemorates a specific milestone or event, like George Brett's 3,000th hit, All-Star games, or division championship winners.

Starting in 1995, the coins were produced in bronze, silver, gold, and 24K versions, as well as proof sets. Mintage for these medallions ranged from 95 for some of the gold medallions to 25,000 for some of the first produced. The coins are individually numbered and are licensed by Major League Baseball.

Two of the most sought-after medallions are the 1990 Nolan Ryan 300th victory (limited to 1,500 coins and selling for $75), and the 1990 Ken Griffey Sr. and Jr. two piece set (3,300, $85).

Prices are for coins in mint condition.

World Series Champions

Year	Team	Mintage	Issue Price	Price
1986	New York Mets	25,000	$29.95	$45.00
1987	Minnesota Twins	25,000	29.95	45.00
1988	Los Angeles Dodgers	25,000	29.95	35.00
1989	Oakland Athletics	6,550	29.95	35.00
1990	Cincinnati Reds	25,000	29.95	35.00
1992	Toronto Blue Jays	25,000	29.95	60.00
1995	Atlanta Braves Silver	10,000	29.95	40.00
1995	Atlanta Braves 24K	5,000	49.95	60.00
1995	Atlanta Braves 3-pc. Proof Set	1,995	125.00	140.00
1995	Atlanta Braves Gold	195	850.00	850.00
1996	New York Yankees Silver	10,000	29.95	40.00
1996	New York Yankees 24K	3,000	49.95	60.00
1996	New York Yankees 3-pc. Proof Set	1,000	125.00	140.00
1996	New York Yankees Gold	96	850.00	850.00
1997	Florida Marlins 6-pc. Photo/Coin Set	500	299.95	300.00
1997	Florida Marlins Silver	25,000	34.95	35.00
1997	Florida Marlins 24K	7,500	49.95	50.00
1997	Florida Marlins 3-pc. Proof Set	1,000	125.00	125.00
1997	Florida Marlins Gold	197	850.00	850.00

American League Champions

Year	Team	Mintage	Issue Price	Price
1987	Minnesota Twins	5,000	$35.00	$45.00
1988	Oakland Athletics	4,250	29.95	32.50
1989	Oakland Athletics	6,550	29.95	32.50
1990	Oakland Athletics	10,000	29.95	30.00
1991	Minnesota Twins	10,000	29.95	30.00
1992	Toronto Blue Jays	10,000	29.95	55.00
1995	Cleveland Indians Silver	10,000	29.95	35.00
1995	Cleveland Indians 24K	3,000	29.95	40.00
1995	Cleveland Indians 3-pc. Proof Set	250	125.00	140.00
1995	Cleveland Indians Gold	95	850.00	850.00
1996	New York Yankees Silver	10,000	29.95	40.00
1996	New York Yankees 24K	3,000	49.95	60.00
1996	New York Yankees 3-pc. Proof Set	250	125.00	140.00
1997	Cleveland Indians Silver	10,000	34.95	35.00
1997	Cleveland Indians 24K	3,000	49.95	50.00
1997	Cleveland Indians 10-pc. Proof Set	500	125.00	125.00
1997	Cleveland Indians 6-pc. WS Photo/Coin Set	500	299.95	300.00

National League Champions

Year	Team	Mintage	Issue Price	Price
1987	St. Louis Cardinals	5,000	$29.95	$45.00
1988	Los Angeles Dodgers	4,050	29.95	32.50
1989	San Francisco Giants	8,100	29.95	32.50
1990	Cincinnati Reds	10,000	29.95	30.00
1992	Atlanta Braves	10,000	29.95	49.95
1994	Atlanta Braves Gold	95	850.00	850.00
1995	Atlanta Braves Silver	10,000	29.95	40.00
1995	Atlanta Braves 24K	3,000	49.95	60.00
1995	Atlanta Braves 3-pc. Proof Set	95	125.00	140.00
1997	Florida Marlins Silver	10,000	34.95	35.00
1997	Florida Marlins 24K	3,000	49.95	50.00
1997	Florida Marlins 10-pc. Proof Set	500	125.00	125.00

American League East Division Winners

Year	Team	Mintage	Issue Price	Price
1987	Detroit Tigers	1,800	$29.95	$35.00
1988	Boston Red Sox	500	29.95	45.00
1989	Toronto Blue Jays	2,300	29.95	75.00
1990	Boston Red Sox	450	29.95	50.00
1991	Toronto Blue Jays	5,000	29.95	75.00
1992	Toronto Blue Jays	5,000	29.95	58.00
1995	Boston Red Sox Silver	5,000	29.95	40.00
1995	Boston Red Sox 24K	1,995	49.95	60.00
1995	Boston Red Sox Bronze	500	14.95	20.00
1995	Boston Red Sox 3-pc. Proof Set	95	125.00	140.00
1997	Baltimore Orioles Silver	1,997	34.95	35.00
1997	Baltimore Orioles 24K	500	49.95	50.00
1997	Baltimore Orioles 3-pc. Proof Set	197	125.00	125.00

American League West Division Winners

Year	Team	Mintage	Issue Price	Price
1987	Minnesota Twins	3,000	$29.95	$35.00
1988	Oakland Athletics	800	29.95	35.00
1989	Oakland Athletics	900	29.95	35.00
1990	Oakland Athletics	150	29.95	75.00
1991	Minnesota Twins	5,000	29.95	30.00
1995	Seattle Mariners Silver	5,000	29.95	40.00
1995	Seattle Mariners 24K	1,995	49.95	60.00
1995	Seattle Mariners Bronze	500	14.95	20.00
1995	Seattle Mariners 3-pc. Proof Set	95	125.00	140.00

Year	Team	Mintage	Issue Price	Price
1996	Texas Rangers Silver	1,996	29.95	35.00
1996	Texas Rangers 24K	500	49.95	55.00
1996	Texas Rangers 3-pc. Proof Set	196	125.00	130.00
1997	Seattle Mariners Silver	1,997	34.95	35.00
1997	Seattle Mariners 24K	500	49.95	50.00
1997	Seattle Mariners 3-pc. Proof Set	197	125.00	125.00

National League East Division Winners

Year	Team	Mintage	Issue Price	Price
1987	St. Louis Cardinals	1,500	$29.95	$35.00
1988	New York Mets	1,100	29.95	35.00
1989	Chicago Cubs	6,200	29.95	35.00
1989	Chicago Cubs	10,000	29.95	35.00
1990	Pittsburgh Pirates	1,300	29.95	40.00
1991	Pittsburgh Pirates	450	29.95	50.00
1995	Atlanta Braves Silver	5,000	29.95	40.00
1995	Atlanta Braves 24K	1,995	49.95	60.00
1995	Atlanta Braves Bronze	500	14.95	20.00
1995	Altanta Braves 3-pc. Proof Set	95	125.00	125.00
1997	Atlanta Braves Silver	1,997	34.95	35.00
1997	Atlanta Braves 24K	500	49.95	50.00
1997	Atlanta Braves 3-pc. Proof Set	197	125.00	125.00

National League West Division Winners

Year	Team	Mintage	Issue Price	Price
1987	San Francisco Giants	1,000	$29.95	$35.00
1988	Los Angeles Dodgers	800	29.95	35.00
1989	San Francisco Giants	600	29.95	35.00
1990	Cincinnati Reds	1,050	29.95	55.00
1991	Atlanta Braves	5,000	29.95	32.50
1992	Atlanta Braves	5,000	29.95	34.50
1995	Los Angeles Dodgers Silver	5,000	29.95	40.00
1995	Los Angeles Dodgers 24K	1,995	49.95	60.00
1995	Los Angeles Dodgers Bronze	500	14.95	20.00
1995	Los Angeles Dodgers 3-pc. Proof Set	95	125.00	125.00
1997	San Francisco Giants Silver	1,997	34.95	35.00
1997	San Francisco Giants 24K	500	49.95	50.00
1997	San Francisco Giants 3-pc. Proof Set	197	125.00	125.00

American League Central Division Winners

Year	Team	Mintage	Issue Price	Price
1995	Cleveland Indians Silver	5,000	$29.95	$40.00
1995	Cleveland Indians 24K	1,995	49.95	60.00
1995	Cleveland Indians 3-pc. Proof Set	95	125.00	125.00
1997	Cleveland Indians Silver	1,997	34.95	35.00
1997	Cleveland Indians 24K	500	49.95	50.00
1997	Cleveland Indians 3-pc. Proof Set	197	125.00	125.00

National League Central Division Winners

Year	Team	Mintage	Issue Price	Price
1995	Cincinnati Reds Silver	5,000	$29.95	$40.00
1995	Cincinnati Reds 24K	1,995	49.95	60.00
1995	Cincinnati Reds Bronze	500	14.95	20.00
1995	Cincinnati Reds 3-pc. Proof Set	95	125.00	125.00
1997	Houston Astros Silver	1,997	34.95	40.00
1997	Houston Astros 24K	500	49.95	60.00
1997	Houston Astros 3-pc. Proof Set	197	125.00	125.00

All-Star Game

Year	Team	Mintage	Issue Price	Price
1988	Cincinnati	2,000	$29.95	$45.00
1989	Anaheim	2,000	29.95	45.00
1991	Toronto	5,000	29.95	60.00
1992	San Diego	5,000	29.95	40.00
1993	Baltimore	5,000	29.95	35.00
1994	Pittsburgh Silver	5,000	29.95	40.00
1994	Pittsburgh 24K	500	49.95	60.00
1995	Texas Silver	5,000	29.95	40.00
1995	Texas 24K	1,000	49.95	60.00
1995	Texas Bronze	5,000	14.95	20.00
1995	Texas 3-pc. Proof Set	95	125.00	125.00
1996	Philadelphia Silver	1,996	29.95	40.00
1996	Philadelphia 24K	500	49.95	60.00
1996	Philadelphia 3-pc. Proof Set	196	125.00	125.00
1996	Philadelphia Ball/Coin	500	49.95	50.00
1996	Philadelphia Ball/Coin with Case	500	79.95	80.00
1997	Cleveland Silver	1,997	29.95	30.00
1997	Cleveland 24K	500	49.95	50.00
1997	Cleveland 3-pc. Proof Set	197	125.00	125.00
1997	Cleveland Ball/Coin with Case	1,997	124.95	125.00
1998	Colorado (Exclusive at field)	1,998	N/A	N/A
1998	Colorado Silver	1,998	34.95	35.00
1998	Colorado 24K	500	49.95	50.00
1998	Colorado 3-pc. Proof Set	198	125.00	125.00

Player Coins

Year	Team	Mintage	Issue Price	Price
1995	Alomar, Roberto Silver	1,500	$29.95	$35.00
1995	Alomar, Roberto 24K	125	49.95	60.00
1995	Alomar, Roberto Bronze	500	14.95	20.00
1995	Alomar, Roberto Silver/All-Star	1,995	29.95	35.00
1995	Alomar, Roberto 24K/All-Star	500	49.95	60.00
1995	Alomar, Roberto Bronze/All-Star	1,995	14.95	20.00
1995	Alomar, Roberto All-Star 3-pc. Proof Set	95	125.00	125.00
1996	Alomar, Roberto All-Star Ball/Coin Set	100	124.95	125.00
1997	Alomar, Roberto All-Star Photo/Coin Set	500	49.95	50.00
1997	Alomar, Roberto 3-pc. Photo/Coin Set	197	150.00	150.00
1997	Alomar, Sandy WS Photo/Coin Set	1,997	49.95	50.00
1997	Alou, Moises All-Star Photo/Coin Set	500	49.95	50.00
1997	Alou, Moises All-Star 3-pc. Proof Set	197	150.00	150.00
1997	Alou, Moises WS Photo/Coin Set	1,997	49.95	50.00

Year	Team	Mintage	Issue Price	Price
1997	Anderson, Brady All-Star Photo/Coin Set	500	49.95	50.00
1997	Anderson, Brady 3-pc. Photo/Coin Set	197	150.00	150.00
1997	Assenmacher, Paul WS Photo/Coin Set	1,997	49.95	50.00
1995	Baerga, Carlos Silver/All-Star	1,995	29.95	35.00
1995	Baerga, Carlos 24K/All-Star	500	49.95	60.00
1995	Baerga, Carlos Bronze/All-Star	1,995	14.95	20.00
1995	Baerga, Carlos All-Star 3-pc. Proof Set	95	125.00	130.00
1996	Bagwell, Jeff Silver	1,996	29.95	30.00
1996	Bagwell, Jeff 24K Select	500	49.95	50.00
1996	Bagwell, Jeff 3-pc. Proof Set	196	125.00	125.00
1996	Bagwell, Jeff All-Star Ball/Coin Set	100	124.95	125.00
1997	Bagwell, Jeff All-Star 3-pc. Photo Set	197	150.00	150.00
1995	Albert Belle Silver	1,500	29.95	35.00
1995	Belle, Albert 24K	125	49.95	60.00
1995	Belle, Albert Bronze	500	14.95	20.00
1995	Belle, Albert Silver/All-Star	1,995	29.95	35.00
1995	Belle, Albert 24K/All-Star	500	49.95	60.00
1995	Belle, Albert Bronze/All-Star	1,995	14.95	20.00
1995	Belle, Albert All-Star 3-pc. Proof Set	95	125.00	130.00
1996	Belle, Albert All-Star Ball/Coin Set	100	124.95	130.00
1996	Belle, Albert Framed Photo/Coin Set	96	125.00	130.00
1997	Belle, Albert Silver	1,997	34.95	35.00
1997	Belle, Albert 24K/All-Star	500	49.95	50.00
1997	Belle, Albert 3-pc. Proof Set	197	125.00	125.00
1997	Belle, Albert All-Star Photo/Coin Set	500	49.95	50.00
1997	Belle, Albert 3-pc. All-Star Photo/Coin Set	197	150.00	150.00
1989	Bench, Johnny Silver/Hall of Fame	15,000	29.95	45.00
1995	Bichette, Dante Silver/All-Star	1,995	29.95	35.00
1995	Bichette, Dante 24K/All-Star	500	49.95	60.00
1995	Bichette, Dante Bronze/All-Star	1,995	14.95	20.00
1995	Bichette, Dante All-Star 3-pc. Proof Set	95	125.00	130.00
1996	Bichette, Dante All-Star Ball/Coin Set	100	124.95	125.00
1996	Bichette, Dante Framed Photo/Coin Set	96	125.00	125.00
1997	Bichette, Dante NL Photo/Coin Set	500	49.95	50.00
1997	Biggio, Craig All-Star Photo/Coin Set	500	49.95	50.00
1997	Biggio, Craig 3-pc. Photo/Coin Set	197	150.00	150.00
1997	Blauser, Jeff All-Star Photo/Coin Set	500	49.95	50.00
1997	Blauser, Jeff All-Star Photo/Coin Set	197	150.00	150.00
1987	Boggs, Wade Batting Title	1,249	29.95	55.00
1993	Boggs, Wade	13,751	30.00	43.00
1995	Boggs, Wade Silver/All-Star	1,995	29.95	35.00
1995	Boggs, Wade 24K/All-Star	500	49.95	60.00
1995	Boggs, Wade Bronze/All-Star	1,995	14.95	20.00
1995	Boggs, Wade All-Star 3-pc. Proof Set	95	125.00	130.00
1996	Boggs, Wade All-Star Ball/Coin Set	100	124.95	130.00
1996	Boggs, Wade WS Reverse	500	29.95	30.00
1996	Boggs, Wade WS 3-pc. Proof Set	96	125.00	125.00
1996	Boggs, Wade WS Combo	196	125.00	125.00
1996	Boggs, Wade Framed Photo/Coin Set	96	125.00	125.00
1993	Bonds, Barry Silver/NL MVP	1,500	29.95	45.00
1993	Bonds, Barry 24K/NL MVP	125	49.95	65.00
1993	Bonds, Barry Bronze/NL MVP	500	14.95	20.00
1995	Bonds, Barry Silver/All-Star	1,995	29.95	40.00
1995	Bonds, Barry 24K/All-Star	500	49.95	60.00
1995	Bonds, Barry Bronze/All-Star	1,995	14.95	20.00
1995	Bonds, Barry All-Star 3-pc. Proof Set	95	125.00	125.00
1996	Bonds, Barry All-Star Ball/Coin Set	100	124.95	125.00
1997	Bonds, Barry All-Star Photo/Coin Set	500	49.95	50.00
1997	Bonds, Barry All-Star 3-pc. Photo/Coin Set	197	150.00	150.00
1997	Bonilla, Bobby WS Photo/Coin Set	1,997	49.95	50.00
1991	Brett, George Silver/3 Decades of Baseball	2,033	29.95	45.00
1992	Brett, George Silver/3,000th Hit	6,273	29.95	45.00
1992	Brett, George/Yount, Robin 2-pc. Set	1,000	82.95	95.00
1992	Brett, George Silver	15,000	29.95	40.00
1992	Brett, George Silver/3,000 Hits	15,000	29.95	40.00
1995	Buhner, Jay Silver	1,995	29.95	35.00
1995	Buhner, Jay 24K	500	49.95	60.00
1995	Buhner, Jay Bronze	1,995	14.95	20.00
1995	Buhner, Jay 3-pc. Proof Set	95	125.00	130.00
1996	Buhner, Jay All-Star Ball/Coin Set	100	124.95	130.00
1996	Caminiti, Ken NL MVP 3-pc. Proof Set	196	125.00	130.00
1997	Caminiti, Ken All-Star Photo/Coin Set	500	49.95	50.00
1997	Caminiti, Ken All-Star 3-pc. Photo/Coin Set	197	150.00	150.00
1990	Canseco, Jose Silver/40-40, Athletics	6,000	29.95	45.00
1992	Canseco, Jose Silver/40-40, Rangers	9,000	29.95	42.00
1995	Canseco, Jose Silver	1,995	29.95	35.00
1995	Canseco, Jose 24K	500	49.95	60.00
1995	Canseco, Jose Bronze	1,995	14.95	20.00
1995	Canseco, Jose 3-pc. Proof Set	95	125.00	125.00
1990	Carlton, Steve 4 Cy Youngs	15,000	29.95	45.00
1995	Carter, Joe Silver	1,500	29.95	35.00
1995	Carter, Joe 24K	125	49.95	60.00
1995	Carter, Joe Bronze	500	14.95	20.00
1995	Carter, Joe Silver	1,995	29.95	35.00
1995	Carter, Joe 24K	500	49.95	60.00
1995	Carter, Joe Bronze	1,995	14.95	20.00
1995	Carter, Joe 3-pc. Proof Set	95	125.00	130.00
1996	Carter, Joe All-Star Ball/Coin Set	100	124.95	125.00
1995	Castilla, Vinny Silver/All-Star	1,995	29.95	35.00
1995	Castilla, Vinny 24K/All-Star	500	49.95	60.00
1995	Castilla, Vinny Bronze/All-Star	1,995	14.95	20.00
1995	Castilla, Vinny All-Star 3-pc. Proof Set	95	125.00	130.00
1990	Clark, Will	2,389	29.95	42.00
1995	Clark, Will Silver	15,000	29.95	35.00
1995	Clark, Will Silver	1,995	29.95	40.00
1995	Clark, Will 24K	500	49.95	60.00
1995	Clark, Will Bronze	1,995	14.95	20.00
1995	Clark, Will 3-pc. Proof Set	95	125.00	130.00
1997	Clark, Will All-Star Photo/Coin Set	500	49.95	50.00
1990	Clemens, Roger Silver/'86-'87 Cy Young	740	29.95	60.00
1995	Clemens, Roger Silver	1,995	29.95	38.00
1995	Clemens, Roger 24K	500	49.95	60.00
1995	Clemens, Roger Bronze	1,995	14.95	20.00
1995	Clemens, Roger 3-pc. Proof Set	95	125.00	135.00
1997	Clemens, R. Cy Young Photo/Coin Set	500	49.95	50.00
1997	Clemens, Roger 24K/Cy Young	1,000	34.95	35.00
1988	Clemente, Roberto Silver/1973 HOF	15,000	29.95	55.00
1994	Clemente, R. Silver/All-Star Game	5,000	29.95	40.00
1994	Clemente, Roberto 24K/All-Star Game	1,000	49.95	75.00
1995	Clemente, Roberto Silver/Career	5,000	29.95	40.00
1995	Clemente, Roberto 24K/Career	1,000	49.95	75.00
1995	Clemente, Roberto Silver/Card	1,973	150.00	225.00

Year	Team	Mintage	Issue Price	Price
1995	Clemente, Roberto 24K/Card	500	199.00	350.00
1995	Clemente, Roberto Silver Coin/Card Set	500	185.00	275.00
1995	Clemente, Roberto 24K Coin/Card Set	100	250.00	400.00
1988	Cobb, Ty	1,093	29.95	45.00
1995	Cobb, Ty Silver	15,000	29.95	30.00
1997	Conine, Jeff WS Photo/Coin Set	1,997	49.95	50.00
1997	Counsell, Craig WS Photo/Coin Set	1,997	49.95	50.00
1995	Daulton, Darren Silver	1,500	29.95	35.00
1995	Daulton, Darren 24K	125	49.95	70.00
1995	Daulton, Darren Bronze	500	14.95	20.00
1995	Daulton, Darren Silver/All-Star	1,995	29.95	30.00
1995	Daulton, Darren 24K/All-Star	500	49.95	60.00
1995	Daulton, Darren Bronze/All-Star	1,995	14.95	20.00
1995	Daulton, Darren All-Star 3-pc. Proof Set	95	125.00	130.00
1989	Davis, Mark 1989 Cy Young	270	29.95	65.00
1990	Dawson, Andre 1987 MVP	10,900	29.95	32.50
1993	Dawson, Andre	4,100	30.00	45.00
1997	Dickson, Jason All-Star Photo/Coin Set	500	49.95	50.00
1997	Dickson, Jason 3-pc. Photo/Coin Set	197	150.00	150.00
1997	Doby, Larry Silver	500	34.95	38.00
1997	Doby, Larry 24K	500	49.95	55.00
1997	Doby, Larry 3-pc. Proof Set	197	125.00	130.00
1995	Dykstra, Lenny 24K	125	49.95	60.00
1995	Dykstra, Lenny Bronze	500	14.95	20.00
1995	Dykstra, Lenny Silver/All-Star	1,995	29.95	40.00
1995	Dykstra, Lenny 24K/All-Star	500	49.95	60.00
1995	Dykstra, Lenny Bronze/All-Star	1,995	14.95	20.00
1995	Dykstra, Lenny All-Star 3-pc. Proof Set	95	125.00	130.00
1992	Eckersley, Dennis 40 saves/3 years	400	29.95	50.00
1992	Eckersley, Dennis 1992 Cy Young	15,000	29.95	35.00
1995	Eckersley, Dennis Silver	1,995	29.95	40.00
1995	Eckersley, Dennis 24K	500	49.95	60.00
1995	Eckersley, Dennis Bronze	1,995	14.95	20.00
1995	Eckersley, Dennis 3-pc. Proof Set	95	125.00	130.00
1997	Estes, Shawn 3-pc. Photo/Coin Set	197	150.00	150.00
1997	Fernandez, Alex WS Photo/Coin	1,997	49.95	50.00
1997	Fernandez, Alex WS Photo/Coin Set	1,997	49.95	50.00
1997	Fernandez, Tony WS Photo/Coin Set	1,997	49.95	50.00
1991	Fielder, Cecil AL HR/RBI Leader	15,000	29.95	35.00
1996	Fielder, Cecil Silver	1,996	29.95	35.00
1996	Fielder, Cecil 24K	500	49.95	50.00
1996	Fielder, Cecil 3-pc. Proof Set	196	125.00	125.00
1996	Fielder, Cecil WS Reverse Silver	500	29.95	30.00
1996	Fielder, Cecil WS 3-pc. Proof Set	96	125.00	130.00
1996	Fielder, Cecil WS Combo	196	125.00	130.00
1996	Fielder, Cecil WS 24K	196	49.95	50.00
1995	Fingers, Rollie Silver/Hall of Fame	15,000	29.95	38.00
1990	Fisk, Carlton Most Hits by Catcher	15,000	29.95	38.00
1995	Gallaraga, Andres Silver	1,500	29.95	40.00
1993	Gallaraga, Andres Bronze	500	14.95	20.00
1993	Gallaraga, Andres 24K	125	49.95	60.00
1995	Gallaraga, Andres Silver	1,995	29.95	40.00
1995	Gallaraga, Andres 24K	500	49.95	60.00
1995	Gallaraga, Andres Bronze	1,995	14.95	20.00
1995	Gallaraga, Andres 3-pc. Proof Set	95	125.00	130.00
1996	Gallaraga, Andres Photo/Coin Set	96	125.00	125.00
1997	Gallaraga, A. All-Star Photo/Coin Set	197	150.00	150.00
1997	Garciaparra, Nomar 24K/ROY	1,000	34.95	35.00

Year	Team	Mintage	Issue Price	Price
1997	Garciaparra, Nomar ROY Bronze Photo/Coin Set	500	49.95	50.00
1989	Garvey, Steve 1,207 Consecutive Games	15,000	29.95	35.00
1987	Gehrig, Lou 2,130 Consecutive Games	1,352	29.95	45.00
1988	Gibson, Kirk 1988 MVP	600	29.95	45.00
1995	Gibson, Kirk Silver	1,995	29.95	40.00
1995	Gibson, Kirk 24K	500	49.95	60.00
1995	Gibson, Kirk Bronze	1,995	14.95	20.00
1995	Gibson, Kirk 3-pc. Proof Set	95	125.00	130.00
1991	Glavine, Tom Silver/'91 Cy Young	15,000	29.95	35.00
1995	Glavine, Tom Silver	1,995	29.95	40.00
1995	Glavine, Tom 24K	500	49.95	60.00
1995	Glavine, Tom Bronze	1,995	14.95	20.00
1995	Glavine, Tom 3-pc. Proof Set	95	125.00	130.00
1996	Glavine, Tom All-Star Ball/Coin Set	100	124.95	12.00
1996	Glavine, Tom Silver/WS	500	29.95	30.00
1996	Glavine, Tom 24K/WS	196	49.95	50.00
1996	Glavine, Tom WS 3-pc. Proof Set	96	125.00	125.00
1996	Glavine, Tom WS Combo Set	196	125.00	125.00
1997	Glavine, Tom All-Star 3-pc. Photo/Coin Set	197	150.00	150.00
1995	Gonzalez, Juan Bronze	500	14.95	20.00
1995	Gonzalez, Juan Silver	1,500	29.95	40.00
1995	Gonzalez, Juan 24K	125	49.95	60.00
1995	Gonzalez, Juan Silver	1,995	29.95	40.00
1995	Gonzalez, Juan 24K	500	49.95	60.00
1995	Gonzalez, Juan Bronze	1,995	14.95	20.00
1995	Gonzalez, Juan 3-pc. Proof Set	95	125.00	130.00
1996	Gonzalez, Juan Silver/AL MVP	1,996	34.95	40.00
1996	Gonzalez, Juan 24K/AL MVP	500	49.95	60.00
1996	Gonzalez, Juan AL MVP 3-pc. Proof Set	196	125.00	130.00
1997	Gonzalez, Juan AL Photo/Coin Set	500	49.95	50.00
1995	Gooden, Dwight Silver	15,000	29.95	35.00
1995	Grace, Mark Silver	1,500	29.95	35.00
1995	Grace, Mark 24K	125	49.95	60.00
1995	Grace, Mark Bronze	500	14.95	20.00
1995	Grace, Mark Silver/All-Star	1,995	29.95	40.00
1995	Grace, Mark 24K/All-Star	500	49.95	60.00
1995	Grace, Mark Bronze/All-Star	1,995	14.95	20.00
1995	Grace, Mark All-Star 3-pc. Proof Set	95	125.00	130.00
1996	Grace, Mark Framed Photo/Coin Set	96	125.00	130.00
1990	Griffey, Ken Jr. & Sr.	3,700	29.95	65.00
1990	Griffey, Ken Jr. & Sr.	3,300	29.95	85.00
1995	Griffey, Ken Jr. & Sr. Silver	15,000	29.95	35.00
1995	Griffey, Ken Jr. Silver	1,500	29.95	45.00
1995	Griffey, Ken Jr. 24K	125	49.95	80.00
1995	Griffey, Ken Jr. Bronze	500	14.95	25.00
1995	Griffey, Ken Jr. Silver/All-Star	1,995	29.95	45.00
1995	Griffey, Ken Jr. 24K/All-Star	500	49.95	65.00
1995	Griffey, Ken Jr. Bronze/All-Star	1,995	14.95	25.00
1995	Griffey, Ken Jr. All-Star 3-pc. Proof Set	95	125.00	140.00
1996	Griffey, Ken Jr. All-Star Ball/Coin Set	100	125.95	140.00
1996	Griffey, Ken Jr. Framed Photo/Coin Set	96	125.00	140.00
1996	Griffey, Ken Jr. All-Star Photo/Coin Set	500	49.95	65.00
1997	Griffey, Ken Jr. MVP Photo/Coin Set	500	49.95	65.00
1997	Griffey, Ken Jr. 24K/MVP	1,000	34.95	45.00
1997	Griffey, K. Jr. HR Leader Photo/Coin Set	500	49.95	65.00

Year	Team	Mintage	Issue Price	Price
1997	Griffey, Ken Jr. 24K/HR Leader	1,000	34.95	45.00
1997	Griffey, Ken Jr. 24K HR/MVP 2-pc. Set	97	129.95	140.00
1997	Griffey, Ken Jr. Bronze HR/MVP 2-pc. Set	197	79.95	95.00
1990	Gwynn, Tony Batting Title '87, '88, '89	1,075	29.95	50.00
1995	Gwynn, Tony Silver/All-Star	1,995	29.95	40.00
1995	Gwynn, Tony 24K/All-Star	500	49.95	60.00
1995	Gwynn, Tony Bronze/All-Star	1,995	14.95	20.00
1995	Gwynn, Tony All-Star 3-pc. Proof Set	95	125.00	130.00
1996	Gwynn, Tony All-Star Ball/Coin Set	100	124.95	125.00
1996	Gwynn, Tony Framed Photo/Coin Set	96	125.00	125.00
1997	Gwynn, Tony Batting Title Photo/Coin Set	500	49.95	50.00
1997	Gwynn, Tony 24K Batting Title	1,000	34.95	35.00
1997	Gwynn, Tony/Frank Thomas 24K 2-pc. Set	97	129.95	130.00
1997	Gwynn, Tony/Frank Thomas Bronze 2pc. Set	197	79.95	80.00
1990	Henderson, Rickey Stolen Bases	7,109	29.95	45.00
1993	Henderson, Rickey	7,981	29.95	40.00
1995	Henderson, Rickey Silver	1,995	29.95	40.00
1995	Henderson, Rickey 24K	500	49.95	60.00
1995	Henderson, Rickey Bronze	1,995	14.95	20.00
1995	Henderson, Rickey 3-pc. Proof Set	95	125.00	130.00
1996	Hentgen, Pat Silver/AL Cy Young	1,996	34.95	35.00
1996	Hentgen, Pat 24K/AL Cy Young	500	49.95	50.00
1996	Hentgen, P. AL Cy Young 3-pc. Proof Set	196	125.00	125.00
1997	Hernandez, Livan WS Photo/Coin Set	1,997	49.95	50.00
1997	Hernandez, Livan WS MVP Photo/Coin Set	1,997	49.95	50.00
1997	Hernandez, Livan 2-pc. Card/Coin Set	197	179.95	180.00
1989	Hershiser, Orel 1988 Cy Young	600	29.95	45.00
1995	Hershiser, Orel Silver	1,995	29.95	40.00
1995	Hershiser, Orel 24K	500	49.95	60.00
1995	Hershiser, Orel Bronze	1,995	14.95	20.00
1995	Hershiser, Orel 3-pc. Proof Set	95	125.00	130.00
1997	Hershiser, Orel WS Photo/Coin Set	1,997	49.95	50.00
1996	Hollandsworth, Todd Silver/ROY	1,996	34.95	35.00
1996	Hollandsworth, Todd 24K/ROY	500	49.95	50.00
1996	Hollandsworth, Todd ROY 3-pc. Proof Set	196	125.00	125.00
1990	Jackson, Bo Raiders/Royals	4,400	29.95	45.00
1991	Jackson, Bo Raiders/White Sox	N/A	29.95	35.00
1993	Jackson, Reggie 1993 HOF Gold	44	850.00	850.00
1993	Jackson, Reggie HOF 2-pc. Set	100	82.95	125.00
1996	Jeter, Derek Silver/WS Reverse	500	29.95	40.00
1996	Jeter, Derek WS Ball/Coin Set	96	125.00	130.00
1996	Jeter, Derek 24K/WS	196	49.95	60.00
1996	Jeter, Derek WS 3-pc. Proof Set	96	125.00	125.00
1996	Jeter, Derek Framed Photo/Coin Set	96	125.00	125.00
1996	Jeter, Derek Silver/ROY	1,996	29.95	30.00
1996	Jeter, Derek 24K/ROY	500	49.95	50.00
1996	Jeter, Derek ROY 3-pc. Proof Set	196	125.00	125.00
1991	Fergie, Jenkins 1991 HOF	15,000	29.95	35.00
1997	Johnson, Charles WS Photo/Coin Set	1,997	49.95	50.00
1991	Johnson, Howard HR/RBI Champ	680	29.95	35.00
1995	Johnson, Randy Silver	1,500	29.95	40.00
1995	Johnson, Randy 24K	125	49.95	60.00
1995	Johnson, Randy Bronze	500	14.95	20.00

Year	Team	Mintage	Issue Price	Price
1995	Johnson, Randy Silver/All-Star	1,995	29.95	40.00
1995	Johnson, Randy 24K/All-Star	500	49.95	60.00
1995	Johnson, Randy Bronze/All-Star	1,995	14.95	20.00
1995	Johnson, Randy All-Star 3-pc. Proof Set	95	125.00	130.00
1995	Johnson, Randy Silver/Cy Young	1,995	29.95	45.00
1995	Johnson, Randy 24K/Cy Young	500	49.95	65.00
1995	Johnson, Randy Bronze/Cy Young	1,995	14.95	25.00
1995	Johnson, R. Cy Young 3-pc. Proof Set	95	125.00	135.00
1996	Johnson, Randy Framed Photo/Coin Set	96	125.00	135.00
1997	Johnson, Randy 3-pc. Photo/Coin Set	197	150.00	160.00
1995	Jones, Chipper Silver	1,995	29.95	40.00
1995	Jones, Chipper 24K	500	49.95	60.00
1995	Jones, Chipper Bronze	1,995	14.95	20.00
1995	Jones, Chipper 3-pc. Proof Set	95	125.00	130.00
1996	Jones, Chipper All-Star Ball/Coin Set	100	124.95	125.00
1996	Jones, Chipper 24K/WS	196	49.95	50.00
1996	Jones, Chipper WS 3-pc. Proof Set	96	125.00	130.00
1996	Jones, Chipper WS Combo	196	125.00	125.00
1996	Jones, Chipper Framed Photo/Coin Set	96	125.00	125.00
1997	Jones, Chipper All-Star 3-pc. Photo/Coin Set	197	150.00	150.00
1997	Jones, Bobby All-Star Photo/Coin Set	500	49.95	50.00
1997	Jones, Bobby All-Star Photo/Coin Set	197	150.00	150.00
1991	Justice, David 1990 Rookie of Year	15,000	29.95	38.00
1995	Justice, David Silver	1,995	29.95	40.00
1995	Justice, David 24K	500	49.95	60.00
1995	Justice, David Bronze	1,995	14.95	20.00
1995	Justice, David 3-pc. Proof Set	95	125.00	125.00
1996	Justice, David Silver/WS	500	29.95	30.00
1996	Justice, David 24K/WS	196	49.95	50.00
1996	Justice, David WS 3-pc. Proof Set	96	125.00	125.00
1996	Justice, David WS Combo	196	125.00	125.00
1996	Justice, David Framed Photo/Coin Set	96	125.00	125.00
1997	Justice, David All-Star Photo/Coin Set	500	49.95	50.00
1997	Justice, David 3-pc. Photo/Coins Set	197	150.00	150.00
1997	Justice, David WS Photo/Coin Set	1,997	49.95	50.00
1991	Killebrew, Harmon 1984 Hall of Fame	15,000	29.95	45.00
1993	Knoblauch, Chuck	15,000	29.95	40.00
1995	Knoblauch, Chuck Silver	1,995	29.95	40.00
1995	Knoblauch, Chuck 24K	500	49.95	60.00
1995	Knoblauch, Chuck Bronze	1,995	14.95	20.00
1995	Knoblauch, Chuck 3-pc. Proof Set	95	125.00	130.00
1996	Knoblauch, Chuck All-Star Ball/Coin Set	100	124.95	130.00
1997	Knoblauch, Chuck 3-pc. Photo/Coin Set	197	150.00	150.00
1995	Larkin, Barry Bronze/All-Star	1,995	14.95	20.00
1995	Larkin, Barry All-Star 3-pc. Proof Set	95	125.00	130.00
1997	Larkin, Barry All-Star Photo/Coin Set	500	49.95	60.00
1997	Larkin, Barry All-Star 3-pc. Photo/Coin Set	197	150.00	150.00
1995	Lofton, Kenny Silver/All-Star	1,995	29.95	40.00
1995	Lofton, Kenny 24K/All-Star	500	49.95	60.00
1995	Lofton, Kenny Bronze/All-Star	1,995	14.95	20.00
1995	Lofton, Kenny 3-pc. Proof Set	95	125.00	130.00
1996	Lofton, Kenny All-Star Ball/Coin Set	100	124.95	130.00
1996	Lofton, Kenny Framed Photo/Coin Set	96	125.00	130.00
1997	Lofton, Kenny All-Star Photo/Coin Set	500	49.95	50.00
1997	Lofton, Kenny 3-pc. Photo/Coin Set	197	150.00	150.00
1992	Maddux, Greg Silver/Cy Young	15,000	29.95	40.00

Year	Team	Mintage	Issue Price	Price	Year	Team	Mintage	Issue Price	Price
1993	Maddux, Greg Silver/Cy Young	1,500	29.95	65.00	1995	McDowell, Jack 24K	500	49.95	60.00
1993	Maddux, Greg Bronze/Cy Young	500	14.95	40.00	1995	McDowell, Jack Bronze	1,995	14.95	20.00
1993	Maddux, Greg 24K/Cy Young	125	49.95	100.00	1995	McDowell, Jack 3-pc. Proof Set	95	125.00	130.00
1995	Maddux, Greg Silver/All-Star	1,995	29.95	45.00	1995	McGriff, Fred Silver/All-Star	1,995	29.95	40.00
1995	Maddux, Greg 24K/All-Star	500	49.95	65.00	1995	McGriff, Fred 24K/All-Star	500	49.95	60.00
1995	Maddux, Greg Bronze/All-Star	1,995	14.95	25.00	1995	McGriff, Fred Bronze/All-Star	1,995	14.95	20.00
1995	Maddux, Greg All-Star 3-pc. Proof Set	95	125.00	140.00	1995	McGriff, Fred 3-pc. Proof Set	95	125.00	130.00
1995	Maddux, Greg Silver/4-Time Cy Young Winner	1,995	29.95	45.00	1996	McGriff, Fred All-Star Ball/Coin Set	100	124.95	125.00
1995	Maddux, Greg 24K/4 Time Cy Young Winner	500	49.95	65.00	1996	McGriff, Fred WS Silver	500	29.95	30.00
1995	Maddux, Greg Bronze/4 Time Cy Young Winner	1,995	14.95	25.00	1996	McGriff, Fred WS 24K	196	49.95	50.00
					1996	McGriff, Fred WS 3-pc. Proof Set	96	125.00	125.00
1995	Maddux, Greg 4 Time Cy Young Winner 3-pc. Proof Set	95	125.00	135.00	1996	McGriff, Fred WS Combo Set	196	125.00	125.00
1996	Maddux, Greg All-Star Ball/Coin Set	100	124.95	135.00	1997	McGriff, Fred NL Photo/Coin Set	500	49.95	50.00
1996	Maddux, Greg WS Combo	196	125.00	135.00	1991	McGwire, Mark 30 HR/4 season	15,000	29.95	45.00
1996	Maddux, Greg Framed Photo/Coin Set	96	125.00	135.00	1995	McGwire, Mark Silver/All-Star	1,995	29.95	45.00
1997	Maddux, Greg All-Star 3-pc. Photo/Coin Set	197	150.00	150.00	1995	McGwire, Mark 24K/All-Star	500	49.95	65.00
1997	Mantle, Mickey Silver	10,000	29.95	45.00	1995	McGwire, Mark Bronze/All-Star	1,995	14.95	25.00
1997	Mantle, Mickey 24K	1,956	49.95	75.00	1995	McGwire, Mark All-Star 3-pc. Proof Set	95	125.00	135.00
1997	Mantle, Mickey Bronze	25,000	14.95	25.00	1996	McGwire, Mark All-Star Ball/Coin Set	100	124.95	125.00
1997	Mantle, Mickey 3-pc. Proof Set	1,000	125.00	150.00	1996	McGwire, Mark Framed Photo/Coin Set	96	125.00	125.00
1997	Mantle, Mickey Gold	100	850.00	850.00	1997	McGwire, Mark 3-pc. All-Star Photo/Coin Set	197	150.00	150.00
1997	Mantle, Mickey Card/Coin 2-pc. Set	1,956	49.95	65.00	1997	McGwire, Mark HR Leader	500	49.95	50.00
1997	Martinez, Pedro All-Star Photo/Coin Set	500	49.95	50.00	1997	McGwire, Mark 24K Bronze/HR Leader	1,000	34.95	35.00
1997	Martinez, Pedro All-Star 3-pc. Photo/Coin Set	197	150.00	150.00	1997	Mesa, Jose WS Photo/Coin Set	1,997	49.95	50.00
					1990	Mitchell, Kevin 1989 MVP	1,200	29.95	35.00
1997	Martinez, Pedro Cy Young 24K Bronze	1,000	34.95	35.00	1992	Mitchell, Kevin	108	29.95	60.00
1995	Martinez, Tino Silver	1,995	29.95	40.00	1993	Mitchell, Kevin	13,692	29.95	32.00
1995	Martinez, Tino 24K	500	49.95	60.00	1990	Molitor, Paul 39-Game Hitting Streak	11,001	29.95	35.00
1995	Martinez, Tino Bronze	1,995	14.95	20.00					
1995	Martinez, Tino 3-pc. Proof Set	95	125.00	130.00	1990	Morgan, Joe 1990 HOF	15,000	29.95	45.00
1997	Martinez, Tino All-Star Photo/Coin Set	500	49.95	50.00	1995	Murray, Eddie Silver/3,000 Hits	3,000	29.95	45.00
1997	Martinez, Tino 3-pc. Photo/Coin Set	197	150.00	150.00	1995	Murray, Eddie 24K/3,000 Hits	1,995	49.95	65.00
1995	Martinez, Edgar Silver/All-Star	1,995	29.95	40.00	1995	Murray, Eddie Gold/3,000 Hits	100	850.00	850.00
1995	Martinez, Edgar 24K/All-Star	500	49.95	60.00	1995	Murray, Eddie 3000 Hits 3-pc. Proof Set	95	125.00	130.00
1995	Martinez, Edgar Bronze/All-Star	1,995	14.95	20.00	1996	Murray, Eddie Silver/500th Home Run	1,996	29.95	35.00
1995	Martinez, Edgar All-Star 3-pc. Proof Set	95	125.00	130.00	1996	Murray, Eddie 24K/500th Home Run	1,000	49.95	55.00
1996	Martinez, Edgar All-Star Ball/Coin Set	100	124.95	125.00	1996	Murray, Eddie 500th Home Run 3-pc. Proof Set	196	125.00	125.00
1996	Martinez, Edgar Framed Photo/Coin Set	96	125.00	125.00					
1997	Martinez, Edgar All-Star Photo/Coin Set	500	49.95	50.00	1996	Murray, Eddie Gold/500th Home Run	33	850.00	850.00
1997	Martinez, Edgar 3-pc. Photo/Coin Set	197	150.00	150.00	1996	Murray, Eddie 500th HR/3,000th Hit 2-pc. Silver	500	82.95	85.00
1995	Martinez, Dennis Silver/All-Star	1,995	29.95	40.00					
1995	Martinez, Dennis 24K/All-Star	500	49.95	60.00	1996	Murray, Eddie 500th HR/3,000th Hit 2-pc. 24K	100	135.00	140.00
1995	Martinez, Dennis Bronze/All-Star	1,995	14.95	20.00					
1995	Martinez, D. All-Star 3-pc. Proof Set	95	125.00	130.00	1995	Myers, Randy Silver/All-Star	1,995	29.95	40.00
1988	Mattingly, Don Most Grand Slams	15,000	29.95	40.00	1995	Myers, Randy 24K/All-Star	500	49.95	60.00
1995	Mattingly, Don Silver	1,995	49.95	60.00	1995	Myers, Randy Bronze/All-Star	1,995	14.95	20.00
1995	Mattingly, Don 24K	500	49.95	80.00	1995	Myers, Randy All-Star 3-pc. Proof Set	95	125.00	130.00
1995	Mattingly, Don Bronze	1,995	14.95	20.00	1997	Nagy, Charles AL Photo/Coin Set	500	49.95	50.00
1995	Mattingly, Don 3-pc. Proof Set	95	125.00	130.00	1997	Nagy, Charles WS Photo/Coin Set	1,997	49.95	50.00
1994	McDowell, Jack Silver/1993 Cy Young	1,500	29.95	40.00	1997	Nagy, C. 3-pc. All-Star Photo/Coin Set	500	150.00	150.00
1994	McDowell, Jack 24K/1993 Cy Young	125	49.95	60.00	1997	Nen, Robb WS Photo/Coin Set	1,997	49.95	50.00
1994	McDowell, Jack Bronze/1993 Cy Young	500	14.95	20.00	1995	Nomo, Hideo Silver/All-Star	1,995	29.95	40.00
1994	McDowell, Jack/Frank Thomas 2-pc. set	100	82.95	85.00	1995	Nomo, Hideo 24K/All-Star	500	49.95	60.00
1995	McDowell, Jack Silver	1,995	29.95	40.00	1995	Nomo, Hideo Bronze/All-Star	1,995	14.95	20.00
					1995	Nomo, Hideo All-Star 3-pc. Proof Set	95	125.00	130.00
					1995	Nomo, Hideo Silver	1,995	N/A	40.00
1995	McDowell, Jack Silver	1,995	29.95	40.00	1995	Nomo, Hideo 24K	500	N/A	60.00

Year	Team	Mintage	Issue Price	Price	Year	Team	Mintage	Issue Price	Price
1995	Nomo, Hideo Bronze	1,995	14.95	20.00	1995	Ripken, Cal Bronze	500	14.95	30.00
1995	Nomo, Hideo Silver/Rookie	1,995	29.95	40.00	1995	Ripken, Cal Silver/All-Star	1,995	29.95	40.00
1995	Nomo, Hideo 24K/Rookie	500	49.95	60.00	1995	Ripken, Cal 24K/All-Star	500	49.95	60.00
1995	Nomo, Hideo Bronze/Rookie	1,995	14.95	20.00	1995	Ripken, Cal Bronze/All-Star	1,995	14.9i5	20.00
1995	Nomo, Hideo Rookie 3-pc. Proof Set	95	125.00	130.00	1995	Ripken, Cal All-Star 3-pc. Proof Set	95	125.00	130.00
1995	Nomo, Hideo Framed Photo/Coin Set	96	125.00	130.00	1996	Ripken, Cal Silver/2,131 Coin	10,000	29.95	40.00
1993	Olerud, John Silver	1,500	29.95	40.00	1996	Ripken, Cal 24K/2,131 Coin	2,131	49.95	75.00
1993	Olerud, John 24K	125	49.95	60.00	1996	Ripken, Cal Jr. Gold/2,131 Coin	95	850.00	850.00
1993	Olerud, John Bronze	500	14.95	20.00	1996	Ripken, Cal 2,131 Coin 3-pc. Proof Set	500	125.00	135.00
1995	Olerud, John Silver	1,995	29.95	40.00	1996	Ripken, Cal All-Star Ball/Card Set	100	124.95	125.00
1995	Olerud, John 24K	500	49.95	60.00	1997	Ripken, Cal All-Star Photo/Coin Set	500	49.95	50.00
1995	Olerud, John Bronze	1,995	14.95	20.00	1991	Robinson, Brooks 1983 HOF	15,000	29.95	35.00
1995	Olerud, John 3-pc. Proof Set	95	125.00	130.00	1996	Rodriguez, Alex All-Star Ball/Coin Set	100	124.95	125.00
1990	Olson, Greg 89 Rookie of the Year	15,000	29.95	35.00	1996	Rodriguez, Alex Silver	1,996	29.95	40.00
1995	O'Neil, Paul Silver/All-Star	1,995	29.95	40.00	1996	Rodriguez, Alex 24K	500	49.95	60.00
1995	O'Neil, Paul 24K/All-Star	500	49.95	60.00	1996	Rodriguez, A. Bat. Champ. 3-pc. Proof Set	196	125.00	125.00
1995	O'Neil, Paul Bronze/All-Star	1,995	14.95	20.00	1997	Rodriguez, Alex All-Star Photo/Coin Set	500	49.95	50.00
1995	O'Neil, Paul All-Star 3-pc. Proof Set	95	125.00	130.00	1995	Rodriguez, Ivan Silver/All-Star	1,995	29.95	40.00
1991	Pendleton, Terry 1991 Batting Title	900	29.95	45.00	1995	Rodriguez, Ivan 24K/All-Star	500	49.95	60.00
1991	Pendleton, Terry 1991 NL MVP	15,000	29.95	40.00	1995	Rodriguez, Ivan Bronze/All-Star	1,995	14.95	20.00
1995	Pendleton, Terry Silver	1,995	29.95	40.00	1995	Rodriguez, Ivan All-Star 3-pc. Proof Set	95	125.00	130.00
1995	Pendleton, Terry 24K	500	49.95	60.00	1996	Rodriguez, Ivan All-Star Ball/Coin Set	100	124.95	125.00
1995	Pendleton, Terry Bronze	1,995	14.95	20.00	1997	Rodriguez, Ivan All-Star Photo/Coin Set	500	49.95	50.00
1995	Pendleton, Terry 3-pc. Proof Set	95	125.00	130.00	1997	Rodriguez, Ivan 3-pc. Photo/Coin Set	197	150.00	150.00
1996	Pettite, Andy Silver WS Reverse	500	29.95	35.00	1997	Rolen, Scott ROY Photo/Coin Set	500	49.95	50.00
1996	Pettite, Andy WS Ball/Coin Set	96	125.00	125.00	1997	Rolen, Scott ROY 24K Bronze	1,000	34.95	35.00
1996	Pettite, Andy WS 24K	196	49.95	55.00	1985	Rose, Pete All Time Hit Leader	25,000	29.95	65.00
1996	Pettite, Andy WS 3-pc. Proof Set	96	125.00	125.00	1987	Ruth, Babe	15,000	29.95	50.00
1993	Piazza, Mike Silver	1,500	29.95	50.00	1989	Ryan, Nolan 5,000th Strikeout	1,500	49.95	75.00
1993	Piazza, Mike 24K	125	49.95	75.00	1990	Ryan, Nolan 300th Victory	1,500	49.95	75.00
1993	Piazza, Mike Bronze	500	14.95	25.00	1991	Ryan, Nolan 7th No-Hitter	1,500	49.95	65.00
1995	Piazza, Mike Silver/All-Star	1,995	29.95	40.00	1993	Ryan, Nolan Silver/Retirement	15,000	29.95	45.00
1995	Piazza, Mike 24K/All-Star	500	49.95	60.00	1993	Ryan, Nolan Gold/Retirement	100	850.00	850.00
1995	Piazza, Mike Bronze/All-Star	1,995	14.95	20.00	1993	Ryan, Nolan Bronze/Retirement	25,000	14.95	20.00
1995	Piazza, Mike All-Star 3-pc. Proof Set	95	125.00	130.00	1993	Ryan, Nolan Retirement 2-pc. set	500	120.00	145.00
1996	Piazza, Mike All-Star Ball/Coin Set	100	124.95	125.00	1993	Ryan, Nolan Bat w/Silver Coin Set	1,993	169.96	175.00
1996	Piazza, Mike Framed Photo/Coin Set	96	125.00	125.00	1993	Ryan, Nolan Bat w/24K Coin Set	500	199.95	250.00
1997	Piazza, Mike 3-pc. Photo/Coin Set	197	150.00	150.00	1996	Ryan, Nolan Silver/Jersey Retirement	1,996	29.95	35.00
1990	Puckett, Kirby AL Batting Champ	2,200	29.95	50.00	1996	Ryan, Nolan 24K/Jersey Retirement	500	49.95	55.00
1995	Puckett, Kirby Silver/All-Star	1,995	29.95	40.00	1996	Ryan, N. Jersey Retirement 3-pc. Proof Set	196	125.00	135.00
1995	Puckett, Kirby 24K/All-Star	500	49.95	60.00	1990	Saberhagen, Bret 1998 Cy Young	300	29.95	65.00
1995	Puckett, Kirby Bronze/All-Star	1,995	14.95	20.00	1995	Saberhagen, Bret Silver	1,995	29.95	40.00
1995	Puckett, Kirby All-Star 3-pc. Proof Set	95	125.00	130.00	1995	Saberhagen, Bret 24K	500	49.95	60.00
1996	Puckett, Kirby Silver/Retirement	1,996	29.95	35.00	1995	Saberhagen, Bret Bronze	1,995	14.95	20.00
1996	Puckett, Kirby 24K/Retirement	500	49.95	55.00	1995	Saberhagen, Bret 3-pc. Proof Set	95	125.00	130.00
1996	Puckett, Kirby Retirement 3-pc. Proof Set	196	125.00	130.00	1989	Sabo, Chris '88 NL ROY	1,315	29.95	45.00
1996	Puckett, Kirby Gold/Retirement	34	850.00	850.00	1993	Salmon, Tim Silver	1,500	29.95	45.00
1996	Puckett, Kirby Framed Photo/Coin Set	96	125.00	125.00	1993	Salmon, Tim 24K	125	49.95	65.00
1995	Ramirez, Manny Silver/All-Star	1,995	29.95	40.00	1993	Salmon, Tim Bronze	500	14.95	25.00
1995	Ramirez, Manny 24K/All-Star	500	49.95	60.00	1995	Salmon, Tim Silver	1,995	29.95	50.00
1995	Ramirez, Manny Bronze/All-Star	1,995	14.95	20.00	1995	Salmon, Tim 24K	500	49.95	60.00
1995	Ramirez, Manny All-Star 3-pc. Proof Set	95	125.00	130.00	1995	Salmon, Tim Bronze	1,995	14.95	20.00
1996	Ramirez, Manny Framed Photo/Coin Set	96	125.00	130.00	1995	Salmon, Tim 3-pc. Proof Set	95	125.00	130.00
1997	Ramirez, Manny WS Photo/Coin Set	1,997	49.95	50.00	1990	Sandberg, Ryne Errorless Streak	15,000	29.95	38.00
1997	Renteria, Edgar WS Photo/Coin Set	1,997	49.95	50.00	1996	Sandberg, Ryne Framed Photo/Coin Set	96	125.00	125.00
1992	Ripken, Cal 1991 MVP	15,000	29.95	40.00	1996	Sandberg, Ryne Silver	1,996	34.95	35.00
1995	Ripken, Cal Silver	1,500	29.95	50.00	1996	Sandberg, Ryne 24K	500	49.95	50.00
1995	Ripken, Cal 24K	125	49.95	80.00	1996	Sandberg, Ryne 3-pc. Proof Set	196	125.00	125.00

Year	Team	Mintage	Issue Price	Price
1997	Sandberg, Ryne Silver/HRs Record	1,997	34.95	35.00
1997	Sandberg, Ryne 24K/HRs Record	500	49.95	50.00
1997	Sandberg, R. HRs Record 3-pc. Proof Set	197	125.00	125.00
1992	Sanders, Deion	15,000	29.95	32.00
1997	Sanders, Deion Silver	1,997	34.95	35.00
1997	Sanders, Deion 24K	500	49.95	50.00
1997	Sanders, Deion 3-pc. Proof Set	197	125.00	125.00
1997	Saunders, Tony WS Photo/Coin Set	1,997	49.95	50.00
1990	Schmidt, Mike Player of Decade	10,000	29.95	45.00
1995	Schmidt, Mike Silver/Hall of Fame	5,000	29.95	65.00
1995	Schmidt, Mike 24K/Hall of Fame	1,995	49.95	85.00
1995	Schmidt, Mike Gold/Hall of Fame	95	850.00	850.00
1995	Schmidt, Mike Bronze/Hall of Fame	5,000	14.95	25.00
1997	Schilling, Curt All-Star Photo/Coin Set	500	49.95	50.00
1997	Schilling, Curt All-Star 3-pc. Photo Set	197	150.00	150.00
1992	Seaver, Tom—1992 HOF	15,000	29.95	40.00
1997	Sheffield, Gary WS Photo/Coin Set	1,997	49.95	50.00
1995	Smith, Ozzie Silver	1,500	29.95	50.00
1995	Smith, Ozzie 24K	125	49.95	70.00
1995	Smith, Ozzie Bronze	500	14.95	25.00
1995	Smith, Ozzie Silver/All-Star	1,995	29.95	40.00
1995	Smith, Ozzie 24K/All-Star	500	49.95	60.00
1995	Smith, Ozzie Bronze/All-Star	1,995	14.95	20.00
1995	Smith, Ozzie All-Star 3-pc. Proof Set	95	125.00	130.00
1996	Smith, Ozzie All-Star Ball/Coin Set	100	124.95	125.00
1996	Smith, Ozzie Framed Photo/Coin Set	96	125.00	125.00
1996	Smoltz, John All-Star Ball/Coin Set	100	124.95	125.00
1996	Smoltz, John Silver	1,996	29.95	35.00
1996	Smoltz, John 24K	500	49.95	55.00
1996	Smoltz, John 3-pc. Proof Set	196	125.00	130.00
1996	Smoltz, John 24K/WS	196	49.95	50.00
1996	Smoltz, John WS 3-pc. Proof Set	96	125.00	125.00
1996	Smoltz, John Silver/NL Cy Young	1,996	34.95	35.00
1996	Smoltz, John 24K/NL Cy Young	500	49.95	50.00
1996	Smoltz, John NL Cy Young 3-pc. Proof Set	196	125.00	125.00
1997	Smoltz, John NL Photo/Coin Set	500	49.95	50.00
1995	Sosa, Sammy Bronze/All-Star	1,995	14.95	20.00
1997	Sosa, Sammy 24K/All-Star	500	49.95	50.00
1990	Strawberry, Darryl	1,200	29.95	45.00
1995	Strawberry, Darryl	13,800	29.95	32.00
1996	Strawberry, Darryl WS	500	29.95	30.00
1996	Strawberry, Darryl WS 3-pc. Proof Set	96	125.00	125.00
1993	Thomas, Frank Silver/AL MVP	1,500	29.95	50.00
1993	Thomas, Frank 24K/AL MVP	125	49.95	80.00
1993	Thomas, Frank Bronze/AL MVP	500	14.95	28.00
1994	Thomas, Frank Silver/MVP	1,500	29.95	50.00
1994	Thomas, Frank 24K/MVP	125	49.95	80.00
1994	Thomas, Frank Bronze/MVP	500	14.95	28.00
1995	Thomas, Frank Silver/All-Star	1,995	29.95	40.00
1995	Thomas, Frank 24K/All-Star	500	49.95	60.00
1995	Thomas, Frank Bronze/All-Star	1,995	14.95	20.00
1995	Thomas, Frank All-Star 3-pc. Proof Set	95	125.00	130.00
1996	Thomas, Frank All-Star Ball/Coin Set	100	124.95	125.00
1997	Thomas, Frank All-Star Photo/Coin Set	197	150.00	150.00
1997	Thome, Jim WS Photo/Coin Set	1,997	49.95	50.00
1995	Vaughn, Mo Silver/All-Star	1,995	29.95	40.00
1995	Vaughn, Mo 24K/All-Star	500	49.95	60.00
1995	Vaughn, Mo Bronze/All-Star	1,995	14.95	20.00

Year	Team	Mintage	Issue Price	Price
1995	Vaughn, Mo All-Star 3-pc. Proof Set	95	125.00	130.00
1996	Vaughn, Mo All-Star Ball/Coin Set	100	124.95	125.00
1997	Vaughn, Mo AL Photo/Coin Set	500	49.95	50.00
1988	Viola, Frank '88 Cy Young	15,000	29.95	32.00
1997	Visquel, Omar WS Photo/Coin Set	1,997	49.95	50.00
1997	Walker, Larry MVP Photo/Coin Set	500	49.95	50.00
1997	Walker, Larry 24K Bronze MVP	1,000	34.95	35.00
1990	Walton, Jerome '89 NL ROY	900	29.95	55.00
1996	Wetteland, John Silver/WS MVP	500	29.95	30.00
1996	Wetteland, John 24K/WS MVP	196	49.95	50.00
1996	Wetteland, John WS MVP 3-pc. Proof Set	96	125.00	125.00
1997	White, Devon WS Photo/Coin Set	1,997	49.95	50.00
1996	Williams, Bernie Silver/WS Reverse	500	29.95	30.00
1996	Williams, Bernie 24K/WS	196	49.95	50.00
1996	Williams, Bernie WS 3-pc. Proof Set	96	125.00	125.00
1997	Williams, Bernie Photo/Coin Set	500	39.95	40.00
1991	Williams, Billy 1987 HOF	15,000	29.95	35.00
1995	Williams, Matt Silver	1,500	29.95	40.00
1995	Williams, Matt 24K	125	49.95	65.00
1995	Williams, Matt Bronze	500	14.95	22.00
1996	Williams, Matt Silver/All-Star	1,995	29.95	30.00
1996	Williams, Matt 24K/All-Star	500	49.95	50.00
1996	Williams, Matt Bronze/All-Star	1,995	14.95	15.00
1996	Williams, Matt All-Star 3-pc. Proof Set	95	125.00	125.00
1997	Williams, Matt AL Photo/Coin Set	500	49.95	50.00
1997	Williams, Matt WS Photo/Coin Set	1,997	49.95	50.00
1992	Winfield, Dave	389	29.95	60.00
1993	Winfield, Dave Twins	14,611	29.95	40.00
1995	Winfield, Dave Silver	1,995	29.95	40.00
1995	Winfield, Dave 24K	500	49.95	60.00
1995	Winfield, Dave Bronze	1,995	14.95	20.00
1995	Winfield, Dave 3-pc. Proof Set	95	125.00	130.00
1997	Witt, Bobby AL Photo/Coin Set	500	49.95	50.00
1997	Wohlers, Mark NL Photo/Coin Set	500	49.95	50.00
1997	Wright, Jaret WS Photo/Coin Set	500	49.95	50.00
1990	Yount, Robin 1989 MVP	2,387	29.95	50.00
1992	Yount, Robin 3,000th Hit	12,632	29.95	35.00

Team Commemorative Coins

Year	Team	Mintage	Issue Price	Price
1998	Arizona Diamondbacks Silver	5,000	$29.95	$30.00
1998	Arizona Diamondbacks 24K	500	49.95	50.00
1998	Arizona Diamondbacks Silver Inaugural	1,998	37.95	38.00
1998	Arizona Diamondbacks 24K Inaugural	500	49.95	50.00
1998	Arizona Diamondbacks Inaugural 3-pc. Proof Set	198	125.00	125.00
1995	New Arlington Stadium Silver	5,000	29.95	40.00
1995	New Arlington Stadium 24K	500	49.95	60.00
1995	New Arlington Stadium Gold	100	850.00	850.00
1995	Old Arlington Stadium Silver	5,000	29.95	40.00
1995	Old Arlington Stadium 24K	500	49.95	60.00
1995	Old/New Arlington Stadium 2-pc. Silver Set	1,000	82.95	85.00
1993	Old/New Arlington Stadium	1,000	29.95	75.00
1995	Old/New Arlington Stadium 2-pc. 24K Set	100	135.00	135.00

Year	Team	Mintage	Issue Price	Price
1995	Atlanta Braves Silver Generic Coin	1,000	29.95	30.00
1995	Baltimore Orioles Silver Generic Coin	1,000	29.95	30.00
1996	Baltimore Orioles Silver/AL Wild Card	1,996	29.95	30.00
1996	Baltimore Orioles 24K/AL Wild Card	500	49.95	50.00
1996	Baltimore Orioles AL Wild Card			
	3-pc. Proof Set	196	125.00	125.00
1996	Camden Yards/Orioles Silver	1,996	29.95	30.00
1991	Chicago Cubs Silver Generic Coin	1,000	29.95	30.00
1990	Chicago Cubs 24K/1984 Division Heir	1,500	49.95	50.00
1990	Chicago Cubs 24K/1989 Division Heir	1,500	49.95	50.00
1988	Chicago Cubs Silver/Wrigley Field			
	First Night Game	39,012	29.95	30.00
1990	Chicago Cubs 24K/Wrigley Field			
	First Night Game	1,500	49.95	60.00
1990	Chicago Cubs/Wrigley 75th Anniversary			
		10,000	29.95	40.00
1995	Chicago White Sox Silver Generic Coin	1,000	29.95	30.00
1995	Cleveland Indians Stadium Silver	10,000	29.95	45.00
1995	Cleveland Indians Stadium Gold	61	850.00	850.00
1995	Cleveland Indians/Eddie Murray			
	2-pc. Silver Set	400	82.95	85.00
1995	Cleveland Indians/Eddie Murray			
	2-pc. 24K Set	100	135.00	135.00
1995	Cleveland Indians Silver Generic Coin	1,000	29.95	30.00
1995	Cleveland Indians Silver	1,000	29.95	40.00
1995	Cleveland Indians 24K	1,000	49.95	60.00
1996	Cleveland Indians Back-to-Back 2-pc. Set	196	82.95	85.00
1991	Colorado Rockies Franchise	10,000	29.95	40.00
1993	Colorado Rockies Inaugural	10,000	29.95	40.00
1995	Colorado Rockies Silver Generic Coin	5,000	29.95	30.00
1995	Colorado Rockies Silver/Record Attendance			
		5,000	29.95	40.00
1995	Colorado Rockies Silver/1995 Wildcard	5,000	29.95	40.00
1995	Colorado Rockies 24K/1995 Wildcard	1,995	49.95	60.00
1995	Colorado Rockies Bronze/'95 Wildcard	500	14.95	20.00
1995	Colorado Rockies 1995 Wildcard			
	3-pc. Proof Set	95	125.00	130.00
1985	Comiskey Park 75th Anniversary	680	29.95	75.00
1990	Old/New Comiskey Park	43,931	29.95	35.00
1995	Coors Field Silver 2-pc. Card/Coin Set	195	185.00	185.00
1995	Coors Field 24K 2-pc. Card/Coin Set	95	250.00	125.00
1995	Coors Field Inaugural Silver	1,995	29.95	50.00
1995	Coors Field Inaugural 24K	500	49.95	75.00
1995	Coors Field Inaugural Gold	95	850.00	850.00
1991	Florida Marlins Franchise	10,000	29.95	40.00
1993	Florida Marlins Inaugural	10,000	29.95	40.00
1997	Florida Marlins Silver/Wild Card	1,997	34.95	40.00
1997	Florida Marlins 24K/Wild Card	500	49.95	60.00
1997	Florida Marlins Wild Card 3-pc. Proof Set	197	125.00	139.00
1997	Florida Marlins 10pc Framed Set	500	399.95	400.00
1995	Houston Astros Silver Generic Coin	1,000	29.95	30.00
1997	Interleague Play Silver/Yankees-Mets	5,000	34.95	40.00
1997	Interleague Play 24K/Yankees-Mets			
	(Yankees side)	1,997	49.95	60.00
1997	Interleague Play/Yankees-Mets 3-pc. Set			
	(Yankees side)	500	125.00	125.00
1997	Interleague Play/Yankees-Mets 24K			
	(Mets side)	1,997	49.95	60.00

Year	Team	Mintage	Issue Price	Price
1997	Interleague Play/Yankees-Mets			
	3-pc. Set (Mets side)	500	125.00	125.00
1997	Interleague Play Silver/Cubs-White Sox	5,000	34.95	40.00
1997	Interleague Play 24K/Cubs-White Sox			
	(Cubs side)	1,997	49.95	60.00
1997	Interleague Play Cubs-White Sox			
	3-pc. Set (Cubs side)	500	125.00	125.00
1997	Interleague Play 24K Cubs-White Sox			
	(White Sox side)	1,997	49.95	60.00
1997	Interleague Play Cubs/White Sox			
	3-pc. Set (White Sox side)	500	125.00	125.00
1993	Kansas City Royals 25th Anniversary	5,000	30.00	40.00
1995	Kansas City Royals Silver Generic Coin	1,000	29.95	30.00
1990	Los Angeles Dodgers 100th Anniversary	5,000	30.00	65.00
1995	Los Angeles Silver Generic Coin	1,000	29.95	30.00
1995	Los Angeles Dodgers Silver/Rookies	1,995	29.95	40.00
1995	Los Angeles Dodgers 24K/Rookies	500	49.95	60.00
1995	Los Angeles Dodgers Bronze/Rookies	1,995	14.95	20.00
1995	Los Angeles Dodgers Rookies			
	3-pc. Proof Set	95	125.00	130.00
1996	Los Angeles Dodgers Silver/Wild Card	1,996	29.95	40.00
1996	Los Angeles Dodgers 24K/Wild Card	500	49.95	60.00
1996	Los Angeles Dodgers Wild Card			
	3-pc. Proof Set	196	125.00	125.00
1993	Montreal Expos 25th Anniversary	5,000	30.00	50.00
1995	Montreal Expos Silver Generic Coin	1,000	29.95	30.00
1995	Milwaukee Brewers Silver Generic Coin	1,000	29.95	30.00
1995	Milwaukee Brewers Silver/25th Anniversary			
		5,000	29.95	30.00
1995	Milwaukee Brewers 24K/25th Anniversary			
		1,000	49.95	50.00
1995	Minnesota Twins Silver Generic Coin	1,000	29.95	30.00
1995	New York Mets Silver Generic Coin	1,000	29.95	30.00
1995	New York Yankees Silver/Wildcard	5,000	29.95	40.00
1995	New York Yankees 24K/Wildcard	1,995	49.95	60.00
1995	New York Yankees Bronze/Wildcard	500	14.95	20.00
1995	New York Yankees Wildcard			
	3-pc. Proof Set	95	125.00	130.00
1997	New York Yankees Silver/Wildcard	1,997	34.95	35.00
1997	New York Yankees 24K/Wildcard	500	49.95	50.00
1997	New York Yankees Wild Card			
	3-pc. Proof Set	197	125.00	125.00
1995	Philadelphia Phillies Silver Generic Coin	1,000	29.95	30.00
1990	Rookies Mark McGwire/Jose Canseco	15,000	30.00	65.00
1995	Seattle Mariners Silver Generic Coin	1,000	29.95	30.00
1992	St. Louis Cardinals 100th Anniversary	5,000	30.00	50.00
1998	Tampa Bay Devil Rays Silver/Inaugural	1,998	37.95	38.00
1998	Tampa Bay Devil Rays 24K/Inaugural	500	49.95	50.00
1998	Tampa Bay Devil Rays Inaugural			
	3-pc. Proof Set	198	125.00	125.00
1995	Texas Rangers Silver Generic Coin	1,000	29.95	30.00
1992	Toronto Blue Jays Alomar/Carter/White			
		15,000	29.95	45.00
1993	Toronto Blue Jays Back-to-Back 2-pc. Set	400	82.95	175.00
1992	WS 3-Piece set	500	125.00	290.00
1993	WS 3-Piece set	500	125.00	255.00

PENNANTS & POSTERS

PENNANTS

The history of baseball pennants is perhaps the most difficult to track of all memorabilia. While a good deal is known about recent pennants, it's virtually impossible to determine how many were produced prior to 1970.

The first known baseball pennants appeared at ballparks around the turn of the century. From 1905-1910 the first pennants bearing team or city names were produced. The first commemorative pennant—celebrating the World Champion Boston Braves—appeared in 1914. By 1986, the market had grown considerably, as fans of the New York Mets had a selection of eight banners to choose from at Shea Stadium souvenir stands. Championship and single-season pennants through the years have evolved to include team rosters, facsimile signatures, and team photos.

But the earliest pennants were not always season-specific. In the early years, fans might find the same pennants for sale at the ballpark for several years in a row. And these pennants were generally made with excess and scrap felt, so sizes and colors would differ at each stadium. Manufacturer labels can often be found sewn on the back of pennants produced before 1940, but between 1940-1970 it's nearly impossible to determine a specific producer.

Technology in the 1970s brought a change to the traditional felt pennants. Synthetics were added to the fabric, making the pennants thinner, more rigid, and less expensive to produce. Two companies—Trench Manufacturers of Buffalo and Wincraft of Winona, Minn.—established licensing agreements and have been the major players in the industry since 1970.

Event-specific and commemorative pennants seem to be the easiest to track, as well as being the most popular with collectors. They're often limited editions sold only at ballparks involved in the event. Pennants from the World Series, ballpark openings, and retirement ceremonies fall into this category.

Attaching values to pennants is extremely difficult. Before the early 1990s there are no checklists available, and previously unknown specimens are continually being discovered. The best places to find vintage pennants are in the traditional baseball cities, at card shows, or through auctions.

In general, collectors prefer attractive pennants that can easily be displayed. Vibrant, colorful pennants, especially of the pre-1970 variety, are the most valuable and hardest to find. Many older pennants are faded, missing tassels, or have pin holes around the tip—all direct results of being hung on bedroom walls.

When collecting current pennants, hobbyists can look to three manufacturers—Mitchell & Ness, Tag Express, and WinCraft. Through extensive research, Mitchell & Ness has produced a line of replica pennants similar to those produced from 1907-1970. Each season, WinCraft produces a new pennant for every major league team, but their specialty is a line of pennants featuring player caricatures. Recently WinCraft has begun to produce wool team pennants that feature current team logos. Tag Express, the company that purchased Trench, specializes in event- and ballpark-specific pennants.

On the following page is a list of some of the WinCraft caricature pennants with their latest secondary market values.

1991-1992 WinCraft

Player	Team	Quantity	Price
George Brett	Royals	Less than 5,000	$10.00
Jose Canseco	A's	Less than 5,000	15.00
Roger Clemens	Red Sox	Less than 5,000	7.00
Ken Griffey Sr & Jr	Mariners	More than 5,000	10.00
Ken Griffey Jr.	Mariners	More than 5,000	10.00
Tony Gwynn	Padres	Less than 5,000	8.00
Don Mattingly	Yankees	More than 5,000	7.00
Mark McGwire	A's	Less than 5,000	6.00
Paul Moliter	Brewers	Less than 5,000	5.00
Cal Ripken Jr.	Orioles	Est. 25,000	8.00
Cal Ripken Jr. (MVP)	Orioles	More than 5,000	10.00
Nolan Ryan	Rangers	Est. 8,922	10.00
Nolan Ryan (Texas Heat)	Rangers	Est. 6,780	10.00
Nolan Ryan (5,000 Ks)	Rangers	Est. 11,093	8.00
World Champ '91	Twins	More than 5,000	8.00
World Champ '92	Blue Jays	Less than 5,000	6.00

1993 WinCraft

WinCraft began numbering its pennants in 1993.

No.	Player	Team	Quantity	Price
100	Kirby Puckett	Twins	More than 5,000	$6.00
103	K. Griffey Jr.	Mariners	More than 5,000	10.00
105	Mark McGwire	A's	Less than 5,000	7.00
106	George Brett	Royals	Less than 5,000	7.00
107	Ozzie Smith	Cardinals	Less than 5,000	6.00
108	Braves Fever	Braves	More than 5,000	5.00
112	Chiefs of Staff	Braves	Less than 5,000	5.00
117	Barry Bonds	Giants	More than 5,000	6.00
118	Nolan Ryan (Farewell)		More than 5,000	8.00
120	G. Brett (Thanks)	Royals	Est. 5,000	8.00

1994-1998 WinCraft

Quantities not available.

No.	Player	Team	Price
121	Miracle Mets 25th Anniversary	Mets	$10.00
123	Frank Thomas (MVP)	White Sox	10.00
128	Dave Winfield	Twins	5.00
129	Mike Piazza	Dodgers	7.00
134	Cleveland Tribe	Indians	5.00
135	Barry Bonds	Giants	6.00
138	David Cone	Royals	5.00
139	Greg Maddux	Braves	8.00
140	Randy Johnson	Mariners	6.00
142	Nolan Ryan	Rangers	8.00
147	Gary Sheffield	Marlins	5.00
148	Roberto Clemente	Pirates	10.00
150	Cal Ripken Jr.	Orioles	10.00
151	Ken Griffey Jr.	Mariners	10.00
156	Cal Ripken Jr.	Orioles	10.00
158	Barry Bonds	Giants	6.00
159	Mike Piazza	Dodgers	7.00
160	Mo Vaughn	Red Sox	5.00
161	Red Schoendienst-Stadium Exclusive	Cardinals	6.00
162	Big Bats II	Rockies	5.00
164	The Big Three	Rockies	5.00
168	Cal Ripken Jr.	Orioles	10.00

No.	Player	Team	Price
169	Cal Ripken Jr.	Orioles	10.00
170	Mo Vaughn (MVP)	Red Sox	6.00
171	Kirby Puckett	Twins	6.00
172	Albert Belle	Indians	6.00
173	Ken Griffey Jr.	Mariners	10.00
174	David Cone	Yankees	5.00
176	Paul Moliter	Twins	5.00
177	Marty Cordova (ROY '95)	Twins	5.00
178	Hideo Nomo (ROY '95)	Dodgers	7.00
179	Barry Larkin ('95 NL MVP)	Reds	5.00
180	Ryne Sandberg	Cubs	6.00
184	Cal Ripken Jr.	Orioles	10.00
186	Chipper Jones	Braves	8.00
189	Greg Maddux (4-time Cy Young)	Braves	8.00
192	Blake Street Bombers	Rockies	5.00
195	Rey Ordonez	Mets	5.00
198	White Sox Signature Pennant	White Sox	8.00
199	Rockies Signature Pennant	Rockies	6.00
200	Reds Signature Pennant	Reds	6.00
203	All-Star Game Signature Pennant		10.00
204	Alex Rodriguez	Mariners	7.00
205	Eddie Murray (3,000 hits)	Orioles	7.00
206	Paul Molitor (3,000 hits)	Twins	7.00
207	Ken Griffey Jr.	Mariners	10.00
208	Cal Ripken Jr.	Orioles	10.00
209	Albert Belle	White Sox	6.00
210	Frank Thomas	White Sox	10.00
211	Mike Piazza	Dodgers	8.00
215	Derek Jeter	Yankees	7.00
216	Cal Ripken Jr. (Stadium Exclusive)	Orioles	12.00
218	Mo Vaughn	Red Sox	6.00
219	Roberto Clemente	Pirates	10.00
220	Mark McGwire	A's	7.00
225	Rockies Signature Pennant	Rockies	6.00
226	Don Mattingly	Yankees	6.00
231	Mark McGwire	Cardinals	5.00
232	Roger Clemens (Cy Young)	Blue Jays	7.00
233	Ken Griffey Jr. (MVP)	Mariners	10.00
235	Nomar Garciaparra	Red Sox	7.00
236	Albert Belle	White Sox	5.00
237	Barry Bonds	Giants	5.00
241	Cal Ripken Jr.	Orioles	10.00
242	Frank Thomas	White Sox	10.00

Providing a price list on older pennants is extremely difficult. However, several older pennants occasionally appear in sports memorabilia auctions across the country. Here is a sampling of pennants featured in several recent auctions.

1910 Boston Red Sox

1954 New York Giants

1958 Milwaukee Braves

1962 San Francisco Giants

1966 Orioles v. Dodgers World Series

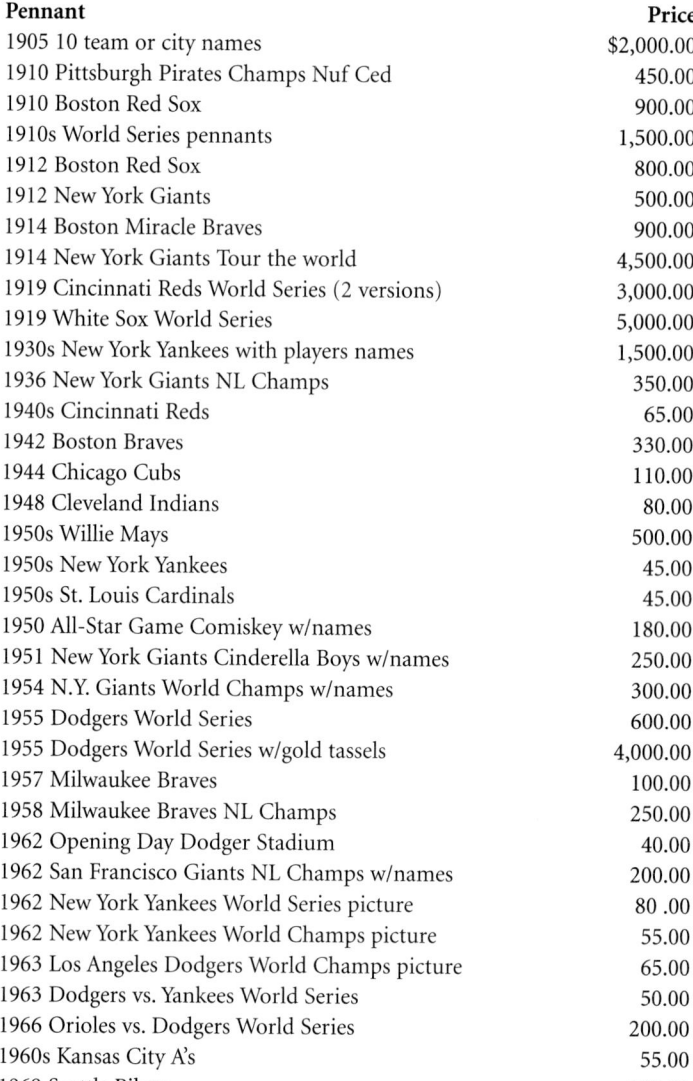

Pennant	Price
1905 10 team or city names	$2,000.00
1910 Pittsburgh Pirates Champs Nuf Ced	450.00
1910 Boston Red Sox	900.00
1910s World Series pennants	1,500.00
1912 Boston Red Sox	800.00
1912 New York Giants	500.00
1914 Boston Miracle Braves	900.00
1914 New York Giants Tour the world	4,500.00
1919 Cincinnati Reds World Series (2 versions)	3,000.00
1919 White Sox World Series	5,000.00
1930s New York Yankees with players names	1,500.00
1936 New York Giants NL Champs	350.00
1940s Cincinnati Reds	65.00
1942 Boston Braves	330.00
1944 Chicago Cubs	110.00
1948 Cleveland Indians	80.00
1950s Willie Mays	500.00
1950s New York Yankees	45.00
1950s St. Louis Cardinals	45.00
1950 All-Star Game Comiskey w/names	180.00
1951 New York Giants Cinderella Boys w/names	250.00
1954 N.Y. Giants World Champs w/names	300.00
1955 Dodgers World Series	600.00
1955 Dodgers World Series w/gold tassels	4,000.00
1957 Milwaukee Braves	100.00
1958 Milwaukee Braves NL Champs	250.00
1962 Opening Day Dodger Stadium	40.00
1962 San Francisco Giants NL Champs w/names	200.00
1962 New York Yankees World Series picture	80 .00
1962 New York Yankees World Champs picture	55.00
1963 Los Angeles Dodgers World Champs picture	65.00
1963 Dodgers vs. Yankees World Series	50.00
1966 Orioles vs. Dodgers World Series	200.00
1960s Kansas City A's	55.00
1969 Seattle Pilots	200.00

1969 Seattle Pilots

POSTERS

Thousands of baseball posters have been printed over the years, and aspiring young ballplayers across the country tacked and taped action images of their heroes on their bedroom walls. But while countless numbers of baseball posters have been issued, only a handful are prized by collectors.

Most older posters sell for just a few dollars, with the game's biggest stars commanding a premium. Tape marks, creases, thumbtack holes, and faded colors all take away from the value of posters, and many are tough to find without any of these imperfections. The price should be adjusted based on the condition of the poster.

Sports Illustrated Posters

The popularity of *Sports Illustrated* has carried over into the magazine's line of baseball posters. These posters are the most collectible in the hobby. From 1968 through 1972 *Sports Illustrated* issued 84 baseball posters, which originally sold for $1.50 each.

In 1983, Marketcom produced 44 baseball posters which were sold through *Sports Illustrated*. Although not as collectible as the original *SI* posters, the Marketcom issues have become more popular in recent years. Common posters book for $10-$15, while star players like Reggie Jackson, Tom Seaver, George Brett, and Mike Schmidt command $25-$50.

In 1987, *Sports Illustrated* teamed with Quaker Chewy Granola Bars to produce a series of mini (3x5-inch) posters similar to the full size posters from 1983. Common players sell for about $5-$10 while star players bring $20-$30.

Sports Illustrated Posters

Year	Name	Price	Year	Name	Price	Year	Name	Price
1968	Hank Aaron	$40.00	1968	Al Kaline	25.00	1968	Earl Wilson	10.00
1968-70	Tommie Agee	12.00	1968	Harmon Killebrew	30.00	1968	Jim Wynn	10.00
1968	Richie Allen	12.00	1968	Jerry Koosman	12.00	1968	Carl Yastrzemski	30.00
1968	Gene Alley	12.00	1969	Let's Go Mets	35.00			
1968	Felipe Alou	12.00	1970	Mickey Lolich	12.00			
1968	Max Alvis	12.00	1968	Jim Lonborg	10.00			
1969	Mike Andrews	10.00	1968	Jim Maloney	10.00			
1968-70	Bob Aspromonte	10.00	1968	Mickey Mantle	200.00			
1968	Ernie Banks	25.00	1968	Juan Marichal	30.00			
1968-70	Glenn Beckert	15.00	1968	Willie Mays	150.00			
1968	Gary Bell	12.00	1968	Bill Mazeroski	15.00			
1970	Bobby Bonds	12.00	1968	Tim McCarver	12.00			
1968	Clete Boyer	10.00	1968	Mike McCormick	10.00			
1968	Lou Brock	20.00	1968	Willie McCovey	100.00			
1968	Johnny Callison	12.00	1970	Sam McDowell	10.00			
1968	Bert Campaneris	12.00	1968	Denny McLain	15.00			
1968	Leo Cardenas	12.00	1968	Don Mincher	12.00			
1970	Rod Carew	35.00	1968	Rick Monday	10.00			
1968	Paul Casanova	10.00	1968-70	Bobby Murcer	12.00			
1968	Orlando Cepeda	14.00	1970	Phil Niekro	20.00			
1968	Roberto Clemente	100.00	1968-70	John Odom	10.00			
1968	Tony Conigliaro	15.00	1968	Tony Oliva	15.00			
1970	Mike Cuellar	12.00	1970	Wes Parker	10.00			
1968	Tommy Davis	12.00	1970	Tony Perez	15.00			
1968	Willie Davis	10.00	1968	Rico Petrocelli	10.00			
1968	Don Drysdale	25.00	1968-70	Boog Powell	12.00			
1970	Mike Epstein	10.00	1968	Rick Reichardt	10.00			
1968	Al Ferrara	10.00	1968	Brooks Robinson	75.00			
1968	Curt Flood	12.00	1968	Frank Robinson	40.00			
1968	Bill Freehan	12.00	1968	Pete Rose	40.00			
1968	Jim Fregosi	12.00	1968	Ron Santo	12.00			
1968	Bob Gibson	20.00	1968	Tom Seaver	75.00			
1968	Bud Harrelson	12.00	1968	Chris Short	12.00			
1970	Ken Holtzman	12.00	1970	Bill Singer	10.00			
1968	Joe Horlen	12.00	1968	Reggie Smith	10.00			
1968	Tony Horton	10.00	1968	Rusty Staub	10.00			
1968	Frank Howard	15.00	1968	Mel Stottlemyre	12.00			
1969	Reggie Jackson	100.00	1968	Ron Swoboda	10.00			
1968-70	Ferguson Jenkins	40.00	1968	Cesar Tovar	10.00			
1968	Tommy John	12.00	1968-70	Roy White	10.00			
1970	Cleon Jones	10.00	1970	Walt Williams	10.00			

Bob Gibson

STADIUM MEMORABILIA

Perhaps more than any other sport, baseball evokes a sense of place. Often the stadium itself is as much a part of a fan's experience as the players and the game on the field. Step inside Yankee Stadium, Wrigley Field, or Fenway Park, and you're not just taking in a ballgame, you're experiencing history and tradition embodied in the very atmosphere of the ballpark.

For many hobbyists, owning a piece of the stadium where some of the game's greatest moments occurred is the ultimate collecting pursuit. Some items—Rickey Henderson's 1,071st stolen base, for example—are tied to a specific player or event. More often than not, however, stadium memorabilia is generic—a seat, a flag, a sign, anything that recalls the experience of being in that particular ballpark.

The following list contains examples of various types of stadium memorabilia featured in recent auctions. Prices given are approximate values for specimens in Excellent to Near Mint, original condition. By its nature, especially in the case of ballparks that have been torn down, stadium memorabilia often shows great signs of wear and use. Beware "original" items that look too good to be true.

Yankee Stadium Cornerstone

Chances are they've been restored to some extent, which decreases their value to collectors.

Pricing Notes

Seats: Unless otherwise noted, prices given are for floor-mounted single seats. Wall-mounted seats generally bring lower prices since they are more difficult to display. Sections of seats attached to one another are also available, and such sections are denoted by the terms "double," "triple," and so forth.

"Figural" seats—aisle seats with decorative scrollwork in the armrests—are the most prized of all stadium seats, and can realize much higher prices than ordinary seats.

Flags/Banners: As every fan knows, each ballpark flies the flags of all of the teams in its league. This can make purchasing stadium flags and banners a bit confusing for collectors. In the list below, all flags and banners are listed with the ballpark in which they originally hung, regardless of the team featured on the flag.

Unless otherwise noted, all dimensions given are in inches.

Arlington Stadium (Arlington, Texas)

Stadium single seat—signed by Nolan Ryan	$900.00

Braves Field (Boston)

Figural seat side	$500.00
Stadium single seat	800.00
Figural stadium seat	1,000.00

Busch Stadium (St. Louis)

1992 clubhouse chair—signed by Joe Torre	$500.00
1967 Cardinals WS banner	500.00
Cardinals stadium banner—7x12 feet	1,000.00

Candlestick/3Com Park (San Francisco)

1989 home plate—from Game 3 of NLCS	$6,000.00
Willie McCovey cardboard locker name plate	300.00
Willie Mays cardboard locker name plate	600.00
Piece of Astroturf—1 sq. foot	100.00

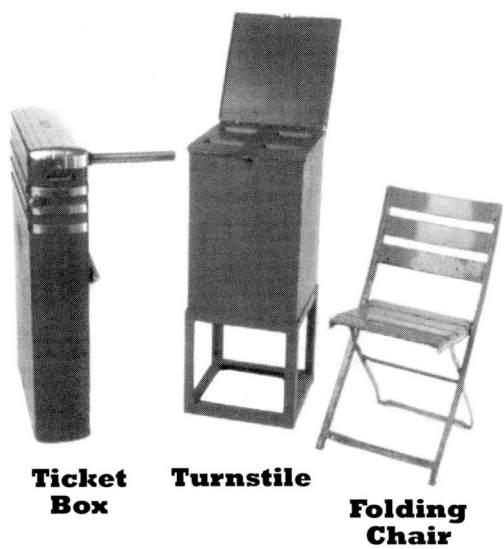

Ticket Box **Turnstile** **Folding Chair**

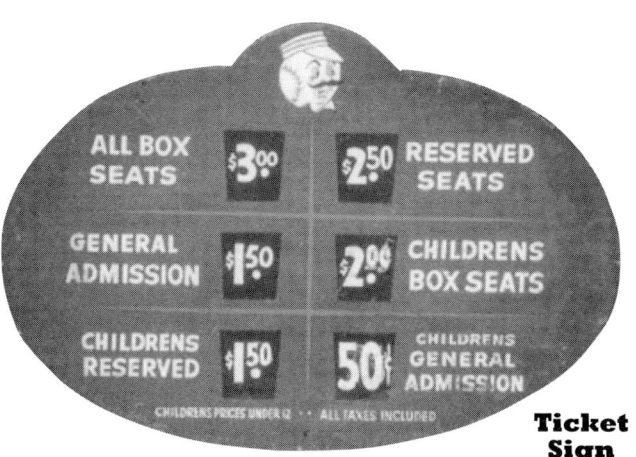

Ticket Sign

Cleveland Municipal Stadium (Cleveland)

Folding chair—metal and wood	$400.00
Stadium bleacher bench—7x84	500.00
Stadium single seat—orange	1,000.00
Bullpen gate—38x32	500.00
Home plate	800.00
Men's Room sign—22x11	300.00
Ticket window sign—17x18	200.00
Ticket box—blue	500.00
Turnstile—4 feet tall, blue	1,000.00
1970s "Basebug" mascot costume—complete	1,500.00

Colt Stadium (Houston)

Colt .45s stadium sign—9x6	$500.00

Cornerstone

Comisky Park (Chicago)

Folding chair	$300.00
Three connected folding seats	800.00
Stadium single seat	900.00
Figural stadium seat	1,000.00
1976 cardboard stadium sign	150.00
White Sox subway sign—18x25	500.00
1910 turnstile—green, brass top	2,500.00
Cast iron cornerstone—12-inch diameter	6,000.00

Crosley Field (Cincinnati)

Stadium single seat—red	$1,000.00
Figural stadium seat—red	3,000.00
1960s Los Angeles Dodgers banner—70x110	500.00
S.F. Giants stadium banner—70x110	500.00
1939 "Baseball Centennial" stadium banner	3,000.00
1939 NL Champions stadium banner—72x56	3,000.00
Cement and brick wall piece—red/white	150.00
Stadium wall brick—red	300.00
Scoreboard number—"1"	300.00
Stadium concessions sign—4x14	200.00
Stadium seating sign—36x24	1,000.00
"Mr. Red" Red Legs ticket sign	600.00
Stadium ticket sign—metal	2,500.00
Short Stop Inn neon sign	7,000.00
Clubhouse locker—74x31x29	3,000.00
Stadium microphone—used by Waite Hoyt	500.00
1960s usher's cap	500.00
1950s usher's uniform	800.00

Stadium Double Seat

Ebbets Field (New York)

Stadium seat slat	$200.00
1912 press box folding chair	1,500.00
Stadium straight-backed seat	1,000.00
Stadium double seat—cast iron and wood	3,000.00
Stadium double aisle seats	5,000.00
Stadium triple seat—Nos. 2, 3, and 4	8,000.00
1949 Dodgers NL Championship banner—31x34	2,000.00

Brooklyn Dodgers banner—118x53	3,000.00
Duke Snider banner—102x21	3,000.00
Stadium light fixture—21 inches	500.00
Rotunda light fixture	800.00
Brick—framed w/print	150.00
Brick—original red w/"1912-1957" stencil	1,000.00
Original on-deck circle	3,500.00
Second base—signed by several Dodgers	1,500.00
1952 WS second base—given to Abbott & Costello	3,000.00
Reserved seating sign—24x4	300.00
Press box typewriter	500.00
Usher's cap and pin	800.00

Stadium Double Seat

Cornerstone

Fenway Park (Boston)

Stadium single seat	$1,800.00
1930s stadium double seat	2,500.00
Center field wall piece—in display case	150.00
Green Monster wall piece—3x5	400.00
Green Monster netting—10x15	400.00
Scoreboard number—"38," 16x16	500.00
1979 Yastrzemski 3,000th Hit first base	2,000.00
1975 home plate	1,500.00
1980s entrance sign—6x6½-feet	1,500.00
1970s Yastrzemski cardboard locker plate	350.00
1930s locker—1½x6½x1½ feet	3,000.00
Door—oak w/brass handle, "Information"	3,000.00
Fenway Station subway lamp	800.00
1912 Park Dedication invitation	1,500.00
1932 renovation blueprints—41x29	4,500.00

Forbes Field (Pittsburgh)

1920s rentable bleacher seat back—steel	$250.00
Folding chair—purple and gray	400.00
Stadium single seat—arch back	1,000.00
Stadium double seat—Nos. 1 and 2	1,000.00
Stadium seats—four, Nos. 14-17	2,000.00
1960 "NL Champs" stadium banner—36x48	600.00
Left field wall brick	300.00
Entry gate baseball ornament	1,500.00
1909 turnstile—red with brass top	6,000.00
Directional street sign—24x24	1,500.00
Forbes Field trolley sign—16x48	1,500.00
Cement cornerstone—24x30	5,000.00

Stadium Double Seat

Fulton County Stadium (Atlanta)

Stadium double seat	$1,000.00
1974 second base—from Aaron's 715th home run	2,000.00
Visitors clubhouse sign—14x28	350.00
Bag of infield/pitcher's mound dirt	10.00

Griffith Stadium (Washington, D. C.)

Stadium single seat	$900.00
Stadium triple seat	2,000.00

Jacob's Field (Cleveland)

1997 All-Star Game folding chair	$500.00

Kansas City Municipal Stadium (Kansas City)

Stadium seat—white and blue	$1,000.00
Donation box—blue, lock top, 13x27x13	1,000.00

League Park (Cleveland)

Figural seat side—iron	$500.00
Folding chair—forest green	1,500.00

Street Sign

Stadium Single Seat

Memorial Stadium (Baltimore)

Stadium single seat—yellow and black	$600.00
AL Champs stadium banner—10x6 feet	700.00
1969 ALCS President's Box bunting	800.00
Stadium seating sign—12x18	300.00
Directional street sign—24x30	600.00

Milwaukee County Stadium (Milwaukee)

St. Louis Cardinals stadium banner	$800.00
Milwaukee Braves stadium banner—64x96	3,000.00
"Screamin' Brave" sign—18-inch diameter	2,000.00

Oakland Coliseum (Oakland)

1989 Team-signed WS Commissioner box chair	$3,500.00
1989 All-Star Game second base	1,200.00
1993 Rickey Henderson 1,071st stolen base (second base)	2,500.00

Oriole Park at Camden Yards (Baltimore)

Stadium double seats	$1,200.00
1993 All-Star Game third base	2,000.00

Polo Grounds (New York)

Stadium single seat	$1,000.00
Figural stadium seat	3,000.00
Harry M. Stevens stadium triple seat	3,500.00
Double figural seat—"DD1"	4,000.00
Giants Sign—from front of park, 32x5 feet	4,500.00
Scoreboard number—"2," 13x20, white & blue	750.00
1957 bullpen home plate—from final game	2,000.00
1930s stadium diagram—6½x9	200.00

Riverfront Stadium (Cincinnati)

Stadium golf cart—w/Reds cap roof	$2,500.00

Robert F. Kennedy Stadium (Washington, D. C.)

1960s Senators stadium banner—8x5 feet	$800.00
"AL Rules" stadium sign	500.00

Seals Stadium (San Francisco)

Stadium seat—blue	$1,000.00

Shea Stadium (New York)

Stadium double seat—18x48, orange and blue	$1,500.00
1969 second base—team-signed, from WS Game 5	10,000.00
Locker tag—Gil Hodges	300.00
Usher's jacket—wool, navy blue	500.00

Shibe Park/Connie Mack Stadium (Philadelphia)

Two-piece stadium sign—78x15, 96x15	$2,500.00
1940s stadium ticket sign—57x18	2,000.00
1960s stadium ticket sign—36x18	1,200.00
1909 turnstile	2,500.00
Stadium street sign—Lee Ave., 4x20	150.00
Stadium street sign—N. 20th St., 4x16	150.00
1950s Phillies usherette uniform	500.00
1908 cornerstone trowel	3,000.00

Skydome (Toronto)

Game-used base	$200.00

Sportsman's Park (St. Louis)

Stool—31 inches, from Browns front office	$800.00
Stadium single seat—wall mount	550.00
Stadium single seat—floor mount	900.00
Turnstile—red	1,000.00

Usher's Hat

Tiger/Briggs Stadium (Detroit)

1950s folding chair—iron, with padding	$425.00
Stadium single seat	600.00
Stadium single seat—wall mount	500.00
Figural stadium seat	2,000.00
Double figural stadium seats	3,500.00
Locker room sign—14x14	400.00
1940s usher's hat	1,000.00
Stadium License—from City of Detroit	300.00

Veterans Stadium (Philadelphia)

Stadium seat—plastic and aluminum	$500.00
Four pieces of Astroturf	50.00

Ernie Banks Stadium Banner

Wrigley Field (Chicago)

1930s folding chair	$450.00
Bleacher plank—green w/white seat numbers	600.00
1930s stadium seat	500.00
Stadium double seat	1,000.00
Stadium double seat—wall-mount	800.00
1945 World Series stadium banner—66x102	1,000.00
Cubs "W" victory banner	600.00
Cincinnati Reds stadium banner—36x64	500.00
Colorado Rockies stadium banner—32x68	150.00
Billy Williams stadium banner—58x93	700.00
Ernie Banks stadium banner—58x93	1,150.00
1940s Cubs stadium banner—6x8 feet	1,500.00

1990 All-Star banner	325.00
Scoreboard letter—"U," 16x32	250.00
Porcelain stadium sign—14x20	450.00
1930s "Please" sign (keep off the infield)	225.00
1945 World Series seating sign—cardboard	400.00
Turnstile—blue, slide-turning style	4,000.00

Stadium Policeman's Badge

Yankee Stadium (New York)

Stadium single seat	$1,000.00
Stadium double seat	1,500.00
1923 wooden seat—slat-backed, No. 13	1,500.00
New York stadium banner—7½ feet long	550.00
1996 ALCS stadium bunting—7x3½ feet	400.00
Original Babe Ruth retired number 3*	30,000.00
Original Lou Gehrig retired number 4*	30,000.00
Original Joe DiMaggio retired number 5*	30,000.00
Bullpen bench—reclining	2,000.00
Stadium "NY" drain grate	600.00
1950s stadium ticket drum	1,200.00
Turnstile—4 feet, blue	3,000.00
Yankee logo clubhouse emblem—41x18	1,500.00
Locker Tag—"Babe Ruth 3," brass	2,500.00
Lighted 3D sign—from Dan Topping's office	1,000.00
Directional street sign—36x42	500.00
Yankee Stadium/Polo Grounds subway sign	100.00
Marble and concrete cornerstone—19x16x4	15,000.00
Yankees vendor shirt—red and white	400.00
1950s usher's jacket	200.00
Stadium policeman's badge	400.00
Stadium policeman's hat	800.00
1922 scoreboard blueprints—hand drawn	500.00

*Actual retired numbers which hung in Yankee Stadium
before its renovation; values are approximate.*

Chadwick Park Stadium Sign

Miscellaneous

1988 Olympic game-used home plate—20 signatures	$400.00
Chadwick Park (Albany, N.Y.) stadium sign	800.00
Bears Stadium (Denver) stadium sign	500.00
Seats (3), Vaughn St. stadium (PCL)	300.00
Pete Rose locker, Lopez Field, spring training	2,000.00

CEREAL BOXES

In 1935, General Mills became the first cereal company to feature athletes on its packaging by picturing Olympians on boxes of Wheaties. Other companies followed suit, and today athletes from all sports regularly adorn a wide range of cereal boxes.

The first athletes appeared on the backs of the cereal boxes, and these images are considered to be cards by collectors. The first athletes appeared on box fronts in 1963. Typically, the standard shot was of a single athlete, until the 1987 Minnesota Twins became the first team commemorated on a single box.

Though Wheaties is the most prominent cereal for athlete appearances, it's far from the only brand endorsed by sports stars. Kellogg's entered the market in 1970 with a Willie Mays release, and resurfaced in 1983 with three issues. In 1991, Kellogg's used athletes on the boxes of three of its major brands: Corn Flakes, Frosted Flakes, and Frosted Mini Wheats. Wheaties may be the most popular with collectors, but the Kellogg's brands certainly have their fans.

OPEN AND SHUT CASE

A debate rages among collectors about whether boxes should be left full of cereal or emptied of their contents for long-term collecting. Full boxes, while mint in the truest sense, come with some problems: they attract mice and bugs that will bite through the box to get to the cereal. Plus, some brands of cereal will eventually eat through their plastic lining.

But removing the cereal doesn't automatically ruin the box. The easiest way to remove the cereal is to heat the glue that seals the bottom of the box. Once the glue has warmed, gently pry the box open with a knife and remove the package of cereal. After filling the box with newspaper or foam peanuts to prevent denting, re-heat the glue and seal the flap.

Some collectors remove the cereal, then carefully flatten the box along its creases. This is something to consider, as flattened boxes take up much less storage space.

Some collectors pursue boxes right off the press, before they are ever folded, glued, and filled with cereal. These boxes carry a slight premium.

While most athlete-adorned boxes are available nationally, a fair number are regional releases in the featured player's home area. Trading regional boxes has become a must in the hobby in order to build a comprehensive collection.

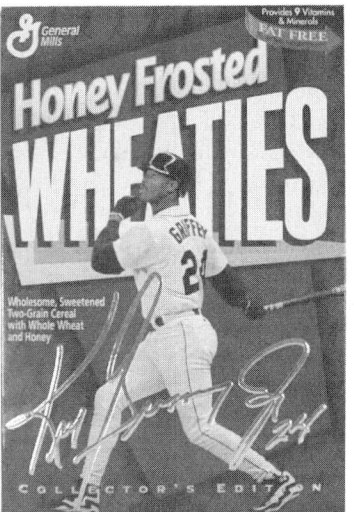

**1996
Honey Frosted
Wheaties**

Ken Griffey Jr.

BASEBALL BOXES

The first baseball players to make Wheaties boxes were Ted Williams, Stan Musial, and Bob Feller in 1951. Again, they appeared on the back of the box, and these pieces are considered cards in the hobby today.

Baseball didn't return to a Wheaties box until 1985, when record-setter Pete Rose graced a box. Since then, past and present stars like Babe Ruth, Johnny Bench, Lou Gehrig, and Cal Ripken Jr. have appeared. The story of Ripken's appearance is particularly interesting.

In 1995, as Ripken approached Gehrig's consecutive games played record, Wheaties was in such a rush to get a Ripken box to market that they acted without permission from Major League Baseball to use the Orioles' logo. So the first boxes, released regionally, had the logo brushed out.

When news of the release hit the hobby, collectors went wild to secure the boxes. Meanwhile, a national release—with the logo—was in the works. Once the boxes hit shelves nationwide, demand for the logo-less boxes dropped, though they still bring a premium compared to the national release.

The following list prices mint, unopened cereal boxes. Original, unfolded boxes are worth 10-20 percent more than the listed price. The year reflects the date when the box was issued. The brand is the type of cereal. An "N" under distribution means the box was distributed nationally, while an "R" indicates regional distribution. We also note which boxes were Canadian issues.

Kellogg's

**1995
Wheaties**

**Atlanta
Braves W.S.
Champs**

Year	Brand	Player/Team	Dist.	Price
1970	Corn Flakes	Willie Mays	N	$50.00
1983	Corn Flakes	Fernando Valenzuela (12oz./18oz.)	N	35.00
1983	Corn Flakes	Mike Reilly, umpire	N	20.00
1983	Corn Flakes	San Diego Chicken	N	25.00
1991	Corn Flakes	Aaron/Berra/Mays/Spahn	N	30.00
1991	Corn Flakes	Bob Gibson	N	25.00
1991	Corn Flakes	Ernie Banks	N	25.00
1991	Corn Flakes	Hank Aaron	N	35.00
1991	Corn Flakes	Lou Brock	N	30.00
1991	Corn Flakes	Steve Carlton	N	25.00
1991	Corn Flakes	Yogi Berra	N	25.00
1992	Corn Flakes	Mike Schmidt	N	30.00
1993	Corn Flakes	Nolan Ryan (18oz./24oz.)	N	25.00
1993	Corn Flakes	Nolan Ryan farewell	R	30.00
1993	Corn Flakes	Philadelphia Phillies WS Champions (phantom)	N	75.00
1993	Corn Flakes	Roberto Clemente portrait	N	35.00
1994	Corn Flakes	Roberto Clemente batting (English)	N	30.00
1994	Corn Flakes	Roberto Clemente batting (Spanish)	N	40.00
1991	Frosted Flakes	Atlanta Braves NL Champions	N	35.00
1991	Frosted Flakes	Atlanta Braves WS (phantom)	N	75.00
1991	Frosted Flakes	Minnesota Twins WS Champions	N	35.00
1992	Frosted Flakes	Atlanta Braves NL Champions	N	35.00
1992	Frosted Flakes	St. Louis Cardinals	N	35.00
1992	Frosted Flakes	Toronto Blue Jays WS Champions	R (Can.)	35.00
1993	Frosted Flakes	Colorado Rockies inaugural	N	18.00
1993	Frosted Flakes	Florida Marlins inaugural	N	18.00
1993	Frosted Flakes	Ken Griffey Jr. (20oz./25oz.)	N	25.00
1995	Frosted Flakes	Carlos Baerga (Spanish; 10oz./15oz.)	N	15.00
1995	Frosted Flakes	Colorado Rockies (Spanish)	N	15.00
1995	Frosted Mini-Wheats	Reggie Jackson (20oz.)	N	30.00
1995	Frosted Bite-Size Mini-Wheats	Reggie Jackson (20 oz.)	N	30.00

**1995
Wheaties**

**Cal Ripken Jr.
No Orioles
Logo**

Post

Year	Brand	Player/Team	Dist.	Price
1995	Honeycomb	Devon White	R (Can.)	$10.00
1995	Sugar Crisps	Devon White	R (Can.)	10.00
1997	Sugar Crisps	Moises Alou	R (Can.)	10.00

General Mills

**1995
Wheaties**

**Cal Ripken Jr.
With Orioles
Logo**

Year	Brand	Player/Team	Dist.	Price
1985	Wheaties	Pete Rose (12oz./18oz.)	N	$40.00
1985	Wheaties	Pete Rose (8oz.)	N	45.00
1985	Wheaties	Pete Rose (24 oz.)	R	50.00
1987	Wheaties	Minnesota Twins WS Champions	R	25.00
1987	Wheaties	Twins WS Champs (w/19 autos)	R	80.00
1989	Wheaties	Johnny Bench HOF	R	35.00
1990	Wheaties	Cincinnati Reds	R	35.00
1990	Wheaties	Jim Palmer HOF	R	50.00
1991	Wheaties	Minnesota Twins WS Champions	R	35.00
1991	Wheaties	Minnesota Twins WS Champions (.75oz)	R	100.00
1991	Wheaties	Rod Carew	R	100.00
1993	Wheaties	Babe Ruth	N	15.00
1993	Wheaties	Lou Gehrig	N	15.00

Year	Brand	Player/Team	Dist.	Price
1993	Wheaties	Willie Mays	N	12.00
1995	Wheaties	Atlanta Braves WS Champions	R	25.00
1995	Wheaties	Cal Ripken Jr. no O's logo	R	15.00
1995	Wheaties	Cal Ripken Jr. w/O's logo	N	12.00
1995	Wheaties	Cleveland Indians AL Champions	R	30.00
1996	Wheaties	Atlanta Braves NL Champions	R	12.00
1996	Wheaties	Kirby Puckett Retirement box	R	25.00
1996	Wheaties	Negro Leagues 75th Anniversary	N	12.00
1996	Wheaties	NY Yankees AL Champions	R	15.00
1996	Wheaties	St. Louis Cardinals NL Champions (phantom)	R	75.00
1997	Wheaties	All-Star: Bonds/Griffey/Gwynn	N	12.00
1997	Wheaties	All-Star: Cone/Maddux/Nomo	N	10.00
1997	Wheaties	All-Star: Griffey Jr./Ripken Jr./Thomas	N	12.00
1997	Wheaties	All-Star: Piazza/Ripken Jr./Sandberg	N	10.00
1997	Wheaties	Jackie Robinson 50th Anniversary (12oz./18oz.)	N	10.00
1997	Wheaties	J.ackie Robinson 50th Anniversary (no book offer) (12oz.)	N	10.00
1997	Wheaties	Seattle Mariners Western Division Champions	R	25.00
1997	Crispy Wheats 'N' Raisins	Jackie Robinson (18oz.)	N	9.00
1996	Honey Frosted Wheaties	Ken Griffey Jr. (1oz.)	N	5.00
1996	Honey Frosted Wheaties	Ken Griffey Jr. (14.75oz.)	N	10.00
1996	Honey Frosted Wheaties	Ken Griffey Jr. (38oz.)	N	15.00
1996	Honey Frosted Wheaties	Ken Griffey Jr. gold emboss (14.75oz.)	N	10.00
1997	Honey Frosted Wheaties	All-Star: Bonds/Griffey Jr./C. Jones	N	12.00
1997	Honey Frosted Wheaties	Jackie Robinson (14.75oz.)	N	10.00

Chapter 12

BOTTLES AND CANS

Cold drinks and baseball naturally go together, but you might be surprised how many people like to collect bottles and cans that commemorate athletes or events.

It's tough to know how many commemorative bottles and cans have been produced in the history of the game. The earliest known examples date to 1906, when six different bottles known as the "Champions of 1906" were released. Featuring Christy Mathewson, John McGraw, Joe McGinnity, Billy Gilbert, Leon "Red" Ames, and Mike Donlin from the 1905 World Champion New York Giants, the set is virtually one-of-a-kind. It's tough to price the entire set, but individually at auction the bottles attracted bids totaling $18,000.

In the 1950s, the Moxie Co. released root beer bottles featuring Ted Williams. These bottles are generally considered the first sports bottles to be widely available to the collecting public.

Through the early- to mid-1970s, miscellaneous sports-related beer and soda cans were issued, but it wasn't until 1977 that a full series of collectible cans was issued. That year, Royal Crown Cola released its first set of baseball cans. The 70-can set pictured many stars of the day, including Johnny Bench, George Brett, Rod Carew, Robin Yount, and Mike Schmidt. In 1978, RC released a second, 100-can set. Some players were repeated

from the previous year, while stars like Nolan Ryan and Reggie Jackson were added. While the cans feature head-shots of the players, the hats don't indicate which teams they play for, meaning RC didn't obtain the proper team licenses. The cans are tough to find in good condition due to rusting and leaks, but demand isn't high.

Coca-Cola baseball bottles and cans seem to be the most popular. Pepsi has also issued commemorative drink containers, but the Coke releases have historically garnered more attention from collectors. The original Coke bottles were 10 ounces, but in 1992 the commemorative issues dropped to eight ounces. The bottles and cans have celebrated World Series champions, team inaugurations, anniversaries, and players.

One of the more intriguing Coke sets in recent years was the 26-can Detroit Tigers set from 1985, featuring stars like Jack Morris, Alan Trammell, Lou Whitaker, and Kirk Gibson.

Cans left full of liquid will eventually rust and disintegrate. To avoid ruining their cans, collectors should open and drain them from the bottom. Prices below are for cans that have been treated in this manner. Bottle collectors obviously don't face this problem, and bottles are worth more with the liquid intact.

"Champions of 1906" Bottles

1977 Royal Crown Cola Cans

Recent Auction Results

Bottle	Price
1906 Christy Mathewson	$6,500.00
1906 John McGraw	3,500.00
1906 Joe McGinnity	3,500.00
1906 Billy Gilbert	1,500.00
1906 Leon "Red" Ames	1,500.00
1906 Mike Donlin	1,500.00
1950s Ted Williams Moxy Co. (unopened)	200.00
1950s Ted Williams Root Beer 6-pack w/Carton (opened)	300.00
1976 Pepsi Cincinnati Reds 1975 World Champions (unopened)	12.00
1976 Hudepohl Brewing Co. Cincinnati Reds World Champions	15.00
1977 Hudepohl Brewing Co. Cincinnati Reds World Champions	15.00
1980 C. Schmidt & Sons Casey's Lager Beer Duke Snider	15.00
1980 C. Schmidt & Sons Casey's Lager Beer Richie Ashburn	15.00
1980 C. Schmidt & Sons Casey's Lager Beer Whitey Ford	15.00
1980 C. Schmidt & Sons Casey's Lager Beer Monte Irvin	15.00

1977 Royal Crown

Bottle	Price
Sal Bando	$3.00
Mark Belanger	1.00
Johnny Bench	10.00
Vida Blue	3.00
Bobby Bonds	3.00
Bob Boone	1.00
Larry Bowa	1.00
Steve Braun	3.00
George Brett	10.00
Lou Brock	10.00
Bert Campaneris	2.00
Bill Campbell	1.00
Jose Cardenal	1.00
Rod Carew	5.00
Dave Cash	1.00
Cesar Cedeño	1.00
Ron Cey	2.00

Bottle	Price
Chris Chambliss	2.00
Dave Concepcion	2.00
Mark Fidrych	2.00
Rollie Fingers	8.00
George Foster	2.00
Wayne Garland	3.00
Ralph Garr	1.00
Steve Garvey	3.00
Bobby Grich	1.00
Ken Griffey	2.00
Don Gullett	1.00
Mike Hargrove	3.00
"Catfish" Hunter	5.00
Randy Jones	1.00
Dave Kingman	4.00
Dave LaRoche	1.00
Ron LeFlore	2.00
Greg Luzinski	2.00
Fred Lynn	2.00
Bill Madlock	1.00
Jon Matlack	1.00
Gary Matthews	1.00
Bake McBride	1.00
Hal McRae	2.00
Andy Messersmith	1.00
Rick Monday	1.00
John Montefusco	1.00
Joe Morgan	10.00
Thurman Munson	6.00
Al Oliver	2.00
Amos Otis	1.00
Jim Palmer	5.00
Dave Parker	2.00
Fred Patek	1.00
Gaylord Perry	10.00
Marty Perez	1.00
Tony Perez	2.00
J. R. Richard	1.00

Bottle	Price
Pete Rose	10.00
Joe Rudi	2.00
Mike Schmidt	10.00
Tom Seaver	10.00
Bill Singer	1.00
Rusty Staub	1.00
Don Sutton	3.00
Gene Tenace	2.00
Luis Tiant	2.00
Ellis Valentine	1.00
Claudell Washington	1.00
Butch Wynegar	1.00
Carl Yastrzemski	10.00
Robin Yount	10.00
Richie Zisk	1.00

1978 Royal Crown

Bottle	Price
1. Don Sutton	$2.00
2. Bill Singer	1.00
3. Pete Rose	10.00
4. Gene Tenace	1.00
5. Dave Kingman	2.00
6. Dave Cash	1.00
7. Joe Morgan	10.00
8. Mark Belanger	1.00
9. Steve Braun	1.00
10. Butch Wynegar	2.00
11. Ken Griffey	2.00
12. Ron LeFlore	1.00
13. George Foster	2.00
14. Tony Perez	4.00
15. Thurman Munson	6.00
16. Bill Campbell	1.00
17. Andy Messersmith	1.00
18. Mike Schmidt	10.00
19. Ron Cey	3.00
20. Chris Chambliss	3.00
21. Ralph Garr	1.00
22. Dave LaRoche	1.00
23. George Brett	10.00
24. Bob Boone	3.00
25. Jeff Burroughs	1.00
26. Bake McBride	3.00
27. Gary Matthews	3.00
28. Don Gullett	1.00
29. Rick Monday	1.00
30. Al Oliver	3.00
31. Ellis Valentine	3.00
32. Mike Hargrove	3.00
33. Hal McRae	2.00
34. Rollie Fingers	7.00
35. Dave Parker	3.00
36. Tom Seaver	10.00
37. Wayne Garland	3.00
38. Jon Matlack	3.00
39. Richie Zisk	3.00
40. Joe Rudi	3.00
41. Sal Bando	3.00

Bottle	Price
42. Greg Luzinski	2.00
43. Vida Blue	3.00
44. Bobby Bonds	2.00
45. Jim Palmer	7.00
46. Claudell Washington	1.00
47. Dave Concepcion	2.00
48. Rod Carew	10.00
49. J. R. Richard	3.00
50. Rich Gossage	2.00
51. Cesar Cedeño	2.00
52. Bert Campaneris	2.00
53. Marty Perez	1.00
54. Bill Madlock	2.00
55. Amos Otis	2.00
56. Robin Yount	10.00
57. Bobby Grich	1.00
58. Catfish Hunter	6.00
59. Butch Hobson	3.00
60. Larry Bowa	2.00
61. Randy Jones	1.00
62. Richie Hebner	1.00
63. Fred Patek	1.00
64. John Denny	1.00
65. Johnny Bench	10.00
66. Doyle Alexander	3.00
67. Dusty Baker	2.00
68. Bert Blyleven	3.00
69. Lyman Bostock	1.00
70. Bill Buckner	1.00
71. Steve Carlton	10.00
72. John Candelaria	1.00
73. Andre Dawson	4.00
74. Al Cowens	1.00
75. Eddie Murray	7.00
76. Dan Driessen	3.00
77. Jim Rice	3.00
78. Garry Maddox	3.00
79. Larry Hisle	3.00
80. Al Hrabosky	3.00
81. Reggie Jackson	10.00
82. Tommy John	3.00
83. Willie McCovey	10.00
84. Sparky Lyle	3.00
85. Tug McGraw	3.00
86. Paul Splittorff	3.00
87. Bobby Murcer	4.00
88. Graig Nettles	4.00
89. Phil Niekro	7.00
90. Lou Piniella	3.00
91. Rick Reuschel	3.00
92. Frank Tanana	3.00
93. Nolan Ryan	30.00
94. Garry Templeton	3.00
95. Reggie Smith	3.00
96. Bruce Sutter	1.00
97. Jason Thompson	3.00
98. Mike Torrez	3.00
99. Rick Wise	1.00
100. Bump Wills	3.00

Coca-Cola Products

Coca-Cola has issued several different regional commemorative bottles and cans over the years. This in not a complete list, but a sampling of issues available on the secondary market.

Bottles

Bottle	Price
1982 St. Louis Cardinals World Series Champs	
Score 10-12 (error) 10 oz.	$20.00
1982 St. Louis Cardinals World Series Champs	
Score 10-17 (correct) 10 oz.	15.00
1983 Baltimore Orioles World Series Champions 10 oz.	10.00
1985 Kansas City Royals World Series Champs 10 oz.	8.00
1989 Ty Cobb—1st in the Hall of Fame 10 oz.	10.00

8 oz.

Bottle	Price
1992 Florida Marlins Inaugural 1993 Season	$5.00
1993 San Diego Padres 25th Anniversary	3.00
1993 Best of the Bay—Oakland A's	3.00
1993 Best of the Bay—San Francisco Giants	3.00
1993 Baltimore Orioles '93 All-Star Game—Camden Yards	4.00
1993 Colorado Rockies—Don Baylor	3.00
1993 Colorado Rockies—Jerry McMorris	3.00
1994 Johnny Mize "The Big Cat HOF '81"	2.00
1994 Cincinnati Reds 1994 First Season in Central	2.00
1994-96 Florida Marlins	2.00
1994 Milwaukee Brewers 25th Anniversary Season	2.00
1994 Cincinnati Reds 1994 World Champs 1919, 1940...	2.00
1995 Ty Cobb—"The Georgia Peach"	5.00
1995 Astrodome 30th Anniversary	2.00
1995 Cincinnati Reds 1869 Logo	2.00
1995 Cincinnati Reds 1907 Logo	2.00
1995 Cincinnati Reds 1911 Logo	2.00
1995 Cincinnati Reds 1939 Logo	2.00
1995 Cincinnati Reds 1995 Logo	2.00
1995 All-Star Fanfest Texas	4.00
1995 Cal Ripken Jr.—Record Breaker	8.00
1996 Atlanta Braves 1995 World Champs	5.00
1996 Cincinnati Reds—20th Anniversary of the Big Red Machine	2.00
1996 St. Louis Cardinals Central Division Champs 1996	2.00
1997 Texas Rangers 1996 West Division Champs	2.00
1997 Jackie Robinson 50th Anniversary #1	5.00
1997 Jackie Robinson 50th Anniversary #2	5.00
1997 Cincinnati Reds—Big Hearts for Little Hearts	2.00

Cans

Cans	Price
1985 Detroit Tigers Team (26)	$35.00
Lou Whitaker	5.00
Alan Trammell	5.00
Marty Castillo	1.00
Doug Baker	1.00
Lance Parrish	1.00
Dave Bergman	1.00
Rusty Kuntz	1.00
Tom Brookens	1.00
Bill Scherrer	1.00
Gary Rozema	1.00
Howard Johnson	2.00
Willie Hernandez	1.00
Kirk Gibson	4.00
Barbaro Garbey	1.00
Aurelio Lopez	1.00
John Grubb	1.00
Ruppert Jones	1.00
Chet Lemon	1.00
Willie Wilcox	1.00
Doug Bair	1.00
Darrell Evans	1.00
Sid Monge	1.00
Juan Berenguer	1.00
Dan Petry	1.00
Jack Morris	4.00
1989 Baseball Collector's Series San Francisco Giants	$2.00
1989 Baseball Collector's Series Kansas City Royals	2.00
1989 Baseball Collector's Series Pittsburgh Pirates	2.00
1991 Atlanta Braves National League Champs	4.00
1992 Braves National League Champs '91 & '92	4.00
1993 All-Star Game Camden Yards	4.00
1993 Phillies 1993 National League Champions	2.00
1993 Royals 25th Anniversary 1969-1993	2.00
1993 Toronto Blue Jays Back-to-back AL Champs	2.00
1993 125 Years Cincinnati Reds	2.00
1993 Cincinnati Reds Play Ball	2.00
1993 Cincinnati Reds Take Flight	2.00
1993 Cincinnati Reds Crosley Field Ladies' Night	2.00
1993 Cincinnati Reds Champions	2.00
1993 Cincinnati Reds On The Air	2.00
1993 Cincinnati Reds 125 Years	2.00
1994 Pittsburgh Pirates—All Star Game July 12, 1994	2.00
1995 Boston Red Sox American League Champions	3.00
1995 Atlanta Braves World Champions	4.00
1995 Texas Rangers Buy 1 Ticket/Get 1 Free (dark blue)	2.00
1995 Texas Rangers Buy 1 Ticket/Get 1 Free (light blue)	2.00

Chapter 13

BASEBALL GAMES

**Baker's Ball Game
For Men & Boys**

Main Street Baseball

**Major League
Indoor Base Ball**

Many collectors believe baseball is the perfect game, and judging from the hundreds of versions released over the last century, it *makes* the perfect game as well. Since the late 1800s, baseball has been the inspiration for countless games designed around the strategies and players of the day. Many of these games were produced just once and are now hard-to-find curiosities. Others, like Strat-O-Matic, have withstood the test of time and still boast strong followings.

This section has been divided into several headings, including "Board Games," "Card Games," and "Miscellaneous Games." At times, these distinctions are completely arbitrary. Some board games, for example, use baseball cards, and some use electronic boards. In general, the distinction "Card Games" is used for games which either aren't played on a board at all, or that collectors prize more for their cards than for the game itself. "Electronic Games" generally refers to handheld digital or computer software games. Certain games, like "Main Street Baseball," combine elements from several categories, and are placed in the "Board Games" section for easier reference.

In general, prices are listed for games in Near Mint/Mint condition with the original packaging intact. For games made before World War II, and especially those made before the turn of the century, the price may be assumed to be for specimens in Excellent/Near Mint to Excellent condition, as few, if any, Mint examples of these games exist.

BASEBALL BOARD GAMES

Baseball board games have been around almost as long as baseball itself. From "mechanical" games with metallic players, to strategy games featuring armloads of stats, game manufacturers have come up with a variety of innovative and entertaining ways to capture the flavor of the national pastime. For collectors, baseball board games offer the best of both worlds—an attractive, eye-catching display piece that also provides hours of fun and enjoyment.

Board game collectors also have an advantage over traditional card collectors in that board games can be found at a variety of different outlets. In addition to baseball card shows and shops, hobbyists can find baseball board games at toy stores, game conventions, and shops devoted to both game and toy collecting.

When pursuing board games, it's important to take several factors into account. Obviously, a game's age and condition factor into its price. Look for complete games with the original pieces, board, and packaging all in good condition. Many games feature either player likenesses, or team and/or Major League Baseball logos, and collectors should expect to pay a premium for these officially-licensed examples.

Name	Company	Year	Price
Action Baseball	Pressman	1965	$75.00
Alexander Baseball Game	Unknown	1930s	500.00
All-Pro Baseball	Ideal	1950	125.00
All-Star Baseball Game	Whitman	1935	200.00
All-Star Baseball	Cadaco	1959	100.00
All-Star Baseball Game	Cadaco	1962	50.00
All-Star Baseball Baseball Game	Cadaco	1968	40.00
All-Star Baseball	Cadaco	1989	30.00
All-Star Electric Baseball & Football	Harett-Gilmar	1955	100.00
All-Time Greats Baseball Game	Midwest Research	1971	35.00
Alpha Baseball Game	Redlich Mfg. Co.	1930s	300.00
American Baseball Game	Unknown	1890s	1,000.00
APBA Baseball Game	APBA	1975	100.00
APBA Baseball Game	APBA	1995	20.00
ASG Baseball	3M	1989	30.00
ASG Major League Baseball	Gerney Games	1973	135.00
A Sports Illustrated Game, Baseball	Time Inc.	1975	75.00
Atkins Real Baseball	Atkins & Co.	1915	900.00
Autograph Baseball Game	F.J. Raff	1948	300.00
Auto-Play Baseball Game	Auto-Play Games Co.	1911	1,000.00
Aydelott's Parlor Baseball	Aydelott's Base Ball Card Co.	1910	500.00
Babe Ruth Baseball Game	Unknown	1933	1,400.00
Babe Ruth National Game of Baseball	Keiter-Fry Mfg. Co.	1929	1,200.00
Babe Ruth's Baseball Game	Milton Bradley	1930s	800.00
Babe Ruth's Official Baseball Game	Toy Town Corp.	1940s	1,000.00
Baker's Ball Game For Men & Boys	Unknown	1919	1,500.00
Ballplayer's Baseball Game	Jon Weber	1955	100.00
Bambino	Johnson Store Equipment Co.	1933	600.00
Bambino Baseball Game	Mansfield-Zesiger	1946	400.00
Base Ball Game	McLoughlin Bros.	1886	1,500.00
Base Ball Game	McLoughlin Bros.	1892	1,400.00
Base Ball Game	McLoughlin Bros.	1897	1,200.00
Baseball	George Parker	1885	1,300.00
Baseball	George B. Doan & Co.	1920	300.00
Baseball	J. Ottman Litho Co.	1915	400.00
Baseball Game	All-Fair	1930	200.00
Baseball	All-Fair	1946	75.00
Baseball	Milton Bradley	1940s	90.00
Baseball	Samuel Lowe Co.	1942	40.00
Baseball, Football & Checkers	Parker Bros.	1957	110.00
Baseball & Checkers	Milton Bradley	1910s	300.00
Baseball Challenge	Tri Valley Games	1980	40.00
Base Ball Dominoes	Evans	1890s	600.00
Baseball Gambling Wheel	Unknown	1930s	2,000.00
Baseball Game	Brinkman Engineering	1925	200.00
Baseball Game	Corey Games	1943	175.00
Baseball Game	Pan-American Toy Co.	1907	800.00
Baseball Game	Parker Bros.	1949	40.00
Baseball Game	Parker Bros.	1950	35.00
Baseball Game, The	Horatio	1988	40.00
Baseball's Greatest Moments	Ashburn Ind.	1979	20.00
Baseball Electro Game Set	Knapp	1929	300.00
Baseball Mania, The Board Game	Baseball Mania	1993	30.00
Baseball Strategy	Avalon Hill	1973	25.00
Baseball Strategy	Avalon Hill	1997	20.00
Baseball Wizard Game	Morehouse Mfg.	1916	600.00
Base Hit	Games Inc.	1944	125.00
Bernco Baseball Game	Bernco	1969	30.00
Bible Baseball	Standard Publishing Co.	1950	35.00

**Mechanical Baseball Game
Anderson**

**Mechanical Baseball Game
Principal Co.**

**Norm Cash
Educational Baseball**

Name	Company	Year	Price
Big Bucks Baseball	Kitchen Table Games	1997	40.00
Big League Baseball Game	J. Chein & Co.	1930s	80.00
Big League Baseball Game	A.E. Gustafson	1938	200.00
Big League Baseball	Saalfield	1959	150.00
Big League Baseball Game	3M Corp.	1967	150.00
Big League Baseball	3M Corp.	1971	35.00
Big Six: Christy Mathewson Indoor Baseball Game	Piroxloid Products Corp.	1922	1,500.00
Big 6 Sports Games	Gardner & Co.	1950s	500.00
Bob Feller's Big League Baseball	Saalfield	1950	300.00
Bobby Shantz's Baseball Game	Realistic Games	1954	275.00
Boston Baseball Game	Boston Game Co.	1906	1,000.00
Broadcast Baseball	J. Pressman & Co.	1938	250.00
Carl Hubbell Mechanical Baseball	Gotham	1950	325.00
Carl Yastrzemski's Action Baseball	Pressman	1962	225.00
Casey on the Mound	Kamm Games Inc.	1947	400.00
Challenge the Yankees	Hasbro	1960s	350.00
Champion Game of Base Ball, The	Schultz	1889	7,500.00
Champion Base Ball Game, The	New York Game Co.	1913	400.00
Champion Game of Baseball, The	Proctor Amusement Co.	1890s	200.00
Championship Baseball	Championship Games Inc.	1966	30.00
Championship Baseball	Milton Bradley	1984	25.00
Championship Base Ball Parlor Game	Grebnelle Novelty Co.	1914	2,000.00
Charlie Brown's All Star Baseball Game	Parker Bros.	1965	75.00
Chicago-Boston Fortune Telling Game	Unknown	1880s	1,500.00
Chicago Game Series Base Ball	George Doan Co.	1890s	2,500.00
Classic Major League Baseball (Green)	Classic	1987	200.00
Classic Major League Baseball (Yellow)	Classic	1987	30.00
Classic Major League Baseball	Classic	1988	15.00
Classic Major League Baseball	Classic	1989	30.00
Classic Major League Baseball (Travel)	Classic	1989	15.00
Classic Major League Baseball	Classic	1989	12.00
Classic Major League Baseball	Classic	1990	12.00
Classic Major League Baseball	Classic	1991	10.00
Classic Major League Baseball	Classic	1992	10.00
College Base Ball Game	Parker Bros.	1898	1,200.00
Computer Baseball	Epoch Playtime	1966	50.00
Danny McFayden's Stove League Baseball Game	National Games Co.	1928	800.00
Dennis the Menace Baseball Game	Unknown	1960	50.00
Diamond Game of Base Ball, The	McLoughlin Bros.	1894	2,500.00
Diceball	Ray-Fair Co.	1938	175.00
Diceball!	Intellijedx	1993	20.00
Dicex Baseball Game, The	Chester S. Howland	1925	450.00
Double Game Board	Parker Bros.	1926	400.00
Double Header Baseball	Redlich Mfg. Co.	1935	400.00
Durgin's New Baseball Game	Durgin & Palmer	1885	1,000.00
Earl Gillispie Baseball Game	Wei-Gill Inc.	1961	60.00
Ebbets Field Pro Baseball Game	Montminy Games	1997	15.00
Electric Baseball	Einson-Freeman	1935	75.00
Electric Baseball	Jim Prentice	1940s	100.00
Electric Baseball	Jim Prentice	1950s	60.00
Ethan Allen's All-Star Baseball	Cadaco Ltd.	1941	200.00
Ethan Allen's All-Star Baseball Game	Cadaco-Ellis	1942	200.00
Ethan Allen's All-Star Baseball Game	Cadaco-Ellis	1946	90.00
Ethan Allen's All-Star Baseball Game	Cadaco-Ellis	1955	75.00
Extra Innings	J. Kavanaugh	1975	40.00
Fan Craze	Unknown	1904	500.00
Fan-I-Tis	C.W. Marsh	1913	225.00

Name	Company	Year	Price
Follow the Stars,			
Watts Indoor Baseball League	H. Allan Watts	1922	500.00
Game of Base Ball	J.H. Singer	1888	800.00
Game of Baseball	Milton Bradley	1910	200.00
Game of Baseball	Milton Bradley	1925	75.00
Game of Baseball	Canada Games	1925	400.00
George Brett's 9th-Inning Baseball	Brett Ball	1981	25.00
Get the Balls Baseball Game	Unknown	1930	40.00
Gil Hodges Pennant Fever	Research Games	1970	125.00
Golden Age of Baseball Chess Set	Longton Crown	1997	850.00
Golden Trivia Game	Western Pub.	1984	15.00
Gonafalon Scientific Baseball Game	General Specialities Corp.	1930	225.00
Goose Goslin's Scientific Base Ball	Wheeler Toy Co.	1935	550.00
Graham McNamee Radio Scoreboard			
World Series Baseball Game	Radio Sports Inc.	1937	550.00
Grand Slam	Sming Game Co.	1979	25.00
Graphic Baseball	North Western	1930s	350.00
Great American Baseball Game, The	William Dapping	1906	450.00
Great American Game, The	Frantz Toys	1925	500.00
Great American Game of Baseball, The	Pittsburgh Brewing Co.	1907	450.00
Great American Game of Baseball, The	Hustler Toy Co.	1923	225.00
Great American Game of Pocket Baseball	Neddy Pocket Game Co.	1910	350.00
Great Pennant Races	Great Pennant Races	1980	25.00
Grebnelle Championship			
Base Ball Parlor Game	Grebnelle Novelty Co.	1914	400.00
Hank Aaron Baseball Game	Ideal	1973	125.00
Hank Aaron's Eye Ball Game	Unknown	1960s	200.00
Hank Bauer's Be A Manager	Bamo Enterprises	1953	200.00
Hatfield's Parlor Base-Ball Game	Hatfield Co.	1914	350.00
Henning's In-Door			
Game of Professional Baseball	Inventor's Co.	1889	1,500.00
Home Baseball Game	McLoughlin Bros.	1900	2,200.00
Home Baseball Game	McLoughlin Bros.	1910	1,500.00
Home Baseball Game	Rosebud Art. Co.	1936	200.00
Home Diamond,			
The Great Baseball Game	Have Diamond Co.	1913	600.00
Home Run Baseball Challenge	Ban Mar	1987	10.00
Home Run King	Selrite Products Inc.	1930s	600.00
Home Run with Bases Loaded	T.V. Morrison	1935	500.00
Home Team Baseball Game	Ben Dickenson	1917	350.00
Home Team Baseball Game	Ben Dickenson	1918	350.00
Home Team Baseball Game	Selchow & Righter	1948	150.00
Home Team Baseball Game	Selchow & Righter	1957	150.00
Home Team Baseball Game	Selchow & Righter	1964	40.00
Houston Astros			
Baseball Challenge Game	Croque Ltd.	1980	25.00
In-Door Baseball	E. Bommer Foundation	1926	250.00
Inside Base Ball Game	Popular Games Co.	1913	750.00
Jackie Robinson Baseball Game	Gotham Pressed Steel Corp	1948	1,000.00
Jacmar Big League Electric Baseball	Jacmar	1952	250.00
JDK Baseball	JDK Baseball	1982	30.00
Jim Thome's Pro Baseball Game	Montminy Games	1997	15.00
Jose Canseco's Perfect Baseball Game	Perfect Game Co.	1991	20.00
Junior Baseball Game	Benjamin-Seller Mfg. Co.	1913	225.00
Kellogg's Baseball Game	Kellogg's	1936	50.00
KSP Baseball	Koch Sports Products	1983	40.00
Las Vegas Baseball	Samar Enterprises	1987	20.00
League Parlor Baseball	Bliss	1880s	2,000.00
League Parlor Baseball	R. Bliss Mfg.	1889	1,200.00

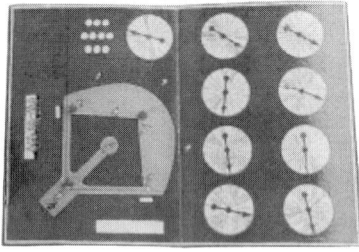

**Pat Moran's
Own Baseball Game**

Peg Baseball

Pro Baseball

Name	Company	Year	Price
Leslie's Base Ball Game	Perfection Novelty & Advertising Co.	1909	400.00
Lew Fonseca, The Carrom Baseball Game	Carrom Co.	1930s	1,000.00
LF Baseball	Len Feder	1980	30.00
Line Drive	Lord & Freber Inc.	1953	150.00
Little League Baseball Game	Standard Toycraft Inc.	1950s	85.00
Longball	Ashburn Industries	1975	90.00
Look All-Star Baseball Game	Progressive Research	1960	125.00
Lucky 7th Baseball Game	All-American Games Co.	1937	125.00
Mac Baseball Game	McDowell Mfg. Co.	1930s	350.00
Main Street Baseball	Main Street Toy Co.	1989	60.00
Major League Ball	National Game Makers	1921	750.00
Major League Baseball	Negamco	1959	30.00
Major League Baseball	Rodaco Ltd.	1973	15.00
Major League Indoor Baseball Game	Philadelphia Game	1912	7,500.00
Manage Your Own Team	Warren	1950s	150.00
Mather's Parlor Base Ball Game	Mathers	1908	750.00
Mechanical Baseball Game	Anderson	1940s	500.00
Mechanical Baseball Game	Principal Co.	1949	400.00
Mickey Mantle's Baseball Action Game	Kohner Bros.	1960s	200.00
Mickey Mantle's Big League Baseball	Gardner Toys and Games	1957	400.00
Mickey Mouse Baseball	Post Cereal	1936	125.00
Monday Night Baseball	Aurora	1960s	25.00
Montreal Expos Super Baseball	Super Sports Games	1979	20.00
MVP Baseball, The Sports Card Game	Ideal	1989	20.00
National Game of Base Ball, The	McLoughlin	1901	1,000.00
National Game, The	National Game Co.	1889	1,750.00
National Game, The	S&S Games Co.	1936	250.00
National League Ball Game	Yankee Novelty Co.	1890	700.00
NBC Baseball Game of the Week	Hasbro	1969	75.00
New Baseball Game	Clark & Martin	1885	400.00
New Parlor Game, Baseball, The	M.B. Summer	1869	12,000.00
New York Recorder Newspaper Supplement Baseball Game	Unknown	1896	1,000.00
Norm Cash Educational Baseball	Norm Cash	1960s	150.00
Numeric Baseball	Unknown	1960s	200.00
Official Baseball Game	Milton Bradley	1953	300.00
Official Baseball Game	Milton Bradley	1970	150.00
Official Denny McLain Magnetik Game	Gotham	1968	325.00
Official Dizzy and Daffy Dean Nok-Out Baseball	Nok-Out Manufacturing Co.	1930	700.00
Our National Ball Game	McGill & Delany	1887	800.00
Our No. 7 Baseball Game Puzzle	Satisfactory Co.	1910	250.00
Parlor Baseball	E.B. Pierce	1878	3,500.00
Parlor Base Ball	American Parlor .	1903	350.00
Parlor Baseball Game, Chicago vs. Boston	Unknown	1880s	5,000.00
Parker Bros. Baseball Game	Parker Bros.	1950	125.00
Pat Moran's Own Baseball Game	Smith Kline & French	1919	700.00
Pee-Wee	Pee Wee Enterprises	1956	500.00
Peg Base Ball	Parker Bros.	1908	250.00
Peg Baseball	Parker Bros.	1961	50.00
Pennant Chasers Baseball Game	Craig Hopkins	1946	80.00
Pennant Drive	Accu-Stat Game Co.	1980	20.00
Pennant Puzzle	L.W. Harding	1909	600.00
Pennant Winner	Wolverine Supply & Manf. Co.	1939	400.00
Philadelphia Inquirer Baseball Game, The	Philadelphia Inquirer	1896	400.00
Photo-Electric Baseball	Cadaco-Ellis	1951	150.00
Pinch Hitter	J&S Corp	1938	250.00
Play Ball	National Game Co.	1920	350.00
Pocket Baseball	Toy Creations	1940	40.00

Name	Company	Year	Price
Pocket Edition Major League Baseball Game	Anderson	1943	175.00
Polar Ball Baseball	Bowline Game Co.	1940	175.00
Popular Indoor Baseball Game	Egerton R. Williams	1896	1,200.00
Pro Baseball	Unknown	1940s	125.00
Pursue the Pennant	Pursue the Pennant	1986	40.00
Psychic Base Ball Game	Parker Bros.	1935	350.00
Radio Baseball	Toy Creations	1939	150.00
Real Action Baseball Game	Real-Action Games	1966	50.00
Realistic Baseball	Realistic Game & Toy Co.	1926	450.00
Red Barber's Big League Baseball Game	G&R Anthony Inc.	1950s	1,000.00
Replay Series Baseball	Bond Sports Ent.	1983	20.00
Right Off the Bat	Grand Slam Baseball Corp.	1997	25.00
Robin Roberts Sports Club Baseball Game	Dexter Wayne	1960	250.00
Roger Maris' Action Baseball	Pressman Toy Co.	1962	200.00
Roll-O Junior Baseball Game	Roll-O Mfg.	1922	700.00
Roulette Base Ball Game	W. Bartholomae	1929	250.00
Rube Bressler's Baseball Game	Unknown	1930s	400.00
Rube Waddell & Harry Davis Baseball Game	Inventors and Investors Corp	1905	1,750.00
St. Louis Cardinals Baseball Card Game	Ed-U-Cards	1964	100.00
Sandlot Slugger	Unknown	1960s	100.00
Say Hey! Willie Mays Baseball Game	Toy Development Co.	1954	600.00
Sher-Co Baseball	Sher-Co	1971	20.00
Slide Kelly! Baseball Game	B.E. Ruth Co.	1936	175.00
Slugger Baseball Game	Marks Bros.	1930	250.00
Snappet Catch Game with Harmon Killebrew	Killebrew Inc.	1960	150.00
Spin Cycle Baseball	Pressman	1965	75.00
Sporting News Baseball	Mundo Games	1986	25.00
Sport-O-Rama	Pin-Bo	1950s	100.00
Sports Illustrated Baseball	Avalon Hill	1972	75.00
Sports Illustrated Pennant Race	Avalon Hill	1982	20.00
Statis Pro Baseball	Avalon Hill	1979	50.00
Statis Pro Baseball	Avalon Hill	1987	15.00
Statis Pro Great Teams	Avalon Hill	1997	30.00
Strategy Manager Baseball	McGuffin-Ramsey	1967	60.00
Strat-O-Matic Baseball	Strat-O-Matic	1961	300.00
Strat-O-Matic Baseball	Strat-O-Matic	1969	35.00
Strat-O-Matic Baseball	Strat-O-Matic	1976	15.00
Strat-O-Matic Baseball	Strat-O-Matic	1992	12.00
Strike-Like	Saxon Toy Corp.	1940s	125.00
Strike Out	All-Fair Inc.	1920s	350.00
Strike 3 by Carl Hubbell	Tone Products Corp.	1946	800.00
Superstar Baseball	Sports Illustrated	1966	90.00
Superstar Baseball	Sports Illustrated	1974	35.00
Swat Baseball	Milton Bradley	1948	60.00
Tiddle Flip Baseball	Modern Craft Ind.	1949	60.00
Time Travel Baseball	Time Travel	1979	20.00
Tom Seaver Game Action Baseball	Pressman Toy Co.	1969	200.00
Triple Play	National Games Inc.	1930s	30.00
Tru-Action Electric Baseball Game	Tudor	1955	100.00
Ty Cobb's Own Game of Baseball	National Novelty Co.	1924	750.00
U-Bat-It	Schultz III Star Co.	1920s	150.00
Ultimate Sports Trivia	Ram Games	1992	40.00
Uncle Sam's Base Ball	J.C. Bell	1890	1,000.00
Wachter's Parlor Base Ball	Wachter	1888	400.00
Walter Johnson Base Ball Game	Unknown	1920s	450.00

Name	Company	Year	Price
Waner's Baseball Game	Waner's Baseball Inc.	1939	700.00
Whiz Baseball	Electric Game Co.	1945	75.00
Wil-Croft Baseball	Wil-Croft	1971	40.00
Willie Mays Push Button Baseball	Eldon Champion	1965	600.00
Willie Mays Say Hey Baseball	Centennial Games	1958	600.00
Win a Card Trading Game	Milton Bradley	1965	1,000.00
Winko Baseball	Milton Bradley	1945	100.00
Wiry Dan's Electric Baseball Game	Harrett-Gilmore	1950	75.00
World's Championship Baseball	Champion Amusement Co.	1910	400.00
World's Championship Baseball	Beacon Hudson Co.	1930s	200.00
World's Greatest Baseball Game	J. Woodlock	1977	100.00
World Series Baseball Game	Radio Sports	1940s	450.00
World Series Big League Baseball Game	E.S. Lowe	1945	250.00
World Series Parlor Baseball	Clifton E. Hooper	1916	350.00
You're Out Baseball Game	Corey Games	1941	200.00
Zimmer Baseball Game	McLoughlin Bros.	1893	12,000.00

BASEBALL CARD GAMES

ard games are another offshoot of collector interest involving all things baseball. The earliest games were produced in the mid-1880s, but aside from sporadic production since then, the majority of baseball card games were created in the 1990s. A sizable portion of the collectible card game market is comprised of playing card sets created regionally for local teams, and sets celebrating milestones like World Series victories and inaugural season team lineups. Most of these recent playing card sets don't command a huge premium, and are easily obtained for $5-$10.

Major League All-Stars Playing Cards 1991

Star Baseball Game

WG4 Polo Grounds Game

Game	Manufacturer	Year	Price
Ask Me Game of Baseball Facts	Quaker Oates	1930s	$300.00
Atlanta Braves Playing Cards	USPC	1992	6.00
Atlanta Braves Playing Cards (Silver)	USPC	1992	8.00
Atlanta Braves Playing Cards	USPC	1994	6.00
Atlanta Braves World Series Playing Cards	USPC	1992	6.00
Baltimore Orioles Playing Cards	USPC	1994	5.00
Baseball Card All-Star Game	Captoys	1987	10.00
Base Ball Card Game	Allegheny	1904	30,000.00
Baseball Card Game	Ed-U-Cards	1950s	35.00
Baseballitis Card Game	Baseballitis Card Co.		
		1909	205.00
Batter Up Card Game	Ed-U-Cards	1949	25.00
Big League Baseball Card Game	Whitman Pub.	1933	35.00
Boston Red Sox Game	Ed-U-Cards	1964	55.00
Boston Red Sox Playing Cards	USPC	1992	4.00
Chicago Cubs Playing Cards	USPC	1992	5.00
Cincinnati Reds Playing Cards	USPC	1993	4.00
Colorado Rockies Playing Cards	USPC	1993	4.00
Detroit Tigers Playing Cards	USPC	1992	4.00
E285 Rittenhouse Candy	Unknown	1933	7,000.00
Egerton R. Williams Baseball Game	The Hatch Co.	1888	8,000.00
Florida Marlins Playing Cards	USPC	1993	5.00
Game of Batter Up	Fenner Game Co.		
		1908	250.00
Joe "Duckey" Medwick Big Leaguer Baseball Game			
	Johnson-Breier Co,		
		1939	125.00
Lawson's Patent Base Ball Playing Cards	T.H. Lawson & Co.		
		1884	350.00
MLB All-Stars Playing Cards	USPC	1990	7.00
MLB All-Stars Playing Cards (Silver)	USPC	1990	8.00
MLB All-Stars Playing Cards	USPC	1991	6.00
MLB All-Stars Playing Cards (Silver)	USPC	1991	8.00
MLB All-Stars Playing Cards	USPC	1992	6.00
MLB Aces Playing Cards	USPC	1993	6.00

Game	Manufacturer	Year	Price
MLB Aces Playing Cards	USPC	1994	6.00
MLB Aces Playing Cards	USPC	1995	6.00
MLB Rookies Playing Cards	USPC	1993	5.00
MLB Rookies Playing Cards	USPC	1994	5.00
Minnesota Twins Playing Cards	USPC	1992	4.00
Minnesota Twins Playing Cards (Silver)	USPC	1992	4.00
National American Base Ball Game	Parker Bros.	1910	500.00
Offical Baseball Game	Milton Bradley	1965	295.00
Philadelphia Phillies Playing Cards	USPC	1994	4.00
Pro Baseball Card Game	Just Games	1980s	10.00
Psychic Base Ball Game	Psychic	1927	150.00
San Francisco Giants Playing Cards	USPC	1994	5.00
Scott's Baseball Card Game	Scott's	1989	20.00
Star Baseball Game	W.P. Ulrich	1941	115.00
T.J. Jordan Card Game	Unknown	1900s	500.00
Topps Blue Backs	Topps	1951	2,500.00
Topps Red Backs	Topps	1951	1,500.00
Topps Dice Game	Topps	1961	5,000.00
Topps Game Cards	Topps	1968	1,000.00
Toronto Blue Jays Playing Cards	USPC	1994	4.00
Toronto Blue Jays Playing Cards	USPC	1995	4.00
W502 Baseball Game	Unknown	1927	700.00
W560 Playing Cards	Unknown	1929	1,500.00
WG1 Baseball Card Game	Unknown	1888	20,000.00
WG2 Fan Craze AL Game	Unknown	1904	5,000.00
WG3 Fan Craze NL Game	Unknown	1906	5,000.00
WG5 The National Game	Unknown	1913	3,500.00
WG4 Polo Grounds Game	Unknown	1910	3,000.00
WG-6 Tom Barker Game	Tom Barker	1913	3,000.00
WG7 Walter Mails Game	Unknown	1923	4,000.00
WG8 National Game	S and S Games	1936	900.00

Donruss
Top of the Order 1996

Complete Set (360)	**$200.00**
Dual Starter Box (5)	90.00
Dual Starter Deck (160)	16.00
Starter Deck (80)	8.00
Booster Box (36)	75.00
Booster Pack (12)	2.50
Unlisted Commons	.20

Atlanta Braves

Chipper Jones (C)	$7.00
Tom Glavine (U)	1.50
Ryan Klesko (U)	1.00
Greg McMichael (U)	1.00
Marquis Grissom (R)	2.00
David Justice (R)	2.00
Greg Maddux (R)	15.00
Fred McGriff (R)	4.00
John Smoltz (R)	4.00
Mark Wohlers (R)	2.00

Baltimore Orioles

Harold Baines (U)	$1.00
Bret Barberie (U)	1.00
Bobby Bonilla (U)	1.00
Ben McDonald (U)	1.00
Mike Mussina (U)	2.00
Curtis Goodwin (R)	2.00
Rafael Palmerio (R)	2.00
Cal Ripken Jr. (R)	15.00

Boston Red Sox

Jose Canseco (U)	$2.00
Mike Greenwell (U)	1.00
Troy O' Leary (U)	1.00
Lee Tinsley (U)	1.00
Tim Naehring (R)	2.00
John Valentin (R)	2.00
Mo Vaughn (R)	5.00

California Angels

Chuck Finley (U)	$1.00
Tony Phillips (U)	1.00
J.T. Snow (U)	1.00
Chili Davis (R)	2.00
Gary DiSarcina (R)	2.00
Jim Edmonds (R)	2.00
Troy Percival (R)	2.00
Tim Salmon (R)	2.00
Lee Smith (R)	2.00

Chicago Cubs

Jim Bullinger (U)	$1.00
Jaime Navarro (U)	1.00
Rey Sanchez (U)	1.00
Steve Trachsel (U)	1.00
Shawon Dunston (R)	2.00
Mark Grace (R)	2.00
Brian McRae (R)	2.00
Randy Myers (R)	2.00
Sammy Sosa (R)	3.00

Chicago White Sox

Mike Devereaux (U)	$1.00
Lance Johnson (U)	1.00
Tim Raines (U)	1.00
Robin Ventura (U)	1.00
Ozzie Guillen (R)	2.00
Frank Thomas (R)	15.00

Cincinnati Reds

Jeff Branson (U)	$1.00
Mariano Duncan (U)	1.00
Jose Rijo (U)	1.00
Pete Schourek (U)	1.00
Bret Boone (R)	2.00
Jeff Brantley (R)	2.00
Ron Gant (R)	2.00
Barry Larkin (R)	3.00
Reggie Sanders (R)	3.00

Cleveland Indians

Jose Mesa (U)	$1.00
Sandy Alomar, Jr. (R)	2.00
Carlos Baerga (R)	4.00
Albert Belle (R)	10.00
Kenny Lofton (R)	6.00
Eddie Murray (R)	3.00
Eric Plunk (R)	2.00
Manny Ramirez (R)	8.00
Jim Thome (R)	3.00

Colorado Rockies

Vinny Castilla (U)	$1.00
Joe Girardi (U)	1.00
Bruce Ruffin (U)	1.00
Bret Saberhagen (U)	1.00
Dante Bichette (R)	3.00
Andres Galarraga (R)	2.00
Steve Reed (R)	2.00
Larry Walker (R)	3.00

Detroit Tigers

Cecil Fielder (U)	$2.00
John Flaherty (U)	1.00
Travis Fryman (U)	1.00
Alan Trammell (U)	1.00
Mike Henneman (R)	2.00
Lou Whitaker (R)	2.00

Florida Marlins

Terry Pendleton (U)	$1.00
Jeff Conine (R)	2.00
Chris Hammond (R)	2.00
Gary Sheffield (R)	3.00

Houston Astros

Jeff Bagwell (U)	$3.00
Craig Biggio (U)	1.00
Tony Eusebio (U)	1.00
Brian Hunter (U)	1.00
Dave Magadan (U)	1.00
Derek Bell (R)	2.00
Todd Jones (R)	2.00

Kansas City Royals

Kevin Appier (R)	$2.00
Vince Coleman (R)	2.00
Tom Goodwin (R)	2.00
Wally Joyner (R)	2.00

Los Angeles Dodgers

Tom Candiotti (U)	$1.00
Jose Offerman (U)	1.00
Ismael Valdes (U)	1.00
Eric Karros (R)	2.00
Raul Mondesi (R)	4.00
Hideo Nomo (R)	7.00
Mike Piazza (R)	8.00
Todd Worrell (R)	2.00

Milwaukee Brewers

Joe Oliver (U)	$1.00
Kevin Seitzer (U)	1.00
B.J. Surhoff (U)	1.00

Minnesota Twins

Alex Cole (U)	$1.00
Chuck Knoblauch (R)	2.00
Kirby Puckett (R)	6.00

Montreal Expos

Sean Berry (U)	$1.00
Wil Cordero (U)	1.00
Carlos Perez (U)	1.00
Mel Rojas (U)	1.00
David Segui (U)	1.00
Tony Tarasco (U)	1.00
Moises Alou (R)	2.00
Pedro Martinez (R)	2.00
Tim Scott (R)	2.00

New York Mets

Joe Orsulak (U)	$1.00
Ryan Thompson (U)	1.00

New York Yankees

David Cone (U)	$1.00
Paul O'Neill (U)	1.00
Wade Boggs (R)	3.00
Don Mattingly (R)	8.00
John Wetteland (R)	2.00

Oakland Athletics

Mike Bordick (U)	$1.00
Rickey Henderson (U)	1.00
Steve Ontiveros (U)	1.00
Mark McGwire (R)	4.00
Todd Stottlemyre (R)	2.00

Philadelphia Phillies

Ricky Bottalico (U)	$1.00
Lenny Dykstra (U)	1.00
Jim Eisenreich (U)	1.00
Tyler Green (U)	1.00
Charlie Hayes (U)	1.00
Mickey Morandini (U)	1.00
Heathcliff Slocumb (U)	1.00
Curt Schilling (R)	2.00

Pittsburgh Pirates

Dave Clark (U)	$1.00
Nelson Liriano (U)	1.00
Al Martin (U)	1.00
Orlando Merced (U)	1.00
Dan Miceli (U)	1.00
Dan Plesac (R)	2.00

San Diego Padres

Andy Ashby (U)	$1.00
Brad Ausmus (U)	1.00
Ken Caminiti (U)	1.00
Steve Finley (R)	2.00
Tony Gwynn (R)	7.00
Bip Roberts (R)	2.00

San Francisco Giants

Rod Beck (U)	$1.00
Mike Benjamin (U)	1.00
Steve Scarsone (U)	1.00
Barry Bonds (R)	8.00
Deion Sanders (R)	3.00
Matt Williams (R)	5.00

Seattle Mariners

Alex Rodriguez (C)	$7.00
Andy Benes (U)	1.00
Jay Buhner (U)	1.00
Joey Cora (U)	1.00
Tino Martinez (U)	1.00
Bobby Ayala (R)	2.00
Ken Griffey, Jr. (R)	15.00
Randy Johnson (R)	4.00
Edgar Martinez (R)	3.00
Billy Risley (R)	2.00

St. Louis Cardinals

Ray Lankford (U)	$1.00
John Mabry (U)	1.00
Ozzie Smith (U)	2.00
Bernard Gilkey (R)	2.00
Tom Henke (R)	2.00
Brian Jordan (R)	2.00

Texas Rangers

Juan Gonzalez (C)	$2.00
Jeff Frye (U)	1.00
Otis Nixon (U)	1.00
Will Clark (R)	2.00
Mark McLemore (R)	2.00
Dean Palmer (R)	2.00
Ivan Rodriguez (R)	2.00

Toronto Blue Jays

Paul Molitor (C)	$1.00
Devon White (U)	1.00
Roberto Alomar (R)	6.00
Joe Carter (R)	3.00

MISCELLANEOUS BASEBALL GAMES

Baseball has inspired innumerable games and gaming paraphernalia including darts, pinball, and—as technology has improved—video games. The more obscure items are frequently prized by niche collectors. As is the case with board games, player likenesses, team and league logos, and official licensing have a direct bearing on a game's value.

The following list provides examples of baseball gaming collectibles that have been featured in several recent auctions. The list is by no means exhaustive, but should give some indication of the wide range of baseball-related games and gaming collectibles available on the secondary market.

CASINO CHIPS

Bally's Grand Atlantic City 60th Anniversary Baseball Hall of Fame

	$75.00
Babe Ruth	18.00
Ty Cobb	18.00
Christy Mathewson	18.00
Walter Johnson	18.00
Honus Wagner	18.00
Bally's Park Place Atlantic City Willie Mays set of Four	60.00
Four Queens Hotel Limited Edition "Perfect Game"	50.00
Don Larsen	14.00
Enos Slaughter	10.00
Hank Bauer	10.00
Andy Carey	10.00
Gil McDougald	10.00

DART GAMES

Game	Manufacturer	Price
1935 Bee Gee Baseball Dart Game	Bee Gee	$70.00
1950s Clown Shoot/Dart Baseball	Bar Zim Toys	50.00
1998 Electronic Baseball Dart Game	QVC	65.00
1958 Major League Baseball Magnetic Darts	Pressman	150.00
1960s Rocky Colavito's Own Baseball 2 in 1 Dart Game		400.00
1950s Safe T Dart Magnetic Dart Game	Unknown	50.00

1938 Play Ball! Punch Board

PUNCH BOARDS/SCRATCH OFFS

Game	Manufacturer	Price
Baseball Tavern Gambling Game	Unknown	$50.00
Baseball One Cent Punch Board	Unknown	20.00

Game	Manufacturer	Price
1950s Diamond Dust (Mantle, Kaline, Berra, Martin, Snider, Ashburn)		425.00
Garcia Grande Very Mild Cigars	Garcia Grande	45.00
1915 National Base Ball Game	National	300.00
1938 Play Ball! Punch Board (Gehrig, Ruth, Cobb, Wagner, Johnson, DiMaggio)		800.00
1920s Two Baseball Games Play Ball Punch Board (Cy Young and Jimmy Foxx)		400.00

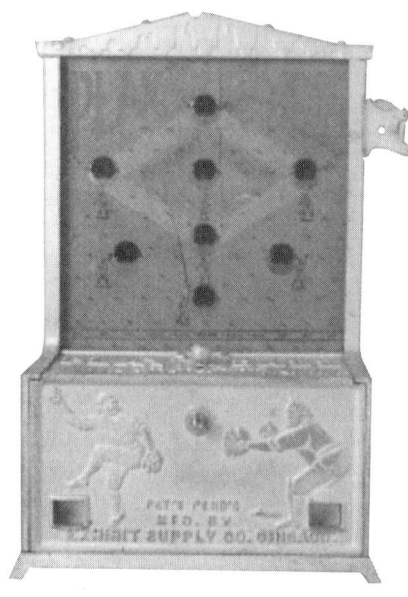

1920s Play Ball Penny Arcade Game

PINBALL/ARCADE GAMES

Game	Manufacturer	Price
1920s Baffle Ball Baseball	Unknown	$1,200.00
1933 Bambino Pinball Machine	Bally	8,000.00
1940s Baseball Coin-Op Machine	Unknown	800.00
1950s Baseball Dexterity Game	Elmar Products	50.00
1950s Baseball Pinball/Gumball Machine	Unknown	800.00
1920s Electric Baseball World Champion Game	Unknown	600.00
Jim Prentice Electric Baseball	Holyoak Electric Toys	200.00
1930s Lou Gehrig's Official Playball	Christy Walsh	1,000.00
Mr. Pinball Game	Marx Toys	20.00
1920s Play Ball Penny Arcade Game	Exhibit Supply	1,200.00
1940s Play Ball Penny Arcade Game	Unknown	200.00
1940s Play Ball Pinball Game	Unknown	100.00
1920s Poosh-M-Up Jr.	Northwestern Products	100.00

Game	Manufacturer	Price
1932 Poosh-M-Up 4 in 1 Game	Northwestern	75.00
1946 Poosh-M-Up Slugger Bagatelle	Northwestern	200.00
1950 Poosh-M-Up Table Pinball	Northwestern	150.00
Poosh-M-Up Streamliner 5 Games in 1	Northwestern	60.00
1930s Skor-It Bagatelle	Northwestern	300.00
1934 World Series Pinball Game	Unknown	2,070.00

Jimmy Piersall's Little Pro Bat A Round

OUTDOOR GAMES

Game	Manufacturer	Price
1880/90s Champion Bean Bag Game	Champion	$1,835.00
Jimmy Piersall's Little Pro Bat A Round	Unknown	600.00
1960 Mickey Mantle's Backyard Baseball	Unknown	300.00
Mickey Mantle's Batmaster Game	Unknown	250.00
Mike Schmidt Pitch 'n' Field Game	Unknown	150.00
Whirly Bird Game with Warren Spahn	Unknown	75.00

VIDEO/ELECTRONIC GAMES

Game	Manufacturer	Price
Atari Real Sports Baseball	Atari (2600)	$10.00
Atari Baseball	Atari (7800)	8.00

Game	Manufacturer	Price
Aaron vs. Ruth	Mindscape	35.00
All-Star Baseball '97 Featuring Frank Thomas	Acclaim	40.00
All-Star Baseball '98	Acclaim	50.00
All-Star Sports	Encore Software	35.00
Backyard Baseball GT	Interactive Software	32.00
Baseball Mogul GT	Value/Wizard Works	33.00
Baseball's Greatest Hits	Voyager	30.00
Cal Ripken Jr. Fantasy Baseball	Fantasy Sports	25.00
Coleco Head-to-Head Baseball	Coleco	30.00
Colecovision Baseball	Coleco	15.00
Dinomight Baseball	Microform Manf.	40.00
Eurekas Sports	Nodtronics PTY LTD	15.00
Fantasy League Baseball	IBM Multimedia	45.00
Frank Thomas Big Hurt Baseball	Acclaim	15.00
Front Page Baseball '98	Sierra On-Line	35.00
Game Gear World Series Baseball '97	Sega	25.00
Hardball 3 Featuring Al Michaels	Accolade	20.00
Hardball 5 Enhanced	Electronic Arts	25.00
High Heat Baseball	3DO Company	40.00
Intellivision Baseball	Mattel	15.00
Intellivision World Championship Baseball	Mattel	25.00
King of Baseball (Japanese)	Nintendo	60.00
Mattel Handheld Baseball	Mattel	20.00
Mego Pulsonic Baseball	Mego	20.00
Mego Pulsonic Baseball II	Mego	15.00
MS Baseball 3D	Microsoft	50.00
Nintendo 8 Bit Baseball	Nintendo	20.00
Odyssey 2 Baseball	Magnivox	10.00
Pro League Baseball '97	Micro League	25.00
Reggie Jackson Baseball	Sega	20.00
Roger Clemens MVP Baseball	Sega	15.00
Sega Championship Baseball	Sega	20.00
Sega Sports Talk Baseball	Sega	15.00
SI Microleague Baseball 6.0	Micro League	40.00
Talking Baseball Handheld Game	VTech	20.00
Tony La Russa Baseball 4	Maxis	50.00
Topps Cybrcards	Topps	
Alex Rodriguez		25.00
Barry Bonds		25.00
Bernie Williams		25.00
Cal Ripken Jr.		25.00
Chipper Jones		25.00
Derek Jeter		25.00
Frank Thomas		25.00
Juan Gonzalez		25.00
Mark McGwire		25.00
Mike Piazza		25.00
Mo Vaughn		25.00
Total Baseball '93	Z Master Prod.	17.00
Triple Play '98	EA Sports	45.00
Ultimate Baseball Series	Electronic Arts	33.00
Virtual Boy Professional Baseball (Japanese)	Kemco	15.00
Virtual Boy League Baseball (American)	Kemco	25.00
VR Baseball '96	Interplay	50.00
VR Baseball '97	Interplay	40.00
World Series Baseball '98	Sega	50.00

BASEBALL MOVIES

MOVIE MEMORABILIA

In the years before television, baseball was America's national pastime, and the movies were the country's most popular form of entertainment—so it's no wonder that enterprising filmmakers often turned to the sport for material. Baseball films began appearing almost simultaneously with the development of movies themselves, the first examples being *Ballgame* (1896) and *Casey at the Bat* (1899), produced by none other than Thomas Edison. Numerous films of varying degrees of quality have followed. From the ridiculous (*The Babe Ruth Story, Roogie's Bump*) to the sublime (*Bang the Drum Slowly, Bull Durham*), Hollywood has chronicled the game for over a century.

For collectors, baseball movies provide a wide variety of desirable memorabilia. From advertising posters to actual props, baseball movie collectibles are as eclectic as those from the game itself.

The following list provides examples of memorabilia from various baseball and baseball-related movies. Each listing provides the film title, principal actors, studio, and year released—except in cases when actual baseball players appeared in a film, in which case they are listed instead of the movie's "stars." Approximate prices are then listed for various collectibles from each film, but remember that auctions often take on a life of their own, and items can fetch prices well above their estimated value.

Notes on price listings:

Video and Laserdiscs: Prices given for new copies only. In cases where the video is out of print, or no longer widely available, no price is listed.

Posters: Prices given for Excellent/Near Mint examples of original posters that hung in movie theaters. Posters are used for advertising purposes, and nearly all examples will show some type of wear from use. Unless otherwise noted, prices are for posters from a film's original run—corresponding with the date given in the header—and not a re-release. Posters bearing later dates are from re-releases, or are replicas, and are worth considerably less.

Photos: Autographed photo prices are given for publicity photos from the film. For example, a Ty Cobb 8x10 signed by Tommy Lee Jones indicates a photo of Jones in character as Ty Cobb, not a Jones-signed picture of Ty Cobb the baseball player.

Jerseys/Uniforms: Prices given are for actual prop uniforms worn by the actors in the movie. The term "replica" is used to avoid confusion in cases where actors portrayed real ballplayers. The Lou Gehrig jersey from *Pride of the Yankees* isn't an actual Lou Gehrig jersey, but a replica made by the Western Costume Company. Manufacturer names have been given, where possible.

Unless otherwise noted, all dimensions given are in inches.

Movie Poster
Angels in the Outfield

Angels in the Outfield (original)—Ty Cobb, Joe DiMaggio; MGM; 1951

Video	$13.00
Laserdisc	25.00
One-Sheet Movie Poster	300.00
Insert Poster	75.00

Angels in the Outfield (remake)—Danny Glover; Disney; 1994

Video	$12.00
One-Sheet Movie Poster	20.00

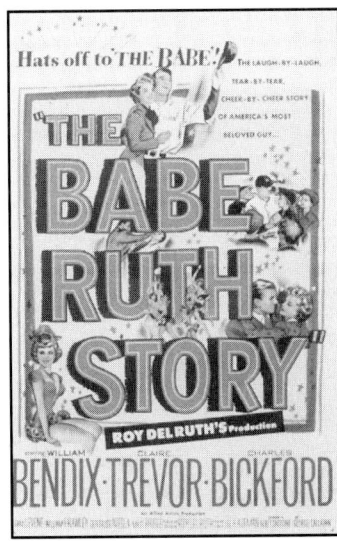

**Movie Poster
The Babe Ruth Story**

**Movie Poster
The Bad News Bears**

**Movie Poster
Bang the Drum Slowly**

The Babe—John Goodman; Universal; 1992

Video	$10.00
Laserdisc	30.00
One-Sheet Movie Poster	20.00
Baseball—signed by Goodman	80.00
Bat—signed by Goodman	200.00
Replica Babe Ruth Uniform—worn by Goodman	3,000.00

The Babe Ruth Story—William Bendix; Allied Artists; 1948

One-Sheet Movie Poster—27x41	$800.00
Six-Sheet Movie Poster—82x41	1,500.00
Half-Sheet Movie Poster and Press Book	900.00
Insert Poster	800.00
Lobby Card	300.00

The Bad News Bears—Walter Mathau, Tatum O'Neal; Paramount; 1976

Video	$15.00
Laserdisc	25.00
One-Sheet Movie Poster	50.00

Bang the Drum Slowly—Robert DeNiro; Paramount; 1973

Video	$15.00
Laserdisc	25.00
One-Sheet Movie Poster	50.00
Baseball—signed by DeNiro	120.00
Bat—signed by DeNiro	300.00
Replica Yankees Jersey—McAuliffe, worn by DeNiro	1,500.00

Big Leaguer—Edward G. Robinson; MGM; 1953

Lobby Card—14x17	$300.00

Bingo Long Traveling All-Stars—Richard Pryor; Universal; 1976

One-Sheet Movie Poster	$50.00
Bingo Long Uniform—worn by Pryor	1,500.00

Bull Durham—Kevin Costner, Susan Sarandon, Tim Robbins; Orion; 1988

Video	$15.00
Laserdisc (remastered)	30.00
One-Sheet Movie Poster—Costner and Sarandon	30.00
One-Sheet Movie Poster—Costner alone	50.00
Promotional Baseball Cards	10.00
Lobby Standee	40.00
Baseball—signed by Costner	100.00
Baseball—signed by Robbins	200.00
Bat—signed by Costner, Sarandon, Robbins	400.00

The Busher—Charles Ray; Paramount; 1919

One-Sheet Movie Poster	$3,000.00

Casey at the Bat—Wallace Beery; Paramount; 1927

Lobby Cards—11x14, set of four	$1,200.00

Cobb—Tommy Lee Jones; Warner Bros.; 1994

Video	$15.00
Laserdisc	35.00
One-Sheet Movie Poster	20.00
Ty Cobb 8x10—signed by Jones	50.00
Baseball—signed by Jones	90.00
Bat—signed by Jones	200.00

**Replica White Sox Jersey
Eight Men Out**

**Video Cover
Field of Dreams**

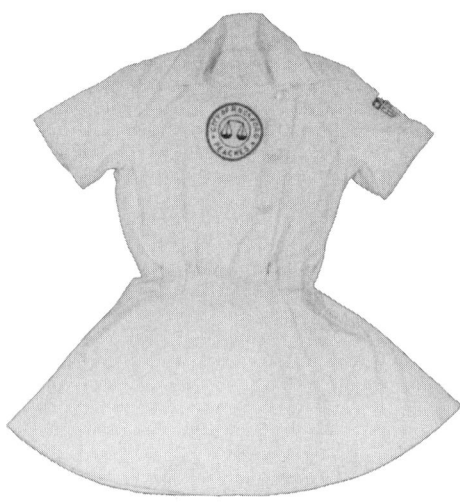

**Madonna's Uniform
A League of Their Own**

Damn Yankees—Ray Walston, Jean Stapleton; Warner Bros.; 1958

Video	$17.00
Laserdisc	20.00
One-Sheet Movie Poster	300.00
Lobby Card	90.00

Eight Men Out—John Cusak, Charlie Sheen; Orion; 1988

Video	$10.00
One-Sheet Movie Poster	40.00
Ring—presented to cast members, "Miller St. Louis Browns"	1,200.00
Replica White Sox Jersey—Western Costume Co., worn by extra	1,000.00

Fear Strikes Out—Anthony Perkins; Paramount; 1957

Video	$15.00
Laserdisc	30.00
One-Sheet Movie Poster	300.00

Field of Dreams—Kevin Costner, Ray Liotta; Universal; 1989

Video	$10.00
Laserdisc	30.00
Laserdisc (Signature Collection)	75.00
One-Sheet Movie Poster	100.00
One-Sheet Movie Poster—signed by Costner	150.00
Joe Jackson 8x10—signed by Liotta	50.00
Ray Kinsella 8x10—signed by Costner	50.00
Baseball—signed by Costner	100.00
Baseball—signed by Liotta	100.00
Baseball—signed by Costner, Liotta	150.00
Bat—signed by Costner, Liotta	300.00

Headin' Home—Babe Ruth; Yankee Pictures; 1920

Theater Give-Away Card—1 $\frac{13}{16}$x3 $\frac{5}{16}$	$5,000.00
Lobby Card—set of eight*	20,700.00

*Only one set known to exist.
Sold in 1995 as a complete set, but has since been broken up.

It Happens Every Spring—Ray Milland; 20th Century Fox; 1949

Video	$17.00
One-Sheet Movie Poster	400.00

The Jackie Robinson Story—Jackie Robinson, Ruby Dee; MGM; 1950

Video	$17.00
One-Sheet Movie Poster—27x41	2,000.00
Half-Sheet Poster—22x28	1,000.00
Insert Poster—14x36	1,000.00
Lobby Card—Robinson in Montreal Royals Uniform	500.00
Lobby Card—Robinson and Minor Watson	200.00
Lobby Cards—set of eight	1,000.00
Baseball—signed by Robinson, 17 other cast members	1,200.00

The Kid From Cleveland—George Brent; Republic; 1949

One-Sheet Movie Poster—27x41	$800.00
Three-Sheet Movie Poster—78x41	1,000.00

A League of Their Own—Tom Hanks, Geena Davis, Madonna; Columbia; 1992

Video	$15.00
Laserdisc	35.00
One-Sheet Movie Poster	50.00
Baseball—signed by Hanks	100.00
Baseball—signed by Davis	100.00

**Video Cover
Major League**

**Movie Poster
The Natural**

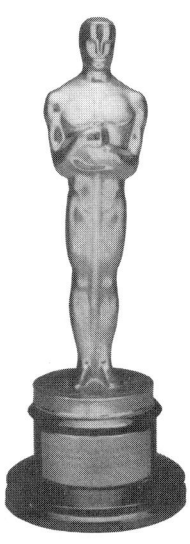

**Oscar for Film Editing
Pride of the Yankees**

Baseball—signed by Madonna	400.00
Bat—signed by Hanks, Madonna, Davis, Rosie O'Donnell	1,000.00
Replica Rockford Peaches Manager's Uniform—worn by Hanks	5,000.00
Replica Rockford Peaches Uniform—worn by Madonna	7,500.00

Major League—**Tom Berenger, Wesley Snipes; Paramount; 1989**

Video	$10.00
One-Sheet Movie Poster	30.00
Baseball—signed by Snipes	200.00
Pedro Cerano Jersey—worn by Dennis Haysbert	1,000.00

Major League 2—**Tom Berenger, Charlie Sheen; Warner Bros.; 1994**

Video	$10.00
One-Sheet Movie Poster	15.00
Replica Cleveland Indians Uniform—worn by David Keith	700.00
Willie Mays Hayes Uniform—worn by Omar Epps	1,200.00

Manhattan Merry-Go-Round—**Joe DiMaggio; Republic; 1938**

Video	$20.00
Lobby Card—signed by DiMaggio	250.00

Mr. Baseball—**Tom Selleck; Universal; 1992**

Video	$15.00
One-Sheet Movie Poster	15.00
Press Kit—10 stills	20.00
Replica Japanese Uniform—Descente, worn by Selleck	1,000.00

The Natural—**Robert Redford, Glenn Close; Tristar; 1984**

Video	$15.00
One-Sheet Movie Poster	40.00
Roy Hobbes 8x10—signed by Redford	100.00
Baseball—signed by Redford	120.00
Bat—signed by Redford	300.00
Prop Tickets—Knights vs. Cubs, Knights vs. Phillies, etc.	10.00 ea.
Prop Scorecards—Knights vs. Braves, Knights vs. Reds, etc.	20.00 ea.
Prop *Life* Magazine—Roy Hobbes on cover	500.00
Cardboard Extras—31x42, 75 photo cutouts used as stadium crowds	800.00
New York Knights Jersey—worn by extra	900.00
Roy Hobbes Jersey—worn by Redford	2,000.00

The Naughty Nineties—**Bud Abbott, Lou Costello; Universal; 1945**

Video	$15.00
"Who's On First?" Video	13.00
"Who's On First?" Lobby Card	200.00

The Pride of St. Louis—**Dan Daily, Joanne Dru; 20th Century Fox; 1952**

Video	$17.00
One-Sheet Movie Poster—29x38	400.00
Lobby Card	50.00

Pride of the Yankees—**Gary Cooper, Babe Ruth; RKO; 1941**

One-Sheet Movie Poster—27x41, Cooper Only (1941 original run)	$3,500.00
One-Sheet Movie Poster—27x41, Cooper and Ruth (1949 reissue)	2,000.00
Half-Sheet Movie Poster—22x28	900.00
Insert Poster—13x30, Cooper and Teresa Wright	800.00
Lobby Card—11x14 (1941 original run)	600.00
Lobby Card—11x14 (1949 reissue)	400.00
Movie Pressbook—22x17, color	800.00
Publicity Stills—set of eight	500.00
Publicity Still—7x9, Ruth with Cooper, signed by Ruth	5,000.00

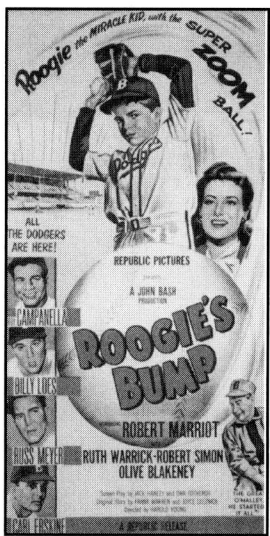

**Movie Poster
Roogie's Bump**

**Movie Poster
Safe At Home**

**Movie Poster
Take Me Out to the Ball Game**

Cast Photo—9½x7½, signed by Cooper, Ruth, Samuel Goldwyn	5,500.00
Yankee Press Statements—signed by Joe DiMaggio, Bill Dickey, others	1,500.00
Letter—signed by Ruth on Samuel Goldwyn stationery	2,500.00
Check Stub—$2,750 to Ruth from Goldwyn Inc.	800.00
Baseball—signed by Cooper, Ruth, Dickey, Walter Brennen, others	4,000.00
Replica Lou Gehrig Jersey—Western Costume Co., worn by Cooper	20,000.00
Replica Lou Gehrig Uniform—WCC, worn by Cooper	30,000.00
Replica Miller Huggins Uniform—WCC, worn by Ernie Adams	1,500.00
Academy of Motion Picture Arts & Sciences Certificate of Nomination	1,500.00
Academy Award "Oscar" Statue—to Daniel Mandell for Film Editing	25,000.00

Rawhide—Lou Gehrig; 20th Century Fox; 1938

One-Sheet Movie Poster—27x41	$3,000.00
Lobby Card	150.00
Movie Press Book—11x17½ cover	500.00
Publicity Stills—8x10, set of eight	250.00
Publicity 8x10—signed by Gehrig	2,000.00
Publicity 9x7½ photo—signed by Gehrig	2,500.00
Publicity 13½x10½photo—signed by Gehrig, Jacob Ruppert	3,000.00

Roogie's Bump—Roy Campanella, Carl Erskine; Republic; 1954

One-Sheet Movie Poster—27x41	$900.00
Advertising Poster—48x24	900.00

Safe At Home—Mickey Mantle, Roger Maris; Columbia; 1962

One-Sheet Movie Poster—27x41	$700.00
Half-Sheet Movie Poster—22x28	500.00
Half-Sheet Movie Poster—signed by Maris	800.00
Movie Poster—14x36	500.00
Movie Poster—60x40	1,500.00
Lobby Cards—11x14, set of eight	800.00
Lobby Card—signed by Maris	300.00
Lobby Card—signed by Mantle, Maris	700.00
Movie Press Book	200.00

Soul of the Game*—Blair Underwood; HBO; 1996

Video	$17.00
Laserdisc	30.00
Replica K. C. Monarchs Jersey—worn by Underwood	800.00

*Also known as *Baseball in Black and White.*

The Stratton Story—James Stewart, June Allyson; MGM; 1949

Video	$15.00
One-Sheet Movie Poster	400.00
Half-Sheet Movie Poster	300.00

Take Me Out to the Ballgame—Frank Sinatra, Gene Kelley; MGM; 1949

Video	$17.00
Laserdisc	30.00
One-Sheet Movie Poster—27x41	600.00
Half-Sheet Movie Poster	400.00

The Winning Team—Ronald Reagan; Warner Bros.; 1952

Video	$15.00
Laserdisc	30.00
Insert Poster	300.00
Baseball—signed by Reagan	300.00

BASEBALL VIDEOS

From actual game footage, to team histories, to highlight films, to instructional videos, to blooper reels, every aspect of baseball has been captured on film. In earlier times, baseball films were largely distributed in 8mm or 16mm "home movie" formats. Modern technology has made VHS video the current format of choice, and most older baseball films have been transferred to videocassettes. While old 8mm and 16mm prints do occasionally come up for sale—generally realizing around $100, depending on the movie and condition—most fans and collectors are content with video copies.

The following is a selection of baseball-related videos available to collectors. Prices are for Near Mint/Mint examples of each movie, including any and all original packaging. In the case of a "series" of videos, each volume is listed as well as a complete set price, except in cases where such listings would be problematic—the MLB official World Series tapes, for example.

Video Cover
Baseball: Funny Side Up!

Video Cover
Super Duper
Baseball Bloopers

A Great Beginning (1993 Florida Marlins)	$20.00
A Tale of Two Cities (New York/San Francisco Giants)	20.00
All-Star Game (single tapes from each year, starting in 1940s)	20.00 ea.
All-Time A's (Oakland A's 25th Anniversary)	20.00
An Amazin' Era (New York Mets 25th Anniversary)	20.00
Angels '62 (Los Angeles Angels)	25.00
An Hour of a Legend (Ted Williams)	35.00
Back to Back Bucs (Pittsburgh Pirates)	20.00
Back 2 Back (Toronto Blue Jays)	20.00
The Baltimore Orioles in Action (1962 Baltimore Orioles)	25.00
Baseball: A Film by Ken Burns (9 tapes)	150.00
Baseball in Boston	25.00
Baseball in the '70s	20.00
Baseball in the '80s	20.00
Baseball in 1990: Review	20.00
Baseball in 1991: Review	20.00
Baseball in 1992: Review	20.00
Baseball Like it Oughta Be (1996 St. Louis Cardinals)	20.00
Baseball's Greatest Games (continuing series of tapes)	
1952 World Series Game 6	20.00
1975 World Series Game 6	20.00
1978 AL East Playoff Game	20.00
1986 World Series Game 6	20.00
1988 World Series Game 1	20.00
1991 World Series Game 7	20.00
Baseball's Greatest Moments	20.00
Baseball's Greatest Pennant Series	15.00
Baseball's Main Street	25.00
Baseball News 1951	25.00
Baseball News 1955-56	25.00
Baseball News 1959	25.00
Battlin' Bucs (Pittsburgh Pirates)	20.00
The Best of Baseball	25.00
The Boys of Zimmer (1988 Chicago Cubs)	20.00
The Braves Family (Boston Braves)	25.00
Bravesland USA (Milwaukee Braves)	25.00
The Brooklyn Dodgers: The Original America's Team (5 tapes)	100.00
The Cardinal Tradition	25.00
Centennial (Philadelphia Phillies 100th Anniversary)	20.00
Century of Success (St. Louis Cardinals)	20.00
Champions by the Bay (1989 San Francisco Giants/Oakland A's)	20.00
Chicago and the Cubs	20.00
Chicago White Sox: A Visual History	20.00
Cleveland Rocks: The Story of the 1995 Cleveland Indians	20.00
Dodgers On-Line (1995 Los Angeles Dodgers)	20.00
Dodger Stadium (Los Angeles Dodgers 25th Anniversary)	20.00

Dusty Baker You Can Teach Hitting (3 tapes)	100.00
Vol. 1: A Systematic Approach to Hitting	30.00
Vol. 2: Ten Common Hitting Mistakes	30.00
Vol. 3: Twenty Hitting Drills	30.00
Expressway to the Big Leagues (New York Mets)	25.00
Ferguson Jenkins: King of the Hill	25.00
The 50 Greatest Home Runs in Baseball History	20.00
The Fighting Braves of '59 (Milwaukee Braves)	25.00
The First Century of Baseball, American League	25.00
The First Century of Baseball, National League	25.00
The First 10 Years (Seattle Mariners)	20.00
The 500 Home Run Club	30.00
Forever Fenway (Boston Red Sox)	20.00
Funny Side Up	10.00
The Game Nobody Saw	25.00
The Glory of Their Times	45.00
The Greatest League Championship Series	15.00
Hall of Fame Weekend 1997	20.00
Hail to the Braves (1957 Milwaukee Braves)	25.00
Hitting the Ted Williams Way Part 1	20.00
Home of the Braves (Milwaukee Braves)	25.00
Jackie Robinson: Breaking Barriers	20.00
The Kansas City A's in Action	25.00
Lefty: The Life and Times of Steve Carlton	20.00
MLB Unbelievable: Bloopers and Great Plays	20.00
The National Pastime (5 tapes)	50.00
Nolan Ryan's 7th No-Hitter	20.00
The Official History of Baseball	15.00
Pinstripe Destiny (1996 New York Yankees)	20.00
Pinstripe Power: The Story of the '61 Yankees	20.00
Play Ball the Major League Way (3 tapes)	50.00
Vol. 1: Pitching and Catching	20.00
Vol. 2: Hitting and Baserunning	20.00
Vol. 3: Infield and Outfield Play	20.00
Play Ball with the Red Sox	25.00
Pride of New England (Boston Red Sox)	25.00
Pride of the Upper Midwest (Minnesota Twins)	25.00
Prime 9 Hosted by Ozzie Smith	20.00
The Reds	20.00
The Red Sox at Home	25.00
Roberto Clemente	20.00
Silver Odyssey (Houston Astros 25th Anniversary)	20.00
The Story of the Washington Nationals (Washington Senators)	35.00
Super Duper Baseball Bloopers	20.00
Super Duper Baseball Bloopers 2	20.00
Super Sluggers	20.00
10 Greatest Moments in Yankee History	20.00
This Week in Baseball: 20 Years of Unforgettable Plays and Bloopers	20.00
Tigertown USA (Detroit Tigers)	25.00
T is for Team (1996 Texas Rangers)	20.00
Wahoo, What a Finish (1995 Cleveland Indians)	20.00
We Had 'Em All the Way (1960 Pittsburgh Pirates)	25.00
Whatever it Takes, Dude (1993 Philadelphia Phillies)	20.00
Winning with the Yankees	25.00
Wire to Wire (1990 Cincinnati Reds)	20.00
World Series Highlights (one tape for each year from 1943-present)	20.00 ea.
Year of Change (New York Mets)	25.00

Video Covers
Baseball: A Film by Ken Burns

Chapter 15

AUCTIONS

RON OSER TELEPHONE AUCTION

A rapidly growing method of obtaining limited and vintage collectibles is through auctions, whether they're live, via telephone, or on the Internet. As authentic vintage collectibles become more scarce, the demand among collectors for memorabilia from the past makes it increasingly difficult to pinpoint values, and auctions look more attractive as a means for assigning values to rare and one-of-a-kind items.

The following list includes all the baseball items auctioned by Ron Oser Enterprises, one of the country's leading auction houses, in a telephone auction held March 14, 1998. The realized price includes a 15 percent buyer's premium. "N/A" indicates that an item didn't reach its reserve bid and wasn't sold.

1941 Joe DiMaggio game-worn spikes from "The Streak"

Final Bid
$36,094.00

1947 Joe DiMaggio New York Yankees autographed game-used home jersey

Final Bid
$82,027.00

Item	Final Bid
1941 Joe DiMaggio game-worn spikes from "The Streak"	$36,094.00
1947 Joe DiMaggio New York Yankees signed game-used home jersey	82,027.00
1913 T200 Fatima Premium Cleveland Team with Joe Jackson	6,325.00
1915 E145-2 Cracker Jack—near set, 173 of 176 cards	13,243.00
1952 Topps—near set, 405 of 407 cards	20,375.00
1942 Joe DiMaggio New York Yankees signed game-used baseball cap	22,188.00
Circa 1949-1951 Joe DiMaggio game-used bat	8,630.00
1942 Joe DiMaggio New York Yankees signed game-used home pants	6,606.00
Complete set of five Joe DiMaggio PM10 stadium pins	3,279.00
1983 Joe DiMaggio signed player model baseball bat with personal notation	2,686.00
1993 signed Limited Edition #45 Joe DiMaggio commemorative baseball bat	2,037.00
1938 Joe DiMaggio store model bat	316.00
Circa 1940s Joe DiMaggio color pennant	1,313.00
Circa 1940s Joe DiMaggio pennant	314.00
Joe DiMaggio (young)—original signed oil painting	1,531.00
Joe DiMaggio (older)—original signed oil painting	633.00

**Philadelphia Phillies
1950 newspaper
scrapbooks**

**Final Bid
$312.00**

**Mickey Mantle—
1966 Fedtro Intercom
advertising display**

**Final Bid
$404.00**

Item	Final Bid
Joe DiMaggio—signed World's Fair Collection	N/A
1940s Joe DiMaggio signed signature model baseball	775.00
Joe DiMaggio 44-Game Hitting Streak ticket stub (NM)	649.00
Joe DiMaggio—Original 1938 signed store model glove box, glove & Spalding premium photos	2,780.00
1944 Joe DiMaggio Diamond Anniversary model glove	370.00
Circa 1945 Joe DiMaggio signed Army model glove	672.00
Circa 1950s Joe DiMaggio signed store model baseball shoes in original box	986.00
Circa 1940s Joe DiMaggio Fan Club premium ring and membership card	505.00
Circa 1940s Joe DiMaggio Charms candy wrapper	616.00
Where Have You Gone, Joe DiMaggio?—hardcover book signed on Marlyn Monroe page	812.00
Joe DiMaggio 2 signed hardcover books: *Baseball for Everyone, Joe DiMaggio: The Yankee Clipper*	370.00
Joe DiMaggio 2 signed *Life* magazines	1,265.00
Joe DiMaggio 2 signed magazines: *Collier's, Sports Illustrated*	978.00
Circa 1940s 6 Japanese magazines and 1 Japanese book, all w/DiMaggio Covers	1,380.00
Joe DiMaggio 7 original wire photographs	230.00
Joe DiMaggio and Ford Frick—original signed Hall of Fame induction photograph	253.00
Joe DiMaggio and Lou Costello—original signed photograph	150.00
Joe DiMaggio—original signed Army photograph	205.00
1989 signed limited edition Gartlan Figurine: "The Yankee Clipper," home uniform	1,808.00
1989 signed limited edition Gartlan Figurine: "The Yankee Clipper," away uniform	421.00
The DiMaggio Albums—signed limited edition two-volume set	591.00
3 Joe DiMaggio license plates (one signed)	840.00
1875 Boston Baseball Association stock certificate	392.00
1887 N690 Kalamazoo Bats—Harry Wright Good condition	994.00
1890 Philadelphia Athletics—season pass	759.00
1922 E120 American Caramel—complete set of 240 cards	5,604.00
1909-11 E90-1 American Caramel near set of 106 cards	3,567.00
1910 E93 Standard Caramel—Ty Cobb Excellent condition	834.00
1912 E270 Colgan's Chips Red Borders—79 Very Good to Excellent/Mint condition cards	4,074.00
1909-11 E254 Colgan's Chips—59 Good to Excellent condition cards	766.00
1911 T3 Turkey Red—4 Excellent to Excellent/Mint condition cabinet cards	575.00
1911 T3 Turkey Red—12 Very Good/Excellent condition cabinet cards	1,205.00
1911 T3 Turkey Red—17 Very Good condition cabinet cards	1,494.00
1911 T3 Turkey Red—27 Fair to Good/Very Good condition cards	759.00
1911 T201 Mecca Double Folders—complete set of 50 cards	1,869.00
1912 T202 Hassan—9 triple folder cards	590.00
1912 T202 Hassan—4 triple folder cards	230.00
1912 T202 Hassan—33 Fair to Good/Very Good condition triple folders cards	729.00
1911 T205 Gold Border complete set of 208 cards	6,722.00
1911 T205 Gold Border 39 Very Good to Very Good/Excellent condition cards	2,538.00
1911 T205 Gold Border 62 Fair to Good/Very Good condition cards	718.00
1909-11 T206 White Border—Ray Demmitt, St. Louis Very Good condition	919.00
1909-11 T206 White Border—Bill O'Hara, St. Louis Good condition	511.00
1909-11 T206 White Border—Kid Elberfield, Washington/Portrait Excellent condition	383.00
1909-11 T206 White Border—Ty Cobb (Portrait, green background) Very Good/Excellent condition	764.00
1909-11 T206 White Border—Ty Cobb (bat off shoulder) Excellent/Mint condition	1,358.00
1909-11 T206 White Border—Ty Cobb (bat off shoulder) Very Good/Excellent to Excellent condition	515.00

Item	Final Bid
1909-11 T206 White Border—32 Excellent condition cards	1,390.00
1909-11 T206 31 Very Good to Excellent condition cards	679.00
1909-11 T206 20 Very Good/Excellent to Near Mint condition cards	840.00
1909-11 T206 White Border—105 Very Good to Very Good/Excellent condition cards	2,315.00
1909-11 T206 White Border—121 Fair to Good/Very Good condition cards	1,127.00
1912 T207 Brown Background—53 Fair to Excellent/Mint condition cards	1,020.00
1912 T207 Brown Background—13 Good to Excellent condition Hall of Famer & tougher cards	631.00
1910 S74 Silk (colored)—Ty Cobb Near Mint/Mint condition	1,122.00
1910 S74 Silk (white)—Ty Cobb Very Good/Excellent condition	407.00
1909-11 E90-1 American Caramel—Napoleon Lajoie Excellent/Mint condition	447.00
1914 B18 Blanket—Joe Jackson (yellow pennants) Excellent condition	575.00
1920's Babe Ruth—4 strip cards	463.00
1922 W575-2—Ty Cobb Excellent condition	407.00
1920 1922, 1933 Mrs. Sherlocks Pins—'20 and '33 complete sets; '22 partial set	633.00
1924 V122 Willard's Chocolate—Sports Champions wrapper Very Good/Excellent condition	127.00
1928 Lou Gehrig exhibit card Excellent condition	476.00
1934-36 Diamond Stars—near set 103 of 108 cards	3,242.00
1934-36 Batter—13 Very Good/Excellent to Near Mint condition cards	498.00
1933 Goudey Sport Kings—near set 46 of 48 cards	4,962.00
1933 Goudey Sport Kings—#1 Ty Cobb Very Good condition	417.00
1933 Goudey—near set of 239 of 240 cards	9,169.00
1933 Goudey—#53 Babe Ruth Very Good/Excellent condition	835.00
1934 Goudey—complete set of 96 cards	3,999.00
1934 Goudey—#61 Lou Gehrig Excellent condition	925.00
1935 Goudey—set of 36 cards	1,850.00
1934 R309-1 Goudey—National League All-Stars and George Herman (Babe) Ruth premiums	522.00
Circa 1938-39 Kansas City Blues—complete set of 10 cards with Phil Rizzuto	964.00
1941 Play Ball—22 Very Good to Excellent/Mint Condition cards	695.00
1941 Play Ball—#71 Joe DiMaggio	475.00
1943 R302-1 M.P. & Co.—uncut strip of 8 cards with Joe DiMaggio	268.00
1946-49 W603 Sports Exchange—Joe Jackson	385.00
Rogers Peet—Herb Pennock, Ty Cobb, and Babe Ruth cards Near Mint/Mint condition	2,445.00
1918-1958 M114 Baseball Magazine 23 Premium Pictures	463.00
Vintage 9 Hall of Famer & star cards	459.00
Ty Cobb—1909 E95 Philadelphia Caramel and 1912 T227 Series of Champions cards Good condition	629.00
1910's Ty Cobb—1909-11 T206 White Border; 1909-11 E90-1 American Caramel	575.00
Ty Cobb—1907 Dietsche postcard, 1913 Tom Barker game, 1912 AL photo schedule.	392.00
Christy Mathewson—1912 T202 Hassan Triple Folder Very Good/Excellent condition; 1911 T205 Gold Border	383.00
1910s-1940s—44 Good to Excellent condition cards	538.00
1910s T205 & T206—54 different Fair to Very Good condition cards	408.00
1910s-1930s—11 Sporting News supplements and Butterfinger premiums	139.00
1948 Bowman complete set of 48 cards	1,962.00
1951 Bowman—119 Very Good to Excellent condition cards	631.00
1951 Bowman—#165 Ted Williams Excellent/Mint condition	560.00
1952 Bowman—complete set of 252 cards	2,720.00
1952 Bowman—63 Very Good to Excellent condition cards	306.00
1953 Bowman color near set of 156 of 160 cards	2,690.00
1953 Bowman black & white—near set 63 of 64 cards	905.00
1954 Bowman —#66 Ted Williams Very Good condition	569.00
1955 Bowman—85 Excellent/Mint to Near Mint condition cards	488.00
1951 Topps Teams—7 cards	247.00
1952 Topps—#311 Mickey Mantle Good condition	3,524.00
1954 Topps—complete set of 250 cards	1,852.00
1954 Topps—#201 Al Kaline Very Good/Excellent to Excellent condition	144.00
1955 Topps—complete set of 206 cards	1,898.00
1955 Topps Doubleheader—Jackie Robinson Near Mint/Mint condition	230.00
1956 Topps—near set 339 of 340 cards	2,105.00
1956 Topps—3 Near Mint condition cards: #31 Hank Aaron, #101 Roy Campanella, #200 Bob Feller	380.00
1956 Topps—No Checklist 1/3 Near Mint/Mint condition	190.00

**1948 Bowman
complete set of 48 cards**

**Final Bid
$1,962.00**

**1952 Topps—#311
Mickey Mantle**

**Final Bid
$3,524.00**

Item	Final Bid
1956 Topps Pins—Ted Williams player pin and display box	542.00
1957 Topps—complete set of 407 cards	2,826.00
1954-56 Spic and Span Braves—complete set of 18 cards	506.00
1962 Salada—near set 258 of 261 coins	N/A
1962 Topps—complete set of 598 cards	1,811.00
1964 Topps Stand Ups—complete set of 77 non die-cut cards	971.00
1965 Topps—complete set of 598 cards	1,784.00
1967 Topps—Who Am I? Mickey Mantle Near Mint condition	185.00
1968 Topps—complete set of 598 cards	1,746.00
1969 Topps—complete set of 664 cards	728.00
1969 Topps—#260 Reggie Jackson rookie card PSA Graded 8 Near Mint/Mint condition	348.00
1969 Topps—# 500 Mickey Mantle (white letter variation) PSA Graded 8 Near Mint/Mint condition	547.00
1969 Topps Super—#24 Mickey Mantle PSA Graded 8 Near Mint/Mint condition	919.00
1969 Topps Super—17 Very Good to Excellent/Mint condition cards	178.00
1969 Milton Bradley—complete set of 296 cards on uncut panels	253.00
1970, '72, '73 Topps—complete or near sets	1,685.00
1970, '72 Topps—complete sets	905.00
1970, '74 Topps—complete sets	764.00
1981-1988—37 Near Mint to Mint condition regular, Update, & rookie sets	695.00
1982 Topps Traded, 1983 Topps Traded, 1984 Fleer Update—complete sets	463.00
1982 Topps Traded—complete boxed set of 132 cards	173.00
1981-1987 Topps, Fleer & Donruss—29 NM/M to Mint condition rookie and star cards	421.00
1984 Nestle and 1984 Donruss—complete sets	348.00
1970's-1980's Humongous Minor League—complete set collection	2,647.00
1968, '77 O-Pee-Chee—complete sets	1,264.00
1973, '75 O-Pee-Chee—complete sets	631.00
1955-1969 Mickey Mantle & Roger Maris—22 Good to Excellent condition cards	1,064.00
1950, '54 Bowman—5 Hall of Famer cards	1,096.00
1950-1955 Bowman—11 Excellent to Near Mint condition cards	421.00
1955-1980 Topps—8 Near Mint /Mint condition Hall of Famer & star cards	380.00
1953-1965 Topps—15 Excellent/Mint to Near Mint condition cards	731.00
1966-1978 Topps—20 Excellent/Mint to Near Mint condition Hall of Famer & star cards	604.00
1952-1956 Topps—17 Very Good to Excellent-Plus condition Hall of Famer & star cards	463.00
1957-1975 Topps—28 Excellent to Excellent-Plus condition Hall of Famer & star cards	731.00
1954-1969 Topps—12 Hall of Famer & star cards	1,390.00
1956-1958 Ted Williams 3 Excellent/Mint to Near Mint condition cards	547.00
1951-1955 Ted Williams—4 Very Good/Excellent to Excellent condition cards	649.00
1941-1955 Cleveland Indians—40 Excellent to Excellent/Mint condition cards	383.00
1910-1955 Cleveland Indians—58 Good to Very/Good Excellent condition cards	707.00
1957-1970 Frank Robinson—10 Excellent to Near Mint condition cards	175.00
1953-1955 Bowman—105 Good to Excellent condition cards	244.00
1960, '69 Topps—partial sets	934.00
1964, '71 Topps Coins—complete sets	764.00
1964-1977 Topps—11 assorted complete sets	696.00
1959 Fleer Ted Williams—complete set of 80 cards	1,390.00
1959 Fleer Ted Williams—# 68 Ted Signs Excellent/Mint condition	616.00
1960 Fleer—complete set of 79 cards	538.00

Item	Final Bid
1961/62 Fleer—complete set of 154 cards	665.00
1961/62 Fleer—complete set of 154 Cards	541.00
1961/62 Fleer Babe Ruth store window display advertising sign	1,323.00
1963 Fleer—complete set of 66 cards plus 2 checklist and an extra Joe Adcock Card	498.00
1963 Fleer—complete set of 66 cards plus checklist	658.00
1963 Fleer checklist Excellent condition	421.00
1963-1965 Bazooka—8 boxes and panels	316.00
1966 Bazooka—10 boxes	383.00
1967-1971 Bazooka—14 boxes and panels	230.00
1954 Johnston Cookies Braves—complete set of 35 cards	658.00
1970, 1972-1983 Kellogg's—16 Near Mint/Mint to Mint condition sets	696.00
1960's Mickey Mantle—4 Bazooka, Post & Jello cards	253.00
1952 Topps Cello box Excellent condition	616.00
1954 Topps wax box Very Good condition	884.00
1956 Topps wax box Very Good/Excellent condition	596.00
1959-1968 Topps—9 different wax boxes	746.00
1959-1968 Topps & Philadelphia—8 baseball & football wax boxes	190.00
1927 W560—complete set of 64 cards on four uncut sheets	463.00
1950 Callahan Hall of Fame—Honus Wagner original artwork	1,097.00
1950 Callahan Hall of Fame—4 original artworks (J. Galvin, K. Cuyler, J. Collins, T. Lyons)	1,117.00
1950 Callahan Hall of Fame—4 original artworks (C. Mack, J. McCarthy, E. Barrow, B. Clem)	574.00
2 Original Mario DeMarco artworks—Babe Ruth, Bill Clem	288.00
Lou Gehrig single-signed baseball	9,492.00
Babe Ruth single-signed baseball	3,279.00
Babe Ruth single-signed baseball	1,643.00
Satchel Paige single-signed baseball	1,531.00
Red Faber, Lefty Gomez, George Kelly signed baseball	574.00
Sam Crawford, Davy Jones signed baseball	431.00
George Kelly & Travis Jackson—2 single-signed baseballs and 2 signed request letters	805.00
Earl Averill, Burleigh Grimes, Red Ruffing single-signed baseballs	886.00
Stanley Coveleski, Red Ruffing, Waite Hoyte single-signed baseballs	821.00
1995 Cal Ripken Jr. 2,131 game-used baseball	3,281.00
500 Home Run & 3000 Hits—19 single signature baseballs	1,015.00
Joe DiMaggio—2 single-signed baseballs	695.00
Mickey Mantle single-signed baseball	447.00
Gil Hodges single-signed baseball	1,326.00
Carl Furillo & Sandy Amoros—single-signed baseballs	554.00
Mickey Mantle, Willie Mays, Duke Snider—single-signed baseballs	330.00
Mike Marshall single-signed baseball	230.00
Al Schacht & Clyde Klutz—single-signed baseballs	454.00
19 assorted single-signed baseballs including Richie Ashburn, Dale Murphy, Pete Rose	633.00
1922 New York Giants signed World Champion team baseball with John McGraw	1,020.00
1929 Philadelphia Athletics signed World Champion team baseball with Babe Ruth	1,852.00
1931 Philadelphia Athletics signed team baseball	903.00
1937 St. Louis Cardinals signed team baseball	192.00
1939 New York Yankees signed World Champions team baseball	3,519.00
1939 Philadelphia Athletics signed team baseball	223.00
1939 National League signed All-Star team baseball	746.00
1940 Cincinnati Reds signed team baseball	2,554.00
1941 National League signed All-Star team baseball	1,252.00
1947 Pittsburgh Pirates signed team baseball	139.00
1948 Boston Red Sox signed team baseball	483.00
1949 National League signed All-Star team baseball	4,078.00
1950 Brooklyn Dodgers signed team baseball	1,020.00
1950 Philadelphia Athletics signed team baseball	370.00
1951 New York Giants signed NL Champions team baseball	463.00
1951 National League signed All-Star team baseball	3,095.00
1952 Brooklyn Dodgers signed team baseball	1,530.00
1954 New York Yankees signed team baseball	920.00

1995 Cal Ripken Jr. 2,131 game-used baseball

Final Bid 3,281.00

1949 National League—signed All-Star team baseball

Final Bid 4,078.00

Item	Final Bid
1955 Brooklyn Dodgers World Champions signed team baseball	2,277.00
1955 American League signed All-Star team baseball	370.00
1955 National League signed All-Star team baseball	1,532.00
1955 Milwaukee Braves signed team baseball	308.00
1954, '56 American League 6 signed team baseballs	741.00
1956 National League 4 signed team baseballs—Pirates, Giants, Cubs, Reds	764.00
1958 New York Yankees World Champions signed team baseball	994.00
1958 Milwaukee Braves NL Champions signed team baseball	542.00
1960 Pittsburgh Pirates World Champions signed team baseball	1,348.00
1960 New York Yankees signed team baseball	920.00
1961 New York Yankees signed team baseball	654.00
1962 New York Yankees World Champions signed team baseball	1,631.00
1963 New York Yankees signed team baseball	988.00
1964 New York Yankees signed team baseball	857.00
1964 National League 8 signed team baseballs—Pirates, Reds, Dodgers, Mets, Braves, Giants, Cubs, Colt .45s	2,433.00
1964 American League 8 signed team baseballs—Yankees, Orioles, Tigers, Red Sox, White Sox, Indians, Angels, Athletics	814.00
1967 St. Louis Cardinals World Champions signed team baseball	612.00
1968 New York Yankees signed team baseball	247.00
1969, '86 New York Mets World Champions signed team baseballs	1,348.00
1970 Pittsburgh Pirates NL Champions signed team baseball	746.00
1972 Oakland Athletics World Champions signed team baseball	383.00
1979 Baltimore Orioles AL Champions signed team baseball	440.00
1982 Milwaukee Brewers AL Champions signed baseball	273.00
1983 New York Yankees signed team baseball	168.00
1984 National League All-Star signed team baseball	139.00
Circa 1930s Babe Ruth & Earl Combs signed baseball	1,358.00
5 assorted signed baseballs—'28 Yankees, '40 Dodgers, '46 Yankees, '56 Pirates, baseball w/11 assorted signatures	949.00
Roger Maris & Mickey Mantle signed baseballs	1,494.00
1960's Chicago White Sox assorted signed baseball including Monty Stratton	380.00
1961 New York Yankees & St. Louis Cardinals signed spring training baseballs	592.00
1969 Hall of Fame Induction signed baseball	695.00
1972 Hall of Fame Induction signed baseball	463.00
1973 Hall of Fame Induction signed baseball	383.00
Circa 1970's Hall of Fame Dinner signed baseball	453.00
Hall of Famers & others signed baseball	324.00
Hall of Famers signed baseball 25 signatures including Mickey Mantle, Frank Robinson, Brooks Robinson	316.00
4 assorted signed baseballs '37 Dodgers, '48 Binghamton Yankees, ball w/9 HOF signatures, Willie McCovey	384.00
500 home run hitters signed baseball	746.00
50 home runs in a season signed baseball	225.00
Billy Sunday signed photograph	407.00
Honus Wagner signed magazine photograph	542.00
Roger Maris signed photograph	475.00
Dizzy Dean signed magazine photograph	168.00
1952 New York Yankees signed photograph	412.00
Brooklyn Dodgers 6 signed photographs	337.00
Circa 1968 New York Yankees 13 signed photographs	N/A
Collection of 4 assorted signed photographs including Don Larsen World Series perfect game, '54 World Series Willie Mays catch	185.00

Item	Final Bid
Hall of Fame Induction weekend signed photograph	601.00
500 home run hitters signed photograph	555.00
1996 New York Yankees signed Sports Illustrated Collectors Edition magazine	224.00
Mickey Mantle framed display signed photograph with 2 World Series tickets	337.00
Mickey Mantle framed display signed photograph with a 1961 World Series ticket	370.00
Mickey Mantle & Joe DiMaggio framed display signed photograph with a 1951 World Series ticket	776.00
Joe DiMaggio framed display signed photograph with a 1936 World Series ticket	408.00
Ted Williams framed display signed photograph with a 1946 World Series ticket	408.00
Mickey Mantle signed Triple Crown photograph	370.00
Mickey Mantle signed photograph	339.00
Mickey Mantle signed photograph	247.00
Ty Cobb four page handwritten letter	1,358.00
Warren Giles & Will Harridge signed letters and a photograph	258.00
Waite Hoyt 10 typewritten letters to a pen pal	288.00
Mickey Mantle 1959 Post Cereal signed consent and release form	2,036.00
Babe Ruth signed personal check	1,792.00
Ty Cobb signed personal check	492.00
Carl Mays & Charles Ruffing New York Yankees paychecks	348.00
1970-1973 Pacific Coast League 54 signed paychecks	286.00
Babe Ruth and Lou Gehrig signed 1933 *Who's Who* book pages	3,128.00
1927 New York Football Giants—Hinkey Haines Testimonial Dinner Program signed By Lou Gehrig, & Others	1,725.00
Ty Cobb signed cut and photographic display	506.00
Vintage autograph collection with a Babe Ruth cut	1,021.00
1929 Loyal Giants Rooters signed sheet music	245.00
1939 Baseball Centennial signed First Day Issue commemorative envelope	300.00
1950 New York Giants signed game scorecard	N/A
Satchel Paige autograph cut and a 1953 Topps baseball card	209.00
Harry Agganis signed government postcard	259.00
1982 Hall of Fame Museum Yearbook signed by over 75 players	498.00
1983 Hall of Fame Museum Yearbook signed by over 80 players	804.00
1983 All-Star Game program signed by over 60 players	616.00
1983 *The National League* Donald Honig hardback book with 156 signatures	631.00
1983 *The American League* Donald Honig hardback book with 76 signatures	547.00
Collection of 79 signed Hall of Fame postcards	1,015.00
Collection of 63 signed Perez-Steele Hall of Fame art postcards	1,455.00
Collection of 48 signed Perez Steele Celebration & Greatest Moments cards	619.00
Collection of 8 signed Otesaga Hotel bills from the 1974 Hall of Fame Induction Ceremonies	316.00
Roger Maris signed magazine cover	306.00
Mickey Mantle signed NY Yankee store model baseball cap	259.00
Mickey Mantle signed Fantasy Camp baseball cap	230.00
1952 Topps Billy Martin signed baseball	124.00
1933-1955 Cleveland Indians 25 signed baseball cards	421.00
1970-1972 Topps 263 signed baseball cards	603.00
1973-1975 Topps 515 signed baseball cards	729.00
1976-1978 Topps 540 signed baseball cards	840.00
1913 World Series Program Philadelphia at New York	1,095.00
1925 World Series Program Washington at Pittsburgh	1,231.00
1942 World Series Program at St. Louis	447.00
1936-1949 10 World Series Programs	978.00
1936-1949 10 World Series Programs	N/A
1950-1959 15 World Series Programs	1,149.00
1950-1959 14 World Series Programs	N/A
1960-1968 15 World Series Programs	675.00
1960-1973 15 World Series Programs	345.00
1944 All-Star Game Program at Pittsburgh	1,358.00
1943-1948 3 All-Star Game Programs	518.00
1950-1959 7 All-Star Game Programs	696.00
1961 All-Star Game Program at San Francisco	348.00
1960-1973 15 All Star Game Programs	822.00

1983 The American League Donald Honig hardback book with 76 autographs

Final Bid
547.00

1944 All-Star Game Program at Pittsburgh

Final Bid
1,358.00

Item	Final Bid
1947-1971 13 All Star Game Programs	696.00
1944-1952 St. Louis Browns—complete set of 3 yearbooks	421.00
1946-1952 Boston Braves—complete set of 5 yearbooks	412.00
1950-1957 Brooklyn Dodgers—6 yearbooks	569.00
1958-1971 Los Angeles Dodgers—13 yearbooks	278.00
1952-1970 New York Yankees—15 yearbooks	627.00
1952-1957 New York Giants—6 yearbooks	294.00
1958-1970 San Francisco Giants—12 yearbooks	370.00
1949-1969 Philadelphia Phillies—15 yearbooks	488.00
1946-1969 Boston Red Sox—13 yearbooks	N/A
1939-1970 Detroit Tigers—14 yearbooks	713.00
1949-1954 Philadelphia Athletics—6 yearbooks	175.00
1955-1967 Kansas City Athletics—9 yearbooks	345.00
1954-1974 Baltimore Orioles—8 yearbooks	288.00
1951-1970 Pittsburgh Pirates—14 yearbooks	N/A
1948-1969 Cleveland Indians—13 yearbooks	575.00
1953-1970 Chicago White Sox—13 yearbooks	314.00
1953-1964 Milwaukee Braves—11 yearbooks	417.00
1951-1970 St. Louis Cardinals—12 yearbooks	230.00
1952-1968 Cincinnati Reds—9 yearbooks	127.00
1948-1957 Chicago Cubs—9 yearbooks	268.00
1953-1968 Washington Nationals & Senators 8 yearbooks	205.00
1963-1969 New York Mets—6 yearbooks	N/A
1952-1970 21 Excellent to Near Mint condition yearbooks	421.00
1939-1970 18 Very Good To Very Good/Excellent condition yearbooks	403.00
1902 Boston Red Sox scorecard	370.00
1903 Boston Red Sox scorecard	450.00
1905 New York Giants scorecard	144.00
1906-1911 Boston Red Sox—5 scorecards	306.00
Baseball publications—*Top Notch* magazine, Lancaster Red Roses yearbook, 1946 Red Sox program, 1948 Tigers program	338.00
1950s Philadelphia Athletics & Phillies—15 yearbooks, programs, and a pennant	253.00
Collection of 19 vintage baseball publications	306.00
Collection of 25 baseball media guides scorecards & Championship programs	N/A
1940s-1950s 21 assorted sports programs and scorecards	306.00
The DiMaggio Albums complete set in original signed slipcase	153.00
Yogi Berra circa 1950 signed game-used bat	1,218.00
Mike Schmidt 1980s signed game-used bat	746.00
Reggie Jackson 1980s signed game-used bat	923.00
Don Zimmer 1950s signed game-used bat	431.00
Gino Cimoli 1950s signed game-used bat	224.00
Carl Yastrzemski 1980s signed game-used bat	324.00
Frank Thomas signed game-used bat	612.00
Dave Winfield & Cecil Fielder signed game-used bats	209.00
Collection of 8 game and non-game used bats including Henry Rodriguez, Bobby Bonilla, Jose Canseco	N/A
1936 New York Yankees World Series brown bat	835.00
1938 New York Yankees World Series black bat	631.00
1951 New York Yankees World Series black bat	522.00

Item	Final Bid
1969, '73, '86 New York Mets—3 World Series black bats	814.00
Joe DiMaggio signed pro model bat	863.00
500 Home Run Club signed commemorative bat	1,684.00
Collection of 3 500 Home Run Club commemorative bats signed by 10 players (not including Mantle)	1,117.00
1989 Hall of Fame commemorative bat signed by 46 Hall of Famers	821.00
1990 All Star Game—signed commemorative bat	255.00
1951 New York Giants of the Grounds team-signed commemorative bat	657.00
1969, '86 New York Mets World Champions team-signed commemorative bats	695.00
1988 Pee Wee Reese & 1994 Duke Snider signed commemorative bats	363.00
Shibe Park & Sportsman's Park signed commemorative bats	273.00
Lou Gehrig store model bat	633.00
George Kelly store model bat	N/A
1950s-1970s 8 store model gloves	N/A
Mickey Mantle signed store model bat	348.00
Vintage catcher's equipment	115.00
Reach & Spalding baseballs in boxes	209.00
Mickey Mantle 1965 New York Yankees signed game-used baseball cap	10,041.00
Casey Stengel 1962 New York Mets game-worn baseball cap plus a signed photograph	1,530.00
Willie Mays 1973 New York Mets game-worn Baseball Cap	1,225.00
Circa 1962-1964 Turk Farrell Houston Colt .45's game-worn baseball cap and warm-up jacket	2,755.00
Pete Rose Cincinnati Reds game-worn baseball cap	509.00
Circa 1940s -1950s 3 game-worn baseball caps	604.00
Wade Boggs 1993 signed All-Star jersey	1,942.00
Barry Bonds 1993 signed All-Star jersey	3,827.00
Jeff Bagwell 1994 signed game-worn jersey	835.00
Frank Thomas 1994 game-worn jersey	1,480.00
Gary Sheffield 1994 game-worn jersey	522.00
Moises Alou 1994 game-worn jersey	N/A
Pete Rose 1988 game-worn jersey	923.00
Larry Walker 1989 rookie game-worn jersey	1,351.00
Cecil Fielder 1994 game-worn jersey	288.00
Todd Hundley 1995 signed game-worn jersey	383.00
Barry Larkin 1993 game-worn jersey	738.00
Matt Williams 1994 game-worn jersey	574.00
Carlos Baerga 1991 game-worn jersey	294.00
Steve Carlton 1986 game-worn jersey	764.00
Steve Rogers 1982 game-worn jersey	N/A
Roger McDowell 1988 game-worn jersey	230.00
Kevin McReynolds 1990 game-worn jersey	209.00
Sid Fernandez 1990 signed game-worn jersey	144.00
Lance Johnson 1996 signed game-worn All-Star warm-up jersey	115.00
Ron Darling 1988 game-worn jersey	307.00
1975 Vida Blue, 1980 Ed Halicki, 1981 Steve Braun game-worn jerseys	633.00
Early 1960s York Pirates (Pittsburgh farm club) baseball jacket	222.00
Joe DiMaggio signed replica jersey	896.00
Mickey Mantle signed replica jersey	812.00
Hank Aaron signed replica jersey	383.00
Willie Mays signed replica jersey	230.00
Frank Thomas game-used glove	1,846.00
Dave Winfield signed game-used glove	766.00
Gary Sheffield signed game-used glove	316.00
Rollie Fingers signed game-used glove	392.00
Barry Bonilla game-used glove	201.00
Robin Ventura game-used glove	621.00
Mark Belanger game-used glove	627.00
Wally Joyner game-used glove	175.00
1913 World Series Philadelphia at New York—Game 1 ticket stub Very Good condition	835.00
1914, '15 World Series—2 ticket stubs Very Good/Excellent condition	1,150.00
1917 World Series New York at Chicago—Game 5 ticket stub Very Good condition	721.00

**Larry Walker
1989 rookie
game-worn
jersey**

**Final Bid
$1,351.00**

**Rickey Henderson
1989 World Series
MVP Trophy**

**Final Bid
$1,682.00**

Item	Final Bid
1921 World Series New York Yankees at New York Giants—Game 7 ticket stub Very Good/Excellent condition	596.00
1922 World Series New York at New York—Game 4 ticket stub Excellent condition	407.00
1956 World Series Don Larson perfect game ticket stub Excellent condition	498.00
Hank Aaron 714 home run ticket stub and scored game program Excellent to Mint condition	713.00
Pete Rose signed 4,156 hit full ticket Excellent/Mint condition	575.00
1967 Chicago White Sox phantom World Series ticket	N/A
1951 Brooklyn Dodgers phantom World Series press pin	278.00
1910s Athletics pennant	184.00
1946 Boston Red Sox pennant	216.00
Early 1950s New York Yankees pennant	175.00
Circa 1950 Cooperstown Hall of Fame pennant	253.00
1955 Brooklyn Dodgers Championship pennant	794.00
1960 Pittsburgh Pirates National League Champions photo pennant	N/A
1960s New York Mets 3 pennants	288.00
Championship pennants: '55 Dodgers, '58 Braves, '67 Red Sox, '69 Mets	320.00
1950s-'60s 11 baseball & football team pennants	465.00
1989 Rickey Henderson World Series MVP trophy	1,682.00
Large 203 original Hartland bats	518.00
Hartland baseball player statues: Mickey Mantle, Hank Aaron, Warren Spahn	370.00
Roberto Clemente Bobbin' Head Doll	1,684.00
Fenway Park double stadium seats	2,467.00
1870 Forest City of Cleveland team photograph	1,719.00
1910s 2 vintage cabinet photographs	407.00
1940-1946 65 original baseball wire photos	821.00
Yogi Berra original photograph identical to his 1950 Bowman baseball card	139.00
1962 "Safe at Home" three sheet	1,265.00
Jackie Robinson Commemorative Cachets impressive 166 different first day issues	N/A
Jackie Robinson signed check, UCLA football program from first collegiate game	459.00
Jackie Robinson signed check	546.00
Jackie Robinson Limited Edition 1993 Joe Wilder lithograph	173.00
1890s-1940s Reach Official Score Book scored with Major League, Negro League, and local league games	508.00
1908 mechanical baseball scorecard/postcard	330.00
1910s Hugh Jennings cigar label	255.00
1911 Philadelphia Athletics Championship plate	679.00
1913 New York Giants *Baseball Magazine* team panorama	294.00
1914 World Series souvenir mini-bat/whistle	331.00
1915 New York Yankees Charles Baumann player's contract	285.00
1917 Brooklyn Ebbets Field season pass	247.00
Circa 1920 Walter Johnson signed baseball game	463.00
1920s *Casey at the Bat* lobby cards	139.00
1929 Cubs vs. Athletics World Series program and ticket stub	1,035.00
1930s Lou Gehrig souvenir mini-bat	N/A
1931 New York Giants sterling silver season pass	440.00
Circa 1930s William Harridge Official American League baseball	139.00
1936 St. Louis Cardinals collection	204.00
1939 Baseball Centennial—4 first day covers	173.00
1943 Bucky Walters Cincinnati players contract	86.00

Item	Final Bid
1944 St. Louis Browns yearbook and a vintage 1940s team stadium pin	127.00
1945 Chicago Cubs paperweight	557.00
1947 Brooklyn Dodgers Ebbets Field banner	1,020.00
1946 & 1951 Brooklyn Dodgers—Two New York Journal-American team photographs	N/A
1950s Ty Cobb—2 Christmas cards	279.00
1934 Babe Ruth Japanese tour photo, circa 1948 pin and baseball	253.00
Babe Ruth Doll in original box	273.00
Ted Williams 1950s Coca-Cola advertising poster, 1950s Moxie Root Beer soda case	201.00
Ted Williams 1954 signed government postcard, 1940s-'50s souvenir bat, 1947 *Sportfolio* magazine	255.00
Joe DiMaggio and Mrs. Joe DiMaggio signed magazine photograph	288.00
Joe DiMaggio PM10 stadium pin, 1950 photo book, 1949 Joe DiMaggio Day scorecard and photograph	222.00
Circa 1948 Satchel Paige stadium pin, signed magazine photo, lobby photo	278.00
1940 Brooklyn Dodgers/Pee Wee Reese Yankees vs. Dodgers scorecard, 1942 Dodgers stadium photopack	N/A
Circa 1940s Lou Boudreau statue	532.00
1940-1970 30 American League season passes and schedules	690.00
1951 Baseball Golden Anniversary jewelry box	115.00
1950 Philadelphia Phillies newspaper scrapbooks	312.00
1950s New York Yankees—2 Ballentine Beer display advertising pieces	278.00
Circa 1955 Hank Aaron Negro League program	185.00
Circa 1962 Red Kress National League scouting reports	306.00
1966 Mickey Mantle Fedtro Intercom advertising display	404.00
1973 Rollie Fingers Fireman of the Year fireman's helmet	532.00
1997 Nomar Garciaparra unused game bat & single-signed baseball	370.00
Tom Seaver 3,000 Strikeout program and ticket stub	115.00
Eight Men Out movie props: scorecard, newspaper, soda bottle, Crackerjack box	337.00
1946-1950 The Sports Exchange Trading Post—33 different early baseball hobby publications	383.00

CARDS

Trading cards have always been the backbone of the baseball collecting hobby. From the T206 Honus Wagner to the '52 Topps Mickey Mantle to the '97 Flair Showcase "Legacy Masterpiece" Ken Griffey Jr., baseball cards have profiled the game's biggest heroes and captured its greatest moments.

For most of their long history, baseball cards were consumer premiums designed to help promote the sale of other products. Before the turn of the century, tobacco manufacturers inserted small, cardboard pictures of baseball players and other popular subjects into tins of chewing tobacco and packages of cigarettes. Later, candy and gum manufacturers followed the idea. Eventually, eveything from Cracker Jack, to cereal, to snack cakes offered baseball cards as an added incentive to spur retail sales.

As the cards themselves became more popular, they ceased to be used as premiums, instead becoming the primary product. Whereas packs of gum may have included one card in earlier times, packs of cards came to include one stick of gum. And then none.

In the 1970s and '80s, the "organized" card hobby came of age, and baseball cards were seen not as interesting curiosities, but valuable collectibles. Prices soared, as the simple keepsakes of childhood blossomed into the investment portfolios of the future. In the early 1990s, card manufacturers faced with flagging sales returned to the idea of cards as premiums, and the age of the insert card was born. Today, "cards" come in a variety of shapes and sizes, and many are no longer made of cardboard. But whether you're a fan of the oldest pre-war tobacco issues, or the latest acetate inserts, no baseball hobbyist's collection can truly be complete without an assortment of baseball cards.

The following pages list prices for a variety of the hobby's most popular baseball cards. We begin with the most noted of the pre-war tobacco issues and follow with a comprehensive list of modern sets. In general, prices are based on Near Mint/Mint examples—that is, cards that show little wear and little or no creasing with centering at least 60/40 from left to right and top to bottom. The older the card, the less likely that truly Mint examples exist, and prices can be assumed to be for cards in Excellent/Near Mint or lesser condition. Now, more than ever, condition is a key factor in the card hobby. So-called "Gem Mint" cards, which have been graded by one of the hobby's numerous third-party grading services, can often bring prices far in excess of accepted market value. The opposite is also true, as lesser-condition cards are worth a fraction of their NM/M cousins.

Notes on price listings:

Each set listed here features a quality rating of one to five stars based on such factors as scarcity, desirability, player selection, key rookie cards, and overall card design. Each listing also contains a set description, which highlights the important facets of the set. Headers also list categories for "Commons" (unlisted players who never achieved star status) and "Unlisted Stars" (unlisted high-caliber players who never reached the "next level" of hobby status). Prices for such players are much lower than their superstar counterparts, but collectors should note that, especially in older sets, regional price variations affect the values of these cards much more than they affect "star" cards.

1869 CINCINNATI RED STOCKINGS

This is considered to be the first baseball card ever issued. It pictures the first professional team and is extremely rare. Estimated value: $10,000.

1909 RAMLY
T204

	EX Price
Complete Set (121)	$30,000.00
Commons	100.00
Unlisted Stars	**100.00-125.00**

This set is easily distinguished with its ornate gold border design around a black-and-white photo. A Ramly or T.T.T. Turkish cigarette ad appears distinctly on the back.

#	Player	EX
8	Bancroft, F. (square)	250.00
12	Bender, C. (HOF)	400.00
17	Bransfield, W. (square)	200.00
18	Bresnahan, R. (HOF)	500.00
20	Brown, M. (HOF)	500.00
22	Burkett, J. (HOF)	700.00
23	Burkett, J. (HOF, square)	700.00
26	Chance, F. (Mgr, HOF)	700.00
28	Cicotte, E.	250.00
31	Collins, J. (HOF)	700.00
32	Collins, E. (HOF)	750.00
40	Dineen, W. (square)	200.00
47	Evers, J. (HOF)	700.00
56	Griffith, C. (Mgr, HOF)	500.00
62	Huggins, M. (HOF)	700.00
64	Johnson, W. (HOF)	3500.00
68	Keeler, W. (HOF)	800.00
87	Moran, P. (square)	250.00
100	Plank, E. (HOF)	1000.00
123	Tinker, J. (HOF)	700.00
126	Wallace, B. (HOF)	700.00

1909–1911
WHITE BORDER
T206

	EX Price
Complete Set (520)	$350,000.00
Commons	50.00
Unlisted Stars	**75.00-100.00**

This is perhaps the most famous of the early tobacco issues, if not for the legendary Wagner card alone. Many players in the set have several pose variations.

Player	EX
Baker, F. (HOF)	150.00
Bender, C. (no trees, HOF)	200.00
Bender, C. (trees, HOF)	150.00
Bender, C. (portrait, HOF)	200.00
Bresnahan, R. (portrait, HOF)	200.00
Bresnahan, R. (bat, HOF)	175.00
Brown, G. (Washington)	400.00
Brown, M. (Cubs, HOF)	250.00
Brown, M. (Chicago, HOF)	150.00
Chance, F. (Cubs, HOF)	250.00
Chance, F. (Chicago, HOF)	175.00
Chance, F. (Batting, HOF)	175.00
Chesbro, J. (HOF)	200.00
Cobb, T. (portrait, green, HOF)	2000.00
Cobb, T. (portrait, red, HOF)	1500.00
Cobb, T. (bat off shoulder, HOF)	1500.00
Cobb, T. (bat on shoulder, HOF)	1200.00
Collins, E. (Phil., HOF)	200.00
Crawford, S. (throwing, HOF)	200.00
Dahlen, B. (Brooklyn)	200.00
Demmitt, R. (St. Louis)	3000.00
Doyle, J. (N.Y. National)	15000.00
Elberfeld, K. (Wash., portrait)	1000.00
Evers, J. (portrait, HOF)	250.00
Evers, J. (bat, Cubs, HOF)	300.00
Johnson, W. (hands/chest, HOF)	700.00
Johnson, W. (portrait, HOF)	800.00
Joss, A. (portrait, HOF)	300.00
Keeler, W. (portrait, HOF)	300.00
Keeler, W. (bat, HOF)	250.00
Kleinow, R. (Boston)	250.00
Lajoie, N. (portrait, HOF)	400.00
Lajoie, N. (throwing, HOF)	250.00
Lajoie, N. (bat, HOF)	300.00
Lundgren, C. (Chicago)	300.00
Magie, S. (Magee)	12000.00
Mathewson, C. (dark hat, HOF)	700.00
Mathewson, C. (portrait, HOF)	800.00
Mathewson, C. (white hat, HOF)	700.00
McGraw, J. (finger in air, HOF)	200.00
McGraw, J. (portrait, HOF)	300.00
O' Hara, B. (St. Louis)	3000.00
Plank, E. (HOF)	20000.00
Smith, F. (Chicago/Boston)	400.00
Speaker, T. (HOF)	500.00
Tinker, J. (hands/knees, HOF)	200.00
Tinker, J. (portrait, HOF)	225.00
Waddell, R. (portrait, HOF)	250.00
Waddell, R. (throwing, HOF)	150.00
Wagner, H. (HOF)	200000.00
Walsh, E. (HOF)	200.00
Young, C. (Cleve., glove, HOF)	400.00
Young, C. (Cleve., bare, HOF)	400.00
Young, C. (Cleve., portrait, HOF)	600.00

1911 GOLD BORDER
T205

	EX Price
Complete Set (208)	$20,000.00
Commons	50.00
Common ML (186-197)	150.00
Unlisted Stars	**60.00-100.00**

These cards were issued in packs of several cigarette brands, all products of the American Tobacco Company. Ads for the various brands appear at the bottom of the cards. There are pose variations for some players.

Player	EX
Baker, F. (HOF)	150.00
Bender, C. (HOF)	150.00
Bresnahan, R. (mouth closed, Mgr)	150.00
Bresnahan, R. (mouth open, Mgr)	300.00
Brown, M. (HOF)	150.00
Chance, F. (Mgr, HOF)	150.00
Chase, H. (left ear, Mgr)	250.00
Cicotte, E.	100.00
Clark, F. (Mgr, HOF)	150.00
Cobb, T.	2500.00
Collins, E. (mouth closed, HOF)	150.00
Collins, E. (mouth open, HOF)	300.00
Donohue, J.	175.00
Duffy, H. (Mgr, HOF)	250.00
Evers, J. (HOF)	175.00
Ford, R. (white cap)	150.00
Graham, G. (Cubs)	300.00
Grant, E.	150.00
Griffith, C. (Mgr, HOF)	150.00
Harmon, B. (left ear)	250.00
Huggins, M. (HOF)	150.00
Jennings, H. (Mgr, HOF)	150.00
Johnson, W. (HOF)	1000.00
Joss, A. (HOF)	500.00
Karger, E.	175.00
Kleinow, R.	200.00
Marquard, R. (HOF)	150.00
Mathewson, C. (HOF)	750.00
McGraw, J. (Mgr, HOF)	200.00
Raymond, A.	175.00
Rowan, J.	150.00
Scanlan, D.	150.00
Shean, D. (Cubs)	300.00
Speaker, T. (HOF)	400.00
Suggs, G.	175.00
Sweeney, J.	150.00
Tinker, J. (HOF)	175.00
Turner, T.	250.00
Vaughn, H.	150.00
Wagner, H.	150.00
Wallace, B. (w/cap, HOF)	150.00
Wallace, B. (1-line 1910, HOF)	300.00
Walsh, E. (HOF)	300.00
Wheat, Z. (HOF)	150.00
White, K. (Pirates)	150.00
Wilhelm, I.	150.00
Wiltse, G. (right ear)	200.00
Young, C. (HOF)	600.00

1911 HELMAR STAMPS
T332

	EX Price
Complete Set (180)	$5,000.00
Commons	18.00
Unlisted Stars	**20.00-25.00**

This is one of only two major "stamp" tobacco sets. The stamps are blank-backed, and at least 50 frame variations on the front are known. There are 25 HOFers in the set. The least expensive cards from this period.

#	Player	EX
5	Baker, (HOF)	50.00
13	Bender, C. (HOF)	50.00
19	Bresnahan, R. (Mgr, HOF)	50.00
22	Brown, M. (HOF)	50.00
28	Carey, M. (HOF)	50.00
30	Chance, F. (Mgr, HOF)	50.00
33	Clark, F. (Mgr, HOF)	50.00
35	Cobb, T. (HOF)	500.00
37	Collins, E. (Phil., HOF)	50.00
41	Crawford, S. (HOF)	50.00
60	Evers, J. (HOF)	50.00
74	Griffith, C. (Mgr, HOF)	50.00
82	Huggins, M. (HOF)	50.00
85	Jennings, H. (Mgr, HOF)	50.00
86	Johnson, W. (HOF)	250.00
93	Lajoie, N. (HOF)	75.00
104	Marquard, R. (HOF)	50.00
105	Mathewson, C. (HOF)	250.00
109	McGraw, J. (Mgr, HOF)	75.00
151	Speaker, T. (HOF)	125.00
162	Tinker, J. (HOF)	50.00
168	Wallace, B. (Mgr, HOF)	50.00
169	Walsh, E. (HOF)	75.00
171	Wheat, Z. (HOF)	50.00
179	Young, C. (HOF)	300.00

1911 MECCA
T201

	EX Price
Complete Set (50)	$3,000.00
Commons	40.00
Unlisted Stars	**45.00**

This issue was one of the first to list the player's statistics. Each double folder portrays two players, but they cannot be viewed simultaneously as each requires the same pair of legs.

Player	EX
Baker/Collins	150.00
Bergen/Wheat	75.00
Bresnahan/Huggins	150.00
Bridwell/Mathewson	300.00
Byrne/Clarke	75.00

Chance/Evers	250.00
Cobb/Crawford	900.00
Dougherty/Lord	250.00
Falkenberg/Lajoie	150.00
Gardner/Speaker	125.00
Hofman/Brown	75.00
Jennings/Summers	70.00
McCarty/McGinnity	70.00
Oldring/Bender	100.00
Payne/Walsh	70.00
Street Johnson	350.00
Wallace/Lake	100.00

1911 TURKEY RED
T3

	EX Price
Complete Set (126)	$30,000.00
Commons	175.00
Unlisted Stars	**200.00-300.00**

One of the most sought after sets of all time. These cabinet cards feature full-color lithos of the players and a plaque for the player's name.

#	Player	EX
1	Brown, M. (HOF)	400.00
4	Bresnahan, R. (Mgr, HOF)	350.00
5	Crawford, S. (HOF)	400.00
8	Clark, F. (Mgr, HOF)	350.00
9	Cobb, T. (HOF)	4000.00
16	Evers, J. (HOF)	400.00
17	Griffith, C. (Mgr, HOF)	350.00
18	Jennings, H. (Mgr, HOF)	500.00
19	Joss, A. (HOF)	450.00
23	Lajoie, N. (HOF)	800.00
26	McGraw, J. (Mgr, HOF)	500.00
27	Mathewson, C. (HOF)	1100.00
35	Tinker, J. (HOF)	500.00
36	Speaker, T. (HOF)	800.00
39	Waddell, R. (HOF)	400.00
40	Willis, V.	350.00
42	Young, C. (HOF)	1200.00
47	Chance, F. (Mgr, HOF)	400.00
52	Attell, A.	300.00
55	Jeffries, J.	500.00
67	Ketchel, S.	500.00
76	Johnson, J.	800.00
78	Baker, F. (HOF)	350.00
80	Bender, C. (HOF)	400.00
87	Collins, E. (HOF)	450.00
99	Johnson, W. (HOF)	1400.00
101	Keeler, W. (HOF)	650.00
124	Wallace, B. (Mgr, HOF)	450.00
125	Walsh, E. (HOF)	400.00

WILSON-NEW YORK-NAT.

1912 BROWN BORDER
T207

	EX Price
Complete Set (208)	$20,000.00
Commons	40.00
Unlisted Stars	**50.00-125.00**

The name of this set is derived from its tan borders and brown backgrounds. The backs have the player's name, a brief biography, and an advertisement for one of several American Tobacco Company issues.

#	Player	EX
11	Bender, C. (HOF)	150.00
20	Bresnahan, R. (Mgr, HOF)	150.00
26	Carey, M. (HOF)	100.00
28	Carrigan, B.	100.00
30	Chance, F. (Mgr, HOF)	200.00
34	Collins, E.	200.00
84	Hooper, H. (HOF)	300.00
87	Johnson, W. (HOF)	800.00
105	Lewis, I. (no emblem)	2000.00
106	Lewis, I. (emblem)	1500.00
107	Livingston, P. (Clev w/ A)	200.00
108	Livingston, P. (Clev w/ C)	200.00
112	Lowdermilk, L.	2000.00
113	Marquard, R. (HOF)	200.00
118	McGraw, J. (HOF)	200.00
121	McKechnie, B. (HOF)	275.00
125	Miller, W.	1200.00
137	Mullin, G.	150.00
153	Ragan, P.	300.00
154	Rasmussen, A.	300.00
159	Saier, V.	700.00
170	Speaker, T. (HOF)	1000.00
183	Tinker, J. (HOF)	200.00
186	Tyler, J.	500.00
189	Wagner, H.	150.00
193	Weaver, B.	500.00
194	Wheat, Z. (HOF)	150.00
205	Works, R.	200.00

1912 HASSAN
TRIPLE FOLDERS
T202

	EX Price
Complete Set (132)	$28,000.00
Commons	100.00
Unlisted Stars	**125.00-175.00**

These unique cards are comprised of two color end cards with a black-and-white action shot between them. Most center shots appear with more than one combination of end cards.

#	Player	EX
2	O'Leary/Cobb	800.00
6	Baker/Collins	250.00
7	Johnson/Street/Birmingham	350.00
8	Birmingham/Turner	400.00
13A	Chance/Foxen	250.00
13E	Chance/Shean	200.00
23	Speaker/Wood	250.00
25B	Baker/Collins	250.00
25C	Collins/Murphy	200.00
29A	Devlin/Mathewson	200.00

#		EX
29B	Devlin/Mathewson	800.00
29C	Fletcher/Mathewson/Devlin	200.00
29D	Meyers/Mathewson/Devlin	300.00
35	Engle/Speaker	200.00
36B	Chance/Evers	250.00
36E	Chance/Tinker/Evers	800.00
37	O'Leary/Cobb	1000.00
39	Moriarty/Cobb	1000.00
48B	Bresnahan/McGraw	250.00
48E	Fletcher/Mathewson	200.00
48G	Jennings/McGraw	250.00
48H	Mathewson/Meyers	300.00
49	Johnson/Knight	400.00
62	Miller/Clark	300.00
63	Speaker/Wood	650.00
64	Engle/Speaker	300.00
74C	Devlin/Mathewson	800.00
74D	Devlin/Mathewson	200.00
75A	Cobb/Jennings	1800.00
75B	Cobb/Moriarty	1800.00
75C	Austin/Stovall/Cobb	1200.00
76	Dahlen/Wheat	200.00

CHICAGO   FATIMA   AMERICAN
CIGARETTES

1913 FATIMA TEAMS
T200

	EX Price
Complete Set (16)	$6,000.00

The set contains eight team cards from both the National and American leagues. The front of the card shows a complete team with each player's name just above or below the photo.

#	Player	EX
1	Boston Nationals	300.00
2	Brooklyn Nationals	250.00
3	Chicago Nationals	250.00
4	Cincinnati Nationals	250.00
5	New York Nationals	400.00
6	Philadelphia Nationals	250.00
7	Pittsburgh Nationals	300.00
8	St. Louis Nationals	400.00
9	Boston Americans	250.00
10	Chicago Americans	300.00
11	Cleveland Americans	800.00
12	Detroit Americans	650.00
13	New York Americans	700.00
14	Philadelphia Americans	250.00
15	St. Louis Americans	500.00
16	Washington Americans	300.00

"OLD JUDGE"

CATCHER,   EWING,   N. Y's

1886 OLD JUDGE
N167

	EX Price
Complete Set (12)	$18,000.00

Issued by Goodwin & Co., this set features players from the New York National League teams.

#	Player	EX
1	Connor, R. (HOF)	2000.00
2	Corcoran, L.	1200.00
3	Dorgan, M.	1200.00
4	Esterbrook, D.	1200.00
5	Ewing, B. (HOF)	2000.00
6	Gerhardt, J.	1200.00
7	Gilespie, P.	1200.00

#		EX
8	Keefe, T. (HOF)	2000.00
9	O'Rouke, J. (HOF)	2000.00
10	Richardson, D.	1200.00
11	Ward, M. (HOF)	2000.00
12	Welch, M. (HOF)	2000.00

TIMOTHY KEEFE,
ALLEN & GINTER'S
RICHMOND   VIRGINIA.

1887 ALLEN & GINTER
N28

	EX Price
Complete Set (10)	$200.00

This is the first mass-produced tobacco set. The ten baseball cards are part of a 50-card set that includes players from other sports.

#	Player	EX
1	Anson, C. (HOF)	2000.00
2	Bennett, C.	250.00
3	Caruthers, R.	300.00
4	Clarkson, J. (HOF)	700.00
5	Comiskey, C. (HOF)	900.00
6	Glasscock, J.	300.00
7	Keefe, T. (HOF)	800.00
8	Kelly, M. (HOF)	1000.00
9	Mulvey, J.	250.00
10	Ward, J. (HOF)	800.00

CRAIG, LEFT FIELDER, WASHINGTON

1887 BUCHNER
N284

	EX Price
Complete Set (152)	$12,000.00
Commons	75.00
Unlisted Stars	**75.00-125.00**

Men from all walks of life were included in the set, but the 152 baseball stars are its most popular feature. The possibility of an additional card (McClellan of Brooklyn) remains, but its existence has not been confirmed.

#	Player	EX
3	Anson, C. (hands out, HOF)	350.00
4	Anson, C. (hands/hip, HOF)	500.00
13	Brouthers, D. (hands out, HOF)	150.00
14	Brouthers, D. (w/bat, HOF)	250.00
25	Clarkson, J. (ball, HOF)	200.00
26	Clarkson, J. (arms out, HOF)	250.00
29	Comiskey, C. (HOF)	300.00
30	Connor, R. (hands out, HOF)	150.00
31	Connor, R. (hands face, HOF)	250.00
48	Ewing, B. (tag, HOF)	150.00
49	Ewing, B. (hands out, HOF)	200.00
77	Keefe, T. (HOF)	150.00
78	Keefe, T. (HOF)	200.00
79	Kelly, K. (RF, HOF)	200.00
80	Kelly, K. (Catcher, HOF)	250.00
101	O'Rourke, J. (HOF)	175.00
102	O'Rourke, J. (hands/thighs, HOF)	200.00

110	Radbourne (hands/chest, HOF)	175.00
111	Radbourne (hands/waist, HOF)	200.00
129	Thompson, S. (HOF)	225.00
130	Thompson, S. (HOF)	225.00
131	Von Der Ahe, C.	250.00
132	Ward, M. (fielding, HOF)	175.00
133	Ward, M. (hands/knee, HOF)	200.00
134	Ward, M. (hands/side, HOF)	200.00

1887-1890
OLD JUDGE
N172

	EX Price
Complete Set (565?)	$125,000.00
Commons	100.00
Unlisted Stars	**125.00-200.00**

Players from more than 40 major and minor league teams are featured in this set. An assortment of variations for almost all the cards exists, putting the total number of cards with variations at more than 3,000.

#	Player	EX
12A	Anson, C. (in uniform, HOF)	12000.00
12A	Anson, C. (no uniform, HOF)	2000.00
28	Beckley, J. (HOF)	500.00
29	Behel, S. (dotted tie)	800.00
43	Brady, S. (dotted tie)	400.00
44	Breckinridge	2000.00
48	Brouthers, D. (HOF)	400.00
76B	Caruthers, B.	250.00
84	Clarkson, J. (HOF)	400.00
92A	Comiskey, C. (HOF)	800.00
92B	Comiskey, C. (Champs)	650.00
94A	Conner, R. (script, HOF)	500.00
94B	Conner, R. (New York, HOF)	500.00
109A	Crotty, J	400.00
114B	Cushman, E.	1000.00
116	Dailey	2000.00
131	Delahanty, E. (HOF)	1000.00
135	Donohue, J. (dotted tie)	2000.00
138	Dooley	2000.00
141	Doyle	2000.00
143	Duffy, H. (HOF)	500.00
158	Ewing, T. (N.Y., HOF)	400.00
159	Ewing & Mascot	400.00
175	Flynn	1000.00
179A	Foster, E. (dotted tie)	350.00
180	Foster, F.W.	400.00
184	Fudger	2000.00
190	Galvin, P. (HOF)	500.00
218	Griffith, C. (HOF)	500.00
228	Hamilton, B. (HOF)	600.00
230A	Hankinson, F. (dotted tie)	350.00
233	Hapeman	2000.00
251A	Holbert, B. (dotted tie)	350.00
260	Hoy, D.	400.00
274	Keefe, T. (N.Y., HOF)	400.00
275	Keefe, T. (HOF)	350.00
278	Kelly, K. (Boston, HOF)	1000.00
293	Kremmeyer, C.	2000.00
304	Levy	2000.00
308	Long, D. (Oakland)	2000.00
311A	Lynch, J. (dotted tie)	400.00
314	Mack, C. (Wash., HOF)	1200.00
328A	Mays, A. (dotted tie)	350.00
330	McCarthy, T. (HOF)	400.00
345	McLaughlin, T. (dotted tie)	350.00
351	Meegan	2000.00
372	Nelson, J.	350.00
373	Nichols, K. (Omaha, HOF)	700.00
391	O'Rourke, J. (N.Y., HOF)	500.00
393A	Orr, D. (dotted tie)	350.00
398	Perrier, H.	2000.00
411	Powers, T.	2000.00
415A	Radbourn, H. (portrait, HOF)	700.00
415B	Radbourn, H. (portrait, HOF)	400.00
425	Ripslager, C. (dotted tie)	350.00

427	Robinson, R. (HOF)	600.00
431	Roseman, C. (dotted tie)	800.00
434	Rusie, A. (HOF)	800.00
465A	Smith, P. (Balti. Athl., portrait)	800.00
485	Stockwell	2000.00
493	Sunday, B.	500.00
499	Sylvester	2000.00
504	Thompson, S. (HOF)	350.00
522	Veach	250.00
523	Veach	2000.00
527	Von Der Ahe, C. (Champs)	250.00
529	Ward, M. (HOF)	400.00
538	Welch, M. (N.Y. HOF)	400.00
563	Wright, H. (HOF)	1200.00

1888 ALLEN & GINTER
N29

	EX Price
Complete Set (6)	$3,000.00

This follow-up to the N28 series, contains only six baseball players as part of a 50-card issue. These cards are similar to those in the first issue. Buck Ewing is the only HOFer.

#	Player	EX
1	Miller, G.	500.00
2	Fogarty, J.	500.00
3	Ryan, J.	500.00
4	Ewing, W. (HOF)	1200.00
5	Getzien, C.	500.00
6	Morrill, J.	500.00

1888 GOODWIN
N162

	EX Price
Complete Set (8)	$6,500.00

This set of "Champions" was the first to compete with the cards produced by Allen & Ginter. It contains stars from several sports, even Buffalo Bill Cody. There are eight baseball players, including four HOFers.

#	Player	EX
1	Andrews, E.	500.00
2	Anson, C. (HOF)	2500.00
3	Brouthers, D. (HOF)	1000.00
4	Caruthers, B.	500.00
5	Dunlap, F.	500.00
6	Glasscock, J.	500.00
7	Keefe, T. (HOF)	1000.00
8	Kelly, K. (HOF)	2000.00

1888-1890 OLD JUDGE
CABINETS
N173

	EX Price
Complete Set (385?)	$?
Commons	175.00
Unlisted Stars	**200.00-450.00**

Issued by Goodwin & Co. from 1888-1890, this large premium set was obtained by exchanging Old Judge and Dogshead cigarettes coupons. Cards exist with both cigarette brand names, but the Dogshead cards are more scarce. It is doubtful that a complete set exists.

#	Player	EX
5A	Anson, C. (HOF)	2500.00
5B	Anson, C. (DH, HOF)	2500.00
24	Breslin, W. (Ewing)	700.00
25	Brouthers, D. (catch, HOF)	800.00
26	Brouthers, D. (bat, HOF)	800.00
27	Brouthers, D. (DH, HOF)	800.00
57	Clarkson, D. (DH, HOF)	2000.00
58	Clarkson, D. (arm out, HOF)	800.00
59	Clarkson, D. (w/bat, HOF)	800.00
67	Comiskey, C. (arms fold, HOF)	800.00
68	Comiskey, C. (DH, HOF)	700.00
69	Conner, R. (catching HOF)	800.00
70	Conner, R. (hands-knee, HOF)	800.00
71	Conner, R. (w/bat, HOF)	800.00
88	Delahanty (bat/shoulder, HOF)	850.00
89	Delahanty (bat/horizontal, HOF)	850.00
97	Duffy, H. (catching, HOF)	800.00
98	Duffy, H. (fielding, HOF)	800.00
99	Duffy, H. (w/bat, HOF)	800.00
111	Ewing, B. (bat/side, HOF)	800.00
112	Ewing, B. (bat/air, HOF)	800.00
113	Ewing, B. (hands/head, HOF)	800.00
114	Ewing, B. (hands/knee, HOF)	800.00
168	Hamilton, B. (fielding, HOF)	800.00
169	Hamilton, B. (w/bat, HOF)	800.00
200	Keefe, T. (DH, HOF)	900.00
201	Keefe, T. (hands/chest, HOF)	750.00
202	Keefe, T. (hand/head, HOF)	750.00
203	Keefe, T. (hand/waist, HOF)	750.00
205	Kelly, K. (Boston, DH, HOF)	825.00
221	Mack, C. (HOF)	2500.00
234	McCarthy, T. (hand/head, HOF)	700.00
235	McCarthy, T. (w/bat, HOF)	700.00
261	Nichols, K. (w/bat, HOF)	900.00
271	O'Rourke, J. (hand/air, HOF)	800.00
272	O'Rourke, J. (w/bat, HOF)	800.00
287	Radbourn, H. (DH, HOF)	900.00
287	Radbourn, H. (HOF)	800.00
296	Robinson, R. (catch)	800.00
297	Robinson, R. (bat)	800.00
334	Sunday, B. (bending)	500.00
335	Sunday, B. (w/bat)	500.00
344	Thompson, S. (Det., HOF)	800.00
345	Thompson, S. (Phil., HOF)	800.00
362	Ward, M. (DH, HOF)	900.00
363	Ward, M. (hands/hip, HOF)	800.00
364	Ward, M. (throwing, HOF)	800.00
385	Wright, H. (HOF)	1800.00

1895
MAYO CUT PLUG
N300

	EX Price
Complete Set (48)	$20,000.00
Commons	300.00
Unlisted Stars	**400.00**

These cards were available in tins of chewing tobacco. Fifteen of the cards portray HOFers.

#	Player	EX
1	Anson, C. (HOF)	2000.00
3A	Brouthers, D. (Baltimore, HOF)	500.00
3B	Brouthers, D. (Louisville, HOF)	750.00
4	Clarkson, J. (HOF)	500.00
7	Duffy, H. (HOF)	500.00
8A	Ewing, B. (Cleveland, HOF)	750.00
8B	Ewing, B. (Cincinnati, HOF)	750.00
21	McCarthy, T. (Mgr, HOF)	500.00
24	Nichols, K. (HOF)	500.00
26A	Rusie, A. (New York, HOF)	1000.00
26B	Rusie, A. (SIC, HOF)	750.00
28A	Ward, M. (2nd base, HOF)	500.00
28B	Ward, M. (Retired, HOF)	750.00
33	Delehanty, J. (HOF)	1000.00
35	Hamilton, B. (HOF)	500.00
36	Robinson, W. (HOF)	500.00

1908 AMERICAN CARAMEL
E91-A

	EX Price
Complete Set (33)	$2,000.00
Commons	25.00
Unlisted Stars	**30.00-80.00**

The producers of this set chose to use lithographs of generic players instead of actual likenesses of the player. Therefore, some collectors don't consider this set to be as collectible as others from the same period. The only players in the set are members of the A's, the Giants, and the Cubs.

#	Player	EX
1	Bender, C. (HOF)	100.00
2	Bresnahan, R. (HOF)	100.00
4	Brown, M. (HOF)	100.00
5	Chance, F. (HOF)	125.00
6	Collins, J. (HOF)	100.00
10	Evers, J. (HOF)	100.00
13	Mathewson, C. (HOF)	200.00
14	McGinnity, J. (HOF)	100.00
15	McGraw, J. (Mgr, HOF)	100.00
20	Plank, E. (HOF)	125.00
32	Tinker, J. (HOF)	100.00
33	Waddell, R. (HOF)	100.00

1909 AMERICAN CARAMEL
E91-B

	EX Price
Complete Set (33)	$2,000.00
Commons	20.00
Unlisted Stars	**25.00-75.00**

This set is similar to its predecessor. Players from the same three teams are included. Eleven are Hall of Famers.

#	Player	EX
2	Baker, F. (HOF)	100.00
4	Bender, C. (HOF)	100.00
6	Brown, M. (HOF)	100.00
7	Chance, F. (HOF)	125.00
8	Collins, E. (HOF)	100.00
13	Evers, J. (HOF)	100.00
18	Marquard, R. (HOF)	100.00
19	Mathewson, C. (HOF)	175.00
20	McGraw, J. (Mgr, HOF)	100.00
25	Plank, E. (HOF)	125.00
32	TInker, J. (HOF)	100.00

1909 PHILADELPHIA CARAMEL
E95

	EX Price
Complete Set (25)	$4,000.00
Commons	50.00
Unlisted Stars	**60.00-75.00**

The fronts of the cards are similar to other early candy issues, featuring a color player with a white border. The E95 can be differentiated by: "This card is one of a set of 25 ballplayers" on the reverse. This is one of the first sets to have a numbered checklist.

#	Player	EX
1	Wagner, H. (HOF)	600.00
5	Bender, C. (HOF)	200.00
9	Cobb, T. (HOF)	1800.00
11	Crawford, S. (HOF)	200.00
12	Mathewson, C. (HOF)	500.00
17	Cicotte, E.	100.00
20	Evers, J. (HOF)	200.00
21	Chance, F. (Mgr, HOF)	200.00
23	Plank, E. (HOF)	200.00
24	Collins, E. (HOF)	200.00

1909-1911 COLGAN CHIPS
E254

	EX Price
Complete Set (310)	$15,000.00
Commons	25.00
Unlisted Stars	**25.00-70.00**

Issued by the Colgan Gum Co., these 1-1/2 inch discs were inserted with gum chips. "Stars of the Diamond" is visible on the reverse. There are 19 HOFers in the set. There are numerous variations because they were issued over the course of three seasons.

#	Player	EX
19	Baker, F. (HOF)	75.00
40	Bresnahan, R. (HOF)	75.00
51	Chance, F. (Mgr, HOF)	100.00
54	Clarke, F. (Pitt, Mgr, HOF)	75.00
57	Cobb, T. (no team, HOF)	500.00
58	Cobb, T. (HOF)	650.00
59	Collins, E. (HOF)	75.00
92	Evers, J. (HOF)	100.00
100	Flick, E. (Clev. HOF)	75.00
101	Flick, E. (Tol., HOF)	75.00
123	Hooper, H. (Nat., HOF)	75.00
124	Hooper, H. (Am., HOF)	75.00
133	Jackson, J.	1500.00
134	Jennings, H. (Mgr, HOF)	75.00
140	Joss, A. (HOF)	100.00
142	Keeler, W. (HOF)	75.00
143	Kelly, J. (HOF)	75.00
153	Lajoie, N. (Mgr, HOF)	200.00
174	Marquard, R. (HOF)	75.00
183	McGinnity, J. (HOF)	75.00
268	Speaker, T. (Nat., HOF)	125.00
269	Speaker, T. (Am., HOF)	125.00
283	Tinker, J. (HOF)	100.00
287	Waddell, R. (St. Lo., HOF)	75.00
288	Waddell, R. (Min., HOF)	75.00
289	Waddell, R. (Newk., HOF)	75.00
290	Wagner, H. (Cvr., Let)	300.00
291	Wagner, H. (horz., Let)	300.00
292	Wagner, H. (Pitt, Let)	300.00
308	Young, C. (HOF)	200.00

1910 STANDARD CARAMEL
E93

	EX Price
Complete Set (30)	$5,500.00
Commons	50.00
Unlisted Stars	**60.00-125.00**

The fronts of the cards are a tinted black-and-white photo of the player with a white border. Blank backs are known to exist. Eighteen HOFers are included.

#	Player	EX
2	Bender, C. (HOF)	150.00
3	Brown, M. (HOF)	150.00
4	Chance, F. (HOF)	150.00
6	Clarke, F. (Mgr, HOF)	150.00
7	Cobb, T. (HOF)	1000.00
8	Collins, E. (HOF)	150.00
13	Evers, J. (HOF)	150.00
15	Griffith, C. (HOF)	150.00
16	Jennings, H. (Mgr, HOF)	150.00
18	Joss, A. (HOF)	175.00
19	Lajoie, N. (HOF)	200.00
21	Mathewson, C. (HOF)	350.00
22	McGraw, J. (Mgr, HOF)	175.00
25	Plank, E. (HOF)	200.00
26	Tinker, J. (HOF)	150.00
27	Wagner, H. (HOF)	500.00
28	Waddell, R. (HOF)	150.00

1912 COLGAN CHIPS RED
E270

	EX Price
Complete Set (158)	$8,000.00
Commons	70.00
Unlisted Stars	**75.00-100.00**

The second in the series from Colgan's Gum Chips ballplayers. These are distiguishable by the red border encircling the discs.

#	Player	EX
7	Baker, F. (HOF)	150.00
16	Bresnahan, R. (Mgr, HOF)	150.00
23	Chance, F. (Mgr, HOF)	125.00
24	Clarke, F. (Mgr, HOF)	150.00
27	Cobb, T (HOF)	700.00
28	Collins, E. (HOF)	150.00
48	Evers, J. (HOF)	150.00
53	Flick, E. (HOF)	150.00
67	Hooper, H. (HOF)	150.00
73	Jennings, H. (Mgr, HOF)	150.00
97	McGinnity, J. (HOF)	150.00
138	Speaker, T. (HOF)	200.00
146	Tinker, J. (HOF)	150.00
148	Waddell, R. (HOF)	150.00
157	Young, C. (HOF)	350.00

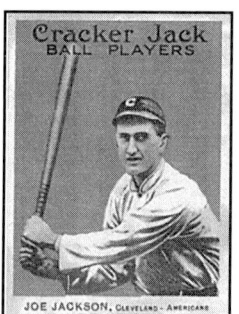

1914 CRACKER JACK
E145-1

	EX Price
Complete Set (144)	$35,000.00
Commons	100.00
Unlisted Stars	**125.00-200.00**

Most famous for its Shoeless Joe Jackson rookie, this set has been reprinted several times. Cards were inserted in boxes of Cracker Jacks. Backs have the card number, followed by a short biography. Most cards exhibit stains from the candy.

#	Player	EX
2	Baker, F. (HOF)	300.00
3	Tinker, J. (HOF)	300.00
6	Plank, E. (HOF)	500.00
7	Collins, E. (HOF)	350.00
12	Mack, C. (HOF)	400.00
14	Crawford, S. (HOF)	250.00
17	Bresnahan, R. (Mgr, HOF)	300.00
17	Bresnahan, R. (Mgr, HOF)	300.00
18	Evers, J. (HOF)	300.00
19	Bender, C. (HOF)	300.00
23	Comiskey, C. (HOF)	250.00
30	Cobb, T. (HOF)	4000.00
32	Brown, M. (HOF)	250.00
35	Hooper, H. (HOF)	250.00
36	Walsh, E. (HOF)	250.00
37	Alexander, G. (HOF)	600.00
43	Marquard, R. (HOF)	250.00
52	Wheat, Z. (HOF)	250.00
57	Johnson, W. (HOF)	1200.00
61	Schalk, R. (HOF)	250.00
65	Speaker, T. (HOF)	500.00
66	Lajoie, N. (HOF)	600.00
68	Wagner, H. (HOF)	1500.00
69	McGraw, J. (Mgr, HOF)	350.00
70	Clarke, F. (Mgr, HOF)	250.00
73	Carey, M. (HOF)	250.00
75	Huggins, M. (Mgr, HOF)	250.00
77	Jennings, H. (Mgr, HOF)	250.00
88	Mathewson, C. (HOF)	2500.00
99	Chance, F. (HOF)	1100.00
103	Jackson, J.	6000.00
133	Rickey, B. (Mgr, HOF)	350.00
136	Maranville, W. (HOF)	250.0

1915 CRACKER JACK
E145-2

	EX Price
Complete Set (176)	$25,000.00
Commons	80.00
Unlisted Stars	**100.00-175.00**

The set is similar to its predecessor, but its distinguishing mark is that the backs are printed upside down in relation to the fronts. These cards have no candy stains as they were available through a redemption offer.

#	Player	EX
2	Baker, F. (HOF)	250.00
3	Tinker, J. (Mgr, HOF)	250.00
6	Plank, E. (HOF)	350.00
7	Collins, E. (HOF)	250.00
12	Mack, C. (Mgr, HOF)	250.00
14	Crawford, S. (HOF)	200.00
17	Bresnahan, R. (Mgr, HOF)	200.00
18	Evers, J. (HOF)	250.00
19	Bender, C. (HOF)	250.00
23	Comiskey, C. (HOF)	200.00
30	Cobb, T. (HOF)	3500.00
32	Brown, M. (Mgr, HOF)	200.00
35	Hooper, H. (HOF)	200.00
36	Walsh, E. (HOF)	200.00
37	Alexander, G. (HOF)	400.00
43	Marquard, R. (HOF)	250.00
52	Wheat, Z. (HOF)	250.00
57	Johnson, W. (HOF)	1000.00
61	Schalk, R. (HOF)	200.00
65	Speaker, T. (HOF)	400.00
66	Lajoie, N. (HOF)	500.00
68	Wagner, H. (HOF)	1000.00
69	McGraw, J. (Mgr, HOF)	250.00
70	Clarke, F. (Mgr, HOF)	200.00

#	Player	EX
73	Carey, M. (HOF)	200.00
75	Huggins, M. (Mgr, HOF)	200.00
77	Jennings, H. (Mgr, HOF)	200.00
88	Mathewson, C. (Mgr, HOF)	1200.00
99	Chase, H. (Mgr, HOF)	250.00
103	Jackson, J. (Mgr, HOF)	5000.00
133	Rickey, B. (Mgr, HOF)	250.00
136	Maranville, R. (Mgr, HOF)	200.00
161	Roush, E. (Mgr, HOF)	250.00
167	Griffith, C. (Mgr, HOF)	250.00

TY COBB
Mgr.—Detroit Americans

1921 AMERICAN CARAMEL SER./120 E121

		EX Price
Complete Set (138)		$8,000.00
Commons		20.00
Unlisted Stars		**25.00-50.00**

These cards are black-and-white, and contain an action shot of the player on the front. A message on the back reads "This set consists of pictures of 120 of the leading BASE BALL STARS…" The figure of 120 is incorrect.

#	Player	EX
1	Alexander, G. (HOF)	125.00
2	Alexander, G. (HOF)	125.00
4	Baker, J. (HOF)	125.00
5	Baker, F. (HOF)	125.00
6	Bancroft, D. (HOF)	60.00
7	Bancroft, D. (HOF)	60.00
12	Carey, M. (HOF, batting)	70.00
13	Carey, M. (HOF, hands on hips)	70.00
15	Cobb, T. (Mgr, HOF, look front)	400.00
16	Cobb, T. (Mgr, HOF, look right)	400.00
17	Cobb, T. (HOF, Mgr, on front)	400.00
18	Collins, E. (HOF)	100.00
29	Faber, R. (HOF)	70.00
30	Faber, R. (HOF)	70.00
33	Frisch, F. (HOF)	60.00
44	Heilmann, H. (HOF)	75.00
44	Heilmann, H. (HOF)	75.00
45	Heilmann, H. (HOF)	75.00
50	Hooper, H. (HOF)	70.00
51	Hornsby, R. (2B, HOF)	125.00
52	Hornsby, R. (OF, HOF)	125.00
53	Hoyt, W. (HOF)	70.00
54	Huggins, M. (Mgr, HOF)	70.00
55	Johnson, W. (throwing, HOF)	150.00
56	Johnson, W. (hands/chest HOF)	150.00
57	Kelly, G. (HOF)	70.00
64	Maranvaille, R. (HOF)	70.00
67	McGraw, J. (Mgr, HOF)	100.00
88	Rice, S. (HOF)	70.00
89	Rixey, E. (HOF)	70.00
90	Rixey, E., (HOF)	70.00
91	Robinson, W. (Mgr, HOF)	70.00
95	Roush, E. (HOF)	70.00
98	Ruth, B. (pose, HOF)	1000.00
99	Ruth, B. (pose, HOF)	1000.00
100	Ruth, B. (hold-bird, HOF)	1000.00
101	Ruth, B. (hold-bird, HOF)	1000.00
102	Ruth, B. (hold-ball, HOF)	1000.00
104	Schalk, R. (catching, HOF)	70.00
105	Schalk, R. (batting, HOF)	70.00
109	Sewell, J. (HOF)	125.00
114	Sisler, G. (batting, HOF)	70.00
115	Sisler, G. (throwing, HOF)	70.00
120	Speaker, T. (large, Mgr, HOF)	125.00
120	Speaker, T. (small, Mgr, HOF)	125.00
133	Wheat, Z. (HOF)	70.00

KENNETH WILLIAMS
OUTFIELD, ST. LOUIS AMERICANS

1922 AMERICAN CARAMEL E120

		EX Price
Complete Set (240)		$9,000.00
Commons		20.00
Unlisted Stars		**25.00-70.00**

American League cards are printed in sepia on a yellow background and the National League cards in blue/green on a green background. Each individual card has that player's team checklist printed on the reverse.

#	Player	EX
4	Alexander, G.	75.00
6	Baker, H.	75.00
29	Cobb, T.	400.00
31	Collins, E.	75.00
64	Frisch, F. (HOF)	75.00
87	Hartnett, G. (HOF)	75.00
97	Hornsby, R. (HOF)	125.00
105	Johnson, W. (HOF)	275.00
127	Marquard, R. (HOF)	75.00
186	Ruth, B. (HOF)	1000.00
194	Sewell, J. (HOF)	75.00
202	Sisler, G. (HOF)	75.00
212	Speaker, T. (HOF)	125.00
231	Wheat, Z. (HOF)	75.00
239	Young, R. (HOF)	75.00

1911 SPORTING LIFE M116

Bender, Philadelphia Americans

		EX Price
Complete Set (310)		$15,000.00
Commons		50.00
Unlisted Stars		**60.00-100.00**

This set consists of 24 series with 12 cards each. The cards were offered to subscribers of the weekly sports paper. Each major league team of the era had several players in the set.

#	Player	EX
10	Baker, F. (HOF)	200.00
20	Bender, C. (HOF, blue)	250.00
21	Bender, C. (HOF, pastel)	150.00
31	Bresnahan, R. (Mgr, HOF)	200.00
34	Brown, M. (Chi., blue, HOF)	250.00
35	Brown, M. (Chi., pastel, HOF)	150.00
42	Chance, F. (blue, Mgr, HOF)	250.00
43	Chance, F. (pastel, Mgr, HOF)	125.00
45	Chase, H. (blue, Mgr)	200.00
47	Cicotte, E.	125.00
48	Clarke, F. (Pitt., Mgr, HOF)	200.00
51	Cobb, T. (blue, HOF)	1500.00
52	Cobb, T. (pastel, HOF)	900.00
53	Collins, E. (blue, HOF)	300.00
54	Collins, E. (pastel, HOF)	150.00
59	Coveleskie, H. (Louisville ML)	150.00

#	Player	EX
61	Crawford, S. (blue, HOF)	250.00
62	Crawford, S. (pastel, HOF)	125.00
87	Duffy, H. (Mgr, HOF)	150.00
95	Evers, J. (HOF)	200.00
103	Foster, E. (Rochester ML)	125.00
105	Frill, J. (Jersey City ML)	125.00
116	Griffith, C. (Mgr, HOF)	150.00
127	Hooper, H. (HOF)	175.00
129	Huggins, M. (HOF)	175.00
130	Hughes, T. (Roch. ML)	125.00
136	Jennings, H. (blue, Mgr, HOF)	250.00
137	Jennings, H. (pastl, Mgr, HOF)	150.00
138	Johnson, W. (HOF)	500.00
143	Joss, A. (HOF)	200.00
153	Kreuger, A. (Sacramento ML)	125.00
154	Lajoie, N. (blue, HOF)	400.00
155	Lajoie, N. (pastel, HOF)	250.00
173	Mack, C. (Mgr, HOF)	200.00
177	Mathewson, C. (blue, HOF)	800.00
178	Mathewson, C. (pastel, HOF)	400.00
183	McConnell, A. (Chi.)	1500.00
185	McGraw, J. (Mgr, HOF)	175.00
194	McQuillan, G. (Cin.)	1500.00
200	Mitchell, F. (Rochester ML)	125.00
217	O'Hara, B. (Toronto ML)	125.00
226	Perring, G. (Columbus ML)	125.00
232	Plank, E. (HOF)	300.00
263	Speaker, T. (HOF)	400.00
285	Tinker, J. (HOF)	150.00
289	Waddell, R. (HOF)	200.00
290	Wagner, H. (blue, HOF)	850.00
291	Wagner, H. (pastel, HOF)	600.00
293	Wallace, B. (Mgr, HOF)	150.00
294	Walsh, E. (Chi., HOF)	150.00
295	Walsh, J. (grey, HOF)	150.00
296	Walsh, J. (white , HOF)	150.00
307	Young, C. (Cleveland, HOF)	350.00

GEO. PIERCE
P.—Chicago Cubs
128

1915 SPORTING NEWS M101-5

		EX Price
Complete Set (202)		$12,000.00
Commons		20.00
Unlisted Stars		**25.00-45.00**

These cards were issued as a premium to "The Sporting News." It features players from the American, National, and Federal leagues. Fronts picture the player, while the backs are an advertisement for the paper.

#	Player	EX
4	Alexander, G. (HOF)	75.00
8	Baker, J. (HOF)	50.00
9	Bancroft, D. (HOF)	50.00
16	Bresnahan, R. (HOF)	75.00
23A	Cady, F.	75.00
23B	Brown, M. (HOF)	50.00
26	Carey, M. (HOF)	50.00
28	Chance, F. (HOF)	75.00
31	Cicotte, E.	50.00
33	Collins, E. (HOF)	75.00
35	Comiskey, C. (HOF)	60.00
42	Crawford, S. (HOF)	50.00
55	Evers, J. (HOF)	50.00
56	Faber, R. (HOF)	50.00
57	Felsch, H.	50.00
83	Hooper, H. (HOF)	50.00
85	Huggins, M. (HOF)	60.00
86	Jackson, J. (HOF)	1500.00
89	Jennings, H. (HOF)	50.00
90	Johnson, W. (HOF)	250.00
95	Lajoie, N. (HOF)	200.00
105	Mack, C. (HOF)	50.00
109	Maranville, R. (HOF)	50.00
110	Marquard, R. (HOF)	50.00
114	McGraw, J. (HOF)	60.00

#	Player	EX
142	Rixey, E. (HOF)	50.00
144	Robertson, W. (HOF)	50.00
146	Roush, E. (HOF)	50.00
151	Ruth, B. (HOF)	2500.00
155	Schalk, R. (HOF)	50.00
166	Sisler, G. (HOF)	50.00
171	Stengel, C. (HOF)	100.00
176	Thorpe, J.	1500.00
177	Tinker, J. (HOF)	50.00
184	Wagner, H. (HOF)	250.00
186	Wheat, Z. (HOF)	50.00
187	Walsh, E. (HOF)	50.00
188	Weaver, B.	50.00

DEL GAINER
1st B.—Boston Red Sox
63

1916 SPORTING NEWS M101-4

		EX Price
Complete Set (200)		$10,000.00
Commons		20.00
Unlisted Stars		**25.00-40.00**

The set is very similar to its predecessor M101-5. Most of the players are the same, but there are some in this issue who did not appear in the first.

#	Player	EX
4	Alexander, G. (HOF)	75.00
9	Baker, J. (HOF)	50.00
10	Bancroft, D. (HOF)	50.00
13	Bender, C. (HOF)	50.00
17	Brown, M. (HOF)	50.00
28	Carey, M. (HOF)	50.00
34	Collins, E. (HOF)	75.00
36	Comiskey, C. (HOF)	50.00
38	Cobb, T. (HOF)	800.00
41	Crawford, S. (HOF)	50.00
54	Evers, J. (HOF)	50.00
55	Faber, R. (HOF)	50.00
64	Gandil, C.	50.00
72	Griffith, C. (HOF)	75.00
84	Hooper, H. (HOF)	50.00
86	Huggins, M. (HOF)	50.00
87	Jackson, J.	1200.00
90	Jennings, H. (Mgr, HOF)	50.00
91	Johnson, W. (HOF)	200.00
97	Lajoie, N. (HOF)	125.00
107	Mack, C. (HOF)	100.00
112	Maranville, R. (HOF)	50.00
113	Marquard, R. (HOF)	50.00
116	McGraw, J. (Mgr, HOF)	50.00
142	Rixey, E. (HOF)	50.00
144	Robertson, W. (Mgr, HOF)	50.00
146	Roush, E. (HOF)	50.00
151	Ruth, B. (HOF)	1500.00
154	Schalk, R. (HOF)	50.00
164	Sisler, G. (HOF)	75.00
169	Stengel, C. (HOF)	100.00
174	Tinker, J. (HOF)	50.00
182	Wagner, H. (HOF)	200.00
184	Walsh, E. (HOF)	50.00
188	Wheat, Z. (HOF)	50.00

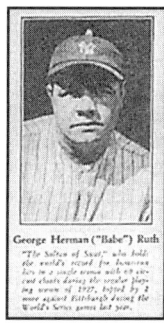

1928 FRO-JOY
BABE RUTH

	EX Price
Complete Set (6)	$500.00

This set was given away with ice cream cones in August of 1928. All cards feature Ruth. This set has been counterfeited many times, so seek expert advice before buying these. According to experts, the fakes in the marketplace outnumber genuine examples by a considerable margin.

#	Player	EX
1	Ruth, B. (George Herman)	100.00
2	Ruth, B. (Look Out)	100.00
3	Ruth, B. (Babe Lines Out)	100.00
4	Ruth, B. (Babe Comes Home)	100.00
5	Ruth, B. (Grip)	75.00
6	Ruth, B. (Fielder)	100.00

1909 WHITE SILKS
S74

	EX Price
Complete Set (92)	$10,000.00
Commons	75.00
Unlisted Stars	**75.00-125.00**

This set features the same players as the T205 set. They were issued as a premium in American Tobacco products. Few silks are found with their brown paperboard backs intact.

#	Player	EX
1	Baker, F. (HOF)	150.00
8	Bender, C. (HOF)	150.00
9	Bresnahan, R. (HOF)	150.00
11	Brown, M. (HOF)	150.00
15	Chance, F. (Mgr, HOF)	175.00
17	Clarke , F. (Mgr, HOF)	150.00
18	Cobb, T. (HOF)	1000.00
19	Collins, E. (HOF)	150.00
30	Evers, J. (HOF)	150.00
38	Griffith, C. (Mgr, HOF)	150.00
47	Marquard, R. (HOF)	150.00
48	Mathewson, C. (HOF)	400.00
51	McGraw, J. (Mgr, HOF)	175.00
76	Smith, H. (HOF)	250.00
78	Speaker, T. (HOF)	250.00
85	Tinker, J. (HOF)	150.00
88	Wallace, B. (HOF)	150.00

1910 COLOR SILKS
S74

	EX Price
Complete Set (120)	$12,000.00
Commons	75.00
Unlisted Stars	**100.00-125.00**

This set is identical to its predecessor, only the silks are full-color. It also features the same players as the T205 set, but they have no paper backs.

#	Player	EX
3	Baker, F. (HOF)	150.00
9	Bender, C. (HOF)	150.00
12	Bresnahan, R. (mouth open, Mgr)	200.00
12	Bresnahan, R. (mouth closed, Mgr)	200.00
15	Brown, M. (HOF)	150.00
19	Chance, F. (Mgr, HOF)	200.00
22	Clarke, F. (Mgr, HOF)	150.00
23	Cobb, T. (HOF)	1000.00
24	Collins, E. (HOF)	150.00
35	Duffy, H. (Mgr, HOF)	150.00
39	Evers, J. (HOF)	150.00
49	Griffith, C. (Mgr, HOF)	150.00
54	Huggins, M. (HOF)	150.00
56	Johnson, W. (HOF)	400.00
65	Marquard, R. (HOF)	150.00
66	Mathewson, C. (HOF)	400.00
69	McGraw, J. (Mgr, HOF)	200.00
102	Speaker, T. (HOF)	250.00
109	Tinker, J. (HOF)	150.00
112	Wallace, B. (HOF)	150.00
113	Wheat, Z. (HOF)	150.00
120	Young, C. (HOF)	350.00

1932 U.S. CARAMEL
R328

	EX Price
Complete Set (27)	$8,000.00
Commons	200.00
Unlisted Stars	**225.00**

This set consists of 27 baseball players and five non-players. These cards were issued for only a brief period and only in the northeast; therefore, this is considered a difficult set. Card number 16 was discovered not too long ago and is not included in the set price.

#	Player	EX
1	Collins, E. (HOF)	250.00
2	Waner, P. (HOF)	250.00
4	Terry, B. (HOF)	250.00
5	Combs, E. (HOF)	250.00
6	Dickey, B. (HOF)	250.00
7	Cronin, J. (HOF)	250.00
8	Hafey, C. (HOF)	250.00
10	Maranville, R. (HOF)	250.00
11	Hornsby, R. (Mgr, HOF)	350.00
12	Cochrane, M. (HOF)	300.00

#	Player	EX
13	Waner, L. (HOF)	250.00
14	Cobb, T. (HOF)	1000.00
16	Lindstrom, L. (HOF)	15000.00
17	Simmons, A. (HOF)	250.00
18	Lazzeri, T. (HOF)	250.00
20	Ruffing, R. (HOF)	250.00
21	Klein, C. (HOF)	250.00
23	Foxx, J. (HOF)	350.00
26	Gehrig, L. (HOF)	1000.00
27	Grove, L. (HOF)	300.00
30	Frisch, F. (HOF)	400.00
31	Gomez, L. (HOF)	250.00
32	Ruth, B. (HOF)	1200.00

1933 DE LONG
R333

	EX Price
Complete Set (24)	$5,000.00
Commons	125.00
Unlisted Stars	**150.00-175.00**

This set features the black-and-white action photo of the player with a colored background. The backs contain tips to help learn about baseball.

#	Player	EX
2	Simmons, A. (HOF)	300.00
4	Terry, B. (Mgr, HOF)	250.00
5	Gehringer, C. (HOF)	250.00
6	Cochrane, M. (HOF)	300.00
7	Gehrig, L. (HOF)	2800.00
8	Cuyler, K. (HOF)	250.00
11	Lindstrom, F. (HOF)	250.00
12	Traynor, P. (HOF)	275.00
13	Maranville, R. (HOF)	250.00
14	Gomez, L. (HOF)	275.00
19	Hafey, C. (HOF)	250.00
21	Foxx, J. (HOF)	400.00
22	Klein, C. (HOF)	250.00
23	Grove, L. (HOF)	400.00
24	Goslin, G. (HOF)	250.00

1933 GOUDEY
R319

	EX Price
Complete Set (239)	$30,000.00
Commons	40.00
Commons (1-40, 45-52)	60.00
Unlisted Stars	**50.00-90.00**

These cards are distinguishable mainly for the words "Big League Chewing Gum" across the bottom front. This is one of the most popular sets for collectors, and it contains a famous Ruth card. The Lajoie card was actually issued in 1934 and is very scarce.

#	Player	EX
1	Bengough, B.	1000.00
2	Vance, D. (HOF)	150.00
7	Lyons, T. (HOF)	125.00
19	Dickey, B. (HOF)	300.00
20	Terry, B. (HOF)	200.00
22	Traynor, P. (HOF)	150.00
23	Cuyler, K. (HOF)	125.00
25	Waner, P. (HOF)	125.00
29	Foxx, J. (HOF)	400.00
31	Lazzeri, T. (HOF)	300.00
35	Simmons, A. (HOF)	300.00
42	Collins, E. (HOF)	125.00
44	Bottomley, J. (HOF)	125.00
47	Manush, H. (HOF)	125.00
49	Frisch, F. (Mgr, HOF)	200.00
53	Ruth, B. (HOF)	3500.00
56	Ruffing, R. (HOF)	125.00
60	Hoyt, W. (HOF)	100.00
63	Cronin, J. (Mgr, HOF)	125.00
64	Grimes, B. (HOF)	100.00
73	Haines, J. (HOF)	125.00
74	Rixey, E. (HOF)	125.00
76	Cochrane, M. (HOF)	150.00
79	Faber, R. (HOF)	100.00
89	Speaker, T. (HOF)	250.00
92	Gehrig, L. (HOF)	2000.00
102	Jackson, T. (HOF)	100.00
103	Combs, E. (HOF)	100.00
106	Lajoie, L. (HOF)	25000.00
107	Manush, H. (HOF)	100.00
109	Cronin, J. (Mgr, HOF)	100.00
110	Goslin, G. (HOF)	100.00
117	Maranville, W. (HOF)	100.00
119	Hornsby, R. (Mgr, HOF)	300.00
125	Terry, B. (Mgr, HOF)	200.00
127	Ott, M. (HOF)	250.00
128	Klein, C. (HOF)	100.00
133	Lindstrom, F. (HOF)	100.00
134	Rice, S. (HOF)	100.00
138	Pennock, H. (HOF)	100.00
144	Ruth, B. (HOF, SP)	2500.00
149	Ruth, B. (HOF, DP)	3500.00
154	Foxx, J. (HOF)	300.00
158	Berg, M.	300.00
160	Gehrig, L. (HOF)	2000.00
164	Waner, L. (HOF)	100.00
165	Sewell, J. (HOF)	100.00
168	Goslin, G. (HOF)	100.00
181	Ruth, B. (HOF)	3500.00
187	Manush, H. (HOF)	100.00
188	Hornsby, R. (HOF)	300.00
189	Cronin, J. . (HOF)	125.00
194	Averill, E. (HOF)	125.00
197	Ferrell, R. (HOF)	100.00
202	Harnett, G. (HOF)	125.00
207	Ott, M. (HOF)	300.00
211	Wilson, H. (HOF)	300.00
216	Gomez, L. (HOF)	300.00
217	Crosetti, F. (HOF)	100.00
220	Grove, L. (HOF)	300.00
222	Gehringer, C. (HOF)	250.00
223	Dean, D. (HOF)	500.00
227	Herman, B. (HOF)	100.00
229	Vaughn, A. (HOF)	100.00
230	Hubbell, C. (HOF)	150.00
234	Hubbell, C. (HOF)	150.00
240	Schumacher, H.	100.00

1933 SPORT KINGS
R338

	EX Price
Complete Set (3)	$3,000.00

This set contains stars from 18 sports, including wrestling, boxing, and tennis. It is distinguishable by the "Sport Kings Gum" banner across the top of the card. Only three cards picture baseball players.

#	Player	EX
1	Cobb, T. (HOF)	1000.00
2	Ruth, B. (HOF)	2000.00
42	Hubbell, C. (HOF)	400.00

1934 GOUDEY
R320

	EX Price
Complete Set (96)	$12,000.00
Commons	40.00
Unlisted Stars	**50.00-75.00**

These cards are most famous for the front design that reads "Lou Gehrig Says…," but some have "Chuck Klein Says…" The Big League Chewing Gum label that was on the fronts of the 1933 set has been moved to the back.

#	Player	EX
1	Foxx, J. (HOF)	600.00
2	Cochrane, M. (Mgr, HOF)	150.00
6	Dean, D. (HOF)	500.00
10	Klein, C. (HOF)	125.00
11	Waner, P. (HOF)	125.00
12	Hubbell, C. (HOF)	150.00
13	Frisch, F. (Mgr, HOF)	125.00
18	Manush, H. (HOF)	125.00
19	Grove, L. (HOF)	200.00
21	Terry, B. (Mgr, HOF)	200.00
22	Vaughan, F. (HOF)	150.00
23	Gehringer, C. (HOF)	150.00
27	Appling, L. (HOF)	150.00
34	Hafey, C. (HOF)	150.00
35	Lombardi, E. (HOF)	125.00
37	Gehrig, L. (HOF)	2200.00
61	Gehrig, L. (HOF)	2200.00
62	Greenberg, H. (HOF)	300.00
90	Cuyler, K. (HOF)	300.00
96	DeShong, J. (HOF)	250.00

1934-1936
DIAMOND STARS
R327

	EX Price
Complete Set (108)	$10,000.00
Commons (1-84)	35.00
Commons (85-96)	60.00
Commons (97-108)	125.00
Unlisted Stars	**50.00-100.00**

These cards from National Chicle are more artsy than others from that time. Some cards are available with different backs. The year can be determined by the stats on the back of each card.

#	Player	EX
1A	Grove, L. (1934, HOF)	600.00
1B	Grove, L. (1935, HOF)	550.00

#	Player	EX
27	Traynor, P. (Mgr, HOF)	125.00
28	Lopez, A. (HOF)	125.00
44	Hornsby, R. (Mgr, HOF)	150.00
50	Ott, M. (HOF)	125.00
54A	Greenberg, H. (HOF, err)	150.00
54B	Greenberg, H. (HOF, cor)	150.00
64	Foxx, J. (HOF)	200.00
77	Gehringer, C. (HOF)	150.00
91	Harris, B. (HOF)	125.00
95	Appling, L. (HOF)	150.00
97	Lopez, A. (HOF)	200.00
99	Traynor, P. (HOF)	250.00
100	Averill, E. (HOF)	200.00
103	Dickey, B. (HOF)	300.00
105	Lombardi, E. (HOF)	200.00

1936 GOUDEY
R322

	EX Price
Complete Set (25)	$1,500.00
Commons	40.00
Unlisted Stars	**45.00-75.00**

This small set contains black-and-white pictures of the players on the fronts. The cards were released as game cards as the backs contain game information. Each player has several different backs. Eight HOFers are included in the set.

#	Player	EX
7	Cochrane, M. (Mgr, HOF)	150.00
14	Gomez, L. (HOF)	125.00
15	Greenberg, H. (HOF)	200.00
20	Klein, C. (HOF)	100.00
24	Waner, P. (HOF)	100.00

JOE DI MAGGIO, Yankees

1938 GOUDEY HEADS-UP
R323

	EX Price
Complete Set (48)	$14,000.00
Commons	75.00
Unlisted Stars	**80.00-100.00**

This set is a continuation of the 1933 set and picks up numbering from that point. You cannot miss this set, with its oversized head shot cropped onto a cartoon body.

#	Player	EX
241	Gehringer, C. (HOF)	300.00
246	Lombardi, E. (HOF)	150.00
249	Foxx, J. (HOF)	350.00
250	DiMaggio, J. (HOF)	4000.00
253	Greenberg, H. (HOF)	350.00
257	Lopez, A. (HOF)	150.00
258	Doerr, B. (HOF)	250.00
262	Medwick, D. (HOF)	200.00
264	Feller, B. (HOF)	500.00
265	Gehringer, C. (HOF)	300.00

#	Player	EX
270	Lombardi, E. (HOF)	150.00
273	Foxx, J. (HOF)	400.00
274	DiMaggio, J. (HOF)	4000.00
277	Greenberg, H. (HOF)	400.00
281	Lopez, A. (HOF)	150.00
282	Doerr, B. (HOF)	300.00
286	Medwick, D. (HOF)	250.00
288	Feller, B. (HOF)	500.00

1939 PLAY BALL
R334

	EX Price
Complete Set (162)	$8,000.00
Commons	20.00
Unlisted Stars	**25.00-60.00**

Some point to this set as the beginning of the modern trading card. The black-and-white fronts feature full-length shots of the players and the backs list complete bios.

#	Player	EX
6	Durocher, L. (HOF)	75.00
7	Doerr, B. (HOF)	75.00
26	DiMaggio, J. (HOF)	2000.00
30	Dickey, B. (HOF)	125.00
48	Gomez, L. (HOF)	100.00
50	Gehringer, C. (HOF)	125.00
51	Ott, M. (HOF)	125.00
53	Hubbell, C. (HOF)	100.00
56	Greenberg, H. (HOF)	150.00
82	Klein, C. (HOF)	100.00
92	Williams, T. (HOF)	2000.00
112	Waner, P. (HOF)	75.00
143	Averill, E. (HOF)	200.00

"SHOELESS JOE" JACKSON

1940 PLAY BALL
R335

	EX Price
Complete Set (240)	$15,000.00
Commons	20.00
Unlisted Stars	**25.00-60.00**

The second year of this series has a picture frame around the player. An advertisement for Superman Card Gum appears at the bottom of the back of the card.

#	Player	EX
1	DiMaggio, J. (HOF)	2200.00
6	Gomez, L. (HOF)	125.00
7	Dickey, B. (HOF)	150.00
27	Williams, T. (HOF)	1500.00
40	Greenberg, H. (HOF)	200.00
41	Gehringer, C. (HOF)	125.00
87	Hubbell, C. (HOF)	100.00
88	Ott, M. (HOF)	150.00
102	Klein, C. (HOF)	75.00
119	Alexander, G. (HOF)	100.00

#	Player	EX
120	Johnson, W. (HOF)	200.00
124	Combs, E. (HOF)	75.00
132	Mack, C. (Mgr, HOF)	200.00
133	Foxx, J. (HOF)	200.00
134	Cronin, J. (Mgr, HOF)	75.00
141	Stengel, C. (Mgr, HOF)	175.00
168	Wagner, H. (HOF)	200.00
170	Speaker, T. (HOF)	150.00
173	Lajoie, L. (HOF)	125.00
175	Mathewson, C. (HOF)	200.00
177	Baker, F. (HOF)	75.00
179	Sisler, G. (HOF)	125.00
180	Cochrane, M. (HOF)	125.00
223	Jennings, H. (HOF)	125.00
224	Traynor, P. (HOF)	150.00
225	Jackson, J.	2000.00
226	Hooper, H. (HOF)	100.00
227	Haines, P. (HOF)	100.00
230	Faber, R. (HOF)	100.00
232	Goslin, G. (HOF)	100.00
234	Chance, F. (HOF)	150.00
235	McGraw, J. (HOF)	150.00
236	Bottomley, J. (HOF)	100.00
237	Keeler, W. (HOF)	200.00
238	Lazzeri, T. (HOF)	125.00

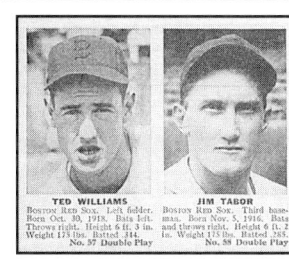

TED WILLIAMS. Boston Red Sox. Left fielder. Born Oct. 30, 1918. Bats left. Throws right. Height 6 ft. 3 in. Weight 175 lbs. Batted .344. No. 57 Double Play

JIM TABOR. Boston Red Sox. Third baseman. Born Nov. 5, 1916. Bats and throws right. Height 6 ft. 2 in. Weight 175 lbs. Batted .285. No. 58 Double Play

1941 DOUBLE PLAY
R330

	EX Price
Complete Set (75)	$4,000.00
Commons	20.00
Unlisted Stars	**25.00-40.00**

The reason for the name of this set is simple—each card contains two players. Each also fills two numbers on the checklist. Fronts feature player and current stats. Backs are blank.

#	Player	EX
23-24	Reese/Higbe	150.00
31-32	Ott/Young	100.00
39-40	Mize/Slaughter	100.00
51-52	Newsome/Greenberg	75.00
53-54	McCosky/Gehringer	75.00
57-58	Williams/Tabor	400.00
59-60	Cronin/Foxx	150.00
61-62	Gomez/Rizzuto	200.00
63-64	DiMaggio/Keller	600.00
65-66	Rolfe/Dickey	75.00
67-68	Gordon/Ruffing	75.00
77-78	Krakauskas/Feller	100.00
81-82	Williams/Cronin	500.00
85-86	Greenberg/Ruffing	150.00
89-90	Ott/Whitehead	70.00
99-100	Mize/Litwhiler	75.00
105-06	Grove/Doerr	125.00
131-32	Campbell/Boudreau	75.00
139-40	Arnovich/Hubbell	75.00

1941 PLAY BALL
R336

	EX Price
Complete Set (72)	$8,000.00
Commons (1-48)	50.00
Commons (49-72)	60.00
Unlisted Stars	**60.00-90.00**

The third Play Ball effort has only 72 cards, but it is the only of the three to appear in full-color. It is considered the pre-cursor to late 1940s Bowman issues. Interestingly, this is the only card set that contains all three DiMaggio brothers.

#	Player	EX
6	Hubbell, C. (HOF)	150.00
8	Ott, M. (HOF)	200.00
13	Foxx, J. (HOF)	250.00
14	Williams, T. (HOF)	1200.00
15	Cronin, J. (Mgr, HOF)	75.00
18	Greenberg, H. (HOF)	250.00
19	Gehringer, C. (HOF)	150.00
20	Ruffing, R. (HOF)	75.00
54	Reese, P.W. (HOF)	500.00
60	Klein, C. (HOF)	175.00
61	DiMaggio, V.	200.00
63	DiMaggio, D.	200.00
64	Doerr, B. (HOF)	150.00
70	Dickey, B. (HOF)	400.00
71	DiMaggio, J. (HOF)	2200.00
72	Gomez, L. (HOF)	400.00

1948 BOWMAN

	NM Price
Complete Set (48)	$3,500.00
Commons (1-36)	20.00
Commons (37-48)	30.00
Unlisted Stars	**35%**
SP (13, 16, 20, 24, 28, 34)	35.00

Quality Rating ★★★
Bowman's premier issue is the first major set of the post-war era. Includes rookies of Musial, Berra, Spahn, Rizzuto, and Kiner.

#	Player	NM
1	Elliott, B. (R)	75.00
2	Blackwell, E. (R)	40.00
3	Kiner, R. (R)	140.00
4	Mize, J.	95.00
5	Feller, B.	210.00
6	Berra, Y. (R)	500.00
7	Reiser, P. (SP)	100.00
8	Rizzuto (R, SP)	300.00
12	Sain, J. (R)	60.00
14	Reynolds, A. (R)	50.00
17	Slaughter, E.	90.00
18	Spahn, W. (R)	325.00
22	Bevens, F. (R, SP)	42.00
29	Page, J. (R, SP)	65.00
30	Lockman, W. (R, SP)	45.00

36	Musial, S. (R)	825.00
38	Schoendienst (R)	135.00
40	Marion, M. (R)	75.00
47	Thomson, B. (R)	75.00
48	Koslo, D. (R)	60.00

1948-49 LEAF

	NM Price
Complete Set (98)	$25,000.00
Commons	20.00
Unlisted Stars	**25.00-30.00**
Short Prints	250.00

Quality Rating ★★★★
This skip-numbered set is the first of the post-war era issued in color. Notable rookies: Musial, Robinson, and Paige.

#	Player	NM
1	DiMaggio, J.	2000.00
3	Ruth, B.	2500.00
4	Musial, S. (R)	800.00
5	Trucks, V. (R, SP)	350.00
8	Paige (R, SP)	2000.00
11	Rizzuto (R)	230.00
20	Sauer, H. (R, SP)	350.00
30	Goodman (R, SP)	275.00
32	Spahn, W. (R)	250.00
38	Kluszewski, T. (R)	110.00
46	Mize, J.	95.00
51	Dark, A. (R, SP)	400.00
55	Henrich, T. (SP)	375.00
59	Appling, L.	85.00
70	Wagner, H.	275.00
75	DiMaggio, D. (SP)	475.00
76	Williams, T.	825.00
79	Robinson, J. (R)	950.00
83	Doerr, B.	100.00
85	Philley, D. (R, SP)	275.00
91	Kiner, R. (R)	175.00
93	Feller, B. (SP)	1200.00
98	Newhouser (R, SP)	500.00
102A	Hermanski, G.(err)	250.00
106	Boudreau, L.	100.00
120	Kell, G. (R, SP)	500.00
121	Pesky, J. (R, SP)	350.00
127	Slaughter, E. (SP)	600.00
133	Holmes, T. (SP)	400.00
136A	Aberson (short sleeve)	250.00
138	Doby, L. (R)	500.00
142	Murtaugh, D. (R)	350.00
146	Reiser, P. (SP)	375.00
158	Brecheen, H. (SP)	350.00
161	Stephens (R, SP)	325.00
163	Hutchinson (R, SP)	325.00
165	Mitchell, D. (R, SP)	325.00
168	Cavarretta, P. (SP)	425.00

LEROY "Satchell" PAIGE

1949 BOWMAN

	NM Price
Complete Set (240)	$14,000.00
Commons (1-36)	15.00
Commons (37-73)	15.00
Commons (74-108)	15.00
Commons (109-144)	15.00
Commons (145-180)	45.00
Commons (181-240)	45.00
Unlisted Stars	**35%**
NOF = name on front,	
NNOF = no name on front,	
SCR = name in script on back,	
PRT = name printed on back.	

Quality Rating ★★★
This set features colorized photos and contains Robinson, Paige, Snider, and Campanella rookies. Scarce high-number series is tuff to find in NM-MT condition.

#	Player	NM
1	Bickford, V. (R)	75.00
4B	Priddy, J. (NOF)	40.00
11	Boudreau, L. (Mgr)	60.00
14	Simmons, C. (R)	35.00
18	Thomson, B.	35.00
19	Brown, B. (R)	40.00
23	Doerr, B.	55.00
24	Musial, S.	450.00
26	Kell, G.	50.00
27	Feller, B.	150.00
29	Kiner, R.	100.00
33	Spahn, W.	160.00
35	Raschi, V. (R)	50.00
36	Reese, P.W.	175.00
46	Roberts, R. (R)	225.00
47	Sain, J.	35.00
50	Robinson, J.	900.00
60	Berra, Y.	300.00
65	Slaughter, E.	65.00
70	Furillo, C.	80.00
78B	Zoldak, S. (NOF)	40.00
83B	Scheffing, R. (NOF)	40.00
84	Campanella, R. (R)	700.00
85A	Mize, J. (NNOF)	90.00
85B	Mize, J. (NOF)	150.00
88B	Salkeld, B. (NOF)	40.00
94	Vernon, M. (R)	32.00
98A	Rizzuto (NNOF)	140.00
98B	Rizzuto, P. (NOF)	215.00
100	Hodges, G. (R)	225.00
104	Stanky, E. (R)	32.00
109B	Fitzgerald, E. (PRT)	40.00
110	Wynn, E. (R)	100.00
111	Schoendienst, R.	60.00
124B	Murtaugh, D. (PRT)	40.00
127B	Majeski, H. (PRT)	40.00
132B	Evans, A. (PRT)	40.00
143B	Dillinger, B. (R, PRT)	40.00
162	Roe, P. (R)	125.00
164	Wertz, V. (R)	60.00
174	Moore, T. (R)	95.00
175	Appling, L.	125.00
185	Reiser, P.	90.00
194	Branca, R. (R)	90.00
196	Hutchinson, F.	80.00
209	Keller, C.	95.00
210	Gordon, J.	100.00
214	Ashburn, R. (R)	500.00
224	Paige, S.	1000.00
225	Coleman, J. (R)	85.00
226	Snider, D. (R)	900.00
229	Lopat, E. (R)	120.00
233	Doby, L.	140.00
238	Lemon, B. (R)	200.00
240	Young, B.	100.00

1950 BOWMAN

	NM Price
Complete Set (252)	$8,600.00
Commons (1-36)	45.00
Commons (37-72)	45.00
Commons (73-108)	15.00
Commons (109-144)	15.00
Commons (145-180)	15.00
Commons (181-216)	15.00
Commons (217-252)	15.00
Unlisted Stars	**35%**

Quality Rating ★★★
These cards include colored drawings taken from photos. Key cards: Williams and Robinson.

#	Player	NM
1	Parnell, M.	150.00
3	DiMaggio, D.	60.00
4	Zernial, G. (R)	50.00
6	Feller, B.	225.00
8	Kell, G.	75.00
10	Henrich, T.	50.00
11	Rizzuto, P.	225.00
16	Sievers, R. (R)	60.00
19	Spahn, W.	215.00
21	Reese, P.W.	215.00
22	Robinson, J.	700.00
23	Newcombe, D. (R)	120.00
28	Thomson, B.	60.00
31	Ennis, D.	50.00
32	Roberts, R.	150.00
33	Kiner, R.	90.00
35	Slaughter, E.	90.00
37	Appling, L.	75.00
39	Doby, L.	65.00
40	Lemon, B.	65.00
43	Doerr, B.	65.00
46	Berra, Y.	350.00
47	Coleman, J.	60.00
56	Crandall, D. (R)	60.00
58	Furillo, C.	60.00
59	Branca, R.	60.00
62	Kluszewski, T.	100.00
64	Dark, A.	65.00
71	Schoendienst, R.	75.00
74	Antonelli, J. (R)	30.00
75	Campanella, R.	250.00
77	Snider, D.	250.00
84	Ashburn, R.	100.00
94	Boudreau, L. (Mgr)	45.00
98	Williams, T.	750.00
100	Raschi, V.	35.00
101	Brown, B.	32.00
112	Hodges, G.	90.00
138	Reynolds, A.	35.00
139	Mize, J.	75.00
142	Lollar, S. (R)	25.00
147	Garcia, M. (R)	30.00
148	Wynn, E.	50.00
167	Roe, P.	35.00
215	Lopat, E.	35.00
217	Stengel, C. (Mgr)	100.00
219	Bauer, H. (R)	50.00
220	Durocher, L. (Mgr)	60.00
221	Mueller, D. (R)	30.00
226	Konstanty, J. (R)	38.00
229	Frisch, F. (Mgr)	38.00
232	Rosen, A. (R)	50.00
234	Shantz, B. (R)	40.00
246	Dropo, W. (R)	25.00
247	Noren, I. (R)	25.00
248	Jethroe, S. (R)	30.00
252	DeMars, B. (R)	35.00

1951 BOWMAN

	NM Price
Complete Set (324)	$16,200.00
Commons (1-36)	15.00
Commons (37-72)	15.00
Commons (73-108)	15.00
Commons (109-144)	15.00
Commons (145-180)	15.00
Commons (181-216)	15.00
Commons (217-252)	15.00
Commons (253-324)	45.00
Unlisted Stars	**35%**

Quality Rating ★★★★
Bowman increased its issue to 324 cards. This popular set contains the "true" rookies of Mantle and Mays.

#	Player	NM
1	Ford, W. (R)	800.00
2	Berra, Y.	350.00
3	Roberts, R.	75.00
6	Newcombe, D.	40.00
7	Hodges, G.	85.00
10	Schoendienst, R.	50.00
14	Dark, A.	25.00
25	Raschi, V.	36.00
26	Rizzuto, P.	125.00
30	Feller, B.	115.00
31	Campanella, R.	225.00
32	Snider, D.	225.00
40	Bell, G. (R)	30.00
46	Kell, G.	50.00
50	Mize, J.	50.00
53	Lemon, B.	45.00
54	Boone, R. (R)	28.00
56	Branca, R.	28.00
58	Slaughter, E.	50.00
62	Boudreau, L. (Mgr)	45.00
78	Wynn, E.	50.00
80	Reese, P.W.	150.00
81	Furillo, C.	38.00
109	Reynolds, A.	30.00
118	Roe, P.	30.00
122	Garagiola, J. (R)	85.00
126	Thomson, B.	28.00
127	Maglie, S. (R)	50.00
134	Spahn, W.	120.00
143	Kluszewski, T.	38.00
151	Doby, L.	30.00
165	Williams, T.	725.00
181	Stengel, C. (Mgr)	75.00
183	Bauer, H.	30.00
186	Ashburn, R.	85.00
196	Pierce, B. (R)	30.00
198	Irvin, M. (R)	100.00
203	Law, V. (R)	30.00
218	Lopat, E.	30.00
219	Woodling, G. (R)	40.00
232	Fox, N. (R)	175.00
233	Durocher, L. (Mgr)	50.00
253	Mantle, M. (R)	8200.00
254	Jensen, J. (R)	100.00
257	Tebbetts, B. (R)	60.00
258	Easter, L. (R)	60.00
259	Dressen, C. (Mgr)	60.00
260	Erskine, C. (R)	110.00
262	Zernial, G.	55.00
275	Harris, B. (Mgr)	55.00
282	Frisch, F. (Mgr)	70.00
290	Dickey, B. (Co.)	100.00
291	Henrich, T. (Co.)	55.00
295	Lopez, A. (Mgr)	110.00
305	Mays, W. (R)	3500.00
306	Piersall, J. (R)	85.00
312	Mauch, G. (R)	55.00
314	Sain, J.	55.00
317	Burgess, S. (R)	70.00
319	Rolfe, R. (Mgr)	55.00
323	Adcock, J. (R)	70.00
324	Pramesa, J. (R)	85.00

1951 TOPPS BLUE BACKS

	NM Price
Complete Set (52)	$2,500.00
Commons	28.00
Unlisted Stars	**32.00-35.00**

Quality Rating ★★★
Designed to be part of a game, these are more scarce than Red Backs. A lack of the day's top stars limits popularity.

#	Player	NM
1	Yost, E.	60.00
3	Ashburn, R.	200.00
6	Schoendienst, R.	100.00
9	Sain, J.	45.00
20	Branca, R.	45.00
30	Slaughter, E.	100.00
37	Doerr, B.	80.00
45	Pierce, B. (R)	45.00
50	Mize, J.	120.00

1951 TOPPS RED BACKS

	NM Price
Complete Set (52)	$1,500.00
Commons	9.00
Unlisted Stars	**10.00-12.00**

Quality Rating ★★★
Identical in design to the Blue Backs, this set contains such stars as Berra, Snider, and Spahn.

#	Player	NM
1	Berra, Y.	125.00
5	Rizzuto, P.	50.00
8	Wynn, E.	25.00
15	Kiner, R.	30.00
22	Feller, B.	50.00
23	Boone, R. (R)	15.00
30	Spahn, W.	50.00
31	Hodges, G.	35.00
36A	Zernial, G. (Chicago)	35.00
36B	Zernial, G. (Philadelphia)	20.00
38	Snider, D.	70.00
39	Kluszewski, T.	20.00
50	Irvin, M. (R)	40.00
52A	Holmes, T. (Boston)	38.00
52B	Holmes, T. (Hartford)	24.00

1952 BOWMAN

	NM Price
Complete Set (252)	$7,500.00
Commons (1-36)	15.00
Commons (37-72)	15.00
Commons (73-108)	15.00
Commons (109-144)	15.00
Commons (145-180)	15.00
Commons (181-216)	15.00
Commons (217-252)	30.00
Unlisted Stars	**35%**

Quality Rating ★★★★
Bowman reduced the number of cards in this attractive and popular set. Top-grade singles such as Mantle, Mays, and Musial are always in demand.

#	Player	NM
1	Berra, Y.	400.00
2	Thomson, B.	35.00
4	Roberts, R.	60.00
5	Minoso, M. (R)	110.00
8	Reese, P.W.	120.00
11	Kiner, R.	50.00
17	Lopat, E.	35.00
21	Fox, N.	70.00
23	Lemon, B.	45.00
24	Furillo, C.	35.00
27	Garagiola, J.	45.00
30	Schoendienst, R.	50.00
33	McDougald, G. (R)	70.00
37	Raschi, V.	25.00
43	Feller, B.	125.00
44	Campanella, R.	200.00
52	Rizzuto, P.	115.00
53	Ashburn, R.	85.00
70	Erskine, C.	28.00
75	Kell, G.	40.00
80	Hodges, G.	75.00
101	Mantle, M.	2500.00
115	Doby, L.	30.00
116	Snider, D.	200.00
128	Newcombe, D.	30.00
142	Wynn, E.	45.00
145	Mize, J.	55.00
146	Durocher, L. (Mgr)	50.00
156	Spahn, W.	120.00
161	Jensen, J.	35.00
162	Irvin, M.	45.00
191	Friend, B. (R)	30.00
196	Musial, S.	550.00
217	Stengel, C. (Mgr)	125.00
218	Mays, W.	1300.00
232	Slaughter, E.	75.00
238	McMillan, R. (R)	38.00
240	Loes, B. (R)	38.00
244	Burdette, L. (R)	50.00
252	Crosetti, F. (Co.)	100.00

1952 TOPPS

	NM Price
Complete Set (407)	$60,000.00
Commons (1-80)	50.00
Commons (81-130)	30.00
Commons (131-190)	25.00
Commons (191-250)	25.00
Commons (251-280)	50.00
Commons (281-300)	50.00
Commons (301-310)	50.00
Commons (311-407)	220.00
Unlisted Stars	**35%**

Quality Rating ★★★★★
First major issue from Topps is tuff, mainly because of scarcity of the cards in the final series. The Mantle is one of the hobby's true treasures.

#	Player	NM
1	Pafko, A.	1000.00
11	Rizzuto, P.	200.00
20	Loes, B. (R, SP)	100.00
22	DiMaggio, D.	85.00
26	Irvin, M.	85.00
29	Kluszewski, T.	85.00
31	Zernial, G.	70.00
33	Spahn, W.	200.00
36	Hodges, G.	150.00
37	Snider, D.	275.00
48A	Page, J. (cor)	70.00
48B	Page, J. (err)	260.00
49A	Sain, J. (cor)	75.00
49B	Sain, J. (err)	260.00
57	Lopat, E.	75.00
59	Roberts, R.	150.00
65	Slaughter, E.	130.00
66	Roe, P.	85.00
67	Reynolds, A.	85.00
88	Feller, B.	200.00
91	Schoendienst, R.	75.00
99	Woodling, G.	50.00
108	Konstanty, J.	35.00
122	Jensen, J.	70.00
129	Mize, J.	100.00
137	McMillan, R. (R)	35.00
151	Post, W. (R)	35.00
168	Silvera, C. (R)	30.00
175	Martin, B. (R)	250.00
180	Maxwell, C. (R)	35.00
191	Berra, Y.	350.00
195	Minoso, M. (R)	140.00
196	Hemus, S. (R)	35.00
200	Houk, R. (R)	65.00
202	Collins, J. (R)	40.00
215	Bauer, H.	50.00
216	Ashburn, R.	160.00
219	Shantz, B.	35.00
227	Garagiola, J.	75.00
233	Friend, B. (R)	50.00
237	Coleman, J.	35.00
243	Doby, L.	60.00
246	Kell, G.	65.00
250	Erskine, C.	75.00
253	Berardino, J.	60.00
261	Mays, W.	2500.00
262	Trucks, V.	60.00
268	Lemon, B.	140.00
274	Branca, R.	90.00
277	Wynn, E.	140.00
311	Mantle, M. (DP)	23000.00
312	Robinson, J. (DP)	1300.00
313	Thomson, B. (DP)	275.00
314	Campanella, R.	2000.00
315	Durocher, L. (Mgr)	375.00
316	Williams, D. (R)	275.00
321	Black, J. (R)	285.00
326	Shuba, G. (R)	300.00
333	Reese, P.W.	1200.00
334	Mizell, W. (R)	275.00
342	Labine, C. (R)	300.00
344	Blackwell, E.	285.00
347	Adcock, J.	285.00
351	Dark, A.	285.00
357	Burgess, S.	285.00
360	Crowe, G. (R)	275.00
365	Lavagetto, C. (Co.)	275.00
369	Groat, D. (R)	350.00
372	McDougald, G. (R)	350.00
373	Turner, J. (R, Co.)	300.00
382	Jones, S. (R)	300.00
384	Crosetti, F. (Co.)	285.00
392	Wilhelm, H. (R)	700.00
394	Herman, B. (Co.)	300.00
396	Williams, D. (R)	300.00
400	Dickey, B. (Co.)	750.00
406	Nuxhall, J. (R)	300.00
407	Mathews, E. (R)	3200.00

1953 BOWMAN B&W

	NM Price
Complete Set (64)	$2,400.00
Commons	28.00
Unlisted Stars	**35%**

Quality Rating ★★
These cards were produced in lesser quantities than their color counterparts. Lack of stars keeps interest low.

#	Player	NM
1	Bell, G.	100.00
15	Mize, J.	125.00
16	Miller, S. (R)	35.00
25	Sain, J.	50.00
26	Roe, P.	45.00
27	Lemon, B.	125.00
28	Wilhelm, H.	125.00
31	Woodling, G.	50.00
36	Piersall, J.	50.00
39	Stengel, C. (Mgr)	300.00
46	Harris, B. (Mgr)	50.00
51	Burdette, L.	50.00
60	Cox, B.	40.00
64	Hansen, A.	55.00

1953 BOWMAN COLOR

	NM Price
Complete Set (160)	$11,000.00
Commons (1-96)	28.00
Commons (97-112)	28.00
Commons (113-128)	65.00
Commons (129-160)	55.00
Unlisted Stars	**35%**

Quality Rating ★★★
Considered one of the best-looking modern era sets. Difficulty of high-numbers makes it a challenge.

#	Player	NM
1	Williams, D.	100.00
8	Rosen, A.	40.00
9	Rizzuto, P.	150.00
10	Ashburn, R.	150.00
18	Fox, N.	90.00
21	Garagiola, J.	50.00
32	Musial, S.	650.00
33	Reese, P.W.	825.00
36	Minoso, M.	55.00
40	Doby, L.	50.00
44	Bauer/Berra/Mantle	650.00
46	Campanella, R.	250.00
51	Irvin, M.	60.00
52	Marion, M. (Mgr)	42.00
55	Durocher, L. (Mgr)	65.00
57	Boudreau, L. (Mgr)	50.00
59	Mantle, M.	3000.00
61	Kell, G.	60.00
62	Kluszewski, T.	50.00
63	McDougald, G.	50.00

#	Player	NM
65	Roberts, R.	80.00
68	Reynolds, A.	45.00
78	Furillo, C.	45.00
80	Kiner, R.	70.00
81	Slaughter, E.	70.00
92	Hodges, G.	160.00
93	Martin/Rizzuto	250.00
97	Mathews, E.	250.00
99	Spahn, W.	210.00
101	Schoendienst, R.	65.00
114	Feller, B.	275.00
117	Snider, D.	550.00
118	Martin, B.	240.00
121	Berra, Y.	550.00
143	Lopez, A. (Mgr)	65.00
146	Wynn, E.	120.00
153	Ford, W.	450.00
160	Abrams, C.	80.00

JOHN MIZE

1953 TOPPS

	NM Price
Complete Set (274)	$13,000.00
Commons (1-165)	25.00
Commons (166-220)	20.00
Commons (221-280)	90.00
Common DP (1-165)	15.00
Common DP (221-280)	45.00
Unlisted Stars	**35%**

Quality Rating ★★★★
This set features color drawings of the players. Contractual problems kept several prominent players out of the set. Cards 253, 261, 267, 268, 271, and 275 don't exist.

#	Player	NM
1	Robinson, J. (DP)	475.00
10	Burgess, S. (SP)	55.00
27	Campanella, R. (DP)	185.00
31	Blackwell, E.	45.00
37	Mathews, E. (DP)	100.00
41	Slaughter, E.	75.00
43	McDougald, G.	45.00
54	Feller, B. (DP)	80.00
61	Wynn, E. (SP)	90.00
66	Minoso, M.	50.00
72	Hutchinson, F. (Mgr, SP)	40.00
76	Reese, P.W.	160.00
77	Mize, J. (DP)	55.00
78	Schoendienst, R.	55.00
81	Black, J. (SP)	60.00
82	Mantle, M.	3200.00
86	Martin, B.	115.00
87	Lopat, E.	40.00
104	Berra, Y.	200.00
114	Rizzuto, P.	150.00
119	Sain, J. (SP)	50.00
138	Kell, G.	45.00
147	Spahn, W.	150.00
149	DiMaggio, D. (DP)	35.00
151	Wilhelm, H.	70.00
162	Kluszewski, T.	40.00
188	Carey, A. (R)	40.00
191	Kiner, R.	70.00
207	Ford, W.	150.00
210	Cerv, B. (R)	50.00
220	Paige, S.	425.00
228	Newhouser, H.	150.00
244	Mays, W.	2800.00
258	Gilliam, J. (R)	265.00
263	Podres, J. (R)	265.00
265	Jensen, J.	110.00
273	Haddix, H. (R)	120.00
280	Bolling, M. (R)	285.00

1954 BOWMAN

	NM Price
Complete Set (224)	$4,000.00
Commons (1-128)	10.00
Commons (129-224)	10.00
Unlisted Stars	**35%**

Quality Rating ★★★★
Plenty of stars in this set. Due to contractual problems, Ted Williams (#66) was pulled and has consequently become a favorite.

#	Player	NM
1	Rizzuto, P.	150.00
2	Jensen, J.	15.00
6	Fox, N.	75.00
10	Erskine, C.	15.00
15	Ashburn, R.	75.00
23	Kuenn, H. (R)	35.00
33A	Raschi, V. (No TR)	15.00
33B	Raschi, V. (TR)	35.00
38	Minoso, M.	15.00
45	Kiner, R.	30.00
50	Kell, G.	30.00
57	Wilhelm, H.	25.00
58	Reese, P.W.	70.00
62	Slaughter, E.	35.00
64	Mathews, E.	50.00
65	Mantle, M.	1400.00
66A	Williams, T.	4500.00
66B	Piersall, J.	70.00
74	Gilliam, J.	28.00
84	Doby, L.	18.00
89	Mays, W.	400.00
90	Campanella, R.	160.00
95	Roberts, R.	45.00
97	McDougald, G.	20.00
101	Larsen, D. (R)	60.00
110	Schoendienst, R.	30.00
113	Reynolds, A.	18.00
122	Furillo, C.	18.00
129	Bauer, H.	18.00
132	Feller, B.	65.00
138	Hodges, G.	75.00
141	Garagiola, J.	35.00
144	Johnson, E. (R)	25.00
145	Martin, B.	65.00
154	Newcombe, D.	25.00
155	Thomas, F. (R)	20.00
161	Berra, Y.	160.00
163A	Philley, D. (No TR)	18.00
163B	Philley, D. (TR)	35.00
164	Wynn, E.	45.00
170	Snider, D.	150.00
177	Ford, W.	80.00
192	Burdette, L.	18.00
196	Lemon, B.	35.00
201	Thomson, B.	18.00
210	Piersall, J.	20.00
218	Roe, P.	18.00
224	Bruton, B.	30.00

1954 TOPPS

	NM Price
Complete Set (250)	$7,500.00
Commons (1-50)	14.00
Commons (51-75)	25.00
Commons (76-125)	14.00
Commons (126-250)	14.00
Unlisted Stars	**35%**

Quality Rating ★★★
Cards contain two photos. Absence of Mantle is a weakness, but three HOF rookies and two Williams cards help.

HENRY AARON
outfield MILWAUKEE BRAVES

#	Player	NM
1	Williams, T.	650.00
3	Irvin, M.	35.00
7	Kluszewski, T.	32.00
10	Robinson, J.	275.00
13	Martin, B.	50.00
14	Roe, P.	20.00
17	Rizzuto, P.	75.00
20	Spahn, W.	70.00
25	Kuenn, H. (R)	35.00
30	Mathews, E.	70.00
32	Snider, D.	125.00
35	Gilliam, J.	25.00
36	Wilhelm, H.	45.00
37	Ford, W.	90.00
43	Groat, D.	20.00
45	Ashburn, R.	65.00
50	Berra, Y.	150.00
52	Power, V. (R)	30.00
70	Doby, L.	60.00
80	Jensen, J.	20.00
85	Turley, B. (R)	25.00
86	Herman, B. (Co.)	25.00
90	Mays, W.	500.00
94	Banks, E. (R)	775.00
98	Black, J.	24.00
101	Woodling, G.	24.00
102	Hodges, G.	65.00
128	Aaron, H. (R)	1400.00
130	Bauer, H.	24.00
132	Lasorda, T. (R)	200.00
137	Moon, W. (R)	28.00
139	O'Brien Brothers	38.00
166	Podres, J.	30.00
201	Kaline, A. (R)	725.00
205	Sain, J.	25.00
210	Buhl, B. (R)	20.00
239	Skowron, B. (R)	90.00
250	Williams, T.	700.00

MAYS

1955 BOWMAN

	NM Price
Complete Set (320)	$4,500.00
Commons (1-96)	7.00
Commons (97-224)	7.00
Commons (225-320)	15.00
Common Umpires	25.00
Unlisted Stars	**35%**

Quality Rating ★★★★
Bowman's final issue exhibits a "TV set" design and features a number of umpires. "The 500 Club" members Mantle, Banks, Aaron, and Mays are top dogs.

#	Player	NM
1	Wilhelm, H.	90.00
2	Dark, A.	12.00
9	McDougald, G.	15.00
10	Rizzuto, P.	60.00
22	Campanella, R.	120.00
23	Kaline, A.	120.00
25	Minoso, M.	18.00
29	Schoendienst, R.	22.00
33	Fox, N.	50.00
37	Reese, P.W.	60.00
38	Wynn, E.	25.00
48B	Bolling, M. (cor)	25.00
59	Ford, W.	75.00

#	Player	NM
60	Slaughter, E.	25.00
65	Zimmer, D. (R)	25.00
67	Larsen, D.	20.00
68	Howard, E. (R)	70.00
89	Boudreau, L. (Mgr)	25.00
97	Podres, J.	18.00
98	Gilliam, J.	20.00
101A	Johnson, D. (err)	12.00
101B	Johnson, D. (cor)	28.00
103	Mathews, E.	40.00
130	Ashburn, R.	35.00
132B	Kuenn, H. (cor)	28.00
134	Feller, B.	65.00
143	Newcombe, D.	18.00
157B	Johnson, E. (cor)	28.00
158	Hodges, G.	35.00
160	Skowron, B.	25.00
168	Berra, Y.	90.00
169	Furillo, C.	18.00
170	Erskine, C.	18.00
171	Roberts, R.	30.00
179	Aaron, H.	225.00
184	Mays, W.	225.00
191	Lemon, B.	20.00
195B	Palica, E. (TR)	30.00
197	Kiner, R.	28.00
202	Mantle, M.	800.00
204B	Bolling, F. (R, cor)	28.00
213	Kell, G.	20.00
229	Brosnan, J. (R)	18.00
242	Banks, E.	300.00
246	Bauer, H.	25.00
259	Mossi, D. (R)	25.00
265	Barlick, A. (R, Umpire)	70.00
267	Honochick, G. (R, Umpire)	70.00
278	Neal, C. (R)	30.00
296	Virdon, B. (R)	30.00
302	Malzone, F. (R)	30.00
303	Conlan, J. (R, Umpire)	70.00
306	Cerv, B.	25.00
308	Lopez, A. (Mgr)	50.00
313	Donatelli, A. (R, Umpire)	38.00
315	Hubbard, C. (R, Umpire)	70.00
320	Susce, G. (R)	50.00

1955 TOPPS

	NM Price
Complete Set (206)	$7,200.00
Commons (1-150)	14.00
Commons (151-160)	18.00
Commons (161-210)	28.00
Unlisted Stars	**35%**

Quality Rating ★★★★

Topps shifts to a horizontal format for its second consecutive Mantle-less issue. High numbers are difficult in a set that features Koufax, Clemente, and Killebrew rookies.

#	Player	NM
1	Rhodes, D.	40.00
2	Williams, T.	450.00
4	Kaline, A.	175.00
5	Gilliam, J.	20.00
22	Skowron, B.	18.00
24	Newhouser, H.	20.00
25	Podres, J.	20.00
28	Banks, E.	175.00
31	Spahn, W.	80.00
47	Aaron, H.	350.00
50	Robinson, J.	275.00
75	Amoros, S. (R)	28.00
92	Zimmer, D. (R)	25.00
120	Kluszewski, T.	35.00
123	Koufax, S. (R)	1000.00
124	Killebrew, H. (R)	250.00
125	Boyer, K. (R)	65.00
152	Agganis, H.	55.00
155	Mathews, E.	80.00
156	Black, J.	35.00
160	Narleski, R.	35.00
164	Clemente, R. (R)	2100.00
166	Bauer, H.	35.00
180	Labine, C.	35.00
187	Hodges, G.	125.00
189	Rizzuto, P.	125.00
193	Sain, J.	40.00
194	Mays, W.	450.00
195	Roebuck, E. (R)	35.00
198	Berra, Y.	200.00
200	Jensen, J.	35.00
210	Snider, D.	450.00

1956 TOPPS

	NM Price
Complete Set (340)	$6,900.00
Commons (1-100)	11.00
Commons (101-180)	11.00
Commons (181-260)	14.00
Commons (261-340)	11.00
Unlisted Stars	**35%**
Team Cards	30.00
Team Cards (Dated)	60.00

Quality Rating ★★★★

Topps' final oversized issue has a design similar to that of its predecessor. The key rookie is Aparicio.

#	Player	NM
1	Harridge, W. (R, Pr.)	90.00
2	Giles, W. (R, Pr.)	22.00
5	Williams, T.	325.00
8	Alston, W. (R, Mgr)	40.00
10	Spahn, W.	60.00
14	Boyer, K.	15.00
15	Banks, E. (DP)	75.00
16	Lopez, H. (R)	14.00
20	Kaline, A.	90.00
25	Kluszewski, T.	25.00
30	Robinson, J. (DP)	140.00
31	Aaron, H.	250.00
33	Clemente, R.	500.00
61	Skowron, B.	15.00
63	Craig, R. (R)	18.00
79	Koufax, S.	350.00
95A	Braves Team (NIC)	40.00
95B	Braves Team (1955)	75.00
95C	Braves Team (NOL)	40.00
100A	Orioles Team (NIC)	35.00
100B	Orioles Team (1955)	75.00
100C	Orioles Team (NOL)	35.00
101	Campanella, R.	140.00
107	Mathews, E.	50.00
109	Slaughter, E.	35.00
110	Berra, Y.	125.00
113	Rizzuto, P.	75.00
118	Fox, N.	50.00
120	Ashburn, R.	60.00
125	Minoso, M.	22.00
130	Mays, W.	350.00
135	Mantle, M.	1400.00
140	Score, H. (R)	50.00
145	Hodges, G.	50.00
150	Snider, D.	100.00
155	Kuenn, H.	18.00
164	Killebrew, H.	100.00
165	Schoendienst, R.	25.00
166	Dodgers Team	200.00
173	Podres, J.	18.00
177	Bauer, H.	18.00
180	Roberts, R.	40.00
181	Martin, B.	50.00
187	Wynn, E.	40.00
188	White Sox Team	40.00
190	Furillo, C.	22.00
191	Lary, F.	20.00
194	Irvin, M.	33.00
195	Kell, G.	35.00
200	Feller, B.	85.00
208	Howard, E.	50.00
213	Tigers Team	50.00
225	McDougald, G.	30.00
226	Giants Team	70.00
233	Erskine, C.	25.00
235	Newcombe, D.	50.00
240	Ford, W.	100.00
250	Doby, L.	30.00
251	Yankees Team	250.00
255	Lemon, B.	30.00
257	Thomson, B.	28.00
260	Reese, P.W.	125.00
268	Mitchell, D.	18.00
280	Gilliam, J.	20.00
288	Cerv, B.	25.00
292	Aparicio, L. (R)	115.00
299	Neal, C.	30.00
304	Malzone, F.	20.00
307	Wilhelm, H.	32.00
332	Larsen, D.	60.00
340	McDermott, M.	45.00
No#	Checklist 1/3	265.00
No#	Checklist 2/4	265.00

1957 TOPPS

	NM Price
Complete Set (407)	$7,200.00
Commons (1-88)	9.00
Commons (89-176)	7.00
Commons (177-264)	6.00
Commons (265-352)	18.00
Commons (353-407)	7.00
Unlisted Stars	**35%**
Common DP (265-352)	12.00
Team Cards	15.00

Quality Rating ★★★★★

First issue of "standard size" cards. Considered one of Topps' best.

#	Player	NM
1	Williams, T.	475.00
2	Berra, Y.	100.00
7	Aparicio, L.	36.00
10	Mays, W.	225.00
15	Roberts, R.	30.00
18	Drysdale, D. (R)	200.00
20	Aaron, H.	220.00
24	Mazeroski, B. (R)	70.00
25	Ford, W.	60.00
29	Herzog, W. (R)	25.00
30	Reese, P.W.	70.00
35	Robinson, F. (R)	180.00
38	Fox, N.	45.00
40	Wynn, E.	25.00
45	Furillo, C.	18.00
50	Score, H.	18.00
55	Banks, E.	115.00
62	Martin, B.	30.00
70	Ashburn, R.	40.00
76	Clemente, R.	300.00
80	Hodges, G.	40.00
82	Howard, E.	18.00
90	Spahn, W.	65.00
95	Mantle, M.	1200.00
97	Yankees Team	80.00
114	Braves Team	18.00
120	Lemon, B.	20.00
121	Boyer, C. (R)	25.00
122	Boyer, K.	15.00
125	Kaline, A.	80.00
130	Newcombe, D.	15.00
135	Skowron, B.	15.00
138	Minoso, M.	15.00
154	Schoendienst, R.	18.00
165	Kluszewski, T.	40.00
170	Snider, D.	100.00
173	Craig, R.	15.00
175	Lemon, B.	18.00
176A	Baker, G. (err)	350.00
200	McDougald, G.	15.00
203	Wilhelm, H.	20.00
210	Campanella, R.	115.00
212	Colavito, R. (R)	150.00
215	Slaughter, E.	22.00
230	Kell, G.	20.00
240	Bauer, H.	15.00
250	Mathews, E.	40.00
270	Senators Team	50.00
272	Shantz, B.	25.00
275	Indians Team	50.00
277	Podres, J. (DP)	40.00
284	Zimmer, D.	25.00
286	Richardson, B. (R)	115.00
302	Koufax, S. (DP)	260.00
312	Kubek, T. (R, DP)	70.00
317	Giants Team	60.00
322	Redlegs Team	60.00
324	Dodgers Team	115.00
328	Robinson, B. (R)	350.00
329	White Sox Team	50.00
338	Bunning, J. (R)	130.00
400	Campanella/Snider	250.00
407	Berra/Mantle	500.00
No#	Checklist 1/2	250.00
No#	Checklist 2/3	400.00
No#	Checklist 3/4	725.00
No#	Checklist 4/5	850.00

1958 TOPPS

	NM Price
Complete Set (494)	$4,800.00
Commons (1-110)	11.00
Commons (111-198)	7.00
Commons (199-352)	5.00
Commons (353-440)	5.00
Commons (441-474)	5.00
Common All-Stars	5.00
Unlisted Stars	**35%**
Yellow Letter Variations	40.00
Yellow Team Variations	40.00
Team Cards	14.00
SP (443, 446, 450, 462)	18.00

Quality Rating ★★★

All-Star cards debut in this colorful set, and the Mantle and Musial All-Star cards are triple-prints. "Yellow letter" variations are more scarce than the "white letter" versions.

#	Player	NM
1	Williams, T.	400.00
2A	Lemon, B.	25.00
2B	Lemon, B. (YT)	50.00
5	Mays, W.	200.00
19	Giants Team	30.00
20B	McDougald, G. (YL)	50.00
25	Drysdale, D.	65.00
30A	Aaron, H.	200.00
30B	Aaron, H. (YL)	425.00
42	Roseboro, J. (R)	20.00
44	Senators Team	20.00
47	Maris, R. (R)	450.00
52A	Clemente, R.	250.00
52B	Clemente, R. (YT)	425.00
70A	Kaline, A.	90.00
70B	Kaline, A. (YL)	150.00
71	Dodgers Team	50.00
85A	Aparicio, L.	28.00
85B	Aparicio, L. (YT)	65.00
88	Snider, D.	65.00
90	Roberts, R.	30.00
100A	Wynn, E.	24.00
100B	Wynn, E. (YT)	55.00
101A	Richardson, B.	22.00
101B	Richardson, B. (YL)	55.00
115	Bunning, J.	28.00
120	Podres, J.	10.00
142	Slaughter, E.	22.00
150	Mantle, M.	825.00
161	Larsen, D.	15.00
162	Hodges, G.	26.00
175	Throneberry, M. (R)	12.00
187	Koufax, S.	200.00
190	Schoendienst, R.	16.00
230	Ashburn, R.	35.00
238	Mazeroski, B.	22.00

240	Skowron, B.	14.00
246	Yankees Team	80.00
270	Spahn, W.	50.00
271	Martin, B.	16.00
275	Howard, E.	15.00
285	Robinson, F.	100.00
288	Killebrew, H.	80.00
296	Duren, R. (R)	14.00
304	Kaline/Kuenn	18.00
307	Robinson, B.	100.00
310	Banks, E.	100.00
314	Snider/Alston	25.00
320	Ford, W.	45.00
321	Kluszewski/Williams	65.00
324	Wilhelm, H.	15.00
340	Newcombe, D.	10.00
343	Cepeda, O. (R)	90.00
350	Boyer, K.	14.00
351	Aaron/Mathews	35.00
352	Score, H.	12.00
368	Colavito, R.	45.00
370	Berra, Y.	80.00
375	Reese, P.W.	50.00
377B	Braves Team (numerical)	80.00
386	Robinson/Tebbetts	12.00
393	Kubek, T.	18.00
397B	Tigers Team (numerical)	85.00
400	Fox, N.	20.00
408B	Orioles Team (numerical)	85.00
418	Mantle/Aaron	250.00
420	Pinson, V. (R)	35.00
428B	Redlegs Team (numerical)	85.00
433A	Herrera, P. (err)	600.00
436	Mays/Snider	70.00
440	Mathews, E.	30.00
464	Flood, C. (R)	24.00
475	Haney/Stengel (AS/Mgr)	20.00
476	Musial, S. (AS, TP)	40.00
480	Mathews, E.	14.00
482	Banks, E. (AS)	32.00
483	Aparicio, L. (AS)	15.00
484	Robinson, F. (AS)	25.00
485	Williams, T. (AS)	100.00
486	Mays, W. (AS)	50.00
487	Mantle, M. (AS, TP)	175.00
488	Aaron, H. (AS)	50.00
494	Spahn, W. (AS)	20.00
495	Score, H. (AS)	15.00

1959 TOPPS

	NM Price
Complete Set (572)	$4,500.00
Commons (1-110)	5.00
Commons (111-198)	4.00
Commons (199-286)	4.00
Commons (287-506)	4.00
Commons (507-550)	15.00
Common All-Stars	15.00
Unlisted Stars	**35%**
Team Cards	13.00
Hi-Lites (461-470)	5.00

Quality Rating ★★★
Eye-catching design and high-number All-Stars contribute to its popularity. Notable rookies include HOFer Bob Gibson and future HOFer Sparky Anderson.

#	Player	NM
1	Frick, F. (Commissioner)	50.00
8	Phillies Team	60.00
10	Mantle, M.	600.00
20	Snider, D.	45.00
30	Fox, N.	25.00
34	Kaline/Maxwell	15.00
35	Kluszewski, T.	15.00
40A	Spahn, W. (err)	80.00
40B	Spahn, W. (err)	100.00
40C	Spahn, W. (cor)	50.00
48	Orioles Team	20.00
50	Mays, W.	130.00

69	Giants Team	20.00
76	Richardson, B.	18.00
90	Skowron, B.	12.00
94	White Sox Team	30.00
102	Alou, F. (R)	32.00
147	Banks/Long/Moryn	20.00
149	Bunning, J.	20.00
150	Musial, S.	125.00
155	Slaughter, E.	18.00
163	Koufax, S.	140.00
166	Minoso/Colavito/Doby	12.00
180	Berra, Y.	35.00
202	Maris, R.	100.00
212	Aaron/Mathews	70.00
237	McDougald/Turley/Richardson	12.00
260	Wynn, E.	15.00
262	Podres/Drysdale/Labine	12.00
270	Hodges, G.	25.00
295	Martin, B.	12.00
300	Ashburn, R.	25.00
310	Aparicio, L.	18.00
316B	Lumenti (no opt.)	75.00
317	Ashburn/Mays	65.00
321B	Giallmbdo, B. (no opt.)	75.00
322B	Hanebrink, H. (no TR)	75.00
336B	Loes, B. (no TR)	75.00
338	Anderson, S. (R)	85.00
349	Wilhelm, H.	15.00
350	Banks, E.	70.00
352	Roberts, R.	18.00
359	White, B. (R)	22.00
360	Kaline, A.	60.00
362B	Nichols, D. (no opt.)	75.00
380	Aaron, H.	125.00
387	Drysdale, D.	40.00
390	Cepeda, O.	18.00
408	Aparicio/Fox	20.00
420	Colavito, R.	30.00
430	Ford, W.	40.00
435	Robinson, F.	45.00
439	Robinson, B.	45.00
450	Mathews, E.	26.00
457	Dodgers Team	25.00
461	Mantle Hits 42nd HR	150.00
462	Colavito's Catch	10.00
463	Kaline Young Champ	15.00
464	Mays' Series Catch	32.00
467	Aaron's Series HR	28.00
468	Snider's Victory	15.00
469	Banks Wins MVP	15.00
470	Musial's 3000th Hit	20.00
478	Clemente, R.	200.00
480	Schoendienst, R.	15.00
509	Cash, N. (R)	60.00
510	Yankees Team	125.00
514	Gibson, B. (R)	250.00
515	Killebrew, H.	120.00
518	Cuellar, M. (R)	30.00
528	Pirates Team	55.00
542	Perry, J. (R)	28.00
543	Clemente/Skinner/Virdon	140.00
550	Campanella, R.	160.00
552	Stengel, C. (AS, Mgr)	35.00
553	Cepeda, O. (AS)	24.00
554	Skowron, B. (AS)	24.00
555	Mazeroski, B. (AS)	24.00
556	Fox, N. (AS)	35.00
557	Boyer, K. (AS)	24.00
559	Banks, E. (AS)	60.00
560	Aparicio, L. (AS)	30.00
561	Aaron, H. (AS)	115.00
562	Kaline, A. (AS)	60.00
563	Mays, W. (AS)	115.00
564	Mantle, M. (AS)	300.00
571	Spahn, W. (AS)	35.00
572	Pierce, B. (AS)	30.00

1960 LEAF

	NM Price
Complete Set (145)	$1,600.00
Commons (1-72)	3.00
Commons (73-144)	28.00
Unlisted Stars	**35%**

Quality Rating ★★★
These cards accompanied a marble instead of a stick of gum. Both versions of card #25 are included in the set price.

#	Player	NM
1	Aparicio, L.	22.00
6	Alou, F.	7.00
12	Boyer, K.	7.00
25A	Grant, J. (err)	15.00
25B	Grant, J. (cor)	20.00
27	Robinson, B.	45.00
37	Snider, D.	40.00
52	Green, D. (R)	10.00
69	Wilhelm, H.	12.00
71	Herzog, W.	7.00
94	Smith/Smith	35.00
125	Anderson, S.	70.00
128	Cepeda, O.	60.00
141	Flood, C.	35.00
144	Bunning, J.	60.00

1960 TOPPS

	NM Price
Complete Set (572)	$3,600.00
Commons (1-110)	3.50
Commons (111-198)	3.50
Commons (199-286)	3.50
Commons (287-440)	3.50
Commons (441-506)	6.00
Commons (507-552)	14.00
Unlisted Stars	**35%**
World Series (385-391)	6.00
All-Stars (553-572)	15.00
Team Cards	8.00

Quality Rating ★★★★
"Rookie Prospects" includes Yastrzemski. Managers appear on individual cards, and each team's coaching staff appears collectively on one card.

#	Player	NM
1	Wynn, E.	30.00
7	Mays/Rigney	20.00
10	Banks, E.	45.00
18	Dodgers Team	35.00
28	Robinson, B.	45.00
34	Anderson, S.	20.00
35	Ford, W.	40.00
50	Kaline, A.	45.00
55	Mazeroski, B.	9.00
72	Tigers Team	14.00
73	Gibson, B.	45.00
100	Fox, N.	15.00
105	Sherry, L (R)	8.00
132	Howard, F. (R)	20.00
136	Kaat, J. (R)	38.00
148	Yastrzemski (R)	130.00
160	Boyer/Mantle	130.00
173	Martin, B.	15.00
200	Mays, W.	100.00
210	Killebrew, H.	25.00
212	Alston, W. (Mgr)	12.00
227	Stengel, C. (Mgr)	15.00
230	Buhl/Burdette/Spahn	10.00
240	Aparicio, L.	15.00
250	Musial, S.	90.00
260	Colavito/Francona	10.00
264	Roberts, R.	12.00
295	Hodges, G.	18.00
300	Aaron, H.	100.00
305	Ashburn, R.	30.00
316	McCovey, W. (R)	120.00

326	Clemente, R.	200.00
332	Yankees Team	50.00
335	Schoendienst, R.	12.00
343	Koufax, S.	140.00
350	Mantle, M.	450.00
352	Robinson/Lynch/Bell	8.00
366	Green, D. (R)	8.00
377	Maris, R.	120.00
388	WS Game 4 (Hodges)	10.00
389	WS Game 5 (Aparicio)	10.00
395	Wilhelm, H.	12.00
400	Colavito, R.	16.00
405	Richardson, B.	12.00
420	Mathews, E.	25.00
445	Spahn, W.	40.00
448	Gentile, J. (R)	18.00
450	Cepeda, O.	18.00
465	Dickey, B. (Co.)	12.00
475	Drysdale, D.	40.00
480	Berra, Y.	70.00
484	Pirates Team	32.00
485	Boyer, K.	15.00
488	Cash, N.	14.00
490	Robinson, F.	45.00
493	Snider, D.	45.00
494	Orioles Team	14.00
502	Bunning, J.	16.00
505	Kluszewski, T.	14.00
509	Davis, T. (R)	25.00
513	Cubs Team	30.00
537	Red Sox Team	30.00
554	McCovey, W. (AS)	45.00
555	Fox, N. (AS)	20.00
558	Mathews, E. (AS)	30.00
559	Aparicio, L. (AS)	25.00
560	Banks, E. (AS)	60.00
561	Kaline, A. (AS)	60.00
563	Mantle, M. (AS)	325.00
564	Mays, W. (AS)	120.00
565	Maris, R. (AS)	90.00
566	Aaron, H. (AS)	120.00
570	Drysdale, D. (AS)	30.00
572	Antonelli, J. (AS)	28.00

1961 TOPPS

	NM Price
Complete Set (587)	$5,000.00
Commons (1-109)	3.00
Commons (110-370)	3.00
Commons (371-446)	3.50
Commons (447-522)	6.00
Commons (523-565)	28.00
Common All-Stars	28.00
Unlisted Stars	**35%**
SP (421,423,428)	16.00
Team Cards	6.50
League Leaders (41-50)	6.00
Thrills (401-410)	6.00
World Series (306-313)	7.50
MVPs (471-486)	6.00
Checklists	9.00

Quality Rating ★★★★
Extremely popular set. With the exception of Billy Williams, it's short on rookies, but HOFers and high-numbers make it desireable.

#	Player	NM
1	Groat, D.	28.00
2	Maris, R.	150.00
10	Robinson, B.	35.00
20	Roberts, R.	12.00
25	Pinson/Robinson/Bell	10.00
35	Santo, R. (R)	55.00
41	Mays/Clemente (LL)	25.00
43	Banks/Aaron/Matthews (LL)	25.00
44	Mante/Maris/Colavito (LL)	100.00
49	Drysdale/Koufax (LL)	15.00
80	Killebrew, H.	20.00
88	Ashburn, R.	12.00

120	Mathews, E.	25.00
141	Williams, B. (R)	60.00
150	Mays, W.	100.00
160	Ford, W.	36.00
180	Richardson, B.	12.00
200	Spahn, W.	30.00
207	Koufax/Podres	24.00
211	Gibson, B.	35.00
228	Yankees Team	50.00
260	Drysdale, D.	28.00
273A	Checklist 4	15.00
287	Yastrzemski, C.	50.00
290	Musial, S.	100.00
300	Mantle, M.	450.00
307	WS Game 2 (Mantle)	85.00
311	WS Game 6 (Ford)	15.00
312	WS Game 7 (Mazeroski)	18.00
313	WS Summary	14.00
327	Alou, M. (R)	10.00
330	Colavito, R.	18.00
344	Koufax, S.	100.00
350	Banks, E.	40.00
360	Robinson, F.	40.00
361B	Checklist 5	15.00
371	Skowron, B. (SP)	50.00
388	Clemente, R.	150.00
401	Ruth Hits 60th HR	40.00
402	Larsen's Perfect Game	22.00
404	Hornsby Tops NL	9.00
405	Gehrig Benched	75.00
406	Mantle's 565' HR	75.00
408	Mathewson's 267 Ks	20.00
409	Johnson's Shutouts	10.00
415	Aaron, H.	100.00
416	Howser, D. (R)	10.00
417	Marichal, J. (R)	125.00
425	Berra, Y.	70.00
426	Braves Team (#463)	10.00
429	Kaline, A.	40.00
430	Mazeroski, B. (SP)	55.00
435	Cepeda, O.	12.00
436	Maloney, J. (R)	18.00
437A	Checklist 6 (err)	12.00
437B	Checklist 6 (cor)	12.00
440	Aparicio, L.	14.00
443	Snider, D.	40.00
455	Wynn, E.	14.00
460	Hodges, G.	15.00
471	Rizzuto, P. (MVP)	15.00
472	Berra, Y. (MVP)	55.00
475	Mantle, M. (MVP)	200.00
477	Fox, N. (MVP)	10.00
478	Maris, R. (MVP)	45.00
480	Campanella, R. (MVP)	35.00
482	Mays, W. (MVP)	45.00
484	Aaron, H. (MVP)	45.00
485	Banks, E. (MVP)	32.00
490	Bunning, J.	15.00
505	Schoendienst, R.	14.00
506	Davis, W. (R)	18.00
516	Checklist 7	13.00
517	McCovey, W.	50.00
525	Perranoski, R. (R)	35.00
540	Jensen, J.	35.00
541	Sheldon, R. (R)	35.00
542	Twins Team	60.00
545	Wilhelm, H.	50.00
554	Pirates Team	65.00
559	Gentile, J.	50.00
563	Cerv, B.	40.00
565	Alou, F.	45.00
568	Skowron, B. (AS)	35.00
570	Fox, N. (AS)	45.00
571	Mazeroski, B. (AS)	35.00
572	Robinson, B. (AS)	80.00
573	Boyer, K. (AS)	35.00
574	Aparicio, L. (AS)	45.00
575	Banks, E. (AS)	90.00
576	Maris, R. (AS)	160.00
577	Aaron, H. (AS)	170.00
578	Mantle, M. (AS)	450.00
579	Mays, W. (AS)	175.00
580	Kaline, A. (AS)	90.00
581	Robinson, F. (AS)	85.00
586	Ford, W. (AS)	85.00
589	Spahn, W. (AS)	100.00

1962 TOPPS

	NM Price
Complete Set (598)	$4,800.00
Commons (1-109)	4.50
Commons (110-196)	4.50
Commons (197-283)	4.50
Commons (284-370)	4.50
Commons (371-446)	5.00
Commons (447-522)	10.00
Commons (523-590)	20.00
Commons (591-598)	42.00
Unlisted SP	30.00
Unlisted Stars	**35%**
Team Cards	7.00
Checklists	10.00
Babe Ruth (135-144)	18.00
World Series (232-237)	5.00
All-Stars (390-399)	6.00
All-Stars (466-475)	12.00

Quality Rating ★★★★
This set contains a 10-card Babe Ruth subset. Woodgrain borders make NM-MT cards difficult. Rookies include Brock, Perry, and "Mr. Baseball," Bob Uecker.

#	Player	NM
1	Maris, R.	185.00
5	Koufax, S.	150.00
10	Clemente, R.	200.00
18	Mantle/Mays	200.00
20	Colavito, R.	18.00
25	Banks, E.	40.00
29	Stengel, C. (Mgr)	20.00
30	Mathews, E.	18.00
31	Tresh, T. (R)	15.00
40	Cepeda, O.	15.00
45	Robinson, B.	40.00
50	Musial, S.	100.00
52	Clemente/Boyer (LL)	15.00
53	Maris/Mantle/Killebrew (LL)	100.00
54	Mays/Robinson (LL)	15.00
60	Koufax/Drysdale (LL)	15.00
65	Richardson, B.	10.00
70	Killebrew, H.	18.00
73	Fox, N.	18.00
85	Hodges, G.	15.00
99	Powell, B. (R)	28.00
100	Spahn, W.	28.00
129B	Walls, L. (left)	25.00
132B	Angels Team (photo)	25.00
134B	Hoeft, B. (left)	25.00
139A	Ruth Hits 60	25.00
139B	Reniff, H. (R, portrait)	12.00
139C	Reniff, H. (R, pitch)	60.00
140	Gehrig & Ruth	50.00
147B	Kunkel, B. (pitch)	25.00
150	Kaline, A.	40.00
167	McCarver, T. (R)	30.00
170	Santo, R.	14.00
174B	Willey, C. (w/cap)	25.00
176B	Yost, E. (bat)	25.00
190B	Moon, W. (bat)	25.00
199	Perry, G. (R)	85.00
200	Mantle, M.	550.00
208	Martin, B.	15.00
209	Fregosi, J. (R)	12.00
213	Ashburn, R.	18.00
218	Torre, J. (R)	30.00
234	WS Game 3 (Maris)	18.00
235	WS Game 4 (Ford)	10.00
243	Roberts, R.	14.00
250	Cash, N.	10.00
251	Yankees Team	50.00
288	Williams, B.	30.00
300	Mays, W.	145.00
310	Ford, W.	35.00
312	Spahn's No-Hit Form	15.00
313	Maris Blasts 61st	35.00
314	Colavito's Power	10.00

315	Ford Tosses Curve	12.00
316	Killebrew In Orbit	12.00
317	Musial's 21st Season	18.00
318	Mantle Connects	150.00
320	Aaron, H.	150.00
325	Aparicio, L.	15.00
340	Drysdale, D.	40.00
350	Robinson, F.	45.00
360	Berra, Y.	75.00
384	A's Team	10.00
385	Wynn, E.	18.00
387	Brock, L. (R)	125.00
390	Cepeda, O. (AS)	10.00
391	Mazeroski, B. (AS)	10.00
394	Aaron, H. (AS)	45.00
395	Mays, W. (AS)	45.00
396	Robinson, F. (AS)	15.00
398	Drysdale, D. (AS)	15.00
399	Spahn, W. (AS)	15.00
400	Howard, E.	10.00
401	Cepeda/Maris	45.00
409	Pirates Team	10.00
425	Yastrzemski, C.	115.00
441	Checklist 6	15.00
458B	Buhl, B. (no emblem)	45.00
461	Hubbs, K. (R)	30.00
462B	Tasby, W. (no emblem)	45.00
468	Robinson, B. (AS)	20.00
470	Kaline, A. (AS)	18.00
471	Mantle, M. (AS)	175.00
472	Colavito, R. (AS)	15.00
475	Ford, W. (AS)	14.00
476	Orioles Team	15.00
500	Snider, D.	45.00
505	Marichal, J.	40.00
516	Checklist 7	15.00
530	Gibson, B. (SP)	140.00
537	Indians Team	45.00
544	McCovey, W. (SP)	120.00
545	Wilhelm, H. (SP)	50.00
552	Cubs Team (SP)	50.00
572	Miller, B. (SP)	32.00
575	Schoendienst, R. (SP)	50.00
584	Twins Team (SP)	50.00
591	McDowell, S. (R)	65.00
592	Bouton, J. (R)	70.00
594	Uecker, B. (R)	70.00
596	Pepitone, J. (R)	60.00
598	Hickman, J. (R)	60.00

1963 FLEER

	NM Price
Complete Set (67)	$1,800.00
Commons	14.00
Unlisted Stars	**15.00-22.00**

Quality Rating ★★★★
A popular set because, with only 67 cards, it's afford-able. Key rookie here is Maury Wills.

#	Player	NM
4	Robinson, B.	90.00
5	Mays, W.	180.00
8	Yastrzemski, C.	100.00
41	Drysdale, D.	60.00
42	Koufax, S.	180.00
43	Wills, M. (R)	115.00
45	Spahn, W.	70.00
46	Adcock, J. (SP)	180.00
56	Clemente, R.	275.00
59	Mazeroski, B.	25.00
61	Gibson, B.	70.00
64	Cepeda, O.	30.00
No#	Checklist (SP)	700.00

1963 TOPPS

	NM Price
Complete Set (576)	$4,900.00
Commons (1-109)	3.00
Commons (110-196)	3.00
Commons (197-283)	4.00
Commons (284-370)	5.00
Commons (371-446)	5.00
Commons (447-522)	18.00
Commons (523-576)	14.00
Unlisted Stars	**35%**
Team Cards	5.00
League Leaders (1-10)	5.50
World Series (142-148)	4.50
Checklists	10.00

Quality Rating ★★★
Cards feature a full color photo along with an inset B&W photo. Rose and Stargell rookies, along with Musial's last card, are keys to the set.

#	Player	NM
1	Musial/Aaron (LL)	40.00
2	Mantle/Runnels (LL)	40.00
3	Mays/Aaron/Banks (LL)	30.00
4	Killebrew/Maris/Colavito (LL)	15.00
5	Koufax/Drysdale/Gibson (LL)	18.00
9	Drysdale/Koufax/Gibson (LL)	15.00
18	Burgess/Clemente	60.00
25	Kaline, A.	32.00
54A	DeBusschere, D. (R, 62)	16.00
68	Hodges/Snider	15.00
108	Wilhelm, H.	10.00
115	Yastrzemski, C.	40.00
120	Maris, R.	50.00
125	Roberts, R.	12.00
126	Uecker, B.	12.00
135	Ashburn, R.	15.00
138	Mays/Musial	50.00
142	WS Game 1 (Ford)	8.00
144	WS Game 3 (Maris)	10.00
169	Perry, G.	24.00
173	Mantle/Richardson/Tersh	175.00
200	Mantle, M.	550.00
205	Aparicio, L.	14.00
210	Koufax, S.	150.00
228	Oliva/Kranepool (R)	45.00
233	Stengel, C. (Mgr)	16.00
240	Colavito, R.	15.00
242	Aaron/Banks	50.00
245	Hodges, G.	18.00
247	Yankees Team	35.00
250	Musial, S.	120.00
275	Mathews, E.	18.00
288	White Sox Team	9.00
300	Mays, W.	125.00
312	Colt 45's Team	20.00
317	McDowell, S.	8.00
320	Spahn, W.	38.00
323	Mazeroski, B.	8.00
337	Dodgers Team	20.00
340	Berra, Y.	65.00
345	Robinson, B.	50.00
347	Torre, J.	8.00
353	Williams, B.	25.00
360	Drysdale, D.	40.00
365	Bunning, J.	10.00
375	Boyer, K.	8.00
377	Orioles Team	9.00
380	Banks, E.	70.00
390	Aaron, H.	130.00
394	McCarver, T.	10.00
397	A's Team	9.00
398	Powell, B.	25.00
400	Robinson, F.	50.00
401	Bouton, J.	12.00
412	Drysdale/Koufax/Padres	38.00
415	Gibson, B.	50.00
417	Giants Team	9.00
420	Richardson, B.	12.00

431B	Checklist 6	18.00
440	Marichal, J.	30.00
446	Ford, W.	40.00
451	Indians Team	35.00
466	Freehan, B. (R, SP)	60.00
470	Tresh, T. (SP)	60.00
472	Brock, L.	100.00
473	Mets Team	90.00
490	McCovey, W.	125.00
500	Killebrew, H. (SP)	135.00
503	Braves Team	35.00
509A	Checklist 7	18.00
509B	Checklist 7	18.00
520	Cepeda, O.	25.00
524	Cardinals Team	25.00
525	Fox, N.	35.00
537	Rose, P. (R)	1000.00
540	Clemente, R.	350.00
544	Staub, R. (R)	40.00
550	Snider, D.	70.00
552	Tigers Team	40.00
553	Stargell, W. (R)	125.00
562	McNally, D. (R)	22.00
576	Temple, J.	22.00

DUKE SNIDER outfield

1964 TOPPS

	NM Price
Complete Set (587)	$3,000.00
Commons (1-109)	3.00
Commons (110-196)	3.00
Commons (197-283)	3.00
Commons (284-370)	3.00
Commons (371-446)	7.00
Commons (447-522)	7.00
Commons (523-587)	14.00
Unlisted Stars	**35%**
Team Cards	5.00
World Series (136-140)	5.00
League Leaders (1-12)	5.00
Checklists	9.00

Quality Rating ★★
Contains many HOFers at reasonable prices. Lack of stars in high numbers hinders popularity.

#	Player	NM
1	Koufax/Friend (LL)	25.00
3	Koufax/Marichal/Spahn (LL)	15.00
4	Bouton/Ford/Pascual (LL)	7.00
5	Drysdale/Koufax (LL)	12.00
7	Aaron/Clemente (LL)	14.00
8	Kaline/Yastrzemski (LL)	10.00
9	Aaron/Mays/McCovey (LL)	25.00
10	Allison/Killebrew (LL)	7.00
11	Aaron/Boyer/White (LL)	10.00
12	Kaline/Killebrew (LL)	7.00
13	Wilhelm, H.	8.00
21	Berra, Y. (Mgr)	30.00
27	Mets Team	7.00
29	Brock, L.	35.00
35	Mathews, E.	20.00
38	Wynn, J. (R)	7.00
41	McCovey/Wagner	7.00
50	Mantle, M.	300.00
55	Banks, E.	35.00
81	Fox/Killebrew	8.00
116	Oliva, T.	12.00
120	Drysdale, D.	20.00
125	Rose, P.	125.00
128	Lolich, M. (R)	20.00
136	WS Game 1 (Koufax)	15.00
146	John, T. (R)	25.00
150	Mays, W.	85.00
155	Snider, D.	25.00
167	Piniella, L. (R)	32.00
175	Williams, B.	12.00
177	Killebrew, H.	18.00
182	Schilling/Yastrzemski	12.00
190	Richardson, B.	7.00
200	Koufax, S.	100.00

205	Fox, N.	12.00
210	Yastrzemski, C.	35.00
225	Maris, R.	60.00
230	Robinson, B.	40.00
243	Allen, R. (R)	28.00
244	LaRussa, T. (R)	28.00
250	Kaline, A.	38.00
260	Robinson, F.	38.00
262	Shannon, M. (R)	8.00
265	Bunning, J.	10.00
267	Wood, W. (R)	7.00
280	Marichal, J.	14.00
285	Roberts, R.	14.00
287	Conigliaro, T. (R)	42.00
300	Aaron, H.	90.00
306	Cepeda/Mays	32.00
320	Colavito, R.	12.00
324	Stengel, C. (Mgr)	15.00
331	Kaline/Mantle/Maris	175.00
337	Torborg, J. (R)	7.50
342	Stargell, W.	28.00
350	McCovey, W.	20.00
368	Buford, D. (R)	7.00
373	Pirates Team	10.00
375	Santo, R.	10.00
380	Ford, W.	32.00
393	Stengel/Kranepool	10.00
400	Spahn, W.	38.00
403	Reds Team	11.00
419	Harrelson, K. (R)	12.00
423	Aaron/Mays	120.00
429	McCarver, T.	10.00
433	Yankees Team	28.00
438	Checklist 6	12.00
440	Clemente, R.	250.00
460	Gibson, B.	38.00
468	Perry, G.	35.00
471	Brown, G. (R)	10.00
473	Orioles Team	10.00
476	Carty, R. (R)	12.00
496	White Sox Team	10.00
509	Alley, G. (R)	10.00
512	Horton, W. (R)	14.00
517A	Checklist 7 (err)	22.00
517B	Checklist 7 (cor)	15.00
531	Dodgers Team	22.00
540	Aparicio, L.	20.00
541	Niekro, P. (R)	80.00
543	Uecker, B.	35.00
547	Hodges, G. (Mgr)	18.00
550	Hubbs, K.	30.00
570	Mazeroski, B.	18.00
579	Red Sox Team	25.00

GIANTS OUTFIELD
WILLIE McCOVEY

1965 TOPPS

	NM Price
Complete Set (598)	$3,400.00
Commons (1-283)	2.00
Commons (284-370)	3.50
Commons (371-446)	6.00
Commons (447-522)	6.00
Commons (523-598)	6.00
Common SP (523-598)	11.00
Unlisted Stars	**35%**
Team Cards	5.00
League Leaders (1-12)	3.50
World Series (132-139)	4.00
Checklists	9.00

Quality Rating ★★★★
This set contains the rookies of Carlton, Hunter, and Morgan and future HOFer Perez.

#	Player	NM
1	Oliva/Robinson (LL)	15.00
2	Aaron/Clemente (LL)	22.00
3	Killebrew/Mantle (LL)	40.00
4	Mays/Williams/Cepeda (LL)	15.00
5	Killebrew/Mantle/Robinson (LL)	40.00
6	Boyer/Mays/Santo (LL)	10.00

8	Drysdale/Koufax (LL)	20.00
12	Drysdale/Gibson (LL)	7.00
15	Roberts, R.	12.00
16	Morgan, J. (R)	75.00
50	Marichal, J.	11.00
55	Conigliaro, T.	12.00
74	Petrocelli, R. (R)	11.00
120	Robinson, F.	30.00
130	Kaline, A.	30.00
134	WS Game 3 (Mantle)	65.00
138	WS Game 7 (Gibson)	10.00
145	Tiant, L. (R)	24.00
150	Robinson, B.	28.00
155	Maris, R.	50.00
160	Clemente, R.	160.00
170	Aaron, H.	80.00
176	McCovey, W.	18.00
187	Stengel, C. (Mgr)	14.00
193	Perry, G.	16.00
205	Spahn, W.	28.00
207	Rose, P.	150.00
208	John, T.	10.00
220	Williams, B.	9.00
236	McLain, D. (R)	28.00
250	Mays, W.	90.00
259	Northrup, J. (R)	6.00
260	Drysdale, D.	18.00
266	Campaneris, B. (R)	10.00
276	Wilhelm, H.	9.00
282	Murakami, M. (R)	20.00
293	Angels Team	7.00
294	McCarver, T.	7.00
300	Koufax, S.	120.00
308	Jones, C. (R)	8.00
316	Reds Team	7.00
320	Gibson, B.	36.00
330	Ford, W.	32.00
335	Lolich, M.	7.00
338	Phillies Team	7.00
340	Oliva, T.	16.00
350	Mantle, M.	600.00
361	Checklist 5	12.00
377	Stargell, W.	27.00
379	Giants Team	10.00
380	Colavito, R.	12.00
385	Yastrzemski, C.	70.00
400	Killebrew, H.	38.00
403	Red Sox Team	10.00
410	Aparicio, L.	10.00
415	Flood, C.	10.00
426	Braves Team	10.00
443	Checklist 6	12.00
460	Allen, R.	36.00
461	Carroll/Niekro (R)	45.00
470	Berra, Y. (Co.)	50.00
473	Blair/Johnson (R)	12.00
477	Carlton, S. (R)	250.00
481	Indians Team	10.00
485	Fox, N.	15.00
500	Mathews, E.	30.00
508	Checklist 7	12.00
510	Banks, E.	75.00
513	Yankees Team	45.00
519	Uecker, B.	28.00
526	Hunter, J. (R, SP)	90.00
527	Torborg, J. (SP)	14.00
533	McGraw/Swoboda (R, SP)	24.00
540	Brock, L. (SP)	50.00
549	Beckert, G. (R, SP)	18.00
550	Stottlemyre (R, SP)	30.00
551	Mets Team (SP)	30.00
556	Schoendienst, R. (Mgr, SP)	22.00
560	Powell, B. (SP)	22.00
561	Lefebvre, J. (R)	10.00
572	Orioles Team (SP)	26.00
573	Lonborg, J. (R, SP)	22.00
581	Perez, T. (R, SP)	90.00
598	Downing, A. (SP)	20.00

1966 TOPPS

	NM Price
Complete Set (598)	$4,000.00
Commons (1-109)	1.50
Commons (110-196)	2.00
Commons (197-283)	2.00
Commons (284-370)	2.50
Commons (371-446)	3.50
Commons (447-522)	8.00
Commons (523-598)	13.00
Common SP (523-598)	28.00
Unlisted Stars	**35%**
Team Cards	4.00
League Leaders (215-226)	4.00
Checklists	8.00

ORIOLES
JIM PALMER pitcher

Quality Rating ★★★★
Exciting set holds rookie's of Palmer, Sutton, and Jenkins. Final series has several short-prints.

#	Player	NM
1	Mays, W.	125.00
24	Kessinger, D. (R)	5.00
28	Niekro, P.	20.00
30	Rose, P. (DP)	40.00
36	Hunter, J. (DP)	18.00
50	Mantle, M. (DP)	200.00
62B	Ranew, M. (sold)	30.00
70	Yastrzemski, C.	30.00
72	Perez, T.	25.00
80	Allen, R.	5.00
90	Aparicio, L.	5.00
91A	Uecker, B. (traded)	10.00
91B	Uecker, B. (no trade)	35.00
92	Yankees Team	15.00
99	Clendenon/Stargell	5.00
100	Koufax, S.	75.00
101A	Checklist 2 (err)	16.00
101B	Checklist 2 (cor)	5.00
103B	Groat, D. (no trade)	30.00
104B	Johnson, D. (no trade)	30.00
110	Banks, E.	28.00
120	Killebrew, H.	16.00
124	McGraw, T.	5.00
125	Brock, L.	18.00
126	Palmer, J. (R)	90.00
132	Cepeda, O.	5.00
150	Colavito, R.	6.00
160	Ford, W.	24.00
167	Powell, B.	5.00
195	Morgan, J.	13.00
200	Mathews, E.	12.00
210	Mazeroski, B.	5.00
215	Aaron/Clemente/Mays (LL)	45.00
217	Mays/McCovey/Williams (LL)	20.00
219	Mays/Robinson (LL)	10.00
221	Koufax/Marichal (LL)	10.00
223	Drysdale/Koufax (LL)	10.00
225	Gibson/Koufax (LL)	10.00
234	White, R. (R)	8.00
254	Jenkins, F. (R)	80.00
255	Stargell, W.	18.00
275	McCarver, T.	5.00
288	Sutton, D. (R)	60.00
290	Santo, R.	5.00
300	Clemente, R.	160.00
310	Robinson, F.	36.00
320	Gibson, B.	25.00
350	Stottlemyre, M.	5.00
363	Checklist 5	10.00
365	Maris, R.	45.00
379	Cardinals Team	10.00
380	Conigliaro, T.	10.00
390	Robinson, B.	36.00
404	Pirates Team	10.00
410	Kaline, A.	36.00
420	Marichal, J.	12.00
424	May/Osteen (R)	10.00
426	White Sox Team	10.00
430	Drysdale, D.	18.00
435	Bunning, J.	12.00
444	Checklist 6	10.00
445	Kaat, J.	10.00
450	Oliva, T.	12.00
463	Phillies Team	12.00
469	Murcer, B. (R)	28.00
486	John, T.	12.00
490	Richardson, B.	12.00
492	A's Team	12.00
500	Aaron, H.	120.00
510	Wilhelm, H.	14.00
515	Howard, F.	12.00
517A	Checklist 7	14.00
517B	Checklist 7	14.00
526	Twins Team (SP)	90.00

#	Player	NM
530	Roberts, R.	50.00
535	Davis, W. (SP)	40.00
540	McLain, D. (SP)	70.00
547	Clarke, H. (R, SP)	30.00
550	McCovey, W. (SP)	90.00
558	Scott, G. (R)	20.00
565	Piersall, J. (SP)	32.00
579	Johnson, D.	20.00
580	Williams, B. (SP)	60.00
583	Tigers Team (SP)	115.00
590	Skowron, B. (SP)	32.00
591	Jackson, G. (R, SP)	32.00
598	Perry, G. (SP)	160.00

1967 TOPPS

	NM Price
Complete Set (609)	$4,500.00
Commons (1-109)	1.50
Commons (110-196)	2.00
Commons (197-283)	2.00
Commons (284-370)	2.50
Commons (371-457)	4.00
Commons (458-533)	6.00
Commons (534-609)	15.00
Unlisted Stars	35%
Teams	4.00
World Series (151-155)	4.00
League Leaders (233-244)	4.00
Checklists	7.00

Quality Rating ★★★★★

Many consider this set to be one of the greatest ever. Sharp design and HOF rookies contribute to its popularity. Hard-to-find high-numbers challenge set builders.

#	Player	NM
1	Bauer/Robinson/Robinson	20.00
5	Ford, W.	18.00
20	Cepeda, O.	6.00
26A	Priddy, B. (no trade)	25.00
30	Kaline, A. (DP)	15.00
33	Bando, S. (R)	4.00
42	Mets Team	6.00
45	Maris, R.	50.00
50	Oliva, T.	5.00
55	Drysdale, D.	14.00
60	Aparicio, L.	5.00
63	Brock/Flood	7.00
86A	McCormick, M. (no trade)	25.00
100	Robinson, F. (DP)	15.00
103	Checklist 2 (Mantle)	15.00
131	Yankees Team	10.00
140	Stargell, W.	18.00
146	Carlton, S.	70.00
150	Mantle, M.	350.00
152	WS Game 2 (Palmer)	7.00
166	Mathews, E.	14.00
191B	Checklist 3 (Mays)	12.00
200	Mays, W.	90.00
210	Gibson, B.	20.00
215	Banks, E.	20.00
216	Cash/Kaline	8.00
228	Hodges, G. (Mgr)	5.00
230	Powell, B.	5.00
234	Koufax/Marichal (LL)	14.00
236	Gibson/Koufax/Marichal/Perry (LL)	25.00
238	Bunning/Koufax (LL)	10.00
239	Kaline/Oliva/Robinson (LL)	8.00
241	Killebrew/Powell/Robinson (LL)	8.00
242	Aaron/Allen/Clemente (LL)	18.00
243	Killebrew/Powell/Robinson (LL)	8.00
244	Aaron/Allen/Mays (LL)	18.00
250	Aaron, H.	85.00
266	Stargell/Clendenon	5.00
280	Conigliaro, T.	10.00
285	Brock, L.	20.00
300	Kaat, J.	5.00
302	Orioles Team	6.00
314	Smith, R. (R)	8.00
315	Williams, B.	10.00
320	Perry, G.	12.00
326	Uecker, B.	8.00
327	Angels Team	6.00
333	Jenkins, F.	18.00
334	Allison/Killebrew	6.00
337	Morgan, J.	13.00
354	Cubs Team	6.00
355	Yastrzemski, C.	30.00
361	Checklist 5 (Clemente)	10.00
369	Hunter, J.	16.00
377	Tiant, L.	6.00
378	Tigers Team	7.00
400	Clemente, R. (DP)	90.00
407	Reds Team	7.00
417A	Bruce, B. (err, DP)	27.00
420	McLain, D.	7.00
422	Wilhelm, H.	7.00
423	Mays/McCovey (DP)	25.00
430	Rose, P.	75.00
437	Senators Team	7.00
445	Sutton, D.	24.00
450	Allen, R.	7.00
456	Niekro, P.	15.00
460	Killebrew, H.	50.00
475	Palmer, J.	90.00
476	Perez, T. (SP)	65.00
477	Braves Team	15.00
480	McCovey, W.	35.00
481	Durocher, L. (Mgr)	14.00
485	McCarver, T.	18.00
492	Pirates Team	15.00
500	Marichal, J.	20.00
503	Dodgers Team	15.00
510	Mazeroski, B.	12.00
512	Schoendienst, R. (Mgr)	12.00
516	Giants Team	15.00
528	Petrocelli, R.	10.00
530	Alou, F.	10.00
531	Checklist 7 (Robinson)	12.00
536	Niekro, J. (R)	30.00
540	Cash, N.	30.00
544	Indians Team	30.00
553	Hegan, M. (R)	25.00
558	Belanger, M. (R)	40.00
560	Bunning, J.	65.00
563	Adcock, J.	20.00
569	Carew (R, DP)	250.00
570	Wills, M.	85.00
573	White Sox Team	30.00
580	Colavito, R.	80.00
581	Seaver, T. (R)	800.00
584	Piersall, J.	24.00
587	Shaw/Sutherland (R)	20.00
600	Robinson, B.	260.00
604	Red Sox Team	100.00
605	Shannon, M.	45.00
607	Stanley, M.	30.00
609	John, T.	65.00

1968 TOPPS

	NM Price
Complete Set (598)	$3,000.00
Commons (1-109)	1.50
Commons (110-196)	1.50
Commons (197-283)	1.50
Commons (284-370)	1.50
Commons (371-457)	1.50
Commons (458-533)	3.00
Commons (534-598)	3.50
Unlisted Stars	35%
Team Cards	3.00
All-Stars (361-380)	2.00
League Leaders (1-12)	3.00
World Series (151-158)	4.00
Checklists	6.00

Quality Rating ★★★★

This offering contains the rookies of Ryan and Bench and second-year Seaver and Carew cards.

#	Player	NM
1	Alou/Clemente (LL)	30.00
2	Kaline/Robinson/Yaz (LL)	12.00
3	Aaron/Cepeda/Clemente(LL)	16.00
4	Killebrew/Robinson/Yaz (LL)	12.00
5	Aaron/McCovey/Santo (LL)	7.50
6	Howard/Killebrew/Yaz (LL)	7.00
16	Piniella, L.	4.00
20	Robinson, B.	25.00
27	Hodges, G. (Mgr)	7.00
30	Torre, J.	4.00
37	Williams, B.	9.00
40	McLain, D.	7.00
45	Seaver, T.	50.00
49B	Brinkman, E. (YT)	40.00
50	Mays, W.	70.00
58	Mathews, E.	12.00
66B	Cox, C. (YT)	85.00
72	John, T.	5.00
80	Carew, R.	50.00
85	Perry, G.	7.00
86	Stargell, W.	10.00
99	Colavito, R.	6.00
100	Gibson, B.	25.00
103	Sutton, D.	8.00
110	Aaron, H.	60.00
130	Perez, T.	10.00
140	Conigliaro, T.	7.00
144	Morgan, J.	12.00
145	Drysdale, D.	12.00
150	Clemente, R.	80.00
151	WS Game 1 (Brock)	9.00
152	WS Game 2 (Yaz)	9.00
154	WS Game 4 (Gibson)	7.00
177	Ryan/Koosman (R)	1000.00
192A	Checklist 3 (Yaz)	7.00
192B	Checklist 3 (Yaz)	7.00
200	Cepeda, O.	5.00
201	Marshall, M. (R)	4.00
205	Marichal, J.	8.00
215	Bunning, J.	5.00
220	Killebrew, H.	15.00
230	Rose, P.	40.00
235	Santo, R.	5.00
240	Kaline, A.	24.00
247	Bench, J. (R)	125.00
250	Yastrzemski, C.	25.00
251	Sanguillen, M. (R)	5.00
256	Cash, N.	5.00
257	Niekro, P.	7.00
275	McCarver, T.	4.00
280	Mantle, M.	275.00
290	McCovey, W.	11.00
310	Aparicio, L.	5.00
330	Maris, R.	40.00
350	Wilhelm, H.	7.00
355	Banks, E.	24.00
361	Killebrew, H. (AS)	7.00
363	Carew, R. (AS)	7.00
364	Morgan, J. (AS)	7.00
365	Robinson, B. (AS)	8.00
369	Yastrzemski, C. (AS)	8.00
370	Aaron, H. (AS)	16.00
372	Brock, L. (AS)	8.00
373	Robinson, F. (AS)	8.00
374	Clemente, R. (AS)	25.00
378	Gibson, B. (AS)	8.00
381	Powell, B.	4.00
384	McRae, H. (R)	7.00
385	Hunter, J.	12.00
400B	McCormck, M. (WT)	125.00
408	Carlton, S.	32.00
410	Jenkins, F.	12.00
414	Lolich, M.	5.00
454A	Checklist 6 (Robinson)	7.00
454B	Checklist 6 (Robinson)	7.00
460	Lonborg, J.	5.00
470	Freehan, B.	5.00
477	Phillies Team	6.00
480	Cardenas/Clemente/Oliva	50.00
488	Tracewski, D.	5.00
490	Killebrew/Mantle/Mays	160.00
497	Cardinals Team	6.00
500	Robinson, F.	28.00
505	Sparma, J.	6.00
518A	Checklist 7 (Boyer)	10.00
518B	Checklist 7 (Boyer)	10.00
520	Brock, L.	22.00
528	Tigers Team	60.00
530	Robinson/Robinson	35.00
532	Tiant, L.	6.00
544	Smith, M. (Mgr)	7.50
554	A's Team	7.00
562	Bouton, J.	6.00
571	LaRussa, T.	10.00
574	Reds Team	7.00
575	Palmer, J.	38.00
579	Hisle, L. (R)	7.00
583	Brown, G.	6.00
598	May, J.	5.00

1969 TOPPS

	NM Price
Complete Set (664)	$2,400.00
Commons (1-109)	1.50
Commons (110-218)	1.50
Commons (219-327)	2.50
Commons (328-425)	1.50
Commons (426-512)	1.50
Commons (513-588)	3.00
Commons (589-664)	3.00
White Letter Variations	20.00
Unlisted Stars	35%
League Leaders (1-12)	3.00
All-Stars (416-435)	2.00
Checklists	6.00
World Series (162-169)	4.00

Quality Rating ★★★★

Reggie's rookie headlines the set. There are two versions of Mantle's last card, and Ted Williams makes his managerial debut.

#	Player	NM
1	Carer/Oliva/Yaz (LL)	12.00
2	Alou/Alou/Rose (LL)	6.00
4	McCovey/Santo/Williams (LL)	5.00
6	Allen/Banks/McCovey (LL)	5.00
10	Gibson/Jenkins/Marichal (LL)	6.00
20	Banks, E.	20.00
35	Morgan, J.	9.00
47B	Popovich, P. (emblem)	20.00
49B	Jones/Rodriguez (R, cor)	22.00
50	Clemente, R.	50.00
75	Aparicio, L.	5.00
77B	Perranski, R. (no emblem)	20.00
82	Oliver, A. (R)	14.00
85	Brock, L.	16.00
90	Koosman, J.	5.00
95	Bench, J.	50.00
99A	Nettles (R, no loop)	20.00
99B	Nettles (R, loop)	18.00
100	Aaron, H.	50.00
107B	Checklist 2 (Gibson, cor)	7.00
120	Rose, P.	25.00
130	Yastrzemski, C.	15.00
150	McLain, D.	5.00
151B	Dalrymple, B. (Phillies)	13.00
162	WS Game 1 (Gibson)	7.00
164	WS Game 3 (McCarver)	6.00
165	WS Game 4 (Brock)	7.00
166	WS Game 5 (Kaline)	7.00
168	WS Game 7 (Gibson)	7.00
175	Bunning, J.	5.00
190	Mays, W.	40.00
200	Gibson, B.	12.00
208B	Clendenon, D. (Expos)	13.00
216	Sutton, D.	5.00
235	Hunter, J.	9.00
237	Cox, B. (R)	7.50
244	Fosse, R. (R)	7.00
250	Robinson, F.	30.00
255	Carlton, S.	35.00
260	Jackson, R. (R)	350.00
270	Lolich, M.	5.00
290	Kaat, J.	5.00
295	Perez, T.	12.00
304	Gaston, C. (R)	10.00
311	Lyle, S. (R)	12.00
330	Conigliaro, T.	5.00
355	Niekro, P.	6.00
370	Marichal, J.	8.00
375	Killebrew, H.	16.00

394	Piniella, L.	4.00
400	Drysdale, D.	12.00
410	Kaline, A.	18.00
412	Checklist 5 (Mantle)	12.00
416	McCovey, W. (AS)	6.00
419	Carew, R. (AS)	8.00
421	Robinson, B. (AS)	7.00
424	Rose, P. (AS)	15.00
425	Yastrzemski, C. (AS)	9.00
428	Brock, L. (AS)	6.00
430	Bench, J. (AS)	9.00
432	Gibson, B. (AS)	6.00
440A	McCovey, W.	16.00
440B	McCovey, W. (WL)	90.00
450	Williams, B.	6.00
465	John, T.	4.00
470B	Stottlemyre, M. (WL)	28.00
476B	Brett, K. (R, WL)	26.00
480	Seaver, T.	75.00
485A	Perry, G.	10.00
485B	Perry, G. (WL)	75.00
500A	Mantle, M.	350.00
500B	Mantle, M. (WL)	1000.00
504	Checklist 6 (Robinson)	7.00
510	Carew, R.	34.00
516	Weaver, E. (R, Mgr)	16.00
533	Ryan, N.	450.00
539	Epstein/Williams	8.00
545	Stargell, W.	12.00
547	Martin, B. (Mgr)	5.00
550	Robinson, B.	28.00
552	Sizemore, T. (R)	5.00
560	Tiant, L.	5.00
562	Watson, B. (R)	6.00
564	Hodges, G. (Mgr)	10.00
565	Wilhelm, H.	6.00
570	Santo, R.	6.00
572	Marichal/McCovey	14.00
573	Palmer, J.	30.00
582B	Checklist 7 (Oliva)	7.00
587	Rudi, J. (R)	5.50
597	Fingers, R. (R)	40.00
600	Oliva, T.	6.00
601	McGraw, T. (SP)	7.00
630	Bonds, B. (R)	35.00
640	Jenkins, F.	20.00
650	Williams, T. (Mgr)	15.00
653	Rodriguez, A. (R)	5.00
657	Murcer, B.	5.00
660	Smith, R.	5.00
664	Hunt, R.	5.00

1970 TOPPS

	NM Price
Complete Set (720)	$1,800.00
Commons (1-132)	.75
Commons (133-263)	.75
Commons (264-372)	.75
Commons (373-459)	1.50
Commons (460-546)	1.75
Commons (547-633)	3.00
Commons (634-720)	8.00
Unlisted Stars	**35%**
League Leaders (61-72)	2.00
Playoffs (195-202)	2.00
World Series (305-310)	3.00
All-Stars (450-469)	2.00
Team Cards	2.50
Checklists	5.00

Quality Rating ★★
This gray-bordered set does little to excite collectors. Lone key rookie is Munson. Bench and Ryan high-numbers and second-year Reggie are popular.

#	Player	NM
1	Mets Team	15.00
9	Checklist 1	8.00

10	Yastrzemski, C.	15.00
17	Wilhelm, H.	4.00
21	Blue/Tenace (R)	7.00
61	Clemente/Rose (LL)	12.00
63	McCovey/Perez/Santo (LL)	4.00
64	Jackson/Killebrew/Powell (LL)	5.00
65	Aaron/Mays/McCovey (LL)	5.00
66	Howard/Jackson/Killebrew (LL)	5.00
67	Carlton/Gibson/Marichal (LL)	6.00
69	Seaver/Marichal/Jenkins (LL)	6.00
71	Gibson/Jenkins/Singer (LL)	4.00
96	Reuss, J. (R)	3.00
140	Jackson, R.	50.00
148	Weaver, E. (Mgr)	4.50
150	Killebrew, H.	8.00
160	Niekro, P.	5.00
170	Williams, B.	6.00
180	John, T.	3.00
181	Anderson, S. (Mgr)	5.00
189	Munson, T. (R)	50.00
195	NLCS Game 1 (Seaver)	13.00
197	NLCS Game 3 (Ryan)	28.00
198	NLCS Smmry (Ryan)	12.00
210	Marichal, J.	6.00
211	Williams, T. (Mgr)	11.00
220	Carlton, S.	12.00
230	Robinson, B.	12.00
240	Jenkins, F.	7.00
250	McCovey, W.	8.00
286	Buckner, B. (R)	7.00
290	Carew, R.	18.00
291	**Durocher, L. (Mgr)**	**3.00**
300	Seaver, T.	38.00
304	Russell, B. (R)	4.00
310	WS Summary	4.00
315	Aparicio, L.	4.00
321	Piniella, L.	3.00
330	Brock, L.	8.00
350	Clemente, R.	70.00
380	Perez, T.	8.00
394	Hodges, G. (Mgr)	5.00
410	Powell, B.	4.00
425	Bonds, B.	6.00
449	Palmer, J.	12.00
450	McCovey, W. (AS)	6.00
453	Carew, R. (AS)	7.00
455	Robinson, B. (AS)	6.00
458	Rose, P. (AS)	12.00
459	Jackson, R. (AS)	12.00
461	Yastrzemski, C. (AS)	10.00
463	Aaron, H. (AS)	14.00
463	Robinson, F. (AS)	7.00
464	Bench, J. (AS)	10.00
466	Marichal, J. (AS)	4.00
470	Stargell, W.	10.00
491	Nettles, G.	5.00
500	Aaron, H.	50.00
502	Fingers, R.	10.00
530	Gibson, B.	12.00
537	Morgan, J.	9.00
539	Bowa, L. (R)	6.00
549	Cardinals Team	6.00
550	Howard, F.	5.00
555	Cepeda, O.	5.00
560	Perry, G.	9.00
563	Red Sox Team	6.00
565	Hunter, J.	10.00
579	Tigers Team	6.00
580	Rose, P.	50.00
588A	Checklist 7 (err)	7.00
593	Cubs Team	6.00
600	Mays, W.	70.00
608	Pirates Team	6.00
610	Koosman, J.	5.00
621	Evans, D. (R)	9.00
622	Sutton, D.	12.00
630	Banks, E.	50.00
631	A's Team	6.00
637	Indians Team	10.00
640	Kaline, A.	50.00
654	Gamble, O. (R)	10.00
657	Padres Team	6.00
660	Bench, J.	90.00
670	Santo, R.	10.00
676	Senators Team	10.00
696	Giants Team	10.00
700	Robinson, F.	50.00
712	Ryan, N.	425.00
713	Pilots Team	25.00
720	Reichardt, R.	12.00

1971 TOPPS

	NM Price
Complete Set (752)	$2,000.00
Commons (1-132)	1.50
Commons (133-263)	1.50
Commons (264-393)	1.50
Commons (394-523)	2.00
Commons (524-643)	3.50
Commons (644-752)	6.00
Unlisted Shortprints	10.00
Unlisted Stars	**35%**
League Leaders (61-72)	2.00
Playoffs & World Series	2.50
Team Cards	2.50
Checklists	5.00

Quality Rating ★★★
Black borders make this set tuff to find in NM-MT, so top-grade stars command a premium.

#	Player	NM
1	Orioles Team	14.00
5	Munson, T.	20.00
14	Concepcion, D. (R)	20.00
20	Jackson, R.	35.00
25	Gaston, C.	3.00
26	Blyleven, B. (R)	10.00
30	Niekro, P.	5.00
45	Hunter, J.	7.00
50	McCovey, W.	9.00
55	Carlton, S.	15.00
64	Bench/Perez/Williams (LL)	5.00
65	Howard/Killebrew/Yaz (LL)	4.50
66	Bench/Perez/Williams (LL)	5.00
70	Gibson/Jenkins/Perry (LL)	5.00
72	Seaver/Gibson/Jenkins (LL)	5.00
100	Rose, P.	35.00
117	Simmons, T. (R)	12.00
140	Perry, G.	7.00
160	Seaver, T.	25.00
180	Kaline, A.	20.00
183	Hodges, G. (Mgr)	5.00
193	Grich, B. (R)	5.00
197	ALCS Game 3 (Palmer)	4.50
208	Martin, B. (Mgr)	4.00
210	Carew, R.	18.00
230	Stargell, W.	8.00
250	Bench, J.	15.00
264	Morgan, J.	7.00
276	Foster, G. (R)	7.00
280	Jenkins, F.	7.50
295	Bonds, B.	4.50
300	Robinson, B.	15.00
325	Marichal, J.	5.00
329	WS Game 3 (F. Robinson)	4.50
331	WS Game 5 (B. Robinson)	5.00
341	Garvey, S. (R)	25.00
350	Williams, B.	5.00
361	Sutton, D.	7.50
370	Torre, J.	3.50
380	Williams, T. (Mgr)	10.00
384	Fingers, R.	6.00
400	Aaron, H.	40.00
402	Dodgers Team	4.00
439	Luzinski, G. (R)	4.00
442	Angels Team	4.00
450	Gibson, B.	15.00
462	Senators Team	4.00
477	Weaver, E. (Mgr)	4.00
482	Padres Team	4.00
502	Cubs Team	4.00
513	Ryan, N.	250.00
520	John, T.	4.00
522	Twins Team	4.00
525	Banks, E.	50.00
529	Buckner, B.	4.00
530	Yastrzemski, C.	30.00
543	Yankees Team	8.00

544	Blue, V.	7.00
550	Killebrew, H.	25.00
563	Giants Team	7.00
570	Palmer, J.	28.00
574	Bunning, J.	4.50
580	Perez, T.	16.00
584	Indians Team	7.00
594	Hrabosky, A. (R)	5.00
599	Cash, N.	5.00
600	Mays, W.	90.00
603	Pirates Team	7.00
605	Cepeda, O.	6.00
609	Durocher, L. (Mgr)	6.00
615	Stottlemyre, M.	6.00
618	McGraw, T.	6.00
619B	Checklist 6 (cor)	10.00
620	Howard, F.	6.00
624	A's Team	7.00
625	Brock, L.	25.00
630	Clemente, R.	100.00
635	Murcer, B.	6.00
640	Robinson, F.	35.00
641	Mets Team	12.00
648	Matlack, J. (R, SP)	20.00
649	Lyle, S. (SP)	18.00
650	Allen, R. (SP)	35.00
652	Braves Team	12.00
665	Swoboda, R. (SP)	15.00
674	Expos Team	12.00
688	Anderson, S. (Mgr, SP)	40.00
698	Brewers Team (SP)	18.00
700	Powell, B. (SP)	22.00
709	Baker/Baylor (R, SP)	80.00
722	Astros Team (SP)	18.00
740	Aparicio, L. (SP)	22.00
742	Royals Team	12.00
750	McLain, D. (SP)	20.00
751	Weis, A. (SP)	12.00

1972 TOPPS

	NM Price
Complete Set (787)	$1,800.00
Commons (1-132)	.50
Commons (133-263)	.75
Commons (264-394)	1.00
Commons (395-525)	1.25
Commons (526-656)	3.50
Commons (657-787)	10.00
Unlisted Stars	**35%**
League Leaders (85-96)	1.50
Playoffs & World Series	1.50
Boyhood Photos	1.25
Awards (621-626)	4.50
Traded Cards (751-757)	10.00
Team Cards	1.50
Checklists	3.00

Quality Rating ★★★
Topps' largest pre-'80s set features various color combinations and a design that exemplifies the early 1970s style. Fisk is the key rookie.

#	Player	NM
1	Pirates Team	6.00
18B	Pizarro, J. (green)	5.00
29B	Bonham, B. (green)	5.00
33	Martin, B. (Mgr)	4.00
37	Yastrzemski, C.	10.00
38	Yastrzemski, C. (IA)	5.00
45B	Beckert, G. (green)	5.00
49	Mays, W.	20.00
50	Mays, W. (IA)	10.00
51	Killebrew, H.	6.00
52	Killebrew, H. (IA)	3.00
79	Fisk/Cooper (R)	70.00
80	Perez, T.	4.00
87	Aaron/Stargell (LL)	3.00
88	Killebrew/Robinson (LL)	3.00

89	Aaron/Stargell (LL)	3.00
93	Carlton/Jenkins/Seaver (LL)	3.00
95	Jenkins/Seaver (LL)	3.00
100	Robinson, F.	6.00
117B	James, C. (green)	5.00
130	Gibson, B.	7.00
132	Morgan, J.	5.00
142	Chambliss, C. (R)	5.00
147	Kingman, D. (R)	5.00
198	Hough, C. (R)	5.00
200	Brock, L.	6.00
222	ALCS (B. Robinson)	3.00
226	WS Game 4 (Clemente)	6.00
241	Fingers, R.	5.00
270	Palmer, J.	8.00
280	McCovey, W.	6.00
285	Perry, G.	5.00
299	Aaron, H.	40.00
300	Aaron, H. (IA)	20.00
309	Clemente, R.	40.00
310	Clemente, R. (IA)	25.00
330	Hunter, J.	4.00
347	Seaver, T. (BP)	3.00
410	Jenkins, F.	6.00
420	Carlton, S.	18.00
433	Bench, J.	25.00
434	Bench, J. (IA)	13.00
435	Jackson, R.	25.00
436	Jackson, R. (IA)	12.00
439	Williams, B.	4.00
441	Munson, T.	15.00
442	Munson, T. (IA)	7.00
445	Seaver, T.	25.00
446	Seaver, T. (IA)	12.00
447	Stargell, W.	6.00
448	Stargell, W. (IA)	3.00
474	Oates/Baylor (R)	15.00
498	Robinson, B. (BP)	3.00
510	Williams, T. (Mgr)	9.00
515	Blyleven, B.	3.00
530	Sutton, D.	6.00
539	Forster, T. (R)	5.00
547	Indians Team	6.00
550	Robinson, B.	25.00
555	Santo, R.	5.00
559	Rose, P.	40.00
560	Rose, P. (IA)	20.00
567	Marichal, J.	10.00
568	Marichal, J. (IA)	5.00
575	Oliver, A.	5.00
576	Durocher, L. (Mgr)	5.00
579	Alexander, D. (R)	5.00
580	Piniella, L.	5.00
582	Expos Team	6.00
590	Nettles, G.	5.00
595	Ryan, N.	225.00
600	Kaline, A.	24.00
604A	Checklist 6	8.00
604B	Checklist 6	8.00
617	Royals Team	6.00
620	Niekro, P.	8.00
651	Reds Team	6.00
668	Rangers Team	20.00
686	Garvey, S.	45.00
688	Cardinals Team	15.00
695	Carew, R.	65.00
696	Carew, R. (IA)	32.00
697	Koosman, J.	15.00
698	Koosman, J. (IA)	12.00
699	Murcer, B.	15.00
700	Murcer, B. (IA)	12.00
709	Kaat, J.	15.00
710	Kaat, J. (IA)	12.00
711	Bonds, B.	18.00
712	Bonds, B. (IA)	12.00
731	Orioles Team	14.00
736	Russell, B.	12.00
741	Hutton/Milner/Miller (R)	12.00
749	Alston, W. (Mgr)	12.00
751	Carlton, S. (TR)	55.00
752	Morgan, J. (TR)	45.00
753	McLain, D. (TR)	18.00
754	Robinson, F. (TR)	42.00
760	Mazeroski, B.	15.00
761	Oglivie/Cey (R)	22.00
764	Baker, D.	18.00
771	Giants Team	15.00
777	Wilhelm, H.	18.00
778	Dempsey, R. (R)	16.00
787	Reed, R.	12.00

1973 TOPPS

	NM Price
Complete Set (660)	$750.00
Commons (1-132)	.50
Commons (133-264)	.50
Commons (265-396)	.60
Commons (397-528)	1.00
Commons (529-660)	3.00
Unlisted Stars	35%
Playoffs & World Series	1.00
Boyhood Photos (341-346)	.75
Rookies (601-616)	3.25
Team Cards	1.00
Checklists	2.50
Team Checklist (No#)	6.00
All-Time Leaders	3.00
Manager Cards	.75

Quality Rating ★★
Plain design contributes to lack of interest in this set. Schmidt rookie is the key.

#	Player	NM
1	Aaron/Ruth/Mays	40.00
10	Sutton, D.	2.00
31	Bell, B. (R)	3.00
50	Clemente, R.	60.00
61	Williams/Carew (LL)	3.00
62	Bench/Allen (LL)	2.00
63	Bench/Allen (LL)	2.00
64	Brock/Campaneris (LL)	2.00
65	Carlton/Tiant (LL)	2.00
66	Carlton/Perry/Wood (LL)	2.00
67	Carlton/Ryan (LL)	25.00
84	Fingers, R.	3.00
90	Robinson, B.	8.00
100	Aaron, H.	30.00
130	Rose, P.	20.00
142	Munson, T.	6.00
145	Bonds, B.	2.00
160	Palmer, J.	6.00
165	Aparicio, L.	3.00
170	Killebrew, H.	5.00
174	Gossage, R. (R)	6.00
175	Robinson, F.	6.00
180	Jenkins, F.	4.00
190	Gibson, B.	6.00
193	Fisk, C.	8.00
200	Williams, B.	3.50
213	Garvey, S.	6.00
215	Baker, D.	2.00
220	Ryan, N.	85.00
230	Morgan, J.	6.00
235	Hunter, J.	3.00
245	Yastrzemski, C.	10.00
255	Jackson, R.	18.00
257A	Berra, Y. (Mgr)	2.50
257B	Berra, Y. (Mgr)	4.50
275	Perez, T.	3.50
280	Kaline, A.	6.00
300	Carlton, S.	8.00
305	Mays, W.	35.00
320	Brock, L.	5.00
330	Carew, R.	7.00
350	Seaver, T.	12.00
370	Stargell, W.	5.00
380	Bench, J.	8.00
384	Baylor, D.	3.00
389	Mets Team	3.00
400	Perry, G.	4.50
410	McCovey, W.	5.00
421B	Winkles, B. (Mgr)	3.00
434	Giants Team	2.50
449B	Aspromonte, K. (Mgr, Spahn)	3.50
471	Cobb, T. (ATL)	7.00
472	Gehrig, L. (ATL)	12.00
473	Aaron, H. (ATL)	9.00
474	Ruth, B. (ATL)	15.00

475	Cobb, T. (ATL)	6.00
480	Marichal, J.	4.00
481	White Sox Team	2.50
486B	Ozark, D. (Mgr)	3.00
497B	Schoendienst, R. (Mgr)	3.50
498	Nettles, G.	3.00
503	Niekro, P.	4.00
517B	Virdon, B. (Mgr)	3.00
530	Kaat, J.	5.00
536	Phillies Team	5.50
545	Cepeda, O.	4.50
549	Herzog, W. (Mgr)	5.00
554	Concepcion, D.	5.00
556	Yankees Team	10.00
560	Howard, F.	5.00
569	Alston, W. (Mgr)	5.00
576	Expos Team	5.00
588	Checklist 5	20.00
596	Red Sox Team	5.00
605	Cabell, E. (R)	5.00
606	Matthews, G. (R)	5.00
608	Busby/Medich (R)	5.00
609	Lopes, D. (R)	5.00
610	Hough, C. (R)	5.00
613	Boone, B. (R)	25.00
614	Bumbry/Evans (R)	25.00
615	Schmidt/Cey (R)	300.00
624	Durocher, L. (Mgr)	5.00
629	Indians Team	5.50
630	McLain, D.	5.00
641	Reds Team	5.00
650	Alou, F.	5.00
654	Twins Team	5.00

1974 TOPPS

	NM Price
Complete Set (660)	$600.00
Complete Fact. Set (660)	625.00
Commons	.50
Unlisted Stars	.60-1.75
Hank Aaron Specials (2-6)	6.00
League Leaders (201-208)	1.00
All-Stars (331-339)	.75
Playoffs & World Series	1.00
Rookies (596-608)	.60
Washington NL Cards	6.00
Team Cards	1.25
Checklists	2.00
Team Checklist (No#)	.75
Manager Cards	.60
Traded Set (44)	14.00

Quality Rating ★
Topps issued all of its cards in one series for the first time. Highlight is the rookie of future HOFer Dave Winfield.

#	Player	NM
1	Aaron, H.	35.00
7	Hunter, J.	3.00
10	Bench, J.	10.00
20	Ryan, N.	75.00
35	Perry, G.	3.00
40	Palmer, J.	7.00
50	Carew, R.	5.00
55	Robinson, F.	5.00
60	Brock, L.	5.00
80	Seaver, T.	10.00
85	Morgan, J.	6.00
87	Jenkins, F.	3.00
95	Carlton, S.	6.00
100	Stargell, W.	4.00
105	Fisk, C.	10.00
110	Williams, B.	3.00
130	Jackson, R.	15.00
160	Robinson, B.	6.00
173B	Jones, R. (R, Washington)	8.00
187	Baylor, D.	2.50

201	Carew/Rose (LL)	5.00
202	Jackson/Stargell (LL)	4.50
203	Jackson/Stargell (LL)	4.50
206	Palmer/Seaver (LL)	4.00
207	Ryan/Seaver (LL)	20.00
212	Fingers, R.	2.50
215	Kaline, A.	5.50
226B	Padres Team (Washington)	8.00
230	Perez, T.	3.00
250A	McCovey, W. (SD)	5.00
250B	McCovey, W. (Washington)	25.00
252	Parker, D. (R)	12.00
280	Yastrzemski, C.	7.00
283	Schmidt, M.	60.00
300	Rose, P.	15.00
309B	Roberts, D. (Washington)	8.00
330	Marichal, J.	2.50
331	Fisk/Bench (AS)	6.00
332	Allen/Aaron (AS)	4.00
333	Carew/Morgan (AS)	3.00
338	Jackson/Williams (AS)	4.00
340	Munson, T.	7.00
350	Gibson, B.	5.00
351	Evans, D.	3.50
364B	Gaston, C. (Washington)	12.00
387B	Morales, R. (Washington)	8.00
400	Killebrew, H.	5.00
456	Winfield, D. (R)	110.00
470	ALCS (Jackson)	5.00
473	WS Game 2 (Mays)	6.00
477	WS Game 6 (Jackson)	5.00
575	Garvey, S.	5.00
598	Griffey, K. (R)	15.00
599B	Freisleben, D. (R, SD)	3.00
599C	Freisleben, D. (R, SD)	5.00
600	Madlock, B. (R)	4.00
601	Downing/McBride (R)	4.00
604	Thornton/White (R)	5.00
605	Tanana, F. (R)	5.00
654A	Alou, J. (err)	6.00

1975 TOPPS

	NM Price
Complete Set (660)	$800.00
Commons	.50
Unlisted Stars	.60-2.00
Highlights (1-7)	.75
MVPs (189-212)	1.00
League Leaders (306-313)	1.00
Playoffs & World Series	1.00
Rookies (614-624)	.60
Team Cards	2.00
Checklists	2.00
Mini's	1x-1.5x

Quality Rating ★★★★
This colorful issue is driven by rookies of future HOFers Brett and Yount. Also included are cards that feature AL and NL MVPs from 1951-1974.

#	Player	NM
1	Aaron, H. (HL)	30.00
2	Brock, L. (HL)	3.00
3	Gibson, B. (HL)	3.00
4	Kaline, A. (HL)	4.00
5	Ryan, N. (HL)	30.00
7	Bosman/Busby/Ryan (HL)	10.00
20	Munson, T.	6.00
21	Fingers, R.	3.00
29	Parker, D.	4.00
50	Robinson, B.	6.00
60	Jenkins, F.	3.00
61	Winfield, D.	40.00
70	Schmidt, M.	50.00
80	Fisk, C.	10.00
100	Stargell, W.	3.00
140	Garvey, S.	6.00
150	Gibson, B.	5.00

#	Player	NM
180	Morgan, J.	6.00
185	Carlton, S.	6.00
189	Berra/Campanella (MVP)	3.00
192	Berra/Mays (MVP)	3.00
193	Berra/Campanella (MVP)	3.00
194	Mantle/Newcombe (MVP)	18.00
195	Mantle/Aaron (MVP)	28.00
200	Mantle/Wills (MVP)	16.00
204	Clemente/Robinson (MVP)	5.00
211	Jackson/Rose (MVP)	5.50
220	Sutton, D.	3.00
223	Yount, R. (R)	100.00
228	Brett, G. (R)	200.00
230	Hunter, J.	3.00
260	Bench, J.	10.00
280	Yastrzemski, C.	6.00
284	Griffey, K.	4.50
300	Jackson, R.	15.00
307	Allen/Schmidt (LL)	3.00
312	Ryan/Carlton (LL)	18.00
320	Rose, P.	18.00
335	Palmer, J.	7.00
370	Seaver, T.	12.00
450	McCovey, W.	4.00
461	WS Game 1 (Jackson)	3.00
500	Ryan, N.	75.00
531	Reds Team (Anderson)	3.00
540	Brock, L.	5.00
545	Williams, B.	3.00
580	Robinson, F.	4.50
600	Carew, R.	5.00
616	Rice, J. (R)	12.00
617	DeCinces/Trillo (R)	2.00
620	Carter, G. (R)	20.00
622	Lynn, F. (R)	7.00
623	Hernandez/Garner (R)	7.50
640	Killebrew, H.	5.00
660	Aaron, H.	30.00

1976 TOPPS

	NM Price
Complete Set (660)	$375.00
Commons	.30
Unlisted Stars	**.40-1.50**
Record Breakers (1-6)	.50
Father and Son (66-70)	.45
League Leaders (191-205)	.65
Playoffs & World Series	.60
Rookies (589-599)	.35
Team Cards	1.25
Checklists	1.25
All-Time Greats	1.00
Traded Set (44)	15.00

Quality Rating ★★
This set offers the last player cards of HR king Hank Aaron.

#	Player	NM
1	Aaron, H. (RB)	15.00
5	Seaver, T. (RB)	4.00
10	Brock, L.	4.50
19	Brett, G.	65.00
55	Perry, G.	2.50
95	Robinson, B.	5.00
98	Eckersley, D. (R)	40.00
100	Hunter, J.	2.50
104	Reds Team (Anderson)	2.00
128	Griffey, K.	2.00
150	Garvey, S.	4.00
160	Winfield, D.	20.00
192	Carew/Munson (LL)	2.50
193	Kingman/Schmidt (LL)	2.50
194	Jackson, R. (LL)	2.50
202	Eckersley/Hunter/Palmer (LL)	4.00
230	Yastrzemski, C.	6.00
240	Rose, P.	15.00
250	Jenkins, F.	2.00

#	Player	NM
270	Stargell, W.	3.00
300	Bench, J.	7.00
316	Yount, R.	30.00
325	Perez, T.	2.00
330	Ryan, N.	70.00
340	Rice, J.	4.00
341	Gehrig, L. (AS)	12.00
342	Hornsby, R. (AS)	3.00
344	Wagner, H. (AS)	3.50
345	Ruth, B. (AS)	12.00
346	Cobb, T. (AS)	7.00
347	Williams, T. (AS)	10.00
349	Johnson, W. (AS)	2.00
355	Carlton, S.	6.00
365	Fisk, C.	8.00
400	Carew, R.	5.00
405	Fingers, R.	2.50
420	Morgan, J.	5.00
441	Carter, G.	7.00
450	Palmer, J.	5.00
480	Schmidt, M.	20.00
500	Jackson, R.	14.00
520	McCovey, W.	3.50
525	Williams, B.	3.00
550	Aaron, H.	25.00
592	Randolph, W. (R)	5.00
599	Guidry, R. (R)	7.00
600	Seaver, T.	7.00
650	Munson, T.	5.00

1977 TOPPS

	NM Price
Complete Set (660)	$375.00
Commons	.20
Unlisted Stars	**.25-.1.50**
League Leaders (1-8)	.30
Record Breakers (231-234)	.30
Playoffs & World Series	.50
Turn Back Clock (433-437)	.35
Rookies (472-479, 487-494)	.25
Big League Brothers (631-634)	.35
Team Cards and Checklists	1.00

Quality Rating ★★★
Dawson and Murphy rookie cards highlight this issue.

#	Player	NM
1	Brett/Madlock (LL)	6.00
6	Ryan/Seaver (LL)	15.00
10	Jackson, R.	10.00
60	Rice, J.	3.00
70	Bench, J.	6.00
100	Morgan, J.	4.00
110	Carlton, S.	4.00
120	Carew, R.	4.00
140	Schmidt, M.	12.00
144	Sutter, B. (R)	2.00
150	Seaver, T.	6.00
170	Munson, T.	4.00
231	Brett, G. (RB)	10.00
234	Ryan, N. (RB)	15.00
265	Fidrych, M. (R)	4.00
280	Hunter, J.	2.00
285	Robinson, B.	4.00
355	Brock, L.	3.00
359	Randolph, W.	2.00
387	Yankees Team (Martin)	2.00
390	Winfield, D.	12.00
400	Garvey, S.	2.50
430	Jenkins, F.	2.00
450	Rose, P.	10.00
460	Stargell, W.	2.00
473	Dawson, A. (R)	50.00
476	Murphy, D. (R)	20.00
480	Yastrzemski, C.	5.00
488	Clark/Mazzilli (R)	4.00
491	Martinez, D. (R)	4.00
525	Eckersley, D.	5.00

#	Player	NM
547	McCovey, W.	3.00
580	Brett, G.	40.00
600	Palmer, J.	3.00
631	Brett Brothers	7.00
635	Yount, R.	20.00
640	Fisk, C.	5.00
650	Ryan, N.	45.00

1978 TOPPS

	NM Price
Complete Set (726)	$275.00
Commons	.20
Unlisted Stars	**.25-1.00**
Record Breakers (1-7)	.30
League Leaders (201-208)	.30
Playoffs (411-412)	.50
Rookies (701-711)	.25
Team Cards	1.00
Checklists	1.00

Quality Rating ★★★★
The Molitor/Trammell rookie is difficult to find without ink smudges. The Murray rookie is also popular with collectors.

#	Player	NM
1	Brock, L. (RB)	2.50
3	McCovey, W. (RB)	1.50
4	Robinson, B. (RB)	1.50
5	Rose, P. (RB)	3.25
6	Ryan, N. (RB)	15.00
7	Jackson, R. (RB)	3.00
20	Rose, P. (DP)	4.50
34	McCovey, W.	2.00
36	Murray, E. (R)	125.00
40	Yastrzemski, C.	4.00
45	Fidrych, M.	1.50
60	Munson, T.	3.50
72	Dawson, A.	12.00
100	Brett, G.	20.00
119	Martinez, D.	2.00
120	Carter, G.	2.50
122	Eckersley, D.	3.50
160	Palmer, J.	3.00
170	Brock, L.	3.00
173	Yount, R.	10.00
200	Jackson, R.	7.00
205	Carlton/Palmer (LL)	1.50
206	Niekro/Ryan (DP, LL)	4.00
270	Fisk, C.	3.00
282	Yankees Team	2.00
300	Morgan, J.	3.00
350	Garvey, S.	1.50
360	Schmidt, M.	10.00
400	Ryan, N.	35.00
413	World Series (Jackson)	2.50
450	Seaver, T.	3.50
460	Hunter, J.	1.50
510	Stargell, W.	1.50
530	Winfield, D.	6.00
540	Carlton, S.	3.00
580	Carew, R.	2.50
670	Rice, J.	2.00
674	Knight, R. (R)	2.00
700	Bench, J.	4.00
703	Morris, J. (R, DP)	5.00
704	Whitaker, L. (R)	15.00
707	Molitor/Trammell (R)	100.00
708	Murphy/Parrish (R)	6.00

1979 TOPPS

	NM Price
Complete Set (726)	$200.00
Commons	.15
Unlisted Stars	**.20-1.00**
League Leaders (1-8)	.30
Record Breakers (201-206)	.20
Rookies (701-726)	.25
Team Cards	.75
Checklists	.75
All-Time Leaders	.25

Quality Rating ★★
The Wizard's rookie is the top card in an average set. Centered versions of this card are difficult.

#	Player	NM
1	Carew/Parker (LL)	2.00
6	Richard/Ryan (LL)	5.00
24	Molitor, P.	25.00
25	Carlton, S.	2.00
30	Winfield, D.	7.00
39	Murphy, D.	4.00
40	Eckersley, D.	1.50
55	Stargell, W.	2.00
95	Yount, R.	10.00
100	Seaver, T. (DP)	2.00
115	Ryan, N.	30.00
116	Smith, O. (R)	100.00
123	Whitaker, L.	5.00
200	Bench, J. (DP)	2.00
204	Rose, P. (RB)	2.50
212	Lansford, C. (R)	2.00
215	McCovey, W.	2.00
300	Carew, R.	2.00
310	Munson, T.	5.00
320	Yastrzemski, C.	3.00
330	Brett, G.	20.00
340	Palmer, J.	2.00
348	Dawson, A.	6.00
358	Trammell, A.	8.00
369A	Wills, B. (err)	2.50
369B	Wills, B. (cor)	2.50
400	Rice, J.	1.50
417	Johnson/Ryan (ATL, DP)	4.00
610	Schmidt, M.	7.00
640	Murray, E.	25.00
650	Rose, P.	5.00
665	Brock, L.	2.00
680	Fisk, C.	2.50
700	Jackson, R. (DP)	2.00

1980 TOPPS

	NM Price
Complete Set (726)	$130.00
Commons	.15
Unlisted Stars	**.20 -1.00**
Team Cards	.50
Checklists	.50
Pack (15)	8.00
Box (36)	250.00

Quality Rating ★★★
Henderson rookie has fallen drastically. Many reasonably priced HOFers are part of this set.

#	Player	NM
1	Brock/Yastrzmski (HL)	2.00
4	Rose, P. (HL)	2.00
40	Fisk, C.	1.50
100	Bench, J.	2.50
160	Murray, E.	15.00
206	Ryan/Richard (LL)	4.00
210	Carlton, S.	1.50
230	Winfield, D.	5.00
232	Trammell, A.	4.00
235	Dawson, A.	4.00
265	Yount, R.	7.00
270	Schmidt, M. (DP)	3.00
274	Murphy, D.	2.00
335	McCovey, W.	1.50
358	Whitaker, L.	3.00
393	Smith, O.	18.00
406	Molitor, P.	15.00
450	Brett, G.	12.00
482	Henderson, R. (R)	40.00
500	Seaver, T.	3.00
540	Rose, P.	4.00
580	Ryan, N.	20.00
590	Palmer, J.	1.50
600	Jackson, R.	3.50
650	Morgan, J.	1.50

1981 DONRUSS

	NM Price
Complete Set (605)	$35.00
Commons	.07
Unlisted Stars	**.10 -.75**
Pack (18)	2.00
Box (36)	60.00

Quality Rating ★
Raines and hoopster Ainge are bright spots in this issue.

#	Player	NM
1	Smith, O.	4.00
5	Trammell, A.	1.00
11	Schmidt, M.	2.00
18	Morgan, J.	1.00
33	Carlton, S.	1.50
62	Bench, J.	1.50
94	Yastrzemski, C.	1.25
96	Eckersley, D.	1.00
100	Brett, G.	3.00
112	Murray, E.	3.00
119	Henderson, R.	4.00
131A	Rose, P. (251)	2.00
131B	Rose, P. (371)	2.00
182	Bench, J.	1.50
203	Molitor, P.	2.00
212	Dawson, A.	1.00
214	Yastrzemski, C.	1.50
228	Jackson, R.	1.50
251	Rose, P.	2.00

#		NM
260	Ryan, N.	8.00
323	Yount, R.	1.50
335	Fisk, C.	1.00
348	Jackson, R.	1.50
364	Winfield, D.	1.50
371	Rose, P.	2.00
422	Seaver, T.	1.50
425	Seaver, T.	1.50
468	Jackson, R.	1.50
491	Brett, G. (MVP)	2.00
537	Brett/Carew	2.00
538	Raines, T. (R)	3.00
569	Ainge, D. (R)	3.00
590	Schmidt, M. (MVP)	1.50

1981 FLEER

	NM Price
Complete Set (660)	$35.00
Commons	.07
Unlisted Stars	**.10 -.75**
"Small-Hand" Variations	.50
Pack (17)	2.50
Box (36)	65.00

Quality Rating ★
Fleer's first mainstream set is unimpressive. All of the day's stars are included.

#	Player	NM
1	Rose, P.	2.00
5	Schmidt, M.	2.00
6A	Carlton, S.	1.50
6B	Carlton, S.	1.50
6C	Carlton, S.	1.50
28	Brett, G.	3.00
57	Ryan, N.	8.00
79	Jackson, R.	2.00
87A	Nettles, G. (err)	9.00
140	Valenzuela, F. (R)	1.50
145	Dawson, A.	1.00
184	Murray, E.	3.00
196	Bench, J.	1.50
200	Seaver, T.	1.50
221	Yastrzemski, C.	1.50
226	Eckersley, D.	1.00
346	Baines, H. (R)	2.00
351	Henderson, R. (Steals)	2.00
418	Ainge, D. (R)	2.00
434	McCovey, W.	1.00
461	Trammell, A.	1.00
481	Gibson, K. (R)	2.00
484	Winfield, D.	1.50
488	Smith, O.	4.00
511	Yount, R.	1.50
515	Molitor, P.	2.00
574	Henderson, R.	3.00
638	Yastrzemski, C.	1.00
640A	Schmidt, M.	2.00
640B	Schmidt, M.	2.00
645	Schmidt/Rose/Bowa	2.00
650	Jackson, R.	2.00
655	Brett, G.	4.00
660A	Carlton, S.	1.00
660B	Carlton, S.	1.00
660C	Carlton, S.	1.00

1981 TOPPS

	NM Price
Complete Set (726)	$50.00
Commons	.07
Unlisted Stars	**.10 -.75**
Pack (15)	3.50
Box (36)	85.00

Quality Rating ★★★
Despite average design, this is the most desired set from 1981.

#	Player	NM
1	Brett/Buckner (LL)	2.50
2	Jackson/Schmidt (LL)	1.00
100	Carew, R.	1.50
110	Yastrzemski, C.	1.50
125	Dawson, A.	1.25
180	Rose, P.	2.00
201	Bench, J. (RB)	1.00
205	Rose, P. (RB)	1.50
206	Schmidt, M. (RB)	2.00
207	Smith, O. (RB)	2.00
220	Seaver, T.	2.00
240	Ryan, N.	10.00
254	Smith, O.	5.00
261	Henderson, R.	2.00
300	Molitor, P.	3.00
302	Scioscia/Valenzuela (R)	2.00
315	Gibson, K. (R)	3.00
347	Baines, H. (R)	3.00
370	Winfield, D.	2.00
400	Jackson, R.	2.00
401	ALCS (Brett)	2.00
479	Raines/Ramos (R)	3.00
490	Murray, E.	4.00
515	Yount, R.	2.50
540	Schmidt, M. (DP)	3.00
560	Morgan, J.	1.00
600	Bench, J.	1.50
620	Eckersley, D.	1.00
630	Carlton, S.	1.50
700	Brett, G.	5.00
709	Trammell, A. (DP)	1.00

1981 TOPPS TRADED

	NM Price
Complete Set (132)	$30.00
Factory Set (132)	35.00
Commons	.25
Unlisted Stars	**.30 -1.00**

Quality Rating ★★
Everybody wants the Winfield card but don't overlook HOFers Fingers and Morgan.

#	Player	NM
727	Ainge, D.	6.00
762	Fisk, C.	5.00

#		NM
807	Morgan, J.	2.50
812	Perry, G.	1.50
816	Raines, T.	6.00
819	Reardon, J.	3.50
839	Sutton, D.	2.00
850	Valenzuela, F.	2.00
855	Winfield, D.	6.00

1982 DONRUSS

	NM Price
Complete Set (660)	$75.00
Factory Set (660)	80.00
Commons	.07
Unlisted Stars	**.10 -.75**
Pack (15)	4.00
Box (36)	90.00

Quality Rating ★★
Ripken's rookie carries the set, which is filled with HOFers.

#	Player	NM
1	Rose, P. (DK)	2.00
13	Ryan, N. (DK)	3.00
15	Brett, G. (DK)	2.00
18	Winfield, D. (DK)	1.50
21	Smith, O. (DK)	2.00
30	Eckersley, D.	1.00
31	Winfield, D.	1.00
34	Brett, G.	2.00
76A	Trammell, A. (err)	1.00
78	Molitor, P.	1.50
88	Dawson, A.	1.00
94	Smith, O.	3.00
113	Henderson, R.	1.50
148	Seaver, T.	1.00
168	Rose, P.	1.50
214	Raines, T.	2.00
252	Smith, L. (R)	3.00
275	Butler, B. (R)	1.50
294	Schmidt, M.	1.50
400	Bench, J.	1.00
405	Ripken, C. (R)	45.00
419	Ryan, N.	8.00
483	Murray, E.	2.00
510	Yount, R.	2.00
535	Jackson, R.	2.00
557	Hrbek, K. (R)	1.50
575	Jackson/Winfield	2.00
585	Rose/Schmidt	1.50
638	Ainge, D.	1.25

1982 FLEER

	NM Price
Complete Set (660)	$75.00
Commons	.07
Unlisted Stars	**.10 -.75**
Pack (15)	4.00
Box (36)	90.00

Quality Rating ★

Set doesn't have much appeal other than Ripken's rookie.

#	Player	NM
39	Jackson, R.	1.50
56	Winfield, D.	1.25
57	Bench, J.	1.00
82	Seaver, T.	1.00
92	Henderson, R.	1.00
148	Molitor, P.	1.50
155	Yount, R.	1.25
174	Murray, E.	2.00
176	Ripken, C. (R)	45.00
187	Dawson, A.	1.25
202	Raines, T.	1.50
229	Ryan, N.	8.00
256	Rose, P.	1.50
258	Schmidt, M.	1.50
292	Eckersley, D.	1.00
405	Brett, G.	2.50
438A	Hrabosky, A. (err)	6.00
555C	Jackson, D. (no emblem)	2.50
576A	Littlefield, J. (err)	225.00
582	Smith, O.	2.00
603A	Smith, L. (R, err)	3.00
603B	Smith, L. (R, cor)	3.00
634	Bench/Seaver	1.00
637	Schmidt, M.	1.00
640	Pete Rose & Son	1.50
641	Schmidt/Carlton	1.00
646	Jackson/Winfield	2.00

1982 TOPPS

	NM Price
Complete Set (792)	$125.00
Commons	.07
Unlisted Stars	**.10 -.75**
Pack (15)	7.00
Box (36)	210.00

Quality Rating ★★★

Ripken is highly sought after. Player selection is quite good.

#	Player	NM
4	Rose, P. (HL)	1.00
5	Ryan, N. (HL)	4.00
21	Ripken, C. (R)	70.00
30	Seaver, T.	2.00
31	Seaver, T. (IA)	1.00
66	Ryan/Howe (TL)	2.00
70	Raines, T.	1.50
90	Ryan, N.	8.00
95	Smith, O.	3.00
100	Schmidt, M.	2.00
101	Schmidt, M. (IA)	1.50
110	Fisk, C.	1.25
125	Ainge, D.	2.00
167	McCatty/Ryan (LL)	2.00
171	Brenly/Davis (R)	2.00
191	Wallach, T. (R)	1.00
195	Molitor, P.	2.00
200	Brett, G.	3.00
201	Brett, G. (IA)	2.00
300	Jackson, R.	2.00
301	Jackson, R. (IA)	1.00
337	Rose, P. (AS)	1.00
339	Schmidt, M. (AS)	1.25
383A	Perez, P. (err)	10.00
390	Murray, E.	3.00
400	Bench, J.	1.25
435	Yount, R.	2.00
452	Smith, L. (R)	4.00
480	Carlton, S.	1.00
502	Bedrosian/Butler (R)	2.00
540	Dawson, A.	1.00
549	Brett, G. (AS)	2.00

#	Player		NM
551	Jackson, R. (AS)		1.00
553	Winfield, D. (AS)		1.50
600	Winfield, D.		2.00
610	Henderson, R.		2.00
650	Yastrzemski, C.		1.25
651	Yastrzemski, C. (IA)		1.00
754	Morgan, J.		1.00
766	Hrbek/Laudner (R)		2.00
780	Rose, P.		2.00
781	Rose, P. (IA)		1.00

1982 TOPPS TRADED

	NM Price
Complete Set (132)	$300.00
Commons	.45
Unlisted Stars	**.50 -.75**

Quality Rating ★★★★

This set has leveled off but is still one of the popular Traded sets ever. Ripken card is a hobby mainstay.

#	Player	NM
23	Davis, C.	5.00
44	Hrbek, K.	4.00
47	Jackson, R.	10.00
98	Ripken, C.	275.00
109	Smith, O.	25.00

1983 DONRUSS

	NM Price
Complete Set (660)	$80.00
Factory Set (660)	90.00
Commons	.07
Unlisted Stars	**.10 -.75**
Pack (15)	5.00
Box (36)	125.00

Quality Rating ★★★★

Gwynn continues to be one of the game's best hitters. Boggs and Sandberg are great choices as well.

#	Player	NM
3	Jackson, R. (DK)	1.00
35	Henderson, R.	1.25
42	Rose, P.	1.50
115	Jackson, R.	1.50
118	Ryan, N.	5.00
120	Smith, O.	2.00
122	Seaver, T.	1.00
168	Schmidt, M.	1.50
258	Yount, R.	1.50
277	Sandberg, R. (R)	15.00
279	Ripken, C.	15.00
338	Brett, G.	2.00
403	Smith, L.	1.00
405	Murray, E.	1.50
409	Winfield, D.	1.00
484	Molitor, P.	1.00
500	Bench, J.	1.00
525	Franco, J. (R)	1.50
586	Boggs, W. (R)	10.00
598	Gwynn, T. (R)	25.00
639A	Jackson, R. (err)	7.00

Alan Trammell SHORTSTOP

1983 FLEER

	NM Price
Complete Set (660)	$90.00
Commons	.08
Unlisted Stars	**.10 -.75**
Pack (15)	5.00
Box (36)	125.00

Quality Rating ★★★

Gray borders detract from the improved photography. Other than the big three rookies, this set contains nothing special.

#	Player	NM
22	Smith, O.	1.50
40	Molitor, P.	1.00
51	Yount, R.	1.50
67	Murray, E.	1.50
70	Ripken, C.	12.00
93	Jackson, R.	1.00
108	Brett, G.	2.00
171	Rose, P.	1.50
173	Schmidt, M.	1.50
179	Boggs, W. (R)	10.00
360	Gwynn, T. (R)	28.00
398	Winfield, D.	1.50
463	Ryan, N.	5.00
507	Sandberg, R. (R)	12.00
508	Smith, L.	1.00
519	Henderson, R.	1.00
584	Bench, J.	1.00
601	Seaver, T.	1.00

WADE BOGGS 1st BASE-3rd BASE RED SOX

1983 TOPPS

	NM Price
Complete Set (792)	$125.00
Commons	.08
Unlisted Stars	**.10 -.75**
Pack (15)	6.00
Box (36)	175.00

Quality Rating ★★★★★

Player selection and attactive design are two reasons this set is popular. Super Vets offer now and then views of top stars.

#	Player	NM
2	Henderson, R. (RB)	1.00
20	Fisk, C.	1.00
49	McGee, W. (R)	2.00
60	Bench, J.	1.25
70	Carlton, S.	1.25
83	Sandberg, R. (R)	20.00
100	Rose, P.	1.50
101	Rose, P. (SV)	1.00
163	Ripken, C.	18.00
180	Henderson, R.	1.00
197	Eisenreich, J. (R)	1.50
270	Eckersley, D.	1.00

#	Player	NM
300	Schmidt, M.	1.50
301	Schmidt, M. (SV)	1.50
350	Yount, R.	1.50
360	Ryan, N.	7.00
361	Ryan, N. (SV)	4.00
388	Brett, G. (AS)	1.50
389	Yount, R. (AS)	1.50
390	Jackson, R. (AS)	1.00
391	Henderson, R. (AS)	1.00
397	Rose, P. (AS)	1.00
482	Gwynn, T. (R)	50.00
498	Boggs, W. (R)	18.00
500	Jackson, R.	1.50
530	Murray, E.	2.50
540	Smith, O.	2.00
580	Seaver, T.	1.25
600	Brett, G.	2.50
630	Molitor, P.	2.00
699	Smith, L.	1.50
704	Henderson/Raines (LL)	1.00
770	Winfield, D.	2.00

JOE MORGAN 2nd BASE PHILLIES

1983 TOPPS TRADED

	NM Price
Complete Set (132)	$32.00
Commons	.20
Unlisted Stars	**.25 -.75**

Quality Rating ★★★

Strawberry had a poor 1997 and this traded set remained stale. Seaver and Morgan cards are bargains.

#	Player	NM
34	Franco, J.	3.00
77	Morgan, J.	2.00
87	Phillips, T.	5.00
101	Seaver, T.	5.00
108	Strawberry, D.	20.00

PADRES TONY GWYNN OF

1984 DONRUSS

	NM Price
Complete Set (658)	$200.00
Factory Set (658)	200.00
Commons	.25
Unlisted Stars	**.30 -.75**
Pack (15)	9.00
Box (36)	300.00

Quality Rating ★★★★★

Mattingly and Carter rookies are the big cards but Gwynn's second-year effort is also a key addition to your set.

#	Player	NM
1A	Yount, R. (DK, err)	4.00
1B	Yount, R. (DK, cor)	5.00
22A	Murray, E. (DK, err)	2.00
22B	Murray, E. (DK, cor)	2.50
23A	Schmidt, M. (DK, err)	4.00
23B	Schmidt, M. (DK, cor)	4.50
26A	Boggs, W. (DK, err)	4.00

#	Player	NM
26B	Boggs, W. (DK, cor)	4.50
30B	Darling, R. (RR, cor)	2.00
32	Fernandez, T. (RR)	2.00
41	Carter, J. (RR)	25.00
44	Fernandez, S. (RR)	2.00
47	Murray, E.	5.00
48	Yount, R.	5.00
51	Winfield, D.	4.00
53	Brett, G.	10.00
54	Henderson, R.	3.00
55	Carter, G.	2.00
57	Jackson, R.	5.00
59	Smith, O.	7.00
60	Ryan, N.	25.00
61	Rose, P.	5.00
66	Murphy, D.	2.00
68	Strawberry, D. (R)	10.00
83	Van Slyke, A. (R)	2.00
97	Dawson, A.	3.00
106	Ripken, C.	30.00
107	Molitor, P.	5.00
111	Carlton, S.	4.00
116	Seaver, T.	5.00
151	Boggs, W.	6.00
183	Schmidt, M.	6.00
227	Whitaker, L.	1.00
248	Mattingly, D. (R)	50.00
278	Phillips, T. (R)	3.00
289	Smith, L.	2.00
293	Trammell, A.	2.00
299	Raines, T.	1.50
302	Fisk, C.	2.00
311	Sandberg, R.	15.00
324	Gwynn, T.	25.00
352	Carew, R.	3.00
355	Morgan, J.	1.50
393	Candiotti, T. (R)	1.00
576	Palmer, J.	3.00
593	Gibson, K.	1.50
625	McGee/Smith/Smith	1.25
639	Eckersley, D.	3.00
A	Perry/Fingers (SP)	4.00
B	Bench/Yaz (SP)	8.00

Steve Garvey
FIRST BASE

1984 FLEER

	NM Price
Complete Set (660)	$90.00
Commons	.10
Unlisted Stars	**.15 -.75**
Pack (15)	5.00
Box (36)	125.00

Quality Rating ★★★★
Another mid-'80s winner. Finding unopened wax is a full-time job.

#	Player	NM
14	Murray, E.	3.00
17	Ripken, C.	15.00
25	Carlton, S.	2.00
46	Rose, P.	3.00
48	Schmidt, M.	3.00
58	Fisk, C.	1.00
131	Mattingly, D. (R)	25.00
143	Winfield, D.	2.00
152	Fernandez, T. (R)	1.50
186	Murphy, D.	1.00
207	Molitor, P.	2.00
219	Yount, R.	4.00
239	Ryan, N.	12.00
273	Dawson, A.	2.00
301	Gwynn, T.	12.00
336	Smith, O.	3.00
344	Brett, G.	3.00
392	Boggs, W.	3.00
412	Yastrzemski, C.	2.00
447	Henderson, R.	2.00
459	Phillips, T. (R)	2.00
462	Bench, J.	2.00
504	Sandberg, R.	4.00
505	Smith, L.	2.00
511	Carew, R.	2.00
520	Jackson, R.	2.00
595	Seaver, T.	2.00
599	Strawberry, D. (R)	5.00
630	Boggs, W.	2.00
638	Brett/Perry	2.00
640	Bench/Yastrzemski	3.00

Kirby Puckett
OUTFIELD

1984 FLEER UPDATE

	NM Price
Complete Set (132)	$450.00
Commons	.75
Unlisted Stars	**1.00-2.00**

Quality Rating ★★★★
Clemens had another monster year and gives this Update set new life. Several stars are undervalued.

#	Player	NM
27	Clemens, R.	225.00
34	Eckersley, D.	8.00
39	Franco, J.	8.00
43	Gooden, D.	20.00
61	Key, J.	15.00
70	Langston, M.	6.00
80	Morgan, J.	6.00
93	Puckett, K.	175.00
102	Rose, P.	20.00
103	Saberhagen, B.	6.00
106	Seaver, T.	12.00

DON MATTINGLY OF-1B

1984 TOPPS

	NM Price
Complete Set (792)	$50.00
Commons	.05
Unlisted Stars	**.10 -.75**
Pack (15)	3.00
Box (36)	80.00

Quality Rating ★★
Player selection is good but Topps is outdone by Fleer and Donruss.

#	Player	NM
4	Ryan, N. (HL)	1.25
8	Mattingly, D. (R)	10.00
10	Yount, R.	1.50
30	Boggs, W.	1.50
60	Molitor, P.	1.00
100	Jackson, R.	1.00
130	Smith, O.	1.50
182	Strawberry, D. (R)	2.00
230	Henderson, R.	1.50
240	Murray, E.	1.50
251	Gwynn, T.	5.00
300	Rose, P.	1.00
309	Phillips, T. (R)	1.00
399	Brett, G. (AS)	1.00
400	Ripken, C. (AS)	2.00
426	Ripken/Boddicker(TL)	1.50
460	Winfield, D.	1.25
470	Ryan, N.	5.00
490	Ripken, C.	5.00
500	Brett, G.	2.00
596	Sandberg, R.	2.00
700	Schmidt, M.	2.00e
707	Seavr/Carllton/Ryan (LL)	1.50
740	Seaver, T.	1.00

DWIGHT GOODEN P

1984 TOPPS TRADED

	NM Price
Complete Set (132)	$35.00
Commons	.20
Unlisted Stars	**.25 -.50**

Quality Rating ★★
A set filled with pitching talent and several future HOFers.

#	Player	NM
34	Eckersley, D.	3.00
42	Gooden, D.	7.00
62	Key, J.	4.00
82	Morgan, J.	3.00
103	Rose, P.	6.00
104	Saberhagen, B.	3.00
108	Seaver, T.	5.00

GOOSE GOSSAGE P

1985 DONRUSS

	NM Price
Complete Set (660)	$125.00
Factory Set (660)	150.00
Commons	.10
Unlisted Stars	**.15 -.75**
Pack (15)	5.00
Box (36)	150.00

Quality Rating ★★★★
Clemens and Puckett join Ryan and Ripken in a loaded set.

#	Player	NM
1	Sandberg, R. (DK)	2.00
7	Mattingly, D. (DK)	3.00
14	Ripken, C. (DK)	4.00
25	Gwynn, T. (DK)	3.00
47	Murray, E.	2.00
48	Yount, R.	2.00
51	Winfield, D.	1.50
53	Brett, G.	4.00
57	Jackson, R.	1.50
59	Smith, O.	2.00
60	Ryan, N.	10.00
61	Schmidt, M.	2.00
63	Gwynn, T.	7.00
67	Sandberg, R.	3.00
169	Ripken, C.	8.00
172	Boggs, W.	2.00
176	Henderson, R.	1.00
190	Gooden, D. (R)	2.00
222	Saberhagen, B. (R)	1.00
254	Rose, P.	2.50
273	Clemens, R. (R)	28.00
295	Mattingly, D.	4.00
312	Strawberry, D.	1.00
325	Davis, E. (R)	1.50
359	Molitor, P.	1.50
421	Dawson, A.	1.00
424A	Seaver, T. (err)	1.50
424B	Seaver, T. (cor)	25.00
438	Puckett, K. (R)	30.00
442	Eckersley, D.	1.00
534A	Pendleton, J. (R, err)	2.00
534B	Pendleton, T. (R, cor)	7.00
557	Langston, M. (R)	1.00
559	Key, J. (R)	2.50
581	Hershiser, O. (R)	3.00
616	Carter, J.	4.00
641	Rose, P.	2.00
651A	Winfield/Mattngly (YL)	3.00
651B	Winfield/Mattngly(WL)	8.00

WADE BOGGS
THIRD BASE

1985 FLEER

	NM Price
Complete Set (660)	$125.00
Commons	.07
Unlisted Stars	**.10 -.75**
Pack (15)	5.00
Box (36)	175.00

Quality Rating ★★★
Gooden no longer carries any status in the hobby, but several future HOFers help this set.

#	Player	NM
34	Gwynn, T.	7.00
65	Sandberg, R.	4.00
82	Gooden, D. (R)	1.00
93	Strawberry, D.	1.00
110	Key, J. (R)	2.00
133	Mattingly, D.	5.00
146	Winfield, D.	1.25
151	Boggs, W.	2.00
155	Clemens, R. (R)	28.00
184	Murray, E.	2.00
187	Ripken, C.	8.00
199	Brett, G.	3.00
212	Saberhagen, B. (R)	1.00
236	Pendleton, T. (R)	1.00
240	Smith, O.	2.00
265	Schmidt, M.	2.50
286	Puckett, K. (R)	25.00
303	Jackson, R.	1.50
359	Ryan, N.	10.00
371	Hershiser, O. (R)	2.00
394	Dawson, A.	1.00
425	Henderson, R.	2.00
443	Carter, J.	3.00
492	Langston, M. (R)	1.00
526	Seaver, T.	2.00
533	Davis, E. (R)	1.50
550	Rose, P.	2.00
588	Molitor, P.	2.00
601	Yount, R.	2.00
626	Ripken, C.	4.00
627	Schmidt, M.	2.00
629	Winfield/Henderson	1.50
630	Schmidt/Sandberg	2.00
640	Rose's 4000th Hit	1.00
641	The Ripkens (F/S)	5.00
647	Tartabull/Kiefer (R)	2.00

1985 FLEER UPDATE

		NM Price
Complete Set (132)		$15.00
Commons		.10
Unlisted Stars		**.15 -.50**

Quality Rating ★★
This Update set hasn't shown much movement as its big-name players have faltered.

#	Player	NM
33	Daulton, D.	6.00
51	Henderson, R.	1.50
119	Tettleton, M.	1.50

1985 TOPPS

		NM Price
Complete Set (792)		$50.00
Commons		.05
Unlisted Stars		**.10 -.75**
Pack (15)		3.00
Box (36)		90.00

Quality Rating ★★★★
As McGwire continues his quest for 61 homers, his rookie is skyrocketing.

#	Player	NM
7	Ryan, N. (RB)	1.25
30	Ripken, C.	3.00
100	Brett, G.	1.50
181	Clemens, R. (R)	10.00
340	Yount, R.	1.00
350	Boggs, W.	1.00
401	McGwire, M. (R, USA)	32.00
460	Sandberg, R.	2.00
493	Hershiser, O. (R)	1.00
500	Schmidt, M.	1.25
522	Molitor, P.	1.00
536	Puckett, K. (R)	8.00
605	Smith, O.	1.00
620	Gooden, D. (R)	1.00
660	Gwynn, T.	2.00
665	Mattingly, D.	2.00
694	Carter, J.	1.25
700	Murray, E.	1.00
704	Ripken, C. (AS)	2.00
713	Sandberg, R. (AS)	1.00
717	Gwynn, T. (AS)	1.00
760	Ryan, N.	4.00

1985 TOPPS TRADED

		NM Price
Complete Set (132)		$10.00
Commons		.10
Unlisted Stars		**.15 -.60**

Quality Rating ★
This traded set has no big-name rookie or superstar.

#	Player	NM
43	Guillen, O.	1.50
49	Henderson, R.	1.00
120	Tettleton, M.	1.50

1986 DONRUSS

		NM Price
Complete Set (660)		$40.00
Factory Set (660)		50.00
Commons		.07
Unlisted Stars		**.10 -.75**
Pack (15)		4.00
Box (36)		90.00

Quality Rating ★★★★
At one time this set was one of the most desired in the market. Prices have fallen and rookies of Canseco and McGriff are more reasonable.

#	Player	NM
28	McGriff, F. (RR)	6.00
33A	Galarraga, A. (RR, err)	8.00
33B	Galarraga, A. (RR, cor)	8.00
37	O'Neill, P. (RR)	3.00
39	Canseco, J. (RR)	8.00
48	Yount, R.	1.50
53	Brett, G.	1.50
59	Smith, O.	1.50
61	Schmidt, M.	1.50
62	Rose, P.	1.00
67	Sandberg, R.	1.50
72	Puckett, K.	4.00
88	Murray, E.	1.00
112	Gwynn, T.	3.00
172	Clemens, R.	3.00
173	Mattingly, D.	2.50
210	Ripken, C.	5.00
224	Carter, J.	2.00
258	Ryan, N.	1.50
371	Boggs, W.	1.50
377	Jackson, R.	1.25
477	Daulton, D. (R)	2.00
482	Dykstra, L. (R)	1.50
512	Fielder, C. (R)	4.00
609B	Seaver, T. (cor)	2.00
653	King of Kings-Rose	1.50

1986 DONRUSS ROOKIES

		NM Price
Complete Set (56)		$30.00
Commons		.10
Unlisted Stars		**.15 -.60**

Quality Rating ★★★★★
A great chance to pick up Bonds and Clark at a reasonable price.

#	Player	NM
7	Galarraga, A.	4.00
11	Bonds, B.	8.00
22	Canseco, J.	4.00
30	Bonilla, B.	2.00
32	Clark, W.	4.00
38	Jackson, B.	2.00

1986 FLEER

		NM Price
Complete Set (660)		$50.00
Factory Set (660)		60.00
Commons		.07
Unlisted Stars		**.10 -.75**
Pack (15)		3.00
Box (36)		70.00

Quality Rating ★★★★
NM sets are difficult to find. Inserts are an added bonus to Fielder and Canseco rookies.

#	Player	NM
5	Brett, G.	2.00
46	Smith, O.	1.25
78	Dykstra, L. (R)	1.25
109	Mattingly, D.	2.00
160	Jackson, R.	1.25
191	Rose, P.	1.00
282	Murray, E.	1.00
284	Ripken, C.	5.00
310	Ryan, N.	5.00
323	Gwynn, T.	3.00
341	Boggs, W.	1.50
345	Clemens, R.	3.00
378	Sandberg, R.	2.00
401	Puckett, K.	4.00
432	Tettleton, M. (R)	1.50
438	Daulton, D. (R)	1.50
450	Schmidt, M.	1.50
506	Yount, R.	1.50
583	Carter, J.	1.50
627	Mattingly, D.	1.00
633	Ripken/Trammell	1.50
634	Boggs/Brett	1.00
639	Boggs/Mattingly	1.00
646	Daniels/O'Neill (R)	2.00
647	Galarraga/Toliver (R)	5.00
649	Canseco/Plunk (R)	8.00
653	Fielder/Snyder (R)	4.00

Fleer All-Stars

		NM
Complete Set (12)		30.00
Commons		.25
1	Mattingly, D.	8.00
3	Brett, G.	8.00
5	Ripken, C.	15.00
7	Henderson, R.	4.00
10	Gooden, D.	1.00

Fleer Future Hall of Famers

		NM
Complete Set (6)		20.00
1	Rose, P.	3.00
2	Carlton, S.	2.00
3	Seaver, T.	2.00
4	Carew, R.	2.00
5	Ryan, N.	12.00
6	Jackson, R.	2.50

1986 FLEER UPDATE

		NM Price
Complete Set (132)		$15.00
Commons		.10
Unlisted Stars		**.15 -.60**

Quality Rating ★★★
Today's biggest stars make this set worth collecting.

1986 TOPPS

		NM Price
Complete Set (792)		$25.00
Factory Set (792)		30.00
Commons		.03
Unlisted Stars		**.05 -.75**
Pete Rose Specials (2-7)		.25
Pack (15)		1.00
Box (36)		25.00

Quality Rating ★★★
A high print run and unpopular design have hurt this set's value.

#	Player	NM
1	Rose, P.	1.00
10	Gwynn, T.	1.00
70	Winfield, D.	.50
100	Ryan, N.	2.00
180	Mattingly, D.	1.00
300	Brett, G.	1.00
329	Puckett, K.	2.00
340	Ripken, C.	2.00
386	Fielder, C. (R)	1.00
661	Clemens, R.	1.50
690	Sandberg, R.	.75
715	Ripken, C. (AS)	1.00

1986 TOPPS TRADED

		NM Price
Complete Set (132)		$10.00
Commons		.05
Unlisted Stars		**.10 -.50**

Quality Rating ★★★★
A huge year by Galarraga has collectors asking for his earlier cards.

#	Player	NM
11	Bonds, B.	2.00
12	Bonilla, B.	1.00
20	Canseco, J.	1.00
24	Clark, W.	1.00
40	Galarraga, A.	1.50
50	Jackson, B.	1.00

1986 FLEER UPDATE price list

#	Player	NM
14	Bonds, B.	5.00
15	Bonilla, B.	2.00
20	Canseco, J.	3.00
25	Clark, W.	3.00
44	Galarraga, A.	2.50

1987 DONRUSS

	NM Price
Complete Set (660)	$30.00
Factory Set (660)	30.00
Commons	.03
Unlisted Stars	**.05 -.75**
Pack (15)	1.50
Box (36)	35.00

Quality Rating ★★★★
Maddux is a must but don't overlook Bonds, Clark, and Palmeiro.

#	Player	NM
35	Jackson, B. (RR)	1.50
36	Maddux, G. (RR)	18.00
38	White, D. (RR)	1.00
43	Palmeiro, R. (RR)	2.00
46	McGwire, M. (RR)	3.00
52	Mattingly, D.	1.00
54	Brett, G.	1.00
64	Gwynn, T.	1.00
66	Clark, W. (R)	1.50
77	Sandberg, R.	1.25
89	Ripken, C.	2.00
97	Canseco, J.	1.00
138	Ryan, N.	2.00
149	Puckett, K.	1.50
276	Clemens, R.	1.00
361	Bonds, B. (R)	4.00
492	Larkin, B. (R)	2.00
502	Cone, D. (R)	1.50
558	Bonilla, B. (R)	1.00
627	Brown, K. (R)	1.50

1987 DONRUSS ROOKIES

	NM Price
Complete Set (56)	$20.00
Commons	.05
Unlisted Stars	**.10 -.60**

Quality Rating ★★
Maddux and a cast of All-Stars make up a set that has great player selection for a modest price.

#	Player	NM
1	McGwire, M.	3.00
14	Jackson, B.	1.00
31	McGriff, F.	1.50
35	Cone, D.	2.00
45	Williams, M.	4.00
47	Palmeiro, R.	2.00
52	Maddux, G.	15.00

1987 FLEER

	NM Price
Complete Set (660)	$40.00
Factory Set (672)	50.00
Tin Set (660)	50.00
Commons	.05
Unlisted Stars	**.10 -.75**
Pack (15)	3.00
Box (36)	70.00

Quality Rating ★★★★
Top-notch rookie selection will make this set a favorite for years.

#	Player	NM
32	Clemens, R.	1.50
67	Ryan, N.	4.00
84	Jackson, R.	1.00
86	Joyner, W. (R)	1.00
104	Mattingly, D.	1.50
187	Schmidt, M.	1.00
204	Larkin, B. (R)	4.00
213	Rose, P.	1.00
269	Clark, W. (R)	4.00
308	Smith, O.	1.00
319	Galarraga, A.	1.25
366	Brett, G.	2.00
369	Jackson, B. (R)	1.50
389	Canseco, J.	1.00
416	Gwynn, T.	2.00
478	Ripken, C.	3.00
549	Puckett, K.	2.50
572	Sandberg, R.	2.00
604	Bonds, B. (R)	18.00
605	Bonilla, B. (R)	1.50
646	Fraser/White (R)	1.00

Fleer All-Stars

Complete Set (12)		20.00
Commons		.25
1	Mattingly, D.	6.00
5	Puckett, K.	8.00
6	Schmidt, M.	3.00
11	Clemens, R.	6.00

Fleer Headliners

Complete Set (6)		7.00
Commons		.50
1	Boggs, W.	2.00
2	Canseco, J.	3.00

World Series Set

Complete Set (12)		3.00
Commons		.20
3	Clemens, R.	1.00
11	Knight/Strawberry	.40

1987 FLEER UPDATE

	NM Price
Complete Set (132)	$15.00
Tin Set (132)	15.00
Commons	.03
Unlisted Stars	**.05 -.60**

Quality Rating ★★★
A great set paced by Maddux, McGriff, and Williams.

#	Player	NM
68	Maddux, G.	10.00
75	McGriff, F.	1.50
76	McGwire, M.	3.00
129	Williams, M.	4.00

1987 TOPPS

	NM Price
Complete Set (792)	$15.00
Factory Set (792)	15.00
Commons	.02
Unlisted Stars	**.05 -.50**
Pack (15)	.50
Box (36)	15.00

Quality Rating ★★★
You can find these cards everywhere. That fact alone has kept values to a minimum.

#	Player	NM
320	Bonds, B. (R)	1.50
340	Clemens, R.	.60
366	McGwire, M.	1.00
400	Brett, G.	.60
420	Clark, W. (R)	1.00
450	Puckett, K.	1.00
606A	Mattingly, D. (AS, err)	.75
609	Ripken, C. (AS)	.60
611	Puckett, K. (AS)	.60
634	Palmeiro, R. (R)	.75
648	Larkin, B. (R)	.75
680	Sandberg, R.	.60
757	Ryan, N.	1.00
784	Ripken, C.	1.00

1987 TOPPS TRADED

	NM Price
Complete Set (132)	$10.00
Commons	.03
Unlisted Stars	**.05 -.50**

Quality Rating ★★
Another over-printed, low-value set. The cards mirror the regular set in design.

#	Player	NM
24	Cone, D. (R)	1.00
70	Maddux, G. (R)	5.00
74	McGriff, F. (R)	1.00
129	Williams, M. (R)	2.00

1988 DONRUSS

	NM Price
Complete Set (660)	$10.00
Factory Set (660)	10.00
Commons	.04
Unlisted Stars	**.05 -.50**
Pack (15)	.45
Box (36)	9.00

Quality Rating ★★
Adequate design makes for a so-so set. Alomar Rated Rookie leads the way.

#	Player	NM
34	Alomar, R. (RR)	1.00
61	Ryan, N.	.75
171	Ripken, C.	1.00
326	Bonds, B.	.75
539	Maddux, G.	1.00
545	Buhner, J. (R)	.75
628	Williams, M. (R, SP)	1.00
644	Glavine, T. (R)	.75

MVP Set

Complete Set (26)		3.00
Commons		.10

1988 DONRUSS ROOKIES

	NM Price
Complet Set (56)	$15.00
Commons	.05
Unlisted Stars	**.10 -.35**

Quality Rating ★★★
Edgar Martinez is the sleeper in this set. Overproduction keeps the value down.

#	Player	NM
1	Grace, M.	1.50
11	Buhner, J.	1.50
14	Anderson, B.	1.50
35	Alomar, R.	4.00
36	Martinez, E.	1.50

1988 FLEER

	NM Price
Complete Set (660)	$25.00
Factory Set (660)	25.00
Factory Set (672)	30.00
Commons	.03
Unlisted Stars	**.05 -.50**
Pack (15)	1.50
Box (36)	35.00

Quality Rating ★★★
Includes rookie cards of Ken Caminiti and Edgar Martinez.

#	Player	NM
19	Puckett, K.	1.00
101	Williams, M. (R)	1.50

#	Player	NM
214	Mattingly, D.	.60
254	Brett, G.	.60
286	McGwire, M.	1.00
322	Bonds, B.	1.50
349	Clemens, R.	.75
378	Martinez, E. (R)	1.50
423	Maddux, G.	3.00
431	Sandberg, R.	1.00
441	Caminiti, K. (R)	1.50
455	Ryan, N.	1.50
462A	Browne, J. (err)	1.50
539	Glavine, T. (R)	1.00
570	Ripken, C.	1.50
585	Gwynn, T.	.75
640	Ripken Bros.	.75
641	Grace/Jackson (R)	2.00

Fleer All-Stars

#	Player	NM
	Complete Set (12)	6.00
	Commons	.20
4	Clemens, R.	2.50
8	Boggs, W.	.75
12	Molitor, P.	1.00

Fleer Headliners

#	Player	NM
	Complete Set (6)	5.00
	Commons	.60
1	Mattingly, D.	2.50
2	McGwire, M.	1.00

World Series Set

#	Player	NM
	Complete Set (12)	2.00
	Commons	.15
4	Smith, O.	.50
8	Puckett, K.	.75
12	Viola, F.	.40

1988 FLEER UPDATE

	NM Price
Complete Set (132)	$10.00
Commons	.03
Unlisted Stars	**.05 -.50**

Quality Rating ★★
Alomar is the talk of this set, but others are worth obtaining.

#	Player	NM
74	Smoltz, J.	3.00
77	Grace, M.	1.50
89	Biggio, C.	2.00
122	Alomar, R.	4.00

1988 SCORE

	NM Price
Complete Set (660)	$12.00
Factory Set (660)	12.00
Commons	.03
Unlisted Stars	**.05 -.40**
Pack (18)	.40
Box (36)	10.00

Quality Rating ★★
Score's first set has a good group of rookies, including Caminiti.

#	Player	NM
1	Mattingly, D.	.50
11	Brett, G.	.50
24	Puckett, K.	.50
26	Sandberg, R.	.50
93A	Walker, G. (err)	2.00
110	Clemens, R.	.50
118	Williams, M. (R)	.60
164	Caminiti, K. (R)	.50
265	Bonds, B.	.75
550	Ripken, C.	1.00
575	Ryan, N.	.75
638	Glavine, T. (R)	.75

1988 SCORE TRADED

	NM Price
Complete Set (110)	$50.00
Commons	.15
Unlisted Stars	**.20 -.50**

Quality Rating ★★★★
Set has rebounded thanks to Brady Anderson and the performances of the other big stars like Buhner.

#	Player	NM
70	Anderson, B.	8.00
80	Grace, M.	7.00
95	Buhner, J.	8.00
103	Biggio, C.	10.00
105	Alomar, R.	25.00

1988 TOPPS

	NM Price
Complete Set (792)	$12.00
Factory Set (792)	$12.00
Commons	.02
Unlisted Stars	**.05 -.40**
Pack (15)	.45
Box (36)	8.00

Quality Rating ★
Williams has had his ups and downs, and so have his cards. Decent design from Topps.

#	Player	NM
10	Sandberg, R.	.50
70	Clemens, R.	.50
120	Puckett, K.	.50
250	Ryan, N.	.75
361	Maddux, G.	1.50
372	Williams, M. (R)	.75
450	Bonds, B.	.75
637	Bell, J. (R)	.75
650	Ripken, C.	1.00
778A	Comstock, K. (err)	2.00
779	Glavine, T. (R)	.75

1988 TOPPS TRADED

	NM Price
Complete Set (132)	$12.00
Commons	.03
Unlisted Stars	**.05 -.50**

Quality Rating ★★★
Stars for Team USA are now players for big league clubs. Few major hobby stars.

#	Player	NM
4	Alomar, R.	4.00
5	Anderson, B.	2.00
21	Buhner, J.	1.50
39	Gant, R.	.75
66	Martinez, T. (USA)	6.00
124	Ventura, R. (USA)	1.50

1989 BOWMAN

	NM Price
Complete Set (484)	$15.00
Factory Set (484)	15.00
Commons	.02
Unlisted Stars	**.05 -.40**
Pack (13)	.45
Box (36)	10.00

Quality Rating ★
Bowman returns, but oversized cards don't interest most collectors.

#	Player	NM
9	Ripken, C.	1.00
18	Anderson, B. (R)	.50
121	Brett, G.	.50
142	Sheffield, G. (R)	.60
162	Puckett, K.	.50
176	Mattingly, D.	.50
211	Martinez, T. (R)	.75
220	Griffey Jr., K. (R)	6.00
225	Ryan, N.	.75
259	Griffey (F/S)	1.00
266	Smoltz, J. (R)	.75
284	Maddux, G.	.50
426	Bonds, B.	.50
458	Alomar, R.	.60

1989 DONRUSS

	NM Price
Complete Set (660)	$12.00
Factory Set (672)	15.00
Commons	.03
Unlisted Stars	**.05 -.40**
Pack (15)	.35
Box (36)	8.00

Quality Rating ★★
Griffey and Sheffield are worth collecting. Bichette could move into that category.

#	Player	NM
4	Alomar, R.	4.00
5	Anderson, B.	2.00
21	Buhner, J.	1.50
39	Gant, R.	.75
66	Martinez, T. (USA)	6.00
124	Ventura, R. (USA)	1.50

#	Player	NM
33	Griffey Jr., K. (RR)	6.00
42	Johnson, R. (RR)	1.50
51	Ripken, C.	1.00
74	Mattingly, D.	.50
92	Bonds, B.	.60
105	Sandberg, R.	.50
154	Ryan, N.	.60
182	Puckett, K.	.50
204	Brett, G.	.50
373	Maddux, G.	.60
561	Biggio, C. (R)	.60
634	Bichette, D. (R)	1.00
642	Smoltz, J. (R)	.75

Grand Slammers Set

#	Player	NM
	Complete Set (12)	1.75
	Commons	.10
1	Canseco, J.	.75
7	McGwire, M.	.50

1989 DONRUSS ROOKIES

	NM Price
Complete Set (56)	$8.00
Commons	.03
Unlisted Stars	**.05 -.35**

Quality Rating ★★
Today's best players are included. Randy Johnson is a great complement to the Griffey card.

#	Player	NM
1	Sheffield, G.	.75
3	Griffey Jr., K.	8.00
6	Sanders, D.	1.00
43	Johnson, R.	1.50

1989 FLEER

	NM Price
Complete Set (660)	$12.00
Factory Set (660)	12.00
Factory Set (672)	12.00
Commons	.03
Unlisted Stars	**.05 -.50**
Pack (15)	.75
Box (36)	15.00

Quality Rating ★★★
Filled with errors and unchallenging inserts, but you should add the Griffey to your collection.

TOMMY JOHN
PITCHER

#	Player	NM
173A	Treadway, J. (err)	5.00
196	Sheffield, G. (R)	.60
299	Alomar, R.	.75
350A	Ashby, A. (err)	2.00
368	Ryan, N.	.75
381	Johnson, R. (R)	1.00
431	Maddux, G.	.60
468	Bichette, D. (R)	1.00
534A	VandeBerg, E. (err)	1.50
548	Griffey Jr., K. (R)	6.00
602	Smoltz, J. (R)	.75
616A	Ripken, B. (FF)	6.00
616B	Ripken, B. (whiteout)	30.00
616C	Ripken, B. (scribble)	6.00
617	Ripken, C.	1.00

Fleer All-Stars

	Complete Set (12)	5.00
	Commons	.15
2	Canseco, J.	1.00
3	Clark, W.	1.00
8	Molitor, P.	1.25

Fleer For The Record

	Complete Set (6)	8.00
	Commons	.20
1	Boggs, W.	1.00
2	Clemens, R.	1.50
3	Galarraga, A.	1.25
5	Maddux, G.	5.00
6	Mattingly, D.	2.50

World Series Set

	Complete Set (12)	1.75
	Commons	.10

KEVIN APPIER
PITCHER

1989 FLEER UPDATE

	NM Price
Complete Set (132)	$8.00
Commons	.03
Unlisted Stars	**.05 -.40**

Quality Rating ★★★
Belle is the headliner. Several of the game's better young arms are included.

#	Player	NM
25	Belle, A. (R)	3.00
53	Sanders, D. (R)	1.00
59	Johnson, R.	1.25
67	Ryan, N.	1.50

RON GANT

1989 SCORE

	NM Price
Complete Set (660)	$15.00
Factory Set (660)	15.00
Commons	.03
Unlisted Stars	**.05 -.40**
Pack (17)	.35
Box (36)	9.00

Quality Rating ★★
Plagued by errors, Score's second effort resembles its first. Rookie crop is fairly weak.

#	Player	NM
15	Ripken, C.	1.00
20	Puckett, K.	.50
35	Sandberg, R.	.50
75A	Brett, G. (err)	.75
100	Mattingly, D.	.50
119	Maddux, G.	.60
127	Bonds, B.	.60
237	Biggio, C. (R)	.60
300	Ryan, N.	.75
350A	Clemens, R. (err)	1.50
507B	Holton, B. (cor)	2.00
563	Anderson, B. (R)	.50
612	Williams, M.	.50
616	Smoltz, J. (R)	.75
625	Sheffield, G. (R)	.60
645	Johnson, R. (R)	1.00
654A	Boggs, W. (HL, err)	2.00

NOLAN RYAN

1989 SCORE TRADED

	NM Price
Complete Set (110)	$8.00
Commons	.03
Unlisted Stars	**.05 -.35**

Quality Rating ★★
A Traded set filled with talent. With such a low price tag, this group should attract attention.

#	Player	NM
2	Ryan, N.	1.50
77	Johnson, R.	1.50
100	Griffey Jr., K. (R)	7.00
106	Belle, A. (R)	3.00

WADE BOGGS

1989 TOPPS

	NM Price
Complete Set (792)	$15.00
Factory Set (792)	15.00
Commons	.03
Unlisted Stars	**.05 -.40**
Pack (15)	.40
Box (36)	9.00

Quality Rating ★★
Get these Sheffield, Biggio, and Johnson rookies at a low prices.

#	Player	NM
49	Biggio, C. (R)	.60
206	Alomar, R.	.75
240	Maddux, G.	.60
250	Ripken, C.	1.00
343	Sheffield, G. (R)	.60
530	Ryan, N.	.75
605A	Welch, B. (err)	2.00
620	Bonds, B.	.60
647	Johnson, R. (R)	1.00
650	Puckett, K.	.50
665A	Oliva, T. (TBTC, err)	1.50
700	Mattingly, D.	.50
761	Bichette, D. (R)	1.00

STEVE BEDROSIAN

1989 TOPPS TRADED

	NM Price
Complete Set (132)	$7.00
Commons	.03
Unlisted Stars	**.05 -.30**

Quality Rating ★★
Griffey accounts for almost all of this set's value.

#	Player	NM
41	Griffey Jr., K. (R)	6.00
57	Johnson, R.	1.25
106	Ryan, N.	1.25
110	Sanders, D. (R)	1.00

1989 UPPER DECK

	NM Price
Complete Set (800)	$120.00
Factory Set (800)	130.00
Low Series Set (1-700)	110.00
High Series Set (701-800)	10.00
Commons	.10
Unlisted Stars	**.15 -.75**
Low Pack (15)	6.00
Low Box (36)	160.00
High Pack (15)	4.00
High Box (36)	120.00

Quality Rating ★★★★★
Smoltz, Bichette, and Johnson join Griffey as the must-have cards in the set.

Eddie Murray

#	Player	NM
1	Griffey Jr., K. (R)	100.00
5	Alomar, S. (R)	2.00
13A	Sheffield, G. (R, err)	4.00
13B	Sheffield, G. (R, cor)	4.00
17	Smoltz, J. (R)	3.00
18	Martinez, R. (R)	1.00
24	Bichette, D. (R)	2.00
25	Johnson, R. (R)	7.00
115	Galarraga, A.	1.00
120	Sandberg, R.	1.50
145	Ryan, N.	4.00
195	Clemens, R.	1.25
200	Mattingly, D.	1.50
215	Brett, G.	1.50
235	Palmeiro, R.	1.00
241	Maddux, G.	4.00
247	Williams, M.	2.00
273	Biggio, C. (R)	3.00
300	McGwire, M.	2.00
321A	Varsho, A. (err)	1.50
357A	Murphy, D. (err)	18.00
376	Puckett, K.	1.50
384	Gwynn, T.	2.00
406	Schmidt, M.	1.50
408	Anderson, B. (R)	2.00
440	Bonds, B.	2.00
467	Ripken, C.	3.00
471	Alomar, R.	3.00
583A	Gallego, M. (err)	1.00
627A	Schroeder, B. (err)	1.00
652A	Sheridan, P. (err)	8.00
669	Astros CL (Ryan)	1.00
682	Ripken, C.	1.00
707	Hayes, C. (R)	1.00
754	Zeile, T. (R)	1.00
768	Martinez, E.	1.25
772	Palmeiro, R.	1.25
774	Ryan, N.	4.00

BREWERS ♦ GREG VAUGHN

1990 BOWMAN

	NM Price
Complete Set (528)	$15.00
Factory Set (528)	15.00
Commons	.03
Unlisted Stars	**.05 -.50**
Pack (15)	.40
Box (36)	10.00

Quality Rating ★★
Player selection is great, but an overabundance of cards will keep this set's value down.

#	Player	NM
117	Walker, L. (R)	1.00
178	Alou, M. (R)	.75
255	Ripken, C.	1.00
275	Vaughn, M. (R)	1.25
312	Sosa, S. (R)	.75
320	Thomas, F. (R)	3.00
333	Belle, A.	1.25
360	Fryman, T. (R)	.60

#	Player	NM
439	Williams, B. (R)	1.00
481	Griffey Jr., K.	2.50
486	Ryan, N.	75
492	Gonzalez, J. (R)	1.50

1990 DONRUSS

	NM Price
Complete Set (716)	$10.00
Factory Set (728)	10.00
Commons	.03
Unlisted Stars	.05 -.50
Pack (16)	.35
Box (36)	8.00

Quality Rating ★★
Juan Gonzalez is the highlight of this set. A Sosa rookie is included.

#	Player	NM
4	Griffey Jr., K. (DK)	75
33A	Gonzalez, J. (RR, err)	4.50
33B	Gonzalez, J. (RR, cor)	1.50
96	Ripken, C.	1.00
158	Maddux, G.	60
166	Ryan, N.	75
365	Griffey Jr., K.	2.50
390	Belle, A.	1.25
489	Sosa, S. (R)	60
578	Walker, L. (R)	60
659A	Ryan, N. (5000, err)	2.00
660A	Baines, H. (AS, err)	75
660B	Baines, H. (AS, cor)	1.00
660C	Baines, H. (AS, cor)	60
665A	Ryan (King/Kings, err)	2.00
676A	Ripken, C. (err.)	1.00
689	Williams, B. (R)	1.00
704	Justice, D. (R)	75
BC12	Smoltz, J.	75

Grand Slammers Set

		NM
Complete Set (12)		2.00
Commons		.10
4	McGwire, M.	50
6	Clark, W.	60

1990 DONRUSS ROOKIES

	NM Price
Complete Set (56)	$2.50
Commons	.03
Unlisted Stars	.05 -.35

Quality Rating ★
Justice had a great 1997 season but this set still has no following.

#	Player	NM
14	Justice, D.	60
45	Grissom, M.	50

1990 FLEER

	NM Price
Complete Set (660)	$10.00
Retail Factory Set (660)	10.00
Hobby Factory Set (672)	10.00
Commons	.03
Unlisted Stars	.05 -.50
Pack (15)	.35
Box (36)	8.00

Quality Rating ★
A decent design but the real attractions are Gonzalez and Sosa.

#	Player	NM
37	Maddux, G.	60
187	Ripken, C.	1.00
297	Gonzalez, J. (R)	1.50
313	Ryan, N.	60
353A	Martinez, D. (err)	2.00
363	Walker, L. (R)	1.00
485	Belle, A.	1.00
513	Griffey Jr., K.	2.50
548	Sosa, S. (R)	75
586	Justice, D. (R)	1.00
621A	Brett, G. (1980 err)	1.50
624A	Ripken, C. (1983, err)	5.00
630A	Clark, W. (1989, err)	75

Fleer All-Stars

		NM
Complete Set (12)		4.00
Commons		.15
7	Puckett, K.	1.50
8	Ripken, C.	3.00
9	Sandberg, R.	1.25

Fleer League Standouts

		NM
Complete Set (6)		5.00
Commons		.60
2	Mattingly, D.	2.50

Fleer Soaring Stars

		NM
Complete Set (12)		25.00
Commons		.50
3	Walker, L.	5.00
6	Griffey Jr., K.	20.00

World Series Set

		NM
Complete Set (12)		1.50
Commons		.15
4	Clark, W.	50
5	Canseco, J.	50

1990 FLEER UPDATE

	NM Price
Complete Set (132)	$5.00
Commons	.03
Unlisted Stars	.05 -.50

Quality Rating ★★
Thomas leads a talented group of players. A chance to pick up Ryan at a reasonable price.

#	Player	NM
87	Thomas, F. (R)	3.50
96	Fryman, T. (R)	75
131	Ryan, N.	75

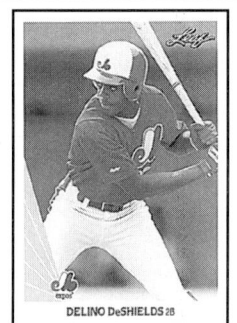

1990 LEAF

	NM Price
Complete Set (528)	$220.00
Series 1 Set (1-264)	90.00
Series 2 Set (265-528)	130.00
Commons	.20
Unlisted Stars	.25 -1.00
Series 1 Pack (15)	6.00
Series 1 Box (36)	160.00
Series 2 Pack (15)	7.00
Series 2 Box (36)	230.00

Quality Rating ★★★★
Still a popular choice among collectors. Rookies includes Sosa, Walker, and Thomas.

#	Player	NM
12	Clemens, R.	3.00
21	Ryan, N.	8.00
25	Maddux, G.	20.00
59	Smoltz, J.	2.50
62	McGwire, M.	5.00
69	Mattingly, D.	3.00
71	Yount, R.	2.00
75	Alomar, R.	2.50
91	Bonds, B.	3.00
94	Williams, M.	4.00
98	Sandberg, R.	4.00
100	Palmeiro, R.	2.00
107	Grissom, M. (R)	4.00
108	Canseco, J.	2.00
123	Puckett, K.	4.00
142	Smith, O.	1.50
154	Gwynn, T.	4.00
157	Sheffield, G.	4.00
178	Brett, G.	4.00
180	Belle, A.	10.00
193	DeShields, D. (R)	2.50
197	Ripken, C.	8.00
220	Sosa, S. (R)	10.00
237	Olerud, J. (R)	2.50
242	Molitor, P.	1.50
245	Griffey Jr., K.	30.00
249	McDonald, B. (R)	2.00
265	Ryan "No Hit King"	4.00
297	Justice, D. (R)	10.00
299	Martinez, E.	2.00
300	Thomas, F. (R)	85.00
325	Walker, L. (R)	15.00
340	Bichette, D.	3.00
353	Gilkey, B. (R)	3.00
359	Sanders, D.	3.00
443	Baerga, C. (R)	3.00
483	Johnson, R.	6.00

1990 SCORE

	NM Price
Complete Set (704)	$15.00
Factory Set (704)	15.00
Factory Set (714)	18.00
Commons	.03
Unlisted Stars	.05 -.50
Pack (16)	.50
Box (36)	15.00

Quality Rating ★★★
Gonzalez, Sosa, and Justice all have rookie cards in this affordable set.

#	Player	NM
2	Ripken, C.	1.00
250	Ryan, N.	75
338B	Griffey, K. (cor)	1.50
403	Maddux, G.	60
508	Belle, A.	1.00
558	Sosa, S. (R)	75
560	Griffey Jr., K.	2.50
561A	Sandberg, R. (err)	7.00
631	Walker, L. (R)	1.00
637	Gonzalez, J. (R)	1.50
650	Justice, D. (R)	1.00
663	Thomas, F. (R, #1 DP)	4.50
672	Knoblauch, C. (R)	75
675	Vaughn, M. (R, #1 DP)	1.00
697	Jackson, B. (FB/BB)	75

Rookie Dream Team

		NM
Complete Set (10)		5.00
Commons		.25
1	Giamatti, B.	75
6	Ventura, R.	1.00
9	Grissom, M.	2.00

1990 SCORE TRADED

	NM Price
Complete Set (110)	$8.00
Commons	.03
Unlisted Stars	.05 -.50

Quality Rating ★★
Lindros and Thomas are not enough to attract people to this Update effort.

#	Player	NM
86	Thomas, F.	5.00
100	Lindros, E.	2.00

1990 TOPPS

	NM Price
Complete Set (792)	$15.00
Factory Set (792)	15.00
Commons	.03
Unlisted Stars	.05 -.40
Pack (16)	.35
Box (36)	10.00

Quality Rating ★★
Doesn't get much attention other than the Thomas error card.

#	Player	NM
1	Ryan, N.	.75
8	Ripken, C. (RB)	.50
283	Belle, A.	1.00
331	Gonzalez, J. (R)	1.25
336	Griffey Jr., K.	2.50
388	Ripken, C. (AS)	.60
414A	Thomas, F. (R, DP, err)	1500.00
414B	Thomas, F. (R, DP, cor)	4.00
570	Ripken, C.	1.00
692	Sosa, S. (R)	.75
715	Maddux, G.	.60
757	Walker, L. (R)	1.00

1990 TOPPS TRADED

	NM Price
Complete Set (132)	$4.00
Factory Set (132)	4.00
Commons	.03
Unlisted Stars	**.05 -.35**

Quality Rating ★★
Overproduction has kept this set's price at a reasonable level.

#	Player	NM
33	Fryman, T. (R)	.75
48	Justice, D. (R)	.75

1990 UPPER DECK

	NM Price
Complete Set (800)	$25.00
Factory Set (800)	25.00
Low Series Set (1-700)	20.00
High Series Set (701-800)	5.00
Commons	.03
Unlisted Stars	**.05 -.50**
Low or High Pack (15)	1.00
Low or High Box (36)	25.00

Quality Rating ★★
Not as popular as the 1989 set, despite Grissom, Gonzalez, and Walker rookies.

#	Player	NM
9	Grissom, M. (R)	1.00
13	Sanders, D.	.75
17	Sosa, S. (R)	1.50
24	Griffey, K. (TC)	.75
34	Ryan, N. (SP)	1.00
54A	McDonald, B. (R, err)	5.00
60A	Tettleton, M. (CL, err)	2.00
72	Gonzalez, J. (R)	3.50
89A	Gott, J. (err)	3.00
124	Brett, G.	.75
156	Griffey Jr., K.	5.00
191	Mattingly, D.	.75
213	Maddux, G.	1.00
227	Bonds, B.	.75
236	Puckett, K.	.75
266	Ripken, C.	1.25
324	Sandberg, R.	.75
344	Gwynn, T.	1.00
446	Belle, A.	1.25
466	Walker, L. (R)	2.00
478A	Garrelts, S. (err)	2.00
544	Ryan, N.	1.25
683A	Weston, M. (err)	2.00
700A	Checklist (err)	2.00
702	Expos Rookies	1.00
711	Justice, D. (R)	2.00
726	Hundley, T. (R)	1.00
734A	Ryan, N. (6/300, err)	4.00
734B	Ryan, N. (6/300, cor)	1.00
737	Baerga, C. (R)	1.00
755	Lankford, R. (R)	.75

Jackson Heroes Set

Complete Set (10)	25.00
Jackson Singles (1-9)	2.50
Cover Card (No#)	4.00
Jackson Autographed (2500)	300.00

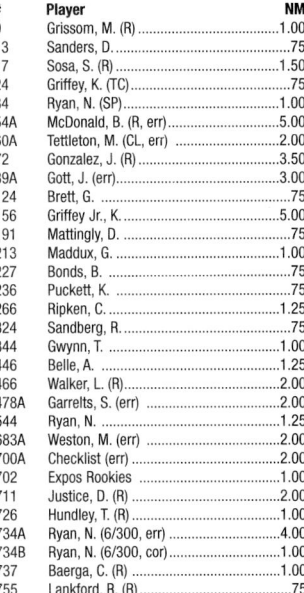

1991 BOWMAN

	NM Price
Complete Set (704)	$25.00
Factory Set (704)	25.00
Commons	.03
Unlisted Stars	**.05 -.40**
Pack (14)	.90
Box (36)	25.00

Quality Rating ★★
Contains such collectible rookies as Mussina and Mondesi. Value is modest due to high production.

#	Player	NM
68	Thome, J. (R)	1.50
81	Belle, A.	.50
97	Mussina, M. (R)	1.25
104	Ripken, C.	1.00
112	Vaughn, M.	.50
180	Gonzalez, J. (MVP)	.75
183	Bagwell, J. (R, MVP)	2.50
203	Salmon, T. (R)	1.00
246	Griffey Jr., K.	1.50
272	Rodriguez, I. (R)	1.25
280	Ryan, N.	.50
366	Thomas, F.	1.50
426	Maddux, G.	.60
450	White, R. (R)	1.00
537	Sanders, R. (R)	.75
565	Lofton, K. (R)	1.50
569	Jones, C. (R)	3.00
587	Lopez, J. (R)	1.00
590	Klesko, R. (R)	1.00
593	Mondesi, R. (R)	1.00

1991 DONRUSS

	NM Price
Complete Set (792)	$8.00
Series 1 Set (1-386)	4.00
Series 2 Set (387-792)	4.00
Factory w/Leaf Previews (796)	12.00
Factory w/Studio Previews (796)	12.00
Commons	.03
Unlisted Stars	**.05 -.40**
Series 1 or 2 Pack (15)	.35
Series 1 or 2 Box (36)	9.00

Quality Rating ★★
The lack of a big rookie card keeps Donruss an affordable option.

#	Player	NM
49	Griffey Jr., K. (AS)	.75
77	Griffey Jr., K.	1.50
89	Ryan, N.	.50
223	Ripken, C.	1.00
371	Gonzalez, J.	.75
374	Maddux, G.	.50
392	Griffey Jr., K. (MVP)	.75
430	Vaughn, M. (RR)	.60
477	Thomas, F.	1.50
BC3	Ryan, N.	.50
BC15	Ryan, N.	.50

Donruss Elite

#		
	Complete Set (8)	500.00
	Commons	25.00
1	Bonds, B.	75.00
2	Brett, G.	120.00
3	Canseco, J.	30.00
8	Williams, M.	60.00
	Ryan Legend	275.00
	Sandberg Autograph	400.00

Grand Slammers

#		
	Complete Set (14)	2.00
	Commons	.10
5	Bonds, B.	.50
11	McGwire, M.	.75

Leaf Previews

#		
	Complete Set (26)	50.00
	Commons	1.50
1	Justice, D.	3.00
2	Sandberg, R.	4.00
3	Larkin, B.	2.00
9	Bonds, B.	6.00
10	Lankford, R.	2.00
11	Gwynn, T.	7.00
12	Clark, W.	2.00
20	Molitor, P.	4.00
21	Puckett, K.	7.00
22	Mattingly, D.	5.00
25	Ryan, N.	15.00

Leaf Studio Previews

#		
	Complete Set (18)	25.00
	Commons	1.50
	Title Card	1.00
2	Clemens, R.	6.00
10	Justice, D.	4.00

1991 DONRUSS ROOKIES

	NM Price
Complete Set (56)	$4.00
Commons	.03
Unlisted Stars	**.05 -.30**

Quality Rating ★
This set features a Bagwell rookie, but the supporting cast is weak.

#	Player	NM
30	Bagwell, J. (R)	3.00
33	Rodriguez, I. (R)	1.25
36	Vaughn, M.	.50

1991 FLEER

	NM Price
Complete Set (720)	$10.00
Retail Set (732)	12.00
Hobby Set (732)	12.00
Commons	.03
Unlisted Stars	**.05 -.30**
Pack (15)	.35
Box (36)	8.00

Quality Rating ★★★
Fleer increases the number of cards in its set, but design problems make more cards less desirable.

#	Player	NM
33	Bonds, B.	.50
138	Thomas, F.	1.50
286	Gonzalez, J.	.75
302	Ryan, N.	.60
426	Maddux, G.	.50
450A	Griffey Jr., K. (err)	1.50
450B	Griffey Jr., K. (cor)	1.50
490	Ripken, C.	1.00
552	Brett, G.	.50
710	Bonds/Griffey (Stars)	.75

Fleer Pro Visions

#		
	Complete Set (12)	3.50
	Commons	.20
1	Puckett, K.	.75
9	Clemens, R.	.75
11	Mattingly, D.	1.00

Fleer Factory Set Pro Visions

#		
	Complete Set (4)	3.00
1	Bonds, B.	1.25
2	Henderson, R.	.50
3	Sandberg, R.	1.25
4	Stewart, D.	.25

Fleer All-Stars

#		
	Complete Set (10)	15.00
	Commons	.35
1	Sandberg, R.	2.50
2	Larkin, B.	1.00
3	Williams, M.	1.25

#		
5	Bonds, B.	2.50
7	Griffey Jr., K.	10.00
10	Clemens, R.	2.50

World Series Set

	Complete Set (8)	1.50
	Commons	.20
3	Canseco, J.	.50

1991 FLEER UPDATE

	NM Price
Complete Set (132)	$5.00
Commons	.03
Unlisted Stars	**.05 -.30**

Quality Rating ★

The names are there, but Fleer Update just can't match the limited run of Ultra Update.

#	Player	NM
7	Vaughn, M.	.75
16	Belle, A.	.75
62	Rodriguez, I. (R)	1.25
87	Bagwell, J. (R)	3.00

1991 FLEER ULTRA

	NM Price
Complete Set (400)	$20.00
Commons	.05
Unlisted Stars	**.10 -.40**
Pack (14)	.60
Box (36)	15.00

Quality Rating ★★★

Lack of inserts and photography may be the reason Ultra doesn't match up with other premium sets from 1991.

#	Player	NM
24	Ripken, C.	2.00
64	Maddux, G.	1.25
66	Sandberg, R.	.75
85	Thomas, F.	5.00
107	Belle, A.	.60
144	Brett, G.	.60
195	Puckett, K.	.50
239	Mattingly, D.	.50
275	Bonds, B.	.60
303	Gwynn, T.	.50
336	Griffey Jr., K.	4.00
355	Ryan, N.	1.50
382	Knoblauch, C.	.75
387	Vaughn, M.	1.00
395	Ryan, N. (EP)	.50

Fleer Ultra Gold

	Complete Set (10)	8.00
	Commons	.30
1	Bonds, B.	1.50
2	Clark, W.	1.00
4	Griffey Jr., K.	5.00
8	Puckett, K.	1.50
10	Sandberg, R.	1.25

1991 FLEER ULTRA UPDATE

	NM Price
Complete Set (120)	$35.00
Commons	.15
Unlisted Stars	**.20 -.45**

Quality Rating ★★★

Gonzalez is just part of this great checklist. Bernie Williams is an undervalued star.

#	Player	NM
4	Mussina, M.	7.00
14	Fernandez, A.	2.00
20	Nagy, C.	1.50
37	Knoblauch, C.	4.00
44	Williams, B.	5.00
55	Gonzalez, J.	20.00
56	Palmer, D.	2.00
58	Rodriguez, I. (R)	10.00
79	Bagwell, J. (R)	15.00
93	Walker, L.	4.00

1991 LEAF

	NM Price
Complete Set (528)	$15.00
Series 1 Set (1-264)	5.00
Series 2 Set (265-528)	10.00
Commons	.05
Unlisted Stars	**.10 -.40**
Series 1 or 2 Pack (15)	1.00
Series 1 or 2 Box (36)	25.00

Quality Rating ★★★

Unlike Leaf's previous issue, this product is widely available.

#	Player	NM
119	Gonzalez, J.	1.00
127	Maddux, G.	1.25
207	Sandberg, R.	.75
208	Puckett, K.	.75
239	Belle, A.	1.00
261	Bonds, B.	.75
281	Thomas, F.	5.00
290	Gwynn, T.	.60
335	Brett, G.	.60
372	Griffey Jr., K.	4.00
396	Knoblauch, C. (R)	.75
423	Ryan, N.	1.50
425	Mattingly, D.	.75
430	Ripken, C.	2.00

Gold Leaf Rookies

	Complete Set (26)	25.00
	Commons	.75
7	Vaughn, M.	7.00
10	Sanders, R.	1.50
12	Mussina, M.	3.00
14	Bagwell, J.	8.00
21	Klesko, R.	4.00
25	Ryan, N.	2.00

1991 LEAF STUDIO

	NM Price
Complete Set (264)	$15.00
Commons	.05
Unlisted Stars	**.10 -.50**
Pack (10)	1.00
Box (48)	25.00

Quality Rating ★★

Leaf had a nice idea, but the black and white photos didn't attract attention.

#	Player	NM
9	Ripken, C.	1.50
20	Vaughn, M.	1.00
40	Thomas, F.	5.00
90	Puckett, K.	.75
97	Mattingly, D.	.75
112	Griffey Jr., K.	4.00
124	Gonzalez, J.	1.00
128	Ryan, N.	1.50
158	Sandberg, R.	.75
172	Bagwell, J. (R)	3.00
222	Bonds, B.	.60
245	Gwynn, T.	.75

1991 OPC PREMIER

	NM Price
Complete Set (132)	10.00
Factory Set (132)	12.00
Commons	.05
Unlisted Stars	**.10 -.50**
Pack (7)	.30
Box (36)	10.00

Quality Rating ★

Player selection is good, but this product can be found everywhere.

#	Player	NM
8	Belle, A.	.60
12	Bonds, B.	.60
54	Gonzalez, J.	.75
56	Griffey Jr., K.	2.00
100	Ripken, C.	1.00
102	Ryan, N.	1.00
121	Thomas, F.	2.00

1991 SCORE

	NM Price
Complete Set (893)	$12.00
Factory Set (900)	15.00
Commons	.03
Unlisted Stars	**.05 -.40**
Pack (16)	.40
Box (36)	10.00

Quality Rating ★

The rookie crop is decent with Mussina and Jones leading the way. Mantle insert set is a hit with collectors.

#	Player	NM
2	Griffey Jr., K.	1.50
4	Ryan, N.	.60
95	Ripken, C.	1.00
317	Maddux, G.	.75
383	Mussina, M. (R, FDP)	1.25
390	White, R. (R, FDP)	.75
396	Griffey Jr., K. (AS)	.75
671	Jones, C. (R, FDP)	3.00
697	Griffey Jr., K. (RF)	1.00
750	Vaughn, M. (RP)	.50
805	Gonzalez, J.	.75
840	Thomas, F.	1.50
841	The Griffeys	1.00
858	Griffey Jr., K. (FRAN)	1.00
874	Thomas, F. (FRAN)	.75
892	Griffey Jr., K. (DT)	1.50

Score Cooperstown

	Complete Set (7)	10.00
1	Boggs, W.	.75
2	Larkin, B.	.75
3	Griffey Jr., K.	6.00
4	Henderson, R.	.75
5	Brett, G.	2.00
6	Clark, W.	.75
7	Ryan, N.	3.00

Score Hot Rookies

	Complete Set (10)	15.00
	Commons	.50
1	Justice, D.	1.50
4	Thomas, F.	10.00
7	Lankford, R.	1.00
9	Gonzalez, J.	4.00

Score Mickey Mantle

	Complete Set (7)	300.00
	Mantle Singles (1-7)	50.00
	Mantle Autograph (1000)	500.00

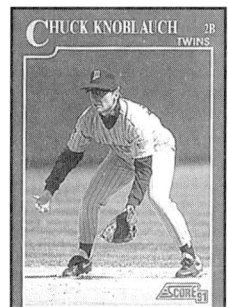

1991 SCORE TRADED

	NM Price
Complete Set (110)	$5.00
Commons	.03
Unlisted Stars	**.05 -.30**

#	Player	NM
82	Rodriguez, I. (R)	1.00
96	Bagwell, J. (R)	3.00

1991 TOPPS

	NM Price
Complete Set (792)	$15.00
Factory Set (792)	18.00
Commons	.03
Unlisted Stars	**.05 -.40**
Pack (15)	.35
Box (36)	9.00

#	Player	NM
1	Ryan, N.	.60
5	Ripken, C. (RB)	.50
35	Maddux, G.	.60
79	Thomas, F.	1.50
150	Ripken, C.	1.00
224	Gonzalez, J.	.75
333	Jones, C. (R, FDP)	3.00
392	Griffey Jr., K. (AS)	.75
790	Griffey Jr., K.	1.50

1991 TOPPS TRADED

	NM Price
Complete Set (132)	$6.00
Factory Set (132)	6.00
Commons	.03
Unlisted Stars	**.05 -.35**

#	Player	NM
4	Bagwell, J. (R)	2.00
45	Giambi, J. (R, USA)	1.00
50	Greene, T. (USA)	1.50
61	Johnson, C. (R, USA)	1.50
101	Rodriguez, I. (R)	1.50
123	Vaughn, M.	.50

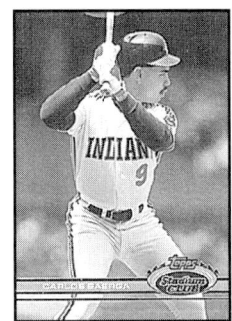

1991 TOPPS STADIUM CLUB

	NM Price
Complete Set (600)	$110.00
Series 1 Set (1-300)	70.00
Series 2 Set (301-600)	40.00
Commons	.20
Unlisted Stars	**.25 -1.00**
Series 1 Pack (13)	3.50
Series 1 Box (36)	90.00
Series 2 Pack (13)	1.75
Series 2 Box (36)	45.00

#	Player	NM
6	Sosa, S.	1.50
21	Mattingly, D.	3.00
57	Thomas, F.	12.00
93	Walker, L.	3.00
95	Sheffield, G.	1.50
110	Puckett, K.	3.00
126	Maddux, G.	6.00
154	Smith, O.	1.50
159	Brett, G.	2.00
200	Ryan, N.	6.00
220	Bonds, B.	2.00
230	Sandberg, R.	2.00
237	Gonzalez, J.	6.00
270	Griffey Jr., K.	10.00
304	Alomar, R.	2.00
308	Gwynn, T.	3.00
349	Hundley, T.	1.50
388	Bagwell, J. (R)	7.00
399	McGwire, M.	3.00
409	Johnson, R.	2.00
430	Ripken, C.	4.00
465	Belle, A.	2.50
537	Lankford, R.	1.50
543	Vaughn, M.	5.00
548	Knoblauch, C.	2.50

1991 TOPPS STADIUM CLUB DOME

	NM Price
Complete Set (200)	$15.00
Commons	.10
Unlisted Stars	**.15 -.45**

#	Player	NM
58	Giambi, J. (USA)	1.00
67	Green, S. (R, DP)	1.00
69	Greene, T. (USA)	1.00
70	Griffey Jr., K. (AS)	2.00
85	Hollandsworth, T. (R)	1.00
91	Johnson, C. (USA)	2.00
146	Ramirez, M. (R, DP)	3.00
154	Ripken, C. (AS)	1.50
162	Sandberg, R. (AS)	.50

1991 UPPER DECK

	NM Price
Complete Set (800)	$25.00
Factory Set (800)	25.00
Low Series Set (1-700)	20.00
High Series Set (701-800)	5.00
Commons	.04
Unlisted Stars	**.05 -.40**
Low or High Pack (15)	.75
Low or High Box (36)	18.00

#	Player	NM
5	Vaughn, M. (SR)	.75
24	Karros, E. (R)	.75
55	Jones, C. (R, TP)	3.50
65	Mussina, M. (R, TP)	1.50
71	Sanders, R. (R, TP)	.75
115	Maddux, G.	.75
154	Bonds, B.	.50
246	Thomas, F.	2.00
345	Ryan, N.	1.00
347	Ripken, C.	1.50
354	Mattingly, D.	.50
525	Brett, G.	.50
555	Griffey Jr., K.	2.00
646	Gonzalez, J.	1.00
702	Bagwell/Gonzalez/Rhodes	.75
755	Bagwell, J. (R)	2.50
764	Belle, A.	.60
HH1	Hank Aaron Hologram	2.00
SP1	Jordan, M.	18.00
SP2	Henderson/Ryan	2.50

Upper Deck Baseball Heroes

	Complete Set (4)	40.00
1	Killebrew, H.	10.00
2	Perry, G.	10.00
3	Jenkins, F.	10.00
4	Header Card	10.00
	Killebrew Autograph	100.00
	Perry Autograph	80.00
	Jenkins Autograph	100.00

Silver Sluggers

	Complete Set (18)	18.00
	Commons	.60
5	Bonds, B.	2.50
8	Sandberg, R.	2.50

Aaron Heroes Set

	Complete Set (10)	6.00
	Aaron Singles (19-27)	.50
	Cover Card (No#)	3.50
	Aaron Autograph (2500)	300.00

Ryan Heroes Set

	Complete Set (10)	6.00
	Ryan Singles (10-18)	.50
	Cover Card (No#)	3.50
	Ryan Autograph (2500)	600.00

1991 UPPER DECK FINAL EDITION

	NM Price
Complete Set (100)	$8.00
Commons	.03
Unlisted Stars	**.05 -.40**

#	Player	NM
2	Martinez, P. (R)	1.50
8	Klesko, R. (R)	1.00
17	Thome, J. (R)	1.50
24	Lofton, K. (R)	2.50
34	Neagle, D. (R)	1.00
55	Rodriguez, I. (R)	1.25
85	Ripken, C. (AS)	.75
87	Griffey Jr., K. (AS)	1.25

1992 BOWMAN

	NM Price
Complete Set (705)	300.00
Commons	.25
Gold Foil Commons	.40
Unlisted Stars	**.30 -1.00**
Pack (15)	9.00
Box (36)	225.00

#	Player	NM
1	Rodriguez, I.	4.00
20	Alomar, R.	2.00
28	Jones, C.	35.00
50	Gwynn, T.	3.00
60	Bonds, B.	2.50
64	Mondesi, R.	8.00
80	Puckett, K.	2.50
82	Martinez, P.	8.00
84	Gonzalez, J.	5.00
100	Griffey Jr., K.	15.00
101	Hundley, T.	1.50
110	Lofton, K.	8.00
114	Thomas, F.	8.00
127	Delgado, C. (R)	8.00
148	Maddux, G.	6.00
151	Estes, S. (R)	4.00
178	Johnson, R.	2.00
200	Bagwell, J.	5.00
222	Ryan, N.	6.00
250	Ochoa, A. (R)	2.00
259	Salmon, T. (R)	7.00
288	Karros, E.	3.00
298	Anderson, G. (R)	3.00
300	Sandberg, R.	2.50
302	Rivera, M. (R)	5.00
311	Sele, A. (R)	2.00
327	Reynolds, S. (R)	3.00
329	Belle, A.	3.00
340	Mattingly, D.	3.00
384	McGwire, M.	3.00
389	Jones, B. (R)	3.00
397	Vaughn, M.	3.00
400	Ripken, C.	8.00
436	White, R.	5.00
452	Lopez, J.	7.00
460	Thome, J.	14.00
461	Piazza, M. (R)	60.00
464	Jordan, B. (R)	4.00

#	Player	NM
500	Brett, G.	2.50
532	Ramirez, M. (R)	20.00
543	Thompson, J. (R)	5.00
549	Klesko, R.	9.00
551	Thomas, F. (Gold)	10.00
590	Bonds, B. (Gold)	3.00
596	Gonzalez, A. (R)	4.00
620	McGwire, M.	4.00
623	Klesko, R. (Gold)	3.00
661	Johnson, C. (Gold)	8.00
676	Ramirez, M. (Gold)	4.00
678	Floyd, C. (R)	3.00
682	Tucker, M. (R, Gold)	4.00
691	Clemens, R.	2.00
696	Hentgen, P.	2.50

1992 DONRUSS

	NM Price
Complete Set (784)	$10.00
Series 1 Set (1-396)	5.00
Series 2 Set (397-784)	5.00
Factory w/Leaf Previews (788)	15.00
Factory w/Updates (788)	15.00
Commons	.03
Unlisted Stars	**.05 -.40**
Series 1 or 2 Pack (15)	.50
Series 1 or 2 Box (36)	15.00

Quality Rating ★★★
Elite Griffey and Thomas cards are always a good choice. Regular set is stale.

#	Player	NM
5	Lofton, K.	1.00
13	Klesko, R. (RR)	.75
22	Ripken, C. (AS)	.75
24	Griffey Jr., K. (AS)	.75
35	Ripken, C.	1.00
154	Ryan, N. (HL)	.60
165	Griffey Jr., K.	1.50
243	Bonds, B.	.50
358	Bagwell, J.	.60
393	Gonzalez, J.	.50
406	Thome, J.	.75
500	Belle, A.	.50
520	Maddux, G.	.75
592	Thomas, F.	1.50
596	Mattingly, D.	.50
707	Ryan, N.	1.00

Donruss Diamond Kings

Complete Set (27)		20.00
Series 1 Set (1-14)		15.00
Series 2 Set (15-27)		5.00
Commons		.50
1	Molitor, P.	2.00
5	Ripken, C.	7.00
8	Thomas, F.	7.00
11	Bagwell, J.	4.00

Donruss Elite

Complete Set (10)		450.00
Commons		15.00
11	Clark, W.	30.00
13	Griffey Jr., K.	150.00
14	Gwynn, T.	65.00
17	Puckett, K.	60.00
18	Thomas, F.	150.00
	Henderson Legend	50.00
	Ripken Autograph	350.00

1992 DONRUSS THE ROOKIES

	NM Price
Complete Set (132)	$6.00
Commons	.03
Unlisted Stars	**.05 -.30**
Pack (12)	1.00
Box (36)	25.00

Quality Rating ★★★
This set is available in wax packs for the first time.

#	Player	NM
83	Mondesi, R.	1.25
98	Ramirez, M.	2.00

Donruss Phenoms

Complete Set (20)		35.00
Foil Set (12)		25.00
Large Set (8)		10.00
Commons		.50
1	Alou, M.	1.00
6	Karros, E.	1.50
8	Lofton, K.	7.00
9	Piazza, M.	20.00
10	Salmon, T.	6.00
15	Klesko, R.	5.00

1992 DONRUSS TRIPLE PLAY

	NM Price
Complete Set (264)	$10.00
Commons	.03
Unlisted Stars	**.05 -.40**
Pack (15)	.40
Box (36)	10.00

Quality Rating ★★
Young collectors like the simple design and affordable price tag.

#	Player	NM
19	Maddux, G.	.75
22	Ryan, N.	1.00
103	Belle, A.	.50
112	Gonzalez, J.	.50
115	Brett, G.	.50
116	Bonds, B.	.50
152	Griffey Jr K.	1.50
159	Mattingly, D.	.50
199	Ripken, C.	1.00
200	Bagwell, J.	.75
206	Thomas, F.	1.50
253	Ripken, C.	.60

Triple Play Gallery

Complete Set (12)		18.00
Foil Set (6)		3.00
Large Set (6)		15.00
Commons (1-6)		.50
Commons (7-12)		1.00
7	Bagwell, J.	3.00
8	Griffey Jr., K.	8.00

#	Player	NM
11	Ripken, C.	6.00
12	Thomas, F.	8.00

1992 DONRUSS UPDATE

	NM Price
Complete Set (22)	$60.00
Commons	1.50
Unlisted Stars	**2.00-3.00**

Quality Rating ★★
Lofton card has fallen off but McGwire, Murray, and Sheffield help make this a desirable set.

#	Player	NM
3	Jordan, B.	8.00
5	Curtis, C.	5.00
6	Lofton, K.	30.00
7	McGwire, M.	15.00
8	Murray, E.	8.00
11	Sheffield, G.	4.00

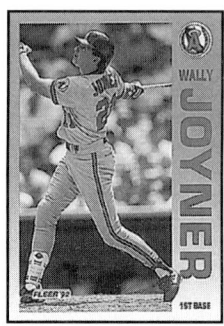

1992 FLEER

	NM Price
Complete Set (720)	$12.00
Factory Set (732)	20.00
Commons	.03
Unlisted Stars	**.05 -.40**
Pack (15)	.75
Box (36)	20.00

Quality Rating ★★
Collectors get six inserts with the regular cards. Look for autographed cards from Roger Clemens.

#	Player	NM
26	Ripken, C.	1.00
100	Thomas, F.	1.50
105	Belle, A.	.50
125	Thome, J.	.75
154	Brett, G.	.50
237	Mattingly, D.	.50
279	Griffey Jr., K.	1.50
304	Gonzalez, J.	.50
320	Ryan, N.	1.00
386	Maddux, G.	.75
425	Bagwell, J.	.60
655	Lofton, K.	.75
682	Ryan, N. (RS)	.50
701	Jones/Thomas	.50
703	Ripken/Carter	.50
709	Griffey Jr., K. (PV)	.75
710	Ryan, N. (PV)	.50
711	Ripken, C. (PV)	.75
712	Thomas, F. (PV)	1.00

Fleer Rookie Sensations

Complete Set (20)		50.00
Commons		1.00
1	Thomas, F.	25.00
4	Bagwell, J.	10.00
10	Knoblauch, C.	4.00
12	Rodriguez, I.	8.00
17	Lankford, R.	2.00

Fleer All-Stars

Complete Set (24)		30.00
Commons		1.00
2	Gwynn, T.	2.50
3	Bonds, B.	2.00
11	Thomas, F.	10.00
14	Sandberg, R.	2.00
20	Ripken, C.	8.00
22	Puckett, K.	2.00
23	Griffey Jr., K.	10.00

Fleer Team Leaders

Complete Set (20)		50.00
Commons		1.00
1	Mattingly, D.	6.00

#	Player	NM
5	Puckett, K.	4.00
7	Gwynn, T.	5.00
15	Griffey Jr., K.	25.00
17	Ripken, C.	20.00

Fleer Lumber Company

Complete Set (9)		12.00
Commons		.75
4	Sandberg, R.	1.50
7	Ripken, C.	8.00
8	Bonds, B.	2.00

Fleer Smoke 'n Heat

Complete Set (12)		12.00
Commons		.50
4	Clemens, R.	1.50
5	Ryan, N.	6.00
11	Johnson, R.	1.50

Fleer Roger Clemens

Complete Set (15)	10.00
Clemens Autograph	150.00

1992 FLEER UPDATE

	NM Price
Complete Set (132)	$130.00
Factory Set (136)	150.00
Commons	.25
Unlisted Stars	**.30 -1.00**

Quality Rating ★★★★
A tough set to find. Lofton, Piazza, and Sosa are just three of the numerous stars included.

#	Player	NM
4	Valentin, J. (R)	3.00
10	Salmon, T.	15.00
17	Lofton, K.	30.00
59	Canseco, J.	3.00
64	Hentgen, P.	6.00
77	Sosa, S.	3.00
92	Piazza, M. (R)	100.00
94	Young, E. (R)	3.00
95	Alou, M.	3.00
104	Kent, J (R)	3.00
112	Schilling, C.	2.50
125	Sheffield, G.	2.00
HL1	Griffey Jr., K.	20.00
HL2	Yount, R.	3.00
HL4	Fielder, C.	2.00

1992 FLEER ULTRA

	NM Price
Complete Set (600)	$30.00
Series 1 Set (1-300)	15.00
Series 2 Set (301-600)	15.00
Commons	.08
Unlisted Stars	**.10 -.75**
Series 1 Pack (14)	1.25
Series 1 Box (36)	40.00
Series 2 Pack (14)	1.00
Series 2 Box (36)	30.00

Quality Rating ★★★
A better card design helps. The usual cast of stars carries the load.

#	Player	NM
11	Ripken, C.	2.00
44	Thomas, F.	3.00
47	Belle, A.	.75
54	Thome, J.	1.50
68	Brett, G.	1.00
97	Puckett, K.	1.00
105	Mattingly, D.	1.00
123	Griffey Jr., K.	3.00
132	Gonzalez, J.	1.00
141	Ryan, N.	2.00
178	Maddux, G.	1.25

#	Player	NM
198	Bagwell, J.	1.25
251	Bonds, B.	.75
350	Lofton, K.	1.50

Fleer Ultra All-Rookie Team

#	Player	NM
	Complete Set (10)	15.00
	Commons	.75
1	Karros, E.	1.50
7	Lofton, K.	10.00

Fleer Ultra All-Stars

#	Player	NM
	Complete Set (20)	20.00
	Commons	.65
3	Ripken, C.	10.00
6	Griffey Jr., K.	10.00
8	Puckett, K.	2.00
9	Thomas, F.	10.00
12	Sandberg, R.	1.50
16	Bonds, B.	2.00

Fleer Ultra Award Winners

#	Player	NM
	Complete Set (25)	35.00
	Commons	.60
2	Knoblauch, C.	1.50
3	Bagwell, J.	8.00
5	Ripken, C.	12.00
6	Clemens, R.	3.00
9	Smith, O.	2.00
11	Bonds, B.	2.00
12	Gwynn, T.	3.00
19	Mattingly, D.	5.00
21A	Ripken, C. (error)	15.00
21B	Ripken, C. (correct)	12.00
22	Griffey Jr., K.	15.00
23	Puckett, K.	4.00
24	Maddux, G.	8.00
25	Sandberg, R.	3.00

Ultra Tony Gwynn

Item	Price
Complete Set (12)	10.00
Gwynn Singles (1-12)	1.00
Gwynn Autograph	150.00

LENNY DYKSTRA CF

1992 LEAF

	NM Price
Complete Set (528)	$12.00
Series 1 Set (1-264)	6.00
Series 2 Set (265-528)	6.00
Commons	.04
Unlisted Stars	**.05 -.40**
Series 1 or 2 Pack (15)	.75
Series 1 or 2 Box (36)	20.00

Quality Rating ★★
After taking the industry by storm in 1990, Leaf increases production and turns collectors toward more limited products.

#	Player	NM
13	Mussina, M.	.50
28	Bagwell, J.	1.00
41	Ryan, N.	1.50
52	Ripken, C.	1.50
57	Mattingly, D.	.60
62	Gonzalez, J.	.75
98	Puckett, K.	.50
206	Gwynn, T.	.75
255	Brett, G.	.50
275	Bonds, B.	.50
294	Maddux, G.	1.25
349	Thomas, F.	2.50
350	Belle, A.	.60
392	Griffey Jr., K.	2.50

Leaf Black Gold

Item	Price
Complete Set (528)	70.00
Series 1 Set (1-264)	35.00
Series 2 Set (265-528)	35.00
Commons	.20
Black Gold Stars	3x

Leaf Gold Rookies

#	Player	NM
	Complete Set (24)	20.00
	Series 1 Set (12)	10.00
	Series 2 Set (12)	10.00
	Commons	.40
3	Martinez, P.	4.50
4	Lofton, K.	6.00
7	Hundley, T.	1.50
16	Mondesi, R.	3.00

Leaf Previews

#	Player	NM
	Complete Set (26)	50.00
	Commons	1.00
2	Sandberg, R.	5.00
4	Bagwell, J.	8.00
13	Ripken, C.	12.00
16	Thomas, F.	15.00
19	Brett, G.	6.00
22	Mattingly, D.	6.00
24	Griffey Jr., K.	15.00
25	Ryan, N.	10.00

ROBERTO ALOMAR PREVIEW
Toronto Blue Jays

1992 LEAF STUDIO

	NM Price
Complete Set (264)	$15.00
Commons	.05
Unlisted Stars	**.10 -.40**
Pack (12)	.75
Box (36)	20.00

Quality Rating ★
This concept was unique in 1991, but collectors like to see action.

#	Player	NM
15	Maddux, G.	1.00
18	Sandberg, R.	.50
31	Bagwell, J.	.60
82	Bonds, B.	.60
104	Gwynn, T.	.50
129	Ripken, C.	2.00
139	Vaughn, M.	.50
159	Thomas, F.	3.00
164	Belle, A.	.60
168	Lofton, K.	.75
181	Brett, G.	.75
216	Mattingly, D.	.50
232	Griffey Jr., K.	3.00
242	Gonzalez, J.	.75
248	Ryan, N.	1.50

Leaf Studio Heritage

#	Player	NM
	Complete Set (14)	25.00
	Foil Set (8)	15.00
	Large Set (6)	10.00
	Commons	1.00
1	Sandberg, R.	3.00
5	Mattingly, D.	4.00
7	Ripken, C.	8.00
12	Bagwell, J.	5.00
14	Puckett, K.	3.00

1992 OPC PREMIER

	NM Price
Complete Set (198)	$10.00
Factory Set (198)	15.00
Commons	.05
Unlisted Stars	**.10 -.50**
Pack (8)	.30
Box (36)	9.00

Quality Rating ★
Same story for Premier as prices are kept down by overprinting.

IVAN RODRIGUEZ CATCHER • RECEIVER RANGERS

#	Player	NM
59	Thomas, F.	1.50
72	Lofton, K.	.75
81	Ryan, N.	1.00
107	Bagwell, J.	.60
137	Ripken, C.	1.50
167	Griffey Jr., K.	1.50

RYNE SANDBERG CUBS

1992 PINNACLE

	NM Price
Complete Set (620)	$40.00
Series 1 Set (1-310)	20.00
Series 2 Set (311-620)	20.00
Commons	.05
Unlisted Stars	**.10 -.50**
Series 1 or 2 Pack (16)	1.00
Series 1 or 2 Box (36)	30.00

Quality Rating ★★★
Score debuts a premium line of cards that includes several rookies.

#	Player	NM
1	Thomas, F.	3.00
20	Puckett, K.	1.00
23	Mattingly, D.	1.00
31	Belle, A.	.75
50	Ryan, N.	2.00
60	Brett, G.	1.00
65	Maddux, G.	1.00
70	Bagwell, J.	1.00
127	Gonzalez, J.	1.00
200	Ripken, C.	1.50
205	Vaughn, M.	.60
247	Thome, J.	1.00
283	Griffey/Henderson (Idols)	.75
290	Lofton, K.	.75
294	Ryan, N. (SL)	1.00
295	Ramirez, M. (R)	4.00
400	Gwynn, T.	.75
500	Bonds, B.	.75
548	Jones, B. (R, DP)	.75
549	Griffey Jr., K.	3.00
582	Lofton, K.	2.00
618	Ryan, N. (TECH)	1.25

Pinnacle Team 2000

#	Player	NM
	Complete Set (80)	35.00
	Series 1 Set (40)	20.00
	Series 2 Set (40)	15.00
	Commons	.10
	Unlisted Stars	.20 -.40
3	Thomas, F.	5.00
10	Bagwell, J.	1.50
18	Belle, A.	1.25
26	Gonzalez, J.	1.50
32	Maddux, G.	2.50
35	Lofton, K.	2.00
37	Thome, J.	1.50
47	Griffey Jr., K.	5.00
54	Vaughn, M.	1.50

Rookie Idols

#	Player	NM
	Complete Set (18)	120.00
	Commons	4.00
1	Sanders/Davis	6.00
3	Cooper/Brett	15.00
4	Wohlers/Clemens	10.00
7	Lofton/Henderson	20.00
11	Zosky/Ripken	30.00
12	Van Poppel/Ryan	25.00
13	Thome/Sandberg	15.00
15	Clayton/Smith	10.00
18	Bell/Winfield	8.00

Pinnacle Slugfest

#	Player	NM
	Complete Set (15)	40.00
	Commons	1.00
2	McGwire, M.	3.00
4	Bonds, B.	2.00
7	Griffey Jr., K.	10.00
9	Sandberg, R.	2.00
11	Thomas, F.	10.00
13	Puckett, K.	2.00
14	Ripken, C.	8.00
15	Bagwell, J.	4.00

Team Pinnacle

#	Player	NM
	Complete Set (12)	90.00
	Commons	5.00
1	Clemens/Martinez	10.00
3	Rodriguez/Santiago	7.00
4	Thomas/Clark	25.00
5	Alomar/Sandberg	10.00
6	Ventura/Williams	8.00
7	Ripken/Larkin	25.00
8	Tartabull/Bonds	8.00
9	Griffey/Butler	25.00

Pinnacle Rookies

#	Player	NM
	Complete Set (30)	8.00
	Commons	.20
3	Lofton, K.	3.00
22	Sanders, R.	1.00
24	Karros, E.	1.00

DAVE JUSTICE BRAVES RIGHT FIELD

1992 SCORE

	NM Price
Complete Set (893)	$16.00
Factory Set (910)	20.00
Series 1 Set (1-442)	8.00
Series 2 Set (443-893)	8.00
Commons	.03
Unlisted Stars	**.05 -.40**
Series 1 or 2 Pack (16)	.40
Series 1 or 2 Box (36)	10.00

Quality Rating ★
An 800-plus card set by Score is bettered by DiMaggio inserts.

#	Player	NM
1	Griffey Jr., K.	1.50
2	Ryan, N.	1.00
11	Gonzalez, J.	.60
23	Mattingly, D.	.50
269	Maddux, G.	.60
425	Ryan, N. (NHC)	.60
433	Ripken, C. (AS)	.75
436	Griffey Jr., K. (AS)	1.00
505	Thomas, F.	1.50
540	Ripken, C.	1.00
576	Bagwell, J.	.60
650	Brett, G.	.75
788	Ripken, C. (MVP)	.75
794	Ripken, C. (MOY)	.75
800	Ramirez, M. (R)	1.50
845	Lofton, K.	.75
884	Ripken, C. (DT)	1.50
893	Thomas, F. (DT)	1.50
	Knoblauch Autograph	50.00

Score Factory Set Specials

	Complete Set (17)	8.00
	Commons	.25
5	Game 5 (Justice)	1.50
6	Game 6 (Puckett)	3.00
9	Smith, O. (COOP)	2.00
10	Winfield, D. (COOP)	1.00
11	Yount, R. (COOP)	1.50
12	DiMaggio, J.	2.00
13	DiMaggio, J.	2.00
14	DiMaggio, J.	2.00

Score Hot Rookies

	Complete Set (10)	10.00
	Commons	.30
3	Lofton, K.	8.00
7	Martinez, T.	4.00

Score Franchise

	Complete Set (4)	35.00
1	Musial, S.	6.00
2	Mantle, M.	15.00
3	Yastrzemski	6.00
4	Franchise Players	10.00
	Mantle Autograph	500.00
	Musial Autograph	250.00
	Yastremski Autograph	175.00
	Mantle/Musial/Yaz Autograph	1300.00

Score Impact Players

	Complete Set (90)	20.00
	Series 1 Set (45)	12.00
	Series 2 Set (45)	8.00
	Commons	.07
	Unlisted Stars	.10-.30
2	Bagwell, J.	1.25
21	Vaughn, M.	.75
27	Gonzalez, J.	1.00
28	Griffey Jr., K.	4.00
32	Lofton, K.	1.00
43	Thomas, F.	4.00
55	Bonds, B.	.60
77	Maddux, G.	2.00

Score Joe DiMaggio

	Complete Set (5)	175.00
	DiMaggio Singles (1-5)	35.00
	DiMaggio Autograph (1000)	550.00

1992 SCORE TRADED

	NM Price
Complete Set (110)	$20.00
Commons	.20
Unlisted Stars	**.25 -.75**

Quality Rating ★★★
Lofton is the top card in this set.

#	Player	NM
14	Lofton, K.	8.00
83	Jordan, B. (R)	2.00
93	Salmon, T.	5.00

1992 TOPPS

	NM Price
Complete Set (792)	$20.00
Factory w/Gold Cards(802)	25.00
Holiday Set (811)	30.00
Commons	.03
Unlisted Stars	**.05 -.40**
Pack (14)	.50
Box (36)	14.00

Quality Rating ★★★
White card stock helps, but Topps' regular issue is up against the ever-popular premium cards.

#	Player	NM
1	Ryan, N.	1.00

27	Gonzalez, J.	.75
40	Ripken, C.	1.50
50	Griffey, Jr., K.	1.50
69	Lofton, K.	.75
156	Ramirez, M. (R)	2.00
300	Mattingly, D.	.50
400	Ripken, C. (AS)	.50
520	Bagwell, J.	.60
551	Jones/Cordero/Arias	2.00
555	Thomas, F.	1.50
580	Maddux, G.	.75

Topps Gold

	Complete Set (792)	175.00
	Factory Set (793)	200.00
	Commons	.45
	Gold Stars	8x-15x
	Gold Rookies	5x-10x
	Taylor Autograph	20.00

Topps Gold Winners

	Complete Set (792)	60.00
	Commons	.20
	Veteran Winners	3x-6x
	Rookie Winners	2x-4x

1992 TOPPS TRADED

	NM Price
Complete Set (132)	$35.00
Commons	.05
Unlisted Stars	**.10 -.30**

Quality Rating ★★★
Garciaparra card has this set on collectors' hot lists. Charles Johnson is also included.

#	Player	NM
39	Garciaparra (R, USA)	30.00
40	Giambi, J. (USA)	.75
56	Johnson, C. (USA)	2.00
66	Lofton, K.	1.00
119	Tucker, M. (R, USA)	.75
123	Varitek, J. (R, USA)	.75

Topps Traded Gold

	Complete Set (132)	40.00
	Commons	.20
	Gold Stars	2x

1992 TOPPS STADIUM CLUB

	NM Price
Complete Set (900)	$60.00
Series 1 Set (1-300)	20.00
Series 2 Set (301-600)	20.00
Series 3 Set (601-900)	20.00
Commons	.08
Unlisted Stars	**.10 -.50**
Series 1,2,3 Pack (15)	1.00
Series 1,2,3 Box (36)	28.00

Quality Rating ★★
Stadium Club's second effort has all the big names and several young stars.

#	Player	NM
1	Ripken, C.	2.00
150	Brett, G.	1.00
220	Belle, A.	1.00
240	Gonzalez, J.	1.00
301	Thomas, F.	3.00
325	Vaughn, M.	.75
330	Bagwell, J.	1.00
360	Thome, J.	.75
400	Griffey Jr., K.	3.00
420	Mattingly, D.	1.00
500	Puckett, K.	.75
591	Thomas, F. (MC)	1.50
595	Ripken, C. (MC)	1.50
603	Griffey Jr., K. (MC)	1.50
605	Ryan, N. (MC)	1.50
620	Bonds, B.	.75
665	Maddux, G.	1.50
695	Lofton, K.	1.00
770	Ryan, N.	2.00
825	Gwynn, T.	.75
SP1	Jones, C.	15.00
SP3	Nevin, P.	1.00

1992 TOPPS STADIUM CLUB SPECIAL

	NM Price
Complete Set (200)	$20.00
Factory Set (212)	25.00
Commons	.08
Unlisted Stars	**.10 -.50**

Quality Rating ★★★
Collectors see a different side of players as many are shown in their college uniforms or street clothes.

#	Player	NM
3	Gwynn, T. (AS)	1.00
12	Clyburn, D. (R)	1.50
28	Puckett, K. (AS)	1.00
44	Sandberg, R. (AS)	1.00
56	Griffey Jr., K. (AS)	3.00
93	Garciaparra, N. (USA)	12.00
117	Jeter, D. (R)	6.00
126	Maddux, G. (AS)	2.50
141	Ripken, C. (AS)	2.50
143	Beamon, T. (R)	1.50
148	Kendall, J. (R)	1.50
161	Bonds, B. (AS)	.75

1992 UPPER DECK

	NM Price
Complete Set (800)	$18.00
Factory Set (800)	25.00
Low Series Set (1-700)	15.00
High Series Set (701-800)	3.00
Commons	.03
Unlisted Stars	**.05 -.40**
Low or Hi Pack (15)	.75
Low or Hi Box (36)	20.00

Quality Rating ★★★
Upper Deck continues to offer great photos and decent player selection. Manny Ramirez and Joey Hamilton highlight a weak crop of rookies. This is the beginning of the insert craze.

#	Player	NM
1	Klesko/Thome (CL)	.50
5	Thome, J.	.75
24	Klesko, R. (SR)	.75
25	Lofton, K. (SR)	1.00
63	Ramirez, M. (R, TP)	2.00
67	Hamilton, J. (R)	.75
82	Ripken Brothers	.60
85	Griffey Family (BL)	.75
87	Thomas, F. (CL)	.75
165	Ripken, C.	1.25
166	Thomas, F.	1.50
243	Gonzalez, J.	.75
276	Bagwell, J.	.60
353	Maddux, G.	.75
424	Griffey Jr., K.	1.50
645	Ripken, C. (DS)	.75
650	Griffey Jr., K. (DS)	.75
655	Ryan, N.	1.00
766	Lofton, K.	1.00
HH2	Ted Williams Hologram	2.00
SP3	Sanders, D.	2.00
SP4	Selleck/Thomas	5.00

Upper Deck Baseball Heroes

	Complete Set (4)	15.00
5	Blue, V.	5.00
6	Brock, L.	6.00
7	Fingers, R.	6.00
8	Header Card	6.00
	Blue Autograph	30.00
	Brock Autograph	70.00
	Fingers Autograph	50.00

Home Run Heroes

	Complete Set (26)	15.00
	Commons	.35
4	Ripken, C.	3.00
8	Thomas, F.	4.00
13	Belle, A.	1.25
19	Gonzalez, J.	1.50
21	Bonds, B.	1.25
25	Bagwell, J.	1.50

Upper Deck Scouting Report

	Complete Set (25)	15.00
	Commons	.35
12	Karros, E.	1.50
15	Lofton, K.	5.00
20	Sanders, R.	1.00
22	Thome, J.	5.00

U.D. Ted Williams Best

	Complete Set (20)	20.00
	Commons	.65
2	Bonds, B.	1.25
6	Gwynn, T.	1.25
9	Puckett, K.	2.00
12	Bagwell, J.	2.00
13	Belle, A.	1.25
14	Gonzalez, J.	2.00
15	Griffey Jr., K.	8.00
19	Thomas, F.	8.00

Williams Heroes Set

	Complete Set (10)	8.00
	Williams Singles (28-36)	.50
	Cover Card (No#)	5.00
	Williams Autograph (2500)	450.00

Bench/Morgan Heroes Set

	Complete Set (10)	14.00
	Bench/Morgan Singles (37-45)	1.00
	Cover Card (No#)	6.00
	Bench/Morgan Autograph	225.00

1993 BOWMAN

	NM Price
Complete Set (708)	$70.00
Commons	.10
Unlisted Stars	**.15 -1.00**
Common Foil	.25
Pack (15)	2.00
Box (24)	40.00

Quality Rating ★★★
The name carries weight because of the 1992 set. Could be a sleeper. Rookies of Pettitte and Jeter are the key cards.

#	Player	NM
12	Hunter, B. (R)	2.50
86	Jones, C.	3.50
103	Pettitte, A. (R)	7.00
140	Bonds, B.	1.25
162	Kendall, J. (R)	2.00
200	Sandberg, R.	1.25
225	Ripken, C.	3.00
265	Brett, G.	1.50
325	Puckett, K.	1.50
345	Cordova, M. (R, Foil)	3.00
347	Jones, C. (Foil)	3.50
353	Mondesi, R. (Foil)	1.00
365	Ramirez, M. (Foil)	2.00
375	Griffey Jr., K.	4.00
405	Ryan, N.	3.00
417	Lofton, K.	1.25
420	Bagwell, J.	1.25
445	Belle, A.	1.25
511	Jeter, D. (R)	8.00
542	Clyburn, D. (R)	1.50
550	Maddux, G.	2.50
555	Thomas, F.	3.00
595	Mattingly, D.	1.50
618	Mondesi, R.	2.00
630	Gwynn, T.	1.50
646	Piazza, M.	3.00
669	Ramirez, M.	1.25
703	Griffeys (Jr/Sr)	1.25

1993 DONRUSS

	NM Price
Complete Set (792)	$30.00
Series 1 Set (1-396)	15.00
Series 2 Set (397-792)	15.00
Commons	.03
Unlisted Stars	**.05 -.40**
Series 1 or 2 Pack (14)	.75
Series 1 or 2 Box (36)	24.00

Quality Rating ★★★
This set offers reasonably priced cards of all of the game's stars.

#	Player	NM
7	Thomas, F.	2.00
126	Gwynn, T.	.50

209	Piazza, M. (RR)	1.50
344	Sandberg, R.	.50
423	Ryan, N.	2.00
428	Bagwell, J.	.60
435	Belle, A.	.50
537	Lofton, K.	.50
553	Griffey Jr., K.	2.00
555	Gonzalez, J.	.60
559	Ripken, C.	2.00
607	Puckett, K.	.50
608	Maddux, G.	1.50
609	Mattingly, D.	.50
678	Bonds, B.	.50
721	Jones, C. (RR)	2.00

Donruss Diamond Kings
Complete Set (31)		35.00
Series 1 Set (1-15)		20.00
Series 2 Set (16-31)		15.00
Commons		.75
1	Griffey Jr., K.	10.00
2	Sandberg, R.	2.00
3	Clemens, R.	3.00
4	Puckett, K.	3.00
7	Gonzalez, J.	3.00
18	McGwire, M.	3.00
20	Alomar, R.	2.00
25	Murray, E.	2.00

Donruss Elite
Complete Set (18)		400.00
Commons		12.00
	Yount Legend	30.00
20	Sandberg, R.	40.00
21	Murray, E.	30.00
22	Molitor, P.	25.00
24	Mattingly, D.	65.00
26	Alomar, R.	30.00
31	Bonds, B.	40.00
33	McGwire, M.	40.00
36	Gonzalez, J.	45.00
	Clark Autograph	150.00

Donruss Elite Dominators
Complete Set (20)		1000.00
Commons		50.00
1	Sandberg, R.	70.00
3	Maddux, G.	125.00
6	Mattingly, D.	100.00
8	Piazza, M.	100.00
10	Ryan, N.	150.00
11	Gonzalez, J.	75.00
12	Griffey Jr., K.	150.00
13	Thomas, F.	150.00
15	Brett, G.	110.00
16	Bonds, B.	65.00
17	Belle, A.	65.00
19	Ripken, C.	150.00
	Ryan Autograph	300.00
	Molitor Autograph	75.00
	Mattingly Autograph	200.00
	Gonzalez Autograph	200.00

Long Ball Leaders
Complete Set (18)		80.00
Series 1 Set (9)		40.00
Series 2 Set (9)		40.00
Commons		2.00
3	Belle, A.	5.00
4	McGwire, M.	8.00
9	Griffey Jr., K.	20.00
10	Thomas, F.	20.00
14	Gonzalez, J.	8.00
15	Sandberg, R.	6.00
17	Bagwell, J.	8.00

Donruss MVP's
Complete Set (26)		35.00
Series 1 Set (13)		10.00
Series 2 Set (13)		25.00
Commons		.50
2	Thomas, F.	9.00
3	Brett, G.	3.00
5	Mattingly, D.	3.00
6	Alomar, R.	2.00
14	Ripken, C.	9.00
15	Clemens, R.	3.00
18	Puckett, K.	3.00
19	McGwire, M.	3.00
20	Griffey Jr., K.	9.00
21	Gonzalez, J.	3.00
22	Sandberg, R.	3.00
24	Bagwell, J.	3.00
25	Bonds, B.	3.00

Donruss Spirit of the Game
Complete Set (20)		25.00
Series 1 Set (10)		10.00
Series 2 Set (10)		15.00

3	Alomar, R.	3.00
5	Gonzalez/Canseco	2.00
6	Bell/Thomas	3.00
11	Lofton, K.	3.00
14	Sandberg, R.	3.00
18	Thomas, F.	10.00

1993 DONRUSS TRIPLE PLAY

	NM Price
Complete Set (264)	$12.00
Commons	.05
Unlisted Stars	**.10 -.40**
Pack (12)	.50
Box (36)	14.00

Quality Rating ★★
Nickname inserts have been popular with stars like Thomas and Griffey getting a lot of attention.

#	Player	NM
1	Griffey Jr., K.	1.50
3	Ripken, C.	1.50
10	Sandberg, R.	.50
26	Thomas, F.	1.50
32	Clinton, B.	1.00
43	Bagwell, J.	.75
51	Gwynn, T.	.50
55	Piazza, M.	1.25
77	Thomas, F. (LH)	1.00
94	Belle, A.	.50
96	Ryan, N.	1.50
120	Mattingly, D.	.75
122	Smith, O.	.50
181	Lofton, K.	.50
214	Brett, G.	.50
221	Gonzalez, J.	.50
260	Puckett, K.	.60

Triple Play Action
Complete Set (30)		8.00
Commons		.20
4	Sandberg, R.	.60
12	Bagwell, J.	.75
17	Ripken, C.	1.50
19	Mattingly, D.	.75
20	Puckett, K.	.75
21	Thomas, F.	1.50
22	Gonzalez, J.	.75
24	Griffey Jr., K.	1.50

Triple Play Gallery of Stars
Complete Set (10)		32.00
Commons		1.50
1	Bonds, B.	5.00
4	Maddux, G.	18.00

Triple Play League Leaders
Complete Set (6)		30.00
1	Bonds/Eckersley (MVP)	7.00
2	Maddux/Eckersley (CY)	15.00
3	Karros/Listach (ROY)	1.50
4	McGriff/Gonzalez (HR)	10.00
5	Daulton/Fielder (RBI)	1.50
6	Martinez/Sheffield (Average)	2.00

Triple Play Nicknames
Complete Set (10)		32.00
Commons		1.00
1	Thomas, F. (Big Hurt)	10.00
2	Clemens, R. (Rocket)	4.00
3	Sandberg, R. (Ryno)	3.00
5	Griffey Jr., K. (Kid)	10.00
7	Ryan, N. (Express)	10.00

1993 FLEER

	NM Price
Complete Set (720)	$40.00
Series 1 Set (1-360)	20.00
Series 2 Set (361-720)	20.00
Commons	.03
Unlisted Stars	**.05 -.40**
Series 1 or 2 Pack (15)	1.00
Series 1 or 2 Box (36)	26.00

Quality Rating ★★★
Insert collectors love this set. Team Leader cards have leveled off.

#	Player	NM
6	Klesko, R.	.60
25	Sandberg, R.	.60
46	Bagwell, J.	.75
112	Bonds, B.	.50
138	Gwynn, T.	.75
210	Thomas, F.	1.50
218	Lofton, K.	.50
236	Brett, G.	.75
273	Puckett, K.	.60
281	Mattingly, D.	.75
307	Griffey Jr., K.	1.50
322	Gonzalez, J.	.75
380	Maddux, G.	1.00
551	Ripken, C.	1.50
590	Belle, A.	.60
690	Ryan, N.	1.50
707	Maddux, G. (LL)	.75
714	Fielder/Thomas (Power)	.50

Fleer Golden Moments I
Complete Set (3)		4.00
1	Brett, G.	4.00
2	Morandini, M.	.50
3	Winfield, D.	1.00

Fleer Golden Moments II
Complete Set (3)		6.00
1	Eckersley, D.	.75
2	Roberts, B.	.50
3	Thomas/Gonzalez	6.00

Fleer Pro Visions I
Complete Set (3)		4.00
1	Alomar, R.	3.00
2	Eckersley, D.	.75
3	Sheffield, G.	1.25

Fleer Pro Visions II
Complete Set (3)		2.00
1	Van Slyke, A.	.50
2	Glavine, T.	1.25
3	Fielder, C.	1.00

Fleer NL All-Stars
Complete Set (12)		15.00
Commons		.75
7	Bonds, B.	3.00
10	Maddux, G.	10.00

Fleer AL All-Stars
Complete Set (12)		30.00
Commons		.75
1	Thomas, F.	10.00
2	Alomar, R.	1.00
6	Gonzalez, J.	5.00
7	Griffey Jr., K.	10.00
9	Puckett, K.	3.00

Fleer Prospects I
Complete Set (18)		25.00
Commons		.75
7	Snow, J.T.	4.00
13	Piazza, M.	20.00

Fleer Prospects II

#	Player	NM
	Complete Set (18)	15.00
	Commons	.75
4	Martinez, P.	3.50
15	Lopez, J.	2.50

Fleer Rookie Sensation I

#	Player	NM
	Complete Set (10)	20.00
	Commons	1.00
1	Lofton, K.	10.00
6	Karros, E.	3.00

Fleer Rookie Sensation II

#	Player	NM
	Complete Set (10)	10.00
	Commons	1.00
1	Alou, M.	2.50

Fleer AL Team Leaders

#	Player	NM
	Complete Set (10)	50.00
	Commons	1.50
1	Puckett, K.	4.00
2	McGwire, M.	7.00
4	Clemens, R.	6.00
5	Thomas, F.	20.00
8	Gonzalez, J.	7.00
9	Alomar, R.	3.00
10	Griffey Jr., K.	20.00

Fleer NL Team Leaders

#	Player	NM
	Complete Set (10)	30.00
	Commons	1.50
6	Sandberg, R.	5.00
9	Bagwell, J.	8.00

Fleer Tom Glavine

		NM
	Complete Set (15)	10.00
	Glavine Singles (1-15)	.75
	Glavine Autograph	75.00

1993 FLEER FINAL EDITION

	NM Price
Complete Set (300)	$8.00
Factory Set (310)	12.00
Commons	.05
Unlisted Stars	**.10-.40**

Quality Rating ★★★
Easy to find at a reasonable price. Offers decent player selection.

#	Player	NM
3	Maddux, G.	2.00
82	Mondesi, R.	1.25
150	Bonds, B.	.75
181	Edmonds, J. (R)	1.50
204	Ramirez, M.	1.25

Diamond Tribute

#	Player	NM
	Complete Set (10)	5.00
	Commons	.25
2	Brett, G.	1.50
5	Molitor, P.	.75
6	Ryan, N.	3.00
8	Smith, O.	1.00

1993 FLEER FLAIR

	NM Price
Complete Set (300)	$60.00
Commons	.30
Unlisted Stars	**.35-1.00**
Pack (10)	2.50
Box (24)	50.00

Quality Rating ★★★
Most collectors seem to like the thicker card stock. Photos are clear and stars can be found at a fraction of the cost of Finest.

#	Player	NM
7	Maddux, G.	5.00
20	Sandberg, R.	3.00
57	Bagwell, J.	3.00
75	Piazza, M.	7.00
128	Smith, O.	1.50
133	Gwynn, T.	3.00
138	Bonds, B.	2.00
157	Ripken, C.	7.00
160	Clemens, R.	3.00
177	Salmon, T.	2.00
189	Thomas, F.	8.00
192	Belle, A.	2.00
195	Lofton, K.	2.00
213	Brett, G.	3.00
242	Puckett, K.	2.50
249	Mattingly, D.	3.00
261	McGwire, M.	3.00
270	Griffey Jr., K.	8.00
280	Gonzalez, J.	4.00
286	Ryan, N.	7.00

Fleer Wave of the Future

#	Player	NM
	Complete Set (20)	50.00
	Commons	1.50
4	Edmonds, J.	8.00
12	Piazza, M.	15.00
13	Ramirez, M.	8.00
15	Salmon, T.	5.00

1993 FLEER ULTRA

	NM Price
Complete Set (650)	$40.00
Series 1 Set (1-300)	20.00
Series 2 Set (301-650)	20.00
Commons	.08
Unlisted Stars	**.10 -.40**
Series 1 or 2 Pack (14)	1.50
Series 1 or 2 Box (36)	45.00

Quality Rating ★★★★
Ultra has the quality to keep collectors interested.

#	Player	NM
60	Piazza, M.	2.50
113	Smith, O.	.50
181	Thomas, F.	3.00
206	Brett, G.	.75
236	Puckett, K.	.75
244	Mattingly, D.	1.00
279	Gonzalez, J.	1.00
307	Maddux, G.	1.50
320	Sandberg, R.	1.00
390	Bagwell, J.	1.00
402	Mondesi, R.	.60
472	Gwynn, T.	1.00
483	Bonds, B.	1.00
501	Ripken, C.	2.00
519	Edmonds, J. (R)	1.50
525	Snow, J.T. (R)	1.00
538	Belle, A.	.75
542	Lofton, K.	1.00
545	Ramirez, M.	1.00
619	Griffey Jr., K.	3.00
636	Ryan, N.	2.00

Ultra Award Winners

#	Player	NM
	Complete Set (25)	45.00
	Commons	.75
1	Maddux, G.	10.00
6	Smith, O.	3.00
7	Bonds, B.	4.00
12	Mattingly, D.	6.00
13	Alomar, R.	2.50
15	Ripken, C.	12.00
16	Griffey Jr., K.	15.00
17	Puckett, K.	5.00
22	Maddux, G.	10.00
24	Bonds, B.	4.00

Ultra Home Run Kings

#	Player	NM
	Complete Set (10)	25.00
	Commons	1.00
1	Gonzalez, J.	5.00
5	Belle, A.	4.00
6	Bonds, B.	4.00

Ultra All-Rookies

#	Player	NM
	Complete Set (10)	18.00
	Commons	.75
7	Piazza, M.	12.00
8	Salmon, T.	4.00
9	Snow, J. T.	3.00

Ultra All-Stars

#	Player	NM
	Complete Set (20)	40.00
	Commons	.75
2	Clark, W.	2.00
3	Sandberg, R.	4.00
6	Bonds, B.	4.00
9	Maddux, G.	8.00
14	Ripken, C.	12.00
16	Gonzalez, J.	5.00
17	Griffey Jr., K.	15.00
18	Puckett, K.	5.00
19	Thomas, F.	15.00
20	Mussina, M.	2.00

Ultra Strikeout Kings

#	Player	NM
	Complete Set (5)	20.00
	Commons	1.00
1	Clemens, R.	4.50
3	Johnson, R.	3.50
4	Ryan, N.	15.00

Ultra Performers

#	Player	NM
	Complete Set (10)	20.00
	Commons	1.00
1	Bonds, B.	2.00
2	Gonzalez, J.	3.00
3	Griffey Jr., K.	7.00
6	Maddux, G.	4.00
10	Thomas, F.	7.00

Ultra Dennis Eckersley

		NM
	Complete Set (10)	5.00
	Eckersley Singles (1-10)	.50
	Eckersly Autograph	55.00

1993 LEAF

	NM Price
Complete Set (550)	$45.00
Series 1 Set (1-220)	20.00
Series 2 Set (221-440)	20.00
Update Set (441-550)	5.00
Commons (1-440)	.10
Commons (441-550)	.15
Unlisted Stars	**.20-.40**
Series 1 or 2 Pack (14)	1.00
Series 1 or 2 Box (36)	30.00
Update Pack (14)	1.50
Update Box (36)	40.00

Quality Rating ★★★★
Wax prices have fallen but this issue is still popular among collectors because of the Thomas inserts.

#	Player	NM
18	Belle, A.	1.00
28	Gwynn, T.	1.25
35	Piazza, M.	2.00
40	Lofton, K.	.75
115	Ryan, N.	2.00
125	Bagwell, J.	1.00
146	Brett, G.	1.25
170	Gonzalez, J.	1.00
195	Thomas, F.	3.00
224	Sandberg, R.	.75
237	Mattingly, D.	1.00
269	Bonds, B.	.75
279	Clemens, R.	1.00
319	Griffey Jr., K.	3.00
323	McGwire, M.	1.25
326	Maddux, G.	2.00
328	Smith, O.	.50
378	Puckett, K.	1.25
431	Ripken, C.	2.50
473	Mondesi, R.	.50
500	Snow, J.T. (R)	.75
DW	Winfield (3000 Hits)	2.00
	Thomas Autograph	250.00

Leaf Gold Rookies

#	Player	NM
	Complete Set (20)	45.00
	Series 1 Set (10)	20.00
	Series 2 Set (10)	25.00
	Commons	1.50
10	Salmon, T.	10.00
17	Snow, J.T.	4.00
19	Jones, C.	25.00

Leaf Heading for the Hall

#	Player	NM
	Complete Set (10)	35.00
	Series 1 Set (5)	20.00
	Series 2 Set (5)	15.00
1	Ryan, N.	15.00
2	Gwynn, T.	5.00
3	Yount, R.	2.00
4	Murray, E.	3.00
5	Ripken, C.	12.00
6	Clemens, R.	5.00
7	Brett, G.	5.00
8	Sandberg, R.	4.00
9	Puckett, K.	4.00
10	Smith, O.	4.00

Leaf Gold All-Stars

#	Player	NM
	Complete Set (20)	38.00
	Series 1 Set (10)	18.00
	Series 2 Set (10)	20.00
	Commons	.75
2	McGriff/Mattingly	2.00
3	Fielder/Bagwell	3.00
4	Baerga/Sandberg	1.50
7	Griffey/Van Slyke	6.00
8	Carter/Justice	1.50
9	Canseco/Gwynn	2.00
11	McGwire/Clark	2.00
12	Thomas/Grace	6.00
14	Ripken/Larkin	6.00
16	Gonzalez/Bonds	5.00
17	Puckett/Grissom	2.00
19	Ryan/Maddux	8.00

Leaf Fasttrack

#	Player	NM
	Complete Set (20)	100.00
	Series 1 Set (10)	60.00
	Series 2 Set (10)	40.00
	Commons	2.00
1	Thomas, F.	35.00
3	Lofton, K.	10.00
4	Mussina, M.	5.00
5	Gonzalez, J.	15.00
17	Bagwell, J.	15.00

Leaf Frank Thomas

		NM
	Complete Set (10)	45.00
	Thomas Singles	5.00

Leaf Update Gold All-Stars

#	Player	NM
	Complete Set (10)	12.00
	Commons	.75
4	Alomar/Sandberg	3.00
6	Ripken/Larkin	5.00
7	Bonds/Puckett	3.00
8	Griffey/Grissom	5.00

Leaf Update Gold Rookies

#	Player	NM
	Complete Set (5)	15.00
	Commons	.75
2	Hammonds, J.	1.00
4	Piazza, M.	15.00

Leaf Update Frank Thomas

		NM
	Complete Set (10)	70.00
	Thomas Singles	7.00

1993 LEAF STUDIO

	NM Price
Complete Set (220)	$15.00
Commons	.05
Unlisted Stars	**.10 -.40**
Pack (12)	1.00
Box (36)	25.00

Quality Rating ★★★
Another set with great pictures. Aside from that, this issue is doing very little with collectors.

#	Player	NM
12	Bonds, B.	.60
25	Brett, G.	1.00
34	Bagwell, J.	.60
71	Ryan, N.	2.00
80	Ripken, C.	2.00
95	Belle, A.	.75
96	Griffey Jr., K.	3.00
100	Gwynn, T.	.75
139	Thomas, F.	3.00
160	Gonzalez, J.	.75
176	Sandberg, R.	.60
180	Lofton, K.	.60
193	Mattingly, D.	1.00
196	Maddux, G.	2.00
201	Piazza, M.	2.50
214	Puckett, K.	1.00
217	Smith, O.	.50

Studio On Canvas

Complete Set (10)		30.00
Commons		1.00
1	Griffey Jr., K.	15.00
4	Mussina, M.	2.00
6	Thomas, F.	15.00
10	Bonds, B.	5.00

Studio Silhouettes

Complete Set (10)		25.00
Commons		.75
1	Thomas, F.	10.00
2	Bonds, B.	3.00
3	Bagwell, J.	3.50
4	Gonzalez, J.	4.00
9	Piazza, M.	5.00
10	Ryan, N.	8.00

Studio Heritage

Complete Set (12)		25.00
Commons		1.00
1	Brett, G.	6.00
2	Gonzalez, J.	4.00
6	Smith, O.	3.00
8	Thomas, F.	15.00

Studio Frank Thomas

Complete Set (5)	28.00
Thomas Singles	6.00

1993 OPC

	NM Price
Complete Set (396)	$30.00
Commons	.10
Unlisted Stars	**.15 -.50**
Pack (9)	1.00
Box (36)	25.00

Quality Rating ★★★
Decent design and player selection helps, but this set has faded.

#	Player	NM
29	Bagwell, J.	1.00
46	Bonds, B.	.75
50	Brett, G.	1.50
66	Belle, A.	.75
91	Griffey Jr., K.	3.00
94	Gwynn, T.	1.00
97	Gonzalez, J.	1.00
103	Mattingly, D.	1.00
135	Maddux, G.	2.00
229	Ryan, N.	2.50
251	Lofton, K.	.75
274	Sandberg, R.	.75
306	Puckett, K.	1.25
313	Smith, O.	.50
314	Piazza, M.	2.00
352	Ripken, C.	2.00
362	Thomas, F.	3.00

OPC Blue Jays Inserts

Complete Set (18)		3.00
Commons		.25
1	Alomar, R.	.75

OPC Series Heroes

Complete Set (4)		1.00
Commons		.25
4	Winfield, D.	.50

1993 OPC PREMIER

	NM Price
Complete Set (132)	$5.00
Commons	.05
Unlisted Stars	**.10 -.40**
Pack (9)	.50
Box (36)	10.00

Quality Rating ★
Draft picks cards are a bonus in an otherwise forgettable set.

#	Player	NM
1	Bonds, B.	.60
26	Piazza, M.	1.50
46	Mattingly, D.	.60
125	Ripken, C.	2.00
126	Maddux, G.	1.50

OPC Star Performers

Complete Set (22)		10.00
Commons		.15
Common Foil		2.00
Foil Stars		10x
1	Thomas, F.	2.00
4	Sandberg, R.	.60
7	Gonzalez, J.	.75
9	Griffey Jr., K.	2.00
11	Puckett, K.	.60
14	Bonds, B.	.60
17	Lofton, K.	.60
19	Maddux, G.	2.00
20	Ryan, N.	2.00

OPC Top Draft Picks

Complete Set (4)		8.00
1	Wallace, B.J.	2.00
2	Stewart, S.	4.00
3	Henderson, R.	2.00
4	Steverson, T.	2.00

1993 PINNACLE

	NM Price
Complete Set (620)	$40.00
Series 1 Set (1-310)	20.00
Series 2 Set (311-620)	20.00
Commons	.08
Unlisted Stars	**.10 -.40**
Series 1 or 2 Pack (15)	1.00
Series 1 or 2 Box (36)	30.00

Quality Rating ★★★
Inserts and big names carry this otherwise dull base set.

#	Player	NM
10	Bagwell, J.	1.00
15	Sandberg, R.	.75
20	Ripken, C.	2.50
23	Mattingly, D.	1.00
40	Lofton, K.	.75
58	McGwire, M.	1.00
75	Ryan, N.	2.50
93	Belle, A.	.75
98	Gwynn, T.	1.00
108	Thomas, F.	3.00
110	Griffey Jr., K.	3.00
131	Brett, G.	1.00
191	Gonzalez, J.	1.00
252	Piazza, M.	2.00
290	Ryan, N. (NT)	1.00
294	Brett, G. (NT)	.50
305	Ripken, C. (HH)	1.50
426	Puckett, K.	1.00
457	Jeter, D. (R, DP)	4.00
470	Mattingly, D. (NT)	.60
471	Ripken, C. (NT)	1.50
484	Bonds, B. (HH)	.50
504	Bonds, B.	.75
517	Maddux, G.	2.00

Pinnacle Expansion

Complete Set (9)		15.00
Commons		1.00
3	Destrade/Galarraga	4.00
7	Conine/Clark	4.00
9	Felix/Bichette	6.00

Rookie Team Pinnacle

Complete Set (10)		100.00
Commons		5.00
3	Piazza/Levis	50.00
4	Klesko/Snow	20.00
8	Hosey/Salmon	15.00

Pinnacle Team 2001

Complete Set (30)		30.00
Commons		.50
3	Mussina, M.	3.00
4	Knoblauch, C.	1.00
9	Bagwell, J.	6.00
13	Gonzalez, J.	7.00
18	Lofton, K.	4.00
20	Salmon, T.	2.50
27	Klesko, R.	2.50
29	Rodriguez, I.	4.00

Pinnacle Slugfest

Complete Set (30)		50.00
Commons		1.00
1	Gonzalez, J.	6.00
2	McGwire, M.	6.00
6	Bonds, B.	4.00
9	Thomas, F.	15.00

11	Belle, A.	5.00
13	Walker, L.	3.00
14	Bagwell, J.	6.00
16	Puckett, K.	5.00
23	Mattingly, D.	6.00
27	Sandberg, R.	5.00
28	Griffey Jr., K.	15.00

Team Pinnacle

Complete Set (10)		100.00
Commons		4.00
1	Maddux/Mussina	25.00
3	Daulton/Rodriguez	10.00
4	McGriff/Thomas	40.00
5	DeShields/Baerga	6.00
7	Smith/Listach	8.00
8	Bonds/Gonzalez	20.00
9	Van Slyke/Puckett	10.00
10	Walker/Carter	7.00

Pinnacle Tribute

Complete Set (10)	70.00
Brett Singles (1-5)	6.00
Ryan Singles (6-10)	10.00

1993 SCORE

	NM Price
Complete Set (660)	$40.00
Commons	.03
Unlisted Stars	**.05 -.40**
Pack (16)	.75
Box (36)	18.00

Quality Rating ★★
Collectors seem to be losing interest in the inserts.

#	Player	NM
1	Griffey Jr., K.	1.50
3	Thomas, F.	1.50
4	Sandberg, R.	.50
6	Ripken, C.	2.00
23	Mattingly, D.	.50
24	Gwynn, T.	.75
51	Gonzalez, J.	.75
57	Brett, G.	.60
58	Lofton, K.	.60
59	Ryan, N.	1.50
84	Belle, A.	.60
89	Bagwell, J.	1.00
286	Piazza, M.	1.50
484	Maddux, G. (CY)	.75
489	Jeter, D. (R, DP)	4.00
490	Kendall, J. (R)	1.00
504	Griffey Jr., K. (AS)	1.00
510	Thomas, F. (AS)	1.00
527	Maddux, G. (AS)	.75
536	Griffey Jr., K. (DT)	1.00
541	Thomas, F. (DT)	1.00
557	McGwire, M.	.75
560	Bonds, B.	.50
562	Smith, O.	.50
576	Maddux, G.	1.50
606	Puckett, K.	.60

Gold Dream Team

Complete Set (12)		5.00
Commons		.25
1	Smith, O.	.75
2	Puckett, K.	1.00
5	Griffey, K.	3.00
10	Thomas, F.	3.00
11	Alomar, R.	.50

Boys of Summer

Complete Set (30)		50.00
Commons		.75
2	Salmon, T.	6.00
3	Martinez, P.	3.00
5	Piazza, M.	25.00
8	Klesko, R.	8.00

The Franchise

	Complete Set (28)	125.00
	Commons	2.00
1	Ripken, C.	30.00
2	Clemens, R.	15.00
4	Thomas, F.	35.00
9	Puckett, K.	10.00
10	Mattingly, D.	15.00
12	Griffey Jr., K.	35.00
13	Gonzalez, J.	15.00
14	Alomar, R.	8.00
16	Sandberg, R.	10.00
18	Bagwell, J.	12.00
20	Walker, L.	6.00

1993 SELECT

	NM Price
Complete Set (405)	$30.00
Commons	.05
Unlisted Stars	**.10 -.40**
Pack (15)	1.25
Box (36)	30.00

Quality Rating ★★★
Jeter rookie has received attention. Chase Rookies have softened.

#	Player	NM
1	Bonds, B.	.75
2	Griffey Jr., K.	2.50
4	Puckett, K.	1.00
5	Gwynn, T.	1.00
6	Thomas, F.	2.50
15	Smith, O.	.50
16	McGwire, M.	1.25
18	Ripken, C.	2.50
24	Mattingly, D.	1.00
31	Maddux, G.	2.00
40	Gonzalez, J.	1.00
50	Belle, A.	.75
78	Brett, G.	.75
90	Ryan, N.	2.00
97	Sandberg, R.	.60
113	Bagwell, J.	1.00
118	Johnson, R.	.60
275	Lofton, K.	.75
304	Thome, J.	.60
339	Salmon, T.	.75
347	Piazza, M.	2.00
359	Kendall, J. (R)	.75
360	Jeter, D. (R)	4.00
405	Klesko, R.	.60

Select Triple Crown

	Complete Set (3)	100.00
1	Mantle, M.	70.00
2	Robinson, F.	25.00
3	Yastrzemski, C.	25.00

Select Chase Rookie

	Complete Set (21)	140.00
	Commons	4.00
3	Sanders, R.	6.00
4	Lofton, K.	50.00
5	Karros, E.	10.00
11	Salmon, T.	30.00
12	Conine, J.	8.00
19	Hundley, T.	12.00

Select Chase Stars

	Complete Set (24)	150.00
	Commons	3.00
2	Sandberg, R.	12.00
3	Smith, O.	10.00
7	Bonds, B.	12.00
8	Gwynn, T.	18.00
9	Maddux, G.	30.00
15	Ripken, C.	40.00
17	Rodriguez, I.	12.00
18	Puckett, K.	15.00
19	Griffey Jr., K.	50.00
21	Clemens, R.	12.00

Select Diamond Aces

	Complete Set (24)	80.00
	Commons	2.50
1	Clemens, R.	15.00
4	Maddux, G.	40.00
20	Mussina, M.	10.00

Select Stat Leaders

	Complete Set (90)	15.00
	Commons	.20
	Unlisted Stars	.40-.75
3	Thomas, F.	2.00
15	Griffey Jr., K.	2.00
33	Thomas, F.	2.00
38	Thomas, F.	2.00
45	Thomas, F.	2.00
49	Thomas, F.	2.00
78	Maddux, G.	1.50
84	Maddux, G.	1.50
88	Glavine/Maddux	1.25

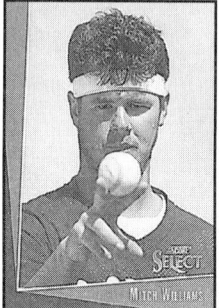

1993 SELECT UPDATE

	NM Price
Complete Set (150)	$20.00
Commons	.20
Unlisted Stars	**.25 -.50**
Pack (12)	2.50
Box (24)	45.00

Quality Rating ★★★
Maddux is garnering most of the attention here.

#	Player	NM
23	Bonds, B.	1.25
44	Snow, J.T.	.75
123	Maddux, G.	5.00

Select Update All-Star Rookies

	Complete Set (10)	150.00
	Commons	6.00
5	Piazza, M.	80.00
8	Salmon, T.	25.00
No#	Salmon, T.	25.00
No#	Piazza, M.	80.00
No#	Ryan, N.	125.00

1993 TOPPS

	NM Price
Complete Set (825)	$25.00
Series 1 Set (1-396)	12.00
Series 2 Set (397-825)	15.00
Retail Set (838)	45.00
Hobby Set (847)	45.00
Commons	.03
Unlisted Stars	**.05 -.40**
Series 1 or 2 Pack (15)	.75
Series 1 or 2 Box (36)	20.00

Quality Rating ★★
Collectors seem to be bored with the inserts. Several rookies, including Jeter help the set.

#	Player	NM
2	Bonds, B.	.60
3	Sandberg, R.	.60
5	Gwynn, T.	.75
32	Mattingly, D.	.60
34	Gonzalez, J.	.75
98	Jeter, D. (R)	4.00
100	McGwire, M.	.75
150	Thomas, F.	2.00
179	Griffey Jr., K.	2.00
183	Maddux, G.	1.00
200	Puckett, K.	.50
227	Bagwell, J.	.60
300	Ripken, C.	2.00
331	Lofton, K.	.50
334	Kendall, J. (R)	.75
397	Brett, G.	.60
401	McGriff/Thomas	.50
405	Griffey Jr., K. (AS)	.50
422	Snow, J.T. (R)	.60
423	Prospects	1.00
529	Prospects	1.25
635	Belle, A.	.50
700	Ryan, N.	2.00
701	Prospects	2.00
710	Mussina, M.	.50
799	Edmonds, J. (R)	1.50

Topps Gold

	Complete Set (825)	80.00
	Series 1 Set (1-396)	40.00
	Series 2 Set (397-825)	40.00
	Commons	.25
	Gold Stars	3x-6x
	Gold Rookies	2x-4x

Topps Black Gold

	Complete Set (44)	15.00
	Series 1 Set (22)	5.00
	Series 2 Set (22)	10.00
	Commons	.25
1	Bonds, B.	.75
8	Gwynn, T.	1.00
12	Maddux, G.	3.00
17	Sandberg, R.	1.00
32	Gonzalez, J.	.75
33	Griffey Jr., K.	3.00
36	Lofton, K.	.75
40	Puckett, K.	1.25
42	Thomas, F.	3.00

1993 TOPPS FINEST

	NM Price
Complete Set (199)	$250.00
Commons	1.00
Unlisted Stars	**1.50-4.00**
Pack (6)	35.00
Box (18)	500.00

Quality Rating ★★★★
Refractors are still hot. Regular set is holding steady with Gwynn and Clemens gaining steam.

#	Player	NM
11	Bagwell, J.	12.00
16	Belle, A.	8.00
28	Smith, O.	7.00
43	Lofton, K.	10.00
47	Rodriguez, I.	12.00
63	Brett, G.	12.00
70	Molitor, P.	5.00
77	Gwynn, T.	15.00
85	Maddux, G. (AS)	25.00
88	Alomar, R. (AS)	6.00
92	McGwire, M. (AS)	12.00
96	Ripken, C. (AS)	25.00
97	Walker, L. (AS)	6.00
98	Mattingly, D. (AS)	12.00
102	Thomas, F. (AS)	30.00
103	Bonds, B. (AS)	8.00
104	Clemens, R. (AS)	12.00
105	Sandberg, R. (AS)	10.00
107	Ryan, N. (AS)	30.00
110	Griffey Jr., K. (AS)	30.00
112	Puckett, K. (AS)	12.00
116	Gonzalez, J. (AS)	15.00
122	Murray, E.	6.00
154	Johnson, R.	6.00
157	Mussina, M.	6.00
163	Salmon, T.	6.00
165	Vaughn, M.	7.00
199	Piazza, M.	25.00

Finest Refractors

	Complete Set (199)	35000.00
	Commons	50.00
	Unlstd Stars	60.00-175.00
1	Justice, D.	225.00
3	Harvey, B.	200.00
10	Schilling, C.	300.00
11	Bagwell, J.	1000.00
12	Cole, A.	200.00
16	Belle, A.	700.00
25	Williams, M.	450.00
28	Smith, O.	300.00
30	Williams, B.	450.00
31	Sheffield, G.	400.00
40	Grissom, M.	350.00
41	Davis, G.	200.00
43	Lofton, K.	400.00
47	Rodriguez, I.	800.00
63	Brett, G.	650.00
70	Molitor, P.	500.00
71	Anderson, B.	300.00
76	Knoblauch, C.	400.00
77	Gwynn, T.	600.00
79	Sosa, S.	500.00
85	Maddux, G. (AS)	1200.00
87	Glavine, T. (AS)	200.00
88	Alomar, R. (AS)	400.00
92	McGwire, M. (AS)	750.00
96	Ripken, C. (AS)	2000.00
97	Walker, L. (AS)	400.00
98	Mattingly, D. (AS)	400.00
99	Canseco, J. (AS)	200.00
102	Thomas, F. (AS)	1200.00
103	Bonds, B. (AS)	650.00
104	Clemens, R. (AS)	550.00
105	Sandberg, R. (AS)	250.00
106	McGriff, F. (AS)	250.00
107	Ryan, N. (AS)	1300.00
108	Clark, W. (AS)	200.00
110	Griffey Jr., K. (AS)	2000.00
112	Puckett, K. (AS)	400.00
116	Gonzalez, J. (AS)	1500.00
119	Biggio, C.	225.00
122	Murray, E.	500.00
124	Buhner, J.	250.00
130	Galarraga, A.	250.00
131	Caminiti, K.	250.00
141	Sanders, D.	200.00
154	Johnson, R.	450.00
157	Mussina, M.	400.00
163	Salmon, T.	350.00
165	Vaughn, M.	400.00
166	Smoltz, J.	250.00
173	Felix, J.	200.00
189	Alou, M.	200.00
190	Martinez, E.	200.00
192	Yount, R.	200.00
199	Piazza, M.	1300.00

All-Star Jumbos

	Complete Set (33)	500.00
	Commons	4.00
	Jumbos	2x-3x

1993 TOPPS TRADED

	NM Price
Complete Set (132)	20.00
Commons	.10
Unlisted Stars	**.15 -.40**

Quality Rating ★★★
Topps chronicles late-season player moves and Team USA members.

#	Player	NM
1	Bonds, B.	.60
12	Hinch, A.J. (R)	3.00
19	Helton, T. (R)	12.00
24	Piazza, M.	2.00
45	Powell, D. (R)	1.00
54	Maddux, G.	1.00
79	Walker, T. (R)	5.00
107	Wilson, P. (R)	1.50
124	Wagner, B. (R)	1.00

1993 TOPPS STADIUM CLUB

		NM Price
Complete Set (750)		$50.00
Series 1 Set (1-300)		20.00
Series 2 Set (301-600)		20.00
Series 3 Set (601-750)		10.00
Commons		.06
Unlisted Stars		**.10 -.40**
Series 1, 2, 3 Pack (15)		1.50
Series 1, 2, 3 Box (24)		25.00

Quality Rating ★★★★
First Day issues are always a hit with hobbyists. With 750 cards this set requires some time.

#	Player	NM
2	Maddux, G.	.2.00
8	Thome, J.	.75
40	Ripken, C.	.2.50
51A	Bonds, B. (err)	.75
51B	Bonds, B. (cor)	.75
102	Belle, A.	.75
200	Thomas, F.	.3.00
277	Lofton, K.	.75
283	Puckett, K. (MC)	1.00
297	Gonzalez, J. (MC)	.50
353	Ryan, N.	.2.50
366	Sandberg, R.	.75
384	Bagwell, J.	1.00
424	Brett, G.	1.00
478	McGwire, M.	1.00
538	Gwynn, T.	1.00
540	Gonzalez, J.	.75
541	Klesko, R.	.60
548	Smith, O.	.50
557	Mattingly, D.	1.00
585	Piazza, M.	.2.00
591	Griffey Jr., K. (MC)	1.50
597	Puckett, K. (MC)	.50
638	Jones, C.	.2.50
665	Maddux, G.	.2.00
684	Bonds, B.	.75
707	Griffey Jr., K.	.3.00
746	Thomas, F. (MC)	1.50
750	Maddux, G. (MC)	1.00

Stadium Club I Inserts

Complete Set (4)		.6.00
1	Yount, R.	.2.00
2	Brett, G.	.5.00
3	Nied, D.	.75
4	Wilson, N.	.75

Stadium Club II Inserts

Complete Set (4)		10.00
1	Clark/McGwire	1.50
2	Gooden/Mattingly	.2.00
3	Sandberg/Thomas	.5.00
4	Griffey/Strawberry	.4.00

Stadium Club III Inserts

Complete Set (2)		1.50
1	Nied, D.	1.00
2	Hough, C.	1.00

First Day Production

Complete Set (750)		2200.00
Series 1 Set (1-300)		800.00
Series 2 Set (301-600)		800.00
Series 3 Set (601-750)		600.00
Commons		3.00
Unlisted Stars		25x-40x
2	Maddux, G.	80.00
40	Ripken, C.	85.00
200	Thomas, F.	100.00
353	Ryan, N.	100.00
384	Bagwell, J.	40.00
424	Brett, G.	40.00
538	Gwynn, T.	40.00
557	Mattingly, D.	50.00

585	Piazza, M.	50.00
591	Griffey Jr., K. (MC)	50.00
638	Jones, C.	75.00
665	Maddux, G.	80.00
707	Griffey Jr., K.	100.00
746	Thomas, F. (MC)	50.00
750	Maddux, G. (MC)	50.00

1993 UPPER DECK

		NM Price
Complete Set (840)		$40.00
Series 1 Set (1-420)		20.00
Series 2 Set (421-840)		20.00
Factory Set (840)		50.00
Commons		.05
Unlisted Stars		**.10 -.40**
Series 1 or 2 Pack (15)		1.00
Series 1 or 2 Box (36)		30.00

Quality Rating ★★★★
Two series and lots of insert cards makes this set a challenge.

#	Player	NM
2	Piazza, M. (SR)	.2.00
24	Jones, C. (SR)	1.50
36	Ripken, C. (CH)	1.00
37	Ryan, N. (CH)	1.00
44	Ripken/Anderson	.75
45	Belle/Lofton	.60
56	Brett, G.	.50
134	Mattingly, D.	.50
155	Ryan, N.	1.50
165	Gwynn, T.	.75
175	Sandberg, R.	.50
256	Bagwell, J.	.75
262	Lofton, K.	.50
355	Griffey Jr., K.	1.50
433	Ramirez, M. (TP)	1.50
449	Jeter, D. (R, TP)	.4.00
452	Bagwell, J. (IN)	.50
459	Jones, C. (IN)	.60
488	Maddux, G. (AW)	.75
535	Maddux, G.	1.50
555	Thomas, F.	1.50
565	Puckett, K.	.50
566	McGwire, M.	.75
567	Bonds, B.	.60
585	Ripken, C.	1.50
586	Belle, A.	.60
755	Gonzalez, J.	.60
813	Bagwell, J.	.60
SP5	Brett/Yount	.2.00
SP6	Ryan, N.	.5.00

Clutch Performers

Complete Set (20)		20.00
Commons		.50
3	Bonds, B.	1.50
10	Gonzalez, J.	.2.50
11	Griffey Jr., K.	.6.00
14	Mattingly, D.	.2.00
17	Puckett, K.	1.50
18	Sandberg, R.	1.50
20	Thomas, F.	.6.00

On Deck

Complete Set (25)		20.00
Commons		.50
4	Belle, A.	1.50
6	Brett, G.	.2.00
12	Gonzalez, J.	.2.50
13	Griffey Jr., K.	.6.00
14	Gwynn, T.	1.50
16	Jones, C.	.2.50
19	Puckett, K.	1.50
20	Ryan, N.	.6.00
22	Sandberg, R.	1.50
24	Thomas, F.	.6.00

Season Highlights

Complete Set (20)		160.00
Commons		.2.50
5	Bonds, B.	10.00
7	Brett, G.	15.00
9	Griffey Jr., K.	50.00
11	Lofton, K.	15.00
13	Murray, E.	.6.00
17	Ryan, N.	50.00
20	Yount, R.	.4.00

Then and Now

Complete Set (18)		50.00
Series 1 Set (9)		25.00
Series 2 Set (9)		25.00
Commons		.50
2	Brett, G.	.4.00
4	Ripken, C.	10.00
5	Ryan, N.	10.00
6	Sandberg, R.	.3.00
7	Smith, O.	.2.00
11	Gwynn, T.	.3.00
13	Mattingly, D.	.3.00
14	Murray, E.	.2.00
16	Jackson, R.	.2.50
17	Mantle, M.	12.00
18	Mays, W.	.8.00

Triple Crown

Complete Set (10)		25.00
Commons		1.00
1	Bonds, B.	.2.50
4	Griffey Jr., K.	10.00
6	Puckett, K.	.4.00
7	Ripken, C.	10.00
9	Thomas, F.	10.00

Home Run Heroes

Complete Set (28)		12.00
Commons		.30
1	Gonzalez, J.	.2.50
2	McGwire, M.	.2.50
5	Belle, A.	1.50
6	Bonds, B.	1.25
9	Griffey Jr., K.	.6.00
11	Sandberg, R.	1.00
21	Williams, M.	1.00
24	Puckett, K.	.2.00

Iooss Collection

Complete Set (26)		20.00
Commons		.50
Header (No#)		1.00
2	Bagwell, J.	.2.50
3	McGwire, M.	.2.50
7	Smith, O.	1.00
12	Belle, A.	1.50
13	Griffey Jr., K.	.6.00
15	Ripken, C.	.7.00
19	Ryan, N.	.6.00
22	Brett, G.	.2.50
24	Puckett, K.	.2.25
25	Thomas, F.	.6.00
26	Mattingly, D.	.2.50

Fifth Anniversary

Complete Set (15)		20.00
Commons		.50
1	Griffey Jr., K. (89)	10.00
5	Ryan, N. (89)	.5.00
6	Gonzalez, J. (90)	.2.50
11	Jones, C. (91)	.2.00
14	Thomas, F. (92)	.6.00

Mays Heroes Set

Complete Set (10)		.4.00
Mays Singles (46-54)		.50
Cover Card (No#)		1.00

Future Heroes

Complete Set (10)		10.00
Commons (55-63)		.50
Header (No#)		1.00
56	Bonds, B.	1.50
58	Gonzalez, J.	.2.50
59	Griffey Jr., K.	.5.00
60	McGwire, M.	.5.00
61	Puckett, K.	.2.00
62	Thomas, F.	.5.00

1993 UPPER DECK SP

		NM Price
Complete Set (290)		75.00
Commons		.20
Unlisted Stars		**.25 -.50**
Pack (12)		6.00
Box (24)		120.00

Quality Rating ★★★★
Wax remains a solid choice, as do singles of Griffey and Thomas.

#	Player	NM
1	Alomar, R. (AS)	1.00
4	Griffey Jr., K. (AS)	10.00
7	Puckett, K. (AS)	.3.00
8	Ripken, C. (AS)	.8.00
10	Bonds, B. (AS)	.2.00
17	Sandberg, R. (AS)	.2.00
25	Salmon, T.	.2.00
26	Snow, J.T. (R)	.2.00
28	Bagwell, J.	.3.00
41	McGwire, M.	.3.00
59	Maddux, G.	.8.00
79	Smith, O.	1.50
96	Mondesi, R.	.2.00
98	Piazza, M.	.7.00
120	Belle, A.	1.50
123	Lofton, K.	.2.00
152	Murray, E.	1.50
167	Gwynn, T.	.3.00
194	Gonzalez, J.	.3.00
198	Ryan, N.	.8.00
199	Clemens, R.	.2.00
206	Vaughn, M.	1.50
227	Brett, G.	.3.00
260	Thomas, F.	10.00
265	Mattingly, D.	.3.00
272	Cedeno, R. (R, PP)	.2.00
273	Damon, J. (R, PP)	.3.00
275	Delgado, C. (PP)	.3.00
279	Jeter, D. (R, PP)	25.00
280	Jones, C. (PP)	10.00
281	Lopez, J. (PP)	.3.00
285	Ramirez, M. (PP)	.5.00
287	Tucker, M. (PP)	1.50
289	White, R. (PP)	.2.00

Platinum Power

Complete Set (20)		150.00
Commons		.4.00
1	Belle, A.	12.00
2	Bonds, B.	10.00
8	Gonzalez, J.	20.00
9	Griffey Jr., K.	50.00
13	McGwire, M.	15.00
15	Piazza, M.	30.00
16	Salmon, T.	.8.00
17	Sandberg, R.	10.00
19	Thomas, F.	50.00
20	Williams, M.	.6.00

1994 BOWMAN

		NM Price
Complete Set (682)		$120.00
Commons		.10
Unlisted Stars		**.15 -.50**
Pack (12)		3.00
Box (24)		65.00

Quality Rating ★★★★

The usual Bowman traits are evident, a ton of cards and a lot of quality. Certain cards are tough to find, causing collectors to purchase several wax boxes to find them.

#	Player	NM
5	Griffey Jr., K.	3.00
12	Benes, A. (R)	4.00
15	Thomas, F.	3.00
25	Mattingly, D.	1.25
45	Gonzalez, J.	1.50
55	Ramirez, M.	1.50
58	Wright, J. (R)	2.00
75	Ripken, C.	2.50
76	Fullmer, B. (R)	4.00
94	Renteria, E. (R)	3.00
98	Park, C. (R)	6.00
118	Bagwell, J.	1.25
120	Gwynn, T.	1.50
135	Bonds, B.	1.00
156	Alfonzo, E. (R)	4.00
166	Orie, K. (R)	3.00
192	McGwire, M.	1.50
195	Lofton, K.	.75
205	D'Amico, J. (R)	1.50
209	Clark, T. (R)	18.00
217	King, A. (R)	.75
232	Lee, D. (R)	8.00
245	Maddux, G.	2.00
250	Sandberg, R.	1.00
282	Perez, N. (R)	2.00
285	Johnson, R.	1.00
315	Vaughn, M.	1.00
326	Isringhausen, J. (R)	1.50
341	Delgado, C. (Foil)	.75
348	Rivera, R. (R, Foil)	4.00
353	Jones, C. (Foil)	2.00
354	Kieschnick, B. (Foil)	1.50
359	Hollandsworth, T. (Foil)	.75
371	Ramirez, M. (Foil)	1.50
373	Damon, J. (Foil)	2.00
374	D'Amico, J.	1.50
376	Jeter, D. (Foil)	3.00
386	Mattingly, D. (Foil)	1.50
387	Piazza, M. (Foil)	1.50
388	Sandberg, R. (Foil)	1.00
391	Suppan, J. (R)	3.00
411	Belle, A.	1.50
413	Spiezio, S. (R)	2.00
424	Smith, O.	.75
433	Dye, J. (R)	3.00
438	Kieschnick, B. (R)	1.50
460	Puckett, K.	1.00
475	Clemens, R.	1.00
489	Jones, C.	2.00
510	Piazza, M.	2.00
586	Hidalgo, R. (R)	8.00
633	Jeter, D.	3.00
637	Delgado, C.	.60
642	Wagner, B. (R)	3.00

1994 BOWMAN'S BEST

	NM Price
Complete Set (180)	$80.00
Commons	.50
Unlisted Stars	**1.00-1.50**
Pack (7)	4.50
Box (24)	90.00

Quality Rating ★★★

Vets and rookies give collectors great player selection. Mirror Image cards are one per pack and feature some stars of the future.

Red Set

#	Player	NM
19	Gonzalez, J.	3.00
36	Maddux, G.	5.00

40	Griffey Jr., K.	8.00
41	Belle, A.	3.00
45	Mattingly, D.	3.00
53	Bagwell, J.	3.00
55	Thomas, F.	8.00
59	Bonds, B.	2.00
68	Lofton, K.	2.00
71	Ripken, C.	6.00
75	Puckett, K.	3.00
78	Gwynn, T.	4.00
81	Piazza, M.	5.00
88	Ramirez, M.	4.00

Blue Set

1	Jones, C.	6.00
2	Jeter, D.	5.00
5	Kieschnick, B. (R)	3.00
13	Alfonzo, E. (R)	4.00
19	Wagner, B. (R)	3.00
25	Park, C. (R)	6.00
55	Fullmer, B. (R)	4.00
61	Benes, A. (R)	4.00
62	Clark, T. (R)	15.00
63	Renteria, E. (R)	3.00
71	Orie, K. (R)	3.00
90	Greer, R. (R)	4.00

Mirror Image

	Complete Set (20)	35.00
	Commons	1.00
91	Thomas/Young	5.00
94	Ripken/Orie	6.00
95	Larkin/Jeter	3.00
96	Griffey/Damon	7.00
97	Bonds/White	2.50
98	Belle/Hurst	2.00
99	Mondesi/Rivera	6.00
101	Maddux/Wasdin	3.00
104	Piazza/Hughes	2.00
107	Ramirez/Malave	3.00
108	Fryman/Jones	1.50

Refractors

	Complete Set (200)	1200.00
	Commons	3.00
	Unlisted Stars	5x-10x
1	Jones, C.	70.00
2	Jeter, D.	70.00
36	Maddux, G.	70.00
40	Griffey Jr., K.	100.00
41	Belle, A.	30.00
45	Mattingly, D.	40.00
53	Bagwell, J.	45.00
55	Thomas, F.	100.00
59	Bonds, B.	35.00
71	Ripken, C.	80.00
75	Puckett, K.	40.00
78	Gwynn, T.	50.00
81	Piazza, M.	70.00
88	Ramirez, M.	50.00

1994 DONRUSS

	NM Price
Complete Set (660)	$40.00
Series 1 Set (1-330)	20.00
Series 2 Set (331-660)	20.00
Commons	.05
Unlisted Stars	**.10 -.30**
Series 1 Pack (13)	1.50
Series 1 Box (36)	45.00
Series 2 Pack (13)	1.25
Series 2 Box (36)	40.00

Quality Rating ★★★

Donruss has nothing flashy, but the inserts are fun to chase and the regular set offers great photos.

#	Player	NM
1	Ryan, N.	2.50
2	Piazza, M.	1.50

4	Griffey Jr., K.	3.00
10	Gwynn, T.	1.25
18	Sandberg, R.	.60
35	Smith, O.	.50
39	Lofton, K.	.75
40	Ripken, C.	2.00
49	Gonzalez, J.	.75
107	Brett, G.	1.00
322	Ramirez, M.	.75
335	McGwire, M.	1.00
340	Mattingly, D.	1.00
341	Thomas, F.	3.00
343	Puckett, K.	1.00
349	Bonds, B.	.75
351	Belle, A.	1.00
365	Bagwell, J.	1.00
380	Maddux, G.	2.00
453	Jones, C.	2.00

Anniversary

	Complete Set (10)	50.00
	Commons	2.00
3	Brett, G.	8.00
5	Ryan, N.	20.00
6	Ripken, C.	15.00
8	Mattingly, D.	8.00
9	Sandberg, R.	6.00
10	Gwynn, T.	7.00

Decade Dominators

	Complete Set (20)	50.00
	Series 1 Set (10)	20.00
	Series 2 Set (10)	30.00
	Commons	.75
	Large Dominators	2x
2	Bonds, B.	2.00
6	Gonzalez, J.	5.00
9	Griffey Jr., K.	10.00
11	Gwynn, T.	4.00
12	Thomas, F.	10.00
15	Puckett, K.	3.00
16	Griffey Jr., K.	10.00
17	Bonds, B.	2.00

Diamond Kings

	Complete Set (30)	50.00
	Series 1 Set (15)	25.00
	Series 2 Set (15)	25.00
	Commons	.75
	Large Diamond Kings	2x
1	Bonds, B.	2.50
2	Vaughn, M.	2.00
8	Belle, A.	2.00
11	Gwynn, T.	4.00
14	Griffey Jr., K.	10.00
15	Piazza, M.	6.00
16	Mattingly, D.	4.00
26	Mussina, M.	2.00
27	Bagwell, J.	3.00
28	Thomas, F.	10.00

Elite

	Complete Set (12)	275.00
	Series 1 Set (6)	150.00
	Series 2 Set (6)	125.00
	Commons	8.00
37	Thomas, F.	50.00
38	Gwynn, T.	30.00
39	Salmon, T.	12.00
40	Belle, A.	12.00
42	Gonzalez, J.	25.00
44	Bonds, B.	18.00
45	Griffey Jr., K.	50.00
46	Piazza, M.	35.00

Large Award Winners

	Complete Set (10)	100.00
	Series 1 Set (5)	50.00
	Series 2 Set (5)	50.00
	Commons	4.00
1	Bonds, B. (MVP)	8.00
2	Maddux, G. (CY)	35.00
3	Piazza, M. (ROY)	15.00
4	Bonds, B. (HR Leader)	8.00
5	Puckett, K. (AS MVP)	12.00
6	Thomas, F. (MVP)	35.00
9	Gonzalez, J. (HR Leader)	15.00

Long Ball Leaders

	Complete Set (10)	45.00
	Common	1.00
5	Griffey Jr., K.	15.00
7	Piazza, M.	8.00
8	Thomas, F.	15.00
9	Bonds, B.	5.00
10	Gonzalez, J.	6.00

MVPs

	Complete Set (28)	70.00
	Series 1 Set (14)	15.00
	Series 2 Set (14)	55.00
	Commons	.75
6	Bagwell, J.	4.00
7	Piazza, M.	6.00
13	Gwynn, T.	4.00
14	Bonds, B.	3.00
15	Ripken, C.	12.00
16	Vaughn, M.	2.50
17	Salmon, T.	2.00
18	Thomas, F.	15.00
19	Belle, A.	4.00
23	Puckett, K.	4.00
24	Mattingly, D.	5.00
26	Griffey Jr., K.	15.00
27	Gonzalez, J.	5.00

Special Edition

	Complete Set (100)	24.00
	Series 1 Set (50)	12.00
	Series 2 Set (50)	12.00
	Commons	.35
1	Ryan, N.	5.00
2	Piazza, M.	2.50
4	Griffey Jr., K.	6.00
10	Gwynn, T.	1.25
18	Sandberg, R.	5.00
40	Ripken, C.	5.00
49	Gonzalez, J.	1.50
60	Mattingly, D.	1.50
61	Thomas, F.	5.00
63	Puckett, K.	1.25
69	Bonds, B.	1.50
71	Belle, A.	1.00

Spirit of the Game

	Complete Set (10)	65.00
	Series 1 Set (5)	35.00
	Series 2 Set (5)	30.00
	Large SOG	2x
	Commons	2.00
2	Bonds, B.	5.00
3	Griffey Jr., K.	18.00
4	Piazza, M.	10.00
5	Gonzalez, J.	5.00
6	Thomas, F.	18.00
9	Mattingly, D.	8.00

1994 DONRUSS TRIPLE PLAY

	NM Price
Complete Set (300)	$15.00
Commons	.10
Unlisted Stars	**.15 -.30**
Pack (12)	.75
Box (36)	20.00

Quality Rating ★★★

Many collectors like Triple Play because it has a simple design and only 300 cards.

#	Player	NM
21	Bagwell, J.	1.00
46	Maddux, G.	1.50
77	Sandberg, R.	.50
88	Piazza, M.	1.25
102	Bonds, B.	.60
113	Belle, A.	.60
115	Lofton, K.	.60
127	Griffey Jr., K.	2.00
159	Ripken, C.	2.00
167	Gwynn, T.	.50
194	Gonzalez, J.	.75
258	Puckett, K.	.60
269	Thomas, F.	2.00
276	Mattingly, D.	.75
281	Jones, C.	1.00

Bomb Squad

#	Player	
	Complete Set (10)	35.00
	Commons	2.00
1	Thomas, F.	10.00
3	Gonzalez, J.	4.00
4	Bonds, B.	3.00
8	Griffey Jr., K.	10.00
9	Belle, A.	3.00

Medalists

#	Player	
	Complete Set (15)	40.00
	Commons	2.00
3	Thomas/Olerud/Palmeiro	10.00
4	Grace/McGriff/Bagwell	4.00
6	Sandberg/Biggio/Thompson	3.00
7	Ripken/Trammell/Fernandez	10.00
11	Griffey/Puck/Belle	10.00
12	Bonds/Dykstra/Van Slyke	3.00
14	Maddux/Rijo/Swift	6.00

Nicknames

#	Player	
	Complete Set (8)	35.00
	Commons	2.00
2	Sandberg, R.	7.00
6	Ripken, C.	25.00

1994 FLEER

	NM Price
Complete Set (720)	$55.00
Commons	.05
Unlisted Stars	**.10 -.30**
Pack (15)	1.00
Box (36)	30.00

Quality Rating ★★★★
Fleer is a favorite among hobbyists as insert sets feature all the best names in the game.

#	Player	NM
19	Ripken, C.	2.50
96	Thomas, F.	3.00
100	Belle, A.	.60
111	Lofton, K.	.75
119	Ramirez, M.	.75
149	Brett, G.	1.00
217	Puckett, K.	.75
239	Mattingly, D.	1.00
268	McGwire, M.	1.25
286	Griffey Jr., K.	3.00
290	Johnson, R.	.50
307	Gonzalez, J.	1.00
321	Ryan, N.	3.00
365	Maddux, G.	2.00
396	Sandberg, R.	.60
483	Bagwell, J.	1.00
520	Piazza, M.	1.50
646	Smith, O.	.50
665	Gwynn, T.	1.25
684	Bonds, B.	.60

All-Rookie Team

#	Player	
	Complete Set (9)	10.00
	Commons	.50
1	Abbott, K.	1.00
3	Delgado, C.	3.00
No#	All-Rookie Exchange	2.00

All-Stars

#	Player	
	Complete Set (50)	25.00
	Commons	.25
3	Belle, A.	1.00
9	Gonzalez, J.	1.50
10	Griffey Jr., K.	4.00
12	Johnson, R.	.75
20	Puckett, K.	1.00
21	Ripken, C.	4.00
23	Thomas, F.	4.00
31	Bonds, B.	1.50
39	Gwynn, T.	1.50
47	Piazza, M.	1.50
48	Sandberg, R.	.75

Award Winners

#	Player	
	Complete Set (6)	15.00
1	Thomas, F.	5.00
2	Bonds, B.	1.25
3	McDowell, J.	.75
4	Maddux, G.	5.00
5	Salmon, T.	1.00
6	Piazza, M.	2.50

Golden Moment

#	Player	
	Complete Set (10)	30.00
	Commons	.50
4	Griffey Jr., K.	10.00
6	Brett, G.	5.00
7	Ryan, N.	10.00
9	Thomas, F.	10.00

League Leaders

#	Player	
	Complete Set (12)	10.00
	Commons	.50
2	Belle, A.	1.50
4	Lofton, K.	1.50
8	Bonds, B.	1.50
12	Maddux, G.	5.00

Lumber Company

#	Player	
	Complete Set (10)	15.00
	Commons	.75
1	Belle, A.	1.50
2	Bonds, B.	1.50
4	Gonzalez, J.	2.50
5	Griffey Jr., K.	7.00
9	Thomas, F.	7.00

Major League Prospects

#	Player	
	Complete Set (35)	15.00
	Commons	.40
6	Cordova, M.	2.00
9	Delgado, C.	2.00
18	Jones, C.	10.00

Pro Visions

#	Player	
	Complete Set (9)	6.00
	Commons	.50
5	Smith, O.	.75
6	Gonzalez, J.	1.50
8	Piazza, M.	2.00
9	Gwynn, T.	1.50

Rookie Sensations

#	Player	
	Complete Set (20)	15.00
	Commons	.75
14	Piazza, M.	10.00
17	Salmon, T.	4.00

Smoke N' Heat

#	Player	
	Complete Set (12)	75.00
	Commons	3.00
1	Clemens, R.	8.00
5	Johnson, R.	6.00
7	Maddux, G.	25.00
8	Mussina, M.	6.00
10	Ryan, N.	30.00

Team Leaders

#	Player	
	Complete Set (28)	25.00
	Commons	.50
1	Ripken, C.	4.00
2	Vaughn, M.	1.50
4	Thomas, F.	6.00
9	Puckett, K.	2.00
10	Mattingly, D.	2.00
12	Griffey Jr., K.	6.00
13	Gonzalez, J.	2.00
16	Sandberg, R.	1.50
20	Bagwell, J.	2.00
21	Piazza, M.	3.00
27	Gwynn, T.	2.00

Tim Salmon

	Complete Set (12)	30.00
	Salmon Singles	3.00
	Salmon Autograph (2000)	65.00

1994 FLEER UPDATE

	NM Price
Complete Set (200)	$15.00
Factory Set (210)	20.00
Commons	.10
Unlisted Stars	**.15 -.30**

Quality Rating ★★★
Fleer Update includes the brightest young star in Rodriguez and veterans like Clark and Sanders.

#	Player	NM
86	Rodriguez, A. (R)	10.00
144	Hunter, B.	.60
151	Park, C. (R)	3.00

Diamond Tribute

#	Player	
	Complete Set (10)	4.00
	Commons	.30
1	Bonds, B.	.75
5	Gwynn, T.	1.00
6	Mattingly, D.	1.25
9	Puckett, K.	1.00
10	Ripken, C.	3.00

1994 FLEER EXTRA BASES

	NM Price
Complete Set (400)	$30.00
Commons	.05
Unlisted Stars	**.10 -.30**
Pack (12)	1.00
Box (36)	30.00

Quality Rating ★★
Collectors didn't respond to this one-time oversized product.

#	Player	NM
12	Ripken, C.	2.50
44	Durham, R. (R)	1.25
53	Thomas, F.	3.00
57	Belle, A.	.75
60	Lofton, K.	.75
66	Ramirez, M.	.75
69	Thome, J.	.50
123	Puckett, K.	1.00
133	Mattingly, D.	1.25
166	Griffey Jr., K.	3.00
168	Johnson, R.	.60
178	Gonzalez, J.	1.00
208	Maddux, G.	1.50
268	Bagwell, J.	1.00
294	Piazza, M.	1.50
363	Smith, O.	.50
372	Gwynn, T.	1.00
383	Bonds, B.	.75

Second Year Stars

#	Player	
	Complete Set (20)	10.00
	Commons	.50
16	Piazza, M.	4.00
18	Salmon, T.	1.50

Rookie Standouts

#	Player	
	Complete Set (20)	15.00
	Commons	.50
5	Delgado, C.	1.50
11	Klesko, R.	1.50
12	Lopez, J.	1.25
13	Mondesi, R.	1.50
16	Ramirez, M.	2.50

Major League Hopefuls

#	Player	
	Complete Set (10)	8.00
	Commons	.50
3	Durham, R.	2.50

Game Breakers

#	Player	
	Complete Set (30)	30.00
	Commons	.50
1	Bagwell, J.	1.25
3	Belle, A.	1.00
4	Bonds, B.	1.00
12	Gonzalez, J.	1.50
14	Griffey Jr., K.	5.00
16	Maddux, G.	4.00
17	Mattingly, D.	2.00
22	Piazza, M.	3.00
23	Puckett, K.	2.00
24	Ripken, C.	5.00
27	Thomas, F.	5.00

Pitchers Duel

#	Player	
	Complete Set (10)	12.00
	Commons	.75
1	Clemens/McDowell.	2.00
2	McDonald/Johnson.	1.50
4	Mussina/Sele	2.50
7	Maddux/Rijo	6.00

1994 FLEER FLAIR

	NM Price
Complete Set (450)	$65.00
Series 1 Set (1-250)	30.00
Series 2 Set (251-450)	35.00
Commons	.15
Unlisted Stars	**.20 -.50**
Series 1 Pack (10)	2.50
Series 1 Box (24)	50.00
Series 2 Pack (10)	3.50
Series 2 Box (24)	70.00

Quality Rating ★★★
Production was lower in the second series making Rodriguez cards more attractive.

#	Player	NM
8	Ripken, C.	4.00
36	Thomas, F.	5.00
38	Belle, A.	1.00
43	Ramirez, M.	1.00
45	Thome, J.	1.00
77	Puckett, K.	1.50
84	Mattingly, D.	1.50
94	McGwire, M.	1.50
103	Griffey Jr., K.	5.00
109	Gonzalez, J.	1.50
130	Maddux, G.	3.00
141	Sandberg, R.	1.00
181	Park, C. (R)	2.50
182	Piazza, M.	3.00
228	Smith, O.	1.00
239	Bonds, B.	1.25
283	Lofton, K.	1.50
337	Johnson, R.	1.25
340	Rodriguez, A. (R)	18.00
385	Bagwell, J.	1.00
436	Gwynn, T.	2.00

Wave of The Future

#	Player	
	Complete Set (20)	80.00
	Series 1 Set (10)	20.00
	Series 2 Set (10)	60.00
	Commons	1.00
4	Klesko, R.	4.00
5	Lopez, J.	3.00
6	Mondesi, R.	4.00
8	Park, C.	3.00
13	Hamilton, J.	3.00
18	Rodriguez, A.	40.00

Outfield Power

#	Player	
	Complete Set (10)	30.00
	Commons	1.00
1	Belle, A.	3.00
2	Bonds, B.	3.00
5	Gonzalez, J.	4.00

6	Griffey Jr., K.	12.00
8	Puckett, K.	4.00

Infield Power
	Complete Set (10)	20.00
	Commons	1.00
1	Bagwell, J.	3.00
4	Mattingly, D.	4.00
7	Piazza, M.	6.00
8	Ripken, C.	8.00
9	Thomas, F.	10.00

Hot Numbers
	Complete Set (10)	100.00
	Commons	5.00
7	Piazza, M.	25.00
8	Ripken, C.	30.00
9	Sandberg, R.	10.00
10	Thomas, F.	40.00

Hot Glove
	Complete Set (10)	200.00
1	Bonds, B.	20.00
2	Clark, W.	10.00
3	Griffey Jr., K.	75.00
4	Lofton, K.	25.00
5	Maddux, G.	50.00
6	Mattingly, D.	30.00
7	Puckett, K.	25.00
8	Ripken, C.	60.00
9	Salmon, T.	15.00
10	Williams, M.	10.00

1994 FLEER ULTRA
	NM Price
Complete Set (600)	$50.00
Series 1 Set (1-300)	25.00
Series 2 Set (301-600)	25.00
Commons	.10
Unlisted Stars	**.15 -.30**
Series 1 or 2 Pack (14)	1.50
Series 1 or 2 Box (36)	45.00

Quality Rating ★★★
On Base Leaders, RBI Kings, and Rising Stars are three of the most difficult to find inserts.

#	Player	NM
9	Ripken, C.	2.50
39	Thomas, F.	3.00
41	Belle, A.	.75
45	Lofton, K.	.75
111	McGwire, M.	1.25
120	Griffey Jr., K.	3.00
127	Gonzalez, J.	1.00
152	Jones, C.	1.50
166	Sandberg, R.	1.00
203	Bagwell, J.	1.00
218	Piazza, M.	1.50
280	Gwynn, T.	1.25
286	Bonds, B.	.75
334	Durham, R. (R)	1.25
351	Ramirez, M.	.75
394	Puckett, K.	1.00
400	Mattingly, D.	1.25
446	Maddux, G.	2.00
568	Smith, O.	.60

Achievements
	Complete Set (5)	10.00
	Commons	2.00
3	Ripken, C.	7.00
4	Sandberg, R.	3.00

All-Rookie Team
	Complete Set (10)	10.00
	Commons	.75
5	Klesko, R.	3.00
6	Lopez, J.	2.00
7	Mondesi, R.	3.00

All-Stars
	Complete Set (20)	20.00
	Commons	.50
2	Thomas, F.	5.00
4	Ripken, C.	4.00
6	Belle, A.	1.50
7	Gonzalez, J.	2.50
8	Griffey Jr., K.	5.00
11	Piazza, M.	3.00
13	Sandberg, R.	1.50
16	Bonds, B.	1.25
20	Maddux, G.	4.00

Award Winners
	Complete Set (25)	20.00
	Commons	.50
2	Mattingly, D.	2.50
3	Alomar, R.	1.50
6	Griffey Jr., K.	5.00
7	Lofton, K.	2.00
15	Bonds, B.	1.50
18	Maddux, G.	4.00
19	Thomas, F. (MVP)	5.00
20	Bonds, B. (MVP)	1.50
21	Molitor, P. (WS MVP)	1.50
23	Maddux, G. (CY)	4.00
24	Salmon, T. (ROY)	1.00
25	Piazza, M. (ROY)	3.50

Firemen
	Complete Set (10)	8.00
	Commons	.75

Hitting Machines
	Complete Set (10)	15.00
	Commons	.50
1	Alomar, R.	1.00
3	Bonds, B.	1.25
5	Gonzalez, J.	2.00
6	Gwynn, T.	2.50
9	Piazza, M.	3.50
10	Thomas, F.	5.00

League Leaders
	Complete Set (10)	5.00
	Commons	.75
3	Lofton, K.	2.50
5	Johnson, R.	1.50

On Base Leaders
	Complete Set (12)	150.00
	Commons	4.00
2	Bonds, B.	15.00
6	Griffey Jr., K.	60.00
9	Molitor, P.	10.00
12	Thomas, F.	60.00

Home Run Kings
	Complete Set (12)	75.00
	Commons	2.00
1	Gonzalez, J.	10.00
2	Griffey Jr., K.	25.00
3	Thomas, F.	25.00
4	Belle, A.	6.00
7	Bonds, B.	6.00
12	Piazza, M.	15.00

RBI Kings
	Complete Set (12)	125.00
	Commons	5.00
1	Belle, A.	15.00
2	Thomas, F.	60.00
3	Gonzalez, J.	25.00
7	Bonds, B.	15.00
10	Piazza, M.	30.00

Rising Stars
	Complete Set (12)	150.00
	Commons	5.00
2	Bagwell, J.	25.00
3	Belle, A.	15.00
4	Lofton, K.	15.00
9	Piazza, M.	30.00
11	Salmon, T.	10.00

Second Year Standouts
	Complete Set (10)	10.00
	Commons	.75
4	Salmon, T.	3.00
9	Piazza, M.	10.00

Strikeout Kings
	Complete Set (5)	5.00
	Commons	.50
1	Johnson, R.	1.50
3	Maddux, G.	5.00

Phillies Finest
	Complete Set (20)	15.00
	Finest Singles (1-20)	.75
	Daulton/Kruk Autograph	50.00

1994 LEAF
	NM Price
Complete Set (440)	$30.00
Series 1 Set (1-220)	15.00
Series 2 Set (221-440)	15.00
Commons	.10
Unlisted Stars	**.15-.30**
Series 1 or 2 Pack (12)	1.25
Series 1 or 2 Box (36)	40.00

Quality Rating ★★★
Another highly collectible Leaf set. Inserts are once again the main attraction.

#	Player	NM
1	Ripken, C.	2.50
46	Jones, C.	1.50
94	Maddux, G.	2.00
121	Mattingly, D.	1.00
164	Johnson, R.	.60
221	Bagwell, J.	1.00
251	Belle, A.	1.00
254	Gwynn, T.	1.25
264	Bonds, B.	.75
294	Puckett, K.	1.00
350	Lofton, K.	1.00
368	Griffey Jr., K.	3.00
391	McGwire, M.	1.25
400	Thomas, F.	3.00
418	Gonzalez, J.	1.00
425	Sandberg, R.	.75
436	Piazza, M.	1.25
No#	Thomas, F. (5th Anniversary)	5.00

Clean-Up Crew
	Complete Set (12)	50.00
	Series 1 Set (6)	15.00
	Series 2 Set (6)	35.00
	Commons	1.00
1	Walker, L.	10.00
7	Gonzalez, J.	18.00
10	Williams, M.	6.00
11	Belle, A.	12.00

Gamers
	Complete Set (12)	180.00
	Series 1 Set (6)	80.00
	Series 2 Set (6)	100.00
	Commons	5.00
1	Griffey Jr., K.	50.00
3	Gonzalez, J.	15.00
4	Mattingly, D.	20.00
7	Thomas, F.	50.00
8	Bonds, B.	12.00
9	Puckett, K.	12.00
12	Piazza, M.	25.00

Gold Leaf Rookies
	Complete Set (20)	20.00
	Series 1 Set (10)	12.00
	Series 2 Set (10)	8.00
	Commons	.50
1	Lopez, J.	2.00
2	White, R.	2.00
6	Ramirez, M.	6.00

Gold Leaf Stars
	Complete Set (15)	250.00
	Series 1 Set (1-8)	150.00
	Series 2 Set (9-15)	100.00
	Commons	8.00
1	Alomar, R.	10.00
2	Bonds, B.	15.00
4	Griffey Jr., K.	70.00
6	Mattingly, D.	25.00
8	Maddux, G.	50.00
11	Thomas, F.	70.00
13	Gonzalez, J.	20.00

AL MVP Contenders
	Complete Set (15)	100.00
	Commons	2.00
	Gold Version	2x
	Thomas Jumbo	15.00
	Note: Contest Has Expired.	
1	Belle, A.	8.00
6	Gonzalez, J.	10.00
7	Griffey Jr., K.	35.00
10	Puckett, K.	8.00
11	Ripken, C.	30.00
12	Thomas, F.	35.00

NL MVP Contenders
	Complete Set (15)	60.00
	Commons	2.00
	Gold Version	2x
	Note: Contest Has Expired.	
2	Bagwell, J.	12.00
4	Bonds, B.	8.00
12	Piazza, M.	15.00

Power Brokers
	Complete Set (10)	25.00
	Commons	1.00
1	Thomas, F.	10.00
3	Bonds, B.	2.00
4	Gonzalez, J.	3.00
5	Griffey Jr., K.	10.00
6	Piazza, M.	5.00
10	Belle, A.	2.00

Slide Show
	Complete Set (10)	65.00
	Series 1 Set (5)	35.00
	Series 2 Set (5)	30.00
	Commons	2.00
1	Thomas, F.	18.00
2	Piazza, M.	10.00
4	Sandberg, R.	4.00
6	Bonds, B.	4.00
7	Gonzalez, J.	5.00
9	Griffey Jr., K.	18.00

Statistical Standouts
	Complete Set (10)	18.00
	Commons	.75
1	Thomas, F.	6.00
2	Bonds, B.	1.50
3	Gonzalez, J.	2.00
4	Piazza, M.	4.00
5	Maddux, G.	4.00
6	Griffey Jr., K.	6.00
9	Gwynn, T.	2.50
10	Ripken, C.	5.00

1994 LEAF LIMITED
	NM Price
Complete Set (160)	$90.00
Commons	.50
Unlisted Stars	**.75-1.50**
Pack (5)	5.00
Box (20)	70.00

Quality Rating ★★★★
Collectors still like Limited's design but overall demand for the set has fallen off.

#	Player	NM
5	Ripken, C.	8.00
7	Clemens, R.	3.00
12	Vaughn, M.	3.00
24	Thomas, F.	10.00
27	Belle, A.	3.00
28	Lofton, K.	3.00
30	Ramirez, M.	2.00

51	Puckett, K.	3.00
61	McGwire, M.	4.00
56	Mattingly, D.	4.00
66	Griffey Jr., K.	10.00
67	Johnson, R.	2.00
72	Gonzalez, J.	5.00
87	Maddux, G.	5.00
110	Bagwell, J.	4.00
120	Piazza, M.	5.00
152	Gwynn, T.	4.00
156	Bonds, B.	3.00

Gold All-Stars

	Complete Set (18)	175.00
	Commons	4.00
1	Thomas, F.	40.00
7	Ripken, C.	30.00
8	Smith, O.	8.00
9	Puckett, K.	12.00
10	Bonds, B.	12.00
11	Griffey Jr., K.	40.00
12	Gwynn, T.	18.00
16	Piazza, M.	25.00
18	Maddux, G.	25.00

1994 LEAF LIMITED ROOKIES

	NM Price
Complete Set (80)	$30.00
Commons	.50
Unlisted Stars	**.75-1.00**
Pack (5)	4.00
Box (20)	60.00

Quality Rating ★★★
Donruss wanted more of a good thing so they developed an extended set.

#	Player	NM
43	Valdes, I. (R)	2.50
49	Edmonds, J.	2.00
66	Greer, R. (R)	5.00
78	Park, C. (R)	5.00

Rookie Phenoms

	Complete Set (10)	175.00
	Commons	8.00
1	Mondesi, R.	20.00
4	Delgado, C.	15.00
7	Klesko, R.	20.00
8	Lopez, J.	15.00
9	Ramirez, M.	30.00
10	Rodriguez, A.	90.00

1994 LEAF STUDIO

	NM Price
Complete Set (220)	$15.00
Commons	.05
Unlisted Stars	**.10-.30**
Pack (12)	1.00
Box (36)	25.00

Quality Rating ★★★
The usual Studio quality and player selection is here, but the Silver and Gold Stars have leveled off.

#	Player	NM
16	Bagwell, J.	.75
39	Maddux, G.	2.00
54	Smith, O.	.50
63	Sandberg, R.	.75
72	Piazza, M.	1.50
83	Bonds, B.	.75
92	Belle, A.	.75
93	Lofton, K.	.75
95	Ramirez, M.	.75
101	Griffey Jr., K.	3.00
102	Johnson, R.	.50
127	Ripken, C.	2.50
132	Gwynn, T.	1.25

154	Gonzalez, J.	1.00
200	Puckett, K.	1.00
209	Thomas, F.	3.00
215	Mattingly, D.	1.00

Editor's Choice

	Complete Set (8)	40.00
	Commons	2.00
1	Bonds, B.	3.00
2	Thomas, F.	15.00
3	Griffey Jr., K.	15.00
5	Gonzalez, J.	5.00
8	Piazza, M.	8.00

Heritage

	Complete Set (8)	20.00
	Commons	.75
1	Bonds, B.	2.50
2	Thomas, F.	8.00
4	Mattingly, D.	4.00
5	Sandberg, R.	3.00
8	Mussina, M.	1.50

Silver Stars

	Complete Set (10)	225.00
1	Gwynn, T.	25.00
2	Bonds, B.	12.00
3	Thomas, F.	50.00
4	Griffey Jr., K.	50.00
5	Carter, J.	6.00
6	Piazza, M.	25.00
7	Ripken, C.	40.00
8	Maddux, G.	25.00
9	Gonzalez, J.	18.00
10	Mattingly, D.	20.00

Gold Stars

	Complete Set (10)	450.00
1	Gwynn, T.	45.00
2	Bonds, B.	25.00
3	Thomas, F.	100.00
4	Griffey Jr., K.	100.00
5	Carter, J.	12.00
6	Piazza, M.	60.00
7	Ripken, C.	80.00
8	Maddux, G.	50.00
9	Gonzalez, J.	35.00
10	Mattingly, D.	35.00

1994 OPC

	NM Price
Complete Set (270)	$15.00
Commons	.10
Unlisted Stars	**.15-.30**
Pack (15)	.75
Box (36)	25.00

Quality Rating ★★
Production was very low on this set, and some of the inserts are becoming increasingly difficult.

#	Player	NM
16	Sandberg, R.	.60
22	Griffey Jr., K.	3.00
28	Gonzalez, J.	1.00
43	Belle, A.	.75
54	Mattingly, D.	.75
57	Jones, C.	1.00
93	Puckett, K.	.75
96	Alomar, R.	.50
101	Maddux, G.	2.00
109	Gwynn, T.	.75
121	Ramirez, M.	1.00
127	Thomas, F.	3.00
147	Piazza, M.	1.00
181	Smith, O.	.50
185	Ripken, C.	2.50
200	Bonds, B.	.75
212	Bagwell, J.	.75
237	Lofton, K.	.60

All-Star Redemptions

	Complete Set (25)	12.00
	Commons	.25
1	Thomas, F.	3.00
3	Bonds, B.	.75
4	Gonzalez, J.	1.00
5	Bagwell, J.	1.00
7	Sandberg, R.	.75
8	Griffey Jr., K.	3.00
9	Piazza, M.	1.00
12	Belle, A.	.75
15	Ripken, C.	3.00
17	Puckett, K.	.60
21	Alomar, R.	.75
22	Maddux, G.	3.00
25	Lofton, K.	.75

Large All-Stars

	Complete Set (25)	40.00
	Commons	.75
1	Thomas, F.	8.00
3	Bonds, B.	2.50
4	Gonzalez, J.	3.00
5	Bagwell, J.	3.00
7	Sandberg, R.	3.00
8	Griffey Jr., K.	8.00
9	Piazza, M.	8.00
12	Belle, A.	2.00
13	McGriff, F.	1.00
15	Ripken, C.	8.00
17	Puckett, K.	2.50
21	Alomar, R.	2.00
22	Maddux, G.	8.00
25	Lofton, K.	2.00

Toronto Blue Jays

	Complete Set (9)	20.00
	Commons	1.00
3	Molitor, P.	3.00
4	Carter, J.	2.50
6	Alomar, R.	5.00

Hot Prospects

	Complete Set (9)	25.00
	Commons	1.00
4	Mondesi, R.	3.00
5	Delgado, C.	2.50
6	Ramirez, M.	8.00
7	Lopez, J.	3.00
9	Klesko, R.	6.00

Diamond Dynamos

	Complete Set (18)	45.00
	Commons	1.50
1	Piazza, M.	20.00
11	Salmon, T.	8.00
12	Conine, J.	3.00

1994 PACIFIC

	NM Price
Complete Set (660)	$35.00
Commons	.10
Unlisted Stars	**.15-.40**
Pack (12)	1.00
Box (36)	25.00

Quality Rating ★★
Some of this product was shipped to Spanish speaking areas thus it can be somewhat difficult to locate. Inserts are nearly impossible to find in any quanity.

#	Player	NM
10	Jones, C.	1.00
15	Maddux, G.	1.50
44	Ripken, C.	2.00
109	Sandberg, R.	.60
138	Thomas, F.	2.00
165	Belle, A.	.75
173	Lofton, K.	.75
183	Ramirez, M.	.75

257	Bagwell, J.	1.00
318	Piazza, M.	1.00
365	Puckett, K.	1.00
430	Mattingly, D.	1.00
456	McGwire, M.	1.00
525	Gwynn, T.	1.25
540	Bonds, B.	.75
570	Griffey Jr., K.	2.00
617	Gonzalez, J.	1.00
655	Bonds, B. (MVP)	.50
656	Maddux, G. (CY)	1.00
658	Piazza, M. (ROY)	.50
660	Thomas, F. (MVP)	1.50

All-Latino Team

	Complete Set (20)	35.00
	Commons	1.50
13	Rodriguez, I.	7.00
14	Gonzalez, J.	10.00
17	Alomar, R.	4.00

Home Run Leaders

	Complete Set (20)	100.00
	Commons	2.00
1	Gonzalez, J.	10.00
2	Griffey Jr., K.	30.00
3	Thomas, F.	30.00
4	Belle, A.	6.00
11	Bonds, B.	5.00
16	Piazza, M.	15.00

Jewels of the Crown

	Complete Set (36)	130.00
	Commons	2.00
2	Gonzalez, J.	10.00
5	Alomar, R.	4.00
7	Johnson, R.	5.00
8	Griffey Jr., K.	25.00
10	Mattingly, D.	8.00
11	Puckett, K.	7.00
12	Salmon, T.	4.00
13	Thomas, F.	25.00
15	Ripken, C.	20.00
17	Lofton, K.	7.00
24	Bagwell, J.	8.00
26	Sandberg, R.	6.00
28	Bonds, B.	6.00
29	Piazza, M.	12.00
30	Maddux, G.	20.00
35	Gwynn, T.	8.00

1994 PINNACLE

	NM Price
Complete Set (540)	$30.00
Series 1 Set (1-270)	15.00
Series 2 Set (271-540)	15.00
Commons	.10
Unlisted Stars	**.15-.35**
Series 1 or 2 Pack (14)	2.00
Series 1 or 2 Box (24)	38.00

Quality Rating ★★★★
Team Pinnacle cards have faded despite great player selection and crisp photography.

#	Player	NM
1	Thomas, F.	3.00
4	Gwynn, T.	1.00
6	Sandberg, R.	.75
11	Maddux, G.	2.00
15	Belle, A.	.75
21	Puckett, K.	1.00
23	Mattingly, D.	1.00
26	Bonds, B.	.75
28	Piazza, M.	1.50
50	Ripken, C.	2.50
100	Griffey Jr., K.	3.00
179	Lofton, K.	.75
236	Jones, Chi.	1.50
242	Mondesi, R.	.60

#	Player	
244	Ramirez, M.	1.00
264	Wagner, B. (R)	.75
270	Nixon, T. (R)	.75
278	Johnson, R.	.50
290	Bagwell, J.	1.00
300	McGwire, M.	1.25
350	Gonzalez, J.	1.00
389	Smith, O.	.50
438	Lee, D. (R)	1.00
527	Park, C. (R)	1.50
SR1	Delgado, C.	6.00

Artist's Proofs

Complete Set (540)		3200.00
Series 1 Set (270)		2200.00
Series 2 Set (270)		1000.00
Commons		3.00
Unlisted Stars		10.00-40.00
1	Thomas, F.	125.00
4	Gwynn, T.	45.00
11	Maddux, G.	100.00
23	Mattingly, D.	50.00
28	Piazza, M.	60.00
50	Ripken, C.	100.00
100	Griffey Jr., K.	125.00
236	Jones, C.	60.00
290	Bagwell, J.	50.00

Museum Collection

Complete Set (540)		900.00
Series 1 Set (270)		500.00
Series 2 Set (270)		400.00
Commons		1.50
Unlisted Stars		5.00-18.00
1	Thomas, F.	50.00
4	Gwynn, T.	20.00
11	Maddux, G.	40.00
23	Mattingly, D.	25.00
28	Piazza, M.	30.00
50	Ripken, C.	45.00
100	Griffey Jr., K.	50.00
236	Jones, C.	30.00
244	Ramirez, M.	25.00
290	Bagwell, J.	20.00

Rookie Team Pinnacle

Complete Set (9)		80.00
Commons		5.00
1	Delgado/Lopez	12.00
5	Jones/Abbott	30.00
6	White/Ramirez	12.00

Run Creators

Complete Set (44)		140.00
Series 1 Set (22)		80.00
Series 2 Set (22)		60.00
Commons		2.00
2	Thomas, F.	20.00
3	Griffey Jr., K.	20.00
7	Gonzalez, J.	7.00
8	Belle, A.	4.00
12	Vaughn, M.	4.00
14	Lofton, K.	5.00
20	Puckett, K.	5.00
23	Bonds, B.	5.00
28	Piazza, M.	8.00
35	Gwynn, T.	7.00
36	Bagwell, J.	7.00

Team Pinnacle

Complete Set (9)		150.00
Commons		8.00
1	Bagwell/Thomas	60.00
4	Ripken/Bell	40.00
5	Rodriguez/Piazza	25.00
6	Dykstra/Griffey	45.00
7	Gonzalez/Bonds	20.00
9	Maddux/McDowell	25.00

Tribute Series

Complete Set (18)		100.00
Series 1 Set (9)		40.00
Series 2 Set (9)		60.00
Commons		2.00
7	Piazza, M.	10.00
8	Bonds, B.	4.00
9	Johnson, R.	4.00
10	Smith, O.	5.00
12	Maddux, G.	15.00
13	Ripken, C.	20.00
14	Thomas, F.	20.00
15	Gonzalez, J.	10.00
16	Alomar, R.	4.00
17	Griffey Jr., K.	20.00

1994 SCORE

	NM Price
Complete Set (660)	$30.00
Series 1 Set (1-330)	15.00
Series 2 Set (331-660)	15.00
Commons	.05
Unlisted Stars	**.10 -.30**
Series 1 or 2 Pack (14)	1.25
Series 1 or 2 Box (36)	36.00

Quality Rating ★★★
Score remains a big sleeper. Putting together a Gold Star set is a real task.

#	Player	NM
1	Bonds, B.	.75
3	Griffey Jr., K.	2.00
4	Bagwell, J.	.75
7	Belle, A.	.60
12	Gwynn, T.	.75
20	Sandberg, R.	.60
21	Puckett, K.	.75
23	Mattingly, D.	.75
27	Gonzalez, J.	.75
41	Thomas, F.	2.00
85	Ripken, C.	1.50
384	Smith, O.	.50
476	Piazza, M.	.75
486	Nixon, T. (R)	.60
524	Maddux, G.	1.50
536	Wagner, B. (R)	.50
550	McGwire, M.	.75
572	Jones, C.	.75
585	Lee, D. (R)	1.00
628	Griffey Jr., K.	1.50
631	Thomas, F.	1.50
634	Maddux, G.	1.00
645	Ramirez, M.	1.00

Boys of Summer

Complete Set (60)		120.00
Series 1 Set (1-30)		60.00
Series 2 Set (31-60)		60.00
Commons		1.25
Unlisted Stars		1.50-2.00
6	Piazza, M.	25.00
20	Lopez, J.	5.00
24	Salmon, T.	5.00
38	Ramirez, M.	12.00
41	Klesko, R.	7.00
45	Delgado, C.	5.00
47	Mondesi, R.	6.00
58	Jones, C.	25.00

Dream Team

Complete Set (10)		70.00
Commons		4.00
1	Mussina, M.	8.00
3	Mattingly, D.	20.00
7	Gonzalez, J.	20.00

Gold Rush

Complete Set (660)		170.00
Series 1 Set (1-330)		85.00
Series 2 Set (331-660)		85.00
Commons		.40
Gold Stars		4x-10x
Gold Rookies		2x-4x

Gold Stars

Complete Set (60)		275.00
Series 1 Set (30)		100.00
Series 2 Set (30)		175.00
Commons		2.00
1	Bonds, B.	10.00
8	Bagwell, J.	12.00
11	Galarraga, A.	5.00
13	Piazza, M.	20.00
23	Gwynn, T.	15.00
27	Walker, L.	6.00

#	Player	
32	Griffey Jr., K.	40.00
33	Gonzalez, J.	15.00
36	Ripken, C.	30.00
41	Lofton, K.	12.00
42	Alomar, R.	5.00
43	Johnson, R.	6.00
44	Salmon, T.	5.00
45	Thomas, F.	40.00
46	Belle, A.	8.00
49	Mattingly, D.	15.00
51	Vaughn, M.	7.00
52	Puckett, K.	10.00
58	Rodriguez, I.	10.00

The Cycle

Complete Set (20)		150.00
Commons		2.00
2	Lofton, K.	15.00
3	Molitor, P.	5.00
9	Bichette, D.	7.00
16	Gonzalez/Bonds	18.00
17	Griffey Jr., K.	50.00
18	Thomas, F.	50.00
20	Williams/Belle	15.00

1994 SCORE TRADED

	NM Price
Complete Set (165)	$10.00
Commons	.05
Unlisted Stars	**.10 -.30**
Pack (10)	1.00
Box (36)	25.00

Quality Rating ★★
The Rodriguez call-up card is the highlight of the set. Player selection is quite good.

#	Player	NM
72	Ramirez, M.	.75
82	Mondesi, R.	.75
136	Park, C (R).	1.25
No#	Rodriguez, A. (Call-Up)	55.00

Gold Rush

Complete Set (165)		50.00
Commons		.30
Unlisted Stars		2x-5x

Changing Places

Complete Set (10)		35.00
Commons		2.00
1	Clark, W.	8.00
10	Sanders, D.	8.00

Super Rookies

Complete Set (18)		60.00
Commons		2.00
1	Delgado, C.	5.00
2	Ramirez, M.	15.00
3	Klesko, R.	10.00
4	Mondesi, R.	6.00
11	Lopez, J.	5.00
14	White, R.	5.00
18	Edmonds, J.	8.00

1994 SELECT

	NM Price
Complete Set (420)	$35.00
Series 1 Set (1-210)	20.00
Series 2 Set (211-420)	15.00
Commons	.10
Unlisted Stars	**.15-.30**
Series 1 Pack (12)	1.50
Series 1 Box (24)	30.00
Series 2 Pack (12)	1.00
Series 2 Box (24)	20.00

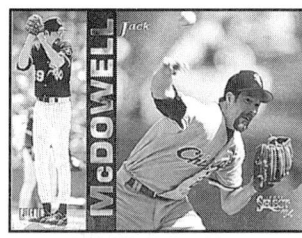

Quality Rating ★★
Select never caught fire as it became just another premium set. Wax prices remain a bargain.

#	Player	NM
1	Griffey Jr., K.	3.00
2	Maddux, G.	2.00
4	Piazza, M.	1.50
6	Thomas, F.	3.00
17	Puckett, K.	1.00
19	Johnson, R.	.60
23	Mattingly, D.	1.00
30	Smith, O.	.50
32	Sandberg, R.	1.00
57	McGwire, M.	1.00
77	Gwynn, T.	1.00
177	Park, C. (R)	1.50
181	Ramirez, M.	1.00
211	Bonds, B.	.75
212	Gonzalez, J.	1.00
231	Lofton, K.	.75
234	Bagwell, J.	1.00
235	Belle, A.	.75
249	Ripken, C.	2.50
309	Salmon, T.	.60
No#	Ripken, C. (Salute)	50.00
No#	Winfield, D. (Salute)	8.00
No#	Molitor, P. (MVP)	10.00
No#	Delgado, C. (ROY)	6.00

Crown Contenders

Complete Set (10)		100.00
Commons		3.00
2	Maddux, G.	20.00
4	Johnson, R.	6.00
5	Thomas, F.	30.00
6	Bonds, B.	6.00
7	Gonzalez, J.	12.00
9	Piazza, M.	18.00
10	Griffey Jr., K.	30.00

Rookie Surge

Complete Set (18)		100.00
Series 1 Set (9)		50.00
Series 2 Set (9)		50.00
Commons		4.00
3	Klesko, R.	10.00
4	Delgado, C.	10.00
6	White, R.	8.00
9	Lopez, J.	10.00
10	Ramirez, M.	20.00
13	Park, C.	15.00
17	Mondesi, R.	12.00

Skills

Complete Set (10)		60.00
Commons		3.00
1	Johnson, R.	10.00
2	Larkin, B.	6.00
4	Lofton, K.	12.00
5	Gonzalez, J.	20.00
6	Bonds, B.	10.00
8	Rodriguez, I.	10.00
9	Walker., L.	10.00

1994 SPORTFLICS

	NM Price
Complete Set (193)	$25.00
Commons	.20
Unlisted Stars	**.25-.60**
Pack (8)	1.50
Box (24)	33.00

Quality Rating ★★★
Inserts are difficult to find and keep collectors busy. The design provides a change of pace.

#	Player	NM
7	Bagwell, J.	1.00
10	Belle, A.	.75
25	Gwynn, T.	1.25
35	Gonzalez, J.	1.25
42	Puckett, K.	.75
43	Lofton, K.	1.00
45	Sandberg, R.	1.00
53	Maddux, G.	2.00
67	Piazza, M.	1.50
69	Ripken, C.	2.50
70	Thomas, F.	3.00
91	Bonds, B.	.75
127	Mattingly, D.	1.00
143	Griffey Jr., K.	3.00
151	Ramirez, M.	1.25
160	Jones, C.	1.25
176	Thomas, F. (SF)	2.00
179	Ripken, C. (SF)	1.50
181	Griffey Jr., K. (SF)	2.00
189	Piazza, M. (SF)	1.00
193	Maddux, G. (SF)	1.00
No#	Cliff Floyd	5.00
No#	Paul Molitor	15.00

Movers

	Complete Set (12)	50.00
	Commons	2.00
2	Sandberg, R.	6.00
4	Puckett, K.	8.00
5	Gwynn, T.	10.00
9	Mattingly, D.	10.00

Shakers

	Complete Set (12)	80.00
	Commons	3.00
1	Lofton, K.	12.00
2	Salmon, T.	6.00
3	Bagwell, J.	12.00
6	White, R.	4.00
11	Piazza, M.	18.00
12	Ramirez, M.	8.00

1994 SPORTFLICS UPDATE

	NM Price
Complete Set (150)	$20.00
Commons	.15
Unlisted Stars	**.20-.50**
Pack (5)	3.00
Box (24)	60.00

Quality Rating ★★★
This set really caused a stir with its retail only release. Rodriguez is available along with hard-to-find inserts.

#	Player	NM
122	Park, C. (R)	2.50
148	Rodriguez, A. (R)	12.00
No#	Ramirez/Klesko (ROY)	10.00

Artist Proofs

	Complete Set (150)	2200.00
	Commons	8.00
	Unlisted Stars	20x-60x
91	Murray, E.	90.00
122	Park, C.	100.00
148	Rodriguez, A.	600.00

3-D Rookies

	Complete Set (18)	175.00
	Commons	6.00
2	Ramirez, M.	25.00
4	Delgado, C.	12.00
5	Lopez, J.	15.00
7	Mondesi, R.	15.00
9	Klesko, R.	15.00
11	Rodriguez, A.	80.00

Going, Going, Gone

	Complete Set (12)	100.00
	Commons	4.00
3	Gonzalez, J.	10.00
4	Griffey Jr., K.	30.00
5	Piazza, M.	15.00
6	Thomas, F.	30.00
8	Bonds, B.	6.00
11	Belle, A.	6.00

1994 TOPPS

	NM Price
Complete Set (792)	$35.00
Series 1 Set (1-396)	18.00
Series 2 Set (397-792)	18.00
Factory Set (808)	50.00
Commons	.05
Unlisted Stars	**.10 -.30**
Series 1 or 2 Pack (12)	.75
Series 1 or 2 Box (36)	18.00

Quality Rating ★★
Rookie selction is decent. Wax prices are very affordable.

#	Player	NM
1	Piazza, M.	1.25
34	Ryan, N.	1.50
40	Bagwell, J.	.75
100	Puckett, K.	.75
149	Lofton, K.	.50
158	Miller/Jeter	2.00
180	Brett, G.	.75
200	Ripken, C.	1.50
202	Benes, A. (R)	.75
205	Kieschnick, B. (R)	.60
209	Wagner, B. (R)	.75
216	Ramirez, M.	1.00
270	Thomas, F.	1.50
300	Sandberg, R.	.75
369	Bell/Arias (R)	.75
384	Thomas/McGriff (AS)	.60
387	Ripken/Blauser (AS)	.60
400	Griffey Jr., K.	1.50
480	Belle, A.	.75
499	Maddux, G.	1.00
600	Mattingly, D.	.75
601	Thomas, F. (ST)	.75
604	Ripken, C. (ST)	1.00
606	Griffey Jr., K. (ST)	.75
620	Gwynn, T.	.75
685	Gonzalez, J.	.75
700	Bonds, B.	.60
777	Jones/Klesko (CA)	2.00
783	Mondesi/Van Ryn (CA)	.50

Topps Gold

	Complete Set (792)	90.00
	Series 1 Set (1-396)	45.00
	Series 2 Set (397-792)	45.00
	Commons	.20
	Gold Stars	3x-5x
	Gold Rookies	2x-4x

Topps Black Gold

	Complete Set (44)	30.00
	Series 1 Set (22)	18.00
	Series 2 Set (22)	12.00
	Commons	.50
	Note: Winner cards have expired.	
1	Alomar, R.	1.00
3	Belle, A.	1.50
7	Gonzalez, J.	1.25
8	Griffey Jr., K.	4.00
11	Lofton, K.	1.00
17	Puckett, K.	1.00
18	Ripken, C.	4.00
21	Thomas, F.	4.00
23	Bagwell, J.	1.00
27	Bonds, B.	1.00

38	Maddux, G.	4.00
41	Piazza, M.	1.50

1994 TOPPS FINEST

	NM Price
Complete Set (440)	$160.00
Series 1 Set (1-220)	80.00
Series 2 Set (221-440)	80.00
Commons	.75
Unlisted Stars	**1.00-2.00**
Series1 or 2 Pack (7)	3.00
Series1 or 2 Box (24)	65.00

Quality Rating ★★★
This set is not as strong as the 1993 issue, but it's worth having.

#	Player	NM
1	Piazza, M.	8.00
78	McGwire, M.	5.00
136	Smith, O.	3.00
201	Gwynn, T.	5.00
203	Thomas, F.	10.00
204	Puckett, K.	3.00
208	Belle, A.	3.00
209	Maddux, G.	8.00
210	Sandberg, R.	3.00
211	Gonzalez, J.	6.00
212	Bagwell, J.	4.00
217	Clemens, R.	4.00
218	Lofton, K.	3.00
230	Bonds, B.	3.00
232	Griffey Jr., K.	12.00
235	Ripken, C.	10.00
392	Mattingly, D.	5.00
426	Park, C. (R)	7.00
430	Ramirez, M.	2.50

Finest Refractors

	Comp. Set (440)	2600.00
	Series 1 Set (1-220)	1300.00
	Series 2 Set (221-440)	1300.00
	Commons	3.00
	Unlisted Stars	10.00-40.00
1	Piazza, M.	80.00
203	Thomas, F.	120.00
209	Maddux, G.	80.00
212	Bagwell, J.	50.00
232	Griffey Jr., K.	120.00
235	Ripken, C.	100.00
392	Mattingly, D.	60.00
430	Ramirez, M.	50.00

Topps Finest Pre-Productions

	Complete Set (40)	150.00
	Commons	3.00
22	Sanders, D.	15.00
59	Bichette, D.	12.00
66	Mussina, M.	15.00
102	Thome, J.	10.00
136	Smith, O.	20.00

Finest Jumbos

	Complete Set (80)	400.00
	Series 1 Set (40)	200.00
	Series 2 Set (40)	200.00
	Commons	2.00
	Jumbos	2x

1994 TOPPS TRADED

	NM Price
Complete Set (132)	$50.00
Factory Set (140)	60.00
Commons	.05
Unlisted Stars	**.10 -.30**

Quality Rating ★★
Rookie cards of Grieve and Konerko make this set one to watch in the near future.

#	Player	NM
1	Wilson, P.	1.00
29	Greer, R. (R)	4.00
33	Long, T. (R)	.75
44	Grieve, B. (R)	35.00
54	Witt, K. (R)	4.00
56	Prospects	.75
70	Park, C. (R)	5.00
101	Ryan, R. (R)	1.00
112	Konerko, P. (R)	25.00
115	Clark, W.	.50
116	Smith, M. (R)	.50
130	Sandberg, R.	1.00
131	Sandberg, R.	1.00

Finest Inserts

	Complete Set (8)	7.00
1	Maddux, G.(MVP)	2.00
2	Piazza, M. (MVP)	2.00
3	Williams, M. (MVP)	.50
4	Mondesi, R. (ROY)	.50
5	Griffey Jr., K. (MVP)	3.00
6	Lofton, K. (MVP)	.75
7	Thomas, F. (MVP)	3.00
8	Ramirez, M. (ROY)	.75

1994 TOPPS STADIUM CLUB

	NM Price
Complete Set (720)	$55.00
Series 1 Set (1-270)	20.00
Series 2 Set (271-540)	20.00
Series 3 Set (541-720)	15.00
Commons	.10
Unlisted Stars	**.15-.35**
Series 1, 2, 3 Pack (12)	1.00
Series 1, 2, 3 Box (24)	20.00

Quality Rating ★★★
Stadium Club gives collectors plenty of stars and inserts that are fun to chase.

#	Player	NM
5	Brett, G.	1.00
34	Ryan, N.	3.00
85	Griffey Jr., K.	3.00
108	Bagwell, J.	1.00
140	Piazza, M.	1.50
151	Gwynn, T.	1.00
195	Mattingly, D.	1.00
219	Belle, A.	.75

#	Player	
238	Bonds, B. (AW)	.75
262	Griffey Jr., K. (35 HR)	1.50
266	Piazza, M. (35 HR)	.75
267	Thomas, F. (35 HR)	1.50
285	Thomas, F.	3.00
301	Lofton, K.	.75
320	Ramirez, M.	.75
358	McGwire, M.	1.25
359	Puckett, K.	1.00
373	Ripken, C.	2.50
397	Sandberg, R.	.75
528	Thomas, F.	1.25
529	Griffey Jr., K.	1.25
532	Bonds, B.	.50
544	Maddux, G.	2.00
568	Gonzalez, J.	.60
638	Jones, C.	1.50
716	Maddux, G.	1.00
718	Thomas, F.	1.50

Dugout Dirt

Complete Set (12)		12.00
Series 1 Set (4)		4.00
Series 2 Set (4)		4.00
Series 3 Set (4)		4.00
Commons		.50
1	Piazza, M.	1.50
4	Ripken, C.	2.50
6	Bonds, B.	1.00
7	Griffey Jr., K.	3.00
9	Thomas, F.	3.00

Super Teams

Complete Set (28)		60.00
Commons		2.00
1	Atlanta Braves	12.00
7	Los Angeles Dodgers	4.00
15	Baltimore Orioles	6.00
16	Boston Red Sox	4.00
19	Cleveland Indians	6.00
24	New York Yankees	4.00

First Day Production

Complete Set (720)		2800.00
Series 1 Set (1-270)		1200.00
Series 2 Set (271-540)		1100.00
Series 3 Set (541-720)		500.00
Commons		3.00
Unlisted Stars		5.00-35.00
5	Brett, G.	60.00
34	Ryan, N.	100.00
85	Griffey Jr., K.	100.00
140	Piazza, M.	50.00
195	Mattingly, D.	40.00
262	Griffey, K. (35 HR)	60.00
267	Thomas, F. (35 HR)	60.00
285	Thomas, F.	100.00
373	Ripken, C.	75.00
528	Thomas, F.	60.00
529	Griffey Jr., K.	60.00
544	Maddux, G.	70.00
638	Jones, C.	50.00
716	Maddux, G.	40.00
718	Thomas, F.	60.00

Golden Rainbow

Complete Set (720)		170.00
Series 1 Set (1-270)		65.00
Series 2 Set (271-540)		65.00
Series 3 Set (541-720)		40.00
Commons		.25
Golden Stars		3x-5x
Golden Rookies		2x-4x

Bowman Previews

Complete Set (10)		45.00
Commons		1.00
1	Thomas, F.	20.00
2	Piazza, M.	10.00
3	Belle, A.	6.00

Finest

Complete Set (10)		35.00
1	Bagwell, J.	3.50
2	Belle, A.	2.50
3	Bonds, B.	3.00
4	Gonzalez, J.	4.00
5	Griffey Jr., K.	12.00
6	Grissom, M.	2.00
7	Justice, D.	3.00
8	Piazza, M.	5.00
9	Salmon, T.	3.00
10	Thomas, F.	12.00

1994 UPPER DECK

	NM Price
Complete Set (550)	$50.00
Series 1 Set (1-280)	30.00
Series 2 Set (281-550)	20.00
Commons	.10
Unlisted Stars	**.15-.35**
Series 1 East/West Pack (12)	1.50
Series 1 East/West Box (36)	40.00
Series 1 Central Pack (12)	2.50
Series 1 Central Box (36)	60.00
Series 2 East/West Pack (12)	1.25
Series 2 East/West Box (36)	30.00
Series 2 Central Pack (12)	1.50
Series 2 Central Box (36)	40.00

Quality Rating ★★★

Another quality issue from Upper Deck is bettered by Jordan and Rodriguez rookies. Regional wax distribution makes for a challenge.

#	Player	NM
16	Hunter, B.	.75
19	Jordan, M. (R)	10.00
23	Ramirez, M.	1.25
24	Rodriguez, A. (R)	10.00
33	Piazza, M.	.75
38	Bonds, B.	.60
47	Piazza, M.	.75
53	Griffey Jr., K.	2.00
55	Thomas, F.	2.00
67	McGwire, M.	1.25
90	Mattingly, D.	1.00
92	Sandberg, R.	.75
131	Belle, A.	.75
155	Gonzalez, J.	1.25
185	Jones, C.	2.00
215	Lofton, K.	.75
219	Gwynn, T.	1.25
224	Griffey Jr., K.	3.00
272	Bagwell, J.	.60
273	Piazza, M.	.75
280	Bonds, B.	.50
281	Ripken, C.	1.50
284	Thomas, F.	1.50
285	Belle, A.	.60
289	Puckett, K.	.50
290	Mattingly, D.	.50
292	Griffey Jr., K.	1.50
298	Rodriguez, A.	4.00
300	Thomas, F.	3.00
320	Maddux, G.	2.00
325	Puckett, K.	1.00
360	Smith, O.	.50
400	Bonds, B.	.75
425	Ripken, C.	2.50
450	Clemens, R.	1.25
480	Bagwell, J.	1.00
500	Piazza, M.	1.25
520	Park, C. (R)	2.00
524	Wagner, B. (R)	1.00
529	Benes, A. (R)	1.00
530	Kieschnick, B. (R)	.75
532	Fullmer, B. (R)	1.25
543	Nixon, T. (R)	.75
550	Jeter, D.	1.50
	Griffey Autograph	250.00
	Mantle Autograph	500.00
	Griffey/Mantle Autogrph	1000.00
	Rodriguez Autograph	200.00

Electric Diamond

Complete Set (550)		130.00
Series 1 Set (1-280)		80.00
Series 2 Set (281-550)		50.00
Commons		.25
Unlisted Stars		2x
19	Jordan, M.	25.00

Diamond Collection

Complete Set (30)		320.00
Central Set (10)		150.00
East Set (10)		70.00
West Set (10)		100.00
Commons		4.00
C1	Bagwell, J.	15.00
C2	Jordan, M.	50.00
C4	Puckett, K.	15.00
C5	Ramirez, M.	10.00
C6	Sandberg, R.	10.00
C7	Smith, O.	10.00
C8	Thomas, F.	50.00
E2	Clemens, R.	10.00
E8	Mattingly, D.	20.00
E9	Ripken, C.	40.00
W1	Bonds, B.	12.00
W3	Gonzalez, J.	15.00
W4	Griffey Jr., K.	50.00
W5	Gwynn, T.	18.00
W9	Piazza, M.	30.00

Mantle's Long Shots

Complete Set (21)		50.00
Commons		1.00
1	Bagwell, J.	4.00
2	Belle, A.	3.00
3	Bonds, B.	3.00
9	Gonzalez, J.	5.00
10	Griffey Jr., K.	12.00
13	McGwire, M.	5.00
15	Piazza, M.	5.00
18	Thomas, F.	12.00
21	Mantle, M.	15.00

Next Generation

Complete Set (18)		130.00
Commons		1.50
1	Alomar, R.	4.00
5	Gonzalez, J.	10.00
6	Griffey Jr., K.	30.00
8	Jordan, M.	40.00
10	Klesko, R.	6.00
12	Mondesi, R.	5.00
13	Piazza, M.	15.00
14	Puckett, K.	10.00
15	Ramirez, M.	10.00
16	Rodriguez, A.	40.00

SP Previews

Complete Set (15)		190.00
Central Set (5)		80.00
East Set (5)		45.00
West Set (5)		65.00
C1	Bagwell, J.	10.00
C2	Jordan, M.	30.00
C3	Puckett, K.	10.00
C4	Ramirez, M.	12.00
C5	Thomas, F.	30.00
E1	Alomar, R.	6.00
E2	Floyd, C.	2.00
E3	Lopez, J.	4.00
E4	Mattingly, D.	12.00
E5	Ripken, C.	30.00
W1	Bonds, B.	8.00
W2	Gonzalez, J.	10.00
W3	Griffey Jr., K.	30.00
W4	Piazza, M.	15.00
W5	Salmon, T.	5.00

Insert Checklists

Complete Set (4)	18.00
Insert Singles	5.00

Mantle Heroes Set

Complete Set (8)	80.00
Mantle Singles (64-71)	10.00
Cover Card (No#)	10.00

1994 U.D. COLLECTOR'S CHOICE

	NM Price
Complete Set (670)	$30.00
Factory Set (675)	35.00
Series 1 Set (1-320)	15.00
Series 2 Set (321-670)	15.00
Commons	.05
Unlisted Stars	**.10-.40**
Series 1 or 2 Pack (12)	1.00
Series 1 or 2 Box (36)	25.00

Quality Rating ★★

UDCC is highlighted by Gold and Silver Signature inserts.

#	Player	NM
16	Ramirez, M.	1.00
65	Brett, G.	.60
117	Griffey Jr., K.	2.00
152	Jones, C.	1.25
183	Maddux, G.	1.50
192	Mattingly, D.	.60
240	Ripken, C.	1.50
249	Ryan, N.	2.00
340	Griffey Jr., K.	1.00
343	Ripken, C.	1.00
354	Thomas, F.	1.00
400	Piazza, M.	.75
425	Puckett, K.	.60
500	Thomas, F.	2.00
555	Sandberg, R.	.60
565	Lofton, K.	.50
590	Bagwell, J.	.60
610	Bonds, B.	.60
620	Belle, A.	.60
634	Griffey Jr., K.	1.00
635	Jordan, M.	4.00
640	Thomas, F.	1.00
644	Jeter, D.	.75
645	Lee, D. (R)	1.00
647	Rodriguez, A. (R)	8.00
661	Jordan, M. (R)	7.00

Silver Signatures

Complete Set (670)	200.00
Series 1 Set (1-320)	100.00
Series 2 Set (321-670)	100.00
Commons	.20
Silver Stars	3x-6x

Gold Signatures

Complete Set (670)	4000.00
Series 1 Set (1-320)	2000.00
Series 2 Set (321-670)	2000.00
Commons	3.00
Gold Stars	40x-75x

Home Run All-Stars

Complete Set (8)		6.00
1	Gonzalez, J.	.75
2	Griffey Jr., K.	3.50
3	Bonds, B.	1.25
4	Bonilla, B.	.50
5	Fielder, C.	.50
6	Belle, A.	1.25
7	Justice, D.	.60
8	Piazza, M.	1.25

1994 UPPER DECK SP

	NM Price
Complete Set (200)	$60.00
Commons	.10
Unlisted Stars	**.15-.50**
Pack (8)	6.00
Box (32)	150.00

Quality Rating ★★★

The Red Holoview cards are still a popular choice. Wax prices are holding steady thanks to the Rodriguez rookie card.

#	Player	NM
3	Damon, J. (PP)	1.00
4	Fullmer, B. (PP)	3.00
5	Hamilton, J. (PP)	1.00
7	Hunter, B. (PP)	1.00
9	Kieschnick, B. (PP, R)	1.00
10	Lee, D. (PP, R)	6.00
11	Nixon, T. (PP, R)	2.00
13	Park, C. (R)	4.00
15	Rodriguez, A. (PP, R)	30.00
16	Silva, J. (PP, R)	1.00
18	Wagner, B. (PP, R)	3.00
19	Williams, G. (PP, R)	1.50
27	Bagwell, J.	1.50
36	McGwire, M.	1.25
54	Maddux, G.	3.00
65	Smith, O.	1.00
71	Sandberg, R.	1.50
80	Piazza, M.	3.00
90	Bonds, B.	1.00
97	Belle, A.	1.00
98	Lofton, K.	1.50
101	Ramirez, M.	1.50
105	Griffey Jr., K.	5.00
106	Johnson, R.	1.00
126	Ripken, C.	4.00
130	Gwynn, T.	2.00
148	Gonzalez, J.	1.50
152	Clemens, R.	1.25
157	Vaughn, M.	1.00
186	Puckett, K.	2.00
193	Thomas, F.	5.00
198	Mattingly, D.	2.00

SP Die-Cuts

Complete Set (200)	150.00
Commons	.50
Unlisted stars	2x-3x

Blue Holoview

	Complete Set (38)	140.00
	Commons	2.50
1	Alomar, R.	6.00
3	Bagwell, J.	10.00
5	Clemens, R.	10.00
11	Gonzalez, J.	15.00
12	Griffey Jr., K.	30.00
13	Gwynn, T.	15.00
16	Jordan, M.	35.00
21	Klesko, R.	8.00
25	Mattingly, D.	12.00
26	McGwire, M.	15.00
29	Piazza, M.	20.00
30	Puckett, K.	10.00
31	Ramirez, M.	10.00
32	Ripken, C.	25.00
33	Rodriguez, A.	25.00
34	Salmon, T.	6.00
36	Smith, O.	6.00

Red Holoview

	Complete Set (38)	1300.00
	Commons	12.00
1	Alomar, R.	35.00
3	Bagwell, J.	80.00
5	Clemens, R.	80.00
6	Delgado, C.	25.00
11	Gonzalez, J.	100.00
12	Griffey Jr., K.	250.00
13	Gwynn, T.	100.00
16	Jordan, M.	300.00
17	Justice, D.	40.00
20	Kieschnick, B.	20.00
21	Klesko, R.	40.00
25	Mattingly, D.	80.00
26	McGwire, M.	100.00
27	Mondesi, R.	30.00
29	Piazza, M.	150.00
30	Puckett, K.	80.00
31	Ramirez, M.	60.00
32	Ripken, C.	200.00
33	Rodriguez, A.	250.00
34	Salmon, T.	40.00
36	Smith, O.	40.00
37	Sosa, S.	30.00

1995 BAZOOKA

	NM Price
Complete Set (132)	$12.00
Factory Set (137)	15.00
Commons	.05
Unlisted Stars	**.10 -.30**
Pack (5)	.50
Box (36)	15.00

Quality Rating ★★

At fifty cents per pack collectors get stars and and a piece of gum. Card design is average but adequate.

#	Player	NM
1	Maddux, G.	1.50
2	Ripken, C.	2.00
20	Bonds, B.	.60
22	Lofton, K.	.60
27	McGwire, M.	.75
30	Gwynn, T.	.75
31	Griffey, K.	2.00
47	Mattingly, D.	.60
61	Bagwell, J.	.75
68	Gonzalez, J.	.75
77	Piazza, M.	1.00
109	Ramirez, M.	.75
113	Puckett, K.	.60
116	Belle, A.	.60
120	Thomas, F.	2.00

Red Hot

	Complete Set (22)	20.00
	Commons	.20
1	Maddux, G.	3.00
2	Ripken, C.	3.50
3	Bonds, B.	1.25
4	Lofton, K.	1.50
6	Gwynn, T.	2.00
7	Griffey, K.	4.00
13	Bagwell, J.	1.50
15	Piazza, M.	1.50
21	Belle, A.	1.50
22	Thomas, F.	4.00

1995 BOWMAN

	NM Price
Complete Set (439)	$230.00
Commons	.10
Unlisted Stars	**.15 -.50**
Pack (10)	8.00
Box (24)	180.00

Quality Rating ★★★

Once again Bowman supplies collectors with many names they may not have heard of before. Card design is a plus.

#	Player	NM
4	Abreu, B. (R)	3.00
22	Colon, B. (R)	3.00
25	Lee, D.	2.00

23	Jones, A. (R)	30.00
36	Wilson, E. (R)	2.00
83	Carpenter, C. (R)	2.00
88	Moss, D. (R)	2.00
90	Guerrero, V. (R)	25.00
92	Garcia, K. (R)	8.00
127	Higginson, B. (R)	6.00
140	Ordonez, R. (R)	2.50
152	Nixon, T.	1.00
157	Gibson, D. (R)	10.00
172	Marrero, E. (R)	4.00
180	Isringhausen, J.	1.50
206	Dye, J.	1.50
224	Grudzielanak, M. (R)	1.00
227	Greene, T.	3.00
229	Jeter, D.	3.00
231	Rivera, R.	2.00
238	Nomo, H. (R)	10.00
240	Payton, J. (R)	3.00
241	Konerko, P.	20.00
242	Elarton, S. (R)	2.00
249	Garciaparra, N.	25.00
253	Clark, T.	2.50
254	Damon, J.	1.00
257	Pettitte, A.	2.00
258	Grieve, B.	25.00
262	Jones, C.	2.00
271	Rolen, S. (R)	25.00
276	Belle, A.	2.00
279	Bagwell, J.	1.50
280	Puckett, K.	1.00
282	Mattingly, D.	1.50
293	Clemens, R.	1.50
303	McGwire, M.	2.00
304	Gwynn, T.	2.00
305	Lofton, K.	1.00
310	Piazza, M.	2.00
321	Griffey, K.	4.00
323	Gonzalez, J.	1.50
351	Thomas, F.	4.00
352	Ramirez, M.	1.00
368	Alomar, R.	.75
370	Smith, O.	.60
376	Bonds, B.	1.00
392	Murray, E.	.75
395	Johnson, R.	.75
406	Maddux, G.	3.00
411	Vaughn, M.	1.00
413	Ripken, C.	3.00

Gold Foil

	Complete Set (54)	150.00
	Commons	1.00
	Gold Foil	1x-2x

1995 BOWMAN'S BEST

	NM Price
Complete Set (180)	$230.00
Commons	.50
Unlisted Stars	**1.00-2.00**
Pack (7)	15.00
Box (24)	325.00

Quality Rating ★★★

Jones, Guerrero, and Rolen rookies are carrying the set. Player selection is great.

Red Set

#	Player	NM
10	Ripken, C.	6.00
12	Ramirez, M.	3.00
13	Bonds, B.	3.00
15	Maddux, G.	6.00
16	Bagwell, J.	3.00
20	Lofton, K.	3.00
21	Gwynn, T.	3.50
23	Clemens, R.	3.00
27	Puckett, K.	2.50
30	Gonzalez, J.	3.50
36	Piazza, M.	5.00

46	Mattingly, D.	4.00
49	Griffey, K.	8.00
50	Belle, A.	4.00
65	Thomas, F.	8.00
69	McGwire, M.	3.00
83	Nomo, H. (R)	12.00

Blue Set

1	Jeter, D.	5.00
2	Guerrero, V. (R)	25.00
3	Abreu, B. (R)	4.00
7	Jones, A. (R)	35.00
10	Sexson, R. (R)	4.00
12	Kieschnick, B.	2.50
18	Greene, T.	4.00
20	Clark, T.	5.00
25	Grieve, B.	30.00
28	Konerko, P.	25.00
29	Garciaparra, N.	30.00
33	Ordonez, R.	3.00
37	Elarton, S. (R)	3.00
42	Rivera, R.	3.00
45	Damon, J.	3.00
49	Encarnacion, J. (R)	10.00
50	Pettitte, A.	2.00
56	Garcia, K. (R)	8.00
62	Payton, J. (R)	2.00
73	Colon, B. (R)	4.00
74	Carpenter, C. (R)	3.00
85	Cruz, J. (R)	5.00
87	Rolen, S. (R)	30.00

Mirror Image

	Complete Set (15)	30.00
	Commons	1.00
	Diffraction Foil	5x-10x
2	Redman/Ramirez	1.50
5	LeBron/Gonzalez	1.50
8	Jenkins/Vaughn	2.00
9	Rivera/Thomas	7.00
10	Goodwin/Lofton	2.00
11	Hunter/Gwynn	2.00
12	Green/Griffey	5.00
13	Garcia/Williams	2.00
15	Watkins/Bagwell	2.00

Refractors

	Complete Set (195)	2400.00
	Commons	3.00
	Unlisted Stars	12x
B1	Jeter, D.	75.00
B2	Guerrero, V.	150.00
B7	Jones, A.	175.00
B25	Grieve, B.	125.00
B28	Konerko, P.	100.00
B29	Garciaparra, N.	140.00
B87	Rolen, S.	140.00
R10	Ripken, C.	80.00
R15	Maddux, G.	60.00
R21	Gwynn, T.	40.00
R30	Gonzalez, J.	40.00
R36	Piazza, M.	60.00
R49	Griffey, K.	120.00
R65	Thomas, F.	100.00

1995 DONRUSS

	NM Price
Complete Set (550)	$35.00
Series 1 Set (1-330)	20.00
Series 2 Set (331-550)	15.00
Commons	.05
Unlisted Stars	**.10 -.30**
Series 1 or 2 Pack (12)	1.25
Series 1 or 2 Box (36)	40.00

Quality Rating ★★★

Donruss adds Press Proofs into the mix of already popular inserts. All-Star cards are hot.

#	Player	NM
5	Piazza, M.	1.50
8	Bonds, B.	.75
20	Bagwell, J.	1.00
42	Gonzalez, J.	1.00
55	Mattingly, D.	1.00
83	Ripken, C.	2.50
114	Rodriguez, A.	2.50
224	Gwynn, T.	1.25
264	Belle, A.	.75
275	Thomas, F.	3.00
331	Maddux, G.	2.00
340	Griffey Jr., K.	3.00
371	Lofton, K.	.75
380	Puckett, K.	1.00
460	McGwire, M.	1.00

Press Proofs
Complete Set (550)		1800.00
Series 1 Set (330)		1000.00
Series 2 Set (220)		800.00
Commons		2.00
Unlisted Stars		5.00-30.00
5	Piazza, M.	70.00
20	Bagwell, J.	40.00
42	Gonzalez, J.	40.00
55	Mattingly, D.	50.00
83	Ripken, C.	80.00
114	Rodriguez, A.	90.00
275	Thomas, F.	125.00
331	Maddux, G.	60.00
340	Griffey Jr., K.	125.00
370	Ramirez, M.	50.00

AL All-Stars
Complete Set (9)		100.00
Commons		3.00
2	Rodriguez, I.	8.00
3	Thomas, F.	35.00
6	Ripken, C.	30.00
8	Griffey Jr., K.	40.00
9	Puckett, K.	10.00

NL All-Stars
Complete Set (9)		60.00
Commons		3.00
1	Maddux, G.	25.00
2	Piazza, M.	20.00
6	Smith, O.	8.00
7	Bonds, B.	10.00
8	Gwynn, T.	15.00

Bomb Squad
Complete Set (6)		30.00
Commons		2.00
1	Griffey/Williams	12.00
2	Thomas/Bagwell	12.00

Diamond Kings
Complete Set (29)		50.00
Series 1 Set (14)		25.00
Series 2 Set (15)		25.00
Commons		1.50
1	Thomas, F.	10.00
2	Bagwell, J.	4.00
11	Lofton, K.	4.00
19	Puckett, K.	3.00
22	Maddux, G.	6.00
24	Gwynn, T.	4.00
27	Griffey Jr., K.	10.00

Dominators
Complete Set (9)		30.00
1	Cone/Mussina/Maddux	7.00
2	Rodriguez/Piazza/Daulton	4.00
3	McGriff/Thomas/Bagwell	10.00
4	Alomar/Baerga/Biggio	3.00
5	Ventura/Fryman/Wlliams	2.00
6	Ripken/Larkin/Cordero	10.00
7	Belle/Bonds/Alou	4.00
8	Griffey/Lofton/Grissom	10.00
9	Puckett/O'Neill/Gwynn	4.00

Elite
Complete Set (12)		375.00
Series 1 Set (6)		200.00
Series 2 Set (6)		175.00
49	Bagwell, J.	30.00
50	O'Neill, P.	10.00
51	Maddux, G.	50.00
52	Piazza, M.	40.00
53	Williams, M.	15.00
54	Griffey Jr., K.	70.00
55	Thomas, F.	60.00
56	Bonds, B.	20.00
57	Puckett, K.	20.00
58	McGriff, F.	10.00
59	Canseco, J.	10.00
60	Belle, A.	15.00

Long Ball Leaders
Complete Set (8)		25.00
1	Thomas, F.	8.00
2	McGriff, F.	1.50
3	Griffey Jr., K.	8.00
4	Williams, M.	2.00
5	Piazza, M.	4.00
6	Canseco, J.	1.00
7	Bonds, B.	2.50
8	Bagwell, J.	3.00

Mound Marvels
Complete Set (8)		20.00
Commons		2.00
1	Maddux, G.	15.00
7	Johnson, R.	3.00

1995 E-MOTION
	NM Price
Complete Set (200)	$40.00
Commons	.20
Unlisted Stars	**.25-.75**
Pack (8)	3.00
Box (36)	75.00

Quality Rating ★★★
Emotion gives the collector alot for the money as player selection is great and inserts are limited and very attractive.

#	Player	NM
8	Ripken, C.	5.00
10	Clemens, R.	1.50
29	Thomas, F.	6.00
32	Belle, A.	1.50
34	Lofton, K.	1.50
37	Ramirez, M.	1.50
58	Puckett, K.	1.50
62	Mattingly, D.	2.50
72	McGwire, M.	2.50
77	Griffey, K.	6.00
82	Rodriguez, A.	5.00
85	Gonzalez, J.	2.50
102	Jones, C.	3.00
106	Maddux, G.	4.00
134	Bagwell, J.	1.50
144	Nomo, H. (R)	6.00
145	Piazza, M.	3.00
187	Gwynn, T.	1.50
192	Bonds, B.	1.25

Cal Ripken Timeless
Complete Set (10)		70.00
Ripken Singles		8.00

Masters
Complete Set (10)		75.00
1	Bonds, B.	4.00
2	Gonzalez, J.	8.00
3	Griffey, K.	20.00
4	Gwynn, T.	8.00
5	Lofton, K.	6.00
6	Maddux, G.	10.00
7	Mondesi, R.	3.00
8	Ripken, C.	15.00
9	Thomas, F.	20.00
10	Williams, M.	3.00

N-Tense
Complete Set (12)		150.00
Commons		6.00
1	Bagwell, J.	20.00
2	Belle, A.	12.00
3	Bonds, B.	10.00
5	Griffey, K.	40.00
7	McGwire, M.	20.00
8	Piazza, M.	25.00
9	Ramirez, M.	10.00
10	Thomas, F.	40.00
11	Vaughn, M.	10.00

Rookies
Complete Set (10)		30.00
Commons		1.25
8	Jones, C.	10.00
9	Nomo, H.	8.00
10	Rodriguez, A.	12.00

1995 FLAIR
	NM Price
Complete Set (432)	$85.00
Series 1 Set (1-216)	50.00
Series 2 Set (217-432)	35.00
Commons	.10
Unlisted Stars	**.15 -.50**
Series 1 or 2 Pack (9)	4.00
Series 1 or 2 Box (24)	75.00

Quality Rating ★★★
These cards are super nice with some of the best photos and overall quality in the hobby. Silver foil is used for the A.L. players and gold foil for the N.L.

#	Player	NM
9	Ripken, C.	4.00
10	Clemens, R.	1.50
15	Vaughn, M.	1.50
27	Thomas, F.	5.00
30	Belle, A.	1.50
35	Ramirez, M.	1.00
62	Puckett, K.	1.50
66	Mattingly, D.	2.00
76	McGwire, M.	2.00
81	Griffey, K.	5.00
85	Rodriguez, A.	5.00
88	Gonzalez, J.	2.00
105	Maddux, G.	2.50
143	Bagwell, J.	1.50
155	Piazza, M.	3.00
195	Smith, O.	1.00
201	Gwynn, T.	2.00
207	Bonds, B.	1.25
258	Higginson, B. (R)	1.50
325	Jones, C.	3.00
368	Nomo, H. (R)	8.00

Cal Ripken
Complete Set (10)		90.00
Ripken Singles		10.00

Hot Gloves
Complete Set (12)		175.00
Commons		8.00
1	Alomar, R.	10.00
2	Bonds, B.	20.00
3	Griffey, K.	70.00
7	Lofton, K.	25.00
8	Mattingly, D.	30.00
9	Ripken, C.	40.00
10	Rodriguez, I.	15.00

Hot Numbers
Complete Set (10)		60.00
1	Bagwell, J.	6.00
2	Belle, A.	4.00
3	Bonds, B.	4.00
4	Griffey, K.	15.00
5	Lofton, K.	4.00
6	Maddux, G.	10.00
7	Piazza, M.	8.00
8	Ripken, C.	10.00
9	Thomas, F.	12.00
10	Williams, M.	3.00

Infield Power
Complete Set (10)		20.00
Commons		1.00
1	Bagwell, J.	3.00
7	Piazza, M.	5.00
8	Thomas, F.	10.00
9	Vaughn, M.	1.50

Outfield Power
Complete Set (10)		20.00
Commons		1.50
1	Belle, A.	2.00
3	Bonds, B.	2.00
6	Gonzalez, J.	3.00
7	Griffey, K.	10.00
8	Puckett, K.	3.00

Today's Spotlight
Complete Set (12)		125.00
Commons		5.00
1	Bagwell, J.	15.00
5	Lofton, K.	10.00
9	Piazza, M.	30.00
10	Ramirez, M.	8.00
12	Thomas, F.	40.00

Wave of the Future
Complete Set (10)		30.00
Commons		1.50
9	Jones, C.	12.00
10	Nomo, H.	8.00

1995 FLEER
	NM Price
Complete Set (600)	$55.00
Commons	.05
Unlisted Stars	**.10 -.30**
Pack (12)	1.25
Box (36)	35.00

Quality Rating ★★★
This Fleer set has a cool design and the usual hoard of insert sets.

#	Player	NM
19	Ripken, C.	2.50
26	Clemens, R.	1.00
76	Mattingly, D.	1.00
128	Thomas, F.	3.00
132	Belle, A.	.75
137	Lofton, K.	.75
145	Ramirez, M.	.75
212	Puckett, K.	1.00
249	McGwire, M.	1.00
269	Griffey Jr., K.	3.00
285	Gonzalez, J.	1.00
311	Maddux, G.	2.00
451	Bagwell, J.	1.00
547	Piazza, M.	1.50
560	Gwynn, T.	1.25
574	Bonds, B.	.75

All-Fleer
Complete Set (9)		10.00
1	Piazza, M.	1.50
2	Thomas, F.	3.00
3	Alomar, R.	.60
4	Ripken, C.	2.50
5	Williams, M.	.60
6	Bonds, B.	1.00
7	Griffey, K.	3.00
8	Gwynn, T.	1.25
9	Maddux, G.	2.00

All-Stars
Complete Set (25)		12.00
Commons		.50
1	Rodriguez/Piazza	2.00
2	Thomas/Jefferies	3.00
5	Ripken/Smith	3.00
6	Carter/Bonds	.60
7	Griffey/Gwynn	5.00
8	Puckett/Justice	1.00
9	Key/Maddux	2.50
13	Molitor/Bagwell	1.00
16	Lofton/Alou	.75
17	Belle/Grissom	.75

Award Winners
Complete Set (6)		12.00
Commons		.50

1	Thomas, F.	5.00
2	Bagwell, J.	2.00
4	Maddux, G.	4.00

League Leaders
	Complete Set (10)	12.00
	Commons	.75
2	Griffey Jr., K.	6.00
6	Gwynn, T.	2.50
8	Bagwell, J.	2.00
9	Maddux/Hill	2.00

Lumber Company
	Complete Set (10)	40.00
	Commons	1.00
1	Bagwell, J.	4.00
2	Belle, A.	4.00
3	Bonds, B.	3.00
6	Griffey Jr., K.	12.00
9	Thomas, F.	12.00

Major League Prospects
	Complete Set (10)	10.00
	Commons	.75
3	Benes, A.	2.00
6	Hunter, B.	2.00
7	Jeter, D.	5.00
10	Rodriguez, A.	10.00

Pro-Visions
	Complete Set (6)	4.00
1	Mussina, M.	.75
2	Mondesi, R.	.75
3	Bagwell, J.	1.50
4	Maddux, G.	2.00
5	Salmon, T.	.75
6	Ramirez, M.	1.25

Rookie Sensations
	Complete Set (20)	40.00
	Commons	1.50
10	Klesko, R.	5.00
11	Lopez, J.	3.00
13	Mondesi, R.	4.00
14	Ramirez, M.	10.00

Team Leaders
	Complete Set (28)	230.00
	Commons	3.00
1	Ripken/Mussina	35.00
2	Vaughn/Clemens	15.00
4	Thomas/McDowell	35.00
5	Belle/Martinez	12.00
9	Puckett/Aguilera	12.00
10	Mattingly/Key	12.00
12	Griffey/Johnson	40.00
15	Justice/Maddux	30.00
20	Bagwell/Drabek	12.00
21	Piazza/Martinez	18.00
27	Gwynn/Benes	15.00

1995 FLEER UPDATE
NM Price
Complete Set (200)	$15.00
Commons	.05
Unlisted Stars	**.10 -.30**
Pack (12)	1.25
Box (36)	35.00

Quality Rating ★★★
This update set has one of the first cards of Hideo Nomo. Player selection includes many veterans.

#	Player	NM
27	Pettitte, A.	.75
77	Rodriguez, A.	3.00
91	Jones, C.	1.00
175	Nomo, H. (R)	3.00

Diamond Tribute
	Complete Set (10)	10.00
	Commons	.50
1	Bagwell, J.	1.50
2	Belle, A.	1.00
3	Bonds, B.	1.25
6	Griffey, K.	4.00
8	Maddux, G.	3.00
9	Thomas, F.	4.00

Headliners
	Complete Set (20)	15.00
	Commons	.25
1	Bagwell, J.	1.00
2	Belle, A.	.75
3	Bonds, B.	.75
10	Gonzalez, J.	1.00
11	Griffey, K.	4.00
12	Lofton, K.	1.00
13	Maddux, G.	3.00
15	Piazza, M.	1.00
16	Puckett, K.	1.00
18	Thomas, F.	4.00

Rookie Update
	Complete Set (10)	20.00
	Commons	.50
5	Jones, C.	5.00
7	Nomo, H.	4.00
9	Rodriguez, A.	8.00

Soaring Stars
	Complete Set (9)	55.00
	Commons	3.00
6	Lofton, K.	12.00
8	Piazza, M.	25.00

Smooth Leather
	Complete Set (10)	30.00
	Commons	1.00
1	Alomar, R.	1.50
2	Bonds, B.	2.50
3	Griffey, K.	10.00
6	Lofton, K.	3.00
7	Mattingly, D.	4.00
8	Ripken, C.	8.00

1995 FLEER ULTRA
NM Price
Complete Set (450)	$35.00
Series 1 Set (1-250)	20.00
Series 2 Set (251-450)	15.00
Commons	.05
Unlisted Stars	**.10 -.30**
Series 1 or 2 Pack (12)	2.00
Series 1 or 2 Box (36)	50.00

Quality Rating ★★★
Ultra has developed the set within a set by having a parallel card for each, including inserts.

#	Player	NM
10	Clemens, R.	1.00
34	Thomas, F.	3.00
36	Belle, A.	.75
38	Lofton, K.	.75
41	Ramirez, M.	.75
76	Puckett, K.	.75
94	McGwire, M.	1.25
101	Griffey Jr., K.	3.00
109	Gonzalez, J.	1.00
129	Maddux, G.	2.00
169	Bagwell, J.	1.00
233	Gwynn, T.	1.25
258	Ripken, C.	2.50
311	Mattingly, D.	1.00
331	Rodriguez, A.	2.50
347	Jones, C.	1.50
399	Piazza, M.	1.50
442	Bonds, B.	1.00

Gold Medallion
	Complete Set (450)	120.00
	Series 1 Set (1-250)	70.00
	Series 2 Set (251-450)	50.00
	Commons	.20

All-Rookies
	Complete Set (10)	10.00
	Commons	.50
	Gold All Rookies	20.00
	Gold Medallion	2x-5x
7	Klesko, R.	2.00
8	Mondesi, R.	1.50
9	Ramirez, M.	2.50

All-Stars
	Complete Set (20)	25.00
	Commons	.50
	Gold All Stars	50.00
	Gold Medallion	2x-5x
2	Belle, A.	1.25
5	Bonds, B.	1.25
7	Griffey, K.	5.00
8	Gwynn, T.	2.00
11	Lofton, K.	1.50
12	Maddux, G.	3.00
15	Piazza, M.	2.50
16	Puckett, K.	1.50
17	Ripken, C.	4.00
19	Thomas, F.	5.00

Award Winners
	Complete Set (25)	20.00
	Commons	.50
	Gold Award Winners	40.00
	Gold Medallion	2x-5x
2	Mattingly, D.	2.00
3	Alomar, R.	1.00
6	Griffey Jr., K.	5.00
7	Lofton, K.	1.50
11	Bagwell, J.	1.50
15	Bonds, B.	1.50
18	Maddux, G.	3.00
19	Thomas, F.	5.00
20	Bagwell, J.	1.50
22	Maddux, G.	4.50

Gold Medallion Rookies
	Complete Set (20)	15.00
	Commons	.50
	Gold Rookies	30.00
	Gold Medallion	2x-5x
10	Damon, J.	1.50
17	Nomo, H.	8.00

Golden Prospects
	Complete Set (10)	12.00
	Commons	1.00
	Gold Prospects	25.00
	Gold Medallion	2x-5x
7	Jeter, D.	8.00
9	Rodriguez, A.	10.00

Hitting Machines
	Complete Set (10)	20.00
	Commons	.75
	Gold Hitting Machines	40.00
	Gold Medallion	2x-5x
1	Bagwell, J.	2.00
2	Belle, A.	1.50
4	Bonds, B.	1.50
6	Griffey, K.	6.00
7	Gwynn, T.	3.00
9	Piazza, M.	3.00
10	Thomas, F.	5.00

Home Run Kings
	Complete Set (10)	30.00
	Commons	1.50
	Gold HR Kings	60.00
	Gold Medallion	2x-5x
1	Griffey Jr., K.	12.00
2	Thomas, F.	10.00
3	Belle, A.	3.00
7	Bagwell, J.	4.00
8	Bonds, B.	3.00

League Leaders
	Complete Set (10)	5.00
	Commons	.50
	Gold League Leaders	10.00
	Gold Medallion	2x-5x
2	Lofton, K.	1.50
6	Gwynn, T.	2.00
8	Maddux, G.	4.00

On Base Leaders
	Complete Set (10)	50.00
	Commons	2.00
	Gold On Base Leaders	100.00
	Gold Medallion	2x-5x
1	Bagwell, J.	6.00
2	Belle, A.	4.00
5	Bonds, B.	4.00
7	Gwynn, T.	7.00
10	Thomas, F.	20.00

Power Plus
	Complete Set (6)	40.00
	Gold Power Plus	80.00
	Gold Medallion	2x-5x
1	Belle, A.	4.00
2	Griffey Jr., K.	25.00
3	Thomas, F.	25.00
4	Bagwell, J.	6.00
5	Bonds, B.	5.00
6	Williams, M.	2.00

RBI Kings
	Complete Set (10)	50.00
	Commons	2.00
	Gold RBI Kings	100.00
	Gold Medallion	2x-5x
1	Puckett, K.	6.00
3	Belle, A.	4.00
4	Thomas, F.	20.00
8	Bagwell, J.	6.00
10	Piazza, M.	10.00

Rising Stars
	Complete Set (9)	75.00
	Commons	4.00
	Gold Rising Stars	150.00
	Gold Medallion	2x-5x
2	Bagwell, J.	10.00
3	Belle, A.	6.00
4	Gonzalez, J.	12.00
6	Lofton, K.	6.00
8	Piazza, M.	15.00
9	Thomas, F.	30.00

Second Year Standouts
	Complete Set (15)	8.00
	Commons	.50
	Gold Standouts	15.00
	Gold Medallion	2x-5x
9	Klesko, R.	2.00
11	Ramirez, M.	4.00

Strikeout Kings
	Complete Set (6)	5.00
	Commons	.25
	Gold Strikeout Kings	10.00
	Gold Medallion	2x-5x
2	Clemens, R.	3.00
4	Maddux, G.	4.00

1995 LEAF
NM Price
Complete Set (400)	$45.00
Series 1 Set (1-200)	20.00
Series 2 Set (201-400)	25.00
Commons	.05
Unlisted Stars	**.10 -.30**
Series 1 or 2 Pack (12)	2.25
Series 1 or 2 Box (36)	60.00

Quality Rating ★★★
One of the most talked about 1995 efforts. Statistical Standouts are becoming collector favorites.

#	Player	NM
1	Thomas, F.	3.00
8	Lofton, K.	.75
115	Maddux, G.	2.00
119	Bagwell, J.	1.00
134	Ripken, C.	2.50
183	Puckett, K.	1.00
202	Gonzalez, J.	1.00

#	Player	Price
211	Griffey, K.	3.00
218	Piazza, M.	1.50
240	McGwire, M.	1.25
255	Clemens, R.	1.25
267	Nomo, H. (R)	4.00
279	Bonds, B.	1.00
284	Belle, A.	.75
299	Gwynn, T.	1.25
303	Mattingly, D.	1.00
313	Rodriguez, A.	2.50
369	Jones, C.	1.50

Checklists

#	Player	Price
	Complete Set (8)	9.00
	Series 1 Set (4)	5.00
	Series 2 Set (4)	4.00
	Commons	.75
3	Thomas, F.	3.00
6	Maddux, G.	2.50
7	Gwynn, T.	1.25
8	Bagwell, J.	1.25

Frank Thomas

Player	Price
Complete Set (6)	25.00
Thomas Singles	5.00

Cornerstones

#	Player	Price
	Complete Set (6)	12.00
	Commons	1.50
1	Thomas/Ventura	8.00
3	Mattingly/Boggs	4.00
4	Bagwell/Caminiti	3.00

Gold Leaf Stars

#	Player	Price
	Complete Set (14)	300.00
	Series 1 Set (8)	150.00
	Series 2 Set (6)	150.00
	Commons	10.00
1	Bagwell, J.	25.00
2	Belle, A.	15.00
3	Gwynn, T.	25.00
4	Griffey, K.	50.00
5	Bonds, B.	15.00
6	Mattingly, D.	30.00
9	Maddux, G.	40.00
10	Thomas, F.	40.00
11	Piazza, M.	30.00
13	Puckett, K.	18.00

Gold Leaf Rookies

#	Player	Price
	Complete Set (16)	8.00
	Commons	.50
1	Rodriguez, A.	8.00

Great Gloves

#	Player	Price
	Complete Set (16)	10.00
	Commons	.50
1	Bagwell, J.	1.00
3	Bonds, B.	1.00
6	Griffey, K.	4.00
8	Lofton, K.	1.00
10	Mattingly, D.	1.00
11	Maddux, G.	3.00
12	Puckett, K.	1.00
14	Ripken, C.	3.00

Heading for the Hall

#	Player	Price
	Complete Set (8)	300.00
	Commons	15.00
1	Thomas, F.	90.00
2	Griffey, K.	100.00
3	Bagwell, J.	25.00
5	Puckett, K.	20.00
6	Ripken, C.	70.00
7	Gwynn, T.	30.00

300 Club

#	Player	Price
	Complete Set (18)	125.00
	Series 1 Set (9)	50.00
	Series 2 Set (9)	75.00
	Commons	2.00
1	Thomas, F.	25.00
3	Piazza, M.	15.00
10	Griffey, K.	30.00
12	Bagwell, J.	12.00
13	Gwynn, T.	15.00
15	Mattingly, D.	15.00
17	Puckett, K.	10.00
18	Lofton, K.	10.00

Statistical Standouts

#	Player	Price
	Complete Set (9)	450.00
	Commons	15.00
2	Griffey, K.	125.00
3	Mattingly, D.	50.00
5	Molitor, P.	25.00
6	Puckett, K.	35.00
7	Ripken, C.	90.00
8	Thomas, F.	100.00

Slideshow

#	Player	Price
	Complete Set (16)	80.00
	Series 1 Set (8)	40.00
	Series 2 Set (8)	40.00
	Commons	3.00
2A	Thomas, F.	18.00
4A	Ripken, C.	15.00
5A	Bagwell, J.	5.00
8A	Griffey, K.	18.00
2B	Thomas, F.	18.00
4B	Ripken, C.	15.00
5B	Bagwell, J.	5.00
8B	Griffey, K.	18.00

1995 LEAF LIMITED

	NM Price
Complete Set (192)	60.00
Series 1 Set (1-96)	30.00
Series 2 Set (97-192)	30.00
Commons	.50
Unlisted Stars	**.75-1.00**
Series 1 or 2 Pack (5)	4.00
Series 1 or 2 Box (20)	65.00

Quality Rating ★★★

Leaf Limited is back for a second year and collectors will like the added inserts and excellent player selection.

#	Player	NM
1	Thomas, F.	7.00
11	Bonds, B.	2.00
12	Lofton, K.	3.00
14	Rodriguez, A.	7.00
48	Clemens, R.	3.00
55	Mattingly, D.	5.00
64	Nomo, H. (R)	6.00
66	Ramirez, M.	3.00
78	Jones, C.	5.00
79	Piazza, M.	5.00
87	Gwynn, T.	3.00
97	Ripken, C.	7.00
115	Maddux, G.	6.00
118	Griffey, K.	8.00
122	Puckett, K.	2.50
132	Bagwell, J.	2.50
147	Belle, A.	2.00
152	Vaughn, M.	2.00
166	McGwire, M.	3.00
176	Gonzalez, J.	2.50

Bat Patrol

#	Player	Price
	Complete Set (24)	30.00
	Commons	1.00
1	Thomas, F.	8.00
2	Gwynn, T.	4.00
5	Griffey, K.	10.00
6	Bagwell, J.	3.00
7	Ramirez, M.	3.00
9	Lofton, K.	3.00
10	Piazza, M.	5.00
12	Vaughn, M.	2.00
15	Bonds, B.	2.00
16	Puckett, K.	2.50
17	Alomar, R.	1.50
21	Mattingly, D.	3.00
23	Belle, A.	2.00

Gold

#	Player	Price
	Complete Set (24)	50.00
	Commons	1.00
1	Thomas, F.	8.00
2	Bagwell, J.	3.00
4	Bonds, B.	2.50
5	Belle, A.	2.00
6	Griffey, K.	8.00
7	Ripken, C.	7.00
11	Puckett, K.	2.50
12	Mattingly, D.	4.00
14	Alomar, R.	1.50
15	Maddux, G.	5.00
16	Piazza, M.	4.00
18	Lofton, K.	2.50
19	Rodriguez, A.	8.00
20	Gwynn, T.	3.00
21	Vaughn, M.	2.00
22	Jones, C.	3.00
23	Ramirez, M.	3.00

Lumberjacks

#	Player	Price
	Complete Set (16)	500.00
	Series 1 Set (8)	250.00
	Series 2 Set (8)	250.00
	Commons	12.00
1	Belle, A.	25.00
2	Bonds, B.	25.00
3	Gonzalez, J.	40.00
4	Griffey, K.	80.00
6	Piazza, M.	50.00
7	Puckett, K.	30.00
8	Vaughn, M.	25.00
9	Thomas, F.	70.00
10	Bagwell, J.	25.00
14	Ramirez, M.	15.00
16	Ripken, C.	70.00

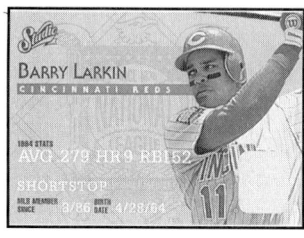

1995 LEAF STUDIO

	NM Price
Complete Set (200)	$40.00
Commons	.05
Unlisted Stars	**.10 -.30**
Pack (5)	1.50
Box (36)	40.00

Quality Rating ★★★

Great player selection mixed in with a complete design change has collectors talking about Studio.

#	Player	NM
1	Thomas, F.	3.00
2	Bagwell, J.	1.00
3	Mattingly, D.	1.00
4	Piazza, M.	1.50
5	Griffey, K.	3.00
6	Maddux, G.	2.00
7	Bonds, B.	.75
8	Ripken, C.	2.50
11	Lofton, K.	.75
15	Belle, A.	.75
16	Clemens, R.	1.25
18	Rodriguez, A.	2.50
21	Gonzalez, J.	1.25
22	Puckett, K.	1.00
25	Gwynn, T.	1.25
32	Ramirez, M.	1.25
41	Smith, O.	.50
48	Johnson, R.	.60
141	McGwire, M.	1.25
160	Jones, C.	1.50

Gold

#	Player	Price
	Complete Set (50)	40.00
	Commons	.50
1	Thomas, F.	5.00
2	Bagwell, J.	1.50
3	Mattingly, D.	2.00
4	Piazza, M.	2.50
5	Griffey, K.	5.00
6	Maddux, G.	4.00
7	Bonds, B.	2.00
8	Ripken, C.	4.00
11	Lofton, K.	1.00
15	Belle, A.	1.00
18	Rodriguez, A.	5.00
21	Gonzalez, J.	2.00
22	Puckett, K.	1.50
25	Gwynn, T.	2.00
32	Ramirez, M.	2.00
41	Smith, O.	1.00

Platinum

#	Player	Price
	Complete Set (25)	125.00
	Commons	1.50
1	Thomas, F.	20.00
2	Bagwell, J.	5.00
3	Mattingly, D.	7.00
4	Piazza, M.	8.00
5	Griffey, K.	20.00
6	Maddux, G.	15.00
7	Bonds, B.	4.00
8	Ripken, C.	15.00
11	Lofton, K.	4.00
15	Belle, A.	4.00
18	Rodriguez, A.	20.00
21	Gonzalez, J.	6.00
22	Puckett, K.	4.00
25	Gwynn, T.	7.00

1995 PACIFIC CROWN COLLECTION

	NM Price
Complete Set (450)	$25.00
Commons	.05
Unlisted Stars	**.10 -.30**
Pack (12)	2.00
Box (36)	60.00

Quality Rating ★★★

A better card design helps Crown as well as three limited insert sets. All the game's best are available.

#	Player	NM
11	Maddux, G.	2.00
30	Ripken, C,	2.50
34	Clemens, R.	1.00
97	Thomas, F.	3.00
118	Belle, A.	.75
122	Lofton, K.	.75
128	Ramirez, M.	.75
180	Bagwell, J.	1.00
224	Piazza, M.	1.25
255	Puckett, K.	.75
299	Mattingly, D.	1.00
316	McGwire, M.	1.25
362	Gwynn, T.	1.25
373	Bonds, B.	.75
398	Griffey, K.	3.00
402	Rodriguez, A.	2.50
416	Smith, O.	.50
426	Gonzalez, J.	1.25

Gold Crown

#	Player	Price
	Complete Set (20)	225.00
	Commons	5.00
1	Maddux, G.	25.00
4	Ripken, C.	30.00
6	Thomas, F.	40.00
7	Belle, A.	10.00
8	Ramirez, M.	10.00
10	Bagwell, J.	15.00
13	Piazza, M.	20.00
14	Puckett, K.	15.00
15	Bonds, B.	10.00
16	Griffey, K.	50.00
17	Rodriguez, A.	40.00
18	Gonzalez, J.	20.00
19	Alomar, R.	6.00

Hot Hispanics

#	Player	Price
	Complete Set (36)	40.00
	Commons	1.00
1	Alomar, R.	3.00
17	Gonzalez, J.	10.00
28	Ramirez, M.	5.00
30	Rodriguez, A.	15.00
31	Rodriguez, I.	5.00

Marquee Prism

#	Player	NM
	Complete Set (36)	150.00
	Commons	2.00
9	Ripken, C.	20.00
10	Mattingly, D.	10.00
11	Gonzalez, J.	10.00
13	Bonds, B.	7.00
14	Belle, A.	8.00
16	Bagwell, J.	10.00
17	Piazza, M.	12.00
19	Thomas, F.	25.00
21	Griffey, K.	25.00
24	Lofton, K.	10.00
26	Puckett, K.	10.00
30	Walker, L.	5.00
32	Ramirez, M.	8.00
36	Gwynn, T.	10.00

1995 PACIFIC PRISM

		NM Price
Complete Set (144)		$150.00
Commons		.50
Unlisted Stars		1.00-2.00
Team Logo Set (28)		5.00
Pack (2)		1.50
Box (36)		48.00

Quality Rating ★★★
Collectors get only one prism card per pack but player selection makes it worth the effort.

#	Player	NM
4	Maddux, G.	12.00
10	Ripken, C.	15.00
12	Clemens, R.	6.00
31	Thomas, F.	20.00
38	Belle, A.	4.00
39	Lofton, K.	4.00
41	Ramirez, M.	4.00
58	Bagwell, J.	6.00
72	Piazza, M.	10.00
82	Puckett, K.	6.00
97	Mattingly, D.	6.00
116	Gwynn, T.	7.00
120	Bonds, B.	5.00
126	Griffey Jr., K.	20.00
127	Johnson, R.	6.00
129	Rodriguez, A.	20.00
133	Smith, O.	4.00
136	Gonzalez, J.	8.00

1995 PINNACLE

		NM Price
Complete Set (450)		$30.00
Series 1 Set (1-225)		15.00
Series 2 Set (226-450)		15.00
Commons		.05
Unlisted Stars		.10 -.30
Series1 or 2 Hobby Pack (12)		2.00
Series1 or 2 Hobby Box (24)		40.00
Series1 or 2 Retail Pack (12)		2.00
Series1 or 2 Retail Box (36)		50.00

Quality Rating ★★★
Pinnacle trims the number of cards, but you still get a lot of quality for your money.

#	Player	NM
1	Bagwell, J.	1.00
2	Clemens, R.	1.00
21	Mattingly, D.	1.00
93	Gwynn, T.	1.25
111	Jones, C.	1.50
128	Griffey Jr., K.	3.00
132	Rodriguez, A.	2.50
170	Konerko, P.	2.50
175	Grieve, B.	2.50
189	Lofton, K.	.75
196	McGwire, M.	1.25
204	Ripken, C.	2.50
226	Thomas, F.	3.00
227	Gonzalez, J.	1.50
233	Belle, A.	.75
237	Piazza, M.	1.50
244	Maddux, G.	2.00
272	Bonds, B.	.75
283	Rodriguez, A.	1.25
295	Mattingly, D.	.50
300	Piazza, M.	.75
301	Bagwell, J.	.50
302	Thomas, F.	1.50
303	Jones, C.	.50
304	Griffey, K.	1.50
305	Ripken, C.	1.50
333	Smith, O.	.50
340	Puckett, K.	.75
350	Ramirez, M.	.75
446	Thomas, F.	1.25
447	Griffey, K.	1.25
448	Piazza, M.	.40
449	Bagwell, J.	.50
450	Checklist	1.50

Artist Proofs

#	Player	NM
	Complete Set (450)	1800.00
	Series 1 Set (1-225)	900.00
	Series 2 Set (226-450)	900.00
	Commons	3.00
	Unlisted Stars	5.00-25.00
1	Bagwell, J.	50.00
21	Mattingly, D.	50.00
93	Gwynn, T.	50.00
111	Jones, C.	60.00
128	Griffey Jr., K.	100.00
132	Rodriguez, A.	90.00
189	Lofton, K.	40.00
204	Ripken, C.	90.00
226	Thomas, F.	100.00
237	Piazza, M.	60.00
244	Maddux, G.	60.00
302	Thomas, F.	60.00
304	Griffey, K.	60.00
305	Ripken, C.	50.00
340	Puckett, K.	50.00
446	Thomas, F.	50.00
447	Griffey, K.	50.00
450	Checklist	90.00

Museum Collection

#	Player	NM
	Complete Set (450)	700.00
	Series 1 Set (1-225)	350.00
	Series 2 Set (226-450)	350.00
	Commons	1.50
	Unlisted Stars	2.00-15.00
1	Bagwell, J.	20.00
21	Mattingly, D.	20.00
111	Jones, C.	25.00
128	Griffey Jr., K.	40.00
132	Rodriguez, A.	40.00
204	Ripken, C.	40.00
226	Thomas, F.	50.00
237	Piazza, M.	30.00
244	Maddux, G.	30.00
302	Thomas, F.	30.00
304	Griffey, K.	30.00
305	Ripken, C.	30.00
446	Thomas, F.	20.00
447	Griffey, K.	20.00
450	Checklist	35.00

E.T.A.

#	Player	NM
	Complete Set (6)	25.00
1	Grieve, B.	25.00
2	Ochoa, A.	2.00
3	Vitiello, J.	2.00
4	Damon, J.	4.00
5	Beamon, T.	2.00
6	Kieschnick, B.	2.00

Gate Attractions

#	Player	NM
	Complete Set (18)	125.00
	Commons	3.00
1	Griffey, K.	30.00
2	Thomas, F.	30.00
3	Ripken, C.	25.00
4	Bagwell, J.	10.00
5	Piazza, M.	15.00
6	Bonds, B.	7.00
7	Puckett, K.	8.00
8	Belle, A.	7.00
9	Gwynn, T.	10.00
12	Mattingly, D.	10.00
13	Clemens, R.	8.00
16	Maddux, G.	20.00
17	Lofton, K.	10.00

New Blood

#	Player	NM
	Complete Set (9)	90.00
	Commons	5.00
1	Rodriguez, A.	50.00
3	Hunter, B.	15.00
6	Jones, C.	50.00

Pinnacle Performers

#	Player	NM
	Complete Set (18)	100.00
	Commons	2.50
1	Thomas, F.	25.00
2	Belle, A.	8.00
3	Bonds, B.	8.00
4	Gonzalez, J.	12.00
9	Piazza, M.	15.00
12	Maddux, G.	25.00
13	Ramirez, M.	10.00
14	Puckett, K.	8.00

Pin Redemption

#	Player	NM
	Complete Set (18)	80.00
	Commons	1.50
1	Maddux, G.	12.00
2	Mussina, M.	3.00
3	Piazza, M.	10.00
5	Bagwell, J.	6.00
6	Thomas, F.	20.00
8	Alomar, R.	3.00
9	Smith, O.	3.00
10	Ripken, C.	20.00
13	Bonds, B.	3.00
14	Griffey, K.	20.00
16	Belle, A.	6.00
17	Gwynn, T.	8.00
18	Puckett, K.	5.00

Red Hot

#	Player	NM
	Complete Set (25)	80.00
	Commons	3.00
	White Hot	2x-4x
1	Ripken, C.	15.00
2	Griffey, K.	20.00
3	Thomas, F.	20.00
4	Bagwell, J.	8.00
5	Piazza, M.	10.00
6	Bonds, B.	6.00
7	Belle, A.	6.00
8	Gwynn, T.	8.00
9	Puckett, K.	8.00
10	Mattingly, D.	9.00
12	Maddux, G.	10.00
15	Ramirez, M.	8.00
18	Clemens, R.	5.00
21	Lofton, K.	5.00
23	Alomar, R.	5.00

Team Pinnacle

#	Player	NM
	Complete Set (9)	250.00
1	Mussina/Maddux	40.00
2	Delgado/Piazza	25.00
3	Thomas/Bagwell	70.00
4	Alomar/Biggio	12.00
5	Ripken/Smith	60.00
6	Fryman/Williams	10.00
7	Griffey/Bonds	60.00
8	Belle/Justice	15.00
9	Puckett/Gwynn	30.00

Upstarts

#	Player	NM
	Complete Set (30)	60.00
	Commons	1.00
1	Thomas, F.	18.00
2	Alomar, R.	3.00

#	Player	NM
3	Piazza, M.	7.00
5	Belle, A.	7.00
8	Salmon, T.	2.00
10	Gonzalez, J.	4.00
11	Ramirez, M.	4.00
25	Sanders, D.	2.00

1995 SCORE

		NM Price
Complete Set (605)		$25.00
Series 1 Set (1-330)		15.00
Series 2 Set (331-605)		10.00
Commons		.05
Unlisted Stars		.10 -.30
Series 1 or 2 Pack (12)		1.00
Series 1 or 2 Box (36)		25.00

Quality Rating ★★★
Score has reduced the number of cards in the second series but the inserts make up the difference.

#	Player	NM
1	Thomas, F.	3.00
3	Ripken, C.	2.50
17	Piazza, M.	1.00
28	Gwynn, T.	.75
30	Bonds, B.	.60
32	Maddux, G.	2.00
221	Bagwell, J.	.60
223	Belle, A.	.60
237	Puckett, K.	.60
239	Mattingly, D.	.75
312	Rodriguez, A.	2.50
377	McGwire, M.	1.00
422	Lofton, K.	.60
437	Griffey, K.	3.00
439	Gonzalez, J.	1.00
445	Ramirez, M.	.60
551	Griffey, K.	1.25
554	Bagwell, J.	.50
556	Ripken, C.	1.25
558	Piazza, M.	.50
559	Puckett, K.	.50
562	Bonds, B.	.50
564	Mattingly, D.	.50
571	Thomas, F.	1.25
No#	Klesko Greatness	6.00
No#	Klesko Greatness (Autograph)	20.00

Air Mail

#	Player	NM
	Complete Set (18)	50.00
	Commons	2.50
9	Klesko, R.	5.00
12	Delgado, C.	5.00
14	Mondesi, R.	5.00
15	Ramirez, M.	6.00
17	Rodriguez, A.	35.00

Gold Rush

#	Player	NM
	Complete Set (605)	140.00
	Series 1 Set (1-330)	70.00
	Series 2 Set (331-605)	70.00
	Commons	.25

Double Gold Champions

#	Player	NM
	Complete Set (12)	120.00
1	Thomas, F.	30.00
2	Griffey, K.	30.00
3	Bonds, B.	6.00
4	Gwynn, T.	10.00
5	Mattingly, D.	10.00
6	Maddux, G.	15.00
7	Clemens, R.	8.00
8	Lofton, K.	6.00
9	Bagwell, J.	8.00
10	Williams, M.	4.00
11	Puckett, K.	8.00
12	Ripken, C.	20.00

Draft Picks

#	Player	NM
	Complete Set (18)	65.00
	Commons	3.00
2	Wagner, B.	5.00
3	Wilson, P.	5.00
5	Booty, J.	4.00
6	Williamson, A.	4.00
7	Konerko, P.	20.00
12	Grieve, B.	20.00
15	Hermanson, D.	5.00

Dream Team Gold

#	Player	NM
	Complete Set (12)	150.00
	Commons	4.00
1	Thomas, F.	40.00
2	Alomar, R.	8.00
3	Ripken, C.	30.00
4	Williams, M.	6.00
5	Piazza, M.	20.00
6	Belle, A.	10.00
7	Griffey Jr., K.	40.00
8	Gwynn, T.	18.00
11	Maddux, G.	30.00

Hall of Gold

#	Player	NM
	Complete Set (110)	90.00
	Series 1 Set (55)	60.00
	Series 2 Set (55)	30.00
	Commons	.75
1	Griffey Jr., K.	10.00
3	Alomar, R.	2.00
4	Bagwell, J.	4.00
6	Ripken, C.	8.00
7	Johnson, R.	2.00
9	Belle, A.	4.00
10	Piazza, M.	6.00
11	Puckett, K.	4.00
14	Gwynn, T.	5.00
15	Clemens, R.	4.00
16	Bonds, B.	3.00
18	Maddux, G.	7.00
22	Mattingly, D.	5.00
24	Smith, O.	2.00
38	Ramirez, M.	3.00
41	Rodriguez, A.	8.00
56	Thomas, F.	10.00
57	Lofton, K.	4.00
58	Gonzalez, J.	5.00

Rookie Dream Team

#	Player	NM
	Complete Set (12)	60.00
	Commons	3.00
3	Rodriguez, A.	50.00
7	Hunter, B.	6.00

Score Rules

#	Player	NM
	Complete Set (30)	125.00
	Commons	2.00
1	Griffey Jr., K.	25.00
2	Thomas, F.	25.00
3	Piazza, M.	12.00
4	Bagwell, J.	10.00
5	Rodriguez, A.	25.00
6	Belle, A.	7.00
8	Alomar, R.	3.00
9	Bonds, B.	5.00
12	Puckett, K.	7.00
14	Lofton, K.	8.00
15	Maddux, G.	15.00
16	Gonzalez, J.	12.00
18	Ripken, C.	20.00
23	Gwynn, T.	12.00
24	Ramirez, M.	6.00
25	Mattingly, D.	10.00

1995 SCORE SUMMIT

	NM Price
Complete Set (200)	$30.00
Commons	.05
Unlisted Stars	**.10-.50**
Pack (7)	2.00
Box (24)	30.00

Quality Rating ★★★
Summit's first effort has alot of what collector's want. Player selection is top notch.

#	Player	NM
1	Griffey, K.	3.00
6	Gwynn, T.	1.25
9	Bonds, B.	.75
11	Belle, A.	.75
18	Ramirez, M.	.75
21	Mattingly, D.	1.00
27	McGwire, M.	1.25
30	Maddux, G.	2.00
32	Puckett, K.	1.00
41	Clemens, R.	1.00
48	Lofton, K.	.75
79	Ripken, C.	2.50
88	Piazza, M.	1.50
90	Gonzalez, J.	1.25
92	Thomas, F.	3.00
96	Bagwell, J.	1.00
115	Jones, C.	1.50
133	Rodriguez, A.	2.50
141	Nomo, H. (R)	4.00
174	Griffey, K. (BS)	1.50
175	Thomas, F. (BS)	1.50
176	Ripken, C. (BS)	1.50
178	Piazza, M. (BS)	.75
181	Mattingly, D. (BS)	.75
189	Maddux, G. (SD)	1.00
194	Thomas, F. (CL)	1.25
195	Griffey, K. (CL)	1.25
196	Ripken, C. (CL)	1.00

Nth Degree

Complete Set (200)	450.00
Commons	2.00
Nth Degree	6x-12x

21 Club

#	Player	NM
	Complete Set (9)	35.00
	Commons	4.00
1	Abreu, B.	6.00
5	Rivera, R.	8.00
6	Park, C.	8.00
8	Valdes, I.	5.00

Big Bang

#	Player	NM
	Complete Set (20)	350.00
	Commons	10.00
1	Griffey, K.	60.00
2	Thomas, F.	50.00
3	Ripken, C.	50.00
4	Bagwell, J.	20.00
5	Piazza, M.	40.00
6	Bonds, B.	15.00
8	Mattingly, D.	30.00
10	Gwynn, T.	30.00
11	Puckett, K.	25.00
14	Belle, A.	15.00
20	Vaughn, M.	20.00

New Age

#	Player	NM
	Complete Set (15)	70.00
	Commons	3.00
2	Ramirez, M.	10.00
3	Mondesi, R.	5.00
4	Rodriguez, A.	30.00
11	Jones, C.	25.00

1995 SELECT

	NM Price
Complete Set (250)	$15.00
Commons	.05
Unlisted Stars	**.10 -.30**
Pack (12)	2.00
Box (24)	40.00

Quality Rating ★★★
Select has great player selection and another effort at the Artist Proof cards.

#	Player	NM
1	Ripken, C.	2.50
14	McGwire, M.	1.25
17	Piazza, M.	1.50
21	Maddux, G.	2.00
22	Thomas, F.	3.00
37	Bagwell, J.	1.00
46	Bonds, B.	.75
60	Belle, A.	.75
72	Clemens, R.	1.00
79	Puckett, K.	1.00
81	Ramirez, M.	1.00
86	Gonzalez, J.	1.00
89	Griffey, K.	3.00
94	Gwynn, T.	1.25
101	Mattingly, D.	1.00
120	Lofton, K.	.75
173	Jones, C.	1.50
203	Rodriguez, A.	2.00
235	Jones, C.	.50
242	Thomas, F.	1.50
243	Griffey, K.	1.50
244	Belle, A.	.75
245	Ripken, C.	1.50
248	Piazza, M.	.75
250	Bagwell/Piazza/Thomas/Griffey (CL)	1.50
251	Nomo, H.	3.00

Artist's Proofs

#	Player	NM
	Complete Set (250)	2000.00
	Commons	5.00
	Unlisted AP's	20x-40x
1	Ripken, C.	100.00
17	Piazza, M.	65.00
21	Maddux, G.	60.00
22	Thomas, F.	125.00
37	Bagwell, J.	50.00
89	Griffey, K.	125.00
94	Gwynn, T.	60.00
101	Mattingly, D.	50.00
173	Jones, C.	60.00
203	Rodriguez, A.	90.00
235	Jones, C.	40.00
241	Rodriguez, A.	40.00
242	Thomas, F.	60.00
243	Griffey, K.	60.00
245	Ripken, C.	50.00
248	Piazza, M.	40.00
250	Checklist	100.00

Big Sticks

#	Player	NM
	Complete Set (12)	150.00
1	Thomas, F.	35.00
2	Griffey, K.	35.00
3	Ripken, C.	25.00
4	Piazza, M.	20.00
5	Mattingly, D.	15.00
6	Clark, W.	5.00
7	Gwynn, T.	12.00
8	Bagwell, J.	12.00
9	Bonds, B.	8.00
10	Molitor, P.	6.00
11	Williams, M.	5.00
12	Belle, A.	8.00

Can't Miss

#	Player	NM
	Complete Set (12)	50.00
	Commons	3.00
2	Klesko, R.	6.00
4	Mondesi, R.	5.00
5	Ramirez, M.	8.00
10	Rodriguez, A.	25.00
11	Jones, C.	20.00

Sure Shots

#	Player	NM
	Complete Set (10)	75.00
	Commons	7.00
1	Grieve, B.	35.00
2	Witt, K.	8.00
4	Konerko, P.	30.00

1995 SELECT CERTIFIED

	NM Price
Complete Set (135)	$40.00
Commons	.20
Unlisted Stars	**.25-.75**
Pack (6)	5.00
Box (20)	70.00

Quality Rating ★★★
One of 1995's final efforts, Select Certified has great player selection and inserts. Certified Gold Team cards are a very tough find.

#	Player	NM
1	Bonds, B.	1.50
5	Thomas, F.	5.00
18	Ripken, C. (Tribute)	4.00
21	Mattingly, D.	2.50
33	Puckett, K.	2.00
39	Piazza, M.	3.50
48	Ramirez, M.	2.00
50	McGwire, M.	2.00
54	Bagwell, J.	2.00
55	Smith, O.	1.25
56	Belle, A.	1.50
59	Maddux, G.	3.00
66	Gwynn, T.	3.00
70	Griffey, K.	6.00
72	Ripken, C.	5.00
75	Alomar, R.	1.50
80	Piazza/Mondesi	1.50
88	Clemens, R.	2.00
91	Lofton, K.	2.00
98	Nomo, H, (R)	6.00
107	Jones, C.	2.00
118	Rodriguez, A.	5.00
135	Anderson, G.	1.25

Mirror Gold

Complete Set (135)	800.00
Commons	3.00
Mirror Gold	4x-10x

Certified Future

#	Player	NM
	Complete Set (10)	70.00
	Commons	6.00
1	Jones, C.	25.00
3	Nomo, H.	15.00
7	Hunter, B.	8.00
10	Rodriguez, A.	25.00

Certified Gold Team

#	Player	NM
	Complete Set (12)	300.00
1	Griffey, K.	70.00
2	Thomas, F.	70.00
3	Ripken, C.	60.00
4	Bagwell, J.	20.00
5	Piazza, M.	40.00
6	Bonds, B.	15.00
7	Williams, M.	6.00
8	Mattingly, D.	30.00
9	Clark, W.	8.00
10	Gwynn, T.	25.00
11	Puckett, K.	20.00
12	Canseco, J.	6.00

Checklist

#	Player	NM
	Complete Set (7)	8.00
1	Griffey, K.	2.00
2	Thomas, F.	2.00
3	Ripken, C.	3.00
4	Bagwell, J.	1.00
5	Piazza, M.	1.50
6	Bonds, B.	1.00
7	Ramirez/Mondesi	1.00

Potential Unlimited

#	Player	NM
	Complete Set (20)	250.00
	Commons	8.00
2	Ramirez, M.	25.00

10	Nomo, H.	50.00
11	Jones, C.	60.00
20	Rodriguez, A.	70.00

1995 SPORTFLIX

		NM Price
Complete Set (170)		$20.00
Commons		.10
Unlisted Stars		**.15 -.30**
Pack (5)		2.00
Box (36)		50.00

Quality Rating ★★★

Sportflix has tough to find inserts and excellent player selection. The 3-D style cards enhance the set.

#	Player	NM
1	Griffey, K.	3.00
13	Mattingly, D.	1.00
14	Belle, A.	.75
16	Gwynn, T.	1.25
20	Thomas, F.	3.00
25	Puckett, K.	1.00
45	Maddux, G.	2.00
48	Bagwell, J.	1.00
51	Clemens, R.	1.00
53	Bonds, B.	.75
73	Gonzalez, J.	1.00
81	Lofton, K.	.75
83	Piazza, M.	1.50
121	McGwire, M.	1.00
122	Ripken, C.	2.50
141	Rodriguez, A.	2.50
162	Jones, C.	1.50
167	Griffey, K. (CL)	1.25
168	Thomas, F. (CL)	1.25
169	Piazza, M. (CL)	.75
170	Bonds/Ripken (CL)	1.25

Artist's Proofs

Complete Set (170)		1000.00
Commons		3.00
Veteran Proofs		20x-40x
Rookie Proofs		15x-30x

3-D Detonators

Complete Set (9)		35.00
1	Bagwell, J.	3.50
2	Williams, M.	2.00
3	Griffey, K.	12.00
4	Thomas, F.	12.00
5	Piazza, M.	6.00
6	Bonds, B.	3.00
7	Belle, A.	3.00
8	Floyd, C.	1.50
9	Gonzalez, J.	4.00

3-D Hammer Team

Complete Set (18)		30.00
Commons		1.00
1	Griffey, K.	5.00
2	Thomas, F.	5.00
3	Bagwell, J.	2.00
4	Piazza, M.	3.00
5	Ripken, C.	4.00
6	Belle, A.	2.00
7	Bonds, B.	1.50
8	Mattingly, D.	2.50
10	Gwynn, T.	2.00
12	Puckett, K.	2.00
15	Gonzalez, J.	3.00
16	Lofton, K.	2.00

Double Take

Complete Set (12)		150.00
1	Bagwell/Thomas	35.00
2	Clark/McGriff	6.00
3	Alomar/Kent	8.00
4	Williams/Boggs	6.00
5	Ripken/Smith	30.00

6	Rodriguez/Cordero	15.00
7	Piazza/Delgado	15.00
8	Lofton/Justice	10.00
9	Bonds/Griffey	30.00
10	Belle/Mondesi	8.00
11	Gwynn/Puckett	15.00
12	Key/Maddux	15.00

ProMotion

Complete Set (12)		150.00
1	Griffey, K.	30.00
2	Thomas, F.	30.00
3	Ripken, C.	25.00
4	Bagwell, J.	12.00
5	Piazza, M.	15.00
6	Williams, M.	5.00
7	Belle, A.	8.00
8	Canseco, J.	4.00
9	Mattingly, D.	15.00
10	Bonds, B.	10.00
11	Clark, W.	5.00
12	Puckett, K.	10.00

1995 SPORTFLIX UC3

		NM Price
Complete Set (147)		$30.00
Commons		.10
Unlisted Stars		**.15-.50**
Pack (5)		2.00
Box (36)		55.00

Quality Rating ★★★

More Sportflix technology for the collector as UC3 hits the market with more action and color.

#	Player	NM
1	Thomas, F.	4.00
18	Bonds, B.	.75
20	Mattingly, D.	1.00
33	Puckett, K.	1.00
39	Piazza, M.	2.00
48	Ramirez, M.	1.00
55	Bagwell, J.	1.00
58	Belle, A.	.75
61	Maddux, G.	2.50
69	Gwynn, T.	1.25
73	Griffey, K.	4.00
74	Gonzalez, J.	1.00
75	Ripken, C.	3.00
85	Lofton, K.	.75
95	Clemens, R.	1.00
97	Nomo, H. (R)	4.00
101	Jones, C.	1.25
115	Rodriquez, A.	3.00
123	Ripken, C. (AD)	1.50
124	Griffey, K. (AD)	2.00
125	Thomas, F. (AD)	2.00
126	Piazza, M. (AD)	.75
129	Maddux, G. (AD)	1.50
134	Ramirez, M. (AD)	.75
144	Bagwell, J. (AD)	.75

Artist's Proofs

Complete Set (147)		1000.00
Commons		3.00
Veteran Proofs		20x-40x
Rookie Proofs		15x-30x

Clear Shots

Complete Set (12)		80.00
Commons		3.00
1	Rodriquez, A.	30.00
3	Nomo, H.	15.00
9	Jones, C.	25.00

Cyclone Squad

Complete Set (20)		30.00
Commons		.75
1	Thomas, F.	6.00
2	Griffey, K.	6.00
3	Bagwell, J.	2.00
4	Ripken, C.	5.00
5	Bonds, B.	1.50
6	Piazza, M.	3.00

8	Puckett, K.	2.00
11	Mattingly, D.	2.50
12	Belle, A.	1.50
13	Gwynn, T.	2.00
19	Lofton, K.	2.00

In Motion

Complete Set (10)		50.00
1	Ripken, C.	10.00
2	Griffey, K.	12.00
3	Thomas, F.	12.00
4	Piazza, M.	6.00
5	Bonds, B.	3.00
6	Williams, M.	2.00
7	Puckett, K.	4.00
8	Maddux, G.	10.00
9	Mattingly, D.	5.00
10	Clark, W.	2.00

1995 TOPPS

		NM Price
Complete Set (660)		$45.00
Series 1 Set (1-396)		25.00
Series 2 Set (397-660)		20.00
Factory Set (677)		50.00
Commons		.05
Unlisted Stars		**.10 -.30**
Series 1 or 2 Pack (15)		1.25
Series 1 or 2 Box (36)		35.00

Quality Rating ★★

Topps adds some flash to the design. Collectors search for All-Star cards and a Babe Ruth tribute.

#	Player	NM
1	Thomas, F.	2.50
3	Ruth, B.	2.00
70	Gonzalez, J.	1.00
100	Bonds, B.	.60
104	Lofton, K.	.75
139	Konerko, P.	2.50
199	Jeter, D.	2.00
212	Grieve, B.	3.00
237	Pullen/ Garcia	2.00
295	Maddux, G.	2.00
347	Smith, O.	.50
360	Clemens, R.	1.00
384	Bagwell/Thomas	.75
387	Cordero/Ripken	.75
388	Bonds/Griffey	.75
397	Griffey Jr., K.	2.50
399	Mattingly, D.	1.00
405	Bagwell, J.	1.00
431	Gwynn, T.	1.00
443	Payton, J. (R)	.75
466	Piazza, M.	1.50
472	McGwire, M.	1.00
503	Belle, A.	.75
521	Cruz, J. (R)	.75
534	Puckett, K.	1.00
535	Jones, C.	1.50
577	Ramirez, M.	1.00
587	Garciaparra, N.	2.50
588	Ripken, C.	3.00
599	Abbott/Damon	.75
640	Rivera/Pettitte	2.00
653	Isringhausen, J.	2.00

League Leaders

Complete Set (50)		60.00
Series 1 Set (25)		25.00
Series 2 Set (25)		35.00
Commons		.50
1	Belle, A.	1.50
4	Gwynn, T.	2.00
8	Bonds, B.	2.00
9	Thomas, F.	7.00
11	Bagwell, J.	2.50
12	Puckett, K.	2.00
14	Belle, A.	1.50

16	Lofton, K.	1.50
24	Maddux, G.	5.00
27	Bagwell, J.	2.50
28	Thomas, F.	7.00
30	Lofton, K.	1.50
31	Griffey, K.	7.00
32	Bagwell, J.	2.50
33	Belle, A.	1.50
39	Thomas, F.	7.00
40	Piazza, M.	2.00
46	Johnson, R.	1.50

Total Bases

Complete Set (15)		70.00
1	Bagwell, J.	6.00
2	Belle, A.	4.00
3	Griffey, K.	20.00
4	Thomas, F.	20.00
7	Bonds, B.	4.00
10	Lofton, K.	6.00
12	Gwynn, T.	8.00
13	Puckett, K.	5.00

Spectralight

Complete Set (396)		90.00
Series 1 Set (198)		45.00
Series 2 Set (198)		45.00
Commons		.25
Unlisted Stars		2x-4x
1	Thomas, F.	10.00
50	Gonzalez, J.	4.00
64	Bonds, B.	2.50
67	Lofton, K.	3.00
116	Johnson, R.	2.00
158	Maddux, G.	6.00
188	Smith, O.	2.00
199	Griffey Jr., K.	12.00
200	Mattingly, D.	3.50
206	Bagwell, J.	2.50
228	Gwynn, T.	3.00
261	Piazza, M.	5.00
293	Belle, A.	2.50
319	Puckett, K.	3.00
351	Ramirez, M.	2.50
360	Ripken, C.	8.00

1995 TOPPS TRADED

		NM Price
Complete Set (165)		$20.00
Commons		.05
Unlisted Stars		**.10 -.30**
Pack (11)		1.25
Box (36)		35.00

Quality Rating ★★

This traded set does include Nomo and several other talented rookies. Power Booster cards are nice additions.

#	Player	NM
1	Thomas, F.	2.00
2	Griffey, K.	2.00
5	Ripken, C.	2.00
6	Piazza, M.	.75
35	Higginson, B. (R)	1.25
40	Nomo, H. (R)	3.00
74	Davis, B. (R)	.75
106	Jenkins, G. (R)	.60
124	Nomo, H.	1.50
128	Jones, C.	1.00
156	Thomas/McGriff (AS)	.75
159	Ripken/Smith (AS)	1.00
160	Griffey/Gwynn (AS)	.75
164	Johnson/Nomo (AS)	2.00

Power Booster

Complete Set (10)		90.00
1	Thomas, F.	20.00
2	Griffey, K.	25.00
3	Bonds, B.	7.00

4	Belle, A.	7.00
5	Ripken, C.	20.00
6	Piazza, M.	12.00
7	Gwynn, T.	12.00
8	Bagwell, J.	8.00
9	Vaughn, M.	5.00
10	Williams, M.	5.00

1995 TOPPS DIII

	NM Price
Complete Set (59)	$25.00
Commons	.40
Unlisted Stars	**.50-.75**
Retail Pack (3)	1.25
Retail Box (24)	25.00
Hobby Pack (5)	2.00
Hobby Box (24)	40.00

Quality Rating ★★
Similar to Flair with the thick card stock and Sportflix with the three dimensional look, DIII does have quite an impressive checklist.

#	Player	NM
2	Ripken, C.	4.00
7	Belle, A.	1.25
24	Bonds, B.	1.25
27	Piazza, M.	2.00
37	Mattingly, D.	2.00
42	Gwynn, T.	1.50
43	Griffey, K.	4.00

DIII Zone

Complete Set (6)		20.00
1	Thomas, F.	10.00
2	Puckett, K.	3.00
3	Bagwell, J.	3.00
4	McGriff, F.	1.50
5	Mondesi, R.	2.50
6	Lofton, K.	3.00

1995 TOPPS EMBOSSED

	NM Price
Complete Set (140)	$30.00
Commons	.10
Unlisted Stars	**.15-.50**
Pack (6)	2.00
Box (24)	40.00

Quality Rating ★★★
Wax prices have taken a huge tumble as Embossed never really caught collector's attention.

#	Player	NM
1	Lofton, K.	1.00
6	Gwynn, T.	1.25
30	Gonzalez, J.	1.25
51	Griffey, K.	4.00
71	Puckett, K.	.75
75	Smith, O.	.75
100	Thomas, F.	4.00

109	Maddux, G.	2.50
110	Piazza, M.	2.00
113	Ripken, C.	3.00
115	Mattingly, D.	1.50
118	Bagwell, J.	1.00
120	Bonds, B.	.75
125	Belle, A.	1.00

Golden Idols

Complete Set (140)	100.00
Commons	.50
Golden Idols	2x-3x

1995 TOPPS FINEST

	NM Price
Complete Set (330)	$120.00
Series 1 Set (1-220)	80.00
Series 2 Set (221-330)	40.00
Commons	.50
Unlisted Stars	**1.00-1.50**
Series 1 Pack (7)	5.00
Series 1 Box (24)	100.00
Series 2 Pack (7)	4.00
Series 2 Box (24)	70.00

Quality Rating ★★★
The third edition of Finest has all the great names to go along with two new insert sets. Flame Throwers looks to be the most difficult to find. As always, the refractors are holding their value.

#	Player	NM
4	Ramirez, M.	3.00
56	Lofton, K.	3.00
82	Belle, A.	3.00
89	Thomas, F.	12.00
113	Piazza, M.	6.00
117	Bagwell, J.	4.00
118	Griffey, K.	12.00
120	Ripken, C.	10.00
126	Mattingly, D.	4.00
158	Gonzalez, J.	5.00
167	Puckett, K.	3.00
169	McGwire, M.	4.00
185	Clemens, R.	3.00
192	Bonds, B.	2.50
196	Gwynn, T.	4.00
213	Maddux, G.	8.00
221	Jones, C.	6.00
228	Nomo, H. (R)	15.00
257	Higginson, B. (R)	7.00
279	Jeter, D.	4.00

Refractors

Complete Set (330)		4000.00
Series 1 Set (1-220)		3000.00
Series 2 Set (221-330)		1000.00
Commons		8.00
Unlisted Refractors		15x-30x
4	Ramirez, M.	60.00
56	Lofton, K.	60.00
82	Belle, A.	60.00
89	Thomas, F.	250.00
113	Piazza, M.	150.00
117	Bagwell, J.	100.00
118	Griffey, K.	300.00
120	Ripken, C.	250.00
126	Mattingly, D.	125.00
158	Gonzalez, J.	125.00
167	Puckett, K.	100.00
169	McGwire, M.	100.00
196	Gwynn, T.	125.00
213	Maddux, G.	200.00
221	Jones, C.	125.00
228	Nomo, H.	150.00
279	Jeter, D.	150.00

Flame Throwers

Complete Set (9)	80.00
Commons	8.00

2	Clemens, R.	25.00
5	Johnson, R.	20.00

Power Kings

Complete Set (18)		200.00
	Commons	5.00
5	Ramirez, M.	10.00
6	Piazza, M.	30.00
7	Bagwell, J.	18.00
8	Vaughn, M.	15.00
9	Thomas, F.	50.00
10	Griffey, K.	50.00
11	Belle, A.	20.00
17	Bonds, B.	15.00

1995 TOPPS STADIUM CLUB

	NM Price
Complete Set (630)	$60.00
Series 1 Set (1-270)	25.00
Series 2 Set (271-495)	20.00
Series 3 Set (496-630)	15.00
Commons	.05
Unlisted Stars	**.10 -.30**
Series1 or 2 Pack (14)	2.25
Series1 or 2 Box (24)	40.00
Series 3 Pack (13)	2.50
Series 3 Box (24)	45.00

Quality Rating ★★★
Phone card inserts and great photos make this set a winner.

#	Player	NM
1	Ripken, C.	2.50
10	Clemens, R.	1.00
46	Maddux, G.	1.50
47	Thomas, F.	1.50
97	Garciaparra, N.	2.50
102	Konerko, P.	2.50
103	Grieve, B.	2.00
145	Gonzalez, J.	1.25
149	Piazza, M.	1.50
212	Mattingly, D.	.75
236	Thomas, F.	1.50
239	Ripken, C.	1.50
240	Bagwell, J.	.60
241	Griffey Jr., K.	3.00
264	Ramirez, M.	.75
271	Bonds, B.	.75
289	McGwire, M.	1.25
314	Ripken, C.	1.50
318	Thomas, F.	1.50
320	Piazza, M.	.50
375	Bagwell, J.	1.00
381	Mattingly, D.	1.25
400	Thomas, F.	3.00
425	Maddux, G.	2.00
450	Puckett, K.	1.00
470	Lofton, K.	.75
475	Gwynn, T.	1.25
489	Belle, A.	.75
502	Piazza, M.	.75
510	Ripken, C.	1.25
513	Thomas, F.	1.50
521	Griffey, K.	1.50
543	Jones, C.	1.25
556	Nomo, H. (R)	4.00
611	Higginson, B. (R)	1.25

Clear Cut

Complete Set (28)		100.00
Series 1 Set (14)		50.00
Series 2 Set (14)		50.00
	Commons	1.50
1	Piazza, M.	15.00
3	Gwynn, T.	10.00
4	Thomas, F.	25.00
12	Puckett, K.	5.00
15	Bagwell, J.	8.00
16	Belle, A.	6.00

18	Griffey, K.	30.00
20	Vaughn, M.	4.00
27	Bonds, B.	4.00

Crunch Time

Complete Set (20)		40.00
	Commons	.75
1	Bagwell, J.	3.50
2	Puckett, K.	4.00
3	Thomas, F.	10.00
4	Belle, A.	4.00
9	Griffey Jr., K.	12.00
19	Bonds, B.	3.00
20	Ripken, C.	10.00

Crystal Ball

Complete Set (15)		70.00
	Commons	3.00
1	Jones, C.	25.00
3	Durham, R.	6.00
12	Rivera, R.	10.00
14	Jeter, D.	25.00

First Day Production

Complete Set (270)		250.00
	Commons	1.00
	First Day	8x-15x
131	Clark, W.	25.00
149	Piazza, M.	7.00

Phone Cards

Regular Set (13)	40.00
Silver Set (13)	125.00
Gold Set (13)	250.00

Power Zone

Complete Set (12)		90.00
	Commons	3.00
1	Bagwell, J.	10.00
2	Belle, A.	7.00
3	Bonds, B.	7.00
7	Griffey, K.	30.00
11	Thomas, F.	30.00

Ring Leaders

Complete Set (40)		200.00
Series 1 Set (20)		80.00
Series 2 Set (20)		120.00
	Commons	2.00
1	Bagwell, J.	10.00
3	Smith, O.	5.00
7	Gwynn, T.	12.00
14	Griffey Jr., K.	30.00
22	Belle, A.	8.00
23	Gonzalez, J.	12.00
24	Puckett, K.	8.00
26	Thomas, F.	30.00
27	Ripken, C.	25.00
30	Bonds, B.	10.00
33	Mattingly, D.	15.00

Super Skill

Complete Set (20)		80.00
Series 1 Set (9)		35.00
Series 2 Set (11)		45.00
	Commons	2.00
2	Bonds, B.	5.00
5	Mattingly, D.	10.00
11	Griffey, K.	30.00
14	Lofton, K.	8.00
20	Johnson, R.	5.00

Virtual Extremists

Complete Set (10)		100.00
	Commons	2.00
1	Bonds, B.	8.00
2	Griffey, K.	35.00
3	Bagwell, J.	12.00
4	Belle, A.	8.00
5	Thomas, F.	35.00
6	Gwynn, T.	15.00
7	Lofton, K.	8.00

Virtual Reality

Complete Set (270)		90.00
Series 1 Set (135)		50.00
Series 2 Set (135)		40.00
	Commons	.25
1	Ripken, C.	5.00
39	Smith, O.	1.00
43	Alomar, R.	1.00
74	Gonzalez, J.	3.00
78	Piazza, M.	3.00
120	Griffey Jr., K.	6.00
132	Ramirez, M.	2.00
136	Bonds, B.	1.50
184	Vaughn, M.	1.50
198	Bagwell, J.	2.00
200	Mattingly, D.	2.00

209	Thomas, F.	6.00
222	Maddux, G.	5.00
241	Puckett, K.	2.00
257	Lofton, K.	1.50
261	Gwynn, T.	2.00
269	Belle, A.	2.00

1995 UPPER DECK

	NM Price
Complete Set (450)	$50.00
Series 1 Set (1-225)	25.00
Series 2 Set (226-450)	25.00
Commons	.05
Unlisted Stars	**.10 -.30**
Series 1 or 2 Pack (12)	2.00
Series 1 or 2 Box (36)	55.00

Quality Rating ★★★
Player selection and predictor cards have collectors excited about UD.

#	Player	NM
3	Grieve, B.	3.00
9	Garcia, K. (R)	2.00
10	Garciaparra, N.	3.00
35	McGwire, M.	1.25
49	Maddux, G.	2.00
90	Lofton, K.	.75
97	Ramirez, M.	.75
100	Griffey Jr., K.	3.00
101	Maddux, G.	1.50
105	Thomas, F.	1.50
110	Griffey Jr., K.	1.50
135	Gwynn, T.	1.25
159	Clemens, R.	1.25
200	Jordan, M.	4.00
210	Mattingly, D.	1.25
215	Rodriguez, A.	2.50
225	Jeter, D.	1.50
226	Nomo, H. (R)	4.00
233	Higginson, B. (R)	1.25
275	Bagwell, J.	1.00
293	Jones, C.	1.50
320	Piazza, M.	1.50
335	Bonds, B.	.75
340	Belle, A.	.75
365	Ripken, C.	3.00
395	Gonzalez, J.	1.25
430	Puckett, K.	1.00
435	Thomas, F.	3.00
448	Ryan, N.	2.00
449	Brett, G.	1.00
450	Schmidt, M.	.60
493	Pettitte, A. (Trade)	5.00
159	Clemens Jumbo Autograph.	35.00
215	A. Rodriguez Jumbo Autograph	75.00
No#	Clemens, R. (Autograph)	50.00
No#	Jackson, R. (Autograph)	35.00
No#	Mays, W. (Autograph)	80.00
No#	Mondesi, R. (Autograph)	40.00
No#	Robinson, F. (Autograph)	40.00

Checklists

	Complete Set (10)	25.00
	Series 1 Set (5)	10.00
	Series 2 Set (5)	15.00
	Commons	1.50
5	Maddux, G.	8.00
7	Gwynn, T.	4.00
8	Maddux, G.	8.00
9	Johnson, R.	2.00

Ruth Heroes Set

Complete Set (10)	100.00
Ruth Singles (73-81)	12.00
Cover Card (No#)	10.00

Electric Diamond

Complete Set (450)	100.00
Series 1 Set (1-225)	50.00

Series 2 Set (226-450)	50.00
Commons	.15
Electric Diamond Stars	3x-5x
Electric Diamond Rookies	2x-4x

Electric Diamond Gold

Complete Set (450)	1500.00
Series 1 Set (1-225)	750.00
Series 2 Set (226-450)	750.00
Commons	3.00
Gold Stars	10x-20x
Gold Rookies	8x-15x

Special Edition

	Complete Set (270)	180.00
	Series 1 Set (1-135)	80.00
	Series 2 Set (136-270)	100.00
	Commons	.20
4	Walker, L.	1.50
5	Jeter, D.	5.00
14	Jones, C.	5.00
20	Thomas, F.	10.00
25	Belle, A.	1.50
33	Garcia, K.	7.00
35	Piazza, M.	5.00
40	Gonzalez, J.	4.00
45	Bagwell, J.	3.00
46	Ripken, C.	8.00
70	Bonds, B.	3.00
78	Garciaparra, N.	8.00
85	Puckett, K.	3.00
107	Grieve, B.	5.00
120	Rodriguez, A.	10.00
144	Rivera, R.	3.00
145	Mattingly, D.	4.00
151	Maddux, G.	7.00
159	Lofton, K.	3.00
161	Ramirez, M.	3.00
168	Nomo, H.	10.00
175	Ryan, N.	10.00
190	Brett, G.	4.00
208	Schmidt, M.	3.00
210	Vaughn, M.	1.50
212	Clemens, R.	3.00
240	Walker, L.	2.00
247	McGwire, M.	4.50
255	Griffey, K.	10.00
258	Sandberg, R.	3.00
270	Gwynn, T.	4.00

Special Edition Gold

Complete Set (270)	2200.00
Series 1 Set (1-135)	1200.00
Series 2 Set (136-270)	1300.00
Commons	3.00
Gold Stars	8x-15x
Gold Rookies	5x-10x

Home Run Predictor

	Complete Set (20)	40.00
	Series 1 Set (10)	20.00
	Series 2 Set (10)	20.00
	Unlisted HR Predictor	2.00
1	Belle, A.	3.00
4	Griffey, K.	12.00
5	Thomas, F.	12.00
6	Bagwell, J.	4.00
35	Ramirez, M.	3.00
37	Piazza, M.	5.00

RBI Predictor

	Complete Set (20)	40.00
	Series 1 Set (10)	20.00
	Series 2 Set (10)	20.00
	Unlisted RBI Predictor	2.00
11	Belle, A.	3.00
15	Thomas, F.	12.00
18	Piazza, M.	6.00
45	Griffey, K.	12.00

Batting Predictor

	Complete Set (20)	50.00
	Series 1 Set (10)	25.00
	Series 2 Set (10)	25.00
	Unlisted Batting Predictor	2.00
22	Lofton, K.	4.00
25	Thomas, F.	12.00
26	Bagwell, J.	5.00
27	Gwynn, T.	8.00
52	Griffey, K.	12.00
53	Mattingly, D.	5.00
55	Puckett, K.	4.00
59	Belle, A.	3.00
60	Piazza, M.	6.00

MVP Predictor

Complete Set (20)	60.00
Series 1 Set (10)	30.00
Series 2 Set (10)	30.00

	Unlisted MVP Predictor	2.00
1	Belle, A.	3.00
3	Griffey, K.	12.00
4	Puckett, K.	4.00
5	Thomas, F.	12.00
8	Piazza, M.	6.00
21	Ripken, C.	10.00
27	Maddux, G.	6.00

ROY Predictor

	Complete Set (20)	40.00
	Series 1 Set (10)	20.00
	Series 2 Set (10)	20.00
	Unlisted ROY Predictor	2.00
14	Jeter, D.	8.00
15	Rodriguez, A.	12.00
38	Nomo, H.	7.00
39	Jones, C.	8.00
40	Cordova, M.	3.00

Steal of a Deal

	Complete Set (15)	100.00
	Commons	3.00
1	Piazza, M.	15.00
3	Lofton, K.	10.00
5	Bagwell, J.	10.00
6	Alomar/Carter	7.00
8	Smith, O.	6.00
13	Mattingly, D.	15.00
15	Jordan, M.	35.00

1995 UPPER DECK COLLECTOR'S CHOICE

	NM Price
Complete Set (530)	$25.00
Factory Set (545)	30.00
Commons	.05
Unlisted Stars	**.10 -.30**
Pack (12)	1.00
Box (36)	30.00

Quality Rating ★★
Collectors Choice returns as one series. Silver and Gold signatures are again popular among collectors.

#	Player	NM
5	Rodriguez, A. (RC)	2.00
15	Jeter, D. (RC)	1.25
29	Garciaparra, N.	2.00
39	Garcia, K. (R)	2.00
40	Grieve, B.	1.50
46	Ryan, N.	1.50
49	Brett, G.	.75
52	Ryan, N.	.75
62	Griffey, K.	1.00
63	Maddux, G.	1.00
64	Thomas, F.	1.00
67	Maddux, G.	1.50
70	Griffey, K.	2.00
73	Gwynn, T.	1.00
75	Thomas, F.	1.00
76	Bagwell, J.	.75
77	Puckett, K.	.75
80	Piazza, M.	1.25
81	Lofton, K.	.60
82	Bonds, B.	.60
83	Belle, A.	.75
84	Gonzalez, J.	.75
85	Ripken, C.	1.50
87	Piazza, M.	.60
88	Griffey, K.	1.00
89	Thomas, F.	1.00
154	Jones, C.	1.25
200	Smith, O.	.50
500	Jordan, M.	2.00
510	Mattingly, D.	.75

Silver Signatures

Complete Set (530)	100.00
Commons	.20
Silver Signatures	2x-4x

Gold Signatures

Complete Set (530)	1300.00
Commons	3.00
Gold Stars	25x-40x

You Crash the Game

	Com. Silver Set (60)	40.00
	Commons	.20
	Golds	4x
	Silver Redeemed Singles	1/2x
	Gold Redeemed Singles	2x
	Silver Redeemed Set	8.00
	Gold Redeemed Set	40.00

Note: Redemption expired.
Three different dates per player.

1	Bagwell, J.	.50
2	Belle, A.	.75
8	Griffey, K.	1.50
15	Piazza, M.	1.00
17	Rodriguez, A.	.75
19	Thomas, F.	1.50

1995 UPPER DECK COLLECTOR'S CHOICE SE

	NM Price
Complete Set (265)	$25.00
Commons	.05
Unlisted Stars	**.10 -.30**
Pack (12)	1.25
Box (36)	35.00

Quality Rating ★★
SE gives hobbyists a nice card for a reasonable price.

#	Player	NM
1	Rodriguez, A. (RC)	2.50
2	Jeter, D. (RC)	1.50
26	Griffey Jr., K. (RP)	1.25
27	Gwynn, T. (RP)	.50
29	Thomas, F. (RP)	1.25
40	Bagwell, J.	1.00
60	Maddux, G.	2.50
90	Piazza, M.	1.25
105	Bonds, B.	.75
117	Ramirez, M.	.75
119	Lofton, K.	.75
120	Belle, A.	.75
125	Griffey Jr., K.	2.50
140	Gwynn, T. (SL)	.50
142	Maddux, G. (SL)	1.50
155	Ripken, C.	2.50
160	Gwynn, T.	1.00
186	Gonzalez, J.	.75
230	Puckett, K.	1.00
235	Thomas, F.	2.50
238	Jordan, M.	3.00
240	Mattingly, D.	1.00
249	Maddux, G. (FT)	1.00
253	Piazza, M. (FT)	.60
258	Lofton, K. (FT)	.50
261	Griffey Jr., K. (CL)	.75
263	Ripken, C. (CL)	1.00

Silver Signatures

Complete Set (265)	70.00
Commons	.20
Silver Signatures	2x-4x

Gold Signatures

Complete Set (265)	1500.00
Commons	3.00
Gold Stars	25x-40x

1995 UPPER DECK SP

	NM Price
Complete Set (207)	$40.00
Commons	.10
Unlisted Stars	**.15-.50**
Pack (8)	3.50
Box (32)	80.00

Quality Rating ★★★★

SP is once again one of the most limited products on the market. Nomo is just one reason collectors pay top dollar for wax products.

#	Player	NM
1	Ripken, C.	4.00
2	Ryan, N.	3.00
3	Brett, G.	1.50
14	Nomo, H. (R)	4.00
16	Clark, T.	1.25
31	Maddux, G.	3.00
34	Jones, C.	2.50
60	Bagwell, J.	1.25
70	Piazza, M.	3.00
105	Gwynn, T.	2.00
115	Bonds, B.	1.00
125	Vaughn, M.	1.00
127	Clemens, R.	1.50
140A	Thomas, F.	7.00
140B	Thomas, F.	5.00
145	Belle, A.	1.25
150	Lofton, K.	1.00
151	Ramirez, M.	1.00
170	Puckett, K.	1.50
175	Mattingly, D.	2.50
185	McGwire, M.	1.50
188	Rodriquez, A.	4.00
189	Johnson, R.	1.50
190	Griffey, K.	5.00
195	Gonzalez, J.	2.50

SuperbaFoil

Complete Set (207)		100.00
Commons		.50
SuperbaFoil		2x-3x

Platinum Power

#	Player	NM
Complete Set (20)		25.00
Commons		.75
1	Bagwell, J.	2.00
2	Bonds, B.	1.50
6	Piazza, M.	3.00
9	Belle, A.	2.00
11	Gonzalez, J.	3.00
12	Griffey, K.	6.00
13	McGwire, M.	2.00
15	Ramirez, M.	2.00
16	Ripken, C.	5.00
18	Thomas, F.	6.00
20	Vaughn, M.	1.50

Special F/X

#		
Complete Set (48)		1200.00
Commons		10.00
2	Clemens, R.	60.00
3	Vaughn, M.	50.00
9	Belle, A.	50.00
10	Lofton, K.	40.00
11	Ramirez, M.	30.00
13	Puckett, K.	50.00
15	Mattingly, D.	70.00
16	Ripken, C.	150.00
18	Griffey, K.	225.00
19	Johnson, R.	25.00
20	Rodriquez, A.	200.00
22	Gonzalez, J.	75.00
23	Alomar, R.	20.00
29	Maddux, G.	125.00
38	Bagwell, J.	60.00
43	Piazza, M.	125.00
46	Gwynn, T.	70.00

1995 UPPER DECK SP CHAMPIONSHIP SERIES

	NM Price
Complete Set (200)	$35.00
Commons	.20
Unlisted Stars	**.25-.40**
Pack (6)	3.00
Box (44)	80.00

Quality Rating ★★★

SP Championship is available at the retail level and gives collectors a chance to pick up a unique Ripken "Ironman" card.

#	Player	NM
1	Nomo, H. (R, Dia.)	5.00
20	Jeter, D.	1.50
25	Maddux, G.	3.00
26	Jones, C.	2.50
50	Bagwell, J. (Profiles)	.75
55	Bagwell, J.	1.25
57	Piazza, M. (Profiles)	1.00
60	Piazza, M.	3.00
85	Smith, O.	1.00
88	Gwynn, T. (Profiles)	.75
90	Gwynn, T.	2.00
96	Bonds, B.	1.00
99	Ripken, C. (CL)	1.50
101	Brett, G. (Legends)	1.50
109	Jackson, R. (Legends)	1.00
115	Ripken, C. (Profiles)	2.50
120	Ripken, C.	3.00
122	Clemens, R.	1.00
136	Thomas, F. (Profiles)	2.00
140	Thomas, F.	4.00
145	Belle, A.	1.50
149	Lofton, K.	1.50
150	Ramirez, M.	1.50
156	Higginson, B. (R)	1.50
170	Puckett, K.	1.50
171	Mattingly, D. (Profiles)	1.00
175	Mattingly, D.	2.00
181	McGwire, M.	1.25
183	Griffey, K. (Profiles)	2.00
184	Rodriguez, A.	3.00
185	Griffey, K.	4.00
186	Johnson, R.	1.00
190	Gonzalez, J.	2.00
	Ripken Tribute	50.00

Die-Cut

Complete Set (200)		150.00
Commons		.50
Die-Cut		2x-4x

Classic Performances

Complete Set (10)		40.00
Commons		2.00
Die-Cut		3x-5x
1	Jackson, R.	5.00
2	Ryan, N.	20.00
5	Brett, G.	8.00
6	Alomar, R.	6.00
7	Smith, O.	5.00
8	Puckett, K.	8.00

Destination Fall Classic

Complete Set (9)		125.00
Die-Cut		3x-5x
1	Griffey, K.	35.00
2	Thomas, F.	35.00
3	Belle, A.	10.00
4	Piazza, M.	20.00
5	Mattingly, D.	15.00
6	Nomo, H.	20.00
7	Maddux, G.	25.00
8	McGriff, F.	5.00
9	Bonds, B.	8.00

1995 ZENITH

	NM Price
Complete Set (150)	$40.00
Commons	.20
Unlisted Stars	**.25-.75**
Pack (6)	4.00
Box (24)	80.00

Quality Rating ★★★

Another product with super quality and great player selection.

#	Player	NM
1	Belle, A.	1.50
5	Bonds, B.	1.50
12	Ripken, C.	4.00
29	Mattingly, D.	3.00
33	Thomas, F.	5.00
37	Maddux, G.	4.00
47	Bagwell, J.	2.00
48	Nomo, H. (Japanese)	5.00
59	Gonzalez, J.	2.50
61	Griffey, K.	5.00
62	Lofton, K.	2.00
65	Puckett, K.	1.50
69	Ramirez, M.	1.50
71	McGwire, M.	2.00
76	Piazza, M.	3.00
91	Clemens, R.	2.00
104	Gwynn, T.	2.50
111	Jones, C.	2.50
131	Higginson, B. (R)	1.50
146	Rodriquez, A.	4.00
149	Nomo, H. (R)	6.00

All-Star Salute

Complete Set (18)		50.00
Commons		1.50
1	Ripken, C.	8.00
2	Thomas, F.	8.00
3	Piazza, M.	5.00
4	Puckett, K.	3.00
5	Ramirez, M.	3.00
6	Gwynn, T.	4.00
7	Nomo, H.	6.00
9	Johnson, R.	3.00
11	Belle, A.	3.00
13	Bonds, B.	3.00
15	Griffey, K.	10.00
17	Thomas, F.	8.00
18	Ripken/ Bonds	7.00

Rookie Roll Call

Complete Set (18)		200.00
Commons		10.00
1	Rodriquez, A.	80.00
2	Jeter, D.	50.00
3	Jones, C.	50.00
7	Nomo, H.	50.00
8	Durham, R.	12.00
10	Hunter, B.	12.00

Z-Team

Complete Set (18)		400.00
Commons		10.00
1	Ripken, C.	60.00
2	Griffey, K.	75.00
3	Thomas, F.	60.00
5	Piazza, M.	40.00
6	Bonds, B.	20.00
8	Maddux, G.	45.00
9	Bagwell, J.	30.00
10	Ramirez, M.	20.00
11	Walker, L.	12.00
12	Gwynn, T.	30.00
14	Belle, A.	20.00
15	Lofton, K.	20.00
17	Mattingly, D.	30.00

1996 BAZOOKA

	NM Price
Complete Set (132)	$12.00
Commons	.05
Unlisted Stars	**.10-.30**
Pack (5)	.50
Box (36)	15.00

Quality Rating ★★

Bazooka is back for a second year and once again is very affordable.

#	Player	NM
1	Griffey, K.	2.00
8	Piazza, M.	1.00
12	Lofton, K.	.60
15	Ripken, C.	1.50
23	Mattingly, D.	.75
24	Puckett, K.	.50
40	Bagwell, J.	.75
59	Belle, A.	.75
61	Thomas, F.	2.00
73	Gonzalez, J.	.75
74	McGwire, M.	.75
79	Maddux, G.	1.00
85	Vaughn, M.	.50
96	Jones, C.	1.00
98	Nomo, H.	.60
106	Ramirez, M.	.60
118	Bonds, B.	.50
124	Gwynn, T.	.75

1996 BOWMAN

	NM Price
Complete Set (385)	$120.00
Commons	.10
Unlisted Stars	**.15-.50**
Mantle Reprint	10.00
Pack (11)	6.00
Box (24)	120.00

Quality Rating ★★★★

This set has an added twist, inserts, as well as a buy back guarantee from Topps that could have a lasting affect on future set availability. Rookie crop is excellent.

#	Player	NM
1	Ripken, C.	3.00
3	Rodriguez, I.	1.00
5	Nomo, H.	1.50
21	Vaughn, M.	1.25
22	McGwire, M.	1.50
27	Piazza, M.	2.50
51	Sandberg, R.	1.00
54	Thomas, F.	4.00
55	Lofton, K.	1.25
67	Maddux, G.	2.50

#	Player	Price
69	Murray, E.	1.00
71	Gwynn, T.	2.00
76	Jones, C.	2.50
77	Bagwell, J.	1.50
78	Bonds, B.	1.00
79	Griffey, K.	4.00
89	Clemens, R.	1.50
92	Belle, A.	1.25
95	Gonzalez, J.	2.50
98	Puckett, K.	1.00
112	Jeter, D.	2.50
114	Rolen, S.	3.00
116	Guillen, J. (R)	10.00
124	Jimenez, D. (R)	2.00
159	Walker, T.	5.00
161	Booty, J. (R)	1.50
164	Clark, T.	1.00
181	Garciaparra, N.	4.00
187	Grieve, B.	1.50
192	Jones, A.	5.00
201	Powell, D.	1.50
204	Lombard, G. (R)	2.00
219	Dickson, J. (R)	3.00
220	Hernandez, R. (R)	3.00
221	Bellhorn, M. (R)	2.00
227	Tomko, B. (R)	2.00
229	Rosado, J. (R)	3.00
248	Estalella, B. (R)	2.50
259	Pavano, C. (R)	6.00
264	Cameron, M. (R)	5.00
266	Hernandez, L. (R)	8.00
301	Morris, M. (R)	2.00
311	Valentin, J. (R)	2.00
334	Sweeney, M. (R)	1.00
337	Wright, R. (R)	5.00
338	Konerko, P.	2.00
342	Branyan, R. (R)	8.00
349	Ordonez, R.	1.00
351	Velazquez, E. (R)	2.00
357	Rose, B. (R)	7.00
361	Guerrero, W. (R)	2.50
374	Guerrero, V.	5.00
378	Helton, T.	10.00
380	Blood, D. (R)	1.50

Foil Set

Complete Set (385)		300.00

Bowman's Best Preview

Complete Set (30)		125.00
Commons		2.00
Refractors		2x-3x
Atomic Refractors		4x-5x
1	Jones, C.	12.00
4	Bonds, B.	5.00
7	Piazza, M.	12.00
9	Jones, A.	12.00
10	Gwynn, T.	10.00
13	Thomas, F.	15.00
14	Maddux, G.	10.00
15	Jeter, D.	10.00
16	Bagwell, J.	6.00
25	Vaughn, M.	5.00
26	Nomo, H.	7.00
27	Garciaparra, N.	10.00
28	Ripken, C.	15.00
30	Griffey, K.	20.00

Minor League POY

Complete Set (15)		40.00
Commons		2.00
1	Jones, A.	15.00
4	Walker, T.	5.00
6	Helms, W.	6.00
14	Guerrero, V.	10.00

1996 BOWMAN'S BEST

	NM Price
Complete Set (180)	$100.00
Commons	.30
Unlisted Stars	**1.00-1.50**
Silver Refractors	6x-12x
Gold Refractors	8x-15x
Atomic Refractors	15x-25x
Pack (6)	7.00
Box (24)	150.00

Quality Rating ★★★
Once again Bowman's Best doesn't disappoint as player selection is good as ever.

BEN GRIEVE

#	Player	NM
1	Nomo, H.	2.50
3	Ripken, C.	6.00
6	Belle, A.	2.00
7	Jones, C.	4.00
8	Sandberg, R.	2.00
10	Bonds, B.	2.00
13	Thomas, F.	7.00
16	Vaughn, M.	2.00
20	Bagwell, J.	3.00
21	Johnson, R.	2.00
23	Lofton, K.	2.50
26	Piazza, M.	4.00
38	Gwynn, T.	4.00
42	Murray, E.	2.00
52	Ramirez, M.	2.50
58	Gonzalez, J.	4.00
71	Griffey, K.	7.00
75	McGwire, M.	2.50
78	Puckett, K.	2.50
79	Jeter, D.	4.00
85	Maddux, G.	4.00
91	Jones, A.	8.00
92	Garciaparra, N.	4.00
96	Rivera, R.	2.00
97	Guerrero, V.	6.00
108	Guerrero, W. (R)	3.00
109	Guillen, J. (R)	12.00
118	Grieve, B.	3.00
130	Renteria, E.	2.00
132	Velazquez, E. (R)	2.00
135	Walker, T.	5.00
136	Jenkins, G. (R)	2.00
137	Morris, M. (R)	4.00
139	Dunwoody, T. (R)	5.00
145	Rolen, S.	5.00
151	Valentin, J. (R)	3.00
152	Helms, W. (R)	5.00
154	Castillo, L. (R)	2.00
156	Konerko, P.	3.00
171	Helton, T.	10.00
	1952 Mantle Chrome	8.00
	1952 Mantle Refractor	20.00
	1952 Mantle Atomic Refractor	40.00

Bowman's Best Cuts

Complete Set (15)		200.00
Commons		5.00
Refractors		2x-4x
Atomic Refractors		4x-6x
1	Griffey, K.	35.00
3	Jeter, D.	20.00
4	Jones, A.	25.00
5	Jones, C.	25.00
8	Nomo, H.	12.00
9	Piazza, M.	25.00
11	Ripken, C.	30.00
14	Thomas, F.	30.00

Mirror Image

Complete Set (10)		175.00
Commons		10.00
Refractors		2x-4x
Atomic Refractors		4x-6x
1	Bagwell/Helton/Thomas/Saxson	30.00
2	Jones/Rolen/Boggs/Arias	25.00
4	Larkin/Perez/Ripken/Bellhorn	25.00
5	Walker/Garcia/Belle/Rivera	15.00
6	Bonds/Jones/Lofton/Sadler	30.00
7	Gwynn/Guerrero/Griffey/Grieve	30.00
8	Piazza/Davis/Rodriguez/Valentine	20.00
9	Maddux/Wright/Mussina/Colon	20.00

1996 CIRCA

	NM Price
Complete Set (200)	$25.00
Commons	.05
Unlisted Stars	**.10-.30**
Pack (8)	2.50
Box (24)	50.00

Quality Rating ★★★
Fleer debuts Circa, a product that features an affordable price and a very limited parallel set.

#	Player	NM
4	Murray, E.	.50
8	Ripken, C.	2.50
10	Clemens, R.	1.00
14	Vaughn, M.	.75
19	Erstad, D. (R)	2.00
29	Thomas, F.	3.00
32	Belle, A.	.75
33	Lofton, K.	.75
37	Ramirez, M.	.75
59	Puckett, K.	.75
65	Jeter, D.	1.50
68	Pettitte, A.	.75
73	McGwire, M.	1.25
78	Griffey, K.	3.00
81	Rodriguez, A.	2.50
86	Gonzalez, J.	1.25
101	Jones, A.	4.00
102	Jones, C.	1.50
105	Maddux, G.	2.50
111	Sandberg, R.	.75
133	Bagwell, J.	1.00
144	Nomo, H.	1.25
146	Piazza, M.	1.50
181	Smith, O.	.50
186	Gwynn, T.	1.25
192	Bonds, B.	.75
198	Griffey, K.	1.50
199	Ripken, C.	1.25
200	Thomas, F.	1.50

Rave

Commons		25.00
Rave		.75x-125x
1	Alomar, R.	50.00
4	Murray, E.	70.00
8	Ripken, C.	300.00
10	Clemens, R.	150.00
14	Vaughn, M.	100.00
19	Erstad, D.	125.00
29	Thomas, F.	275.00
32	Belle, A.	90.00
33	Lofton, K.	90.00
37	Ramirez, M.	70.00
59	Puckett, K.	125.00
65	Jeter, D.	200.00
68	Pettitte, A.	90.00
73	McGwire, M.	150.00
78	Griffey, K.	350.00
81	Rodriguez, A.	225.00
86	Gonzalez, J.	150.00
101	Jones, A.	150.00
102	Jones, C.	200.00
105	Maddux, G.	200.00
111	Sandberg, R.	100.00
133	Bagwell, J.	125.00
144	Nomo, H.	200.00
146	Piazza, M.	200.00
181	Smith, O.	100.00
186	Gwynn, T.	150.00
192	Bonds, B.	100.00
198	Griffey, K.	200.00
199	Ripken, C.	125.00
200	Thomas, F.	125.00

Access

Complete Set (30)		125.00
Commons		1.50
1	Ripken, C.	15.00
2	Vaughn, M.	6.00
4	Thomas, F.	20.00
5	Belle, A.	6.00
6	Lofton, K.	7.00
7	Ramirez, M.	6.00
9	Puckett, K.	6.00
11	McGwire, M.	8.00
12	Griffey, K.	15.00
13	Johnson, R.	4.00
14	Maddux, G.	15.00
19	Bagwell, J.	7.00
20	Nomo, H.	8.00
21	Piazza, M.	12.00
26	Smith, O.	3.00
27	Gwynn, T.	8.00
29	Bonds, B.	6.00

Boss

Complete Set (50)		100.00
Commons		2.00
2	Ripken, C.	12.00
4	Vaughn, M.	4.00
6	Thomas, F.	12.00
8	Belle, A.	5.00
9	Lofton, K.	5.00
10	Ramirez, M.	4.00
14	Puckett, K.	5.00
18	McGwire, M.	5.00
20	Griffey, K.	15.00
21	Johnson, R.	4.00
23	Gonzalez, J.	6.00
27	Maddux, G.	10.00
29	Sandberg, R.	4.00
37	Bagwell, J.	6.00
38	Nomo, H.	7.00
39	Piazza, M.	10.00
46	Smith, O.	3.00
47	Gwynn, T.	7.00
49	Bonds, B.	4.00

JOHN VALENTIN

1996 DONRUSS

	NM Price
Complete Set (550)	$35.00
Series 1 Set (1-330)	20.00
Series 2 Set (331-550)	15.00
Commons	.05
Unlisted Stars	**.10-.35**
Series 1 Pack (12)	1.50
Series 1 Box (36)	45.00
Series 2 Pack (12)	2.00
Series 2 Box (18)	30.00

Quality Rating ★★★
Player selection is decent. Donruss will again remain popular with the insert collector.

#	Player	NM
1	Thomas, F.	2.50
8	Rodriguez, A.	2.50
40	Ramirez, M.	.75
50	Puckett, K.	1.00
81	Bagwell, J.	1.00
110	Ripken, C. (CL)	1.50
145	Ripken, C.	2.00
216	Bonds, B.	.75
222	Belle, A.	.75
301	Mattingly, D.	1.00
338	Griffey, K.	2.50
375	Gonzalez, J.	1.25
378	Cameron, M. (R)	1.00
390	Nomo, H.	1.50
394	Maddux, G.	2.00
396	Lofton, K.	.75
424	Piazza, M.	1.50

437	Jones, C.	1.50
490	Checklist	1.00
505	Vaughn, M.	.60
511	McGwire, M.	1.00
525	Gwynn, T.	1.25
539	Clemens, R.	1.00

Press Proofs

Complete Set (550)	1700.00
Series 1 Set (1-330)	1000.00
Series 2 Set (331-550)	700.00
Commons	3.00
Press Proofs	10x-20x

Diamond Kings

	Complete Set (31)	300.00
	Series 1 Set (14)	150.00
	Series 2 Set (17)	150.00
	Commons	5.00
1	Thomas, F.	40.00
2	Vaughn, M.	15.00
3	Ramirez, M.	10.00
4	McGwire, M.	20.00
5	Gonzalez, J.	20.00
8	Bonds, B.	12.00
9	Gwynn, T.	20.00
15	Maddux, G.	30.00
16	Mattingly, D.	25.00
22	Puckett, K.	20.00
27	Nomo, H.	20.00
28	Mussina, M.	10.00
29	Murray, E.	12.00
30	Ripken, C.	35.00

Elite

	Complete Set (12)	300.00
	Series 1 Set (6)	150.00
	Series 2 Set (6)	150.00
	Commons	12.00
61	Ripken, C.	50.00
62	Nomo, H.	40.00
64	Vaughn, M.	25.00
66	Jones, C.	50.00
67	Ramirez, M.	20.00
68	Maddux, G.	50.00
69	Thomas, F.	60.00
70	Griffey, K.	70.00
72	Gwynn, T.	30.00

Freeze Frame

	Complete Set (8)	200.00
1	Thomas, F.	40.00
2	Griffey, K.	50.00
3	Ripken, C.	35.00
4	Nomo, H.	25.00
5	Maddux, G.	30.00
6	Belle, A.	12.00
7	Jones, C.	30.00
8	Piazza, M.	30.00

Hit List

	Complete Set (16)	130.00
	Series 1 Set (8)	65.00
	Series 2 Set (8)	65.00
	Commons	5.00
1	Gwynn, T.	15.00
2	Griffey, K.	35.00
4	Piazza, M.	25.00
6	Vaughn, M.	12.00
8	Puckett, K.	10.00
9	Thomas, F.	35.00
10	Bonds, B.	10.00
11	Bagwell, J.	15.00
15	Mattingly, D.	15.00
16	Murray, E.	8.00

Long Ball Leaders

	Complete Set (8)	150.00
	Commons	10.00
1	Bonds, B.	15.00
3	McGwire, M.	30.00
6	Griffey, K.	70.00
8	Thomas, F.	60.00

Power Alley

	Complete Set (10)	150.00
	Commons	6.00
	Die-Cuts	5x
1	Thomas, F.	60.00
2	Bonds, B.	15.00
4	Belle, A.	20.00
7	Vaughn, M.	15.00
9	Ramirez, M.	15.00
10	Griffey, K.	65.00

Pure Power

	Complete Set (8)	200.00
1	Mondesi, R.	10.00
2	Bonds, B.	20.00
3	Belle, A.	20.00
4	Thomas, F.	70.00
5	Piazza, M.	40.00
7	Ramirez, M.	12.00
8	Vaughn, M.	20.00

Round Trippers

	Complete Set (10)	150.00
1	Belle, A.	10.00
2	Bonds, B.	10.00
3	Bagwell, J.	15.00
4	Salmon, T.	8.00
5	Vaughn, M.	10.00
6	Griffey, K.	45.00
7	Piazza, M.	30.00
8	Ripken, C.	35.00
9	Thomas, F.	45.00
10	Bichette, D.	5.00

Showdown

	Complete Set (8)	150.00
1	Thomas/Nomo	50.00
2	Bonds/Johnson	12.00
3	Maddux/Griffey	50.00
4	Clemens/Gwynn	18.00
5	Piazza/Mussina	30.00
6	Ripken/Martinez	30.00
7	Wakefield/Williams	5.00
8	Ramirez/Perez	8.00

1996 E-MOTION XL

	NM Price
Complete Set (300)	$75.00
Commons	.10
Unlisted Stars	**.15-.75**
Pack (7)	4.00
Box (24)	60.00

Quality Rating ★★★
XL Baseball has alot to offer collectors with it's unique design and great player selection.

#	Player	NM
9	Ripken, C.	4.00
12	Clemens, R.	2.00
20	Vaughn, M.	1.50
42	Thomas, F.	6.00
46	Belle, A.	2.00
49	Lofton, K.	2.00
85	Puckett, K.	1.50
104	McGwire, M.	2.50
113	Griffey, K.	6.00
117	Rodriguez, A.	5.00
121	Gonzalez, J.	2.50
142	Jones, C.	3.50
146	Maddux, G.	3.50
159	Sandberg, R.	1.50
184	Bagwell, J.	2.50
214	Nomo, H.	3.00
215	Piazza, M.	4.00
277	Gwynn, T.	3.00
286	Bonds, B.	1.50

D-Fense

	Complete Set (10)	35.00
	Commons	1.00
2	Bonds, B.	2.50
4	Griffey, K.	10.00
5	Lofton, K.	3.00
6	Maddux, G.	7.00
8	Ripken, C.	8.00

Legion of Boom

	Complete Set (12)	200.00
	Commons	8.00
1	Belle, A.	15.00
2	Bonds, B.	15.00
3	Gonzalez, J.	25.00
4	Griffey, K.	50.00
6	Piazza, M.	35.00
7	Ramirez, M.	12.00
10	Thomas, F.	50.00
11	Vaughn, M.	15.00

N-Tense

	Complete Set (10)	100.00
1	Belle, A.	7.00
2	Bonds, B.	7.00
3	Canseco, J.	3.00
4	Griffey, K.	30.00
5	Gwynn, T.	12.00
6	Johnson, R.	5.00
7	Maddux, G.	20.00
8	Ripken, C.	20.00
9	Thomas, F.	30.00
10	Williams, M.	4.00

Rare Breed

	Complete Set (10)	200.00
	Commons	6.00
6	Jones, C.	60.00
7	Mondesi, R.	10.00
8	Nomo, H.	50.00
9	Ramirez, M.	20.00

1996 FLEER

	NM Price
Complete Set (600)	$80.00
Commons	.05
Unlisted Stars	**.10-.35**
Pack (11)	1.50
Box (36)	45.00

Quality Rating ★★★
Fleer features a great card design and a one series set is always a nice change. This issue has all the best names in baseball.

#	Player	NM
20	Ripken, C.	2.00
25	Clemens, R.	1.00
38	Vaughn, M.	.60
77	Thomas, F.	3.00
83	Belle, A.	.75
89	Lofton, K.	.75
99	Ramirez, M.	.75
172	Puckett, K.	.75
184	Jeter, D.	1.50
189	Mattingly, D.	1.25
238	Griffey, K.	3.00
240	Johnson, R.	.60
243	Rodriguez, A.	2.50
250	Gonzalez, J.	1.00
293	Jones, C.	1.50
299	Maddux, G.	2.00
328	Sandberg, R.	.50
400	Bagwell, J.	1.00
442	Nomo, H.	1.25
445	Piazza, M.	1.50
567	Gwynn, T.	1.25
583	Bonds, B.	.75

Checklist

	Complete Set (10)	6.00
	Commons	.50
2	Griffey, K.	2.00
3	Jones, C.	1.00
4	Maddux, G.	1.00
5	Piazza, M.	1.00
7	Ripken, C.	1.00
8	Thomas, F.	1.50

Golden Memories

	Complete Set (10)	10.00
	Commons	1.00
1	Belle, A.	2.00
2	Bonds/Sosa	1.50
3	Maddux, G.	3.00
6	McGwire, M.	2.50
8	Ripken, C.	3.00
9	Thomas, F.	5.00

Lumber Company

	Complete Set (12)	30.00
	Commons	1.50
1	Belle, A.	2.00
3	Bonds, B.	2.00
4	Griffey, K.	12.00
5	McGwire, M.	4.00
6	Piazza, M.	6.00
7	Ramirez, M.	2.00
10	Thomas, F.	10.00
11	Vaughn, M.	2.00

Post Season Glory

	Complete Set (5)	2.00
	Commons	.25
2	Griffey, K.	2.00
4	Johnson, R.	.50

Prospects

	Complete Set (10)	5.00
	Commons	.50
5	Garcia, K.	3.00
8	Rivera, R.	2.00

Road Warriors

	Complete Set (10)	15.00
	Commons	.75
2	Gwynn, T.	3.00
3	Maddux, G.	4.00
4	McGwire, M.	2.50
5	Piazza, M.	4.00
6	Ramirez, M.	2.00
8	Thomas, F.	6.00
9	Vaughn, M.	2.00

Rookie Sensations

	Complete Set (15)	25.00
	Commons	1.00
2	Cordova, M.	1.00
10	Jones, C.	8.00
12	Nomo, H.	5.00
14	Pettitte, A.	3.00

Smoke 'N Heat'

	Complete Set (10)	8.00
	Commons	.50
2	Clemens, R.	1.50
5	Johnson, R.	1.00
6	Maddux, G.	4.00
8	Nomo, H.	2.00

Team Leaders

	Complete Set (28)	90.00
	Commons	1.00
1	Ripken, C.	15.00
2	Vaughn, M.	7.00
4	Thomas, F.	15.00
5	Lofton, K.	6.00
9	Puckett, K.	5.00
10	Mattingly, D.	8.00
11	McGwire, M.	6.00
12	Griffey, K.	20.00
13	Gonzalez, J.	8.00
15	Maddux, G.	10.00
20	Bagwell, J.	6.00
21	Piazza, M.	10.00
27	Gwynn, T.	7.00
28	Bonds, B.	4.00

Tiffany

Complete Set (600)	200.00
Commons	.50
Tiffany Stars	3x-5x
Tiffany Rookies	2x-4x

Tomorrow's Legends

	Complete Set (10)	12.00
	Commons	.75
6	Jones, C.	5.00
8	Nomo, H.	3.50
9	Ramirez, M.	2.00

Zone

	Complete Set (12)	200.00
	Commons	5.00
1	Belle, A.	12.00
2	Bonds, B.	12.00
3	Griffey, K.	45.00
4	Gwynn, T.	20.00
5	Johnson, R.	10.00
6	Lofton, K.	12.00
7	Maddux, G.	25.00
9	Piazza, M.	25.00

| 10 | Thomas, F. | 40.00 |
| 11 | Vaughn, M. | 10.00 |

1996 FLEER UPDATE

		NM Price
Complete Set (250)		$30.00
Commons		.05
Unlisted Stars		**.10-.35**
Pack (11)		1.50
Box (24)		30.00

Quality Rating ★★★
Rookie talent is average. Design is an added bonus to names like Maddux and Gonzalez.

#	Player	NM
24	Cameron, M. (R)	1.50
145	Guerrero, W. (R)	.75
215	Bonds, B.	.50
221	Gonzalez, J.	.75
223	Griffey, K.	1.50
224	Gwynn, T.	.60
228	Jones, C.	.75
232	Maddux, G.	1.00
234	Nomo, H.	.50
235	Piazza, M.	1.00
237	Ripken, C.	1.50
243	Thomas, F.	1.50
247	Griffey, K.	1.50
250	Thomas, F.	1.50

Diamond Tribute

Complete Set (10)		150.00
Commons		4.00
2	Bonds, B.	12.00
3	Griffey, K.	40.00
4	Gwynn, T.	20.00
6	Maddux, G.	30.00
7	Murray, E.	12.00
8	Ripken, C.	40.00
9	Smith, O.	10.00
10	Thomas, F.	35.00

Headliners

Complete Set (20)		40.00
2	Bagwell, J.	2.00
3	Belle, A.	1.50
4	Bonds, B.	1.00
6	Gonzalez, J.	2.00
7	Griffey, K.	6.00
8	Gwynn, T.	2.50
10	Jones, C.	2.50
12	Lofton, K.	1.00
13	Maddux, G.	4.00
14	Nomo, H.	2.00
15	Piazza, M.	4.00
16	Ramirez, M.	1.50
17	Ripken, C.	4.00
19	Thomas, F.	6.00

New Horizons

Complete Set (20)		12.00
Commons		.25
9	Guerrero, W.	2.00
10	Hildalgo, R.	2.00
14	Kendall, J.	1.50

Smooth Leather

Complete Set (10)		12.00
1	Alomar, R.	2.00
2	Bonds, B.	1.50
3	Clark, W.	.50
4	Griffey, K.	5.00
5	Lofton, K.	2.00
6	Maddux, G.	3.00
7	Mondesi, R.	1.00
8	Ordonez, R.	1.00
9	Ripken, C.	5.00
10	Williams, M.	.60

Soaring Stars

Complete Set (10)		30.00
1	Bagwell, J.	4.00
2	Bonds, B.	3.00
3	Gonzalez, J.	5.00
4	Griffey, K.	10.00
5	Jones, C.	7.00
6	Maddux, G.	7.00
7	Piazza, M.	8.00
8	Ramirez, M.	3.00
9	Thomas, F.	10.00
10	Williams, M.	1.50

Tiffany Set

Complete Set (250)		100.00
Commons		.20
Tiffany		3x-6x

1996 FLEER FLAIR

		NM Price
Complete Set (400)		$180.00
Commons		.30
Unlisted Stars		**.40-.60**
Pack (9)		5.00
Box (18)		75.00

Quality Rating ★★★★
Great looking set bettered by the ever popular Hot Glove insert. One series is a nice change.

#	Player	NM
12	Ripken, C.	6.00
16	Clemens, R.	3.00
29	Vaughn, M.	2.50
60	Thomas, F.	8.00
64	Belle, A.	2.50
67	Lofton, K.	2.50
71	Murray, E.	2.00
74	Ramirez, M.	2.00
120	Puckett, K.	2.00
129	Jeter, D.	5.00
134	Pettitte, A.	2.50
150	McGwire, M.	3.00
160	Griffey, K.	8.00
162	Johnson, R.	2.00
164	Rodriguez, A.	6.00
169	Gonzalez, J.	4.00
178	Rodriguez, I.	2.50
200	Jones, C.	5.00
205	Maddux, G.	6.00
223	Sandberg, R.	2.00
272	Bagwell, J.	3.50
297	Nomo, H.	4.00
298	Piazza, M.	5.00
374	Gwynn, T.	4.00
384	Bonds, B.	2.00

Diamond Cuts

Complete Set (12)		150.00
1	Bagwell, J.	12.00
2	Belle, A.	8.00
3	Bonds, B.	8.00
4	Gonzalez, J.	15.00
5	Griffey, K.	30.00
6	Maddux, G.	20.00
7	Murray, E.	8.00
8	Piazza, M.	20.00
9	Ripken, C.	25.00
10	Thomas, F.	25.00
11	Vaughn, M.	10.00
12	Williams, M.	5.00

Hot Gloves

Complete Set (10)		500.00
1	Alomar, R.	20.00
2	Bonds, B.	40.00
3	Clark, W.	15.00
4	Griffey, K.	150.00

5	Lofton, K.	40.00
6	Maddux, G.	100.00
7	Piazza, M.	100.00
8	Ripken, C.	120.00
9	Rodriguez, I.	35.00
10	Williams, M.	20.00

Powerline

Complete Set (10)		30.00
Commons		1.00
1	Belle, A.	3.00
2	Bonds, B.	3.00
3	Gonzalez, J.	3.00
4	Griffey, K.	10.00
5	McGwire, M.	5.00
6	Piazza, M.	7.00
7	Ramirez, M.	3.00
9	Thomas, F.	10.00

Wave of the Future

Complete Set (20)		250.00
Commons		10.00
1	Abreu, B.	15.00
4	Benes, A.	25.00
8	Dye, J.	15.00
10	Garcia, K.	35.00
13	Hidalgo, R.	18.00
15	Kendall, J.	20.00
18	Ordonez, R.	15.00
19	Rivera, R.	20.00
20	Wilson, P.	20.00

1996 FLEER METAL

		NM Price
Complete Set (250)		$40.00
Commons		.10
Unlisted Stars		**.15-.50**
Pack (8)		2.00
Box (24)		40.00

Quality Rating ★★★
Fleer Metal hits the market with its high-tech style and design. The checklist has all the names collectors want.

#	Player	NM
9	Ripken, C.	2.50
21	Vaughn, M.	.75
40	Thomas, F.	3.00
44	Belle, A.	.75
46	Lofton, K.	.75
80	Puckett, K.	1.00
87	Jeter, D.	2.00
90	Mattingly, D.	1.25
101	McGwire, M.	1.25
107	Griffey, K.	3.00
108	Johnson, R.	.75
110	Rodriguez, A.	2.50
113	Gonzalez, J.	1.50
129	Jones, C.	2.00
134	Maddux, G.	2.00
145	Sandberg, R.	.75
172	Bagwell, J.	1.50
186	Nomo, H.	1.50
187	Piazza, M.	2.00
229	Smith, O.	.75
235	Gwynn, T.	1.25
241	Bonds, B.	1.00

Heavy Metal

Complete Set (10)		30.00
Commons		1.50
1	Belle, A.	3.00
2	Bonds, B.	3.00
3	Gonzalez, J.	5.00
4	Griffey, K.	10.00
5	McGwire, M.	4.00
6	Piazza, M.	5.00

8	Thomas, F.	10.00
9	Vaughn, M.	3.00

Mining for Gold

Complete Set (12)		50.00
Commons		2.00
6	Jeter, D.	20.00
8	Jones, C.	25.00
9	Nomo, H.	20.00
11	Pettitte, A.	8.00

Mother Lode

Complete Set (12)		70.00
Commons		2.00
1	Bonds, B.	5.00
3	Griffey, K.	20.00
4	Lofton, K.	6.00
8	Ripken, C.	15.00
10	Sandberg, R.	6.00
11	Thomas, F.	20.00

Platinum Portraits

Complete Set (10)		15.00
Commons		.50
5	Jones, C.	4.00
7	Nomo, H.	3.00

Titanium

Complete Set (10)		150.00
1	Belle, A.	8.00
2	Bonds, B.	8.00
3	Griffey, K.	30.00
4	Gwynn, T.	10.00
5	Maddux, G.	20.00
6	Piazza, M.	15.00
7	Ripken, C.	25.00
8	Thomas, F.	30.00
9	Vaughn, M.	8.00
10	Williams, M.	4.00

1996 FLEER ULTRA

		NM Price
Complete Set (600)		$50.00
Series 1 Set (1-300)		25.00
Series 2 Set (301-600)		25.00
Commons		.05
Unlisted Stars		**.10-.35**
Series 1 or 2 Pack (12)		2.00
Series 1 or 2 Box (24)		45.00

Quality Rating ★★★
Ultra is released before the base Fleer set and once again features limited production with the rare Gold Medallion inserts.

#	Player	NM
11	Ripken, C.	2.50
16	Clemens, R.	1.00
22	Vaughn, M.	.75
44	Thomas, F.	3.00
46	Belle, A.	.75
48	Lofton, K.	.75
53	Ramirez, M.	.75
92	Puckett, K.	1.00
101	Mattingly, D.	1.00
115	McGwire, M.	1.25
126	Griffey, K.	3.00
130	Rodriguez, A.	2.50
135	Gonzalez, J.	1.25
156	Jones, C.	1.50
160	Maddux, G.	2.00
205	Bagwell, J.	1.00
223	Nomo, H.	1.50
224	Piazza, M.	1.50
279	Smith, O.	1.00
284	Gwynn, T.	1.25
290	Bonds, B.	.60
386	Jeter, D.	1.50
457	Sandberg, R.	.75
498	Guerrero, W. (R)	.75
574	Bagwell, J.	.50

579	Griffey, K.	1.50
580	Gwynn, T.	.60
582	Jones, C.	.75
585	Maddux, G.	1.50
587	Piazza, M.	.75
588	Ripken, C.	1.50
590	Thomas, F.	1.50
596	Jones, C.	.75

Gold Medallion
	Complete Set (600)	180.00
	Series 1 Set (1-300)	90.00
	Series 2 Set (301-600)	90.00
	Commons	.25
	Gold Medallion	2x-4x

Series One Checklists
	Complete Set (10)	10.00
	Commons	.75
	Gold Checklist	20.00
	Gold Medallion	2x-4x
1	Bagwell, J.	1.00
2	Bonds, B.	1.00
4	Griffey, K.	3.00
5	Jones, C.	1.50
6	Piazza, M.	1.50
7	Ramirez, M.	1.00
8	Ripken, C.	2.50
9	Thomas, F.	3.00

Series Two Checklists
	Complete Set (10)	10.00
	Commons	.75
	Gold Checklists	20.00
	Gold Medallion	2x-4x
1	Belle, A.	1.00
3	Griffey, K.	3.00
4	Gwynn, T.	1.25
8	Maddux, G.	2.50
9	Ripken, C.	2.50
10	Thomas, F.	3.00

Call to the Hall
	Complete Set (10)	80.00
	Commons	2.00
	Gold Call to the Hall	160.00
	Gold Medallion	2x-4x
1	Bonds, B.	6.00
2	Griffey, K.	25.00
3	Gwynn, T.	10.00
5	Maddux, G.	15.00
6	Murray, E.	5.00
7	Ripken, C.	20.00
8	Sandberg, R.	6.00
9	Smith, O.	6.00
10	Thomas, F.	25.00

Diamond Producers
	Complete Set (12)	70.00
	Gold Producers	140.00
	Gold Medallion	2x-4x
1	Belle, A.	5.00
2	Bonds, B.	4.00
3	Griffey, K.	15.00
4	Gwynn, T.	8.00
5	Maddux, G.	10.00
6	Nomo, H.	7.00
7	Piazza, M.	10.00
8	Puckett, K.	5.00
9	Ripken, C.	10.00
10	Thomas, F.	15.00
11	Vaughn, M.	5.00
12	Williams, M.	3.00

Fresh Foundations
	Complete Set (10)	6.00
	Commons	.25
	Gold Foundations	12.00
	Gold Medallion	2x-4x
5	Jones, C.	2.00
8	Nomo, H.	2.00
9	Ramirez, M.	1.00

Series One Golden Prospects
	Complete Set (10)	5.00
	Commons	.50
	Golden Prospects	10.00
	Gold Medallion	2x-4x
8	Jeter, D.	5.00

Series Two Golden Prospects
	Complete Set (15)	120.00
	Commons	6.00
	Gold Prospects	240.00
	Gold Medallion	2x-4x
1	Abreu, B.	10.00
4	Cameron, M.	20.00
7	Guerrero, W.	12.00
8	Hidalgo, R.	12.00

Hitting Machines
	Complete Set (10)	450.00
	Commons	15.00
	Gold Hitting Mchnes	900.00
	Gold Medallion	2x-4x
1	Belle, A.	30.00
2	Bonds, B.	30.00
3	Gonzalez, J.	65.00
4	Griffey, K.	125.00
7	Piazza, M.	80.00
9	Thomas, F.	100.00
10	Williams, M.	20.00

Home Run Kings
	Complete Set (12)	70.00
	Commons	3.00
	Gold HR Kings	140.00
	Gold Medallion	2x-4x
1	Belle, A.	6.00
3	Bonds, B.	6.00
5	Gonzalez, J.	10.00
6	Griffey, K.	25.00
7	McGwire, M.	10.00
8	Ramirez, M.	6.00
10	Thomas, F.	25.00
11	Vaughn, M.	5.00

On Base Leaders
	Complete Set (10)	8.00
	Commons	.50
	Gold On Base Ldrs	16.00
	Gold Medallion	2x-4x
2	Bonds, B.	1.50
3	Gwynn, T.	2.00
7	Piazza, M.	3.00
9	Thomas, F.	5.00

Power Plus
	Complete Set (12)	30.00
	Commons	1.50
	Gold Power Plus	60.00
	Gold Medallion	2x-4x
1	Bagwell, J.	4.00
2	Bonds, B.	3.00
3	Griffey, K.	12.00
6	Piazza, M.	6.00
7	Ramirez, M.	4.00
10	Thomas, F.	12.00

Prime Leather
	Complete Set (18)	30.00
	Commons	1.50
	Gold Prime Leather	80.00
	Gold Medallion	2x-4x
4	Ripken, C.	10.00
6	Griffey, K.	12.00
7	Lofton, K.	4.00
8	Puckett, K.	3.00
10	Piazza, M.	6.00
15	Bonds, B.	3.00
16	Gwynn, T.	4.00

Rawhide
	Complete Set (10)	20.00
	Commons	1.00
	Gold Rawhide	40.00
	Gold Medallion	2x-4x
2	Bonds, B.	2.00
4	Griffey, K.	7.00
5	Lofton, K.	3.00
6	Maddux, G.	5.00
8	Piazza, M.	4.00
9	Ripken, C.	5.00

RBI Kings
	Complete Set (10)	35.00
	Commons	3.00
	Gold RBI Kings	70.00
	Gold Medallion	2x-4x
2	Belle, A.	6.00
4	Bonds, B.	6.00
5	Ramirez, M.	6.00
9	Thomas, F.	20.00
10	Vaughn, M.	6.00

Respect
	Complete Set (10)	70.00
	Gold Respect	140.00
	Gold Medallion	2x-4x
1	Carter, J.	3.00
2	Griffey, K.	20.00
3	Gwynn, T.	7.00
4	Maddux, G.	10.00
5	Murray, E.	4.00
6	Puckett, K.	5.00
7	Ripken, C.	15.00
8	Sandberg, R.	5.00
9	Thomas, F.	20.00
10	Vaughn, M.	6.00

Rising Stars
	Complete Set (10)	5.00
	Commons	.50
	Gold Rising Stars	10.00
	Gold Medallion	2x-4x
6	Jones, C.	3.00
8	Nomo, H.	2.50
9	Ramirez, M.	1.50

Season Crowns
	Complete Set (10)	40.00
	Commons	1.00
	Gold Season Crowns	80.00
	Gold Medallion	2x-4x
1	Bonds, B.	3.00
2	Gwynn, T.	4.00
4	Lofton, K.	4.00
5	Maddux, G.	8.00
7	Nomo, H.	6.00
8	Ripken, C.	10.00
9	Thomas, F.	12.00

Thunderclap
	Complete Set (20)	450.00
	Commons	10.00
	Gold Thunderclap	900.00
	Gold Medallion	2x-4x
1	Belle, A.	20.00
2	Bonds, B.	20.00
10	Gonzalez, J.	35.00
11	Griffey, K.	85.00
13	McGwire, M.	40.00
14	Murray, E.	20.00
16	Puckett, K.	40.00
17	Ripken, C.	60.00
18	Sandberg, R.	25.00
19	Thomas, F.	75.00

1996 LEAF

	NM Price
Complete Set (220)	$20.00
Commons	.05
Unlisted Stars	.10-.35
Pack (12)	2.50
Box (30)	55.00

Quality Rating ★★★
Great looking cards mixed in with the fact this is the final baseball product for Donruss has collectors talking.

#	Player	NM
15	McGwire, M.	1.25
21	Ripken, C.	2.50
24	Rodriguez, A.	2.00
28	Jones, C.	1.50
41	Griffey, K.	3.00
69	Clemens, R.	1.00
77	Puckett, K.	1.00
78	Bonds, B.	.75
94	Belle, A.	.75
99	Gwynn, T.	1.25
107	Gonzalez, J.	1.25
127	Lofton, K.	.75
130	Vaughn, M.	.75
148	Nomo, H.	1.25
150	Thomas, F.	3.00
163	Smith, O.	.50
192	Maddux, G.	2.00
199	Bagwell, J.	1.00
200	Piazza, M.	1.00
211	Jeter, D.	1.50

Bronze Proofs
	Complete Set (220)	600.00
	Commons	1.00
	Star Proofs	6x-12x
	Rookie Proofs	4x-8x

Silver Proofs
	Complete Set (220)	1200.00
	Commons	5.00
	Star Proofs	12x-25x
	Rookie Proofs	8x-15x

Gold Proofs
	Complete Set (220)	2500.00
	Commons	5.00
	Star Proofs	25x-50x
	Rookie Proofs	15x-30x

All-Star MVP Contenders
	Complete Set (20)	40.00
	Commons	1.00
1	Thomas, F.	5.00
2	Piazza, M. (W)	6.00
4	Ripken, C.	4.00
5	Bagwell, J.	3.00
8	Gwynn, T.	3.00
11	Jones, C.	4.00
12	Lofton, K.	2.00
13	Ramirez, M.	2.00
14	Bonds, B.	3.00
17	Belle, A.	2.00
18	Griffey, K.	6.00
19	Maddux, G.	3.00

Frank Thomas
	Complete Set (8)	125.00
	Thomas Singles	20.00

Gold Leaf Stars
	Complete Set (15)	500.00
1	Thomas, F.	60.00
2	Bichette, D.	10.00
3	Sosa, S.	12.00
4	Griffey, K.	75.00
5	Piazza, M.	50.00
6	Salmon, T.	10.00
7	Nomo, H.	40.00
8	Ripken, C.	60.00
9	Jones, C.	50.00
10	Belle, A.	30.00
11	Gwynn, T.	40.00
12	Vaughn, M.	20.00
13	Larkin, B.	10.00
14	Ramirez, M.	20.00
15	Maddux, G.	50.00

Hats Off
	Complete Set (8)	200.00
1	Ripken, C.	30.00
2	Larkin, B.	6.00
3	Thomas, F.	35.00
4	Vaughn, M.	12.00
5	Griffey, K.	40.00
6	Nomo, H.	20.00
7	Belle, A.	12.00
8	Maddux, G.	25.00

Picture Perfect
	Complete Set (12)	250.00
1	Thomas, F.	40.00
2	Ripken, C.	40.00
3	Maddux, G.	35.00
4	Ramirez, M.	12.00
5	Jones, C.	30.00
6	Gwynn, T.	20.00
7	Griffey, K.	50.00
8	Belle, A.	15.00
9	Bagwell, J.	20.00
10	Piazza, M.	30.00
11	Vaughn, M.	15.00
12	Bonds, B.	12.00

Statistical Standouts
	Complete Set (8)	450.00
1	Ripken, C.	80.00
2	Gwynn, T.	50.00
3	Thomas, F.	80.00
4	Griffey, K.	100.00
5	Nomo, H.	50.00
6	Maddux, G.	60.00
7	Belle, A.	30.00
8	Jones, C.	60.00

Total Bases
	Complete Set (12)	150.00
	Commons	4.00
1	Thomas, F.	30.00
2	Belle, A.	10.00
4	Bonds, B	8.00
5	Puckett, K.	10.00
9	Griffey, K.	35.00
11	Gonzalez, J.	15.00
12	Ripken, C.	30.00

1996 LEAF
LIMITED

		NM Price
Complete Set (90)		$50.00
Commons		.30
Unlisted Stars		**.40-1.00**
Pack (5)		4.00
Box (14)		50.00

Quality Rating ★★★

Leaf Limited features one of the coolest inserts of the year in Pennant Craze. Lumberjacks are again in demand.

#	Player	NM
2	Clemens, R.	3.00
8	Ramirez, M.	2.00
9	Bagwell, J.	3.00
10	Maddux, G.	5.00
11	Griffey, K.	8.00
13	Piazza, M.	5.00
15	Ripken, C.	6.00
21	McGwire, M.	2.50
23	Thomas, F.	8.00
27	Jones, C.	4.00
29	Lofton, K.	2.50
31	Rodriguez, A.	5.00
34	Gonzalez, J.	3.50
41	Belle, A.	2.50
47	Vaughn, M.	2.00
53	Gwynn, T.	3.00
65	Nomo, H.	3.00
70	Puckett, K.	2.00
71	Bonds, B.	2.00
77	Sandberg, R.	2.00
81	Pettitte, A.	2.50

Gold

Complete Set (90)		450.00
Gold		8x

Lumberjacks

Complete Set (10)		225.00
Limited Edition		5x
1	Griffey, K.	50.00
2	Sosa, S.	12.00
3	Ripken, C.	30.00
4	Thomas, F.	35.00
5	Rodriguez, A.	30.00
6	Vaughn, M.	15.00
7	Jones, C.	30.00
8	Piazza, M.	30.00
9	Bagwell, J.	20.00
10	McGwire, M.	20.00

Pennant Craze

Complete Set (10)		500.00
1	Gonzalez, J.	50.00
2	Ripken, C.	70.00
3	Thomas, F.	70.00
4	Griffey, K.	90.00
5	Belle, A.	25.00
6	Maddux, G.	50.00
7	Molitor, P.	20.00
8	Rodriguez, A.	60.00
9	Bonds, B.	25.00
10	Jones, C.	50.00

Rookies

Complete Set (10)		75.00
Commons		3.00
Gold		4x
2	Erstad, D.	15.00
4	Jeter, D.	20.00
8	Jones, A.	15.00

1996 LEAF
PREFERRED

		NM Price
Complete Set (150)		$30.00
Commons		.10
Unlisted Stars		**.20-.50**
Pack (6)		3.00
Box (24)		50.00

Quality Rating ★★★

Leaf debuted a new product to mixed reviews. Inserts gain the most attention with Staremaster numbered out of 2,500.

#	Player	NM
1	Griffey, K.	4.00
5	Ramirez, M.	.75
8	Bagwell, J.	1.50
12	Maddux, G.	3.00
13	Thomas, F.	4.00
15	McGwire, M.	1.50
19	Clemens, R.	1.25
22	Ripken, C.	3.50
24	Lofton, K.	1.25
25	Piazza, M.	2.50
31	Smith, O.	.60
35	Rodriguez, A.	2.00
40	Jones, C.	2.00
43	Gonzalez, J.	1.50
46	Belle, A.	.75
49	Vaughn, M.	.75
52	Johnson, R.	.60
63	Puckett, K.	.75
64	Nomo, H.	1.50
72	Pettitte, A.	.75
79	Gwynn, T.	1.50
91	Sandberg, R.	1.00
94	Bonds, B.	1.00
116	Jeter, D.	2.00

Press Proofs

Complete Set (150)		1800.00
Commons		3.00
Press Proofs		25x-40x

Leaf Steel

Complete Set (77)		100.00
Commons		.50
Gold		4x
1	Thomas, F.	10.00
3	Lofton, K.	3.00
6	Bonds, B.	2.50
8	Rodriguez, A.	8.00
11	Nomo, H.	4.00
14	McGwire, M.	4.00
17	Ripken, C.	8.00
20	Gonzalez, J.	4.00
22	Vaughn, M.	2.50
33	Jones, C.	5.00
39	Bagwell, J.	3.00
40	Jeter, D.	5.00
41	Puckett, K.	2.50
48	Gwynn, T.	4.00
51	Piazza, M.	6.00
52	Griffey, K.	10.00
53	Maddux, G.	5.00
60	Johnson, R.	2.00
63	Clemens, R.	3.00
66	Sandberg, R.	2.50
68	Belle, A.	2.50
77	Ramirez, M.	2.50

Staremaster

Complete Set (12)		450.00
1	Jones, C.	50.00
2	Rodriguez, A.	50.00
3	Jeter, D.	40.00

4	Gwynn, T.	40.00
5	Thomas, F.	60.00
6	Griffey, K.	70.00
7	Ripken, C.	60.00
8	Maddux, G.	50.00
9	Belle, A.	20.00
10	Bonds, B.	20.00
11	Bagwell, J.	25.00
12	Piazza, M.	50.00

Steel Power

Complete Set (8)		150.00
1	Belle, A.	10.00
2	Vaughn, M.	10.00
3	Griffey, K.	40.00
4	Ripken, C.	30.00
5	Piazza, M.	25.00
6	Bonds, B.	10.00
7	Bagwell, J.	20.00
8	Thomas, F.	30.00

1996 LEAF
SIGNATURE SERIES

		NM Price
Complete Set (150)		$90.00
Series One (100)		60.00
Extended Series (50)		30.00
Commons		.25
Unlisted Stars		**.50-.75**
Pack (4)		10.00
Box (12)		100.00

Quality Rating ★★★

Collectors love to get autographs in packs and here's the chance. Player selection is top notch.

#	Player	NM
1	Piazza, M.	4.00
2	Gonzalez, J.	2.50
3	Maddux, G.	5.00
7	Thomas, F.	6.00
10	Griffey, K.	6.00
11	Ramirez, M.	1.50
15	Ripken, C.	5.00
16	Rodriguez, A.	4.00
22	Bagwell, J.	2.00
23	McGwire, M.	2.00
26	Jones, C.	4.00
28	Clemens, R.	1.50
51	Nomo, H.	2.00
52	Smith, O.	1.00
54	Pettitte, A.	1.25
55	Lofton, K.	2.00
59	Belle, A.	2.00
67	Jeter, D.	3.00
73	Vaughn, M.	2.00
84	Sandberg, R.	1.50
89	Bonds, B.	2.00
94	Erstad, D. (R)	4.00
98	Gwynn, T.	3.00
99	Puckett, K.	1.50
101	Jones, A.	5.00
110	Guerrero, V.	4.00
116	Murray, E.	2.00
117	Walker, T.	5.00
122	Rolen, S.	4.00
150	Thomas, F. (CL)	4.00
No#	Thomas, F. (Auto. promo, 500)	300.00

Press Proofs

Complete Set (150)		1000.00
Unlisted Stars		6x-12x
Gold (50)		2x-5x
Platinum (150)		8x-10x
1	Piazza, M.	50.00
2	Gonzalez, J.	50.00
3	Maddux, G.	60.00

7	Thomas, F.	70.00
10	Griffey, K.	90.00
15	Ripken, C.	60.00
16	Rodriguez, A.	80.00
59	Belle, A.	30.00
67	Jeter, D.	40.00
94	Erstad, D.	30.00
101	Jones, A.	50.00
110	Guerrero, V.	30.00
117	Walker, T.	25.00
122	Rolen, S.	30.00
150	Thomas, F. (CL)	50.00

Bronze Autographs

Complete Set (251)		2000.00
Minor Stars		5.00
Unlisted Stars		12.00
Silver		2x
Gold		4x
Silver SP		2.5x
Gold SP		5x

Note: 700 Bronze sigs for short prints.
200 Silver sigs for short prints.
100 Gold sigs for short prints.

Alomar, R. (SP)		100.00
Boggs, W. (SP)		200.00
Clark, W.		20.00
Cordova, M.		20.00
Jeter, D. (SP)		150.00
Lofton, K. (SP)		100.00
Molitor, P. (SP)		100.00
Mondesi, R. (Bronze)		70.00
Mondesi, R. (Silver)		80.00
Mondesi, R. (Gold)		100.00
Pettitte, A.		40.00
Ramirez, M. (SP)		50.00
Rodriguez, A. (SP)		250.00
Thomas, F. (SP)		250.00
Thome, J. (Gold)		90.00
Thome, J. (Silver)		80.00
Vaughn, M. (SP)		100.00

Extended Series Autographs

Complete Set (217)		3000.00
Minor Stars		5.00
Unlisted stars		10.00
Century Marks		4x

Note: A. Rodriguez and Maddux only signed 500 cards ea.

Jones, A. (SP)		90.00
McGriff, F. (SP)		40.00
Maddux, G. (SP)		400.00
Dye, J. (SP)		40.00
Smoltz, J. (SP)		50.00
Klesko, R. (SP)		50.00
Palmeiro, R. (SP)		40.00
Vaughn, M. (SP)		60.00
Clemens, R. (SP)		170.00
Erstad, D.		40.00
Sosa, S. (SP)		50.00
Thomas, F. (SP)		200.00
Lofton, K. (SP)		70.00
Garcia, K. (SP)		30.00
Puckett, K. (SP)		160.00
Knoblauch, C. (SP)		60.00
Molitor, P. (SP)		75.00
Pettitte, A. (SP)		50.00
Jeter, D. (SP)		150.00
Caminiti, K. (SP)		60.00
Gwynn, T. (SP)		150.00
Williams, M. (SP)		40.00
Rodriguez, A. (SP)		350.00
Buhner, J. (SP)		50.00
Johnson, R. (SP)		75.00
Gonzalez, J. (SP)		150.00
Rodriguez, I. (SP)		80.00
Thomas, F. (Jumbo)		80.00

1996 LEAF STUDIO

		NM Price
Complete Set (150)		$18.00
Commons		.05
Unlisted Stars		**.10-.35**
Pack (7)		2.50
Box (24)		45.00

Quality Rating ★★★

Pinnacle puts its stamp on the highly anticipated Studio set. Two parallel sets add to the excitement.

#	Player	NM
1	Ripken, C.	2.50
6	Sandberg, R.	.75
11	Clemens, R.	1.00
18	Maddux, G.	2.00
33	Jeter, D.	1.50
45	Lofton, K.	1.00
49	Bagwell, J.	1.00
63	Nomo, H.	1.25
65	Rodriguez, A.	2.50
72	Jones, C.	1.50
74	Puckett, K.	.75
76	Bonds, B.	.75
80	Piazza, M.	2.00
93	Thomas, F.	3.00
114	Ramirez, M.	.75
116	Griffey, K.	3.00
118	McGwire, M.	1.00
143	Belle, A.	.75
145	Gwynn, T.	1.25

Bronze Proofs

Complete Set (150)		400.00
Common Bronze		1.00
Common Silver		20.00
Common Gold		5.00
Bronze Proofs		8x
Silver Proofs		100x
Gold Proofs		40x

Hit Parade

Complete Set (10)		100.00
1	Gwynn, T.	10.00
2	Griffey, K.	30.00
3	Thomas, F.	25.00
4	Bagwell, J.	12.00
5	Puckett, K.	10.00
6	Piazza, M.	18.00
7	Bonds, B.	10.00
8	Belle, A.	10.00
9	Salmon, T.	4.00
10	Vaughn, M.	10.00

Masterstrokes

Complete Set (8)		150.00
1	Gwynn, T.	25.00
2	Piazza, M.	30.00
3	Bagwell, J.	20.00
4	Ramirez, M.	12.00
5	Ripken, C.	35.00
6	Thomas, F.	40.00
7	Griffey, K.	50.00
8	Maddux, G.	25.00

Stained Glass Stars

Complete Set (12)		100.00
1	Ripken, C.	15.00
2	Griffey, K.	20.00
3	Thomas, F.	20.00
4	Maddux, G.	12.00
5	Jones, C.	10.00
6	Piazza, M.	10.00
7	Belle, A.	4.00
8	Bagwell, J.	6.00
9	Nomo, H.	5.00
10	Bonds, B.	4.00
11	Ramirez, M.	4.00
12	Lofton, K.	4.00

1996 PACIFIC CROWN COLLECTION

	NM Price
Complete Set (450)	$30.00
Commons	.05
Unlisted Stars	**.10-.35**
Pack (12)	2.00
Box (36)	60.00

Quality Rating ★★★
Crown Collection's photography gets better every year. Roberto Alomar is this year's spokesman.

#	Player	NM
4	Jones, C.	1.50
6	Maddux, G.	2.00
18	Maddux, G.	1.00
89	Bagwell, J.	1.00
100	Nomo, H.	1.25
103	Piazza, M.	1.50
184	Gwynn, T.	1.25
198	Gwynn, T. (Bat. Chp.)	.50
202	Bonds, B.	.60
230	Ripken, C.	2.50
248	Vaughn, M.	.75
258	Clemens, R.	1.00
287	Thomas, F.	3.00
301	Ramirez, M.	.75
303	Lofton, K.	.75
307	Belle, A.	.75
365	Puckett, K.	.75
376	Mattingly, D.	1.25
383	Jeter, D.	1.50
385	McGwire, M.	1.00
401	Johnson, R.	.60
410	Griffey, K.	3.00
416	Rodriguez, A.	2.00
423	Gonzalez, J.	1.25

Cramer's Choice

Complete Set (10)		1200.00
Commons		30.00
3	Ripken, C.	200.00
4	Maddux, G.	175.00
5	Thomas, F.	250.00
6	Gwynn, T.	120.00
7	Piazza, M.	150.00
8	Griffey, K.	250.00
9	Ramirez, M.	70.00

Gold Crown Die-Cuts

Complete Set (36)		400.00
Commons		4.00
1	Alomar, R.	6.00
4	Mattingly, D.	15.00
6	Ramirez, M.	10.00
7	Piazza, M.	25.00
10	Bagwell, J.	15.00
13	Griffey, K.	45.00
15	Ripken, C.	30.00
18	Thomas, F.	30.00
19	Nomo, H.	20.00
23	Vaughn, M.	12.00
25	Puckett, K.	12.00
26	Belle, A.	10.00
28	Maddux, G.	25.00
31	Jones, C.	25.00
33	Johnson, R.	8.00
34	McGwire, M.	20.00
35	Gwynn, T.	20.00
36	Bonds, B.	10.00

Great Latinos

Complete Set (36)		50.00
Commons		1.00
1	Alomar, R.	3.00
12	Gonzalez, J.	8.00

25	Ramirez, M.	4.00
26	Rodriguez, A.	15.00
27	Rodriguez, I.	4.00

Hometown of the Players

Complete Set (20)		120.00
Commons		2.00
1	Piazza, M.	15.00
2	Maddux, G.	15.00
3	Gwynn, T.	10.00
5	Mattingly, D.	12.00
6	Ripken, C.	20.00
7	Jones, C.	15.00
9	Ramirez, M.	5.00
11	Griffey, K.	25.00
13	Thomas, F.	20.00
17	Puckett, K.	6.00
19	Nomo, H.	10.00

Milestones

Complete Set (10)		75.00
Commons		3.00
1	Belle, A.	6.00
2	Mattingly, D.	10.00
3	Gwynn, T.	10.00
7	Maddux, G.	12.00
9	Griffey, K.	25.00
10	Ripken, C.	18.00

October Moments

Complete Set (20)		150.00
Commons		4.00
2	Belle, A.	8.00
6	Griffey, K.	35.00
8	Jones, C.	20.00
11	Lofton, K.	8.00
13	Maddux, G.	20.00
15	Mattingly, D.	15.00
16	Nomo, H.	15.00
17	Piazza, M.	20.00
18	Ramirez, M.	8.00

1996 PACIFIC PRISM

	NM Price
Complete Set (144)	$150.00
Commons	.50
Unlisted Stars	**1.00-2.00**
Pack (2)	1.50
Box (36)	48.00

Quality Rating ★★★
Prism cards get better every year. Player selection is top notch and at one player card per pack it will take a while to complete a set.

#	Player	NM
2	Jones, C.	10.00
6	Maddux, G.	12.00
29	Bagwell, J.	7.00
37	Nomo, H.	8.00
38	Piazza, M.	10.00
61	Gwynn, T.	8.00
65	Bonds, B.	5.00
72	Smith, O.	4.00
77	Ripken, C.	15.00
79	Clemens, R.	6.00
81	Vaughn, M.	5.00
91	Thomas, F.	15.00
94	Belle, A.	5.00
95	Lofton, K.	5.00
98	Ramirez, M.	4.00
117	Puckett, K.	5.00
126	McGwire, M	6.00
119	Mattingly, D.	7.00
131	Griffey, K.	20.00
136	Gonzalez, J.	8.00
138	Rodriguez, I.	4.00

Gold

Complete Set (144)		500.00
Commons		3.00
Gold		2x-4x

Fence Busters

Complete Set (20)		200.00
Commons		4.00
1	Belle, A.	12.00
3	Bonds, B.	12.00
6	Griffey, K.	40.00
7	Jones, C.	20.00
11	McGwire, M.	18.00
13	Piazza, M.	20.00
14	Puckett, K.	12.00
15	Ripken, C.	30.00
18	Thomas, F.	30.00
19	Vaughn, M.	12.00

Flame Throwers

Complete Set (10)		150.00
Commons		6.00
1	Johnson, R.	25.00
3	Clemens, R.	25.00
5	Nomo, H.	40.00
7	Maddux, G.	50.00

Red Hot Stars

Complete Set (20)		300.00
Commons		4.00
1	Alomar, R.	8.00
3	Jones, C.	25.00
4	Piazza, M.	25.00
6	Bagwell, J.	15.00
7	Griffey, K.	40.00
8	Maddux, G.	25.00
9	Puckett, K.	12.00
10	Thomas, F.	30.00
11	Belle, A.	12.00
12	Gwynn, T.	18.00
14	Ramirez, M.	12.00
15	Bonds, B.	12.00
17	Johnson, R.	8.00
18	Mattingly, D.	15.00
19	Ripken, C.	30.00
20	Vaughn, M.	12.00

1996 PINNACLE

	NM Price
Complete Set (399)	$30.00
Series 1 (1-200)	15.00
Series 2 Set (201-399)	15.00
Commons	.10
Unlisted Stars	**.15-.50**
Series 1 or 2 Pack (10)	2.50
Series 1 or 2 Box (24)	45.00

Quality Rating ★★★
The 1996 version of Pinnacle has a great card design and inserts that feature new names like Sosa and Sanders.

#	Player	NM
1	Maddux, G.	2.00
4	Piazza, M.	1.50
10	Bagwell, J.	1.00
38	Gonzalez, J.	1.25
46	Ramirez, M.	1.00
78	Vaughn, M.	.75
99	Mattingly, D.	1.00
103	Pettitte, A.	.75
105	Lofton, K.	.75
114	Jones, C.	1.50
122	Griffey, K.	3.00
130	McGwire, M.	1.25
131	Nomo, H.	1.50
134	Griffey, K.	1.50
135	Thomas, F.	1.50

136	Ripken, C.	1.50
137	Belle, A.	.75
138	Piazza, M.	.75
171	Jeter, D.	2.00
194	Thomas, F. (CL)	1.00
195	Griffey, K. (CL)	1.00
196	Ripken, C. (CL)	1.00
198	Piazza, M. (CL)	.75
201	Thomas, F.	3.00
203	Puckett, K.	.75
205	Gwynn, T.	1.25
207	Belle, A.	.75
208	Bonds, B.	.75
214	Ripken, C.	2.50
247	Clemens, R.	1.00
254	Maddux, G.	1.25
255	Griffey, K.	1.50
256	Nomo, H.	.75
257	Thomas, F.	1.00
258	Ripken, C.	1.50
265	Piazza, M.	.75
266	Jones, C.	.75
275	Rodriguez, A.	1.00
301	Griffey, K.	1.50
322	Piazza, M.	.75
323	Thomas, F.	1.00
372	Hernandez, L. (R)	1.50
383	Guerrero, W. (R)	.75
393	Ripken, C.	1.50
394	Griffey, K.	1.50
395	Thomas, F.	1.00
396	Jones, C.	1.00
397	Maddux, G.	1.00
398	Piazza, M.	1.00
399	Checklist	1.50
	Ripken Tribute	20.00

Essence of the Game

	Complete Set (18)	150.00
	Commons	3.00
1	Ripken, C.	25.00
2	Maddux, G.	20.00
3	Thomas, F.	25.00
5	Jones, C.	15.00
7	Griffey, K.	30.00
8	Puckett, K.	6.00
9	Nomo, H.	10.00
10	Piazza, M.	15.00
11	Bagwell, J.	8.00
12	Vaughn, M.	6.00
13	Belle, A.	7.00
15	Mattingly, D.	10.00
17	Murray, E.	5.00
18	Bonds, B.	6.00

First Rate

	Complete Set (18)	125.00
	Commons	3.00
1	Griffey, K.	35.00
2	Thomas, F.	30.00
3	Vaughn, M.	10.00
4	Jones, C.	20.00
5	Rodriquez, A.	30.00
6	Puckett, K.	10.00
9	Bonds, B.	8.00
13	Jeter, D.	15.00
14	Ramirez, M.	6.00
18	McGwire, M.	12.00

Pinnacle Power

	Complete Set (20)	120.00
	Commons	3.00
1	Thomas, F.	35.00
2	Vaughn, M.	6.00
3	Griffey, K.	35.00
5	Bonds, B.	6.00
7	Piazza, M.	20.00
11	Bagwell, J.	10.00
13	Belle, A.	8.00
16	Ramirez, M.	8.00
17	Murray, E.	5.00
19	Walker, L.	5.00
20	Gonzalez, J.	15.00

Project Stardom

	Complete Set (18)	150.00
	Commons	5.00
2	Jeter, D.	30.00
3	Garcia, K.	8.00
5	Rodriguez, A.	40.00
6	Jones, C.	30.00
9	Benes, A.	8.00
11	Ramirez, M.	12.00
15	Dye, J.	8.00
17	Mondesi, R.	8.00
18	Klesko, R.	8.00

Skylines

	Complete Set (18)	250.00
	Commons	4.00
1	Griffey, K.	50.00
2	Thomas, F.	50.00
3	Maddux, G.	30.00
4	Ripken, C.	35.00
5	Belle, A.	12.00
6	Vaughn, M.	12.00
7	Piazza, M.	25.00
10	Bonds, B.	12.00
12	Nomo, H.	18.00
13	Gwynn, T.	20.00
14	Puckett, K.	15.00
15	Jones, C.	25.00
16	Bagwell, J.	15.00
17	Ramirez, M.	8.00

Slugfest

	Complete Set (18)	200.00
	Commons	3.00
1	Thomas, F.	40.00
2	Griffey, K.	40.00
3	Bagwell, J.	18.00
4	Bonds, B.	12.00
5	Vaughn, M.	12.00
6	Belle, A.	12.00
7	Piazza, M.	25.00
13	Ramirez, M.	10.00
14	Murray, E.	10.00
15	Gonzalez, J.	15.00

Starburst

	Complete Set (200)	550.00
	Series 1 Set (100)	275.00
	Series 2 Set (100)	275.00
	Commons	1.00
	Artist Proof Set (200)	1800.00
	AP Series 1 Set (100)	900.00
	AP Series 2 Set (100)	900.00
	Common AP	3.00
	Unlisted Stars	2.00-6.00
	Starburst AP's	2x-4x
1	Maddux, G.	20.00
4	Piazza, M.	20.00
7	Bagwell, J.	12.00
28	Vaughn, M.	8.00
37	Mattingly, D.	15.00
40	Lofton, K.	10.00
41	Griffey, K.	30.00
45	Jones, C.	20.00
54	Nomo, H.	15.00
57	Gonzalez, J.	12.00
61	Griffey, K.	20.00
62	Thomas, F.	20.00
63	Ripken, C.	20.00
65	Piazza, M.	10.00
76	Ramirez, M.	5.00
78	Bagwell, J.	7.00
82	Puckett, K.	5.00
84	Mattingly, D.	8.00
97	Jeter, D.	15.00
101	Thomas, F.	30.00
103	Puckett, K.	6.00
105	Gwynn, T.	18.00
107	Belle, A.	10.00
108	Bonds, B.	10.00
114	Ripken, C.	25.00
147	Clemens, R.	10.00
154	Maddux, G.	12.00
155	Griffey, K.	20.00
156	Nomo, H.	10.00
157	Thomas, F.	20.00
158	Ripken, C.	15.00
159	Bagwell, J.	8.00
165	Piazza, M.	10.00
166	Jones, C.	10.00
167	Gwynn, T.	10.00
175	Rodriguez, A.	12.00
185	Griffey, K.	20.00
190	Bagwell, J.	8.00
192	Mattingly, D.	8.00
197	Piazza, M.	10.00
198	Thomas, F.	20.00
200	Gwynn, T.	10.00

Team Pinnacle

	Complete Set (9)	150.00
	Commons	10.00
1	Thomas/Bagwell	40.00
4	Larkin/Ripken	40.00
5	Bonds/Salmon	15.00
6	Griffey/Sanders	40.00
7	Belle/Sosa	10.00
8	Rodriguez/Piazza	30.00
9	Maddux/Johnson	30.00

Team Spirit

	Complete Set (12)	275.00
1	Maddux, G.	30.00
2	Griffey, K.	50.00
3	Jeter, D.	25.00
4	Piazza, M.	25.00
5	Ripken, C.	40.00
6	Thomas, F.	40.00
7	Bagwell, J.	20.00
8	Vaughn, M.	12.00
9	Belle, A.	10.00
10	Jones, C.	25.00
11	Damon, J.	5.00
12	Bonds, B.	10.00

Team Tomorrow

	Complete Set (10)	100.00
1	Rivera, R.	6.00
2	Damon, J.	4.00
3	Mondesi, R.	6.00
4	Ramirez, M.	12.00
5	Nomo, H.	20.00
6	Jones, C.	30.00
7	Anderson, G.	5.00
8	Rodriguez, A.	40.00
9	Jeter, D.	25.00
10	Garcia, K.	10.00

The Christie Brinkley Collection

	Complete Set (16)	80.00
	Commons	3.00
1	Maddux, G.	20.00
5	Jones, C.	15.00
10	Belle, A.	8.00
11	Ramirez, M.	8.00
16	Lofton, K.	10.00

1996 PINNACLE AFICIONADO

	NM Price
Complete Set (200)	$50.00
Commons	.20
Unlisted Stars	**.30-.75**
Pack (5)	2.00
Box (16)	28.00

Quality Rating ★★★
Pinnacle has taken on a new look with Aficionado. Cards have a great feel and smell like bubble gum.

#	Player	NM
5	Smith, O.	1.00
6	McGwire, M.	2.00
9	Clemens, R.	2.00
10	Johnson, R.	1.00
16	Sandberg, R.	1.50
18	Ripken, C.	4.00
22	Maddux, G.	3.00
24	Puckett, K.	1.50
30	Gwynn, T.	2.50
58	Vaughn, M.	1.50
59	Thomas, F.	5.00
69	Rodriguez, I.	1.50
73	Bagwell, J.	2.00
75	Griffey, K.	5.00
77	Belle, A.	1.50
80	Bonds, B.	1.50
99	Gonzalez, J.	2.50
109	Ramirez, M.	1.25
114	Lofton, K.	1.50
124	Piazza, M.	3.50
127	Jones, C.	2.50
132	Nomo, H.	2.00
136	Rodriguez, A.	4.00
163	Jeter, D.	3.00
180	Guerrero, W. (R)	1.50
196	Griffey, K. (CL)	3.00
198	Piazza, M. (CL)	2.00
199	Maddux, G. (CL)	2.00
200	Thomas, F. (CL)	3.00

Artist Proofs

	Complete Set (200)	2000.00
	Commons	4.00
	Artist Proofs	10x-20x

Magic Numbers

	Complete Set (10)	250.00
	Commons	6.00
1	Griffey, K.	50.00
2	Maddux, G.	30.00
3	Thomas, F.	40.00
4	Vaughn, M.	12.00
5	Bagwell, J.	18.00
6	Jones, C.	30.00
7	Belle, A.	15.00
8	Ripken, C.	40.00

Rivals

	Complete Set (24)	250.00
1	Griffey/Thomas.	20.00
2	Thomas/Ripken	20.00
3	Ripken/Vaughn	15.00
4	Vaughn/Griffey	15.00
5	Griffey/Ripken	20.00
6	Thomas/Vaughn	15.00
7	Ripken/Griffey	20.00
8	Vaughn/Thomas	15.00
9	Griffey/Vaughn	15.00
10	Thomas/Griffey	20.00
11	Ripken/Thomas	15.00
12	Vaughn/Ripken	15.00
13	Piazza/Bagwell	15.00
14	Bagwell/Bonds	10.00
15	Bagwell/Piazza	15.00
16	Gwynn/Piazza	18.00
17	Piazza/Bonds	12.00
18	Bagwell/Gwynn	15.00
19	Bonds/Piazza	12.00
20	Gwynn/Bagwell	15.00
21	Piazza/Gwynn	15.00
22	Bonds/Bagwell	12.00
23	Gwynn/Bonds	15.00
24	Bonds/Gwynn	15.00

Slick Picks

	Complete Set (32)	150.00
	Commons	2.00
1	Piazza, M.	15.00
2	Ripken, C.	20.00
3	Griffey, K.	25.00
5	Thomas, F.	20.00
6	Vaughn, M.	5.00
7	Bonds, B.	5.00
8	Belle, A.	5.00
9	Bagwell, J.	10.00
11	Nomo, H.	10.00
13	Ramirez, M.	5.00
14	Maddux, G.	15.00
15	Gwynn, T.	15.00
16	Sandberg, R.	5.00
18	Jeter, D.	15.00
20	Rodriguez, A.	15.00
21	Klesko, R.	5.00
23	Lofton, K.	10.00
25	Johnson, R.	5.00
27	Gonzalez, J.	12.00
28	Puckett, K.	8.00
30	Jones, C.	12.00
32	Murray, E.	5.00

1996 SCORE

	NM Price
Complete Set (510)	$20.00
Series 1 Set (1-275)	10.00
Series 2 Set (276-510)	10.00
Commons	.05
Unlisted Stars	**.10-.35**
Series 1 or 2 Pack (10)	1.00
Series 1 or 2 Box (36)	28.00

Quality Rating ★★★
These cards are super nice for a base set. Ripken Tribute is an added bonus.

#	Player	NM
8	Mattingly, D.	1.00
16	Gwynn, T.	1.00
20	Rodriguez, A.	2.00
21	Thomas, F.	2.00
52	Puckett, K.	.75
60	Ripken, C.	2.00
61	Smith, O.	.50
72	Belle, A.	.75
194	Maddux, G.	1.00
195	Nomo, H.	.75
240	Jeter, D.	1.50
272	Thomas, F. (CL)	.75
273	Griffey, K. (CL)	.75
274	Ripken, C. (CL)	1.00
275	Maddux/Belle (CL)	.75
276	Maddux, G.	2.00
282	Griffey, K.	2.50
304	Bagwell, J.	.75
305	Ramirez, M.	.60
310	McGwire, M.	1.00
317	Piazza, M.	1.50
320	Nomo, H.	1.25
322	Jones, C.	1.50
325	Lofton, K.	.75
333	Clemens, R.	1.00
340	Bonds, B.	.75
356	Ripken, C.	1.25
373	Thomas, F.	1.00
384	Jeter, D.	.60
396	Pettitte, A.	.60
	Ripken Tribute	25.00

All-Stars
#	Player	NM
	Complete Set (20)	75.00
	Commons	2.00
1	Thomas, F.	12.00
2	Belle, A.	4.00
3	Griffey, K.	15.00
4	Ripken, C.	10.00
5	Vaughn, M.	3.00
7	Bonds, B.	4.00
9	Gwynn, T.	8.00
10	Maddux, G.	10.00
11	Johnson, R.	3.00
12	Nomo, H.	6.00
14	Bagwell, J.	5.00
18	Jones, C.	8.00
19	Ramirez, M.	4.00
20	Murray, E.	4.00

Big Bats
#	Player	NM
	Complete Set (20)	150.00
	Commons	3.00
1	Ripken, C.	25.00
2	Griffey, K.	30.00
3	Thomas, F.	25.00
4	Bagwell, J.	10.00
5	Piazza, M.	15.00
6	Bonds, B.	6.00
9	Gwynn, T.	10.00
10	Belle, A.	6.00
11	Ramirez, M.	6.00
13	Vaughn, M.	6.00
16	Lofton, K.	6.00
19	Murray, E.	6.00
20	Jones, C.	15.00

Diamond Aces
#	Player	NM
	Complete Set (30)	150.00
	Commons	2.00
1	Nomo, H.	10.00
4	Thomas, F.	20.00
5	Ripken, C.	20.00
6	Bonds, B.	6.00
7	Maddux, G.	20.00
8	Jones, C.	12.00
10	Piazza, M.	12.00
11	Jeter, D.	12.00
14	Griffey, K.	25.00
15	Rodriguez, A.	20.00
16	Ramirez, M.	6.00
17	Vaughn, M.	5.00
21	Belle, A.	6.00
22	Murray, E.	4.00
23	Gwynn, T.	12.00
24	Bagwell, J.	10.00

Dream Team
#	Player	NM
	Complete Set (9)	100.00
1	Ripken, C.	25.00
2	Thomas, F.	25.00
3	Baerga, C.	2.00
4	Williams, M.	5.00
5	Piazza, M.	18.00
6	Bonds, B.	7.00
7	Griffey, K.	30.00
8	Ramirez, M.	7.00
9	Maddux, G.	20.00

Dugout Collection
#	Player	NM
	Complete Set (220)	100.00
	Series 1 Set (110)	50.00
	Series 2 Set (110)	50.00
	Commons	.75
	Unlisted Stars	1.00-2.00
	Artist's Proof	4x-8x
8	Mattingly, D.	3.00
15	Gwynn, T.	3.00
20	Thomas, F.	7.00
52	Ripken, C.	6.00
59	Belle, A.	2.00
106	Jeter, D.	5.00
276	Maddux, G.	4.00
282	Griffey, K.	7.00
304	Bagwell, J.	2.50
317	Piazza, M.	3.50
320	Nomo, H.	3.00
322	Jones, C.	3.50
356	Ripken, C.	3.50
373	Thomas, F.	3.50

Future Franchise
#	Player	NM
	Complete Set (16)	125.00
	Commons	3.00
2	Jones, C.	30.00
3	Jeter, D.	30.00
4	Rodriguez, A.	30.00
6	Ramirez, M.	8.00
8	Rivera, R.	6.00
9	Garcia, K.	8.00
11	Cordova, M.	5.00
13	Nomo, H.	20.00
16	Mondesi, R.	8.00

Gold Stars
#	Player	NM
	Complete Set (30)	60.00
	Commons	1.00
1	Griffey, K.	12.00
2	Thomas, F.	10.00
5	Piazza, M.	7.00
6	Gwynn, T.	6.00
11	Belle, A.	4.00
12	Jones, C.	6.00
15	Bonds, B.	3.00
16	Bagwell, J.	5.00
17	Maddux, G.	8.00
18	Vaughn, M.	4.00
24	Nomo, H.	5.00
25	Ripken, C.	10.00
29	Johnson, R.	4.00
30	Ramirez, M.	4.00

Numbers Game
#	Player	NM
	Complete Set (30)	60.00
	Commons	1.00
1	Ripken, C.	10.00
2	Thomas, F.	10.00
3	Griffey, K.	12.00
4	Piazza, M.	6.00
5	Bonds, B.	3.00
6	Maddux, G.	8.00
7	Bagwell, J.	4.00
9	Gwynn, T.	5.00
10	Nomo, H.	5.00
13	Belle, A.	3.00
17	Vaughn, M.	3.00
19	Jones, C.	6.00
21	Gonzalez, J.	5.00
22	Lofton, K.	3.00
23	Mattingly, D.	5.00
26	Jeter, D.	5.00
30	Rodriguez, A.	10.00

Power Pace
#	Player	NM
	Complete Set (18)	100.00
	Commons	3.00
1	McGwire, M.	10.00
2	Belle, A.	6.00
4	Thomas, F.	20.00
7	Piazza, M.	12.00
9	Vaughn, M.	6.00
12	Griffey, K.	25.00
13	Bonds, B.	5.00
14	Ramirez, M.	6.00

Reflextions
#	Player	NM
	Complete Set (20)	130.00
	Commons	2.00
1	Ripken/Jones	25.00
2	Griffey/Rodriguez	35.00
3	Thomas/Vaughn	25.00
4	Lofton/Hunter	8.00
5	Mattingly/Snow	10.00
6	Ramirez/Mondesi	8.00
7	Gwynn/Anderson	8.00
8	Alomar/Baerga	5.00
10	Larkin/Jeter	8.00
11	Bonds/Sanders	6.00
12	Piazza/Belle	15.00
15	Clark/Bagwell	8.00
16	McGwire/Fielder	7.00
17	Maddux/Mussina	15.00
18	Johnson/Nomo	10.00

Titantic Taters
#	Player	NM
	Complete Set (18)	100.00
	Commons	3.00
1	Belle, A.	6.00
2	Thomas, F.	25.00
3	Vaughn, M.	6.00
4	Griffey, K.	30.00
6	McGwire, M.	10.00
9	Bagwell, J.	10.00
11	Piazza, M.	15.00
15	Ramirez, M.	8.00
17	Bonds, B.	6.00

1996 SELECT

	NM Price
Complete Set (200)	$15.00
Commons	.05
Unlisted Stars	**.10-.35**
Pack (10)	2.00
Box (24)	45.00

Quality Rating ★★★
Select continues to be a collector favorite. Look for ESPN's Dan Patrick on his own En Fuego card.

#	Player	NM
6	Griffey, K.	3.00
7	Maddux, G.	2.00
8	Ramirez, M.	.75
11	Thomas, F.	3.00
12	Bagwell, J.	1.00
14	Lofton, K.	.75
19	Ripken, C.	2.50
20	Clemens, R.	1.00
22	Piazza, M.	1.50
31	McGwire, M.	1.25
36	Belle, A.	.75
41	Jones, C.	1.50
45	Rodriguez, A.	2.00
48	Vaughn, M.	.75
56	Gonzalez, J.	1.25
59	Gwynn, T.	1.50
64	Puckett, K.	1.00
73	Nomo, H.	1.25
101	Bonds, B.	.75
140	Sandberg, R.	.75
151	Griffey, K.	1.50
152	Thomas, F.	1.50
153	Ripken, C.	1.25
155	Piazza, M.	.75
159	Maddux, G.	1.00
161	Jeter, D.	1.50
174	Hernandez, L. (R)	1.00
182	Guerrero, W. (R)	.75
196	Thomas, F.	1.50
197	Griffey, K.	1.50
198	Maddux, G.	1.00
199	Piazza, M.	.75
200	Ripken, C.	1.25

Artist Proofs
#	Player	NM
	Complete Set (200)	2000.00
	Commons	4.00
	Unlisted AP's	25x-50x
6	Griffey, K.	100.00
7	Maddux, G.	60.00
11	Thomas, F.	100.00
19	Ripken, C.	75.00
22	Piazza, M.	60.00
41	Jones, C.	50.00
45	Rodriguez, A.	80.00
151	Griffey, K.	50.00
152	Thomas, F.	50.00
153	Ripken, C.	40.00
159	Maddux, G.	30.00
196	Thomas, F.	50.00
197	Griffey, K.	50.00
199	Piazza, M.	30.00
200	Ripken, C.	40.00

Claim to Fame
#	Player	NM
	Complete Set (20)	275.00
	Commons	3.00
1	Ripken, C.	30.00
2	Maddux, G.	30.00
3	Griffey, K.	40.00
4	Thomas, F.	30.00
5	Vaughn, M.	10.00
6	Belle, A.	10.00
7	Bagwell, J.	15.00
10	Nomo, H.	20.00
11	Jones, C.	25.00
12	Piazza, M.	25.00
14	Gwynn, T.	25.00
17	Puckett, K.	10.00
18	Bonds, B.	10.00

En Fuego
#	Player	NM
	Complete Set (25)	250.00
	Commons	3.00
1	Griffey, K.	30.00
2	Thomas, F.	25.00
3	Ripken, C.	25.00
4	Maddux, G.	25.00
5	Bagwell, J.	15.00
6	Bonds, B.	10.00
7	Vaughn, M.	10.00
8	Belle, A.	10.00
11	Piazza, M.	20.00
12	Jones, C.	20.00
13	Gwynn, T.	15.00
14	Puckett, K.	10.00
16	Patrick, D.	7.00
21	Rodriguez, A.	20.00
24	Ramirez, M.	8.00
25	Nomo, H.	18.00

Team Nucleus
#	Player	NM
	Complete Set (28)	90.00
	Commons	2.00
1	Belle/Ramirez/Baerga	6.00
4	Bichette/Galaraga/Walker	5.00
8	Clemens/Vaughn/Canseco	5.00
9	Griffey/Martinez/Johnson	20.00
11	Piazza/Mondesi/Nomo	15.00
12	Maddux/Jones/Klesko	20.00
14	Rodriguez/Clark/Gonzalez	8.00
15	Sandberg/Sosa/Grace	6.00
18	Bonds/Williams/Beck	6.00
19	Puckett/Knoblauch/Cordova	6.00
20	Ripken/Bonilla/Mussina	12.00
22	Gwynn/Caminiti/Newfield	8.00
26	Bagwell/Biggio/Bell	8.00
27	Thomas/Ventura/Fernandez	15.00

1996 SELECT CERTIFIED

	NM Price
Complete Set (144)	$45.00
Commons	.20
Unlisted Stars	**.25-.75**
Pack (6)	9.00
Box (20)	160.00

Quality Rating ★★★★
Certified returns for a second season. For those of you that like parallel sets you will find Mirror Golds especially tough at 1 per 300 packs.

#	Player	NM
1	Thomas, F.	5.00
4	Lofton, K.	2.00
6	Rodriguez, A.	4.00
7	Jones, C.	3.00
8	Clemens, R.	2.00
13	Nomo, H.	3.00
17	Johnson, R.	2.00
20	McGwire, M.	2.00
21	Gwynn, T.	2.00

22	Belle, A.	1.50
28	Sandberg, R.	1.50
30	Piazza, M.	4.00
31	Bonds, B.	1.50
32	Maddux, G.	4.00
47	Griffey, K.	7.00
53	Ripken, C.	5.00
54	Bagwell, J.	2.00
56	Gonzalez, J.	2.50
62	Puckett, K.	1.50
67	Vaughn, M.	1.50
100	Jeter, D.	3.00
113	Guerrero, W. (R)	1.00
135	Thomas, F.	2.50
136	Griffey, K.	3.00
137	Maddux, G.	2.00
138	Piazza, M.	2.00
139	Ripken, C.	2.50
141	Vaughn, M.	1.00
142	Jones, C.	2.00
143	Nomo, H.	2.00

Artist Proofs
Complete Set (144) 2000.00
Artist Proofs 10x-20x

Certified Red
Complete Set (144) 300.00
Certified Red 4x-8x

Certified Blue
Complete Set (144) 4000.00
Certified Blue 30x-60x

Mirror Red
Commons 15.00
Mirror Red 75x-125x

Mirror Blue
Commons 35.00
Mirror Blue 150x-250x

Mirror Gold
Commons 100.00
Mirror Gold 250x-500x

Interleague Preview
Complete Set (25) 300.00
Commons 5.00

1	Griffey/Nomo.	50.00
2	Maddux/Vaughn	30.00
3	Thomas/Sosa	35.00
4	Piazza/Edmonds	30.00
5	Klesko/Clemens	12.00
6	Jeter/Ordonez	25.00
8	Ramirez/Sanders	12.00
9	Bonds/Buhner	12.00
11	Cone/Jones	25.00
12	Bagwell/Clark	20.00
13	Gwynn/Johnson	25.00
14	Ripken/Glavine	30.00
15	Puckett/Benes	15.00
16	Sheffield/Mussina	12.00
19	Fielder/Sandberg	10.00
20	Lofton/Hunter	12.00
23	Williams/McGwire	12.00
24	Belle/Larkin	15.00

Select Few
Complete Set (18) 250.00
Commons 6.00

2	Jeter, D.	25.00
3	Griffey, K.	40.00
4	Belle, A.	12.00
5	Ripken, C.	30.00
6	Maddux, G.	25.00
7	Thomas, F.	40.00
8	Vaughn, M.	12.00
9	Jones, C.	25.00
10	Piazza, M.	30.00
12	Nomo, H.	15.00
14	Ramirez, M.	10.00
16	Bonds, B.	12.00

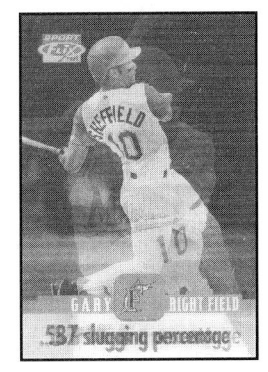

1996 SPORTFLIX

	NM Price
Complete Set (144)	$25.00
Commons	.05
Unlisted Stars	**.10-.35**
Pack (5)	1.50
Box (36)	40.00

Quality Rating ★★★
You will only find SportFlix on retail shelves. Some collectors love the concept, some don't.

#	Player	NM
5	Bonds, B.	.75
6	Puckett, K.	1.00
7	Belle, A.	.75
8	Maddux, G.	2.00
9	Gwynn, T.	1.25
10	Piazza, M.	1.50
13	Thomas, F.	3.00
16	McGwire, M.	1.25
18	Griffey, K.	3.00
19	Jones, C.	1.50
20	Rodriguez, A.	2.50
21	Bagwell, J.	1.00
31	Vaughn, M.	.75
39	Lofton, K.	.75
48	Nomo, H.	1.50
54	Ripken, C.	2.50
58	Clemens, R.	1.00
95	Gonzalez, J.	1.50
97	Jones, C.	.75
98	Griffey, K.	1.50
99	Thomas, F.	1.50
100	Ripken, C.	1.25
102	Piazza, M.	.75
139	Jeter, D.	1.50
142	Griffey, K. (CL)	1.50
143	Maddux, G. (CL)	1.25
144	Ripken, C. (CL)	1.25

Artist Proofs
Complete Set (144) 1000.00
Commons 3.00
Star Proofs 20x-40x
Rookie Proofs 15x-30x

Double Take
Complete Set (12) 125.00

1	Larkin/Ripken.	20.00
2	Alomar/Biggio	5.00
3	Jones/Williams	15.00
4	Griffey/Rivera	25.00
5	Maddux/Nomo	20.00
6	Thomas/Vaughn	25.00
7	Piazza/Rodriguez	12.00
8	Belle/Bonds	8.00
9	Rodriguez/Jeter	20.00
10	Puckett/Gwynn	15.00
11	Ramirez/Sosa	6.00
12	Bagwell/Brogna	8.00

Hit Parade
Complete Set (16) 125.00
Commons 3.00

1	Griffey, K.	25.00
2	Ripken, C.	20.00
3	Thomas, F.	25.00
4	Piazza, M.	12.00
5	Vaughn, M.	6.00
6	Belle, A.	6.00
7	Bagwell, J.	10.00
10	Puckett, K.	7.00
13	Gwynn, T.	10.00
15	Jones, C.	12.00
16	Bonds, B.	7.00

PowerSurge
Complete Set (25) 200.00
Commons 3.00

1	Jones, C.	15.00
2	Griffey, K.	30.00
3	Thomas, F.	30.00
4	Ripken, C.	25.00
5	Belle, A.	8.00
6	Piazza, M.	15.00
9	Vaughn, M.	7.00
16	Bonds, B.	8.00
17	Ramirez, M.	7.00
19	Bagwell, J.	10.00
21	McGwire, M.	10.00
23	Murray, E.	8.00
25	Puckett, K.	8.00

ProMotion
Complete Set (20) 100.00
Commons 1.50

1	Ripken, C.	12.00
2	Maddux, G.	10.00
3	Vaughn, M.	5.00
4	Belle, A.	5.00
5	Piazza, M.	8.00
6	Griffey, K.	15.00
7	Thomas, F.	15.00
8	Bagwell, J.	6.00
9	Nomo, H.	6.00
10	Jones, C.	8.00
11	Gwynn, T.	8.00
12	Mattingly, D.	6.00
15	Ramirez, M.	4.00
16	Bonds, B.	4.00

1996 SUMMIT

	NM Price
Complete Set (200)	$30.00
Commons	.05
Unlisted Stars	**.10-.35**
Artist Proofs	15x-40x
Pack (7)	2.50
Box (18)	40.00

Quality Rating ★★★
Another great set from Pinnacle. Summit has it all, player selection, design, and affordability.

#	Player	NM
1	Piazza, M.	2.00
7	Bagwell, J.	1.00
19	Ripken, C.	2.50
20	McGwire, M.	1.25
31	Vaughn, M.	.75
39	Lofton, K.	.75
40	Nomo, H.	1.25
60	Gonzalez, J.	1.25
70	Sandberg, R.	.75
77	Puckett, K.	1.00
82	Belle, A.	1.00
84	Rodriguez, A.	2.50
86	Griffey, K.	3.00
88	Thomas, F.	3.00
91	Maddux, G.	2.00
101	Clemens, R.	1.25
107	Bonds, B.	.75
126	Jones, C.	1.50
134	Gwynn, T.	1.25
154	Ripken/Jeter	1.50
156	Piazza/Kendall	1.00
157	Klesko/Thomas	1.50
158	Damon/Griffey	1.50
161	Jones/Williams	.75
171	Jeter, D.	2.00
172	Hernandez, L. (R)	1.50
180	Guerrero, W. (R)	1.00
197	Griffey, K.	1.50
198	Thomas, F.	1.50
199	Maddux, G.	1.00
200	Ripken, C.	1.25

Ballparks
Complete Set (18) 125.00
Commons 3.00

1	Ripken, C.	15.00
2	Belle, A.	6.00
4	Vaughn, M.	6.00
5	Griffey, K.	25.00
6	Jeter, D.	12.00
7	Gonzalez, J.	10.00
8	Maddux, G.	12.00
9	Thomas, F.	15.00
10	Sandberg, R.	6.00
11	Piazza, M.	15.00
13	Bonds, B.	6.00
14	Bagwell, J.	8.00
17	Puckett, K.	6.00
18	Gwynn, T.	8.00

Big Bang
Complete Set (16) 700.00
Mirage 2x

1	Thomas, F.	80.00
2	Griffey, K.	100.00
3	Belle, A.	30.00
4	Vaughn, M.	25.00
5	Bonds, B.	25.00
6	Ripken, C.	80.00
7	Bagwell, J.	40.00
8	Piazza, M.	70.00
9	Klesko, R.	15.00
10	Ramirez, M.	25.00
11	Salmon, T.	10.00
12	Bichette, D.	8.00
13	Sosa, S.	15.00
14	Mondesi, R.	12.00
15	Jones, C.	70.00
16	Anderson, G.	6.00

Hitters, Inc.
Complete Set (16) 200.00
Commons 5.00

1	Gwynn, T.	18.00
2	Vaughn, M.	10.00
4	Griffey, K.	40.00
6	Thomas, F.	30.00
8	Belle, A.	10.00
9	Ripken, C.	30.00
10	Ramirez, M.	10.00
13	Piazza, M.	25.00
14	Jones, C.	25.00
15	Sandberg, R.	10.00

Positions
Complete Set (9) 300.00

1	Bagwell/Vaughn/Thomas	50.00
2	Alomar/Biggio/Knoblach	18.00
3	Williams/Thome/Jones	30.00
4	Larkin/Ripken/Rodriguez	75.00
5	Piazza/Rodriguez/Johnson	35.00
6	Nomo/Maddux/Johnson	35.00
7	Bonds/Belle/Klesko	15.00
8	Damon/Edmonds/Griffey	45.00
9	Ramirez/Sheffield/Sosa	20.00

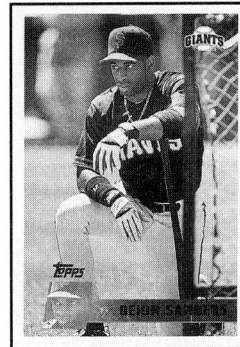

1996 TOPPS

	NM Price
Complete Set (440)	$35.00
Series 1 Set (1-220)	20.00
Series 2 Set (221-440)	15.00
Factory Set (449)	45.00
Commons	.05
Unlisted Stars	**.10-.35**
Series 1 Pack (12)	2.50
Series 1 Box (36)	70.00
Series 2 Pack (12)	2.00
Series 2 Box (36)	60.00

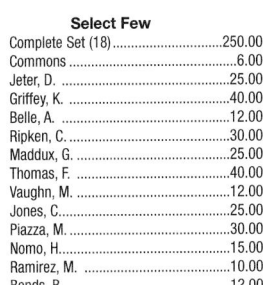

Quality Rating ★★★

Mantle inserts, especially the refractors have the hobby excited over regular Topps again.

#	Player	NM
1	Gwynn, T. (SP)	.50
2	Piazza, M. (SP)	.75
3	Maddux, G. (SP)	.75
7	Mantle, M. (Tribute)	3.50
13	Helton, T.	2.00
25	Casey, S. (R)	1.00
45	Belle, A.	.75
50	Puckett, K.	1.00
96	Ripken, C. (Tribute)	2.50
100	Thomas, F.	2.50
136	Nomo, H.	1.50
145	McGwire, M.	1.25
177	Jones, C.	1.50
185	Mattingly, D.	1.00
200	Ripken, C.	2.00
205	Griffey, K.	2.50
211	Garciaparra, N.	1.50
219	Jeter, D.	1.50
222	Ripken, C.	1.00
229	Thomas, F. (SP)	1.50
230	Griffey, K. (SP)	1.50
246	Piazza, M.	1.50
250	Gwynn, T.	1.25
274	Vaughn, M.	.60
300	Bonds, B.	.75
318	Maddux, G.	1.50
325	Gonzalez, J.	.75
356	Sandberg, R.	.60
380	Bagwell, J.	.75
420	Lofton, K.	.50
424	Wright, R. (R)	1.00
432	Konerko, P.	1.00
434	Rolen, S.	1.00
435	Jones, A. (AS)	2.50
436	Gibson/Grieve	1.00
	Mantle Last Day	10.00

Classic Confrontations

#		NM
	Complete Set (15)	5.00
	Commons	.20
1	Griffey, K.	1.25
2	Ripken, C.	1.00
4	Puckett, K.	.40
5	Thomas, F.	1.25
6	Bonds, B.	.30
9	Gwynn, T.	.75
10	Piazza, M.	.50
15	Maddux, G.	1.00

Mantle Case

Complete Set (19) 1000.00
Singles 50.00

Mantle Insert

Complete Set (19) 125.00
Singles 8.00

Mantle Finest Insert

Complete Set (19) 175.00
Singles 10.00
Refractors 4x

Masters of the Game

#		
	Complete Set (20)	50.00
	Commons	1.00
3	Murray, E.	2.50
5	Smith, O.	2.00
9	Ripken, C.	8.00
12	Gwynn, T.	5.00
13	Mattingly, D.	4.00
15	Puckett, K.	3.00
18	Bonds, B.	3.00
19	Maddux, G.	8.00
20	Thomas, F.	10.00

Mystery Finest

#		
	Complete Set (21)	150.00
	Commons	3.00
	Refractors	4x
1	Nomo, H.	12.00
2	Maddux, G.	15.00
4	Jones, C.	12.00
7	Ripken, C.	20.00
8	Puckett, K.	6.00
9	Gwynn, T.	8.00
10	Ramirez, M.	5.00
12	Piazza, M.	12.00
13	Bonds, B.	6.00
16	Griffey, K.	25.00
17	Belle, A.	6.00
19	Vaughn, M.	6.00
20	Bagwell, J.	8.00
21	Thomas, F.	20.00

Five Star Mystery Finest

#		
	Complete Set (5)	60.00
	Refractors	4x
22	Nomo, H.	10.00
23	Ripken, C.	20.00
24	Piazza, M.	12.00
25	Griffey, K.	25.00
26	Thomas, F.	20.00

Power Boosters

#		
	Complete Set (25)	80.00
	Commons	2.50
1	Gwynn, T.	7.00
2	Piazza, M.	8.00
3	Maddux, G.	15.00
4	Bagwell, J.	6.00
10	Bonds, B.	5.00
13	Helton, T.	15.00
16	Davis, B.	6.00
22	Bellhorn, M.	4.00
24	Jenkins, G.	5.00
25	Casey, S.	10.00

AL Profiles

#		
	Complete Set (20)	35.00
	Series 1 Set (10)	20.00
	Series 2 Set (10)	15.00
	Commons	.75
3	Belle, A.	1.50
5	Griffey, K.	6.00
6	Johnson, R.	2.00
8	Ripken, C.	5.00
9	Thomas, F.	6.00
10	Vaughn, M.	2.50
14	Gonzalez, J.	2.00
15	Lofton, K.	2.50
17	Mattingly, D.	3.00

NL Profiles

#		
	Complete Set (20)	30.00
	Series 1 Set (10)	15.00
	Series 2 Set (10)	15.00
	Commons	.75
1	Bagwell, J.	2.00
3	Bonds, B.	1.50
5	Maddux, G.	4.00
7	Piazza, M.	2.00
15	Jones, C.	4.00
17	Larkin, B.	1.00
18	Nomo, H.	3.00

Road Warriors

#		
	Complete Set (20)	10.00
	Commons	.25
2	Belle, A.	1.00
4	Bonds, B.	1.00
11	McGwire, M.	1.50
12	Piazza, M.	2.00
13	Ramirez, M.	1.00
16	Thomas, F.	4.00
18	Vaughn, M.	1.00

Wrecking Crew

#		
	Complete Set (15)	70.00
	Commons	2.00
1	Bagwell, J.	8.00
2	Belle, A.	6.00
3	Bonds, B.	6.00
8	Gonzalez, J.	10.00
9	Griffey, K.	25.00
11	McGwire, M.	10.00
12	Piazza, M.	12.00
13	Thomas, F.	20.00
14	Vaughn, M.	6.00

1996 TOPPS CHROME

	NM Price
Complete Set (165)	$80.00
Commons	.20
Unlisted Stars	**.25-.75**
Refractors	12x-25x
Pack (4)	5.00
Box (24)	90.00

Quality Rating ★★★

Checklist is filled with young and veteran talent. Masters of the Game features some of baseball's all-time best.

#	Player	NM
1	Gwynn, T. (SP)	1.50
2	Piazza, M. (SP)	2.00
3	Maddux, G. (SP)	2.00
7	Mantle, M. (Commemorative)	8.00
13	Helton, T.	10.00
17	Belle, A.	2.00
19	Puckett, K.	1.50
28	Ripken, C. (Tribute)	5.00
29	Thomas, F.	6.00
34	Murray, E.	1.50
37	Nomo, H.	3.50
39	Rodriguez, I.	1.50
41	McGwire, M.	2.50
52	Jones, C.	4.00
56	Mattingly, D.	3.00
65	Clemens, R.	3.00
67	Ripken, C.	4.00
70	Griffey, K.	6.00
73	Garciaparra, N.	5.00
80	Jeter, D. (FS)	4.00
82	Ripken, C. (SP)	2.50
83	Belle, A. (SP)	1.00
89	Thomas, F. (SP)	3.00
90	Griffey, K. (SP)	3.00
92	Morris, M. (R)	3.00
93	Piazza, M.	4.00
97	Gwynn, T.	3.00
110	Vaughn, M.	1.50
119	Bonds, B.	1.25
120	Smith, O.	1.00
125	Maddux, G.	4.00
129	Gonzalez, J.	3.00
144	Sandberg, R.	1.25
153	Bagwell, J.	2.00
164	Lofton, K.	1.50

Masters of the Game

#		
	Complete Set (20)	70.00
	Commons	2.00
	Refractors	3x-4x
3	Murray, E.	4.00
4	Molitor, P.	3.00
5	Smith, O.	4.00
9	Ripken, C.	18.00
12	Gwynn, T.	10.00
13	Mattingly, D.	10.00
15	Puckett, K.	7.00
17	Clemens, R.	8.00
18	Bonds, B.	7.00
19	Maddux, G.	12.00
20	Thomas, F.	20.00

Wrecking Crew

#		
	Complete Set (15)	80.00
	Commons	2.00
	Refractors	3x-4x
1	Bagwell, J.	10.00
2	Belle, A.	8.00
3	Bonds, B.	8.00
8	Gonzalez, J.	10.00
9	Griffey, K.	30.00
11	McGwire, M.	10.00
12	Piazza, M.	20.00
13	Thomas, F.	25.00
14	Vaughn, M.	8.00

1996 TOPPS FINEST

	NM Price
Series 1 Common Set (110)	30.00
Series 1 Uncommon Set (55)	130.00
Series 1 Rare Set (26)	600.00
Series 2 Common Set (110)	30.00
Series 2 Uncommon Set (36)	100.00
Series 2 Rare Set (22)	250.00
Commons	.25
Common Uncommons	2.00
Common Rare	10.00
Common Unlisted	.30-.75
Uncommon Unlisted	**3.00-5.00**
Series 1 Pack (6)	5.00
Series 1 Box (24)	90.00
Series 2 Pack (6)	3.50
Series 2 Box (24)	60.00

Quality Rating ★★★★

Finest is one of the most talked about sets this year. Player selection is a mix of new and current stars.

#	Player	NM
1	Maddux, G. (U.)	20.00
6	Gwynn, T. (R)	40.00
9	Belle, A. (R)	15.00
11	Piazza, M. (U)	20.00
16	Jones, C. (C)	4.00
18	Puckett, K. (R)	30.00
24	Griffey, K. (C)	6.00
25	Ripken, C. (R)	60.00
33	Nomo, H. (R)	35.00
39	Sandberg, R. (R)	20.00
42	Bagwell, J. (R)	30.00
48	Thomas, F. (C)	4.00
59	Nomo, H. (U)	12.00
61	Gwynn, T. (C)	3.00
64	Vaughn, M. (R)	20.00
74	McGwire, M. (R)	30.00
79	Puckett, K. (U)	8.00
81	Lofton, K. (U)	20.00
92	Jeter, D. (C)	5.00
105	Bonds, B. (R)	20.00
113	Piazza, M. (C)	5.00
115	Gonzalez, J. (U)	10.00
135	Griffey, K. (R)	80.00
141	Jones, C. (R)	35.00
145	Maddux, G. (R)	35.00
146	Bonds, B. (C)	2.00
151	Vaughn, M. (U)	6.00
161	Bagwell, J. (U)	8.00
165	Ripken, C. (U)	20.00
186	Thomas, F. (R)	65.00
188	Belle, A. (U)	3.00
191	Checklist	10.00
192	Jones, C. (R)	35.00
214	Belle, A. (C)	3.00
232	Nomo, H. (R)	30.00
233	Lofton, K. (C)	2.00
234	Sandberg, R. (U)	5.00
235	Maddux, G. (U)	12.00
236	McGwire, M. (C)	3.00
240	Bonds, B. (C)	2.00
253	Gonzalez, J. (C)	4.00
271	Puckett, K. (C)	2.50
275	Piazza, M. (C)	3.00
279	Molitor, P. (R)	15.00
281	Ripken, C. (C)	4.00
294	Hernandez, L. (R)	25.00
299	Bagwell, J. (C)	2.00
305	Griffey, K. (U)	25.00
320	Gwynn, T. (C)	3.00
322	Thomas, F. (C)	4.00
327	Lofton, K. (U)	8.00
347	Sosa, S. (R)	15.00
350	Jeter, D. (U)	12.00
354	Gonzalez, J. (R)	40.00
359	Checklist	10.00

Refractors

	Series 1 Common Set (110)	500.00
	Series 1 Uncommon Set (55)	900.00
	Series 1 Rare Set (26)	3000.00
	Series 2 Common Set (110)	600.00
	Series 2 Uncommon Set (36)	650.00
	Series 2 Rare Set (22)	1200.00
	Commons	3.00
	Common Uncommon	8.00
	Common Rare	30.00
1	Maddux, G. (U)	90.00
6	Gwynn, T. (R)	175.00
9	Belle, A. (R)	70.00
11	Piazza, M. (U)	90.00
16	Jones, C. (C)	40.00
18	Puckett, K. (R)	150.00
22	Salmon, T. (U)	20.00
24	Griffey, K. (C)	70.00
25	Ripken, C. (R)	225.00
33	Nomo, H. (R)	160.00
39	Sandberg, R. (R)	100.00
42	Bagwell, J. (R)	150.00
48	Thomas, F. (C)	50.00
59	Nomo, H. (U)	60.00
61	Gwynn, T. (C)	30.00
64	Vaughn, M. (R)	100.00
74	McGwire, M. (R)	125.00
77	Johnson, R. (U)	25.00
79	Puckett, K. (U)	40.00
81	Lofton, K. (R)	90.00
92	Jeter, D. (C)	30.00
95	Ramirez, M. (U)	25.00
105	Bonds, B. (R)	100.00
113	Piazza, M. (C)	30.00
115	Gonzalez, J. (U)	70.00
135	Griffey, K. (R)	400.00
141	Jones, C. (R)	200.00
145	Maddux, G. (R)	200.00
146	Bonds, B. (C)	15.00
151	Vaughn, M. (U)	20.00
161	Bagwell, J. (U)	50.00
162	McGwire, M. (C)	20.00
165	Ripken, C. (U)	100.00
186	Thomas, F. (R)	350.00
188	Belle, A. (U)	25.00
192	Jones, C. (R)	200.00
214	Belle, A. (C)	25.00
232	Nomo, H. (R)	160.00
233	Lofton, K. (C)	15.00
234	Sandberg, R. (U)	20.00
235	Maddux, G. (U)	70.00
236	McGwire, M. (C)	25.00
240	Bonds, B. (C)	15.00
253	Gonzalez, J. (C)	30.00
258	Rodriguez, I. (C)	15.00
270	Johnson, R. (R)	50.00
271	Puckett, K. (C)	20.00
275	Piazza, M. (C)	30.00
279	Molitor, P. (R)	70.00
281	Ripken, C. (C)	40.00
288	Vaughn, M. (C)	15.00
298	Ramirez, M. (C)	15.00
299	Bagwell, J. (C)	20.00
305	Griffey, K. (U)	130.00
320	Gwynn, T. (C)	20.00
322	Thomas, F. (C)	70.00
327	Lofton, K. (U)	30.00
347	Sosa, S. (R)	50.00
350	Jeter, D. (U)	70.00
354	Gonzalez, J. (R)	200.00

1996 TOPPS GALLERY

	NM Price
Complete Set (180)	$35.00
Commons	.10
Unlsted Stars	**.20-.50**
Pack (8)	3.00
Box (24)	60.00

Quality Rating ★★★
Add another new set to the growing list from Topps. Gallery is an attractive issue with all the big names.

#	Player	NM
38	Sandberg, R.	1.00
92	Nomo, H.	2.50
100	Jones, C.	2.50
143	Jeter, D.	2.50
145	Maddux, G.	3.00
146	Griffey, K.	5.00
147	Gwynn, T.	2.00
150	Vaughn, M.	1.00
152	Puckett, K.	1.50
155	McGwire, M.	1.50
156	Bonds, B.	1.00
157	Belle, A.	1.00
161	Lofton, K.	1.50
163	Gonzalez, J.	2.00
164	Bagwell, J.	1.50
166	Piazza, M.	2.50
168	Ripken, C.	3.50
174	Clemens, R.	1.50
175	Thomas, F.	4.00
	Mantle Masterpiece	25.00

Private Issue

	Complete Set (180)	800.00
	Commons	1.50
	Star Private Issue	8x-15x
	Rookie Private Issue	5x-10x

Expressionists

#		NM
	Complete Set (20)	100.00
	Commons	2.00
1	Piazza, M.	18.00
3	Griffey, K.	25.00
4	Puckett, K.	10.00
6	Jones, C.	18.00
7	Nomo, H.	12.00
8	McGwire, M.	10.00
10	Johnson, R.	6.00
15	Gwynn, T.	10.00
19	Belle, A.	8.00

Photo Gallery

#		NM
	Complete Set (15)	100.00
	Commons	2.00
1	Murray, E.	5.00
2	Johnson, R.	5.00
3	Ripken, C.	25.00
5	Thomas, F.	25.00
8	Clemens, R.	8.00
9	Belle, A.	8.00
10	Griffey, K.	30.00
11	Puckett, K.	8.00

1996 TOPPS LASER

	NM Price
Complete Set (128)	$100.00
Series 1 Set (64)	50.00
Series 2 Set (64)	50.00
Commons	.30
Unlsted Stars	**.40-.75**
Series 1 or 2 Pack (4)	4.00
Series 1 or 2 Box (24)	80.00

Quality Rating ★★★
Laser breaks onto the scene with a very unique design. Player selection does include young stars in Jeter and Paul Wilson.

#	Player	NM
8	Gonzalez, J.	4.00
34	Bagwell, J.	3.00
37	Bonds, B.	2.00
42	Griffey, K.	8.00
43	Gwynn, T.	4.00
45	Jones, C.	4.00
46	McGwire, M.	3.00
48	Sandberg, R.	2.00
52	Clemens, R.	3.00
56	Johnson, R.	2.00
60	Nomo, H.	4.00
82	Jeter, D.	5.00
89	Piazza, M.	6.00
90	Ripken, C.	7.00
92	Thomas, F.	7.00
94	Vaughn, M.	2.50
99	Belle, A.	2.50
108	Lofton, K.	2.00
109	Puckett, K.	2.00
121	Maddux, G.	6.00

Bright Spots

	Complete Set (16)	120.00
	Series 1 Set (8)	50.00
	Series 2 Set (8)	70.00
	Commons	4.00
2	Jeter, D.	20.00
13	Jeter, D.	20.00
14	Jones, C.	20.00
15	Nomo, H.	18.00

Power Cuts

	Complete Set (16)	200.00
	Series 1 Set (8)	100.00
	Series 2 Set (8)	100.00
	Commons	6.00
1	Belle, A.	10.00
4	Piazza, M.	25.00
6	Thomas, F.	30.00
7	Vaughn, M.	10.00
9	Bagwell, J.	20.00
10	Bonds, B.	10.00
13	Gonzalez, J.	20.00
14	Griffey, K.	50.00

Stadium Stars

	Complete Set (16)	250.00
	Series 1 Set (8)	125.00
	Series 2 Set (8)	125.00
	Commons	6.00
2	Bonds, B.	15.00
4	Griffey, K.	60.00
7	Puckett, K.	20.00
8	Ripken, C.	40.00
10	Clemens, R.	18.00
11	Gwynn, T.	25.00
12	Johnson, R.	10.00
13	Lofton, K.	12.00
15	Sandberg, R.	12.00
16	Thomas, F.	50.00

1996 TOPPS STADIUM CLUB

	NM Price
Complete Set (450)	$60.00
Series 1 Set (1-225)	30.00
Series 2 Set (226-450)	30.00
Commons	.05
Unlisted Stars	**.10-.35**
Series 1 or 2 Pack (10)	2.00
Series 1 or 2 Box (24)	40.00

Quality Rating ★★★
Stadium Club has an impressive checklist as well as Mantle cards sure to attract collectors.

#	Player	NM
1	Nomo, H.	1.25
9	Gonzalez, J.	1.25
10	Jones, C.	1.50
23	Puckett, K.	1.00
73	Mattingly, D.	1.00
104	McGwire, M.	1.25
105	Griffey, K.	3.00
123	Jeter, D.	2.00
132	Maddux, G.	2.00
182	Thomas, F.	2.50
183	Bagwell, J.	.75
198	Ripken, C.	2.50
201	Belle, A.	.75
208	Lofton, K.	.75
216	Piazza, M.	1.00
226	Jones, C.	1.00
245	Maddux, G.	2.00
247	Nomo, H.	1.00
260	Jeter, D.	2.00
285	Thomas, F.	3.00
301	Gwynn, T.	1.25
303	Vaughn, M.	.75
325	Lofton, K.	.75
402	Bonds, B.	.75
424	Ripken, C.	2.50
429	Bagwell, J.	1.00
442	Piazza, M.	1.00

Bash & Burn

	Complete Set (10)	30.00
	Commons	2.00
2	Bonds, B.	10.00
5	Mondesi, R.	5.00

Extreme Players

	Complete Set (180)	250.00
	Series 1 Set (90)	125.00
	Series 2 Set (90)	125.00
	Commons	1.00
	Unlisted Stars	2.00-5.00
	Silver	2x
	Gold	5x
1	Nomo, H.	8.00
9	Gonzalez, J.	8.00
10	Jones, C.	12.00
23	Puckett, K.	6.00
73	Mattingly, D.	10.00
105	Griffey, K. (W)	35.00
123	Jeter, D.	8.00
132	Maddux, G. (W)	20.00
285	Thomas, F.	20.00
301	Gwynn, T.	8.00
303	Vaughn, M.	6.00
325	Lofton, K.	6.00
402	Bonds, B. (W)	8.00
424	Ripken, C.	15.00
429	Bagwell, J.	8.00
442	Piazza, M. (W)	20.00

Extreme Winners

	Complete Set (10)	25.00
	Commons	.50
	Unlisted Stars	.75-1.50
	Silver	3x

	Gold	15x
1	Maddux, G.	5.00
2	Piazza, M.	5.00
7	Bonds, B.	2.00
8	Griffey, K.	10.00

Megaheroes
	Complete Set (10)	60.00
	Commons	2.00
1	Thomas, F.	25.00
2	Griffey, K.	30.00
3	Nomo, H.	12.00
4	Smith, O.	5.00
8	Clemens, R.	6.00
10	Vaughn, M.	6.00

Metalists
	Complete Set (8)	60.00
	Commons	2.00
1	Bagwell, J.	8.00
2	Bonds, B.	6.00
4	Clemens, R.	5.00
6	Maddux, G.	12.00
7	Ripken, C.	20.00
8	Thomas, F.	20.00

Midsummer Matchups
	Complete Set (10)	100.00
	Commons	4.00
1	Nomo/Johnson	10.00
2	Piazza/Rodriguez	20.00
3	McGriff/Thomas	30.00
6	Larkin/Ripken	25.00
7	Bonds/Belle	8.00
8	Dykstra/Lofton	8.00
9	Gwynn/Puckett	18.00

Power Packed
	Complete Set (15)	90.00
	Commons	3.00
1	Belle, A.	8.00
2	McGwire, M.	10.00
4	Piazza, M.	15.00
6	Griffey, K.	30.00
7	Vaughn, M.	8.00
10	Thomas, F.	25.00
11	Gonzalez, J.	12.00

Power Streak
	Complete Set (15)	75.00
	Commons	3.00
1	Johnson, R.	4.00
2	Nomo, H.	12.00
3	Belle, A.	6.00
6	Thomas, F.	25.00
7	McGwire, M.	10.00
9	Vaughn, M.	8.00
14	Bonds, B.	7.00

Prime Cuts
	Complete Set (8)	70.00
	Commons	3.00
1	Belle, A.	6.00
2	Bonds, B.	5.00
3	Griffey, K.	25.00
4	Gwynn, T.	8.00
7	Piazza, M.	12.00
8	Thomas, F.	20.00

TSC Awards
	Complete Set (10)	50.00
	Commons	2.00
1	Ripken, C.	15.00
2	Belle, A.	6.00
5	Griffey, K.	20.00
6	Nomo, H.	10.00
7	Maddux, G.	10.00
8	Jones, C.	10.00
9	Johnson, R.	3.00

Mantle Retrospective
	Complete Set (19)	200.00
	Series 1 Set (1-9)	100.00
	Series 2 Set (10-19)	100.00
	Mantle Singles	10.00

1996 UPPER DECK
	NM Price
Complete Set (480)	$65.00
Series 1 Set (1-240)	35.00
Series 2 Set (241-480)	30.00
Factory Set (510)	75.00
Commons	.05
Unlisted Stars	**.10-.35**
Series 1 Pack (10)	2.00
Series 1 Box (28)	45.00
Series 2 Pack (12)	2.00
Series 2 Box (32)	50.00

GARRET ANDERSON
Angels™ of

Quality Rating ★★★
Upper Deck once again mixes great player selection with an an attractive design. Ripken collection continues.

#	Player	NM
1	Ripken, C.	2.50
5	Jones, C.	1.50
10	Maddux, G.	2.00
18	Vaughn, M.	.75
20	Clemens, R.	1.25
55	Ramirez, M.	.75
80	Bagwell, J.	1.00
95	Nomo, H.	1.50
115	Ripken, C.	1.25
116	Gwynn, T.	.60
130	Puckett, K.	1.00
145	Piazza, M.	.75
149	Jones, C.	.75
150	Nomo, H.	.75
151	McGwire, M.	1.25
154	Mattingly, D.	1.00
156	Jeter, D.	1.50
195	Bonds, B.	.75
200	Griffey, K.	3.00
202	Rodriguez, A.	1.25
206	Gonzalez, J.	1.25
244	Hernandez, L. (R)	2.00
254	Guerrero, W. (R)	1.00
280	Ripken, C.	2.50
300	Thomas, F.	3.00
319	Lofton, K.	.75
360	Piazza, M.	1.50
376	Griffey, K.	1.50
377	Gwynn, T.	.60
379	Maddux, G.	1.25
383	Piazza, M.	.75
387	Thomas, F.	1.50
422	Maddux, G.	1.50
425	McGwire, M.	.75
450	Gwynn, T.	1.25
486U	Sandberg, R.	1.25
500U	Molitor, P.	1.00

Blue Chip Prospects
	Complete Set (20)	200.00
	Commons	5.00
1	Nomo, H.	30.00
8	Garcia, K.	12.00
10	Jones, C.	40.00
15	Rodriguez, A.	40.00
17	Jeter, D.	40.00
20	Ramirez, M.	15.00

Cal Ripken Collection
	Complete Set (9)	55.00
	Series 1 Set (4)	25.00
	Series 2 Set (5)	30.00
	Ripken Singles	7.00

Diamond Destiny
	Complete Set (40)	130.00
	Commons	2.00
	Silver	3x-5x
	Gold	10x-20x
1	Jones, C.	10.00
5	Maddux, G.	10.00
6	Ripken, C.	15.00
7	Alomar, R.	5.00
10	Vaughn, M.	4.00
11	Clemens, R.	5.00
12	Erstad, D.	8.00
14	Thomas, F.	15.00
16	Belle, A.	5.00
17	Ramirez, M.	4.00
18	Lofton, K.	5.00
21	Bagwell, J.	5.00
22	Nomo, H.	7.00
23	Piazza, M.	10.00
24	Puckett, K.	4.00

28	Jeter, D.	10.00
30	McGwire, M.	6.00
32	Gwynn, T.	7.00
33	Bonds, B.	4.00
35	Griffey, K.	20.00
38	Rodriguez, A.	15.00
39	Gonzalez, J.	8.00

Future Stock
	Complete Set (20)	12.00
	Commons	1.00
6	Clark, T.	5.00

Gameface
	Complete Set (10)	10.00
	Commons	.25
1	Griffey, K.	2.00
2	Thomas, F.	2.00
3	Bonds, B.	.50
4	Belle, A.	.75
5	Ripken, C.	1.50
6	Piazza, M.	1.25
7	Jones, C.	1.00
10	Maddux, G.	1.25

Hot Commodities
	Complete Set (20)	150.00
	Commons	4.00
1	Griffey, K.	35.00
2	Nomo, H.	12.00
5	Belle, A.	8.00
6	Ramirez, M.	8.00
7	Puckett, K.	10.00
10	Maddux, G.	20.00
11	Jones, C.	20.00
12	Bonds, B.	8.00
13	Vaughn, M.	8.00
14	Piazza, M.	20.00
15	Ripken, C.	25.00
18	Lofton, K.	10.00
19	Gwynn, T.	12.00
20	Thomas, F.	25.00

Nomo Highlights
	Complete Set (5)	18.00
	Nomo Singles	4.00

Power Driven
	Complete Set (20)	120.00
	Commons	4.00
1	Belle, A.	8.00
2	Bonds, B.	8.00
6	Gonzalez, J.	12.00
7	Griffey, K.	30.00
10	McGwire, M.	10.00
12	Piazza, M.	15.00
13	Ramirez, M.	10.00
17	Thomas, F.	25.00
18	Vaughn, M.	8.00

Run Producers
	Complete Set (20)	200.00
	Commons	5.00
1	Belle, A.	10.00
3	Bonds, B.	10.00
6	Gonzalez, J.	18.00
7	Griffey, K.	40.00
8	Gwynn, T.	18.00
9	Lofton, K.	10.00
12	McGwire, M.	15.00
14	Piazza, M.	30.00
15	Ramirez, M.	10.00
18	Thomas, F.	30.00
19	Vaughn, M.	12.00

Hobby Predictor
	Complete Set (60)	110.00
	Series 1 Set (30)	60.00
	Series 2 Set (30)	50.00
	Commons	2.00
1	Belle, A.	4.00
2	Lofton, K.	4.00
4	Griffey, K.	12.00
6	Ripken, C.	8.00
7	McGwire, M.	4.00
8	Thomas, F.	12.00
9	Vaughn, M.	3.00
11	Clemens, R.	4.00
25	Jeter, D.	8.00
31	Bagwell, J.	4.00
32	Bichette, D.	2.50
33	Bonds, B.	3.00
34	Gwynn, T.	6.00
35	Jones, C.	7.00
38	Piazza, M.	7.00
44	Maddux, G.	7.00

Retail Predictor
	Complete Set (60)	160.00
	Series 1 Set (30)	100.00
	Series 2 Set (30)	60.00
	Commons	2.00
	Unlisted Stars	3.00-4.00
4	Griffey, K.	12.00
8	Thomas, F.	12.00
15	Griffey, K.	12.00
18	Thomas, F.	12.00
24	Griffey, K.	12.00
29	Thomas, F.	12.00
34	Jones, C.	6.00
36	Piazza, M.	6.00
46	Piazza, M.	6.00
59	Piazza, M.	6.00

V. J. Lovero Collection
	Complete Set (20)	30.00
	Commons	.50
2	Nomo, H.	2.50
3	Jeter, D.	3.00
4	Bonds, B.	1.50
5	Maddux, G.	6.00
6	McGwire, M.	3.00
10	Griffey, K.	7.00
12	Johnson, R.	1.50
13	Clemens, R.	3.00
15	Thomas, F.	7.00
17	Piazza, M.	4.00
19	Gwynn, T.	4.00

KEN GRIFFEY JR. outfield

1996 U.D. COLLECTOR'S CHOICE
	NM Price
Complete Set (790)	$30.00
Series 1 Set (1-395)	15.00
Series 2 Set (396-790)	15.00
Commons	.05
Unlisted Stars	**.10-.35**
Series 1 Pack (12)	1.00
Series 1 Box (36)	28.00
Series 2 Pack (14)	1.00
Series 2 Box (40)	30.00

Quality Rating ★★★
The 1996 baseball card season gets underway with Collectors Choice and other base sets. A Ripken insert set is included.

#	Player	NM
1	Ripken, C. (AS)	2.00
7	Johnson/Nomo (SL)	.75
8	Johnson/Maddux (SL)	1.25
40	Maddux, G. (AS)	1.00
42	Jones, C.	1.25
90	Thomas, F. (AS)	1.50
105	Thomas, F. (TT)	1.00
127	Lofton, K.	.75
160	Bagwell, J.	.75
180	Nomo, H.	1.25
185	Piazza, M.(AS)	.75
200	Puckett, K.	.75
231	Jeter, D.	1.25
237	Mattingly, D.	.75
268	Maddux, G. (FT)	.75
272	Piazza, M. (FT)	.50
279	Belle, A. (FT)	.50
290	Gwynn, T. (AS)	.60
310	Griffey, K.	2.00
316	Rodriguez, A.	1.50
332	Nomo, H. (IF)	.75
359	Nomo, H. (CL)	.75
362	Ripken, C. (CL)	1.00
368	Mattingly, D.	1.50
370	Griffey, K.	3.00
374	Jones, C.	1.50

#		
386	Maddux, G.	2.00
396	Maddux, G.	1.00
412	Thomas, F.	1.00
415	Griffey, K.	1.00
421	Ripken, C.	1.00
500	Ruth, B.	.75
507	Cameron, M. (R)	1.25
640	McGwire, M.	.75
709	Maddux, G.	1.00
740	Gonzalez, J.	1.00
754	Maddux, G. (CY)	1.00
759	Thomas, F. (HR)	1.00

Cal Ripken Collection

Complete Set (9)	30.00
Series 1 Set (5)	15.00
Series 2 Set (4)	15.00
Headers	5.00
Singles	5.00

Nomo Scrapbook

Complete Set (5)	8.00
Singles	2.00

Silver Signatures

Complete Set (730)	130.00
Series 1 Set (1-365)	70.00
Series 2 Set (396-760)	60.00
Commons	.20
Silver Signature	2x-4x

Gold Signatures

Complete Set (730)	1600.00
Series 1 Set (1-365)	900.00
Series 2 Set (396-760)	700.00
Commons	2.00
Gold Signature	15x-30x

You Crash the Game

Complete Silver Set (90)		50.00
Commons		.20
Unlisted Stars		.75-2.00
Gold		4x
1A	Jones, C. (W)	3.00
1B	Jones, C. (W)	3.00
4A	Ripken, C.	3.00
4B	Ripken, C. (W)	5.00
4C	Ripken, C.	3.50
10A	Thomas, F. (W)	5.00
10B	Thomas, F.	3.00
10C	Thomas, F. (W)	5.00
21A	Piazza, M. (W)	5.00
21B	Piazza, M.	2.50
21C	Piazza, M. (W)	5.00
26A	Griffey, K. (W)	5.00
26B	Griffey, K. (W)	5.00
26C	Griffey, K. (W)	5.00

1996 UPPER DECK SP

	NM Price
Complete Set (188)	$40.00
Commons	.10
Unlisted Stars	**.15-.50**
Pack (8)	4.00
Box (30)	90.00

Quality Rating ★★★★
Once again a great group of young players makes SP a fun set to collect. Die-Cut inserts are a tough find.

#	Player	NM
4	Erstad, D. (R)	5.00
25	Maddux, G.	3.00
26	Jones, C.	2.50
30	Ripken, C.	4.00
40	Vaughn, M.	1.25
39	Clemens, R.	1.50
53	Sandberg, R.	1.00

#		
60	Thomas, F.	4.00
70	Belle, A.	1.25
73	Lofton, K.	1.00
74	Ramirez, M.	1.00
95	Bagwell, J.	1.50
105	Piazza, M.	3.00
106	Nomo, H.	2.00
115	Puckett, K.	1.25
135	Jeter, D.	2.50
140	McGwire, M.	1.50
160	Gwynn, T.	1.50
166	Bonds, B.	1.25
170	Griffey, K.	5.00
171	Rodriguez, A.	3.00
175	Gonzalez, J.	2.00
186	Nomo, H.	1.00
187	Ripken, C.	2.00
188	Griffey, K.	2.50

Baseball Heroes

Complete Set (10)		275.00
81	Griffey, K. (Header)	50.00
82	Thomas, F.	40.00
83	Belle, A.	15.00
84	Bonds, B.	15.00
85	Jones, C.	30.00
86	Nomo, H.	30.00
87	Piazza, M.	30.00
88	Ramirez, M.	10.00
89	Maddux, G.	30.00
90	Griffey, K.	50.00

Marquee Matchups

Complete Set (20)		45.00
Commons		1.50
Die-Cuts		3x-5x
1	Griffey, K.	10.00
2	Nomo, H.	4.00
3	Jeter, D.	4.00
6	Piazza, M.	6.00
7	McGwire, M.	3.00
8	Bonds, B.	2.50
9	Ripken, C.	8.00
10	Maddux, G.	6.00
11	Belle, A.	3.00
13	Bagwell, J.	3.00
14	Gonzalez, J.	4.00
15	Thomas, F.	8.00
18	Jones, C.	5.00

Ripken Collection

Complete Set (5)	35.00
Ripken Singles (18-22)	8.00

Special F/X

Complete Set (48)		200.00
Commons		2.00
Die-Cuts		3x-5x
1	Maddux.	12.00
3	Piazza, M.	15.00
5	Nomo, H.	10.00
10	Griffey, K.	20.00
15	Jones, C.	10.00
16	Puckett, K.	6.00
20	Ripken, C.	15.00
23	Lofton, K.	7.00
25	Bonds, B.	6.00
27	McGwire, M.	10.00
29	Gonzalez, J.	10.00
30	Belle, A.	7.00
35	Thomas, F.	15.00
38	Clemens, R.	7.00
40	Gwynn, T.	10.00
41	Vaughn, M.	6.00
43	Ramirez, M.	6.00
44	Bagwell, J.	7.00
48	Jeter, D.	10.00

1996 UPPER DECK SPX

	NM Price
Complete Set (60)	$100.00
Commons	1.50
Unlisted Stars	**2.00-2.50**
Pack (1)	3.50
Box (36)	100.00

Quality Rating ★★★
SPX reaches the baseball market with the usual excitement. Player selection is great!

#	Player	NM
1	Maddux, G.	7.00
2	Jones, C.	6.00
5	Ripken, C.	10.00
9	Clemens, R.	3.50
10	Vaughn, M.	3.00
14	Sandberg, R.	3.00
16	Thomas, F.	10.00
18	Lofton, K.	3.00
19	Belle, A.	3.00
29	Bagwell, J.	4.00
33	Piazza, M.	7.00
35	Nomo, H.	5.00
36	Puckett, K.	3.00
43	Jeter, D.	5.00
45	McGwire, M.	3.00
49	Gwynn, T.	4.00
51	Bonds, B.	3.00
55	Griffey, K.	12.00
57	Rodriguez, A.	8.00
58	Gonzalez, J.	4.00
KG1	Griffey, K.	20.00
MP1	Piazza, M.	15.00
	Griffey Autograph	400.00
	Piazza Autograph	250.00

Gold

Complete Set (60)	300.00
Gold	3x-4x

Bound for Glory

Complete Set (10)		150.00
1	Griffey, K.	35.00
2	Thomas, F.	25.00
3	Bonds, B.	6.00
4	Ripken, C.	25.00
5	Maddux, G.	20.00
6	Jones, C.	20.00
7	Alomar, R.	6.00
8	Ramirez, M.	6.00
9	Gwynn, T.	20.00
10	Piazza, M.	20.00

1996 ZENITH

	NM Price
Complete Set (150)	$45.00
Commons	.20
Unlisted Stars	**.25-.75**
Pack (6)	3.50
Box (24)	70.00

Quality Rating ★★★
Zenith returns with another quality effort. Mozaics is the coolest looking of the inserts.

#	Player	NM
1	Griffey, K.	5.00
3	Maddux, G.	3.00
5	McGwire, M.	2.00
12	Piazza, M.	3.00
16	Sandberg, R.	1.50
22	Thomas, F.	4.00
24	Bagwell, J.	3.00
29	Bonds, B.	1.50
30	Vaughn, M.	1.50
55	Jones, C.	2.50

#		
61	Gonzalez, J.	2.50
66	Lofton, K.	1.50
76	Ripken, C.	4.00
83	Clemens, R.	2.00
84	Nomo, H.	3.00
90	Puckett, K.	1.50
91	Gwynn, T.	2.50
93	Jeter, D.	2.50
95	Belle, A.	2.00
99	Rodriguez, A.	3.00
130	Erstad, D. (R)	4.00
131	Belle, A.	1.25
132	Ripken, C.	2.00
133	Thomas, F.	2.50
134	Maddux, G.	1.50
135	Griffey, K.	2.50
137	Jones, C.	1.25
138	Piazza, M.	1.50

Artist Proofs

Complete Set (150)	2000.00
Artist Proofs	10x-25x

Diamond Club

Complete Set (20)		250.00
Commons		5.00
With Diamonds		4x-8x
1	Belle, A.	8.00
2	Vaughn, M.	8.00
3	Griffey, K.	35.00
4	Piazza, M.	20.00
5	Ripken, C.	25.00
6	Bagwell, J.	12.00
8	Thomas, F.	30.00
9	Rodriguez, A.	25.00
11	Alomar, R.	6.00
16	Erstad, D.	20.00
18	Maddux, G.	15.00
20	Jones, C.	20.00

Mozaics

Complete Set (25)		200.00
Commons		3.00
1	Maddux/Jones/Klesko	25.00
2	Gonzalez/Clark/Rodriguez	12.00
3	Thomas/Ventura/Durham	25.00
4	Williams/Bonds/Fernandez	8.00
5	Griffey/Johnson/Rodriguez	35.00
6	Sosa/Sandberg/Grace	6.00
8	Ripken/Alomar/Mussina	25.00
9	Vaughn/Clemens/Valentine	8.00
13	Piazza/Nomo/Mondesi	20.00
18	Belle/Ramirez/Baerga	10.00
19	Puckett/Molitor/Knoblach	10.00
20	Gwynn/Henderson/Joyner	10.00
21	McGwire/Burdick/Brosius	8.00
25	Bagwell/Biggio/Bell	10.00

Z-Team

Complete Set (18)		500.00
Commons		12.00
1	Griffey, K.	90.00
2	Belle, A.	25.00
3	Ripken, C.	70.00
4	Thomas, F.	70.00
5	Maddux, G.	60.00
6	Vaughn, M.	25.00
7	Jones, C.	40.00
8	Piazza, M.	40.00
10	Nomo, H.	40.00
11	Alomar, R.	15.00
12	Ramirez, M.	20.00
14	Bonds, B.	20.00
17	Puckett, K.	20.00

1997 BOWMAN

	NM Price
Complete Set (440)	$150.00
Series 1 Set (221)	100.00
Series 2 Set (222-440)	50.00
Commons	.05
Unlisted Stars	**.10-.40**
Series 1 Pack (10)	5.00
Series 1 Box (24)	90.00
Series 2 Pack (10)	4.00
Series 2 Box (24)	80.00

Quality Rating ★★★★
This highly anticipated set was worth the wait. Young stars and autographed cards are the attraction.

#	Player	NM
1	Jeter, D.	2.00
3	Jones, C.	2.00
4	Nomo, H.	1.50
8	Clark, T.	1.00
15	McGwire, M.	1.25
16	Griffey, K.	3.00
18	Ripken, C.	2.50
22	Sandberg, R.	.75
29	Gonzalez, J.	1.50
64	Clemens, R.	1.00
67	Belle, A.	1.25
71	Trammell, B. (R)	2.00
75	Ledee, R. (R)	4.00
80	Green, C. (R)	1.00
87	Hermanson, C. (R)	6.00
92	Erstad, D.	1.50
100	Cruz, J. (R)	20.00
106	Guillen, J.	2.00
107	Jones, A.	3.00
108	Kotsay, M. (R)	5.00
109	Guerrero, W.	1.00
123	Saunders, T. (R)	2.00
127	Sanders, A. (R)	1.00
130	Konerko, P.	1.50
131	Simon, R. (R)	2.50
145	Bradley, M. (R)	2.00
159	Milton, E. (R)	1.50
170	Wilder, P. (R)	2.00
175	Benson, K. (R)	4.00
179	Bocachica, H. (R)	2.00
184	Pickering, C. (R)	3.00
192	Blood, D.	1.00
194	Beltre, A. (R)	12.00
195	Sapp, D. (R)	1.50
196	Wood, K. (R)	4.00
197	Rolison, N. (R)	1.50
198	Tatis, F. (R)	4.00
210	Chavez, E. (R)	6.00
212	Chen, B. (R)	2.00
221	Irabu, H. (R)	3.00
224	Lofton, K.	.75
243	Bagwell, J.	1.00
244	Bonds, B.	.75
256	Maddux, G.	2.00
261	Rodriguez, I.	.75
266	Piazza, M.	2.00
274	Gwynn, T.	1.50
277	Vaughn, M.	.60
290	Thomas, F.	3.00
294	Rolen, S.	2.00
295	Helms, W.	1.50
298	Gonzalez, A. (R)	1.50
309	Gonzalez, J. (R)	1.50
310	Ramirez, A. (R)	7.00
311	Brown, D. (R)	3.00
328	Garciaparra, N.	2.50
329	Jones, J. (R)	2.00
331	Helton, T.	2.00
333	Sanchez, A. (R)	1.00
335	Branyan, R.	1.50
336	Ward, D.	1.50
339	Witt, K.	1.50
362	Nunez, A. (R)	1.50
367	Casey, S.	3.00
384	Zapp, A.J. (R)	3.00
386	Grieve, B.	2.00
389	Lee, T. (R)	20.00
396	Cloude, K. (R)	2.00
398	Wright, J. (R)	12.00
409	Butler, B. (R)	3.00
410	Peoples, D. (R)	1.50
411	Tejada, M. (R)	5.00
416	Guerrero, V.	2.00
417	Liniak, C. (R)	2.00
424	Wells, V. (R)	3.00
425	Caradonna, B. (R)	2.00
427	Garland, J. (R)	2.00
433	Werth, J. (R)	2.50
436	Cameron, T. (R)	2.50

#	Player	NM
437	Davis, J.J. (R)	3.00
438	Berkman, L. (R)	5.00
441	Irabu, H.	1.50

Blue Ink Autographs

	Complete Set (90)	2300.00
	Black	2x
	Gold	3x
	Commons	12.00
5	Benson, C.	50.00
6	Blood, D.	15.00
8	Brown, K.	15.00
11	Cameron, M.	30.00
15	Colon, B.	25.00
17	Cruz, J.	25.00
18	Cruz, J. Jr.	140.00
20	Davis, B.	20.00
22	Elarton, S.	25.00
23	Erstad, D.	50.00
27	Fullmer, B.	25.00
29	Garcia, K.	30.00
31	Green, T.	20.00
32	Grieve, B.	70.00
33	Guerrero, V.	70.00
34	Guillen, J.	50.00
36	Helms, W.	40.00
37	Hermanson, C.	50.00
38	Hildago, R.	25.00
39	Hollandsworth, T.	25.00
41	Jeter, D.	120.00
42	Jones, A.	80.00
45	Konerko, P.	60.00
47	Lee, D.	35.00
48	Lee, T.	120.00
58	Orie, K.	25.00
60	Pavano, C.	50.00
62	Perez, N.	25.00
70	Rolen, S.	75.00
71	Saunders, T.	25.00
73	Sexson, R.	25.00
74	Spiezio, S.	25.00
77	Tatis, F.	50.00
78	Tejada, M.	50.00
79	Thompson, J.	30.00
81	Wagner, B.	30.00
82	Walker, T.	25.00
84	Wilder, P.	25.00
86	Wood, K.	50.00
88	Wright, R.	25.00
89	Young, D.	20.00

International

	Complete Set (440)	300.00
	International	2x-3x

Bowman's Best Preview

	Complete Set (20)	100.00
	Commons	2.00
	Refractor	2x
	Atomic Refractor	4x
1	Thomas, F.	15.00
2	Griffey, K.	18.00
3	Bonds, B.	4.00
4	Jeter, D.	8.00
5	Jones, C.	8.00
6	McGwire, M.	6.00
7	Ripken, C.	12.00
8	Lofton, K.	5.00
10	Bagwell, J.	7.00
12	Rolen, S.	7.00
15	Jones, A.	7.00
16	Garciaparra, N.	8.00
17	Guerrero, V.	6.00
18	Tejada, M.	6.00

Bowman's International Best

	Complete Set (20)	90.00
	Commons	2.00
	Refractor	2x
	Atomic Refractor	5x
1	Thomas, F.	10.00
2	Griffey, K.	12.00
3	Gonzalez, J.	6.00
5	Nomo, H.	6.00
11	Garciaparra, N.	10.00
12	Walker, T.	2.00
13	Jones, A.	7.00
14	Guerrero, V.	6.00
19	Cruz, J.	15.00

1998 Rookie of the Year Candidates

	Complete Set (15)	45.00
	Commons	1.50
3	Helton, T.	5.00
7	Konerko, P.	5.00
8	Kotsay, M.	6.00
9	Ledee, R.	6.00
10	Lee, T.	15.00
15	Tatis, F.	4.00

Scouts' Honor Roll

	Complete Set (15)	50.00
	Commons	1.50
3	Guerrero, V.	6.00
4	Konerko, P.	4.00
7	Grieve, B.	5.00
8	Erstad, D.	4.00
10	Cruz, J.	20.00
11	Rolen, S.	5.00
12	Lee, T.	20.00
13	Jones, A.	6.00
15	Garciaparra, N.	6.00

1997 BOWMAN'S BEST

	NM Price
Complete Set (200)	$100.00
Commons	.30
Unlisted Stars	**1.00-1.50**
Pack (6)	6.50
Box (24)	135.00

Quality Rating ★★★★
The young stars on this checklist are exceptional. Beltre, Lee, and Cruz Jr. are just three of the best.

#	Player	NM
1	Griffey, K.	5.00
3	Belle, A.	1.50
5	Piazza, M.	3.00
7	Vaughn, M.	1.25
8	Sandberg, R.	1.25
9	Jones, C.	3.00
11	Lofton, K.	1.25
29	Gwynn, T.	2.00
38	Thomas, F.	4.00
40	Maddux, G.	3.00
45	McGwire, M.	2.00
58	Bagwell, J.	2.00
64	Ripken, C.	4.00
73	Bonds, B.	1.50
74	Gonzalez, J.	2.50
78	Nomo, H.	2.50
82	Jeter, D.	3.00
86	Clemens, R.	2.00
93	Johnson, R.	1.00
101	Guerrero, V.	2.50
103	Konerko, P.	2.00
104	Gonzalez, A. (R)	1.50
109	Helton, T.	.75
114	Tejada, M. (R)	7.00
115	Erstad, D.	2.00
116	Benson, C. (R)	4.00
117	Beltre, A. (R)	10.00
129	Hermanson, C. (R)	6.00
131	Martinez, W. (R)	2.00
132	Wilder, P. (R)	3.00
145	Tatis, F. (R)	5.00
149	Irabu, H. (R)	2.50
151	Helms, W.	2.00
154	Wood, K. (R)	5.00
162	Cloude, K. (R)	2.50
164	Nunez, A. (R)	1.50
169	Grieve, B.	2.00
177	Garciaparra, N.	3.50
182	Bocachica, H. (R)	2.50
186	Jones, A.	3.00
187	Lee, T. (R)	20.00
188	Cruz, J. (R)	20.00
189	Guillen, J.	2.00
191	Ledee, R. (R)	5.00
194	Rolen, S.	2.00
197	Kotsay, M. (R)	5.00
198	Milton, E. (R)	2.00
199	Branyan, R.	2.00
200	Sanchez, A. (R)	2.00

Autographs

	Complete Set (10)	500.00
	Commons	20.00
	Refractor	2x
	Atomic Refractor	3x-6x
29	Gwynn, T.	120.00
33	Molitor, P.	40.00
82	Jeter, D.	120.00
98	Salmon, T.	40.00
107	Walker, T.	25.00
188	Cruz, J.	125.00
194	Rolen, S.	75.00

Refractors

	Complete Set (200)	1200.00
	Commons	3.00
	Refractors	5x-10x
	Atomic Refractors	10x-20x

Best Cuts

	Complete Set (20)	200.00
	Commons	4.00
	Refractor	2x
	Atomic Refractor	4x
1	Jeter, D.	15.00
2	Jones, C.	15.00
3	Thomas, F.	20.00
4	Ripken, C.	25.00
5	McGwire, M.	12.00
6	Griffey, K.	30.00
7	Bagwell, J.	10.00
8	Piazza, M.	15.00
10	Belle, A.	8.00
11	Cruz, J.	20.00
13	Erstad, D.	12.00
14	Jones, A.	12.00
15	Rolen, S.	10.00
18	Guerrero, V.	10.00
20	Garciaparra, N.	12.00

Mirror Image

	Complete Set (10)	150.00
	Refractor	2x
	Atomic Refractor	4x
1	Garciaparra/Jeter/Larkin	25.00
2	Lee/Thomas/Lee/Bagwell	35.00
3	Wood/Maddux/Benson/Smoltz	20.00
4	Brown/Rodriguez/Piazza	15.00
5	Cruz/Griffey/Jones/Bonds	45.00
6	Gullen/Gonzalez/Sheffield	12.00
7	Konerko/McGwire/Helton/Palmeiro	20.00
8	Guerrero/Biggio/Sadler/Knoblach	6.00
9	Branyan/Williams/Beltre/Jones	25.00
10	Abreu/Lofton/Guerrero/Belle	12.00

1997 BOWMAN CHROME

	NM Price
Complete Set (300)	$350.00
Common Red	.30
Common Blue	.75
Unlisted Stars	**.40-.50**
Pack (3)	15.00
Box (24)	285.00

Quality Rating ★★★★★
Bowman Chrome jumps into the market and looks to have the same collectibility as regular Bowman. Look for cards of Nomar Garciaparra and Travis Lee.

#	Player	NM
1	Jeter, D.	3.00
2	Jones, C.	4.00
3	Nomo, H.	4.00
11	McGwire, M.	3.00
12	Griffey, K.	7.00
14	Ripken, C.	5.00
18	Sandberg, R.	1.50
25	Gonzalez, J.	4.00
46	Clemens, R.	3.00
48	Belle, A.	2.00

#	Player	NM
54	Lofton, K.	2.00
55	Johnson, R.	1.00
68	Bagwell, J.	2.50
69	Bonds, B.	1.50
72	Pettitte, A.	1.00
79	Maddux, G.	4.00
85	Piazza, M.	4.00
91	Gwynn, T.	2.50
93	Vaughn, M.	2.00
100	Thomas, F.	5.00
101	Trammell, B. (R)	4.00
103	Ledee, R. (R)	6.00
105	Loper, B. (R)	1.50
111	Hermanson, C. (R)	15.00
116	Erstad, D.	3.00
121	Greisinger, S. (R)	1.50
122	Cruz, J. (R)	35.00
124	Towle, J. (R)	3.00
125	Rose, B.	2.50
126	Guillen, J.	3.00
127	Jones, A.	4.00
128	Kotsay, M. (R)	10.00
135	Drumright, M. (R)	2.00
137	Saunders, T. (R)	3.00
139	Sanders, A. (R)	3.50
142	Konerko, P.	3.00
143	Simon, R. (R)	7.00
153	Hernandez, L.	7.00
154	Nunez, V. (R)	2.00
157	Milton, E. (R)	4.00
159	Pavano, C.	2.50
165	Wilder, P. (R)	5.00
167	Benson, K. (R)	7.00
171	Bocachica, H. (R)	3.00
174	Pickering, C. (R)	9.00
178	Rodriguez, N. (R)	1.50
180	Blood, D.	2.00
182	Beltre, A. (R)	28.00
183	Wood, K. (R)	12.00
184	Rolison, N. (R)	3.00
185	Tatis, F. (R)	9.00
186	Westbrook, J. (R)	2.50
190	Clement, M. (R)	3.00
192	Chavez, E. (R)	12.00
194	Chen, B. (R)	4.00
198	Irabu, H. (R)	4.00
202	Rolen, S.	4.00
205	Patterson, J. (R)	3.00
206	Gonzalez, A. (R)	3.00
207	Roberts, G. (R)	3.00
211	Caruso, M. (R)	3.00
212	Halladay, R. (R)	2.50
213	Gonzalez, J. (R)	2.50
214	Ramirez, A. (R)	20.00
215	Brown, D. (R)	9.00
224	Garciaparra, N. (R)	4.00
225	Jones, J. (R)	4.00
227	Helton, T.	2.00
229	Sanchez, A. (R)	3.00
230	Branyan, R.	2.50
231	Ward, D.	4.00
232	Witt, K.	5.00
238	Bell, R.	3.00
245	Casey, S.	7.00
247	Johnson, A. (R)	1.50
250	Lee, C. (R)	2.00
253	Zapp, A.J. (R)	8.00
255	Grieve, B.	5.00
256	Vazquez, J. (R)	2.50
257	Lee, T. (R)	30.00
258	Reyes, D. (R)	3.00
260	Escobar, K. (R)	2.00
262	Cloude, K. (R)	5.00
264	Bruner, c. (R)	2.00
265	Marquis, J. (R)	3.00
268	Garrrett, J. (R)	2.00
271	Butler, B. (R)	7.00
272	Peoples, D. (R)	4.00
273	Tejada, M. (R)	12.00
276	Guerrero, V.	3.00
277	Liniak, C. (R)	5.00
282	Barnes, J. (R)	2.00
284	Wells, V. (R)	9.00
285	Caradonna, B. (R)	4.00
287	Garland, J. (R)	4.00
288	Hayes, N. (R)	2.00
290	Kennedy, A. (R)	3.00
293	Werth, J. (R)	7.00
294	Davis, J.J. (R)	3.00
296	Cameron, T. (R)	5.00
297	Davis, J.J. (R)	7.00
298	Berkman, L. (R)	12.00
299	Standridge, J. (R)	2.50
300	Dellaero, J. (R)	2.50

Refractors
Complete Set (300)		3200.00
Commons		4.00
Unlisted Stars		5x-10x

#	Player	NM
	Rookies	5x
1	Jeter, D.	40.00
2	Jones, C.	50.00
3	Nomo, H.	50.00
11	McGwire, M.	40.00
12	Griffey, K.	100.00
14	Ripken, C.	70.00
18	Sandberg, R.	25.00
25	Gonzalez, J.	40.00
46	Clemens, R.	35.00
48	Belle, A.	25.00
54	Lofton, K.	20.00
68	Bagwell, J.	35.00
69	Bonds, B.	20.00
79	Maddux, G.	60.00
85	Piazza, M.	50.00
91	Gwynn, T.	50.00
93	Vaughn, M.	20.00
100	Thomas, F.	75.00
101	Trammell, B.	20.00
103	Ledee, R.	35.00
111	Hermanson, C.	70.00
116	Erstad, D.	25.00
122	Cruz, J.	150.00
127	Jones, A.	35.00
128	Kotsay, M.	50.00
142	Konerko, P.	30.00
143	Simon, R.	40.00
165	Wilder, P.	20.00
167	Benson, K.	35.00
174	Pickering, C.	30.00
182	Beltre, A.	120.00
183	Wood, K.	50.00
185	Tatis, F.	50.00
192	Chavez, E.	60.00
198	Irabu, H.	20.00
202	Rolen, S.	30.00
214	Ramirez, A.	80.00
215	Brown, D.	30.00
224	Garciaparra, N.	40.00
227	Helton, T.	20.00
232	Witt, K.	30.00
245	Casey, S.	30.00
253	Zapp, A.J.	40.00
255	Grieve, B.	30.00
257	Lee, T.	150.00
262	Cloude, K.	20.00
271	Butler, B.	35.00
272	Peoples, D.	25.00
273	Tejada, M.	60.00
276	Guerrero, V.	30.00
284	Wells, V.	40.00
293	Werth, J.	40.00
296	Cameron, T.	20.00
297	Davis, J.J.	40.00
298	Berkman, L.	70.00

International
Complete Set (300)		950.00
Stars		2x
Rookies		1.5x
Refractors		2x

Scout's Honor Roll
#	Player	NM
	Complete Set (15)	70.00
	Commons	2.00
	Refractors	2x
3	Guerrero, V.	5.00
4	Konerko, P.	5.00
6	Walker, T.	3.00
7	Grieve, B.	6.00
8	Erstad, D.	5.00
10	Cruz, J.	20.00
11	Rolen, S.	6.00
12	Lee, T.	20.00
13	Jones, A.	6.00
15	Garciaparra, N.	8.00

1998 ROY Candidates
#	Player	NM
	Complete Set (15)	60.00
	Commons	2.00
	Refractors	2x
2	Garcia, K.	3.00
3	Helton, T.	6.00
7	Konerko, P.	6.00
8	Kotsay, M.	8.00
9	Ledee, R.	7.00
10	Lee, T.	25.00
14	Rose, B.	5.00
15	Tatis, F.	8.00

1997 CIRCA

	NM Price
Complete Set (400)	$40.00
Commons	.05
Unlisted Stars	**.10-.40**
Pack (8)	1.50
Retail Box (18)	25.00
Hobby Box (36)	45.00

Quality Rating ★★★
Circa still features those ever-popular "Rave" parallel cards. Only 400 cards makes for a popular set.

#	Player	NM
1	Lofton, K.	1.00
8	Ripken, C.	2.50
15	Nomo, H.	1.50
21	Clemens, R.	1.25
23	Sandberg, R.	.75
24	Griffey, K.	3.00
25	Bonds, B.	.75
42	Vaughn, M.	.60
45	Thomas, F.	3.00
50	McGwire, M.	1.25
100	Rodriguez, A.	2.00
102	Bagwell, J.	1.00
148	Garciaparra, N.	1.25
150	Gwynn, T.	1.25
200	Jeter, D.	1.50
241	Erstad, D.	1.25
250	Belle, A.	.75
280	Ramirez, M.	.60
283	Rolen, S.	1.00
313	Guerrero, V.	1.50
329	Jones, A.	1.50
337	Maddux, G.	2.00
356	Piazza, M.	1.50
373	Gonzalez, J.	1.25
381	Jones, C.	1.50
394	Jones, A. (CL)	1.25
395	Griffey, K. (CL)	1.50
396	Thomas, F. (CL)	1.50
397	Rodriguez, A. (CL)	1.25
398	Ripken, C. (CL)	1.25
399	Piazza, M. (CL)	1.00
400	Maddux, G. (CL)	1.00

Rave
#	Player	NM
	Commons	15.00
1	Lofton, K.	50.00
8	Ripken, C.	175.00
15	Nomo, H.	150.00
21	Clemens, R.	90.00
23	Sandberg, R.	60.00
24	Griffey, K.	250.00
25	Bonds, B.	60.00
42	Vaughn, M.	60.00
45	Thomas, F.	175.00
50	McGwire, M.	90.00
100	Rodriguez, A.	125.00
102	Bagwell, J.	90.00
148	Garciaparra, N.	100.00
150	Gwynn, T.	100.00
163	Alomar, R.	30.00
200	Jeter, D.	100.00
241	Erstad, D.	70.00
250	Belle, A.	50.00
259	Rodriguez, I.	50.00
276	Johnson, R.	50.00
280	Ramirez, M.	50.00
283	Rolen, S.	90.00
313	Guerrero, V.	80.00
329	Jones, A.	80.00
337	Maddux, G.	125.00
356	Piazza, M.	125.00
373	Gonzalez, J.	100.00
381	Jones, C.	100.00
394	Jones, A. (CL)	40.00
395	Griffey, K. (CL)	125.00
396	Thomas, F. (CL)	100.00
397	Rodriguez, A. (CL)	70.00
398	Ripken, C. (CL)	70.00
399	Piazza, M. (CL)	60.00
400	Maddux, G. (CL)	60.00

Boss
#	Player	NM
	Complete Set (20)	50.00
	Commons	1.00
	Super Boss	2x-3x
1	Bagwell, J.	2.00
2	Belle, A.	1.50
3	Bonds, B.	1.50
5	Gonzalez, J.	2.00
6	Griffey, K.	6.00
7	Gwynn, T.	3.00
8	Jeter, D.	3.00
9	Jones, A.	5.00
10	Jones, C.	3.00
11	Maddux, G.	3.00
12	McGwire, M.	1.50
13	Piazza, M.	3.00
14	Ramirez, M.	1.50
15	Ripken, C.	5.00
16	Rodriguez, A.	5.00
18	Thomas, F.	6.00
19	Vaughn, M.	1.50

Emerald Autograph Exchange
#	Player	NM
	Complete Set (6)	350.00
1	Erstad, D.	60.00
2	Hollandsworth, T.	20.00
3	Ochoa, A.	15.00
4	Rodriguez, A.	150.00
5	Rolen, S.	75.00
6	Walker, T.	25.00

Fast Track
#	Player	NM
	Complete Set (10)	60.00
	Commons	3.00
1	Guerrero, V.	8.00
3	Jeter, D.	10.00
4	Jones, A.	12.00
5	Jones, C.	10.00
6	Rodriguez, A.	12.00
9	Rolen, S.	6.00
10	Walker, T.	3.50

Icons
#	Player	NM
	Complete Set (12)	90.00
1	Gonzalez, J.	10.00
2	Griffey, K.	25.00
3	Gwynn, T.	10.00
4	Jeter, D.	12.00
5	Jones, C.	12.00
6	Maddux, G.	12.00
7	McGwire, M.	10.00
8	Piazza, M.	12.00
9	Ripken, C.	18.00
10	Rodriguez, A.	20.00
11	Thomas, F.	20.00
12	Williams, M.	3.00

Limited Access
#	Player	NM
	Complete Set (15)	150.00
1	Bagwell, J.	8.00
2	Belle, A.	6.00
3	Bonds, B.	6.00
4	Gonzalez, J.	10.00
5	Griffey, K.	25.00
6	Gwynn, T.	10.00
7	Jeter, D.	12.00
8	Jones, C.	12.00
9	Maddux, G.	12.00
10	McGwire, M.	10.00
11	Piazza, M.	12.00
12	Ripken, C.	15.00
13	Rodriguez, A.	15.00
14	Thomas, F.	20.00
15	Vaughn, M.	6.00

Rave Reviews
#	Player	NM
	Ccmplete Set (12)	550.00
1	Belle, A.	30.00
2	Bonds, B.	30.00
3	Gonzalez, J.	50.00
4	Griffey, K.	120.00
5	Gwynn, T.	60.00
6	Maddux, G.	60.00
7	McGwire, M.	50.00
8	Murray, E.	25.00
9	Piazza, M.	60.00
10	Ripken, C.	90.00
11	Rodriguez, A.	70.00
12	Thomas, F.	100.00

PAUL O'NEILL

1997 DONRUSS

	NM Price
Complete Set (450)	$50.00
Series 1 Set (270)	25.00
Update Set (180)	25.00
Commons	.05
Unlisted Stars	**.10-.40**
Pack (10)	2.00
Hobby Box (18)	32.00
Retail Box (36)	60.00
Update Pack (10)	2.00
Update Box (24)	45.00

Quality Rating ★★★
Donruss is back with numbered inserts and a good looking design. Checklist is filled with young stars.

#	Player	NM
1	Gonzalez, J.	1.25
3	Gwynn, T.	1.25
7	Maddux, G.	2.00
12	McGwire, M.	1.00
21	Griffey, K.	3.00
34	Jones, C.	1.50
36	Nomo, H.	1.25
44	Rodriguez, A.	2.50
49	Jeter, D.	1.50
50	Lofton, K.	.75
72	Sandberg, R.	.75
108	Vaughn, M.	.60
121	Ripken, C.	2.50
134	Piazza, M.	2.00
138	Thomas, F.	2.50
146	Bagwell, J.	1.00
160	Belle, A.	.75
167	Bonds, B.	.75
273	Clemens, R.	1.25
276	Lofton, K.	1.00
289	Belle, A.	.75
355	Guerrero, V.	.75
356	Erstad, D.	1.25
357	Rolen, S.	1.00
358	Jones, A.	1.50
361	Irabu, H. (R)	1.50
362	Garciaparra, N.	1.25
396	Cruz, J. (R)	6.00
398	Thomas, F.	1.00
399	Griffey, K.	1.50
400	Ripken, C.	1.25
401	Jones, C.	.75
402	Piazza, M.	.75
404	Rodriguez, A.	1.25
406	Gonzalez, J.	.60
415	Jeter, D.	.75
423	Maddux, G.	.75
428	Clemens, R.	.60
439	Griffey, K.	1.50
448	Ripken, C.	1.00
449	Maddux, G.	.60
450	Griffey, K.	1.25

Press Proofs
Press Proofs	10x-20x
Die-Cut	40x-75x

Armed and Dangerous
	Complete Set (15)	150.00
	Commons	5.00
1	Griffey, K.	30.00
3	Jones, C.	15.00
4	Rodriguez, I.	8.00
6	Rodriguez, A.	25.00
8	Ripken, C.	25.00
9	Lofton, K.	8.00
10	Bonds, B.	6.00
11	Jeter, D.	20.00
13	Maddux, G.	20.00

Diamond Kings
	Complete Set (10)	150.00
	Commons	5.00
	Canvas	3x-5x
1	Griffey, K.	40.00
2	Ripken, C.	30.00
3	Vaughn, M.	8.00
5	Bagwell, J.	10.00
7	Piazza, M.	30.00
8	Rodriguez, I.	10.00
9	Thomas, F.	30.00
10	Jones, C.	20.00

Dominators
	Complete Set (20)	150.00
	Commons	4.00
1	Thomas, F.	20.00
2	Griffey, K.	25.00
3	Maddux, G.	12.00
4	Ripken, C.	20.00
5	Rodriguez, A.	20.00
6	Belle, A.	7.00
7	McGwire, M.	10.00
8	Gonzalez, J.	10.00
9	Jones, C.	12.00
10	Nomo, H.	10.00
11	Clemens, R.	10.00
13	Piazza, M.	12.00
16	Lofton, K.	7.00

Elite
	Complete Set (12)	500.00
1	Thomas, F.	70.00
2	Molitor, P.	15.00
3	Sosa, S.	15.00
4	Bonds, B.	25.00
5	Jones, C.	50.00
6	Rodriguez, A.	60.00
7	Griffey, K.	90.00
8	Bagwell, J.	35.00
9	Ripken, C.	70.00
10	Vaughn, M.	20.00
11	Piazza, M.	60.00
12	Gonzalez, J.	50.00

Franchise Features
	Complete Set (15)	250.00
	Commons	7.00
1	Griffey/Jones, A.	40.00
2	Thomas/Erstad	30.00
3	Rodriguez/Garciaparra	40.00
5	Gonzalez/Cruz, Jr.	30.00
6	Jones, C./Walker	20.00
7	Bonds/Guerrero	18.00
8	McGwire/Young	18.00
9	Piazza/Sweeney	20.00
10	Vaughn/Clark	10.00
12	Lofton/Stewart	10.00
13	Ripken/Rolen	30.00
14	Jeter/Reese	20.00
15	Gwynn/Abreu	15.00

Longball Leaders
	Complete Set (15)	125.00
	Commons	3.00
1	Thomas, F.	30.00
2	Belle, A.	10.00
3	Vaughn, M.	10.00
6	Griffey, K.	35.00
8	Gonzalez, J.	20.00
9	Piazza, M.	25.00
10	Bagwell, J.	15.00
12	McGwire, M.	15.00

Power Alley
	Common Green	5.00
	Common Blue	10.00
	Common Gold	18.00
	Die-Cut	5x
1	Thomas, F.(Gold)	70.00
2	Griffey, K. (Gold)	90.00
3	Ripken, C. (Gold)	70.00
4	Bagwell, J. (Blue)	20.00
5	Piazza, M. (Blue)	35.00
6	Jones, A. (Green)	25.00
7	Rodriguez, A. (Gold)	60.00
8	Belle, A. (Green)	8.00
9	Vaughn, M. (Green)	8.00
10	Jones, C. (Blue)	35.00
11	Gonzalez, J. (Blue)	25.00
13	Ramirez, M. (Green)	10.00
14	McGwire, M. (Green)	20.00
15	Lofton, K. (Blue)	20.00
16	Bonds, B. (Green)	12.00
18	Gwynn, T. (Green)	20.00
19	Guerrero, V. (Blue)	20.00
20	Rodriguez, I. (Blue)	15.00
24	Jeter, D. (Green)	30.00

Rated Rookies
	Complete Set (30)	50.00
	Commons	1.00
3	Rolen, S.	10.00
20	Jones, A.	15.00
24	Erstad, D.	8.00
25	Walker, T.	6.00
27	Guerrero, V.	10.00

Rocket Launchers
	Complete Set (15)	125.00
	Commons	4.00
1	Thomas, F.	30.00
2	Belle, A.	10.00
3	Jones, C.	25.00
4	Piazza, M.	25.00
5	Vaughn, M.	10.00
6	Gonzalez, J.	20.00
8	Bagwell, J.	15.00
11	Bonds, B.	10.00
15	Ripken, C.	30.00

Rookie Diamond Kings
	Complete Set (10)	80.00
	Commons	4.00
1	Jones, A.	15.00
2	Guerrero, V.	15.00
3	Rolen, S.	15.00
4	Walker, T.	8.00
7	Garciaparra, N.	20.00
8	Erstad, D.	12.00

Donruss Team Sets
	Braves Set	5.00
	Orioles Set	5.00
	Red Sox Set	3.00
	White Sox Set	4.00
	Rockies Set	3.00
	Dodgers Set	3.00
	Yankees Set	5.00
	Mariners Set	10.00
	Cardinals Set	2.50
	Commons	.10
	Pennant Edition	5x-15x
16	Maddux, G.	1.50
18	Jones, C.	1.50
24	Lofton, K.	.75
28	Jones, A.	1.50
35	Ripken, C.	2.00
48	Vaughn, M.	.75
60	Garciaparra, N.	1.50
64	Thomas, F.	3.00
70	Belle, A.	1.00
107	Nomo, H.	1.00
111	Piazza, M.	1.50
123	Jeter, D.	1.50
135	Irabu, H.	1.50
136	Griffey, K.	3.00
137	Rodriguez, A.	2.50
148	Cruz, J.	5.00

Team Sets MVP's
	Complete Set (18)	500.00
	Commons	5.00
1	Rodriguez, I.	20.00
2	Piazza, M.	50.00
3	Thomas, F.	60.00
4	Bagwell, J.	25.00
5	Knoblauch, C.	10.00
7	Rodriguez, A.	50.00
8	Larkin, B.	10.00
9	Ripken, C.	60.00
10	Jones, C.	40.00
11	Belle, A.	25.00
12	Bonds, B.	25.00
13	Griffey, K.	75.00
14	Lofton, K.	20.00
15	Gonzalez, J.	35.00
16	Walker, L.	10.00
17	Clemens, R.	25.00
18	Maddux, G.	40.00

The Only Way I Know
Complete Set (10)	100.00
Commons	15.00

1997 DONRUSS ELITE

	NM Price
Complete Set (150)	$40.00
Commons	.15
Unlisted Stars	**.20-.50**
Pack (6)	3.50
Box (18)	55.00

Quality Rating ★★★
Cards are similar looking to Leaf Limited. Inserts are individually numbered and are very tough to find.

#	Player	NM
1	Gonzalez, J.	1.50
2	Rodriguez, A.	3.00
3	Thomas, F.	4.00
4	Maddux, G.	2.00
5	Griffey, K.	4.00
6	Ripken, C.	3.00
7	Piazza, M.	2.50
8	Jones, C.	2.00
9	Belle, A.	1.25
10	Jones, A.	2.50
11	Guerrero, V.	2.50
12	Vaughn, M.	1.00
14	Pettitte, A.	1.00
15	Gwynn, T.	1.50
16	Bonds, B.	1.00
17	Bagwell, J.	1.25
21	McGwire, M.	1.25
24	Jeter, D.	2.00
30	Johnson, R.	1.00
32	Nomo, H.	1.25
57	Rolen, S.	1.50
58	Erstad, D.	1.50
70	Sandberg, R.	1.00
95	Puckett, K.	1.25
150	Nomo, H.	1.50

Gold
	Complete Set (150)	1000.00
	Gold	8x-15x

Leather & Lumber
	Complete Set (10)	1000.00
	Commons	30.00
1	Griffey, K.	200.00
2	Rodriguez, A.	125.00
3	Thomas, F.	150.00
4	Jones, C.	125.00
5	Rodriguez, I.	50.00
6	Ripken, C.	150.00
7	Bonds, B.	50.00
10	McGwire, M.	70.00

Passing the Torch
	Complete Set (12)	550.00
	Commons	20.00
1	Ripken, C.	90.00
2	Rodriguez, A.	70.00
3	Ripken/Rodriguez	125.00
4	Puckett, K.	50.00
5	Jones, A.	60.00
6	Puckett/Jones	70.00
8	Thomas, F.	70.00
9	Fielder/Thomas	90.00
10	Smith, O.	30.00
11	Jeter, D.	70.00
12	Smith/Jeter	70.00

Passing the Torch Autographs
	Complete Set (12)	5000.00
	Commons	100.00
1	Ripken, C.	500.00
2	Rodriguez, A.	500.00
3	Ripken/Rodriguez	1000.00
4	Puckett, K.	350.00
5	Jones, A.	350.00

6	Puckett/Jones	600.00
8	Thomas, F.	500.00
9	Fielder/Thomas	600.00
10	Smith, O.	250.00
11	Jeter, D.	300.00
12	Smith/Jeter	450.00

Turn of the Century

	Complete Set (20)	175.00
	Commons	5.00
	Die-Cut	3x
1	Rodriguez, A.	30.00
2	Jones, A.	25.00
3	Jones, C.	30.00
4	Walker, T.	15.00
5	Rolen, S.	20.00
7	Jeter, D.	30.00
8	Erstad, D.	20.00

1997 DONRUSS LIMITED

	NM Price
Complete Set (200)	1800.00
Common Counterpart	.50
Common Double Team	2.50
Common Star Factor	8.00
Common Unlimited Potential	8.00
Limited Exposure	10x-15x
Unlisted Stars	**.20-.50**
Pack (5)	5.00
Box (24)	100.00

Quality Rating ★★★★

This set is just that, limited. Player selection is awesome and the "Fabric of the Game" inserts are a great find.

#	Player	NM
1	Griffey/White. (C)	5.00
2	Maddux/Cone (C)	2.50
4	Thomas, F. (S)	65.00
5	Ripken/Orie (C)	4.00
6	Guerrero/Bonds (U)	35.00
8	Ramirez/Grissom (D)	6.00
9	Piazza, M. (S)	50.00
11	Bagwell/Karros (C)	2.00
13	Rodriguez/Renteria (C)	4.00
18	Cruz/Griffey (U)	100.00
19	Griffey, K. (S)	90.00
22	Jeter/Collier (C)	2.50
23	Jones/Ventura (C)	2.50
26	Piazza/Mondesi (D)	20.00
27	Erstad/Bagwell (U)	25.00
28	Rodriguez, I. (U)	20.00
36	Rolen/Ripken (U)	70.00
37	Ripken (S)	70.00
40	Garciaparra/Grudzielanek (C)	3.00
43	Nomo/Nagy (C)	3.50
44	Rodriguez/Greer (D)	8.00
45	Walker/Jones (C)	40.00
46	Maddux, G. (S)	50.00
51	Belle/Green (C)	1.50
53	Nomo/Park (D)	18.00
55	Jones, C. (S)	50.00
63	Belle, A. (S)	25.00
64	McGwire/Galarraga (C)	2.00
68	Sosa/Sandberg (D)	10.00
69	Garciaparra/Rodriguez (U)	75.00
70	Bagwell, J. (S)	35.00
71	Erstad/Grace (C)	1.50
72	Rolen/Alfonzo (C)	2.00
73	Lofton/Johnson (C)	1.50
77	Gonzalez, J. (S)	40.00
78	Thomas/Clark (C)	4.00
82	Piazza/Green (U)	50.00
83	Jeter, D. (S)	50.00
88	Kotsay/Gonzalez (U)	40.00
89	Bonds, B. (S)	20.00
91	Gwynn/Butler (C)	2.00

94	Jones/Lofton (U)	40.00
95	Vaughn, M. (S)	20.00
100	Thomas/Lee (U)	60.00
101	McGwire, M. (S)	30.00
106	Clark/McGwire (U)	35.00
107	Gwynn, T. (S)	40.00
110	Clemens/Delgado (D)	10.00
111	Garcia/Belle (U)	20.00
116	Reese/Jeter (U)	40.00
117	Ramirez, M. (S)	15.00
118	Gonzalez/Brown (C)	2.00
120	Johnson/Martinez (D)	8.00
121	Irabu/Maddux (U)	40.00
122	Rodriguez, A. (S)	50.00
123	Bonds/McCracken (C)	1.50
124	Clemens/Benes (C)	2.00
128	Jones/Mondesi (C)	2.50
135	Irabu/Pettitte (D)	5.00
136	Guillen/Gwynn (U)	40.00
137	Nomo, H. (S)	45.00
138	Guerrero/Edmonds (C)	2.00
141	Lofton, K. (S)	20.00
165	Clemens, R (S)	35.00
177	Pettitte, A. (S)	15.00
187	Johnson, R. (S)	15.00
193	Williams, M. (S)	15.00
196	Cruz/Buhner (D)	30.00
198	Erstad/Dickson (D)	10.00
200	Trammell/Higginson (D)	6.00

Fabric of the Game

	Complete Canvas Set (23)	
	Common	25.00
	Bonds, B.	50.00
	Lofton, K.	50.00
	Alomar, R.	35.00
	Sandberg, R.	50.00
	Gwynn, T.	60.00
	Walker, L.	30.00
	Griffey, K.	120.00
	Mondesi, R.	30.00
	Jeter, D.	50.00
	Garciaparra, N.	50.00
	Erstad, D.	40.00
	Complete Leather Set (23)	
	Commons	25.00
	Ripken, C.	150.00
	Gwynn, T.	100.00
	Rodriguez, I.	30.00
	Thomas, F.	80.00
	Bagwell, J.	40.00
	Belle, A.	30.00
	Jones, C.	50.00
	Rolen, S.	40.00
	Guillen	30.00
	Cruz, J.	70.00
	Complete Wood Set (23)	
	Commons	25.00
	Ripken, C.	150.00
	Bonds, B.	50.00
	McGwire, M.	70.00
	Griffey, K.	150.00
	Belle, A.	30.00
	Thomas, F.	125.00
	Gonzalez, J.	50.00
	Piazza, M.	50.00
	Bagwell, J.	40.00
	Vaughn, M.	30.00
	Ramirez, M.	30.00
	Jones, A.	40.00
	Guerrero, V.	40.00

1997 DONRUSS PREFERRED

	NM Price
Complete Set (200)	900.00
Complete Bronze Set (100)	25.00
Complete Silver Set (60)	125.00
Complete Gold Set (30)	250.00
Complete Platinum Set (10)	500.00
Common Bronze	.20
Common Silver	1.50
Common Gold	10.00
Unlisted Stars	**.30-.50**
Tin (5)	5.50
Box (24)	120.00

Quality Rating ★★★

Donruss continues to create new and exciting products. Preferred features cards in a tin. The tins themselves have become very collectible.

#	Player	NM
1	Thomas, F. (P)	60.00
2	Griffey, K. (P)	70.00
6	Maddux, G. (P)	45.00
13	Belle, A. (G)	12.00
22	Gonzalez, J. (P)	35.00
24	Lofton, K. (G)	12.00
28	Nomo, H. (G)	25.00
38	Ramirez, M. (G)	12.00
46	Gwynn, T. (P)	35.00
49	Rodriguez, I. (G)	12.00
50	McGwire, M. (G)	20.00
52	Clemens, R. (B)	2.00
60	Murray, E. (G)	5.00
69	Bagwell, J. (G)	20.00
92	Rodriguez, A. (P)	50.00
93	Jones, C. (P)	45.00
94	Bonds, B. (G)	15.00
96	Sandberg, R. (S)	7.00
98	Ripken, C. (G)	60.00
103	Vaughn, M. (G)	15.00
107	Piazza, M. (G)	45.00
125	Jeter, D. (G)	35.00
133	Erstad, D. (B)	2.50
143	Jones, A. (P)	30.00
147	Garciaparra, N. (G)	25.00
155	Guerrero, V. (G)	25.00
160	Rolen, S. (G)	20.00
167	Rodriguez, A. (B)	2.50
168	Thomas, F. (B)	3.00
169	Ripken, C. (B)	2.00
170	Jones, C. (B)	2.00
171	Piazza, M. (B)	2.00
172	Gwynn, T. (S)	15.00
173	Gonzalez, J. (B)	1.50
174	Lofton, K. (S)	8.00
175	Griffey, K. (B)	3.00
176	McGwire, M. (B)	1.00
177	Bagwell, J. (B)	1.00
179	Jones, A. (B)	2.00
182	Bonds, B. (B)	1.00
184	Jeter, D. (B)	2.00
187	Belle, A. (B)	6.00
194	Nomo, H. (S)	12.00
196	Maddux, G. (B)	2.00
197	Guerrero, V. (CL) (B)	2.50
198	Rolen, S. (CL) (B)	2.00
200	Garciaparra, N. (CL) (B)	2.00
	Tin Set (25)	25.00

Cut To The Chase

	Commons	4.00
	Unlisted Stars	5x-10x

Precious Metals

	Complete Set (25)	6000.00
	Commons	100.00
1	Thomas, F. (P).	550.00
2	Griffey, K. (P)	650.00
3	Maddux, G. (P)	450.00
4	Belle, A. (G)	200.00
5	Gonzalez, J. (P)	325.00
6	Lofton, K. (G)	150.00
7	Gwynn, T. (P)	325.00
8	Rodriguez, I. (G)	150.00
9	McGwire, M. (G)	300.00
12	Murray, E. (G)	100.00
13	Bagwell, J. (G).	250.00
15	Rodriguez, A. (P)	450.00
16	Jones, C. (P)	400.00
17	Bonds, B. (G)	150.00
18	Ripken, C. (P)	500.00
19	Vaughn, M. (G)	150.00
20	Piazza, M. (P)	400.00
21	Jeter, D. (G)	400.00
23	Jones, A. (P)	300.00
24	Guerrero, V. (G)	250.00

Staremasters

	Complete Set (20)	650.00
	Commons	12.00

1	Rodriguez, A.	60.00
2	Thomas, F.	70.00
3	Jones, C.	50.00
4	Ripken, C.	70.00
5	Piazza, M.	50.00
6	Gonzalez, J.	40.00
7	Jeter, D.	40.00
8	Bagwell, J.	30.00
9	Griffey, K.	90.00
10	Gwynn, T.	50.00
11	Bonds, B.	20.00
12	Belle, A.	20.00
13	Maddux, G.	50.00
14	McGwire, M.	35.00
16	Nomo, H.	30.00
18	Jones, A.	40.00
19	Vaughn, M.	20.00
20	Rodriguez, I.	20.00

X-Ponential Power

	Complete Set (20)	300.00
	Commons	6.00
1A	Ramirez, M.	10.00
1B	Thome, J.	10.00
2A	Molitor, P.	10.00
3A	Rodriguez, I.	10.00
3B	Gonzalez, J.	20.00
4A	Belle, A.	12.00
4B	Thomas, F.	40.00
5A	Alomar, R.	8.00
5B	Ripken, C.	40.00
6A	Salmon, T.	7.00
7A	Griffey, K.	50.00
7B	Rodriguez, A.	40.00
8A	Jones, C.	25.00
8B	Jones, A.	35.00
9A	Piazza, M.	25.00
9B	Mondesi, R.	7.00
10A	Gwynn, T.	20.00

1997 DONRUSS SIGNATURE SERIES

	NM Price
Complete Set (100)	$50.00
Commons	.25
Unlisted Stars	**.50-.75**
Pack (5)	15.00
Box (12)	160.00

Quality Rating ★★★★

Signature Series is back and the autograph checklist is filled with big-name stars. Look for sigs from HOFers as well.

#	Player	NM
1	McGwire, M.	2.50
2	Lofton, K.	1.50
3	Gwynn, T.	2.50
6	Griffey, K.	6.00
7	Piazza, M.	3.00
8	Maddux, G.	3.00
11	Clemens, R.	2.00
16	Thomas, F.	5.00
18	Jones, C.	3.00
19	Bagwell, J.	2.00
20	Ramirez, M.	1.25
21	Sandberg, R.	1.50
30	Bonds, B.	1.50
31	Vaughn, M.	1.50
40	Cruz, J. (R)	8.00
43	Gonzalez, J.	2.50
44	Guerrero, V.	2.00
49	Kotsay, M. (R)	2.50
50	Rolen, S.	2.00
51	Jeter, D.	3.00
54	Belle, A.	1.50
58	Ripken, C.	4.00

Column 1

#	Player	Price
61	Rodriguez, A.	4.00
67	Erstad, D.	2.00
70	Jones, A.	2.00
72	Garciaparra, N.	3.00
84	Nomo, H.	2.50
99	Griffey, K. (CL)	3.00
100	Thomas, F. (CL)	2.50

Platinum Press Proofs
Complete Set (100)	2800.00
Commons	8.00

Red Autographs
Complete Set (117)	2000.00
Commons	6.00
Century Marks	2x-3x
Millennium Marks	2x
Ripken, C.	300.00
Maddux, G.	350.00
Rodriguez, A.	200.00
Piazza, M.	200.00
Jones, C.	150.00
Nomo, H.	120.00
Bonds, B.	60.00
Belle, A.	60.00
Bonilla, B.	40.00
Helton, T.	30.00
Knoblauch, C.	70.00
Larkin, B	60.00
Martinez, T.	40.00
Mussina, M.	40.00
Pettitte, A.	60.00
Walker, L.	40.00
Gonzalez, J.	125.00
Bagwell, J.	90.00
McGwire, M.	100.00
Gwynn, T.	150.00
Clemens, R.	250.00
Jeter, D.	250.00
Molitor, P.	75.00
Lofton, K.	70.00
Murray, E.	75.00
Ramirez, M.	50.00
Vaughn, M.	100.00
Alomar, R.	90.00
Sandberg, R.	100.00
Larkin, B.	60.00
Guerrero, V.	50.00
Williams, M.	50.00
Boggs, W.	100.00
Johnson, R.	60.00
Klesko, R.	50.00
Irabu, H.	50.00
Jones, A.	125.00
Thomas, F.	200.00
Garciaparra, N.	150.00
Rolen, S.	60.00
Cruz, J. Jr.	125.00
Erstad, D.	50.00
Kotsay, M.	40.00
Konerko, P.	30.00
Wright, J.	50.00
Chavez, E.	40.00
Grieve, B.	50.00
Galarraga, A.	35.00
Glavine, T.	50.00
Justice, D.	35.00
Martinez, E.	50.00
Martinez, P.	35.00
Mondesi, R.	35.00

Notable Nicknames
Complete Set (10)	1500.00
Commons	50.00
Thomas, F.	400.00
Vaughn, M.	150.00
Rodriguez, I.	200.00
Clemens, R.	300.00
Wagner, B.	70.00
Clark, T.	125.00
Jackson, R.	225.00
Banks, E.	200.00
Musial, S.	250.00
Johnson, R.	150.00

Significant Signatures
Complete Set (22)	1000.00
Commons	25.00
Brett, G.	70.00
Schmidt, M.	75.00
Yastrzemski, C.	70.00
Bench, J.	60.00
Mattingly, D.	90.00
Carew, R.	50.00
Carlton, S.	50.00
Fisk, C.	50.00
Musial, S.	70.00
Palmer, J.	50.00
Seaver, T.	70.00

Column 2

	Banks, E.	60.00
	Doby, L.	40.00
	Killebrew, H.	50.00
	Kaline, A.	60.00
	Robinson, B.	50.00
	Robinson, F.	50.00
	Brock, L.	50.00
	Berra, Y.	70.00
	Gibson, B.	50.00
	Jackson, R.	70.00
	Snider, D.	70.00

1997 FLAIR SHOWCASE

	NM Price
Pack (5)	8.00
Box (24)	150.00
Legacy	50x-75x

Quality Rating ★★★★
Multiple parallel sets makes for a challange. Look for redemption cards good for autographed gloves of Alex Rodriguez.

Style Showtime Set
#	Player	NM
	Style Showtime Set (60)	70.00
	Style Showtime Commons	30
	Grace Showstopper Set (60)	130.00
	Grace Showstoppers Singles	1.25x-1.5x
	Showcase Showpiece Set (60)	1200.00
	Showcase Showpiece Singles	15x-25x
1	Jones, A.	3.00
2	Jeter, D.	4.00
3	Rodriguez, A.	5.00
5	Bagwell, J.	2.50
6	Rolen, S.	3.00
7	Lofton, K.	2.00
8	Ripken, C.	5.00
10	Jones, C.	3.00
16	Nomo, H.	2.50
19	Gonzalez, J.	2.50
21	Clemens, R.	2.00
23	Sandberg, R.	1.50
24	Griffey, K.	6.00
25	Bonds, B.	1.50
26	Garciaparra, N.	4.00
27	Guerrero, V.	2.50
31	Piazza, M.	3.00
33	Ramirez, M.	1.00
35	Thomas, F.	6.00
37	Gwynn, T.	2.50
39	Erstad, D.	2.00
42	Vaughn, M.	1.50
44	Maddux, G.	3.00
48	Belle, A.	2.00
52	McGwire, M.	2.00
57	Rodriguez, I.	1.00

Style Showpiece Set
#		
	Style Showpiece Set (60)	35.00
	Style Showpiece Commons	50
	Grace Showtime Set (60)	30.00
	Grace Showtime Singles	1x
	Showcase Showstopper Set (60)	200.00
	Showcase Showstopper Singles	6x-12x
100	Murray, E.	2.00

Style Showstop Set
#		
	Style Showstopper Set (60)	12.00
	Style Showstopper Commons	25
	Grace Showpiece Set (60)	40.00
	Grace Showpiece Singles	1.5-2x
	Showcase Showtime Set (60)	75.00
	Showcase Showtime Singles	5x-10x
173	Clark, T.	2.50

Diamond Cuts
Complete Set (20)	300.00
Commons	5.00

Column 3

#	Player	
1	Bagwell, J.	12.00
2	Belle, A.	8.00
4	Gonzalez, J.	15.00
5	Griffey, K.	40.00
6	Gwynn, T.	15.00
8	Jones, A.	18.00
9	Jones, C.	20.00
10	Maddux, G.	20.00
11	McGwire, M.	15.00
12	Piazza, M.	20.00
13	Jeter, D.	20.00
14	Ramirez, M.	8.00
15	Ripken, C.	30.00
16	Rodriguez, A.	25.00
17	Thomas, F.	30.00
18	Vaughn, M.	8.00
20	Williams, M.	6.00

Hot Gloves
	Complete Set (15)	700.00
	Commons	15.00
1	Alomar, R.	20.00
2	Bonds, B.	30.00
3	Gonzalez, J.	50.00
4	Griffey, K.	100.00
6	Jeter, D.	60.00
7	Jones, C.	60.00
9	Lofton, K.	30.00
10	Maddux, G.	60.00
11	Piazza, M.	60.00
12	Ripken, C.	90.00
13	Rodriguez, A.	70.00
14	Rodriguez, I.	30.00
15	Thomas, F.	90.00

Wave of the Future
	Complete Set (27)	80.00
	Commons	2.00
1	Greene, T.	3.00
2	Jones, A.	8.00
3	Simon, R.	3.00
9	Trammell, B.	5.00
12	Walker, T.	3.00
14	Guerrero, V.	8.00
15	Ledee, R.	8.00
19	Rolen, S.	8.00
21	Guillen, J.	4.00
24	Tatis, F.	4.00
WF1	Cruz, J.	35.00
WF2	Irabu, H.	10.00

1997 FLEER

	NM Price
Complete Set (761)	$80.00
Series 1 Set (500)	50.00
Series 2 Set (261)	30.00
Commons	.05
Unlisted Stars	**.10-.40**
Series 1 or 2 Pack (10)	1.50
Series 1 or 2 Box (36)	50.00

Quality Rating ★★★★
Another great looking Fleer base set. The 761 card set makes for tons of collectibility and super player selection.

#	Player	NM
13	Ripken, C.	2.50
19	Clemens, R.	1.25
22	Garciaparra, N.	2.00
32	Vaughn, M.	.60
41	Erstad, D.	1.25
72	Thomas, F.	3.00
75	Belle, A.	.75
80	Lofton, K.	.75
154	Puckett, K.	.75
168	Jeter, D.	1.50
193	McGwire, M.	1.00

Column 4

#	Player	
206	Griffey, K.	3.00
213	Rodriguez, A.	2.00
221	Gonzalez, J.	1.25
257	Jones, A.	2.00
258	Jones, C.	1.50
263	Maddux, G.	2.00
282	Sandberg, R.	.75
339	Bagwell, J.	1.00
368	Nomo, H.	1.50
371	Piazza, M.	2.00
418	Rolen, S.	1.00
462	Gwynn, T.	1.25
477	Bonds, B.	.75
492	Griffey, K. (CL)	1.50
493	Jones, A. (CL)	1.00
494	Jones, C. (CL)	.75
497	Piazza, M. (CL)	1.00
498	Ripken, C. (CL)	1.25
499	Rodriguez, A. (CL)	1.25
500	Thomas, F. (CL)	1.50
501	Lofton, K.	1.00
510	Trammell, B. (R)	.75
512	Ortiz, D. (R)	.75
524	Tatis, F. (R)	1.00
560	Ledee, R. (R)	1.25
569	Clemens, R.	1.25
589	Cruz, J. (R)	6.00
600	Belle, A.	1.00
653	Simon, R. (R)	1.00
701	Griffey, K.	1.50
703	Jeter, D.	.75
704	Jones, A.	1.00
705	Jones, C.	.75
707	Maddux, G.	.75
712	Piazza, M.	.75
714	Ripken, C.	1.25
715	Rodriguez, A.	1.25
718	Thomas, F.	1.50
722	Maddux, G.	.75
723	Ripken, C.	1.00
726	Thomas, F.	1.25
734	Piazza, M.	.75
739	Jeter, D.	.75
743	Gwynn, T.	.60
745	Griffey, K.	1.25
751	Irabu, H. (R)	1.50
756	Wright, J. (R)	5.00
No#	Jones, A. (Autograph)	100.00

Tiffany
Tiffany	20x-35x

Bleacher Blaster
	Complete Set (10)	90.00
1	Belle, A.	5.00
2	Bonds, B.	5.00
3	Gonzalez, J.	10.00
4	Griffey, K.	25.00
5	McGwire, M.	10.00
6	Piazza, M.	12.00
7	Rodriguez, A.	20.00
8	Thomas, F.	20.00
9	Vaughn, M.	5.00
10	Williams, M.	3.00

Decade of Excellence
	Complete Set (12)	70.00
	Commons	3.00
2	Bonds, B.	6.00
3	Clemens, R.	8.00
4	Gwynn, T.	10.00
6	Maddux, G.	12.00
7	McGwire, M.	10.00
8	Molitor, P.	4.00
9	Murray, E.	5.00
10	Ripken, C.	20.00
11	Sandberg, R.	6.00
12	Williams, M.	4.00

Diamond Tribute
	Complete Set (12)	600.00
1	Belle, A.	30.00
2	Bonds, B.	25.00
3	Gonzalez, J.	45.00
4	Griffey, K.	100.00
5	Gwynn, T.	40.00
6	Maddux, G.	50.00
7	McGwire, M.	40.00
8	Murray, E.	20.00
9	Piazza, M.	50.00
10	Ripken, C.	75.00
11	Rodriguez, A.	70.00
12	Thomas, F.	80.00

Golden Memories
	Complete Set (10)	12.00
	Commons	.50
1	Bonds, B.	1.50
4	McGwire, M.	2.50

#		
7	Nomo, H.	3.00
8	Piazza, M.	4.00
9	Ripken, C.	5.00
10	Smith, O.	1.50

Goudey Greats
	Complete Set (15)	35.00
1	Bonds, B.	1.50
2	Griffey, K.	6.00
3	Gwynn, T.	2.50
4	Jeter, D.	3.00
5	Jones, C.	3.00
6	Lofton, K.	1.50
7	Maddux, G.	3.00
8	McGwire, M.	2.00
9	Murray, E.	1.00
10	Piazza, M.	3.00
11	Ripken, C.	4.00
12	Rodriguez, A.	4.00
13	Sandberg, R.	1.50
14	Thomas, F.	6.00
15	Vaughn, M.	1.50

Headliners
	Complete Set (20)	15.00
	Commons	.25
1	Bagwell, J.	1.00
2	Belle, A.	.75
3	Bonds, B.	.75
5	Gonzalez, J.	1.50
6	Griffey, K.	3.00
7	Gwynn, T.	1.00
8	Jeter, D.	1.50
9	Jones, A.	1.50
10	Jones, C.	1.50
11	Maddux, G.	1.50
12	McGwire, M.	1.00
13	Molitor, P.	.50
14	Murray, E.	.50
15	Piazza, M.	1.50
16	Ripken, C.	2.00
17	Rodriguez, A.	2.00
18	Sandberg, R.	.75
20	Thomas, F.	3.00

Lumber Company
	Complete Set (18)	200.00
	Commons	5.00
2	Bagwell, J.	15.00
3	Belle, A.	10.00
4	Bonds, B.	10.00
8	Gonzalez, J.	15.00
9	Griffey, K.	35.00
12	McGwire, M.	10.00
13	Piazza, M.	25.00
14	Rodriguez, A.	25.00
17	Thomas, F.	30.00
18	Vaughn, M.	10.00

Million Dollar Moments
	Complete Set (45)	10.00
	Commons	.10

New Horizons
	Complete Set (15)	15.00
	Commons	.50
2	Cruz, J.	6.00
3	Erstad, D.	2.00
4	Garciaparra, N.	3.00
5	Guerrero, V.	3.00
8	Irabu, H.	1.00
9	Jones, A.	3.00
11	Rolen, S.	3.00
13	Trammell, B.	1.00
14	Walker, T.	1.00

Night & Day
	Complete Set (10)	350.00
1	Bonds, B.	25.00
2	Burks, E.	12.00
3	Gonzalez, J.	40.00
4	Griffey, K.	90.00
5	McGwire, M.	30.00
6	Piazza, M.	50.00
7	Ramirez, M.	20.00
8	Rodriguez, A.	60.00
9	Smoltz, J.	15.00
10	Thomas, F.	70.00

Rookie Sensations
	Complete Set (20)	25.00
	Commons	.75
5	Erstad, D.	4.00
7	Jeter, D.	6.00
13	Garciaparra, N.	6.00
16	Jones, A.	5.00
18	Rolen, S.	4.00

Soaring Stars
	Complete Set (12)	40.00
	Commons	2.00
	Glowing	5x-8x
3	Gonzalez, J.	4.00
4	Griffey, K.	8.00
5	Jeter, D.	5.00
6	Jones, A.	5.00
7	Jones, C.	5.00
8	Maddux, G.	5.00
9	McGwire, M.	3.00
10	Piazza, M.	5.00
11	Rodriguez, A.	6.00
12	Thomas, F.	6.00

Team Leaders
	Complete Set (28)	120.00
	Commons	2.00
1	Ripken, C.	20.00
2	Vaughn, M.	6.00
4	Thomas, F.	20.00
5	Belle, A.	6.00
11	McGwire, M.	6.00
12	Griffey, K.	25.00
13	Gonzalez, J.	10.00
15	Jones, C.	12.00
20	Bagwell, J.	10.00
21	Piazza, M.	15.00
27	Gwynn, T.	10.00
28	Bonds, B.	6.00

Zone
	Complete Set (20)	275.00
	Commons	5.00
1	Bagwell, J.	15.00
2	Belle, A.	12.00
3	Bonds, B.	12.00
6	Gonzalez, J.	20.00
7	Griffey, K.	40.00
8	Gwynn, T.	18.00
9	Jones, C.	20.00
10	Maddux, G.	25.00
11	McGwire, M.	15.00
13	Pettitte, A.	12.00
14	Piazza, M.	25.00
15	Rodriguez, A.	25.00
18	Thomas, F.	30.00

1997 FLEER METAL

	NM Price
Complete Set (250)	$40.00
Commons	.10
Unlisted Stars	**.15-.50**
Pack (8)	2.50
Box (24)	50.00

Quality Rating ★★★
Metal's checklist included some of the game's best young players in Todd Walker, Bob Abreu, and Andruw Jones.

#	Player	NM
8	Ripken, C.	2.50
14	Sandberg, R.	.75
20	Clemens, R.	1.25
21	Garciaparra, N.	2.00
26	Vaughn, M.	.60
30	Jones, A.	3.00
31	Jones, C.	1.50
33	Maddux, G.	2.00
40	Erstad, D.	1.25
55	Belle, A.	.75
61	Thomas, F.	3.00
82	Lofton, K.	1.00
104	Nomo, H.	1.25
105	Piazza, M.	3.00
118	Jeter, D.	1.50
131	McGwire, M.	1.00
134	Bagwell, J.	1.00
145	Griffey, K.	3.00
149	Rodriguez, A.	2.50
156	Guerrero, V.	1.50
162	Gonzalez, J.	1.25
219	Gwynn, T.	1.25
242	Bonds, B.	.75

Blast Furnace
	Complete Set (12)	200.00
	Commons	4.00
1	Bagwell, J.	15.00
2	Belle, A.	12.00
3	Bonds, B.	10.00
5	Gonzalez, J.	20.00
6	Griffey, K.	45.00
8	McGwire, M.	12.00
9	Piazza, M.	30.00
10	Rodriguez, A.	35.00
11	Thomas, F.	45.00
12	Vaughn, M.	10.00

Emerald Autographs
	Complete Set (6)	300.00
	Commons	15.00
1	Erstad, D.	50.00
4	Rodriguez, A.	150.00
5	Rolen, S.	75.00
6	Walker, T.	25.00

Magnetic Field
	Complete Set (10)	40.00
	Commons	1.50
2	Bagwell, J.	3.00
3	Bonds, B.	2.50
4	Griffey, K.	12.00
5	Jeter, D.	6.00
6	Lofton, K.	3.00
8	Ripken, C.	8.00
9	Rodriguez, A.	10.00

Mining for Gold
	Complete Set (10)	25.00
	Commons	1.00
3	Garciaparra, N.	6.00
4	Guerrero, V.	6.00
6	Jones, A.	8.00
9	Rolen, S.	5.00
10	Walker, T.	3.00

Mother Lode
	Complete Set (12)	800.00
1	Alomar, R.	20.00
2	Bagwell, J.	50.00
3	Bonds, B.	35.00
4	Griffey, K.	130.00
5	Jones, A.	70.00
6	Jones, C.	75.00
7	Lofton, K.	40.00
8	Piazza, M.	80.00
9	Ripken, C.	100.00
10	Rodriguez, A.	80.00
11	Thomas, F.	100.00
12	Williams, M.	20.00

Platinum Portraits
	Complete Set (10)	70.00
	Commons	2.00
4	Jeter, D.	15.00
5	Jones, C.	15.00
8	Pettitte, A.	5.00
10	Rodriguez, A.	25.00

Titanium
	Complete Set (10)	100.00
1	Bagwell, J.	8.00
2	Belle, A.	6.00
3	Griffey, K.	25.00
4	Jones, C.	12.00
5	Maddux, G.	15.00
6	McGwire, M.	8.00
7	Piazza, M.	15.00
8	Ripken, C.	20.00
9	Rodriguez, A.	20.00
10	Thomas, F.	25.00

1997 FLEER ULTRA

	NM Price
Complete Set (553)	$50.00
Series 1 Set (300)	25.00
Series 2 Set (253)	25.00
Commons	.05
Unlisted Stars	**.10-.40**
Series 1 or 2 Pack (10)	2.00
Series 1 or 2 Box (24)	45.00

Quality Rating ★★★
Ultra hits the streets early again this year and card fronts are filled with color. Backs have complete stats.

Ken Caminiti SAN DIEGO PADRES-3B

#	Player	NM
11	Ripken, C.	2.50
13	Clemens, R.	1.25
21	Vaughn, M.	.60
26	Erstad, D.	1.50
44	Thomas, F.	3.00
46	Belle, A.	.75
50	Lofton, K.	.75
93	Puckett, K.	.75
99	Jeter, D.	1.50
114	McGwire, M.	1.00
121	Griffey, K.	3.00
126	Rodriguez, A.	2.50
132	Gonzalez, J.	1.25
153	Jones, A.	1.50
154	Jones, C.	1.50
157	Maddux, G.	2.00
168	Sandberg, R.	.75
204	Bagwell, J.	1.00
221	Nomo, H.	1.50
223	Piazza, M.	2.00
255	Rolen, S.	1.00
283	Gwynn, T.	1.25
290	Bonds, B.	.75
327	Garciaparra, N.	2.00
377	Clemens, R.	.75
406	Lofton, K.	1.00
411	Belle, A.	1.00
458	Ledee, R. (R)	2.00
495	Guillen, J.	.75
508	Simon, R. (R)	1.50
509	Guerrero, V.	2.00
518	Ortiz, D. (R)	1.00
527	Trammell, B. (R)	1.00
538	Tatis, F. (R)	2.00
551	Cruz, J. (R)	7.00
553	Irabu, H. (R)	2.00

Autographstix Emeralds
	Complete Set (6)	1200.00
	Commons	50.00
2	Walker, T.	100.00
3	Rolen, S.	350.00
4	Erstad, D.	275.00
5	Rodriguez, A.	750.00
5	Hollandsworth, T.	75.00

Gold Medallion
	Complete Set (553)	250.00
	Gold Medallion	2x-4x
	Platinum Medallion	30x-60x

Baseball Rules
	Complete Set (10)	125.00
1	Bonds, B.	8.00
2	Griffey, K.	30.00
3	Jeter, D.	20.00
4	Jones, C.	20.00
5	Maddux, G.	20.00
6	McGwire, M.	10.00
7	Percival, T.	4.00
8	Piazza, M.	20.00
9	Ripken, C.	25.00
10	Thomas, F.	25.00

Checklists
	Complete Set (10)	10.00
	Commons	.50
2	Bonds, B.	.75
3	Griffey, K.	3.00
4	Maddux, G.	2.00
5	McGwire, M.	.75
6	Piazza, M.	2.00
7	Ripken, C.	2.50
10	Thomas, F.	3.00

Series Two Checklists
	Complete Set (10)	15.00
1	Jones, A.	2.00

#	Player	Price
2	Griffey, K.	3.00
3	Thomas, F.	3.00
4	Rodriguez, A.	3.00
5	Ripken, C.	2.50
6	Piazza, M.	2.00
7	Maddux, G.	2.00
8	Jones, C.	1.50
9	Jeter, D.	1.50
10	Gonzalez, J.	1.25

Diamond Producers

#	Player	Price
	Complete Set (12)	600.00
1	Bagwell, J.	40.00
2	Bonds, B.	30.00
3	Griffey, K.	100.00
4	Jones, C.	70.00
5	Lofton, K.	30.00
6	Maddux, G.	70.00
7	McGwire, M.	50.00
8	Piazza, M.	70.00
9	Ripken, C.	90.00
10	Rodriguez, A.	80.00
11	Thomas, F.	90.00
12	Williams, M.	15.00

Double Trouble

#	Player	Price
	Complete Set (20)	15.00
	Commons	.50
1	Alomar/Ripken	3.00
4	Baines/Thomas	3.00
5	Lofton/Belle	1.00
7	Pettitte/Jeter	2.00
8	Giambi/McGwire	2.00
9	Griffey/Rodriguez	6.00
10	Gonzalez/Clark	2.00
11	Maddux/Jones	3.00
14	Bagwell/Bell	2.00
15	Nomo/Piazza	3.00
19	Gwynn/Henderson	2.00
20	Bonds/Williams	1.00

Fielder's Choice

#	Player	Price
	Complete Set (18)	300.00
	Commons	7.00
1	Alomar, R.	10.00
2	Bagwell, J.	25.00
4	Bonds, B.	15.00
6	Griffey, K.	70.00
11	Lofton, K.	20.00
12	Maddux, G.	40.00
15	Ripken, C.	50.00
16	Rodriguez, A.	50.00
17	Rodriguez, I.	20.00

Golden Prospects

#	Player	Price
	Complete Set (10)	8.00
	Commons	.50
1	Jones, A.	3.00
2	Guerrero, V.	3.00
3	Walker, T.	.75
8	Guillen, J.	1.50

Hitting Machines

#	Player	Price
	Complete Set (18)	175.00
	Commons	3.00
1	Jones, A.	12.00
2	Griffey, K.	25.00
3	Thomas, F.	20.00
4	Rodriguez, A.	15.00
5	Ripken, C.	20.00
6	Piazza, M.	15.00
7	Jeter, D.	15.00
8	Belle, A.	10.00
9	Gwynn, T.	15.00
10	Bagwell, J.	10.00
11	McGwire, M.	10.00
12	Lofton, K.	6.00
13	Ramirez, M.	6.00
14	Alomar, R.	5.00
15	Sandberg, R.	6.00
16	Murray, E.	5.00

HR Kings

#	Player	Price
	Complete Set (12)	100.00
	Commons	4.00
1	Belle, A.	8.00
2	Bonds, B.	8.00
3	Gonzalez, J.	15.00
4	Griffey, K.	30.00
7	McGwire, M.	12.00
8	Piazza, M.	20.00
10	Thomas, F.	25.00
11	Vaughn, M.	8.00

Leather Shop

#	Player	Price
	Complete Set (12)	25.00
	Commons	.75
1	Griffey, K.	6.00
2	Rodriguez, A.	4.00

#	Player	Price
3	Ripken, C.	4.00
4	Jeter, D.	3.00
5	Gonzalez, J.	3.00
6	Gwynn, T.	3.00
7	Bagwell, J.	2.00
9	Sandberg, R.	1.50
11	Lofton, K.	1.50

Power Plus

#	Player	Price
	Complete Set (12)	90.00
1	Bagwell, J.	10.00
2	Bonds, B.	6.00
3	Gonzalez, J.	12.00
4	Griffey, K.	25.00
5	Jones, C.	12.00
6	McGwire, M.	10.00
7	Piazza, M.	15.00
8	Ripken, C.	20.00
9	Rodriguez, A.	15.00
10	Sosa, S.	4.00
11	Thomas, F.	20.00
12	Williams, M.	3.00

Series Two Power Plus

#	Player	Price
	Complete Set (12)	40.00
1	Griffey, K.	8.00
2	Thomas, F.	8.00
3	Rodriguez, A.	6.00
4	Ripken, C.	6.00
5	Piazza, M.	4.00
6	Jones, C.	4.00
7	Belle, A.	2.00
8	Gonzalez, J.	3.00
9	Bagwell, J.	3.00
10	McGwire, M.	3.00
11	Vaughn, M.	2.00
12	Bonds, B.	2.00

RBI Kings

#	Player	Price
	Complete Set (10)	50.00
	Commons	2.00
1	Bagwell, J.	6.00
2	Belle, A.	5.00
4	Bonds, B.	4.00
6	Gonzalez, J.	10.00
7	Griffey, K.	20.00
9	Thomas, F.	15.00
10	Vaughn, M.	4.00

Rookie Reflections

#	Player	Price
	Complete Set (10)	5.00
	Commons	.25
3	Erstad, D.	1.50
5	Jeter, D.	3.00
10	Rolen, S.	2.00

Season Crowns

#	Player	Price
	Complete Set (12)	20.00
	Commons	1.00
1	Belle, A.	2.00
3	Bonds, B.	2.00
4	Lofton, K.	2.00
6	McGwire, M.	3.00
8	Piazza, M.	4.00
9	Rodriguez, A.	4.00
12	Thomas, F.	6.00

Starring Role

#	Player	Price
	Complete Set (12)	650.00
1	Jones, A.	50.00
2	Griffey, K.	100.00
3	Thomas, F.	80.00
4	Rodriguez, A.	70.00
5	Ripken, C.	70.00
6	Piazza, M.	60.00
7	Maddux, G.	60.00
8	Jones, C.	60.00
9	Jeter, D.	60.00
10	Gonzalez, J.	50.00
11	Belle, A.	25.00
12	Gwynn, T.	60.00

The Fame Game

#	Player	Price
	Complete Set (18)	70.00
	Commons	2.00
1	Griffey, K.	10.00
2	Thomas, F.	10.00
3	Rodriguez, A.	8.00
4	Ripken, C.	8.00
5	Piazza, M.	7.00
6	Maddux, G.	7.00
7	Jeter, D.	7.00
8	Bagwell, J.	4.00
9	Gonzalez, J.	4.00
10	Belle, A.	3.00
11	Gwynn, T.	5.00
12	McGwire, M.	4.00
14	Lofton, K.	3.00
17	Bonds, B.	2.50

Thunderclap

#	Player	Price
	Complete Set (10)	75.00
1	Bonds, B.	3.00
2	Vaughn, M.	3.00
3	McGwire, M.	5.00
4	Bagwell, J.	5.00
5	Gonzalez, J.	7.00
6	Rodriguez, A.	12.00
7	Jones, C.	8.00
8	Griffey, K.	15.00
9	Piazza, M.	10.00
10	Thomas, F.	12.00

Ultra Top 30

#	Player	Price
	Complete Set (30)	25.00

1997
FLEER WORLD SERIES FEVER

		NM Price
Complete Set (180)		$35.00
Commons		.10
Unlisted Stars		**.10-.40**
Pack (6)		2.00
Box (24)		42.00

Quality Rating ★★★

Fleer and Sports Illustrated team up to produce a set that features baseball's best veterans and young stars like Jose Cruz Jr.

#	Player	NM
4	Cruz, J. (R.)	5.00
6	Garciaparra, N.	2.00
8	Guerrero, V.	1.50
11	Irabu, H. (R)	1.25
13	Jones, A.	1.50
22	Rolen, S.	1.50
25	Trammell, B. (R)	.75
28	Griffey, K. (SH)	1.50
33	Jones/Ripken (SH)	1.50
61	Erstad, D. (SV)	.75
62	Jeter, D. (SV)	.75
70	Rodriguez, A. (SV)	1.25
75	Maddux, G.	1.50
76	Jones, C.	1.50
77	Lofton, K.	.75
95	Sandberg, R.	.75
101	Bagwell, J.	1.00
112	Piazza, M.	1.50
116	Nomo, H.	1.25
119	Gwynn, T.	1.25
121	Bonds, B.	.75
124	Ripken, C.	2.50
128	Jeter, D.	1.50
133	Clemens, R.	1.25
139	Vaughn, M.	.60
148	Thomas, F.	3.00
149	Belle, A.	.75
157	Griffey, K.	3.00
158	Rodriguez, A.	2.50
168	McGwire, M.	1.25
170	Rodriguez, A.	1.25
172	Griffey, K.	1.50
173	Maddux, G.	.75
174	Piazza, M.	.75
177	Ripken, C.	1.25
178	Griffey/Thomas	1.50
179	Rodriguez/Jeter	1.00

Extra Edition

Extra Edition	12x-25x

Autographed Mini-Covers

#	Player	Price
1	Rodriguez, A.	250.00
2	Ripken, C.	300.00
3	Puckett, K.	150.00
4	Mays, W.	150.00

#	Player	Price
5	Robinson, F.	75.00
6	Aaron, H.	150.00

Great Shots

#	Player	Price
	Complete Set (25)	10.00
	Commons	.50
No#	Jones, C.	1.50
No#	Maddux, G.	1.50
No#	Ripken, C.	1.50
No#	Belle, A.	.75
No#	Thomas, F.	1.50
No#	Piazza, M.	1.50
No#	Jeter, D.	1.50
No#	McGwire, M.	1.00
No#	Rodriguez, A.	1.50
No#	Gonzalez, J.	1.00
No#	Griffey, K.	2.00

Cooperstown Collection

#	Player	Price
	Complete Set (12)	50.00
	Commons	4.00
1	Aaron, H.	8.00
2	Berra, Y.	5.00
6	Kaline, A.	5.00
8	Robinson, B.	5.00
10	Puckett, K.	8.00
11	Mays, W.	10.00
12	Robinson, F.	5.00

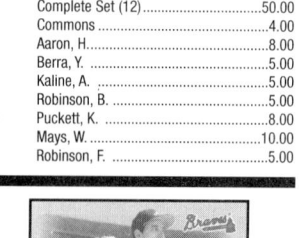

1997 LEAF

	NM Price
Complete Set (400)	$50.00
Series 1 Set (200)	25.00
Series 2 Set (201-400)	25.00
Commons	.05
Unlisted Stars	**.10-.40**
Series 1 Pack (12)	3.00
Series 1 Box (18)	50.00
Series 2 Pack (12)	3.00
Series 2 Box (24)	60.00

Quality Rating ★★★

Fractal Matrix system gives you the chance to build several different sets.

#	Player	NM
16	Rodriguez, A.	2.50
17	Gwynn, T.	1.25
38	McGwire, M.	1.00
54	Bagwell, J.	1.00
65	Bonds, B.	.75
85	Maddux, G.	2.00
99	Nomo, H.	1.25
101	Gonzalez, J.	1.00
105	Ramirez, M.	.75
107	Thomas, F.	3.00
110	Lofton, K.	1.00
149	Erstad, D.	1.50
151	Vaughn, M.	.60
165	Jeter, D.	1.50
168	Jones, A.	2.00
170	Walker, T.	.75
174	Rolen, S.	.75
184	Guerrero, V.	1.50
185	Garciaparra, N.	2.00
188	Ripken, C.	1.25
189	Jones, C.	.75
190	Belle, A.	.75
191	Piazza, M.	1.50
193	Griffey, K.	1.50
199	Jones, A.	1.00
200	Jeter, D.	.75
201	Jones, C.	1.50
202	Belle, A.	.75
203	Piazza, M.	1.50
204	Griffey, K.	3.00
205	Sandberg, R.	.75
208	Clemens, R.	1.25
218	Ripken, C.	2.50
322	Trammell, B. (R)	.75

324	Irabu, H. (R)	1.50
330	Cruz, J. (R)	6.00
348	Thomas, F.	1.50
349	Jones, A.	.75
350	Rodriguez, A.	1.25
351	Maddux, G.	.75
353	Gonzalez, J.	.60
355	McGwire, M.	.60
356	Gwynn, T.	.60
358	Jeter, D.	.75
360	Nomo, H.	.50
368	Rodriguez, A.	1.25
369	Thomas, F.	1.50
370	Ripken, C.	1.25
371	Griffey, K.	1.50
372	Maddux, G.	.75
373	Piazza, M.	.75
374	Jones, C.	.75
398	Guerrero, V.	.75
399	Erstad, D.	.75
400	Garciaparra, N.	1.00
	1948 Leaf Robinson (Reprint)	40.00

Fractal Matrix

	Common Bronze	2.00
	Common Silver	5.00
	Common Gold	10.00
	Die-Cuts	2x-3x
14	Alomar, R. (Gold Y)	25.00
16	Rodriguez, A. (Gold Z)	100.00
17	Gwynn, T.(Gold Z)	70.00
38	McGwire, M. (Gold Z)	50.00
54	Bagwell, J. (Gold Z)	50.00
65	Bonds, B. (Gold Z)	25.00
85	Maddux, G. (Gold Z)	85.00
99	Nomo, H. (Silver Y)	60.00
101	Gonzalez, J. (Gold Z)	70.00
107	Thomas, F. (Gold Z)	100.00
110	Lofton, K. (Gold Z)	30.00
136	Pettitte, A.(Gold Z)	25.00
149	Erstad, D. (Gold Z)	40.00
151	Vaughn, M. (Gold Z)	30.00
165	Jeter, D. (Gold Z)	85.00
168	Jones, A. (Gold Z)	65.00
170	Walker, T. (Gold Z)	25.00
174	Rolen, S. (Gold Z)	50.00
184	Guerrero, V. (Gold X)	100.00
185	Garciaparra, N. (Gold X)	100.00
188	Ripken, C. (Bronze Z)	20.00
189	Jones, C. (Silver Z)	40.00
190	Belle, A. (Silver Z)	20.00
191	Piazza, M. (Bronze Z)	20.00
193	Griffey, K. (Bronze Z)	25.00
199	Jones, A. (Bronze Y)	25.00
200	Jeter, D. (Silver Y)	40.00
201	Jones, C. (Gold X)	300.00
202	Belle, A. (Gold Y)	45.00
203	Piazza, M. (Gold Y)	125.00
204	Griffey, K. (Gold X)	500.00
205	Sandberg, R. (Gold Z)	35.00
208	Clemens, R. (Gold Z)	40.00
218	Ripken, C. (Gold X)	400.00
221	Rodriguez, I. (Gold Y)	40.00
238	Walker, L. (Gold Z)	30.00
319	Guillen, J. (Gold Z)	30.00
324	Irabu, H. (Gold X)	60.00
330	Cruz, J. (Gold X)	250.00
348	Thomas, F. (Silver Y)	90.00
349	Jones, A. (Silver X)	50.00
350	Rodriguez, A. (Bronze Y)	25.00
351	Maddux, G. (Silver Y)	50.00
352	Bagwell, J. (Bronze Y)	15.00
353	Gonzalez, J. (Silver Y)	50.00
355	McGwire, M. (Bronze Y)	15.00
356	Gwynn, T. (Bronze Y)	15.00
358	Jeter, D. (Silver X)	75.00
360	Nomo, H. (Gold Z)	75.00
366	Clemens, R. (Silver Y)	25.00
368	Rodriguez, A. (Silver X)	80.00
369	Thomas, F. (Bronze X)	40.00
370	Ripken, C. (Silver Y)	75.00
371	Griffey, K. (Silver Y)	100.00
372	Maddux, G. (Bronze X)	20.00
373	Piazza, M. (Silver X)	75.00
374	Jones, C. (Bronze Y)	20.00
375	Belle, A. (Bronze X)	15.00
398	Guerrero, V. (Silver Z)	25.00
399	Erstad, D. (Silver Y)	25.00
400	Garciaparra, N.(Silver Z)	30.00

Banner Season

	Complete Set (15)	300.00
	Commons	5.00
1	Bagwell, J.	25.00
2	Griffey, K.	60.00
3	Gonzalez, J.	30.00
4	Thomas, F.	50.00
5	Rodriguez, A.	40.00
6	Lofton, K.	15.00

8	Vaughn, M.	12.00
9	Jones, C.	30.00
14	Jeter, D.	30.00

Dress for Success

	Complete Set (18)	300.00
	Commons	5.00
1	Maddux, G.	25.00
2	Ripken, C.	35.00
3	Belle, A.	12.00
4	Thomas, F.	40.00
7	Bagwell, J.	15.00
8	Piazza, M.	25.00
9	McGwire, M.	15.00
11	Rodriguez, A.	40.00
12	Griffey, K.	50.00
13	Gonzalez, J.	20.00
15	Vaughn, M.	12.00
17	Jones, A.	30.00
18	Jones, C.	25.00

Get-A-Grip

	Complete Set (16)	250.00
	Commons	6.00
1	Griffey/Maddux	50.00
2	Smoltz/Thomas	30.00
3	Piazza/Pettitte	20.00
4	Johnson/Jones, C.	20.00
5	Glavine/Rodriguez	30.00
6	Hentgen/Bagwell	15.00
7	Brown/Gonzalez	15.00
8	Bonds/Mussina	15.00
9	Nomo/Belle	15.00
10	Percival/Jones, A.	20.00
14	Leiter/Jeter	20.00
15	Pulsipher/Ripken	25.00

22K Gold Leaf Stars

	Complete Set (36)	600.00
	Commons	6.00
1	Thomas, F.	50.00
2	Rodriguez, A.	50.00
3	Griffey, K.	70.00
4	Jones, A.	30.00
5	Jones, C.	40.00
6	Bagwell, J.	25.00
7	Jeter, D.	30.00
9	Rodriguez, I.	12.00
10	Gonzalez, J.	30.00
11	Maddux, G.	40.00
12	Pettitte, A.	12.00
13	Clemens, R.	25.00
14	Nomo, H.	35.00
15	Gwynn, T.	35.00
16	Bonds, B.	20.00
17	Lofton, K.	15.00
20	Belle, A.	20.00
21	Ripken, C.	50.00
22	McGwire, M.	30.00
24	Piazza, M.	40.00
25	Erstad, D.	30.00
27	Guerrero, V.	30.00
29	Rolen, S.	30.00
30	Garciaparra, N.	30.00
32	Sandberg, R.	20.00
34	Murray, E.	15.00
36	Guillen, J.	15.00

Leagues of the Nation

	Complete Set (15)	300.00
1	Gonzalez/Bonds	30.00
2	Ripken/Jones	40.00
3	McGwire/Caminiti	20.00
4	Jeter/Lofton	30.00
5	Rodriguez/Piazza	35.00
6	Griffey/Walker	60.00
7	Thomas/Sosa	50.00
8	Molitor/Larkin	8.00
9	Belle/Sanders	12.00
10	Williams/Bagwell	25.00
11	Vaughn/Sheffield	8.00
12	Rodriguez/Gwynn	40.00
13	Martinez/Rolen	25.00
14	Erstad/Guerrero, W.	25.00
15	Clark/Guerrero, V.	25.00

Knot-Hole-Gang

	Complete Set (12)	150.00
	Commons	4.00
2	Griffey, K.	35.00
3	Thomas, F.	30.00
4	Gwynn, T.	15.00
5	Piazza, M.	20.00
6	Bagwell, J.	15.00
8	Ripken, C.	25.00
9	Jones, C.	20.00

Statistical Standouts

	Complete Set (15)	900.00
	Commons	25.00
1	Belle, A.	40.00
2	Gonzalez, J.	70.00
3	Griffey, K.	150.00
4	Rodriguez, A.	90.00
5	Thomas, F.	125.00
6	Jones, C.	85.00
7	Maddux, G.	85.00
8	Piazza, M.	85.00
9	Ripken, C.	100.00
10	Mcgwire, M.	60.00
11	Bonds, B.	40.00
12	Jeter, D.	100.00

Thomas Collection

	Complete Set (6)	2400.00
1	Thomas Hat	350.00
2	Thomas Home Jersey	500.00
3	Thomas Batting Glove	350.00
4	Thomas Bat	350.00
5	Thomas Sweatband	350.00
6	Thomas Away Jersey	500.00

Warning Track

	Complete Set (18)	125.00
	Commons	4.00
1	Griffey, K.	35.00
2	Belle, A.	10.00
3	Bonds, B.	10.00
4	Jones, A.	20.00
5	Lofton, K.	8.00
6	Gwynn, T.	20.00
11	Gonzalez, J.	20.00

1997 LEAF STUDIO

	NM Price
Complete Set (165)	$55.00
Commons	.10
Unlisted Stars	**.15-.40**
Pack (5)	3.00
Box (18)	50.00

Quality Rating ★★★

Leaf introduces 8x10 trading cards. Signed 8x10 from Todd Walker, Scott Rolen, and Vladimir Guerrero highlight the set.

#	Player	NM
1	Thomas, F.	3.00
8	McGwire, M.	1.00
16	Griffey, K.	3.00
17	Clemens, R.	1.25
21	Piazza, M.	2.00
36	Vaughn, M.	.60
41	Sandberg, R.	.75
43	Rodriguez, A.	2.50
51	Ripken, C.	2.50
55	Gonzalez, J.	1.50
59	Bonds, B.	.75
73	Nomo, H.	1.50
79	Jones, C.	1.50
85	Lofton, K.	.75
88	Maddux, G.	2.00
91	Jeter, D.	2.00
98	Belle, A.	.75
102	Bagwell, J.	1.00
124	Gwynn, T.	1.50
149	Jones, A.	1.50
151	Guerrero, V.	1.00
155	Rolen, S.	1.25
160	Garciaparra, N.	1.50
162	Erstad, D.	1.50
163	Griffey, K.	1.50
164	Thomas, F.	1.50
165	Rodriguez, A.	1.50
	Guerrero, V. Autograph (500)	125.00
	Rolen, S. Autograph (1000)	90.00
	Walker, T. Autograph (1250)	30.00

Silver Press Proofs

	Complete Set (165)	500.00
	Silver Press Proofs	8x-15x
	Gold Press Proofs	25x-40x

Studio Portraits

	Complete Set (24)	30.00
	Portraits	2x

Hard Hats

	Complete Set (24)	225.00
	Commons	3.00
1	Rodriguez, I.	10.00
2	Belle, A.	10.00
3	Griffey, K.	35.00
5	Thomas, F.	35.00
6	Ripken, C.	25.00
7	Walker, T.	6.00
8	Rodriguez, A.	25.00
10	Piazza, M.	20.00
12	Jones, C.	20.00
13	Jeter, D.	20.00
20	Gonzalez, J.	15.00
22	Rolen, S.	15.00
23	Erstad, D.	12.00

Master Strokes

	Complete Set (24)	550.00
	Commons	8.00
	8x10 version	1/2x
1	Jeter, D.	35.00
2	Bagwell, J.	25.00
3	Griffey, K.	70.00
4	Bonds, B.	15.00
5	Thomas, F.	60.00
7	Vaughn, M.	15.00
8	Rodriguez, A.	50.00
9	Jones, A.	30.00
10	Lofto11n, K.	15.00
11	Ripken, C.	50.00
12	Maddux, G.	35.00
13	Ramirez, M.	15.00
14	Piazza, M.	35.00
15	Guerrero, V.	25.00
16	Belle, A.	20.00
17	Jones, C.	35.00
18	Nomo, H.	30.00
20	Gwynn, T.	30.00
22	McGwire, M.	20.00
23	Gonzalez, J.	30.00

1997 NEW PINNACLE

	NM Price
Complete Set (200)	$25.00
Commons	.05
Unlisted Stars	**.10-.40**
Pack (10)	3.00
Box (18)	45.00

Quality Rating ★★★

Interleague Encounter insert pairs the best players from both the American and National Leagues.

#	Player	NM
1	Griffey, K.	3.00
3	Maddux, G.	1.50
12	Belle, A.	.75
21	Clemens, R.	1.00
25	Lofton, K.	1.00
29	Nomo, H.	1.25
45	Piazza, M.	2.00
53	Jeter, D.	1.50
57	Bagwell, J.	1.00
68	Gonzalez, J.	1.25
71	Gwynn, T.	1.25
81	Rodriguez, A.	2.50
91	Ripken, C.	2.50
98	Vaughn, M.	.60
115	Erstad, D.	1.50
117	Bonds, B.	.75
118	Thomas, F.	3.00
123	Jones, C.	1.50
140	Sandberg, R.	.75

142	McGwire, M.	1.00
169	Guerrero, V.	1.50
170	Garciaparra, N.	2.00
172	Rolen, S.	1.50
175	Jones, A.	1.50
178	Ripken, C.	1.25
180	Rodriguez, I.	1.50
190	Rodriguez, A.	1.50
191	Piazza, M.	1.00
194	Jones, C.	.75
195	Gonzalez, J.	.60
197	Thomas, F.	1.50
198	Guerrero, V.	.75
200	Rolen, S.	.75

Artist Proofs
Artist Proofs (200) 15x-40x

Museum Collection
Complete Set (200) 500.00
Museum Collection 8x-15x

Interleague Encounter
	Complete Set (10)	600.00
1	Belle/Jordan	35.00
2	Jones, A/Anderson	50.00
3	Griffey/Gwynn	125.00
4	Ripken/Jones, C.	100.00
5	Piazza/Rodriguez, I.	80.00
6	Jeter/Guerrero	90.00
7	Maddux/Vaughn	80.00
8	Rodriguez, A/Nomo	100.40
9	Gonzalez/Bonds	70.00
10	Thomas/Bagwell	100.00

Keeping the Pace
	Complete Set (18)	650.00
	Commons	8.00
1	Gonzalez, J.	50.00
2	Maddux, G.	50.00
3	Rodriguez, I.	25.00
4	Griffey, K.	90.00
5	Rodriguez, A.	60.00
6	Bonds, B.	25.00
7	Thomas, F.	70.00
9	Jeter, D.	50.00
10	Clemens, R.	30.00
11	Lofton, K.	25.00
12	Gwynn, T.	50.00
14	Ripken, C.	70.00
16	Nomo, H.	50.00
17	Johnson, R.	20.00
18	Piazza, M.	60.00

Spellbound
Common Griffey (6)	25.00
Common Jones, A. (6)	15.00
Common Ripken (6)	20.00
Common Jones, C. (7)	15.00
Common Thomas (5)	20.00
Common Piazza (6)	15.00
Common Rodriguez, I. (5)	6.00
Common Rodriguez, A.(4)	25.00
Common Belle, A. (5)	8.00

1997 PACIFIC CROWN COLLECTION

	NM Price
Complete Set (450)	$35.00
Commons	.05
Unlisted Stars	**.10-.40**
Pack (12)	2.00
Box (36)	60.00

Quality Rating ★★★
Regular cards are once again improved. A silver foil parallel set is available at 1 per 73 packs.

#	Player	NM
6	Erstad, D.	1.50
29	Ripken, C.	2.00
35	Clemens, R.	1.25
39	Garciaparra, N.	2.00
48	Vaughn, M.	.75
64	Thomas, F.	3.00
67	Belle, A.	.75
73	Lofton, K.	.75
152	Jeter, D.	2.00
173	McGwire, M.	1.25
186	Griffey, K.	3.00
192	Rodriguez, A.	2.50
200	Gonzalez, J.	1.25
234	Jones, A.	1.50
235	Jones, C.	1.50
240	Maddux, G.	1.50
257	Sandberg, R.	.75
311	Bagwell, J.	1.00
336	Nomo, H.	1.25
339	Piazza, M.	2.00
424	Gwynn, T.	1.00
440	Bonds, B.	.75

Blue
	Complete Set (450)	250.00
	Blue	3x-6x
	Silver	60x-120x

Card-Supials
	Complete Set (36)	300.00
	Commons	2.00
1	Alomar, R.	5.00
3	Murray, E.	6.00
4	Ripken, C.	25.00
6	Vaughn, M.	8.00
7	Thomas, F.	25.00
8	Belle, A.	8.00
13	Jeter, D.	20.00
14	Pettitte, A.	6.00
15	McGwire, M.	12.00
17	Griffey, K.	30.00
18	Rodriguez, A.	20.00
19	Gonzalez, J.	15.00
21	Jones, A.	20.00
22	Jones, C.	15.00
24	Maddux, G.	20.00
25	Sandberg, R.	8.00
28	Bagwell, J.	10.00
30	Nomo, H.	12.00
31	Piazza, M.	20.00
35	Gwynn, T.	15.00
36	Bonds, B.	8.00

Cramer's Choice
	Complete Set (10)	1000.00
1	Alomar, R.	40.00
2	Thomas, F.	200.00
3	Belle, A.	70.00
4	Pettitte, A.	50.00
5	Griffey, K.	250.00
6	Rodriguez, A.	175.00
7	Jones, C.	125.00
8	Smoltz, J.	50.00
9	Piazza, M.	175.00
10	Gwynn, T.	120.00

Fireworks Die-Cuts
	Complete Set (20)	400.00
	Commons	5.00
3	Murray, E.	10.00
4	Ripken, C.	40.00
5	Thomas, F.	40.00
6	Belle, A.	15.00
7	Jeter, D.	30.00
8	Pettitte, A.	10.00
10	McGwire, M.	15.00
11	Griffey, K.	50.00
12	Rodriguez, A.	35.00
13	Gonzalez, J.	25.00
14	Jones, A.	30.00
15	Jones, C.	30.00
16	Nomo, H.	25.00
17	Piazza, M.	40.00
19	Gwynn, T.	25.00
20	Bonds, B.	15.00

Gold Crown Die-Cuts
	Complete Set (36)	400.00
	Commons	3.00
5	Ripken, C.	25.00
7	Thomas, F.	30.00
8	Belle, A.	15.00
11	Jeter, D.	20.00
15	McGwire, M.	15.00
16	Griffey, K.	35.00
18	Rodriguez, A.	25.00
19	Gonzalez, J.	15.00
20	Rodriguez, I.	10.00

21	Jones, A.	20.00
22	Jones, C.	20.00
25	Sandberg, R.	10.00
28	Bagwell, J.	12.00
30	Nomo, H.	15.00
31	Piazza, M.	25.00
35	Gwynn, T.	20.00
36	Bonds, B.	10.00

Latinos of the Major Leagues
	Complete Set (36)	90.00
	Commons	1.00
20	Rodriguez, A.	15.00
21	Gonzalez, J.	8.00
23	Jones, A.	12.00

Triple Crown Die-Cuts
	Complete Set (20)	700.00
	Commons	10.00
3	Vaughn, M.	25.00
4	Thomas, F.	90.00
5	Belle, A.	30.00
8	McGwire, M.	35.00
9	Griffey, K.	120.00
10	Rodriguez, A.	80.00
11	Gonzalez, J.	50.00
12	Jones, A.	70.00
13	Jones, C.	60.00
17	Bagwell, J.	40.00
18	Piazza, M.	70.00
20	Bonds, B.	25.00

1997 PACIFIC PRISM

	NM Price
Complete Set (150)	$175.00
Commons	.50
Unlisted Stars	**.75-2.00**
Pack (3)	1.50
Box (36)	48.00

Quality Rating ★★★
Insert cards are available in Prism baseball as well as a bonus set named "Gems of the Diamond."

#	Player	NM
3	Erstad, D.	7.00
12	Ripken, C.	10.00
14	Clemens, R.	6.00
15	Garciaparra, N.	10.00
17	Vaughn, M.	4.00
22	Thomas, F.	10.00
25	Belle, A.	6.00
26	Lofton, K.	6.00
51	Jeter, D.	8.00
59	McGwire, M.	4.00
63	Griffey, K.	15.00
65	Rodriguez, A.	8.00
68	Gonzalez, J.	6.00
78	Jones, A.	6.00
79	Jones, C.	8.00
82	Maddux, G.	8.00
88	Sandberg, R.	5.00
105	Bagwell, J.	6.00
114	Nomo, H.	8.00
115	Piazza, M.	8.00
144	Gwynn, T.	6.00
147	Bonds, B.	4.00

Platinum
	Complete Set (150)	700.00
	Platinum	3x-5x

Gate Attractions
	Complete Set (32)	550.00
	Commons	5.00
3	Ripken, C.	40.00
4	Thomas, F.	40.00
5	Lofton, K.	12.00

9	Jeter, D.	35.00
10	Pettitte, A.	10.00
13	McGwire, M.	20.00
14	Griffey, K.	50.00
15	Rodriguez, A.	40.00
16	Gonzalez, J.	25.00
17	Jones, A.	30.00
18	Jones, C.	30.00
19	Maddux, G.	30.00
20	Sandberg, R.	10.00
23	Bagwell, J.	20.00
25	Nomo, H.	30.00
26	Piazza, M.	30.00
29	Smith, O.	10.00
31	Gwynn, T.	25.00
32	Bonds, B.	12.00

Gems of the Diamond
	Complete Set (220)	60.00
	Commons	.20
	Unlisted Stars	.50-1.50
16	Ripken, C.	5.00
32	Thomas, F.	6.00
64	Puckett, K.	2.50
80	McGwire, M.	2.00
86	Griffey, K.	6.00
91	Rodriguez, A.	5.00
95	Gonzalez, J.	2.50
112	Jones, C.	3.00
113	Maddux, G.	3.00
160	Nomo, H.	2.50
161	Piazza, M.	3.00
186	Rolen, S.	2.00
207	Gwynn, T.	2.50

Sizzling Lumber
	Complete Set (36)	350.00
	Commons	3.00
1A	Ripken, C.	25.00
2A	Thomas, F.	25.00
3A	Belle, A.	10.00
3C	Lofton, K.	8.00
4A	Jeter, D.	20.00
5A	McGwire, M.	15.00
6A	Griffey, K.	30.00
6B	Rodriguez, A.	25.00
7A	Gonzalez, J.	15.00
8B	Jones, C.	20.00
8C	Jones, A.	20.00
10A	Bagwell, J.	12.00
11A	Piazza, M.	20.00
12A	Gwynn, T.	18.00

Sluggers & Hurlers
	Complete Set (24)	850.00
	Commons	6.00
1A	Ripken, C.	70.00
1B	Mussina, M.	18.00
2B	Clemens, R.	30.00
3A	Thomas, F.	90.00
4A	Lofton, K.	25.00
5A	Jeter, D.	50.00
5B	Pettitte, A.	20.00
6A	Griffey, K.	90.00
6B	Johnson, R.	18.00
7A	Rodriguez, A.	80.00
8A	Jones, A.	70.00
8B	Maddux, G.	50.00
9A	Jones, C.	50.00
10A	Bagwell, J.	30.00
11A	Piazza, M.	50.00
11B	Nomo, H.	40.00
12A	Gwynn, T.	40.00

1997 PINNACLE

	NM Price
Complete Set (200)	$20.00
Commons	.05
Unlisted Stars	**.10-.40**
Pack (10)	2.50
Box (24)	50.00

Quality Rating ★★★
Pinnacle includes several tough insert sets, including Team Pinnacle and Passport to the Majors.

#	Player	NM
18	Gonzalez, J.	1.25
42	Gwynn, T.	1.25
52	McGwire, M.	.75
55	Clemens, R.	1.25
76	Bagwell, J.	1.00
92	Rodriguez, A.	2.50
96	Jones, C.	1.50
97	Bonds, B.	.75
99	Sandberg, R.	.75
100	Belle, A.	.75
102	Thomas, F.	3.00
103	Piazza, M.	2.00
139	Jeter, D.	1.50
161	Erstad, D.	1.50
163	Jones, A.	2.00
172	Garciaparra, N.	2.00
189	Maddux, G.	1.00
191	Ripken, C.	1.25
193	Griffey, K.	1.50
198	Jones, A.	1.50
199	Erstad, D.	.75

Artist's Proofs

	Common Bronze	10.00
	Common Silver	15.00
	Common Gold	25.00
14	Pettitte, A. (G)	60.00
18	Gonzalez, J. (G)	150.00
42	Gwynn, T. (S)	90.00
47	Rodriguez, I. (G)	50.00
52	McGwire, M. (S)	70.00
55	Clemens, R. (B)	50.00
65	Murray, E. (S)	40.00
76	Bagwell, J. (G)	90.00
78	Molitor, P. (G)	50.00
92	Rodriguez, A. (G)	150.00
96	Jones, C. (S)	90.00
97	Bonds, B. (S)	50.00
99	Sandberg, R (S)	50.00
100	Belle, A. (G)	50.00
102	Thomas, F. (G)	200.00
103	Piazza, M. (S)	125.00
139	Jeter, D. (G)	125.00
161	Erstad, D. (G)	90.00
163	Jones, A. (G)	100.00
172	Garciaparra, N. (B)	75.00
189	Maddux, G. (S)	90.00
191	Ripken, C. (G)	125.00
192	Nomo, H. (G)	75.00
193	Griffey, K. (G)	200.00
198	Jones, A. (B)	50.00
199	Erstad, D. (B)	45.00

Museum Collection

	Complete Set (200)	400.00
	Museum Collection	6x-12x

Cardfrontations

	Complete Set (20)	250.00
	Commons	4.00
	Unlisted Stars	8.00-12.00
1	Maddux/Piazza	25.00
3	Johnson/Ripken	25.00
4	Appier/McGwire	15.00
7	Nomo/Jones.	20.00
14	Rivera/Griffey	30.00
15	Gooden/Thomas	25.00
16	Wetteland/Erstad.	15.00
19	McDowell/Rodriguez	25.00

Home/Away

	Complete Set (24)	350.00
1/2	Jones, C.	20.00
3/4	Griffey, K.	40.00
5/6	Piazza, M.	25.00
7/8	Thomas, F.	30.00
9/10	Bagwell, J.	15.00
11/12	Rodriguez, A.	30.00

13/14	Bonds, B.	10.00
15/16	Vaughn, M.	10.00
17/18	Jeter, D.	25.00
19/20	McGwire, M.	15.00
21/22	Ripken, C.	30.00
23/24	Belle, A.	10.00

Passport to the Majors

	Complete Set (25)	300.00
	Commons	5.00
	Unlisted Stars	8.00-15.00
1	Maddux, G.	30.00
2	Griffey, K.	45.00
3	Thomas, F.	40.00
4	Ripken, C.	35.00
5	Piazza, M.	30.00
6	Rodriguez, A.	30.00
8	Jones, C.	25.00
13	Gonzalez, J.	20.00
21	Nomo, H.	20.00

Shades

	Complete Set (10)	120.00
	Commons	3.00
1	Griffey, K.	30.00
2	Gonzalez, J.	15.00
5	Ripken, C.	25.00
6	Vaughn, M.	8.00
8	Piazza, M.	20.00
9	Thomas, F.	25.00
10	Rodriguez, A.	25.00

Team Pinnacle

	Complete Set (10)	300.00
	Commons	10.00
1	Thomas/Bagwell	50.00
4	Rodriguez/Jones	50.00
5	Piazza/Rodriguez	40.00
6	Belle/Bonds	25.00
7	Griffey/Burks	60.00
8	Gonzalez/Sheffield	25.00
10	All Players	50.00

1997 PINNACLE CERTIFIED

	NM Price
Complete Set (150)	$45.00
Commons	.20
Unlisted Stars	**.25-.75**
Pack (6)	6.00
Box (20)	100.00

Quality Rating ★★★
Certified is once again a very popular product with collectors. Production is low and the card quality is a highlight.

#	Player	NM
1	Bonds, B.	1.50
2	Vaughn, M.	1.50
4	Sandberg, R.	1.50
5	Bagwell, J.	2.00
17	Belle, A.	1.50
22	Rodriguez, A.	3.50
26	Piazza, M.	3.00
28	Ripken, C.	5.00
31	Erstad, D.	2.50
39	Clemens, R.	2.00
41	Thomas, F.	5.00
45	Gwynn, T.	2.00
49	McGwire, M.	2.00
51	Jeter, D.	3.00
53	Griffey, K.	6.00
58	Lofton, K.	2.00
59	Jones, C.	3.00
63	Nomo, H.	2.00
69	Gonzalez, J.	2.50
83	Maddux, G.	3.00
106	Jones, A.	3.00
111	Guerrero, V.	2.50

112	Rolen, S.	3.00
114	Garciaparra, N.	4.00
127	Trammell, B. (R)	1.50
129	Irabu, H. (R)	2.00
136	Griffey, K.	3.00
141	Jeter, D.	1.50
142	Gonzalez, J.	1.25
143	Maddux, G.	1.50
144	Rodriguez, A.	2.00
145	Bagwell, J.	1.00
146	Ripken, C.	2.50
147	Gwynn, T.	1.00
148	Thomas, F.	3.00
149	Nomo, H.	1.00
150	Jones, A.	2.00
151	Cruz, J.	25.00
No#	Cruz, J. (Exchange)	25.00

Certified Red
Certified Red (150)	4x-8x

Mirror Red
Mirror Red (150)	25x-50x

Mirror Blue
Mirror Blue (150)	40x-80x

Mirror Gold
Mirror Gold (150)	60x-150x

Certified Team

	Complete Set (20)	250.00
	Commons	4.00
	Certified Gold Team	5x
1	Thomas, F.	30.00
2	Bagwell, J.	12.00
3	Jeter, D.	20.00
4	Jones, C.	20.00
5	Rodriguez, A.	30.00
7	Ripken, C.	25.00
8	Vaughn, M.	8.00
10	Piazza, M.	20.00
11	Gonzalez, J.	15.00
12	Bonds, B.	8.00
13	Griffey, K.	35.00
14	Jones, A.	20.00
15	Belle, A.	10.00
18	Nomo, H.	20.00
19	Maddux, G.	20.00

Lasting Impressions

	Complete Set (20)	200.00
	Commons	4.00
1	Ripken, C.	30.00
2	Griffey, K.	35.00
3	Vaughn, M.	8.00
5	McGwire, M.	15.00
9	Thomas, F.	30.00
10	Gwynn, T.	15.00
11	Clemens, R.	10.00
12	Rodriguez, A.	30.00
14	Lofton, K.	10.00
17	Johnson, R.	8.00
18	Sandberg, R.	10.00
19	Ramirez, M.	10.00
20	Mussina, M.	8.00

1997 PINNACLE INSIDE BASEBALL

	NM Price
Complete Set (150)	$35.00
Commons	.10
Unlisted Stars	**.15-.40**
Pack (10)	3.00
Box (48)	120.00

Quality Rating ★★★
Cards in a can, that's what this set is all about. The cans are just as collectible as the cards.

#	Player	NM
4	Gonzalez, J.	1.50
5	Nomo, H.	1.50
8	Rodriguez, A.	2.50
13	Thomas, F.	3.50
16	Maddux, G.	2.00
19	Griffey, K.	3.50
23	Ripken, C.	2.50
27	Piazza, M.	2.00
31	Jones, C.	2.00
35	Belle, A.	.75
36	Clemens, R.	1.25
37	Sandberg, R.	.75
44	Vaughn, M.	.75
56	Gwynn, T.	1.50
60	Bonds, B.	.75
63	Bagwell, J.	1.25
71	Lofton, K.	.75
78	McGwire, M.	1.25
87	Jeter, D.	2.00
110	Erstad, D.	1.50
128	Jones, A.	2.00
129	Guerrero, V.	2.00
132	Rolen, S.	2.00
144	Walker, T.	.75
146	Garciaparra, N.	3.00
148	Jeter/Hollandsworth	.75

Club Edition

	Complete Set (150)	500.00
	Club Edition	5x-10x
	Diamond Edition	25x-60x

Cans

	Complete Set (24)	20.00
	Unlisted Stars	.75-1.25
2	Thomas, F.	3.00
5	Rodriguez, A.	2.50
8	Griffey, K.	3.00
10	Maddux, G.	1.50
15	Jones, C.	1.50
16	Jeter, D.	1.50
18	Jones, A.	2.00
19	Piazza, M.	2.00
22	Ripken, C.	2.50

Dueling Dugouts

	Complete Set (20)	450.00
	Commons	8.00
1	Rodriguez/Ripken	50.00
2	Bagwell/Caminiti	20.00
3	Bonds/Belle	20.00
4	Piazza/Rodriguez	25.00
5	Knoblauch/Alomar	15.00
6	Griffey/Jones, A.	50.00
7	Jones, C./Thome	25.00
8	Thomas/Vaughn	35.00
9	McGriff/McGwire	20.00
10	Jordan/Gwynn	15.00
11	Larkin/Jeter	20.00
12	Lofton/Williams	15.00
13	Gonzalez/Ramirez	15.00
15	Maddux/Clemens	25.00
16	Smoltz/Pettitte	15.00
18	Nomo/Mussina	20.00
19	Hollandsworth/Erstad	12.00
20	Guerrero/Garcia	18.00

Fortysomething

	Complete Set (16)	350.00
	Commons	6.00
1	Gonzalez, J.	40.00
2	Bonds, B.	20.00
4	McGwire, M.	35.00
6	Belle, A.	30.00
11	Vaughn, M.	20.00
12	Griffey, K.	90.00
16	Thomas, F.	70.00

1997 PINNACLE MINT COLLECTION

	NM Price
Complete Set (30)	$25.00
Commons	.25
Unlisted Stars	**.30-.60**
Pack (3/2)	4.50
Box0 (16)	60.00

Quality Rating ★★
Coins hit the baseball card market. Player selection and several parallel sets help.

#	Player	NM
1	Griffey, K.	3.00
2	Thomas, F.	3.00
3	Rodriguez, A.	2.50
4	Ripken, C.	2.00
6	Gonzalez, J.	1.25
7	Piazza, M.	2.00
8	Belle, A.	1.00
9	Jones, C.	1.50
10	Jones, A.	1.50
11	Maddux, G.	1.50
12	Nomo, H.	1.50
13	Bagwell, J.	1.00
15	McGwire, M.	1.25
16	Jeter, D.	1.25
18	Bonds, B.	.75
21	Gwynn, T.	1.25

Coins

Complete Set (30)		60.00
Commons		1.00
Unlisted Stars		1.50-3.00
Nickel Silver		2x-5x
Solid Silver		50x
Gold Plated		4x-8x
Gold Redemption		100x-125x
1	Griffey, K.	10.00
2	Thomas, F.	10.00
3	Rodriguez, A.	10.00
4	Ripken, C.	8.00
6	Gonzalez, J.	4.00
7	Piazza, M.	6.00
8	Belle, A.	4.00
9	Jones, C.	5.00
10	Jones, A.	8.00
11	Maddux, G.	5.00
13	Bagwell, J.	4.00
16	Jeter, D.	5.00
21	Gwynn, T.	5.00

Bronze Cards

Complete Set (30)		50.00
Commons		.50
Unlisted Stars		2x

Silver Cards

Complete Set (30)		200.00
Commons		2.00
Unlisted Stars		5x-10x

Gold Cards

Complete Set (30)		450.00
Commons		5.00
Unlisted Stars		12x-20x

1997 PINNACLE X-PRESS

	NM Price
Complete Set (150)	$25.00
Commons	.05
Unlisted Stars	**.10-.40**
Pack (8)	2.00
Box (24)	42.00

Quality Rating ★★

Horizontal cards give a different look at baseball's best players. Melting Pot inserts are a tough find at 1 per 288 packs.

#	Player	NM
4	Gonzalez, J.	1.25
5	Thomas, F.	3.00
6	Lofton, K.	1.00
7	Griffey, K.	3.00
9	Maddux, G.	1.50
10	Nomo, H.	1.25
13	Gwynn, T.	1.25
15	Rodriguez, A.	2.00
16	Piazza, M.	1.50
23	Jones, C.	1.50
30	Bonds, B.	.75
32	Jeter, D.	1.50
42	McGwire, M.	1.25
45	Sandberg, R.	.75
47	Belle, A.	.75
54	Clemens, R.	1.00
57	Ripken, C.	2.50
61	Ramirez, M.	.75
78	Bagwell, J.	1.00
82	Erstad, D.	1.50
116	Jones, A.	1.50
117	Garciaparra, N.	2.00
120	Trammell, B. (R)	.75
123	Guerrero, V.	1.00
134	Rolen, S.	1.50
137	Irabu, H. (R)	1.00
139	Griffey, K.	1.50
140	Thomas, F.	1.50
143	McGwire, M.	.75
146	Piazza, M.	.75
147	Rodriguez, A.	1.25
149	Maddux, G.	.75

Men of Summer

Men of Summer		8x-15x

Far & Away

Complete Set (18)		100.00
Commons		2.00
1	Belle, A.	5.00
2	McGwire, M.	7.00
3	Thomas, F.	15.00
4	Vaughn, M.	4.00
5	Bagwell, J.	6.00
6	Gonzalez, J.	8.00
7	Piazza, M.	10.00
8	Jones, A.	8.00
9	Jones, C.	10.00
12	Erstad, D.	6.00
14	Griffey, K.	20.00
18	Rodriguez, A.	12.00

Melting Pot

Complete Set (20)		700.00
Commons		10.00
1	Guillen, J.	20.00
2	Guerrero, V.	60.00
3	Jones, A.	60.00
4	Walker, L.	20.00
5	Ramirez, M.	30.00
6	Griffey, K.	125.00
7	Rodriguez, A.	80.00
8	Thomas, F.	90.00
9	Gonzalez, J.	50.00
10	Rodriguez, I.	20.00
11	Nomo, H.	50.00
14	Garciaparra, N.	70.00
18	Ripken, C.	90.00
19	Jeter, D.	60.00

Bronze Metal Works

Commons		5.00
Silver		3x-6x
Gold		8x-12x
1	Griffey, K.	20.00
3	Jones, A.	10.00
5	Jeter, D.	12.00
6	Ripken, C.	15.00
7	Piazza, M.	15.00
14	McGwire, M.	10.00
15	Garciaparra, N.	12.00
16	Vaughn, M.	6.00
20	Clemens, R.	10.00
	Gold Redemption Card	90.00
	Silver Redemption Card	45.00

Swing For the Fences

Complete Set (60)		70.00
Commons		.25
Upgrade Set (60)		175.00
1	Griffey, K. (W)	20.00
5	McGwire, M. (W)	15.00
9	Gonzalez, J.	2.00
10	Thomas, F.	5.00
18	Ripken, C.	4.00
31	Walker, L. (W)	10.00
39	Piazza, M.	3.00
42	Bagwell, J.	2.00

#		
44	Jones, C.	3.00
53	Guerrero, V.	2.00
U26	Griffey, K.	25.00
U41	McGwire, M.	10.00
U57	Walker, L.	5.00
No#	Jones, A. (Autograph)	45.00

1997 SCORE

	NM Price
Complete Set (551)	$45.00
Series 1 Set (330)	20.00
Series 2 Set (221)	25.00
Factory Set (550)	50.00
Commons	.05
Unlisted Stars	**.10-.40**
Series 1 or 2 Pack (10)	1.00
Series 1 or 2 Box (36)	32.00

Quality Rating ★★★

Score features a white bordered design, with Artist Proof and Premium Stock parallels.

#	Player	NM
1	Bagwell, J.	1.00
12	Belle, A.	.75
22	Piazza, M.	2.00
24	Erstad, D.	1.00
26	Thomas, F.	3.00
35	Jeter, D.	1.25
91	Bonds, B.	.75
95	Rodriguez, A.	2.00
151	Ripken, C.	2.50
156	Griffey, K.	3.00
157	Lofton, K.	.75
159	Nomo, H.	1.25
181	Clemens, R.	.75
187	McGwire, M.	1.00
193	Jones, C.	1.50
198	Gonzalez, J.	1.25
215	Maddux, G.	2.00
249	Gwynn, T.	1.25
310	Jones, A.	1.00
340	Lofton, K.	.75
473	Garciaparra, N.	2.00
474	Rolen, S.	1.25
489	Guerrero, V.	.75
498	Gonzalez, J.	.75
499	Griffey, K.	1.25
500	Jones, A.	.75
501	Piazza, M.	.75
507	Rodriguez, A.	1.25
508	Thomas, F.	1.25
509	Jones, C.	.75
520	Maddux, G.	.75
545	Jeter, D.	.75
546	Ripken, C.	1.00
548	Griffey, K.	1.00
549	Thomas, F.	1.00
550	Piazza, M.	.50
551A	Irabu, H. (R, English)	12.00
551B	Irabu, H. (R, Japanese)	12.00

Artist Proofs

Artist Proofs		15x-25x
Premium Stock		3x-5x
Showcase		4x-8x

Blastmasters

Complete Set (18)		125.00
Commons		2.00
1	Vaughn, M.	5.00
2	McGwire, M.	8.00
3	Gonzalez, J.	10.00
4	Belle, A.	6.00
5	Bonds, B.	5.00
6	Griffey, K.	25.00
7	Jones, A.	15.00
8	Jones, C.	15.00

9	Piazza, M.	15.00
10	Bagwell, J.	8.00
12	Rodriguez, A.	15.00
16	Guerrero, V.	12.00

Heart of the Order

Complete Set (36)		125.00
Commons		2.00
1	Rodriguez, I.	5.00
3	Gonzalez, J.	8.00
4	Thomas, F.	15.00
5	Belle, A.	6.00
7	Rodriguez, A.	15.00
8	Griffey, K.	20.00
12	Ripken, C.	15.00
17	Jeter, D.	10.00
19	Jones, C.	10.00
20	Jones, A.	10.00
23	Piazza, M.	10.00
25	Gwynn, T.	10.00
31	Erstad, D.	10.00

Pitcher Perfect

Complete Set (15)		80.00
Commons		2.00
1	Ripken, C.	15.00
2	Rodriguez, A.	15.00
3	Rodriguez/Ripken	20.00
6	McGwire, M.	8.00
10	Thomas, F.	15.00
12	Vaughn, M.	5.00
14	Griffey, K.	20.00

Stand & Deliver

Complete Set (24)		300.00
Commons		4.00
1	Jones, A.	25.00
2	Maddux, G.	25.00
3	Jones, C.	25.00
5	Griffey, K.	50.00
6	Rodriguez, A.	30.00
9	Jeter, D.	25.00
13	Piazza, M.	25.00
14	Nomo, H.	25.00
21	Gonzalez, J.	20.00
22	Bagwell, J.	15.00
23	Ripken, C.	40.00
24	Thomas, F.	40.00

Stellar Season

Complete Set (18)		90.00
Commons		3.00
1	Gonzalez, J.	10.00
3	Bagwell, J.	8.00
5	McGwire, M.	8.00
6	Griffey, K.	25.00
7	Thomas, F.	20.00
8	Rodriguez, A.	15.00
9	Piazza, M.	12.00
10	Belle, A.	6.00
13	Vaughn, M.	5.00

The Franchise

Complete Set (9)		125.00
Glowing Franchise		2x
Commons		5.00
1	Griffey, K.	35.00
3	Ripken, C.	25.00
4	Jones, C.	15.00
5	Piazza, M.	20.00
6	Belle, A.	10.00
7	Thomas, F.	30.00

The Highlight Zone

Complete Set (18)		200.00
Commons		4.00
1	Thomas, F.	30.00
2	Griffey, K.	35.00
3	Vaughn, M.	10.00
4	Belle, A.	10.00
5	Piazza, M.	20.00
6	Bonds, B.	10.00
7	Maddux, G.	25.00
9	Bagwell, J.	12.00
10	Rodriguez, A.	30.00
11	Jones, C.	15.00
15	Ripken, C.	30.00

Titanic Tators

Complete Set (18)		125.00
Commons		3.00
1	McGwire, M.	10.00
2	Piazza, M.	20.00
3	Griffey, K.	30.00
4	Gonzalez, J.	12.00
5	Thomas, F.	25.00
6	Belle, A.	8.00
8	Bagwell, J.	10.00
12	Vaughn, M.	8.00

#	Player	NM
14	Jones, C.	15.00
15	Bonds, B.	8.00
17	Rodriguez, A.	25.00

1997 SCORE BOARD
MANTLE SHOE BOX

	NM Price
Complete Set (75)	$75.00
Commons (1-50, 70-74)	1.00
Pack (3)	3.00
Box (16)	42.00

Quality Rating ★★★
If you are a fan of Mickey Mantle, this set's for you. Die-Cut versions are also available. For prices on vintage insert cards, check the regular set listings.

#	Player	NM
51-69	Mantle, M.	2.00

Die-Cut

Complete Set (5)	45.00
Singles (1, 6, 7, 70, 74)	10.00

Mickey Mantle 7

Complete Set (7)	120.00
Singles	20.00

1997 SELECT

	NM Price
Complete Set (200)	$80.00
Series 1 Set (150)	50.00
Hi-Series (50)	30.00
Common Red	.10
Unlisted Red Stars	**.15-.40**
Common Blue	.25
Unlisted Blue Stars	**.50-.75**
Pack (6)	3.00
Box (24)	55.00

Quality Rating ★★★
Blue foil cards are more difficult to find than the regular set. Autographs are also a challenge.

#	Player	NM
1	Gonzalez, J.	2.00
2	Vaughn, M.	1.00
3	Gwynn, T.	1.50
8	Thomas, F.	5.00
17	Belle, A.	1.50
23	Maddux, G.	3.00
24	Clemens, R.	1.50
25	Rodriguez, I.	1.00
26	Bonds, B.	1.00
27	Lofton, K.	1.00
29	Nomo, H.	3.00
32	Piazza, M.	3.50
47	Griffey, K.	5.00
51	Bagwell, J.	2.00
53	Rodriguez, A.	4.00
60	Jeter, D.	3.00
63	Jones, C.	3.00
71	Ripken, C.	4.00
75	McGwire, M.	2.00
78	Johnson, R.	1.00
100	Erstad, D.	2.00
101	Jones, A.	4.00
102	Rolen, S.	2.00
105	Guerrero, V.	2.50
106	Garciaparra, N.	3.00
141	Rodriguez, A.	2.00
142	Gonzalez, J.	1.00
144	Thomas, F.	2.00
145	Griffey, K.	2.50
147	Piazza, M.	1.50
148	Jeter, D.	1.50

#	Player	NM
149	Thomas, F.	1.25
150	Griffey, K.	1.25
151	Cruz, J. (R)	8.00
153	Irabu, H. (R)	1.50
156	Gonzalez, J. (R)	.75
157	Tatis, F. (R)	2.50
166	Kotsay, M. (R)	2.50
172	Helton, T.	1.50
182	Womack, T. (R)	.75
194	Wright, J. (R)	5.00
	Guillen, J. Autograph (3000)	40.00
	Guerrero, W. Autograph (3000)	15.00
	Walker, T. Autograph (3000)	25.00
	Jones, A. Autograph (2500)	70.00

Artist Proofs

Red	30x-50x
Blue	75x-100x

Registered Gold

Red	8x-15x
Blue	25x-35x

Rookie Revolution

Complete Set (20)	150.00
Commons	6.00

#		
1	Jones, A.	25.00
2	Jeter, D.	30.00
10	Guerrero, V.	20.00
12	Walker, T.	8.00
13	Rolen, S.	25.00
14	Garciaparra, N.	30.00
16	Erstad, D.	15.00

Tools of the Trade

Complete Set (25)	150.00
Commons	2.00
Mirror Blue	8x-12x

#		
1	Griffey/Jones, A.	20.00
2	Maddux/Pettitte	10.00
3	Ripken/Jones, C.	18.00
4	Piazza/Kendall	10.00
5	Belle/Garcia	7.00
7	Gonzalez/Guerrero	12.00
8	Gwynn/Dye	8.00
10	Bagwell/Giambi	8.00
11	Lofton/Erstad	10.00
12	Sheffield/Ramirez	5.00
17	Boggs/Rolen	5.00
19	Mcgwire/Thomas	20.00
20	Rodriguez/Johnson	5.00
22	Clemens/Percival	5.00
24	Rodriguez/Ordonez	15.00
25	Jeter/Garciaparra	15.00

1997 SKYBOX E-X2000

	NM Price
Complete Set (100)	$100.00
Commons	.75
Unlisted Stars	**1.00-1.50**
Pack (2)	4.00
Box (24)	80.00

Quality Rating ★★★
A 100-card checklist is reasonable and makes for great player selection. Credentials and Emerald Autograph Redemptions are the hot inserts. E-X2000 was a hobby only release.

#	Player	NM
2	Erstad, D.	3.50
8	Ripken, C.	8.00
10	Garciaparra, N.	7.00
11	Vaughn, M.	2.00
12	Belle, A.	2.50
15	Thomas, F.	7.00
33	Jeter, D.	5.00
38	McGwire, M.	4.00

#		
40	Griffey, K.	10.00
43	Rodriguez, A.	6.00
46	Gonzalez, J.	4.00
47	Rodriguez, I.	2.00
49	Clemens, R.	3.00
53	Jones, A.	5.00
54	Jones, C.	5.00
56	Lofton, K.	2.00
57	Maddux, G.	5.00
62	Sandberg, R.	2.00
76	Bagwell, J.	3.00
81	Nomo, H.	4.00
82	Piazza, M.	5.00
83	Guerrero, V.	5.00
89	Rolen, S.	5.00
93	Gwynn, T.	4.00
95	Bonds, B.	2.00

Credentials

Credentials	10x-20x
Essential Credentials	25x-50x

A Cut Above

Complete Set (10)	500.00

#		
1	Thomas, F.	90.00
2	Griffey, K.	125.00
3	Rodriguez, A.	80.00
4	Belle, A.	35.00
5	Gonzalez, J.	60.00
6	McGwire, M.	50.00
7	Vaughn, M.	30.00
8	Ramirez, M.	30.00
9	Bonds, B.	30.00
10	McGriff, F.	20.00

Emerald Autograph Redemptions

Complete Set (6)	400.00
Commons	20.00

#		
1	Erstad, D.	65.00
2	Hollandsworth, T.	25.00
4	Rodriguez, A.	200.00
5	Rolen, S.	85.00
6	Walker, T.	30.00

Hall or Nothing

Complete Set (20)	250.00
Commons	4.00
Unlisted Stars	5.00-8.00

#		
1	Thomas, F.	30.00
2	Griffey, K.	35.00
4	Ripken, C.	25.00
7	Clemens, R.	10.00
8	Gwynn, T.	15.00
9	Rodriguez, A.	25.00
10	McGwire, M.	12.00
12	Maddux, G.	20.00
13	Gonzalez, J.	15.00
14	Belle, A.	12.00
15	Piazza, M.	20.00
16	Bagwell, J.	12.00

Star Date 2000

Complete Set (15)	70.00
Commons	1.50

#		
1	Rodriguez, A.	10.00
2	Jones, A.	6.00
3	Pettitte, A.	3.00
5	Jones, C.	8.00
6	Erstad, D.	6.00
7	Jeter, D.	8.00
11	Rolen, S.	7.00
13	Walker, T.	3.00
14	Clark, T.	3.00
15	Guerrero, V.	6.00

1997 TOPPS

	NM Price
Complete Set (496)	$35.00
Series 1 Set (1-276)	20.00
Series 2 Set (277-496)	15.00
Factory Set (497)	45.00
Commons	.05
Unlisted Stars	**.10-.40**
Series 1 or 2 Pack (11)	1.50
Series 1 or 2 Box (36)	45.00

Quality Rating ★★★
Topps still delivers complete stats and this year's set has a special Jackie Robinson Tribute card.

#	Player	NM
1	Bonds, B.	.75
13	Jeter, D.	1.50
20	Piazza, M.	2.00
42	Robinson, J.	3.00
62	McGwire, M.	1.00
69	Belle, A.	.75
104	Piazza, M.	1.00

#		
108	Thomas, F.	3.00
124	Gonzalez, J.	1.25
130	Maddux, G.	1.50
206	Trammell, B. (R)	.75
268	Rolen, S.	1.25
277	Jones, A.	1.50
293	Garciaparra, N.	1.50
295	Bagwell, J.	1.00
300	Griffey, K.	3.00
350	Lofton, K.	.75
400	Ripken, C.	2.00
410	Gwynn, T.	1.25
433	Guerrero, V.	1.50
440	Nomo, H.	1.25
450	Vaughn, M.	.75
455	Jones, A.	1.50
481	Benson/Koch (R)	1.00
483	Johnson/Kotsay (R)	.75
489	Konerko/Lee (R)	.75
	Jeter Autograph	125.00

All-Stars

Complete Set (22)	65.00
Commons	2.00

#		
1	Rodriguez, I.	5.00
3	Thomas, F.	12.00
8	Jones, C.	5.00
9	Ripken, C.	12.00
11	Belle, A.	5.00
12	Bonds, B.	5.00
13	Griffey, K.	15.00
15	Gonzalez, J.	8.00
17	Pettitte, A.	4.00

Awesome Impact

Complete Set (20)	90.00
Commons	2.00

#		
2	Clark, T.	5.00
4	Garciaparra, N.	15.00
5	Guerrero, V.	10.00
7	Jeter, D.	15.00
8	Jones, A.	10.00
9	Jones, C.	15.00
18	Rolen, S.	10.00
20	Walker, T.	4.00

Hobby Masters

Complete Set (20)	110.00
Series 1 Set (10)	60.00
Series 2 Set (10)	50.00
Commons	3.00

#		
1	Griffey, K.	20.00
2	Ripken, C.	15.00
3	Maddux, G.	10.00
4	Belle, A.	5.00
5	Gwynn, T.	7.00
6	Bagwell, J.	6.00
9	Gonzalez, J.	8.00
10	Lofton, K.	5.00
11	Thomas, F.	15.00
12	Piazza, M.	12.00
13	Jones, C.	10.00
16	Bonds, B.	5.00
17	Vaughn, M.	5.00
18	Jeter, D.	10.00

Inter-League MatchUps

Complete Set (14)	70.00
Commons	3.00
Refractors	4x

#		
1	McGwire/Bonds.	7.00
2	Salmon/Piazza	10.00
3	Griffey/Bichette	15.00
4	Gonzalez/Gwynn	10.00
5	Thomas/Sosa	12.00
6	Belle/Larkin	5.00
12	Ripken/Jefferies	12.00
13	Vaughn/Jones	12.00

Mantle Reprints

Complete Set (16)	120.00
Mantle Singles	8.00
Finest	2x
Finest Refractor	6x

Mays Reprints

Complete Set (27)	85.00
Mays Singles	4.50
Finest	2x
Finest Refractor	6x
Mays Autograph (1000)	150.00

Season's Best

Complete Set (25)	30.00
Commons	.50

#		
1	Gwynn, T.	3.00
3	Thomas, F.	5.00
6	McGwire, M.	2.50
8	Griffey, K.	6.00

9	Belle, A.	2.00
12	Belle, A.	2.00
13	Gonzalez, J.	2.50
21	Lofton, K.	2.00

Sweet Strokes

	Complete Set (15)	50.00
	Commons	2.00
2	Bagwell, J.	4.00
3	Belle, A.	3.00
4	Bonds, B.	3.00
6	Griffey, K.	12.00
7	Gwynn, T.	5.00
8	Jones, C.	6.00
10	McGwire, M.	4.00
12	Piazza, M.	6.00
14	Thomas, F.	10.00
15	Vaughn, M.	3.00

Team Timber

	Complete Set (16)	80.00
	Commons	3.00
1	Griffey, K.	20.00
4	Bagwell, J.	7.00
5	Thomas, F.	15.00
7	Bonds, B.	5.00
10	Gonzalez, J.	8.00
11	Vaughn, M.	5.00
12	McGwire, M.	6.00
14	Belle, A.	5.00
15	Jones, C.	10.00
16	Piazza, M.	12.00

1997 TOPPS CHROME

	NM Price
Complete Set (165)	$75.00
Commons	.25
Unlisted Stars	**.30-.75**
Pack (4)	4.50
Box (24)	85.00

Quality Rating ★★★
A Jackie Robinson tribute card is a great addition to refractors.

#	Player	NM
1	Bonds, B.	1.50
7	Jeter, D.	4.00
9	Piazza, M.	4.00
21	McGwire, M.	2.50
24	Belle, A.	2.00
41	Thomas, F.	5.00
42	Robinson, J. (Trib.)	5.00
47	Gonzalez, J.	4.00
49	Maddux, G.	4.00
67	Sandberg, R.	1.50
96	Rolen, S.	4.00
97	Jones, C	4.00
99	Garciaparra, N.	5.00
100	Bagwell, J.	3.00
101	Griffey, K.	7.00
117	Lofton, K.	2.00
126	Clemens, R.	3.00
140	Ripken, C.	5.00
145	Gwynn, T.	4.00
153	Guerrero, V.	3.00
156	Nomo, H.	4.00
159	Vaughn, M.	2.00
160	Jones, A.	3.00

Refractor

	Complete Set (165)	1800.00
	Refractor	10x-20x

All-Stars

	Complete Set (22)	130.00
	Commons	2.00
	Refractors	3x

1	Rodriguez, I.	6.00
3	Thomas, F.	15.00
8	Jones, C.	15.00
9	Ripken, C.	20.00
11	Belle, A.	8.00
12	Bonds, B.	8.00
13	Griffey, K.	25.00
15	Gonzalez, J.	12.00
17	Pettitte, A.	5.00

Diamond Duos

	Complete Set (10)	100.00
	Refractors	3x
1	Jones/Jones	15.00
2	Jeter/Williams	12.00
3	Griffey/Buhner	25.00
4	Lofton/Ramirez	6.00
5	Bagwell/Biggio	10.00
6	Gonzalez/Rodriguez	12.00
7	Ripken/Anderson	20.00
8	Piazza/Nomo	18.00
9	Galarraga/Bichette	5.00
10	Thomas/Belle	12.00

Season's Best

	Complete Set (25)	100.00
	Refractors	3x
	Commons	2.00
1	Gwynn, T.	10.00
2	Thomas, F.	15.00
6	McGwire, M.	8.00
8	Griffey, K.	20.00
9	Belle, A.	6.00
12	Belle, A.	6.00
13	Gonzalez, J.	10.00
14	Vaughn, M.	6.00
17	Pettitte, A.	6.00
21	Lofton, K.	6.00

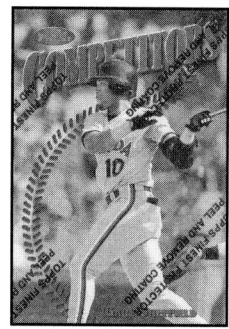

1997 TOPPS FINEST

	NM Price
Series 1 Common Set (100)	$35.00
Series 1 Uncommon Set (50)	150.00
Series 1 Rare Set (25)	450.00
Series 2 Common Set (100)	35.00
Series 2 Uncommon Set (50)	200.00
Series 2 Rare Set (25)	400.00
Commons	.25
Common Uncommons	2.00
Common Rare	10.00
Unlisted Stars	**.30-.75**
Uncommon Unlisted	**3.00-5.00**
Series 1 or 2 Pack (6)	4.00
Series 1 or 2 Box (24)	70.00

Quality Rating ★★★
Similar to last year's set with different levels of collecting. Player selection is top notch.

#	Player	NM
1	Bonds, B. (C)	1.50
10	Bagwell, J. (C)	2.50
15	Jeter, D. (C)	3.50
29	Thomas, F. (C)	5.00
30	McGwire, M. (C)	2.50
37	Erstad, D. (C)	2.00
41	Garciaparra, N. (C)	3.50
50	Piazza, M. (C)	3.00
100	Jones, A. (C)	3.00
108	Jones, C. (U)	15.00
133	Rolen, S. (U)	12.00
135	Ripken, C. (U)	20.00
139	Griffey, K. (U)	30.00
143	Nomo, H. (U)	12.00
150	Gonzalez, J. (U)	12.00
151	Piazza, M. (R)	50.00
153	Vaughn, M. (R)	20.00
155	McGwire, M. (R)	30.00
158	Maddux, G. (R)	60.00
159	Bagwell, J. (R)	30.00

160	Thomas, F. (R)	60.00
162	Jones, A. (R)	40.00
166	Jeter, D. (R)	50.00
167	Guerrero, V. (R)	50.00
169	Gwynn, T. (R)	30.00
174	Lofton, K. (R)	25.00
175	Bonds, B. (R)	20.00
202	Vaughn, M. (C)	1.50
212	Gonzalez, J. (C)	2.50
233	Clemens, R. (C)	2.50
238	Griffey, K. (C)	6.00
240	Belle, A. (C)	2.00
252	Ripken, C. (C)	5.00
265	Ramirez, M. (C)	2.00
273	Jones, C. (C)	3.00
276	Erstad, D. (U)	10.00
279	Thomas, F. (U)	25.00
283	Lofton, K. (U)	10.00
286	Helton, T. (U)	10.00
287	Pettitte, A. (U)	4.00
289	Rodriguez, I. (U)	7.00
292	Piazza, M. (U)	15.00
294	Maddux, G. (U)	15.00
298	Gwynn, T. (U)	10.00
303	Sandberg, R. (U)	8.00
305	McGwire, M. (U)	10.00
306	Jones, A. (U)	15.00
310	Jeter, D. (U)	15.00
311	Vaughn, M. (U)	7.00
313	Bonds, B. (U)	7.00
315	Guerrero, V. (U)	10.00
318	Bagwell, J. (U)	10.00
319	Belle, A. (U)	8.00
320	Irabu, H. (U)	12.00
330	Jones, C. (R)	50.00
332	Gonzalez, J. (R)	35.00
334	Ripken, C. (R)	60.00
337	Cruz, J. (R)	70.00
342	Griffey, K. (R)	80.00
344	Clemens, R. (R)	25.00
345	Nomo, H. (R)	35.00
347	Belle, A. (R)	25.00
349	Ramirez, M.	20.00

Embossed

Embossed (100)		3x
Die-Cut Embossed (50)		5x

Refractors

Series 1 Common Set (100)		500.00
Series 1 Uncommon Set (50)		700.00
Series 1 Rare Set (25)		2200.00
Series 2 Common Set (100)		500.00
Series 2 Uncommon Set (50)		700.00
Series 2 Rare Set (25)		1900.00
Commons		4.00
Common Uncommons		10.00
Common Rare		50.00
1	Bonds, B. (C)	20.00
2	Sandberg, R. (C)	20.00
10	Bagwell, J. (C)	30.00
15	Jeter, D. (C)	40.00
29	Thomas, F. (C)	60.00
30	McGwire, M. (C)	25.00
37	Erstad, D. (C)	25.00
41	Garciaparra, N. (C)	40.00
50	Piazza, M. (C)	50.00
100	Jones, A. (C)	30.00
108	Jones, C. (U)	80.00
133	Rolen, S. (U)	60.00
135	Ripken, C. (U)	125.00
138	Ramirez, M. (U)	30.00
139	Griffey, K. (U)	125.00
143	Nomo, H. (U)	60.00
150	Gonzalez, J. (U)	70.00
151	Piazza, M. (R)	250.00
152	Rodriguez, I. (R)	100.00
153	Vaughn, M. (R)	100.00
155	McGwire, M. (R)	125.00
158	Maddux, G. (R)	250.00
159	Bagwell, J. (R)	150.00
160	Thomas, F. (R)	275.00
162	Jones, A. (R)	150.00
166	Jeter, D. (R)	200.00
167	Guerrero, V. (R)	100.00
169	Gwynn, T. (R)	175.00
175	Bonds, B. (R)	100.00
202	Vaughn, M. (C)	20.00
212	Gonzalez, J. (C)	35.00
233	Clemens, R. (C)	25.00
238	Griffey, K. (C)	70.00
240	Belle, A. (C)	20.00
252	Ripken, C. (C)	50.00
265	Ramirez, M. (C)	20.00
273	Jones, C. (C)	50.00
276	Erstad, D. (U)	50.00
279	Thomas, F. (U)	100.00
283	Lofton, K. (U)	30.00
286	Helton, T. (U)	30.00

289	Rodriguez, I. (U)	30.00
292	Piazza, M. (U)	90.00
294	Maddux, G. (U)	90.00
298	Gwynn, T. (U)	50.00
303	Sandberg, R. (U)	30.00
305	McGwire, M. (U)	50.00
306	Jones, A. (U)	50.00
310	Jeter, D. (U)	70.00
311	Vaughn, M. (U)	35.00
313	Bonds, B. (U)	35.00
315	Guerrero, V. (U)	50.00
318	Bagwell, J. (U)	50.00
319	Belle, A. (U)	25.00
320	Irabu, H. (U)	25.00
330	Jones, C. (R)	200.00
332	Gonzalez, J. (R)	175.00
334	Ripken, C. (R)	250.00
337	Cruz, J. (R)	300.00
341	Walker, T. (R)	80.00
342	Griffey, K. (R)	350.00
344	Clemens, R. (R)	125.00
345	Nomo, H. (R)	200.00
347	Belle, A. (R)	100.00
348	Johnson, R. (R)	70.00
349	Ramirez, M.	70.00

1997 TOPPS GALLERY

	NM Price
Complete Set (180)	$40.00
Commons	.05
Unlisted Stars	**.10-.40**
Pack (8)	4.00
Box (24)	70.00

Quality Rating ★★★
Peter Max artwork is an added bonus to collectors of Gallery baseball. Checklist is great.

#	Player	NM
4	Ripken, C.	3.00
5	Gwynn, T.	2.00
26	Maddux, G.	2.50
29	Sandberg, R.	1.00
37	McGwire, M.	1.50
41	Clemens, R.	1.50
42	Bonds, B.	1.00
73	Gonzalez, J.	2.00
79	Griffey, K.	4.00
82	Belle, A.	.75
90	Thomas, F.	4.00
109	Vaughn, M.	.75
111	Rodriguez, I.	.75
116	Ramirez, M.	.75
117	Lofton, K.	1.25
126	Bagwell, J.	1.50
133	Piazza, M.	2.50
137	Jones, C.	2.50
139	Nomo, H.	2.00
144	Guerrero, V.	2.00
146	Jones, A.	2.00
147	Erstad, D.	2.00
151	Garciaparra, N.	3.00
154	Rolen, S.	2.50
161	Jeter, D.	2.50

Players Private Issue

	Complete Set (180)	1800.00
	Private Issue	20x-30x

Gallery of Heroes

	Complete Set (10)	150.00
1	Jeter, D.	20.00
2	Jones, C.	20.00
3	Thomas, F.	30.00
4	Griffey, K.	35.00
5	Ripken, C.	30.00
6	McGwire, M.	15.00
7	Piazza, M.	20.00

#	Player	NM
8	Bagwell, J.	12.00
9	Gwynn, T.	18.00
10	Vaughn, M.	8.00

Peter Max Paintings

#	Player	NM
	Complete Set (10)	100.00
	Autographs	10x-20x
1	Jeter, D.	12.00
2	Belle, A.	8.00
3	Caminiti, K.	4.00
4	Jones, C.	12.00
5	Griffey, K.	25.00
6	Thomas, F.	20.00
7	Ripken, C.	18.00
8	McGwire, M.	10.00
9	Bonds, B.	6.00
10	Piazza, M.	12.00

Photo Gallery

#	Player	NM
	Complete Set (16)	160.00
	Commons	3.00
2	Molitor, P.	8.00
3	Murray, E.	8.00
4	Griffey, K.	35.00
5	Jones, C.	20.00
6	Jeter, D.	20.00
7	Thomas, F.	30.00
8	McGwire, M.	12.00
9	Lofton, K.	8.00
11	Piazza, M.	20.00

1997 TOPPS SCREEN PLAYS

	NM Price
Complete Set (20)	$125.00
Commons	3.00
Pack (1)	10.00
Box (21)	150.00

Quality Rating ★★★
The quality of Kodak is mixed with baseball cards. 26 different cards makes up one of the most unique sets to date.

#	Player	NM
1	Bagwell, J.	8.00
2	Belle, A.	5.00
3	Bonds, B.	5.00
5	Garciaparra, N.	12.00
6	Gonzalez, J.	10.00
7	Griffey, K.	20.00
8	Gwynn, T.	10.00
9	Jeter, D.	10.00
10	Johnson, R.	5.00
11	Jones, A.	10.00
12	Jones, C.	12.00
13	Lofton, K.	6.00
14	McGwire, M.	8.00
16	Nomo, H.	10.00
17	Ripken, C.	15.00
19	Thomas, F.	15.00

Private Screening

#	Player	NM
	Complete Set (6)	300.00
1	Griffey, K.	75.00
2	Jones, C.	50.00
3	Piazza, M.	50.00
4	Ripken, C.	60.00
5	Thomas, F.	65.00
6	Walker, L.	20.00

1997 TOPPS STADIUM CLUB

	NM Price
Complete Set (390)	$70.00
Series 1 Set (1-195)	35.00
Series 2 Set (196-390)	35.00
Commons	.05
Unlisted Stars	.10-.40
Series 1 or 2 Pack (9)	2.50
Series 1 or 2 Box (24)	50.00

Quality Rating ★★★
Checklist has fewer cards but that doesn't take away from another attractive TSC set.

#	Player	NM
1	Jones, C.	1.50
3	Lofton, K.	1.00
5	McGwire, M.	1.25
8	Ripken, C.	2.50
13	Bagwell, J.	1.00
15	Bonds, B.	.75
20	Gonzalez, J.	1.25
31	Piazza, M.	2.00
42	Vaughn, M.	.75
50	Griffey, K.	3.00
55	Jeter, D.	1.50
157	Garciaparra, N.	2.00
172	Rolen, S.	1.25
181	Jones, A. (2000)	5.00
182	Walker, T. (2000)	1.50
185	Guerrero, V. (2000)	4.00
187	Helton, T. (2000)	2.50
188	Garciaparra, N. (2000)	4.00
190	Branyan, R. (2000)	1.25
193	Rolen, S. (2000)	3.00
196	Maddux, G.	2.00
209	Clemens, R.	1.25
210	Guerrero, V.	1.00
212	Nomo, H.	1.50
213	Thomas, F.	3.00
219	Gwynn, T.	1.25
227	Belle, A.	.75
229	Sandberg, R.	.75
248	Erstad, D.	1.00
255	Jones, A.	1.00
376	Jones, C.	3.00
378	Thomas, F.	4.00
383	Piazza, M.	3.00
385	Griffey, K.	5.00
387	Gonzalez, J.	2.00

Co-Signers

#	Player	NM
	Complete Set (10)	700.00
	Series 1 Set (5)	350.00
	Series 2 Set (5)	350.00
	Commons	50.00
1	Pettitte/Jeter	150.00
4	Rolen/Jefferies	100.00
5	Hollandsworth/Kendall	50.00
7	Karros/Mondesi	70.00
8	Ordonez/Garciaparra	120.00
10	Gwynn/Garcia	100.00

Firebrand

#	Player	NM
	Complete Set (12)	150.00
	Commons	5.00
1	Bagwell, J.	15.00
2	Belle, A.	10.00
3	Bonds, B.	10.00
5	Griffey, K.	35.00
7	McGwire, M.	15.00
8	Jones, C.	20.00
9	Thomas, F.	30.00
10	Piazza, M.	20.00
11	Vaughn, M.	10.00
12	Gonzalez, J.	20.00

Instavision

#	Player	NM
	Complete Set (22)	90.00
	Series 1 Set (10)	40.00
	Series 2 Set (12)	50.00
	Commons	3.00
4	Clemens, R.	7.00
5	Bonds, B.	6.00
6	McGwire, M.	8.00
10	Nomo, H.	12.00
12	Gonzalez, J.	12.00
14	Belle, A.	10.00
17	Jeter, D.	15.00
21	Jones, A.	12.00

Millennium

#	Player	NM
	Complete Set (40)	225.00
	Commons	2.00
	Series 1 Set (20)	100.00
	Series 2 Set (20)	125.00
1	Jeter, D.	20.00
6	Jones, C.	20.00
21	Jones, A.	15.00
22	Walker, T.	10.00
36	Guerrero, V.	15.00
37	Garciaparra, N.	25.00
38	Rolen, S.	15.00

Patent Leather

#	Player	NM
	Complete Set (13)	120.00
	Commons	2.50
1	Rodriguez, I.	8.00
3	Bonds, B.	8.00
4	Griffey, K.	40.00
5	Maddux, G.	20.00
8	Lofton, K.	8.00
13	Jeter, D.	20.00

Pure Gold

#	Player	NM
	Complete Set (20)	450.00
	Series 1 Set (10)	200.00
	Series 2 Set (10)	250.00
	Commons	8.00
2	Belle, A.	15.00
4	Bonds, B.	20.00
6	Gwynn, T.	25.00
7	Jones, C.	35.00
8	McGwir e, M.	20.00
10	Thomas, F.	60.00
11	Gonzalez, J.	30.00
13	Lofton, K.	20.00
14	Bagwell, J.	25.00
15	Griffey, K.	70.00
16	Ripken, C.	60.00
17	Vaughn, M.	15.00
18	Piazza, M.	35.00
19	Jeter, D.	35.00

TSC Matrix

#	Player	NM
	Complete Set (120)	500.00
	Series 1 Set (60)	250.00
	Series 2 Set (60)	250.00
	Commons	2.00
1	Jones, C.	20.00
3	Lofton, K.	8.00
5	McGwire, M.	10.00
8	Ripken, C.	30.00
13	Bagwell, J.	12.00
15	Bonds, B.	8.00
20	Gonzalez, J.	15.00
31	Piazza, M.	25.00
42	Vaughn, M.	8.00
50	Griffey, K.	40.00
55	Jeter, D.	20.00
196	Maddux, G.	25.00
210	Guerrero, V.	12.00
212	Nomo, H.	15.00
213	Thomas, F.	30.00
219	Gwynn, T.	15.00
227	Belle, A.	10.00
229	Sandberg, R.	10.00
244	Ramirez, M.	8.00
248	Erstad, D.	12.00
255	Jones, A.	25.00

1997 TOPPS STARS

	NM Price
Complete Set (125)	$40.00
Commons	.10
Unlisted Stars	**.20-.50**
Always Mint	8x-15x
Pack (7)	3.00
Box (24)	60.00

Quality Rating ★★★★
This set has great veteran names and young stars like Kris Benson ans Travis Lee.

#	Player	NM
3	Ripken, C.	2.50
4	Griffey, K.	3.00
5	Jones, C.	2.00
7	Piazza, M.	2.00
8	Bagwell, J.	1.25
11	Gwynn, T.	1.50
13	Thomas, F.	2.50
17	Maddux, G.	2.00
27	Vaughn, M.	.75
37	Gonzalez, J.	1.50
39	Belle, A.	.75
42	Bonds, B.	.75
50	Clemens, R.	1.25
51	McGwire, M.	1.25
59	Sandberg, R.	1.00
64	Lofton, K.	1.00
71	Nomo, H.	1.50

#	Player	NM
93	Garciaparra, N.	2.50
103	Benson, K. (R)	2.00
105	Konerko, P.	1.50
106	Lee, T. (R)	10.00
108	Kotsay, M. (R)	3.00
110	Wood, K. (R)	3.00
115	Wells, V. (R)	2.00
119	Werth, J.(R)	1.50
121	Cameron, T. (R)	1.50
122	Davis, J.J. (R)	1.50
125	Berkman, L. (R)	3.00

All-Stars

#	Player	NM
	Complete Set (20)	275.00
	Commons	5.00
1	Maddux, G.	35.00
2	Johnson, R.	10.00
4	Bagwell, J.	20.00
6	Piazza, M.	35.00
7	Ripken, C.	45.00
9	Gwynn, T.	25.00
15	Bonds, B.	12.00
16	Griffey, K.	60.00

All-Star Game Memories

#	Player	NM
	Complete Set (10)	70.00
	Commons	2.00
1	Ripken, C.	20.00
3	Piazza, M.	12.00
5	Griffey, K.	25.00
8	Nomo, H.	10.00

Future All-Stars

#	Player	NM
	Complete Set (15)	50.00
	Commons	2.00
1	Jeter, D.	10.00
2	Jones, A.	7.00
3	Guerrero, V.	7.00
4	Rolen, S.	7.00
6	Cruz, J. Jr.	20.00
7	Erstad, D.	6.00
15	Irabu, H.	4.00

Rookie Reprints

#	Player	NM
	Complete Set (15)	35.00
	Commons	3.00
7	Kaline, A.	5.00
9	Mathews, E.	5.00
13	Robinson, B.	5.00

Rookie Reprints Autographs

#	Player	NM
	Complete Set (14)	300.00
	Commons	20.00
7	Kaline, A.	50.00
9	Mathews, E.	40.00
13	Robinson, B.	50.00

1997 TOTALLY CERTIFIED BASEBALL

	NM Price
Complete Set (150)	$450.00
Commons	2.00
Unlisted Stars	**2.50-3.00**
Blue	2x
Gold	40x-60x
Pack (3)	10.00
Box (20)	150.00

Quality Rating ★★★★
Another set with an extremely limited print run. There are three different version, Platinum Red, Platinum Blue, and Platinum Gold.

#	Player	NM
1	Bonds, B.	6.00
2	Vaughn, M.	6.00
4	Sandberg, R.	6.00

#	Player	NM
5	Bagwell, J.	10.00
17	Belle, A.	6.00
22	Rodriguez, A.	20.00
26	Piazza, M.	20.00
28	Ripken, C.	25.00
31	Erstad, D.	8.00
39	Clemens, R.	10.00
41	Thomas, F.	20.00
45	Gwynn, T.	12.00
49	McGwire, M.	10.00
51	Jeter, D.	12.00
53	Griffey, K.	25.00
58	Lofton, K.	6.00
59	Jones, C.	15.00
63	Nomo, H.	15.00
68	Ramirez, M.	4.00
69	Gonzalez, J.	12.00
79	Rodriguez, I.	6.00
83	Maddux, G.	15.00
106	Jones, A.	10.00
111	Guerrero, V.	10.00
112	Rolen, S.	10.00
114	Garciaparra, N.	15.00
129	Irabu, H. (R)	8.00
136	Griffey, K.	20.00
137	Guerrero, V.	5.00
138	Clemens, R.	5.00
139	McGwire, M.	5.00
140	Belle, A.	6.00
141	Jeter, D.	8.00
142	Gonzalez, J.	6.00
143	Maddux, G.	10.00
144	Rodriguez, A.	10.00
145	Bagwell, J.	5.00
146	Ripken, C.	12.00
147	Gwynn, T.	6.00
148	Thomas, F.	15.00
149	Nomo, H.	5.00
150	Jones, A.	8.00

1997 UPPER DECK

	NM Price
Complete Set (520)	$170.00
Series 1 Set (1-240)	30.00
Update Set (241-270)	40.00
Series 2 Set (271-520)	100.00
Commons	.05
Unlisted Stars	**.10-.40**
Series 1 or 2 Pack (12)	2.50
Series 1 or 2 Box (28)	60.00

Quality Rating ★★★
Great looking cards! Design, inserts, and collectibility make Upper Deck a winning set.

#	Player	NM
10	Jones, C.	2.00
20	Ripken, C.	2.50
25	Vaughn, M.	.60
26	Clemens, R.	1.25
40	Thomas, F.	3.00
50	Belle, A.	.75
52	Lofton, K.	1.00
65	Maddux, G.	1.00
83	Bagwell, J.	1.00
94	Nomo, H.	1.50
95	Piazza, M.	2.00
105	Puckett, K.	1.00
137	Maddux, G.	1.00
147	Ripken, C.	1.25
150	Griffey, K.	1.50
175	Griffey, K.	3.00
196	Jones, A.	1.25
229	Rolen, S.	1.50
230	Erstad, D.	1.50
234	Garciaparra, N.	2.00
240	Jones, A.	1.50
246	Jones, C.	5.00

#	Player	NM
247	Gonzalez, J.	5.00
260	Maddux, G.	5.00
262	Jones, A.	4.00
263	Maddux, G.	5.00
271	Guerrero, V.	1.50
302	Maddux, G.	2.00
325	Sandberg, R.	.75
385	Griffey, K.	1.50
414	Puckett, K.	1.00
415	Jones, A.	7.00
416	Jones, C.	6.00
417	Vaughn, M.	3.00
418	Thomas, F.	10.00
419	Belle, A.	3.00
420	McGwire, M.	5.00
421	Jeter, D.	7.00
422	Rodriguez, A.	8.00
423	Gonzalez, J.	5.00
424	Griffey, K.	12.00
440	Jeter, D.	2.00
450	McGwire, M.	1.25
492	Gwynn, T.	1.25
500	Rodriguez, A.	2.50
510	Gonzalez, J.	1.25
520	Clemens, R.	1.25
525	Lofton, K. (Trade)	1.00
542	Guillen, J. (Trade)	1.00
547	Cruz, J. (Trade)	10.00
550	Irabu, H. (Trade)	2.00

Robinson Tribute
Complete Set (9) 8.00

Amazing Greats

Complete Set (20)		600.00
Commons		15.00
1	Griffey, K.	90.00
2	Alomar, R.	20.00
3	Rodriguez, A.	70.00
5	Jones, C.	50.00
6	Gwynn, T.	40.00
7	Lofton, K.	25.00
8	Belle, A.	25.00
10	Thomas, F.	80.00
11	Maddux, G.	50.00
13	Puckett, K.	25.00
14	Bagwell, J.	35.00
15	Ripken, C.	65.00
16	Ramirez, M.	20.00
17	Bonds, B.	25.00
18	Vaughn, M.	25.00
20	Piazza, M.	60.00

Blue Chip Prospects

Complete Set (20)		550.00
Commons		10.00
1	Jones, A.	70.00
2	Jeter, D.	80.00
3	Rolen, S.	70.00
4	Ramirez, M.	25.00
7	Garciaparra, N.	80.00
8	Erstad, D.	50.00
10	Guerrero, V.	60.00
15	Jones, C.	90.00
20	Rodriguez, A.	90.00

Game Jersey

Complete Set (3)		800.00
1	Griffey, K.	600.00
2	Gwynn, T.	250.00
3	Ordonez, R.	100.00

Hot Commodities

Complete Set (20)		100.00
Unlisted Stars		3.00
1	Rodriguez, A.	10.00
2	Jones, A.	8.00
3	Jeter, D.	8.00
4	Thomas, F.	12.00
5	Griffey, K.	15.00
6	Jones, C.	8.00
7	Gonzalez, J.	6.00
8	Ripken, C.	12.00
10	McGwire, M.	6.00
12	Belle, A.	4.00
13	Piazza, M.	8.00
16	Gwynn, T.	6.00
17	Guerrero, V.	5.00
18	Nomo, H.	7.00
19	Maddux, G.	8.00
20	Puckett, K.	6.00

Long Distance Connection

Complete Set (20)		200.00
Commons		6.00
1	McGwire, M.	12.00
3	Griffey, K.	35.00
4	Belle, A.	8.00
5	Gonzalez, J.	15.00

8	Vaughn, M.	8.00
9	Bonds, B.	8.00
12	Thomas, F.	30.00
15	Rodriguez, A.	25.00
16	Piazza, M.	20.00
18	Jones, C.	20.00
20	Jones, A.	15.00

Memorable Moments

Complete Set (10)		20.00
Commons		.75
1	Jones, A.	2.00
2	Jones, C.	2.00
3	Ripken, C.	3.00
4	Thomas, F.	4.00
6	Piazza, M.	2.00
7	McGwire, M.	1.50
9	Griffey, K.	4.00
10	Rodriguez, A.	3.00

Power Package

Complete Set (20)		120.00
Commons		3.00
1	Griffey, K.	25.00
7	Bagwell, J.	8.00
8	Belle, A.	6.00
10	McGwire, M.	10.00
14	Ramirez, M.	6.00
15	Piazza, M.	15.00
16	Bonds, B.	6.00
17	Vaughn, M.	6.00
19	Gonzalez, J.	12.00
20	Thomas, F.	25.00

Predictor

Complete Set (30)		35.00
Commons		.50
Unlisted Stars		.75-1.50
1	Jones, A.	3.00
2	Jones, C.	3.00
3	Maddux, G. (W)	3.00
7	Ripken, C. (W)	4.00
10	Belle, A. (W)	1.50
11	Thomas, F.	5.00
18	Piazza, M. (W)	3.00
19	Jeter, D.	3.00
26	Griffey, K. (W)	5.00
27	Rodriguez, A. (W)	4.00
28	Gonzalez, J. (W)	3.00

Rock Solid Foundation

Complete Set (20)		45.00
Commons		1.00
1	Rodriguez, A.	10.00
3	Jeter, D.	8.00
4	Erstad, D.	6.00
5	Jones, C.	8.00
10	Ramirez, M.	3.00
11	Rodriguez, I.	3.00

Run Producers

Complete Set (24)		325.00
Commons		8.00
1	Griffey, K.	55.00
2	Bonds, B.	12.00
3	Belle, A.	12.00
4	McGwire, M.	20.00
5	Thomas, F.	50.00
6	Gonzalez, J.	25.00
10	Rodriguez, A.	50.00
15	Piazza, M.	35.00
17	Lofton, K.	12.00
18	Vaughn, M.	12.00
20	Jones, C.	35.00
23	Bagwell, J.	20.00

Ticket to Stardom

Complete Set (20)		125.00
Commons		2.00
1	Jones, C.	20.00
5	Jeter, D.	20.00
9	Erstad, D.	15.00
10	Rodriguez, A.	30.00
14	Jones, A.	25.00

1997 UPPER DECK SP

	NM Price
Complete Set (184)	$50.00
Commons	.10
Unlisted Stars	**.20-.50**
Pack (8)	4.50
Box (30)	100.00

Quality Rating ★★★
Collectors have the chance at autographed vintage SP cards, and several of these cards are extremely difficult to find.

#	Player	NM
1	Jones, A.	2.00
3	Garciaparra, N.	2.50
10	Guerrero, V.	2.00
15	Cruz, J. (R)	10.00
17	Erstad, D.	2.00
23	Maddux, G.	2.50
24	Lofton, K.	1.25
25	Jones, C.	2.50
34	Ripken, C.	3.00
35	Vaughn, M.	2.00
43	Sandberg, R.	1.00
45	Belle, A.	1.00
50	Thomas, F.	4.00
60	Ramirez, M.	1.00
85	Bagwell, J.	1.50
92	Nomo, H.	2.00
95	Piazza, M.	2.50
125	Jeter, D.	2.50
128	Pettitte, A.	1.00
130	McGwire, M.	1.50
135	Rolen, S.	2.00
155	Gwynn, T.	2.00
160	Bonds, B.	1.00
165	Griffey, K.	4.00
166	Rodriguez, A.	3.00
175	Gonzalez, J.	2.00
180	Clemens, R.	1.50
184	Irabu, H. (R)	2.00

SP Vintage Autographs

Commons		20.00

Player Name (Year/# Signed)

Bagwell, J. ('95/173)	200.00
Bagwell, J. ('96/292)	150.00
Bagwell, J. ('96/MM23)	400.00
Buhner, J. ('95/57)	80.00
Buhner, J. ('96/79)	80.00
Buhner, J. ('96/FX27)	150.00
Griffey, K. ('93/16)	2300.00
Griffey, K. ('94/103)	900.00
Griffey, K. ('95/38)	1200.00
Griffey, K. ('96/312)	400.00
Gwynn, T. ('93/17)	700.00
Gwynn, T. ('94/367)	175.00
Gwynn, T. ('94/HV31)	400.00
Gwynn, T. ('95/64)	350.00
Gwynn, T. ('96/20)	500.00
Jones, C. ('93/94)	400.00
Jones, C. ('95/60)	350.00
Jones, C. ('96/102)	300.00
Rodriguez, A. ('94/94)	400.00
Rodriguez, A. ('95/63)	450.00
Rodriguez, A. ('96/73)	450.00
Sheffield, G. ('94/130)	100.00
Sheffield, G. ('95/221)	75.00
Sheffield, G. ('96/58)	125.00
Vaughn, M. ('97/250)	75.00

Baseball Heroes

Complete Set (10)	275.00
Common Griffey	30.00

Die-Cut Special F/X

Complete Set (48)		300.00
Commons		2.00
Unlisted Stars		3.00-5.00
1	Griffey, K.	25.00
2	Thomas, F.	20.00
4	Belle, A.	8.00
5	Piazza, M.	12.00
6	Maddux, G.	12.00
7	Jones, C.	12.00
8	Ripken, C.	20.00
9	Bagwell, J.	10.00
10	Rodriguez, A.	20.00
11	McGwire, M.	12.00
13	Gonzalez, J.	12.00
16	Jeter, D.	15.00

#	Player	NM
17	Gwynn, T.	15.00
24	Clemens, R.	10.00
27	Nomo, H.	12.00
42	Erstad, D.	10.00
45	Jones, A.	12.00
46	Rolen, S.	10.00
47	Guerrero, V.	12.00
49	Rodriguez, A. (1996)	25.00

Game Film
	Complete Set (10)	1000.00
1	Rodriguez, A.	150.00
2	Thomas, F.	150.00
3	Jones, A.	100.00
4	Ripken, D.	125.00
5	Piazza, M.	100.00
6	Jeter, D.	100.00
7	McGwire, M.	70.00
8	Jones, C.	100.00
9	Bonds, B.	40.00
10	Griffey, K.	175.00

Inside Info
	Complete Set (25)	325.00
	Commons	4.00
1	Griffey, K.	35.00
2	McGwire, M.	15.00
3	Lofton, K.	6.00
5	Thomas, F.	30.00
6	Maddux, G.	20.00
7	Vaughn, M.	6.00
8	Ripken, C.	25.00
9	Bagwell, J.	15.00
10	Rodriguez, A.	25.00
14	Guerrero, V.	12.00
15	Belle, A.	10.00
16	Piazza, M.	20.00
17	Jeter, D.	20.00
18	Rolen, S.	15.00
19	Gwynn, T.	20.00
20	Bonds, B.	8.00
22	Jones, C.	20.00
23	Gonzalez, J.	20.00
24	Clemens, R.	10.00
25	Jones, A.	20.00

Marquee Matchups
	Complete Set (20)	60.00
	Commons	1.00
	Unlisted Stars	2.00
1	Griffey, K.	10.00
3	Bonds, B.	3.00
4	McGwire/Canseco	4.00
5	Piazza, M.	6.00
7	Gwynn, T.	5.00
8	Rodriguez/Caminiti	7.00
9	Jones, C.	6.00
10	Jeter/Jones, A.	6.00
12	Bagwell/Williams	4.00
13	Maddux, G.	7.00
14	Ripken/Anderson	7.00
19	Thomas, F.	8.00

SPX Force
	Complete Set (10)	1000.00
1	Griffey/Buhner/Galarraga/Bichette	150.00
2	Belle/Anderson/McGwire/Fielder	70.00
3	Vaughn/Caminiti/Thomas/Bagwell	150.00
4	Sheffield/Sosa/Bonds/Canseco	50.00
5	Maddux/Clemens/Smoltz/Johnson	125.00
6	Rodriguez/Jeter/Jones/Ordonez	150.00
7	Hollandsworth/Piazza/Modesi/Nomo	85.00
8	Gonzalez/Ramirez/Alomar/Rodriguez	85.00
9	Gwynn/Boggs/Murray/Molitor	85.00
10	Jones/Guerrero/Walker/Rolen	125.00

SPX Force Autographs
	Complete Set (10)	3000.00
	Commons	125.00
1	Griffey, K.	1000.00
2	Belle, A.	175.00
3	Vaughn, M.	175.00
4	Sheffield, G.	150.00
5	Maddux, G.	500.00
6	Rodriguez, A.	600.00
8	Alomar, R.	150.00
9	Gwynn, T.	400.00
10	Jones, A.	300.00

1997 UPPER DECK SPX

		NM Price
	Complete Set (50)	$70.00
	Commons	1.00
	Unlisted Stars	**1.50-2.00**
	Bronze	1x
	Silver	2x
	Steel	2x
	Gold	5x-10x
	Grand Final	15x-30x
	Pack (3)	6.00
	Box (18)	100.00

Quality Rating ★★★★
Five different parallel sets add to the chase. "Bound for Glory" inserts are limited to 1,500 made and include names like Sheffield, Griffey, and Bagwell.

#	Player	NM
2	Erstad, D.	2.50
4	Jones, A.	4.00
5	Jones, C.	5.00
7	Lofton, K.	2.50
8	Maddux, G.	5.00
12	Ripken, C.	6.00
13	Garciaparra, N.	6.00
15	Sandberg, R.	2.00
17	Thomas, F.	6.00
18	Belle, A.	2.00
27	Bagwell, J.	2.50
29	Nomo, H.	4.00
30	Piazza, M.	5.00
33	Guerrero, V.	4.00
36	Jeter, D.	5.00
38	McGwire, M.	3.00
39	Rolen, S.	4.00
42	Gwynn, T.	4.00
43	Bonds, B.	2.00
45	Griffey, K.	8.00
46	Rodriguez, A.	6.00
47	Cruz, J. (R)	12.00
48	Gonzalez, J.	3.00
50	Clemens, R.	3.00

Bound for Glory
	Complete Set (20)	400.00
	Commons	8.00
1	Jones, A.	30.00
2	Jones, C.	30.00
3	Maddux, G.	30.00
5	Ripken, C.	40.00
7	Thomas, F.	50.00
8	Belle, A.	15.00
11	Bagwell, J.	20.00
12	Piazza, M.	35.00
13	Jeter, D.	35.00
14	McGwire, M.	25.00
15	Gwynn, T.	25.00
18	Rodriguez, A.	40.00
19	Griffey, K.	60.00
20	Gonzalez, J.	25.00

Supreme Signatures
	Complete Set (5)	1000.00
	Bagwell, J.	200.00
	Griffey, K.	500.00
	Jones, A.	200.00
	Rodriguez, A.	350.00
	Shefield, G.	100.00

Cornerstones of the Game
	Complete Set (10)	600.00
1	Griffey/Bonds	125.00
2	Thomas/Belle	100.00
3	Jones/Maddux	70.00
4	Gwynn/Molitor	40.00
5	Jones/Guerrero	50.00
6	Bagwell/Sandberg	40.00
7	Piazza/Rodriguez	60.00
8	Ripken/Murray	90.00
9	Vaughn/McGwire	40.00
10	Rodriguez/Jeter	80.00

1997 UPPER DECK UD3

		NM Price
	Complete Set (60)	$50.00
	Commons	.40
	Unlisted Stars	**.50-.75**
	Pack (3)	4.00
	Box (24)	75.00

Quality Rating ★★★
With only 60 cards, UD3 is easier to collect but still has a $50 price tag. Player selection is quite good. "Generation Next" and Marquee Attraction" inserts are well designed and fun to chase.

#	Player	NM
1	McGwire, M.	2.00
3	Griffey, K.	5.00
4	Belle, A.	1.50
6	Gonzalez, J.	2.50
8	Vaughn, M.	1.50
9	Bonds, B.	1.50
16	Thomas, F.	5.00
18	Piazza, M.	3.00
21	Clemens, R.	2.00
25	Ripken, C.	4.00
27	Nomo, H.	3.00
31	Maddux, G.	3.00
35	Gwynn, T.	2.50
37	Lofton, K.	1.50
38	Bagwell, J.	2.00
40	Puckett, K.	2.00
41	Jones, A.	3.00
42	Guerrero, V.	3.00
45	Erstad, D.	2.00
46	Garciaparra, N.	4.00
50	Rodriguez, A.	4.00
55	Jeter, D.	3.00
58	Rolen, S.	3.00
60	Jones, C.	3.00

Generation Next
	Complete Set (20)	125.00
	Commons	2.00
1	Rodriguez, A.	20.00
2	Guerrero, V.	12.00
5	Jones, A.	15.00
6	Erstad, D.	10.00
10	Jones, C.	15.00
15	Jeter, D.	15.00
18	Garciaparra, N.	20.00
19	Rolen, S.	15.00

Marquee Attraction
	Complete Set (10)	500.00
1	Griffey, K.	120.00
2	McGwire, M.	50.00
3	Gonzalez, J.	50.00
4	Bonds, B.	30.00
5	Thomas, F.	90.00
6	Belle, A.	30.00
7	Piazza, M.	50.00
8	Ripken, C.	90.00
9	Vaughn, M.	30.00
10	Rodriguez, A.	90.00

Superb Signatures
	Complete Set (4)	900.00
No#	Griffey, K.	600.00
No#	Guerrero, V.	150.00
No#	Jeter, D.	250.00
No#	Caminiti, K.	90.00

1997 U.D. COLLECTOR'S CHOICE

		NM Price
	Complete Set (506)	$35.00
	Series 1 Set (246)	18.00
	Series 2 Set (260)	18.00
	Commons	.05
	Unlisted Stars	**.10-.40**
	Series 1 or 2 Pack (12)	1.00
	Series 1 or 2 Box (36)	30.00

Quality Rating ★★★
Collector's Choice has alot to offer. A simple but attractive design makes for fun collecting. Several insert set are very affordable and fun to collect.

#	Player	NM
1	Jones, A.	1.50
5	Erstad, D.	1.00
10	Guerrero, V.	1.00
15	Rolen, S.	.75
25	Garciaparra, N.	1.50
41	Ripken, C.	2.00
55	Robinson, J.	.75
56	Gwynn/Rodriguez	.75
76	Belle, A.	.75
125	Bagwell, J.	.75
141	Nomo, H.	1.00
180	Jeter, D.	1.25
190	McGwire, M.	1.00
210	Gwynn, T.	1.00
225	Bonds, B.	.75
230	Griffey, K.	2.50
235	Rodriguez, A.	2.00
240	Gonzalez, J.	1.00
244-246	Griffey, K. (CL)	.75
247-249	Griffey, K. (CL)	.75
264	Lofton, K.	.75
266	Maddux, G.	1.50
270	Jones, C.	1.50
300	Thomas, F.	2.50
325	Jones, A.	.75
326	Jones, C.	.75
328	Thomas, F.	1.50
331	Jeter, D.	.75
332	Rodriguez, A.	1.50
334	Griffey, K.	1.50
365	Piazza, M.	1.50
500	Clemens, R.	.75

All-Star Connection
	Complete Set (45)	40.00
	Commons	.50
	Unlisted Stars	1.00
1	McGwire, M.	1.50
4	Rodriguez, A.	4.00
5	Griffey, K.	5.00
7	Belle, A.	1.00
10	Thomas, F.	5.00
13	Ripken, C.	4.00
14	Gonzalez, J.	2.00
19	Bagwell, J.	1.50
23	Gwynn, T.	2.00
26	Piazza, M.	2.50
30	Jones, C.	2.50
36	Maddux, G.	2.50
40	Jeter, D.	2.50

Big Shots
	Complete Set (20)	50.00
	Commons	1.00
	Gold Signature	10x
1	Griffey, K.	8.00
2	Garciaparra, N.	3.00
4	Rolen, S.	3.00
5	Rodriguez, A.	6.00
8	Ripken, C.	6.00
10	Thomas, F.	8.00
13	Jeter, D.	4.00
14	Clemens, R.	2.50
15	Jones, C.	4.00
18	Piazza, M.	4.00
19	Gwynn, T.	4.00
20	Bonds, B.	2.00

Clearly Dominant
	Complete Set (5)	100.00

New Frontier
	Complete Set (40)	400.00
	Commons	5.00
1	Rodriguez, A.	40.00

#	Player	Price
2	Gwynn, T.	20.00
4	Nomo, H.	15.00
5	McGwire, M.	12.00
6	Bonds, B.	8.00
7	Gonzalez, J.	18.00
10	Piazza, M.	25.00
11	Griffey, K.	50.00
15	Thomas, F.	40.00
17	Clemens, R.	10.00
18	Jones, A.	30.00
25	Belle, A.	12.00
26	Bagwell, J.	15.00
29	Jeter, D.	25.00
30	Jones, C.	25.00
31	Vaughn, M.	8.00
34	Guerrero, V.	20.00
35	Ripken, C.	40.00
36	Maddux, G.	25.00
40	Rolen, S.	20.00

Premier Power

Complete Set (20)		50.00
Commons		1.50
Gold Version		4x
1	McGwire, M.	4.00
3	Griffey, K.	12.00
4	Belle, A.	3.00
5	Gonzalez, J.	5.00
8	Vaughn, M.	3.00
9	Bonds, B.	3.00
12	Thomas, F.	10.00
18	Rodriguez, A.	8.00
19	Piazza, M.	6.00

Stick'Ums

Complete Set (30)		15.00
Commons		.25
Unlisted Stars		.50-3.00

The Big Show

Complete Set (45)		20.00
Commons		.10
Unlisted Stars		.20-2.00

Toast of the Town

Complete Set (30)		175.00
Commons		4.00
1	Jones, A.	15.00
2	Jones, C.	10.00
3	Maddux, G.	10.00
5	Lofton, K.	8.00
7	Ripken, C.	15.00
8	Vaughn, M.	6.00
10	Belle, A.	6.00
11	Thomas, F.	15.00
14	Bagwell, J.	8.00
15	Piazza, M.	10.00
17	Guerrero, V.	8.00
19	Jeter, D.	10.00
22	McGwire, M.	8.00
23	Rolen, S.	8.00
25	Gwynn, T.	8.00
26	Bonds, B.	6.00
27	Griffey, K.	20.00
28	Rodriguez, A.	15.00
29	Gonzalez, J.	8.00
30	Clemens, R.	7.00

Update Set

Complete Set (30)		5.00
Commons		.05
20	Irabu, H.	1.00
27	Cruz Jr., J.	3.50

You Crash the Game

Complete Set (90)		50.00
Commons		.20
Unlisted Stars		.50-1.50
3A	Jones, A. (W)	3.00
6A	Ripken, C. (W)	4.00
6B	Ripken, C. (W)	4.00
6C	Ripken, C.	2.00
10A	Thomas, F.	3.00
10B	Thomas, F.	3.00
10C	Thomas, F. (W)	4.00
20B	Piazza, M.	2.50
20C	Piazza, M. (W)	2.50
24C	McGwire, M. (W)	2.00
28A	Griffey, K. (W)	5.00
28B	Griffey, K.	2.50
28C	Griffey, K. (W)	5.00
29A	Rodriguez, A.	2.00
29B	Rodriguez, A.	2.00
29C	Rodriguez, A.	2.00
30A	Gonzalez, J. (W)	2.00
30C	Gonzalez, J. (W)	2.00

1997 ZENITH

	NM Price
Complete Set (50)	$45.00
Commons	.20
Unlisted Stars	**.25-.75**
Pack (5 cards/2 8x10)	10.00
Box (12)	100.00

Quality Rating ★★★
Zenith follows in line with Studio and includes a larger pack with 8x10s.

#	Player	NM
1	Thomas, F.	4.00
2	Gwynn, T.	2.00
3	Bagwell, J.	1.50
6	Piazza, M.	2.50
7	Belle, A.	1.25
8	Maddux, G.	2.50
12	Jones, C.	2.50
13	Gonzalez, J.	2.00
14	Bonds, B.	1.25
17	Jeter, D.	2.50
18	Nomo, H.	2.00
19	Clemens, R.	1.50
20	Griffey, K.	5.00
22	Rodriguez, A.	4.00
28	McGwire, M.	2.00
35	Ripken, C.	4.00
36	Erstad, D.	2.00
37	Lofton, K.	1.25
42	Sandberg, R.	1.25
43	Jones, A.	2.00
44	Garciaparra, N.	4.00
45	Irabu, H. (R)	2.00
47	Cruz, J. (R)	10.00
48	Guerrero, V.	2.50
49	Rolen, S.	3.00

8 x 10

Complete Set (24)		60.00
Commons		2.00
Dufex		1.5x
1	Thomas, F.	7.00
2	Gwynn, T.	4.00
3	Bagwell, J.	3.00
4	Griffey, K.	8.00
5	Piazza, M.	5.00
6	Maddux, G.	5.00
8	Belle, A.	2.00
11	McGwire, M.	4.00
12	Clemens, R.	4.00
13	Rodriguez, A.	7.00
14	Jones, C.	5.00
15	Gonzalez, J.	4.00
16	Bonds, B.	2.00
17	Jeter, D.	5.00
18	Nomo, H.	4.00
19	Ripken, C.	8.00
20	Irabu, H.	3.00
21	Jones, A.	5.00
22	Garciaparra, N.	7.00
23	Guerrero, V.	5.00
24	Rolen, S.	5.00

8 x 10 V-2

Complete Set (8)		500.00
1	Griffey, K.	90.00
2	Jones, A.	40.00
3	Thomas, F.	70.00
4	Piazza, M.	50.00
5	Rodriguez, A.	60.00
6	Ripken, C.	70.00
7	Jeter, D.	50.00
8	Guerrero, V.	30.00

Z-Team

Complete Set (9)		600.00
1	Griffey, K.	125.00
2	Walker, L.	25.00
3	Thomas, F.	100.00
4	Rodriguez, A.	90.00
5	Piazza, M.	75.00
6	Ripken, C.	100.00
7	Jeter, D.	65.00
8	Jones, A.	50.00
9	Clemens, R.	50.00

1998 DONRUSS

	NM Price
Complete Set (170)	$18.00
Commons	.05
Unlisted Stars	**.10-.40**
Pack (10)	2.00
Box (24)	42.00

Quality Rating ★★★
Base cards are well designed and feature a ton of stats on the back. Diamond Kings look great this year.

#	Player	NM
2	Gonzalez, J.	1.25
12	Thomas, F.	2.50
16	Lofton, K.	.75
21	Jones, C.	1.50
22	Gwynn, T.	1.25
23	Clemens, R.	1.25
26	Bagwell, J.	1.00
28	Griffey, K.	3.00
31	Piazza, M.	1.50
34	Rodriguez, A.	2.50
35	Maddux, G.	1.50
36	Belle, A.	.75
37	Bonds, B.	.75
38	Vaughn, M.	.60
57	Garciaparra, N.	1.50
61	Ripken, C.	1.50
62	McGwire, M.	1.00
67	Erstad, D.	.60
81	Wright, J.	1.00
85	Rolen, S.	1.00
100	Jeter, D.	1.50
103	Nomo, H.	1.25
104	Jones, A.	1.00
115	Cruz, J.	2.50
131	Ramirez, M.	.75
140	Guerrero, V.	1.00
144	Grieve, B.	1.00
156	Griffey, K.	1.50
157	Thomas, F.	1.25
158	Jones, C.	.75
159	Piazza, M.	.75
160	Ripken, C.	1.25
161	Maddux, G.	.75
162	Gonzalez, J.	.60
163	Rodriguez, A.	1.00
164	McGwire, M.	.60
165	Jeter, D.	.75
167	Gwynn, T. (CL)	.60
169	Rolen, S. (CL)	.50
170	Garciaparra, N. (CL)	.75

Crusade Green

Commons		10.00
Purple		1.5x
Red		5x
6	Greene, T.	15.00
7	Alomar, R.	40.00
8	Ripken, C.	200.00
12	Vaughn, M.	50.00
13	Garciaparra, N.	125.00
16	Cameron, M.	20.00
21	Justice, D.	30.00
25	Thompson, J.	25.00

#	Player	Price
33	Martinez, T.	35.00
36	Irabu, H.	25.00
37	Canseco, J.	25.00
39	Griffey, K.	250.00
42	Martinez, E.	25.00
45	Clark, W.	25.00
47	Greer, R.	15.00
51	Cruz, J. Jr.	125.00
52	Lofton, K.	50.00
53	Jones, C.	125.00
65	Sanders, D.	20.00
67	Walker, L.	50.00
68	Bichette, D.	15.00
71	Helton, T.	50.00
78	Biggio, C.	25.00
85	Martinez, P.	30.00
88	Rolen, S.	100.00
90	Guillen, J.	35.00
93	McGwire, M.	100.00

Gold Press Proofs

Complete Set (170)		2000.00
Singles		8x-12x

Silver Press Proofs

Complete Set (170)		750.00
Singles		3x-5x

Diamond Kings

Complete Set (20)		225.00
Commons		5.00
Canvas		3x-5x
1	Ripken, C.	30.00
2	Maddux, G.	20.00
3	Rodriguez, I.	8.00
4	Gwynn, T.	15.00
6	Lofton, K.	10.00
8	Erstad, D.	10.00
9	Johnson, R.	8.00
10	Jeter, D.	20.00
11	Nomo, H.	15.00
14	Clemens, R.	12.00
16	Jones, A.	10.00
17	Piazza, M.	20.00
18	Thomas, F.	35.00
19	Rodriguez, A.	30.00
20	Griffey, K.	40.00

Longball Leaders

Complete Set (24)		175.00
Commons		3.00
1	Griffey, K.	35.00
2	McGwire, M.	10.00
4	Bonds, B.	7.00
5	Thomas, F.	25.00
6	Belle, A.	6.00
7	Piazza, M.	18.00
8	Jones, C.	18.00
9	Guerrero, V.	8.00
14	Bagwell, J.	10.00
15	Vaughn, M.	7.00
16	Ramirez, M.	6.00
20	Garciaparra, N.	18.00
21	Gonzalez, J.	18.00
22	Rolen, S.	10.00

Production Line

On Base Commons		15.00
1	Thomas, F.	125.00
3	Bonds, B.	40.00
5	Piazza, M.	90.00
6	Bagwell, J.	50.00
8	Vaughn, M.	30.00
10	Lofton, K.	35.00
11	Gwynn, T.	70.00
15	McGwire, M.	70.00
18	Griffey, K.	200.00
19	Jones, C.	100.00
20	Jeter, D.	90.00
	Power Index Commons	10.00
2	Piazza, M.	50.00
3	Thomas, F.	75.00
4	McGwire, M.	45.00
5	Bonds, B.	20.00
6	Griffey, K.	100.00
7	Bagwell, J.	35.00
10	Vaughn, M.	20.00
11	Gwynn, T.	40.00
12	Ramirez, M.	20.00
16	Jones, C.	40.00
17	Rolen, S.	35.00
18	Rodriguez, A.	70.00
19	Guerrero, V.	25.00
20	Belle, A.	20.00
	Slugging Commons	12.00
2	Griffey, K.	150.00
3	McGwire, M.	50.00
4	Piazza, M.	75.00
5	Thomas, F.	100.00

#	Player	NM
6	Bagwell, J.	50.00
7	Gonzalez, J.	60.00
9	Bonds, B.	35.00
12	Vaughn, M.	30.00
14	Ramirez, M.	30.00
15	Garciaparra, N.	70.00
18	Cruz, J.	90.00
19	Rodriguez, A.	100.00
20	Ripken, C.	125.00

Rated Rookies

#	Player	NM
	Complete Set (30)	70.00
	Commons	1.00
	Medalist	8x
1	Kotsay, M.	6.00
3	Konerko, P.	8.00
4	Cruz, J.	12.00
5	Irabu, H.	3.00
11	Tejada, M.	6.00
12	Guillen, J.	4.00
17	Wright, J.	8.00
18	Helton, T.	5.00
20	Garciaparra, N.	10.00
22	Tatis, F.	3.00
28	Grieve, B.	10.00

1998 DONRUSS ELITE

	NM Price
Complete Set (150)	$35.00
Commons	.15
Unlisted Stars	**.20-.75**
Pack (5)	4.00
Box (18)	60.00

Quality Rating ★★★
Autographs and plenty of other inserts should excite you about Elite Baseball. Thomas and Ortiz signed only 100 "Back to the Future" cards.

#	Player	NM
1	Griffey, K.	3.50
2	Thomas, F.	3.00
3	Rodriguez, A.	2.50
4	Piazza, M.	2.50
5	Maddux, G.	2.50
6	Ripken, C.	3.00
7	Jones, C.	2.50
8	Jeter, D.	2.50
9	Gwynn, T.	2.00
10	Jones, A.	2.00
11	Gonzalez, J.	2.00
12	Bagwell, J.	1.50
13	McGwire, M.	1.50
14	Clemens, R.	1.50
15	Belle, A.	1.00
16	Bonds, B.	1.00
17	Lofton, K.	1.00
18	Rodriguez, I.	1.00
29	Vaughn, M.	1.00
35	Nomo, H.	2.00
77	Cruz, J. Jr.	3.00
80	Guerrero, V.	1.50
81	Rolen, S.	2.00
82	Garciaparra, N.	2.00
83	Erstad, D.	1.50
93	Wright, J.	2.00
97	Grieve, B.	1.50
98	Konerko, P.	1.00
118	Griffey, K.	2.00
119	Thomas, F.	1.50
120	Rodriguez, A.	1.25
121	Piazza, M.	1.25
122	Maddux, G.	1.25
123	Ripken, C.	1.50
124	Jones, C.	1.25
125	Jeter, D.	1.25
126	Gwynn, T.	1.25
128	Gonzalez, J.	1.00
130	McGwire, M.	1.00
143	Cruz Jr., J.	1.25
146	Rolen, S.	1.00
147	Garciaparra, N.	1.00
148	Garciaparra, N.	1.00

Elite Status

Complete Set (150)	9000.00
Commons	20.00
Elite Status	40x-80x

Back to the Future

#		
	Complete Set (8)	350.00
	Commons	40.00
1	Ripken/Konerko	75.00
2	Bagwell/Helton	40.00
3	Mathews/Jones	50.00
4	Gonzalez/Grieve	50.00
5	Aaron/Cruz Jr	50.00
6	Thomas/Ortiz	50.00
7	Ryan/Maddux	75.00
8	Rodriguez/Garciaparra	60.00

Back to the Future Autographs

#		
	Complete Set (7)	3000.00
	Commons	300.00
1	Ripken/Konerko	500.00
2	Bagwell/Helton	350.00
3	Mathews/Jones	400.00
4	Gonzalez/Grieve	400.00
5	Aaron/Cruz Jr	500.00
6	Thomas/Ortiz (100)	450.00
7	Ryan/Maddux	1000.00
8	Rodriguez/Garciaparra	500.00
No#	Ripken Exchange	500.00

Elite Craftsman

#	Player	NM
	Complete Set (30)	225.00
	Commons	4.00
	Master Craftsman	10x
1	Griffey, K.	25.00
2	Thomas, F.	20.00
3	Rodriguez, A.	20.00
4	Ripken, C.	20.00
5	Maddux, G.	20.00
6	Piazza, M.	20.00
7	Jones, C.	15.00
8	Jeter, D.	15.00
9	Gwynn, T.	15.00
10	Garciaparra, N.	15.00
11	Rolen, S.	10.00
12	Cruz, J. Jr.	15.00
14	Guerrero, V.	8.00
15	Helton, T.	8.00
16	Grieve, B.	10.00
17	Jones, A.	10.00
18	Bagwell, J.	10.00
19	McGwire, M.	12.00
20	Gonzalez, J.	12.00
21	Clemens, R.	12.00
22	Belle, A.	8.00
23	Bonds, B.	8.00
24	Lofton, K.	8.00
25	Rodriguez, I.	7.00
28	Vaughn, M.	8.00
29	Walker, L.	5.00
30	Martinez, T.	5.00

Prime Numbers

#	Player	NM
	Complete Set (36)	4800.00
	Commons	35.00
1A	Griffey, K.	400.00
1B	Griffey, K.	200.00
1C	Griffey, K.	175.00
2A	Thomas, F.	400.00
2B	Thomas, F.	125.00
2C	Thomas, F.	125.00
3A	McGwire, M.	200.00
3B	McGwire, M.	75.00
3C	McGwire, M.	75.00
4A	Ripken, C.	1000.00
4B	Ripken, C.	125.00
4C	Ripken, C.	125.00
5A	Piazza, M.	225.00
5B	Piazza, M.	75.00
5C	Piazza, M.	75.00
6A	Jones, C.	200.00
6B	Jones, C.	50.00
6C	Jones, C.	50.00
7A	Gwynn, T.	175.00
7B	Gwynn, T.	75.00
7C	Gwynn, T.	75.00
8A	Bonds, B.	100.00
9A	Bagwell, J.	350.00
9B	Bagwell, J.	50.00
9C	Bagwell, J.	50.00
10A	Gonzalez, J.	200.00
10B	Gonzalez, J.	50.00
10C	Gonzalez, J.	50.00
11A	Rodriguez, A.	350.00
11B	Rodriguez, A.	75.00
11C	Rodriguez, A.	75.00
12A	Lofton, K.	100.00

Prime Numbers Die-Cuts

#	Player	NM
	Commons	35.00
1A	Griffey, K.(200)	150.00
1B	Griffey, K.(90)	350.00
2A	Thomas, F. (400)	100.00
2B	Thomas, F. (50)	350.00
3A	McGwire, M. (300)	75.00
3B	McGwire, M. (80)	150.00
4A	Ripken, C. (500)	100.00
5A	Piazza, M. (500)	75.00
5B	Piazza, M. (70)	250.00
6A	Jones, C. (400)	50.00
6B	Jones, C. (80)	200.00
7A	Gwynn, T. (300)	75.00
7B	Gwynn, T. (70)	200.00
8B	Bonds, B. (70)	100.00
9A	Bagwell, J. (400)	50.00
9B	Bagwell, J. (20)	450.00
10A	Gonzalez, J. (500)	50.00
10B	Gonzalez, J. (80)	200.00
11A	Rodriguez, A. (500)	75.00
11B	Rodriguez, A. (30)	450.00
12B	Lofton, K. (50)	100.00

1998 FLEER

	NM Price
Complete Set (350)	$75.00
Commons	.10
Unlisted Stars	**.20-.75**
Pack (10)	1.75
Box (36)	55.00

Quality Rating ★★★★
This years set has an old-time feel with "Decade of Excellence" and 'Vintage '63' inserts.

#	Player	NM
1	Griffey, K.	3.00
2	Jeter, D.	1.50
5	Garciaparra, N.	2.00
8	Ripken, C.	2.50
10	Jones, C.	1.50
19	Gonzalez, J.	1.25
20	Grieve, B.	1.25
21	Clemens, R.	1.25
25	McGwire, M.	1.25
31	Maddux, G.	1.50
35	Thomas, F.	2.50
50	Bagwell, J.	1.00
64	Wright, J.	1.25
69	Konerko, P.	1.00
100	Rodriguez, A.	1.25
104	Lofton, K.	.75
150	Rolen, S.	1.25
170	Rodriguez, I.	.60
190	Helton, T.	.60
200	Piazza, M.	1.50
236	Tejada, M.	.60
244	Guerrero, V.	1.00
250	Gwynn, T.	1.25
271	Jones, A.	1.25
275	Cruz, J. Jr.	2.50
300	Bonds, B.	.75
305	Maddux, G.	.75
312	Cruz, J. Jr.	4.00
313	Garciaparra, N.	3.00
314	Griffey, K.	5.00
315	Gwynn, T.	2.00
318	McGwire, M.	2.00
321	Bagwell, J.	1.00
322	Belle, A.	1.25
323	Bonds, B.	1.25
326	Cruz, J. Jr.	4.00
328	Gonzalez, J.	2.50
329	Griffey, K.	5.00
330	Jones, A.	2.00
332	McGwire, M.	2.50
334	Piazza, M.	4.00
336	Rodriguez, A.	4.00
337	Thomas, F.	4.00
339	Vaughn, M.	1.25
341	Cruz, J. Jr.	1.50
342	Griffey, K.	1.50
343	Jeter, D.	1.00
345	Jones, C.	1.00
346	Maddux, G.	1.00
347	Piazza, M.	1.00
348	Ripken, C.	1.25
349	Rodriguez, A.	1.25
350	Thomas, F.	1.25

Decade of Excellence

#	Player	NM
	Complete Set (12)	100.00
	Commons	3.00
	Rare Traditions	2x-4x
1	Alomar, R.	6.00
2	Bonds, B.	8.00
3	Clemens, R.	12.00
7	Gwynn, T.	20.00
8	Johnson, R.	8.00
9	Maddux, G.	25.00
10	McGwire, M.	20.00
12	Ripken, C.	30.00

Diamond Standouts

#	Player	NM
	Complete Set (20)	50.00
	Commons	1.00
1	Bagwell, J.	3.00
2	Bonds, B.	2.00
3	Clemens, R.	3.50
4	Cruz, J. Jr.	5.00
6	Garciaparra, N.	5.00
7	Gonzalez, J.	3.50
8	Griffey, K.	8.00
9	Jeter, D.	4.00
11	Jones, C.	4.00
12	Lofton, K.	2.00
13	Maddux, G.	4.00
15	McGwire, M.	4.00
16	Piazza, M.	4.00
17	Rodriguez, A.	5.00
19	Thomas, F.	7.00
20	Walker, L.	2.00

Power Game

#	Player	NM
	Complete Set (20)	100.00
	Commons	2.00
1	Bagwell, J.	8.00
2	Belle, A.	5.00
3	Bonds, B.	5.00
5	Clemens, R.	10.00
6	Cruz, J. Jr.	12.00
8	Garciaparra, N.	12.00
9	Gonzalez, J.	10.00
10	Griffey, K.	25.00
11	Johnson, R.	4.00
12	Maddux, G.	15.00
15	McGwire, M.	12.00
16	Piazza, M.	15.00
18	Thomas, F.	20.00
19	Thome, J.	4.00
20	Walker, L.	4.00

Rookie Sensations

#	Player	NM
	Complete Set (20)	50.00
	Commons	1.00
1	Cameron, M.	1.50
2	Cruz, J. Jr.	10.00
5	Garciaparra, N.	10.00
6	Grieve, B.	7.00
7	Guerrero, V.	5.00
9	Guillen, J.	2.00
10	Helton, T.	3.00
11	Hernandez, L.	3.00
12	Irabu, H.	1.50
13	Jones, A.	5.00
17	Rolen, S.	8.00
18	Tatis, F.	2.00
20	Wright, J.	7.00

Zone

#	Player	NM
	Complete Set (15)	550.00
1	Bagwell, J.	40.00
2	Bonds, B.	20.00
3	Clemens, R.	40.00
4	Cruz, J. Jr.	50.00
5	Garciaparra, N.	50.00
6	Gonzalez, J.	40.00
7	Grifffey, K.	100.00
8	Gwynn, T.	50.00
9	Jones, C.	50.00
10	Maddux, G.	50.00
11	McGwire, M.	50.00
12	Piazza, M.	50.00
13	Rodriguez, A.	60.00

14	Thomas, F.	75.00
15	Walker, L.	20.00

Vintage '63
	Complete Set (64)	30.00
	Commons	.25
	Unlisted Stars	.50-1.00
	Classic	50x-100x
3	Jones, A.	2.00
4	Jones, C.	3.00
6	Maddux, G.	3.00
8	Ripken, C.	3.00
9	Garciaparra, N.	2.50
12	Thomas, F.	3.00
18	Wright, J.	1.50
29	Bagwell, J.	1.50
32	Piazza, M.	2.50
35	Guerrero, V.	1.50
38	Jeter, D.	2.50
44	Grieve, B.	2.00
45	Rolen, S.	2.00
50	McGwire, M.	2.00
52	Gwynn, T.	2.00
55	Griffey, K.	4.00
58	Rodriguez, A.	3.00
59	Gonzalez, J.	2.00
62	Clemens, R.	2.00
63	Cruz, J. Jr.	3.00

1998 FLEER ULTRA

	NM Price
Complete Set (250)	$110.00
Commons	.10
Unlisted Stars	**.15-.40**
Gold Medallion	1x-2x
Platinum Medallion	25x-50x
Pack (10)	2.75
Box (24)	55.00

Quality Rating ★★★
This is the first release in 1998. Wow, these cards look great. There are a ton of inserts and the parallel sets are fun to chase.

#	Player	NM
1	Griffey, K.	3.00
3	Clemens, R.	1.25
30	Nomo, H.	1.50
31	Bagwell, J.	1.00
33	Garciaparra, N.	2.00
49	Jones, A.	1.50
50	Bonds, B.	.75
53	Piazza, M.	1.50
63	Thomas, F.	3.00
70	Rolen, S.	1.50
83	Rodriguez, A.	2.00
100	Gonzalez, J.	1.25
108	Gwynn, T.	1.25
122	Maddux, G.	1.50
134	Guerrero, V.	1.25
143	Ripken, C.	2.50
148	Vaughn, M.	.60
150	Jeter, D.	1.50
160	Sandberg, R.	.75
164	Erstad, D.	1.25
194	Cruz, J. Jr.	2.50
202	Jones, C.	2.00
203	Lofton, K.	.75
205	Ramirez, M.	.75
208	McGwire, M.	1.25
210	Rodriguez, I.	.60
211	Bagwell, J. (SC)	4.00
212	Bonds, B. (SC)	2.00
213	Clemens, R. (SC)	4.00
214	Garciaparra, N. (SC)	7.00
215	Griffey, K. (SC)	10.00
216	Gwynn, T. (SC)	5.00
218	McGwire, M. (SC)	5.00

219	Rolen, S. (SC)	5.00
220	Thomas, F. (SC)	8.00
222	Helms, W. (Pros.)	1.00
224	Helton, T. (Pros.)	3.00
225	Rose, B. (Pros.)	1.50
233	Konerko, P. (Pros.)	4.00
238	Ledee, R. (Pros.)	2.00
239	Grieve, B. (Pros.)	5.00
246	Griffey, K. (CL)	3.00
247	Rodriguez, A. (CL)	2.00
249	Thomas, F. (CL)	2.00
250	Ripken, C. (CL)	2.00

Artistic Talents
	Complete Set (18)	70.00
1	Griffey, K.	8.00
2	Jones, A.	4.00
3	Rodriguez, A.	6.00
4	Thomas, F.	8.00
5	Ripken, C.	6.00
6	Jeter, D.	4.00
7	Jones, C.	4.00
8	Maddux, G.	4.00
9	Piazza, M.	4.00
10	Belle, A.	2.00
11	Erstad, D.	3.00
12	Gonzalez, J.	4.00
13	Bagwell, J.	3.00
14	Gwynn, T.	4.00
15	McGwire, M.	4.00
16	Rolen, S.	4.00
17	Bonds, B.	2.00
18	Lofton, K.	2.00

Back to the Future
	Complete Set (15)	25.00
	Commons	1.00
1	Jones, A.	3.00
2	Rodriguez, A.	5.00
3	Jeter, D.	4.00
4	Erstad, D.	2.00
6	Rolen, S.	4.00
7	Garciaparra, N.	5.00
8	Irabu, H.	2.00
9	Cruz, J. Jr.	6.00
10	Guerrero, V.	3.00
11	Kotsay, M.	3.00
14	Guillen, J.	2.00
15	Clark, T.	2.00

Big Shots
	Complete Set (15)	15.00
	Commons	.50
1	Griffey, K.	4.00
2	Thomas, F.	4.00
3	Jones, C.	2.00
4	Belle, A.	1.00
5	Gonzalez, J.	1.50
6	Bagwell, J.	1.25
7	McGwire, M.	1.50
14	Piazza, M.	2.00

Diamond Producers
	Complete Set (15)	900.00
1	Griffey, K.	125.00
2	Jones, A.	50.00
3	Rodriguez, A.	90.00
4	Thomas, F.	100.00
5	Ripken, C.	100.00
6	Jeter, D.	60.00
7	Jones, C.	60.00
8	Maddux, G.	60.00
9	Piazza, M.	60.00
10	Gonzalez, J.	50.00
11	Bagwell, J.	40.00
12	Gwynn, T.	50.00
13	McGwire, M.	50.00
14	Bonds, B.	25.00
15	Cruz, J. Jr.	80.00

Double Trouble
	Complete Set (20)	20.00
	Commons	1.00
1	Griffey/Rodriguez	5.00
3	Jones, A/Lofton	1.50
4	Jones, C/Maddux	3.00
5	Jeter/Martinez	2.00
6	Thomas/Belle	4.00
7	Ripken/Alomar	3.00
8	Piazza/Nomo	3.00
10	Gonzalez/Rodriguez	2.00
12	Gwynn/Finley	1.50
13	McGwire/Lankford	1.50
16	Vaughn/Garciaparra	3.00
19	Clemens/Cruz Jr.	3.00

Fall Classics
	Complete Set (15)	100.00
1	Griffey, K.	15.00

2	Jones, A.	6.00
3	Rodriguez, A.	10.00
4	Thomas, F.	12.00
5	Ripken, C.	12.00
6	Jeter, D.	10.00
7	Jones, C.	10.00
8	Maddux, G.	10.00
9	Piazza, M.	10.00
10	Belle, A.	3.00
11	Gonzalez, J.	8.00
12	Bagwell, J.	6.00
13	Gwynn, T.	10.00
14	McGwire, M.	10.00
15	Bonds, B.	3.00

Kid Gloves
	Complete Set (12)	25.00
	Commons	.50
1	Jones, A.	6.00
2	Rodriguez, A.	6.00
3	Jeter, D.	4.00
4	Jones, C.	4.00
5	Erstad, D.	2.00
7	Rolen, S.	4.00
8	Garciaparra, N.	6.00
9	Cruz, J. Jr.	6.00
12	Guerrero, V.	3.00

Power Plus
	Complete Set (10)	125.00
1	Griffey, K.	30.00
2	Jones, A.	12.00
3	Rodriguez, A.	20.00
4	Thomas, F.	25.00
5	Piazza, M.	15.00
6	Belle, A.	6.00
7	Gonzalez, J.	12.00
8	Bagwell, J.	8.00
9	Bonds, B.	6.00
10	Cruz, J. Jr.	25.00

Prime Leather
	Complete Set (18)	500.00
1	Griffey, K.	70.00
2	Jones, A.	30.00
3	Rodriguez, A.	50.00
4	Thomas, F.	70.00
5	Ripken, C.	60.00
6	Jeter, D.	40.00
7	Jones, C.	40.00
8	Maddux, G.	40.00
9	Piazza, M.	40.00
10	Belle, A.	15.00
11	Erstad, D.	25.00
12	Gonzalez, J.	35.00
13	Bagwell, J.	25.00
14	Gwynn, T.	40.00
15	Alomar, R.	10.00
16	Bonds, B.	15.00
17	Lofton, K.	15.00
18	Cruz, J. Jr.	50.00

1998 PACIFIC CROWN COLLECTION

	NM Price
Complete Set (450)	$45.00
Commons	.10
Unlisted Stars	**.15-.40**
Pack (12)	2.50
Box (36)	75.00

Quality Rating ★★★
Base set is great because cards from lesser known stars are available. "In the Cage Laser Cuts" are a must-have insert.

#	Player	NM
6	Erstad, D.	1.00
33	Ripken, C.	2.50
39	Garciaparra, N.	2.00
49	Vaughn, M.	.60
52	Belle, A.	.75
63	Thomas, F.	3.00
78	Ramirez, M.	.75

82	Wright, J.	1.00
150	Irabu, H.	.50
151	Jeter, D.	1.50
166	Grieve, B.	1.00
186	Griffey, K.	3.00
188	Johnson, R.	.50
193	Rodriguez, A.	2.50
202	Gonzalez, J.	1.25
215	Clemens, R.	1.25
217	Cruz, J.	2.50
234	Jones, A.	1.00
235	Jones, C.	1.50
238	Lofton, K.	.75
241	Maddux, G.	1.50
256	Sandberg, R.	.75
312	Bagwell, J.	1.50
336	Nomo, H.	1.25
339	Piazza, M.	1.50
346	Guerrero, V.	1.00
386	Rolen, S.	1.00
416	McGwire, M.	1.25
427	Gwynn, T.	1.25
437	Bonds, B.	.75

Red
	Complete Set (450)	300.00
	Red	3x-5x

Silver
	Complete Set (450)	225.00
	Silver	2x-4x
	Platinum	50x-100x

Cramer's Choice Awards
	Complete Set (10)	900.00
1	Maddux, G.	125.00
2	Alomar, R.	40.00
3	Ripken, C.	175.00
4	Garciaparra, N.	125.00
5	Walker, L.	50.00
6	Piazza, M.	125.00
7	McGwire, M.	100.00
8	Gwynn, T.	100.00
9	Griffey, K.	225.00
10	Clemens, R.	100.00

Gold Crown Die-Cuts
	Complete Set (36)	400.00
	Commons	3.00
1	Jones, C.	15.00
2	Maddux, G.	20.00
6	Ripken, C.	20.00
7	Garciaparra, N.	15.00
8	Vaughn, M.	8.00
9	Thomas, F.	30.00
12	Ramirez, M.	8.00
16	Hernandez, L.	7.00
18	Bagwell, J.	12.00
20	Nomo, H.	18.00
21	Piazza, M.	20.00
22	Jeter, D.	20.00
25	Grieve, B.	15.00
26	McGwire, M.	12.00
27	Gwynn, T.	15.00
28	Bonds, B.	8.00
29	Griffey, K.	35.00
32	Rodriguez, A.	25.00
33	Gonzalez, J.	15.00
35	Clemens, R.	15.00
36	Cruz, J.	20.00

Home Run Hitters
	Complete Set (20)	275.00
	Commons	5.00
2	Vaughn, M.	10.00
4	Belle, A.	10.00
5	Thomas, F.	45.00
7	Thome, J.	8.00
10	Galarraga, A.	8.00
11	Walker, L.	8.00
12	Bagwell, J.	15.00
13	Piazza, M.	25.00
15	McGwire, M.	20.00
16	Bonds, B.	10.00
18	Griffey, K.	50.00
19	Rodriguez, A.	40.00
20	Gonzalez, J.	20.00

In the Cage Laser-Cuts
	Complete Set (20)	650.00
	Commons	10.00
1	Jones, C.	50.00
2	Alomar, R.	20.00
3	Ripken, C.	70.00
4	Garciaparra, N.	50.00
5	Thomas, F.	70.00
8	Walker, L.	20.00
10	Piazza, M.	50.00
13	McGwire, M.	40.00

#	Player	NM
14	Gwynn, T.	40.00
15	Bonds, B.	25.00
16	Griffey, K.	90.00
18	Rodriguez, A.	60.00
19	Gonzalez, J.	40.00
20	Rodriguez, I.	20.00

Latinos of the Major Leagues

#	Player	NM
	Complete Set (36)	75.00
	Commons	1.00
1	Jones, A.	6.00
6	Garciaparra, N.	8.00
10	Ramirez, M.	3.00
16	Hernandez, L.	4.00
33	Rodriguez, A.	10.00
34	Gonzalez, J.	8.00
36	Cruz, J.	10.00

Team Checklists Laser-Cuts

#	Player	NM
	Complete Set (30)	250.00
	Commons	2.00
2	Ripken/Alomar	20.00
3	Garciaparra/Vaughn	15.00
4	Thomas/Belle	20.00
5	Alomar/Ramirez	5.00
10	Martinez/Jeter	12.00
11	Grieve/Canseco	10.00
12	Griffey/Rodriguez	35.00
13	Gonzalez/Rodriguez	10.00
14	Cruz/Clemens	20.00
15	Maddux/Jones	20.00
18	Walker/Galarraga	5.00
20	Bagwell/Biggio	10.00
21	Piazza/Nomo	20.00
24	Schilling/Rolen	10.00
26	McGwire/Eckersley	12.00
27	Gwynn/Joyner	12.00
28	Bonds/Snow	6.00

1998 PINNACLE

	NM Price
Complete Set (200)	$25.00
Commons	.05
Unlisted Stars	**.10-.40**
Pack (10)	2.50
Box (18)	40.00

Quality Rating ★★★
Photography in the base set is awesome. Some players have complete stats and some have home or away numbers. That's different.

#	Player	NM
1	Gwynn, T.	1.25
3	Lofton, K.	75
7	Piazza, M.	1.50
14	Maddux, G.	1.50
18	Jones, C.	1.50
23	Bonds, B.	75
28	Bagwell, J.	1.00
30	Erstad, D.	1.00
37	Jones, A.	1.00
39	Rolen, S.	1.00
44	Nomo, H.	1.25
45	Ramirez, M.	75
52	Cruz, J.	2.50
62	Guerrero, V.	1.00
63	McGwire, M.	1.25
64	Jeter, D.	1.50
70	Gonzalez, J.	1.25
159	Konerko, P.	1.00
160	Grieve, B.	1.00
163	Wright, J.	1.25
182	Rodriguez, A.	1.25
183	Ripken, C.	1.25
184	Clemens, R.	60
185	Jeter, D.	75
186	Thomas, F.	1.25
187	Griffey, K.	1.50
188	McGwire, M.	60
192	Bagwell, J.	50
193	Griffey, K.	1.50
194	Jones, C.	1.00
197	Garciaparra, N.	1.00

Museum Collection

	Complete Set (200)	500.00
	Commons	1.50

Artist's Proofs

	Complete Set (200)	1200.00
	Commons	4.00

Epix

#	Player	NM
	Common Play	1.00
	Common Game	4.00
	Common Season	8.00
	Purple	1.5x
	Emerald	2x
1	Griffey, K. (Game)	40.00
2	Gonzalez, J. (Game)	20.00
3	Bagwell, J. (Game)	15.00
5	Garciaparra, N. (Game)	20.00
6	Sandberg, R. (Game)	10.00
7	Thomas, F. (Season)	70.00
8	Jeter, D. (Season)	40.00
9	Gwynn, T. (Season)	40.00
10	Belle, A. (Season)	20.00
11	Rolen, S. (Season)	35.00
13	Rodriguez, A. (Moment)	90.00
14	Ripken, C. (Moment)	100.00
15	Jones, C. (Moment)	75.00
16	Clemens, R. (Moment)	50.00
17	Vaughn, M. (Moment)	30.00
18	McGwire, M. (Moment)	70.00
19	Piazza, M. (Play)	15.00
20	Jones, A. (Play)	8.00
21	Maddux, G. (Play)	15.00
22	Bonds, B. (Play)	6.00
24	Murray, E. (Play)	5.00

Hit it Here

#	Player	NM
	Complete Set (10)	70.00
1	Walker, L.	4.00
2	Griffey, K.	20.00
3	Piazza, M.	12.00
4	Thomas, F.	18.00
5	Bonds, B.	5.00
6	Belle, A.	5.00
7	Martinez, T.	3.00
8	McGwire, M.	8.00
9	Gonzalez, J.	8.00
10	Bagwell, J.	7.00

Spellbound

	Common McGwire (7)	10.00
	Common Clemens (6)	10.00
	Common Thomas (7)	20.00
	Common Rolen (5)	8.00
	Common Griffey (7)	25.00
	Common Walker (6)	5.00
	Common Garciaparra (5)	12.00
	Common Ripken (3)	20.00
	Common Gwynn (4)	10.00

1998 SCORE

	NM Price
Complete Set (270)	$18.00
Commons	.05
Unlisted Stars	**.10-.40**
Pack (10)	1.00
Box (36)	30.00

Quality Rating ★★★
Score has upgraded card fronts with some great photography. Artist Proofs are back.

#	Player	NM
1	Jones, A.	1.00
3	Nomo, H.	75
5	Bonds, B.	75
7	Belle, A.	75
9	Maddux, G.	1.50
10	Rodriguez, A.	2.50
14	Irabu, H.	50
22	Jeter, D.	1.50
24	Piazza, M.	1.50
34	Griffey, K.	3.00
38	Bagwell, J.	1.00
41	McGwire, M.	1.25
43	Ripken, C.	2.50
49	Clemens, R.	1.25
50	Gwynn, T.	1.25
51	Jones, C.	1.50
68	Rolen, S.	60
91	Garciaparra, N.	1.50
93	Erstad, D.	1.00
94	Lofton, K.	1.00
105	Thomas, F.	2.00
227	Vaughn, M.	60
233	Cruz, J.	2.00
244	Grieve, B.	1.00
252	Wright, J.	1.00
257	Ripken, C.	1.00
259	Piazza, M.	75
265	Maddux, G.	75
268	Ripken, C. (CL)	1.00
269	Griffey, K. (CL)	1.25

Artist Proofs

	Complete Set (160)	350.00
	Commons	1.50

Showcase Series

	Complete Set (160)	100.00
	Commons	50

All-Stars

#	Player	NM
	Complete Set (20)	125.00
	Commons	2.00
1	Piazza, M.	12.00
2	Rodriguez, I.	7.00
3	Thomas, F.	20.00
4	McGwire, M.	10.00
5	Sandberg, R.	6.00
7	Ripken, C.	20.00
11	Puckett, K.	8.00
12	Gwynn, T.	10.00
13	Griffey, K.	25.00
14	Gonzalez, J.	10.00
15	Bonds, B.	7.00
16	Jones, A.	7.00
17	Clemens, R.	10.00
18	Johnson, R.	6.00
19	Maddux, G.	12.00

Complete Players

#	Player	NM
	Complete Set (30)	225.00
1ABC	Griffey, K.	20.00
2ABC	McGwire, M.	8.00
3ABC	Jeter, D.	10.00
4ABC	Ripken, C.	15.00
5ABC	Piazza, M.	10.00
6ABC	Erstad, D.	5.00
7ABC	Thomas, F.	15.00
8ABC	Jones, A.	7.00
9ABC	Garciaparra, N.	10.00
10ABC	Ramirez, M.	4.00

Epix

#	Player	NM
	Common Game	4.00
	Common Moment	20.00
	Purple	1.5x
	Emerald	2x
1	Griffey, K. (Play)	35.00
2	Gonzalez, J. (Play)	15.00
3	Bagwell, J. (Play)	10.00
4	Rodriguez, I. (Play)	8.00
5	Garciaparra, N. (Play)	20.00
6	Sandberg, R. (Play)	10.00
7	Thomas, F. (Game)	35.00
8	Jeter, D. (Game)	20.00
9	Gwynn, T. (Game)	20.00
10	Belle, A. (Game)	10.00
11	Rolen, S. (Game)	15.00
13	Rodriguez, A. (Season)	70.00
14	Ripken, C. (Season)	80.00
15	Jones, C. (Season)	50.00
16	Clemens, R. (Season)	35.00
17	Vaughn, M. (Season)	20.00
18	McGwire, M. (Season)	40.00
19	Piazza, M. (Moment)	90.00
20	Jones, A. (Moment)	65.00
21	Maddux, G. (Moment)	90.00
22	Bonds, B. (Moment)	30.00
24	Murray, E. (Moment)	30.00

1998 SPORTS ILLUSTRATED THEN AND NOW

	NM Price
Complete Set (150)	$30.00
Commons	.05
Unlisted Stars	**.10-.40**
Pack (5)	2.00
Box (24)	42.00

Quality Rating ★★★
When you mix a card set with photography from SI you get a great looking set. If you want up close action, this is for you.

#	Player	NM
3	Banks, E.	50
19	Mathews, E.	50
20	Mays, W.	1.00
21	McCovey, W.	50
22	Morgan, J.	50
24	Puckett, K.	1.00
28	Robinson, B.	50
29	Robinson, F.	50
38	Maddux, G.	75
40	Ripken, C.	1.25
42	Thomas, F.	1.25
43	Bagwell, J.	50
48	Gwynn, T.	75
50	Griffey, K.	1.50
52	McGwire, M.	60
53	Clemens, R.	60
54	Cruz, J. Jr.	1.50
59	Bagwell, J.	1.00
60	Belle, A.	75
63	Bonds, B.	75
72	Clemens, R.	1.25
74	Cruz, J. Jr.	2.50
78	Erstad, D.	1.25
83	Garciaparra, N.	2.00
85	Gonzalez, J.	1.25
88	Griffey, K.	3.00
89	Guerrero, V.	1.00
90	Gwynn, T.	1.25
93	Jeter, D.	1.50
96	Jones, A.	1.25
97	Jones, C.	1.50
106	Lofton, K.	75
107	Maddux, G.	1.50
113	McGwire, M.	1.25
118	Nomo, H.	1.25
121	Piazza, M.	1.50
124	Ripken, C.	2.50
125	Rodriguez, A.	2.00
127	Rodriguez, I.	75
128	Rolen, S.	1.25
134	Thomas, F.	2.50
136	Vaughn, M.	75
141	Wright, J.	1.25
145	Grieve, B.	1.00
146	Helton, T.	75
147	Konerko, P.	75

Extra Edition

	Commons	5.00
	Extra Edition	15x-25x

Autographs

#	Player	NM
No#	Clemens, R.	200.00
No#	Gibson, B.	75.00
No#	Gwynn, T.	225.00
No#	Killebrew, H.	80.00
No#	Mays, W.	200.00
No#	Rolen, S.	150.00

Art of the Game

#	Player	NM
	Complete Set (8)	20.00
	Commons	1.00
2	Rodriguez, A.	6.00

#	Player	
3	Piazza, M.	6.00
6	Ripken, C.	8.00
8	Bonds, B.	2.00

Covers

#	Player	
	Complete Set (12)	50.00
	Commons	2.00
2	Puckett, K.	5.00
5	Mays, W.	4.00
6	Robinson, F.	3.00
7	Ripken, C.	12.00
8	Clemens, R.	6.00
9	Griffey, K.	15.00
10	McGwire, M.	7.00
11	Gwynn, T.	7.00
12	Rodriguez, I.	4.00

Great Shots

#	Player	
	Complete Set (25)	12.00
	Commons	.25
	Unlisted Stars	.50-1.00
1	Griffey, K.	2.00
2	Thomas, F.	1.50
3	Rodriguez, A.	1.25
5	Jones, C.	1.25
6	Ripken, C.	1.50
9	Maddux, G.	1.25
11	Piazza, M.	1.50
12	Rolen, S.	1.25
13	Garciaparra, N.	1.25
14	Cruz, J. Jr.	1.25

Road to Cooperstown

#	Player	
	Complete Set (10)	60.00
	Commons	1.50
1	Bonds, B.	2.00
2	Clemens, R.	6.00
3	Griffey, K.	15.00
4	Gwynn, T.	7.00
6	Maddux, G.	8.00
8	Piazza, M.	10.00
9	Ripken, C.	12.00
10	Thomas, F.	12.00

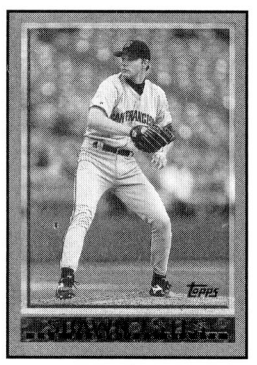

1998 TOPPS

	NM Price
Complete Set (282)	$20.00
Commons	.05
Unlisted Stars	**.10-.40**
Pack (11)	1.50
Box (36)	45.00

Quality Rating ★★★
Topps includes a tribute to Roberto Clemente and a great card design. Inserts will be listed next month.

#	Player	NM
1	Gwynn, T.	1.25
5	Guerrero, V.	.75
20	Thomas, F.	2.00
21	Clemente, R.	1.50
25	Rolen, S.	1.25
30	Gonzalez, J.	1.25
35	Bagwell, J.	1.00
100	Piazza, M.	1.50
160	Jeter, D.	1.50
167	Nomo, H.	1.25
175	Lofton, K.	.75
254	Beltre, A.	1.00
255	Grieve, B.	1.00
262	Chavez/Branyan	.50
268	Garciaparra, N.	.75
273	Gonzalez, J.	.75

Minted

#		
	Complete Set (282)	250.00
	Commons	.75

Baby Boomers

#	Player	
	Complete Set (15)	80.00
	Commons	2.00
1	Jeter, D.	10.00
2	Rolen, S.	10.00
3	Garciaparra, N.	15.00
4	Cruz, J.	20.00
5	Erstad, D.	5.00
6	Helton, T.	5.00
9	Jones, A.	8.00
10	Guerrero, V.	7.00
11	Kotsay, M.	6.00
13	Pettitte, A.	3.00

Clemente Reprint

#		
	Complete Set (10)	50.00
	Common	6.00
	Finest (9 Cards)	3x
	Refractor	10x

Clemente Finest

#		
	Complete Set (9)	75.00
	Commons	10.00
	Refractors	3x

Clemente Tribute

#		
	Complete Set (5)	10.00
	Common	2.00

Etch-A-Sketch

#	Player	
	Complete Set (9)	50.00
1	Belle, A.	3.00
2	Bonds, B.	3.00
3	Griffey, K.	15.00
4	Maddux, G.	8.00
5	Nomo, H.	8.00
6	Piazza, M.	8.00
7	Ripken, C.	10.00
8	Thomas, F.	12.00
9	Vaughn, M.	3.00

Flashback

#	Player	
	Complete Set (10)	75.00
	Commons	3.00
1	Bonds, B.	6.00
2	Griffey, K.	30.00
5	Ripken, C.	20.00
6	Gwynn, T.	12.00
7	Lofton, K.	8.00

Hallbound

#	Player	
	Complete Set (15)	90.00
	Commons	1.00
2	Gwynn, T.	8.00
4	Clemens, R.	6.00
6	Ripken, C.	12.00
7	Maddux, G.	10.00
9	Griffey, K.	15.00
10	Thomas, F.	12.00
11	McGwire, M.	8.00
12	Bonds, B.	4.00
13	Piazza, M.	10.00
14	Gonzalez, J.	8.00

Inter-League Mystery Finest

#	Player	
	Complete Set (20)	125.00
	Commons	2.00
	Refractors	3x
1	Jones, C.	10.00
2	Ripken, C.	15.00
3	Maddux, G.	10.00
4	Jeter, D.	10.00
10	Griffey, K.	20.00
13	Piazza, M.	10.00
18	Thomas, F.	15.00
20	Belle, A.	6.00

1998 TOPPS CHROME

	NM Price
Complete Set (282)	$70.00
Commons	.20
Unlisted Stars	**.25-.60**
Pack (4)	3.50
Box (24)	70.00

Quality Rating ★★★★
Chrome products all over the hobby are super hot. Expect this set to continue the trend. Watch for wax prices to possibly soar.

#	Player	NM
1	Gwynn, T.	4.00
5	Guerrero, V.	2.50
14	Vaughn, M.	2.00
20	Thomas, F.	6.00
21	Clemente, R.	3.50
25	Rolen, S.	4.00
30	Gonzalez, J.	3.50
35	Bagwell, J.	3.00
100	Piazza, M.	5.00
125	Ramirez, M.	2.00
150	Johnson, R.	1.50
160	Jeter, D.	4.50
167	Nomo, H.	4.00
175	Lofton, K.	2.50
181	Irabu, H.	1.50
246	Davis/Berkman	2.00
254	Beltre/Minor	5.00
255	Grieve/Brown	3.00
256	Pavano/Wood	2.00
260	Hermanson/Butler	2.00
262	Chavez/Branyan	2.00
268	Garciaparra, N.	2.00
273	Gonzalez, J.	1.50

Refractors

	Refractors	6x-12x

Baby Boomers

#	Player	
	Complete Set (15)	80.00
	Commons	2.00
	Refractors	3x
1	Jeter, D.	10.00
2	Rolen, S.	10.00
3	Garciaparra, N.	15.00
4	Cruz, J. Jr.	18.00
5	Erstad, D.	4.00
6	Helton, T.	5.00
8	Guillen, J.	3.00
9	Jones, A.	7.00
10	Guerrero, V.	6.00
11	Kotsay, M.	6.00
13	Pettitte, A.	3.00

Flashback

#	Player	
	Complete Set (10)	45.00
	Commons	2.00
	Refractors	3x
1	Bonds, B.	3.00
2	Griffey, K.	15.00
5	Ripken, C.	12.00
6	Gwynn, T.	8.00
7	Lofton, K.	3.00

Hallbound

#	Player	
	Complete Set (15)	80.00
	Commons	2.00
	Refractors	3x
2	Gwynn, T.	8.00
4	Clemens, R.	7.00
6	Ripken, C.	12.00
7	Maddux, G.	8.00
9	Griffey, K.	15.00
10	Thomas, F.	12.00
11	McGwire, M.	8.00
12	Bonds, B.	3.00
13	Piazza, M.	10.00
14	Gonzalez, J.	7.00

1998 TOPPS STADIUM CLUB

	NM Price
Complete Set (200)	$35.00
Commons	.10
Unlisted Stars	**.15-.40**
Pack (10)	3.00
Box (24)	65.00

Quality Rating ★★★★
The odds series of Stadium Club features that, all odd numbered cards. Photos are some of the best you will see this year.

#	Player	NM
1	Jones, C.	1.50
3	Guerrero, V.	1.00
43	Bonds, B.	.75
77	Belle, A.	.75
83	Ripken, C.	2.50
101	Clemens, R.	1.25
105	Erstad, D.	1.00
113	Gwynn, T.	1.25
139	Helton, T.	.75
171	Garciaparra, N.	2.00
191	Wright, J.	1.25
199	Griffey, K.	3.00
203	McGwire, M.	1.25
223	Rodriguez, I.	.75
255	Cruz, J. Jr.	2.50
315	Rolen, S.	1.25
337	Piazza, M.	1.50
361	Beltre, A.	3.00
363	Hinch, A.J.	1.00
367	Stoner, M. (R)	1.00
371	Benson, K.	1.00
373	Brown, D.	1.00
379	Lee, T.	4.00
381	Wells, V.	1.00
383	Davis, J.J.	1.00
No#	Ripken Sound Chip	12.00

Bowman Previews

#	Player	
	Complete Set (10)	35.00
1	Garciaparra, N.	5.00
2	Rolen, S.	5.00
3	Griffey, K.	10.00
4	Thomas, F.	8.00
5	Walker, L.	4.00
6	Piazza, M.	6.00
7	Jones, C.	5.00
8	Martinez, T.	2.00
9	McGwire, M.	4.00
10	Bonds, B.	3.00

Co-Signers

#	Player	
1	Garciaparra/Rolen (A)	N/A
2	Garciaparra/Jeter (B)	250.00
3	Garciaparra/Karros (C)	100.00
4	Rolen/Jeter (C)	125.00
5	Rolen/Karros (B)	150.00
6	Jeter/Karros (A)	N/A
7	Lee/Cruz (B)	300.00
8	Lee/Kotsay (C)	125.00
9	Lee/Konerko (A)	N/A
10	Cruz/Kotsay (A)	N/A
11	Cruz/Konerko (C)	125.00
12	Kotsay/Konerko (B)	125.00
13	Gwynn/Walker (A)	N/A
14	Gwynn/Grudzielanek (C)	100.00
15	Gwynn/Galarraga (B)	200.00
16	Walker/Grudzielanek (B)	100.00
17	Walker/Galarraga (C)	75.00
18	Grudzielanek/Galarraga (A)	N/A

In the Wings

#	Player	
	Complete Set (15)	90.00
	Commons	2.50
1	Encarnacion, J.	5.00

#	Player	NM
2	Fullmer, B.	4.00
3	Grieve, B.	12.00
4	Helton, T.	8.00
7	Konerko, P.	10.00
8	Kotsay, M.	8.00
9	Lee, D.	4.00
10	Lee, T.	20.00
13	Simon, R.	4.00
15	Tatis, F.	8.00

Never Compromise

	Complete Set (20)	90.00
	Commons	2.00
1	Ripken, C.	10.00
2	Rodriguez, I.	3.00
3	Griffey, K.	12.00
4	Thomas, F.	10.00
5	Gwynn, T.	7.00
6	Piazza, M.	8.00
7	Johnson, R.	3.00
8	Maddux, G.	8.00
9	Clemens, R.	7.00
10	Jeter, D.	7.00
11	Jones, C.	8.00
12	Bonds, B.	4.00
13	Walker, L.	3.00
14	Bagwell, J.	6.00
17	McGwire, M.	7.00
18	Ramirez, M.	3.00
20	Molitor, P.	3.00

One of a Kind

One of a Kind	25x-50x

1998 TOPPS STARS 'N STEEL

	NM Price
Complete Set (44)	$150.00
Commons	1.50
Unlisted Stars	2.00-3.00
Pack (3)	10.00
Box (12)	100.00

Quality Rating ★★★★
Checklist is great but you have to like metal cards. Complete stats are a major help to the set.

#	Player	NM
1	Alomar, R.	3.50
2	Bagwell, J.	8.00
3	Belle, A.	4.00
5	Bonds, B.	4.00
9	Clemens, R.	8.00
10	Cruz, J. Jr.	10.00
12	Garciaparra, N.	10.00
13	Gonzalez, J.	10.00
15	Griffey, K.	20.00
16	Gwynn, T.	10.00
18	Jeter, D.	10.00
19	Johnson, R.	3.50
20	Jones, A.	7.00
21	Jones, C.	10.00
25	Lofton, K.	4.00
26	Maddux, G.	10.00
29	McGwire, M.	10.00
32	Piazza, M.	10.00
33	Ramirez, M.	4.00
34	Ripken, C.	15.00
35	Rodriguez, I.	4.00
36	Rolen, S.	8.00
40	Thomas, F.	15.00
41	Thome, J.	3.50
42	Vaughn, M.	4.00
43	Walker, L.	4.00

Gold

Complete Set (44)	750.00
Gold	2x-3x

Holographic

Complete Set (44)	1800.00
Holographic	4x-8x

1998 UPPER DECK

	NM Price
Complete Set (270)	$25.00
Commons	.05
Unlisted Stars	.10-.40
Pack (12)	2.50
Box (24)	50.00

Quality Rating ★★★
Game Jersey cards highlight the inserts. Base set is always fun to collect and highly sought-after. Griffey "Home Run Chronicles" is a must have for fans of "The Kid."

#	Player	NM
5	Maddux, G.	.75
9	McGwire, M.	1.00
10	Griffey, K.	3.00
13	Piazza, M.	1.50
14	Cruz, J. Jr.	3.00
15	Gwynn, T.	1.25
16	Maddux, G.	1.50
17	Clemens, R.	1.00
18	Rodriguez, A.	1.50
22	Erstad, D.	1.25
27	Lofton, K.	.75
30	Maddux, G.	1.50
42	Vaughn, M.	.60
50	Sandberg, R.	.75
60	Belle, A.	.75
118	Nomo , H.	1.25
135	Guerrero, V.	1.00
136	Gwynn, T.	.75
137	Clemens, R.	.60
140	Griffey, K.	1.50
141	Jeter, D.	.75
143	Thomas, F.	1.25
145	Ripken, C.	1.25
146	Rodriguez, A.	1.25
147	Maddux, G.	.75
149	Piazza, M.	.75
150	McGwire, M.	.60
151	Jones, A.	.75
176	Irabu, H.	.50
205	McGwire, M.	1.25
225	Griffey, K.	3.00
245	Griffey, K.	1.50
267	Wright, J.	2.00

10th Anniversary

	Complete Set (60)	100.00
	Commons	1.00
	Unlisted Stars	1.50-2.00
1	Maddux, G.	6.00
3	Clemens, R.	4.00
4	Nomo, H.	5.00
14	Piazza, M.	6.00
18	Thomas, F.	8.00
20	McGwire, M.	4.00
25	Bagwell, J.	4.00
36	Jones, C.	7.00
40	Ripken, C.	8.00
41	Jeter, D.	6.00
42	Rodriguez, A.	6.00
46	Ramirez, M.	2.00
48	Griffey, K.	10.00
49	Gonzalez, J.	5.00
55	Gwynn, T.	5.00

Amazing Greats

	Complete Set (30)	700.00
	Commons	10.00
	Die-Cuts	3x
1	Griffey, K.	75.00
2	Jeter, D.	35.00
3	Rodriguez, A.	50.00
5	Bagwell, J.	25.00
7	Lofton, K.	20.00
8	Ripken, C.	50.00
9	Gonzalez, J.	30.00
10	Jones, C.	40.00
11	Maddux, G.	40.00
13	Piazza, M.	40.00
15	Bonds, B.	20.00
17	Garciaparra, N.	40.00
19	Gwynn, T.	40.00
20	Thomas, F.	60.00
21	Clemens, R.	25.00
23	Cruz, J.	50.00
24	Ramirez, M.	20.00
25	McGwire, M.	35.00
27	Vaughn, M.	20.00
29	Jones, A.	30.00
30	Belle, A.	20.00

A Piece of the Action

Complete Set (10)	1800.00
Buhner Bat	100.00
Gwynn Bat	225.00
Gwynn Jersey	275.00
Hollandsworth Bat	75.00
Hollandsworth Jersey	100.00
Maddux Jersey	350.00
Rodriguez Bat	300.00
Rodriguez Jersey	350.00
Sheffield Bat	100.00
Sheffield Jersey	125.00

HR Chronicles

Complete Set (30)	120.00
Common Griffey	5.00

National Pride

	Complete Set (42)	325.00
	Commons	3.00
7	Hernandez, L.	6.00
8	Jones, A.	10.00
14	Guerrero, V.	10.00
16	Nomo, H.	20.00
27	Gonzalez, J.	20.00
33	Thomas, F.	35.00
34	Bonds, B.	10.00
35	Piazza, M.	25.00
36	Jones, C.	25.00
37	Ripken, C.	35.00
38	Rodriguez, A.	25.00
39	Griffey, K.	40.00

1998 UPPER DECK COLLECTOR'S CHOICE

	NM Price
Complete Set (265)	$20.00
Commons	.05
Unlisted Stars	.10-.40
Pack (14)	1.25
Box (36)	40.00

Quality Rating ★★★
Inserts are a great addition to a well designed base set. Pack price is a little higher but the quality is great.

#	Player	NM
1	Garciaparra, N.	.75
2	Clemens, R.	.60
4	Piazza, M.	1.00
5	McGwire, M.	.60
6	Gwynn, T.	.60
7	Cruz, J.	1.00
8	Thomas, F.	1.00
10	Griffey, K.	1.50
20	Garciaparra, N. (CL)	.75
21	Checklist	.75
22	McGwire/Ripken (CL)	1.00
25	Erstad, D.	.75
35	Jones, A.	.75
40	Ripken, C.	2.00
55	Sandberg, R.	.75
60	Thomas, F.	2.00
110	Grieve, B.	.75
125	Wright, J.	.75
145	Piazza, M.	1.25
166	Guerrero, V.	.75
185	Piazza, M.	.75
220	McGwire, M.	1.00
240	Griffey, K.	2.50
245	Gonzalez, J.	1.00
253	Thomas/Gwynn	1.25
254	McGwire/Griffey/Walker	1.50
255	Griffey/Galarraga	1.25
261	Garciaparra/Rolen	1.00

Evolution Revolution

	Complete Set (28)	50.00
	Commons	.50
2	Maddux, G.	5.00
3	Ripken, C.	8.00
4	Vaughn, M.	2.00
6	Thomas, F.	8.00
9	Walker, L.	1.50
12	Bagwell, J.	3.00
14	Piazza, M.	5.00
17	Guerrero, V.	2.50
21	Rolen, S.	3.00
23	McGwire, M.	4.00
24	Gwynn, T.	4.00
25	Bonds, B.	2.00
26	Griffey, K.	10.00
27	Gonzalez, J.	4.00
28	Clemens, R.	4.00

Starquest

	Complete Delivery Set (45)	15.00
	Delivery Commons	.10
	Complete Student Set (20)	50.00
	Student Commons	1.50
	Complete Powers Set (15)	100.00
	Powers Commons	3.50
	Complete Superstar Set (10)	250.00
	Superstar Commons	8.00
1	Garciaparra, N.	1.25
2	Rolen, S.	1.25
4	Wright, J.	1.00
10	Cruz, J.	2.00
15	Grieve, B.	1.00
20	Konerko, P.	.50
25	Maddux, G.	1.50
27	Ripken, C.	2.00
30	Griffey, K.	3.00
35	Rodriguez, A.	1.50
37	Bagwell, J.	1.00
38	Gonzalez, J.	1.00
40	McGwire, M.	1.00
41	Thomas, F.	2.00
43	Gwynn, T.	1.00
44	Piazza, M.	1.50
46	Garciaparra, N.	8.00
50	Ripken, C.	10.00
52	Rolen, S.	8.00
53	Jeter, D.	8.00
55	Johnson, R.	3.00
57	Lofton, K.	3.50
59	Sandberg, R.	3.50
61	Erstad, D.	4.00
64	Rodriguez, I.	3.50
65	Gwynn, T.	8.00
69	Ramirez, M.	8.00
70	Belle, A.	8.00
72	Vaughn, M.	8.00
73	Bonds, B.	8.00
74	Jones, C.	20.00
75	Bagwell, J.	12.00
81	Cruz, J.	40.00
82	Thomas, F.	50.00
83	Gonzalez, J.	25.00
84	Piazza, M.	35.00
85	Rodriguez, A.	35.00
86	Walker, L.	10.00
87	Martinez, J.	10.00
88	Maddux, G.	40.00
89	McGwire, M.	30.00
90	Griffey, K.	60.00

"Stick-Ums"

	Complete Set (30)	15.00
	Commons	.25
	Unlisted Stars	.50-.75
1	Jones, A.	1.00
2	Jones, C.	1.50
3	Ripken, C.	2.50
4	Garciaparra, N.	2.00
8	Thomas, F.	2.50
14	Bagwell, J.	1.00
15	Piazza, M.	2.00
19	Jeter, D.	1.25
22	McGwire, M.	1.25
23	Gwynn, T.	1.25
25	Griffey, K.	3.00
26	Rodriguez, A.	2.00
27	Gonzalez, J.	1.25
29	Clemens, R.	1.25
30	Cruz, J.	2.00

ABOUT THE AUTHORS

Jim Warren II

Senior price guide editor Jim Warren II joined *Tuff Stuff* in 1991 to take over hockey pricing. He became manager of the price guide department in 1994 and earned his current title in 1995. A native of Buffalo, Jim graduated from Canisius College and brings extensive hobby experience to *Tuff Stuff.* Known nation-wide as an expert in sports figures, Jim authored *Tuff Stuff's Complete Guide to Starting Lineup,* which came out in 1996. Outside the collecting hobby, he enjoys playing pool and listening to the music of Pink Floyd, Led Zeppelin, and Jethro Tull. His prized baseball possession is a Roger Maris store model glove handed down from his father. Jim and his wife, Cindi, live in Chesterfield, Va.

Melanie Haynie

Associate price guide editor Melanie Haynie, a lifelong collector, came to *Tuff Stuff* in 1996. She has since worked with all aspects of the price guide, currently heading up the football, limited edition collectibles, and racing price guides, as well as the autograph and memorabilia sections. After growing up in Reedville, Va., Mel graduated from Mary Washington College and is currently close to earning her master's degree in mathematics. In addition to attending shows throughout the Mid-Atlantic region and feverishly collecting autographs, Mel enjoys playing softball, movie collecting, and fantasy sports. Her prized possession is a signed copy of Cal Ripken's *The Only Way I Know.* She lives on the lake in Ruther Glen, Va.

Dennis Madigan

Associate price guide editor Dennis Madigan came to *Tuff Stuff* in 1993. His responsibilities include the baseball card price guide. Prior to joining *Tuff Stuff,* Dennis was a photographer and reporter for a Richmond television station. A graduate of Radford University, Dennis represents *Tuff Stuff* on numerous hobby-related radio call-in shows. When he's not tending to his collection, Dennis enjoys traveling to the country's newest baseball parks with his wife, Nina. He has been a collector for 20 years, and his prized baseball possession is a 1914 T206 Ty Cobb baseball card. The Madigans live in Richmond.

Jerry Shaver

Jerry Shaver's *Tuff Stuff* career began in 1996 when he came aboard as non-sports price guide editor. He joined the editorial staff in 1997, and his current projects as a copy editor include *Tuff Stuff, Tuff Stuff's Sports Figures,* and *Collect!.* He also writes frequently for several publications in the *Tuff Stuff* family. Jerry graduated from James Madison University and did graduate work in English at the University of Mississippi. In addition to collecting signed baseballs at spring training, Jerry enjoys writing fiction and watching classic movies. He counts a 1971 Baltimore Orioles yearbook signed by both Brooks and Frank Robinson as his prized possession. Jerry is single and lives in Richmond.